22648

D1493947

From Oxford to the People

From Oxford to the People

Reconsidering Newman & the Oxford Movement

Edited by Paul Vaiss

First Published in 1996

Gracewing
Fowler Wright Books
Southern Avenue, Leominster
Herefordshire HR6 0QF

ISBN 0 85244 269 6

Typesetting by Action Typesetting Limited,
Gloucester, GL1 1SP

Printed by Redwood Books,
Trowbridge, Wiltshire, BA14 8RN

Contents

Fourth Part
PERSONALITIES AND INFLUENCES

Foreword

The Oxford Movement has long been studied as one of the formative movements of the Church of England and of the Anglican Communion. It was an important influence in the shaping of much Victorian literature, and its theological and liturgical influence left an enduring monument in great Victorian churches which are now recognised as significant parts of the English national heritage. Part of its enduring fascination is in the intertwining of the stories of personal religious pilgrimage, most notably that of John Henry Newman, with deep issues of theological principle and ecclesial identity. In a remarkable way some of the latter issues have come to have a late twentieth-century theological resonance as ecumenical convergence between Anglicans and Roman Catholics exists in tension with controversies over Anglican ecclesial identity provoked by the ordination of women to the priesthood in many parts of the Anglican Communion.

In recent years much new ground has been broken in reassessing the historiography of the Oxford Movement and evaluating its theology. The stature of Newman as a theologian has been increasingly recognised both within the Roman Catholic Church and beyond. As well as two major new biographies, by Ian Ker and Sheridan Gilley (both contributors to this collection of essays) there have been many doctoral theses and published monographs on aspects of Newman's theology and spirituality. Dr Peter Nockles, another contributor, has drawn out both the continuities and the contrasts between the Tractarians and the older generation of High Churchmen.

This collection of essays is the fruit of a conference outside England organised by Professor Paul Vaiss at the University of Nanterre to mark the one hundred and sixtieth anniversary of John Keble's Assize Sermon in 1833. It would have been a matter of some astonishment to the Tractarians to be commemorated in Paris, associated for them with the Revolution, and for the twentieth century with student revolt in 1968. But that the conference should have taken place when and where it did is itself a signal of new appreciation of the Oxford Movement and its historical, cultural and theological significance.

vii

Dr Gilley poses sharp questions about Anglican ecclesiology and the way it was re-shaped (in his view not altogether convincingly) by the Tractarians. The problems of the 'paper church' and the 'ecclesiogical Noah's Ark' he suggests still remain. There are real challenges for Anglicans here, even if the grape-shot is fired with a touch of romantic nostalgia. Peter Nockles puts us further in his debt by reminding us of the political concerns of the Tractarians, made the more powerful because, as he puts it, Newman was 'a political conservative and a spiritual revolutionary.' It is good to have the Oxford movement set in the context of broader nineteenth-century change, which demanded retrenchment from all churches as the older confessional states were modified. Ultramontanism and Tractarianism both sought to re-affirm apostolic authority within their respective churches. Dr Garrard's contribution on Archbishop William Howley, an old High Churchman generally sympathetic to many of the Oxford Movement's concerns, enables us to see more clearly a shadowy figure, and the essays by Jeremy Morris and Frances Knight continue the work that is still needed on charting the spread of Oxford Movement ideas from Oxford into the parishes. They remind us also that there were powerful lay patrons of the Oxford Movement, and without them Tractarian ideas would not have spread as quickly as they did. The importance of parochial guilds and confraternities in channelling Tractarian principles into parochial life must also not be overlooked.

The group of essays on Newman, includes a vintage meditation by Professor Owen Chadwick on Newman's conversion as it is reflected in his concerns in the *Apologia*, and it is good to set this alongside Ian Ker's question, 'What kind of a book is the *Apologia?*'. Dr Douglas Hedley contributes a piece on Coleridge, of whom Newman wrote that he laid 'a philosophical basis' for Church feelings and opinions, while indulging 'a liberty of speculation which no Christian can tolerate.' It was Coleridge, Newman said, who had 'succeeded in interesting' the genius of the age in 'the cause of Catholic truth.'

This collection of essays is thus a further contribution to the scholarly reassessment of the Oxford Movement and its ideas, an aid to reflection and deeper understanding and a spur to further scholarly work.

GEOFFREY ROWELL

Introduction

Paul Vaiss

The views of the academic world concerning the Oxford Movement and its leaders have undergone a series of changes and evolutions since the middle years of the past century. After an initial series of critical and in some cases hostile Anglican books and pamphlets of which William Palmer's *Narrative of Events* and Tom Mozley's *Reminiscences* are the most famous, Dean Church published his celebrated work *The Oxford Movement, Twelve years* (1891) which, even today, no serious student of Tractarian history can dispense with. H. P. Liddon's massive four volume *Life of E. B. Pusey* (1893–94) complemented Church's work and between them gave an interpretation of the Oxford Movement that was broadly accepted for half a century or more. A similar wish to vindicate Newman against antagonistic biographers like Edwin Abbott, whose *Anglican career of Cardinal Newman* was published in 1892, motivated Wilfred Ward's lengthy *Life of John Henry Newman* published in 1913. Some years before, in 1890, Ann Mozley had given Newman scholars what was to remain the only printed collection of his letters and diaries for almost a century.

As the celebration of the Oxford Movement's centenary approached, a number of studies were produced. Of these the most important were Yngve Brilioth's *The Anglican Revival* in 1925, Christopher Dawson's *The Spirit of the Oxford Movement* (1933), and E. A. Knox's *The Oxford Movement: 1833–1845* (1933). Brilioth's was a ground-breaking study that showed how powerfully Evangelicalism had influenced the movement and especially its main leader, John Henry Newman. Dr. Brilioth drew attention to some of the high church precursors of the movement such as Alexander Knox and Bishop Jebb. He was also the first to undertake a systematic study of Newman's sermons. Dawson had written his small but remarkably insightful book primarily as a reaction to Geoffrey Faber's *Oxford Apostles* (1933) which was an extreme and hostile psycho-analytical study of the movement's leaders. Knox, a not altogether unsympathetic evangelical, attempted to situate the movement in the wider context of a more general

1

religious revival in Europe. Special mention should also be made of
a work of more limited scope – W. E. Houghton's The Art of
Newman's Apologia (1945), as well as of Charles Harrold's *John*
Henry Newman (1945).

A few years later, new light was cast on Newman's early life by
Maisie Ward's *Young Mr. Newman* (1948), and by Sean O'Faolain's
Newman's Way (1952) which went a little further in the chronology.
Both had the merit of giving us a vivid picture of the Newman family
and of interpreting some more personal aspects of Newman's life.
Mention must also be made of R. D. Middleton's *Newman at*
Oxford (1950) which contains a number of interesting details, as
well of A. D. Culler's *The Imperial Intellect* (1955) which gave
a synthetic view of the Oxford Movement's leaders in their age.
In the 1960's, the first volumes (there will be 31 in all when the
series is completed) of Newman's exhaustive *Letters and Diaries*
were published by the Birmingham Oratory and Oxford University
Press (beginning in 1961 with the Catholic period), and a full two
volume biography appeared in 1962 by Meriol Trevor, *The Pillar*
of the Cloud and *Light in Winter*. These volumes gave new details
on Newman's Catholic period, but were generally disappointing on
his Anglican years. Owen Chadwick's study of Newman's theory of
the development of Christian doctrine, *From Bossuet to Newman*
(1957), brought to the fore Newman's contribution to a central
theological issue. Among other works on the subject a special
mention must be made of Nicholas Lash's *Newman on Devel-*
opment (1975).

In 1969 the first full history of the Oxford Movement since R.
W. Church's and E. A. Knox's – Marvin O'Connell, *The Oxford*
Conspirators was published in the United States and may be considered as a sum of whatever was known on the subject at the
time. At the same period new biographies of Keble and Froude
were published, the first by G. Battiscombe, *John Keble: a study*
in limitations (1963), the second by Piers Brendon, *The Life of*
Richard Hurrell Froude (1974). Robert Isaac, Henry Wilberforce
and Henry Manning also had the history of their Anglican years
written by David Newsome in his admirable book, *The Parting*
of Friends (1969). In his own way, he took up Yngve Brilioth's
insistence on the continuity of the Evangelical and Oxford Movements. J. Coulson and A. M. Allchin published the papers of
two important symposiums, *Newman: a portrait restored* (1965)
and *The Rediscovery of Newman* (1967). Two books deserve to
be mentioned here, first Härdelin's *The Tractarian Understanding*

of the Eucharist (1965) and Peter Toon's *Evangelical theology, the response to Tractarianism* (1979), each opening up a new field of investigation.

For over four decades, from 1948 to 1989, Werner Becker and Günther Biemer published the papers of the International Newman Conferences they organised in Germany as well as other studies in the thirteen volumes of their invaluable series *Newman Studien*.

In the 1980's Geoffrey Rowell with *The Vision Glorious* (1983) tried to bring alive the main figures of the Oxford Movement, their teaching and their ideals in an age when many are bewildered. Ian Ker, on the other hand, with his massive *John Henry Newman: a biography* (1988), gave us a specimen of Newman's own idea of what a biography should be like (i.e. ordering primary sources and leaving the subject speak for himself through his own correspondence and diaries) and the gist of his in depth studies of Newman's main works (he has recently published scholarly editions of the *Idea of a University* and the *Grammar of Assent*). In 1987 Lund University Press, Sweden, published Rune Imberg's *In Quest of Authority* with its companion volume, a thorough study of all the editions of the *Tracts for the Times* showing that the progression of Catholic notions in Newman's mind went at a swifter pace than is apparent in the *Apologia*. There were still the important publications by G. Rowell and I. Ker of the 1985 and 1990 Oxford symposium papers and those of yet another one that helped revive interest in E. B. Pusey, *Pusey rediscovered* (1983) by Perry Butler. In 1990 also Sheridan Gilley published his indispensable *Newman and his age*.

As the symposium for which the papers in this collection were originally produced took place in France, I think it only proper that I give a brief overview of Newman and Oxford Movement studies in this country. The first work of note to appear was the perceptive but highly subjective book by Henri Brémond, *Newman, essai de biographie psychologique* in 1905 (translated under the misleading title *The Mystery of Newman*). Then followed F. Thureau-Dangin's monumental study *La Renaissance Catholique en Angleterre* (three volumes 1908–1910) which to this day remains the only French history of the Oxford Movement. It contains vivid and remarkably sensitive sketches of its main leaders. The philosopher Jean Guitton has ever been an admirer of Newman and wrote *La Philosophie de Newman* and *La doctrine du développement [...] chez Newman*, both in 1933. For several decades the leading Newmanist in France was Maurice Nédoncelle who wrote a lengthy introduction to *Newman: Oeuvres Philosophiques* (1945), a translation of selected chapters from

Newman's leading works, especially the *Essay on the Development of Christian Doctrine* and the *Grammar of Assent*. In the 1950s and 60s the publisher Désclées de Brouwer had a number of Newman's works translated in a new collection *Textes Newmaniens*. Worthy of notice are Louis Bouyer's biography of Newman (1948) translated into English (Burns & Oates 1958, Meridian Books 1960), Jean Honoré's beautifully written *L'Itinéraire spirituel de Newman* (1963) and Louis Cognet's perceptive *Newman, ou la recherche de la vérité* (1967). Pierre Gauthier's masterly comparative study of Newman's and Blondel's theories on the development of Christian doctrine was published in 1988. The 'Association Française des Amis de Newman' is very active, organising symposiums every second year and publishing a valuable periodical *Etudes Newmaniennes* (ten issues so far − publication date: November of each year). It is also committed to a programme of publishing translations of Newman's major works.

Among the most recent contributions to Newman and Oxford Movement scholarship four books, at least, deserve to be mentioned. Stephen Thomas' *Newman and Heresy* (1991) which shows how a new understanding of the issue of heresy played a major role in Newman's conversion to Roman Catholicism, my own *Newman, sa vie, sa pensée et sa spiritualité* (1991), a complete reconsideration of his religious development until he left for his Mediterranean tour, Peter Nockles', *The Oxford Movement in Context* (1994) which lays a new emphasis on the High Church tradition between 1760 and 1857, how it shaped the Oxford Movement while remaining largely distinct from it and even antagonistic to it. David Newsome's superb *The Convert Cardinals* was published in 1993. In his work he examines the delicate subject of the differences between Newman and Manning. One further book worthy of mention, especially because it is representative of a new trend in Oxford Movement research, is Jeremy Morris' *Religion and Urban Change: Croydon 1840−1914* (1992). Finally I must draw attention to a work that will henceforth prove indispensable for whoever wishes to enter this field of studies, Lawrence Crumb's two volume exhaustive bibliography, *The Oxford Movement and its Leaders,* ATLA publication, Scarecrow Press 1988 and 1993.

My list is far from being exhaustive, yet it serves my purpose which was to highlight the successive stages of Oxford Movement and Newman studies, up to the time when I felt it necessary to organise a symposium that would make known the significant results of a considerable amount of research done on the subject over the past few years. Bishop Rowell provided his invaluable assistance to trace those scholars who belong to the new generation of specialists that has contributed to rendering a reappraisal of the Oxford Movement possible. Just reading their papers and their footnotes will help find the many books, articles and unpublished theses exploring various aspects of the subject which I couldn't possibly mention here.

As I cite the names of the participants (unfortunately not all those who were invited could come) and give an idea of what their contributions have been, I by no means wish to provide abstracts of their papers lest the less courageous readers should be content to stop there. My aim is simply to make it easier for the non-specialist to approach a vast and most rewarding field of investigation, possibly also to whet his appetite.

It is fitting and highly symbolical that Bishop Geoffrey Rowell's paper should open this series of studies on different aspects of the religious revival that had such a lasting effect on the Church of England a century and a half ago. Both in its Evangelical and High Church wings there are certainly many who would welcome a spiritual and a theological renewal that might save it from its present divisions and cause it to recover its influence on a society that has lost most of its moral and religious moorings. Bishop Rowell studies some of the too often neglected figures of the High Church tradition who prepared the way for the Oxford Movement and inspired its leaders. Until not so long ago they were hardly mentioned by the movement's historiographers.

In a way, Sheridan Gilley's paper should have been placed at the end of this book for it brings the issues raised by the Oxford Movement to bear on the present situation of the Church of England. That I have not done so is a reflection of the very personal nature of his work which could have given the impression of being the conclusion to a collective work by scholars who do not all necessarily share Sheridan Gilley's opinion. Nobody can read what he writes without being deeply moved since he very discreetly gives us a glimpse of his own heartaches over problems largely similar to those Newman and his friends experienced a century and a half ago. The starting point of his paper is provided by the results of recent research that has given us a new picture of the Anglican Church in the eighteenth and early nineteenth centuries. It has shown that there was throughout a dominant High Church tradition, which in the days of Newman was embodied by Archbishop Howley, 'holding together Church and State with the two main streams in the Anglican tradition'. It was Newman and his friends who, by insisting on the Catholic non-Protestant nature of the Church of England, were responsible for the violent confrontations between Anglo-Catholics and radicalised Protestant Evangelicals.

Gilley is convinced that the disappearance of the old High Church tradition and the resulting partisan conflict opened the way for theological liberalism 'simply because that conflict creates intractable problems which only liberalism can resolve by bypassing them altogether'. As a consequence Christian doctrine was diluted, the eventual result being a general decline of religion and morals in the nation as a whole.

I hope it won't be considered presumptuous that I should intervene here as a mere observer. If liberalism has indeed made deep inroads in the Church of England, the rise of Evangelicalism dramatised by the accession to the primacy of a moderate evangelical, seems to show that liberal theologians haven't yet become 'the real victors in the war for the soul of the Church of England'. And there is still among the bishops and the clergy an active High Church movement which is not exclusively composed of bewildered Anglo-Catholics whose reception into the Roman fold in the near future seems inevitable.

At first sight, Nicholas Lossky's paper may seem to divert our attention from contemporary issues and to draw us back to the early centuries of the Christian Church. Yet the attentive reader will find in it much that bears on our present needs and some fresh insight, not only into the 'spirit' of the Oxford Movement, but also into the attempts at recovering the visible unity of the Church. Lossky shows us how deeply Patristic theology influenced Tractarian spirituality and its cast of mind. It taught them that theology is practical and not merely speculative in that it calls men to salvation and a new life in Christ. It also opened up a new vista and a new dimension in their understanding of the christian life, i.e. that it is not a self-sufficient individual life (a notion they received from their Evangelical upbringing), but a salvation and a sanctification to be lived in the communion of the Church, the Body of Christ. It gave them 'a deeply incarnational apprehension of the reality of the Church', which led them to an insistence on the central doctrine of 'theosis' (or deification). It was also through the Fathers that the Tractarians rediscovered the importance of worship and the role of the liturgy as nourishing and deepening the life of the Church.

Peter Nockles' paper cannot be fully appreciated unless it is set in the context of a debate raised by John Griffin, in three articles written in the 1970s and a later book. His main assertion was that the Oxford Movement leaders had broken with the traditional alliance between the tory party and the Church of England, pleading for a separation between Church and State.[1] According to him, the main inspiration behind his radical stance was John Keble:

> For a period of about six or seven years, John Keble was a political Radical, as he understood that term. That is, he looked forward to the separation of the Church of England from the State and every other lay controlling force, a gesture he believed was the first object of the Radical party.[2]

Among the material Griffin collects to prove his point is a letter written by R. H. Froude to A. P. Perceval upon the petition to be sent to the bishops in which he lists the 'points to be put forward' especially:

> IV. We protest against all efforts directed to the subversion of existing Institutions, or to the separation of Church and State.
> V. We think it a duty to steadily contemplate such a separation.
>
> Keble demurs to this because he thinks the union of Church and State, as it is now understood, actually sinful.[3]

A passage which he comments on in the following words:

> Froude was not mistaken in his summary of Keble's political views at the time, and perhaps some of his more extreme measures derive from his friendship and admiration for Keble.

A little further on, we read this statement:

> Thus by the year 1833, Keble had moved away from his position of a scared Conservative to that of a zealous Radical on this issue of Church and State relations.[4]

In his later articles, as well as in his book, Griffin was to extend his view of Keble's politics in that period to the whole Tractarian movement.

If Nockles' aim is to refute Griffin's assertions, his article is much more than simply that. It is an attempt at delineating the

Oxford Movement's political position, insisting on its continuity with the Church and King principle of traditional High Church toryism, and acknowledging the differences between the movement's position and that of the older highchurchmen. Nockles also shows that, contrary to the views of most historians of the movement, 'Tractarian political thought [. . .] was more integral to its theology than is usually recognised'. Peter Nockles draws on his extensive research on the subject, part of which was recently published in a fundamental book, *The Oxford Movement in Context*.[5]

If one paper only were to justify the title that was given to the symposium: 'The Oxford Movement, a reappraisal', it would have been Stephen Prickett's for it gives us a totally unprecedented view of the movement's social conscience. And, surprisingly enough, he has chosen the most unworldly of the tractarian leaders, John Keble, to prove his point that there was among them one at least who was aware of the condition of the poor, who accepted the social and political reforms of his age and who pressed for education to be made available to the lower classes, not only primary or econdary education but university education as well. A modern biographer of Keble has written:

> The pity was that, in spite of his sympathy with the working class [. . .] Keble never sought to identify himself [. . .] with the efforts made to improve social conditions as a whole. His blindness, in this respect, must be accounted one of Keble's greatest limitations [. . .] and the Oxford Movement's in particular.[6]

And yet Prickett shows, studying his Crewian oration of 1839, how concerned Keble was with 'the efforts made to improve social conditions as a whole', especially in the field of learning, advocating the creation of provincial universities with adequate provision to enrol the able young people from among the poorer classes of society.

With Frances Knight we enter a fairly recent field of research which has to do with the real impact of the Tractarian Movement outside Oxford, among the parish clergy and their flock. Most historians of the movement take it for granted that the Oxford students who had been so deeply influenced by Newman's preaching and had more or less embraced his ideas, tried once in their parishes to propagate tractarian teaching and practices 'converting more or less their Rectors and brother curates',[7] as the *Apologia* tells us. A painstaking study of the diocese of Lincoln[8] allows Knight to give a very different picture of the situation showing that, when Tractarian or, later, Ritualist innovations were made the initiative had often been taken by church wardens rather than by curates. Another erroneous notion Frances Knight dispels is that the Oxford Movement leaders were not really interested in ritualistic or ceremonial changes. Finally, contrary to a widespread opinion mainly due to Dean Church's influential history of the Tractarian Movement, Newman's conversion had no fatal effect on its propagation. Paradoxically, it seems that it is in the 1850s and 1860s, even before the rise of the Ritualist Movement, that it really made headway in the parishes.

Jeremy Morris' paper is partly based on his recently published thesis on the parishes of Croydon[9] and partly on similar research about other urban centres. He shows that, in most cases, the Tractarian and Ritualist movements (the distinction between the two currents appears difficult to make in practice) progressed mainly through the support of patrons and trustees who funded the erection of new churches in expanding urban areas and were vigilant as to the opinions of their incumbents. He then contends, contrary to the traditional view, that those movements were not restricted to a party, however numerous, of clergymen but commanded sizeable popular support.

Any collection of papers on the Oxford Movement is bound to be dominated by the overbearing figure of John H. Newman and this one is no exception. Certainly, Owen Chadwick's contribution is particularly welcome for his great perception and what might be called his capacity of communing with Newman's mind and sensitivity. This doesn't prevent him from seeing the faults in an otherwise admirably built demonstration. For he doubts whether Newman's opinions were really built up the way he wants us to believe in the *Apologia,* as if each of his friends or colleagues 'added his own brick to the edifice'. I would just observe that what Newman wanted to impress on his readers was that all his opinions originated in the teaching of either a great name in Oxford or a respected Anglican divine or else the Church Fathers. Using this strategy he was cutting the grass from under his critics' feet, but at the same time he was running the risk of making his account sound artificial and improbable. No wonder that an American scholar analysing a computerised text of the *Apologia* should have concluded that Newman was a passive agent altogether.[10] In his presentation of the Tract 90 episode, Chadwick insists on the particular atmosphere of those days rather than on what appears to him as an innocuous interpretation of Anglican doctrine. The originality of the *Apologia* and the reasons why it had such an impact are examined as well as Newman's wider, more impersonal motive for writing what he viewed as part of his contribution to give Christianity 'a sound intellectual basis' in 'an age of difficulty'.

Ian Ker's approach is quite different again, yet, at times, he comes very close to Owen Chadwick's conclusions. He admits that, although the Apologia is a sincere and truthful account, Newman left out important facts of his life giving the false impression that his conversion to Roman Catholicism was a purely intellectual process. Yet that was a deliberate choice, for Newman didn't want feelings and emotions to interfere with his narrative. His model was the Evangelical Thomas Scott's story of his conversion. But, as Ker shows, there is much more to it than simply that. For, even though it is an intellectual autobiography, the *Apologia* has always gripped and moved its readers. Why and how this effect was achieved is precisely what Ian Ker tries to convey.

A third paper by Rune Imberg is also devoted to the *Apologia,* its tone is very unlike that of Owen Chadwick and also Ian Ker. Imberg does not share their sympathy for Newman. Yet, from a different viewpoint and with a different purpose, all three agree that the *Apologia* poses a number of problems, that it is a highly selective autobiography and, at least Chadwick and Imberg doubt the reliability of Newman's account. However, Rune Imberg goes far beyond this. His paper is based on some of the findings of his thesis.[11] I have read it and found much in it that is both surprising and challenging. Actually, my own research on the period 1801–1832 brought me to question the accuracy of the *Apologia,* although my conclusions are more reserved than his. On one point especially one must be very cautious. For, interpreting Newman's mind and sensitivity as being fundamentally those of a sceptic leaves out much of what he says in his sermons about the nature of faith. This interpretation was suggested by Owen Chadwick in his *From Bossuet to Newman*: '[to him] scepticism was no bogy; it was his personal terror, the dead hand which scrabbled at him when his faith was sleeping'.[12] Yet it was Thirlwall who had first judged his mind as 'essentially sceptical and sophistical'.

It is always an uncomfortable task to introduce one's own

work since one is seldom able to be objective. Let me only say that my paper tries to convey the surprise at the unexpected conclusions I had to draw when faced with the overwhelming evidence that Newman's development between 1824 and 1832 was very different than what I thought. Instead of the progressive deconversion from evangelicalism (the phrase is used in Ian Ker's paper) which the *Apologia* has depicted, Newman's course appears to have continually oscillated between thoroughly evangelical positions and the high church notions which Froude and Keble brought to him.[13] This highly unstable situation lasted until the eve of his Italian tour. In this paper I have selected more particularly his unmistakably evangelical period lasting from mid-January to late November 1832. There are some attempts at explaining this late reconversion to evangelicalism which was by no means his first, but possibly his last return to the fullness of his calvinistic early youth.

Roderick Strange brings in the fundamental dimension of faith in Newman's preaching. Drawing from various sermons, mostly found in the first two volumes of the *Parochial and Plain Sermons* series, Strange shows us how Newman built his theory of faith. Faith is first viewed as a common attitude in any man's everyday life (a notion he had found already in Bishop Butler's *Analogy*), then it is seen in its relationship to conscience, to God, to obedience and fidelity, to love and all the virtues and, finally, to the divinization of the believer. This paper comes as a welcome corrective to the opinion that Newman's mind was 'essentially sceptical'. There is a richness and a liveliness in those sermons about faith that goes far beyond merely proving anything about the preacher's own fullness of faith, it strengthens and refreshes the reader's faith. It is a real delight to be given here ample portions of some of Newman's very best spiritual resources.

Douglas Hedley's paper offers a fitting complement to Strange's study of Newman's preaching on faith and opens up an altogether new perspective. He presents us first with a very different Coleridge than we had so far been used to know. Hedley shows convincingly that Coleridge had fought against the socinian tendencies in Anglican theology, rehabilitating the dogmatic principle. Then he describes his incarnational theology, replacing it in the Augustinian mystic tradition. Finally he reminds us that for him, as for Newman, the existence of a visible Church is central to christianity. Far from being the sceptic philosopher we were used to take him for, S. T. Coleridge then appears as a precursor of Newman's own particular theological emphases. Hedley's paper is one of those in this collection that fully justify the title it was given, for it is certainly a thorough 'reappraisal' of the background and the philosophical setting of most of the fundamental aspects of Oxford Movement teaching.

The last part of this collection is devoted to three very different persons whose influence on the Oxford Movement varied both in nature and intensity. If Froude may be considered a key figure in the movement, Archbishops Howley and Wiseman are only indirectly associated with its history. Yet their influence was far from negligible. Pierre Gauthier wrote a thesis on Richard Hurrell Froude[14] which is especially interesting for its study on his 'Essay on Rationalism' (vol. III of *The Remains)* and, more generally, of Froude's influence on Newman. In his paper, Gauthier shows us how far in advance of Newman he was as far as Catholic doctrine is concerned. He acknowledges the strength and cogency of the Roman Catholic Church's positions at a time when his friend was still battling with the difficulties of his 'Via Media'. Froude's part appears then as that of an exacting critic as well as that of a stimulus. In 1835, for instance, his position on the 39 Articles anticipated on Newman's Tract 90 written in 1841. His view of tradition and his inklings as to a development of christian doctrine also posed a threat to Newman's conceptions and prepared the way for the soul searchings that were ultimately to lead to his 1845 conversion.

James Garrard who wrote a doctoral thesis on Archbishop Howley selects some examples that illustrate how close he was to the Oxford Movement leaders while disapproving of their methods and strategies. He shows how little the primate's attitude was understood and produces a number of documents that lift part of the veil and allow us to set the climactic events of 1838 – 1841 in their proper perspective. With Peter Nockles, Garrard is convinced that the Tractarian Movement was no revival of an all but dead High Church tradition. For it was very much alive in the Church of England of Howley's times and was upheld by most of its dignitaries who formed a powerful party that had reached the climax of its power in the 1830s.

The last paper in this series is Paul Asveld's. It provides us with the very documents of the Newman-Wiseman controversy over the 1839 – 1841 period. Their interest lies in the fact that they show us how much more Wiseman's articles in the *Dublin Review* influenced Newman than he was prepared to own in the *Apologia* or, at least, to convey to his readers. Instead of a few short excerpts, we have extended portions that give the debate greater scope and allow us to get a more correct appreciation of the workings of Newman's mind in those fateful years.

Summing up in a few lines the extent of the reappraisal of the Oxford Movement undertaken in this book is no easy task. I shall simply list the issues addressed and the erroneous opinions redressed:

- The vitality and influence of the High Church tradition in the first half of the XIXth century so long neglected or even bypassed.
- The Patristic roots of Tractarian theology.
- The so often distorted view of Tractarian social and political positions.
- The too long unexplored religious influence of the Oxford Movement in the parishes.
- The real nature and aim of Newman's *Apologia* as well as the issue of its dependability.
- The permanence of the central teachings of Evangelicalism in Newman's preaching long after he was supposed to have renounced them.
- The largely unsuspected agreement over many fundamental points of Coleridge's philosophic theology with Newman's.
- Archbishop Howley's so far misunderstood attitude to the Tractarians.
- The extent of the influence exerted by Froude and by Wiseman's writings over Newman.

Paul Vaiss, Spring 1995.

Notes

1   J. R. Griffin, 'John Keble: Radical', *Anglican Theological Review* (53), 1971, p. 167–175; 'The Anglican Politics of Cardinal Newman', ibid. (55), 1973, p. 431–439; 'The Radical phase of the Oxford Movement', *Journal of Ecclesiastical History* (27), 1976, p. 47–56; *The Oxford Movement: A Revision,* Front Royal (Va.), 1980 and Edinburgh 1984, revised 1985. In fact the book is a reprint of six articles published in *Faith and Reason* in 1979 and 1980.
2   'John Keble: Radical', p. 169.
3   Ibid., p. 170–171.

4   Ibid., p. 172.
5   The sub-title is: 'Anglican High Churchmanship 1760–1857', Cambridge University Press 1994.
6   G. Battiscombe, *John Keble: a study in limitations,* New York 1964, p. 134.
7   *Apologia,* Norton edition, p. 58.
8   See her forthcoming book to be published by Cambridge University Press.
9   J. N. Morris, *Religion and Urban Change: Croydon 1840–1914,* Boydell & Brewer 1992.
10 E. A. Shanahan, *Newman as instrument in the Apologia,* unpubl. PhD dissertation, University of Wisconsin 1982.
11 Rune Imberg, *In Quest of Authority: The Tracts for the Times and the development of the Tractarian Leaders,* Lund University Press 1987.
12 Owen Chadwick, *From Bossuet to Newman,* Cambridge University Press 1957 (2nd ed. 1987), p. 126.
13 See my book: *Newman, sa vie, sa pensée, sa spiritualité (1801–1832),* L'Harmattan, Paris 1991.
14 Pierre Gauthier, *La pensée religieuse de R. H. Froude,* Beauchesne, Paris 1977.

Part One

Reconsidering some fundamentals
of the Oxford Movement

'Church Principles' and 'Protestant Kempism', Some theological forerunners of the Tractarians

Geoffrey Rowell

The men of the Oxford Movement did not see themselves as innovators in either worship or theology, but as those recalling the English Church to an awareness of its identity as part of the Catholic Church. They were conscious that they stood in a theological tradition, which acknowledged that it was rooted in Scripture and in the faith and practice of the Fathers of the early centuries, and which had found its classic Anglican expression in the Caroline divines of the seventeenth century. That tradition had enjoyed a more recent flowering in the theology of the non-jurors, men who, like the Tractarians themselves, had protested against the encroachments of the state upon the authority of the Church. They recognized a kinship also with those who, in the thirty or so years preceding the *Tracts,* had professed a similar theology, giving a high place to the church and sacraments, opposing both a destructive individualism which allowed no place for a corporate creed, and the reductionist liberalism with which such individualism was frequently combined, and rooting their theology in a strongly sacramental spirituality of the heart.

Not all who described themselves as High Churchmen were looked on with approval by the men of the Oxford Movement, but in this essay consideration will be given to those with whom they had a considerable degree of kinship. Of these there are three main groups, the 'Hutchinsonian' theologians, who professed an imaginative, symbolic theology, grounded in Scripture, in opposition to the rationalism of the Deists and latitudinarians; Anglicans of the non-established episcopal churches in Scotland and America, most notably, perhaps, Bishop Hobart of New York; and the Irishmen, Alexander Knox and John Jebb, Bishop of Limerick, whose importance as precursors of the Oxford Movement was particularly recognised by Archbishop Brilioth in his study of the Oxford Movement, *The Anglican Reveival* (1925). Each of these

17

groups contributed something to the theological matrix out of which the Oxford Movement was most immediately fashioned, though it would be wrong to view the Tractarians as doing little more than re-iterating what had been said by these earlier divines. There were important divergences as well as continuities, in ecclesiology, spirituality, and sacramental theology. Nonetheless the kinship was a real one, even though it would be wrong to look for direct influence in each and every particular.

As Newman acknowledged, many of these more immediate precursors showed the close links between Tractarian themes and the characteristic emphases of the Romantic movement.

> In truth there is at this point a great progress of our Church to something deeper and truer than satisfied the last century. I have always contended, and will contend, that it is not satisfactorily accounted for by any particular movements of individuals on a particular spot. The poets and philosophers of the age have borne witness to it for many years. Those great names in our literature, Sir Walter Scott, Mr Wordsworth, Mr Coleridge, though in different ways and with essential differences one from another, still all bear witness to it. Mr Alexander Knox in Ireland bears a most surprising witness to it. The system of Mr Irving is another witness to it. The age is moving towards something . . .[1]

What that 'something' was Newman characterized as 'the feelings of awe, mystery, tenderness, reverence, devotedness, and other feelings which may be especially called Catholic.' It was a sense of holiness and a search for a spirituality as much as a renewal and reconstruction of theology.

If Newman believed the Oxford Movement to be part of a broader rediscovery of elements of human experience which had been unduly neglected by the characteristic theology and philosophy of the eighteenth century − 'the time when love was cold', it was a rediscovery prompted in part by the re-valuation of old traditions in the wake of the French Revolution. The end of the *ancien régime,* which the Revolution betokened, prompted, in different countries in different ways, the re-examination of the relation of church and state and a re-consideration of the values to which the state publicly and constitutionally adhered. The structure and organisation of the Church, in so many respects feudal in character and reflecting the ordering of a pre-industrial society, could not but be affected by the questioning of the nature of the state and its method of government. The

occasion of Keble's 1833 Assize Sermon, the Irish Church Temporalities Act, could only seem to many part of a necessary reform of a
church establishment which no longer matched either the pastoral or
political realities of the situation, but it was interpreted by Keble as a
sign of national apostasy. The willingness of the state unilaterally to
alter the way in which it was bound to the church signalled an alarm
for those who were aware of what had happened to the church on
the other side of the Channel. The practice of occasional conformity
in order to qualify for secular office where the Dissenters were concerned had at least preserved the unitary concept of a Christian state
and a single church, however strained it had been in practice. By
1833 the young Oxford churchmen felt this had broken down and
that there might be worse to follow. The character of the state had
changed; what did that have to say about the identity of the church?
As Hurrell Froude put it:

> The joint effect of three recent and important Acts (1) the Repeal
> of the Test and Corporation Acts, (2) the Concessions to the
> Roman Catholics, (3) the late Act for Parliamentary Reform,
> has most certainly been to efface in at least one branch of our
> Civil Legislature, that character which, according to our great
> Authorities, qualified it to be at the same time our Ecclesias-
> tical Legislature, and thus to cancel the conditions on which it
> has been allowed to interfere in matters spiritual.[2]

Those with a high doctrine of the church were bound as a consequence to reconsider the grounds on which they stood; the nature
of the church's authority; the character of the Christian ministry;
the limits and appropriateness of parliamentary interference in the
affairs of the church. For the clergy it was a serious and urgent
question; as Newman put it in the first of the Tracts:

> Should the government and the country so far forget their God
> as to cast off the Church, to deprive it of its temporal honours
> and substance, *on what* will you rest the claim of respect and
> attention which you make upon your flocks? Hitherto you have
> been upheld by your birth, your education, your wealth, your
> connexions; should these secular advantages cease, on what must
> Christ's ministers depend? Is not this a serious and practical ques-
> tion ...*on what* are we to rest our authority when the state
> deserts us? ...I fear we have neglected the real ground on which
> our authority is built – OUR APOSTOLICAL DESCENT.[3]

As relations between state and church altered, the question of Anglican identity became more pressing, the more so because the Church of England, unlike the Churches of the Reformation on the Continent, was not a confessional church. The Prayer Book stood in the place of the Reformed confessions of faith; the thirty-nine articles bound the clergy; and the articles appealed to Scripture and the church of the Fathers. It was not surprising that those concerned with Anglican identity stressed the importance of the liturgy and the continuity of the Church of England with the undivided church, as well as emphasising the importance of baptism, and baptism reverently and carefully administered. However much some would have liked to make regular communion the badge of Anglican profession it did not reflect the realities of church practice. As a writer in the *Quarterly Review* commented in 1847:

> Is it, or is it not, an exaggeration to say that more than half of all the adult persons who belong to the communion of the Church of England, live and die without ever participating of the Holy Eucharist?[4]

Questions of church discipline flowed naturally from a concern with the locus of authority both theological and ecclesiastical, and these were often sharpened by the suspicion and hostility with which the Dissenters were regarded. They were frequently spoken of as the enemies of the church, and their principles were held to animate those in the state who were only too ready to interfere in the organisation, worship and doctrine of the church. Dr. Nancy Murray has commented, with reference to the attitude of High Churchmen to the French Revolution: 'It seemed to them axiomatic that the fatal "liberal" priciples embraced by the enemies of the Church, by Locke and the rational Dissenters, had produced rebellion in America', and if there was rebellion in France then it was likely to be connected with similar principles.[5] So in the wake of the French Revolution we find many churchmen making a connection between schism and sedition, and stressing the need to return to church principles. The pamphlets circulated by the Society for the Reformation of Principles, founded by William Jones of Nayland, often bore this hallmark. Even among these High Churchmen there were at times apocalyptic overtones:

> I am now convinced that I have lived to see the man of sin revealed and that the way is now open, or opening, to the final judgement. I am in expectation of another event; for now there

has been a formal renunciation of Christianity among the Gentiles, the conversion of the Jews may be at hand.[6]

That concern with Church principles which was so characteristic of the Tractarians was already a marked characteristic of that earlier group of High Churchmen known as the 'Hackney Phalanx', and the 'Hutchinsonian' school of theology to which many of them belonged. Moreover, Anglicans outside England, both in America and in the Episcopal Church of Scotland, had already wrestled with the question of Anglican identity, and the members of the Hackney Phalanx were in close contact with the defenders of 'Church principles' in both Scotland and America. Despite their relatively small numbers (Dr Murray estimates that they were 'probably not more than one hundred in all'), the Hackney Phalanx was able to exert a not inconsiderable influence because of the positions members of the group held within the church, and the fact that they were generally highly articulate.[7] Eight bishops were said to count themselves as friends of the Phalanx: Horne, Van Mildert, Horsley, Douglas, Marsh, Manners Sutton, Randolph and Middleton.

Theologically, Bishop Horne was one of the most notable of these. Born in Kent in 1730, he came up to University College, Oxford, in 1745. He was elected a Fellow of Magdalen in 1750; became President in 1768 — an office which he held until 1791, combining it for the last ten years with the Deanship of Canterbury; and was made Bishop of Norwich, only to die in 1792. During his student days he was much influenced by George Watson, one of the Fellows of University College, and through him aligned himself with the Hutchinsonian group in the University. His biographer, William Jones of Nayland, also belonged to the same school of thought.

'Hutchinsonianism' was in part a protest against the rational religion of the eighteenth century. John Hutchinson (1674–1737) from whom the school took its name, is a rather shadowy figure, who had no universtity education. Having secured a place in the household of the Duke of Somerset, he devoted himself to the exposition of 'Scripture philosophy', the revealed and only true philosophy, which he contrasted with deist religion and certain aspects of Newtonian science.[8] 'The Demonstration of the Being and Attributes of God by a Parcel of Words called Metaphysicks', he wrote, 'we look on as presumptuous in the Attempt, the being wiser than God.'[9] He argued, in a way reminiscent of Bishop Butler, that the natural order of creation is an order of types and analogies: 'All the Ideas of Divinity are formed from the Ideas in Nature; evey description of Divinity in the Scripture is taken from natural Things.'[10] A summary of Hutchinson's theology is provided by Jones in the preface to the second edition of his life of Horne, in which he sought to defend Horne in his espousal of Hutchinsonian teaching. Jones lists twelve points as characteristic:

i)   God is given the pre-eminence.
ii)   There is one way of salvation through Jesus Christ.
iii) In both Testaments divine things are explained and confirmed by allusions to the natural creation.
iv)   A strong and definite Trinitarianism.
v)   Everything in religion is derived from revelation; natural religion is deism in disguise.
vi)   An important place is given to types and figures.
vii) There is strong disagreement with Newton over his method of proving a vacuum.
viii) A strong interest in fossils, and an appeal to fossil evidence as supporting the Biblical account of the Flood.
ix)   Great care is to be exercised in utilising secular learning derived from heathen books.
x)   The Jews are to be regarded as the inveterate enemies of Christianity.
xi)   Hebrew is the primary and original language, and has a divine structure.
xii) The Cherubim are mystical figures, from which derived the animal worship of antiquity.[11]

Although it would be quite wrong to see the somewhat idiosyncratic Hutchinsonian theology as having much influence on the Tractarians, there are certain features which they have in common. There is an insistence that Christianity is a revealed religion; there is a strong Trinitarianism; and there is a recognition of the sacramental character of the world, and of the part played by typology in Scripture. Jones, for instance, in 1773, published a series of treatises on passages of Scripture which admitted of a figurative interpretaion. He argues that figurative language is a necessary characteristic of revealed religion because, firstly, it is adapted to our understanding, and, secondly, it transcends the limitations of particular dispensations, or, as we might say, cultures.

> Words are changeable; language has been confounded; and men in different parts of the world are as unintelligible to one another as barbarians; but the visible works of nature are not subject to any such confusion; they speak to us now in the same sense as

they spoke to Adam in Paradise ... Thus, for example, if we take the word *God,* we have a sound which gives us no idea; and if we trace it through all the languages of the world, we find nothing but arbitrary sounds, with great variety of dialect and accent, all of which still leave us where we began, and reach no farther than the ear. But when it is said, *God is a sun and a shield,* then *things* are added to words, and we understand that the being signified by the word *God,* is bright and powerful; unmeasurable in height, inaccessible in glory; the author of light to the understanding, the fountain of life to the soul; our security against all terror, our defence against all danger. See here the difference between the language of words and the language of things. If an image is presented to the mind when a sound is heard by the ear, then we begin to understand; and a single object of our sight, in a figurative expression gives us a large and instructive lesson; such as could never be conveyed by all possible combinations of sounds.[12]

Greek philosophy, Jones proceeds to argue, derived its power through the imagery of its poetry, and poetry likewise assists revealed religion. Philosophy instructs by words, poetry by images, and in this very fact poetry is religious.[13] And the poet can use images in this way because the world is sacramental. 'Nature itself is christian, and the world a daily miracle; the heavens speak to us and the earth and all things therein join in the same testimony: so that if all nations were to disbelieve, nature itself would still continue a faithful witness to the truth.'[14] The Bible itself assumes, Jones maintains, that the creation is a mirror in which we are invited to behold the figurative expression of spiritual realities.[15] It is not surprising that with this emphasis on imagery and symbol in the natural world and in Scripture, that Jones should also give an importance to sacramental worship.

Sacraments and ceremonies in religion are significant actions, which all nations and all ages have observed in their worship; and the church still retains them: though these latter times (and this unhappy country in particular) have produced a spurious race of Christians, who have thrown off sacraments and ceremonies all together; as if they had consulted with some evil spirit of beggarly taste.[16]

The state of man's mind is such that if it is not raised 'by the help of sensible objects and bodily gestures' it is in danger 'of sinking into sullenness and stupidity'. The neglect of the sacramental is part and parcel of the insipid and indefinite natural religion of the philosophers.

> Modern times have been refining upon the reformation, till by degrees they have conceived and brought forth a sort of philosophical religion, distinct from every thing the world had seen before; because it is *religion without faith.* The scheme of the Deists, as they call themselves, has nothing in it of things past; no fact or tradition to ground itself upon; it has no sacraments, nor services of any kind to keep up its intercourse with heaven; it expects no predicted judgment, and has no particular view of any thing after this life.[17]

The sacramentalism of Jones' Hutchinsonian theology can be paralleled in some contemporary Evangelical writers. Legh Richmond, the author of the celebrated tract, *The Dairyman's Daughter,* could exclaim:

> What do they not lose, who are strangers to serious meditation on the wonders and beauties of created nature! How gloriously the God of creation shines in his works! Not a tree, nor flower; not a bird, nor insect, but proclaims in glowing language, 'God made me'.[18]

And James Hervey could write: 'Surely Nature is a book and every page rich with sacred hints'.[19]

These words are of course strongly reminiscent of Keble's hymn, 'There is a book who runs may read', which powerfully stresses the symbolic character of the natural world, a theme which Keble explores in relation to the Fathers of the Church in Tract LXXXIX, *'On the Mysticism attributed to the Early Fathers of the Church'.* In that Tract Keble contrasts the symbolic understanding of Christian antiquity with 'the speculations of mere natural philosophy' and strongly urges 'the way of regarding external things, either as fraught with imaginative associations, or as parabolical lessons of conduct, or as a symbolical language in which God speaks to us of a world out of sight: which three might, perhaps, be not quite inaptly entitled, the Poetical, the Moral and the Mystical, phases or aspects of this visible world.'[20] Keble argues that the symbolic interpretation of the natural order charateristic of the Fathers is not to be viewed as the result of arbitrary comparison: 'so many analogies *selected by themselves,* from the course of human life or external nature, to render some truth or precept more forcible and vivid.[21] The symbolic character of the natural order is that which is inherent in it because that order is sustained and created by God and so is 'charged with the grandeur of God'.

> The works of GOD in creation and providence, besides their immediate uses in this life, appeared to the old writers as so many intended tokens from the ALMIGHTY, to assure us of some spiritual fact or other, which it concerns us in some way to know. So far, therefore, they fulfilled half at least of the nature of sacraments, according to the strict definition of our Catechism: they were pledges to assure us of some spiritual thing, if they were not means to convey it to us. They were in a very sufficient sense, *Verba visibilia.*[22]

In the same way Pusey in his 1836 Lectures on Types and Prophecies speaks of created things as standing in 'a continual harmony with an order of things above them; they possess in themselves a relation to things unseen.' Because they are derived from God they bear an 'impress and image of himself and an analogy, or proportion, or relation to other existences derived from God.' This means, writes Pusey, 'that the province of the true poet has been not to invent likenesses, but to trace out the analogies, which are actually impressed upon the creation.'[23] The correspondences traced by poets are recognised 'as *true* not as *beautiful* only, and so not belonging to their minds subjectively, but as actually and really existing (objective).'

It is worth observing that both Pusey and the Hutchinsonian divines had a particular concern with Hebrew studies, and his preference for the symbolic language of typology over that of theological abstraction would have been enthusiastically endorsed by them.

> 'When moderns then attempt to translate into plain terms the figurative language of Holy Scripture, and to substitute abstract, and as they would fain have it, clearer terms for the types and typical language of the O.T., they uniformly by this transmutation evaporate much of their meaning ... He who would lay aside these types and typical language, and understand the mysteries of God without them, would be acting contrary to the teaching of Scr. and so very wrongly and foolishly. Men think that they gain in clearness, but they lose in depth; they would employ definite terms, in order to comprehend that which is infinite!'[24]

As Newman recognised, in a letter of 1835 concerning the liturgical practice of Bishop Butler, the rites and ceremonies of the church communicate more directly than the abstractions of theology.

'I conceive his wonderfully gifted intellect caught the idea which had actually been the rule of the Primitive Church, of teaching the more sacred truths by rites and ceremonies. No mode of teaching can be imagined, so public, constant, impressive, permanent, and at the same time reverential than that which makes devotion the memorial and declaration of doctrine – reverential, because the very posture of the mind in worship is necessarily such. In this way Christians receive the Gospel literally on their knees, and in a temper altogether different from that critical and argumentative spirit which sitting and listening engender.'

Newman above all realized that images and symbols were not an inadequate medium of communication of theological ideas, which ought to be superseded by the abstractions of rational theology; nor yet to be dismissed for their lack of precision. Image and symbol, rite and ceremony, were a consequence of man's bodiliness, and were the very means by which God revealed himself to men. As he said forcefully in a University sermon of 1830:

Revelation meets us with simple and distinct *facts* and *actions,* not with painful inductions from existing phenomena, not with generalized laws or metaphysical conjectures, but with *Jesus and the Resurrection;* and *if Christ be not risen* . . . then is our preaching vain, and your faith also in vain. Facts such as this are not simply evidence of the truth of the revelation, but the media of its impressiveness . . . the philosopher aspires towards a divine *principle:* the Christian, towards a Divine *Agent.*[26]

And that Divine Agent has revealed himself through the material order of creation, and through the dispensation, or economy, of a particular series of historical acts. The Christian indwells a co-ordinated, coherent, and divinely grounded universe of images and symbols intended to evoke from him the response of faith in the God in whom those images and symbols ultimately inhere. So there must be rites and ceremonies:

'Religion must be realized in particular acts, in order to its continuing alive . . . There is no such thing as abstract religion. When persons attempt to worship in this (what they call) more spiritual manner, they end, in fact, in not worshipping at all ... Scriptures give the *spirit,* and the Church the *body,* to our worship, and we may as well expect that the spirits of men might be seen by us without the intervention of their bodies, as suppose that the Object of faith can be realized in a world of sense and excitement, without the instrumentality of an outward form to arrest and fix attention, to stimulate the careless, and to encourage the desponding.[27]

Such a concern motivated the theological enterprise of Syriac Christianity, which continued the semitic cultural tradition of the Bible, and a recent scholar in this field has both pointed to the possibility of influence from this tradition on Pusey's thought, and commented on the broader significance of a primarily symbolic theology. There is, he suggests, 'a moment of optimum equilibrium when, without violating the veils of a divine mystery, religious symbols are intelligently presented in such a way as to evoke a heuristic response leading to valid conviction and action — valid, even though the believer could not give a full rational account of what he understands. When that equilibrium is lost the way is open to inconoclasm, demythologisation, rationalism, and the other mental troubles more characteristic of the west than of the east.'[28]

Besides their awareness of the importance of the language of imagery and symbol in theology the Hutchinsonian divines were strongly Trinitarian. Jones attacked the relegation of the doctrine of the Trinity to the realm of speculation. Those who regarded it as 'nothing but a mere lifeless theory, an empty subject for the mind to exercise its curiosity upon, and concerning which, it may think and imagine for itself with as great freedom, as it does about any baseless and airy fabric of modern metaphysics,' had no scriptural warrant for such a rigid distinction between the speculative and the practical in Christian doctrine.[29] Such an attitude was only too characteristic of those who, whilst they pretend 'some zeal of a sort of universal religion common to believers and infidels,' betray 'a sad indifference for the Christian religion in particular.' Such men treat articles of faith as merely speculative, and hold it to be 'of little significance what a man believes, if he is but hearty and sincere in it.'[30]

There was also a strong emphasis on the doctrine of the church. Sometimes this derived from a sense of the threat to the church from Dissenters or from revolutionary ideas from across the Channel. More often it was a positive recognition that the doctrine of the church was unduly neglected and was an integral part of the

Christian gospel. Thomas Sikes of Guilsborough wrote in 1812 that 'the subject of the CHURCH, considered as *a spiritual society, invested with authority from Jesus Christ* to regulate all the affairs of religion, it is but too manifest, is little regarded.'[31] Sikes believed that this failure to pay attention to the doctrine of the church destroyed the proportion of the Christian faith, and went so far as to say that contemporary confusion was 'chiefly owing to the want of asserting this one article of the Creed', and to prophesy that there would be 'yet more confusion attending its revival, when it is thrust on minds unprepared, and on an uncatechized Church.'[32] William Jones wrote of 'this subject of the Church, now so much neglected and almost forgotten by those who are concerned to understand it', a neglect which he attempted to remedy in his *Essay on the Church*.[33] He told the widow of Bishop Horne that it was the troublesome lawsuits initiated by the Dissenters in his parish which had provoked him into writing the *Essay*.

> I owe to their malignity the considerations and searchings of heart, which produced my Essay on the Church: and my zeal is thereby sharpened to the promoting of a great design now on foot, for the preservation of our Church and Government against their devices, of which no man can well be less ignorant than myself.[34]

Disputes with Dissenters may have been the occasion of the *Essay on the Church,* but in it Jones is concerned to present a positive theology. He stresses that the church is holy 'from its relation to God'.

> It is a society or body, of which the Holy Spirit is the life; and this life being communicated to those who are taken into the church, they are thereby made partakers of a holy life, which is elsewhere called the *life of God;* from which life they are alienated who are out of this society. It is holy in its sacraments; our baptism is an holy baptism from the Holy Spirit of God; the Lord's Supper is an holy sacrifice: the ordinance of absolution is for the forgiveness of past sin, that the members of the church may be recovered from sin to a state of holiness, and peace with God. The church is holy in its priesthood; all the offices of which are for the sanctification of the people.[35]

Jones' friend, William Kirby, urged in 1798 that the times demanded of the clergy clear teaching on 'the nature of the Christian Church as a society' and a stress on 'the doctrine of regeneration by baptism, of grace received in confirmation, and at the sacrament of the Lord's Supper'. 'These are topics become more necessary than ever to be inculcated upon our people, who in this respect are often miserably ignorant.'[36]

William Stevens, another Hutchinsonian, and an influential layman, who edited the works of Jones of Nayland, was himself the author of an earlier exposition of ecclesiology, *A Treatise on the Nature and Constitution of the Church* (1773), in which he insisted that the church was not 'a meer voluntary society'. It was a spiritual society; an outward and visible society; and a universal society, with officers and a succession of officers. Stevens was in close contact with the Scottish Episcopalians, and this meant that, unlike some High Churchmen, he recognised that a high doctrine of the church did not necessarily have to be linked with establishment. As he wrote to Bishop Skinner in 1797: '*Making establishment necessary to the existence of the Church, as many are apt to do, is a grievous mistake*; but to be sure it is a convenient appendage; and there is no harm in kings being *nursing fathers* − if they will *nurse it properly.*' Stevens' biographer notes that bishops Horne and Horsley took the same line.[37] W. F. Hook, who had close connections with the Scottish Episcopalians, and with Bishop Hobart of New York, also showed himself alert to the drawbacks of establishment. He wrote in the preface which he contributed to the English edition of the life of Bishop Hobart that the establishment of the Church tended 'to encourage Erastian Heretics within the pale, who, thinking only of the temporalities of the Establishment, impede the proceedings of the Church.' Such concerns, he believed, motivated the general disinterest of English Churchmen in the Scottish Episcopalians. There was an Erastian concern not to offend the Presbyterians.[38]

The stress on the holiness of the church, and the church as a spiritual society, was reflected in a concern that the church's ministry and sacraments should be understood in this way. Jones was critical of some Evangelical attitudes in this respect.

There is a fashion of inviting people to *come to Christ,* without telling them where and how he is to be found. Besides, it is a great mistake to suppose that the whole of our religion consists in our taking of Christ; it is beginning at the wrong end: for Christ is to take us ... Christians are united to God, and to one another, by the services of prayer, and the participation of the sacraments, more than by the hearing of the word of God without them; which many hear for reasons of vanity and uncharitableness.[39]

He blamed Locke's philosophy for the dissemination of low views of the priesthood and the sacraments. The offices of the church are to be regarded as holy in themselves, quite apart from the personal qualifications of the individuals holding those offices, and bishops have authority because they are the successors of the apostles. They are, Jones implies, of the *esse* of the church.

> Bishops have succeeded to that character with which the Apostles were invested ... A church without a Bishop was never heard of till the fifteenth century.[40]

The laying on of hands in confirmation is an appropriate and effectual sign, and we are reminded that we 'can form no idea of spiritual things without the mediation of bodily objects.'[41]

The same emphasis is found in the work of William Van Mildert, the Bishop of Durham, of whom Charles Lloyd said that 'he was so great in his knowledge of the exact doctrines of the Church of England, that orthodoxy oozed out of his pores, and that he would talk of it in his dreams.'[42] In his *Inquiry into the General Principles of Scripture Interpretation* (1815) he wrote strongly of the inadequacy of Socinian, rationalist theology when applied to the sacraments.

> The Socinian, always solicitous to divest Christianity of every thing mysterious, regards the Eucharist as a bare commemorative act of devotion. He thus effectually removes the absurdity of the literal sense: but, at the same time, he reduces the figurative sense almost to a nullity, by setting aside the *sacramental* meaning of the institution, which consists in a right apprehension of what the symbols themselves were intended to represent.

The 'enthusiast', on the other hand, admits both the literal and figurative senses, but reduces everything to the immediate action of the Holy Spirit.

> By both these the spiritual or mystical application of our Lord's words is overlooked; the ordinance being reduced to a bare commemorative rite or a sign unaccompanied by the benefits of the things signified. But ...the full sense of the words of Institution is undoubtedly *mystical;* that is, it has reference to some deeper signification than the words abstractedly import.[43]

Van Mildert's twofold criticism is to a degree an anticipation of Pusey's objections to the theology of both the 'carnal man' and 'the pseudo-spiritualist' in his Lectures on Types and Prophecies.[44] If we turn to Thomas Sikes we again find a high doctrine of episcopacy, but one free from secular considerations. 'Secular dignities and duties', he wrote, 'are entirely adventitious to the episcopal character.'[45] Episcopal authority is based on apostolic succession, for Christ had left with his apostles 'his commission and his Spirit for their natural life, entailing them upon that succession of men, upon whom they should lay their hands according to his direction.' Like Jones he observed that 'scarcely in any country is Christianity known but in connection with Bishops.'[46] Sikes is willing to admit that 'the Apostles, *as such,* cannot have succesors', nonetheless there is clear succession in jurisdiction, and he appeals to Ignatius, Cyprian, Irenaeus and Jerome as teaching this doctrine. The ministry is thus an appointment of God, not of the people, as it appeared to be in Dissenting congregations, and Sikes in consequence warned his people of their duty to attend their parish church rather than going to hear 'edifying' ministers of their own choosing.[47]

Like Sikes, Van Mildert was clear that valid sacraments and apostolic ministry went together, and that they were of the *esse* of the church. 'If the sacraments,' he wrote, 'be not only signs or emblems of spiritual benefits, but the instituted means of conveying those benefits − and if the ministration of the Priesthood, as a Divine ordinance, be necessary to give the Sacraments their validity and effect; then are these interwoven into the very substance of Christianity and inseparable from its general design.'[48] This continues the line of non-juring theology represented in the works of Charles Leslie, George Hickes and William Law, which were a continuing inspiration to both many of the Tractarians and their immediate predecessors in the High Church tradition. Horne read with warm approval the works of Leslie, which he said might be considered 'a library in themselves to any young student of the Church of England.' He also read William Law, welcoming his ascetic devotion but being critical of Law's enthusiasm for the mysticism of Jacob Boehme, a suspicion he shared with John Wesley.[49]

In John Keble's library this whole tradition is, as one would expect, well represented by such works as the following: Kettlewell's *Works* (inscribed, Oriel, 20 Mar. 1820); Law's *Works:* and also separate copies of the *Practical Treatise on Christian Perfection* (1707 ed.) and the *Serious Call* (1823 edition) − presumably the copy that Robert Wilberforce was surprised to see Keble locking away in a drawer, instead of leaving it about to do people good;[50] Hickes' *Sermons* and *Devotions in the Antient Way of Offices;* Ken's *Works* and *Exposition of the Church Catechism.*[51] It is interesting that Hurrell Froude read the devotional *Serious Call* in 1826, but only came to Law's attack on Hoadly in 1834, when he owned himself 'quite astonished' by Law's brilliance.[52] The same forcefulness of Law in this controversy also struck W. F. Hook, who cited the following pungent passage from Law's *First Letter to the Bishop of Bangor* in his preface to the *Life* of Bishop Hobart of New York.

> If there be no uninterrupted succession, then there are no authorized ministers of Christ, if no such ministers, then no Christian sacraments; if no Christian sacraments, then no Christian covenant, whereof the Sacraments are the stated and visible Seals.[53]

It was appropriate that Hook should cite Law in his preface for Bishop Hobart was not only a staunch defender of the apostolic succession but looked to Law and the non-juring divines as a chief source of inspiration. At the same time he stood strongly for the religion of the heart, and in this respect can be reckoned as another instance of that 'neo-Anglicanism' or 'High Church pietism', fusing a High sacramental theology with an inward spirituality, which Archbishop Brilioth saw as characteristic of the Oxford Movement and as witnessing to an affinity with certain important aspects of Evangelicalism.[54] Hobart stood for 'the gospel in the church' and 'primitive faith and apostolic order'. He strove to combine church principles and warm piety in such a way that 'sentiments . . . condemned by Churchmen as *enthusiastic* would be 'approved by them as *evangelical.'* It was said that his detractors were uncertain 'whether to call him 'High Churchman' or 'Methodist', in his striving for the union of heart and head, enthusiasm and principle, zeal and sound judgement.[55] Narrow, high and dry ecclesiasticism, and sectarian disregard of the apostolic order of the church were alike destructive, and he attacked equally 'those baneful principles which are reducing the Gospel to a cold, unfruitful and comfortless system of heathen morals,' and 'that wild spirit of enthusiasm and irregular zeal which, condemning the divinely-constituted government and priesthood of the Church, is destroying entirely her order, unity and beauty, and undermining the foundations of sound and sober piety.'[56] In his *Apology for*

Apostolic order and its Advocates (1807) he stressed the apostolic succession, episcopacy authority, and the necessity of the visible church. As one of his students commented:

> The indispensable character of the apostolic priesthood, the necessity of an unbroken succession; the efficacy of sacraments; the incomparable excellence of the liturgy of the Church; the danger and criminality of a *temporizing policy* in these things; the sacred obligation of vows of conformity and obedience taken at the ordination of the priesthood: these were points which he hesitated not to recommend with all the force of his mind, and to insist upon with all the authority of his office.[57]

Just as Christ received the anointing of the Spirit, so by the laying on of hands in episcopal ordination the Spirit is given as 'the gift of office' by which those ordained became 'vested with power to minister in holy things.'[58]

The titles of bishop and priest were, Hobart maintained, in the very earliest years of the church not clearly distinguished, but 'when the title *Bishops* became appropriate to the first order of the ministry, the second order became known by their other title, Presbyters, and afterwards by the term *Priests,'* and Hobart specifically connects this with a sacrificial understanding of the Eucharist.

> This last appellation has respect to their spiritual oblation of the body and blood of Christ, under the symbols of bread and wine; and this oblation was regarded as equivalent and analogous, in the Gospel, to the sacrifices of the Jewish law, the offering of which appertained to the priests.[59]

It was through the apostolic priesthood that the grace of Christ was sacramentally bestowed: 'the merits and grace of (the) Redeemer are applied to the soul of the believer by devout and humble participation in the ordinances of the Church, administered by a priesthood who derive their authority, by regular transmission from CHRIST, the divine Head of the Church, and the source of all the power in it.[60] Ministry and sacraments are alike the gift of God and 'any reasoning which should prove human authority to be competent to the alteration of the one, will prove to be no less competent to the alteration of the other.'[61] He re-emphasised this in 1815 in his charge on the *Nature of Christian Ministry.*[62]

Hobart drew on many of the resources of the High Church tradition for the establishment of his theological position. In

1805 he published an edition of the non-juring Robert Nelson's *Fasts and Festivals,* expanded with material from William Stevens' *Treatise on the Church,* Potter on *Church Government,* Archdeacon Daubeny's *Directions for a devout and decent Behaviour in the Public Worship of God,* and Dean Hickes' *Devotions in the Ancient Way of Offices.*[63] In the same year, 1805, he listed the books of divinity which he considered most valuable to read and study for the young William Berrian, who later edited Hobart's works. As well as standard works of Divinity, such as those by Paley and Butler, we find the following: Campbell on Miracles; Leland on the Deistical writers; Porteus: *Summary of the evidences of the Christian Revelation;* Newton: *On the Prophecies;* Gray: *Key to the Old Testament;* Percy: *Key to the New Testament;* Collyer; *Sacred Interpretaion;* Prideaux: *Connections;* Lowth: *Hebrew Poetry;* Jones of Nayland; Stackhouse: *Body of Divinity;* Daubeny: *Guide to the Church;* Wilberforce: *Practical View;* Secker; Barrow; Horne; Porteus; Massillon; Seabury; Wilson: *Sermons;* Sherlock *On Death;* Wilson: *Sacra Privata;* Reeves; Shepherd or Wheatley on the Book of Common Prayer; Stanhope on the epistles and gospels; Nelson's *Companion for the Feasts and Fasts.*[64] It is noteworthy that Wilberforce's *Practical View* appears alongside works by Daubeny, Horne and Jones of Nayland, not to mention Bishop Wilson of Sodor and Man, who was held in such high regard by John Keble.

Bishop Hobart did not only stand as a representative of the Catholic tradition in Anglicanism in America, he also maintained links with English High Churchmen. When his *Apology for Apostolic Order* was published in 1807 he sent a copy to Archdeacon Daubeny, acknowledging the extent to which he had made use of his writings and saying how greatly the cause of apostolic order was indebted to him.[65] Hugh James Rose made extensive use of Hobart's *Apology* in his own *Commission and Consequent Duties of the Clergy,* and corresponded with Hobart about the need for patronage to be concentrated in the hands of the bishops.[66] Rose dissented, however, from Hobart's criticisms of the evil effects of English class structure, countering Hobart's suggestion that the penury and hardship of the poor in England was the direct result of the existence of privileged classes, with the argument that it was the result of the poor law discouraging prudent habits and allowing the poor to subsist on a bare sufficiency.[67] This social criticism of Hobart was not appreciated by many of the English High Churchmen. When Hobart visited in England in 1823–4, Sikes of Guilsborough commented how funny it was 'to see honest democracy and sincere episcopacy fast yoked in the man's mind, and perpetually struggling for his heart.'[68]

In England Hobart met not only with Sikes, but with other High Churchmen, such as J. H. Spry of Birmingham; Archdeacon Watson; Coleridge, the editor of the *Christian Remembrancer; and secretary of the S.P.C.K.;* and Campbell, the editor of the *British Critic* as well as Archdeacon Norris and others at Hackney. W. F. Hook wrote enthusiastically of the Hackney meeting both to his mother and the young Pusey, describing Hobart as 'that great and good man' and commenting on 'his sober but zealous piety; his strong, vehement, but tempered orthodoxy; his veneration for our Church,' 'a *worthy* successor – as far as uninspired men can be so – of the Holy Apostles.'[69] In March of the following year Newman met Hobart over dinner with Provost Hawkins and observed to his sister, Jemima, that Hobart was 'an intelligent man' but 'I fear dirty – so at least were his hands and neck-cloth,'[70] though he admitted to learning much of the American Church. Norris lamented to Hobart that the Church in England lacked any effective synod of its own. 'Our great grievance is, that we have not like you, a Convention. Our Convocation is only the pageantry of what formerly so materially contributed to the purity and consolidation of the Church.'[71] In the January of 1824 Hobart visited Scotland, calling on the way on Southey and Wordsworth in the Lakes, and met with bishops Skinner and Jolly. Along with many others Hobart was struck by Jolly's manifest holiness and simplicity.[72]

For their part a concern for the Anglican churches outside England, in Scotland and in North America in particular, was characteristic of many English High Churchmen. Churches which maintained episcopacy because it was the apostolic ordering of the church's ministry, and not because it was bound up with a position in the state Establishment, were an encouragement to the defence of a catholic view of the ministry and sacraments in the Church of England. William Stevens, Judge Park and others, formed a committee to look after the interests of the Episcopal Church in Scotland in the 1790's following a visit of three Scottish bishops to London to seek relief from the disabilities under which the Scottish church laboured. It was from reading the account of the Scottish church in Park's memoir of William Stevens that the young W. F. Hook first had his interest in the Scottish church aroused. It seemed to him to embody the principles of the reformed, primitive, and apostolic catholicism, which he regarded as characteristic of Anglicanism, and in which he was well grounded through the extensive course of reading he set himself in 1824–26.[73] When Hook journeyed to Scotland in 1825 to preach at the consecration of his father's friend, Dr. Luscombe, as a missionary bishop to the Anglican congregations on the Continent, he wrote with strong indignation of the treatment of the Scottish Episcopalians, not only by the British government, but also by English bishops, recounting how two of them had opposed an application by the Scottish church to the S.P.C.K. for assistance for Highland congregations, on the grounds that the Episcopal Church was a dissenting church in Scotland.[74] The Tractarians, likewise, looked sympathetically towards the Scottish Church, having a personal link with it in Bishop Forbes of Brechin, and even seeing it as a possible haven of refuge at the time of the Gorham judgement, when some thought they might 'have to come North for a Church before long'.[75]

The anti-Erastianism of the Tractarians made them look favourably on the bishops of the colonial church, and Pusey was very anxious that they should not be corrupted by close links with the state.[76] In 1847 Manning told John Strachan, the first bishop of Toronto, that 'I can truly declare that the most heartening character about the Church of England to my eyes is the Colonial branch of Our Communion.'[77] In Nova Scotia, Bishop John Inglis, who first introduced Bishop Hobart to H. H. Norris, strove to establish church discipline and wrote that his great object was 'to make our members understand our scriptural and evangelical doctrines in the real meaning of the word, and our apostolic order, from a conviction that, as these are better known, they well be more loved.'[78] He kept in close touch with Joshua Watson and showed himself critically sympathetic to the developments of the Oxford Movement:

> I am only able to gain a very slight knowledge of particulars in reference to Oxford movements. But this I know, all my soundest men feel grateful to them. Still I wish they would not write so much that requires explanation, nor speak so tenderly of Trent.[79]

His father, Bishop Charles Inglis, had been concerned about the equation of Anglican clergy and dissenting ministers implied by certain government policies in Nova Scotia and indicated that he, like his son, had a high doctrine of the ministry:

> If the Bible Society has a tendency to increase the influence of Dissenters in England, the danger would be greater here, where the members of the Church of England scarcely compose a fourth

part of our Population . . . if it be injudicious in England to raise Dissenting Teachers to an equality with the Clergy, it would be still more so here, where the sanctity and importance of the Christian Priesthood is but imperfectly understood.[80]

Charles Inglis was grateful for the support of George Prevost, Lt. Governor of Nova Scotia from 1808–11, whose son, likewise George Prevost, was a close associate of the Kebles, Samuel Wilberforce and Isaac Williams, whose sister he married.[81] Another Canadian bishop, George Medley of Fredericton, witnesses to a Tractarian concern for holiness: writing in his primary visitation charge: 'our great business seems to be, to teach men, not to study controversy, but to study holiness.'[82]

In his account of Hugh James Rose in his *Lives of Twelve Good Men* Dean Burgon is at pains to underline that the response to the *Tracts for the Times* was the consequence of the labours of a good many earlier High Churchmen. He cites from the American church not only Bishop Hobart, but also bishop Doane of New Jersey and Bishop Whittingham of Maryland. In Britain he cites too a long list of divines: Thomas Randolph, Thomas Townson, George Horne, William Jones, Samuel Horsley, William Stevens, John Randolph, William Cleaver, John Frere, John Shepherd, Thomas Middleton, John Bowdler, Charles Daubeny, Reginald Heber, Charles Lloyd, Alexander Knox, John Jebb, John Davison, Thomas Sikes, Richard Laurence, William Van Mildert, William Howley, Christopher Wordsworth, H. H. Norris, Martin Routh, John Oxlee, John Kaye, Joshua Watson, C. J. Blomfield, and Hugh James Rose.[83] Not all of these can be said to have occupied exactly the same theological position, but it is interesting to note how many of them were members of the club known as 'Nobody's Friends', which William Stevens founded in 1800, and the extent to which these, and other members of the club prominent in the High Church revival, were inter-related. Apart from Stevens himself we find the following as members: John Bowdler, Joshua Watson, H. H. Norris, John Frere, Thomas Sikes, William Van Mildert, Thomas Middleton, Charles Lloyd, and C. J. Blomfield. Other members of the club, who do not gain a mention in Burgon's list, were also clearly identified with High Church position. For instance we may note the following: Sir James Park (biographer of William Stevens, and a staunch defender of the Scottish church); Jonathan Boucher, Vicar of Epsom; William Horne (Rector of Otham, and brother of George Horne); John Randolph; Archdeacon Watson, (brother of Joshua Watson); George Downing (a close friend of Stevens and William Jones); Baden Powell (brother-in-law of J. J. Watson and H. H. Norris); Peter Gunning (Rector of Farnborough, Somerset, and brother-in-law of F. Randolph); John Skinner (Bishop of Aberdeen); Thomas Bowdler (son of J. Bowdler); Archdeacon Cambridge; Charles Crawley and George Abraham Crawley; John Lonsdale (later Bishop of Lichfield); J. T. Coleridge; W. H. Coleridge (later Bishop of Barbados); Samuel Wix (described as 'among the last of the old High Church school of Divines, a genuine follower of Robert Nelson and the founders of the Christian Knowledge Society'); John Inglis (Bishop of Nova Scotia); J. H. Spry (Canon of Canterbury and Rector of St. Marylebone); Christopher Benson (Master of the Temple); Edward Copleston (Bishop of Llandaff); George Jelf and R. W. Jelf; Lord Henley (brother-in-law of Sir Robert Peel); George Henry Gibbs (of the Gibbs family, major benefactors of Keble College, Oxford); Sir Robert Inglis.[84] The list could be considerably extended. What is, perhaps, noteworthy, however, is that no Tractarians appear in this list, neither does Bishop Jebb who, along with Alexander Knox, is counted by Burgon as contributing significantly to the pre-Tractarian revival of church principles.

Knox and Jebb, as Archbishop Brilioth rightly noted, have a special significance in the pre-history of Tractarianism. G. T. Stokes in the 1880's went so far as to claim that they were 'the onlie begetters' of the Oxford Movement, writing that 'Wesley begat Knox, and Knox begat Jebb, and Jebb begat Rose and Pusey and Newman', and describing Knox as 'above all the mediator or channel connecting John Wesley and the Wesleyan movement of the last century with the Tractarian movement ... of which latter movement, indeed, I consider Alexander Knox the secret, the unacknowledged, but none the less the real fount and origin.'[85] Stokes argued that Wesley transmitted to Knox the understanding of justification found in the seventeenth-century divines, and Knox passed it on to the Oxford Tractarians. Although there are resemblances between the teaching of Knox and that of Newman on justification it is difficult to assert any very direct dependence. Newman, illustrating the doctrine that in Scripture 'God's word effects what it announces', refers to God's word as 'the consecrating principle' in the Sacraments, and notes that Knox uses the same example. Later, in speaking of G. S. Faber's opposition to Knox's teaching, Newman describes Knox as 'that original and instructive writer.'[86] His appreciation was, however, very cautious. A letter to Rickards of 1835 links Knox with Coleridge, whom Newman read for the first time in that year, as having a place 'in the growth and restoration of

Church principles', a point which Newman also made, as we have seen, in his *Letter to Jelf* at the time of Tract XC. Knox was, he said, 'a remarkable instance of a man searching for and striking out the truth by himself' but whilst the emphasis placed by both Knox and Coleridge on the 'mystical side' of religion was to be welcomed, Knox's eclecticism, which emphasised the good in many different systems was very suspect in Newman's eyes.[87] He wrote more sharply to Robert Wilberforce in 1838:

> I do not know enough of Knox to speak. He seems to say dangerous things, but then his works are private letters, and his words can hardly be taken by the inch. I should be unwilling to think him more than an eclectic, though that is bad enough. Froude did not like him. I think his works on the Eucharist have done much good.[88]

Much the same emphasis is found in a letter of Keble's of the same year, written to J. T. Coleridge, who confesses to having been 'much struck' by Knox's *Remains*. Keble acknowledges that he has great admiration for Knox in some respects, and praises particularly the *Treatise on the Eucharist* but again it is Knox's apparent eclecticism which Keble condemns, as well as his attitude to Wesley.

> I cannot admit his symbolizing with Methodists to be at all Catholic; quite the contrary, for Catholic means, 'according to the rule of the whole uncorrupt Church from the beginning;' and Mr Knox's admiration of Wesley and Co., was founded first on his own private personal experience, and then justified by his own personal interpretation of Church History. Surely it was a great fallacy of his, that where he saw the good effect of a thing, the thing itself is to be approved ... It is rather an arrogant position in which Mr. K. delighted to imagine himself, as one on the top of a high hill, seeing which way different schools tend — (the school of Primitive Antiquity being but one among many) and passing judgment upon each how far it is right, and how well it suited its time — himself superior to all, exercising the royal right of eclecticism over all. It does not seem to me to accord very well with the notion of a faith 'once for all delivered to the saints.' I speak the more feelingly because I know I was myself inclined to eclecticism at one time; and if it had not been for my father and my brother, where I should have been now, who can say?[89]

Benjamin Harrison reports that Pusey read Knox 'very attentively', but Liddon is emphatic that Pusey never claimed Knox as the teacher of the Tractarians in matters concerning Catholic antiquity or Catholic truth.[90] R. W. Church, replying to Stokes in the *Guardian,* was likewise insistent that Knox was not the source of Tractarian theology. 'The Oxford men', he wrote, 'found their doctrines where Wesley in his earlier days found them, and where Knox afterwards found them; but they assuredly did not find them through either Knox or Wesley', but first 'in the writing of great and classic English divines', and then in the Fathers.[91]

It would be wrong, therefore, to look for any very direct influence of Alexander Knox on the Oxford men, though Knox's close associate, Bishop Jebb, was looked to as a definite precursor of Tractarian ideas, and was cited on several occasions in the *Tracts.* Both Newman and Keble, however, refer warmly to Knox's *Treatise on the Eucharist,* which Knox compiled in 1826.[92] In this Knox argues for the 'instrumental efficacy' of the eucharistic elements in conveying the grace of Christ to the faithful receiver of the sacrament. Härdelin would appear to be not quite accurate in his account of Knox's teaching as being that 'the gift is Christ's body and blood in power and effect, but the elements are only considered to be the signs of this gift, and not the actual instruments and vehicles of its conveyance.[93] Knox is certainly opposed to what he calls 'a literal transubstantiation', for he believes this was not taught by the Fathers of the Church. But the Fathers were agreed, he maintained, 'in ascribing to the consecrated elements in the Eucharist an unutterable and efficacious mystery, in virtue of our Saviour's words of institution, by which he had made those elements when consecrated after his example, the vehicles of his saving and sanctifying power; and, in that respect, the permanent representatives of his incarnate person.'[94] Where eucharistic theology has excluded 'the instrumental efficacy of the sacramental symbols', he notes, 'the ordinance itself has appeared to lose its interest and attractiveness.'[95] In the sacrament there is a 'peculiar effluence of supernatural grace, mysteriously united with the consecrated symbols, so as to make them the vehicles of heavenly benediction to the capable communicant.'[96]

Knox specifically connects eucharistic and incarnational theology.

Let us recognise the same spirit of meek majesty which veiled its transcendent brightness in the mystery of the incarnation, as still continuing the like gracious condescension in the mystery of the Eucharist.[97]

Although God does not need to communicate himself by sacramental means, such means are appropriate to human weakness, which needs a visible medium: 'accordingly, the cup of blessing and the broken bread, are made the conduits of influence, in compliance with our animal feelings.'[98] Eucharistically the body of Christ is 'his operative presence, as the incarnate and suffering Messiah, uniting itself with and acting by and through, the consecrated symbols.' And again Knox stresses that the eucharistic elements are 'divine instruments of conveying what they represent.'[99] They correspond to the image of the hill of Zion with the temple of God's presence as the Old Testament image of paradise restored. So a similar honour should be paid to the eucharistic symbols, but even more than the reverence accorded to the Temple, for 'the representative body of Incarnate Deity is, necessarily, a nobler and more exalted thing, than the structure in which he specially manifested himself before he became incarnate.'[100]

We find the same sense of the holiness and awe with which the Eucharist is invested in both Knox and the Tractarians:

> The Eucharist ...is guarded by terrors strictly akin to those of Mount Sinai ... The sacrament of the Eucharist, thus apprehended, would, of necessity, be valued, venerated and loved; it would be all but adored.

We should therefore:

> ...delight in the institution to which those impressive symbols give character and meaning; and love the society, and even the place, in which this mystery is transacted − the mystery of Him, who liveth, and was dead, and is alive for everyone − revisiting his people as effectually, though invisibly, as he came to his Apostles, when the doors were shut, for fear of the Jews; coming − as it becomes Emmanuel, God with us, to come, − for a purpose, in which all his former acts are made effectual; ...coming with a glory, which were it unveiled, would be insupportable by our feeble nature.[101]

What is 'supernaturally communicated in the Eucharist, to those who are capable of receiving it,' is, 'as far as it is in the nature of things communicable, the virtuality of himself.'[102] A true understanding of the Eucharist, Knox wrote to Jebb, leads men to a recognition of a mystery going beyond any dogmatic system.

This sacred ordinance, contemplated in the light of our blessed Lord's institution, and St. Paul's interpretation, implies an interiority, so divine, so simple, and so independent of, and superior to, all doctrinal dogma, as to evince an experimental depth in Christianity, as much beyond the semi-Socinian conceptions of the one party, as it is uncongenial with the low forensic theories of the other.[103]

The stress of 'experimental religion', the religion of the heart, and its close connection with sacramentalism, is characteristic of the teaching of both Knox and Jebb. It was for their witness to the centrality of spirituality that Knox particularly valued the Evangelicals. 'To be *evangelical* is to FEEL that the Gospel is the POWER of God unto salvation', and the Evangelicals have thus been 'the chief instruments of maintaining *experimental* RELIGION in the reformed churches.'[104] '*Whatever errors might be mingled* with the *views* of the grace of our Lord Jesus Christ, when really devout . . . they had a *cordial,* and, as it were, a *vital* apprehension of our blessed Saviour.'[105] That was the positive side, but Knox was critical of some Evangelicals for allowing their '*feeling* system' to become a system of thought, replacing actual experience by a technical phraseology, so converting Christianity into a 'notional religion.' What was necessary was not 'to *look at* what was done by our Saviour on the cross,' but to *look for* such inward effects of that great transaction as would imply *realization* rather than *recollection.*'[106] He rejected Calvinism as a 'selfish, mercenary view of Christianity', and, whilst not following Wesley in every respect, believed him to be an outstanding example of the two great traditions and emphases of early Christianity, the Greek and the Latin, symbolised by the figures of Augustine and Chrysostom. As Augustine was to be seen as 'the great teacher of efficient grace' so Chrysostom was the teacher of 'consummate holiness', and, Wesley, Knox believed, had been 'wonderfully led to the union of grace with holiness.'[107] He disagreed with Wesley in what he saw as Wesley's failure to regard justification as something effected in man's moral nature:

J. Wesley, in conformity with so many others supposed . . . that in justification, something is done in our circumstances; and in sanctification something is done in our moral nature . . . I think, rather, that justification, in the N.T., means our attaining the substance of true and genuine righteousness, such as God approves of; and sanctification, our after advancement and maturity. The one I conceive to be as strictly inward and moral as the other ...[108]

In the Protestant tradition Knox regarded Lutheranism as the continuation of the inward religion represented by Chrysostom and the Greek Fathers, and Calvinism as a continuation of the Latin tradition of Augustine. In John Wesley a basically 'Chrysostomian' religion was combined with a powerful sense of the importance of Augustine's teaching on grace.

> Mr Wesley ... had most certainly every feature of Chrysostom's system and spirit ... but he had more; he had, also, a more direct apprehension of the converting energy of Divine grace, as taught by Augustine, than seems to me to have been possessed by any of the modern Protestant followers of that Father.[109]

Knox saw in Wesley one who stood quite clearly within the spiritual tradition stemming from the Greek Fathers, and believed that his great contribution was to have 'simplified, systematised, rationalised and evangelised ... the very spirit of Macarius and Chrysostom, of Smith and Cudworth, of De Sales and Fénelon.'[110]

Like Wesley, Knox had both a deep appreciation of the Christian mystics, and at the same time a suspicion of the esoteric forms of religion which could characterise those of mystical enthusiasm. Knox believed that much that went under the head of mysticism was really a distortion of Christianity in a Platonist direction, just as scholasticism was a distortion of Christianity by aristotelian philosophy.[111] Nonetheless the main thrust of Knox's writing was in the direction of Christian platonism and the mystical tradition, and we find in the *Remains* a continual appreciation of both the Greek Fathers and other later writers in the same tradition of theology and spirituality. 'The English Church', he wrote, 'is most certainly at this day the only substantial representation of Christianity in the genuine Greek spirit.' For this reason he welcomed such links as there were with the Russian Church, and believed that there was a natural affinity between Orthodoxy and Anglicanism.[112] He described himself as being 'somewhat unpuritanic in doctrine ... being much more engaged by the subtle piety of St. Chrysostom, than by the devotional dogmas of St. Austin or any of his followers.'[113] Knox's protégé, Bishop Jebb, shared his enthusiasm for the Greek church: 'I conceive it may be proved that the Greek church has a far greater leaning to us, than to any other,' Jebb wrote, and in the course of another long letter, he cites a whole series of books which he describes as having 'served as a sort of ecclesiastical heralds; especially as far as Greek philosophy and experimental religion are concerned.' The coupling of Greek philosophy and experimental religion is itself interesting, and Jebb goes on to state that he believes 'the Chrysostomian school' can be traced to Philo, 'who was, merely, the patriarch of later Platonism, as it was modified by the Alexandrine eclectics; but, I also think, that Ephrem Syrus, Macarius, and other fathers of the desert, drank deeply of the same fountain; through them Platonism assumed a more mystical form than that of Clement Alexandrinus, Chrysostom, or even Origen himself.'[114]

Christianity could never be for Knox something formal and external, though its rites and ceremonies were significant and important. Like Erskine and McLeod Campbell his understanding of the Atonement was personal and not forensic, and in this too, he was supported by Bishop Jebb. He wrote to Knox that, 'at the era of the Reformation, there was in the protestant church, a springtide in favour of forensic justification; which, perhaps, was, the only counter-action then attainable, to the popish exaggerations of human merit: but which, it must be admitted, threatened to overwhelm the pure and holy principles of communicated righteousness and spiritual regeneration.'[115] Grace was a real communication of the Divine life. As Knox told a correspondent in 1801: 'my definition (of grace) is almost in the same words with Henry Scougal in "The Life of God in the Soul of Man".'[116] The reference to Scougal echoes John Wesley's comment to Knox's father, that 'true religion is not a negative or an external thing, but the life of God in the soul of man, the image of God stamped upon his heart.'[117] It is interesting to note that Knox was an admirer of Bishop Gilbert Burnet, who contributed a preface to the first edition of Scougal in 1677, and observed that the 'class to which Bishop Burnett belonged' had done justice to the cause of inward religion, and had excellently described 'the radical change which the influences of God's grace produce where they are cordially implored and vigilantly improved.'[118] This religion of the heart was the distinguishing mark of Christianity. 'This real and felt influence, this transmutative and regenerative energy,' Knox wrote, 'is the very thing which places Christianity above all philosophy and all mere law': and yet this central concern had been all but abolished by the 'established divines' who explained Christianity as 'little, if anything, more than a system of rules and motives which we are to follow, as far as the frailty of human nature will allow.'[119] Religion is experience, and not speculation'; it consists in 'affection and principle, and not in any theoretical views or opinions.' Hence the object of the Gospel is not to subdue our understandings to the reception of abstract propositions, or intricate dogmas, of whatever kind, but to possess our hearts with penetrating, vital facts; the due impression of which is religion, let a man theorise upon them ever so little.'[120]

In this stress on the importance of inward religion Knox is, as he acknowledged, the heir of Wesley, and it is remarkable how many of the spiritual writers, such as de Sales, Fénelon, Madame Guyon, á Kempis, de Renty, and Nicole, which Professor Orcibal has shown as having had a powerful influence on Wesley, are also commended and discussed by Knox, particularly in his correspondence with Jebb.[121] Like Wesley, Knox discovered Poiret's compendious *Bibliotheca Mysticorum*.[122] He also knew Henry Brooke, the nephew of the author of *The Fool of Quality* and a man in contact with many students of mysticism, and visited him on his deathbed.[123] Like Wesley also Knox's appreciation of the mystics was a cautious one. John Wesley can describe the mystics as 'those poisonous writers', but can at the same time urge that the greatest thing of all is 'the religion of the heart; the religion which Kempis, Pascal, Fénelon enjoyed: that life of God in the soul of man, the walking with God and having fellowship with the Father and the Son.'[124] On the one hand he appreciated the mystics because they were convinced of the centrality of the life of prayer; on the other he was all too well aware that many of their writings were religiously solipsistic and idiosyncratic, and could inculcate an elitist view of Christianity that had little regard for the ordinances of the Church. He liked to contrast 'the plain religion of the Bible' with the 'refined' religion of Mysticism.[125] So Knox can be appreciative of the mystics, and particularly catholic ones, and also critical. Mysticism was valuable as a counterpoise to dogmatism, and in the Church of Rome it had been of particular importance in acting as a leaven in respect of scholasticism. ('Roman Catholic pietism,' Knox observed, 'had a very methodistical turn; looking for raptures and collapses, . . . gushes of joy, which possibly, could not be analyzed.')[126] In dogmatics, Knox believed, reason had acted too much without love, whereas in the mystics all too often love had acted without reason, and he cited his hero, Chrysostom, as a supreme example of one who had maintained the balance.[127] As he wrote to Jebb:

Much as I value the use mystics have been, I own, I no more relish *them* for myself on the one hand, than I do *calvinists* on the other . . . *we* belong to neither class; neither creep with dogmatists, nor soar, with mystics. By the way, are not the predestinarian class the same transcendentalists on the philosophy of Aristotle, that the mystics are in that of Plato? And have they not both, in their several ways, been efficient out-guards, the one of truth, the other of love?[128]

Jebb replied that he recognised this distinction between Aristotelian philosophy, which frequently went 'as far as precise definition, accurate discrimination, and subtle reasoning can go', and the 'nameless charm' of platonism, 'which makes us feel and love virtue.'[129]

Jebb continued Knox's cautious appreciation of the mystics, welcoming their stress on inward religion, critical of their individualism. In 1830 he endeavoured to provide a manual of balanced spirituality by publishing *Piety without asceticism, or the Protestant Kempis,* which contained selections from Scougal, Charles How, and Cudworth. Amongst those who received this appreciatively was the Episcopal Church in America, which issued an American edition of this, as of Jebb's other works. Like other High Churchmen Jebb had made the acquaintance of Bishop Hobart on his visit to England, and later corresponded with Bishop Doane of New Jersey.[130] Some Evangelicals were suspicious. A reviewer in the *Christian Observer,* noting the extensive discussions of mysticism in the published correspondence of Knox and Jebb, commented that 'Protestant Kempism and refined Popery mean nearly the same thing: a sort of pious mysticism, not, grounded upon clear views of the Evangelical economy.'[131]

Jebb and Knox, however, both had a warm appreciation of Evangelicalism, particularly for much of Wesley's teaching, as we have noted, and also for the piety of the Clapham Sect. Jebb told his biographer that it was to Wilberforce's *Practical View* that he 'owed his *first* personal impressions of experimental religion.'[132] They both corresponded quite extensively with Hannah More, whose *Practical Piety* (subtitled *The Influence of the Religion of the Heart on the Conduct of the Life)* reveals many similar emphases to those found in the teaching of Jebb and Knox. The religion which Hannah More seeks to commend 'is not a religion of forms, and modes, and decencies.' 'It is being transformed into the image of God. It is being like-minded with Christ.' The religion of the heart, she writes, 'has been the support and consolation of the pious believer in all ages of the Church', even though 'it has been perverted by both the cloystered and the un-cloystered mystic, not merely to promote abstraction of mind, but inactivity of life.' The distortions of 'dry speculatists' and 'frantic enthusiasts' ought not to stand in the way of an appreciation of the centrality of the spiritual life, and a remarkably catholic list of those who recognised this is given: Horne, Porteus, Beveridge, Hooker, Taylor, Herbert, Hopkins, Leighton, Usher, Howe, Doddridge, Baxter, Jewell and Hooper, not to mention the Reformers and the Fathers, amongst whom she singles out Knox's representative figures, Augustine and Chrysostom.[133] In one of her letters to Knox she mentions an encounter with a High Churchman 'of the Daubenian school', 'a very respectable correct man' who, nevertheless had an 'unrelenting hatred of those writers whom it is the fashion to call evangelical: but which you and I had rather distinguish by the name of spiritual.'

> When I spoke of spiritual religion, and the sort of writers whom I thought likely to promote it, he declared he had never read one devotional book. I ventured to recommend Pascal upheld as his reputation is by mathematics on one side and brilliant wit on the other, and Nicole, whose strength of argument I hoped might gain some quarter for his serious piety; but he will soon find out that talents will not cover the multitude of sins which their spirituality involves and that Jansenism is but methodism in French.[134]

In a later letter to Knox, Hannah More admits that she read 'a portion of Nicole, or some other good Jansenist' each day, and that this devotional reading had led her to take a much more charitable view of the Church of Rome, agreeing with Knox that 'Popery, in spite of its aggregate mass of religious and political mischiefs, has not precluded individual instances of the most sublime and exalted piety,' so much so that 'in that part of religion which comes under the name of devotion, *we* on our side should probably be at a loss to produce instances as numerous and as elevated as the Romish.'[135]

Although Jebb and Knox were prepared to describe Hannah More, William Wilberforce, Henry Thornton and their friends, as 'the best people and the best school in England', this did not mean theological agreement.[136] There were other matters to be taken into account, which did not figure largely in the theology of the Clapham Sect, most particularly a stress on tradition, and on the importance of the Fathers as embodying in an authoritative way both Christian doctrine and Christian spirituality. Knox stated that he was 'a Christian of the first three centuries as respects the Catholic Church of Christ', though 'a Christian of the seventeenth century' as respects Anglicanism.[137] Jebb wrote that he saw the Fathers as 'a great treasury of spiritual wisdom,' and he gave a warm welcome to Routh's *Reliquiae Sacrae*.[138] He applauded Routh's preface:

He shows that those foreigners, who vilify Christian antiquity, not only neglect and deride the fathers, but even attack the Scripture itself, describing its books as of uncertain origin; denying that they contain a rule of faith; and reducing all necessary beliefs to the bare and dry limits of moral precepts.

Routh's work promised a school of Christian antiquity 'altogether different from that of Michaelis and March.'[139]

Jebb in particular devoted himself to an exposition of the Anglican reverence for the church of the Fathers in an important appendix to a volume of his sermons published in 1815.[140] Jebb notes that Mosheim had described the English Church as 'that correction of the old religion, which separates the Britons equally from the Roman Catholics, and from the other communitites who have renounced the Pope.'[141] Part of this distinctive character arises from the refusal to follow the Church of Rome in fettering the judgment 'by implicit submission to authority', or the foreign reformed churches which gave 'unbounded licence to the fancy, by the unrestricted exercises of private interpretation.'

Our national Church inculcates a liberal, discriminative, yet undeviating reverence for pious antiquity: a reverence, alike sanctioned by reason inspired by feeling, and recommended by authority. This principle, is, in truth, our special Characteristic a principle, which has ever enabled our Church to combine discursiveness, with consistency; freedom of enquiry with orthodoxy of belief; and vigorous good sense with primitive and elevated piety.[142]

Whilst Scripture alone is the source of all necessary Christian doctrine, it is important that it should be studied with 'the concurrent sense of the Church Catholic.' This both supplies appropriate assistance in matters of interpretation, and gives guidance where Scripture is silent. The 'subordinate reverence' of Anglicanism for 'pious antiquity' is clearly witnessed to, Jebb argues, by the liturgy, the Elizabethan Act setting up the Court of High Commission, and the canon of 1571 laying down the rule of doctrine to be observed by public preachers. The liturgy, he notes, is 'derived ...for the most part from the actual forms,' and is 'accordant ...in all parts with the spirit and feeling, of Christian antiquity,' and this is explicitly acknowledged in the preface to the Book of Common Prayer, with its reference to the 'godly and decent order of the ancient Fathers. Anglicans, moreover, have always maintained that the standard of worship is the standard of faith. The commissioners set up to restrain heresy were ordered to test doctrine not only by the authority of Scripture, but by the decisions of the first four councils, and the decisions of any other council 'founded on the express and plain words of holy Scripture.' The canon of 1571 laid down that the rule of doctrine was not the text of Scripture alone, but doctrine deduced therefrom by the Catholic Fathers and the ancient bishops.[143] Episcopacy is the guarantee of this public unity of doctrine with that of the primitive church.[144] In contrast with the Anglican position the continental Protestant churches appeared to wish to divest the church of all authority. 'By sending the candidate for Christian instruction to the Bible alone' in effect they oblige 'every man to begin anew for himself.' Likewise the principle of interpreting Scripture only by itself could all too frequently lead to a neglect of the deeper passages.

Simple truths are simply expressed; majestic truths, are clothed in appropriate majesty of language; and mysterious truths, are invested with that sacred veil, which they alone may penetrate, who are at once illuminated by Christian grace, animated by Christian love, and regulated by Christian humility.[145]

This parallels the Tractarian emphasis that only the pure in heart can see God, and that there is a necessary reserve in the communication of knowledge about holy things demanding holiness of those who would approach God. 'Where the less appropriate and peculiar part of revelation,' Jebb suggests, has been made 'the limits of the rest, the system commonly terminates in Socinianism.' The Church of England has only been preserved from this because of its appeal to Catholic consent.[146]

Jebb cites with approval the Vincentian canon of doctrine, as that which has been believed always, everywhere, and by all, and these criteria of the universality, antiquity and consent of the Catholic and Apostolic Church provide contemporary Christians with a reliable standard of doctrine. It means that the 'integrity of the whole must be preferred to the corruption of a part, antiquity to novelty; (and) in antiquity decrees of councils to rashness of individuals.'[147] This reverence for antiquity does not mean that the Church of England agrees with the Church of Rome in acknowledging two sources of doctrine: scripture and tradition. The authority of tradition for Anglicans is secondary and interpretative; Catholic antiquity assists, and does not supersede, the faculty of private judgement.

The appeal to antiquity is directed against innovation, and Vincent's object in laying down his canon is, as a Catholic Christian, to 'fix our view on the Christian cloud of witnesses.' In doctrine as in devotion the Christian belongs to the communion of saints. The Protestant communions have failed to reverence antiquity; the Church of Rome has usurped the place that should be given to Catholic consent; the Church of England 'has adopted a middle course; moving in the same delightful path, and treading in the same hallowed footsteps, with Vincentius, and the Catholic bishops, and the ancient Fathers.'[148] 'This retrospective unity with the Church of old', Jebb goes on to argue, 'is the only solid ground for present unity with contemporaries, and for prospective unity with the Church progressive upon earth, and consummate in heaven.'[149] That Anglicans have in practice had regard to catholic consent and the teaching of the primitive church Jebb shows both by citing the restoration of a commemoration of the departed at the end of the prayer for the church in the Prayer Book of 1662, and by referring to representative Anglican divines, such as Ridley, Jewel, Overall, Hall, Mede, Beveridge, Hammond, Bull and Leslie. He concludes by summarising the Anglican position:

> It is not, merely his own judgment; it is not by any means the dictatorial mandate of an ecclesiastical dictator, which is to silence his scruples, and dissolve his doubts. His resort is, that concurrent, universal, and undeviating sense of pious antiquity, which he has been instructed, and should be encouraged, to embrace, to follow and revere.[150]

Knox shared the view of tradition defended by Jebb in this important discussion, as he acknowledged in a letter of 1826, in which he refers to the Vincentian canon as of great significance for the rebuttal of 'the extravagant doctrine of tradition taught by the Church of Rome,'[151] The Church of Rome, Knox maintained, had only been prepared to appeal to the Vincentian Canon just so long as it suited its purpose, and had in practice made antiquity subservient to the authority of the contemporary church.[152]

When Jebb's article appeared it was criticised in both the *Christian Observer* and the *Anti-Jacobin Review*. The *Christian Observer* maintained that to make tradition a necessary guide for the interpretation of Scripture would have the consequence that only the learned who were able to compare Scripture and antiquity would be able to read Scripture.[153] Another correspondent claimed that Jebb had misrepresented the position of the continental Reformed churches, by understating 'the degree of respect and deference they profess for the authority of pious antiquity,' as evidenced, for instance, by the reformed confessions of faith. Despite differences of order, the writer claimed, the continental confessions both acknowledge the importance of the visible church, and look back on the church of antiquity as at one with themselves.[154] Jebb replied that the 'Socinianism' of so many foreign professors of theology hardly indicated such a reverence for the authority of catholic antiquity as was claimed.[155] He exemplified his position further, in response to the strictures of the *Anti-Jacobin Review,* in a letter to his friend, Dr. Nash:

> The truth is, that we would guard against the abuse of human authority, more cautiously, than the advocates of private judgement. With them, we reject the domination of the Pope; but we do not, with them, erect 5,000 Popes in his room; and the voice of *antiquity, universality* and *consent,* to which we listen, we take not to be the voice of man, but the voice of God; speaking that, by his providence and gracious guidance of the minds of men in all ages, which no private individual, nor any contemporary body of witnesses, could, of their own wisdom, be competent to pronounce, or to discover.[156]

Brilioth recognised the importance of this work of Jebb's as an anticipation of the Tractarian concern with the church of the Fathers and with the view of Anglicanism as *Via Media* between Rome and Protestantism. He noted Jebb's influence in this respect on men like W. P. Hook.[157] More recently Professor Louis Allen has shown the extent to which the correspondence between Newman and the Abbé Jager, which had a powerful shaping influence on Newman's *Lectures on the Prophetical Office of the Church,* was concerned with issues first raised by Jebb's article, a copy of which Benjamin Harrison had supplied to Jager.[158] As Allen points out, the controversy raised for Newman the issue of change and development, and it was the working out of this issue which brought him eventually to join the Church of Rome.[159] In Jager's second letter Jebb is challenged on three points. Jager argues first, that St. Paul and the Fathers admit an unwritten tradition; secondly, that Jebb's thesis appears to demand that every Christian is compelled to make a scholarly study of the Fathers in order to arrive at Christian truth – the same point made by the *Christian Observer;* and, thirdly, that the doctrinal decisions of the contemporary church must be seen as having a pastoral intent – they are 'a guide to lead us' and 'a torch to light our way', and do not attempt to set forth anything new.[160]

When Newman took over the correspondence with Jager from Benjamin Harrison in 1834–5 he entered the lists in defence of Jebb, though in both his letters to Jager and in his subsequent *Lectures on the Prophetical Office* he went considerably beyond Jebb's position.[161] Most particularly was this the case in his imaginative distinction between 'Episcopal Tradition' and 'Prophetic Tradition', the Episcopal Tradition being 'the outline of sound words', formally stated and enunciated and delivered from hand to hand, 'a collection of definite articles'; the Prophetic Tradition being as it were the *ethos* of the church, 'a vast system, not to be comprised in a few sentences, not to be embodied in one code or treatise, but consisting of a certain body of Truth, pervading the Church like an atmosphere, irregular in its shape from its very profusion and exuberance'. It is, Newman continues, 'partly written, partly unwritten, partly the interpretation, partly the supplement of Scripture, partly preserved in intellectual expressions, partly latent in the spirit and temper of Christians; poured to and fro in closets and upon the housetops, in liturgies, in controversial works, in obscure fragments, in sermons, in popular prejudices, in local customs.'[162] As Allen has shown this important passage is taken almost verbatim from Newman's second letter to Jager.[163]

Like the Tractarians Knox and Jebb gave a high place to baptism. Knox argues that baptism is certainly to be understood as regeneration, 'when by regeneration is merely meant the relative and circumstantial change implied in becoming a member of Christ's visible church, and a professing subject of his mystical kingdom.'[164] In the case of adult baptism faith is a necessary precondition for this regeneration; in the case of infants baptismal regeneration is to be understood as the implanting of 'a vital germ of all virtuous dispositions, and pious affections', which if 'sincerely, however weakly, obeyed and guarded,' will continue and grow. But such baptismal grace may in fact be lost, for, Knox continues, 'it would be as reasonable to maintain, that he, who was once possessed of piety and righteousness, must still possess them, after having apostasised into irreligion and profligacy, as to assert, that spiritual regeneration ...should continue, after spiritual and animal wickedness has become predominant in the heart and life.' Baptismal regeneration cannot be represented as a merely external matter.[165] So, likewise, Jebb insists that in baptism 'we behold the divine seed, the essential elements, the ensured progress of our inward Christianity', and the grace so received is continued in the Eucharist.

In Baptism, we originally received this gift of God: by the Sacrament of the Lord's Supper, the gift then received is renewed, enlarged, confirmed, strengthened, perfected. By Baptismal Grace we first became, properly, Temples of the Holy Ghost: by the Grace of the Eucharist we are made special temples, also, of the Son: an habitation meet for the whole three Persons of the ever-blessed Trinity.[166]

Growth in grace is the manifestation of the Christian's baptism.[167]

In the same way the church must be seen not as 'a simple accumulation of individuals', but as a 'regulated society, an organized body; preserving through successive ages, its identity of essence and unity of spirit.' And members of the church, and above all its ministers, must be marked by 'a spirit of prayer' and 'a spirit of devotedness to God.' It is a real, and not an unreal, righteousness with which the Christian is concerned.

The Fathers were by no means satisfied, either with an imaginary, or merely outward, righteousness: they sought after a real, an intrinsic change. It was not enough, that a man should be *accounted* just; he must really *be made so*. And, while all self-fabricated righteousness was unequivocally discarded, the righteousness of God, the righteousness communicated by God, was invariably described, not as notional, but as solid, substantial, and proceeding from that Spirit which giveth inward life.[168]

It is the same emphasis and concern that we find in Newman's *Lectures on Justification,* in which he argues that justifying faith 'is not ...a shadow or phantom, which flits about without voice or power ...not a mere impression, or gleam upon the soul, or knowledge, or emotion, or conviction, which ends with itself, but the beginning of that which is eternal, the operation of the Indwelling Power which acts from within outwards and round about, works in us so mightily, so intimately with our will as to be in a true sense one with it.'[169] A merely imputed righteousness belonged in Newman's view to a shadowy, visionary system, which had the effect of abolishing sacraments 'to introduce barren and dead ordinances; and for the real participation of Christ, and justification through His Spirit, would, at the very marriage feast, feed us on shells and husks, who hunger and thirst after righteousness.[170]

Because Jebb believed that men were led to this inward reality by a sacramental way, he was careful to insist upon the care of churches and the reverent performance of services in his diocese of Limerick.

Those to be ordained were examined on their knowledge of the Liturgy, and their ability to read the services, which were to be read with 'a chastened hilarity'. There was to be no slovenliness in the conduct of worship; all clergy were to have decent black gowns, and beneficed clergy who were MA's scarves and tippets in addition. He encouraged the building of vestries to avoid the common situation of the clergyman walking up the aisle 'in spattered boots' and robing 'in the reading-desk before the people.'[171] Not only theologically, but practically, Jebb anticipated the Tractarians, with their concern for reverence and for the beauty of holiness.

'The great progress of our Church to something deeper and truer than satisfied the last century' noted by Newman in 1899, we can now see to have been rooted in the fertile seed-bed prepared by the older High Churchmen of the Hackney Phalanx, and the Hutchinsonian divines, not to mention the creative theology of Alexander Knox and Bishop Jebb. The Tractarians did not simply take over this inheritance for they took issue at some important points with the representatives of this tradition. But we misunderstand the significance of the Oxford Movement if view it in isolation from these earlier High Churchmen, and from the search in the context of disestablished Anglican churches in Scotland and America, for Anglican identity. We misunderstand it also if we regard it as concerned solely with the re-affirmation of certain doctrines about the church and sacraments, without seeing that re-affirmation as also being a re-discovery of Catholic spirituality; and this again we find anticipated in these precursors of Tractarianism.

Notes

1   J. H. Newman, *A letter addressed to the Revd. R. W. Jelf, D. D ...in explanation of the Ninetieth Tract in the series called Tracts for the Times.* (1841), *The Via Media of the Anglican Church* 2 vols (first published in this form in 1877; edition of London, 1891) II, p. 386.

2   R. H. Froude, *Remains,* (1838)

3   *Tracts for the Times,* Tract I, (1833), pp. 1–2.

4   q. in J. E. Pinnington, 'Anglican Reactions to the Challenge of a multi-confessional Society with special reference to British North America, 1760–1830' (unpublished D. Phil. dissertation, University of Oxford, 1975), p. 565.

5   N. U. Murray, 'The Influences of the French Revolution on the Church of England and its rivals, 1789–1802' (unpublished D. Phil. dissertation, University of Oxford, 1975), p.55

6   William Jones in 1793, q. J. Freeman, *Life of the Rev. William Kirby, M.A.,* (1852), pp. 43–44.

7   Murray, p. 4.

8   See R. Spearman, *Life of J. Hutchinson,* prefixed to *A Supplement to the Works of John Hutchinson, Esq.,* (1765).

9   *The Philosophical and Theological Works of John Hutchinson, Esq.,* (1748 edition), I, p. xvi. Hutchinson's *Works* run to twelve volumes. The copy in the Bodleian Library is that of William Van Mildert.

10 Hutchinson, *Works,* III, p. ix.

11 *W. Jones, Memoirs of the Life, Studies and Writings of the Rt. Revd. George Horne, D. D., late Lord Bishop of Norwich.* (1799 edition). Preface.

12 W. Jones, *Works,* (1801), III, pp. 239–40.

13 p. 242.

14 p. 244.

15 II, p. 116.

16 III, p. 266.

17 p. 330.

18 See T. R. Grimshawe, *A Memoir of the Revd. Legh Richmond, A. M.,* (1828).

19 See James Hervey, *Meditations and Contimplations* (1814).

20 J. Keble, 'On the Mysticism attributed to the early Fathers of the Church', *Tracts for the Times,* LXXXIX, (1841), p. 143.

21 p. 146.

22 p. 148.

23 J. Coulson and A. M. Allchin, *The Rediscovery of Newman: an Oxford Symposium,* (1967), p. 64.

24 pp. 70–71.

25 q. R. C. Selby, *The Principle of Reserve in the Writings of John Henry Cardinal Newman,* (Oxford, 1975), p. 25.

26 J. H. Newman *Fifteen Sermons preached before the University of Oxford between A.D. 1826 and 1843,* (1872). pp. 27–28.

27 J. H. Newman, *Parochial and Plain Sermons,* (1873), II, pp. 74–75.

28 Couslon and Allchin, p. 69 n.: R. Murray, *Symbols of Church and Kingdom: a study in early Syriac tradition,* (Cambridge, 1975), pp. 346–347.

29 Jones, *Works,* II, p. 70.

30 I, pp. lxxxv–lxxxvi, xciii–xciv.

31 T. Sikes, *A Discourse on Parochial Communion,* (1812), p. v.

32 E. Churton, *Memoir of Joshua Watson,* (1861), I, p. 52.

33 Jones, *Works,* IV, pp. 389–90.

34 Horne MSS., Magdalen College, Oxford, f.38. Letter of 7 June 1792 from William Jones to Mrs Horne.

35 Jones, *Works,* IV, pp. 402–3.

36 *Life of Kirby,* p. 125.

37 J. A. Park, *Memoirs of the late William Stevens, Esq., Treasurer of Queen Anne's Bounty,* (1859 edition), p. 106; see also, W. Stevens, *Treatise on the Nature and Constitution of the Christian Church,* 1772.

38 J. McVic(k)ar, *The Early Life and Professional Years of Bishop Hobart,* (Oxford, 1838), p. iii (from the preface by W. F. Hook).

39 Jones, *Works,* IV, pp. 452–53.

40 III, pp. 404–405.

41 pp. 416–417.

42 Churton, I, p. 73.

43 W. Van Mildert, *An Inquiry into the General Principles of Scriptural Interpretation,* (Oxford, 1815), pp. 225–227.

44 See Coulson and Allchin, pp. 69–70.

45 T. Sikes, *Discourse,* p. 3.

46 pp. 5, 9.

47   p. 127; see also, *A Dialogue between a minister of the Church and his parishioner concerning the Christian's liberty of choosing his teacher,* (1802 edition).

48   Van Mildert, pp. 151–152.

49   Jones, *Memoir of Horne*, pp. 71–74. Horne published *A Caution to the Readers of Mr Law.* It should also be noted that John Wesley was strongly critical of many aspects of Law's teaching as is evident from a number of entries in his journal and letters.

50   *The Autobiography of Isaac Williams,* B. D., edited by George Prevost, (1892), p. 28.

51   Other works of interest preserved in John Keble's library at Keble College, Oxford, include the following; John Locke, *Works* (apparently a prize from Keble's undergraduate days); Jeremy Taylor, *Works;* Sir Walter Scott, *Marmion; Ballads; The Lay of the Last Minstrel;* Archbishop King, *Essay on Evil?* John Milton, *Prose Works;* John Jebb, *Burnet's Lives and Characters;* Alexander Knox, *Remains;* William Wilberforce, *A Practical View;* Tasso, *Gerussaleme Liberate;* John Milton, *Paradise Lost and Re-gained* (a gift from G. J. Cornish in 1818); *Eikon Basilike* (a gift from George Prevost); Waterland, *Works;* Bishop Horne, *Works; A Manual for the Parish Priest* (1815); George herbert, *Poems;* George Hodder, *Works;* Richard Baxter, *A Treatise of Knowledge and Love;* E. Sparke, *vel Scintilla Altaris, Primitive Devotions in the Feasts and Fasts;* William Beveridge, *Sermons.* So far as can be ascertained most of these works belonged to Keble before 1833 – with one or two exceptions of works such as Knox's Remains.

52   Froude, *Remains,* I, pp. 202–203, 336–337.

53   William Law, *Works,* (Brockenhurst, privately reprinted, 1892), I, p. 9; q. in Hook's preface to McVic(k)ar's *Life of Hobart,* pp. x–xi.

54   Y. Brilioth, *The Anglican Revival, studies in the Oxford Movement (London, 1925).*

55   J. H. Hobart, *A Companion for the Altar, or Week's Preparation for the Holy Communion,* (New York, 1804), pp. 205, 207.

56   pp. 202–203.

57   W. E. Wyatt cited in *The Correspondence of J. H. Hobart,* edited by A. Lowndes, *Archives of the General Convention,* (1911), I, p. clxix.

58   W. Berrian, *The posthumous Works of the late Rt. Revd. John Henry Hobart, D.D . . . with a memoir of his life,* (New York, 1833 edition), II (Sermons), pp. 13–14.

59   pp. 21–22.

60   Hobart, *Companion to the Altar,* p. 202.

61   Berrian, I, p. 92. Written when Hobart was working on the *Companion to the Altar.*

62   I, p. 181.

63   *The Correspondence of J. H. Hobart,* III, p. 340.

64   J. McVic(k)ar, *Life of Hobart,* III, p. 340.

65   p. 262.

66   p. 464; Berrian, I, pp. 319–320.

67   Berrian, I, pp. 350–351.

68   Churton, I, p. 244.

69   W. R. W. Stephens, *The Life and Letters of Walter Farquhar Hook, D.D., F.R.S.,* (London 1878), D. W. F. Forrester, 'The Intellectual Development of E. B. Pusey, 1800–1850' (Unpublished D. Phil. disertation, University of

Oxford, 1977), p. 288. Letter of 31 December 1823; Berrian, I, pp. 292–293. Cf. *Life of Hook,* I, pp. 100–101, for his endeavours to meet Bishop Hobart.

70 *The Letters and Diaries of John Henry Newman,* edited by ...Ian Ker and Thomas Gornall, S.J., I, (Oxford, 1978), p. 173.

71 Berrian, I, p. 235.

72 Stephens, *Life of Hook,* I, pp. 72–73; M. Lochhead, *Episcopal Scotland in the 19th Century,* 1966, pp. 42–44; Berrian, I, pp. 288–289.

73 Park, *Memoir of Stevens;* Stephens, *Life of Hook,* I, p. 71 and pp. 64–65, where Hook's extensive reading list is given.

74 Stephens, Life of Hook I, p. 79.

75 W. Perry, *Alexander Penrose Forbes: Bishop of Brechin, the Scottish Pusey,* (1939), p. 55. But see also the comment of Maning: 'We got out of the boat at the Reformation, but I am not going to get out of the boat into a tub.'

76 Forrester, p. 300.

77 Manning to Strachan, 18 October 1847. Ontario Archives (Strachan papers), q. Pinnington, p. 262.

78 Churton, II, p. 99.

79 II, p. 103, Letter of 1841.

80 J. Fingard, *The Anglican Design in Loyalist Nova Scotia, 1783–1816,* (1972), p. 145. Letter of Inglis to Gaskin, 1814.

81 p. 80; O. W. Jones, *Isaac Williams and his circle,* (1971), pp. 16–17.

82 q. E. R. Fairweather, 'A Tractarian Patriarch: John Medley of Fredericton', *Canadian Journal of Theology,* VI, (1960), p. 26.

83 J. W. Burgon, *Lives of Twelve Good Men,* (1888), I, pp. 154–155.

84 Biographical Sketches in: *The Club of Nobody's Friends: a biographical list of the members since its foundation 21 June 1800 to September 1885,* (privately printed, 1935), 2 Volumes. Molesworth refers to 'the Canterbury party' surrounding Howley as including Rose, Molesworth, Lonsdale, and Mill. 'All these were working together on the lines of the pre-Jacobite Church.' (*History of the Church of England from 1660,* (18??), p. 317).

85 G. T. Stokes, 'Alexander Knox and the Oxford Movement', *Contemporary Review,* LII, (1887), pp. 182–205. See also Brilioth, pp. 331–333.

86 J. H. Newman, *Lectures on Justification,* 1828, p. 396 (in the 1874 edition).

87 A. Mozley, *Letters and correspondence of John Henry Newman during his life in the English Church,* (1891), II, p. 93. See also H. Coulson, *Newman and the Common Tradition: a study in the language of church and society,* (Oxford, 1970), pp. 58, 254–255.

88 D. Newsome, *The Parting of Friends: a study of the Wilberforces and Henry Manning,* (1966), p. 197.

89 J. T. Coleridge *A Memoir of the Rev. John Keble, M.A.,* (1869), pp.??

90 Mozley, II, p. 133. Benjamin Harrison to J. H. Newman, 3 October 1835; H. P. Liddon, *Life of Edward Bouverie Pusey,* I, (London, 1893–97), pp. ??

91 *Guardian,* 7 September 1887.

92 *Remains of Alexander Knox, Esq.,* (1836 edition), II, pp. 154–285, (including a prefatory letter to J. S. Harford and a postscript).

93 A Härdelin, *The Tractarian Understanding of the Eucharist,* Uppsala, (1965), p. 126.

94 Knox, *Remains,* II, p. 155.

95 p. 233.

96 p. 233–4.

97 p. 220.

98   p. 414.

99   pp. 415–416.

100 p. 426. Knox wrote to Bishop Jebb that the Eucharistic elements were 'the actual elements thro' wh. (the) blessing is conveyed', and he speaks of the 'analogical equivalence of the Christian Eucharist and the Israelitish ark.' (*Thirty years Correspondence between John Jebb . . . and Alexander Knox,* edited by C. Forster, (1834), II, p. 357).

101 pp. 432–433.

102 IV, p. 311.

103 *Jebb-Knox Correspondence,* II, p. 502.

104 Knox, *Remains,* III, pp. lxi–lxii.

105 p. lxx.

106 pp. xcv, xcvii, xcix.

107 pp. 77–78.

108 p. 27.

109 pp. 129, 135–136.

110 p. 138.

111 p. 145.

112 III, pp. 211–212.

113 IV, pp. 206–207.

114 *Jebb-Knox Correspondence,* I, pp. 350, 301–302.

115 pp. 369–370.

116 Knox, *Remains,* IV, p. 81.

117 *The Letters of John Wesley,* edited by J. Telford, (1931), IV, p. 302, 30 May 1765.

118 Knox, *Remains,* IV, p. 145; G. D. Henderson, *Mystics of the North-East,* (Aberdeen, 1934, published for the Third Spalding Club), p. 13.

119 Knox, *Remains,* IV, pp. 127, 145.

120 pp. 458, 209.

121 See J. Orcibal, 'The Theological Originality of John Wesley' in *A History of the Methodist Church in Great Britain,* edited by R. Davies and G. Rupp, I, (1965), pp. 83–111.

122 In 1806. *Jebb-Knox Correspondence,* I, p. 270.

123 I, p. 263 & N. For Brooke see Desiree Hirst, *Hidden Riches: Traditional Symbolism from the Renaissance to Blake,* (1964), pp. 227ff.

124 Wesley, *Letters,* VIII, p. 218. (To Samuel Wesley, 29 April 1790).

125 VI, p. 233.

127 *Jebb-Knox Correspondence,* I, p. 278.

128 I, p. 285.

129 pp. 283–284.

130 C. Forster, *The Life of John Jebb, D.D., F.R.S.,* (London, 1837) pp. ??

131 *Christian Observer,* 1837.

132 *Life of Jebb,* pp. 303–304.

133 H. More, *Practical Piety: or, the Influence of the Religion of the Heart on the Conduct of the Life,* (1811), I. pp. 12–13.

134 W. Roberts, *Memoirs of the Life and Correspondence of Mrs Hannah More,* (London, 1834), III, pp. ??

135 pp. 304–305.

136 *Jebb-Knox Correspondence,* II, pp. 104–105; See also *Life of Jebb,* p. 468; Churton, II, p. 83.

137 Knox, *Remains,* III, p. cxiii.

138 *Life of Jebb,* p. 523; *Jebb-Knox Correspondence,* II, p. 260.
139 It was reprinted in 1839 by Francis Huyshe as *A Tract for All Times, but most eminently for the present.*
140 Jebb, *Sermons on subjects chiefly practical, (1815).*
141 Jebb, *Sermons,* p. 357.
142 p. 357.
143 p. 359.
144 p. 362.
145 pp. 364–365.
146 p. 367.
147 p. 375.
148 p. 378.
149 p. 381.
150 p. 398.
151 Knox, *Remains,* IV, p. 463.
152 III, pp. 322–333.
153 Christian Observer, (1816), XV, p. 655.
154 pp. 421, 490ff., 556.
155 XVI, (1817), pp. 78–91.
156 *Life of Jebb,* p. 529.
157 Brilioth, pp. 54–55.
158 L. Allen, *John Henry Newman and the Abbe Jager; a controversy on Scripture and Tradition (1834–1836),* (1975), pp. 4–6.
159 p. 12.
160 pp. 22–24.
161 p. 34.
162 J. H. Newman, *The Via Media of the Anglican Church,* (1891 edition), I, pp. 249, 250. (A reprint of the *Lectures on the Prophetical Office*).
163 Allen, pp. 94–95.
164 Knox, *Remains,* I, p. 490.
165 pp. 514–515 – but see the comments of W. F. Hook. (*Life of Hook).*
166 *Jebb, Practical Theology, (1830),* pp. 94, 105.
167 See S. Tugwell, *Did you receive the Spirit?* (1971), pp. 50ff.
168 Newman, *Lectures on Justification,* p. 343–344, 356–357.
169 Newman, *Lectures on Justification,* pp. 343–344.
170 p. 63
171 Jebb, *Practical Theology,* pp. 372, 376–377, 407.

The Ecclesiology of the Oxford Movement: a Reconsideration

Sheridan Gilley

There is a convention of beginning modern history with the French Revolution in 1789, when a new kind of popular politics made the first decisive challenge to the social and spiritual order of the *ancien régime,* a regime built upon the triple pillars of a monarchy, an aristocracy and an Established Church. The odd thing about English history, however, was that until Jonathan Clark published his book on eighteenth-century England a few years ago,[1] the historiography of the period usually stressed the liberal and Whiggish aspect of the Augustan era in England, and the degree to which English society was rationalist and enlightened, and unlike the continental norm. Dr. Clark attempted a bold reversion of such emphases to the extent of defining the dominant ideology of Georgian England as Trinitarian orthodoxy, with the Established Church as the principal source of values and sanction of social and political order in continuity with a tradition going back to the conversion of the nation to Christianity. Clark's argument has an obvious plausibility when it is considered that the three eighteenth-century pillars of monarchy, aristocracy and church establishment have probably more completely survived in England than in any other European country. Indeed for all the destruction of a traditional Catholicism from above in the sixteenth century, it could be argued that the English are among the most conservative people in Europe; a people among whom the Tory Party, with a clear continuous history going back to the seventeenth century, seems to possess an inbuilt majority. This survival has much to do with the strength and vigour of the English reaction against the whole revolutionary idea, a reaction in which Anglican Christianity has played an important part.

Yet the Church of England, like other traditional English institutions, is now deeply troubled, and it is tempting to trace its troubles to the very nineteenth-century movement which did most for its revival. The High Church Oxford Movement began in 1833, under the aegis of John Keble, John Henry Newman and Richard Hurrell Froude, in a conservative reaction against the radical forces, political and religious, which even then seemed to threaten the Church of England's destruction. The crisis of the European confessional state, which began in Paris with the Civil Constitution of the Clergy, had at last reached English shores, as the repeal of the Test and Corporation Acts in 1828 and Catholic Emancipation in 1829 gave Protestant Dissenters and Roman Catholics full rights of membership in the very parliament which had supreme power over the Church. Then in 1830 a new administration of Whigs, successors to decades of rule by Tory Churchmen, seemed poised to reform and to redistribute the Church's ill-distributed properties and possessions. This 'crisis of the Church' continued through the opposition of a number of the bishops in the House of Lords to the Reform Bill passed in 1832, and when the government proposed the abolition of ten useless and overendowed Church of Ireland bishoprics in 1833, the Oxford Professor of Poetry John Keble declared this a National Apostasy.[1]

Yet such a moderate reform seemed long overdue. The second half of the eighteenth century had exacerbated the inequalities of income between rich and poor clergy, making the Church an ever more conservative institution, a precise image of the traditional hierarchical society which it served, especially in its heartlands in the English rural south and midlands. It is true that a large number of Evangelical Protestants, under the aegis of the Clapham Sect, led by William Wilberforce, did much in the generation before 1830 to improve the Church's pastoral witness, while a body of strongly principled High Churchmen, the Hackney Phalanx, had exercised considerable influence on both Church and State during the long Prime Ministership of the Tory Lord Liverpool between 1812 and 1827, when the government voted a million and a half pounds to build new churches. There was, however, a negative side to the Church's close association with the Tory Party and the civil power, in the authority exercised by clerical magistrates and poor law guardians and the closed Anglican Tory corporations which controlled the towns and cities. The number of executions for crime in England attained its peak in 1830, when the proportion of clerical magistrates reached its zenith. Indeed the hostility of radicals to the corruption of a venal State went hand in hand with their hostility to the abuses of simony, pluralism, absenteeism and nepotism in the Church, while there was an increasing disparity between the Church's apparent political power and its diminishing pastoral influence. The notable growth in the number of Protestant Dissenters after 1790, the incursion of pauper Catholics from Ireland into the English slums and the huge increase in the semi-pagan populations of the new northern industrial cities for whom there had been no provision of new priests and churches, had greatly weakened the Church of England's claim to be the Church of the English people, with an authority automatically deriving from the consent of the nation as a whole.

The new High Churchmen in Oxford like Newman and Hurrell Froude were political conservatives with a hearty contempt for majorities, and with an even stronger dislike of the liberalism and rationalism to which they traced the radical utilitarian critique of the Church as a corrupt and worldly institution. Yet they were more than conservatives; in ecclesiastical terms, they were right-wing radicals who transformed the very tradition that they set out to renew. Froude is arguably the nearest thing that the Oxford Movement possessed to a continental radical of the right, and with his affection for the theocratic medieval Church, could be called the Anglican de Maistre or founder of Anglican Ultramontanism. More importantly, Newman's developing polemic from the 1820s against philosophical liberalism and rationalism has been a main pillar of Anglican theological orthodoxy ever since; and indeed his views collided head on with the liberal rationalism which was even then emerging among churchmen. Indeed Newman argued that because the Church was a divine society and not merely a human one, it was not to be judged by merely liberal or rational criteria; while against the State's attempt to reform or despoil the Church, he and Keble appealed to the Church's God-given independent authority from her foundation by Christ, as the Catholic Church in England.

In this Newman and Keble were heirs to a High Church tradition going back to the sixteenth century, which saw the Church of England as a true part of the Church Catholic, holding fast to the teachings of the Scriptures and the ancient Fathers. It was thought to be the special virtue of the Church of England among the major Churches of the Reformation to have retained a valid Catholic sacramental order and ordinances through her providential preservation of an Apostolic Succession of bishops, in an unbroken chain from the age of the Apostles; from that succession there came the Church's claim to a continuity of apostolic teaching and ministry divinely guaranteeing her sacramental and spiritual life. The doctrine is sometimes ridiculed as the 'drain pipe theory', of grace coming down from the apostles as through a drain pipe; it was, however, the Church's assurance of its living organic link through its ministers to its crucified Lord. In the words of one old High Churchman, the Church of England was 'essentially Catholic as being on all vital points of constitution, doctrine, and practice in harmony with the primitive Church, and on the other hand essentially Protestant, as opposed to the pretensions of the Papal power and to the corruption in teaching and practice of the Middle Ages.'[2]

This old High Church view was as militantly hostile to the English Dissenting Churches, Congregationalist, Baptist, Quaker and Methodist, as it was anti-Roman Catholic. Dissenters did not have Churches or valid sacraments as they did not have an Apostolic Succession, while Roman Catholics, though having an Apostolic Succession and valid sacraments, had fallen short of the purity of the Church of England by their corruptions. This was the basis of an ecclesiology older than Newman's *via media,* that the Church of England, is a Protestant and Catholic body which lies midway between popery and radical Protestantism or Dissenting Puritanism. Its obvious attraction and defect is that it presumes that the Church of England is the ideal Church, being manifestly superior to the corrupt Greek and Roman Churches, and to all those other Protestant bodies which lack an Apostolic Succession of bishops and are not really or fully Churches. Moreover the theory has the oddity of declaring the Greek and Roman Churches outside Britain to be true Churches though corrupt; and denies that Protestant or Dissenting Churches are Churches, however pure. Some thought that Sweden and Denmark might have true Churches, and that the Lutherans were not at least originally to blame for their loss of episcopal order, seventeenth-century High Churchmen acknowledging that there was some merit in German or Genevan silver, though these were inferior to Anglican episcopal gold. Yet even by 1790, the High Church tradition had generally come to the view that the episcopate was part of the *esse* or being or essence of the Church, not simply a part of its *bene esse;* and that the rule was no bishop, no church. Or, as the hoary anti-episcopal Anglo-Catholic joke has it, bishops are part of the *esse* of the Church, but not its *bene esse.* There is no obvious reason except English national smugness and the English suspicion that God was an Englishman why England should have been so graced with the *only* major true and pure Church in Christendom. But in accepting the theory, the Oxford Movement men arguably acted upon it with more consistency than their High Church predecessors, by doing what High Churchmen had generally not done, declaring that in possessing bishops, the Church of England was Catholic and not Protestant; so that as Newman put it, the Anglican *via media* was not the old High Anglican Protestant middle way between popery and radical Protestantism or

Puritanism; rather Anglicanism properly understood was a middle way between popery and Protestantism itself.

Here, it seems to me, lies the heart of the matter: Newman's redefinition of an older *via media* out of a repudiation of the Church of England's Protestant inheritance. He awakened the Church of England from the condition in which it could blithely assume that it was both Protestant and Catholic, by asking the question of identity which has plagued it ever since; is it essentially Catholic *or* Protestant *or* Liberal? The points were connected, for Newman thought that the Protestant doctrine of *sola scriptura* led inevitably to the liberalism which denied the authority of Scripture altogether, a point which seems to me to be proven by New Testament scholars daily. The Protestant rule of *sola scriptura* implies either an absolutisation of the book's authority in fundamentalism, or a denial of its authority in liberalism, or the discovery of its true interpreter in Catholicism. It was Newman's genius, in the very different words of a recent liberal Anglican writer, to insist 'that Anglicans cannot claim exemption from the sociological rule which determines that authoritative texts require authoritative interpreters', that the Thirty-Nine Articles and Ordinal give this authority to the Church, 'and that it pertains particularly to the episcopate.'[3] With that conclusion, and the rejection of *sola scriptura,* the days of High Anglican Protestantism were numbered.

Newman's rejection of Protestantism, however, was bound to precipitate controversy between the Oxford Movement men and both old High Churchmen who still thought themselves Protestant, and the Evangelicals, of whom Newman had been one, and who were to grow in power and influence in the Church of England at least until the 1870s. Moreover the new High Churchmen were in conflict with something much more fundamental, the folk-Protestantism of the English people, whose religion was essentially the reading of the Bible and little more. Just by calling themselves Catholic rather than Protestant, the Oxford Movement men awakened these folk-fears of Rome; while by setting out to recover the devotional life and discipline of contemporary Catholicism, they seemed to be supplementing rather than interpreting the teaching of their own *Book of Common Prayer*. Their *Tracts for the Times,* issued between 1833 and 1841, won them notoriety as Tractarians, and culminated and concluded in Newman's *Tract 90* in 1841 in which he tried to reconcile some of the Protestant 39 Articles of Religion, the Church's summary of its Protestant faith, with his own conception of Catholicism, and even with some of the teachings of the Council of Trent. Many Protestants distrusted his appeal to the

Fathers, implicit in the new *Library of the Fathers;* many distrusted the appeal to the more Catholic writers of the Anglican tradition, explicit in the new *Library of Anglo-Catholic Theology.* Thus the Oxford Movement was embattled within and without. Internally, it was set against the older Protestant High Churchmen and Evangelicals in the Church, as well as against the liberals. Externally, it was opposed to both Rome and Protestant Dissent.

This was the basis of the polemical feuding which shook the University of Oxford in the 1830s and '40s, which began when Newman and Pusey joined with High Church Protestants and Evangelicals to exclude the liberal Renn Dickson Hampden from an Oxford chair. The liberals discovered, however, that they could cry popery where Newman had cried heresy; and by 1841, and the affair of *Tract 90,* most of the old High Churchmen and Evangelicals and liberals were united against him.

These affairs in the 1830s and '40s seem to me to be the earliest proper rehearsal of the modern condition of the Church, of its threefold division among High Church Anglo-Catholics, Low Church Evangelicals and Broad Church Liberals, in which two of the parties unite in conflict with the third; and I would argue that it does represent a kind of fall from the Church's prelapsarian condition before 1830, in which the dominant school of Protestant High Churchmen, the school of William Howley[4], held together Church and State with the two main streams in the Anglican tradition. In this I believe I am following the work of Dr. Peter Nockles[5]: and of course I do not mean to deny that the Catholic, Protestant and even liberal traditions all in some way go back to the sixteenth century, so that it is not their mere mutual presence which has made Anglicanism an ecclesiological Noah's Ark, containing beasts both clean and unclean. What does seem to me to be novelly early-Victorian is their self-definition as sharply discrete, partisan, even warring positions. Newman and his friends were responsible for the situation in which the older Protestant High Churchmen were increasingly isolated, as Anglican Protestantism became an anti-Anglo-Catholic Evangelicalism, and as High Churchmanship became an anti-Protestant Anglo-Catholicism. It is a further proof of this postlapsarian condition after 1830 that it was in the 1830s that Newman and his friends gave a novel currency to the terms 'Anglicanism' and 'Anglo-Catholicism'; it was the first time that the Church of England was to be known as an 'ism' describing its identity as a third way between Protestantism and Rome. The *locus classicus* defining the new Anglican positions, W. J. Conybeare's essay on the High, Low and Broad Church schools, appeared in

1853[6]. It is true that there remained High Anglicans like William Ewart Gladstone, Samuel Wilberforce and Walter Hook who retained a strong element of Protestantism in their Anglican Catholicism; but the general tendency of Anglo-Catholicism was towards a repudiation of the Protestant inheritance. And with that, it can be argued that a portion of the Church of England, which was in fact really Protestant, embraced an incompatible Catholic doctrine of the Church, with the consequence, as Bishop Sykes has suggested, that Anglicanism is bound to look as if it is based on an incoherence, on rival Protestant and Catholic conceptions of the Church which simply do not cohere.

The consequence of internal division is external weakness, and the result of the weakening of the old High Church Protestant ascendancy of Oxford in the 1840s by Anglo-Catholicism gave the liberals their chance, and led inexorably to the secularisation of the University in the second half of the nineteenth century. Indeed secularisation was a wider consequence of the Church's departure from a national Protestantism, and the tendency was exacerbated by the Church's competition with an expanding Nonconformity, as even the Wesleyan Methodists, the most pro-Anglican of the Dissenting bodies, increasingly repudiated a Church contaminated by popish Anglo-Catholicism, and as Mats Selén has shown[7], reedited the Methodist Hymnal to purge from it the Catholic teachings on Baptismal Regeneration and the Eucharistic Sacrifice taught by their High Church founders the Wesleys. In the second half of the nineteenth century, English politics was increasingly polarised between Tory Church and Liberal Chapel, as the Liberal chapelgoers strained to achieve further measures of disestablishment of the national Church, measures in which they were partly successful. Moreover the very dynamism of the Oxford Movement contributed to its instability and unpopularity with Protestants. Newman himself regarded his conception of Anglo-Catholicism as a paper church, still needing to be built, and in the end declared that his whole movement pointed inexorably to Rome. His secession to Roman Catholicism in 1845, with some of his brightest followers, left his remaining Anglican disciples under a cloud, as secret papists who might even yet secede, even while their sheer learning and spiritual and intellectual gifts drew to them increasing numbers of the best and brightest in the Church of England.

That was the paradox: that the extension and revival of the Victorian Church of England owed so much to clergy and laity who were widely regarded as traitors to the national Protestant tradition. The Church was convulsed in the second half of the

nineteenth century by the attempts by parochial clergy to introduce
a higher doctrine of the real presence in the sacrament, auricular
confession, prayer to the saints and a large part of medieval
and modern Roman ritual, to give outward and visible liturgical expression to the doctrine which they taught. In the end,
the Public Worship Regulation Act of 1874, under which four
priests were sent to prison for ritual offences, was acknowledged to be null and void, and the refusal of preferment or
promotion to the strong-minded saints of the ritualist movement
only seemed to encourage them, even while the new conventual
sisterhoods and monastic brotherhoods earned a wider respect
for their good works, most famously in times of cholera. Yet
the theory on which they acted might be thought to be wanting,
of obedience, not to the Protestant State and its courts, but to the
undefined practice and cultus of the universal Catholic Church.
There were to be some extraordinary examples of general flouting
of constituted authority, as in the career of the gifted mission
preacher and eccentric self-styled Benedictine Fr. Ignatius Lyne,
and in the circumstances in which Dom Aelred Carlyle founded
an Anglican Benedictine monastery on Caldey Island; here the
extremes of the movement were a byword as a law unto themselves.

The weakness of their ecclesiological position was especially pronounced in relation to the doctrine of the episcopate. The Oxford
Movement began by exalting the bishops as the successors to the
Apostles. The Movement was nourished on the Ignatian-Cyprianic
doctrine of the monarchical episcopate, and Newman's Anglican
bishop, Dr. Bagot of Oxford, was, he declared, his pope. There
was, it is true, a paradox about the Tractarian insistence that the
bishops were the successors of the Apostles and the Angels of the
Churches when some of the bishops did not believe this themselves;
though this was no more paradoxical than the movement's insistence
that their Protestant clerical brethren were, whatever their opinions,
really Catholic priests. Confronted, however, with Protestant or liberal bishops, the Anglo-Catholic clergy defied them with gusto, and
secure in their private incomes or family connections or parson's
freehold, from which they could only be removed by wearisome
litigation, they tended to practise a kind of Presbyterianism with
an infallible priest-Pope in every parish, loyal not to his immediate
bishop but to Catholic Christendom in some vaguer, wider sense.

The result was that having begun by reclaiming the doctrine of the
Church, the Anglo-Catholics ended up believing in every doctrine of
the Church except the doctrine of the Church. In effect, they lacked

a convincing living authority, and therefore lived on past authority, invoking the decisions of the undivided Church of the first five or ten Christian centuries, though there was obvious disagreement, probed by Newman in his *Lectures on the Prophetical Office*,[8] about when exactly the decisions of the undivided Church ceased to carry an ecumenical authority. Any excesses at the Reformation could be attributed to the usurpations of the temporal power, so that the ultimate authority of a predominantly lay and Protestant Parliament became a convenient Anglo-Catholic excuse for ignoring any heretical ecclesiastical pronouncements in the present. The best defence of this anomalous position seems to me to be still Newman's, that in the divided state of the Church all ecclesiological theories are bound to be unsatisfactory because the Church through human sin has fallen short of what God wishes it to be. Yet the gulf remained between the theory of the Church's authority and Anglo-Catholic practice: you called your bishop an angel of the Church and ignored or defied him; you called your bishop an angel of the Church, and the angel bashed you up.

Informing this practical anticlericalism was the active role which the Movement assigned to the laity, in Newman's insistence on the right of private judgement of the individual lay Catholic to correct heretical bishops; an idea which he took into the Roman Communion, in his fatal essay on consulting the faithful, for which he was delated to Rome. In fact what sustained Anglo-Catholicism was the good Protestant principle of voluntary association, of both clergy and laymen. The Catholic movement in the Church of England developed its own central body in the Church Union, founded in 1859–60. It had its own internal divisions, subtle gradations and styles, as a remarkably learned, devoted and sometimes eccentric English sub-culture, which controlled its own seminaries, presses and party newspapers. It reached its full flowering in the 1920s and '30s with the great Anglo-Catholic Congresses, culminating on the movement's centenary in 1933 with a Pontifical High Mass celebrated in the White City stadium with a congregation of fifty thousand people.

Yet from 1850, the movement was influential in a far wider sense, in persuading the greater part of the Church to build its new churches in medieval Gothic, with a Eucharistic altar as the central focus of worship, and increasingly after 1900, with the Eucharist as the main service on a Sunday. Moreover the movement's theory gave a justification to the Church of England's missionary outreach through the creation of a world-wide Anglican episcopal communion, some of whose dioceses, far beyond the ecclesiastical power of the English parliament, could implement the whole Catholic sacerdotal and sacramental system. It is true that bishops in the British colonies were created by Letters Patent from the Crown, and that the British courts were to pass judgement on a notable scandal concerning the heretical Bishop of Natal; but outside the British Isles, the authority of Parliament was nothing beside the local bishop's. The decennial Lambeth Conferences held from 1867 seemed to give point to the medieval pope's description of the Archbishop of Canterbury as the pope of another world, even though his primacy was no more than titular, while the emergence of an international Anglican episcopate gave substance to the High Anglican claim that theirs was a great international episcopal communion, constituting another branch of the Catholic Church beside the Orthodox and Rome.

Even at the extremes, however, Anglo-Catholicism flourished because the authority of the Protestant State was unable to control it, and because the Church itself lacked any such control on the doctrinal teaching of its clergy. The internal paradoxes of the Church of England multiplied, as from the mid-Victorian era, a three party system took form, and Anglo-Catholics, Evangelicals and even liberals opened their own theological colleges, so that until the 1960s, within a stone's throw of my own Department in Durham, there were two wholly distinct Anglican theological colleges cheek by jowl, teaching diametrically opposing Catholic and Protestant theologies. That, in the long term, could only benefit theological liberalism, for it made the defining character of Anglicanism neither Protestantism nor Catholicism but a liberal comprehensiveness including them both and claiming to be broader, more inclusive, than either. The present Bishop of Ely, Dr Sykes, himself a liberal, has derived the theory of comprehension from that fluffy-minded Prayer Book fundamentalist F. D. Maurice, and described it as a substitute for hard thought and as an intellectual fudge[9]. I would call it a way of diluting both Catholic and Protestant dogma, so that in the end, neither Protestants nor Catholics but the theological liberals have proved to be the real victors in the war for the soul of the Church of England.

Yet that end could not have been predicted in the first half of this century, when Anglo-Catholicism did seem to be refashioning the Church: not merely in liturgical and ecclesiological externals, where a creeping Catholicism continued to remake church interiors right up to the 1960s, but in the realms of social justice; scholarship; spirituality, where Catholic writings still have an edge; and ecclesiastical politics. It is easy, however, now to see that the Anglo-Catholic movement has been in decline since the 1940s, and that it was unprepared for the renaissance of Anglican Evangelicalism. I once asked Michael Ramsey how he regarded Evangelicals; he replied that it was only to the end of his long ministry that they came to be of any importance. This seemed to me to show an extraordinary indifference to their sheer historic importance within the Church of England, which was especially astonishing in a man who had been reared a Nonconformist. To this must be added the liberalisation of a large section of the Anglo-Catholic movement, and its departure from the doctrinal and moral teachings of mere Christianity. My own view of Ramsey, and even more of Robert Runcie, is that they were rather less Catholic than liberal, a view in which I see I have the support of Fr. Aidan Nichols[10], and that both Primates bear a heavy responsibility for the Church's loosening hold on the traditional morality which once held Anglican Protestants and Catholics together.

Indeed it seems to me that liberalism is bound to come as a victorious *tertius gaudens* in the conflict between Anglican Catholic and Protestant, simply because that conflict creates intractable problems which only liberalism can resolve by bypassing them altogether. One solution to the Church's divisions, on the basis of the theory of comprehension or inclusiveness, is to appoint an Evangelical, an Anglo-Catholic and a liberal representative to everything, almost along the lines of the old genre joke, 'there was an Englishman, a Scotsman and an Irishman'. The trouble is that anything that a Protestant, a Catholic and a liberal can agree will be only the highest liberal common factor of all three. As the last of the great Anglo-Catholic theologians, Eric Mascall says, 'It is quite ridiculous to envisage the Church as a tricorporate society, each of whose parts is committed to holding one third of the truth'[11]. Again, as Fr. Aidan Nichols had pointed out, far from being well-placed to function as an ecumenical body, the Church of England in fact has special difficulties in ecumenical dialogue when any agreement which it reaches with other Christian communions is bound to be suspect to all three parties within it. Thus on the ARCIC statement on the Eucharist, an 'Evangelical may be suspicious of its attempt to vindicate the language of sacrifice in regard to the Eucharist ... An Anglo-Catholic may share (Roman) Catholic anxieties about the statement's glossing over the cultus of the Blessed Sacrament outside the Mass ... A Broad Churchman may object to the entire enterprise on the grounds that propositional statements about the content of revelation are an inappropriate vehicle in communicating the Christian life'[12]. Yet again, the Church of England has turned down both an Anglican-Methodist unity scheme and a plan for covenanting with Protestant bodies, while the ARCIC agreements with Roman Catholics have been rejected by the Church's militant Protestants and were ruthlessly dissected as insufficient in 1982 and 1991 by the Roman Sacred Congregation for the Doctrine of the Faith. Yet it was supposed to be the great merit of the Anglican Communion that as the Second Vatican Council put it in its Decree on Ecumenism, it was a bridge Church between the Catholic and Protestant Churches, containing both within itself. It is perhaps sufficient to point out that a bridge is merely a span for traffic across a river or ravine, not a place of residence. No one in the modern world lives on bridges.

Indeed the latest Anglican dissensions still concern the central matter of ecclesiology itself. There is a popular impression that there has been a debate in the Church of England over the ordination of women to the priesthood, but there really has been no such debate, simply because Anglican Catholics and Protestants do not agree about what priesthood is. All Christians believe in the Pauline doctrine of the priesthood of all believers. But for many Anglican Protestants, as for Protestants outside the Church of England, the doctrine excludes the kind of Eucharistic ministerial priesthood in which Anglican Catholics, like Roman Catholics and Eastern Orthodox and Oriental Christians, also believe. The difference between Anglo-Catholic and liberal conceptions of ministry is even more glaring. In 1947, Hensley Henson, from his own liberal perspective, drew attention to two books by Anglican bishops, K. E. Kirk's classic Anglo-Catholic *The Apostolic Ministry* and the Modernist E. W. Barnes's *Rise of Christianity*. Henson described the first, Kirk's, as virtually Roman in 'type, temper and tendency' and the second as 'not even, in any tolerable sense, Christian', adding 'I do not think it possible that any Church can long cohere when such radical divergence on essentials is tolerated'.[13]

There are obvious difficulties created for sensible discussion when the disputants do not agree on the meaning of their terms. Anglo-Catholics would not reject the ministry of women in Protestant Churches, precisely because they do not claim to be Catholic priests, and because their communion service contains no more than a representative or spiritual presence of Christ and not a substantial sacramental and sacrificial one. The problem arises because so many Anglo-Catholics do not think of their Church as a Protestant Church. They share their notions of priesthood and sacrament with Catholics in other Churches, and therefore cannot admit the Church of England's right to admit women to the priesthood without the consent of the whole Catholic Church. The Catholic priesthood belongs to the whole Catholic Church, Roman and Orthodox as well as Anglican, so that only the whole Catholic Church can change it. Protestant and liberal doctrines of ministry suffer from no such vaunting ecumenical inhibitions. Under the circumstances, the liberals who reject the Catholic doctrine of priesthood and hold a strong feminist belief in women's rights were bound to give the Protestant view its majority in General Synod, even given a minority of conservative Evangelicals who remain committed to a Biblical doctrine of male headship. But the real victor in the vote for women priests was not Protestantism: it was liberalism, which having fatally wounded the Anglo-Catholic party in the Church, will find it far easier to obscure and bury the dogmatic and moral teachings which Protestants and Anglo-Catholics used to combine to defend, so fulfilling Newman's prophecy, that the Church of England will become a liberal institution after all. It does seem to me possible that the Church of England has now chosen to take its position beside the definitely Protestant and increasingly liberal Churches of northern Europe, in opposition to the Catholic and Orthodox ones. If that is so, then Fr. Ian Ker is correct in his statement that the Oxford Movement is at an end.

Indeed the latest situation contains further paradoxes. The Church of England has traditionally been held together by its connection with the State and its conception of itself as a great English national institution: not by a theological unity which it does not possess. Now that the State's control is slackening, one may wonder what will preserve its unity, and prevent its elements from tearing it apart. The centre itself has been weakened with the decline in the number of merely Anglican parishes without a definite party loyalty. Yet it was the liberals who traditionally appealed to the Erastian, lay and national elements in the Church's constitution, as their protection from Anglo-Catholics and Evangelicals. The loosening of the Church's connection to the State, however, has increasingly given the Church precisely the kind of independence which Anglo-Catholics have always demanded, and deprived them of their old excuse of blaming the State for the Church's heresies. In a recent period, however, senior appointments in the Church have been dominated by liberals, who can see the Church falling into their hands and are increasingly hostile to the state establishment themselves, especially as the General Synod has chosen to use its authority to make a liberal dogmatic definition of the right of women to be ordained. To Anglo-Catholics, this implies that the Church of England is asserting the kind of teaching authority to define new dogmas which the Church of England has always regarded as a Roman corruption, or at least as only to be justified on the Roman understanding of the development of doctrine in the hands of an infallible pope and councils. Given the domination of General Synod by liberals, a Synod no older than 1970, with no particular claims on their respect, the attention of Anglo-Catholics has been called to their lack of a living teaching authority, and pointed up the strength of the Roman position in always having claimed one. The ordination of women has, moreover, revealed further difficulties in their theory of the episcopate. The Anglo-Catholic Bishop of London has decided to allow the ordination of women to the priesthood in his diocese while opposing such ordinations in principle. Never, I think, except in America, in twenty centuries of Christianity, has a bishop sanctioned the ordination of a body of clergy whom he is unable conscientiously to ordain himself. This is, I submit, at least outside the United States, a conception of the episcopal office unknown in the history of the Church. Again, the Anglican hierarchy has spoken of two 'integrities' in the Church, one accepting of ordained women and the other rejecting. It would take a genius to find a more euphemistic term than two 'integrities' for two flat incompatibilities or contradictions.

How, then, did the Church of England find itself in this position? It might have partly to do with the conservative English love of preserving forms when their inner meaning has departed. It is notable that the external splendour of the British monarchy has actually increased with its diminishing powers, and it is liberal bishops who seem keenest in showing their skills with a thurible. The Tudor historian F. M. Powicke remarked that the 'Church of England is the most striking example in European history of the capacity of institutions to maintain an unbroken, almost complete, continuity in structure while undergoing a thorough change in spirit.'[14] There are some splendid examples of such external continuities in Eamon Duffy's new magisterial history of the English Reformation, *The Stripping of the Altars,* as in the diocese of Lincoln, where the bells which had once been rung on the feast of its great bishop, St. Hugh, continued to be rung on that very same day in honour of Queen Elizabeth's accession.[15] A Catholic occasion had been transformed into a Protestant one, but at least the Catholic form, the ringing of bells, had been preserved. The Caroline divines and later the Oxford Movement tried to show that the old forms conserved in the episcopate and Prayer Book could be given their old meanings, and in doing so found themselves increasingly at odds with the nation which they sought to serve. Now, however, it seems that many of the outer forms will be made a vehicle for the propagation of theological liberalism: and that has its implications not only for the mere Christianity of the Church of England, but for the relationship of the English nation to Christianity, with a National Church that is no longer Christian. That in turn has further implications for the English conservative tradition with which I began, because conservatism in England has drawn so strongly on the strong waters of the wells of Christian morality and Christian doctrine. The fate of the Church of England is still bound up with that of the monarchy which supplies the Church's Supreme Governor, and the House of Lords, which contains the senior bishops, and many other parts of the traditional English Constitution. At the very least, for conservative Englishmen, the Church of England is a nostalgic part of a dear familiar landscape, to be there to give a blessing at birth and marriage and death. It is not only Christians who fear the Church of England's fall.

Yet the decline of Anglo-Catholicism seems to me to be a serious impoverishment of Christianity. No one who has not known the High Church tradition from the inside can appreciate its seductive fascinations. It took all that is best and most beautiful in the Church of England, the King James Bible, the Book of Common Prayer, with its wonderful Cranmerian cadences, the ancient English cathedrals and parish churches, a tradition of literature and a tradition of learning, and the kindness, gentleness and tolerance of English life, and enriched them with judicious borrowings from the doctrine, devotion and scholarship of the wider Catholic world. It seemed the perfect meeting place between Catholicity and Englishness, without the harshness or philistinism of English Roman Catholicism, which has spent a generation destroying everything that was most beautiful about itself. Now that whole Anglican Gothic world has come to grief. Yet in voicing these criticisms of its ecclesiology, I am not merely deconstructing my former Anglicanism, for I discovered having written this paper that my reservations about the Anglo-Catholic doctrine of the Church remain very much what they were in 1983 when I wrote with Professor Stephen Sykes a lecture for the hundred and fiftieth anniversary of the Oxford Movement, which was published in the collection *Tradition Renewed* edited by Dr. Geoffrey Rowell[16]. At the time, I was tending under Professor Sykes's influence to a kind of Liberal Protestantism myself. I was saved from this in 1984 by the appointment of the Bishop of Durham, which showed me precisely what the consequences of such Liberal Protestantism must be. Indeed as Newman said, we cannot stand still, and Professor Sykes has gone further into liberalism as I have gone on to Rome. But this seems merely to prove to me that Anglo-Catholicism, the most culturally attractive form of Christianity that I have ever encountered, is bound to be no more than a *preparatio evangelica* to positions more coherent than itself. In its learning, its devotion, its sheer beauty, it is a preparation without equal, but no more. The matter can be put more positively. If I might paraphrase an old Anglo-Catholic, G. W. E. Russell, *Sit anima mea cum sanctis:* may my lot be with the Anglo-Catholic saints from whose lips I first learned of the doctrine of the Church.

Notes

I am grateful to my research student, Dr Michael Peterburs, for his assistance with this paper.

1   Jonathan C. D. Clark, *English Society, 1688–1832: Ideology, Social Structure and Political Practice during the Ancien Régime*, Cambridge 1985.
2   Walter Farquhar Hook, Vicar of Leeds, cited in W. R. W. Stephens, *The Life and Letters of Walter Farquhar Hook D.D. F.R.S.,* 2 vols, fourth edition, London, 1880, I, p. 66.
3.   Stephen Sykes, 'The Genius of Anglicanism' in Geoffrey Rowell (ed), *The English Religious Tradition and the Genius of Anglicanism,* Wantage, 1992, p. 238.
4.   Clive Dewey, *The Passing of Barchester: A Real Life Version of Trollope,* London and Rio Grande, 1991: E. A. Varley, *The Last of the Prince Bishops: William Van Mildert and the High Church Movement of the early nineteenth century,* Cambridge, 1992.
5.   Peter B. Nockles, *The Oxford Movement in Context: Anglican High Churchmanship, 1760–1857,* Cambridge, 1994.
6.   W. J. Conybeare, 'Church Parties', *Edinburgh Review,* 98 (October 1853), pp. 301–330.
7.   Mats Selén, *The Oxford Movement and Wesleyan Methodism in England 1833–1882: A Study in Religious Conflict,* Lund, 1992. See also David Hempton, *Methodism and Politics in British Society 1750–1850,* London, 1984, p. 166.
8.   Oxford, 1837.
9.   Sykes, 'Genius', p. 233.
10. Fr Aidan Nichols, O.P., *The Panther and the Hind: A Theological History of Anglicanism,* Edinburgh, 1993, p. 128.
11. *Ibid.*, p. 176.
12. *Ibid.*, pp. 173–4.
13. Cited Sykes, 'Genius', p. 230.
14. F. M. Powicke, *The Reformation in England,* Oxford, 1941, p. 119. I am grateful for this reference to Fr Charles Praeger, S. J.
15. Eamon Duffy, *The Stripping of the Altars: Traditional Religion in England 1400–1580,* New Haven and London, 1992, p. 590.
16. S. W. Sykes and S. W. Gilley, 'No Bishop, No Church!' The Tractarian impact on Anglicanism', in Geoffrey Rowell (ed), *Tradition Renewed: The Oxford Movement Conference Papers,* London, 1986, pp. 120–39.

The Oxford Movement and the Revival of Patristic Theology

Nicolas Lossky

It is perhaps of some interest to note the very fact that the present symposium, commemorating the hundred and sixtieth anniversary of the Oxford Movement, should be taking place in the English Department of a French University and with the participation of French scholars. This seems to be the sign of an evolution in two areas. First, there has recently appeared a renewed interest for the religous dimension of history, on the part of students and scholars who tend to acknowledge the importance of this dimension in the evolution of mentalities. Secondly, French specialists in religious studies have recently begun to have a better understanding of the very specific nature of the English Reformation which for a long time they tended either to ignore or to consider solely in the light of the Continental Reformation or Counter-Reformation. Only twenty, or twenty-five years ago, such a symposium would hardly have been thinkable at the University of Nanterre.

The slight alteration in the title of my contribution requires an explanation, which, it is hoped, will help to bring us into the heart of the subject. (We had originally agreed on 'something to do with the Fathers' ...). The change from 'Patristic Studies' to 'Patristic Theology' might appear to some to be hardly worth the mention. In fact, the difference is considerable.

The revival of Patristic studies in connexion with the Oxford Movement would imply a consideration of how some of the Tractarian divines actually discovered, studied, published the works of those we call Church Fathers. It would imply, for instance, a consideration of J. H. Newman's lifelong research and meditation on Athanasius of Alexandria; of J. Keble's interest for Irenaeus of Lyons; of E. B. Pusey's presentation of Augustine; and more generally of all that was printed in the *Library of the Fathers* series, making patristic literature known to the educated public. To this should be added a study of the patristic quotations and allusions in the *Tracts for the Times,* accessible, at least at the beginning, to a more general audience. Such an approach, however useful, runs the risk of becoming a rather tedious nomenclature.

The revival of patristic theology in the Oxford Movement is in many ways a totally different subject (although, of course, it is based upon the reading of patristic literature, the 'archaeological' study, the 'philological' approach ...). It implies a certain conception of patristics, of theology, of the Church. And this conception is, – at least so it seems to me – a striking feature, nay, perhaps the most characteristic one of the Oxford Movement.

William Chillingworth wrote in 1638:

> 'I see plainly and with mine own eyes that there are Popes against Popes, Councils against Councils, some Fathers against others, the same Fathers against themselves, a Consent of Fathers of one Age against a Consent of Fathers of another Age, the Church of one Age against the Church of another Age.'[1]

To this well known statement, anyone who reads the Fathers and who has some knowledge of Church history would at least in part subscribe. At a certain level, it is certainly true that the Fathers are not always in full agreement among themselves, that they can change their minds, that Councils clarify, complete or modify earlier Councils (to paraphrase one of J. H. Newman's letters). The Tractarians certainly read the Fathers and undoubtedly knew something of Church History. However, it is not very likely that they would have subscribed wholeheartedly to William Chillingworth's conclusion, namely that therefore only the Bible which 'is the Religion of Protestants' can be trusted.

Indeed, beyond the inevitable human limitations, contradictions, purely contextual emphases, the men of the Oxford Movement, like the great divines of what they termed the 'Golden Age' of Anglicanism, received from the Fathers – in the strong, ecclesial sense of 'reception' – a theological method, a specific sense of the very nature of theology, in which the Fathers are unanimous. They did not content themselves with reading and studying the Fathers; they made their very approach to theology their own.

One of the first and main characteristics of this patristic approach to theology is that it is 'practical', not speculative. This, of course, is not to say that there is never any speculation in the writings of such theologians; but the speculative developments always aim at redirecting people's attention to the essential truth of the Christian faith which is Christ Himself and the salvation offered in Him. Patristic theology is 'practical', one might even say 'utilitarian', in that it is salvational. Now, the sense of urgency in calling people to rediscover the salvational aspect of forgotten traditions and means of grace is, in my opinion, very strongly felt in the 'Advertisement' introducing the first Volume of *Tracts for the Times* (1833–34, reprinted in 1839; this can also be said of Volumes II, 1835, and III, 1836, and of the early *Tracts* themselves).

Another outstanding feature of patristic theology, closely linked with the previous one, is the fact that for the Fathers, theological thinking is no mere intellectual exercise. Certainly, the intellect is called upon to play a part in the process — it is also believed to be God's creation — bu the intellect is incapable of turning to God without experience. Patristic theology is profoundly experiential. One of the best expressions of this is to be found in the famous 'Text' of Evagrius Ponticus: 'If you are a theologian, you pray truly. And if you pray truly, you are a theologian'.[2] This means that the theologian must necessarily be constantly seeking the experience of life in Christ. It is a form of permanent conversion which concerns all aspects of life.

Many might be tempted to say that there is nothing specifically 'patristic' in this manner of conceiving theology, and that it is very familiar to the Evangelical tradition. There is no doubt about this.

If there *is* a difference, it probably lies in a different understanding of the notion of *'personal* conversion'. To be more precise, there is probably a different conception of the very notion of the 'person'. It seems clear to me that most of the Tractarians inherited a strong sense of personal commitment in their adherence to a christian life, from their Evangelical background. They owe it to their fathers and mothers in the flesh.

However in integrating the patristic approach to theology, they discovered, sometimes not quite consciously, the very important difference which exists between the person understood as an individual and what patristic theologians would be tempted to call 'true personhood'. In the Evangelical perspective, an individual, as the very term indicates, is an atom of humanity, a self-sufficient being defined by his or her limits ('where I end, you begin'). The relation with God will therefore tend to be purely 'vertical': God and me. And the conversion will be understood in an individualistic sense.

In the patristic perspective, on the other hand, 'personhood' does not belong to the *natural* experience of the human being. (By 'natural' I mean a human being in his or her autonomous self, without reference to God). Personhood for the Fathers — and this is what the Tractarians rediscovered — is revealed by God to humankind. The revelation comes from Jesus Christ when

He speaks of His relation with the Father and with the Spirit (in particular in the Gospel according to John: 14–17). The three Persons of the Trinity, as many Fathers have said 'share the unsharable', i.e. divinity; they abide in eternal communion, being both absolutely inseparable and absolutely distinct, which is a perfect paradox or a philosophical absurdity, or again a 'crucifixion' for the christian believer's mind (I am paraphrasing Gregory of Nazianzus, also known as 'the Theologian' because he spoke of the Trinity). God, in His trinitarian life, thus becomes the perfect prototype of unity in diversity, of personhood. For in this perspective, a 'person' is by definition a being-in-communion, a relational being who cannot be saved by himself alone.

Personhood is not given once for all, like individuality. It is a call and is to be achieved through a baptismal-eucharistic life. Such a life — and this is precisely what the Tractarians discovered and taught — is a life to be lived as a community (since it must needs be in communion), to be lived as Church (which is communion with Christ and in Christ with all creation). The Church is the community of the People of God, that is a community of persons (or rather of individuals striving, with the help of the grace of God, to grow in personhood), co-responsible for the purity of the faith, each one in his or her capacity, according to the gifts of the Holy Spirit.

We are very far from a conception of the Church as a purely human political organisation, 'as by law established'. And we all know that the Oxford Movement began precisely with the discovery and the very strong affirmation of the specific nature of the Church, the Body of Christ, the Spouse of Christ, in this world but not of this world, a divine-human institution existing since the sending of the Holy Ghost at Pentecost.

Being in this world, it is bound to have an organisation, an institutional dimension. Yet the latter cannot be other than the outward expression of the innermost nature of the Church. It cannot be in contradiction with its divine-human character. Hence a call to all faithful to become conscious churchmen, or 'lively stones' of the 'spiritual house' (1 Peter 2:5). A call to strengthen their deep roots in the life of the Church as it has been essentially since the time of the Apostles.

They called it the 'undivided Church'. The phrase is a little ambiguous. If this means a time when all Christians were fully united, there never was such a time: even in the Apostolic age there were divisions (cf e.g. Acts 20: 29–30). If on the other hand it is meant to refer to the Church as the Bride 'without spot or wrinkle' ... 'holy and without blemish' (Eph. 5: 27), then it is not to be sought only in the past, a 'golden' past. It is therefore not surprising that the Tractarians claimed (and sought) authority for the Church of England of today, as a 'branch' of that Church. (May I suggest that to my mind the use of this phrase in the *Tracts* does not mean that the authors necessarily adhered to the famous 'branch theory'; the context seems to suggest rather that the word is used in the same sense in which St. Paul spoke to e.g. 'the Church of God which is at Corinth', 1 Cor. 1: 2, etc.).

Ecclesiology at this non-institutional level implies quite naturally the discovery and development of another essential feature of patristic theology, understood as an 'economical', almost reluctant expression of the ecclesial experience of God (you speak of the mystery only for purposes of communication and when the challenges of the times force you). This is a deeply incarnational apprehension of the reality of the Church and that means of all creation of which the Church is the heart (the heart irrigates all). In simpler terms, this means taking very seriously the reality of the incarnation and of all its consequences for salvation. In other words, it implies that the dogma of Chalcedon is of primary importance and should be perpetually received by every generation in the Church.

The mystery of the divine-human Person of Christ, this union without confusion yet without division of the human and the divine nature in the Hypostasis (or Person) of the Son of God results in a total change in the status of the human beings. God has assumed humanity and humanity sits 'at the right hand of the Father'. Or, as the Fathers have often put it, both in the East and in the West, 'God became man so that man may become God'. This is not a form of pantheism; the creature does not cease to be a creature. But being penetrated by divine grace, in Christ, the creatures become 'sons and daughters', or, as St. Peter put it in a very bold way 'become partakers of the divine nature' (2 Peter 1: 4). In Christ, the believers are called to become by grace what Christ is by nature. Christ took on flesh and through His Passion and Resurrection, deified humanity. Receiving the gift of the Holy Spirit, human beings are: a) invited to accept the gift through faith, and b) are enabled to progress on the way to what the Greek Fathers call 'theosis' with the Holy Spirit calling in their hearts 'Abba, Father' (Gal. 4: 6).

How central the doctrine of 'theosis' (or deification) is to the Oxford Movement will appear to anyone who reads the very remarkable book of a modern English theologian, Canon A. M. Allchin who writes among other things:

No less central to the concerns of the Oxford Movement is the subject of this book, the reaffirmation of the doctrine of *theosis,* seen as an immediate consequence of the doctrine of the incarnation, and the foundation of a new and transformed vision of the calling and destiny of man. For man is lifted up into participation in God by the loving movement of God's coming to share in the very nature and predicament of man. [. . .] This doctrine, which was at the heart of the Christianity of East and West in the first millennium of the Christian era [. . .] suddenly came to new life with unexpected power in the middle of nineteen-century England. It was as if there were a veritable epiphany of patristic spirituality and theology in the midst of our divided western Christendom.[3]

It was said earlier that the patristic theologian will not separate theology from experience. Spirituality and theology are inseparable and imply a perpetual deepening of the theologian's rooting in the life of the Church. This deepening is lived in a privileged manner in the liturgy. It was therefore inevitable that the men of the Oxford Movement should rediscover the importance of worship. This rediscovery, which encouraged interest in ancient liturgies, led to the complementing of Prayer Book services that produced the 1928 version (not accepted by Parliament but used by many) and eventually, in 1980, *The Alternative Service Book.* Above all, this emphasis laid on the importance of worship represents the expression of another patristic principle, this time of liturgical theology: it is usually expressed in the famous adage *lex orandi, lex credendi* which means that the rule of prayer can in no way differ from, or contradict the rule of faith. The implications of this principle are of great importance for the manner in which the Church prays. However rich the diversity of liturgies may be, they can never differ in the faithfulness to the central truth of God confessed by the Church catholic.

This notion of the Church Catholic, a major rediscovery of the Oxford Movement – what the Greek Fathers call *eccleiasticon phronema* and what an orthodox theologian of the twentieth century, Fr. George Florovsky has rendered in English as the 'mind' of the Church – has become a central theme of reflection among Christians seeking the restoration of visible unity today. May I suggest as a conclusion that to this reflection the Oxford Movement has condiserably contributed. This brings me to believe, with Canon Allchin and many others, that the Oxford Movement is not really confined to a dozen years in the nineteenth century but is an attitude of constant reconversion to the 'one thing needful' (Luke 10: 42). This implies total intellectual honesty in adhering to the conviction that the sole criterion of truth is truth itself, that is Christ who said 'I am the truth' (John 14: 6) and the Holy Spirit who 'will guide you into all truth' (John 16: 13).

The Oxford Movement with its patristic revival is still here and is playing a leading part in the Ecumenical Movement of today.

Notes

1   *The Religion of Protestants. A Safe Way to Salvation,* From the extracts in P. E. More and F. L. Cross, *Anglicanism; the Thought and Practice of the Church of England, illustrated from the Religious Literature of the Seventeenth Century,* London, S.P.C.K., 1962, p. 104.

2   'On Prayer: One Hundred and Fifty Three Texts', in *The Philokalia,* vol, 1, London, 1979, p. 62, text no 61.

3   A. M. Allchin, *Participation in God: A Forgotten Strand in Anglican Tradition,* London, Darton, Longman and Todd, 1988. See in particular chapter 4: 'A Life which is both His and Theirs: E. B. Pusey and the Oxford Movement'.

The Social Conscience of the Oxford Movement: A Reappraisal

Stephen Prickett

The Tractarians hardly dominate most histories of nineteenth-century social reform. When the not inconsiderable role played by the Church is mentioned, it is the evangelicals, the Christian Socialists, and even the Catholics, led by the formidable figure of Manning who tend to take pride of place. This is not to say that many of the Tractarians were not personally philanthropic, but rather that in many cases their vision of social reform tended to stop at personal philanthropy. For men whose minds were quick to think ecclesiastically on a national scale, it is noticeable that their social thought was usually parochial. A 1875 sermon of Pusey's captures both the best and the worst of Tractarian charity:

> What shall we have to say to our Lord when he comes down to be our Judge − when we shall behold him whom our sins have pierced? 'True, Lord, I denied myself nothing for thee; the times were changed, and I could not but change with them. I ate and drank, for thou too didst eat and drink with the publicans and sinners. I did not give to the poor, but I paid what I was compelled to to the poor-rate, of the height of which I complained. I did not take in little children in thy name, but they were provided for. They were sent, severed indeed from father and mother, to the poorhouse, to be taught or not about thee, as might be. I did not feed thee when hungry. Political economy forbade it; but I increased the labour market with the manufacture of my luxuries. I did not visit thee when sick, but the parish doctor looked in on his ill-paid rounds. I did not clothe thee when naked. I could not afford it, the rates were so high, but there was a workhouse for thee to go to. I did not take thee in as a stranger, but it was provided that thou mightest go to the casual ward. Had I known that it was thou' − and he shall say, Forasmuch as thou didst it not to one of the least of these, thou didst it not to me.[1]

In its recognition of the social role of the Gospel, this could rank with the best of the great nineteenth-century statements by Church

83

leaders; but Pusey's words here were part of a campaign not for reforming the poor-law (which, after all had been an object of liberal attack and derision since before Dickens' *Oliver Twist* twenty years before) but for promoting a revival of *private* charity. Pusey himself, of course, is beyond reproach personally: by far the wealthiest of the Tractarians, gave away almost all his fortune in charitable enterprises of one kind or another. But in his inability to recognise that the relief of poverty might at least be as universal and well-organised as the other work of his beloved Church, he was typical of his movement. He was typical in another way. As the rhetoric of the sermon demanded, that list of modes of alleviating poverty and deprivation is, of course, openly scriptural. There is in it no mention of another form of poverty which, by the nineteenth century, was perhaps more disabling, and more difficult to deal with by piecemeal charity, than any of the listed scriptural ones; cognitive poverty. Among the twentieth-century charges thrown at the Oxford Movement, the elitism of its origins, and its failure to address the problems of education have been among the most damaging. Thus S. C. Carpenter, writing sixty years ago in one of the early twentieth century's most thorough discussions of the social conscience of the Victorian Church, can sum up the origins of the Oxford Movement in these terms:

> It is remarkable, and disappointing, that with so many signs of anti-Christ plain to be seen, irreligion and ignorance among the poor, irreligion and pride among the rich, vast areas of misery complacently regarded by the more comfortable as a thing inevitable, a penal system and a Poor Law full of cruelty, an almost complete lack of national education, Keble found National Apostacy in a point so purely ecclesiastical.[2]

Carpenter, of course, came from another tradition of Anglicanism not likely to be overly sympathetic to the ecclesiology of the Tractarians, but, his point has some force, and by and large it has been taken as the judgement of history. In spite of heroic efforts by particular individuals or groups – including the work of Edward King in Lincoln,[3] Nathaniel Woodard of the Woodard Schools, and even the foundation of Keble College – on the evidence given by the leaders of the Movement themselves, the verdict has to be that they were more interested in liturgical and ecclesiastical reform, than in social problems, including education. Or to put it another way, for them the resolution to social problems lay primarily in reform of the Church: the root from which everything else must grow. Here, for instance, is Liddon in cne of the 1866 Bampton Lectures revealingly entitled 'Charity, a Product of Faith in Christ's Divinity':

> The hospital, in which the bed of anguish is soothed by the hand of science under the guidance of love; the penitentiary, where the victims of a selfish passion are raised to a new moral life by the care and delicacy of an unmercenary tenderness; the school, which gathers the ragged outcasts of our great cities, rescuing them from the ignorance and vice of which else they must be the prey; — what is the fountain-head of these blessed and practical results, but the truth of His Divinity, who has kindled man into charity by giving Himself for man?[4]

An argument that apparently takes as its evidence for the divinity of Christ the 'care ... delicacy' and 'tenderness' of the treatment of criminals in Victorian prisons would have been unlikely to make much headway with contemporary members of the Howard League. Perhaps as telling, in its own way, is the vision of the role of charitable schools as rescuing the 'ragged outcasts of our great cities ... from ... ignorance and vice'. That given the right conditions, some of the ragged outcasts might find their way to university was still unthinkable. By implication, the divinity of Christ is the authority not for social change, or for the creation of a more just society, but for making the existing system more acceptable.

For a practical example of the non-ecclesiastical philanthropy of the Tractarians we can turn to Thomas Mozley's *Reminiscences*. Among its estates, Oriel College owned one at Wadley, near Faringdon, which in 1830 had been unoccupied for some years. In view of this, some labourers from a hamlet on the estate asked permission to have cottage gardens on the vacant land for their own cultivation. Their approach was however apparently couched in 'language which indicated a theoretical right rather than an appeal to benevolence'. 'This', Mozley tells us, 'promised some sport'. The Provost and senior fellows (including, we must suppose some prominent future Tractarians) rode out to confront this impudence. 'A labourer's best chance is wages,' they explained; 'his time and strength are due to his employer', and, rather oddly in view of the fact that they had only been asked for 'gardens': 'land above the scale of a garden is an encumbrance. Who is to pay rates and taxes upon it? What is to be done when the holders increase and multiply?' Hardly surprisingly, we are told that the dialogue was 'one-sided'. All the poor labourers could do was to 'repeat that they would like some land to do what they pleased with, and they had been told manors were for the poor as well as for the rich. Oriel College was a very great body . . . it could do anything.'[5] Anything, it seemed, except giving the men their gardens. A few years later one of the Fellows of the College devoted himself to building a pretty little church there.

Certainly there was need to look to the later Pusey or Liddon for evidence of this lack of interest in social as distinct from ecclesiastical reform. We have it, it seems, from the original first phase of the Movement in the words of Keble himself. In 1839 it was his role, as Professor of Poetry, to give the Crewian Oration at the Oxford Commemoration ceremony at which William Wordsworth was presented for an honorary degree. The account of this occasion is given by Keble's first biographer: J. T. Coleridge.

> The Oration commences with pointing out a close analogy between the Church and the University as institutions, and after tracing this out in several particulars, notices a supposed and very important failure of the analogy in respect to the poorer classes, to whom the gates of the latter are not practically open, nor instruction afforded. This failure the orator then proceeds to explain and neutralize so far as he is able . . .[6]

This passage, concluding with Keble's graceful tribute to Wordsworth himself as the poet of the poor, and its tumultuous reception, has become one of the most famous accounts of Keble's attitude not merely towards poverty, but in particular towards the virtual exclusion of the poor from higher education in general and Oxford in particular. Its ambiguity has been read as symptomatic of an ambiguity towards education and social privilege that was endemic in the Oxford Movement right from its beginnings.

When, in 1992 Geoffrey Rowell very generously invited me to give the paper on Keble in a series of lectures in the Chapel of Keble College, Oxford, to mark the bi-centenary of Keble's birth,[7] I decided to take another look at that Crewian Oration of 1839. It did not surprise me overmuch that Glasgow University library turned out not to have a copy; I was disappointed by Scottish parochialism when I discovered that there was no copy in the National Library of Scotland. By the time that I had ascertained that there was no copy in the British Library I began to wonder just where J. T. Coleridge's own source had been. In the end of course, I did what I should have done much earlier: I phoned the librarian at Keble College who, after some investigations of his own, confirmed that the speech had not merely never been published, but that all we have of it is Keble's own lecture notes – 21 pages of them – which he obligingly faxed to me that day. What I received was a series of sheets covered in the most illegible scrawl which, on close study, turned out to be not merely, as one might expect, in Latin, but in Keble's own private abbreviated form of Latin: not so much a continuous piece of prose, as a series of jottings from which he could speak. Here I must record my undying gratitude to my colleague, Paul Jeffries-Powell of the Glasgow Department of Humanity who sat up all one night to produce from these notes a readable Latin text. The final stage of an English translation was then a comparatively simple matter. What emerged from this text was startling and for me quite unexpected.

In the first place it was now clear that J. T. Coleridge himself must have been the source of all previous references to this speech. Though in passing he refers to Dr. Wordswoth's printing of 'it in the original' this seems only to refer to the paragraph directly concerned with William Wordsworth. For the rest we are apparently reliant either on Coleridge's own recollections of the occasion twenty-six years later, or on notes he had made at the time. Either way, his summary of its contents was selective to the point of being totally misleading. Keble had indeed noted that Oxford was in no sense open to the poor, but so far from proceeding to 'explain and neutralize' this failure, as Coleridge suggests, he had gone on to say something very much more pertinent:

> First, I pray you, recall and re-imagine what was the shape and figure of academic things, at the time when we began to enjoy a firm succession of records. There were more than thirty thousand Clerks: some attended to learning here, some wandered all over England, in such a condition of life, for the most part, that the phrase became proverbial: Oxford means poor; while meantime aristrocratic youth despised and detested all pusuits except soldiering.

Poverty, moreover, was never an accidental quality of Oxford in its early days. Keble then proceeds to cite page after page of evidence showing that poverty, and its concomitant, unworldliness, was actually an ideal for the founding patrons of the various colleges: as it were, part of the platonic *idea* of Oxford. Here he is on the foundation of his own college:

And I have a superstitious dread of leaving out at this point the name of the founder of Oriel; who of his piety made sure that this eloquent rule was sworn to, that none should be received into his number 'except the decent, the chaste, the lowly, and the needy'. No need for more: alsmost everybody bears witness that it was for the sake of the poor that they had these houses founded; right up to the time when the ceremonies of religion, and the whole spirit of literature and politics was changed, and the custom gradually grew up of allowing access to the Academy for the talented rich ...

Once again, ecclesiology is paramount: the mediaeval idea of a university, centering on poverty and learning, was fatally undermined by the materialism of the Reformation. Nonetheless, Keble's roll-call of poverty, godliness, and good learning does not stop at the sixteenth century. Samuel Johnson, who 'was not so far removed from true piety and ancient faith' stands as a shining witness that even in the eighteenth century the old ideals had not been quite extinguished.

Significantly, there is absolutely no attempt whatsoever to 'neutralize' the failure of nineteenth century Oxford to open its doors to the poor.

Immediately after the encomium to Wordsworth, somewhat floridly translated and quoted by Coleridge, Keble returns to his main theme of the true calling of the University:

So he who would pay his debt of gratitude, let him to the best of his ability defend that part especially of our discipline which is contained in a worthy and thrifty mode of life; let nothing profuse, nothing immoderate, nothing voluptuary be readily allowed to cross this threshold, within which dwell the poor; and in the tutelage of the poor are honoured the testaments of the dead.

That Alfred Doolittle might have been somewhat sceptical of this sentimentalized portrait of the 'deserving poor' is beside the point. As the following paragraphs make clear, Keble is not just paying lip-service to a lost ideal. Contained within the rhetoric of a peroration is a perfectly practical programme to realise this dream.

Therefore we will call such people back as best we can, and devote ourselves to ensuring that since the waters have been, as it were, divided, our Academy may share its blessings with the commonality and the tribe of the needy. I would wish there to go forth from this place men who shall lead colonies, so to speak, (planted) on every shore of our (native) Britain, nay, and of her provinces. Let the Academy join itself more closely with the views of those who, at this very moment, have by divine inspiration (for I shall speak boldly) formed the plan of propagating in each town not only elementary schools or places to learn a profitable trade, leaving aside the lecture-rooms of a wordy and empty philosophy, and creating those schools which nurture servants and children worthy of Holy Church.

At this very moment, I say, there have gone forth from the bosom of this Academy – and may they succeed and prosper – distinguished architects of this policy; and I pray that our Lord may favour their enterprise, and that he may bring it about, day by day, that this dear and kindly mother of ours may reflect the (true) image of his Church.

For Keble the time has come. Through poets like Wordsworth, the Reform Bill, and the whole process of early nineteenth-century social agitation that was yet to culminate in Chartism, the poor, like a new Israel, have been led out of bondage to the shores of the Red Sea. Social change has begun, and there is no return to the old order. The university must reform itself, in the first place by a system of scholarships to allow scholars from any class of society to attend it. But there is more to this than merely opening up Oxford. As Keble has already made clear, admitting the poor with a desire to learn has an inevitable concomitant: excluding the idle rich, who have no such desire. Oxford must be re-invigorated academically from top to bottom. Moreover, it is clear from that metaphor of 'colonies' that the Latin *Academia* is not simply to be translated by the word 'University' let alone by implication, 'Oxford University'. What he seems to mean by 'colonies' is nothing short of a nationwide system of provincial universities, presumably on the lines of Durham and King's College, London, which will make the ideal of godliness and good learning available to all who really wanted it sufficiently to take the path of academic poverty.

A marginal note to the manuscript, presumably of later date, in Keble's handwriting, clarifies the reference to the 'distinguished architects of this policy' who are named as 'Mr. Acland, Mr. Mathieson, Mr. Wood and others'. The first of these is easy to identify. Thomas Dyke Acland, was the son of a reforming and philanthropic west country M.P., a graduate of Christ Church, who had been a Fellow of All Souls from 1831–39. His plans for such a national educational system reaching out from his university were to lead to the establishment of the Oxford Local Examinations syndicate in the 1850s. Mathieson is a mystery — unless he be an aging Scottish radical from Fife who, in his youth, when his fiancee mistakenly married his rival, went out into the street and proposed to the first girl he met. Samuel F. Wood, the brother of the Earl of Halifax, had been a pupil of both Keble and Newman at Oriel; but as an active Tractarian he has come down to us more for his desire to translate the Latin Breviary[8] than to extend educational provision.

Though, since it was in Latin, it could hardly have been meant as a popular rallying call, Keble's Oration was clearly intended to give a force and direction to the social conscience of his University, and of the Movement, that the former never, and the latter hardly ever achieved. The intention was clearly to support the efforts of Acland and his associates to extend the influence and ethos of Oxford to a much wider circle: and, going beyond their immediate and practically limited objectives, to give a vision of plain living and high thinking that for Keble was essential to the original conception of what a university should be, and the direct equivalent for Oxford of the recovery of first principles that he wished to see in the Church. No matter that it was not immediately achievable; neither was his goal of a re-generated Church. One day indeed, in God's time, there might flourish a Church of England, true to its ancient principles, and co-extensive with a system of national university education, also true to its ancient statutes, and bringing the benefits of university education, as Keble understood it, to all serious minded scholars. In the meantime, the Oration was on record in much the same way as the Assize Sermon of 1833: a prophetic call for reform and a return to primitive purity. It provided a programme that, with hindsight, suddenly begins to draw together what might otherwise seem to be scattered, unco-ordinated, and spasmodic attempts to improve not just primary, but secondary and university education. Nathaniel Woodard's systematic attempt from 1847 onwards to found church schools in every region of the country may have been a personal crusade, but it was also no more than Keble's ambitious programme had already laid down.

What went wrong? Why, if this were so, did the Oration fail to ignite his peers in the way the 1833 Sermon had? Why was it later so carefully edited as to make it lose all its revolutionary thrust? The short answer is almost certainly Newman. It was the very next morning after that fateful Commemoration, the 13th of

June 1839, that Newman began reading about the Monophysites. 'It was during this course of this reading,' he tells us in the *Apologia* 'that for the first time a doubt came upon me of the tenableness of Anglicanism.'[9] The rest, as they say, is history ... Writing to Bishop Selwyn in December 1845, just after Newman's defection to Rome, Charles Marriott, sub-Dean of Oriel, commented 'There has been much talk of extending Education in Oxford. Had it been eighteen months ago, I could have raised money to found a college on strict principles. Now, people are so shaken that I do not think anything can be effected.' But history is not the story of inevitabilities. Another fortuitous tragedy had also distracted the energies of the Movement: less than three weeks before that Commemoration of 1839, on May 26, Pusey's wife had died, and with her much of his personal energy and vitality. With both Pusey and Newman otherwise occupied, Keble's call to reform Oxford and the education system it represented scarcely stood a chance. Samuel Wood – if it was he mentioned in the marginal note – died tragically young in 1843. The crisis into which Newman was to plunge the Oxford Movement was to last for the whole of the 1840s, and the Movement that was finally to emerge as the High Church of the 1850s was, in some ways, a very different creature. Not merely had it lost Newman, its most charismatic leader, it had also lost Manning – perhaps the only one of the Tractarians to have any real understanding of, or sympathy for the working-classes. Pusey was by then a shadow of his former self. Moreover, the world of the 1850s was also itself a very different place. Any faint chance there might have been of creating a reformed Anglican Oxford in 1839 was finally dispelled by the Royal Commission of 1851 that was effectively to secularize the institution and to hand control of it from the clergy to a new generation of career dons who were to totally transform it within a generation.

In view of this, the fate of Keble's address at the hands of J. T. Coleridge in 1868 is the more significant. Coleridge's *Memoir* is the first of a whole series of works that display the old unreformed Oxford in a golden haze of nostalgia. Its purpose is not to show a lost moment of opportunity, but to eulogize a vanished era. Money was already being raised to build the Oxford College that was to bear Keble's name. In a sense, Coleridge's book was less a biography than a hagiography – a fund-raiser for the memorial of a saint, not a plea for allowing the working-class into Oxford. By switching the focus of the address specifically to Wordsworth, Keble's biographer is able to make it seem that it was primarily the tribute of one poet to his master. Wordsworth's death in 1850 was yet another finality sealing off the present from the vanished past. The statement that Keble 'explains and neutralises' the 'supposed failure' of Oxford to admit the poorer clases is part of the process of gilding a past whose importance is already more symbolic than actual. In so doing, of course, he is, consciously or unconsciously, re-writing the history of the movement and making his hero less worldly, less socially aware, less prophetic than in fact he turns out to have been. It is a disservice that only now we are in a position to redress.

Notes

1   Cited by S. C. Carpenter, *Church and People 1789–1889,* SPCK 1933. p. 306.
2   Ibid., p. 114.
3   See John A. Newton, *Search for a Saint: Edward King,* London, Epworth Press, 1977.
4   Carpenter, op.cit. pp. 306–7.
5   Thomas Mozley, *Reminiscences, Chiefly of Oriel College and the Oxford Movement,* Longman, 1882. Vol. 1, pp. 200–201.
6   J. T. Coleridge, *Memoir of the Rev. John Keble,* Parker, Oxford, 1869, p. 248.
7   Now published as *The English Religious Tradition and the Genius of Anglicanism,* ed. Geoffrey Rowell, Wantage, Ikon Press, 1992.
8   See Ian Ker, *John Henry Newman*, Oxford University Press, 1988, pp. 167–8.
9   J. H. Newman, *Apologia Pro Vita Sua,* ed. M. J. Svaglic; Oxford, 1967, p. 108.

'Church and King': Tractarian Politics Reappraised

Peter Nockles

> There is now in France a High Church Party who are Repub-
> licans, and wish for universal suffrage, on the ground that in
> proportion as the franchise falls lower, the influence of the
> Church makes itself more felt . . . Don't be surprised if one of
> these days . . . [we turn] Radicals on similar grounds'.[1]

Hurrell Froude's comment in May 1833 identifies the nascent
Oxford Movement with the movement associated with Lamennais
in France, in a repudiation of the civil as well as ecclesiastical
status quo. Froude believed that the Church in France as well as
in England was oppressed by the state. Like Lamennais, Froude
maintained that captivity would cease if the Church's power basis
was widened. The young James Mozley in 1833 referred to the
Oxford divines as 'the Democratical High Church school',[2] and considered that Froude had imported his notions of popular power from
France. In a letter to Matthew Arnold in 1871, Newman confirmed
the impact on Froude of Lamennais's notion that the Church must
embrace democratic ideas. 'It was', he commented, 'one of Hurrell
Froude's main views that the Church must alter her position in the
political world – and, when he heard of la Mennais, he took up
his views with great eagerness'.[3]

Both Newman and Lamennais were inspiring and approximately
contemporaneous leaders of great religious movements. Both had
enthusiastic followers; Tractarians and Mennaisians respectively.
The parallel between Lamennais's call to the French clergy in 1829
to exert 'the liberty of your ministry' and Newman's message to the
Anglican clergy in *Tract 1* in 1833, 'magnify your office', is clear
enough. Lamennais demanded a free Church in a free State, and the
logic of Tractarian anti-Erastianism pointed in the same direction.
Christopher Dawson and others have stressed Froude's knowledge
of Lammenais's writings and the kinship between the two.[4] Professor J. R. Griffin has argued that having imbibed Lamennais's

93

vision Froude drew the early Tractarians into a position of political as well as ecclesiastical radicalism.[5] Professor Marvin O' Connell, however, cautions against pressing the links between the ideas of Froude and Lamennais too far.[6] This paper seeks to build on O'Connell's reappraisal of Tractarian politics. I will argue that far from countenancing political radicalism, the Oxford Movement at least in its early phase entailed a positive enhancement of the Tory political inheritance of an older High Church tradition, although gradually constitutional realities forced the Tractarians to modify their stance. Apart from Froude, Lamennais had limited influence on Tractarian political thought. The authors of the *Tracts for the Times* remained more wedded to the spirit of the old political order than did the author of *L'Avenir*. Newman's diagnosis of the Church's thralldom to the state was similar to that of Lamennais, but his solution was not. Lamennais's ultimate error, in Newman's eyes, was his failure 'to recognize, nay to contemplate the idea, that rebellion is a sin'.[7] In fact, there was a close French parallel with Tractarian political attitudes, but it was between Newman and the Legitimist writers De Maistre and Bonald, rather than between Newman and Lamennais.

The High Church religious connotations of 'Toryism' were recognised from an early date. 'High Church' and 'Tory' were almost synonymous terms during the reign of Queen Anne.[8] In his *Dictionary* (1755), Samuel Johnson defined a 'Tory' as 'one who adheres to the ancient constitution of the state, and the apostolic hierachy of the Church of England'.[9] Jacobitism, which coloured early eighteenth-century Toryism, no longer represented a viable political grouping after the 1750s and 'Tory' ceases to be a precise descriptive label from between about 1760 and 1812.[10] Recent scholarship, however, points to the continuity of a set of 'Throne and Altar' values which survived the Stuart-Brunswick conflict. According to Jonathan Clark in his influential *English Society,* these values which he characterises as Anglican 'orthodox political theology' continued to underpin the English *ancien regime* throughout the eighteenth century to an extent hitherto unrecognised by secular historians.[11] Moreover, a non-Erastian Caroline ideal of church and state that had been enunciated by Richard Hooker also characterised Hanoverian Anglicanism to a degree until recently underestimated.

Nevertheless, there was a shift in the mode and expression of the High Church Tory tradition in Anglicanism. In the three decades prior to the Oxford Movement, High Churchmen became the strongest opponents of Rome, linking theological objections to various Catholic beliefs and practices, with an exaltation of the Royal Supremacy and attacks on divided allegiance.[12] From having been identified with closet Jacobitism as late as the 1750s, Anglican High Churchmanship by the 1820s had become identified with a robust defence of the Protestant Constitution and the House of Brunswick. Anti-Catholicism became the defining principle of what became known as Ultra-Toryism.[13]

Traditional Anglican political theology, misleadingly described by Griffin as 'Tory erastianism',[14] survived the constitutional crisis of 1828–32, and was restated and only gradually modified by the early Tractarians in a new political context. Tractarian populism was subservient to Tractarian patristicism. It was not only with the ecclesiastical weapon of a call to apostolicity that the Tractarians challenged the Erastian threat to the Church of England in 1833; it was also with the political weapon of a call to monarchical authority, passive obedience and non-resistance. The two elements were not in tension. Tractarian anti-erastianism entailed a repudiation not of the role of the state *per se* in matters ecclesiastical, but true to the Caroline model, repudiated only a secular or infidel and indifferent state enslaving the Church.

The early *Tracts for the Times* stressed 'apostolical descent' and exalted priestly and episcopal authority against the intrusion of the state. Yet the purely political origins of the rise of the Oxford Movement are too often overlooked. Tractarianism represented a revolt of Oxford Toryism as well as an assertion of ecclesiastical independence against the reformist mesures which the Grey ministry brought into Parliament in the early-1830s. Dean Stanley offended Anglo-Catholics when he made this point, but most historians taking their cue from Tractarian historiography regard the Movement as having been unconcerned with constitutional and political questions.[15] Pusey encouraged this misconception. When William Molesworth in 1864 asked Pusey for information on the political background to the Oxford Movement, he was dismayed that such a question should even be posed. Pusey shared the view expressed by his Tractarian friend William Copeland, 'that the political element, the Reform Bill, had not any effect in producing the "Tracts for the Times" '.[16] Copeland maintained that Tractarianism had not been a response to the political crisis of the early-1830s. He could not 'imagine how the two subjects could be brought into any intelligible relation to each other'.[17] Later writers have seen a dichotomy between politics and theology in the Oxford Movement. Edward Norman has emphasised Newman's relative lack of concern for purely political questions. Holding that the sickness of human society was spiritual, Newman was sceptical of political solutions that neglected a transcendent dimension.[18] But it is not true that the Tractarians in time retreated from the political sphere to the 'innermost sanctuary of religion'. John Rowlands has shown how Tractarian political thought was enshrined in the sermons and meditations of the Movement's leaders, and was thus more integral to Tractarian theology than is usually recognized.[19] For the early Tractarian Newman, the institutions of church, state and university were real bulwarks of true religion against the forces of secularity; only gradually did he lose faith in them. Newman stressed the link between apostolicity and Toryism when he objected to the proposed introduction of modern history into Oxford's curriculum in the mid-1830s. As he told Charles Anderson in 1836, the difficulty as to modern history was 'the introduction of modern politics. The present school of philosophers are disgusted with our teaching religion on a positive basis – would they be better pleased if we taught Toryism as well? and it is quite certain that, if we taught the history of the last three centuries, we should interpret it in our own way'.[20]

At the root of Tractarian attitudes to politics, however, was what Rowlands calls an 'Otherworldliness', which contrasted with the mentality of many contemporary Tory High Churchmen. Newman's religious individualism led him to foresee and brand as 'apostacy' our modern preoccupation with politics. Lamennais himself complained that the Tractarians treated political questions too theologically,[21] while Newman regarded Lamennais's vision as too political and naturalistic in texture. Certainly party politics was eschewed. Newman maintained: 'we have nothing to hope or fear from Whig or Conservative governments. We must trust upon our own ethos'.[22] Tractarian theological views increasingly cut across the political spectrum, with the liberal Conservative Roundell Palmer and even the Radical Whig politician Sir William Page Wood coming under the Movement's influence. The Toryism of the early Tractarians was primarily a moral Toryism that was distinct from the more political Ultra-Toryism espoused by Lord Eldon, the pillar of the pre-Reform Protestant constitution in church and state. It also differed from what Copeland called 'the semi-infidel Conservatism of many of the maintainers of our so-called happy establishment'.[23]

It was a political episode, Oxford University's repudiation of Peel in 1829, that marks more accurately the true origin of the Oxford Movement than Keble's 1833 Assize Sermon condemning the suppression of the Irish bishoprics. For it was the compaign against Peel which first brought together the future Tractarian constellation on the basis of political discontent underpinned by moral principle. The campaign drew on the 'Church and King' traditions of the University, with Newman appealing to Romantic sensibility as well as religious principle in conjuring up potent images of historic Tory Oxford as a 'place set apart' to 'witness to the nation'. Thus, Newman recalled that as he walked along the 'old road' from Oxford to visit his mother in the autumn of 1829, 'King Charles and his Bishop [Laud] seemed to rise before him'.[24] The anti-Peel lobby essentially represented the reassertion of an older anti-establishment tradition in Toryism that had been in abeyance since the accession of George III in 1760. For Newman, the defeat of Peel, 'proved the independence of the Church and of Oxford. So rarely is either of the two in opposition to Government, that not once in fifty years can independent principle be shown'.[25] Since the 1770s, Oxford had been a pillar of the establishment in the broadest sense. The defeat of the Home Secretary and Leader of the Commons represented a reversion to the University's eighteenth-century traditions of independence and opposition, in which a strong party within the University insisted upon Oxford's detachment from the political nation. Like Oxford Jacobitism in an earlier period, the Tractarian Movement for many years was to depend for its life-blood on the non-resident Tory country clergy and gentry represented in the University's Convocation. It was the Peel election which inaugurated the anti-liberal alliance on which early support for the Movement in the University rested. Newman invested the Peel election, in itself a merely political contest, with the character of an almost apocalyptic struggle against the forces of darkness. Oxford's orthodox Anglican consensus broke down. A moderate 'liberalism', which had been part of the earlier influence of Oriel *Noetics* such as Whately on Newman, was now branded as one of the satanic forces imperilling Church and University.[26]

Martin Svaglic has maintained that 'Newman's early political thought was a blend of the conservatism of Burke, which dominated Oxford, with the Nonjuring principle taught in the Anglican Homily on Wilful Disobedience (1569)'.[27] In the note on 'Liberalism' in the appendix to his *Apologia,* Newman included among the eighteen propositions that he had 'denounced and abjured', the tenets that 'the people were the legitimate source of power', and that 'it is lawful to rise in arms against legitimate princes. Therefore, e.g. the Puritans in the 17th century, and the French in the 18th, were justified in their Rebellion and Revolution respectively'.[28] In the face of the challenge of democratic ideas, Newman in 1833 was prepared to defend Church establishment as an instrument of the state. He even invoked a military analogy. The Church, Newman declared, was not only on the side of loyalty and civil order, but represented 'a standing army, insuring the obedience of the people to the Laws by weapons of persuasion'.[29]

The religious roots of Newman's politics were explicit. His Burkean scepticism about abstract political panaceas that overlooked original sin shaped his critique of Lamennais's ideas. Thus, he criticized Lamennais's belief in 'certain indefeasible rights of man, which certain forms of government incroach upon, and against which a rising is at any time justified', as flattering 'what we, in our English theology, should call the lawless and proud lusts of corrupt nature'. For Newman, Lamennais adopted the tempter's motto: 'Ye shall be gods', so that he drew 'close to the democratical party of the day in that very point in which they most resemble antichrist'.[30] Newman's attitude here, like Froude's, was much closer to that of De Maistre and Bonald than to Lamennais.

Newman also assailed Benthamite Utilitarianism, with its Liberal theory of Education and glorification of natural and physical science as 'norms of truth'. The root of what Newman perceived as the false idols of Benthamism, which in his *Letters on the Tamworth Room* he condemned Peel for taking up, lay in 'the cheerful, hopeful view of human nature, which prevails at all times (especially since the 'Glorious' 1688!). Such was Paley's, Addison's, Blair's, and now Maltby's and the Liberals'.[31] There was also continuity with the recent High Church past. In the 1790s, Bishop Horsley, Jones of Nayland and other Tory High Churchmen had indulged in prophetical interpretations of Scripture which branded Jacobinism as partaking of Antichrist. It was in similar vein in the 1830s, that Newman identified prevailing forces of rebellion, sedition and insubordination with that same spirit of Antichrist 'which scared the world some forty or fifty years ago'.[32] Newman wished for 'a rumpus' such as the Jacobin convulsion of the 1790s. This would 'shake people and make them talk sense . . . Half the men one now meets would then turn Tories, e.g. just as your Tories at the beginning of the French Revolution'.[33] Froude agreed and also highlighted the link between the 1830s and 1790s. He gave his enthusiastic support in 1833 to a short-lived monthly, the *New Anti-Jacobin Review,* which advocated high Tory principles.[34] His private correspondence was full of diatribes against the evils of Whiggery as well as Protestant Latitudinarianism.[35]

With Keble, the link with the High Church political heritage was explicitly acknowledged. Tory High Churchmen in earlier generations had equated Whig politics with Latitudinarian theology. The

Tractarians echoed this critique. As late as 1841, Keble devoted a review in the *British Critic* to castigating not only what he regarded as the lax theology but also the lax politics of the Whig school of the divine William Warburton in the preceding century. For Keble, Warburton's 'proud spirited' abstract notions of liberty were deemed to emanate from the same tainted source as his claims for religious enquiry and doctrinal latitude. It was a spirit which Keble detected and lamented even in some High Church and later Ultra-Tory eulogizers of the Protestant constitution and Revolution settlement. As Keble put it, 'in this overweening talk of human dignity and civil liberty, Warburton was but following the fashionable quasi-idolatry of that era, perhaps we might say, of our country, for a century and a half: a superstition not confined to any one school in theology'.[36] The Nonjurors had been different. They had invoked the true spirit of the primitive Christians first in passively obeying King James II and then at the Revolution of 1688 heroically refusing to compromise their principles and suffering for conscience's sake. For Keble as for Newman, an insistence on the duty of obedience and on the horror of rebellion as a form of blasphemy, stemmed from theological principle; it was but 'one inseparable branch of the universal doctrine of resignation and contentment'.[37] Rebellion was akin to heresy; both were breaches of the natural moral order and forms of sacrilege. As Pusey's biographer Liddon observed, it was Keble's 'moral temper' which 'led him to view reform and change with distrust: his faith in God's presence and guidance made all high-handed self-willed action on man's part appear more or less irreverent'.[38] Of course this message served political purposes. But Keble's political theology was not deterministically controlled by the dynamics of the *ancien regime,* but transcended the particular constitutional order under which it had been nurtured.

With Pusey, under the formative influence of Keble, an abandonment of a youthful political liberalism in favour of a 'moral Toryism', precisely coincided with his jettisoning of an early moderate latitudinarianism and emergence as one of the leaders of the Oxford Movement.[39] Given the popular historical assumption that Tractarianism was born out of its leaders having bade a 'farewell to Toryism', there was a paradox here, though one more apparent than real. A striking passage in a letter of Pusey's to Edward Churton in 1865 has been cited to demonstrate Pusey's own 'farewell to Toryism'. Pusey told Churton, 'I could have been a Tory; but 1830 ended Toryism. I could not be a mere Conservative, i.e. I could not bind myself, or risk the future of the Church on the fidelity or wisdom of persons whose principle is to keep what they think they can, and part with the rest'.[40] Yet the real implication of this passage, was that Pusey actually regarded his theological volte-face into the vanguard of the Movement in the 1830s as a different expression of that deeper philosophical Toryism which the triumph of Reform appeared to have overthrown. Pusey rightly sensed that it was almost impossible in the wake of the events of 1828 – 33 again to translate such Tory principles into political reality. It was only when external political conditions had changed, and when the Tractarians regarded party politics as no longer a fitting forum for the pursuit of the High Church cause, that the tradition of Orthodox political theology gained in Pusey a wholehearted convert.

The early Tractarians were also heirs of the Orthodox political tradition in their espousal of a sacral or mystical theory of monarchy. Froude's reading of Clarendon's influential *History of the Great Rebellion* (posthumously published in 1702) in 1825 led him to 'adore King Charles and Bishop Laud'.[41] Keble shared such sentiments. His Toryism was infused by a romantic reverence for the House of Stuart and the potent symbol of Charles I as 'the Royal Martyr'. For Keble, the office of monarch represented the 'annointed of the Lord, a living type of the supreme dominion of Jesus Christ'.[42] Like pre-Tractarian High Churchmen, Keble's sacral royalism was reflected in a theological understanding of the Royal Supremacy. Against Whig ministerial interference in matters ecclesiastical in 1833 – 34, Keble sought part refuge in the ideal of the godly prince, as expressed in the text from Isaiah xlix, 23, 'And Kings shall be thy nursing fathers'. As the crown failed in the 1830s to protect the Church from secular encroachment, however, Keble's sense of the dangers of such reliance increased. Yet as with the Non-jurors with whom Keble identified, this did not diminish his faith in the old theory rightly interpreted. As he explained in 1839, for some, the phrase 'nursing father' had 'acquired a trite and almost proverbial use . . . in a very different sense: as though the church were a helpless infant in the arms of some Defender of the Faith'. The true imagery of the text from Isaiah was of the church as a mother with her children lodged in her arms; 'monarchs were essentially foster fathers and mothers'.[43]

Pusey acknowledged his conversion to Keble's brand of Toryism, by his own changed attitude to the cult symbols of the royalist tradition in High Churchmanship. As he told Keble in November 1837,

It was at Fairford, many years ago, when I was thoughtlessly or rather I must say confidently taking for granted that the Stuarts were rightly dethroned, that I heard for the first time a hint to the contrary from you; your seriousness was an intended reproof to my petulant expression about it, and so it stuck by me, although it was some time before it took root, and burst through all the clouds placed upon it'.[44]

Pusey's November 5th sermon in 1837, *Patience and Confidence the Strength of the Church,* symbolized by its dedication to Keble, was a fruit of the latter's influence.

The example of the Jacobite Nonjurors lurked as a potential reproach to the Tractarians. James Anthony Froude, mockingly complained that his brother Hurrell and his Tractarian cohorts were guilty of a reconstruction of history which not only canonised and spoke of Charles I 'as the holy and blessed Martyr St. Charles', but which led them 'to speak of James III instead of The Pretender'.[45] Pusey's repudiation of the 'Glorious Revolution' of 1688 led some to treat the sermon as an anachronistic piece of neo-Jacobite polemic, comparable to Sacheverell's notorious sermon in 1709, *In Peril among False Brethren*.[46] Just as Warburton and Samuel Parr had denounced the 'Jacobite' or 'Tory' politics of the sermons of Horne and Horsley in the 1760s and 1790s respectively, Thomas Arnold in January 1838 was complaining that Pusey had quoted texts 'which appear to advocate pure despotism'.[47] It was true that Pusey cited such authorities as Filmer, Overall's *Convocation Book,* Sanderson and Horsley in favour of the 'high doctrine of Non-Resistance',[48] but it was moral and religious lessons not party politics that concerned him. Those who accused Pusey of wishing to restore the Stuarts missed the point. As Pusey made clear, 'with regard to the special instance of the English Revolution of 1688, the question is now happily of practical importance only, as relates to men's feelings and principles, not to any political mode of acting'.[49] 'Non-resistance or passive obedience, in the sense to which they are generally limited' were 'but two sides of the same doctrine' – faith and humility in religion, obedience and submission in political allegiance.[50] The contrast with Lamennais's approach, which Newman criticized as one of hurrying and thereby disrupting God's providential designs, could not have been greater. Far from contradicting the basic themes of the Oxford Movement as Griffin suggests,[51] the moral emphasis of Pusey's sermon was a genuine product of Tractarian spiritual teaching and *ethos*.

Keble's influence on Pusey was also exhibited by the latter's adherence to the notion of the monarch as 'nursing father' of the church. In a sermon of 1838, Pusey stressed the role of the crown in the church's missionary endeavour, declaiming that the 'princes of this world shall reverence the Church, and shall find their glory and their joy in ministering to her necessities'.[52] Far from complaining of the monarch's interference, Pusey faulted the crown's occasional failure to fulfil her duties of protection and succour. An instance of neglect was the failure in the previous century to introduce episcopacy to the North American colonies. The old theme of American Loyalists such as Jonathan Boucher that this failure had contributed to the revolt of the 1770s was reiterated by Pusey. But Pusey blamed ministerial advisers rather than the crown itself.[53] Pusey criticized state interference in church matters partly because it stifled the true role of the monarch as 'nursing father'. For Pusey, the 'blessed influence of George the Third' was a worthy model. But Pusey lamented, 'even he could not undo the evil which had been done by the ministers of the first two sovereigns of his line'.[54] Pusey complained that politicians had prostituted the episcopal office, but took comfort in the fact that 'their interference grew only with the weakness of the House of Hanover, and even Pitt could not carry his own Archbishop of Canterbury (Tomline)'.[55] Pusey maintained that 'this modern plan, wherein ministers are virtually the patrons, and the king a cypher, did not come in until the middle of the last century'. He hoped that 'with a struggle we might again recover the old system'.[56] Pusey's desire for a veto by the chapter and consecrating bishop in the case of bad episcopal appointments was not intended to restrict royal authority. He agreed with Keble that 'His Majesty's Prerogative would gain more than it would lose by taking from him the nominal appointment and giving the real one to that party who we know are always surest to stand by him'.[57]

Pusey remained committed to the ideal of sacral monarchy as a bulwark of the church. In the Gorham crisis of 1850, it was an emphasis which divided him from other Tractarians and allied him with old High Churchmen with whom on sacramental teaching he had come to differ. In his *The Royal Supremacy not an Arbitrary Authority* (1850), Pusey appealed to that tradition of Orthodox political theology which 'owned the ancient authority of the Crown' and which provided him with precedents to 'justify the principles which the Church had conceded'.[58]

Newman's royalist instincts were no less marked. He had a notorious horror of 'republicanism'[59] which was represented on the index of eighteen 'Liberal' propositions which he anathematised. Griffin is mistaken in his assertion that Newman ignored Anglican political liturgies as a Tractarian.[60] On the contrary, while he appears to have given up the November 5th service in

1834, Newman took up the traditional High Church cult of the Royal Martyr and like High Churchmen of an earlier generation scrupulously observed January 30th as the day of the Martyrdom.[61] Moreover, Newman shared the theoretical neo-Jacobitism of Froude and Keble. In contrast to the Ultra-Tory idolisers of the 1688 Constitution with whom he found himself in temporary alliance, by 1830 Newman had doubts as to 'whether we can consider our King as a proprietor of land in the old Tory theory'. Newman was convinced that 'the rightful heir was lost in the Revolution — then the nation took (usurped?) the property of the island (time has sanctioned their violence) and gave it to William and then to George on certain conditions, i.e. that of being their chief magistrate. Has not the constitution since that time been essentially a republic?'[62]

In spite of private misgivings over the legitimacy of the House of Brunswick, as with Keble and Pusey, Newman's royalist feelings found expression in a passionate appeal to the Crown to use her Supremacy to defend the Church against ministerial thraldom. When Bishop Phillpotts in a fighting speech in the House of Lords in June 1833 urged the Crown to veto Whig legislation by recourse to the coronation oath, thereby clashing with Lord Grey, Newman rallied to the former's side. After Newman's old mentor, Richard Whately, had defended Grey's interpretation of the coronation oath, Newman exploded, 'as to Whately and his evasions about the Coronation Oath, it is quite distressing to think about him'.[63] Newman still regarded the Royal Supremacy as a guarantor of the spiritual rights of the Church. Although William IV might not appear credible in the role of Christ's earthly Vicar, when Whig legislation threatened to infringe the Church's rights in 1833, it was natural for Newman to appeal to him as 'Defender of the Faith'. As Newman explained in a letter to the *British Magazine* in 1834

> If it be said that the Act of Settlement secures to the people certain liberties, I reply that the Coronation Oath has secured to the Church its liberties also to the utter annulment of all former precedents of tyranny — and that we stand by that oath as our law as well as our Sovereign's sanction and acknowledgment of it, and that any power in the state that innovates on the spirit of that oath tyrannises over us'.[64]

When it became clear that William IV in 1833–34, unlike George II in 1801, was not prepared to stand by his oath in the way Tractarian leaders urged, Newman's disillusionment was patent. William IV's acquiescence in Peel's creation of the Ecclesiastical Commission in 1835 further deepened Newman's feeling that the Church was being betrayed by the Crown as well as by the Conservative party, and that she would have to confide her trust elsewhere.[65] For Newman, William IV had proved as frail a reed for the Church to lean upon as the Bourbon monarch Charles X had proved in Lamennais' eyes.

Froude had never shared such illusions. His own devotion to the Royal Martyr had not been accompanied by any faith in a Royal Supremacy. His influence in lessening Newman's trust in the Supremacy was evident as early as the autumn of 1833, when Newman confided to a friend:

> 'It is most natural and right that the Monarchy and Aristoc- racy should be our secular instruments of influence − but if these powers will not, lo! we turn to the people. The King has tied his own hands − he has literally betrayed us ... Our first duty is the defence of the Church. We have stood by Monarchy and Aristocracy till they have refused to stand by themselves'.[66]

By 1837, Newman could sarcastically reflect that 'the gridiron of St. Laurence would be found a more effectual guarantee of church property than a coronation oath or an act of parliament'.[67] After all, the fact that since 1707 the monarch presided as head of a Presbyterian Kirk north of the Tweed represented a serious con- stitutional anomaly and long-standing embarrassment for High Churchmen. Ultimately, Newman had to ask the question, which mattered more, monarchy or church? As Jonathan Clark puts it, 'in 1688−9 the political classes ultimately chose the second; in 1828−9 they reversed that choice'.[68] Newman could not respect that reversal. Consequently, he sought new 'secular instruments'. Yet as he insisted to Froude, 'theoretically and historically' he remained 'a Tory'. It was only altered external political circumstances that forced him to 'begin to be a radical practically'.[69] Thus, he told Rose in 1836,

> Now suppose one had been born 30 years sooner, I think one should have kept quiet. But the times will not allow of this ...outward circumstances are changing ... we have a reason for being bolder ... men like Hooker, Andrewes, and Laud, acted in the system they found themselves. The single dif- ference between their views and those I seem to follow is this −

they had a divine right king — we in matter of fact have not'.[70]

Robert Wilberforce was to make a similar point in 1854 in a work marking his final abandonment of Tractarian Anglicanism for Roman Catholicism. Wilberforce retained, even at this time, a certain nostalgia for the Caroline ideal. He now believed that while the notion of the monarch as 'Spiritual Governor' was an innovation of the Reformation, yet in the seventeenth-century context it had retained a certain spiritual integrity. But Wilberforce insisted that in the nineteenth century when there was a parliamentary Sovereign with Parliament representing a divided nation, and with Presbyterianism established in Scotland, such a notion had lost all meaning. As Wilberforce put it, 'in the times of the Tudors and Stuarts, the Church seemed to come before the world as a living body, because the Royal Supremacy was alive and active; at present, the Church does nothing as a body, but leaves individuals to act as they will for themselves'.[71]

Froude helped undermine the basis of Newman's Toryism as a practical outlet for his ecclesiastical principles. But Newman's historical and emotional attachment to a Laudian monarchical and hierachical ideal lingered on even into his later Tractarian years. This attachment was exemplified in Newman's article on the *Court of James I* in the *British Critic* in 1840. On reading the article, the Tractarian Charles Marriott confided to Newman, 'the very broad avowal of the Anglican notion of Royal Supremacy . . . made me open my eyes an eighth of an inch wider than usual. But I think facts bear you out'.[72] Of course, there had been no stauncher Legitimist than Lamennais until his perception that the Church's interests had been sacrificed by the state led him to react against the politics of the *ancien regime*. Yet in spite of Newman's similar disillusionment with the Crown for failing to protect the church from Whig encroachments, he refrained from following Lamennais into a repudiation of the 'Throne and Altar' principle. Although Newman felt the same outrage at the Church's subjection to state concerns, he actually criticised Lamennais for being too ready to forsake the House of Bourbon with whom the French clergy had returned in 1815. 'One might suppose', he complained, 'there were some old recollections of loyalty, or even vows of allegiance to attach them and to excuse their attachment to the sons of St. Louis. Far from it; he [Lamennais] measures the unfortunate family only according to their power of advancing the interests of the church; and considers they may be cast off without pity, if he does but succeed in proving that it is inexpedient to hold by them'.[73] In the spirit of traditional

Tory Anglicanism, Newman regarded the challenge to the hereditary monarchical principle as an aspect of secularisation rather than as an assertion of ecclesiastical liberty.

Newman's Tory and royalist sympathies acted as a brake in his drift towards Rome, even as his theological objections were overcome. The apparent identification of the Church of Rome with the cause of Daniel O'Connell in Ireland and of the Whigs in England in the late-1830s especially troubled him, as it also did Gothic-minded Roman Catholic advocates of reunion such as Ambrose Phillips de Lisle.[74] The antipathy was reciprocated. As Sheridan Gilley has pointed out, the Ultramontane and O'Connellite editor of the *Tablet,* Frederick Lucas who advocated that the Roman Catholic church 'ally herself with the reforming and popular party in every nation', regarded the Tractarians as 'some of the most Hibernophobe High Tory members of the Anglican Church'.[75] On the other hand, if English Roman Catholics would break ranks with Whigs and Irish nationalists, Newman conceded that 'strong temptations will be placed in the way of individuals, already imbued with a tone of thought congenial to Rome, to join her communion'.[76] Certainly, Newman never found the political iconoclasm of some of the younger 'Romanising' adherents of the Movement such as W. G. Ward congenial. Wilfrid Ward later revealed the shock which his father caused when he declared at a dinner of Puseyites that Charles I had been rightly executed.[77] Newman's own comment about Ward on his joining the Movement in 1838 is a revealing mixture of spiritual empathy and political distaste: 'I cannot help liking him very much, in spite of his still professing himself a Radical in politics'.[78]

As Paul Misner, Sheridan Gilley and Rowlands have demonstrated, however, Newman's Toryism would be softened, and his passage towards Rome eased, by his rediscovery and reappropriation after 1840 of the 'Evangelical prophetical tradition' in which he had been educated.[79] As 'the World' and its secular princes and powers began to assume the guise of Antichrist rather than Whiggery or Popery in Newman's always active eschatology, so his political Toryism was modified by an 'Otherworldliness'.[80] This drew out of Newman that latent sense of the satanic significance of contemporary events which Sheridan Gilley has aptly described as the 'Protestant brimstone element' in his teaching about liberalism.[81] This element was not peculiar to Evangelical Protestantism but also characterized much Ultramontane Roman Catholicism in the wake of the French Revolution. Nonetheless, it represented in Newman one of several Evangelical traits that never left him. On the one hand, this trait had an anti-radical tendency, making it impossible for him to sympathize with a key theme in Lamennais's later teaching, the social regeneration of society as an end in itself. Yet, on the other hand, as Edward Norman argues, the same trait also had a radical tendency.[82] Newman's Anglican Toryism ultimately was undermined by his very detachment from worldly values and consequent view that all political ideas and institutions were unstable and transient.

The anti-establishment stance of the Tractarians increasingly qualified their authoritarian political attitudes. Froude's message was, 'let us tell the truth and shame the devil; let us give up a national church, and have a real one'.[83] Establishment was an incubus and ought to be jettisoned; all 'secular' interference in the Church even by the Crown was a 'usurpation'. Froude's *Remarks on State interference in matters Spiritual* published in November 1833, in suggesting the possibility of the Church breaking its alliance with an Erastian state and appealing for popular support, echoed the radical line advocated in *L'Avenir*. Froude, however, sought to persuade rather than provoke Tory high Churchmen. In advocating that the Church face constitutional reality and adopt a new line of policy in relation to the state, Froude appealed to the very principles of Hooker's church-state theory. It was only because 'Parliament was a lay synod of the Church, that Hooker justified himself in consenting to its interference in matters spiritual'.[84] For Froude, the logic of the constitutional revolution of 1828–33 was that 'the CONDITIONS on which our predecessors consented to parliamentary interference in matters spiritual are CANCELLED'.[85] This enabled Froude to turn the tables on Tory High Churchmen with the retort, 'open your eyes to the fearful change which has been so noiselessly effected; and acknowledge that BY STANDING STILL YOU BECOME A PARTY TO REVOLUTION'.[86]

Yet Froude's church-state ideal was not the constitutionalism of Hooker nor the Laudian theocracy of the Caroline Divines or early Nonjurors. His vision was of ecclesiastical supremacy over the civil power in all capacities as symbolised by Becket and the twelfth-century church dictating to monarchs.[87] Tory High Churchmen condemned the late-medieval church's claim to spiritual dominion over the secular power as championed by Hildebrand.[88] In contrast, Froude faulted the church for alienating too many of her ecclesiastical powers to the domain of temporal rulers in the fourteenth century. Froude argued that the 'usurpations' of Roman Pontiffs by the end of the fourteenth century, were 'usurpations, not on the rights of Kings and Governors, but on the rights of the Church itself, of the congregations of Christ's little ones, the poor, the halt, the lame and the blind'.[89] Froude lamented that fourteenth-century bishops had 'shrunk from asserting their station as successors of the Apostles, for fear of losing their station in society'.[90]

In the context of the High Church stand in the 1830s against Protestant Dissent, Froude's late-medieval frame of reference rendered him an unreliable ally. Froude's radical objection to the payment of tithes on the ground that it was enforced by the civil power and thus partook of 'desecration',[91] appeared to put him in league with Dissenters. To the dismay of Tory High Churchmen, Froude's brand of anti-Erastianism led him to identify with the anti-church and state views of the early Puritans in their struggle with 'High Church' episcopal opponents such as Whitgift and Bancroft.[92]

Froude remained in one sense a Tory and 'romantic reactionary' in the continental rather than John Bull mould, but the radical implications of his anti-establishment mentality seeped into the bloodstream of later Anglo-Catholicism and overshadowed the Tory and royalist character of the original Oxford Movement. By the late-1850s, the new spirit had inspired objections even to that Tory High Church red-letter day of the liturgical calendar, the Book of Common Prayer's January 30th Thanksgiving rite, on the ground that it was but a 'state service' imposed by the civil power.

Froude's influence in modifying Tractarian attitudes to establishment was potent. During the 1820s, Keble's constant refrain was of the 'danger to the Church Establishment'.[93] Even his *National Apostasy* sermon was conservative in tone. In private correspondence by 1833, however, Keble began to sound more like Froude, eschewing compromise and even threatening dramatic gestures such as in August 1833 threatening to refuse the Oath of Supremacy 'in the sense which the legislature now puts upon it'.[94] But Keble did not put himself to the ultimate test, though again in 1850 he would contemplate the prospect of lay communion. Keble frequently acknowledged his personal debt to Froude in his later thinking on Church and state, for example, in his review of Gladstone's *The State in its Relations with the Church* (1838) which he regarded as 'exceptionally well-meant' but wanted 'a little reconciling with Froude's view.[95] On the other hand there were limits to Froude's influence on Keble. It was Nonjurors such as Leslie rather than Becket or even Ambrose, who remained his ultimate guides on church-state matters.[96]

Newman's initially conservative attitude to establishment was eroded by Froude's influence. The message which Newman sought to impress upon contemporary churchmen in articles such as 'The Church of the Fathers' in the *British Magazine,* was that following the example of the age of Ambrose and the Church of Milan, the Church of England might have to take a 'popular' course, and 'flee to the moutains'. Yet this was not in itself an index of political radicalism. The Nonjurors and Scottish episcopalians had followed just such a path. Stephen Thomas suggests that Newman's conservative rhetoric such as his references to 'good King George' had only been designed to soothe his Tory country clerical readership which might otherwise baulk at the innovative and disturbing message he was delivering.[97] Whatever the truth of this, Froude encouraged Newman to re-read the whole history of church-state relations in England with a new and more jaundiced eye, so that his tone changed. But in the Tractarian Newman there remained a tension between genuine nostalgia for the *ancien regime,* and the pull of a patristic ideal. He came to regard the Church of Henry VIII and William III as a 'law church', as might be proved by the ready acquiesence in the establishment of Presbyterianism in Scotland in 1707. But he took consolation in the fact that Lamennais had represented the Church of Rome 'as much more of a law church in practice, than our own'. He even concluded that the main difference between the two churches was that 'we have hitherto been well-treated, and Romanists ill-treated by the civil power'.[98] Newman's line, however, became increasingly subversive of the assumptions of Tory High Churchmanship. Thus whereas Tory High Churchmen rejoiced that by the mid-1830s the spectre of disestablishment was receding, Newman found little consolation in this development. Newman now concluded that the Liberals did not want disestablishment.

> They fear the church too much to let her go; at present they are but weakening her, as they hope, while they retain her. It is the kind and considerate office you perform to birds when you clip their wings, that they may hop about on a lawn, and pick up worms and grubs. Liberals do but want a tame church'.[99]

By 1836, Newman had reached the view which underpinned his *Lectures on Anglican Difficulties* (1851), that 'Erastianism' was the Church of England's natural condition.[100]

In conclusion, disillusionment with establishment modified the inherited Toryism of the early Tractarians. As C. K. Gloyn has argued, the Tractarians embraced a dynamic or progressive as well as a static concept of church authority.[101] This entailed a reaction against the associations of wealth and privilege and the political entaglements of the older Tory High Churchmanship, symbolized by Froude's strictures on the 'gentleman heresy'.[102] This reaction, which reached an apogee with W. G. Ward's *Ideal of a Christian Church* (1845), up to a point mirrored that of the 'Liberal Catholic' or Ultramontane reaction in Roman Catholicism against the Gallican Church's compromises with the pre-revolutionary order of wealth and privilege. Although the links between Newman and Lamennais were tenuous, with both displaying physical insularity, the Oxford Movement itself was not an insular phenomenon.[103] On the contrary, at a political level it can be viewed as part of a pan-European disengagement from the idea of a confessional state towards religious pluralism that was evident not only in France but in Belgium and the Prussian Rhineland.[104] Impressed by the 'popularity of High Churchism among the lower orders at the time of the Sacheverell trial', Froude hoped that Anglo-Catholicism could become populist like contemporary Ultramontane Roman Catholic movements on the continent.[105] In Anglo-Catholic historiography the slum priest and Sisters of Mercy would become symbols of later Tractarian social concerns. But the ideal of the *pauperes christi* and a romantic view of the corporate collective character of medieval society destroyed by the Reformation and overthrow of monasticism, had already found expression in a series of articles by Frederick Oakeley in the *British Critic* in the early-1840s. Tractarian social teaching enshrined in those articles and in Pusey's sermons on almsgiving and riches deserves further consideration.[106]

The Tractarian reaction against the political *status quo* extended to a growing disenchantment with the world of royal favour and patronage. This disenchantment was encouraged by Queen Victoria's early *penchant* for Whig Latitudinarian advisers and later support for the Presbyterian Kirk in Scotland. By the 1860s, the loyalty to the Queen exhibited in Presbyterian Scotland was being contrasted unfavourably with the tendency among some clergy in England to dispense with prayers for the Sovereign. The Evangelical chaplain of Jesus College, Oxford, Peter Maurice, could even exclaim to Dr. MacBride, Evangelical Principal of Magdalen Hall in 1867:

> You could scarcely expect . . . that in a place like Oxford, once so renowned for its loyalty and orthodoxy, that such a departure from the externals of both church and state symbolism should have been permitted, and that so many of its churches should have neither the Royal Arms nor the Tables of the Ten Commandments, as prescribed by law and ancient custom, for out

of the eighteen there are only two in which the Royal Arms are visible.[107]

There was also a reaction against putting the trust of Church and University in the hands of even well-intentioned politicians such as Lord Eldon or the Duke of Wellington. This reaction was reflected in the private suspicion of the role of Wellington as Chancellor of Oxford University after 1834. Wellington was accused of sacrificing the Church and University's religious principles on the altar of academic order.[108] The experience of being at the receiving end of the University authorities in the early-1840s encouraged a more critical view of the 'powers that be' among even the most moderate supporters of the Movement. The process of disenchantment was such that one Tractarian writer in 1844 in a critique of what he regarded as the limitations of Eldonian political philosophy, was provoked into condemning Toryism as 'the ingenious device whereby politicians have endeavoured to enlist in their unholy warfare of partisanship those sentiments and feelings, whose rightful place is to be found in the blessed ranks, and among the sacred forces of our true Mother [the Church]'. Toryism was dismissed as 'the child of the world, the congenial offspring of a worthless parent'.[109]

Tractarian political disengagement was also aided by the continued identification of parliamentary Toryism with the fortunes of Protestantism. The Tractarians who had allied themselves with Ultra-Tory Protestantism in 1829, found themselves in dispute with it as the theological principles of the Movement developed in the direction of Rome. Not only were the Tractarians suspected of a theological leaning towards 'popery', but Tractarian strictures on the Revolution of 1688 put them in political conflict with the archaic brand of Whiggery hitherto espoused by the Ultra-Tory defenders of the Protestant constitution. The wonder is that the uneasy alliance between the neo-Jacobite Tractarians and neo-Orangeist or Eldonite Ultra-Tories survived so long. However, the Protestantism that partly underpinned the reconstruction and revival of the Conservative party in parliament between 1838–41 was increasingly directed against the Tractarians.[110] Moreover, the role of the state as a partisan legal engine of Protestantism brought it into increasing conflict with Tractarian claims. In various ritual cases from the 1850s onwards, Anglo-Catholics found themselves in direct constitutional opposition to the decisions of a Protestant state.

Edward Norman's assertion that Newman's Toryism did not derive 'from the after-glow of the old world' is open to question.[111]

Newman's Tractarian political ideology was infused by a roman-
ticised historical identification with Caroline Anglicanism. Yet
Newman's politics retained a pragmatic element. His espousal
of modified divine-right monarchy theory well into the 1830s
might seem anachronistic, but perhaps owed something to a sub-
conscious doubt about Anglicanism which needed shouting down.
For Newman in 1845, however, the transcendent order of God's
way finally triumphed over the politics of national establishment.
Conversion entailed political as well as religious liberation. This liberation is vividly apparent in a letter written from Rome in 1847,
wherein he likens the Jesuits there to the 'Conservatives of the
political world' who had been dominant in the Oxford of 16 or
17 years previously. He was thinking of 'the Kebles, Perceval, etc
and Froude before his eyes were opened to see through the hollowness of the then so-called Toryism'.[112]

Clearly, Newman had outlived the Anglican political lumber of
1829–32. The Roman Catholic Newman gratefully conceded that
the rise of social pluralism had destroyed 'the whole theory of
Toryism' which had underpinned confessional Oxford and historic
Anglicanism. The Tory theory, he exulted in 1851, 'came to pieces
and went the way of all flesh'.[113] The Wardite wing of the
Movement went further still. W. G. Ward, for whom the politics
of Anglican confessionalism were always anathema, insisted that
the Church's ordinary position must be on the side of the poor,
who were accorded a quasi-sacramental status, and in opposition
to those high in worldly station.[114] in his letter to Matthew Arnold
in 1871 following the republication of his essay on Lamennais,
Newman even conceded that 'perhaps la Mennais will be a true
prophet after all'.[115]

As Professor Ward has shown, these trends encouraged the rise
of 'Liberal Catholicism' among the later Tractarians.[116] A combination of High Churchmanship and Liberal opinions in politics was
much less unusual by the 1870s than it had been in the 1830s.[117]
Yet Anglican 'Liberal Catholicism' remained a fragile plant. Not
all Tractarians supported Gladstone's means of reasserting the lib-
erties of the church at the expense of old Tory High Church ideals
of Anglican confessionalism. Some still regarded various outworks
of the old constitutional order as firmer guarantors of doctrinal
orthodoxy than unfettered church liberty. The anti-establishmentism
of the Tractarians was essentially episodic in character. It only
became pronounced at times of crisis in church-state relations, as
in 1833, 1847 and 1850. As Gloyn argues, the dynamic concept
of church authority in Tractarianism actually fostered a concern

to preserve a residual spiritual character to the state. The state's claim to sovereignty was a challenge to be overcome, rather than in effect conceded by the church's retreat to the margins of society.[118] Ironically, from the 1850s onwards it was Pusey who often upheld against Gladstone the ideals of the old orthodox political theology, opposing the transition from what he called 'the Catholic to the infidel idea of the state'.[119] For Pusey, fears of the triumph of secularism outweighed any disadvantages of establishment. The Tractarians were not so much concerned with the Tory High Church rationale for establishment, that the church should consecrate the nation, than with the idea that the church should 'ensoul' society. The hope was that the church could lead the state back into acknowledging her supremacy rather than alienating the state entirely by pressing for a premature divorce.

The uncompromising anti-Erastianism of the *Tracts for the Times* was not, as Griffin suggests, tantamount to political radicalism, any more than the anti-Erastianism of the Nonjurors had been. The early Tractarian appeal to the people, unlike in the case of Lamennais, had been largely rhetorical. Nor was Pusey the odd man out in his political conservatism. Those who were most strident in their political conservatism such as Robert Wilberforce, Bishop Forbes and George Anthony Denison, upheld a Tory philosophy that spurned both ecclesiastical and political democracy.[120] The Gladstonian 'liberal catholicism' espoused by the *Guardian* was also assailed as a betrayal of the Catholic cause by the extreme Anglo-Catholic *Union Review* in the 1860s. The *Union Review* advocated 'uncompromising Toryism allied with untainted Catholicity', and asserted that the 'Catholic remembers the time when the state was in good sooth the protector of the church, and eagerly looks for a return of those golden days'.[121] Of course, the Anglo-Catholic had to be selective in his invocation of old-style Toryism. The political creed which was advocated was one 'not hampered with certain Protestant prejudices, thought by our ancestors to be inseparable from Toryism'.[122] A devotion to an historic Toryism which transcended and went behind the narrow Protestant constitutionalism of the 1820s remained a bond between old High Churchmen such as Edward Churton and Tractarians such as Robert Wilberforce even when the theological gulf between them was widening. Both chafed under the Whig ministerial regime of Lord John Russell. But as Churton commented to Wilberforce, in a conscious echo of an earlier era: 'under a Whig dynasty, "sufferance is the badge of all our tribe" '.[123]

Newman himself is perhaps best regarded as both a political conservative and a spiritual revolutionary. He was a prophet who, no
less than radical Evangelicals with whom he retained residual points
of affinity, believed that political events had to be interpreted
theologically. While his spiritual journey inevitably reshaped the
outward form and expression of his earlier political notions, there
remained a degree of continuity in his political outlook. Even in
1875 in his *Letter to the Duke of Norfolk,* Newman was able to
wax lyrical about 'Toryism, that is loyalty to persons', springing
'immortal in the human breast'.[124] Newman retained the conviction,
expressed in his critique of Lamennais, that the spirit which could
throw off civil authority might also deny the authority of religion
itself.[125] As applied to Lamennais, this proved to be a prophetic
utterance.

The 1828–33 period witnessed the shipwreck of the old constitution in church and state. The Oxford Movement represented a
response and heralded a new beginning. Toryism ceased to be the
secular domicile of church feeling, loyalty and patriotism that it had
hitherto been. Yet for many Tractarians, post-Reform politics presented an opportunity for new wine in old bottles. For as Thomas
Mozley noted in 1839,

> though the objective part of the Tory system seemed thus to pass
> away, the sentiment could not, as it had deeper root than in the
> voices of a multitude, or the suffrages of a chamber of worldly
> statesmen. The feelings remained, though hopeless, orphaned
> and widowed. They could find no political centre . . . Politically
> speaking, the greater part of the nation were become as sheep
> without a shepherd'.[126]

The Oxford Movement initially harnessed and found a home for
such Tory sentiments. It is in this context that Newman regarded
Froude as having turned from being a Tory to an Apostolical,[127]
and Frederic Rogers judged Froude as being too High Church to be
a Tory.[128] Clearly, Tractarianism transcended Toryism even while it
subsumed it.

In retrospect, the Tractarians regretted that the Tory High
Churchmanship of preceding generations had become, in their eyes,
'alloyed with faction'. But the fact that the battles of the Church
had been fought, according to Mozley, 'in election committees
and hustings; in pamphlets, popular addresses and newspapers',
was blamed on circumstances rather than individuals. As Mozley

argued, Tory churchmen of the pre-Refom era 'could not choose their own ground, or their own mode of warfare'. The Oxford Movement, however, in embracing the principles underlying the 'Church and King' tradition, acted, in Mozley's words, as 'the fan of the Winnower perpetually separating the chaff from the wheat — purifying mixed motives, and testing the solidity and durability of principles'.[129] Religious truth had ceased to be bound up with dynastic legitimacy and other political questions, but the values which had underpinned adherence to such causes endured precisely because they transcended the causes themselves. Tractarianism signalled no 'farewell to Toryism' as such, but represented the spiritual refashioning and reapplication of a sacred political creed.

Notes

1   *Remains of Richard Hurrell Froude,* 4 vols, (London & Derby, 1838–9), vol. I (London, 1838), p. 312.

2   J. B. Mozley, *Essays Historical and Theological,* 2 vols, (London, 1878), vol. I, p. xix.

3   J. H. Newman to M. Arnold, 3 December 1871, C. S. Dessain & T. Gornall, eds, *Letters and Diaries of John Henry Newman,* vol. 25, (Oxford, 1973), p. 442.

4   C. Dawson, *The Spirit of the Oxford Movement* (London, 1933), pp. 59–65; W. G. Roe, *Lamennais and England: the Reception of Lamennais's Religious Ideas in England in the Nineteenth Century* (Oxford, 1966), p. 95; P. Brendon, *Hurrell Froude and the Oxford Movement* (London, 1974), p. 120. According to Bishop Knox, the real influence of Lamennais on Froude was in inculcating a hostile attitude to the Reformation, the impiety of which Lamennais had stressed in his *Essai sur l'Indifference en Religion.* E. A. Knox, *The Tractarian Movement, 1833–1845: a Study of the Oxford Movement as a Phase of the Religious Revival in Western Europe in the Second Quarter of the Nineteenth Century.* (London, 1933), pp. 49–51.

5   J. R. Griffin, 'The Radical Phase of the Oxford Movement', *Journal of Ecclesiastical History,* 27, (1976), 47–56; J. R. Griffin, 'John Keble: Radical', *Anglican Theological Review,* 53 (1971), 167–175.

6   M. O'Connell, 'Politics and Prophecy: Newman and Lamennais', in I. Ker & A. G. Hill, eds, *Newman After a Hundred Years* (Oxford, 1990), pp. 175–91.

7   [J. H. Newman], 'Affairs of Rome', *British Critic,* 22, (1837), 274. The review article was reprinted as 'The Fall of de la Mennais', in J. H. Newman, *Essays, Critical and Historical,* 2 vols, (London, 1878), vol. I, pp. 102–36.

8   G. Every, *The High Church Party, 1688–1718* (London, 1956), p. 1; G. V. Bennett, 'Conflict in the Church', in G. Holmes, ed, *After the Glorious Revolution, 1689–1714* (London, 1969), p. 166.

9   See J. Sledd & G. Kalb, 'Johnson's definitions of Whig and Tory', *PMLA,* 67, (September, 1952), p. 882.

10   J. Sack, *From Jacobite to Conservative. Reaction and Orthodoxy, c. 1760–1832* (Cambridge, 1993), chs. 3–4.

11   J. C. D. Clark, *English Society, 1688–1832: Ideology, Social Structure and*

Political Practice During the Ancien Regime (Cambridge, 1985), especially ch. 4; R. Hole, *Pulpits, Politics and Public Order in England, 1760–1832* (Cambridge, 1989), pp. 12–21.

12   G. Best, 'The Protestant Constitution and its Supporters, 1800–29', *TRHS,* 5th Series, 8, (1958), 105–27. For an example of the genre of Protestant High Churchmanship, see H. Phillpotts, *Letters to Charles Butler on the Theological Parts of his Book of the Roman Catholic Church* (London, 1825).

13   Sack, *From Jacobite to Conservative,* ch. 9. See also D. G. S. Simes, 'The Ultra Tories in British Politics, 1824–1834', D. Phil. thesis (Oxford, 1975). Sack (pp. 224–5) detects a more cordial attitude to Catholicism among Jacobite-orientated High Churchmen of the early and mid-eighteenth century.

14   J. R. Griffin, *The Oxford Movement: a Revision* (Edinburgh, 1984), p. 1.

15   See G. Best, ed, R. W. Church, *The Oxford Movement, Twelve Years, 1833–45,* (Chicago, 1970), pp. xxix–xxx. For Stanley's view, see *Edinburgh Review,* 43, 'The Oxford School', (April 1881), 305–35.

     In contrast to later Tractarian historiography, Hurrell Froude's brother, James Anthony, described the Oxford Movement as 'Toryism in ecclesiastical costume'. J. A. Froude, 'The Oxford Counter-Reformation', in *Short Studies on Great Subjects,* Series IV (New edn, 1893), p. 249.

16   Pusey House, Pusey Papers (Liddon Bound Volumes), W. J. Copeland to E. B. Pusey, 30 October 1864.

17   PH, Pusey Papers, (LBV), W. J. Copeland to W. N. Molesworth, 2 November 1864.

18   E. Norman, 'Newman's Social and Political Thinking', in *Newman After a Hundred Years,* pp. 153–73. Newman certainly produced no systematic treatise of political thought. T. Kenny, *The Political Thought of John Henry Newman* (London, 1957), p. 144. On Newman's politics, see also A. Ryan, 'The Development of Newman's Political Thought', *Review of Politics,* 7 (1945), 210–17.

19   J. H. L. Rowlands, *Church, State and Society: the Attitudes of John Keble, Richard Hurrell Froude and John Henry Newman* (Worthing, 1989), p. x. For an alternative, crudely reductionist view of Tractarian politics, see V. Pitt, 'The Oxford Movement: a case of cultural distortion?', in K. Leech & R. Williams, eds, *Essays Catholic and Radical* (london, 1983), pp. 205–24.

20   J. H. Newman to C. Anderson, 24 January 1836, G. Tracey, ed, *Letters and Diaries of John Henry Newman,* vol. 6, (Oxford, 1984), pp. 212–13. Hurrell Froude was an admirer of the Tory histories of Clarendon and the Nonjuror, Jeremy Collier. He wished for a continuation of Collier's two-volume *Ecclesiastical History of Great Britain* (1708–14). *Remains of Hurrell Froude* vol. I, p. 339. See also n. 41.

21   Roe, *Lamennais and England* p. 92.

22   J. H. Newman to Miss M. R. Giberne, 3 December 1837, Tracey, ed, *Letters and Diaries of John Henry Newman,* vol. 6, p. 174.

23   Pusey House, Pusey Papers, W. J. Copeland to Miss M. A. Copeland, 3 May 1836. For John Scott, 1st Earl of Eldon (1751–1838), see H. Twiss, *The Public and Private Life of Lord Chancellor Eldon With Selections from his Correspondence,* 3 vols, (2nd edn., London, 1844). For Tractarian strictures on Eldon's type of churchmanship, see *Christian Remembrancer,* 8, 'Life of Lord Eldon', (September, 1844), 274–86. Eldon was notoriously neglectful of

his churchly duties. See Twiss, *Life of Eldon,* vol. III, p. 488; W. E. Surtees, *Sketch of the Lives of Lords Stowell and Eldon* (london, 1846), p. 143.

24 J. H. Newman to J. W. Bowden, 17 January 1830, T. Gornall & I. Ker, eds., *Letters and Diaries of John Henry Newman,* vol. 2, (Oxford, 1979), p. 189.

25 J. H. Newman to Mrs Newman, 1 March 1830, *ibid.,* p. 125.

26 P. B. Nockles, 'An Academic Counter-Revolution: Newman and Tractarian Oxford's Idea of a University', *History of Universities,* 10, (1991), pp. 148−50. 'Ultra-Tory' Evangelicals such as Sir Robert Harry Inglis (1786−1855), M.P. for Oxford University, in the 1830s allied themselves with the Tractarians against the Whig-latitudinarian ministerial interest.

27 J. H. Newman, *Apologia Pro Vita Sua,* J. Svaglic, ed, (Oxford, 1967), p. 506.

28 Ibid., pp. 260−2.

29 J. H. Newman, *The Via Media of the Anglican Church Illustrated in Lectures, Letters and Tracts Written Between 1830 and 1841,* 2 vols, (London, 1877), vol. II, p. 84.

30 [Newman], 'Affairs of Rome', 274.

31 Gornall & Ker, eds, *Letters and Diaries of John Henry Newman,* vol. 2, p. 35.

32 J. H. Newman, *Discussions and Arguments on Various Subjects* (London, 1885), p. 68.

33 J. H. Newman to R. H. Froude, 10 September 1830, Gornall & Ker, *Letters and Diaries of John Henry Newman,* vol. 2, p. 289.

34 L. I. Guiney, *Hurrell Froude. Memoranda and Comments* (London, 1904), p. 127. The original *Anti-Jacobin Review,* a literary vehichle of Tory High Churchmanship had run from 1798 till 1821.

35 For example, see his comment in 1834: 'I have been much surprised to find that the first Latitudinarians were Tories: e.g. Hales, Chillingworth, and that set. How Whiggery has by degrees taken up all the filth that has been secreted in the fermentation of human thought! Puritanism, Latitudinarianism, Popery, Infidelity; they have it all now, and good luck to them'. *Remains of Hurrell Froude,* vol. I, p. 339.

36 [J. Keble], 'Unpublished Papers of Bishop Warburton', *British Critic* 29, (April, 1841), 427.

37 J. Keble, 'The Danger of Sympathising with Rebellion', Sermon V, 'Preached before the University of Oxford on 30th January 1831, being the Day of King Charles' Martyrdom', in *Sermons Academical and Occasional* (Oxford, 1843), p. 124.

38 Liddon, *Life of Pusey,* vol. II, p. 29.

39 On Pusey's early political liberalism, see D. Forrester, *Young Doctor Pusey: a Study in Development* (London, 1989), pp. 14−18.

40 Quoted in Liddon, *Life of Pusey,* vol. IV, p. 199.

41 *Remains of Hurrell Froude,* vol. I, p. 177.

42 J. Keble, 'Kings to be Honoured for their Office's Sake' [Accession Day Sermon, 1836], in *Plain Sermons by Contributors to the 'Tracts for the Times',* vol. I, (London, 1839), p. 243; J. Keble, 'On the Death of a King' [9 July, 1837], in *Plain Sermons,* vol. IV, (London, 1842), pp. 76−7.

43 [J. Keble], 'Gladstone − the State in its relations with the Church', *British Critic,* 26, (October, 1839), 374−5.

44 PH, (LBV), E. B. Pusey to J. Keble, 15 November 1837.

45 J. A. Froude, 'Oxford Counter-Reformation', p. 248.

46 Liddon, *Life of Pusey,* vol. II, p. 27. Even prior to the delivery of Pusey's sermon, the Evangelical *Christian Observer* accused Pusey of wishing 'to restore the doctrines and practices of Laud and Sacheverell'. Among these doctrines were included high notions of monarchical authority and non-resistance. *Christian Observer,* 37, 'Oxford Saintology', (September, 1837), 586; R. Fisher, *Tractarianism Opposed to the Truth* (London, 1843), pp. 15–16. Moderate High Churchmen also raised the spectre of Jacobitism. See J. Beaven, *Warnings from History, Political and Ecclesiastical. A Discourse Delivered before the University of Oxford on the 30th January 1838, being the Day of King Charles' Martyrdom* (Oxford, 1838).

The status of the 'Glorious Revolution' remained a source of contention among High Churchmen into the 1840s. Edward Churton cautioned his friend William Gresley in 1845: 'those who submitted to the change of Government [in 1688], having no share in the guilt of the Revolution, acted on the old principles. I wish you therefore to speak with more moderation on this doubtful question'. Churton rejected the Tractarian tendency 'to attribute all the subsequent evils to this ancient date of the Revolution'. PH, Gresley Papers, Gres 3/7/57, E. Churton to W. Gresley, 17 November 1845.

47 Quoted in A. P. Stanley, ed, *The Life and Correspondence of Thomas Arnold D.D.* (4th edn., London, 1845), vol, II, p. 93.

48 E. B. Pusey, *Patience and Confidence the Strength of the Church: a Sermon Preached on the Fifth of November, before the University of Oxford at St. Mary's* (Oxford, 1837), p. xv.

49 *Ibid,* p. vi. Liddon described the sermon as 'imbued with the old moral as well as political temper of Toryism'. Liddon, *Life of Pusey,* vol. II, p. 27.

50 Pusey, *Patience and Confidence,* p. v. The sermon was praised by a friendly reviewer for invoking the example of 'the saints and martyrs of our own church, exhibited in all the beauty, dignity and loveliness of passive obedience and non-resistance'. [N. Goldsmid], 'Pusey's Sermon on the Fifth of November', *British Critic,* 23, (January, 1838), 144.

51 Griffin misinterprets the sermon as 'more a political treatise than a sermon'. Griffin, *Oxford Movement,* pp. 64–5. It is also interesting that a current historian of Jacobitism maintains 'that the last Oxford Jacobite sermon was preached by Dr. Pusey on 5 November 1837'. P. K. Monod, *Jacobitism and the English People, 1688–1788* (Cambridge, 1989), p. 152.

52 E. B. Pusey, *the Church, the Converter of the Heathen. Two Sermons Preached in Conformity with the Queen's Letter in Behalf of the SPG* (Oxford, 1838), p. 23.

53 *Ibid,* p, 56. For an earlier statement of this view, see J. Boucher, *View of the Causes and Consequences of the American Revolution in Thirteen Discourses* (London, 1797).

54 E. B. Pusey, *Remarks on the Prospective and Past Benefits of Cathedral Institutions, in the Promotion of Sound Religious Knowledge, and of Clerical Education* (London, 1833), p. 96.

55 Bodleian Library, Ms Wilberforce d. 17, fol. 336, E. B. Pusey to S. Wilberforce, 9 September 1836.

56 PH, (LBV), E. B. Pusey to W. E. Gladstone, March 1836.

57 Bodleian Library, Ms Wilberforce d. 17, fol. 338, J. Keble to S. Wilberforce, 19 September 1836.

58 E. B. Pusey, *The Royal Supremacy Not an Arbitrary Authority but Limited*

by the Laws of the Church, of which Kings are Members (Oxford, 1850), p. 159.

59 On his Mediterranean journey in 1832–3, Newman refused even to look at the tricolor on a French vessel in the port of Algiers. Newman, *Apologia,* p. 97. For both Newman and Froude's defence of the Bourbon monarchy, see n. 67. Sack (*From Jacobite to Conservative,* pp. 246–7) contrasts Newman's attitude with that of contemporary English Ultra-Tories whose inveterate anti-Catholicism inclined them, unlike their French counterparts, to take the liberal side in continental politics. On the other hand, according to the unreliable Tom Mozley, 'all Oxford' was for the Bourbons and opposed to 'the Orleanist machinations'. T. Mozley, *Reminiscences Chiefly of Oriel College and the Oxford Movement,* 2 vols, (London, 1882), vol. I, p. 252. See also n. 73.

60 J. R. Griffin, 'The Anglican Politics of Cardinal Newman', *Anglican Theological Review,* 55, (October, 1973), 435.

61 The entry in Newman's diary for 30 January 1836 reads: 'Saturday 30th January. The Martyrdom. I tried to find a church open in vain'. T. Gornall, ed, *Letters and Diaries of John Henry Newman,* vol. 5, (Oxford, 1981), pp. 220, 302. On the cult of the Royal Martyr in the High Anglican tradition, see H. W. Randall, 'The Rise and Fall of a Martyrology: Sermons on Charles I', *Huntington Library Quarterly,* 10, (1946/7), 164–5; Sack, *From Jacobite to Conservative,* pp. 126–30.

62 J. H. Newman to R. H. Froude, 7 January 1830, Gornall & Ker, eds, *Letters and Diaries of John Henry Newman,* vol. 2, p. 186.

63 J. H. Newman to H. A. Woodgate, 7 July 1833, T. Gornall, ed, *Letters and Diaries of John Henry Newman* vol. 4 (Oxford, 1981), pp. 26–7. Newman's attitude here mirrored that of conservative High Church supporters of the Oxford Movement such as Arthur Philip Perceval, later Chaplain to Queen Victoria. In 1833, Perceval accused the Whig Premier, Lord Grey of undermining the monarchy. A. P. Perceval, *A Letter to the Rt. Hon. Earl Grey on the Obligation of the Coronation Oath* (London, 1833), pp. 6–7. On the religious symbolism of the coronation service, see E. C. Ratcliff, *The English Coronation Service* (London, 1937).

64 Gornall & Ker, eds, *Letters and Diaries of John Henry Newman,* vol. 4, p. 164.

65 J. H. Newman to J. W. Bowden, 5 February 1835, Gornall, ed, *Letters and Diaries of John Henry Newman,* vol. 5, p. 24.

66 J. H. Newman to R. F. Wilson, 8 September 1833, Gornall & Ker, eds, *Letters and Diaries of John Henry Newman,* vol. 4, p. 44. The reluctant nature of the shift is clear from Newman's avowal: 'It is not we who desert the government, but the government that has left us; we are forced back upon those below us, because those above us will not honour us. There is no help for it, I say'. J. H. Newman, *The Church of the Fathers* (London, 1840), p. 3.

67 [Newman], 'Affairs of Rome', 270.

68 Clark, *English Society,* p. 419.

69 J. H. Newman to R. H. Froude, 31 August 1833, *Letters and Correspondence of Newman,* 2 vols, (London, 1891), vol. I, p. 450.

70 J. H. Newman to H. J. Rose, 23 May 1836, Gornall, ed, *Letters and Diaries of John Henry Newman,* vol. 5, p. 304.

71 R. I. Wilberforce, *An Inquiry into the Principles of Church Authority; or*

Reasons for Recalling My Subscription to the Royal Supremacy (London, 1854); R. I. Wilberforce, *A Sketch of the History of Erastianism* (London, 1851), pp. 58–61. As Wilberforce explained: 'the Tudors had required all persons to agree with themselves; the Stuarts, with their Bishops; but William of Orange was indifferent what men believed, provided they differed from the Pope'. Wilberforce, *Church Authority*, p. 277.

72   PH, Ollard Papers, C. Marriott to J. H. Newman, 15 January 1840. See [J. H. Newman], 'The Court of James I', *British Critic* 27, (January, 1840), 34–5.

73   [Newman], 'Affairs of Rome', 276. Froude's pro-Bourbon attitude was also akin to that of the French Legitimist 'Ultras' and in contrast to the pro-Orleanism of the English 'Ultra-Tories'. Froude had been serious in 1830 when he expressed the hope that 'the march of mind in France may yet prove a bloody one'. *Remains of Hurrell Froude*, vol. I, p. 244.

74   'I was driven, by my state of mind, to insist upon the political conduct, the controversial bearing, and the social methods and manifestations of Rome ... I had an unspeakable aversion to the policy and acts of Mr. O'Connell, because, as I thought, he associated himself with men of all religions and no religion against the Anglican Church, and advanced Catholicism by violence and intrigue'. Newman, *Apologia*, p. 223. The Tractarian Gothicist, Lord John Manners likewise accused Catholics of 'shamelessly casting away your Stuart memories, your Jacobite predilections, your aristocratic sympathies, and your old English associations, to league yourselves with the legitimate descendants of those, who through long years of bitterness and reproach, ceased not to persecute your fathers'. [Lord John Manners], *What are the English Roman Catholics to do? The Question Considered in a Letter to Lord Edward Howard, by 'Anglo-Catholicus'* (London, 1841), p. 9.

On Phillipps de Lisle, a Tory Leicestershire squire who converted to Catholicism, see E. S. Purcell & E. de Lisle, *Life and Letters of Ambrose Phillipps de Lisle*, 2 vols, (London 1900).

75   S. W. Gilley, 'Frederick Lucas, *The Tablet* and Ireland – A Victorian Forerunner of Liberation Theology', S. Mews, ed, *Modern Religious Rebels, Presented to John Kent* (London, 1993), p. 65.

76   Newman, *Apologia*, p. 237. Even when opposing Catholic Emancipation in 1829 Keble had looked to Catholics 'as possible allies instead of enemies in the struggles which seem to await us. It was so in the days of Charles I'. Bodleian Library, Ms Eng Lett d. 124, fols. 23–4, J. Keble to C. A. Ogilvie, 14 March 1829. But English Catholic nobles such as the Earl of Shrewsbury disappointed the Tractarians in their continued adherence to the Whig cause. See Earl of Shrewsbury, *A Second Letter to Ambrose Lisle Phillipps Esq. on the Present Position of Affairs* (London, 1841). However, the *Catholic Magazine* shared the neo-Jacobite and Tory sympathies of the Tractarians. See *Catholic Magazine* I, New Series, 'the last of the Stuarts', (March, 1843), 184.

77   W. Ward, *William George Ward and the Oxford Movement* (London, 1889), p. 214.

78   J. H. Newman to J. W. Bowden, May 1839, Mozley, ed, *Letters and Correspondence of Newman*, vol. II, p. 282.

79   See 'The Protestant Idea of Antichrist', in J. H. Newman, *Essays, Critical and Historical*, 2 vols, (London, 1871), Ess. II, pp. 112–85.

80   S. W. Gilley, 'Newman and Prophecy, Evangelical and Catholic', *The Journal of the United Reformed Church Society,* 3, (March, 1985), 160–183; P. Misner, *Papacy and Development: Newman and the Primacy of the Pope* (London, 1976), pp. 50–77; Rowlands, *Church State and Society,* pp. 181–96.

81   S. W. Gilley, *Newman and His Age* (London, 1990), p. 175.

82   E. Norman, 'Newman's Social and Political Thinking', pp. 165–6.

83   *Remains of Hurrell Froude,* vol. III, (Derby, 1838), p. 274.

84   *Ibid,* pp. 199–200. Froude, however, used Hooker's views as an *argumentum ad hominem.* Privately, he conceded that he was 'out of conceit with old Hooker's notion of a lay synod: it is unecclesiastical and Whig. We must only be popular in the choice of church officers'. *Remains of Hurrell Froude,* vol. I, p. 333. As early as 1836, one critic argued that the Oxford party had 'secretly discovered Hooker's doctrines [on church and state] to be dangerous, though it is willing to shelter under his name still'. *State of Parties in Oxford* (Oxford, 1836). p. 16.

85   *Remains of Hurrell Froude,* vol. III, p. 207.

86   *Ibid,* p. 196.

87   See Froude's article on Becket in the *British Magazine,* 2, (September, 1832), especially 34–5. The article was reprinted as volume IV of the *Remains* (Derby, 1839). Even Newman thought that the 'Becket papers might frighten people considerably – on church and state'. J. H. Newman to J. Keble, 13 September 1838, G. Tracey, ed, *Letters and Diaries of John Henry Newman,* vol. VI, p. 317. The most zealous lay participant in the early Movement, James William Bowden, was also sympathetic to Becket's standpoint. See J. W. Bowden, *The Life and Pontificate of Gregory the Seventh,* 2 vols, (London, 1840), vol. I, pp. 113–117.

88   For example, see W. F. Hook, *On the Church and Establishment. Two Plain Sermons* (London, 1834), p. 44; J. H. Pott, *The Rights of Sovereignty in Christian States Defended in Some Chief Particulars* (London, 1821). William Sewell later reminded his Tractarian friends that the Caroline Divines 'show no sympathy with Hildebrand ...still less would they hold up Becket to reverence, or allow him to be a martyr'. [W. Sewell], 'Divines of the Seventeenth Century', *Quarterly Review,* 69, (March, 1842), 500–01.

89   *Remains of Hurrell Froude,* vol. IV, p. 273.

90   *Ibid,* p. 227.

91   *Ibid,* vol. I, pp. 414, 434.

92   *Ibid,* vol. I, pp. 325–8. Frederic Rogers told Newman in 1837 that Froude had 'said to me ...that all our divines since the Reformation had been very dark about church independence'. F. Rogers to J. H. Newman, 21 January 1839, G. E. Marindin, ed, *Letters of Frederic, Lord Blachford* (London, 1896), pp. 45–6.

93   PH, (LBV), J. Keble to A. P. Perceval, 29 June 1837.

94   J. Keble to J. H. Newman, 8 August 1833, Mozley, ed, *Letters and Correspondence of Newman,* vol. I, p. 441.

95   Keble College Archives, Keble Papers, J. Keble to J. H. Newman, 31 March 1839.

96   In his *Case of the Regale and of the Pontificate* (1700), the Nonjuror Charles Leslie had limited the Royal Supremacy to civil matters.

97   Thomas, *Newman and Heresy,* p. 52.

98   [Newman], 'Affairs of Rome', p. 261.

99 *Ibid,* 278.

100 Newman asserted in 1851, 'that the established religion was set up in erastianism, that erastianism was its essence'. J. H. Newman, *Certain Difficulties Felt by Anglicans in Catholic Teaching* (London, 1851), p. 223. But as early as 1836, Newman privately conceded to Pusey, 'that the English church subsists in the state, and has no internal consistency . . . to keep it together'. J. H. Newman to E. B. Pusey, 24 January 1836, Gornall, ed, *Letters and Diaries of John Henry Newman,* vol. 5, p. 214. Even by 1834–5, Newman had questioned the legitimacy of the church's surrender of her juridical powers to the state in 1534. [J. H. Newman], 'The Convocation of the Province of Canterbury', *British Magazine,* 6, (October, 1834), 517–24, 637–47; 7, (January-March, 1835), 33–41, 145–54, 259–68.

101 C. K. Gloyn, *The Church in the Social Order: a Study of Anglican Social Theory from Coleridge to Maurice* (Forest Grove, Oregon), pp. 49–54.

102 By 1847, the High Churchman William Gresley was cautioning the more advanced Tractarians not to 'set down the old cry of "Church and King" as altogether Erastian. Good men used it as well as mere politicians'. W. Gresley, *A Second Statement on the Real Danger of the Church of England* (London, 1847), p. 14. Tractarian disenchantment with the world of royal favour and patronage was encouraged by Queen Victoria's early *penchant* for Whig latitudinarians and later support of the Presbyterian Kirk in Scotland. See Thomas Mozley's comment in 1839: 'that times are changed in this respect is evinced by our being unable to estimate the feeling which made a Herbert, or a Laud, such zealous competitors for royal favour'. [T. Mozley], 'Church and King', *British Critic,* 25, (April, 1839), 325–6.

103 O'Connell, 'Newman and Lamennais', p. 177.

104 See Knox, *Tractarian Movement,* ch. 3.

105 *Remains of Hurrell Froude,* vol. I, p. 339. On popular Tory Jacobitism in the era of the Whig trial of Doctor Henry Sacheverell (1709) for supposedly libelling the Revolution of 1688, see Monod, *Jacobitism and the English People,* ch. 6.

106 Important research on this topic is currently being carried out by Dr. Simon Skinner of Mansfield College, Oxford, to whom I am indebted for drawing my attention to the work by C. K. Gloyn.

107 P. Maurice, *The Ritualism of Oxford Popery. A Letter to Dr. MacBride, Principal of Magdalen Hall, Oxford* (London, [1867]), p.

108 See my forthcoming, 'The Great Disruption: the University and the Oxford Movement, 1829–54', M. Brock & M. C. Curthoys, *History of the University of Oxford,* vol. 6.

109 *Christian Remembrancer,* 8, 'Life of Lord Eldon', 285–6.

110 J. Wolffe, *The Protestant Crusade in Great Britain, 1829–1860* (Oxford, 1991), ch. 3.

111 Norman, 'Newman's Social and Political Thinking', p. 165.

112 C. S. Dessain, ed, *Letters and Diaries of John Henry Newman,* vol. 12, (London, 1962), pp. 103–4.

113 Newman, *Difficulties of Anglicans,* p. 267.

114 W. G. Ward, *The Ideal of a Christian Church Considered in Comparison with Existing Practice* (London, 1844), pp. 26–33.

115 Newman to Arnold, 3 December 1871, Dessain & Gornall, eds, *Letters and Diaries of John Henry Newman,* vol. 25, p. 442.

116 W. R. Ward, 'Oxford and the Origins of Liberal Catholicism in the Church of England', *Studies in Church History,* 1, (1964), 234–9.
117 J. Parry, *Democracy and Religion: Gladstone and the Liberal Party, 1867–1875* (Cambridge, 1986), p. 182.
118 Gloyn, *Church in the Social Order,* pp. 66–9.
119 P. B. Nockles, 'Pusey and the Question of Church and State', in P. Butler, ed, *Pusey Rediscovered* (London, 1983), p. 291.
120 For Denison's political Toryism, see G. A. Denison, *Notes of My Life, 1805–1878* (Oxford, 1878), p. 64. Denison avowed, 'I am an old Tory. I never liked a Whig ...I am not fond of a Conservative either, as a Conservative'. G. A. Denison, *Mr Gladstone. With Appendix, Containing the Accumulated Evidence of Fifty-Five Years. A Retrospect and Prospect. With Summary* (London, 1885), p. 9.
121 *Union Review,* I (1863), 32.
122 *Ibid,* 38.
123 PH, Churton Papers, Chur 2/4/20, E. Churton to R. I. Wilberforce, 5 June 1849.
124 J. H. Newman, *A Letter to His Grace, the Duke of Norfolk on Occasion of Mr. Gladstone's Recent Expostulation* (London, 1875), p. 72.
125 [Newman], 'Affairs of Rome', 283.
126 [Mozley], 'Church and King', 322.
127 J. H. Newman to F. Rogers, 5 July 1837, Tracey, ed, *Letters and Diaries of John Henry Newman,* vol. 6, p. 89.
128 Birmingham Oratory, Newman Papers, B.12.1.220, F. Rogers to J. H. Newman, 14 August 1833. But for Thomas Mozley, Froude remained 'a Tory with that transcendental ideal of the English gentleman which forms the basis of Toryism'. Mozley, *Reminiscences,* vol. I, p. 228. It is significant that Froude never used 'Tory' in a pejorative sense as he did with the term 'Conservative'. See, *Remains of Hurrell Froude,* vol, I, p. 366.
129 [Mozley], 'Church and King', 324–5.

Part Two

From Oxford to the People

The Influence of the Oxford Movement in the Parishes c. 1833–1860: A Reassessment

Frances Knight

Amongst students of Anglican history, there is a widely-articulated belief that the Oxford Movement's most enduring legacy was to be found in the impact of Ritualism in the parishes of England. This tends to be understood in terms of a new emphasis on devotion, liturgy and ceremonial, which became prominent in the period after 1860. Assessing the results of the Oxford Movement, Owen Chadwick has claimed that no one did more than the Tractarians to drive Anglican worshippers out of formalism, and to enable sympathetic hearts to perceive the beauty and poetry of religion.[1] In a similar vein, W. S. F. Pickering has argued that the Ritualistic component of the Oxford Movement was enormous in bringing about a revolutionary change in the practical conduct of the Church of England,[2] and his point has been echoed by the bold claims of Nigel Yates and Adrian Hastings. Yates suggests that the Movement transformed not only the devotional, liturgical and theological aspects of the established Church, but its social outlook as well, and through it the lives of many British citizens.[3] Hastings reminds us that by the 1920s the Anglo-Catholics were beginning to enter into their inheritance, no longer a barely tolerated party, but the central moving force within the Church, reshaping its ethos and symbolism. The 'moderate' Anglo-Catholicism adopted in theological colleges at the heart of the establishment, such as Westcott and Cuddesdon, was effectively fashioning the Anglican clerical norm, and promoting a standard which was to become almost uniform in the parishes.[4] Despite Parliament's rejection of the Prayer Book measure in 1928, Anglican liturgy and devotion began to assume a fairly fixed identity which would have won unqualified approval from the first generation of persecuted Ritualists.

If the consensus among historians seems to be that in its secondary phase the impact of the High Church revival was principally liturgical and therefore parochial, the assumption is that in its first, 'Oxford' phase, the Movement was anything but liturgical, and that its leaders were essentially indifferent to such matters. Chadwick tells us that Newman and Pusey were not sympathetic to changes in trivial detail which might offend, and that Pusey thought that the simplicity of English practice was appropriate to the penitential state of divided Christendom.[5] Yates remarks that the leaders of the Oxford Movement were liturgically conservative;[6] Louis Weil observes that the first leaders demonstrated no great interest in ceremonial.[7] Pickering also makes explicit the contention that for the leaders of the Oxford Movement in 1833 'the battle immediately became one of ideas. It had very little to do with ritual worship'.[8] It was the Cambridge Camdenians, we are told, who were the first to attempt the transposition of Tractarian theology into a liturgical and ecclesiological key.

The purpose of this article is not to argue, *contra* the weight of scholarly opinion cited above, that the leaders of the Oxford Movement did regard ritual and ceremonial as particularly important, or to deny that one of the major legacies of the Movement was the establishment of a watered-down Anglo-Catholicism as more or less normative in Anglican worship. Rather, the purpose is to shed some light upon the little studied question of the way in which the ideas associated with the Oxford Movement were received in the parishes in the years before the onset of Ritualism. To do this, the article begins by outlining some older and some more recent trends in historiography. It then examines evidence from primary sources chiefly relating to rural areas, and in particular to parishes within the massive diocese of Lincoln.

Very little seems to be known about Tractarianism in places outside Oxford in the period before about 1860. This is perhaps a reflection of the way in which the entire Oxford Movement has been studied, rather as a heroic narrative focused on the lives and thoughts of a handful of Oxford men — Keble, Pusey, Froude and above all Newman. Perhaps every movement needs to identify its heroes if it is to capture the popular imagination. Indeed, John Kent has suggested that some of the older historians of Evangelicalism attempted to package the Wesleys, the Venns, Charles Simeon and J. C. Ryle as Evangelical heroes to rival Keble, Pusey and Gore.[9] Certainly, the ripping accounts of the saintliness of Keble, the scholarly austerity of Pusey, the boyish flamboyance of Froude and at centre stage, the mounting tension of the personal drama of Newman, make for far more compelling reading than any abstract account of their theological principles could ever do. R. W. Church, S. L. Ollard and other historians who have assumed their mantle surely knew that this was so. But this approach also led to a tendency, unconscious perhaps, to overplay the crisis of the Oxford Movement's 'wilderness period', which was seen as resulting from the loss of leadership after 1845. George Herring's work on Tractarianism outside Oxford has questioned whether the loss of Newman and his followers did in fact have the devastating impact on the Movement which has generally been assumed. Indeed, he argues that it may rather have had a rejuvenating than a shattering effect.[10]

Herring's work is the only recent attempt to provide a systematic examination of Tractarianism in the parishes during the period 1845 − 1867, and it is a valuable resource. It is harder to glean information for the period 1833 − 1845. The older histories provide the reader with snippets, which, as the following examples show, seem to have passed into the common stock which is the historical imagination. In the *Apologia* Newman refers to students who, upon graduation, 'went down to the country, and became curates of parishes. Then they had down from London parcels of the Tracts and other publications. They placed them in the shops of local booksellers, got them into newspapers, introduced them to clerical meetings, and converted more or less their Rectors and brother curates'.[11] A few pages later he adds, 'In a very few years a school of opinion was formed, fixed in its principles, indefinite and progressive in their range; and it extended itself into every part of the countryside'.[12] R. W. Church, whose history is predicated on the assumption that what is being described is essentially an 'Oxford' phenomenon, is correspondingly vague about developments outside the University. In a rare reference, he suggests that 'From the end of 1835, or the beginning of 1836, the world outside Oxford began to be alive to the force and the rapid growth of this new and, to the world at large, not very intelligible movement. The ideas which had laid hold so powerfully on a number of the leading minds in the University began to work with a spell, which seemed to many inexplicable, on others unconnected with them'.[13] Ollard provided a characteristically more highly embellished account of the Movement's transition into the countryside, loosely based on a passage in the *Apologia* 'The real campaign began. Mr Newman, in 1833, in the Long Vacation, rode round to country vicarages carrying parcels of the Tracts and begging the clergy to read them. His friends did the same ... The Tractarians, as they were called, were popular. Recruits poured in'.[14]

Beyond reworking some of the little vignettes from the older histories, most recent historians have tended to overlook the possibility of early Tractarian activity outside Oxford. Instead, they have favoured an interpretation which focuses first on the Movement's heroic leadership and then, only after the heroes have come tumbling from their pedestals, on the assimilation of Tractarianism countrywide. Nigel Yates has been almost alone in attempting local studies of the Oxford Movement, and George Herring is the only person to have concentrated systematically on the Movement's second phase, the period 1845–1867.

A corrective to the rosiness of the interpretation favoured by Church and Ollard, which saw the Movement catching hold in the countryside like a bush fire, is appropriate. It is the contention of this article that true Tractarians were few and far between at this period, and that many who were accused of harbouring Tractarian sympathies were in fact old fashioned high churchmen of varying types. George Herring drew up a list of 958 clergy active during the period 1840–1870 to whom he assigned the label Tractarian. This figure includes Anglican priests who converted to Rome. Whilst Herring is the first to admit that further research would uncover further names, and that attempting to reconstruct the churchmanship of individual clergy from a distance of 130 years is in any case fraught with pitfalls, it seems unlikely that his figure is a serious under representation. W. J. Conybeare, (although clearly not an impartial source), provided a contemporary estimate of 1,000 Tractarian clergy in his essay on 'Church Parties' in 1853,[15] and this within an estimated clerical cohort of 18,000. Implicit within Conybeare's essay is the contention that the importance of the Movement had been grossly exaggerated. He dismissed the bulk of the Tractarian party as 'young and silly partisans ...they have learnt by rote a set of phrases for which they shout ...the noise made by all this astonishes those who know how few are the makers of it ...in this multiplying mirror the image of a single Tractarian is transformed into a assembly of divines; and a little knot of ambitious curates pass themselves off on a dazzled public as the leaders of ecclesiastical opinion.'[16]

Arguments for the extremely limited impact of Tractarianism are borne out by investigation of the diocese of Lincoln. The diocese's most celebrated Tractarians, both of whom became Roman Catholics, were Richard Waldo Sibthorpe[17] and Bernard Smith.[18] Neither, however, and the point should be stressed, could be described as remotely representative of Anglican clergy as a whole. Sibthorpe was readmitted to Anglican orders in 1847, but seceded again in 1865. He was however buried with the Anglican liturgy in 1879. Bernard Smith is perhaps better known than Sibthorpe because he figures obliquely as 'Mr B.S.' in chapter four of

Newman's *Apologia*. Smith provoked the ire of some of the parishioners of Leadenham, Lincolnshire, when he appointed A. W. Pugin to refurbish the interior of his church in 1841. Then followed the introduction of two 'colossal and gaudy candlesticks, and candles in front of the communion table', which, according to one enraged parishioner, gave the chancel 'the precise semblance of a popish place of worship'.[19] Smith began to cross himself and bow to the altar, and taught the Sunday school children to do the same. He adopted the eastward position, and at his weekly early communions used wafers in place of bread.[20] At Christmas 1842, Smith was received into the Church of Rome at Oscott. After a few years, he was reordained, and worked as a parish priest from 1853 until his death in 1903.

Conversions to Rome were of course highly unusual. In the Lincoln diocese in the period up to 1860, only one other has come to light — that of William G. Penny who resigned the perpetual curacies of Ashendon and Dorton in Buckinghamshire in November 1844.[21] Whilst departure from the Anglican communion was almost unheard of in the countryside, unease amongst high churchmen about its character and constitution probably lurked not infrequently below the surface — even if seldom publicly acknowledged — particularly during the unsettled period between the publication of Tract 90 in 1841 and Newman's conversion in 1845. Francis Massingberd, rector of South Ormsby in Lincolnshire, confided to his diary shortly after news had reached him of Newman's secession: 'Today, low in spirits . . . Tempted for the first time in my life to be discontented with ye Ch: of E.'[22]

It is striking that in the diocese of Lincoln at least, the terms 'Tractarian', 'Puseyite' or 'supporter of the Oxford party' were not readily owned, even by those to whom they seem most applicable. Henry Bull, perpetual curate of Lathbury in Buckinghamshire, advocated more frequent but shorter services, greater ecclesiastical discipline and spiritual guidance, a stricter rule of life for the clergy and the adoption of distinctive clerical dress. Yet he described his 'friends at Oxford' as rash and unscriptual.[23] John Wolley, vicar of Beeston, Nottinghamshire, found himself unexpectedly at the centre of controversy after he introduced changes in his church in 1843. 'I am called a Puseyite, tho' in fact I have never read any one of the Tracts. Turning to the East in the Reading desk at the Creeds has always been my custom'.[24] This in itself is interesting, for Wolley had been vicar of Beeston since 1822. Despite having always turned east, he admitted to some liturgical innovations, including a third service aimed at the poor, the dismissal of the choir, with the parish

clerk taking their place by leading the singing and responses from
the gallery; the acquisition of a new altar cloth and carpet, and the
adoption of surplices. He also introduced a monthly communion,
at which 'no longer is the bread and wine placed on the table in a
black bottle and a crockery plate covered over with a napkin at the
beginning of the service. They are now stored in the ancient but
broken niche for holy water within the rails'.[25] It is significant that
hostile observers accused Wolley of Tractarianism, despite his rigorous denials. Also interesting is the attitude of his bishop, the
High Church John Kaye, who by 1843 was no friend of Tractarians.
Rather than censuring Wolley, Kaye commended him warmly for
his innovations. 'Far from finding anything liable to just objection
in the changes which you have made, I find much to approve; and
the charge of Puseyism can only originate in great ignorance of the
intentions of our Church in framing its Services and Rubrics'.[26]

   This evidence from Lathbury and Beeston — and indeed also from
Leadenham — suggests that although historians have not regarded
the Oxford Movement in its first phase as primarily liturgical in
character, this was not a perception shared by contemporaries in
the parishes. From the early 1840s, liturgical innovation seems to
have been regarded as a clear indication of Tractarian sympathies —
in fact its most distinguishing feature — even when those accused
disowned all connection with the Movement.

   Who then were the real Tractarians, the men who were prepared
to admit their association with the Oxford Movement? George Herring's interesting chapter on the way in which Tractarian ideas were
disseminated has questioned the assumption that large numbers of
the young men who had sat at Newman's feet in Oxford were in
the vanguard when it came to introducing Tractarian theology into
the parishes. Among his sample of 958 Tractarian clergy, only
112 were resident in Oxford during the Movement's first phase.[27]
Herring refers also to such noted Tractarians as G. A. Dension,
who despite having been a Fellow of Oriel from 1828–38 claimed
to owe nothing either to Tractarian writings or to Tractarian personalities.[28] In a further departure from conventional wisdom, Herring
suggests that in the decade 1856–65, Cambridge actually produced
more Tractarian clergy than Oxford.[29] No doubt Newman's sermons
at the university church were well attended, but it is clearly unwise
to assume that all the ordinands who heard him were set alight
with Tractarian fervour. And of those who had been enthusiastic as
undergraduates, perhaps some began to take a lower key approach
as curates, finding that their newly-minted Oxford theology could
not be so readily assimilated into the realities of rural parish life.

This theory would seem to be strengthened by the evidence that after 1841, public admission of Tractarian sympathies could in itself severely damage the prospects of employment. In 1848 at Donnington, Lincolnshire, the Vicar John Wilson rejected a Mr. Whiteford for a curacy on the grounds of his 'extreme' Tractarian views. He expressed his position succinctly: 'The inhabitants are of a very mercurial temperament, and would soon reach boiling point, if a curate under the influence of 'Newmania' came amongst them to introduce new doctrines and new plans'.[30] A similar victim of such treatment may perhaps have been James Trevor White, who was passed over for the incumbency of the new church of St. John the Baptist, Nottingham, in 1844, allegedly on account of his Tractarian principles. However, his case is complicated by the fact that he had briefly been gaoled for debt, and this may well have been seen as a blacker mark against him. Whatever the exact circumstances, he was destined to remain unbeneficed for the rest of his life, and his alleged Tractarianism proved to be a convenient excuse for by-passing him. At Epworth in Lincolnshire in 1850, the curate was accused of being a Jesuit, despite the fact that he was married. Epworth's non-resident rector wrote scornfully from Bologne to scotch the rumour. He admitted that his curate was 'High Church', but remarked that 'anybody who at all insists on church principles in Epworth is sure to be called High Church if not *Tractarian* ... particularly at this moment when the whole country is gone mad about the pope, and visions of Jesuits present themselves in abundance, I dare say, to the excellent people of Epworth'.[31] Here again is evidence of the term 'Tractarian' being used in a loose and pejorative sense to describe someone who might more properly be seen as a high churchman.

Self-confessed Tractarian incumbents were evidently few and far between. Herring estimates that there were 141 in 1845, although the numbers did begin to increase steadily.[32] Amongst the clergy, the majority of Tractarian sympathizers were to be found amongst the unbeneficed. Newman's description, cited earlier, of the curates who 'converted more or less their Rectors and brother curates' appears apt, as indeed is Conybeare's rather venomous reference to 'a little knot of ambitious curates'. Of Herring's sample, the majority were young, graduating in the 1840s, 1850s and 1860s. A large number seem to have led an almost itinerant lifestyle, changing parishes and often also dioceses every few years. Christopher Thompson, for example, was ordained in 1859, and served curacies at St John's, Leicester from 1859–61, St Mary, Roade from 1861–62, St Bartholomew, Cripplegate from 1862–64 and St Paul's Brighton in 1864, after which nothing more is known of him. Edwards Pearson, ordained in 1852, served curacies at St Nicholas, Great Yarmouth from 1852–54, Barrow in Suffolk from 1854–55, St Martin's Liverpool from 1855–56, Alverstoke from 1856–57, St Paul's Birmingham in 1857, Christ Church Westminster in 1858, St Peter's Normanton from 1859–66 and finally All Saints North Street in York from 1866. Like Thompson, Pearson was never beneficed. Although these two men did perhaps move around rather more than the average, their careers were not untypical. In Herring's list, it is apparent that the same parishes keep reappearing: St Paul's Knightsbridge, St Anne's Soho, St Augustine's Haggerston, Christ Church Clapham, and away from the capital, Clewer, Wantage, Alverstoke, St Paul's Brighton, St Peter's Plymouth. These were regarded as highly desirable Tractarian parishes, and they clearly had a relatively high turnover of curates.

In some cases at least, newly ordained Tractarian curates arrived in their parishes and began to court controversy. W. T. Mossman arrived at Donington-on-Bain from St. Edmund Hall, Oxford in 1849, and within months had fallen out with George Tomline of Riby Grove, who was the largest landowner in the parish. The curate informed Tomline that he was *'morally* bound' to give money towards a National school at Donington, and he complained about him to the bishop when Tomline ignored his increasingly strongly worded letters.[33] As Herring has argued, reminding the gentry that their social responsibilities were divinely ordained was part of the Anglican ethos, and in this Tractarians differed little from other clergymen.[34] One distinctive difference, however, was in the Tractarian emphasis on the Eucharist as a model for transforming relations in a refashioned social community. It is significant that Mossman also wrote to the bishop to ask if he could be admitted to priest's orders before the end of his diaconal year, on the grounds that he was in sole charge of two parishes, and found it inconvenient to be unable to administer the sacrament of the Lord's Supper.[35]

Weekly celebration of the Eucharist, which was the Tractarian ideal, was itself a cause of controversy.[36] The Bishop of Salisbury, Walter Kerr Hamilton, who was known for his Tractarian sympathies, noted in his diary that a complaint had been made against the clerical meetings orgainized by Anthony Huxtable, one of his rural deans, commenting that the 'clergy are themselves startled at finding how great the differences are between them', and that some disliked having Holy Communion before the meeting.[37] This awareness of the division of clerical opinion, which was becoming manifest by the 1840s, was clearly an unintended by-product of the move towards greater clerical contact through societies and meetings. Rather than fostering unity between clergy, as was originally hoped, the Eucharist, and indeed the meetings, became a focus for contention. In some dioceses, the fear that the clergy would provoke controversy if they were permitted to give public expression to their opinions seems to have made it harder for them to say anything very much at all. Arthur Burns has suggested that the visitation sermon, which was traditionally the occasion at which one of the brighter of the younger clergy was invited to preach to his peers, began to disappear from visitations, and that it was a casualty of tensions caused by intensified party feeling.[38] Burns argues that whereas Claphamite Evangelicals and orthodox High Churchmen had achieved a fair degree of cooperation, particularly over such matters as the revival of diocesan institutions, the impact of the Tractarians was more ambivalent. Like the Recordite Evangelicals, Tractarians were less concerned with pragmatic considerations or unity, unless founded on a narrow theological basis. Rather than being the unifying occasions that they were intended to be, visitations and episcopal charges became marred by division.[39] As a correspondent put it to Walter Kerr Hamilton after the reception accorded to his charge of 1864, 'What a blessing you must think it to be, that your Charge does not occur every year, or you would never be out of hot water'.[40] When a clergyman admitted Tractarian sympathies, he tended to provoke distrust and hostility. That so very few openly avowed the Tractarian position served to increase the notoriety of those who did. Of the rest, it seems clear that party sympathy or identity was not as differentiated or divisive at this period as it later became, and that cooperation, rather than conflict, was still the norm amongst Anglican clergy.

If the Tractarian clergy were regarded as oddities who failed to conform to the prevailing ethos of the Church of England, how then were the Tractarian laity regarded? From the diocese of Lincoln comes evidence of some apparently Tractarian laymen who were considerably in advance of the more conservative clergy. Two particular groups merit special attention here: churchwardens and architects. Once again, the evidence suggests that their interventions were chiefly over liturgical matters.

Church wardening, with its onerous responsibilites for maintaining the church's fabric and attempting to levy the church rates, was not generally regarded as a suitable occupation for a gentleman at this period, and most wardens tended to be tradesmen or farmers. It is significant, therefore, that the people's churchwarden at St James', Standard Hill in Nottingham was described by a clergyman in a letter to the bishop as 'highly respectable' but 'of late years [he has] unfortunately drank in Tractarianism'.[41] In 1847, the warden in question, John Horsefall, began to make detailed complaints about the way in which the sacrament was celebrated at St James', although he appears to have been doing nothing more than attempting to enforce the rubrics.[42] The more Horsefall criticized the clergy, the more determined they seemed to become to hold out against him, in what became a ferocious battle of wills. Matters came to a head when the curate commenced a communion service by walking up to the altar with a black bottle in one hand and bread wrapped in a paper in the other.[43] Tractarian churchwardens were also apparently active in Boston, Lincolnshire, a town which was racked by religious controversy of one sort or another for much of the first half of the nineteenth century. In 1850, the wardens outraged the clergy when they purchased a deep puce altar cloth embroidered with a large white cross, and draped it over the altar at the beginning of Lent. As at Epworth, allegations of romanizing were made, but this time by a clergyman against a layman. William Simmonds, one of the wardens in question, was accused of being married to a Roman Catholic, and of having entertained a Jesuit at his house.[44] These cases from Nottingham and Boston are suggestive of wardens who were beginning to move beyond their traditional realm of responsibility for leaking guttering and pew allocations into more directly liturgical matters. Given that they enjoyed a high degree of autonomy once they had been elected and inducted into office, and could not be subject to either parochial or clerical restraint, Tractarian churchwardens may have played a significant role in the reshaping of Anglican worship, and one which has not previously been acknowledged.[45]

It would be a mistake to imply that one had to be a Tractarian to be committed to church restoration and the principles of the Gothic revival, though some Tractarian laymen were undoubtedly attracted to careers in architecture, a profession which was beginning to offer unrivalled possiblities for the hardworking, the ambitious and the talented. Whilst Butterfield and Gilbert Scott, the great show-piece architects, remain the best known, there were other local architects at work, whose lives remain obscure even when their buildings live on. When the present generation looks at churches which have undergone Gothic revival restoration, perhaps they should bear in mind that the initiative to restore did not always come from the clergy alone. Nor did the money, which was derived in large amounts from the purses of lay people. Christopher Neville, who was patron and Vicar of Thorney in Nottinghamshire, employed

Nockalls Johnson Cottingham to restore his church. Cottingham was a pre-Camdenian Gothic revivalist who was later to design the reredos at Hereford cathedral.[46] Later Neville admitted to Bishop Kaye that his own indifference to architectural matters had resulted in his paying insufficient attention to the details of the project. Suddenly he found the persuasive architect about to transform his church in a manner which did not reflect his views. Among the many alterations 'I find he proposes to place the commandments on the Communion Table in what he calls a *triptic,* a word I never saw, or heard. The outer leaves or doors are to be opened during service and shut afterwards, and the whole highly ornamented and gilt'.[47] Bishop Kaye advised against the adoption of Cottingham's plan, and Neville seemed relieved. He decribed himself as the last clergyman in the diocese to whom could be ascribed Romish or Tractarian views.[48]

In the diocese of Salisbury, the very high church Bishop Hamilton was predictably more sympathetic to Tractarian styles of architecture than was Kaye at Lincoln. At Fosbury, in Wiltshire, the architect was Samuel Saunders Teulon, an architect with some evangelical connections, and in this respect typical of other Tractarians. On 30 September 1856, Hamilton noted in his diary: 'A district has been made out of Shalbourn parish in Tidcombe . . . Mr. Teulon is Architect. House and Church have cost abt. £4000 – the Church has no chancel – It is one long building – but the East End is made what Mr. Teulon calls a Ritualist Chancel, by rising two steps and placing the seats stall ways. The Effect is very good and suits our Service'.[49] Here again, it seems to have been the architect, rather than the local clergy, who took the initiative in setting the tone for the building.

Several points may be made in conclusion. The first is that there is some evidence of Tractarian activity in places outside Oxford in the first thirty years of the Movement, and that more work needs to be done, not so much on the 'show piece' Tractarian parishes like St Saviour's Leeds or St. Paul's Knightsbridge, but on ordinary towns and rural districts, where the occasional adherent to Tractarianism may be viewed in his proper context – against a complex canvas in which the vast number of Anglicans, if they professed any party allegiance at all, owed it to some shade of old fashioned high churchmanship or to Evangelicalism.

There is also a need to treat with caution those who at first sight seem to embrace the Tractarian ideal, and to remember that the term was often applied in a loose and pejorative manner. Some of those falsely accused were high churchmen who had never read the

Tracts, and who had little sympathy for the Oxford divines. Some were essentially indifferent to ecclesiological matters but had come under the influence of others − perhaps churchwardens, architects or influential patrons. Among those clergy who were willing to be identified with Tractarianism, many were curates, and many were destined to remain unbeneficed. Yet, in the Lincoln diocese at least, of those who did succeed in becoming incumbents, the majority had to thank a lay person for their preferment. Of the 36 Tractarian incumbents who have been identified in the diocese at this period, 20, (or 55%) had been presented by a lay person. This statistic seems to confirm the point that at parish level, it was lay people who were sometimes in the vanguard of promoting Tractarianism. Tractarians may have been justified in sensing hostility and prejudice from bishops and brother clergy, but perhaps this charge could not be fairly levelled at the generality of lay Anglicans.

A letter which the Rector of St. Mary's Lambeth wrote to the Bishop of Lincoln in 1851 illustrates the way in which even avowedly high church clergy could be deeply suspicious of Tractarian colleagues. C. B. Dalton, the Rector, was toying with the possibility of having Robert Gregory (a future Dean of St. Paul's) as his curate, and asked the bishop for his advice.

> I am anxious to have a sound Churchman, who will appreciate daily service and weekly Communion, and who will aid me in teaching the doctrine and carrying out the discipline of our Church.
> But any tendency to Rome, or any extremes of ritualism wd. be most painful to me personally and fatal to the success of my ministry at Lambeth.
> I like the tone of Mr Gregory's letters, but I am a little afraid of *his entire concurrence* with Mr John Keble, and of his words about the sacramental system.[50]

Dalton hesitated for some months before deciding to appoint Gregory for a trial period.

> I heard so much of his readiness to receive and follow advice that I have at length made an arrangement with him to come to me for three months. He speaks most strongly, and so do his friends, of his steadiness to the Church of England, and he assures me of his desire in future to abstain from all agitation . . . I feel I am making rather a *venture* for the sake of securing a man of zeal and talent.[51]

This little vignette serves to illustrate something of the character of the existing high church tradition, and of the sense of apprehension, tinged perhaps also with curiosity, which was evident when high churchmen came face to face with Tractarians. The sheer vigour and variety of high church attitudes in early Victorian England have tended to be eclipsed by the tendency to magnify Tractarianism, which was but one of the strands, out of all proportion to its real importance. Tractarian historiography has propagated an interpretation of nineteenth-century Anglicanism which continues to be widely accepted, by focusing on the hostilities of opposing church parties, and portraying a Church riven by Tractarian and Evangelical controversy. Rather, evidence from outside Oxford suggests that party allegiance, where it may be discerned at all, was simply one among a number of determining influences on the Victorian Church, and that Tractarianism, where it occurs, should be seen as but a single thread in a tapestry of high churchmanship.

Notes

1   Owen Chadwick, *The Victorian Church* Vol. 1 (London 1971) p. 231.
2   W.S.F. Pickering, *Anglo-Catholicism: A Study in Religious Ambiguity* (London 1989) p. 21.
3   Nigel Yates, *Leeds and the Oxford Movement* (Thoresby Society, Leeds 1975, Vol. LV No. 121) p. 68.
4   Adrian Hastings, *A History of English Christianity 1920–1985* (London 1986) pp. 195, 199.
5   Chadwick, p. 212.
6   Yates, p. 4.
7   Louis Weil, 'The Tractarian Liturgical Inheritance Re-assessed' in *Tradition Renewed: The Oxford Movement Conference Papers* ed. G. Rowell (London 1986) p. 110.
8   Pickering, p. 17.
9   John Kent, *The Unacceptable Face: The Modern Church in the Eyes of the Historian* (London 1987) pp. 85–6.
10   G. W. Herring, 'Tractarianism to Ritualism: A Study of some Aspects of Tractarianism outside Oxford, from the time of Newman's Conversion in 1845 until the first Ritual Commission in 1867' (Oxford D.Phil 1984).
11   J. H. Newman, *Apologia pro Vita Sua* (London 1864) Sheed & Ward 'Spiritual Masters' edition, 1984 p. 39.
12   Ibid. p. 51.
13   R. W. Church, *The Oxford Movement: Twelve Years 1833–1845* (London 1892) p. 196.
14   S. L. Ollard, *A Short History of the Oxford Movement* (London 1915) pp. 45–6.
15   W. J. Conybeare, 'Church Parties' *Edinburgh Review* October 1853 p. 338.
16   Ibid. pp. 314–318.
17   See *DNB* Vol. LII pp. 190–1; also R. D. Middleton, *Magdalen Studies* (London 1936) pp. 193–228.

18　See Middleton, pp. 229–255. The best account of Smith's conversion is in *Lincolnshire History and Archaeology* Vol. 14 (1979) pp. 57–61: R. W. Ambler, 'The Conversion to Roman Catholicism of Bernard Smith of Leadenham, 1842'.

19　Lincolnshire Archives Office (LAO) CorB5/1 Lord Bayning to Bishop Kaye, n.d.

20　LAO CorB5/1 Kaye to B. Smith, 11 Nove 1841.

21　LAO CorB5/3/3/5 Kaye to W. G. Penny, 7 Nov 1844.

22　LAO MASS8/1 25 Oct 1845.

23　LAO CorB5/3/37 H. Bull to Kaye 22 Dec 1845.

24　LAO CorB5/8A/2 J. Wolley to Kaye 3 Jan 1843.

25　Ibid.

26　Ibid. Kaye to Wolley 5 Jan 1843.

27　Herring p. 42.

28　Ibid. p. 19.

29　Ibid. pp. 40–2.

30　LAO CorB5/4/21/2 J. Wilson to Kaye 15 Dec 1848.

31　LAO CorB5/4/78/3 Hon. C. Dundas to Kaye 20 Dec 1850.

32　Herring p. 45.

33　LAO CorB5/4/14/3 W. T. Mossman to Kaye 18 Oct 1850.

34　Herring p. 154.

35　LAO CorB5/4/14/3 Mossman to Kaye 14 Nov 1849.

36　See Frances Knight, *The Experience of Anglicanism: The Church in English Society c.1800–c.1870* (Cambridge University Press, forthcoming, 1995) for a detailed discussion of attitudes to the Eucharist.

37　Pusey House Mss HAM/1/1/4 7 Jan 1856.

38　R. A Burns, 'The Diocesan Revival in the Church of England, c.1825–1865' (Oxford D.Phil. 1990) pp. 33, 48.

39　Ibid. pp. 6–7, 36.

40　Ibid. p. 37.

41　LAO CorB5/8/5 H. Bolton to Kaye 21 April 1847.

42　Ibid. G. Wilkins to Kaye 29 March 1847; J. Horsefall to Kaye 16 April 1847; Coleman to Kaye 24 May 1847.

43　Ibid. G. Wilkins to Kaye 30 June 1847.

44　LAO CorB5/4/130 J. H. Oldrid to Kaye 29 April 1850.

45　See Knight, *Experience of Anglicanism* for a discussion of the role of churchwardens.

46　Howard Colvin, *Biographical Dictionary of British Architects 1600–1840* (London 1978) pp. 234–5 (see L. N. Cottingham). I am grateful to Dr. Colin Cunningham for discussions on Cottingham and Teulon.

47　LAO Cor B5/8A/3 C. Neville to Kaye 9 May ny.

48　Ibid. Neville to Kaye 17 Sep ny.

49　Pusey House Mss HAM/2/1/1 30 Sep 1856.

50　LAO Cor B5/4/38/1 C. B. Dalton to Kaye, 10 July 1851.

51　LAO Cor B5/4/38/1 Dalton to Kaye 14 Oct 1851.

The Regional Growth of Tractarianism: Some Reflections

Jeremy Morris

The purpose of this paper may appear too ambitious since I have tried to draw a number of important conclusions about the High Church revival as a whole from the study of one particular area of South London during the second half of the nineteenth century. Yet, it seems to me that many of the more interesting, unanswered questions about the influence of the Oxford Movement – such as What was its parochial impact? What was its distinctive role in the High Church revival? What kind of popular support (and opposition) did it attract? – can only be examined in the light of local studies, and that sufficient local studies do now exist for some tentative answers to be attempted.[1] So, wherever possible, I have attempted to pursue parallels to my own suggestions through previously published work.

The paper falls into three main sections. The first attempts to identify particular, relevant historiographical issues concerning principally the relationship of Tractarianism to Ritualism, and the ways in which both movements – if indeed they were separate – implanted themselves and grew within the Church of England. The second section is a detailed examination of a series of Tractarian and Ritualist parishes in South London, that is in Croydon and Norwood, and concentrates on their foundation. The third attempts to assess the strength and nature of opposition to Tractarianism and Ritualism, and the strength of their lay support. Here I will also draw to a limited extent on some research I have begun into local communicants' guilds. Finally, the last section will try to draw these strands together, offering several conclusions about the regional dynamics of the High Church revival.

1

It is now perhaps no more than a historical commonplace to acknowledge that, until recently, our understanding of the Oxford

Movement tended to be dominated by a perspective in which the
'crisis' of the Movement in the mid-1840s was seen from a vantage
point — the early twentieth century — when Anglo-Catholicism
seemed to be on the verge of becoming the largest and most vigorous wing of the Established Church. If, as Owen Chadwick has
suggested, the first, influential series of studies of the movement
were those, not by 'its heirs but its critics and renegades',[2] which
appeared in the 1880s and prompted the posthumous publication
of R. W. Church's history, nevertheless it was books such as
Ollard's *Short History* (1915), Webb's *Religious Thought in the
Oxford Movement* (1928), Brilioth's *Anglican Revival* (1925) and
Faber's *Oxford Apostles* (1933) which for two generations or so
heavily influenced historians' views. These studies were all published around what has been called the 'triumphal period' of
Anglo-Catholicism, when numbers of clergy and laity enrolled at
the Anglo-Catholic congresses, for example, jumped from 13,000
in 1920 to some 70,000 in 1933.[3] They tended to reinforce a view
of the High Church revival both as a crescendo from a rather
isolated 'rump' in the mid-1840s and, paradoxically, as a direct
consequence of the inspiration and actions of the early Tractarian
leaders. There appeared to be numerical and other evidence to back
up this view. Palmer's *Narrative* describes how the petition to archbishop Howley in 1834 raised apprehension and opposition from
some clergy who might otherwise have sympathized with its views;
nevertheless, some 7,000 did sign, and in the *Apologia* Newman
described his own efforts to rally clergy 'in favour of the Church'.[4]
Again, both Newman's and Palmer's narratives, from differing perspectives, coincided in depicting 1845 as a watershed, a crisis from
which the Movement took many years to recover. The sense of
Tractarianism as embattled in mid-century was underlined, on this
view, by the Gorham judgement, further secessions, and popular
hostility exemplified by the surplice riots at Exeter. George Herring's research appears to confirm the picture of Tractarianism as
a relatively small, albeit growing clerical movement in mid-century,
some 81 Tractarian incumbents in 1840 rising to 442 by 1870.[5] It
was a very different picture by the end of the Victorian period; the
Tourist's Church Guide of 1902 reckoned some 1,526 churches in
England and Wales as possessing and using Eucharistic vestments,
for example.[6]

But for all the apparent precision of such figures, measurements
of the real strength of Anglo-Catholicism throughout this period
are extraordinarily elusive, and arguably assume a monolithic ecclesiastical movement which can be sharply differentiated from the

rest of the Established Church. In practice, the controversial nature of Tractarianism and Ritualism itself probably would have encouraged many who shared some similar views to distance themselves from such labels, thus concealing or blurring the doctrinal distinctions between Tractarians and Ritualists and others.[7] W. J. Conybeare's survey of 'Church Parties' in the *Edinburgh Review* in 1853 reckoned that some 7,000 clergymen out of 18,000 could be described as 'High Church', though of these only 1,000 were the 'more noisy than numerous' Tractarians.[8] This is nothing more than an estimate, based on an extrapolation from 500 clergymen on the *Clergy List* whom Conybeare happened to know. But it does at least indicate the nature of the problem.[9] If there were indeed some thousands of clergymen who could be described as High Church in the 1840s and '50s – a proposition that is of a piece with Peter Nockles's work on the High Church party and its relationship to Tractarianism – is it possible to describe the High Church revival in terms of a numerical advance in the late nineteenth century? If, again, it is not possible to argue either that the High Church was moribund in the 1820s and '30s – and in addition to Peter Nockles's work, that of Nigel Yates and Peter Virgin suggests that it was not – or, as seems equally likely, it did not wither in mid-nineteenth century in the wake of secessions, then the relationship of all these apparently divergent strands within the High Church in the late nineteenth century is much more problematic than has often been assumed.[10] At the local level it is generally possible to identify distinctively Tractarian or Ritualist churches, but the influence of the revival or development of Anglo-Catholic doctrines, of liturgical renewal, of greater provision of services, especially communion, was far wider and far more diffuse. Croydon Parish Church, for example, was scarcely in the forefront of Ritualist innovation in the 1860s and '70s, and yet it introduced a surpliced choir, used altar candles, and introduced weekly communion and then daily offices, all of which modest changes led to accusations that the vicar of Croydon had compromised his opposition to Ritualism.[11] What precisely was the relationship between this kind of moderate change, and the sharper, more focused practice and ecclesiology of Tractarianism and Ritualism? A simple assumption of continuous, numerical expansion as itself sufficient to describe the High Church revival can scarcely be satisfactory.

For this reason, whilst not ruling out altogether some limited notion of High Church expansion within the Church of England as a whole, the revival is much more helpfully characterized in terms of distinctive changes and shifts within what has come to be called

'Anglo-Catholicism'. Two issues in particular require attention, the specific nature of the relationship of Tractarianism to Ritualism, and the question of the extent to which the High Church was indeed the clerical, or elitist, movement it has so often been alleged to have been.[12] The second issue will be approached later in this paper; the first demands some attention here. A common view is that Ritualism was simply a natural development from Tractarian sacramental theology, 'the logical outcome', as Nigel Yates has put it.[13] This view has been strongly criticized in the unpublished thesis of George Herring, who argues that the very extremism of Ritualist clergy in the late 1850s and 1860s marked them out from the Tractarians, who had elevated the practice of caution and moderation almost into a distinctive pastoral technique.[14] Herring points out that many Tractarian clergymen were critical of Ritualist innovations and did not themselves see these as a 'logical outcome' of their own views.[15] Ritualism chiefly arose, as he sees it, in the wake of the publication of the first edition of the *Directorium Anglicanum* in 1858.[16]

Herring thus sharpens up a distinction between Tractarianism and Ritualism which arguably needs to be blunted again. As he acknowledges, both Protestant and Roman Catholic critics drew a direct connection between the two, on both accounts ironically because Tractarian teaching was assumed to lead to Rome.[17] Furthermore, whilst citing Tractarian critics of Ritualism such as Pusey, Butler, William Gresley, and Thomas Stevens, he also supplies a number of instances of Tractarians who supported Ritualism and did assume a direct connection: J. M. Neale, T. T. Carter, W. J. E. Bennett, and J. W. H. Molyneux, amongst others.[18] If caution and moderation are to be taken as distinctive Tractarian hallmarks, then where do Neale and Bennett fit in? Herring uses what is essentially a pastoral distinction to prise apart liturgical practice from sacramental theology, but there is much evidence to suggest that contemporaries recognized this could not be done. Take Newman, in the *Apologia*, for example, looking back on his views in the 1840s:

'I considered that to make the *Via Media* concrete and substantive, it must be much more than it was in outline; that the Anglican Church must have a ceremonial, a ritual, and a fulness of doctrine and devotion, which it had not at present, if it were to compete with the Roman Church with any prospect of success. Such additions would not remove it from its proper basis (presumably the Prayer Book), but would merely strengthen and beautify it: such, for instance, would be confraternities, particular devotions, reverences for the Blessed Virgin, prayers for the dead, beautiful churches, rich offerings to them and in them, monastic houses, and many other observances and institutions, which I used to say belonged to us as much as to Rome.'[19]

James Bentley quotes Newman, again, writing to Manning in 1839: 'Give us more services, more vestments and decorations in worship.'[20]

Furthermore, it does not seem convincing to argue that Ritualism represented a distinctly new, essentially innovative approach to liturgical matters. Liturgical revival and reform was well under way before the publication of the *Directorium Anglicanum*; works such as William Palmer's *Origines Liturgicae* (1832) and William Maskell's *Monumenta Ritualia Ecclesiae Anglicanae* (1846) drew attention to continuities between the Prayer Book and historic rites and liturgies of the Western Church. J.M. Neale's *Hierurgia Anglicana* (1843), itself a principal soruce for the *Directorium,* assembled a battery of evidence about the rites and ceremonies of the post-Reformation Church. Even the word 'ritualist' was commonly in use from the 1830s to describe someone who favoured more elaborate ceremonial in worship: Palmer, for example, used it in the Preface to *Origines Liturgicae* as early as 1832, and Maskell used it in his letters *On the Present Position of the High Church Party* in 1850.[21] It seems likely that the *Directorium* no more than focused ritualistic tendencies which were already in existence by the late 1850s. Two sources or trends in particular served to intensify the movement towards ritual revival and innovation. One, quite simply, was the response to controversy and particularly to legal prosecution. The Denison and Westerton versus Liddell cases, for example, prompted a flurry of publications on either side, including Thomas Perry's *Lawful Church Ornaments* (1857), yet another of the principal sources for the *Directorium*.[22] Perry's enormous volume anticipated the *Directorium's* assertion that the Ornaments Rubric of the Prayer Book referred to existing common practice in the second year of Edward VI, and not solely to the ordinances of the First Prayer Book; it and the Denison case illustrate the other trend, namely the developing Tractarian understanding of the eucharist, particularly the doctines of real presence and eucharistic sacrifice.[23] Indeed it may have been not so much the ritual directions contained in the *Directorium* which caused so much offence, thoroughly in line in the main with published Tractarian teaching as they were, as its uncompromising language of eucharistic sacrifice.[24] If, as Härdelin argues, the change was marked by the appearance of Robert Wilberforce's *Doctrine of the Holy Eucharist* in 1853, nevertheless this was not in itself a novel or isolated theological stance.[25]

In Herring's argument, then, Ritualism seems to become simply shorthand for liturgical extremism, detached to some degree from the sacramental theology to which it was supposed to be an expression. It is not surprising, on this view, that evidence can be found for contemporary Tractarian clergymen wishing to distance themselves from the stance of avowed Ritualists. But these distinctions do not seem to have carried much weight for local clergymen and parishioners, nor indeed for local church historians. The terms 'Tractarian' and 'Ritualist', and then later 'Anglo-Catholic' seem to have been largely interchangeable at the local level. In retrospect, there were many differences between certain Anglo-Catholic 'Romish' positions. Prayer Book Catholicism, and Tractarianism proper, but they scarcely constituted discrete, firmly defined 'parties within a party'. Thus the patterns of interaction were extremely complicated, and perhaps the best that can be said, along with the Royal Commission on Ecclesiastical Discipline, is the vague but adequate statement that "If on the one hand it is true to say that what is called Ritualism is a development of the Tractarian Movement, it is on the other hand as true to say that it represented a great change, an unforeseen phase, a new departure in that movement."[26]

The question of the relationship of different strands within the High Church revival in turn has a bearing on a further issue, the relationship of the High Church to the rest of the Established Church, because if we must − as I would argue we must − assume something of a 'ripple' effect within the High Church, whereby liturgical practices originally advocated by a seeming minority gradually became adopted throughout that wing of the Church, then we must presumably assume a continuation of that effect throughout the rest of the Church, weakening as it worked its way through the Broad Church to liberal Evangelicalism, and disappearing altogether at the Evangelical or Low Church extreme. This is a thoroughly limited image, mechanistic even; nevertheless its appropriateness in some contexts − the spread of surpliced choirs, the increasing frequency of communion, for example − is undeniable. The complexity of the inter-party relationships to which I have drawn attention means that to understand this process, at the heart of the High Church revival, it is necessary to attempt to delineate both the forms of resistance to Tractarianism, and their effectiveness or lack of effectiveness, and the peculiar methods by which its influence was conducted. Thus there is a significant role for local studies in attempting to understand the dynamics of the High Church revival. My justification for assuming that the urban context has much to say in this regard is simply that urban expansion presented all denominations in the Victorian period with almost unparalleled opportunities for growth and mission, so that an examination of how the High Church in particular responded to these opportunities may be especially fruitful for understanding the revival as a whole.

2

The area of South London once covered by the old parish of Croydon was indeed an area of spectacular urban growth in the nineteenth century, its population leaping from some 12,000 in 1831 to over 134,000 by 1901.[27] The old parish was enormous, thirty-six miles in circumference, largely rural apart from the market town of Croydon itself at the beginning of the nineteenth century, and almost entirely urban and suburban by 1914, integrated into the London sprawl. Its one parish, with its parish church and two district churches in the 1830s, had subdivided to form twenty-nine Anglican churches in nineteen parishes by 1901. In these nineteen parishes the High Church was a powerful presence: six of them could be described as Ritualist, and a further one as moderate High Church. On the face of things, then, this was precisely the kind of area, urban and suburban, in which contemporaries assumed Tractarianism and Ritualism to be embedding themselves, so much so that many regarded London and its suburbs almost as natural soil for the High Church revival.[28] It is significant, then, that the growth of the High Church in this part of South London occurred largely in spite of powerful opposition from local clergy, including successive vicars of Croydon until the 1880s, with their powers of patronage, and Archbishops of Canterbury.

Anglican church extension in this area was extremely piecemeal, not at all of the systematic, planned kind that Hook, for example, was able to execute in Leeds.[29] The seven High Church parishes in existence by the end of the century formed in effect three clusters, the churches within them partly linked by ties of patronage. In and around the centre of Croydon were St. James', St. Saviour's, and St. Michael and All Angels, the last two springing indirectly from the first; to the north, at Upper Norwood and South Norwood, were St. John the Evangelist and its daughter parish of St. Albans; south of the town centre were St. Peter's and its daughter parish of St. Augustine's. The seven fall broadly into two different groups,

namely those where Tractarian or Ritualist views came as a result
of clergymen being appointed to already existing non-Tractarian
churches (and it was in this instance that local controversy was usually most intense), and the establishment of new churches explicitly
on Tractarian or Ritualist lines.

Only two churches really fall into the first group, that of
existing churches subsequently 'Tractarianized'. St. Peter's, in
South Croydon, was formed directly out of the old parish of
Croydon to cater for a growing, largely middle class suburban
population; initially a district church, it was formed into a separate
parish in 1853, the patronage of the benefice remaining in the
hands of the vicar of Croydon.[30] Nothing in its early years leads
one to suspect that it was at that stage anything other than conservative High Church at most; its second vicar, John White,
appointed in 1854, seemed happy for many years to continue the
established pattern of morning and evening prayer, with monthly
communion.[31] Some time in the late 1870s, however, he began to
adopt more overtly Ritualistic practices, increasing the frequency of
communion, adopting altar lights and a crucifix, and even fitting up
a cubicle similar to a confessional at the door of the church, all of
which in 1878 prompted the resignation of his churchwardens and
the usual critical letters in the local press from 'Anti-Rome' and
others.[32] The vicar of Croydon, as patron, was unable to control
what happened at St. Peter's; he had not appointed a known
Tractarian or Ritualist priest, and White's views began to change,
so far as one can tell, at a time when powerful lay opposition to
Ritualism − despite the actions of his churchwardens − had begun
to recede. Even more controversial, and far more complex, was the
case of St. Saviour's church, built in 1865 east of the town centre as
a chapel of ease to St. James' church. Here the conservative High
Church of St. James appointed as incumbent-designate of the new
church William Cameron, a moderate Tractarian who fell ill within
two years and appointed one Richard Hoare as his curate.[33] Hoare
was to occupy a pivotal role in the High Church revival in this part
of South London, and his Ritualist sympathies became apparent
very quickly. Here the story parts company with the seeming parallel
of St. Peter's; Hoare seems to have attracted a large congregation
and sympathetic churchwardens, so that, as Cameron lay dying in
early 1869, they memorialized the patron, the vicar of St. James,
and also the vicar of Croydon and the Archbishop of Canterbury
to appoint Hoare as Cameron's successor.[34] The subsequent correspondence, both private and in the local press, is too complex to
summarize here; the gist of the conflict was that the patron refused

to appoint Hoare and gave only limited guarantees about preserving the character of the services at St. Saviour's.[35]

The controversy at St. Saviour's provides an appropriate bridge to the second group of churches, namely those founded explicitly on Tractarian or Ritualist lines, because the result of the controversy was to prompt a group of influential, wealthy laity to press for the establishment of a new church for Richard Hoare.[36] This they were able to achieve, despite the opposition of the vicar of Croydon, by appeal to Archbishop Tait and the use of Peel's Church Building Act of 1843. As Tait is reported to have said, 'The matter is in your own hands, gentlemen. You have only to provide the money and a new parish can be formed.'[37] The parish of St. Michael and All Angels was formed by Order in Council in July 1871, and the patronage vested in five lay trustees, as yet without any building or even a site for one. The church of St. Michael's eventually built, described by Cherry and Pevsner as 'one of [J. L.] Pearson's finest', became a highly visible centre for Ritualism in the area, and the host church for the Croydon branch of the English Church Union; Richard Hoare was incumbent for almost fifty years, and occupied a position of some national influence in Anglo-Catholicism, particularly as Warden of the Confraternity of the Blessed Sacrament.[38] This pattern of establishing a church using lay patronage under the Church Building Act was repeated in the foundation of St. John the Evangelist in Upper Norwood, another Pearson church, and paralleled to some extent by the establishment of St. Andrew's as a Tractarian church in South Croydon under the patronage (and with the financial aid) of a rural Tractarian clergyman, J. H. Randolph, pluralist rector of Sanderstead in Surrey.[39] Two other churches in this group demonstrate entirely uncontroversial patterns of foundation, since they were daughter churches of existing Tractarian or Ritualist parishes: St. Alban's in South Norwood, and St. Augustine's in South Croydon.[40]

What do these patterns of Tractarian and Ritualist growth suggest about the nature of the High Church revival? Clearly in an area such as South London, urban growth provided the underlying justification for church extension, and thus provided the opportunity for the establishment of churches along distinctive, doctrinal or party lines. This was true, however, for all shades of Anglicanism, and the above account could be matched to some extent by a consideration of Evangelicalism in the area.[41] Two observations seem particularly appropriate. First, the characteristic mechanisms by which the Church of England sought to make its parochial machinery more flexible and responsive to demographic change in the nineteenth century could weaken, rather than strengthen, control over church affairs in urbanizing districts. Despite the apparent 'mildness' of Peel's 1843 Act, in particular, its consequences were far-reaching when set in the context of party divisions in the church.[42] Churches of one 'party allegiance' could be intruded into the parish of another, provided there was sufficient need and sufficient money. Furthermore, the failure of Parliament to institute even a moderate reform of the patronage system before 1898 meant that it was relatively easy for church parties to perpetuate their influence in parishes they had established, through the use of patronage trusts. Initial Tractarian and Ritualist suspicion of such trusts, presumably of a piece with their overall suspicion of private patronage, appears to have receded by the 1870s; by this period, as M. J. D. Roberts suggests, the Ecclesiastical Commissioners and many bishops 'had come to regard trust patronage as 'normal' in new urban parishes'.[43] The use of patronage to advance High Church views is well attested in numerous local cases: Yates, for example, cites the establishment of St. Barnabas's church in Tunbridge Wells, with its patronage vested in the Warden, Council and Scholars of Keble College, Oxford, despite the opposition from the rural dean, the evangelical vicar of Holy Trinity, who asserted: 'I can scarcely imagine a body of men less fitted for the appointment of a parochial clergyman'; other cases Yates mentions are St. Saviour's in Leeds, and churches in Frome and Bovey Tracey.[44] Patronage could also be used the other way round, to resist Tractarianism: Yates again describes how, in large parts of Wales, episcopal control of most patronage severely contained the growth of Tractarianism; Cobb demonstrates similarly how the evangelical Bristol Church Trustees were able to do so in Bristol.[45]

Linked to the question of the patronage system is a second observation on these patterns of High Church growth, and that is the important – and in some cases crucial – role of lay supporters and patrons. The importance of aristocratic and gentry patrons in this respect is widely acknowledged – Lord Halifax and his relations in Leeds and surrounding areas, for example, the Beresford Hopes in various Kentish and London churches, the Thynnes in Cornwall and at Wells Theological College, the Baths at Frome.[46] But the South London cases I have described suggest that there was a humbler and yet still significant class of lay patrons and other supporters, for whom the patronage trust was a useful way of combining to support High Church views, if not the only one. These were middle class, professional people, relatively wealthy but not outstandingly so, who were prepared to take offices and responsibilities in Tractarian churches and societies − men such as William Drummond, solicitor, chairman of the Local Board of Health, and active layman at St. Saviour's.[47] Again, in urbanizing areas, and perhaps particularly the suburbs, where there was a constant pressure for the formation of new parishes in this period, the influence of such people would have been especially strong.

3

The consideration of lay patrons and supporters leads directly to the question of opposition to and support for the High Church revival. They did not, and could not, stand simply as an isolated, elitist group apart from the bulk of other churchgoers; in controversies such as that at St. Saviour's in Croydon, the actions of such people received support and encouragement from a wider circle of the congregation; over 750 people signed one of the memorials to the patron urging the appointment of the Ritualist Richard Hoare as incumbent.[48] But how strong really was this support, and how necessary to the High Church revival?

It is easier to answer the second question first, and that by reference to a highly unusual, indeed bizarre case of Ritualism in South London − one which can serve as a sort of test case for my assertions about the importance of lay supporters. In the thoroughly middle-class suburb of Addiscombe in the 1860s an evangelical curate from the church of St. Matthew's, Croydon, attracted such popularity that he drew worshippers away from nearby St. James.[49] His name was Maxwell Machluff Ben-Oliel; he was a Scottish Jew who had converted to Anglicanism and later was to convert again to the Roman Catholic church. His supporters, led by his own father-in-law, procured a site for a church for him in Addiscombe, despite opposition from the incumbent of the parish, who sponsored his own, rival, official church in the same district. All of this was accompanied by a public correspondence of extraordinary rancour, involving both Archbishops Longley and then Tait. Ben-Oliel's unofficial church of St. Paul's was able to survive for some two and a half years, however, on its high level of lay support and reliance on offertories. Then in June 1872, quite unexpectedly and unaccountably, Ben-Oliel dramatically switched theological views, and one Sunday introduced a ritualistic form of service. All of his congregation fled to the nearby official church, his position became impossible, and he was forced to submit immediately to Archbishop Tait and eventually to sell the church to his rival.

Arguably, as priest-in-charge of an unofficial Anglican church, his position was more akin to that of a Nonconformist minister than to other Anglican clergy, since he was reliant on voluntary offerings; in this instance, too, profound local support for him (as an evangelical, that is) nevertheless was not able to prevail against a local incumbent so determined to resist that he would even finance a largely empty official church as an alternative. But then this is the point: if sometimes, as here, lay support could not overcome opposition, nevertheless without it, in most cases Tractarian and Ritualist clergy in urbanizing areas at least could hardly have made much headway.

To propose such a view is to run counter, admittedly, to common perceptions of the popular standing of Tractarianism and Ritualism in the mid and late-nineteenth century. Protestant, anti-Tractarian historians have always had an interest in depicting the mass of churchgoers as hostile to Tractarian theology and ritual innovation in this period. High Church writers have frequently concurred in this, tempted by the scale of popular opposition on some occasions and by the history of anti-Ritualist prosecutions to read Anglo-Catholic history as a narrative of heroic individuals. In this connection, priests such as Lowder, Mackonochie and Stanton spring to mind. Thus the High Church revival has frequently been seen as a sort of clerical fad, imposed upon congregations at worst hostile but at best only passive.[50] So some unravelling to the different strands of opposition and support needs to be undertaken.

First, it does not seem necessary to add much to existing accounts of ritual prosecutions, except to make two observations.[51] The existence of national organizations such as the Church Association and later the Protestant Truth Society is some evidence of continuing anti-Catholic and anti-Ritualist hostility, but it does not necessarily say anything about the extent of real popular hostility to ritualism at the local level. Despite the notoriety of these cases, they were relatively few in number and in some dioceses (particularly London) their decisions were widely flouted. Furthermore, there is some evidence to suggest that the Church Association was obliged to plant supporters or stooges − outsiders, in other words − simply in order to mount a case. For example, attempts to prosecute R. W. Randall, the incumbent of All Saints', Clifton under the Public Worship Regulation Act failed when one of the three aggrieved parishioners was demonstrated to have no connection with the parish, another died, and the third refused to proceed.[52]

Secondly, setting these prosecutions to one side, what is interesting about supposed popular agitation against Tractarianism and

Ritualism is its relative infrequency. Certainly it is striking that disturbances of the kind which afflicted St. Barnabas', Pimlico in 1850, and then St. George's-in-the-East in 1859-60 were extremely rare, and had almost disappeared by the 1870s, even though, as many historians now accept, crowd violence on an uproarious scale – including that directed against street missionaries and the Salvation Army – did not disappear until around the 1890s.[53] Simplistic though it may sound, it is hard to escape the conclusion that this was because of a subtle process of 'privatization' of religious practice: street missionaries were a threat because they invaded working-class areas and criticized their modes of living, whereas Ritualists largely confined their activities to churches; interestingly, though, not even ritual processions seem to have sparked much popular hostility. An important dimension of this process was undoubtedly what has been described as the 'partial disestablishment' of the Church of England, and in particular the abolition of church rate in 1868.[54] In many parishes before that date the cry of 'No Popery on the Rates!' could seem to encapsulate a legitimate objection, since even district churches could receive a proportion of church rate. Vestry meetings were a focus for genuine local conflicts of interest, even when, on occasions, a church rate *per se* was not at issue. William Butler's early difficulties in Wantage came to a head at a vestry meeting in early 1852, to which he submitted proposals for a complete restoration of his church; the meeting was packed with Dissenters, and if his despair at its overwhelming rejection of his proposals seems understandable in the light of his refusal to ask for a church rate, nevertheless the hostility of his opponents itself seems understandable given the behaviour of Butler's predecessor, the pluralist Dean of Windsor, who 'arrived with a carpet bag at the Bear Inn, received his tithes, and returned, without leaving either his carpet bag or his blessing behind him.'[55]

Thirdly, as I have already implied in talking of the St. Saviour's case in Croydon, in other controversial cases – all those accounts of Tractarian and Ritualist disputes which involved neither prosecution nor crowd violence – it is possible to invert the common view and lay the emphasis instead on those who were prepared to support High Church clergymen against their critics. Evidence of congregational acquiescence in ritual innovations is extremely widespread, if difficult to quantify. Herring refers to the phenomenon of affluent residents in non-Tractarian parishes touring Tractarian churches (using the various church guides that appeared from mid-century), and rightly points out that in towns it was far easier to ignore parochial boundaries and shop around for a church which suited your taste.[56] The highly controversial W. J. E. Bennett was supported in his appointment to Frome by a petition of 1,039 parishioners, and subsequently built up his Sunday congregations to some 2,000.[57]

This method of accumulating evidence − not all of it numerically reliable − does suggest that there is a case for saying that Tractarianism and Ritualism attracted substantial congregational support in some areas. Fourthly, then, very briefly I want to examine some of the ways in which this support was organized. There were of course national societies promoting particular doctrinal and ritual interests, such as the Confraternity of the Blessed Sacrament, the Guild of the Holy Cross, the Guild of St. Alban, the English Church Union, and so on. Since Walter Walsh's hostile treatment, few historians have paid these much more than passing attention, and many of them were principally clerical organizations.[58] However, some were aimed at laity and attracted a moderately sizeable membership; the Guild of All Souls, for example, by 1902 had 92 branches in England and Wales, with a membership of between five and six and a half thousand, of whom only about a thousand were clergy.[59] Parallel to these organizations was a plethora of local communicants' guilds, often organized under a church's patronal name and usually with the explicit intention of uniting communicant members of a church in spiritual fellowship. Simon Green has recently described these as part of the initiative whereby Sunday scholars were induced 'to assume the duties of adult worship', but they were surely much more than that.[60] They were evidence of that greater emphasis on the importance of the eucharist in church life which was characteristic of the High Church in the late nineteenth century. They also, however, again qualify the picture of Ritualism as simply a clerical, elitist movement, because in many cases they functioned as advisory and consultative bodies for clergy, a generation before the formation of parochial church councils. At St. Augustine's in South Croydon, for example, the guild discussed the provision of altar frontals, arrangements for times of services, the formation of a Band of Hope, resolutions and petitions on the education issue, and the foundation of a Men's Institute.[61] At the moderate Tractarian All Saints' church, in Cambridge, the Guild was sub-divided into four branches, each of which was assigned a particular range of responsibilities, the Branch of St. Agnes, for example, taking charge of the ornaments and vestments of the church, the Branch of St. Gabriel assistance with daily worship at the church.[62] Urban church guilds seemed to fare better than those in rural churches, perhaps once again because of the greater likelihood that the congregation was self-selected on doctrinal lines. In the village of Barrington in Cambridgeshire, for example, shortly after its formation the communicants' guild seems to have become largely a social organization holding tea meetings for women of the parish.[63] By the 1900s communicants' guilds were being more widely adopted and were ceasing to be a peculiarly High Church phenomenon; nevertheless their role in promoting High Church views and strengthening High Church support at parochial level was considerable.

4

This discussion of various aspects of the local dynamics of the High Church revival may have seemed rather piecemeal and unwieldy. It may sound lame to suggest that an understanding of the regional strengths and weaknesses of Tractarianism and Ritualism can only come about by the patient accumulation of detailed case studies, but I suspect nevertheless that that is true. It is unfortunate, for example, that so little research has been undertaken on the growth of Ritualism in the diocese of London, one of the great areas of Anglo-Catholic strength. Furthermore I have not considered here a number of other important factors – above all episcopal policy, and the reform of theological education. Existing local studies demonstrate at the very least that there is no easy, overall regional pattern. However, in summary several conclusions can be drawn.

First, areas of urban development do seem to have provided special opportunities for the High Church revival. Growing areas demanded more churches, and, given the nature of the patronage system, it was generally easier to establish new churches in urban areas than to 'Tractarianize' existing churches elsewhere. The very mechanisms by which new churches could be established tended to limit the degree of control hostile clergymen could exercise over an area. This conclusion applies as much to small but expanding market towns as it does to large urban conglomerates. Also, in urban areas the possibility of choosing between different churches undoubtedly assisted the development of distinctively Tractarian and Ritualist congregations.

Second, the High Church was able to seize the opportunities thus presented to it because it attracted a substratum of genuine lay support, ranging from wealthy aristocratic patrons to middle-class professionals to organized voluntary associations of communicants. Plainly, Tractarianism and Ritualism did not amount to a mass movement; nevertheless it did represent a genuinely popular church movement in the sense that it attracted considerable lay support within the High Church wing, and was far from being simply a movement of self-preoccupied clerics. To say this is not to prejudge many other questions, such as to what extent was it a movement of lay women rather than men, or how active really were the majority of High Church attenders, and so on.

Finally, resistance to the High Church revival was generally ineffective not just in the courts but in the localities as well. On the clerical side, church structures and procedures provided plenty of opportunities for High Church clergy to resist attempts to discipline or control them. Popular hostility was of little avail, either; it was rarer than sometimes assumed, and seems to have withered in the 1860s and '70s. The changing public profile of Establishment almost certainly assisted this, along with the reform and redefinition of church government; particularly relevant was the reduction in the role of the vestry meeting and the eventual emergence of alternative agencies, to which the guilds themselves were a precursor.

Notes

1   Particularly important are: G. W. Herring, 'Tractarianism to Ritualism: A Study of Some Aspects of Tractarianism outside Oxford, from the time of Newman's Conversion in 1845 until the First Ritual Commission in 1867' (Oxford Univ., D.Phil., 1984); H. M. Brown, *The Catholic Revival in Cornish Anglicanism*: A Study of the Tractarians of Cornwall 1833–1906 (1980);W.N. Yates, 'Bells and Smells'; London, Brighton and South Coast Religion reconsidered', *Southern History*, 5 (1983), and other articles footnoted elsewhere in this paper; P. G. Cobb, *The Oxford Movement in Nineteenth-Century Bristol* (1988).

2.   W. O. Chadwick, *The Spirit of the Oxford Movement* (1990), p. 139.

3.   W. S. F. Pickering, *Anglo-Catholicism, A Study in Religious Ambiguity* (1989), pp. 48 & 56.

4.   W. Palmer, *A Narrative of events connected with the publication of the Tracts for the Times* (1843; 1883 ed.), pp. 108–9; J. H. Newman, *Apologia Pro Vita Sua* (1864; Fontana ed., 1959), p. 127.

5.   Herring, op. cit., p. 43.

6.   Cited in the *Report of the Royal Commission on Ecclesiastical Discipline* (1906), para. 88.

7.   Precisely what seems to have happened in the case of W. F. Hook, for example: W. N. Yates, *Leeds and the Oxford Movement: A Study of 'High Church' Activity in the Rural Deaneries of Allerton, Armley, Headingley and Whitkirk in the Diocese of Ripon 1836–1934* (Thoresby Society Publications, 55, 1975), p.13.

8.   W. J. Conybeare, 'Church Parties', *Edinburgh Review*, 200 (1853), pp. 322 & 338.

9.   There is a strong likelihood that Herring's identification of 958 Tractarian clergymen in the period 1845 to 1867 is itself a severe underestimate: since he includes figures such as Charles Lowder and Alexander Mackonochie, it must be assumed that his Appendix listing these clergymen embraces both

Ritualism and Tractarianism, movements which in the main body of his thesis he tends to distinguish from each other, and yet of eleven priests-in-charge and five incumbents at Tractarian and Ritualist churches in Croydon and Norwood before 1870, none are listed; Herring, *op. cit.*, pp. 37–9 & Appendix.

10. W. N. Yates, *Buildings, Faith and Worship: the Liturgical Arrangement of Anglican Churches 1600–1900* (1991), esp. ch. 6, 'A Return to Liturgical Orthodoxy'; P. Virgin, *The Church in an Age of Negligence: Ecclesiastical Structure and Problems of Church Reform 1700–1840* (1989), pp. 258–67.

11. Rev. John Hodgson defended the use of a surpliced choir, for example, on the grounds that it met 'an advance of taste'; one of the strongest criticisms of his conduct for his (alleged) Ritualistic sympathies is in Anon., *Croydon Crayons* (1873), p. 10.

12. For example, by H. M. Brown: 'Tractarianism was largely a clerical movement, at least as far as Cornwall is concerned'; *op. cit.*, p. 5.

13. W. N. Yates, *The Oxford Movement and Anglican Ritualism* (1983), p. 22.

14. Herring, *op. cit.*, esp. ch. 13, 'Tractarianism and Ritualism'.

15. See, for example, his citation of W. J. Butler's view that Alexander Mackonochie was 'trying to force into the use of the Church of England that which the Church in no way authorizes'; Herring, *op. cit.*, p. 203, quoting A.J. Butler (ed.), *Life and Letters of William John Butler* (1897).

16. Herring, *op. cit.*, p. 286.

17. Ibid., pp.309 & 399.

18. See, for example, T. T. Carter's assertion in 1878 that 'there were real, vital links binding the one to the other, – a substantial unity of faith and purpose'; ibid., p. 312.

19. Newman, *op. cit.*, pp. 223–4.

20. J. Bentley, *Ritualism and Politics in Victorian Britain: the Attempt to Legislate for Belief* (1978), p.26.

21. W. Palmer, *Origines Liturgicae or Antiquities of the English Ritual* (2nd ed., 1846; Preface to 1st ed.), p. iv; W. Maskell, *A Second Letter on the Present Position of the High Church Party in the Church of England* (1850), p. 61.

22. T. W. Perry, *Lawful Church Ornaments: being an historical examination of the Judgment of the Right Hon. Stephen Lushington* (1857).

23. Ibid., p. 7; see A. Härdelin, *The Tractarian Understanding of the Eucharist* (1965).

24. See, for example: 'The Ritual of Heaven is objective, and the principal worship of the Church on earth is equally so by reason of its being identical with the Normal and Apocalyptic ritual, and thus containing a great action, even the perpetuation of the Sacrifice made on the Cross, in an unbloody manner on the altar'; J. Purchas (ed.), *Directorium Anglicanum; being a Manual of Directions for the Right Celebration of the Holy Communion* (1858), p. x.

25. As David Newsome reminds us, 'to Manning, Gladstone, Phillpotts and others like them it came as manna in the wilderness'; *The Parting of Friends* (1966), p. 380.

26 *Report of the Royal Commission on Ecclesiastical Discipline* (1906), para. 302.

27. Details in this paragraph are taken from J. N. Morris, *Religion and Urban Change: Croydon. 1840–1914* (1992), ch. 3, 'The churches in Victorian Croydon I'.

28. See, for example, the comments in the anti-Ritualist volume edited by Linden Heitland, *Ritualism in Town and Country: a Volume of Evidence* (1902): 'The energetic ritualist curates found greater scope for work in large and crowded populations; there was a disinclination on their part to vegetate in quiet country places.'; *ibid.*, p. 3.

29. W. R. W. Stephens, *Life and Letters of W. F. Hook* (1878), ch. 6; see also W. N. Yates, *Leeds and the Oxford Movement*.

30. Anon., *St. Peter's, Croydon: The First Hundred Years* (1951).

31. Service details in this and following paragraphs are from advertisements in *Gray's Commercial and General Directory for Croydon* (annually, 1851–61), and its successors, *Warren's Directory* (1865–9) and *Ward's Directory* (1874–1914).

32. *Croydon Chronicle*, 30 March 1878.

33. Anon (ed.), *Memorials and Correspondence respecting the recent appointment of an Incumbent for St. Saviour's Church, Croydon* (1869), p. 5.

34. Ibid., pp. 8–11.

35. Ibid., p. 24.

36 F.N. Heazell, *The History of St. Michael's Church, Croydon: A Chapter in the Oxford Movement* (1934), pp. 4–9.

37. Ibid., p. 7.

38. B. Cherry & N. Pevsner, *The Buildings of England: London 2: the South (1983)*, p.210; *Croydon Chronicle*, 21 September 1878.

39. H. W. Bateman, *A Short History of the Church of St. John the Evangelist, Upper Norwood 1871–1937* (1937); see also W. F. La Trobe-Bateman, *Memories Grave and Gay* (1927); Anon., *St. Andrew's Church for the Poor* (1858).

40. Bateman, *op. cit.*, ch. 2, 'Expansion and Consolidation'; J. H. White, *A Short History of the Foundation and Progress of the Church of St. Augustine's,* South Croydon (1909).

41. Morris, *op. cit.*, p. 52.

42. G. F. A. Best, *Temporal Pillars: Queen Anne's Bounty, the Ecclesiastical Commissioners and the Church of England* (1964), pp. 356–8.

43. M. J. D. Roberts, 'Private Patronage and the Church of England, 1800–1900', *Journal of Ecclesiastical History*, 32 (1981), p. 213.

44. W. N. Yates, *Kent and the Oxford Movement* (1983), p.98; *ibid., Leeds and the Oxford Movement*, p.28; *ibid.*, 'Bells and Smells', pp. 130 & 132.

45. W. N. Yates, 'The Parochial Impact of the Oxford Movement in South West Wales', in T. Barnes & W. N. Yates (eds.), *Carmarthenshire Studies* (1974), p. 223; Cobb, *Oxford Movement*, p. 31.

46. Yates, Leeds and the Oxford Movement, pp. 12, 40 & 43; *ibid., Kent and the Oxford Movement*, p. 7; Brown, *The Catholic Revival in Cornish Anglicanism*, p. 66; W. M. Jacob, 'The Diffusion of Tractarianism: Wells Theological College 1840–49', *Southern History*, 5 (1983), p. 1934.

47. Morris, *Religion and Urban Change*, p. 112; Anon., *Memorials and Correspondence*, p. 10.

48. Ibid., p. 19.

49. Details in this paragraph are extracted from J. N. Morris, 'Religion and Urban Change in Victorian England: A Case Study of the Borough of

Croydon 1840–1914' (Oxford Univ., D.Phil. thesis, 1985), pp. 125–32, where specific references can be found.

50. Even Herring, whilst citing J. D. Chambers' view that 'the present Ritual movement could not have lived a day if it had not been largely countenanced by the laity', nevertheless goes on to describe Ritualism as a movement of parochial clergy, contrasting it with Tractarianism as a movement of young academic clergy; *op. cit.*, pp. 326–7.

51. The most useful account of these prosecutions and the issues they involved is the 'Historical Survey' in chapters 9 and 10 of the *Report of the Royal Commission on Ecclesiastical Discipline* (1906); also useful are P. T. Marsh, *The Victorian Church in Decline* (1969) and J. Bentley, *op. cit.*

52. Cobb, *op. cit.*, p.23.

53. I cannot accept, then, what John Wolffe implies, namely that the 'largely spontaneous growth of resistance to ritualism' continued beyond 1860 because 'the practices and values which provoked it were a new, objective and verifiable challenge to the existing religious order', whereas 'Roman Catholicism seemed less of a threat than it had twenty years earlier': J. Wolffe, *The Protestant Crusade in Great Britain, 1829–1860* (1991), p. 288. See also P. T. Smith, 'The London Police and the Holy War: Ritualism and St. George's-in-the-East, London, 1859–60', *Journal of Church and State*, 28 (1986). For continuing crowd hostility to popular evangelists and the Salvation Army, see for example: V. Bailey, 'Salvation Army Riots, the "Skeleton Army" and Legal Authority in the Provincial Town', in A. P. Donajgrodski (ed.), *Social Control in Nineteenth Century Britain* (1977); C. Hare, 'The Skeleton Army and the Bonfire Boys, Worthing, 1884', *Folklore*, 99 (1988); J. N. Morris, 'A Disappearing Crowd? Collective Action in Late Nineteenth Century Croydon', *Southern History*, 11 (1989).

54. On 'partial disestablishment' and its consequences, see A. D. Gilbert, *Religion and Society in Industrial England* (1976), ch. 7, 'Church and chapel in denominational relationship'.

55. *Bristol Times*, December 1847, quoted in Butler, *Life and Letters*, p. 56.

56. Herring, *op. cit.*, pp. 104 & 332.

57. Yates, 'Bells and Smells', pp. 129–30.

58. W. Walsh, *The Secret History of the Oxford Movement* (1898), chapters 7 (the Confraternity of the Blessed Sacrament') and 8 ('Some Other Ritualistic Societies').

59. *Report of the Royal Commission on Ecclesiastical Discipline* (1906), paras. 8817–8821.

60. S. J. D. Green, 'Religion and the Rise of the Common Man: Mutual Improvement Societies, Religious Associations and Popular Education in Three Industrial Towns in the West Riding of Yorkshire c.1850–1900', in D. Fraser (ed.), *Cities, Class and Communication* (1990), p. 31.

61 Surrey Record Office, Guild of St. Augustine, Croydon, Minute Book, entries for 1886–6, *passim*.

62. Cambridgeshire Record Office, Guild of All Saints, Cambridge, Minute Book for 1889 to 1892, 1889 Prospectus.

63. Cambridgeshire Record Office, Barrington Church Guild, Minute Book for 1888 to 1897, entries for 1888–9, *passim*.

Part Three

About Newman and the *Apologia*

A Consideration of Newman's
Apologia Pro Vita Sua

Owen Chadwick

The attack by Charles Kingsley upon Newman in the winter of 1863 – 4 was an unprovoked attack. It was also unpleasant. Kingsley made capital out of Newman's low reputation. For part of public opinion Newman was one who had been a secret Roman Catholic while he was an Anglican priest and therefore was associated with underhand behaviour. Kingsley, confident in public applause, used this reputation in a wider Protestant onslaught on Roman Catholicism. He said, in effect, Father Newman is underhand, and in this is typical of Roman Catholic priests. Moreover he used in the course of the quarrel plenty of epithets about Newman: silly, credulous, knave or fool, eccentric, affected, paradoxical, a cunning logician.

Newman was hurt to the quick. The first part of his answer is that of a man who is angry; not only at the personal nature of the attack, but at its injustice; all the more so since it did not come from a contemptible hack writer but from one of the most famous of English clergymen. He used equally strong language in retort. He described Kingsley as shallow, inaccurate, narrow-minded, a person furiously carried away by his feelings, one who poisoned the public mind against him, a base and cruel controversialist – 'Away with you, Mr Kingsley, and fly into space'.

The importance of the *Apologia* does not lie in this quarrel, where giants banged away at each other with ping-pong bats. Newman saw that far bigger questions were at stake than his own personal integrity, or the prejudice of Charles Kingsley's mind. The real issue of this conflict was the belief of Protestants that Roman Catholics did not care about truth.

Yet within this general issue came the question of Newman's past. He was accused of being a secret Roman Catholic while he was a Protestant clergyman. Did that mean that the leaders of the religious movement of 1833, who attempted to make the Church of England Catholic, had been disloyal to their Anglican inheritance? Or were they rather honourably trying to carry out the teaching

163

and practice of the Church of England as they saw it? In other words, was the Catholic inheritance within the Church of England an authentic expression of Anglican faith?

Since this question was posed by his opponent in a personal way, he had to give a personal answer:

'I am accused of having been a Catholic while an Anglican clergyman. Is it wrong to be a Catholic while one is an Anglican clergyman? How did I come to perceive the Catholic dimension in the Anglican inheritance? And how was I to feel, eventually, that to be a truly faithful Catholic I had to leave the Church of England? Was this an honourable episode in my life?'

Newman had long needed to be able to explain to the public why this was honourable. Kingsley gave him that chance.

That meant, he must write an autobiography. 'I wish to be known as a living man, and not as a scarecrow which is dressed up in my clothes.' Yet it is not an autobiography, for he does not even tell us when he was born, or who were his father and mother, nor whether he was older or younger than his brother, or whether he had any sisters. It is the history of a religious mind, and its development from a sort of Calvinism in childhood to Roman Catholicism in the forties of adult life. The notion of autobiography was out of keeping with the devotional ideals of the Oxford Movement. They preached reserve, and practised it. We cannot imagine Keble or Pusey writing an autobiography, whether religious or not. And Newman professed that this self-exposure to the public in print was painful: 'how great a trial', '[one should] keep one's secrets to oneself', '[it is] not pleasant ... to be egotistical ... not pleasant to reveal to high and low ... what has gone on within me'. 'It is not pleasant to be giving to every shallow or flippant disputant the advantage over me of knowing my most private thoughts, I might even say the intercourse between myself and my Maker.' The reader will not doubt that he felt this pain of exposure. But he will not doubt either that he enjoyed part of the process: writing good English on a theme where he cared; recapturing the characters of people whom he had loved, or scenes of long ago which still lived in his memory; and to thinking again in this personal way, about the nature of the Christian faith and the structure of the Christian Church. Newman had a long life ahead of him, but already he was curiously old. He supposed that he had one foot in the grave. And in this mood, he looked back to childhood with clarity of vision. He astonishes us by saying at a time when he still had twenty-six more years to live: 'As men draw towards their end they care less for disclosures.'

Once embarked upon self-disclosure he must be entirely honest. He was accused of credulity because of his attitude to miracles and saints. So he must speak of his early simplicities; how the boy wished the Arabian Nights Tales were true, and how he felt himself surrounded by invisible angels, and was so superstitious at the age of fifteen that he used to cross himself when going into the dark; how, though a very Protestant little boy, he drew for himself a picture of a rosary; how he felt isolated from the material objects which surrounded him; and so rested in the 'thought of two and two only supreme and luminously self-evident beings, myself and my Creator'; how he professed the belief that the Pope is Antichrist; and how he felt so early called to live in the world unmarried – not without hesitation and scruples, but he thought that he might be called to some vocation which needed single men, like the work of a missionary among the heathen.

Like all people who look back on their lives he was sometimes confused. When he thought about himself he realized that he was no leader. He did not think that he had the gravitas that went with it. 'I had a lounging, free-and-easy way of carrying on.' He admitted only that he was the leading author in a school of religious writers. In his memory it was not he who influenced his friends but his friends who influenced him. In retrospect he thought that the Oxford Movement would never have become a power in the land if he had remained its leader. And yet – when he looked back upon his young followers, he could remember them imitating him, and how his pupils took his ideas, and how young dons in the university and distributors of the tracts spread them, and how they went out among the curates of parishes, or even into clerical meetings in the country.

Certainly he was the leading thinker of the Oxford Movement. But he felt the need, and there was no insincerity about it, to show that others were the real source of those ideas: how John Keble was 'the true and primary author of them', how he taught him of the sacramental system of the Church, and how material objects can be the instruments of things that are unseen; and that from Keble he learnt of 'The Communion of the Saints', and of the certainty of faith, through its working in love, though the evidence for faith was only probable. From Hurrell Froude he says that he learnt to look with admiration towards the Church of Rome (did he? for Newman was still fierce against the Church of Rome after Hurrell Froude died – but someone may not realize the idea shown by another until that other has gone). He says that Froude taught him the idea of devotion to the Blessed Virgin, and gradually to believe in the Real Presence (but he learnt the language of Real Presence in the

Holy Communion from the Catechism which he knew perfectly as a child). To Hugh James Rose of Cambridge he likewise attributed much, too much, in the origins of the Oxford Movement; and here is another person, though no intimate, of whom he wrote with public affection. He says that it was Pusey who gave the movement a position and a name – 'a man who could be the head and centre of the zealous people in every part of the country'; a man who gave a personality to what was without him a sort of mob – that word *mob* is the sign of a rhetorical overstatement.

Something is effusive about his professions. He wrote about the Provost of his College, Dr Hawkins, with whom he quarrelled over a tutorship, and who was his most powerful enemy in the University of Oxford: 'I can say with a full heart that I love him, and that I have never ceased to love him'. It may be true, he must have felt it to be true, but when we know so much about Dr Hawkins it reads oddly, almost absurdly. He broke with Whately over Whately's liberalism; and 35 years later he says, 'I loved him too much to bid him farewell without pain' (p. 37)[1]. He writes of 'my dear and true friend Dr Pusey' (p. 40), and so he was in the early twenties, and now in the early sixties he has become the defender of the doctrine of eternal punishment. He says that as a young Fellow he was rather solitary and had few friends; but evidently they were soon an affectionate circle; John Bowden, 'my great friend' (p. 41); Hurrell Froude, with whom 'I was in the closest and most affectionate friendship' from about 1829, and others.

By 1836 his Anglican doctrine was thus said to be built up, block by block:

- the truth of the Bible, in childhood;
- the truth of the Catechism, in childhood;
- God's mercy to himself – aged 15 (in his Catechism also);
- The Holy Trinity – aged 15 (Thomas Scott but in his Catechism also);
- eternal punishment – aged 15–16;
- warfare between the City of God and the powers of darkness – (Thomas Scott, William Law);
- The Pope is Antichrist – aged 15 – from Newton on the Prophecies – modified before 1830 into the doctrine that the Pope teaches error in a way that is harmful to Christians;
- the rightness for some of the unmarried life – his own idea aged 15–16;
- regeneration in the sacrament of baptism – learnt from a book (*Apostolical Preaching*) by J. B. Sumner (originally published

in 1817, fifth and sixth editions 1826) − but he had it in his Catechism as a child;

- tradition − that is, learn Christian doctrine from the teaching of the Church and go to the Scripture to prove its truth − said to be learnt by him from a sermon of his Provost, Dr. Hawkins;
- apostolic succession of bishops − taught by William James, 1823;
- the certainty that some miracles had happened and therefore that others might happen − learnt from his Bible and his own thinking, at least by 1826, no doubt long before then;
- the Church has rights which the State cannot touch − said to be learnt from Dr Whately, 1826 − but it might more naturally have been learnt from his New Testament with 'Render unto Caesar ...';
- the sacramental system − said to be owed to John Keble, but so far as the two gospel sacraments were concerned he had it in the Catechism from his childhood;
- the certainty of faith though its evidence can only be probable − he ascribes his insight into this to John Keble, but it is much more probable that he thought it out for himself, especially under the hammering of liberal minds like that of his colleague Whately;
- devotion to the Blessed Virgin Mary − (from Hurrell Froude);
- the Real Presence in the Holy Communion (from Hurrell Froude − but it is there, or very nearly there, in the catechism of his childhood).

Something is artificial in this scheme; as though his mind were constructed out of a lot of different bricks, each added to the edifice by the trowel of one of his friends or colleagues. It cannot really have happened so tidily, nor so architecturally. At heart he knew that the minds of human beings seldom develop logically. But the form of this neat description was a symbol of two truths which needed to be put over: first, how much he owed in faith to the Anglicans; and second, how much more widely based were the ideas of the Oxford Movement than in the notions of a single mind.

The one addition needed to his Anglican doctrine was due to the study of the Early Christian writers, which rapidly became his field of academic study. This addition was a crux. *Antiquity is the guide to the doctrine of the Church of England.* We must understand the Bible as the earliest Christians understood it. We must model our Church government upon their pattern, our way of worship, our way of Church life upon theirs. He believed that this conviction came through his own reading and he must be right, though the idea was in the air of the time. For the first time in the *Apologia* his prose became lyrical as he thought of it. He was excited, like any student who makes for himself a discovery that is new to him; 'Some portions of their teaching, magnificent in themselves, came like music to my inward ear'; their sacramental sense, their love of allegory, and poetry, and parable; and 'Holy Church in her sacraments and her hierarchical appointments will remain even to the end of the world, only a symbol of those heavenly facts which fill eternity'.

When he announced the principle that the Church of England must model itself on the Early Fathers, he did not yet know all that the Fathers said or taught. 'I spoke vaguely and imperfectly, of what I thought they said, or what some of them said.' The Fathers might surprise. But if so, it would fit into the historic pattern of continuous faith from the apostles. He surprised himself as his studies continued. H. J. Rose wanted to arrange for the translation of the French Church History by Fleury, which had the reputation of being moderate, unpartisan history without comment. Newman organized it. What Fleury recorded about the Early Fathers surprised Newman: the angels − he had them with him in childhood; he had them with him still as an adult; the Fathers of the Church had them; they guided the world; the real causes of motion, light and life and the elementary principles of the physical universe. He remembered how in one of his sermons he drew out with poetic power a quasi-Platonic doctrine − how 'every breath of air and ray of light and heat, every beautiful prospect is, as it were, the skirts of their garments, the waving of the robes of those whose faces see God'.

Such was his faith when the Conservative government was overthrown, the Reform Bill became law, and there began to be a threat of revolution in Church and State − confiscation of some Church property at the least, of much Church property if worse, total separation of Church and State at worst, if it came to worst. He felt 'passionately' that the Church must be defended. He did not trust Bishop Blomfield of London, nor the evangelicals, nor the old Protestants who followed the principles of the Reformation, nor the old Church-and-State men, to defend his Church. It must be defended, not because it was the Church of England, but because it was the English part of the Church of all the centuries; 'his' Church, the Ancient Church, the Church of martyrs and ascetics and bishops with their faith and their power against a persecuting State. Immediately the Reform Act was passed he was not well and went for his health to Italy and Sicily, where he nearly died. He reached England again in July 1833, and began the work of his life.

The reader may not have noticed a feature of the *Apologia* which astonished the readers of 1864. A Roman Catholic priest, writing about his Protestant past, was expected to denounce it as heretical, boring, inadequate, and dangerously untrue. This Roman Catholic priest says that he was truly converted to authentic faith at the age of fifteen, and that he learnt all the main truths of the Christian religion from his home and then from a series of books or people, none of which, or none of whom, was a modern Roman Catholic; and he described all these books and people with a memory filled with affection, gratitude, and generosity. Nothing in English literature or religion had ever happened like this before. It made the general public sit up, and look upon the author in a new light.

His next task was to explain the Oxford Movement of 1833, or rather his personal part in it. There is the liveliest self-portrait as he looked back at that moment; a man of exuberant and bounding health; conscious not only of a cause but a great cause; a cause which he could without a feeling of absurdity compare to a cause like that of Martin Luther, to change the Church and the world; a new reformation of the Church of England by recalling it to the primitive Christian Church, a recall which in its own past would make it nearer to the Church of the seventeenth century, to the Church of Lancelot Andrewes and George Herbert and George Bull, than to the Church of Latimer and Ridley and the Puritans. He was sure that such a movement must be led by free individuals, writing as they wished; and it could not be the work of organizations, associations, committees; and he could not care to be prudent, or to think what was practicable, or to wonder whether bishops would accept what was said.

And here came the first sign in the *Apologia* of something deeper than modesty; a hint in the self-portrait of public penitence, or public confession. Confident in his cause, he *despised* anyone who disagreed with him. He had 'a thorough contempt for the evangelicals', and hardly thought better of the old conservative high-churchman. He wanted disciples but did not care if they refused to be disciples. He found that stories began to circulate about him, gossip that was untrue or exaggerated. He scorned it, no doubt rightly; but with such assurance that he did not bother to correct what might with advantage have been corrected. Sometimes he fed the gossip by the language of irony, which the recipient took to be sincere. He realized that he made himself unpopular with some. He did not mind in the least. And looking back thirty years later, he doubted his own conduct. He used about it the over-strong word, *wantonness*. It is not quite a public confession; but nearly; at least it is a half-penitential explanation.

He asked himself, now, whether some of the language was too strong; whether it was right to say so loudly that the country would be better if it were vastly more superstitious and bigoted and gloomy and fierce in its religion than it is; or to say that heretics should receive no mercy; or whether it was right to refuse to have any social intercourse with his own brother Frank whose opinions were more like those of the Plymouth Brethren. 'A sort of guilt attaches to me, not only for that vain confidence, but for my multiform conduct in consequence of it.' And yet − whatever penitence or shades of penitence were demanded − in essentials, he thought as he looked back, the confidence was right and the attitude had something right. Religion is dogmatic. It must be dogmatic if it is to have force; if religion is only a sentiment, it is a mockery. There is a visible Church with its creeds and its orders of ministry and its sacraments, which bear grace to humanity.

There stood the Church of England, modelled upon the early Christian Church; with a Prayer Book of Sacramental rites, and allowing confession, and teaching the creeds and the body of early Christian doctrine − but there was a snag; the XXXIX articles, to which every clergyman must subscribe. They were dated 1571. They were therefore a document of the Reformation. In their most obvious interpretation they taught that man is justified by faith alone; that some men are predestined to eternal life; that the invocation of saints, widely practised in the Church of the Fathers, is a fond thing vainly invented. Newman's Anglican predecessors of the seventeenth century had trouble stretching these articles to fit their Catholic view of the Church of England. But they had done it. It was now incumbent upon Newman to do it again; in a new and ardent generation of young Anglicans. He had to show that the XXXIX Articles could be interpreted in a way agreeable to the faith and practice of the Church of the Fathers. This was not a game. It was essential to him personally. Unless he did this his whole plea for a Catholic Anglicanism seemed to him to fall to the ground. It was even more essential to some of his young disciples.

Tract XC of early 1841, in which he did this, was not well drafted. He provoked unnecessarily, by playing with two or three formulas making them mean what few people of common sense could ever think that they meant. And then, these two or three contortions were not necessary to support his case. But the essence of the case was no more contorted than similar attempts by earlier Anglicans, and it was honest.

If this Tract were condemned by the Church of England – that is, the Tract as a whole, for the correction of an odd phrase or two would not matter to him – his case for Anglicanism collapsed. It meant contradiction between his Church and the early Church which in his eyes was sovereign over his Church.

If Newman's opponents wanted to condemn Tract XC and declare that the positions in it were untenable for an Anglican, they had more than one way open to them. The effective way was to prosecute Newman for heresy before an ecclesiastical court. But such a prosecution was unlikely to succeed, for no one could doubt that Newman's mind was in the essentials very 'orthodox'. It would have needed the assent of Newman's bishop, Bagot of Oxford, a gentle humane person unlikely to allow the prosecution of anybody, let alone a clergyman who had done a lot of good. And it would have allowed an appeal to a secular court, the Judicial Committee of the Privy Council; the verdict of which Newman would be likely to despise, and the composition of which was disliked even by the possible prosecutors. Newman could not be legally prosecuted with any hope of success. No one could legally 'eject' him from his parish of St. Mary's, Oxford.

Therefore Newman was secure – legally. A harder, less sensitive person might have sat tight, and scorned whatever abuse might be thrown. It was his doctrine that truth is likely to be unpopular.

The pressure was too great. (1) Ireland was in a terrible state socially and politically, and Englishmen held Roman Catholics largely responsible. Therefore there was a rising anti-Catholic sentiment among the English people. They were more intolerant about Roman Catholicism. The idea of an Anglican leader being 'a secret Catholic' was not to be born. And by now this tide of popular feeling had as its vehicle an effective Press. In a way, Newman's Anglican faith was one of the early victims of pressure from modern media. 'I was quite unprepared for the outbreak, and was startled at its violence.'

For (2) that was the way he was represented. When Kingsley said libellously in 1864 that Newman was a secret Roman Catholic for several years while he was an Anglican, he said no more than what gossip and malice said from the time of Tract XC onwards. Newman was a sincere person and to know that he was portrayed in his university and in society as a hypocrite was worse than troubling to his mind. If there was no legal authority in the Church of England

which would condemn his teaching, perhaps it was condemned by
the consensus of the people – by a crude rather ignorant repudiation of what he said or what they fancied that he said. He
saw at once, or fancied that he saw, that his place as leader of
a movement (if that was what he was) was gone. Most people now
did not trust him.

But (3) if there was an authority, it did not exist in a court
which could hardly sit, nor in a Convocation which could not
meet, perhaps it consisted in the bishops; if not all the bishops,
yet bishops; and above all the bishop to whom he owed obedience,
Richard Bagot the Bishop of Oxford.

To the Provost of Oriel, as the head of his college, he had no
special sense of any duty of obedience. But his bishop was the representative of the apostles to him. He felt that he ought to obey him
as he would have obeyed if St. Paul had asked him to do something. He did not think much of 'bishops' as a bench; or of synods,
whether diocesan or general. What commanded his allegiance was
his bishop, as *his* apostle; and his bishop happened to be kind aristocratic Bagot of Oxford, whom everyone liked but who was not very
exacting in his demands on his clergy, and who came to consecrate
the little church which Newman built in the village of Littlemore at
the country end of the parish of St. Mary's. Newman looked back
and saw how fortunate he was that Bagot was his bishop. For his
memory, he said, 'I have a special affection' – 'may his name ever
be blessed!'. It was a new thing in English literature that a Roman
Catholic priest should bless the memory of a bishop of the Church
of England.

But – if the bishops elsewhere in England fulminated against
Newman – could Richard Bagot stay silent? He was under the
same pressure from popular gossip. He had one of his clergy under
a grave accusation. He would be irresponsible if he did not speak.

He asked that Tract XC be withdrawn. That was impossible for
Newman if he wished to stay a loyal Anglican. Bishop Bagot gave
way. The Tract remained, uncondemned. But in return the bishop
asked Newman to stop the publication of the *Tracts for the Times*,
and to publish his opposition to the Church of Rome. And out of
pure obedience to his bishop, and mistakenly if he thought his place
in the Oxford Movement important, he consented to stop the Tracts.
He was pleased with the outcome. The Tract that was so important
to him was still a permissible opinion to him or to anyone else who
was a member of the Church of England. But he was not pleased for
long. Bishops started condemning Tract XC – 24 of them by three
years later, which was a large majority of the bishops of the Church

of England. Even Bishop Bagot, despite his promise, found that he could not stand aside. He made his condemnation very mild. But it was a condemnation.

The fascination of the *Apologia* reaches its climax in Newman's attempt to describe his state of mind during the four years after the publication of Tract XC. He loved the Church of England. To it he owed his soul. In it he found friendships of the heart. In it he was fulfilled as a reformer, a kind of prophet who recalled his Church to half-forgotten truths, to prayer and sacrament and self-discipline and force of truth. But public opinion, and most university opinion, and the bishops, repudiated him and his teaching. His Church was unfaithful to what he understood his Church must stand for to be the true Church. Was it possible then that the other great Church of the West, the Church of Rome, was the truly apostolic Church? How could it be so? − it varied from the Church of the Fathers like the Puritans, though in different ways. It taught, or at least allowed, practices which he thought to be superstitious and unwarranted. And it was associated politically with Liberalism and agitation in Ireland and nothing could make him accept that a Church should be linked with political agitation. The Church of England was sensible, reasonable and cool − the Church of Rome might be superstitious but it was warm. Yet the Church of England was his home, and the house of his friends. Two Churches − each now with a pull at his heart, and each with an appeal to his intellect. Soon it was near a torment as he was pulled this way and that − perplexity and dismay, he said, weighed upon him, and even to think about it he felt like a ripping of the bowels, 'a cruel operation' − a miserable time in which the stars of his life one by one went dark. Yet he must try to say how he felt in this misery, because Kingsley made his vacillation the ground of the charge that he was really a secret Roman Catholic while he was an Anglican.

This description, or part of it, moves the reader to this day. For it is a true attempt, perhaps the first attempt in the history of literature, to describe the condition of a divided heart. Arguments float in and out − arguments weighty with the author but unintelligible to most of the readers − the ancient Monophysites, or the ancient Donatists, or the too modern Jerusalem bishopric − but he knew that these arguments were not near the centre of the debate − 'it was not logic that carried me on . . . pass a number of years and I find my mind in a new place; how? . . . All the logic in the world would not have made me move faster towards Rome than I did.'

In 1841 he went to live in the village part of his parish, Littlemore. This rightly confirmed the press and the university in their impression that his mind was unsettled. They kept asking questions. 'Who would ever dream of making the world his confidant?' He only wanted to be left alone to think and say some prayers. He was not given the chance. The quiet of the hermitage which he expected was put under the spotlight of publicity. 'I cannot walk into or out of my house, but curious eyes are upon me. Why will you not let me die in peace? Wounded brutes creep into some hole to die in, and no one grudges it them. Let me alone, I shall not trouble you long.'

Perhaps in the circumstances he failed in prudence. Parents with sons who thought of becoming Roman Catholics, tutors with pupils who thought of becoming Roman Catholics, sent them to him to learn how to be a Catholic without being a Roman, and he accepted their presence and company, out of a sense of duty to his Church. Naturally one or two or three of them became Roman Catholics, for no one could have held them. And in the suspicion of that time, when Newman was fancied to be a crypto-Roman, this fed the illusion: he sits at Littlemore pretending to be Anglican, and at the same time he is enticing young people into his net to make them Roman Catholics. One of these conversions caused him to resign his parish of St. Mary's (September 1843). He had done what he could; he had failed; he felt he must resign. He preached his last sermon at Littlemore in September 1843; and then remained as a 'layman' for the two following years (actually for four years); not preaching, administering no sacraments. The only thing he kept was his Fellowship at Oriel College, though he hardly used it.

One scruple afflicted him, though much less sorely than the tug of the heart between the Churches. He stood for the dogmatic principle against 'liberalism' − against individuals choosing religion as they liked. Yet if he became a Roman Catholic he did just that; he encouraged the private judgement against which he was sworn to defend the faith. If he disappeared from the Church of England, the Liberals would profit. And if he had taught a creed with a total confidence and a total commitment, and gained many disciples, and then he abandoned the creed, would anyone ever believe him again? 'How could I ever hope to make them believe in a second theology when I had cheated them in the first?' Besides, deceived once, why might he not be deceived again? And in answer he could only say that a mind will go on seeking truth and be obedient to it if it is thought to be found. He had a horror of sowing the seed of doubt in other people, and of unsettling their consciences.

John Keble did not like him to resign his parish and go back to acting as a layman. In Keble's view he needed pastoral care and its responsibility to have a sane view of the Churches. In 1840 Newman tried to get Oriel College to separate from St. Mary's the Littlemore end of the parish and let him go on as the parish priest of Littlemore. But Oriel College and its Provost would not countenance the idea. And thenceforward he tried to turn in upon himself, to his own prayers and thoughts, and not to be any more a guru to the young. 'How could I in any sense direct others, who had to be guided in so momentous a manner myself?' Dr. Pusey, rock-like in his faith, could not understand all this vacillation in a friend's mind. He seems not to have believed what he was told about it. There were moments when Newman laboured under a sense of guilt; that he was destroying friendships; that he was not worthy of the friends who looked to him. 'I could not come to see you' he wrote to his close friend J. W. Bowden, another who would not understand doubt. 'I am not worthy of friends. With my opinions, to the full of which I dare not confess, I feel like a guilty person with others, though I trust I am not so.'

In September 1844 Bowden died. Newman saw how good an Anglican he was, how he had grace from the sacraments, how he was evidence for all the best that Newman felt about the Church of England. He went to Bowden's funeral expecting that the death would settle this tug that divided the heart. 'I sobbed bitterly over his coffin, to think that he left me still dark.'

So he started to write the Essay on Development, as a way of settling his mind. Was it possible that the Church of the Apostles developed, part naturally and part by the leading of God, into the Church of Rome that we know? It was enough to persuade his mind. He never finished the book. He asked to be received into the Roman Catholic Church and was received at Littlemore 9 October 1845.

It is hard to narrate the story of a conversion without bitterness. Conversions may be a form of divine leading, but humanly speaking they are also a betrayal of the past. They are a knock in the eye for one's parents, a parting from valued friends, the destruction of affection. They are the sackcloth and the ashes of saying that one taught doctrines with all one's force but that now it must be admitted that one was the worst of guides and misled one's pupils grossly. It is a turning upside down of sympathies. It is starting to talk of things which were once declared to be very good as though they were bad, and to talk of things which were once declared to be bad as though they were very good; and then sincerity is pain, the words do not trip off the tongue with a comfortable ease. In such circumstances the events that surround the change of allegiance cannot be other than emotional, sometimes emotional in the extreme.

The soul has the consolation that it has a feeling of coming home; like a man who has been in prison and now is free; or like an Odysseus driven by winds into exile and now at last at his own hearth. But this consolation and gratitude also carries its danger for a person trying to explain what is happening. For his feelings are indeed emotional, and he looks back upon the stormy seas where, as he now thinks, he was in peril of his life, and he looks back upon his cell which he now thinks to be cramped and shackled. And he cannot help therefore but exaggerate the contrast between his former life and his new life.

All this has to be explained both to the soul itself and to the former friends and colleagues. This can hardly be done without telling one's former allies and disciples that they are as wrong as one has been oneself; that they are all at sea and tossed about when they could be at rest in harbour; that they are fools to like their narrow cell when all the wide world is out of the window. The attempt to explain cannot but take the form of an onslaught on old friends — to burn what was once adored.

During the first years after his change of allegiance, from 1846 to about 1852, Newman did precisely that. He assailed his former Church, and former friends, with ability and with power. He had to defend himself from what would look like a betrayal; and naturally he hoped that some of them would follow him into what he now saw to be the truth. And the whole process is distasteful to read, to this day. The commandment, Honour thy father and mother, is not so easy to harmonize with a satirical onslaught upon the religion of one's childhood.

And there was a further difficulty in writing. This was no private person, led quietly from one denomination to another. This was a priest who tried to lead his people up towards the God of Sinai by a certain path through the desert. A lot of people had felt the rightness of the guidance. They felt that they owed him a better understanding of God and the demands of the conscience in relation to God. And now he has to tell them: 'everything I did was failure; I tried my best and it did not work, it would not do, the people were being led further into wilderness, I longed and my longing ended in frustration'. Therefore, if he wrote the account of his own conversion, he was also writing the history of the smashing of hope, and a description of how a high plan ended in nothing. The history of a failure is never the easiest or the most enjoyable thing to write, especially when that failure is so personal and so public and so passionate.

This is the key to the extraordinary difficulty of the task which Newman set himself. He was now mellow. He did not wish to pillory his past or his former colleagues. On the contrary he realized, in a longer perspective, all that he owed to those Anglicans. Part of his wish was to say how grateful he was. Yet he must express this gratitude without seeming for a single instant to suggest that he regretted what he had done when he left his former Church. And he never did regret it, and could be fierce with people who suggested that he did regret. He had to show himself thankful for past happiness and past insights into truth and past affections, and still to show that nevertheless he could have done no other than what he did, that when he did it he felt that he was coming home, and that he had never since then ceased to think of it as home.

So here is a person whose past and present contradict each other, and even excommunicate each other. Yet he writes as though past and present are friends; and he writes it in such a way that the reader feels no incompatibility and no incongruity. Never before had a convert to the Roman Catholic Church written about his past with such generosity to Protestants. It was something new in the history of the Church. Yet there was nothing self-conscious about it, and nothing artificial.

A description of doubt was a relatively new thing. The old Calvinist devotional writers found warnings of souls which doubted their salvation and tried to guide their troubled spirits through the valley of darkness to an assured faith. In a strange way that was what Newman was doing for himself in quite another context. The atmosphere is very new. We have entered the age of Victorian doubt, where Thackeray agonized about the moral standards of God in the Old Testament, or Clough yearned for the truth which he could never attain. In all these essentials of Christian faith Newman acquired too intimate a conviction as a child ever again to doubt in that way. His doubt was not that kind of doubt. But still he was full of doubt; and part of the interest of his autobiography was the description of a mind struggling with its doubts. This did not commend his book to some readers, who were still incapable of thinking that doubt could be anything but wickedness. But to other Victorians − the kind of Victorians who were to love his doubting hymn *Lead kindly light*, a conviction of faith achieved through darkness − these descriptions of hesitancy were the most gripping parts of the book. The power in the book was

the indecision of someone who came through to decision. Rome or
Canterbury – the argument sways to and fro, all is not black nor
white, the scales go up and down.

In this way the *Apologia* came to be bigger than an individual's
account of his own struggles with faith. At first sight the book is a
defence of his personal sincerity. But at second view that defence
is taken up into a far bigger question – the truth of the Christian
religion. Here is a man who was brought up to revere the Bible;
and who then learnt to see the Bible through the eyes of the early
Church and the early Christian Fathers; a boy for whom religion
was the ruling passion in life from early years; a boy for whom, at
least at times, God was more real than the world. Thus he learnt
to value historic Christianity and to accept its substantial truth. He
learnt to look to the ethos and the creeds of primitive Christianity
as the way of understanding his Bible. And then he finds himself
in a world of modernity – with critical history, and challenges to
the texts of the Bible, and suspicion of miracles, and people who
say that man was never created but evolved out of apes. What
then is the relation of historic Christianity to this new world? Has
historic Christianity to be adapted and adjusted if it is to survive as
a force among mankind? And if it has to be adapted and adjusted,
how is that to be done? The authority of the Bible we know, the
authority of the early Church we know. We know nothing about
the authority of professors of Christian history. Why should we
believe what someone like Dr. Whately, with all his logic, tells us
of the way in which we must adapt our faith?

It was a struggle, in an age of difficulty though not of such difficulty as a generation later, to find a sound intellectual basis for a
Church. The mind behind the *Apologia* thinks of this quest as in
large part a fight against 'Liberalism'. This word Liberalism was a
very confusing word. In the modern sense of the term, which has a
sense of open-mindedness, it was certain that no one could find an
intellectual basis for a Church without some element of liberalism
in his mode of enquiry. At the time the *Apologia* was written Pope
Pius IX condemned Liberalism in unmeasured language. The Pope
meant, first, the idea that a democracy was the only good kind of
government and therefore that his autocracy (which was more an
autocracy of show than of reality) in the Papal States in Central
Italy was a bad kind of government; and second, that religion was
a matter of any individual's opinion and that the idea that God
revealed a truth to the world was false. Newman did not mind
about Central Italy. He was a loyal person who accepted what
was taught by the teaching authority of his Church; and if the

Pope condemned Liberalism Newman condemned Liberalism. But he happened to agree with the Pope that God revealed truth to the world and that religion was more than a matter of individual opinion. Most Anglicans, most nonconformists, agreed with him in this attitude. If that was what Liberalism meant, a majority of the professing Christians in Britain were in agreement.

In this way Newman's appeal against Liberalism appealed to the better Christian sentiments of many outside the Roman Catholic church because, even if they were Liberals in politics or humane studies, they wanted the truth about God and his revelation. Some non-Roman Catholics would in this context see Newman as an ally. But they could only see him as an ally if he were not too extreme in his statement of the case. If he had said, for example, the only way to find the truth about God in the world is to listen to what the Pope says, they would laugh at him or despise him. To influence them he must be seen to be seeking the truth as they understood the way to seek truth. Newman's moderation was essential if he was to influence more than a handful outside his Church.

Yet it was the purpose of his argument to show that in this sceptical world of the middle nineteenth century, where everyone's ideas were at sea, the authority of Rome was the only reliable safeguard against the dissolvents of Liberalism, when that word is taken in its sense to mean that religious truth was not to be found. It was the purpose of his argument to show, Rome or nothing; either accept authority, or find yourself in scepticism. This sounds like an extreme position, and in a manner it was. Some people, like Liddon, saw that it was an extreme position and rejected it, however they admired the *Apologia*. Yet the subtlety and delicacy of Newman's mind was somehow able to lead up to this Either-Or without ferocity, or provocation, or mere dogmatism.

This feat was achieved because he could put himself into Anglican shoes. He well knew what it felt like, as an Anglican, to cope with people who said that this bit of the faith, or those bits, were now proved untrue and must be dropped. And in a manner he was still trying to cope in the old way. We must show how the conscience leads us to an immediacy of God. We must look into the Bible to see how the message there is delivered; and we must continue to understand the Bible by seeing it through the eyes of the apostolic men and their successors. Thereby we have an anchor of faith; and how this will be affected by the sober or wilder enquiries of our age, with that we must be patient, and take time to work it out, knowing that we shall be led onward by a Spirit higher than ourselves. But the anchor of Bible-in-the-Church is still unshaken.

The *Apologia* is in one of its sides the story of how this conviction of the Anglican Newman was shaken, was then weakened, and finally despaired of; how a soul came to feel that the anchor, as it was presented to him in his Church, was dragging along the sea-bed. He came to a sentiment, which was at first only half-conscious, that the anchor was not tough enough, nor big enough, for the gales that beat upon the ship. *Securus* − if there is a key word of this personal narrative it is that Latin word. Secure. Safe at anchor. If Dr. Whately tells us something why should we believe him? But if the Church tells us something − and we know that the Church is being led by the Spirit of God − it is secure. If the Anglican Church tells us something, is that secure? He spent a decade believing that it was secure; for his Anglicans had the Bible, and the valuing of apostolic men, and the respect for the ethos of the early Christian Church, and the continuity through the centuries. But now − he came to feel that something stronger, and bigger, was necessary amid these dissolvent quicksands of the European mind; and that something bigger must be a whole Church, not an insular Church; an international Church and not a national Church.

There was another semi-articulate feeling which we can only guess at from little signs in the *Apologia* but which we know of more fully from other writings of Newman. He had written a classical book of lasting weight − the six volumes of sermons preached as an Anglican vicar. In those sermons he was uncompromising in his challenge to the comfortable state of his Church. He compared its moderation with the absolute call to perfection and sanctity which according to Newman the early Church heard and strove to attain. Of course he recognized that in any Church, in any human institution with ideal objectives, there would be a wide gap between what was professed and what was achieved. He had not idealized the Roman Catholic Church before he became a Roman Catholic. One of the reasons for his long pause after he lost faith in the Church of England was a doubt whether the Church of Rome was any better. When after 1846 he got to know the Church of Rome better, increased knowledge brought still more reasons for contrasting the ideals professed with the moral performance of the institution.

But during those years which he was trying to explain in the *Apologia*, the years of growing doubt about his Church, the contrast had something in it of the contrast between prose and poetry. Steadiness versus excitement; suspicion of miracle versus a revelling in miracle; formal family prayers versus the long nights of prayer among contemplative nuns; suggestion that the sanctity of tradition was an extremism of the past with nothing to say to modern society, versus the admiration for strange excesses of sanctity; carelessness about the Virgin contrasted with affection for our Blessed Lady; rational prosaic faith versus faith in the improbable – these were nothing exactly to do with the truth or otherwise of religion. If the object was to persuade modern society of the intellectual truth of Christianity it was not likely that the Catholic way was better than the Anglican way, for there were a lot of modern men and women whom miracles and improbabilities and even excitement were sure to repel. But although the *Apologia* was dealing in the base of religion in a disturbed world, it was also an account of personal mood. We cannot quite say that he felt Anglicanism boring and Roman Catholicism exciting. Yet there is a touch of that feeling evident in his private temperament, from time to time. Such excitement about aspects of a Church to which he did not belong, taken by itself, could not move him. Novels may be exciting but are not therefore true. The question of truth was what mattered to him. But in the quest for truth he knew that a person moves not with the top of the head but with the whole being; and part of Newman's whole being, at that moment, contained the sensation that he was being summoned to a higher aspiration than his own Church could easily supply.

Yet this feeling was no unsubtle mood of black and white. It was not the feeling, I must get away from what bores me to what stirs me. He had been stirred too deeply in his Anglican way. Facing his past with his sincerity, he could see what vast debts in religion and life he owed to it.

This sense of debt keeps coming out in the *Apologia*. It took two forms. The first was gratitude. The second was nostalgia, or sadness about a never-to-be-recovered past.

The gratitude comes out in his generosity to Keble and Pusey and Froude; even to his old enemies Whately and Hawkins. It comes out also in the sense that what he did in those Anglican years was not wrong. He looked back and found it a great work which really helped the Churches to fulfil their true vocation in the modern world. Therefore the book has sadness. The nostalgia for the past had in it a touch of melancholy. He had done what he had to do because he could not do other. He left the Church of his childhood, to which he knew that he owed so much, because he was sure that he had to do so if he was to be faithful to the divine leading which he sought, or to the moral obedience which he wished to practise. But that did not force him to say that the change was all happiness. In some respects he preferred where he was before to where he was now — that is, from the human or worldly point of view. He told everyone in the *Apologia* that the Anglican years, from 1837 to 1841, when he led the Oxford Movement, were the happiest times of his life.

So the sadness was composed of three elements. First to part from friends was pain; and these were not just friends of the common room, they were friends of the soul. Secondly, to part from the ideals which he loved and which he represented was pain — when he owed them so much himself and when he seemed to desert not what was low and trivial but what was high and influential. This form of pain was bearable because he felt he still represented the same ideals, though in a better or fuller way. And thirdly the mood was bound to be sad because it was a story of a crashing failure. It recounted how he and a group of like-minded souls pinned their hopes on an ascent to the stars and rose up and up on Jacob's ladder and the ladder cracked under their feet and they were tumbling about in a heap and a disorder. The sadness is part of the sorrow of a parting; and part the rueing of a failure.

'From the time that I became a Catholic, of course I have no further history of my religious opinions to narrate.' The sentence is wonderful. Was it irony? The insertion of that tremendous pair of words *of course*, when he is stating something which nobody could believe, suggests humour. Here was a person who knew well that the mind of a Church, the mind of humanity, the mind of an individual, is always on the move. He then withdrew the 'of course' by defining the sentence to mean, not that his mind did not move, but that his mind had no anxiety about faith. The sting in the sentence is in the first clause; 'since I became a Catholic', for despite everything he had said over 200 pages in praise of and affection for the Church of England, the sentence denied its claim to be Catholic.

He had one more task; which did not fit the rest of the book. Kingsley said that to be a Roman Catholic was to be either credulous or a hypocrite. Newman needed to say why he and others could believe in the infallibility of the Church, and therefore in the doctrine of transubstantiation in the holy communion, and in the authority of the Pope; and therefore in the freedom of the Blessed Virgin Mary from the taint of original sin, without being hypocrites. The chapter which he devoted to this vast theme is too short to be weighty. But really the charge was too vague and too general to be worth answering. For the best answer was very brief. If Roman Catholic priests are so hypocritical, why did more than thirty of them die ministering to the epidemic in Liverpool and Leeds?

Yet underneath 'the general answer to Mr. Kingsley', concealed at first sight, Newman had a target that was neither Kingsley nor the prejudice of Protestants, but the authorities of the Roman Catholic Church.

For several years he knew that people in the Curia at Rome, and some Roman Catholics in England like Manning, distrusted him as not quite a loyal Roman Catholic; not devoted enough to the Pope; still too Anglican in his ways of thinking; not accepting Italian influence on English Roman Catholicism. Bits of the *Apologia* would do nothing to dispel, and something to confirm, this suspicion.

His doctrine that faith rested on probabilities was contrary to the doctrine of the Roman schools. And he made admissions that were not welcome. He granted how impossible the doctrine of transubstantiation is to imagine; he talked of the 'enormous mass of sin and ignorance' which of necessity exists in a communion so world-wide; he confessed that sometimes the authority of the Church had been harshly used, and hinted at tyranny. He spoke of 'a violent ultra party' which exalts opinions into dogmas. He showed that he did not want the Roman Catholic Church in England to copy Italian habits of devotion too closely.

Therefore he also needed to show his own Catholics that he was a truly loyal member of their Church. He needed to make a public profession of his faith, which sits uncomfortably within the *Apologia*, that infallibility is a tremendous power to check the wild intellect of man, and to profess his absolute submission to its claim, and to the rulings of the Holy See even on matters which could not claim any infallible authority. He needed to profess allegiance to the great system of Catholic theology from the Fathers to St. Thomas Aquinas, for some Catholics suspected him of wanting to 'break it up'. So strongly did he feel this necessity that he included in the final stages of the *Apologia* two extraordinary paragraphs, one of which is out of keeping with the rest of the book.

This one is a postscript, dated 4 June 1864. It was a letter from the Bishop of Birmingham, *his* bishop, Ullathorne, which took the form of a testimonial to Newman. To print a testimonial to oneself is a sign of weakness. Here is a modest and sometimes insecure man, printing in a book to be widely read a statement thanking him for all the good he has done to the Church since he has been a Catholic. Nothing that Bishop Ullathorne could say could make Newman any bigger than he was. It is a sign of a bizarre form of modesty, and of a measure of self-delusion, that Newman could think it worth-while to publish Ullathorne's letter. He needed to say that the Roman

Catholic Church approved of him; because some people thought that it did not.

The second extraordinary paragraph is on friendship. It is the most personal paragraph which Newman ever wrote for print in all his life, and no one else would have dared to put it into print. He offered his book to the members of his Oratory at Birmingham:

> and to you especially, dear Ambrose St. John; whom God gave me, when He took everyone else away; who are the link between my old life and my new; who have now for twenty-one years been so devoted to me, so patient, so zealous, so tender; who have let me lean so hard upon you; who have watched me so narrowly; who have never thought of yourself, if I was in question.

The paragraph must have embarrassed Ambrose St. John and needs a lot of explanation. According to normal thinking it is wrong for the superior of a monastic house to select one of his community for a special expression of affection in private, let alone in public. The portrait of a man being a staff and prop to another man, with a steady personal devotion to him, who watches him narrowly and tenderly – the portrait is not without its discomfort to the reader. And yet in this portrait there is a key to the whole nature of the *Apologia*.

Ambrose St. John had been the Anglican curate of Newman's friend Henry Wilberforce. He joined the little Anglican community with Newman at Littlemore during the summer of 1843. He became a Roman Catholic a week before Newman. Therefore his person was the only surviving link between the Anglican Newman and the Roman Catholic Newman. When Newman became a Roman Catholic some of the Anglican friends would no longer speak to him; and from others, who were as friendly as ever, like Church or Marriott, the roads parted, and Newman went away to Rome and Birmingham and their paths ceased to cross. Others who had been with him in Littlemore went different ways, either into liberalism like Mark Pattison, or into some other order or way of life within the Roman Catholic Church. Only one remained – 'whom God gave me when he took everyone else away . . . the link between my old life and my new'.

And really that is what the *Apologia* is about; the unity of Newman's personality. It started in a quarrel with a professor of history. Then Kingsley flew away into the limbo where papers are heaped when they interest no one but professors of history; and the book grew into a personal reflexion upon the English religious movement of the nineteenth century; and by that route it at last explained a course which looked to the outer eye to be divided into two contradictory parts, and showed, to himself as much as to others, the unity of a soul in its vocation before its Maker.

Notes
1   Page references to Everyman edition, 1912.

What Kind of a Book is the *Apologia?*

Ian Ker

Newman was anxious to disclaim any suggestion that the *Apologia* purported to be a history of the Oxford movement. And yet it obviously is to some extent at least a historical account, and seen from the point of view of the man who effectively inspired and led the movement until he began to be assailed by serious doubts. But it is this very fact that may easily be disguised by Newman's modest narrative, in which obviously he does not make clear how crucial his own role and influence were. So closely documented is his account by letters and quotations from published writings that there is little room for any serious factual error, while the author's comments on and interpretation of the facts tend to be so carefully expressed as simply his own personal opinions as to disarm in advance any doubts concerning their objectivity. After all, the point of the *Apologia* was to try and describe as far as possible the development of the narrator's theological views which led to his conversion to Rome. As such a purely subjective account, which is fully supported by the wealth of autobiographical materials (now partially published), the book has never been challenged, although of course the actual ideas and their evolution have been held up to plenty of critical scrutinies, especially from apologists for the Church of England.[1]

This in turn brings us to what the *Apologia* essentially is, namely an autobiography. But unlike that other Victorian classic, John Ruskin's *Praeterita*, the *Apologia* is an austerely intellectual work, purporting merely to be what its subtitle 'A History of his Religious Opinions' indicates it is. Certainly it is often called a 'spiritual' autobiography, but in the strictly narrow sense of the word it is very far from being a spiritual work like St. Augustine's *Confessions*, with which it is indeed often compared. If it is at all confessional, it is virtually only in its theological revelations, and such disclosures as there are of the writer's soul are made almost incidentally in connection with the former. Thus, for example, Newman tells us nothing of his prayer life, there is no mention of his Anglican confirmation and first communion, nor is his ordination ever referred to, or the parochial work he did as a curate in the Oxford parish of St. Clement's, or his strongly held convictions about the pastoral responsibilities of a college tutor. Central autobiographical themes like these, of great importance for understanding Newman's spiritual life, are simply ignored. In at least two cases the silence is practically misleading, as there were important effects on his theological development. I refer in the first place to Newman's gradual deconversion from Evangelicalism. In his 'Autobiographical Memoir' which he wrote in the 1870s, he records that after receiving Anglican orders he discovered from 'personal experience' that the kind of Christianity he had imbibed from reading books by Evangelicals like John Newton and Thomas Scott 'would not work in a parish; that it was unreal; that this he had actually found as a fact ... that Calvinism was not a key to the phenomena of human nature, as they occur in the world'. In other words, it was not only through the kind of theological discussion and study which he records in the *Apologia* that he became disenchanted with Evangelicalism, but also as a result of the actual pastoral work he undertook in the working class parish of St. Clement's. But to this practical experience − 'the teaching of facts'[2] − he makes no reference at all in the *Apologia*.

That the silence was quite deliberately self-imposed can be shown by the even more glaring omission of any real description of the imaginative effect on his religious imagination of his momentous Mediterranean cruise of 1832−3, immediately prior to the formal beginning of the Oxford movement. Newman's visits to Italy, Malta, and the Greek islands are almost dismissed in six paragraphs in the first chapter in the *Apologia*, and yet the letters and verses he wrote on his travels, as well as the extraordinarily vivid account he later wrote of his near-fatal illness in Sicily, show how crucial this intense period of his life was for his subsequent religious development. In this regard, too, then, the *Apologia* is quite misleading autobiographically.

Actually, in a later passage in the second chapter of the *Apologia* Newman does let drop a hint that his earlier brief account of his foreign travels was less than complete. In the course of discussing his theological position in 1833, he alludes to his ingrained prejudice that the Pope was the antichrist predicted in Scripture, which had been deeply impressed on him by his adolescent Evangelical reading. Remarking that 'My imagination was stained by the effects of this doctrine up to the year 1843', he qualifies this by adding, 'it had been obliterated from my reason and judgment at an earlier date'.[3] This contrast reappears later in the same chapter when he retraces the gradual diminution of his antipathy to the papacy.

But this time it is his imagination which becomes less anti-papal than his reason. When he went abroad for the first time to Catholic countries, 'the sight of so many great places, venerable shrines, and noble churches, much impressed by imagination'. His 'heart was touched also', he recalled by Catholic devotions and worship, and although his 'reason was not affected at all', for his 'judgment was against her, when viewed as an invitation, as truly as it ever had been', nevertheless he 'learned to have tender feelings towards her'.[4]

There may appear to be an obvious contradiction between these two passages, but the discrepancy is more apparent than real. Keenly sensitive as he always was to the complex interaction of the imaginative and the rational elements in the human mind, Newman was well aware that just as the imagination may anticipate ideas only later embraced by the reason, so too the imagination may refuse to keep up with the intellect's progress. Thus, while a view of the Pope as the antichrist may leave a 'stain' on the imagination which the intellect finds itself unable to expunge, so too the imagination may be impressed by ideas which are not yet entertained by the reason.

As Newman's great philosophical work the *Grammar of Assent* (1870) shows so profoundly, the so-called intellect and imagination are in his view integrally connected; nevertheless, the *Apologia*, in its scrupulous concern with the intellectual development of its author's religious views, seriously downplays the powerful impressions he received during those eventful months abroad before the commencement of the movement. It is, however, of course true that the two traumatic shocks that Newman suffered in the summer of 1839 could be called as much imaginative as intellectual, as he describes them in the *Apologia*. But such is the force of those celebrated pages that a reader would conclude that Newman's deconversion from Anglicanism only really began in that fateful long summer vacation. In fact, what the travel letters of 1832–3 reveal so graphically is that the imaginative seeds of Newman's eventual conversion to Rome were sown during his visits to the countries of southern Europe, where he experienced at first-hand for the first time the two forms of Christianity which had never been 'reformed' by the Reformation of the sixteenth century and which could trace their origins directly and uninterruptedly back to the primitive church of apostles and martyrs. There was a sense in which eastern Orthodoxy interested him more than Roman Catholicism, as after all it was the Greek rather than the Latin Fathers who were his real theological mentors, especially his hero St. Athanasius. Witnessing Orthodox devotion to the Virgin Mary – more prominent in their liturgy than in the Latin Mass – and to the saints clearly disconcerted Newman, as such idolatry and superstition were supposed to be the peculiar marks of the Church of Rome. It also seemed that the various Protestant sects with which Newman was familiar in England were far more heretical than either Constantinople or Rome. Most perplexing of all were his very mixed emotions on reaching Rome — the city of the antichrist but the city also where Peter and Paul were martyred, the city to which England owed its Christian faith but the city too where the most famous church in Christendom, St. Peter's, had been built partly by the sale of indulgences, the city full of superstition but also full of churches and shrines conspicuous for their devotion. It was all very confusing when he had been taught to believe that Rome was one of the four beasts of the Apocalypse. He was impressed by the devoutness of the seminarians he saw, and yet he knew (as all Protestants knew) that the Roman Catholic priesthood was deeply corrupt — but then again he found himself wondering if the pompous Anglican chaplain in Rome was really closer to Christian truth than the Italian priests he saw. In the end he came to the somewhat contradictory conclusion that while Roman Catholicism itself was hopelessly corrupt, nevertheless individual Roman Catholics could be very impressive indeed. But what, he dared wonder, if this in reality was an example of the principle that the corruption of the best is the worst? He was beginning to glimpse that the argument from corruption was a two-edged weapon, which could be fatally turned on itself. As he waited in Palermo for a ship to take him home he put into verse his new attitude to Roman Catholicism, full of ambivalence and of significance for a decision that was still twelve years away:

> Oh that thy creed were sound!
> For thou dost soothe the heart, Thou Church of Rome,
> By thy unwearied watch and varied round
> Of service, in thy Saviour's holy home.[5]

In both Newman's deconversion from Evangelicalism, then, and in his conversion to Roman Catholicism personal experience of a very concrete kind was a key contributory factor, as well as the more theological aspects to which the *Apologia* largely confines itself.[6] It is time now to look more positively at what kind of an autobiography the *Apologia* is, rather than what it is not.

First of all, it clearly stands within a recognizable genre, as its author practically indicates when he acknowledges his enormous debt to the Evangelical Thomas Scott (1747–1821), who recounted his own religious pilgrimage in his little, best-selling autobiography

The Force of Truth (1779), a book which Newman says deeply impressed him because it showed how Scott 'followed truth wherever it led him, beginning with Unitarianism, and ending in a ...faith in the Holy Trinity'.[7] Scott's own autobiography, of course, belonged to the English Protestant autobiographical tradition, beginning with John Bunyan's *Grace Abounding to the Chief of Sinners* (1666). The autobiography of conversion was naturally especially dear to Evangelicals whose spirituality and theology were so overwhelmingly centred on personal conversion to Christ. The typical Evangelical pattern of conversion was to be found, for example, in the extremely popular *Rise and Progress of Religion in the Soul* (1745) by Philip Doddridge (1702–51), a book which Newman lent to his parishioners.[8] It was a book that his own Evangelical mentor, Walter Mayers had recommended to him after his conversion in 1816 in a letter which accompanied the gift of a copy of *Private Thoughts upon Religion and Private Thoughts upon a Christian Life* by William Beveridge (1637–1708). It is significant that nearly sixty years later Newman himself testified to the exclusively intellectual nature of his own autobiography when he noted that he had not mentioned Beveridge's *Private Thoughts in the Apologia*, because he was 'speaking there of the formation of my doctrinal opinions, and I do not think they were influenced by it. I had fully and eagerly taken up Calvinism into my religion before it came into my hands [.] But no book was more dear to me, or exercised a more powerful influence over my devotion and my habitual thoughts. In my private memoranda I even wrote in its style.'[9]

Unlike the autobiographies of Bunyan, Cowper, Newton, and Whitefield, Scott's *The Force of Truth* was, like the *Apologia,* devoid of emotional introspection, being wholly concerned with giving a strictly theological account of the author's religious development. Scott also avoided the personal details of his life – although in this reticence he was only following Bunyan and Newton. Again, as if to prove that his conversion was based on intellectual rather than merely emotional grounds, Scott emphasised that the Trinitarian Christianity he eventually embraced was derived ultimately from his reading of orthodox Anglican divines. Similarly, as if to show that he was not influenced by subjective considerations, Newman stressed that his conversion had little or nothing to do with reading or meeting Roman Catholics. Whereas the Protestant autobiographical tradition naturally depended on Biblical motifs, particularly that of the exodus of the Israelites, Newman is influenced by the analogies he finds in his study of the primitive Church and the early heresies.

As has recently been shown,[10] Newman's autobiography was not only the culmination of the English Protestant tradition but also bears marked resemblances to the most famous of all spiritual autobiographies, the Confessions of St. Augustine. Indeed, it was, Newman tells us, a sentence from another of Augustine's writings that triggered off his own eventual conversion to Catholicism, just as, he reminds us, Augustine himself had been converted to Catholic Christianity from Manichaeism by hearing some chance words of a child – an event which is also the dramatic turning point of the Confessions. Rather like Augustine's depiction of his conversion, in terms of a transition from death to life, so too Newman finds himself on his Anglican death-bed, an image which in effect replaces the traditional Protestant idea of the religious seeker wandering in the desert like the Israelites in search of the promised land. Like Augustine, too, Newman has to recant his misconceptions of Catholicism. And again rather like Augustine, who commends his mother St. Monica to the prayers of his readers at the end of bk.IX, so Newman prays at the end of ch.v for all his old Oxford friends, a finale which contrasts with the traditional Protestant closure that concerns the salvation of the individual Christian. Finally, just as the last four books (X-XIII) of the *Confessions* abandon narrative, with the achievement of conversion, for reflective exposition, so too the last chapter of the *Apologia* turns to a different kind of 'apologia' where Newman defends Catholicism against the traditional Protestant charges, in the same way that Augustine ends by defending the Catholic doctrine of creation against the Manichean heresy he had previously himself held.

But if it is true that Newman has in the *Apologia* drawn, however unconsciously, from a Catholic model, thus modifying the Protestant or Evangelical tradition from within which he is clearly and more or less consciously writing, it is also the case, as I have already indicated, that the *Apologia* is much more drily theological, like Scott's *The Force of Truth*, than the introspective, spiritual *Confessions*. So, it may be asked, how is it that the *Apologia* has continued to grip readers even in the latter part of the twentieth century when ecumenism on the one hand and secularization on the other may seem to have combined to rob so much of Newman's theological pilgrimage of the compelling interest it once had?

First of all, the austere, largely documentary form that Newman employs paradoxically only serves to highlight the few personal details that are divulged. For instance, a large number of people appear in the first chapter whom Newman acknowledges as formative influences, but because he wishes for his own apologetic reasons to confine himself to their theological significance, such description of them as even his uncompromising narrative demands is fleetingly and tantalizingly elusive. For example, in his generously detailed account of the influence of the provost of Oriel, Edward Hawkins, he alludes with extreme politeness to the fact that 'he provoked me very much from time to time, though I am perfectly certain that I have provoked him a great deal more'.[11] This is all that he says about the celebrated row over the college office of tutor, which was not only germane to future developments of the famous Oxford tutorial system but also highly relevant to the formation of Newman's own views on education which would achieve their classic expression in *The Idea of a University* (1873). The sparsity of the text gives a certain dramatic resonance to the narrative as the reader picks up the vibrations of the carefully controlled voice of the narrator. Similarly, there is no attempt to convey the actual atmosphere of the famous Oriel common room, but small details are allowed to escape: for example, it was on a walk round Christ Church meadow that the Rev. William James taught Newman the doctrine of apostolical succession, while on another solitary walk as a new, shy fellow of Oriel, he encountered the then provost, Edward Copleston, who 'turned round, and with the kind courteousness which sat so well on him, made me a bow and said 'that one was never less alone than when alone'.[12] It is little, apparently incidental touches like these that give the narrative a personal immediacy which is the more strongly felt precisely because of the sense of suppressed emotion. Moreover, the reader is affected by the sense that it is only the author's overriding desire to present as frankly and squarely as possible his developing doctrinal views that restrains him from more personal revelations. And it is this very impression of severe self-restraint that helps the actual theological story that is being told to be even more dramatically tense as our attention is focused relentlessly and unremittingly on the pressure of ideas on a mind both alertly responsive to new problems and questions and keenly aware of its own moral responsibility to follow the truth wherever it may lead.

It was, as we have seen, this single-minded pursuit of the truth which had so impressed Newman in Scott's *The Force of Truth*. However, it would be quite misleading to imply that the only passion to be found in the *Apologia* lies in a kind of repressed intellectual excitement. Perhaps the great triumph of the book, is the way in which Newman not only holds our attention by the detached documentary report of his theological pilgrimage but also draws us into the dim historical events of the early church against the background of which he resolves his own religious identity. We find ourselves as surprised at our own interest in the Monophysites ('I saw my face in that mirror, and I was a Monophysite'[13]) as Newman himself was astonished that a particularly unsavoury episode in the history of the early church should have caused his first really serious doubt about the Anglican position. The dramatic passage that he then quotes from a later controversial writing in which he revisited this moment of crisis reminds us that the *Apologia* consists to a very large extent of lengthy quotations from private letters as well as published works, and that this sets in relief the limpid tone of the narrative which itself is a kind of connecting commentary on those (largely contemporary) documents. For there is plenty of excitement in the *Apologia*, but the difference from Newman's other writings is that the argument and polemic are now recollected at a distance – if not exactly in tranquillity, at least in relative detachment.

It is a curious anomaly that the book on which Newman's literary reputation is usually presumed principally to rest, itself so strikingly differs from his other works of controversy, which give him so distinctive a place in the history of English literature. Its power largely indeed lies in the (almost) disconcertingly calm tone of the author's conversational, even sometimes colloquial, voice. Flashes of eloquence are rare (and all the more effective for the rarity), for eloquence is nearly as rigorously excluded as explicit self-defence: 'I am not setting myself up as a pattern of good sense or of any thing else: I am but giving a history of my opinions, and that, with the view of showing that I have come by them through intelligible processes of thought and honest external means.'[14] Nor is there any claim that his history will be of any great human interest – 'I have no romantic story to tell.'[15] The *Apologia* is indeed unique among Newman's published works, not only in its form and content, but also in its style and tone. Nearly all Newman's writings were 'occasional' in the sense of being responses to particular occasions, and of course the *Apologia* is no exception, for it is an extended answer to the attack of Kingsley, which itself was only representative of many others. But what makes the *Apologia* so different is that, with the exception of the last chapter, the actual argument, debate, and polemic are now all in the recorded past tense. And the main *'apologia'* persuades not by overt argument but by the narration of past facts, albeit to a large extent of past controversies and polemic.

As we have already seen, it is to those parts of the original *Apologia* that Newman later omitted or drastically abridged that we must turn for the polemic that makes Newman probably the greatest controversialist in the English language. Newman was certainly right to omit what would not only have looked excessively vindictive to an audience that had already recognized his victory over Kingsley, but which would have been not so much irrelevant as prejudicial to the purpose of the history he had decided to tell in refutation not only of Kingsley but of the prejudiced Protestant public. However, from another point of view we can only regret the undoubted literary loss of writing that recalls the exuberant satire that flowered in the years after Newman's conversion, pre-eminently in *Lectures on Certain Difficulties felt by Anglicans in submitting to the Catholic Church* (1850) and *Lectures on the Present Position of Catholics in England* (1851). Newman not only echoes ideas from the latter work, but employs similar imagery to express the blind power of prejudice:

> He [Kingsley] need not commit himself to a definite accusation against me, such as requires definite proof and admits of definite refutation; for he has two strings to his bow; − when he is thrown off his balance on the one leg, he can recover himself by the use of the other. If I demonstrate that I am not a knave, he may exclaim, 'Oh, but you are a fool!' and when I demonstrate that I am not a fool, he may turn round and retort, 'Well, then, you are a knave.'[16]

The superb invective of some of the passages that Newman eventually omitted may startle, even shock, modern readers unused to the kind of hard-hitting religious controversy that came naturally to the Victorians. We should notice, however, that Newman explicitly makes the point it is 'very difficult to get up resentment towards persons whom one has never seen', and so 'I wish to impute nothing worse to Mr. Kingsley than that he has been furiously carried away by his feeling'.[17] When Kingsley died ten years later, Newman felt he could honestly say he had never felt angry personally with him. But at the time he was so convinced that it was only by speaking out strongly that people would believe him, that he had decided 'it would not do to be tame, and not to show indignation'. Anyway, the fact was that by his 'passionate attack' on him Kingsley had inadvertently become one of his 'best friends, whom I always wished to shake hands with when living, and towards whose memory I have much tenderness'.[18] This claim is supported by an examination of Newman's satirical method which (except in one very serious and justifiable instance that Newman always acknowledged) invariably avoided the kind of moral personalizing that is usually the stock-in-trade of the satirist. Instead, what Newman's satire fastens upon

here (as elsewhere) is the absurdity of the inconsistency and incoherence of Kingsley's blustering indictment. It is not Kingsley's
moral character that is under sarcastic scrutiny but the superfici-
ality of his intelligence and understanding.[19]

Finally, the *Apologia* is not only an autobiography that grew
out of controversy and satire; it is also a book that is not just
a theological record but is, at least in its last chapter, a very
important contribution to ecclesiology, the theology of the church.
The modern development or revival of Catholic understanding of
the nature of the church, to which Newman contributed so significantly, would eventually culminate in the great reforming Second
Vatican Council (1962–5) that effectively closed the Tridentine era
and opened a new chapter in the history of Christianity. It would
be impossible and inappropriate here to attempt to offer any close
study of the key issue that Newman examines with such sensitivity
and subtlety in chapter v, a rhetorical *tour de force* which may be
easily read as an essay in its own right.[20]

The central issue that Newman is considering in his general
defence of the Roman Catholic Church, is really the question
of authority and freedom. As against the modern assumption
that freedom by definition means the absence of checks and
limitations (except such as may incidentally be imposed by conflict between opposing freedoms), Newman's case is that in order
to avoid its own self-destruction freedom actually demands those
boundaries which in fact define its nature; otherwise it degenerates
into anarchy. The post-Enlightenment mind is deeply impressed with
the idea of the individual mind seeking truth in a kind of splendid
isolation both from tradition and the community of other minds.
Now although Newman did not live to see philosophers of science
themselves 'cast doubt upon the credentials of science itself as an
avenue to truth'[21] he did seriously challenge the epistemology of the
Enlightenment in other areas of human knowledge. And in this last
chapter of the *Apologia* he insists that the authority of an infallible
church, far from destroying reason, actually sustains it by protecting
it from its own 'suicidal excesses'.[22] Not only that, he argues, but
paradoxically the 'energy of the human intellect ...thrives and is
joyous, with a tough elastic strength, under the terrible blows of
the divinely-fashioned weapon [infallibility], and is never so much
itself as when it has lately been overthrown'.[23] Newman claims that
the reason for the vitality of Catholic theology is precisely because
it has to work within the constraints and discipline of an authoritative Church, and the resulting tension, indeed conflict, far from
being debilitating or frustrating, is actually creative and liberating:

... it is the vast Catholic body itself, and it only, which affords
an arena for both combatants in that awful, never-dying duel.
It is necessary for the very life of religion, viewed in its large
operations and its history, that the warfare should be incessantly
carried on. Every exercise of infallibility is brought out into act
by an intense and varied operation of the Reason, both as its ally
and as its opponent, and provokes again, when it has done its
work, a re-action of Reason against it; and, as in a civil polity
the State exists and endures by means of the rivalry and collision,
the encroachments and defeats of its constituent parts, so in like
manner Catholic Christendom is no simple exhibition of religious
absolutism, but presents a continuous picture of Authority and
Private Judgment alternately advancing and retreating as the ebb
and flow of the tide ... [24]

Newman does not purport to be able to provide any kind of schematic theology for the relation between authority and freedom in
the church, and indeed the whole implication of his rhetoric is that
no such blueprint is possible for what after all is a living rather than
a static relationship. But he does proceed, with pointed examples
from church history, to show, as against the authoritarianism of
the Ultramontanes − at whom this chapter is aimed at least as
much as at Kingsley − how important theology is for the life of
the church. And it is the careful balance with which he asserts both
the right of theologians to free inquiry and at the same time the pre-
rogatives of the hierarchical teaching authority that still makes his
discussion highly pertinent to the perennial problem of reconciling
the conservative and the innovative elements in the church.

Notes

1   Sometimes by simply ignoring what Newman actually says, as when Owen
     Chadwick claims that he was in search of 'an ideal' church, to which
     the closest he believed was the Roman Catholic Church (Introduction to
     Susan Foister, *Cardinal Newman 1801−90: A centenary Exhibition* [London:
     National Portrait Gallery Publications, 1990], 7). In his *Newman* (Oxford:
     Oxford University Press, 1983) 14, Chadwick virtually attributes his con-
     version to intellectual isolation at Littlemore.
2   *Newman's Autobiographical Writings* AW 79.
3   Apo.
4   Apo.
5   *Verses on Various Occasions* 153.
6   For a fuller account of these experiential factors in Newman's religious
     development, see Ian Ker, 'Newman's Conversion to the Catholic Church:
     Another Perspective', *Renascence*, 43 (1990/1), 17−27.
7   *Apo* [18].

8   Letters and Diaries of J H Newman i. 196.

9   *LD* i. 30 n.1.

10   Linda H. Peterson, *Victorian Autobiography: The Tradition of Self-Inter-pretation* (New Haven and London: Yale University Press, 1986), 93–119, a study to which I am indebted for the foregoing and following remarks, although I cannot agree with the unconvincing parallel she attempts (on the basis of a flimsy and unpersuasive piece of secondary evidence) to draw between Augustine's mother, who was profoundly involved in his conversion, and Newman's mother, who (unlike his grandmother and aunt) can safely be said to have had no significant effect whatsoever on his religious development nor indeed any sympathy with it.

11   *Apo.* [21].

12   *Apo.* [27].

13   *Apo.* [108].

14   *Apo.* [39].

15   *Apo.* [44].

16   *Apo.* [388].

17   *Apo.* [394].

18   *LD* xxvii. 219; xxix. 388.

19   For a fuller consideration of Newman's satire, see Ian Ker, 'Newman the Satirist', *Newman After a Hundred Years*, ed. Ian Ker and Alan G. Hill (Oxford: Clarendon Press, 1990), 1–20.

20   For a full discussion, see Ian Ker, *John Henry Newman: A Biography*, Clarendon Press, Oxford 1988, 549–59.

21   Basil Mitchell, 'Newman as a Philosopher', *Newman After a Hundred Years,* 237.

22   *Apo.* [220].

23   *Apo.* [225].

24   *Apo.* [226].

Who, then, was Dr. Newman? – The Man and the Myth

Dr. Rune Imberg

Anyone with even a modicum of insight knows that Newman was a giant – as a theologian, a thinker, a writer. But how and why?

It has been said about some English writer, perhaps about Oscar Wilde, that he never wrote a dull line in his life. Something similar can also be said about Newman. His mastery of the English language can be rivalled by very few men. His autobiography, the *Apologia*, is in world literature compared with the Confessiones by St. Augustin and then with – little else. There is a beauty in whatever he wrote – sermons, theological treatises, letters – which can be appreciated even a century after his death.[1] This is also one reason why many of his books are still reprinted and studied today.

This cannot be said about Pusey, Newman's friend and fellow-leader of the Oxford Movement. In their own lifetime both were almost larger-than-life – but what has then become of Pusey? He is *known* as an important personality in the incipient Anglo-Catholic movement, but *read* by very, very few. He seems to have passed in the shadow of Newman. One reason is, of course, stylistic. His letters are interesting to read, but most of his books and treatises are quite dull.

This is one explanation, but hardly the most important one. Perhaps the reason why Newman stands out today, while others like Pusey and Keble have faded into oblivion, is the question of personality. There is something timeless in the way Newman put his questions and gave his answers, integrating them into his personal situation. Even if you don't agree with what he said, you can all the same appreciate his way of expressing it!

Saying this, it is necessary to face the fact: One of the major problems in the research concerning him and the Oxford Movement revolves around this question:

Do we meet the real Newman in his writings?[2]

One problem with Newman, according to many scholars, is that he was a little 'too clever'. The best example is, perhaps, Tract 90 where he used all his logic to defend a quite untenable theological position. This tract gives a sad impression to many readers. Some of his arguments are so strained, not to say false, that the reader asks himself: Did Newman, himself, in fact believe everything he had written in it?[3]

But a still more important question is this: Haven't many scholars been misled by Newman himself?

The best example to me is his *Apologia*. Of course it belongs to the classical pieces in the history of world literature, also giving a very interesting insight into Newman's development – *as he believed himself, or as he wanted people to believe, it had occurred.* But how reliable is it as an historical document? That is the question which should never be forgotten.

In my thesis, this was one of the major topics I dealt with. There I have shown (especially through an analysis of different editions of *Tracts for the Times*) that the description of Newman's drift toward Rome as it appears in the *Apologia* is not correct. I believe that he wrote in good faith – but that is no guarantee of correctness! The importance of the events in 1839 was not that he started to doubt his position (as he himself thought), because that had already been theologically undermined for quite some time, but that he *had become aware of it*. Many scholars have missed the psychological aspect and been satisfied with his own, more theological, statement. His own interpretation has been accepted at its face value instead of being examined critically.

I would also like to take another example concerning his private life. In part III of the *Apologia*, dealing with his religious opinions up to 1833, he writes about his celibate life:

'I am obliged to mention, though I do it with great reluctance, another deep imagination, which at this time, the autumn of 1816, took possession of me, – there can be no mistake about the fact; – viz, that it was the will of God that I should lead a single life. This anticipation, which has held its ground almost continuously ever since, – with the break of a month now and a month then, up to 1829, and, after that date, without any break at all, – was more or less connected, in my mind, with the notion that my calling in life would require such a sacrifice as celibacy involved; as, for instance, missionary work among the heathen, to which I had a great drawing for some years. It also strengthened my feeling of separation from the visible world, of which I have spoken above.'[4]

This gives an interesting insight into a special area of his life. It becomes evident that he was not only unmarried by chance, he was also celibate by purpose. His statement in itself is also quite easy to follow – but what really lies behind it?

A careful reading of Newman's letters concerning family matters gives, in fact, a rather strange impression. His relationship with male friends often remained very stable over the years, even decades – as long as they were unmarried. But if they became engaged and married, especially if they also had been considering living a celibate life, it almost always strained the relationship with Newman. One of the few marriages he approved of was Pusey's. There are even cases where some of his nearest friends didn't dare to mention to him their engagements; instead the news was broken through go-betweens, etc.[5]

It is surprising that this element in Newman's life hasn't been studied psychologically, when so many others have been analyzed in detail. Is it connected with his 'sensitiveness', which many of his nearest friends complained of?[6] Many other elements in his behaviour also remain enigmatic. What does it mean, e.g., that he was buried in the same grave as his old friend Ambrose St. John? – an event which is duly mentioned in many accounts of Newman's life, but never fully explained.

In short, the questions related to Newman's personality cannot be answered through just reading the *Apologia* once more – what is needed is careful study using all relevant sources.

Concerning Pusey, it has become evident that the picture painted by Liddon was partly distorted. In this four-volume biography Pusey is presented as a saint, but later research has definitely made some important corrections to this work which otherwise deserves much praise. His theological development is now partly painted with other, but more realistic, colours.[7]

It is also evident that Pusey as well ought to be made the object of a careful psychological study. He was definitely hurt in different ways during his youth, and it seems that these sores never really healed. They are seen in his rather strange behaviour towards his wife and children, but also towards himself, and they had certain theological implications.[8]

The recent revaluation of Pusey needs to go further. Much more can be said about his theological development, both as a young liberal, influenced by Germany, and as an elderly, very influential conservative. The Rediscovery of Pusey has only started!

But in a similar way Newman needs to be rediscovered — the *real Newman* behind the *public Newman*. Although hundreds of books have been written about him, and many of them very good, this is the big flaw in most of them in my opinion.[9] The problem is to get behind the public Newman.

Here it is interesting for different reasons to compare Newman with Luther. They resemble each other — at the same time they are totally different.

Both were theological fighters, engaged in hundreds of theological debates, very often successful at least in silencing their opponents. But they used different weapons — if Luther can be depicted as using a club, Newman's weapon would be a rapier; Luther is forceful, Newman elegant.

Both of them produced dozens of books, often written in the heat of a controversy, and in most cases very readable. But then a great difference appears. In general, Luther let his writings be as they were while Newman was very interested in the impression he wanted to make on others. For instance, he did not only keep the letters he had received, and there was many thousands of them, but he also tried to get his own letters returned or at least have a chance to copy them.

This is a memento in Newman research. No one can deny his importance both for the High Church movement, in England and abroad, and for the Roman Catholic church (Vatican II etc.) and certainly his sermons directly or indirectly influenced thousands of people, etc.

However, it must also be said that no one has influenced our understanding of Newman more than — Newman himself. This ought, naturally, to make all scholars a bit suspicious. All the same, behind this public Newman, whose monument he partly raised himself, there is a still more interesting Newman, the *real* one!

In my research I concluded that Newman was, in fact, a sceptic who found refuge in the claims of authority proclaimed by the Roman Catholic Church. It was then interesting for me to note that Newman almost acted like a paradigm for many of the converts in Sweden who converted from the Lutheran Church of Sweden in the 1980s, becoming Roman Catholics. In many cases they often used exactly the same arguments as Newman without having read one single sentence written by him!

The last word about the Oxford Movement has not been said yet. Much more research needs to be done and, presumably, will be done.

Notes

1. The only exception in my opinion, where Newman can be both dull and unconvincing is – in his two novels!
2. See my dissertation 'In Quest of Authority' and its companion volume 'Tracts for the Times. A Complete Survey of All the Editions,' both published 1987 by Lund University Press.
3. For practical reasons I just refer to p. 134 ff, esp. note 55, in my thesis 'In Quest of Authority'.
4. *Apologia*, p. 100 (Fontana ed. 1977).
5. See Newman's *Letters and Diaries*.
6. Cf. Imberg, 'In Quest of Authority', p. 190 f.
7. Especially through Forrester and the volume *Pusey Rediscovered*.
8. His resolve, e.g., never to smile except in the presence of children ought, of course, to have theological implications, e.g., concerning his understanding of the atonement. In the same way, his enormous guilt feelings for the death of some relatives must partly account for his personal sternness.
9. I deal more with these matters in my thesis, 'In Quest of Authority', e.g. p. 137.

Newman's state of mind on the eve of his Italian tour

Paul Vaiss

To the reader of the *Apologia*, Newman's spiritual development appears to be a very smooth process which is quite easy to follow. After his first conversion of 1816, he was for some time a staunch Evangelical, preaching the gospel of instantaneous conversion and believing in the sharp distinction between the elect and the damned which his Calvinist mentors had taught him. During his final year as curate of St. Clement's, in 1826, he is supposed to have abandoned most of his Evangelical notions and to have embraced a more sacramental view of religion, some sort of a moderate High Church position, under the combined influence of Whately, Froude and Keble. Yet, a chronological reading of the sermons he preached between 1828 and 1832, particularly those he did not publish later on, gives a far different picture. In them, Newman appears torn between his early Evangelical convictions, he has by no means relinquished, and the High Church notions of his new friends. If his religious position is to be determined through the sermons he preached at the time, one can single out several periods that can be graded from definitely evangelical to clearly High Church, with middle of the way stages when both traditions seemed to coexist in an uneasy *modus vivendi*. Now, such a study leads to a most surprising result. For, in the last ten months before he left for Italy, Newman turns out to be in a most definitely Evangelical phase.

This unexpected discovery must of course be tested in light of the other documents available so as to establish our judgement on a firm basis. The most important witness to Newman's state of mind at the time is his correspondence. We shall see that it largely confirms the impression that 1832 might be called his late Evangelical period before the Oxford Movement began.

I. A study of Newman's unpublished sermons

The first difficulty to overcome is methodological. Is it legitimate to call such a sermon Evangelical, another High Church and a

203

third in-between? While I was deciphering Newman's unpublished sermon manuscripts, trying to recover the different stages of their texts – for he used to preach some of them several times, altering a word here, a whole sentence there or even rewriting two or three pages on occasions – I found a few clues. I first realised that when Newman was very much taken up with Froude's ideas on tradition, the Church, the apostolical succession, the sacraments, the liturgy, those notions would inevitably appear in most, if not all, the sermons he preached at the time. At other periods, for some reason, most of his sermons give us the Evangelical view of christian doctrine, of salvation, sanctification and even, at times, the Calvinist teaching on predestination.

This poses a further problem. When the sermons Newman delivered at a given period are filled with Evangelical doctrines, does that necessarily mean that he had repudiated his former High Church positions? It would be too rash to go to such lengths. Obviously Newman rarely managed to strike a satisfactory balance between his Evangelical convictions and the doctrines and ethos he had received through Froude and Keble. There were some circumstances in his life that seem to have been more favourable to the former and others to the latter.

The last difficulty to be addressed is simply a definition of the main points of Evangelical doctrine and a clarification as to what is meant by 'High Church' notions, in this paper at least. In Newman's days the distinction between High Churchmen and Evangelicals was still rather blurred. Some were even called 'High Church Evangelicals', others 'Evangelical High Churchmen' and others were accused of being 'liberal Evangelicals'. So that there is always a risk of choosing the wrong criteria to distinguish between the two traditions. The safest course is to give greater importance to such teachings and emphases which characterised those extreme Evangelicals that were later called the 'recordites' after the name of the paper that set forth their opinions. Newman, by the way, subscribed to *The Record* until the mid-thirties. On the other hand, defining what I call in this paper, as well as in my book on Newman, 'High Church' doctrines is more difficult. Some of those, such as baptismal regeneration, were held by Evangelicals like William Wilberforce but most were certainly foreign to Evangelicalism. Many churchmen who would have been surprised to be called 'High Church', and had no sympathy for the Evangelical party either, believed in the efficiency of the sacraments and in the value of tradition. Yet, for someone who, like Newman, had been taught by Walter Mayers, Thomas Scott, or William Romaine, there was no doubt as to what 'High Church' teaching was. So that, once again, for the sake of clarity, our viewpoint must be that of radical Evangelicals.

It is impossible within the limits of such a paper to give a satisfactory account of Newman's preaching in the last year or two before he left for Italy. Yet, I hope to convey a fair idea of the evolution of his thought at the time through a selection of significant examples. Between 17th October 1830 and 25th November 1832, Newman preached a hundred and twenty-nine sermons, not including his university sermons.[1] Sixty-seven were new sermons, sixty-two had already been preached before and, among those, fifty-eight were typically Evangelical. A more detailed investigation allows us to distinguish three periods:

First a High Church period lasting until March 1831. Most of the twenty-seven sermons delivered over those five months contained many elements of High Church teaching and practically nothing that could be called Evangelical. A few examples may serve to illustrate this. In a sermon on the Virgin Mary dated 25th March 1831, Newman declares:

> Now, if divine blessings were displayed without consideration of our obedience and faith, then indeed there is no reason the Virgin should have been better than other daughters of Adam − but if, as is the way of providence, He rewardeth according to our works, what untold holiness in the Virgin Mary is intimated to us by the favour of this mysterious blessing from God?[2]

Here we have a statement no Evangelical might ever have made, a statement that clearly denies that salvation is only through grace and unequivocally proclaims that it is as much through good works and personal virtues. Of course, if such a position is not necessarily High Church, it is obviously un-Evangelical. In February of the same year he had said: 'The Spirit was given you in baptism. It is given you whenever you come for it in the celebration of the Lord's Supper'[3] − which is a high view of the sacraments which later sermons seem no longer to entertain. A few weeks afterwards he asserted:

> God's grace is promised, not through preaching, but through the Sacraments and through whatever has a sacramental character, and public prayer is of this kind.[4]

Another aspect of High Church teaching which the Oxford movement will adopt is its elevated conception of the One Holy Catholic

Apostolic Church. In a sermon preached on 28th November 1830 Newman declares:

> A thousand and seven hundred years are gone and still that same society, which the Apostles once set up, remains throughout the world in its several branches. It has never been dissolved; never been refounded. Does not this very fact carry with it something of an evidence of a divine power lodged in it? [. . .] Our own branch, descended from the Roman Church a thousand years since, still declares the glory of God [. . .]. Nor is there in these branches of the one christian body, nor has there ever been for any time, error or corruption of faith, sufficient to impair its authority [. . .] − we are looking to the Church as a guide.[5]

Surprisingly enough, Newman doesn't seem here to find much fault with the Church of Rome.

A second period from March 1831 to January 1832 may be called a middle of the way period. Out of fifty sermons, sixteen had been preached before, among those, fourteen are clearly Evangelical and at least ten of the new ones have many mildly Evangelical passages.

But by far the most interesting period is the last one which covers practically the whole year 1832. It is the second most thoroughly Evangelical stage of Newman's preaching after the time of his curacy of St. Clement's. There is little recognisable High Church elements in the sermons he delivered during those ten months before he left for Italy, at least in those he did not publish later. Out of the fifty-two sermons of that period, nineteen were published after 1834 (among those, only eight were written in 1832, the others were old sermons re-used). Since there is no way of tracing their original text − for once he published his sermons Newman used to destroy the manuscripts − I have looked through the published sermons he wrote in 1832. Two of those are Evangelical and the clear High Church teachings I found in two others are a sacramental view of the Lord's supper as well as an implicit belief in baptismal regeneration. It is impossible to be sure that the sacramental passages are not later additions or, possibly, alterations of earlier statements so as to adjust them to Newman's opinions at the time of publication. This is why I felt safer to limit this study to the unpublished sermons of the period.[6] More than half of my quotations are taken from the eleven sermons he wrote at the time, rather than from those he re-used, so as to express with greater certainty his position then. For the sake of clarity I have isolated five typically Evangelical teachings that will be illustrated by two or three examples each.

* The first characteristic theme is the emphasis on the total corruption of human nature and on its utter inability to do any good:

> The forbidden fruit poisoned the soul of man, and it died – and
> ever after man could bring into existence man to succeed him, but
> they all had dead souls – souls dead to religion, which is the true
> life of the soul. And were it not for the Holy Spirit, they would con-
> tinue, one and all, dead to religion, disliking the thought of it, and
> living here as children of wrath, predestined to eternal misery.[7]

> What should we think of ourselves, if we could see ourselves
> as God sees us? What if we could see the real state of our
> souls, marked as they are, and scarred with the multitude of
> our sins?[8]

And the sermon continues along this line, on and on for five pages.
Six months later, in November 1832, Newman insisted:

> It is not enough to confess we are corrupt, merely because Scripture
> says we are – we must feel we are corrupt, or we shall not embrace
> heartily those further doctrines concerning our redemption which
> are built upon our previous admission of our sinful state.[9]

The emphasis on the emotions, on feeling one's misery and guilt, is one
of the main characteristics of evangelical religion. Here Newman is
closer to the more radical wing of the Movement and certainly not in
the 'Evangelical High Church' or 'High Church Evangelical' mood.

* A second character of Evangelical preaching is the call to conversion and the belief in salvation through faith alone. Most evangelicals also believed in the possibility, or rather in the necessity, of
entertaining a real assurance of one's personal salvation. The whole
subject was often greatly dramatised and set in the context of the
day of judgment:

> I well know [. . .] that I shall one day answer for what I have said
> to you and what I am now saying. At the day of judgment, when
> I hear the fate of each of you, I shall hear my own sentence too
> [. . .]. Joy and fear indeed, both must be intense when an eternity
> is at stake [. . .] – You ask 'What must I do to be saved?' (Acts
> 16) – I answer in St. Paul's words 'Believe on the Lord Jesus
> Christ' – Make him your God – choose Him for your portion
> – His grace is sufficient for you [. . .] in every time of need pray
> to Him for aid who died on the Cross to save you.[10]

Four months later, in October 1832, Newman mentioned conversion in a slightly different way:

> It is evident that [. . .] to have the full privileges of the gospel, to be acknowledged as the true sons of God, His true elect, [. . .] we must be consistent and confirmed believers [. . .] and converted in the nature of our souls from sin to holiness.[11]

Conversion here is seen as an introduction into the way of holiness, an experience that makes all the difference between the 'true elect' and the others. Newman's view of justification also remains at that late date as specifically Evangelical as it was in his sermons at St. Clement's:

> This acceptance of man in God's sight, this restoring to His favour is called [. . .] justification by faith only. A doctrine of infinite importance, containing in it the substance of all true religion. Expressed in a sentence it is this: that those whom God saved are saved on the ground of their confessing to Him they are not worthy to be saved and must owe it entirely to Him [. . .]. 'To him that worketh not', or more accurately [Vide Bull] 'who worketh not to purchase a reward but believeth on the justifier, the accepter of the ungodly, his faith is imputed, is counted, is taken for righteousness'.[12]

This is, clearly stated, the doctrine of imputed righteousness as well as the need for men to undergo a conscious process of conversion in order to be saved. There is nothing about either baptismal regeneration or the means of grace.

Evangelicals insisted also on the vast difference between a mere intellectual knowledge of the doctrine of salvation and the real experimental apprehension of it that alone can get a man to heaven:

> Shut your eyes to the world and turn resolutely to God − take no half measures − if you are secretly conscious you are making His service but part of your daily employment, not the chief object of your thoughts and actions, you must be converted, it is plain [. . .]. You must retire into your secret chamber and pray him to have mercy upon you [. . .] and though you know well that Christ saves you wholly, you will learn the meaning of this great doctrine experimentally.[13]

Here we have an insistent call to immediate conversion which was unpalatable to High Churchmen such as Keble or Froude.

* The doctrine of imputed righteousness is another recognisable tenet of Evangelicalism. I shall give only one of the many instances when Newman expounded it in his sermons of 1832. One other example I have already given in the quotation above illustrating the Evangelical view of justification:

> Viewed in Him we are all that He is, having all His excellence imputed to us, yet it is only as found in Him, for we have nothing of good inherent in ourselves [. . .] in St. Paul's words. He is made unto us and for us and upon us without any merit of ourselves righteousness and sanctification and redemption.[14]

* The necessity of new birth considered as a post-baptismal phenomenon following conversion was not a doctrine all Evangelicals held. Conservative or 'High Church Evangelicals' such as William Wilberforce had kept the traditional view of baptismal regeneration, insisting only on the necessity of conversion to enter fully into the privileges and reality of new birth. In a sermon preached in October 1832, Newman appears to side with the advocates of regeneration as following conversion rather than baptism:

> Were we but slightly wrong, a slight influence would be enough − but since a marvellous and vast change is necessary, we must know, it is clear, some load of sin within us − Scripture does not tell us we must be merely amended, strengthened, improved − but that we must be changed − in its own expressive language that we must be born again if we would enter into life.[15]

Such a text shows that even at that late date Newman had not definitely adopted the doctrine of baptismal regeneration.

* Although all Evangelicals made a distinction between saved and unsaved christians, only the Calvinists expressed the divide in terms of the elect and the reprobate:

> Scripture seems to divide christians into two classes, those who at the last day have not done more than just save themselves − and those who, through God's blessing, are made the instruments of good to others [. . .]. He who has faith sufficient for his justification, though it be sufficient for nothing besides, yet is infinitely removed above the mass of the world.[16]

In May 1832, the distinction between the real christians and the others is as clearly drawn as ever:

The great mass of Christians indeed (so called) think not of religion at all – but live in wilful sin – but even the better sort, how far are they from rising to the full knowledge of the gospel of Christ! Of resting their hopes on Him, making Him their Guide and Teacher – their Redeemer and Sanctifier.[17]

In January of the same year Newman's words have a definite Calvinistic ring:

How many men (we may humbly hope) will be saved at the last day – yet much greater is the number for whom He has died and whom He has put in the way of salvation than the number of the elect, His tried and indefectible servants![18]

Now these last words concerning the elect and their indefectibility is an addition he made to the original 1829 text of the sermon which read only: 'how many more has Christ died for and put in the way of salvation than will eventually be saved'. Clearly then, in 1832 Newman was closer to the Calvinist tradition than in 1829.

* The last characteristic of Evangelical religion is fundamental but slightly misleading. Historically, the call to a holy life, to a process of sanctification, is by no means confined to their tradition. William Law, Lancelot Andrewes and the Caroline divines as well as many others in the High Church tradition had also preached on the necessity of holiness. Yet in Newman's early years, before the Oxford Movement began, the emphasis on holiness, or sanctification, was generally assumed to be a characteristic feature of Evangelicalism. As such it may be safely considered as a reliable indicator. All the more so since in those sermons Newman uses unmistakable Evangelical vocabulary, notably the words: 'serious' – 'seriousness'; 'conscientious' – 'conscientiousness'; 'strict'; 'diligent'. Here are a few examples:

The seriousness and strict conscientiousness are despised [by the world] as the marks of a gloomy and narrow mind.[19]

Let us from this day begin a stricter profession and a holier life [...]. Let us learn to be serious and not be ashamed of being so.[20]

If you would be a true saint, go about your daily duties better – pray more seriously – keep your thoughts from wandering –

desire and seek what you pray for – this is a beginning for the morning. As the day goes on, curb your temper – be diligent in your calling whatever it be.[21]

This is an apt description of the 'practical holiness' the great evangelical leaders of the day valued so much. The very language used in the last quotation is Beveridge's, a favourite author among Evangelicals.

II. The University sermons

Before we leave Newman's preaching to turn to his letters and diaries, a brief look at the university sermons he delivered in 1832 may shed a significant light on this study. Generally this type of preaching was more formal, more academic than the ordinary Sunday morning or afternoon sermons. They often addressed great religious, theological or even philosophical questions. So that, if ever Newman wished to express his High Church opinions and insist on a recovery of a lost tradition, the university pulpit he spoke from on five occasions in 1832 could have provided him with the ideal platform. Yet, excepting the last sermon he delivered on the very eve of his departure, one hardly ever finds a mention of High Church notions in these sermons while Evangelical views abound. This is all the more striking since two of them are clear calls to a spiritual awakening and to a restoration of the dignity and independence of the Church which were to be the main emphases of the Oxford movement. Now, anyone listening to Newman or reading his university sermons of 1832 could well have believed he was yearning for a third Evangelical revival.

Just a few quotations from Newman's university sermons will be enough to make us sense their tone and intent. The most famous is certainly 'Personal influence, the means of propagating the truth', a sermon that set forth so admirably the spirit and methods of the Oxford movement that some, such as the late Charles Stephen Dessain, believed that it represented the real start of the movement.[22] If the main thrust of the sermon is a call to a revival of spiritual stamina in the Church, so as to restore its beneficent influence on the world, the main line of the argument is that the real strength of the Church has ever been dependent on the faithfulness of the few.

Nor can it be satisfactorily maintained that the visible church, which the miracles formed, has taken their place in the course of Divine Providence, as the basis, strictly speaking, on which the Truth rests [. . .] the Epistle to the Corinthians sufficiently showing, that, in all ages true christians, though contained in it, and forming its life and strength, are scattered and hidden in the multitude, and, but partially recognizing each other, have no means of combining and co-operating.[23]

This is a clear declaration of the conservative Evangelical view of the church, a mixed society whose strength is derived from the small company of true believers, those who have been through a process of conversion followed by a commitment to a life of holiness. The distinction between the great mass of professing christians and the little flock of the saved could hardly be stated more explicitly. Now, he further adds, commenting on the power of the Truth:

And if such be the personal influence exerted by the Teacher of Truth over the mixed crowd of men whom he encounters, what (think we) will be his power over that select number, just referred to, who have already, in a measure, disciplined their hearts after the law of holiness [. . .]. These are they whom our Lord especially calls His 'elect', and came to 'gather in one' for they are worthy.[24]

There is nothing more typically Evangelical or even Calvinistic, than such a vision of the visible Church within which a 'select number' of 'elect' is ready to answer Christ's call and defend His interests. We may even notice that they are those whom the Lord 'came to gather into one' which, apparently, voices the opinion of some of the most radical Evangelicals who believed in a church exclusively composed of converts and eventually seceded from the Church of England. Christopher Dawson used to say that Newman's emphasis was not so much on 'the hierarchical principle of the episcopal succession than on the more mystical notion of an apostolical succession of saints'.[25]

In the university sermon he preached on the 8th April of the same year it is the Evangelical view of human nature and sin which comes to the fore:

The gospel is in its very name a message of peace, but it must never be separated from the bad tidings of our fallen nature [. . .].
To see truly the cost and misery of sinning, we must quit the public haunts of business and pleasure, and be able, like the Angels, to see the tears shed in secret; to witness the anguish of pride and impatience, where there is no sorrow; the stings

of remorse, where yet there is no repentance, the wearing, never ceasing struggle between conscience and sin; the misery of indecision; the harassing, haunting fears of death, and a judgment to come [...]. Who can name the overwhelming total of the world's guilt and suffering [...]?[26].

The insistence on our sinful nature and on the heinousness of sin takes up over three fourths of this sermon written to disprove the liberal humanistic view of man's moral improvement.

Newman's last university sermon for 1832 has a decidedly political turn. He firmly denounces the new spirit of the age which was manifest in the events surrounding the failure of the Reform Bill in 1831 and the unprecedented torrent of abuse it unleashed against the bishops of the Church of England who had voted against it. Newman reasserts the duties of obedience and the sacred character of the priesthood. Of course, such reaction was, by no means, restricted to High Churchmen. Many conservative Evangelicals were outraged by what had happened and they had a notion of the sacredness of the Church and of its ministers, as well as a sense of duty of obedience, that was as developed as Newman's own. Yet, in a study such as this, the emergence of a theme generally associated with Newman's high church periods is a sure sign of a changing position. Ian Ker and others have recently shown how important Newman's Italian tour had been in the development of his attraction towards a more sacramental view of religion coupled with a growing interest in Roman Catholicism.

III. Newman's Letters and Diaries

Since the Birmingham Oratory began their remarkably precise and exhaustive publication, the study of Newman's diaries and correspondence has become a most rewarding occupation. For my present purpose it has not only confirmed his Evangelical stance in 1832, but it has also provided precious information that may help explain this return to the religion of his youth.

I shall begin with the evidences of a late Evangelical stage in 1832. Although the conflict that had opposed him to John Hill and his circle at the end of 1829 over the C.M.S. (Church Missionary Society) had cut him from some of the more radical Evangelicals, Newman maintained a solid friendship with the main leaders of the movement. He often met Benjamin P. Symons whom he congratulated on his becoming Master of Wadham College in June 1831.[27]

He spent much time also with William Garbett, possibly their ablest polemicist, and kept up the activities of the inter-college club they had both founded. In November 1830 he had spent several evenings with William Wilberforce who was on a visit to his sons in Oxford. A few months later, this admirable Evangelical leader sent him a warm letter of thanks for the influence he exerted on his sons, expressing his desire to continue their nascent friendship.[28] In December 1831, Newman was invited to dinner at Benjamin Symons to meet E. G. Mash, a well known Evangelical preacher of the day, a visit he renewed three days later.[29] Between 1830 and 1832 he often met and wrote to Henry Ryder, the Evangelical Bishop of Lichfield whose son had been one of his students.[30]

Until March 1831, he continued to attend regularly the meetings of the C.M.S. in spite of the conflict that had opposed him to its leaders in 1829. He also kept the habit of organising periodical collections in favour of the society at St. Mary's. Newman's feelings towards the Evangelicals at the time were rather mixed. He certainly appreciated the sincere spirituality and moral integrity of a great number among them. But he also deplored the excesses, the disregard of ecclesiastical discipline and of the respect due to the authorities and principles of the Established Church as well as the ultra-Calvinistic dogmatism of the most radical brand of Evangelicals. He also shunned their party spirit which he considered a first step towards schism.

Yet, in spite of his reservations, Newman's attitude to the evangelicals was more favourable than hostile and, at times, he definitely felt attracted to them. In January 1831 he wrote a letter to Golightly in which he broached the subject of the 'propheticals', those evangelicals who had taken to the study of the prophecies on Christ's second coming, giving their unbridled imagination free play:

> The Propheticals, by the bye, look like a hopeful progeny from the Evangelicals. I wish they could discard some of their notions and they should have my sanction. I do not despair, if there were a general break-up, of their becoming better Churchmen.[31]

In a letter he wrote five months later to Henry Wilberforce, he again alluded to the same:

> I am far from wishing to be disrespectful to any expounders of Prophecy, to go on to your question, and really want light.[32]

In August 1832, writing to Jemima, his sister, Newman tells her of his preaching at Tunbridge Wells:

Woodgate has made me preach for him three times — two sermons being written for the occasion — and I fancy, as at Brighton, my hearers give me more criticisms than thanks for my pains. I believe they think me an Evangelical — which is natural enough.[33]

This passage, in which he alludes to the series on the epistle to the Romans he had given at Brighton in 1829, is a valuable testimony as to the impression his sermons made on his hearers. Their feeling was definitely that he was to be counted among the Evangelicals since his preaching was so close to theirs, and this feeling was 'natural enough'. This reminds us of a remark made by some undergraduates in 1831 on seeing him at the theatre: 'There is that Methodist, Newman, here!'.[34] A letter to Froude dated 4th October 1832, is quite significant in this respect:

I have had from time to time diverse thoughts about turning Evangelical so far — only I am afraid.[35]

The letter's style is too loose, and most of what Newman writes there too vague and disconnected, to allow us to understand fully what he means. Yet, this statement undeniably evidences a strong pull towards Evangelicalism.

I would like now to address a question that had been neglected until recently and has some bearing on Newman's attitude to the evangelicals. In February 1835 he exchanged a series of letters about his first volume of sermons with Samuel Wilberforce who was to become bishop of Oxford. As Wilberforce had quoted some criticism made by James Stephen, a respected Evangelical leader, Newman replied:

I acquiesce in much that Mr. Stephen says, or rather have anticipated it in my own mind. Not indeed that I will allow the weakness he charges against me of wishing to separate myself from the Peculiars [as the Evangelicals were then called], as he would confess did he know either me or my doctrine better — for in truth I look most hopefully towards numbers of them. They are a very heterogeneous party, but contain some of the highest and noblest elements of the christian character among them.[36]

A little later, as he entered a correspondence with James Stephen directly, he further wrote about Evangelical preachers:

As far indeed as [they] put before the mind the simple elementary Verities of the Gospel, they aim at what is right. Doubtless

saving Truth[37] lies in a narrow compass, and is all we want and is
all that can possibly satisfy. In attempting to put the Atonement,
etc ... before the mind, they are but natural witnesses to its need
and its remedy [...]. In this spirit I would receive the Incarnation as the great doctrine of the Gospel, and do not desire
to go beyond it and its development. Now the (so called) Evangelicals feel this by a natural instinct, the instinct of spiritual life,
which [...] all of them, I would hope, have in a measure [...].
Yet what I shrink from is their rudeness, irreverence, and almost
profaneness; the profaneness of making a most sacred doctrine a
subject of vehement declamation, or instrument of exciting the
feelings.[38]

Now what is particularly interesting in this correspondence is the
extent to which Newman approved of Evangelical doctrine and his
unwillingness to dissociate himself from their movement. His only
objection, and it was a very serious one, had to do with the tone
used by too many Evangelical preachers which tended to cheapen and
debase the most sacred truths as they tried to play on their hearers
emotions. David Newsome, in his excellent book, The *Parting of
Friends*, insists on the continuity most Tractarians saw between the
Evangelical revival of the early nineteenth century and the Oxford
movement. I can't possibly find the courage to resist quoting him:

In many ways the Tractarians appeared − in the early stages of
the Oxford Movement − to be the continuators of the Evangelicals
[...]. At this stage it was not at all clear that sacramentalism, and
all that followed from high sacramental teaching, might become
a dividing factor. After all, the Evangelicals were pioneers in
recalling christians to the importance of the sacraments [...]. The
tightest knot which bound the Evangelicals and the Tractarians
together, however, in these early years was the common pursuit
of holiness [...]. Appreciation of John Keble's religious poetry,
admiration for Newman's sermons, and a sense of the common
endeavour in urging upon a worldly generation the virtues and
duties of holiness, could all go together with a distaste for the
teaching and principles of the traditional High Church party. The
Tractarians seemed most truly the heirs of the Evangelicals when
one compared their teaching and sentiments with the traditional
tenets of the old High Church school.[39]

He further observes that they had another common cause which
was their resistance to liberalism in religion as embodied in Thomas

Arnold's ideas and to what they considered as the unacceptable interference of the State in Church affairs. Now, those considerations may
explain to some extent why Newman could remain faithful to the main
lines of Evangelical preaching while reverting, for some periods, to
more typically High Church doctrine. Yet, such explanation is, at
best, uncomplete. A close examination of Newman's circumstances
and state of mind at that period may help us discover other reasons
for his changing opinions.

IV. Personal circumstances and health condition

The years 1830 to 1832 were particularly trying for Newman. His
relations with his mother and sisters were strained. In July 1829,
Mrs. Newman and her daughters moved to a cottage in the vicinity
of Oxford, thinking that they would see John more often than before.
They were to be sorely disappointed and Harriet wrote to him a bitter
letter in November. At the same time the new High Church ideas he
expressed in the sermons of that period caused a misunderstanding
that soured their relationship.[40] This must certainly have disturbed
Newman and caused him to isolate himself even more from his family.
This situation doesn't seem to have improved with the years since we
have a very strong letter of October 1832 in which Harriett tries to
explain the causes for her resentment:

> I think it is right to point out some causes which have prevented
> the entire and unreserved confidence which it has ever been my
> most earnest wish and intention to have reposed in you. And first,
> is your own manner, which I am sure you must know is sometimes
> very trying to me, and which I cannot always understand [. . .].
> Another difficulty I have felt in speaking to you freely is the great
> difference I see in our opinions on many points [. . .]. Then think
> how few opportunities there have been for our talking together
> and at ease, for years past I may almost say [. . .]. I wished to
> show you, that, however I might respect etc. persons who were
> your friends, I will not feel towards them as my own.[41]

This last sentence shows that Harriett and, possibly, Mrs. Newman
and Jemima, did not appreciate some of John's most intimate friends
he used to take with him almost each time he paid a visit to them.
They particularly resented Froude and his overbearing attitude, to
women especially.

There was also another cause for torment and disappointment. The conflict with Hawkins over the tutorship had resulted in an agreement according to which Newman was to withdraw progressively as his pupils were getting their degree. Now, 1831–1832 was the academic year when this withdrawal was to be complete. When we know how much he valued this occupation, what high hopes he had built on it, how fully he had devoted himself to what he considered as his specific mission and service to God, even more so than the duties of his parish, it is no wonder that he should have felt his withdrawal from the tutorship as a singular failure and a heart rending experience. Louis Cognet has these words:

> There was in him [...] this need to dominate over a company of men, both to influence and shape them, and to find in their midst the affection he was after. Newman was deeply attached to the pastoral duties of his parish, but he didn't find in them what could satisfy desires that were certainly unconscious. When he realised that his role as a tutor was to become impossible and that he would soon have to give it up, the feeling of frustration grew more painful still.[42]

We know through his diary of the period of his illness in Sicily that the conflict with Hawkins over the tutorship had left him with uneasy feelings and nagging remorse at his arrogant attitude on that occasion. Although his sense of guilt may not have taken the same dramatic proportions before the Sicilian episode, there must have been some unsettlement somewhere, deep down in his conscience.

Now, his disappointment with his mother and sisters, with the tutorship and with his own self, was not the end of the story. There was disappointment in other quarters as well. We know, through the correspondence he exchanged at the time with several friends and former students, that he was already preparing some kind of a response to what he considered the spiritual and moral declension of his country and the impending threats upon the Church of England. The method he intended to follow he had already expounded in his famous university sermon on 'Personal Influence ...'. Now some of the men on whom he relied most for his as yet rather vague project had proved a bitter disappointment. Robert I. Wilberforce had just married Agnes Wrangham and his brother Henry was clearly too weak to resist the charm of the Sargent sisters. He wrote Robert disillusioned letters, blaming him also for having accepted a living offered by the arch-liberal, Lord Brougham. This, Newman felt, was akin to downright betrayal. George Ryder could not wait to get married. For Newman the coming fight in defence of the Church called for men who would be totally free of any worldly entanglement and marriage, he felt, was possibly the most paralysing of those. So that, for him, the Wilberforce brothers were lost to the sacred cause. Another of his hopeful disciples, Tom Mozley, was proving despairingly lazy and idle and Frederick Rogers seemed to be taking the same way. Even Keble had married. Still, there was the faithful Froude, but his best friend was suffering from a disease that already appeared incurable.

There was still another disappointment that must have hurt him sorely. He had spent a whole year working very hard at his study of the Arian heresy that was to be published in the Theological Library Hugh James Rose and Archdeacon Lyall were responsible for. He exerted himself so much that he almost ruined his health. And now Lyall refused to take his book with objections on form and contents. This was quite a shock!

As to his health problems, his diary is a good guide. In June 1831 he began a treatment, taking blue pills for he was 'unwell'.[43] In October he records a visit to the doctor. In December, then in February 1832 and in July he sleeps very poorly, collapses, must stay in bed, etc.[44]

The time has now come to interpret those events and the influence they had on Newman's preaching. Strikingly enough his evangelical periods coincide with hard times and illness whereas his high church periods are those when the future seems promising and his mood is optimistic or even euphoric. The beginning of his studies of the Fathers of the Church corresponds to a moderately high church period. That was the time when he discovered the dauntless resistance of Ambrose and Athanasius to secular power, Anthony and Augustin's asceticism and praise of celibacy, their utter unworldiness and their high notion of the Church. Yet, the realities of his difficult life, his frustrations and misgivings, his fragile health developed in him feelings of discouragement and distress. He knew no other solution then but to turn to the Evangelical religion of his youth. There he could find comfort and hope, the solace of forgiveness for an uneasy conscience a restored vision of an all-sufficient Saviour and Lord, the reassuring certainty of his election and eternal salvation. There also he found new strength to turn his back on the vain glories of this world and to consider that one thing only was necessary: the pursuit of holiness and surrender to Christ. Evangelicalism brought to him a soothing sense of God's all-sufficient grace, the comforting and strengthening feeling that the divine Master had his eye on his elect, on 'those who are called according to his purpose'[45] and that all hardships and trials are meant to prepare them for high destinies. Now, once he found his own need to be met by evangelical spirituality, he naturally felt his parishioners needed to be reminded of the simple truths of the gospel, what the evangelicals called 'saving truth' or 'vital truth'. He would apply to them the same remedies he felt were able to cure and appease him.

Yet this return to evangelical religion was by no means a rejection of all the ideas he had received through Froude and Keble. They simply lay dormant in some unconscious strata of his mind. *The Arians of the Fourth century* expresses many aspects of High Church teaching and even some notions that were so close to some Roman Catholic principles (especially economy in imparting religious knowledge and the *disciplina arcani*) that Archdeacon Lyall felt they were utterly foreign to Anglican tradition. As most of the book was already written before late January 1832, when his new Evangelical period began, this poses no difficulty to our study. Yet it may serve to show how Newman's religious mind and sensitivity worked. For as soon as he left for his Mediterranean tour with the Froudes, his poems, the few sermons he preached and his letters evidence a forceful re-emergence of High Church, or rather of 'Apostolical' notions, to use the vocabulary Froude will coin in the days of the Oxford Movement.

When Newman came back to Oxford with the sense of a mission to accomplish, he was to live an exceptional period of intense activity and euphoria. It wasn't before Froude's death and his fateful study of the Donatist and Monophysite controversies coupled with several disappointments that he found himself in a situation comparable to his circumstances in 1832. But he had gone a long way into the Catholic ethos and the Evangelical moorings of the past had lost their comforting and strengthening virtues for him. On the other hand his intellectual development no longer allowed him to be satisfied with Evangelical teaching nor with its *Sola Biblia* as the exclusive and final source of authority.

Conclusion

The purpose of this paper was to show how much of an evangelical Newman was less than a year before the Oxford Movement began. Although Yngve Brilioth and David Newsome have already showed how powerfully evangelical sensitivity and teaching informed the Tractarian revival, it was necessary to gather fresh evidence to their argument and extend it somewhat further. For we now have the picture of an unreservedly 'High Church Evangelical', Newman, initiating a movement that was later to be associated with a rejection of some of the very notions he seemed so keen to convey to his parishioners and friends from the pulpit of St. Mary's in 1832. Among those were the belief in the necessity of a definite conversion followed by a regeneration apparently unconnected to baptism, a calvinist conception of election, a radical evangelical view of the Church as well as an insistence on a life of holiness derived from the same body of teaching.

Notes

1 See my book: *Newman, sa vie, sa pensée et sa spiritualité – première période* – L'Harmattan, Paris 1991, pages 396 to 400.
2. Sermon n°291 (25/3/1831), pages 14–15, A50–4: *Containing Saints day Sermons* (Reel 23). Newman's unpublished sermons are presented here as follows:
   Number, date when first preached followed by the date of second preaching, pages in the manuscript, code number in the Birmingham Oratory Archives, Reel number in the microfilm collection at Yale University Library (U.S.A.).
3. Sermon n°286 (24/2/1831), page 14, A50–4 (Reel 23).
4. Sermon n°290 (20/3/1831), page 9, A50–5: *Personal* (Reel 24).
   The passage can be found in Placid Murray's recent *John Henry Newman – Sermons 1824–1843* (Vol.I), Clarendon Press, Oxford 1991, Sermon n°4, page 26.
5. Sermon n°270 (28/11/1830), pages 16–17, A50–2: *Some on the doctrine of the Church* (Reel 23).
6. There is a published sermon given on the 25/03/1832 that greatly praises the Virgin Mary but doesn't exceed the veneration Protestants may feel towards her. Anyhow, it was probably revised by Newman to adapt it to his feelings at the period of publication, in March 1835.
7. Sermon n°339 (Pentecost 1832), page 8, A17–1: *St Clement's and later* (Reel 13).
8. Sermon n°332 'On National Apostasy' (21/03/1832), page 1, B3 Box IV: *General Theology* (Reel 28).
9. Sermon n°192 (29/03/1829 – 04/11/1832), page 4, A50–6: *Sin and Justification* (Reel 24).
10. Sermon n°255 (24/08/1830 – 11/06/1832) pages 18–20, A50–4 (Reel 23).
11. Sermon n°343 (21/10/1832), page 14, B3 Box IV: *General Theology* (Reel 28).
12. Sermon n°188 (18/01 and 26/04/1829 – 15/01/1832), pages 6–7, A50–6 (Reel 24).
13. Sermon n°202 (12.07/1829 – 29/01/1832) pages 30–32, B3 Box IV: *Biblical* (Reel 29).
14. Sermon n°224 (31/01/1830 – 07/10/1832), pages 16–17, A50–3: *Mostly on the Sacraments and Liturgy* (Reel 23).
15. Sermon n°192, page 19.
16. Sermon n°343, pages 4 and 21.

17. Sermon n°337 (01/05/1832), pages 9–10, A50–1: *On General Theology* (Reel 22).
18. Sermon n°202, page 14.
19. Sermon n°323 (18/12/1831), page 14, A50–2 (Reel 23).
20. Sermon n°332, pages 20–21.
21. Sermon n°339, pages 20–21.
22. C. S. Dessain, *Newman's Spiritual Themes*, Dublin 1977, page 31.
23. J. H. Newman, *Fifteen Sermons preached before the University of Oxford*, Christian Classics, Westminster (Md.), 1966, page 77.
24. Ibid., page 95.
25. Christopher Dawson, *The Spirit of the Oxford Movement*, London 1933, page 41.
26. *Fifteen Sermons*, op. cit., pages 101 then 115.
27. *The Letters and Diaries of John Henry Newman* ed. by Ian KER and Thomas Gornall at the Birmingham Oratory, Oxford 1979 – Vol. II, page 336.
28. Ibid., page 325.
29. Ibid., page 375.
30. Ibid., pages 193, 346, 349, 377 and vol. III, page 72.
31. Ibid., vol. II, page 308.
32. Ibid., page 331.
33. Ibid., vol. III, page 82.
34. Ibid., vol. II, page 319.
35. Ibid., vol. III, page 100.
36. Ibid., vol. V, page 21.
37. This is how the Evangelicals called the body of teaching on the different aspects of Christ's death (atonement, propitiation, substitution ...) and of their appropriation by the repenting and believing sinner.
38. Ibid., page 45.
39. David Newsome, *The Parting of Friends*, John Murray, London 1966.
40. *Letters and Diaries*, op. cit., vol. II, pages 172–173.
41. Ibid., vol. III, pages 107–108.
42. Louis Cognet, *Newman, ou la recherche de la vérité*, Paris 1967.
43. *Letters and diaries*, op. cit., vol. II, page 337.
44. Ibid., page 365 and vol. III, pages 13, 63, 65, 66 and 75.
45. Romans 8:28.

Newman at Oxford:
Preaching a Living Faith

Roderick Strange

I

Imagine that it is about five minutes to four one Sunday afternoon in Oxford in the late eighteen thirties. You are an undergraduate and, as your custom is, walking briskly with a group of your friends across Broad Street, down the Turl, and into Radcliffe Square, anxious to reach the University Church by four o'clock. Your College has moved the hour of its evening meal so that it clashes with the service in an attempt to dissuade you and your companions from going to St. Mary's at that time, but that manoeuvre has, if anything, only fuelled your enthusiasm to attend. You reach the Church and take your place in one of the pews. You try to pray, but feel distracted, as you wait for the preacher to arrive. You are waiting for John Henry Newman.

In old age you will look back on these regular Sunday afternoon occasions as golden memories. Your thoughts will echo Matthew Arnold's:

Forty years ago, when I was an undergraduate at Oxford, voices were in the air there which haunt my memory still. Happy the man who in that susceptible season of youth hears such voices! they are a possession to him for ever ... The name of Cardinal Newman is a great name to the imagination still, his genius and his style are still things of power. But he is over eighty years old ... Forty years ago, he was in the very prime of life; he was close at hand to us at Oxford; he was preaching in St. Mary's pulpit every Sunday; he seemed about to transform and to renew what was for us the most national and natural institution in the world, the Church of England. Who could resist the charm of that spiritual apparition, gliding in the dim afternoon light through the aisles of St. Mary's, rising into the pulpit, and then, in the most entrancing of voices, breaking the silence with words and thoughts which were

223

a religious music – sweet, subtle, mournful? I seem to hear him still ...[1]

And so, in reflecting on Newman at Oxford as we reappraise the Tractarian Movement, I propose to draw on those afternoon sermons almost exclusively. Whatever other tasks Newman may have had, he was supremely a pastor and, as such, had the responsibility of expounding a spiritual vision to those who heard him preach. I shall extract just one vital theme and try to show what you and the others who went with you to St. Mary's during those momentous years would have learnt about faith.

The subject, of course, preoccupied Newman on many occasions, notably in his formal University sermons, in his *Grammar of Assent*, and in the various papers in which he hammered out his thought over the years. Such a rich body of material has created a minor industry for philosophers of religion, but I do not propose to add to it unduly here. My concern is more spiritual and I am encouraged to concentrate on the sermons in this way by the esteem in which they have always been held, an esteem which is indicated by Professor Owen Chadwick's rhetorical question: '... are not the Parochial Sermons of Newman the "typical" doctrine of the [Oxford] Movement at its highest ...? It is of the essence of the Movement that its best writing should be enshrined in parochial sermons.'[2] My choice is not arbitrary.

II

To appreciate the content of the sermons it is helpful to remember their context: they were directed in part against the religious fashion of the day; that fashion was sometimes rationalistic, sometimes evangelical. Newman had had experience of both. His first conversion was cast in the evangelical mould and the vivid impression it made on him lasted throughout his life. He paid tribute to its influence in the eighteen eighties when he was an old man and a cardinal. He spoke of 'those great and burning truths, which I learned when a boy from evangelical teaching', and which he had found 'impressed upon my heart with fresh and ever increasing force by the Holy Roman Church'.[3] All the same, when he first became a fellow of Oriel in 1822, he fell in with the highly logical temper of that distinguished Senior Common Room. One man in particular, Richard Whately, who became later the Anglican Archbishop of Dublin, was renowned for his dialectical skills, and so was asked to draw out the shy young Newman. Whately liked to beat out his ideas on people like a hammer on an anvil. Newman responded well to that treatment, came to co-operate with Whately academically, and, on Whately's appointment as head of St. Alban Hall, accepted the invitation to become his Vice-Principal. Although Newman always retained his personal affection for Whately, after some years their diverging theological views separated them and cooled their friendship. A different circle of Oriel friends, Hurrell Froude, Edward Pusey, and John Keble, a severe illness as the result of overworking, and the experience of personal grief at the death of Mary, his youngest and dearest sister, forced Newman to reexamine his priorities. Illness and bereavement drew him away from the rationalism associated with Whately, and Froude and the others pointed out to him a more Catholic path.

It is ironical, but true, that evangelical enthusiasm and liberal rationalism came to a common conclusion, in so far as both were opposed to dogma. There is a sermon Newman wrote early in 1835 called, 'Self-Contemplation', in which he described the evangelical insistence on 'a certain state of heart', while it disparaged 'the revealed doctrines of the Gospel'. Newman could mock: '. . . when they find men possessed of [right religious affections] (as they conceive), yet not altogether orthodox in their belief, then they relax a little, and argue that an admission of (what they call) the strict and technical niceties of doctrine, whether about the Consubstantiality of the Son or the Hypostatic Union, is scarcely part of the definition of a spiritual believer.' He went on: 'In order to support this position, they lay it down as self-evident, that the main purpose of revealed doctrine is to affect the heart, − that that which does not seem to affect it does not affect it, − that what does not affect it is unnecessary, − and that the circumstances that this or that person's heart seems rightly affected, is a sufficient warrant that such Articles as he may happen to reject, may safely be universally rejected, or at least are only accidentally important.' And so he concluded that this emphasis on a right state of heart 'tends legitimately to obliterate the great objects brought to light in the Gospel and to darken . . . the eye of faith'.[4]

The rationalist makes the same journey, but follows a different route. At the end of the previous year, 1834, Newman had composed another sermon. He dwelt upon 'The Gospel, a Trust committed to us', and began by speaking of the views to which he was opposed. He observed: 'It is a fashion of the day, then, to suppose that all insisting upon precise Articles of Faith is injurious to the cause of spiritual religion, and inconsistent with an enlightened view of it; . . .' It may seem at first glance that it is the evangelical approach which Newman has in mind once more. But that is not the case. He continued: 'Accordingly, instead of accepting reverently the doctrinal Truths which have come down to us, an attempt is made by the reasoners of this age to compare them together, to weigh and measure them, to analyze, simplify, refashion them; to reduce them to system, to arrange them into primary and secondary, to harmonize them into an intelligible dependence upon each other.'[5] Here then it is the rationalists, the reasoners of this age, who neglect to unfold the mysteries of the Gospel and concentrate instead on analysis, 'the use of the message', its practical effects; 'they say that the great end of the Gospel is the union of hearts in the love of Christ and of each other, and that, in consequence, Creeds are but fetters on souls which have received the Spirit of Adoption; that Faith is a mere temper and a principle, not the acceptance for Christ's sake of a certain collection of Articles'.[6] There is more in the same vein.

It is important to appreciate this context for Newman's preaching. From an early age he had been a champion of the principle of dogma. The anti-dogmatic tendency common to evangelicalism and rationalism naturally aroused his opposition. By contrast, the approach in so many of his sermons was one of unadorned exposition. Questions were raised, difficulties were probed, but not as critical analysis of the doctrine under consideration; he sought only to make possible their more lucid presentation.

That suggestion may make us suspicious and it is true that those days were innocent of much of the critical apparatus with which we are familiar, but we should not therefore dismiss what he was doing out of hand as fundamentalist or positivistic. As fine music calls for musicological ability, if it is to be appreciated, and yet even deep learning of that kind will be inadequate without an ear for music – a sensitivity to what we may properly call its mystery – so indeed Christian doctrine cannot be grasped without exegesis and hermeneutics, and yet its content must never be restricted to their results; at some stage we must contemplate the mystery. Newman's sermons were regularly an invitation to contemplate.

He felt keenly his obligation to preach the faith, the Gospel as a trust committed to us. Father Stephen Dessain used to say that it was this devotion to revealed religion which gave his life its unity.[7] So as you listened in St. Mary's each Sunday, you would have heard teaching on the three Persons in the one God, on the incarnation, death, and resurrection of the divine and human Saviour, on the indwelling of the Holy Spirit, on the Church, on the sacraments, on sin and forgiveness, and on much else besides. As a regular member of that congregation, you would have received a thorough grounding in the content of your faith. Moreover, you would have heard it presented in a way that sought consistently to make its content real for you. Here is the major distinction between Newman and the evangelicals and rationalists. The man who was to take for his cardinal's motto, 'Heart speaks to heart', was not being inconsistent in opposing the place given to the heart in evangelical and rationalist preaching. For them the effect on the heart was the primary test of a doctrine's significance, which for him it could never be. Newman's was never a religion of the heart; he preached a revealed religion, but he always tried to do so in a way that engaged the heart, so that the revelation could be recognized as real by those who heard him, and come alive for them. He wished to kindle in them a living faith, that sensitivity to mystery which he once described as 'colourless, like air or water; it is but the medium through which the soul sees Christ; and the soul as little really rests upon it and contemplates it, as the eye can see the air'.[8] As you sat in St. Mary's Sunday after Sunday you would have learnt much too about this response to revelation, about the nature of a life lived by this faith.

III

It seems natural to turn now to one of Newman's earliest sermons. He called it, 'Religious Faith Rational', and preached it on 24 May 1829. It is interesting, first of all, because already Newman can be seen adopting the approach which was to become so characteristic of him: he eschewed theory and settled for empirical observation. 'To hear some men speak', he noticed, '(I mean men who scoff at religion), it might be thought we never acted on Faith or Trust, except in religious matters, whereas we are acting on trust every hour of our lives.'[9] He gave the examples of our memory and our powers of reasoning. 'And what I wish you particularly to observe,' he went on, 'is, that we continually trust our memory and our reasoning powers in this way, though *they often deceive us*.'[10] That is a very typical Newman touch. If in daily life our continued trust in our memory and reason, despite errors, does not make us irrational or credulous, then neither should it do so in religion, for 'When faith is said to be a religious principle, it is (I repeat) the things believed, not the act of believing them, which is peculiar to religion'.[11] To believe, to trust, is not only possible for human beings; it is unavoidable.

Next he took the argument a stage further. Remarking that reliance on memory or reasoning powers might be seen as no more than trust in ourselves, he went on to illustrate that reliance on another, on testimony, which is integral to religious faith, is an everyday experience as well. We acknowledge the existence of certain towns, though we have never seen them, and the British, for example, accept that they live on an island, though they have never toured the coastline. We are convinced, Newman observed, by 'the *report of others*'. And he commented that this faith in testimony is called irrational only 'when religion is concerned'.[12] And after further examples he concluded that Scripture 'only bids us act in respect to a future life, as we are every day acting at present'.[13] We are guided by faith.

One reason for the interest in this sermon is the way it anticipates his approach in the *Grammar of Assent*, published forty-one years later, in 1870. There too Newman insisted on the human constitution as a principle and starting-point: 'If I may not assume that I exist, and in a particular way, that is, with a particular mental constitution, I have nothing to speculate about, and had better let speculation alone.'[14] The example that Great Britain is an island also finds a place in the argument,[15] but it is worth noting that Newman's misgiving about the other examples has hardened. His view that 'it may be said . . . that to trust our senses and reason is in fact nothing more than to trust ourselves',[16] has become a 'reluctance to speak of our trusting memory or reason, except indeed by a figure of speech'. Why? 'It seems to me unphilosophical', he explained, 'to speak of trusting ourselves. We are what we are, and we use, not trust our faculties.'[17] In other words, his later, more explicit adherence to the principle of working from the human constitution had revealed the weakness or the inappropriateness of those particular illustrations. It had not, of course, affected the conclusion that human beings, whether religious or not, necessarily live by faith.

In his 1829 sermon, Newman went on to consider a further question, namely the reason for trusting in God. It led him to declare: 'It is a mistake to suppose that our obedience to God's will is merely founded on our belief in the word of such persons as tell us Scripture came from God. We obey God primarily because we actually feel His presence in our consciences bidding us obey Him.'[18] The authority of the Bible derives from God, perceived through conscience. At this early date, Newman was already placing specific emphasis on the role of conscience. He was to write about it at length in the *Grammar*[19] and to preach on it with memorable power and beauty in Dublin on the fourth Sunday of Advent, 1856,[20] but it was a prominent theme in the *Parochial Sermons* as well. You would have heard the preacher mention it on various occasions, as you sat listening each week.

There was a sermon he called 'Faith without Sight', which he preached on St. Thomas's Day, 21 December 1834; in fact it was the forerunner of the Dublin sermon. He explained:

... a man of religious mind is he who attends to the rule of conscience, which is born with him, which he did not make for himself, and to which he feels bound in duty to submit. And conscience immediately directs his thoughts to some Being exterior to himself, who gave it, and who evidently is superior to him; for a law implies a lawgiver, and a command implies a superior. Thus a man is at once thrown out of himself, by the very Voice which speaks within him; and while he rules his heart and conduct by his inward sense of right and wrong, not by the maxims of the external world, still that inward sense does not allow him to rest in himself, but sends him forth again from home to seek abroad for Him who has put His word in him ... He looks out of himself for that Living Word to which he may attribute what has echoed in his heart; ...[21]

To live by faith is to live in obedience to conscience. The voice of conscience alerts the believer to the authority on which that faith rests.

There is similar teaching in another sermon, 'Faith without Demonstration', which Newman first preached on 21 May 1837. There too he argued against those who sought rational proof for belief. He maintained that we commonly trust the opinions of others, for example, in legal matters, without becoming experts ourselves. We rely on authority. Accordingly it is not unreasonable to do the same in religion. And to the objection that the law of the land is not improbable or difficult, while, for instance, the Catholic teaching on the Trinity is mysterious and unlikely, Newman retorted that that is just what we should expect: 'I do not say that it *is* true, *because* it is mysterious; but if it *be* true, it cannot help being mysterious.[22] And he pursued the point further. In the end, however, he acknowledged that the Being of God cannot be proved. There may be much to impress us, to strengthen us in faith, to enliven our devotion, but the unbeliever will not be moved to faith by formal evidence. It has not that power. Instead, Newman urged, we must learn to walk by faith, and he returned to the role of conscience:

There is a voice within us, which assures us that there is something higher than earth. We cannot analyze, define, contemplate what it is that thus whispers to us. It has no shape or material form. There is that in our hearts which prompts us to religion, and which condemns and chastises sin. And this yearning of our nature is met and sustained, it finds an object to rest upon, when it hears of the existence of an All-powerful, All-gracious Creator. It incites us to a noble faith in what we cannot see.[23]

In these sermons, therefore, Newman argued for the reasonableness of faith, not by supplying a proof, but by pointing to the common practice of the exercise of trust amongst human beings. He was directing attention to reality, to the actual experience of ordinary life. At the same time, he indicated the authority upon which religious faith rests, by appealing to the way conscience alerts us to God's existence and the reality of his presence. And, in passing, we should notice that Newman recognized the rights of erroneous conscience as well. Although he was emphatic about the existence of right and wrong, he also affirmed that fidelity to conscience, to the religious principle, was supreme. Thus in 1835 he declared: 'I had rather the Church were levelled to the ground by a nation, really, honestly, and seriously, thinking they did God service in doing so (fearful indeed as the sin would be), than that it should be upheld by a nation on the *mere* ground of maintaining property, for I think this a much greater sin.'[24] Erroneous conscience has rights.

These themes of faith, of obedience, and of conscience recur constantly in Newman's preaching. In 1830 he spoke about 'Faith and Obedience', in order to illustrate their identity. He argued that these two states of mind 'are altogether one and the same'. He continued:

> ... it is quite indifferent whether we say a man seeks God in faith, or say he seeks Him by obedience; and whereas Almighty God has graciously declared He will receive and bless all that seek Him, it is quite indifferent whether we say, He accepts those who *believe*, or those who *obey*. To believe is to look beyond this world to God, and to obey is to look beyond this world to God; to believe is of the heart, and to obey is of the heart; to believe is not a solitary act, but a consistent habit of trust; and to obey is not a solitary act, but a consistent habit of doing our duty in all things. I do not say that faith and obedience do not stand for separate ideas in our minds, but they stand for nothing more; they are not divided one from the other in fact. They are but one thing viewed differently.[25]

Later the same year Newman returned to these twin themes with an eye to their relationship when he preached on 'Obedience to God the way to Faith in Christ',[26] and ten years later he referred to a 'familiar illustration, obedience is the *road* to heaven, and faith the *gate*'.[27] But these themes of faith and obedience are woven together in a way which rewards particular study in his sermon, 'Saving Knowledge'. It was composed early in 1835, as the Oxford Movement, then eighteen months old, was beginning to gather momentum. It is set down as a sermon for Easter Monday.

The 'saving knowledge' of the title is the knowledge of God manifest in the flesh, the incarnate Lord. But if the knowledge of God is eternal life, how are we to know that we know him? That is the question which Newman posed. What assurance do we have that we are not in a dream or mistaken? Some Christians, he observed, believed their faith to carry with it its own evidence. He was not convinced so easily. He quoted St. John: 'Hereby do we know that we know Him, if we keep His commandments' (1 Jn. 2:3), and commented: 'Obedience is the test of Faith'. These two, faith and obedience, he saw as 'the whole duty and work of a Christian'.[28]

Next, he referred again to that fashion of the day which regarded 'all true and careful consideration of the Object of faith [God manifest in the flesh], as barren orthodoxy, technical subtlety, and the like, and all due earnestness about good works as a mere cold and formal morality', while it insisted on 'what is called a spiritual state of heart'.[29] It is the kind of teaching we were noticing earlier. Newman turned rather to faith and obedience: '. . . deeds of obedience', he suggested, 'are an intelligible evidence, nay, the sole evidence possible, and, on the whole, a satisfactory evidence of the reality of our faith.[30] He had in mind general obedience, not just one good quality or another: 'Various deeds, done in different departments of duty, support and attest each other.'[31] The habit of obedience is necessary. 'The more we *do*, the more shall we trust in Christ'. 'Disobedience blinds the conscience; obedience keeps it keen-sighted and sensitive.'[32] The habit of obedience leads to faith and then becomes its fruit and guarantee, just as an unselfish disposition will lead to love which then bears fruit in and is confirmed by generous service. At the same time, that obedience keeps conscience alert, enabling it to perceive more clearly the one in whom we believe.

This insistence on obedience may fall rather oddly on our ears. Some years ago in Oxford I thought I would preach on it myself and called in at the local bookshop, which is well stocked with theology. 'What have you got on obedience?' I asked. With a wry smile I was told, 'Nobody's writing about obedience these days.' Yet, for the Christian, obedience is not a matter of a regulated reaction to a command, but of a life lived in fidelity to the demands of the Gospel. For an illustration of such fidelity we need look no further than Newman himself, not the relatively young man at the height of his influence in Oxford, who is preaching these sermons, but the man he had become more than thirty years later, not yet a cardinal, who could survey a life shredded by disappointments.

He had had his hopes for the Church of England overturned and his reception into the Catholic Church had brought about a sorrowful parting from many of his dearest friends. He had been asked to found a University in Dublin, but his efforts had been constantly thwarted. He had been invited to translate the Bible and had made plans, but the invitation dissolved: his work was undermined through lack of support. He had been urged to save the Catholic periodical, *The Rambler*, by taking over as editor, but then almost at once encouraged to resign. His hopes for an Oratory in Oxford had been systematically frustrated. He knew himself to be an object of pity and contempt. It comes as no surprise to find this entry in his Journal in 1863: 'O how forlorn and dreary has been my course since I have been a Catholic! ...since I made the great sacrifice, to which God called me, He has rewarded me in ten thousand ways, O how many! but He has marked my course with almost unintermittent mortification ...since I have been a Catholic, I seem to myself to have had nothing but failure, personally.'[33] Newman was all too familiar with disappointments and the sense of defeat which is the guise in which the cross has often to be carried. They lowered his spirits, but, as the gratitude expressed in his Journal showed, they could not conquer his faithfulness. And, of course, there is more to the disposition of living faith than fidelity.

IV

Central to Newman's understanding of that disposition was his refusal to concentrate on any one virtue or quality exclusively. The sermon on saving knowledge was careful to avoid the pitfall which assumed that a single good quality could be the guarantee of true holiness. General obedience, many qualities together, make up the whole. On 25 February in 1838 you would have heard Newman speaking about the relationship between faith and love.

'Love', he pointed out, 'is the material (so to speak) out of which all graces are made, the quality of mind which is the fruit of regeneration, and in which the Spirit dwells; ...Faith and hope are the graces of an imperfect state, and they cease with that state; but love is greater, because it is perfection.'[34] Love is 'the seed of holiness, and grows into all excellences, not indeed destroying their peculiarities, but making them what they are.'[35] 'Faith is the first element of *religion*, and love, of *holiness*; and as holiness and religion are distinct, yet united, so are love and faith.'[36] 'Moreover it is plain', he went on, 'that, while love is the root out of which faith grows, faith by receiving the wonderful tidings of the Gospel, and presenting before the soul its sacred Objects, the mysteries of the faith, the Holy Trinity, and the Incarnate Saviour, expands our love, and raises it to a perfection which otherwise it could never reach. And thus our duty lies in faith working by love; . . .'[37] There is much more packed into this sermon which handles so delicately this life-giving relationship. We break off at this phrase, 'faith working by love', in effect, 'fides charitate formata'.

Let us suppose that your enthusiasm for Mr. Newman is such that not only do you attend his weekly sermons in St. Mary's; the previous year, 1837, you had also gone along to his *Lectures on Justification*, delivered in the Adam de Brome Chapel in the University Church. That phrase, faith working by love, might well have stirred in your memory one of those lectures' most captivating passages. Newman had declared:

I would treat of faith as it is actually found in the soul; and I say it is as little an isolated grace, as a man is a picture. It has a depth, a breadth, and a thickness; it has an inward life which is something over and above itself; it has a heart, and blood, and pulses, and nerves, though not on the surface. All these indeed are not *spoken* of, when we make mention of faith; nor are they painted on the canvas; but they are implied in the word, because they exist in the thing . . . Love and fear, and heavenly-mindedness, and obedience, and firmness, and zeal, and humility, are as certainly one with justifying faith, considered as a thing existing, as bones, muscle, and vital organs, are necessary to that outward frame of man which meets the eye, though they do not meet it. Love and fear and obedience are not really posterior to justifying faith for even a moment of time, unless bones and muscles are formed after the countenance and complexion. It is as unmeaning to speak of living faith, as being independent of newness of mind, as of solidity as divisible from body, or tallness from stature, or colour from landscape. As well might it be said that an arm or a foot can exist out of the body, and that man is born with only certain portions, head or heart, and the rest accrues afterwards, as that faith comes first and gives birth to other graces.[38]

The virtues weave together to become a seamless web of holiness.

Of course, the Anglican Newman gave a place to the teaching about faith alone being justifying. He added a qualification to that very passage, namely 'that faith, though connatural with other graces, has a power of reacting upon them, by placing more constraining objects before them, as motives to their more vigorous exercise'.[39] Elsewhere, in his sermon on 'Faith and Obedience' in 1830, he allowed faith 'a certain prerogative or dignity under the Gospel',[40] and in January, 1841, he preached on faith as our title for justification,[41] while he still asked the question whether the granting of right and title means that they are possessed forthwith. He answered no. What faith has begun still needs to be brought to perfection. It seems probable, as one scholar has suggested, that Newman presented this teaching because he believed it to be revealed.[42] All the same, it is difficult to feel that this particular teaching carried much significance for him, as the very attempt to isolate one virtue is so out of character with his general, unified approach.

V

If we now ask how Newman thought of the condition of a person in whom these qualities and virtues had come together, we can turn to the beginning of the sermon he entitled, 'The State of Salvation'. He preached it on 18 March 1838, which was only six days after he had composed the Advertisement for his volume of *Lectures on Justification*. He observed:

As that which is created differs from what is not yet created, so the Christian differs from the natural man. He is brought into a new world, and as being in that new world, is invested with powers and privileges which he absolutely had not in the way of nature. By nature his will is enslaved to sin, his soul is full of darkness, his conscience is under the wrath of God; peace, hope, love, faith, purity, he has not; nothing of heaven is in him; nothing spiritual, nothing of light and life. But in Christ all these blessings are given: the will and the power; the heart and the knowledge; the light of faith, and the obedience of faith. As far as a being can be changed without losing his identity, as far as it is sense to say that an existing being can be new created, so far has man this gift when the grace of the

Gospel has its perfect work and its maturity of fruit in him.[43]

To be thus new created is to share the divine nature. In a Christmas sermon, Newman set out his teaching on this condition plainly: 'Men we remain, but not mere men, but gifted with a measure of all those perfections which Christ has in fullness, partaking each in his own degree of His Divine Nature so fully, that the only reason (so to speak) why His saints are not really like Him, is that it is impossible − that He is the Creator, and they His creatures; yet still so, that they are all but Divine, all that they can be made without violating the incommunicable majesty of the Most High.'[44] This is the deep doctrine of divinization, learnt from Athanasius.

However, it would be a mistake to presume that this privileged condition was a panacea. For Newman the contrary was closer to the truth. A fortnight after he had described the state of salvation in such exalted terms, he preached a sermon which is amongst his most moving. It displays notable psychological perceptiveness. It was called 'Sins of Infirmity'. On this occasion Newman indicated that the results of faith 'are righteous and holy', but he also acknowledged that 'the process through which they are obtained is one of imperfection'. From a distance, he remarked, the soul of the righteous appears 'youthful in countenance, and bright in apparel; but approach him, and his face has lines of care upon it, and his dress is tattered'. His righteousness has been 'wrought out of sin, the result of a continual struggle, − not spontaneous nature, but habitual self-command'. And he went on: 'True faith is not shown here below in peace, but rather in conflict; ... As we gain happiness through suffering, so do we arrive at holiness through infirmity, because man's very condition is a fallen one, and in passing out of the country of sin, he necessarily passes through it.'[45] Those who 'venture much with their talents,' he added a little later, 'gain much ...[but they] cannot believe that they are making any progress; and though they do, yet surely they have much to be forgiven in all their services. They are like David, men of blood; they fight the good fight of faith, but they are polluted with the contest.'[46] These few sentences can convey only slightly the effect of the whole; still they may be enough to show that Newman did not regard believing as immunity from conflict. Indeed, in 1836, you would have heard him urging you to seek out conflict, when he told you that, as faith is the essence of a Christian life, so there is a duty 'in risking upon Christ's word what we have, for what we have not'.[47] We need to make 'ventures of faith'. What virtue is there in living in such a way that it would make no difference to us if Christ's word proved to be false? But I must draw to a close.

V

It has been my intention to give you an account of the teaching on faith contained in Newman's parochial sermons. In doing so I hope I have given you glimpses of his spirituality as well.

From the start it was important to appreciate the circumstances of those times which influenced what he had to say, rationalism and evangelicalism, while it was also necessary to be aware of the convictions which guided him as a preacher. Notably we have found him throughout attentive to human experience so that his words would be real, his sermons come alive. We have seen the emphasis he placed on faith as common to everyone, not something peculiar to the religious; we have considered the role of conscience as the authority on which faith rests; and we have listened to his account of the bond between faith and obedience, and not only obedience, but the other virtues as well which are woven together, a seamless robe, an entire disposition, which establishes us in a privileged condition before God, which gives us indeed a share in the divine nature, and which bestows on us perfection at the last, but which at first is experienced as conflict. There should be much in this teaching which can speak to us still.

At the beginning I compared your memories to Matthew Arnold's. Let us return to him at the end. What Arnold had said he had seemed to hear was a passage from a sermon called, 'Peace in Believing'. Newman preached it first in May, 1839. He offered comfort, the reward of a living faith: 'After the fever of life; after weariness and sicknesses; fightings and despondings; languor and fretfulness; struggling and succeeding; after all the changes and chances of this troubled unhealthy state, at length comes death, at length the White Throne of God, at length the Beatific Vision.'[48] Now it has been suggested that Arnold would have heard Newman only rarely, but that matters little to us. Rather the contrary. For, if it is true, the vividness of his memory reveals the power of the impression which the preacher made on him. And we know that such impressions are not commonly caused by sermons composed out of theory. Arnold's clear memory bears witness to the reality of Newman's experience.

Notes

1   Matthew Arnold, 'Emerson', in R.H. Super (ed.), *Philistinism in England and America*, (University of Michigan Press, 1974), p. 165.
2   Owen Chadwick, *The Mind of the Oxford Movement*, (London, 1960), p. 42.
3   *LD*.xxxi.189. The abbreviations are those laid down in C. S. Dessain (ed.), *The Letters and Diaries of John Henry Newman* xi, (London, 1961), pp. xxv − xxvi.

4   *PS*.ii.166−8.
5   *PS*.ii.259−60.
6   *PS*.ii.260,261.
7   See C. S. Dessain, *John Henry Newman*, (Oxford, 1980), p. xii.
8   *Jfc*.336.
9   *PS*.i.191.
10 *PS*.i.192.
11 *PS*.i.192.
12 *PS*.i.195.
13 *PS*.i.195.
14 *GA*.347; I. T. Ker (ed.), (Oxford, 1985), p. 224.
15 See *GA*.294−6; Ker, pp. 191−2.
16 *PS*.i.193.
17 *GA*.61; Ker, p. 46
18 *PS*.i.199−200.
19 See *GA*.105−18; Ker, pp. 73−81.
20 See *OS*. 64−6, 74.
21 *PS*.ii.18.
22 *PS*.vi.333.
23 *PS*.vi.339−40.
24 *PS*.iii.213.
25 *PS*.iii.80−1.
26 See *PS*.viii.201−16.
27 *PS*.v.166; see also v.183−4.
28 *PS*.ii.153.
29 *PS*.ii.54.
30 *PS*.ii.157.
31 *PS*.ii.158.
32 *PS*.ii.160.
33 *AW*.254−5.
34 *PS*.iv.309.
35 *PS*.iv.311.
36 *PS*.iv.312.
37 *PS*.iv.314−15.
38 *Jfc*.265−6.
39 *Jfc*.266.
40 *PS*.iii.87.
41 See *PS*.vi.153−73.
42 See Thomas Sheridan, *Newman on Justification*, (New York, 1967), p. 254.
43 *PS*.v.178−9. For an account of the basis of this teaching in Newman's under-
    standing of the Christ, see Roderick Strange, *Newman and the Gospel of
    Christ*, (Oxford, 1981), pp. 134−56.
44 *PS*.viii.253.
45 *PS*.v.210.
46 *PS*.v.214.
47 *PS*.iv.299.
48 *PS*.vi.369−70.

Participation in the divine life: Coleridge, the vision of God and the thought of John Henry Newman

Douglas Hedley

1. The enigma of Coleridge

Why should we discuss Coleridge at a conference on the Oxford Movement? The obvious reason is that Newman refers to the contemporary climate of thought in his biography and in particular Coleridge as contributing to the Catholic revival in the Church of England:

> 'While history in prose and verse was thus made the instrument of Church feelings and opinions, *a philosophical basis* for the same was laid in England by a very original thinker, who, while he indulged a liberty of speculation, which no Christian can tolerate, and advocated conclusions which were often heathen rather than christian, yet after all instilled *a higher philosophy in inquiring minds*, than they had hitherto been accustomed to accept. In this way he made a trial of his age, and succeeded in interesting its genius in the cause of *Catholic truth*.'[1] (My italics D.H.)

Was not Newman later accused of communicating German infidelity through the music and perfume of St Peter's?[2] And do we not sense Coleridge's influence behind such accusations – particularly given Newman's ignorance of German? I do not wish to address the complex issue of Coleridge's influence upon Newman,[3] but to consider what Newman could have meant by the 'higher philosophy' which Coleridge 'instilled' in 'inquiring minds'. Any judgement about the *extent* of the influence of Coleridge upon Newman is unduly rash if we do not first consider *what* the 'philosophical basis' which Newman refers to might reside in.

This may seem to be merely stating the obvious. Yet Coleridge is perhaps even more of an enigma than he was in Newman's day. Today, we are still not at all sure about the nature and import of Coleridge's thought – despite the editorial work of Kathleen

Coburn and many other Coleridge scholars. In the face of the variety of conflicting interpretations of Coleridge in the secondary literature, the student of his thought is very much on his own with some of the most forbidding primary sources in English.

The matter is further complicated by Coleridge's plagiarism. First of all this has been a source of embarrassment. Secondly, it undermines the strong claims for Coleridge's originality: to what extent can we see Newman as being really influenced by a cheat and a fraud. I think this problem has been vastly overemphasized but it remains a difficulty.[4] In particular, the relation of Coleridge's thought to German idealism is a problem because many of the Anglo-Saxon critics are either unduly impressed by the German influence or ignore it altogether.[5]

Coleridge's most influential work for the Victorians was *Aids to Reflection* (1825, second corrected ed.1831). Newman was in his mid twenties when the book first appeared. This work has been neglected in the 20th century; it seemed too theological and old fashioned to inspire much interest. If we reflect upon the salient thoughts and arguments of this work, we may be able to reconstruct something of the impact of Coleridge upon his contemporaries.

The most serious problem for our reception of Coleridge, I contend, is the decline of Anglican theology in this century.[6] The heart of Anglican theology is the doctrine of the *incarnation*. Anglicanism flourished in the 19th century despite the challenge of Darwin. But in this century is has not really recovered from the shock of the First World War and Anglican theology has lost much of its traditionally close relationship to philosophy evident in Berkeley or Butler. Coleridge is a genuinely English mind; rooted in the likes of Hooker and Cudworth, he is the source of the great tradition of Anglican thought which we see in Newman, Hort, Wescott, Gore and William Temple.[7] The uncertainties in modern Anglican thought are reflected in the strange limbo of one of her greatest sons. I shall not try to link Newman and Coleridge directly but try to suggest what I see as strikingly Coleridgean in Newman. My main point is quite simple: Coleridge revived the idea of the *dogmatic* in English *philosophical* theology. Whereas 18th century Anglicans of a philosophical persuasion like Paley tended to avoid dogma, since Coleridge English philosophical theologians have been concerned to interpret and defend dogma. The tendency in Anglicans like Newman or Maurice to combine an insistence upon dogma within philosophical theology has its roots, I suggest, in Coleridge's idiosyncratic reception of German Idealistic theology and his emphatic avowal of 17th century Anglicanism.[8]

The cardinal dogma for Coleridge is that of the *Trinity*. It is plain that this dogma is not seen as mere notional doctrine but the basis of manly character.[9] The doctrine of the Trinity is seen in eminently practical terms: the vision of God, the participation in the divine and holiness or godliness are bound in the Trinitarian theology of both Coleridge and Newman. This trinitarian dogmatic religion is, I propose, the root of the most significant link between Coleridge and Newman. Once we grasp this affinity between the two, we can see good reasons for the influence of the enigmatic and oracular Coleridge upon the mind of Newman.

2 The Church of England and Socinianism

'While history in prose and verse was thus made the instrument of *Church* feelings and opinions, a *philosophical basis* for the same was laid in England by a very original thinker . . .'

One does not have to read *Aids to Reflection* or the *Lay Sermons* with any great care in order to see that the Christian religion in its Anglican form and the tenets of Unitarianism play a central, I dare say *the* central role. What is Coleridge's **target**? He had heard that the intellectual atmosphere in Cambridge in the 1820s was one of rampant atheism. Coleridge decided to provide an apology for the Christian faith aimed at undergraduates. He believed that Socinianism had exerted a baneful influence upon the Church of England and he wanted to attack Socinian tendencies both with the Church of England (Paley) as well as in Unitarianism.[10] Formally he presented his argument in the form of beauties from Archbishop Leighton and other great Anglican divines of the 17th century, Jeremy Taylor and the Cambridge Platonists, Hackett and 16th century Divines like Hooker. Coleridge believed that since 1688 the intellectual fabric of England had changed radically, and that the source of the intellectual problems which beset Theology in the 19th century arose from the tacit acceptance of Socinianism, and the loss of Trinitarian thought.

Coleridge's nostalgia for the 'spiritual platonic old England'[11] and his hostility to Socinianism is often treated with scepticism or indifference by recent writers. Yet Socinianism played a vital role in the history of theology in the period leading up to the Enlightenment. Troeltsch pointed out acutely that whereas the thought of Luther and Calvin effectively belongs to the Middle ages, the intellectual roots of modernity are to be found in the radical wings of the Reformation such as Socinianism.[12] Faustus Socinus (1539–1604) was a radical in continental Protestant thought who denied the validity of the doctrine of the Trinity. His theology was marked by a curious mixture of scriptural positivism and empiricism. Socinianism was very influential in Holland and England in the 17th century.

Socinianism was particularly potent as an intellectual force in the English 18th century because of the influence and prestige of Locke. John Locke spent time in exile in Holland and we know that he possessed Socinian works in his library. Bishop Stillingfleet attacked Locke in his *Vindication of the Trinity*, contending that Locke did not possess an *instrumentarium* with which he might accommodate the doctrine of the Trinity: concepts like substance or person.[13] Indeed, Locke's theology is, albeit unavowedly, Socinian.[14] For Locke the essence of Christianity is not dogma but an essentially rational or ethical religion which is *proved* to be divinely sanctioned by the existence of miracles. This (Socinian) combination of an ethical rationalism and a scriptural positivism is, of course, a bone of contention for Hume and the very foundation of Paley's theology.[15]

In order to consider the impact of anti-Trinitarian thought in England in the 18th century we ought to remind ourselves of the historical background of the Established Church in England. Since the period of Elizabeth I many members of the Anglican Church were unsatisfied with the Elizabethan settlement and in the 17th century there were two great waves of dissent (particularly in 1662 under Charles II's Act of Uniformity when 2500 priests out of a total of 9000 left the Church and became dissenters). The conflict between the Church and dissent was an excellent basis for the development of Unitarianism because the anti-dogmatic biblicism of many of the dissenters encouraged Unitarianism within their ranks. The formularies of the Church prevented general change within its ranks and Protestant dissent disavowed dogmatic creeds. This is the specific English context. Consider the difference in Europe. The Lutherans, Reformed and the Roman Church all agreed on the issue of the Trinity. This was common ground – quite unlike the issues of the sacraments, ecclesiology, justification etc. which were the grounds of contention. Between Anglicans and Dissenters the Trinity seemed a genuine issue because the doctrine was clearly not entirely biblical; particularly not in its dogmatic formulation. The status of dogma was a real issue in England on account of the Trinitarian controversies, and Coleridge repeatedly praised the manly efforts of Bull and Waterland to defend the Nicene creed.

Socinianism in both its Unitarian and Anglican forms became a particularly potent force in English theology. The status of dogma and the dogma of the Trinity in particular had a special significance in England. For Coleridge – especially as a former Unitarian – the connection between the dogma and the Church was both natural and pressing. Indeed if the content of *Aids to Reflection* is trinitarian, the form, in its commentaries upon the 17th century Anglican divines, is a sort of homage to the glories of the 'most apostolic Church'.

3 Aids to Reflection

Coleridge '. . . instilled a *higher philosophy* in inquiring minds, than they had hitherto been accustomed to accept' (my italics D.H.).

Aids to Reflection is an emphatic rejection of the claim that the essence of Christianity lies in rational ethics and in miracles. For Coleridge the essence of Christianity is dogmatic. Warburton's attack upon the Methodists and their enthusiasm led to his claim that the spirit is merely a metaphor.[16] Paley's Utilitarianism and his Socinian theology was barely better than the materialism of Priestley – the foremost Utilitarian of the age. Coleridge's attack on Paley's rationalism might be more accurately described as an attack upon the decay of dogma in Anglican thought, in particular the loss of the doctrine of the Trinity. There are two aspects which we should observe. Firstly, Coleridge's appropriation of German thought, and secondly his interest in the 17th century Anglican Divines.

The German Enlightenment differed from the English on the point of *dogma*. In place of a timeless religion of reason we can see the attempt to rehabilitate and reinterpret exactly those dogmas reviled by the Anglo-Gallic Enlightenment. Lessing in *Das Christentum der Verunft* (1758) sees Christianity not as the morally interpreted gospel of Jesus but in its dogmatic form and interprets it as such. This is a vague beginning in Lessing, but it is developed by Kant in *Die Religion innerhalb der Grenzen der Blossen Vernunft* (1793). This tradition culminates in Schelling and Hegel both of whom emphasize the doctrines of the Trinity and the Incarnation. One of Coleridge's main interests in going to Germany was to write a life of Lessing, and his interest for Schelling is well documented.[17] Most Coleridge commentators get side tracked by complex issues like pantheism and miss the simple point: the German Idealist tradition as opposed to the Romanticism of say Schleiermacher was thoroughly dogmatic (albeit in a manner with which Newman would have had little sympathy!). Nonetheless we have to say that the essence of Christianity for the Idealists rests in an interpretation of dogma not in feeling or ethics.

Yet in its salient points Coleridge's theology is rooted in the English 17th century and is mystical. By mystical I mean a concentration upon the vision of God as within the Christian philosophical mystical tradition. Four tenets are central for this tradition and temper of thought:

1. The soul can attain to the vision of God.
2. Man is made in the image of God and it is his vocation to participate in the divine nature.
3. Without holiness the vision is unattainable.
4. Culmination of the vision is love.

Coleridge's distinction between Reason as the divine light and Understanding as the faculty of discursive thought is an instance of his mystical metaphysics which concentrates upon the idea of the vision of God. This distinction is essentially a thought about revelation: God does not reveal propositional information but reveals Himself. Coleridge presents an Augustinian argument. Revelation is not to be judged by the standards of the human understanding because human understanding presupposes the divine Light.[18] Religion is marked by the conscious participation in that divine light in which all men participate unconsciously and is essentially practical in the sense of being the renewal of the human into the divine form through the spirit.[19] This is a theology which is theocentric and anti-liberal. Its aim is to lose all self in God and thereby to gain genuine selfhood: 'We proceed from the SELF, in order to lose and find all self in GOD.'[20] This Augustinianism is equally evident in Newman. Consider Newman on the same theme: 'The soul of man is made for the contemplation of its Maker; and that nothing short of that high contemplation is its happiness; that, whatever it may possess besides, it is unsatisfied till it is vouchsafed God's presence, and lives in the light of it.'[21]

It is important to bear in mind that the mystical tradition is intensely practical in its orientation. Coleridge's Christian mysticism revolves not just around the vision but the participation in the

Divine life: participation in the death and rising of the incarnate Christ.

Coleridge's attainment of this position was the result of his own spiritual experience. As a young man he was deeply influenced by Unitarianism. Jesus college, Cambridge was notorious for its Unitarianism. Coleridge became a Unitarian effectively although he does not seem to have taken the materialist metaphysics of Priestley seriously. He was in his youth a Trinitarian *ad normam Platonis* while he was Unitarian in religion.[22] This means he accepted the notion of the logos but not that the logos became flesh, suffered died and rose. He seems to have become a Trinitarian while in Malta after the breakdown of his marriage. The decisive development was in a period at the end of 1813 during a profound personal spiritual crisis.[23] In that moment of crisis he turned to Leighton. 'To feel the full force of Christian Religion, it is necessary, for many tempers, that they should be made to feel, experimentally, the hollowness of human friendship, the presumptuous emptiness of human hopes.'[24] At the heart of the mystical theology is a rejection of humanism in favour of theocentric metaphysics.

At this period Coleridge sees the need to consider the centrality of the cross and the resurrection – the atonement as at the heart of Christianity, and not in the evangelical sense of imputed righteousness, but in the sense of the sonship which arises from participation in the way of the cross: an incarnational theology of redemption. Coleridge insists that when we look at the philosophic apostle, i.e. Paul, we do not see an appeal to miracles or evidences of any sort other than those of the spiritual life of man: Paul, Coleridge insists, argues from the fact of man's sinfulness and his need for renewal. At the centre of Leighton's theology is the idea of the renewal in the image of Christ this is 'Plato glorified by St. Paul.'[25] The contrast is with Socininan thought which lays emphasis upon external evidence i.e. *proofs*.[26]

The logos in the flesh is not an isolated miracle which *proves* anything from *without* ... The Logos attested to by John is the same who lives in mankind when they die to their old selves and live as sons of God. Coleridge is concerned to show that the essence of Christianity does not consist in miracles which prove the validity of a teaching (Socinianism) but the dying and rising to the new man in Christ through the Spirit as the fruits of the indwelling Logos.[27] The essence of Christianity is not the *evidence from without* but the *mystery of the Trinity as experienced within*.

We tend to miss the point of such utterances. We take them to be flat rejections of philosophy; Coleridge means rather a rejection of the false philosophy of Socinianism. The emphasis upon proofs is a denial of the importance of dogmas and the substitution of human judgement for divine revelation. The incarnation is not a singular miracle but the living principle of renewal and sonship. In other words, Christianity is a religion of godliness in the strict sense of god-likeness: a full blooded religion of the incarnation. The aids of the spirit which Coleridge refers to are meant to be aids for the discovery of a deeper self in *Christo*. In contrast to the humanist position that many interests as objects are valuable, Coleridge insists that there should be *one* dominant pursuit: a manly character based on godliness or god*likeness*: in Christ. The Christian faith maintains both that God cannot be adequately described in our language and yet there is an intelligible manifestation of God: for Coleridge only those in whom the Logos dwells can attain to an intuition of the Son of God — in the light of the Word men are *logikoi*. Both grace and holiness are inextricably bound together for a mystic like Coleridge: the mystical path of negation is transformed into the path of affirmation through the conviction that the best contemplation of God is the life of holiness: here is the Word of God and this Word must be perpetually renewed. This life of renewal or reflection is called godliness by Coleridge and holiness by Newman.[28]

4. The meaning of Enlightenment

'. . . he made a *trial* of his age . . .' (my italics D.H.)

Newman saw the mistake of Enlightenment in subjecting divine revelation to human judgement. Coleridge believes that en*light*enment begins when we become aware of our need for enlightening: for grace. In *Aids to Reflection* Coleridge considers and attacks the Arminianism or semi-pelagianism of Jeremy Taylor. Taylor was reluctant to admit the doctrine of original sin. Coleridge senses here the roots of a humanistic liberalism which wishes to subject the Divine to the canons of the human Understanding and to dispense with grace. Real *enlightenment*, Coleridge thinks, starts from the fact of man's need for illumination and renewal. In his attack upon an older kind of High Churchmanship, Coleridge was laying down hints for the new movement with Newman.

Coleridge believed that scrupulous attention to the meanings of words was a prerequisite of genuine thought. Let us consider the word 'reflection'.

The word reflection has three primary meanings:

1. Thought.
2. Reflection as in a mirror *imago dei*.
3. As the translation of the Neoplatonic terminus ἐπιστροφέ.

All these meanings are connected. Coleridge has no sympathy for the fideism which has dominated German theology from Schleiermacher to Barth. Reflection, i.e. thought, for Coleridge is an integral element of religion: he is in agreement with the Enlightenment on this. He differs from the Enlightenment insofar as it denies the ancient Christian Platonic belief in the Logos as the power of Reason in which we participate; the light of which empowers our discursive Understanding. Finally, he differs from the Enlightenment in insisting that man needs must reflect or turn back from his natural state towards God and this requires a supernatural renewal of his will. The turning from sin i.e. the state of being asunder from God to atonement at-one-ment to God is the result of the *aids* of the Spirit. The spirit is the advocate who has been called to aid man's participation in him who is consubstantial with the Father.

The *soi disant* Enlightenment is actually **blind** on account of three premises:

1. The cogito 'I think' of Descartes as the beginning of philosophy.
2. The contractual atomistic view of society in Locke.
3. The mechanical view of the universe of Descartes and Newton.

Coleridge's objection to 1 is that the 'I think' presupposes a community background. We cannot start from self evident premises: least of all is the subject, the ego or self, transparent or self evident but dark confused and can only follow a dim light which it senses to be revealed. Conscience is the voice of a wider and greater spirit than our self: the awakening of a wider vision through the renewal of the will in Christ. Coleridge says that conscience is the ground of consciousness, and conscience is the voice of the indwelling Christ. Consider Newman's thoughts on this matter: 'there is a power given to us Christians, which 'worketh in us,' a special hidden mysterious power, which makes us its instruments. We do not see our souls; but we see in others and we are conscious in ourselves of a principle which rules our bodies, and makes them what the brutes are not.'[29] Our eyes must be enlightened in order to recognise it. This is Newman's denial of the transparency of the self and his insistence upon the primacy of the ethical in consciousness: 'Lead, kindly light, amid the encircling gloom, . . .' is profoundly Coleridgean in its temper.

2. Coleridge criticises the idea of contract — the central concept of Enlightened theories of society presupposes deeper sacral bonds. Human life, Coleridge insists, depends upon the recognition of duties which have little or nothing to do with our consent.[30] This is what Coleridge means when he says that without the *vision* a people will perish.[31] He means that people have to learn to *perceive* the divine ideas and the Church's role is to foster and nurture that which is not a product of human contract but of divine furnishing. Coleridge provided a philosophical basis for the idea of the Church as a 'frontal mirror' of the Divine and the divinely instituted aid to reflection *ex umbris et imaginibus in veritatem*.

3. Nature is the cloak and the vehicle of the spiritual and as such speaks to mankind. In contrast to the deistic views of God Coleridge is concerned to see a Trinitarian concept of God as involved and evolving in his creation as well as redeeming it. The central message of the Christian Platonic vision is that the material world imperfectly represents the ideal world: because the world is created it does not share God's incomprehensibility or his necessity, but the phenomenal universe is nonetheless a communication. This is '. . . the doctrine that material phenomena are both the types and the instruments of real things unseen.'[32] Within a sacramental — as opposed to a purely mechanical — universe faith in the unseen as the ground of the seen is both pious and rational. In his *Treatise on Method* Coleridge shows that artist only succeeds when an obscure impulse becomes a clear idea. Thus the artist is impelled by a great power of which he is only barely aware. So too is the complex act of inference and assent which is faith: ultimately it is fidelity to our own renewed being. Consider Newman: 'Let us not deny Him the glory of His life-giving holiness, that diffusive grace which is the renovation of our whole race, a spirit quick and powerful and piercing, so as to leaven the whole mass of human corruption, and make it live. He is the first-fruits of the Resurrection: we follow Him each in his own order, as we are hallowed by his inner presence. And in this sense, among others, Christ, in the Scripture phrase, is 'formed in us'; that is, the communication is made to us of His new nature, which sanctifies the soul, and makes the body immortal.'[33] The same creative Word who is the source of the endless manifold of objects is also the high priest of the universe who beckons mankind to search their own hearts and He enlightens them: *cor ad cor loquitur*. This is neither a sentimental religion of feelings about God nor a systematic religion of notions. *Reflection* means the transformation

through the indwelling Logos in the spirit. Our subjective realm is but a dark *glass* of the Divine life which is continually offering the possibility of participation in the vision glorious.[34]

Conclusion

'... and succeeded in interesting its genius in the cause of *Catholic truth*.' (My italics D.H.)

Coleridge marks a watershed in English theology. He insists that the essence of Christianity is dogmatic and he connected this insistence with a very subtle philosophical apology for the Christian religion. Genuine Christianity, for Coleridge, lies in the doctrinal proclamation of the Church catholic that the risen Lord lives on in his Church through the communication of his nature. The one true philosophy is incarnational, and it leads to the conviction in the renewal and sonship in the Triune life, and to a view of the Church as a divine institution. The consequence of Coleridge's view of the essence of Christianity as dogmatic is his insistence in *Aids to Reflection* that CHRISTIANITY WITHOUT A CHURCH EXERCISING SPIRITUAL AUTHORITY IS VANITY AND DISSOLUTION.[35] The relevance of this chain of thought for Newman's thinking is, I think, evident.

Coleridge believed that one of the reasons for the modern decline of theology in the 18th century was the failure of churchmen to understand and unfold the riches of their metaphysical heritage. Newman was quite right to point to the dangers of such a project: dangers as evident in Origen as in Coleridge. Yet I suspect Newman to have been equally aware that Coleridge was an *anima naturlaiter christiana* and much closer to the spirit of the Fathers than the admirably robust intellect of Butler. Newman was temperamentally averse to recognizing, or perhaps admitting, the depth of his affinity to Coleridge's theology: an affinity which rests in the conviction that only a dogmatic catholic, i.e. *kat-holon*, Christianity with its insistence upon the necessity of holiness or godliness for the attainment of the vision could wind up the Church of England to its vocation. Coleridge's endeavour was essentially apologetic in the name of the Anglican and in the spirit of the Alexandrine Divines. The genius of English theology in the 19th and early 20th century was deeply interested in catholic truth: in a sacramental religion rooted in the Word who became flesh, *lux mundi*. Coleridge is the threshold between Paley and Warburton *and* Newman and Gore.

Once we can understand Coleridge's project properly as the attack aimed at the Socinianism and Liberalism of the 18th century, rehabilitation of Christian dogma and the revival of the mystical Trinitarian theology which the 16th and 17th century Divines of the Church of England inherited from the Fathers, we are in a much better position to begin the work of saying how much Newman owed to Coleridge. Not only did he, like Coleridge, write his own apologetic biography: only a *dogmatic* religion demands assent. Further, the defence of the development of *doctrine* and the exultation of the *ideas* is a task which Newman pursued with a force and temper quite his own, but the task itself shows Newman thinking in the wake of Coleridge.

Notes

1   *Apologia pro vita sua* (Oxford 1967) p. 94.
2   Reardon, *Religious Thought in the Victorian Age.* p. 150.
3   Coleridge had a particular influence in Oriel – upon Thomas Arnold, R. W. Church and Mark Pattison. Newman was inclined to deny any influence of Coleridge on his own mind. Yet certain connections are obvious. Coleridge attacks the narrower rationalism of the day, stresses the role of the symbolic and the Church, and lays great weight upon the ethical in religion. These affinities have struck a number of commentators from the 19th century onwards, those who saw Coleridge as the indirect source of spectral Puseyism with his talk of the Church. John Coulson in *Newman and the Common Tradition* (Oxford 1970) has emphasized the link between Newman and Coleridge on the issue of faith. Coulson, however employs a complex, and I don't think very plausible, argument about fiduciary language. Reardon's excellent text book *Religious thought in the 19th century*, sees Newman as presenting a continuation of an appeal to the inner life which begins with Coleridge and which dominates the best English religious thought up to Gore.
4   This is a very complicated issue: Coleridge did plagiarize, but he often does the opposite! More often than not, Coleridge attributes his own writing to others. *Aids to Reflection* has the form of a commentary on other writers; especially Archbishop Leighton. When the editorial work of the new edition is finished I think that it will be possible to see how often Coleridge attributes to Leighton his own phrases, thoughts and ideas.
5   G. Steiner in his book *After Babel* (Oxford 1975) p. 69 speaks of the Coleridgean notion of 'reticulation'. This word is actually not Coleridgean at all but a term used by Thomas McFarland in a – to say the very least – curious justification of Coleridge's plagiarisms in: *Coleridge and the Pantheist Tradition* (Oxford 1969) p. 49ff. There are various other examples of the manner in which Coleridge is vaguely and fashionably present but little understood in modern literary criticism. The work of Friedrich Uehlein *Die Manifestation des Selbstbewusstseins im konkreten 'Ich bin'* (Hamburg 1982) is the best book on the subject. Uehlein's is the *only* book on Coleridge written by a philosopher who knows the German tradition, but it has been almost entirely ignored by Anglo-Saxons.
6   Coleridge's work was revived at a time when his influence was waning in theology and Coleridge became particularly closely associated with English

literature through I. A. Richards. This appropriation by English literature has concentrated upon the *Biographia Literaria*. This is Coleridge's most confused book and it was written at a time of severe depression. It is also unsuitable for understanding Coleridge because not aesthetics but theology and metaphysics are at the heart of his thought. It is much better to move from the centre of Coleridge's thought (i.e. *Aids to Reflection*) to the outskirts, even if the outskirts seem more hospitable for the modern or post-modern mind.

7　Coleridge is a mysterious figure and yet is obviously the source of the really interesting religious thought in England in the 19th century. One is hard pressed to notice the terminological influence of Hegel in the mid and late 19th century in England among writers who are often thought of as Hegelians. Coleridge's influence in England in 19th and 20th theology in books like *Lux Mundi* or *Foundations* is more tangible than that of Hegel.

8　This is not really a theme of Coleridge scholarship in the faculties of English Literature. On the contrary, during the 1980s the theory that Coleridge was an *anti-dogmatic* ironist was very popular, and is still quoted and put forward. I have to say quite plainly that I think this is an exegetical mistake and reflects modern or post-modern preoccupations far more than Coleridge himself. See for example David Jasper, *Coleridge as Poet and Religious Thinker* (London 1985) p18f. Kathleen Wheeler and Elinor Shaffer are other well known proponents of the irony view. The position is based upon a rather nebulous conviction that as a Romantic Coleridge *should* be expected to share continental Romantic interests like 'higher irony'. As a matter of *fact* Coleridge does not.

9　*Aids to Reflection for the formation of a manly character.* The 'manly' character is a central Victorian notion and as important for Newman as it was for Thomas Arnold, Hughes and Kingsley.

10　See the informative article by J. E. Carpenter, 'Unitarianism' in the *Encyclopedia of Religion and Ethics*, (Edinburgh 1921) ed. J.Hastings,vol.XII p. 519–527, and the article by W. M. Clow 'Socinianism' also in *Encyclopedia of Religion and Ethics*, vol XI p. 650–654.

11　Coleridge Collected Notes (London 1961) note 2598.

12　Ernst Troeltsch, Die Bedeutung des Protestantismus für die Enstehung der modernen Welt (Berlin 1911). See W. Pannenberg, 'Reformation und Neuzeit', in: Troeltsch-Studien. Protestantismus und Neuzeit, (Gütersloh 1984), p. 21–34.

13　See Walter Dahrendorf, *Lockes Kontroverse mit Stillingfleet und ihre Bedeutung für seine Stellung zur anglikanischen Kirche*, (Hamburg 1932).

14　I am using the term Socinian in the broad sense employed by Coleridge to denote a kind of theology rather than to designate a strict pupil of Socinus.

15　The miracle as a rational proof of the Christian religion may seem counter-intuitive to the modern mind, but in the 18th century the emphasis upon miracles was linked to a rationalist defence of religion in writers like Priestley, Paley and Warburton.

16　Warburton, *The Doctrine of Grace*, (London 1788) (repr. Olms Hildesheim 1978). Cf. *Aids to Reflection* (Princeton 1994) p.81.

17　German Idealism redeveloped the kind of God talk which a full blooded metaphysical theology needs. One might consider Stillingfleet's objection to

Locke and reflect upon the extent to which unity, simplicity, difference, sameness, substance, relation and spirit are necessary for a comprehension of say Augustin's or Boethius' *De Trinitate*. Moreover, there are striking affinities between German Idealism and the Alexandrine tradition of theology. Hegel's *Logic* is, for example, quite simply the description of the movement of ideas of the Godhead (the logos) into the world.

18 See Coleridge *On the Constitution of Church and State* (Princeton 1976) p. 165 where a mystic is defined as one who '... *muses* with closed lips, as meditating on *Ideas* ...' and Coleridge's intellectual heroes, Plato and Bacon are designated as mystics. On p.120 of the same work he defines 'IDEAL, i.e. mystic and supersensual ...' Coleridge sees the real mystic as primarily a speculative philosopher like Plotinus. See the conclusion of *Aids to Reflection* for his views about philosophically less capable mystics like Boehme.

19 See Nicholas Lossky, *Lancelot Andrewes The Preacher* (Oxford 1991).

20 *Biographia Literaria I* (Princeton 1983) p. 283 cf. Acts 17.28.

21 *Parochial and Plain Sermons*, 8 vols (London 1917–24),V p. 315.

22 *Biographia Literia l* (Princeton 1983) p. 179.

23 At this time Coleridge had lost virtually his friendship with Wordsworth and Sarah Hutchinson. See John Beer 'Coleridge's Religious Thought' in: *The Interpretation of Belief* (London 1986) ed. D. Jaspers p. 55ff.

24 Coleridge *Collected Letters* (Oxford 1956–71) IV, 893.

25 Coleridge *Marginalia* (Princeton 1992) III p. 511.

26 The Leighton passage reads: 'It was doubtless fit time: but notwithstanding the schoolmen offer at Reasons to prove the Fitness of it, as their Humour is to prove all things, . . .
Coleridge comments 'The True Spirit of modern Philosophy i.e. Psilosophy.' Coleridge *Marginalia* (Princeton 1992) III p. 511. He means the Socinian-Empiricist concern for empirical proofs.

27 Though Paul does not use the *terminus* Logos, for Coleridge there is no paradox in speaking of the Logos of St. Paul: '... St. Paul's Christ (as the Logos) the eternal *Yea* (Cor. 2.1.) is the frontal idea.' Coleridge, *The Friend* (London 1969) II p. 76. Paul's doctrine of the mystical life in Christ e.g. 'I am crucified with Christ: nevertheless I live; yet not I, but Christ liveth in me.' (Gal. 2.20.) lends weight to Coleridge's language.

28 For a modern Anglican philosophical theology of a plainly mystical and Platonic nature see Stephen Clark's Trilogy *Limits and Renewals* (Oxford 1989–1991) 3 vols.

29 *Parochial and Plain Sermons* V p. 344.

30 See Coleridge on Burke: *Biographia Literia I* p. 191.

31 *On the Constitution of Church and State* p. 58. See also Proverbs 29:18 (Editor's note).

32 *Apologia pro vita sua* (Oxford 1967) p. 29.

33 *Parochial and Plain Sermons* II p. 147.

34 See also 2 Corinthians 3:18 'But we all, with open face beholding as in a glass the glory of the Lord, are changed into the same image from glory to glory, even as by the Spirit of the Lord' [Editor's note].

35 *Aids to Reflection*, p. 298.

Part Four

Personalities and Influences

Richard Hurrell Froude's influence on Newman and the Oxford Movement

Pierre Gauthier

The English friend who takes you round on your first visit to Oxford shows you in St. Giles square a monument in the shape of a small neo-gothic tower erected in memory of the Reformers who perished on the stake on that very spot in the reign of Queen Mary Tudor. He would add, changing his tone and feeling a little embarrassed, that the monument was built about a hundred and fifty years ago to vindicate the memory of those Reformers whom Richard Hurrell Froude is supposed to have vilified. You then discover that, in the minds of Anglicans, this monument is associated with the 'succès de scandale' caused by the publication of Froude's *Remains* which many considered a blow dealt the Church of England by one of its members – or rather that the monument reminds them of a family tragedy one had better not dwell too much upon.

As a foreigner you then feel you should be discreet, yet you wish you could know more about this matter. Then, after you have visited the university church of St. Mary's and crossed High Street, your guide takes you to Oriel College. The memory of Froude then is recalled in greater detail and with less constraint as you enter the buildings, first the old library, then the Common Room which more than any other place, still retains something of the atmosphere that suffused it when Froude was a young tutor. Among the numerous pictures and portraits hung on the wall, a small sketch portrays three persons among whom Newman and Froude: it is almost sufficient to give you the feeling of a presence which the passage of time hasn't completely obliterated from those venerable precincts. We must pause here and get better acquainted with those figures.

Who was Richard Hurrell Froude?

He was born on 25th March 1803 and died in the bloom of youth at 32, on 28th February 1836, of a lung disease. His father was the Anglican Rector of Dartington and Archdeacon of Totnes in Devon.

255

He belonged to the High Church party which held numerous Catholic doctrines within Anglicanism, but had gradually conformed to the pattern of the Establishment informed by Thomas Erastus' ideas on the interdependence of Church and State. Richard Hurrell's younger brother, James Anthony, who became an eminent historian wrote:

> My father was a highchurchman of the old school. The Church itself, he regarded as part of the constitution, and the Prayer Book as an Act of Parliament which only folly or disloyalty could quarrel with.[1]

The same witness tells us that their father was a typical representative of the established order and ranked among the local gentry:

> My father was a fair representative of the old order. He was arch-deacon, he was justice of the peace. He had a moderate fortune of his own, consisting chiefly in land, and belonged therefore to the 'landed interest'. Most of the magistrates' work of the neighbourhood passed through his hands. If anything was amiss, it was his advice which was most sought after.[2]

The younger son appears to have insisted more on the gentleman than on the pastor in his father. As for Hurrell he was very much attached to the Catholicity of his Church, which is one of the main traits of a High Churchman. Yet he was averse to the links with the State it had developed throughout its history and to the official character that usually went with the office of Anglican parson.

Hurrell's talents were evident very early in his life and he soon became an object of admiration for the numerous household whose eldest son he was:

> We adored Hurrell. He was sparkling, brilliant, moved as a sort of king in the element that surrounded us. My father was infinitely proud of him, and let him do as he pleased.[3]

On 13th April 1821 he entered Oxford University as a resident student. He was matriculated at Oriel College and entrusted to John Keble's care as to the master who was to follow him throughout his training according to the tutorial system which is so profitable to a diligent student. So that the exuberant youngster he was found himself under the guidance of a tutor who was so unlike him in temperament as could ever be imagined. Yet they shared the same religious ideas, but those High Church notions in Keble received new stamina and were rejuvenated by the quality of his affections and his spiritual elevation which were a strong contrast to the cold formalism that too often characterised High Churchmen in those days. If we are to believe Isaac Williams who was one of Keble's pupils at Oriel at the same time as Froude, nothing less than the master's moderation and gentle firmness was needed to soften and control the young man's fiery but not wayward nature, to contain, develop and channel an energy and a talent that might have been otherwise wasted or improperly used.

He [Froude] was considered a very odd fellow at college, but clever and original: Keble alone was able to appreciate and value him. If he had not at this time fallen into such hands, his speculations might have taken a very dangerous turn; but, as his father, the archdeacon told me, from this time it was much otherwise, he continued to throw paradoxes, but always for good.[4]

The master pupil relationship soon developed into real friendship, and the influence of the one over the other was exerted both ways.

Meeting Newman

When Froude completed his studies, he stood for the fellowship of Oriel College and was elected on 31st March 1826. Keble had left the university then to become vicar of a country parish while Newman had been elected fellow of Oriel two years before. He was put in Newman's care for his probational year. The latter was two years his senior. This is how he recalls their first meeting:

I knew him first in 1826, and was in the closest and most affectionate friendship with him from 1829 till his death in 1836.[5]

Newman had many friends throughout his life whom he considered as gifts of God's providence. Every friend holds a unique place in our existence which is due to what he is. So that comparing friendships is, to some extent, comparing what is uncomparable, unless we simply acknowledge that they belong to that category we call friendship, i.e. that they are based on the principle of reciprocity. I may love somebody who doesn't love me and vice versa; yet I cannot say I am the friend of somebody who doesn't reciprocate my friendship. This being so, there are different modes of friendships: Aristotle had already seen it in the *Nicomachian Ethics* he devotes two books of which to the study of this type of human relationship. Contrary to what is generally thought, friends do not necessarily share in every-thing: there are areas that are off limits, which one keeps to oneself or opens up to other friends. There are also higher levels of inter-course that have to do with the lives of the intellect and of the spirit and, possibly, even higher ones where words give way to silence. There were certainly affectionate feelings in the friendship between Newman and Froude, yet its strength lay primarily and found its fullest expression in the realm of the intellect and of the inter-change of ideas. It is indeed a privileged area of human intercourse, yet one which it is difficult to attain and to keep unscathed, for dif-ferences of opinions may be kept hidden so as to spare the bonds of affection or, on the contrary, left unrestrained and consequently destroy a friendship. Not so with Newman and Froude: respect for truth was part of the esteem they felt for each other and those two qualities were to combine to strengthen their friendship. The old Aristotelian saying, *amicus Plato sed magis amica veritas*, could certainly apply to them, but differences of opinions by no means cast a shadow between the two friends. Yet, before they reached that state, Froude wrote to Robert Isaac Wilberforce, his friend, on 7th September 1828:

> He [Newman] is a fellow that I like more, the more I think of him, only I would give a few odd pence if he were not a heretic.[7]

Those reservations soon gave way to a great friendship the first con-sequence of which was to cause Keble and Newman to meet and to understand each other. Froude who had been the instrument of that meeting puts it this way:

> Do you know the story of the murderer who had done one good thing in his life? If I were asked what good deed I have ever done, I should say I had brought [Keble] and [Newman] to understand each other.[8]

No doubt it was a good thing he did! For this mutual understanding prepared the movement of religious and intellectual renewal they were to initiate within the Church of England. While Froude and Keble had become Newman's friends they were showing him, in their own char-acters, the very best of the High Church tradition.

Oriel College, at the time, was dominated by a school of thought, logicians that were called the Noetics; their leader was Richard Whately. Their theology was rather liberal, a mild latitudinarianism, but on the Church viewed as an institution with a life of its own, its distinct powers, its freedom from the state, Whately held firm positions our friends, especially Froude, found most interesting. They were equally impressed by the exactness of his logical mind. When debating with someone, he would compel his companion to build up a consistent defence of his views or else to renounce them. When he came to the doctrine of the Church, he led him back to its true foundations, i.e. the Fathers and the Councils. Froude was enthusiastic about Whately's ideas on the independence of the Church but he also adopted his celebrated mentor's truly noetic or socratic mind which led him to put repeatedly Newman to the test of his questions and of his objections. The correspondence between Froude and Newman illustrates the former's influence on the latter as to the intellectual rigour and the clearness in formulating one's ideas required in the quest for truth.

First intimations of the Via Media

The tendency to refer to the 'ancient Chuch of England' as to an ideal is characteristic of High Churchmen. To them the seventeenth century is the period when the Anglican Church reached its greatest glory for then its highest Catholic idea was a living reality: King Charles I, Archbishop Laud, and, after 1688, the Non-Jurors represented the greatest figures of that ideal. Later on the divide between the Churches had widened due to the Catholic Counter-Reformation but, even more so, due to the growing influence of continental protestantism favoured by the 1688 revolution and the fall of the Stuart Kings. Newman also referred to the seventeenth century Church and to the great Caroline divines and the Non-Jurors, but they were only good examples for him. The true foundation of the Anglican theology he wanted to systematise was Christian antiquity, i.e. the conformity the Church had maintained with the first Christian centuries. For, contrary to Froude, he had had no High Church background.

Froude and the 39 Articles of Anglican faith

Yet, Froude also privileged the most ancient expressions of doctrine which brought him, many years before Newman ever reached that stage, to wonder whether 'ancient Catholic thought' was embodied in the 39 Articles and in the formularies of the Church of England and to try and assess their authority. He wrote to Newman on 17th November 1833: 'I should be content to waive the Articles, keeping the Creeds'.[9] And, a few months later, in another letter dated 8th April, he told him how he had overcome his perplexity:

> I got over my scruples about the Articles by considering the preface to them in which it is said that we are to understand them in their grammatical sense; which I interpret into a permission to think nothing of their framers.[10]

By which he meant understanding the Articles literally without taking into account their framers' opinions. In the sharp formula we quoted just before, a formula that was apt to scandalise many a churchman, Froude was appealing to the creeds of the apostolic and patristic faith and, more generally, to the writings of ancient Christianity to give the Articles a Catholic interpretation. Moreover, he remembered that a similar interpretation had been given in the XVIIth century by the franciscan Francis Sancta Clara — who was not a jesuit as Froude thought — ; he wrote to Newman on 4th March 1835:

> It occurred to me the other day that one might send a Latin petition to the Pope confessing one's interpretation of the 39 Articles (which by the by the jesuit Francis Sancta Clara showed to be 'patient if not ambitious of a Catholic meaning'), and apparently Laud did not think the interpretation 'overstretched'.[11]

By this appeal to christian antiquity as a proponent of a Catholic interpretation of the 39 Articles, Froude was not really keeping company with Newman, he was actually ahead of him. For, appealing to the creeds of the Christian faith to interpret the Articles was using the argument from antiquity; appealing to the Fathers was using the argument from Tradition; suggesting a Catholic interpretation of the Articles was anticipating on Newman's Tract 90.

Froude and the role of Tradition

Actually it was on the authority of Christian antiquity in matters of doctrine and on the role of Tradition that Froude was to embarrass Newman when, at his friend's request he was associated to the controversy he had taken up with the French priest, Abbé Jean-Nicholas Jager. The occasion offered Newman the opportunity to expound the main lines of the *Via Media* which, for him, represented Anglicanism standing between Roman Catholicism and Continental Protestantism: the only Rule of faith is the Holy Scriptures for in them are all the fundamental doctrines — by this he meant all the doctrines necessary to

salvation as also to communion in the Church — Scriptures as interpreted by Tradition which, in this respect, only has a subordinate role
to the Scriptures. Beside these doctrines, there are others that have
come to us through Tradition alone which is the reason why they are
called non-fundamental doctrines or articles of religion the Churches
have promulgated throughout their history. Non-fundamental doctrines are not part of the Rule of faith, but accepting them is a godly
attitude; they are not necessary to be received into the Church but
they are a privilege the christian enjoys once he is received. The fundamental doctrines are the common ground of the Churches for they
expressed their common faith before they divided up into branches,
the Roman Catholic, the Orthodox and the Anglican: they are the
expression of primitive faith. The Protestants have tended, Newman
adds, to deviate from primitive faith by dropping or forgetting some
of those doctrines; while the Roman Catholics tend to add new doctrines unduly and to impose them on the faithful, on an equal footing
with the former. Such distinction between two types of doctrines was
of capital importance in the system Newman held at the time for, as
the Abbé Jager observed, if ever it were challenged or forsaken, the
whole system was threatened.

When Newman invited Froude to give his opinion on the controversy that opposed him to the French priest, he rather took sides
with the Abbé. For Froude criticised two major stays of the system:
the insufficient part ascribed to Tradition and the notion of fundamental doctrines. Although he was keeping to the Anglican view of
the *Via Media* according to which Christian antiquity represented
the authority in matters of doctrine, Froude intervened in his appreciation of that period over which Newman thought his church was
immune from criticism. Those 'Roman corruptions' Newman had
denounced did not affect him: he struck, in his own way, at the
very principle of Newman's thought which, according to him, was
merely a truncated version of the Protestant principle of the sufficiency of Scripture. He wrote to his friend on 2nd July 1835:

> Your trumpery principle about 'Scripture being the sole rule of
> faith in fundamentals' (I nauseate the word) is but a muti-
> lated edition, without the breadth and axiomatic character of
> the original.[12]

His criticism of the *Sola Scriptura* principle is clear; he doesn't
spare the principle of fundamental doctrines as distinct from non-
fundamental ones either — 'I nauseate the word' —. Moreover
Froude insisted on the role Newman ascribed to Tradition in

christian antiquity, yet he observed he didn't allow it the same role to interpret all doctrines; on 3rd September he wrote to him:

> Of course if the Fathers maintain that 'nothing not deducible from the Scriptures ought to be insisted on as terms of communion', I have nothing more to say. But again if you allow Tradition an interpretative authority, I cannot see what is gained. For surely the doctrine of the Priesthood and the Eucharist may be proved by Scripture interpreted by Tradition; and if so, what is to hinder our insisting on them as terms of communion? [. . .] Also you lug in the Apostles' Creed a talk about expansions? Will not the Rs [Romanists] say that their whole system is an expansion of 'the H.C.C. [Holy Catholic Church] and the communion of Saints?' Also what are the Nicene and the Athanasian Creeds but expansions? Also to wh. [which] class of Tradition do you refer the Athanasian C. [Creed]? For I suppose you admit that it carries in its different forms the assertion of its fundamentality. In short why treat a subject of great perplexity and deep and general interest on a narrow and unsufficient ground?[13]

So that Froude was clearly showing the role of Tradition as the authorised interpreter of Scripture since the beginnings of christianity. At the time when the two friends were sharing their ideas in the correspondence they regularly kept up — Froude was then far away from Oxford — their positions as to the authority of christian authority was the same, as was, with little 'nuances', their positions on the role of Tradition as interpreter of Scripture. But their viewpoints were different: Froude wished to know — as Newman a few years later — whether 'ancient catholic truth' were really part of the Articles of Anglican faith, and beyond, of the Church of England, no matter if his quest were to lead him, or lead his church, nearer to that of Rome, nor if taking antiquity as the authority would turn to the advantage of the Roman Catholics. He did not deny that his Church should get closer to Rome which had preserved the apostolical succession uninterrupted. As to Newman, the confidence he had then in the *Via Media* was unshakeable; purity of doctrine was to be preferred to apostolic continuity: hence it was useless to take the Roman Church into account since it had added to ancient doctrine, thereby forfeiting doctrinal purity. One might as well say that Newman was still keeping to the Protestant cast of mind, the latter referring to the Bible only as the source of authority while Newman added to the Bible the Church of the first centuries. And this in spite of Froude's hint: 'Also you lug in the Apostles'

Creed a talk about expansions? Will not the Rs say that their whole system is an expansion of the H.C.C. . . .'.

Froude and Newman agreed in their common concern for doctrinal continuity, in other words they prized conformity to origins. This was Newman's guiding concern while he was devising the *Via Media*, the starting point and deepest burden of which was the will to remain faithful to Christian antiquity: a quality which he considered to be the distinctive characteristic of his Church as opposed to the Roman Catholic Church who, according to him, had added new doctrines to the primitive creed. Conformity to ancient Christianity was the argument of the Anglican Church while the argument of the Church of Rome was universality, as he clearly states in an article he wrote in the March and April 1836 issues of the *British Magazine* under the title 'Home Thoughts Abroad',[14] which embodied the discussions and reflections Newman and Froude had during their Mediterranean voyage and in Rome. This conformity to origins was primarily a reflection over the relationship between Scripture and Tradition, as the controversy with the Abbé Jager as well as the debate upheld against the other side — those who kept to the principle of Scripture as sole Rule of faith — evidence. Newman considered that the revealed trust was indeed in a text, but that it consisted in a series of truths, a doctrine, and in a text as well as in the meaning of that text. Even when considering this truth as it had been transmitted as entirely objective and distinct from the Church, as Christ on the Cross or Christ risen from the dead, with the Church being present yet relegated to the background — to use the image he had developed in a review of William Palmer's treatise on the Church[15] — it represented a teaching, not merely a combination of words or a written text. This truth was a message and a thought that had been committed to writing, for the most part, and hence were to be used as guidelines to the ideas and practices that informed the life of the christian.

In his controversy with the Abbé Jager and in his *Lectures on the Prophetical Office of the Church* which are his most important contributions to the elaboration of the *Via Media*, Newman had moved from the distinction, commonly admitted in Anglicanism, between fundamental and non-fundamental doctrines to the less rigid and more practical one between an episcopal and a prophetic tradition. By episcopal tradition he meant the mere transmission of creeds through the Apostolical succession. Prophetic tradition, on the other hand, was the presentation and the exposition of those doctrines, an office performed by teachers, preachers, theologians and catechists: it was based on Scripture and Tradition as its foundation but it went beyond them to systematise, interpret and adapt them to the times. In short, it was the exposition of episcopal tradition at a given period as applied to a given public. This is the reason why some of its components could well become obsolete or even corrupt; it could change whereas Scripture and Episcopal tradition were immutably set and were transmitted unchanged.

Such distinction between two traditions allowed Newman to get closer to the actual life of the Church than the distinction between fundamental and non-fundamental doctrines permitted, yet it by no means resolved the difficulty since the difference between the two traditions was very important. For, if prophetic tradition was quite elastic and open to adaptations, episcopal tradition remained immutable in its contents; the commentaries prophetic tradition made of it could by no means cause it to evolve for it was actually impossible to add them up, they did not represent together a progressive understanding of doctrine. Of course, they provided a new and better adapted way of understanding episcopal tradition, yet they could be forgotten or set aside without any loss incurred since they neither added new riches to the fundamentals, nor provided the disclosure of anything essential. Newman found himself pressed by his opponents on both sides: those who blamed him for not allowing Tradition enough scope, such as the Abbé Jager and Froude, and those who denied Tradition any value whatsoever, as Renn Dickson Hampden, an Oriel College noetic, had done in a booklet which narrated the imaginary debate between a Unitarian and an Anglican. In the article he wrote to answer him, Newman sums up Hampden's position in this way:

> There is no such thing as a succession of preaching and hearing [...]. Tradition, he [Hampden] says, is nothing more than expositions of Scripture, reasoned out by the Church, and embodied in a code of doctrine. It is but the gold and silver of inspired writers taken out in coppers.[16]

In this article, having been challenged on both sides, Newman was modifying his idea of Tradition: he admitted its unity and its authoritative role as interpreter of Scripture. His new position is summed up clearly enough in the following passage:

> But as Anglicans, we maintain that it [Scripture] is not its own interpreter, and that, as an historical fact, it has ever been furnished for individuals with an interpreter which is external to

its reader and infallible; that is, with an ecclesiastical Tradition, derived in the first instance from the Apostles — a Tradition illuminating Scripture and protecting it —; moreover that this Tradition, and not Scripture itself, is our immediate and practical authority for much high doctrines as these friends discuss. To attempt to prove against adversaries our Lord's Divinity and Incarnation by Scripture without Tradition, seems to me a mistake as great as that of attempting to speak a living language by studying its classics, or to ascertain physical facts by pure mathematics without experiment or observation.[17]

Now Newman's position was the outcome of both Froude's observations and the Abbé Jager's criticisms, as well as a reaction to Hampden's radically antagonistic position. All of Froude's comments tended to one object, underlining:

— First that scripture alone doesn't provide us with the contents of doctrinal truths, in the same way as the mere sight of the starry skies cannot disclose to an observer ignorant of Newton's discoveries the secrets of celestial mechanics: one is in need of an interpreter in the former case as of a scientist in the latter. This is precisely what he was telling Newman in a letter written on 2nd July 1835:

I must say a word or two on your casual remark about the impopularity of our notions among 'Bible Christians'. Don't you think Newton's system would be impopular with 'sky astronomers', just in the same way. The phenomena of the heavens are repugnant to Newton, just in the same way as the letter of Scripture to the Church; i.e. on the assumption that they contradict every notion that they do not make self-evident; which is the basis of Bible-Christianity, and also of Protestantism.[18]

— Then that, if some doctrines appear to rest on Tradition only, such as those concerning the priesthood or the eucharist, they may be found in Scripture as interpreted by Tradition, which was what Froude had told in the 3rd September 1835 letter we quoted an extract of above.[19]

The position Newman had rached in this article written in answer to Dr. Hampden was already indicative of the idea of doctrinal development which he was to expand so much, first in his fifteenth *University Sermon*, he preached on 2nd February 1843, for the Feast of the Purification of the Blessed Virgin Mary, but which he had already written out the year before, and then in his *Essay on the Development of Christian Doctrine*. For in the

article against Hampden the notion of Tradition as a trust to which
Newman had come round, benefited from the distinction between
episcopal and prophetic traditions without suffering from its limitations and rigidity, allowed the Anglican and the Catholic views of
Tradition almost to coincide, explained in a more satisfactory way
the relationship between the Church and revealed truth and, finally,
contained the idea of doctrinal development. There again if Froude
hadn't given the very word to his friend, he at least had suggested
the reality it accounts for when, in his 3rd September 1835 letter, he
pointed out to Newman's own use of the word 'expansions' to characterise the Apostles' Creed in relation to Scripture and asked him
whether the Nicean and Athanasian Creeds could be considered as
anything but 'expansions'.

Conclusion

In an article which dates back to a number of years now since
it was published in *The Church Quarterly Review* of April and
June 1966 with the title 'Froude's Remains', Herbert Clegg, its
author, drew an assessment of Froude's theological influence on
Newman and, we may add, of Newman's influence on the Tractarian
movement. According to him, Froude brought Newman to realise
that the Reformers were not on their side, which Newman admitted
readily; he suggested to him the idea of the *Via Media* by giving him
as a model the XVIIth century English Church; he inspired him the
interpretation of the 39 Articles which was embodied in Tract 90;
in a letter to Keble, he pleaded for the true tradition the Church
of Rome had retained, which Newman was to become convinced of
later on; finally when it came to the Prayer Book, which was then
considered sacrosanct, Froude believed it was possible to get back
before the time when it was composed and retrace the traditional
books that had inspired it. He had written on this subject the 9th
and the 63rd of the *Tracts for the Times*, with the titles: 'On shortening the Church services' and 'The antiquity of existing liturgies'.[20]
Without ascribing to Froude a greater part in shaping Newman's
ideas than he really had, we may admit that, on these points, he
influenced his friend who was better prepared and better equipped
to give them their full impact and development.

Froude wished the Anglican Church to recover her Catholic character, or better still, to use the word by which the Tractarians liked
to be known: her apostolical character. For Newman, Froude represented Catholicism as it could legitimately be found within the bounds

of Anglicanism. This is the reason why he took, with Keble, the initiative of publishing their common friend's writings after he died in 1836. '*The Remains* had to be published as marking out the broad limits of Anglicanism and the differences of opinion which are allowed in it',[21] as Newman was to observe later on. It was the gist of his answer to Dr. Fausset who had preached at St. Mary's, on 20th May 1838, a sermon on the revival of popery; that was after the first two volumes of Froude's *Remains* had been published. In the next two days, Newman wrote out a 98 page answer in which he expounded the main lines of Froude's thought and refuted the accusations levelled against him. He showed that Froude had not gone beyond the limits of Anglicanism and had never been unfaithful to his church. He was especially using Froude's own argument that to interpret the Articles of Anglican faith one shouldn't take into account the opinions of those who drew them up. If ever there was a time when the Church of England was in any danger to fall into Romanism, Newman explained, it was when the Articles were promulgated. Their authors were so much aware of the fact that they left everyone a sufficient margin of freedom of thought. If today the Church wishes to limit the meaning of the Articles, she may do so; but until then, she must respect the freedom of interpretation she had allowed at the time.[22] This is where the link Newman found between the publication of Froude's *Remains and Tract 90* takes its full meaning:

As to the *Remains*, Froude had said that the Reformers had set wrong a broken leg, and it must be broken again in order to be set rightly. The *Remains* and *N° 90* were the rebreakening (or breakaway). It is a painful process: perhaps we are cross with the surgeon.[23]

Notes

1. This passage is quoted in the book by L. Imogen Guiney, *Hurrell Froude, Memoranda and comments*, London, Methuen & Co., 1904.
2. J. Anthony Froude, *Short Studies on great Subjects*, Fourth series, 'The Oxford Counter-Reformation', London, Longmans 1883, p. 170.
3. This passage is quoted in W. H. Dunn, *James Anthony Froude, a Biography*, Oxford, Clarendon Press, vol. 1, 1963, p. 18.
4. *Autobiography of Isaac Williams*, ed. by Sir George Prevost, London, Longmans 1892, p. 22–23.
5. J. H. Newman, *Apologia pro vita sua*, London, Longmans 1873 (standard edition), p. 23.
6. Ibid., p.18.
7. *Remains of the late Reverend Richard Hurrell Froude*, London, Rivington 1838, vol. I, I, p. 232–233, letter n°37.

8.　Ibid., p. 438.
9.　*Froude's Remains*, vol.I, I, p. 332, letter n°90; see also *The Letters & Diaries of J. H. Newman*, Oxford, Clarendon Press, vol. IV (1980), p. 212.
10.　Froude's *Remains*, ibid., p. 363, letter n°98; *L.&D. of J.H.N.*, ibid., p. 254.
11.　*L. & D.*, vol. V, p. 68.
12.　Froude's *Remains*, vol. I, I, P. 412–413, letter n°113; *L. & D., vol. V, p. 97–98.*
13.　Froude's *Remains*, ibid., p. 419–420, letter n°117; *L. & D.*, ibid., p. 128.
14.　Later, Newman included this article in the collection *Discussions and Arguments*, London, Longmans 1872 (standard edition), p. 1–36 with the title 'How to accomplish it'.
15.　Later, Newman included this review in his *Essays* critical and historical, Longmans 1871 (standard edition), Essay n°5 with the title 'Palmer's view of Faith and unity'.
16.　The article's original title is 'The Brothers Controversy'; Newman published it later in *Essays critical and historical*, vol. I, Essay n°3 with the title 'Apostolical Tradition'. Our quotation is found page 117 of that volume.
17.　Ibid., p. 103.
18.　Froude's *Remains*, vol. I, I, letter n°113, p. 421–423; *L. & D.*, vol. V, p. 97–98.
19.　Vide supra note 13.
20.　Later published in the *Remains*, vol. I, II, p. 375–382.
21.　Quoted in Ann Mozley, *Letters and Correspondence of John Henry Newman*, London, Longmans 1891, vol. II, p. 252.
22.　The document, 'A Letter addressed to the Reverend Godfrey Fausset on certain points of faith and practice' was published by Newman in *The Via Media of the Anglican Church*, London 1877 (standard edition), vol. II, n°6, p. 191–248.
23.　Manuscript at the Bodleian Library, Notes by Cardinal Newman on R. W. Church's account of Richard Hurrell Froude, Eng mw d 624.

Archbishop Howley and the Oxford Movement

James Garrard

Having spent five years in writing and submitting a thesis on William Howley, I feel something like an ecclesiastical door-to-door salesman in propagating further thought about him. What follows is a selection and, I hope, a distillation of some of the things I said in my thesis about Howley and the Oxford Movement. It is inevitably less complete than is desirable and where I have chosen to focus on an issue, there are usually two or three others which would have illustrated my point just as well.

As *prolegomena*, I shall talk about Howley very briefly. He was born in 1766 and was educated at Winchester and New College, Oxford. He became Domestic Chaplain to Lord Abercorn in 1792 and was elected Fellow of Winchester in 1794. After various parochial appointments he became Canon of Christ Church in 1804 and Regius Professor of Divinity in 1809. In 1813, at the age of 47, he was consecrated Bishop of London (the first man since the Restoration to be made Bishop of London without holding previously a more junior See). While at London he was involved in various controversies with Unitarians, with Jeremy Bentham and was pilloried as a blind supporter of the King against Queen Caroline in 1820. His politics were of the extreme conservative type.

Somewhat against Wellington's wishes, he was appointed Archbishop of Canterbury in 1828, at the age of 62 after the death of Charles Manners Sutton. He was adamantly opposed to the Repeal of the Test and Corporation Acts, the Emancipation of the Catholics and the first Reform Bill, for all of which (but especially opposition to the Reform Bill) he was roundly pilloried.

Howley owed everything to that style of government in both Church and State which is most conveniently characterised as *ancien regime*. He was the most successful of all those able clergy who manipulated this most intricate system of patronage. It is all the more surprising therefore that he should have embraced the cause of Church Reform in the mid-1830s, when in his late sixties, since it appeared to threaten that very system to which he owed everything.

269

No biography of him was ever published, either in the nineteenth century, when episcopal biography was a commonplace, or later. As more recent research has provided a more nuanced view of the Church of England in the eighteenth and nineteenth centuries and in particular of the 'old High Churchmen' who looked back to the Fathers and to the Caroline Divines for their inspiration, interest in Howley's 'party' has been revived and, as a consequence, interest in him as Archbishop of Canterbury during its swan-song.

Peter Nockles has attacked the distorting historiography of Tractarianism which gained currency with the widespread success of the movement in the latter part of the nineteenth and the first half of the twentieth century. The suggestion that the original Tractarians were responsible for a rekindling of the long dead flame of Catholicism within the Church of England and the characterisation of the late eighteenth and early nineteenth century Church as arid and suffering from spiritual *rigor mortis* found its most influential expression in Dean Church's *The Oxford Movement: Twelve Years 1833–1845* (1891).

Following Nockles' 'elastic' definition of the High Church has the advantage of allowing for the fact that several protagonists of the 'party' did hold differing views, notably on the correct relationship of the Church with the State. The question will arise about whether it is possible to ascribe particular strategies to the 'party' as a whole. David Newsome's *The Parting of Friends. A Study of the Wilberforces and Henry Manning* (1966) holds to a similarly loose definition of High Churchmanship and his book shows how complex were relationships both within the High Church 'party' and between the High Church and the evangelical 'party'.[1]

The two most important works to deal with the High Church in the nineteenth century, Edward Churton's *Memoir of Joshua Watson* (1861) and J. W. Burgon's *Lives of Twelve Good Men* (1888) presupposed that a 'party' could be identified. Burgon, writing of Hugh James Rose (Howley's Domestic Chaplain) identified those men of 'the old fashioned piety' who 'had retained their hold on Catholic Truth amid every discouragement.' Amongst these he listed Howley.[2] Churton refers to Howley's strong espousal of the doctrine of baptismal regeneration, noted above as a hall mark of High Church views.[3] In addition to this, W. N. Molesworth, the son of a Domestic Chaplain of Howley's, spoke in his *History of the Church of England from 1660* (1882) of the 'Canterbury party', mainly comprised of Howley's past and present Domestic Chaplains, which surrounded him during his time at Lambeth. Its members, who included Rose and Benjamin Harrison (about whom more anon), were uniformly 'old High Church'.[4] All of Howley's most senior appointments were exclusively from this 'party'. Dr Arthur Burns has shown that in this Howley was more devoted to party than many bishops, who were not always guided by such partisan considerations.[5] There is no doubt that these men exercised a remarkable monopoly over the preferment available in the Church.

Judging from the number of its adherents who held positions in the episcopate, the archidiaconate and as members of Cathedral Chapters, the High Church party was at its zenith during Howley's archiepiscopate. Howley's tenure of the See of Canterbury had seen the high point of the old High Churchmen's influence in the central counsels of the Church. Clive Dewey, whose book *The Passing of Barchester* (1991) focuses on the patronage network of W. R. Lyall, Dean of Canterbury 1845–57 and one of Howley's *protegés* has traced how quickly his lieutenants lost their influence after the Archbishop's death. After Sumner moved to Lambeth, Tait moved to London to replace Blomfield in 1856. At Canterbury, Lyall was replaced in the Deanery by the Evangelically educated Henry Alford.

Hugh James Rose's name is frequently cited to support the contention that there was much interest in matters which the later historiography of the Oxford Movement claimed as the exclusive preserve of the Tractarians.[6] Rose performed something of a liaising role between Howley as Archbishop and the Oxford leaders. Burgon attempted some kind of corrective to the more extreme claims for a Tractarian rediscovery of Catholicity.

> To read of the great Church Revival of 1833 as it presents itself to the imagination of certain writers, one would suppose that in their account the publication of the earliest of the *Tracts for the Times* had the magical effect of kindling into glory the dead embers of an all-but-extinct Church. The plain truth is that the smouldering materials for the cheerful blaze which followed the efforts made in 1832–34 had been accumulating unobserved for many years: had been the residuum of the altar-fires of a long succession of holy and earnest men.[7]

Rose's premature death was universally regarded as a disaster. William Palmer (of Worcester College, Oxford), another High Churchman who was initially involved with the Tractarians and who dropped back when they became too radical for him, thought that Rose had been the Church's best chance of peace.[8] Newman made his affection for him abundantly plain in the *Apologia*.

The Address to the Primate, 1834

The Tractarians' view of Howley was profoundly ambivalent. There were many occasions on which their reaction to him was confused. Pusey tended to be the most positive of the three leaders of the Movement towards Howley. Newman was inclined to be well disposed towards him whereas Keble was generally mistrustful. It must be re-iterated that the multiplicity of 'High Church' views could also account for some 'old High Churchmen' being dissatisfied with Howley from time to time as well. For example, after the Hadleigh Conference, William Palmer of Worcester was keen that an Association of the Friends of the Church should be established to propagate some of the principles which had been expounded at Hadleigh. As is well known, Keble and Newman shied away from such a plan. The *Address to the Primate* undertook to assist him in any measures which preserved the apostolical polity of the Church and the doc-trine of the Prayer Book and which revived primitive discipline. The collection of the seven thousand clergy signatures was, in some ways, an additional bonus. Joshua Watson also regarded the *Address* with mixed feelings. Not only did he have qualms about the Oxford school from the beginning, he was also chary of Howley, whom he suspected of having allowed far too much lay interference in the Ecclesiastical Commission. His reaction on hearing of the planned *Address* was cautious.

Yet if we follow Liddon's view of events we have a different picture of the old High Churchmen's view: he contrasted Rose and Palmer's desire for calculated and combined action with Newman, Froude and Keble's eventual claim for 'personal liberty'. The 'laboured appeals of committees from which all the sting had been extracted' did not appeal to Newman.[9] Liddon also thought that Palmer had been subjected to strong-arm tactics by H. H. Norris and his friends in London, who had forced him to abandon his support of the Tracts. Newman noted Rose, Pusey and Harrison as Tract supporters.[10] So, on this issue we see Joshua Watson, the archetypal old High Churchman, at least superficially appearing to fall on the anti-Howley side of the argument. At the same time when Newman had declared that he rejoiced to hear that Howley was on the Tractarians' side, he was also decrying the point of an *Address to the Primate* at all.[11]

Newman betrayed such ambivalence to J. W. Bowden

I wish the Archbishop had somewhat of the boldness of the old Catholic Prelates; no one can doubt he is a man of the highest principle, and would willingly die a Martyr; but if he had but the little finger of Athanasius, he would do us all the good in the world.[12]

Such varying reactions would characterise Keble, Newman and Pusey's attitude to Howley in the forthcoming years. There was a suggestion that Howley be nominated for the Chancellorship of the University of Oxford after the death of Lord Grenville in 1834, but it came to nothing and was never a practical suggestion. Its primary motive seems to have been that election would 'athanasize' Howley (a favourite concept for Newman).

The Regius Professor of Divinity, 1836

Liddon believed that 1836 was the most important year in the history of the Oxford Movement, several causes combining to make it so, but none more than the controversy surrounding Renn Dickson Hampden's appointment as Regius Professor of Divinity. Hampden's 1834 pamphlet *Observations on Religious Dissent* had caused controversy. Liddon characterised Hampden as saying that moral and theological truths were things distinct from religion and that no 'inferences' ought to be drawn from Scripture; that the language of the Creeds themselves was thus a mistake, even though they expressed only what was taught by Holy Scripture. He had called for the abolition of the subscription to the Articles by newly arriving undergraduates.

No less than the Tractarians did Howley's circle object to Hampden's new book, *Lectures on Moral Philosophy*. Rose thought the lectures were so mischievous and un-Christian that it was a public calamity that they should pass with nothing more than an anonymous review. He had watched with growing anxiety as a selection of books had come out and had not been publicly reproved for fear of exciting more interest in them than they would create on their own. If obscurity, harshness and vagueness could cause a writer to be neglected, the defence would in some degree be valid. The problem came when one who held high official station in the University published, for he did so with the apparent authority of the entire University.[13] It was all the more alarming when Edward Burton, Regius Professor of Divinity and a leading old High Churchman died in January 1836 at the age of 42.

Newman's immediate fear was that H. H. Milman, Thomas Arnold or Hampden would be appointed.[14] Burton had represented better than anyone the 'middle party'. Equally appalled at the prospect, Howley had submitted a list of names to Melbourne for consideration for appointment:

1. E. B. Pusey, Regius Professor of Hebrew
2. P. N. Shuttleworth, Warden of New College
3. C. A. Ogilvie, former Fellow of Balliol and Domestic Chaplain to Howley
4. J. H. Newman, Fellow of Oriel
5. John Keble, Fellow of Oriel
6. John Miller, fellow of Worcester
7. T. V. Short, Rector of St George's, Bloomsbury
8. C. Goddard, Archdeacon of Lincoln

Newman heard about Howley's list from Rose and told Keble of his outside chance. He wanted to ensure that Keble would not reject the offer if it came because it was given by Melbourne. Keble would not take such an appointment. Intriguingly, he neither told Keble that Pusey was Howley's first choice, nor does he appear to have corresponded with Pusey on the news. Howley was in touch with Newman over the matter. Liddon wrongly thought that Howley had agreed to the appointment and then regretted it when fully conversant with Hampden's writings. He was opposed to him from the start.[15]

Pusey attempted a last ditch appeal to Melbourne.[16] First, he stressed the importance of professors agreeing amongst themselves since opposing professors either cancel each other out, or one is crushed, or they both have small cliques of supporters and the mass of students wander aimlessly. Neither he nor Faussett, the Margaret Professor of Divinity, had any principles in common with Hampden. Many Colleges would probably ban students from attending Hampden's lectures. He might even be prohibited from preaching. While Burton was alive there had been plans to enlarge and improve theological instruction; now instead of more instruction, effectively there would only be two professors. A rumour had gone round Oxford that Melbourne had allowed the Archbishop a negative voice upon the appointment. It was all the more of a shock when Hampden's name was announced, since all knew that Howley would not suggest him.

Hampden began a correspondence with Howley, later published. He protested that his Bampton Lectures of 1832 were nothing more than a history of the technical terms of theology; his *Observations on Religious Dissent* had no other design than to include a charitable construction of the views of those who differed from the Anglican

Church. He rather weakly admitted that he might not always have been as clear in his publications as he might have been.[17] Howley gave him an unequivocal answer. He felt it no less painful than useless to enter into such a discussion. He accepted Hampden's protestations that he had no intention of impugning the vital truths of Christianity, but the question turned rather on the undoubted impression to the contrary which certain parts of his writings had made. Explanations should, if needed, be given to the University.

The Library of the Fathers

The most important literary result of the Hampden controversy was the creation of the 'Library of the Fathers'. Newman and Pusey had sketched out a general *schema* for the publication of selected writings of the 'Catholic Fathers' before communicating with Keble. Keble's attitude towards dedicating the Library to Howley was remarkable. Frederic Rogers told Newman that Keble would object to it mentioning Howley at all. Newman believed that Howley would refuse a dedication in any case.[18] Rose felt that Howley might be chary of aligning himself with the three leaders because of their high profile in the Hampden controversy.[19] This seems an extraordinary thing to say after Howley's attacks on Hampden had aligned him more closely with the Tractarians than ever before. Keble did not want to let Howley think that the Church was satisfied with him. He was even rumoured to be planning to avoid meeting Howley on his visit to Sir William Heathcote's home in Hursley.[20]

Pusey was disturbed by reports of Keble's opinion. He believed that Howley had made a good stand in the Hampden business on the theological issues alone. Rose said that he had done all that a man could and Pusey was inclined to believe him.[21] Newman left the matter to be resolved between Pusey and Keble. Keble said that Rogers' claim was mere speculation. Yet his grounds for accepting Howley were so unenthusiastic as to make the presumption entirely understandable.

I should suppose it is a proper compliment to the ABp and may make the work a little more useful. But on many accounts I should wish as little as possible to be said in the way of praise or expression of confidence. I certainly do not feel the least of *that* towards the ABp. We are told that he has remonstrated privately about H[ampden], but what public steps has he taken? What has he done that has the least tendency to warn the Church against the results of such teaching? And unless he has been belied in all the newspapers, the whole of his proceedings in Parliament about these Church Bills is only to be accounted for on the notion of his being thoroughly Erastian.

Keble wished to restrict the expression in the dedication to 'respect for his high spiritual office'. He feared the time was coming when it would be impossible personally to compliment bishops with a good conscience. By August 1838, Howley was listed as a patron of the Library, and there were seven episcopal subscribers – London, Exeter, Rochester, Chichester, Lincoln, Gloucester and Bangor. The final version of the dedication to Howley showed only minor changes from Pusey's original draft to Newman. Keble felt it most appropriate to avoid all personal compliments – both he and Newman had excised a reference to Howley's 'private graces'. Keble liked the suggestion of paying tribute to Howley's 'episcopal kindness' even though Newman thought it sounded strange.[22] Pusey pointed out that the original suggestion was Benjamin Harrison's and although those who did not value episcopacy would think it strange, it was the strongest word he could think of.[23]

The final form of the dedication read:

TO THE
MOST REVEREND FATHER IN GOD
WILLIAM
LORD ARCHBISHOP OF CANTERBURY
PRIMATE OF ALL ENGLAND
formerly Regius Professor of Divinity
in the University of Oxford

THIS LIBRARY
OF
ANCIENT BISHOPS, FATHERS, DOCTORS, MARTYRS,
CONFESSORS, OF CHRIST'S MOST
HOLY CATHOLIC CHURCH
IS
WITH HIS GRACE'S PERMISSION
RESPECTFULLY INSCRIBED
IN TOKEN OF
REVERENCE FOR HIS PERSON AND SACRED OFFICE
AND OF
GRATITUDE FOR HIS EPISCOPAL KINDNESS

Harrison, Howley, Bishop Bagot and Froude's *Remains*

Benjamin Harrison's appointment as Chaplain to the Archbishop was greeted with astonishment and delight by the Tractarian leaders. As Pusey's assistant lecturer in Hebrew he was closely associated with them, at least in public perception. Howley was keen to replace C. A. Ogilvie (later the first Regius Professor of Pastoral Theology) with another definite High Churchman and Harrison fitted his needs well. Harrison regretted the enforced absence but told Gladstone in Pusey's words that 'the invisible bond remains'.[24]

Harrison told Newman and Pusey that Howley had said that the position would give a person so disposed, a considerable insight and influence in what was going on regarding the Church and its operations 'which were daily becoming more and more important and extensive.' The Archbishop had expressed his high regard for 'the Oxford Divines' and how he fully understood that he would be generally regarded as giving them his unqualified sanction by the appointment. Howley paid fulsome tribute to Pusey, Keble and Newman by name whilst holding that some opinions had already been carried too far and feared that certain practices, like the wearing of crosses 'would be apt to be regarded by uninstructed persons as an approach to Popery'. The worst thing that the Oxford school had done was to publish Hurrell Froude's *Remains*; Howley's own view of the necessity of calling man's attention to neglected truths was one which did not conform to Froude's dramatic presentation.

Howley's primary grounds for regretting the publication was the leverage it gave 'to parties of whose designs and motives he highly disapproved'. To counter this, Howley himself mentioned how difficult it was to know oneself and to draw the line between moderation and lukewarmness and that a person might seem lukewarm where he would desire to guard anxiously against it. Nonetheless Howley could not accept that everything enjoined in antiquity was necessary to be observed to the letter in the present day, hinting that some of the fuss about the neglecting of fasting and the stated times of prayer by the Tractarians was rather affected.

Howley had asked for no confession of faith on Harrison's part but had wished to make it clear where he differed from the views of those with whom Harrison was identified; so that he would not be understood, by making the appointment, to be expressing an unqualified approbation of their whole system. This sits curiously with his happy acceptance of the confusion that the appointment would make publicly.[25] Pusey was thrilled by the appointment and urged immediate acceptance but was aware of the division of loyalties which Harrison might face.

> I suppose, that you will feel that you will have a good deal of tri-al . . . the very amiableness of the Archbishop's character would render it naturally the more difficult to hold a line different from him, whose firm character, age, and station you are bound to, and must, respect.

Pusey welcomed the publication of the *Remains*, thinking that they might well be a check but that might be very good for the Movement, preventing a too rapid and weakening growth. Pusey later admitted to Newman that he had not known how he was thinking of the Reformers, since he never read the 'Preface' to the *Remains*, which was Keble's work in any case.[26] Keble was delighted by the news, thinking Harrison less likely to be corrupted than almost any one whom Howley might have chosen. The appointment would bring much comfort to Rose.[27]

Pusey was caused considerable embarrassment three years later when he confided to Lord Morpeth that he considered that the Tractarians were teaching nothing new and were regarded by the older men whose warfare was over as taking up the same ground, and that he knew no difference between his own view and Harrison's. Morpeth took this to mean that bishops and their chaplains were in acquiescence with the Tractarians, and broadcast the news. Pusey reassured Harrison that he had laid no undue stress on Howley's name, insisting that he had in no way implied that Howley sanctioned the details of the Tracts when he appointed Harrison his chaplain. Nevertheless, the damage was done.[28]

Liddon's comments on Harrison's later attitude to the Tractarians sums up how quickly the 'invisible bond' was dissolved and how betrayed they felt.

> It can hardly be added that Pusey's sanguine anticipation of the results of his appointment at Lambeth were realized. Perhaps no one could have realized them: certainly Harrison did not. The traditional caution of Lambeth was too much for him: his tone became gradually more official and less sympathetic; he was, as years went on, less the friend of the Movement than its critic. Pusey felt the change deeply . . . although they remained on terms of affectionate friendship . . . (he) always referred in later years to the move to Lambeth as an 'unfortunate experiment'.[29]

F. E. Paget, former Chaplain to Bishop Bagot of Oxford wrote in 1879 to Bishop Robert Eden, Primus of the Scottish Episcopal Church.

In those days there were no recalcitrant Bishops. A word from Lambeth was taken as a command – and no doubt was often a relief from responsibility, and did not necessarily imply weakness on the yielding Bishop's part.

A MS. addition to the transcription, perhaps by W. J. Copeland, quotes Joshua Watson: 'you must make allowance for Lambeth "atmosphere"'. Paget believed that Bagot's intense humility, his conviction that he was not worthy to loosen Pusey or Newman's shoe-strings, had saved him from shipwreck. Bagot had been adamant that he would not move from the deanery of Canterbury when offered Oxford by Wellington. Howley and Wellington were both keen in urging him to accept. Howley had assured him that the diocese would never give him trouble.

Howley had been only one of many churchmen horrified by the publication of Hurrell Froude's *Remains* in 1838 after his untimely death. So extreme had some of his views been that the loyal High Churchman Edward Churton told Pusey that he would rather have lost his right hand than see whole sentences and pages of the volumes pulbished.[30] Newman and Keble were clear about the effect that publication would have; Copeland thought Pusey only swallowed the publication with a gulp as an act of homage to Newman.[31] Nothing caused greater offence in the *Remains* than disparaging comments about the English Reformers.

Really I hate the Reformation more and more, have almost made up my mind that the rationalist spirit they set afloat is the *pseudoprophetes* of the Revelation.[32]

Bagot believed that it would have been invaluable (a term he stressed several times to Pusey) for the Tractarians if they had subscribed to the Memorial.[33] Pusey suggested that he could subscribe if it were made clear that Bagot had enjoined it, 'Dr Pusey by the Bp of Oxford'. Howley agreed with Bagot's view that any degree of support for the memorial which contained such a formula would be unsatisfactory both to Bagot and to Pusey and would do neither of them any good. If Pusey could not subscribe in the normal way to the Memorial, Bagot urged him to make a declaration of his attachment to the Reformed Church to stop the accusations of his hostility to the Reformation. Howley had previously written to Bagot that the editors of the *Remains* should take the opportunity of declaring that they were not hostile to the Reformation since the greatest part of the benefit that derived from their talent, learning and industry would otherwise in all probability be lost to the Church. He acquitted them entirely of the charge.[34]

Pusey's fears were that the English Reformers were so mixed up with the Continental Reformers that they might well have strayed from the doctrines of the Primitive Church. He told Harrison: 'I cannot feel assured that those who put the Reformers to death, were not intending to suppress what was really erroneous.' The errors of the foreign reformers seemed to him far greater than those of the Romanists.[35] Harrison felt that Bishop Bull's writings were authority enough to describe the bishops of Queen Mary's time as 'Martyrs'. Bull was well enough aware of the evils of ultra-Protestantism for him to be a reliable guide.[36]

Howley was very keen on Pusey's plan of building in the parish of St. Ebbe's for the destitute population. Secondary motives were to set the Tractarians straight with the country and pave the way for right principles and third to protect friends in the country in a state of perplexity whether to subscribe or not. Pusey wanted a fine church to make a good impression and had proposed that the sum of 10,000 be raised.[37] As early as October 1838 Edward Churton had talked of making the Church a 'little cathedral with cenotaphs'.[38] The Committee in charge of the Memorial rejected Pusey's proposals wholesale. The Bricknell Papers in Pusey House Library contain an extraordinary proposal for a Church to relieve St. Ebbe's which would have entailed removing St. Mary Magdalen Church to the site originally proposed for the monumental Church in St. Ebbe's and building the latter on the site of the former.[39]

The ever widening chasm between the Tractarians and the increasingly cautious Harrison and Pusey's uncomfortable connections with both camps are well illustrated by Harrison's advice on the same matter. He encouraged Pusey to publish a brief description of Catholic views, summarising the lines which separated Romanism from Catholicism. Harrison was not at all surprised that the Memorial Committee refused to change its purpose from a Memorial of the Martyrs who died in Oxford to a Memorial of the blessings of the Reformation.

The final scheme, which involved the Memorial built in St. Giles' and the addition of the Martyrs' aisle to the untransported Church of St. Mary Magdalen, had an inscription unequivocal in its message

TO.THE.GLORY.OF.GOD
AND.IN.GRATEFUL.COMMEMORATION
OF.HIS.SERVANTS
THOMAS.CRANMER
NICHOLAS.RIDLEY
HUGH.LATIMER
PRELATES.OF.THE.CHURCH
OF.ENGLAND
WHO.NEAR.THIS.SPOT
YIELDED.THEIR.BODIES
TO.BE.BURNED
BEARING.WITNESS
TO.THE.SACRED.TRUTH
WHICH.THEY.HAD
AFFIRMED.AND.MAINTAINED
AGAINST.THE.ERRORS
OF.THE.CHURCH.OF.ROME
AND.REJOICING.THAT
TO.THEM.IT.WAS.GIVEN
NOT.ONLY.TO.BELIEVE.IN.CHRIST
BUT.ALSO.TO.SUFFER.FOR.HIS.SAKE
THIS.MONUMENT.WAS.ERECTED
BY.PUBLIC.SUBSCRIPTION
IN.THE.YEAR.OF.OUR.LORD.GOD
MDCCCXLI

Tract 90

Tract 90 was either the rankest sophistry or a honest attempt for a Catholic to remain an Anglican. To whichever of these views one subscribed, it was probably most painful for High Churchmen like Howley who had expended considerable efforts to affirm the views of the Tractarians as a valid, although perhaps excessive, perspective on Anglicanism. They were presented with a document that would be read widely (*pace* Newman's genuine hopes) as an attack on Anglicanism and all it stood for.[40]

Bagot realized that *Tract 90*, if left unexplained, would be a fatal blow to the promotion of Church principles though the *Tracts*. This he deeply regretted since it would destroy the influence which was gradually leavening the church from within. He knew that the extreme Low Church party would be the beneficiary by it and that Romanism, as distinct from and opposed to 'Catholic truth', would be promoted by the refusal of a *clear* and *hearty* explanation. He was specially concerned that, at a time when the Church of England was seeking friendly communion with the Churches of the East, and founding branches in the Colonies, unity among her members and an unsuspected doctrine were particularly important. Both these considerations were, of course, very close to Howley's heart as well.[41] Bagot and Howley kept in very close touch and Bagot passed on Howley's advice, often unacknowledged and *verbatim* in his letters to Pusey and Newman.

Benjamin Harrison wrote to Thomas Gaisford, Dean of Christ Church, to report that Howley was very unwilling to take any public part in the matter and that he was adamant that any action by University Convocation would be disastrous. Howley thought that it would inevitably lead to 'a general agitation across the country'.[42] Howley was delighted by the resolution of the Heads of Houses of 16 March 1841 that the *Tracts* did not embody the teaching of the University of Oxford. This he thought would avoid the 'general excitement' which he had feared.[43]

Bagot wrote to Pusey with advice for Newman. He believed that the alarm in the Church could be more effectively allayed by the Tract's author than by himself or any of his brethren on the bench. What he wanted was Newman to declare certain of the most obnoxious opinions to be opposed to the *spirit* if not the *letter* of the Articles. What was required was respectful language in speaking of the formularies. Howley was opposed to Newman publishing. If anything, Newman's own expressions lessened the prospect of a *satisfactory* explanation. An *un*satisfactory explanation would do irreparable damage. Bagot appreciated what Newman had been trying to achieve and was more understanding of the attempt than Howley, who thought it mischievous.[44]

Copeland noted that the anxiety which the events caused for Bagot was evidenced by the numerous duplicate copies of letters he had made. They were doubtless sent to bishops and others for advice. Howley supported Bagot's actions over the Tract to the hilt. He agreed with the exceptions Bagot had. Peter Nockles analyses Newman's reactions to episcopal comments on *Tract 90* and concludes that his kindly words about Bagot in the *Apologia* masked a shifty account of a 'supposed' understanding between himself and the bishops. Newman certainly thought that by withdrawing *Tract 90* from sale, he would avoid censure. Pusey said the same in his *Historical Preface* to the work in 1866. Some correspondence which Nockles does not mention adds to the impression of confusion. Writing to J. D. Coleridge in 1864, Newman said that he had never defended it, but Pusey and Ward had done so — from different perspectives. He claimed to have kept silent in the belief of saving it from condemnation. He understood at the time that the undertaking was said 'from authority' though he would not divulge how he had heard this. In a note to Copeland of 1868, explaining that the sixth volume of the *Tracts* never had a dedication, he was explicit.

> Jelf came to me, on the beginning of the row . . . from Archbishop Howley to say that, if my friends would consent not to move, nothing should be done on the other side.[45]

It is difficult to find a corollary for Newman's memory of a definite deal beyond the exhortations of Howley and Bagot mentioned above. The evidence of episcopal Charges would suggest that Newman had inferred an understanding which never existed or had, at the very most, not been discouraged from believing that one existed.

In the aftermath of *Tract 90*, Howley had suggested that there be a period when the Tractarians did not publish new work nor even respond to their critics in print. This advice had been ignored. Having defended themselves thus, Howley felt it incumbent on the Tractarians to make some formal statement declaratory of their true theological position. He used the specific example of William Goode's recently published *Divine Rule of Faith and Practice*. Peter Toon describes Goode as probably the most learned Evangelical of his day in the areas of historical theology and ecclesiastical history and law. A future editor of the *Christian Observer* (1847–49), Goode's habit of taking the Tractarians on their own ground, by quoting from the Fathers and others, called in question the Tractarian understanding and Howley believed such passages would have to be answered.[46] *The Divine Rule of Faith and Practice* was an enormous undertaking of 1446 pages. Volume I was dedicated to Howley and Blomfield and systematically discussed the doctrine of the Rule of Faith; Pusey, Newman and Keble's view of 'patristical' tradition, comparing this with the view of the 'Romish Church' and a view of the authority of the Fathers' writings against Scripture. He incorporated the work of the Caroline and earlier Divines. In Volume II, Goode considered the sufficiency and fullness of Divine Revelation in Scripture, again producing *catenae* of the Fathers, Carolines and others to support his conclusions.[47]

Such examples give some indication of the range of disputes into which Howley and the Tractarians were to fall. I regret particularly not discussing the furore over the Anglo-Prussian Bishopric at Jerusalem since that issue also sharpened divisions between what Froude described as the Ys (the Apostolicals) and the Zs, the old high churchmen. Had I further space I would have ventured some remarks on Howley's handling of the beginning of the ritualist controversies which were so to dog the next sixty years. Howley's *Letter addressed to the Clergy and Laity of His Province* (1845) was published when he was 79 and already frail, three years before his death.

Only with the benefit of hindsight does it become clear how closely Howley was involved in the immediate situation of dealing with the Tractarians in Oxford. The advice which Bagot followed slavishly, even to the point of the direct and unattributed transcription of it into correspondence with Pusey and others, can only be assessed at some distance of time. Some polemical Tractarian judgments were inevitably partial; yet they have retained their sting. I conclude by commenting that it was precisely because so many of the Tractarians' aims were close to Howley's own heart that the conflict opposing him to them erupted: their strategies for achieving the same ends were very different.

Notes

1. David Newsome, *The Parting of friends. A Study of the Wilberforces and Henry Manning*, London, 1966, esp. p. 318
2. J. W. Burgon, *Lives of Twelve Good Men*, London, 1888, I, pp. 154–55
3. Edward Churton (ed), *Memoir of Joshua Watson*, London, 1861, II, p. 279.
4. W. N. Molesworth, *History of the Church of England from 1660*, London, 1882, p. 313.
5. R. A. Burns, *The Diocesan Revival in the Church of England c 1825 – c 1865*, unpubl. Oxford D.Phil. thesis, 1990, p. 63
6. Peter Nockles discusses the historiography of the Oxford Movement in the introduction to *The Oxford Movement in Context, Continuity and Change in Anglican High Churchmanship, 1792–1850*, Cambridge 1994.
    Yngve Brilioth, *The Anglican Revival. Studies in the Oxford Movement*, London, 1925 and J. H. Overton, *The English Church in the Nineteenth Century (1800–1833)*, London, 1894, pp. 24–50 are earlier examples of discussion of the differences between the 'High Church' and the Tractarians in some detail.
7. J. W. Burgon, *Lives of Twelve Good Men*, London, 1888, I, p. 153–54
8. *Ibid*, I, p. 161.
9. H. P. Liddon, *Life of Edward Bouverie Pusey*, 3rd ed, 1893, I, p. 269
10. 'Fragmentary Diary', 6 December 1833 in Ian Ker *et al.* (eds), *The Letters and Diaries of John Henry Newman*, Oxford, 1980, IV, p. 11 [hereafter *LD*]
11. Newman to H. A. Woodgate, 7 August 1833 in *LD*, IV, p. 27.
12. Newman to Bowden, 31 August 1833 in *LD*, IV, p. 33.
13. Rose to Newman, [1 January 1836], Pusey House Archives, Pusey MS [hereafter *PH*].
14. Newman to Henry Wilberforce, 21 January 1836 in *LD*, V, p. 209.
15. H. P. Liddon, *op cit*, I, p. 370.

16. Pusey to Melbourne, 22 February 1836, Melbourne Ps, Bodleian Library, [Microfilm of Royal Archives collection], Box 79, f 28.
17. [Copy] Hampden to Howley, 27 February 1836, Melbourne Ps, Box 79, f 32.
18. Newman to Keble, [22 September 1836] in *LD*, V, 1984, p. 359.
19. Pusey to Newman, 3/9 October 1836, *PH*, Pusey MS.
20. Newman to Pusey, 23 September 1836, *PF*, Pusey MS.
21. Pusey to Newman, 23 September 1836, *PH*, Pusey MS.
22. Keble to Pusey, 2 October 1838, *PH*, Pusey MS.
    Keble to Pusey, 6/8 October 1838, *PH*, Pusey MS.
23. Pusey to Newman, 19th Sunday after Trinity, 1838, *PH*, Pusey MS.
24. Harrison to Gladstone, 29 August 1838, British Library, Add MS 44204 f 92.
25. Harrison to Pusey, 11 August 1838, *PH*, Pusey MS.
26. Pusey to Harrison, [13 August 1838], *PH*, Pusey MS.
    Pusey to Newman, 9 August 1841, *PH*, Pusey MS.
    Newman to Pusey, 13 August 1841, *PH*, Pusey MS.
27. Keble to Newman, 23 August 1838, Keble College Library, Keble MS.
28. Pusey to Harrison, 14 March 1841, *PH*, Pusey MS
29. *Liddon*, II, pp 45–46
30. Piers Brendon, *Hurrell Froude and the Oxford Movement*, London, 1974, p. 180
31. *Ibid*, p. 187.
32. [R. H. Froude], *Remains of the late Reverend Richard Hurrell Froude, M.A.*, Oxford 1838, Part One, Vol. I, p. 389.
33. Richard Mead, *Richard Bagot, Bishop of Oxford and the Oxford Movement, 1833–1845*, Univ. of Oxford unpubl. B.Litt. thesis, p. 62 f.
34. Bagot to Pusey, 18 January 1839, *PH*, Pusey MS.
35. Pusey to Harrison, 15 January 1839, *PH*, Pusey MS.
36. Harrison to Pusey, 16 January 1839, *PH*, Pusey MS.
37. Pusey to Keble, 24 January 1839, *PH*, Pusey MS.
38. Pusey to Newman, 23 October 1838, *PH*, Pusey MS.
39. 'Monument to Cranmer, Ridley and Latimer', *PH*, Bricknell MS.
40. R. Mead, *op cit*, pp. 94–110.
41. 'Memorandum', March 1841, *PH*, Pusey MS.
42. Harrison to Thomas Gaisford, 15 March 1841, Bodleian Library, Oxford University Archives, NW 21.5, no. 54.
43. Harrison to Gaisford, 17 March 1841, Bodleian Library, Oxford University Archives, NW 21.5, no. 56.
44. Bagot to Pusey, 17 March 1841, *PH*, Pusey MS
45. Newman to J. D. Coleridge, 16 October 1864, *LD*, XXI, 1971, p. 262. For this question see Peter Nockles, op. cit., pages 294–298 [Editor's addition.]
46. Peter Toon, *Evangelical Theology 1833–1856: A response to Tractarianism*, London, 1979, p. 6.
47. William Goode, *The Divine Rule of Faith and Practice*, 2 vols, London, 1842.

Newman and Wiseman in the days of the Oxford Movement

Paul Asveld

Over the period covered by the present paper, Newman met Wiseman only once, in Rome, in April 1833. The correspondence between the two men is practically unexistent during those years. Yet Newman is often mentioned in Wiseman's letters of the period as well as Wiseman in Newman's. But their contacts were most important, much more than the reader of the *Apologia* may infer, when they began to review each other's publications, the 'juris publici', those that pertained to the literary genre of polemical writings.

To our knowledge no important study on this theme, using the primary sources, has ever been done so far. Similarly, during the special occasions that celebrated the hundred and fiftieth anniversary of the Oxford movement, one important aspect was all but neglected, i.e. the political aspect. In this short essay on the relations between those two men in the days of the Oxford Movement, we would underline this aspect among others.

I − The first contacts

1 − The details of the long talk Hurrell Froude and Newman had with Mgr. Wiseman at the English College during the Holy week of 1833 are too well known to need to be recalled here. Newman tells us in the *Apologia* how he had taken leave of Wiseman as his anxiety over the political and religious developments in England since the advent of the liberal party was growing:

> When we took leave of Monsignore Wiseman, he had courteously expressed a wish that we might make a second visit to Rome; I said with gravity, 'We have a work to do in England'.[1]

The incidents of the return journey are well known. Taken ill with a malignant fever in Sicily, Newman had spent several days between life and death. He saw in it a divine punishment, but he knew he would not die for an important struggle was awaiting him in England. He resumed his journey as soon as he could and composed, as we know, the famous poem known as 'Lead, Kindly Light'[2] as his ship was being detained in the straits of Bonifacio for a whole week. But what is less known is that he composed a short poem on France called 'Apostasy' as he was off Marseille on 26th June. The first stanza begins with the words: 'France! I will think of thee as what thou wast'; the second with the words: 'France! I dare not think of thee as what thou art'; and the poem ends as follows: 'And so in silence I will now proclaim, hate of thy present self, and scarce will be thy name'.[3]

From Lyon he had hurried towards England, taking hardly any sleep over the seven days the journey lasted and reached Oxford on 1st July. Later on, in the *Apologia*, he would recall this journey in the following words:

> It was the success of the Liberal cause which fretted me inwardly. I became fierce against its instruments and manifestations. A French vessel was at Algiers; I would not even look at the tricolor. On my return, though forced to stop twenty four hours at Paris, I kept indoors the whole time, and all that I saw of that beautiful city was what I saw from the Diligence.[4]

One of Newman's and his Oxford friends' 'bête noire' then was undoubtedly the religious policies of the liberal government that had come to office in the early 1830s, suppressing Anglican bishoprics in Ireland and taking steps to remove the monopoly the established Church enjoyed in the universities. A. D. Culler very well studied this aspect of the Oxford Movement. Let us not forget the starting signal of the movement was, to a large extent, the celebrated Assize Sermon Keble delivered on 14th July 1833 on 'National Apostasy'.[5]

2 – Wiseman took a vivid interest in the Oxford Movement since its very outset. As far as its literary production is concerned, he first mentioned it in the famous conferences he gave in London in 1835 and 1836 on the nature of Catholicism. Newman is described as a learned Oxford theologian who had written a very valuable book on Arianism, as Möhler had in Germany. The conferences were mainly devoted to the discussions between Catholics and Protestants over the 'Regula Fidei' and they were published straight away with the title: *Lectures on the principal Doctrines and Practices of the Catholic Church*, 2 volumes, 1836.

Newman mentioned the book several times in his correspondence and he devoted a long review to it in *The British Critic* of October 1836, pages 373–403. As all articles in the periodical, this review was anonymous. Newman bitterly blamed Wiseman for having based his theory on the opposition between Roman Catholicism and Ultra-Protestantism, entirely neglecting the 'Via Media Anglicana'.

Wiseman wasn't long replying in *The Dublin Review*, the new catholic quarterly he had helped create in that very year 1836 on the model of *The British Critic*. In a long review, published in volume 3, 1837, pages 43–79 under the title: 'The High Church Principle of Dogmatic Authority', he availed himself of Newman's article and of a sermon by Keble to return to his exposition of the 'Regula Fidei', arguing that the theory of the 'High Church Divines' was, in the first place, at best a particular theory within the Church of England, and then that it didn't hold together. As in *The British Critic*, the main articles in *The Dublin Review* remained anonymous and respected the anonymity of the writings they reviewed.

3 – *The Dublin Review* was to play an important part in the discussions between Wiseman and the Oxford Movement's theologians. In the record of *The Letters and Diaries*, Newman alludes for the first time to the creation of the Review in a letter addressed to Thomas Dyke Acland dated 27th April 1836. He writes:

> Dr. Wiseman has just begun what he calls the *Dublin Review*, under the auspices of himself and O'Connell. Really, if one wished a plain practical direction as to one's behaviour towards Romanism, this surely would seem a sufficient one. As no one can suppose O'Connell is to *write* for the Review, it is plainly but his *name* which is put forward.[6]

In his biography of Wiseman, W. Ward informs us that he had set as a condition to his collaboration – a condition rendered necessary due to O'Connell's political activities – that no extreme political position would be expressed in the review. Wiseman himself indicated that one of the main motives that drew him to join the venture was the burning interest he had for the Oxford Movement as he felt the new quarterly would give him a possibility to follow it very closely.[7] Actually, in the very first issue that came out in May 1836, there is an anonymous article by him on 'The Oxford Controversy', i.e. on Dr. Hampden's Case.

II – The Debate over the Apostolical Succession in the Anglican Church.

1 – Newman did not fail, year after year, to republish the *Tracts for the Times* in bound volumes and Wiseman very soon began to devote to them long reviews in *The Dublin Review*.

A first review was published in the April 1838 issue, but the most notorious was undoubtedly an article in two parts which, using the title of Tract 15, attacked 'The Anglican claim of Apostolical Succession'. In the October 1838 number, Wiseman reviewed under that title the first three volumes of the Tracts, as well as the new edition of Hooker's works by Keble. In the second part of the article, published in the July 1839 issue (pages 139–180), he drew that well known parallel between the Anglicans and the Donatists.

2 – In order to understand fully how this article disturbed Newman, one must not only refer to *The Apologia* written twenty- five years after the event, but also directly to the long article in *The British Critic* of January 1840 (pages 40–88) in which Newman expressed the equilibrium he had temporarily recovered. This article took the form of a review that was, as usual, anonymous of a recent book by A. P. Perceval, *An Apology for the Doctrine of Apostolical Succession, with an Appendix on the English Orders*, 1839.

Newman's article offers us an interesting view of the theories concerning the unity of the Catholic, – i.e. the universal – Church. Concerning the question that underpins the argument of Wiseman's articles, Newman reaches the point when he must ask:

> How do we escape from the conclusion which would seem to follow, and which St. Austin especially as the spokesman of other Fathers seems to urge upon us, that the English Church is cut off from the Catholic body, a ray from the sun, a branch from the tree, a channel from the fountain?[8]

He then comes to the conclusion that Augustin's dictum cannot be taken as a first principle:

> On the whole then, it being considered that the dicta of the Fathers upon the temporal state of the Church are not to be taken as first principles, and from the happy circumstances of their times the Fathers may have been led to lay an extreme stress upon the necessity of intercommunion as a condition of churchmanship, and that the Church may possibly be intended to bear a different appearance in different ages, and to wear her bridal ornaments and

the signs of her rank, some at one time, some at another, and in consequence that branches estranged from the rest of the body, may, nevertheless be part of the body, let us proceed to show that what *may possibly* be, is *probably*, as regards the English Church.[9]

The notes of the Church are diverse, Newman declares, and the Church of England is not devoid of them. He then comments Bellarmine at length on the question of the notes and writes:

While we are on the subject we will notice another note of the Church, which Bellarmin doesn't explicitly mention, but is equal to any, *life*.[10]

In the extracts we would like to quote in relation with this theme there is fierce criticism of the practical attitude of Roman Catholics generally, and of the political alliances of English and Irish Catholics particularly:

At all times, since Christianity came into the world, an open contest has been going on between religion and irreligion and the true Church, of course, has ever been on the religious side. This then is a sure test in every age, *where* the Christian should stand [...]. Now applying this simple criterion to the public parties of this day, it is very plain that the English Church is at present on God's side, and therefore so far God's Church; we are sorry to be obliged to add that there is as little doubt on which side English Romanism is. It must be a very galling thought to serious minds who profess it to feel that they are standing with the enemies of God, co-operating with the haters of truth and haters of the light, and thereby prejudicing religious minds even against those verities which Rome continues to hold.[11]

The final considerations in the article deserve our attention. Newman writes:

Much as Roman Catholics may denounce us at present as schismatical, they could not resist us, if the Anglican communion had but that one note of the Church upon it, to which all these instances point: sanctity.[12]

The author would be delighted to set the issue of the debate on that ground. But so would, obviously, be the Roman Catholics. At this point Newman launches a fierce attack as he writes that so long as

Anglicans won't be able to see in the Roman Catholics less of the reproaches they have traditionally charged them with, among others 'less indulgence of [men's] low and carnal superstitions, less intimacy with the revolutionary spirit of the day, we will keep aloof from them as we do'.[13] Following suit, Newman describes what Anglicans dislike in the Catholic Church, first abroad in catholic countries, then at home:

> We see it associated everywhere with the low democracy, pandering to the spirit of rebellion, the lust of change, the unthankfulness of the irreligious, and the enviousness of the needy. We see its grave theologians connecting their names with men who are convicted by the common sense of mankind of something very like perjury, and its leaders in alliance with a political party notorious in the 'orbis terrarum' as a sort of standard in every place for liberalism and infidelity [. . .].[14]
> Till she ceases to be what she practically is, a union is impossible between her and England; but if she does reform (and who shall presume to say that so large a part of Christendom never can?) then it will be our Church's duty at once to join in communion with the Continental Churches, whatever politicians at home may say to it, and whatever steps the civil power may take in consequence.[15]

3 – Newman was not the only one to react to Wiseman's articles. William Palmer of Worcester College also attacked them, calling their author by his name. He devoted a whole book to them, analysing Wiseman's argument in detail. His style was harsh and muscular. It bore the title: *The Apostolical Jurisdiction and Succession of the Episcopacy in the British Churches vindicated against the Objections of Dr. Wiseman in the Dublin Review*, June 1840, 253 pages. As far as the accusation of schism is concerned he defended, contrary to Newman, the traditional Anglican thesis which turns the tables on the Roman Church accusing it of having gone into schism.[16]

III – Tract 90 and its aftermath

Tract 90 which came out on 27th February 1841 followed by the series of open letters it occasioned led Wiseman to react publicly for a very good motive.

1 – Actually Tract 90 and, even more, the letters of explanation Newman addressed to Dr. Jelf and to the Bishop of Oxford had

very harsh words about the doctrinal corruptions and practices the Roman Catholic Church was traditionally blamed for.

The first reaction of the university of Oxford to the publication of Tract 90, a protest by four tutors issued on 8th March, had these words:

> The Tract has in our apprehension a highly dangerous tendency from its suggestion that certain very important errors of the Church of Rome are not condemned by the Articles of the Church of England; for instance that those articles do not contain any condemnation of the doctrines, 1, of Purgatory; 2, of Pardons; 3, of the worship and adoration of Images and Relics; 4, of the Invocation of Saints; 5, of the Mass, as they are taught authoritatively by the Church of Rome, but only of certain absurd practices and opinions which intelligent Romanists repudiate as much as we do.[17]

Contrary to what the tutors had written Newman, in his letter to Dr. Jelf considers that:

> The Articles do contain a condemnation of the authoritative teaching of the Church of Rome on these points; I only say that, whereas they were written before the decrees of Trent, they were not directed against those decrees [. . .]. Those decrees expressed her authoritative teaching, and they will continue to express it, while she so teaches. The simple question is, whether, taken by themselves in their mere letter, they express it; whether in fact other senses, short of the sense conveyed in the present authoritative teaching of the Roman Church will not fulfil their letter, and may not even now in point of fact be held in that Church.[18]

Wiseman then published a pamphlet entitled: 'A letter respectfully addressed to the Rev. J. H. Newman, upon some passages in his letter to the Rev. Dr. Jelf, by N. Wiseman D.D., Bishop of Melipotamus'. The booklet, dated 27th March is 32 pages long.

2 – Since Newman had decided not to engage into an open debate with Wiseman, it was once more W. Palmer of Worcester who led the attack. In a few months he was able to publish no less than six open letters written in the same muscular style he had used before, a style verging on rudeness, for which Newman apologised. Wiseman only answered the first letter.

Let us just recall three titles. The letter issued on 12th April was styled: 'A letter to N. Wiseman D.D., calling himself Bishop of

Melipotamus, containing Remarks on his letter to Mr. Newman', 40 pages. Palmer meant to express in his title that he considered Wiseman an intruder who held no episcopal jurisdiction in England. Wiseman replied in late April: 'Remarks on a letter from the Rev. W. Palmer M.A., of Worcester College, Oxford, By N. Wiseman D.D., Bishop of Melipotamus', 88 pages. On 8th June: 'A fifth Letter to N. Wiseman D.D., containing a Reply to his Remarks on Letter 1, with additional Proofs of the Idolatry and Superstitions of Romanism', 91 pages.

3 – Newman eventually intervened, anonymously as usual, in the debate by means of a review for *The British Critic* of July 1841, pages 100–134. Under the general title: 'Private Judgment', he reviewed several books and among those: 'Letters 1, 2, 3, 4, 5 to Nicholas Wiseman D.D., containing Remarks on his Letter to Mr. Newman etc., by the Rev. W. Palmer M.A... .'.

(a) Among the eight works he reviewed, the first four are analyses of conversions, 'one to Protestantism, and three to Rome, differing in most points from one another; but all of them illustrating the operation of private judgement in matters of faith'.[19]

The reviewer added some 'pamphlets' or booklets the Oxford controversy had occasioned. Among those, Newman chose one writing by Pusey, two booklets by W. G. Ward and also W. Palmer's pamphlets we just noticed. Concerning the latter, Newman writes:

Mr. Palmer's booklets are eminently learned and useful compositions as is everything he writes. As to their tone, which grieved me, I cannot help passing on them a severe judgment, for these booklets are very little in keeping with his kind and amiable character, or rather, they are like a man in other respects very amiable, who feels it is his duty to show himself nasty. Nevertheless, we are happy to be able to add that in his fifth letter he has thrown his artificial trappings overboard to reveal his true character to us.[20]

(b) Within the limits of our paper, we are content to single out a point which, according to the reviewer, 'is so often felt as a difficulty by members of our Church' and upon it he wishes to enlarge in conclusion to his article. He writes:

It cannot be denied, then, that a very plausible ground of attack may be taken up against our Church from the circumstance that she is separated from the rest of Christendom [...]. We are in fact, it may be objected, cut off from the whole of the Christian world;

nay far from denying, in a certain sense we glory in that excommunication, and that under a notion that we are so very pure that it must soil our fingers to touch any other Church whatever upon the earth, in north, east or south.[21]

How should the situation of the Church of England be reconciled with St. Paul's and our Lord's announcements on the unity of the Body? Moreover:

What increases the force of this argument is, that St. Augustin seems, at least at first sight, virtually to urge it against us in his controversy with the Donatists, whom he represents as condemned, simply because separate from the 'orbis terrarum', and styles the point in question 'quaestio facillima', and calls on individual Donatists to decide it by their private judgment.[22]

Newman is far from under-estimating the force of the objection. Yet he immediately adds that when taking it in a practical view:

It can have legitimately no effect whatever in leading us from England to Rome. We do not say no legitimate tendency in itself, but no actual influence on any legitimate ground with serious men, who wish to know how their duty lies. For this reason: because if the note of schism on the one hand lies against England, an antagonist disgrace lies upon Rome, the note of idolatry.[23]

He continues, further on, along the same line:

Now whether or not what we see in the church of Rome be sufficient to warrant a religious person to leave her (a question, we repeat, about which we have no need here to concern ourselves), we certainly think it sufficient to deter him from joining her; and whatever be the perplexity and distress of his position in a communion so isolated as the English, we do not think he would mend the matter, by placing himself in a communion so superstitious as the Roman; especially considering, agreeably to a remark I have already made, that even if he be schismatical at present, he is so by the act of Providence, whereas he would be entering into superstition by his own. Thus an Anglo-Catholic is kept at a distance from Rome, if not by our own excellences, at least by her errors.[24]

Now, Newman concedes:

If Anglicans are almost unchurched by the Protestantism which has mixed itself up with their ecclesiastical proceedings, Romanists also are almost unchurched by their superstitions.[25]

Newman proceeds to borrow, page after page, from Pusey, Ward and Palmer compromising examples for the Roman Church, recent as well as ancient instances condemning its idolatrous practices. He observes:

It is then a note of the Christian Church, as decisive as any, that she is not idolatrous; and any semblance of idolatrous worship in the Church of Rome as plainly dissuades a man of Catholic feelings from her communion, as the taint of a Protestant or schismatical spirit in ours may tempt him to depart from ours. This is the Via Media which we would maintain, and thus without judging Rome on the one hand, or acquiescing in our own state on the other, we may use what we see, as a providential intimation to *us* not to quit what is bad for what may be worse, not (if so be) to mend schism with idolatry, but to learn resignation to what we inherit, nor seek to escape into a happier state by suicide.[266]

Newman wished to avoid by all means the secession of individual tractarians. So he continues:

And in such a state of things, certain though it be that St. Austin invites individual Donatists to the Church, on the simple ground that the larger body must be the true one, he is not, he cannot be, a guide to *our* conduct here. The Fathers are our teachers, but not our confessors or casuists; they are the prophets of great truths, not the spiritual directors of individuals [. . .].
We have not St. Austin to consult; we cannot go to him with his works in our hand, and ask him whether they are to be taken to the letter under our altered circumstances? We cannot explain to him that, as far as the appearance of things go, there are, besides our own, at least two Churches, one Greek the other Roman; and that they both are marked by a peculiarity which does not appear in his own times, or in his own writings, and which much resembles what Scripture condemns as idolatry [. . .].
Much more may it be maintained, without any want of reverence to so great a saint, that private letters which he wrote fourteen hundred years ago, do not take into consideration the present circumstances of Anglo-Catholics. Are we sure that had he known

them, they would not have led to an additional chapter in his *Retractationes*?

And again, if ignorance would have been an excuse, in his judgement, for the Catholic world's passing over the crime of the Traditiors, had Caecilian and his party been such, much more in so nice a question as the Roman claim to the 'orbis terrarum' at this day, in opposition to England and Greece, may we consider that he who condemned the Donatists only in the case of 'quaestio facillima', would excuse us, even if mistaken, from the notorious difficulties which lie in the way of true judgment. Nor, moreover, would he, who so constantly sends us to Scripture for the notes of the Church Catholic, condemn us for shunning communions which had been so little careful themselves from what he would have considered, after Scripture, misprision of idolatry.

But even let us suppose him, after full cognizance of our case, to give judgement against us; even then we shall have the verdict of St. Chrisostom, St. Basil, and others virtually in our favour, supporters and canonizers as they were of Meletius, Bishop of Antioch, who in St. Augustine's own day lived and died out of the communion of Rome and Alexandria.[27]

Such is the gist of Newman's answer to Wiseman in this article. Yet, he concludes it with a warning to the Anglican Church:

There is only one quarter from which a cloud can come over us, and darken and bewilder our course. If 'nefas dictus', our Church is by any formal acts rendered schismatical, while Greek and Roman idolatry remains not of the church, but in it merely, denounced by councils, though admitted by authorities of the day; if our own communion were to own itself Protestant, while foreign communions still disclaimed the superstitions of which they are too tolerant; if the profession of ancient truth were to be persecuted in our Church, and its teaching forbidden, then, doubtless, for a season, Catholic minds among us would be unable to see their way.[28]

IV – 1841–1845: Newman, Wiseman and the Romeward Movement

The article we have expounded at length was Newman's last public contribution to the controversy that had intermittently opposed him and his Oxford friends to Mgr. Wiseman over a five year period.

Newman was to meet Wiseman for the second time in his life after his conversion to Roman Catholicism, when he went to Oscott with some of his companions to be confirmed by him. For first hand information as to the relations between the two men from 1841 to 1845, one has first to look into Newman's correspondence as Ann Mozley published it or as it is preserved in the Birmingham Oratory's collections and second to consult W. Ward's biography of Wiseman.[29]

Newman kept reducing his participation in Oxford life and retired ever more completely to Littlemore, where he was trying to check among his companions the desire to convert individually to the Roman Church, for he considered such moves unappropriate and premature.

Wiseman, who had been rector of the English College in Rome from 1828 to 1840, had returned to England at that time to take up his new duties as rector of the Oscott Theological College as well as auxiliary bishop of the Central District which was part of the missionary organisation of English Catholicism in those days.

Wiseman's correspondence allows us to see how he tried to follow from Oscott the evolution of the Tractarians who had gathered round Newman. It also shows the pains he took to alter the attitude of the Catholics and their Press towards the Oxford Movement as well as his preoccupation with the political attitude of the Irish Catholics and their loyalty to the British Crown.

The sources W. Ward had at his disposal enabled him to draw a vivid description of the last months Newman spent in the Anglican Church and of the first meeting between the two men after 1833.

With Newman's conversion to Roman Catholicism, an altogether new and radically different chapter in the relations between the two men begins as well as in their relations with the Oxford Movement.

Notes

1 J. H. Newman, *Apologia pro Vita Sua*, Norton edition, page 40.
2 The poem 'The Pillar of the Cloud' was published first in the *Lyra Apostolica* and was then included in *Verses on various Occasions* in 1869, under number 79.
3 See *Verses* ... , op. cit., page 112.
4 *Apol.*, op. cit., page 39.
5 See A. D. Culler, *The Imperial Intellect*, 1955.
6 *The Letters and Diaries of J. H. Newman*, O.U.P., Volume V, page 290.
7 W. Ward, *The Life and Times of Cardinal Wiseman*, Vol. I, pages 248–249.
8 *The British Critic*, January 1840, page 67.
9 Ibid., page 72.
10 Ibid., page 76.

11 Ibid., page 79. In the chapter of the Apologia devoted to the years 1839−1841, Newman tries to explain why he used such a violent tone in his 1840 article in the *British Critic*. He also recalls the excessive rudeness he had shown 'that zealous and most charitable man, Mr. Spencer, when he came to Oxford in January 1840, to get Anglicans to set about praying for Unity' (*Apol.*, page 103). Newman refused to have dinner with him, for, he writes: 'I considered him in loco apostatae from the Anglican Church, and I hereby beg his pardon for it. I wrote afterwards with a view to apologize, but I dare say he must have thought that I made the matter worse, for these were my words to him' (ibid. pages 103−104). Why couldn't Newman join him? For the only reason, he writes:

that your acts are contrary to your words. You invite us to a union of hearts, at the same time that you are doing all you can, not to restore, not to reform, not to re-unite, but to destroy our Church. You go further than your principles require. You are leagued with our enemies [. . .] this is what we cannot understand; how christians like yourselves, with the clear view that you have that a warfare is ever waging in the world between good and evil, should in the present state of England, ally yourselves with the side of evil against the side of good [. . .]. Break off, I would say with Mr. O'Connell in Ireland and the liberal party in England, or come not to us with overtures for mutual prayer and religious sympathy'. (ibid., page 104).

12 Op. cit., page 86.
13 Ibid., page 87.
14 Ibid., pages 87−88.
15 Ibid., page 88.
16 Dr. Maguire, in the October 1837 issue of *The Dublin Review*, pages 468−525, had already given a review of A. P. Perceval's book published in 1836 with the title: *The Roman Schism, Illustrated from the Records of the Catholic Church*.
17 *The Via Media of the Anglican Church, illustrated in Lectures, Letters and Tracts, written between 1830 and 1841 by John Henry Cardinal Newman*, Vol. II, 1885, page 359.
18 Ibid., page 368.
19 The British Critic, July 1841, 'Private Judgment', page 100.
20 Ibid., page 101.
21 Ibid., page 121.
22 Ibid., page 122
23 Ibid., page 123.
24 Ibid., page 124
25 Ibid., page 131.
26 Ibid., page 132.
27 Ibid., page 132−133.
28 Ibid., page 134.
29 Cf. *Letters and Correspondence of John Henry Newman during his Life in the English Church*. Edited at Cardinal Newman's request by Ann Mozley, 2 volumes, 1891.
Correspondence of John Henry Newman with John Keble and Others . . . 1839−1845. Edited at the Birmingham Oratory, 1917.
The Life and Time of Cardinal Wiseman, by W. Ward, Volume I, 1897.

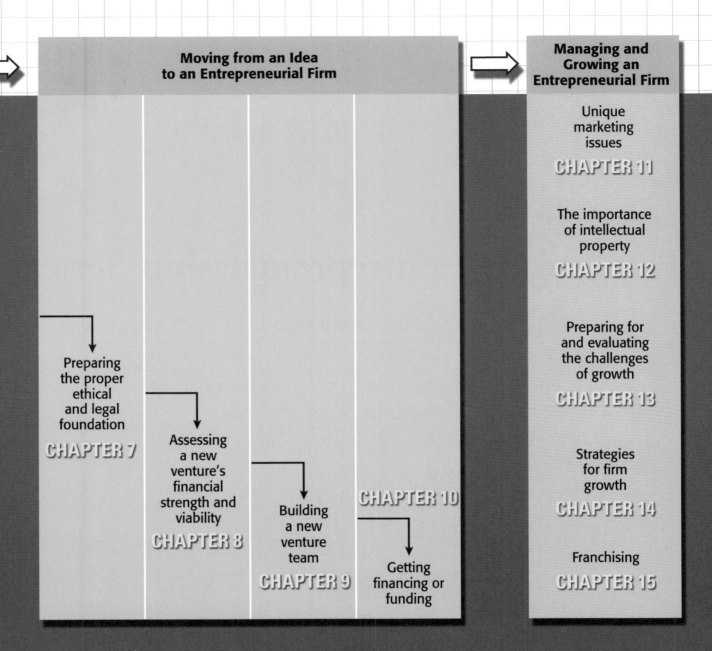

Moving from an Idea to an Entrepreneurial Firm

Preparing the proper ethical and legal foundation

CHAPTER 7

Assessing a new venture's financial strength and viability

CHAPTER 8

Building a new venture team

CHAPTER 9

CHAPTER 10

Getting financing or funding

Managing and Growing an Entrepreneurial Firm

Unique marketing issues

CHAPTER 11

The importance of intellectual property

CHAPTER 12

Preparing for and evaluating the challenges of growth

CHAPTER 13

Strategies for firm growth

CHAPTER 14

Franchising

CHAPTER 15

passion **plus**

WHERE A GREAT IDEA MEETS A GREAT PROCESS

Introducing the

Prentice Hall Entrepreneurship Series...

The Entrepreneurship series by Prentice Hall is a compilation of brief, practical, and engaging titles that focus on the latest research findings, issues, and trends that guide successful entrepreneurs today. Written by experts of selected areas of entrepreneurship, each title is perfect for covering a special topic or to enhance your textbook material.

Series Editors
R. Duane Ireland, Mays Business School, Texas A&M University
Michael H. Morris, Whitman School of Management, Syracuse University

New for 2008:
Bruce R. Barringer, *Effective Business Plans*, ISBN 0-13-231832-6

Arthur C. Brooks, *Social Entrepreneurship: A Modern Approach to Social Venture Creation*, ISBN 0-13-233076-8

Gerard George and Adam J. Bock, *Inventing Entrepreneurs: Technology Innovators and their Entrepreneurial Journey*, ISBN 0-13-157470-1

Donald F. Kuratko and Jeffrey S. Hornsby, *New Venture Management*, ISBN 0-13-613032-1

Minet Schindehutte, Leland Pitt, and Michael H. Morris, *Rethinking Marketing: The Entrepreneurial Imperative*, ISBN 0-13-239389-1

Future Titles in the Series*:
Africa Ariño, Paul M. Olk, and Jeffrey J. Reuer, *Entrepreneurial Alliances*, ISBN 0-13-615636-3

David L. Deeds, *Exploring Entrepreneurial Finance*, ISBN 0-13-157457-4

Frank Hoy and Pramodita Sharma, *Entrepreneurship & Family Businesses*, ISBN 0-13-157711-5

*After 2008, we will be publishing new titles every year

Interested?
For more information on these titles or to request an examination copy for adoption consideration, please contact your local Prentice Hall sale srepresentative, visit www.prenhall.com, or call Faculty Services at 1-800-526-0485.

Entrepreneurship
Successfully Launching New Ventures

Second Edition

Bruce R. Barringer
University of Central Florida

R. Duane Ireland
Texas A&M University

PEARSON
Prentice
Hall

Pearson Education International

If you purchased this book within the United States or Canada you should be aware that it has been wrongfully imported without the approval of the Publisher or the Author.

LEN
338.04
p84

Acquisitions Editor: Mike Ablassmeir
VP/Editorial Director: Jeff Shelstad
Product Development Manager: Ashley Santora
Project Manager: Claudia Fernandes
Editorial Assistant: Kristen Varina
Marketing Manager: Anne Howard
Marketing Assistant: Susan Osterlitz
Associate Director, Production Editorial: Judy Leale
Managing Editor: Renata Butera
Permissions Coordinator: Charles Morris
Associate Director, Manufacturing: Vinnie Scelta
Manufacturing Buyer: Arnold Vila
Design/Composition Manager: Christy Mahon

Composition Liaison: Suzanne Duda
Art Director: Steven Frim
Interior design: Atelier De Zin
Cover Photo: Shayle Keating
Cover design: Steven Frim
Director, Image Resource Center: Melinda Patelli
Manager, Rights and Permissions: Zina Arabia
Manager, Visual Research: Beth Brenzel
Image Permission Coordinator: Kathy Gavilanes
Composition/Full-Service Project Management:
GGS Book Services
Printer/Binder: Quebecor World-Dubuque
Typeface: 10/12 Times

Credits and acknowledgments borrowed from other sources and reproduced, with permission, in this textbook appear on appropriate page within the text.

Microsoft® and Windows® are registered trademarks of the Microsoft Corporation in the U.S.A. and other countries. Screen shots and icons reprinted with permission from the Microsoft Corporation. This book is not sponsored or endorsed by or affiliated with the Microsoft Corporation.

Pearson Education LTD., London
Pearson Education Australia PTY, Limited
Pearson Education Singapore, Pte. Ltd
Pearson Education North Asia Ltd
Pearson Education Canada, Inc.
Pearson Educación de Mexico, S.A. de C.V.
Pearson Education -- Japan
Pearson Education Malaysia, Pte. Ltd
Pearson Education, Upper Saddle River, New Jersey

10 9 8 7 6 5 4 3 2 1
ISBN 10: 0-13-505282-3
ISBN 13: 978-0-13-505282-2

Dedication

To my wife Jan. Thanks for your never ending encouragement
and support. Without you, this book would have never
been possible. Also, thanks to all the student entrepreneurs who
contributed to the chapter opening features in the book.
Your stories are both insightful and inspiring.

Bruce R. Barringer

To our son Scott:
We are so proud of you and your commitment to help others
learn how to visualize and then pursue their dreams.
Your strength gives all of us strength and your hopes bring
all of us hope. Always follow your hungry heart to make your
own dreams a reality, Scott. Your Mother and I love you.

R. Duane Ireland

Brief Contents

Contents

Preface

Introduction

We are truly excited about this book and the promise we believe it brings to you. The main reason for our excitement is that there has never been a more invigorating time to study entrepreneurship. Across the world, entrepreneurial ventures are creating and bringing to market new products and services that make our lives easier, enhance our productivity at work, improve our health, and entertain us in new and fascinating ways. As you will see from reading this book, entrepreneurs are some of the most passionate and inspiring people you'll ever meet. This is why successful firms have been launched in a variety of unexpected places such as garages and an array of coffee houses with wireless hot spots. Indeed, we never know the amount of success the person sitting next to us drinking coffee might achieve after launching an entrepreneurial venture!

As you might anticipate, the passion an entrepreneur has about a business idea, rather than fancy offices or other material things, is typically the number-one predictor of a new venture's success. Conversely, a lack of passion often leads to entrepreneurial failure.

The purpose of this book is to provide you, our readers and students of entrepreneurship, a thorough introduction to the entrepreneurial process. We do this because evidence suggests that it is important for entrepreneurs to thoroughly understand the entrepreneurial process. The fact that in the United States alone roughly one-third of new firms fail within the first 2 years while another 20 percent fail within 4 years of their launching is the type of evidence we have in mind. These failure rates show that while many people are motivated to start new firms, motivation alone is not enough; indeed, motivation must be coupled with good information, a solid business idea, an effective business plan, and sound execution to maximize chances for success. In this book, we discuss many examples of entrepreneurial ventures and the actions separating successful firms from unsuccessful ones.

This book provides a thoughtful, practical guide to the process of successfully launching and growing an entrepreneurial venture. To do this, we provide you with a thorough analysis of the entrepreneurial process. We model this process for you in the first chapter and then use the model's components to frame the book's remaining parts. Because of its importance, we place a special emphasis on the beginnings of the entrepreneurial process—particularly opportunity recognition and feasibility analysis. We do this because history shows that many entrepreneurial ventures struggle or fail not because the business owners weren't committed or didn't work hard, but because the idea they were pushing to bring to the marketplace wasn't the foundation for a vibrant, successful business.

How Is This Book Organized?

To explain the entrepreneurial process and the way it typically unfolds, we divide this book into four parts and 15 chapters. The four parts of the entrepreneurial process model are:

Part 1: Decision to Become an Entrepreneur

Part 2: Developing Successful Business Ideas

Part 3: Moving from an Idea to an Entrepreneurial Firm

Part 4: Managing and Growing an Entrepreneurial Firm

We believe that this sequence will make your journey towards understanding the entrepreneurial process both enjoyable and productive. The model is shown here. The step in the model that corresponds to the chapter being introduced is highlighted to help you, our readers, form a picture of where each chapter fits in the entrepreneurial process.

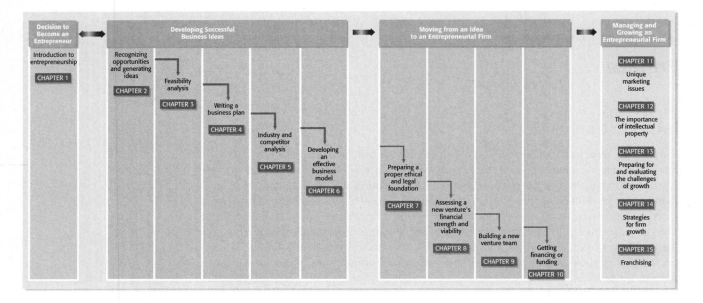

What Are the Book's Beneficial Features?

To provide as thorough and meaningful an introduction to the entrepreneurial process as possible, we include several features, as follows, in each chapter of this book:

FEATURE INCLUDED IN EACH CHAPTER	BENEFIT
Learning objectives	Help focus the reader's attention on the major topics in the chapter
Chapter opening profile	Introduces the chapter's topic by focusing on a company that was started while its founder or founders were still in college
Boldfaced key terms	Draw the reader's attention to key concepts
Examples and anecdotes	Liven up the text and provide descriptions of both successful and unsuccessful approaches to confronting the challenges discussed in each chapter
End-of-chapter summary	Integrate the key topics and concepts included in each chapter
20 review questions	Allow readers to test their recall of chapter material
15 application questions	Allow readers to apply what they learned from the chapter material
Four discussion questions following each case	Provide opportunities to use concepts examined in each chapter to evaluate situations faced by entrepreneurs
Two application questions following each case	Provide opportunities to use a chapter's materials to situations readers might face as entrepreneurs

What Are Some Other Unique Features of This Book?

While looking through your book, we think you'll find several unique features, as presented next, that will work to your benefit as a student of entrepreneurship and the entrepreneurial process.

UNIQUE FEATURE OF THE BOOK	EXPLANATION
Focus on opportunity recognition and feasibility analysis	The book begins with strong chapters on opportunity recognition and feasibility analysis. This is important, because opportunity recognition and feasibility analysis are key activities that must be completed early when investigating a new business idea.
What Went Wrong? boxed feature	Each chapter contains a boxed feature titled "What Went Wrong?" We use these features to explain the missteps of seemingly promising entrepreneurial firms. The purpose of these features, as you have no doubt already guessed, is to highlight the reality that things can go wrong when the fundamental concepts in the chapters aren't carefully followed.
Partnering for Success boxed feature	Each chapter contains a boxed feature titled "Partnering for Success." The ability to partner effectively with other firms is becoming an increasingly important attribute for successful entrepreneurial ventures.
Savvy Entrepreneurial Firm boxed feature	Each chapter contains a boxed feature titled "Savvy Entrepreneurial Firm." These features illustrate the types of business practices that facilitate the success of entrepreneurial ventures. As such, these are practices you should strongly consider putting into play when you are using the entrepreneurial process.
You Be the VC end-of-chapter features	Two features, titled "You Be the VC," are provided at the end of each chapter. These features present a "pitch" for funding from an emerging entrepreneurial venture. The features are designed to stimulate classroom discussion by sparking debate on whether a particular venture should or shouldn't receive funding. All of the firms featured are real-life entrepreneurial start-ups. Thus, you'll be talking about real—not hypothetical or fictitious— entrepreneurial ventures.
A total of 30 original end-of-chapter cases	Two medium-length cases, written by the authors of the book, are featured at the end of each chapter. The cases are designed to stimulate classroom discussion and illustrate the issues discussed in the chapter.
A total of six comprehensive cases	Six comprehensive cases, authored by leading entrepreneurship writers and scholars, are included at the end of the book. Each case deals with topics from several chapters. These cases are suitable for individual assignments, group assignments, or exams. A notation is made at the end of each chapter alerting you and your professor to the comprehensive cases that complement that particular chapter.

What Is New to This Edition?

We are committed to presenting you with the most up-to-date and applicable treatment of the entrepreneurial process available in the marketplace. While serving your educational interests, we want to simultaneously increase the likelihood that you will become excited by entrepreneurship's promise as you read and study current experiences of entrepreneurs and their ventures as well as the findings springing from academic research.

To verify currency, thoroughness, and reader interest, we have made several important changes, as presented next, while preparing this second edition of our book:

Opening Profile.   Each chapter opens with a profile of an entrepreneurial venture that was started by one or more students while completing their university-level educational experience. These descriptions of real-life entrepreneurs demonstrate that many of us have the ability to be entrepreneurs even while enrolled as a college student. Each profile is specific to a chapter's topic. We completed extensive interviews with each student entrepreneur(s) to obtain required materials.

Student Entrepreneurs' Insights.   At the bottom of each Opening Profile, we present entrepreneurs' answers to a series of questions. In providing answers to these questions, the entrepreneurs who launched their venture while enrolled in school express their perspectives about various issues. An important benefit associated with thinking about these responses is that those reading this book today have opportunities to see that they, too, may indeed have the potential to launch an entrepreneurial venture quicker than originally thought.

Updated Features.   Over 75 percent of the "What Went Wrong?," "Savvy Entrepreneurial Firm," "Partnering for Success," and "You be the VC" features are new to this edition. The features we did retain have been updated. The newness shown by these features benefits readers by allowing them to consider contemporary issues facing today's entrepreneurial ventures. The new and updated "You be the VC" features allow readers to decide if the potential of a proposed entrepreneurial venture is sufficient to warrant funding.

New and Updated Cases.   Virtually all of the pairs of two cases per chapter appearing at the ends of chapters are new to this edition. Those retained have been updated. Comprehensive in nature, these cases were written with the purpose of presenting readers with opportunities to use chapter-specific concepts to identify problems and propose solutions to situations facing actual entrepreneurial ventures. Questions appearing at the end of each case can be used to stimulate classroom discussions.

Updated References.   The amount of academic research examining entrepreneurship topics continues to grow. To provide you, our readers, with the most recent insights from the academic literature, we draw from newly published articles. Similarly, we relied on the most current articles appearing in business publications such as *The Wall Street Journal*, *Entrepreneur*, and *Business 2.0*, among others, to present you with examples of the actions being taken by today's entrepreneurial ventures.

Instructor Support Material

A full package of support material for instructors is provided with the book to enhance the overall learning experience. We, the authors of this book, prepared all of the instructor support materials.

Instructor's Resource Center

www.prenhall.com/irc is where instructors can access a variety of print, media, and presentation resources available with this text in downloadable, digital format. Resources are also available for course management platforms such as Blackboard, WebCT, and CourseCompass.

After registering at www.prenhall.com/irc, instructors do not need to fill out any additional forms nor do they need to be able to recall multiple usernames and passwords in order to access new titles and/or editions. As a registered faculty member, instructors can log in directly to download resource files and receive immediate access and instructions for installing course management content to their campus server.

The Prentice Hall dedicated Technical Support team is ready to assist instructors with questions about the media supplements that accompany this text. Instructors can visit http://247.prenhall.com/ for answers to frequently asked questions and toll-free user support phone numbers.

For detailed descriptions of all of the supplements listed below, please visit: www.prenhall.com/irc

POWERPOINT SLIDES (AVAILABLE ON CD-ROM) A full set of PowerPoint slides is provided. The slides are divided by chapter and are suitable for leading class lectures and discussion. The slides contain the relevant material from each chapter along with reproductions of key tables and figures.

INSTRUCTOR'S MANUAL An instructor's manual, which includes both traditional and new value-added material, includes the following:

- Chapter outlines.
- Sample answers for each of the questions for critical thinking (within the boxed features), end-of chapter review questions, application question, and questions following the cases.
- A full analysis of each of the "You Be the VC" features that appear at the end of each chapter.
- Case notes for the six comprehensive cases included in the book.
- A short summary of each video segment that is included in the video package that accompanies the book.
- Sample course outlines.
- Additional student and instructor resources.

TESTBANK A testbank that includes the following for each chapter in the book:

- 50 multiple-choice questions
- 20 true-false questions
- 5 short-answer questions

VIDEO A collection of video segments is provided to supplement the course material. A short summary of each video segment is provided in the Instructor's Manual.

- Instructor's Resource Center (IRC) on CD-ROM—ISBN: 0-13-224062-9
- Printed Instructor's Manual—ISBN: 0-13-224058-0
- Printed Test Item File—ISBN: 0-13-224069-6
- TestGen test-generating software—Visit the IRC (both online and on CD-ROM) for this text.
- PowerPoint Slides—Visit the IRC (both online and on CD-ROM) for this text.
- Videos on DVD—ISBN: 0-13-224070-X

Student Resources

- **Companion Website:** www.prenhall.com/barringer contains free access to a student version of the PowerPoint package, chapter quizzes, and links to featured websites.
- **Business Feasibility Analysis Pro**—ISBN: 0136132014. This wizard-based software is a step-by-step guide and an easy-to-use tool for completing a feasibility analysis of a business idea. The program allows instructors the flexibility to assign each step in the feasibility analysis separately or to assign the entire feasibility analysis as a semester-long project. It can be packaged with the textbook at a nominal cost.
- **VangoNotes.com.** Students can study on the go with VangoNotes—chapter reviews from this text in downloadable MP3 format. Students can purchase VangoNotes for the entire textbook or for individual chapters. For each chapter, VangoNotes contains:
  - Big Ideas: The "need to know" for each chapter.

- Practice Test: A gut check for the Big Ideas—indicates if students need to keep studying.
- Key Terms: Audio "flashcards" to help students review key concepts and terms.
- Rapid Review: A quick drill session—to use right before taking a test.

Feedback

Your authors and their book's product team would appreciate hearing from you! Let us know what you think about this textbook by writing to: college_marketing@prenhall.com. Please include "Feedback about Barringer/Ireland 2e" in the subject line.

    If you have questions related to this book about entrepreneurship, please contact our customer service department online at www.247.prenhall.com.

Acknowledgments

We are pleased to express our sincere appreciation to four groups of people for helping bring both editions of our book to life.

Prentice Hall Professionals. A number of individuals at Prentice Hall have worked with us conscientiously and have fully supported our efforts to create a book that will work for those both studying and teaching the entrepreneurial process. From Prentice Hall, we want to extend our sincere appreciation to our editors Jennifer Simon, David Parker, and Mike Ablassmeir, our director of marketing Eric Frank, and our project manager, Claudia Fernandes. We would also like to thank Jeff Shelstad, Editorial Director, for his overall leadership of the project. Each individual provided us invaluable guidance and support and we are grateful for their contribution.

Student Entrepreneurs. We want to extend a heartfelt "thank you" to the student entrepreneurs who contributed to the opening features in our book. Our conversations with these individuals were both informative and inspiring. We enjoyed getting to know these bright young entrepreneurs, and wish them nothing but success as they continue to build their ventures.

Amy Appleyard, Boston University

David Bateman, Brigham Young University

Anthony Casalena, University of Maryland

Anand V. Chhatpar, University of Wisconsin

Erica Fand, Syracuse University

Evan Fieldman, University of Florida

Derek Gregg, Marshall University

Matt Hedges, University of Mississippi

Mitch Hintze, University of Florida

Luke Hooper, Tulane University

Vail Horton, University of Portland

Joseph Keeley, St. Thomas University

Shelly Kohan, Syracuse University

Christian Martin, Case Western Reserve University

Ryan O'Donnell, Rensselaer Polytechnic Institute

Sarah Schupp, University of Colorado at Boulder

Del Segura, Tulane University

Evan Shapiro, Emory University

Jan Stephenson, Boston University

Justin Swick, Marshall University

Mitch Towbin, Emory University

Academic Reviewers. We want to thank our colleagues who participated in reviewing individual chapters of the book while they were being written. We gained keen insight from these individuals (each of whom teaches courses in entrepreneurship) and incorporated many of the suggestions of our reviewers into the final version of the book.

Thank you to these professors who participated in reviews:

David C. Adams, Manhattanville College

Rose Bednarz, Gateway Community College

Stephen Braun, Concordia University

Martin Bressler, Houston Baptist University

Debbi Brock, Berea College

John Callister, Cornell University

Jason Duan, Midwestern State University

Brooke Envick, St. Mary's University

Mark Fenton, University of Wisconsin–Stout

Cathy Folker, University of St. Thomas

Eugene Fregetto, University of Illinois at Chicago

Vance H. Fried, Oklahoma State University

Connie Marie Gaglio, San Francisco State University

Michael Goldsby, Ball State University

Mihalis Halkides, Bethune Cookman College

Kirk C. Heriot, Columbus State University

John Lofberg, South Dakota School of Mines and Technology

Avinash V. Mainkar, James Madison University

Morgan Miles, Georgia Southern University

William Pinchuk, Rutgers University

Darrell Scott, Idaho State University

Richard L. Smith, Iowa State University

Robert Tosterud, University of South Dakota

Nancy Upton, Baylor University

Monica Zimmerman-Treichel, Temple University

Academic Colleagues.   We thank this large group of professors whose thoughts about entrepreneurial education have helped shape our book's contents and presentation structure:

David C. Adams, Manhattanville College

Sol Ahiarah, SUNY—Buffalo State College

Frederic Aiello, University of Southern Maine

James J. Alling Sr., Augusta Technical College

Jeffrey Alstete, Iona College

Jeffrey Alves, Wilkes University

Joe Aniello, Francis Marion University

Mary Avery, Ripon College

Jay Azriel, Illinois State University

Richard Barker, Upper Iowa University

Jim Bell, Texas State University

Robert J. Berger, SUNY Potsdam

Jenell Bramlage, University of Northwestern Ohio

Barb Brown, Southwestern Community College

James Burke, Loyola University—Chicago

Lowell Busenitz, University of Oklahoma

John Butler, University of Texas—Austin

Jane Byrd, University of Mobile

Art Camburn, Buena Vista University

Carol Carter, Louisiana State University

Gaylen Chandler, Utah State University

James Chrisman, Mississippi State University

Delena Clark, Plattsburgh State University

Dee Cole, Middle Tennessee State University

Roy Cook, Fort Lewis College

Andrew Corbett, Rensselaer Polytechnic Institute

Simone Cummings, Washington University School of Medicine

Suzanne D'Agnes, Queensborough Community College

Douglas Dayhoff, Indiana University

Frank Demmler, Carnegie Mellon University

David Desplaces, University of Hartford/Barney

Vern Disney, University of South Carolina—Sumter

Dale Eesley, University of Toledo

Alan Eisner, Pace University

Susan Everett, Clark State Community College

Henry Fernandez, North Carolina Central University

Charles Fishel, San Jose State University

Dana Fladhammer, Phoenix College

Brenda Flannery, Minnesota State University

John Friar, Northeastern University

Barbara Fuller, Winthrop University

Barry Gilmore, University of Memphis

Caroline Glackin, Delaware State University

Cheryl Gracie, Washtenaw Community College

Frederick Greene, Manhattan College

Lee Grubb, East Carolina University

Brad Handy, Springfield Technical Community College

Carnella Hardin, Glendale College

Ashley Harmon, Southeastern Technical College

Steve Harper, University of North Carolina at Wilmington

Alan Hauff, University of Missouri—St. Louis

Gordon Haym, Lyndon State College

Andrea Hershatter, Emory University

Richard Hilliard, Nichols College

Jo Hinton, Copiah Lincoln Community College

Dennis Hoagland, LDS Business College

Frank Hoy, University of Texas at El Paso

Jeffrey Jackson, Manhattanville College

Grant Jacobsen, Northern Virginia Community College–Woodbridge

Susan Jensen, University of Nebraska—Kearney

Alec Johnson, University of St. Thomas

James M. Jones, Univ. Incarnate Word, ERAU, Delmar College

Jane Jones, Mountain Empire Community College

Joy Jones, Ohio Valley College

Tom Kaplan, Fairleigh Dickinson University—Madison

Elizabeth Kisenwether, Penn State University

James Klingler, Villanova University

Edward Kuljian, Saint Joseph's University

James Lang, Virginia Tech University

Allon Lefever, Eastern Mennonite University

Anita Leffel, University of Texas—San Antonio

Gary Levanti, Polytechnic University—LI Campus

Benyamin Lichtenstein, University of Massachusetts, Boston

Bruce Lynskey, Vanderbilt University

Janice Mabry, Mississippi Gulf Coast Community College

Jeffrey Martin, University of Texas—Austin

Greg McCann, Stetson University

Elizabeth McCrea, Pennsylvania State—Great Valley

Brian McKenzie, California State University—Hayward

Chris McKinney, Vanderbilt University

Dale Meyer, University of Colorado

Steven C. Michael, University of Illinois Urbana—Champaign

Angela Mitchell, Wilmington College

Bryant Mitchell, University of Maryland—Eastern Shore

Rob Mitchell, University of Oklahoma

Charlie Nagelschmidt, Champlain College

William Naumes, University of New Hampshire

Connie Nichols, Odessa College

Gary Nothnagle, Nazareth College

Edward O'Brien, Scottsdale Community College

Haesun Park, Louisiana State University

Joseph Picken, University of Texas at Dallas

Emmeline de Pillis, University of Hawaii—Hilo

John Pfaff, University of the Pacific

Carol Reeves, University of Arkansas

John Richards, Brigham Young University

Christo Roberts, University of Minnesota—Twin Cities

George Roorbach, Lyndon State College

Janice Rustia, University of Nebraska Medical Center

James Saya, The College of Santa Fe

William Scheela, Bemidji State University

Gerry Scheffelmaier, Middle Tennessee State University

Gerald Segal, Florida Gulf Coast University

Cynthia Sheridan, St. Edward's University

Donald Shifter, Fontbonne University

C. L. J. Spencer, Kapi'olani Community College

Joseph Stasio, Merrimack College

Deborah Streeter, Cornell University

Dara Szyliowicz, University of Denver

Craig Tunwall, Empire State College

Clint B. Tankersley, Syracuse University

Barry Van Hook, Arizona State University

George Vozikis, University of Tulsa

David Wilemon, Syracuse University

Charlene Williams, Brewton Parker College

Doug Wilson, University of Oregon

Diana Wong, Eastern Michigan University

Finally, we want to express our appreciation to our home institutions (University of Central Florida and Texas A&M University) for creating environments in which ideas are encouraged and supported.

We wish each of you—our readers—all the best in your study of the entrepreneurial process. And, of course, we hope that each of you will be highly successful entrepreneurs as you pursue the ideas you'll develop at different points in your careers.

About the Authors

Bruce R. Barringer Bruce R. Barringer is an Associate Professor in the Department of Management at the University of Central Florida. He obtained his PhD from the University of Missouri and his MBA from Iowa State University. His research interests include feasibility analysis, firm growth, corporate entrepreneurship, and the impact of interorganizational relationships on business organizations. He also works closely with the University of Central Florida technology incubator.

He serves on the editorial review board of *Entrepreneurship Theory and Practice* and the *Journal of Small Business Management*. His work has been published in *Strategic Management Journal, Journal of Management, Journal of Business Venturing, Journal of Small Business Management, Journal of Developmental Entrepreneurship*, and *Quality Management Journal*.

His outside interests include running, swimming, and reading.

R. Duane Ireland R. Duane Ireland holds the Foreman R. and Ruby S. Bennett Chair in Business in the Mays Business School, Texas A&M University, where he also serves as the head of the management department. Previously, he served on the faculties at University of Richmond, Baylor University, and Oklahoma State University. His research interests include strategic entrepreneurship, corporate entrepreneurship, strategic alliances, and effectively managing organizational resources.

Duane's research has been published in journals such as *Academy of Management Journal, Academy of Management Review, Academy of Management Executive, Strategic Management Journal, Administrative Science Quarterly, Journal of Management, Journal of Business Venturing, Entrepreneurship Theory and Practice, Long Range Planning, Human Relations*, and *British Journal of Management*. He is a co-author of both scholarly books and textbooks, including best-selling strategic management texts. Along with Professor Mike Morris (Syracuse University), Duane serves as a co-editor for the Prentice Hall Entrepreneurship Series. These soon-to-be-released books offer in-depth treatments of specific entrepreneurship topics, such as *Business Plans for Entrepreneurs* (authored by Bruce Barringer).

Duane has served or is serving on the editorial review boards for a number of journals, including *AMJ, AMR, AME, JOM, JBV, ETP, European Management Journal*, and *Journal of Business Strategy*. Currently, he is serving as an associate editor for *AMJ*. He has completed terms as an associate editor for *AME* and as a consulting editor for *ETP* and has served as a guest co-editor for special issues of *AMR, AME, SMJ, Journal of Engineering and Technology Management*, and *JBV*. He is a Fellow of the Academy of Management and has served as a member of the Board of Governors for the Academy. He is the recipient of both teaching and research awards.

Running, reading, listening to a variety of music, and playing with his grandson are Duane's outside interests.

Entrepreneurship
Successfully Launching New Ventures

Second Edition

introduction to *entrepreneurship*

THE GUIDE TO BOULDER

Getting Personal

with

SARAH SCHUPP

Currently in my iPod

Norah Jones

Best advice I've received

Be persistent

My biggest worry as an entrepreneur

Losing a customer

niversity Parent:

The Classic Entrepreneurial Story

As a college student at the University of Colorado (CU), in Boulder, Colorado, Sarah Schupp invited her parents to visit her a couple times a year to see where she was living and see the campus and its various attractions. Although she enjoyed her parent's visits, one challenge she always encountered was helping them plan their stay and make it enjoyable. "My parents would visit me from Dallas and they wanted to know where to shop, eat, and stay in Boulder," Schupp remembers.[1] She always felt hesitant to give her parents too much advice. After all, as a college student she wasn't familiar with the hotels and motels in Boulder, for example, and, as a dormitory resident, didn't know a lot about the restaurants in different parts of town. After muddling through helping her parents plan several visits, it occurred to Schupp that what CU needed was a magazine that would provide parents a directory of hotels, motels, restaurants, and shops to help them plan their trips to Boulder.

At the same time that Schupp started thinking about this idea, she was enrolled in the entrepreneurship program at the Leeds School of Business at CU. Fortunately for her, as she was thinking about her idea, she was scheduled to take a business plan course taught by Frank Moyes. Reflecting back on her business idea, Schupp recalls, "I knew what I wanted to do, but I didn't know how to do it."[2] Schupp entered the class, which required the students to break up into teams, think of a business idea, and prepare a business plan to describe how the idea would be turned into a commercial reality. Schupp became part of a five-person team and persuaded her teammates to help her flesh out her parent magazine business idea. Schupp remembers that the class taught her to look at each step in the business plan carefully. The class culminated with a business plan competition—which Schupp and her teammates won. Reflecting back on the class, Schupp remarked, "His class (Frank Moyes) is a lot of work. We won the competition and we didn't even get an 'A'. But he really knows what he's doing."[3]

After the class concluded, Schupp became increasingly convinced that her idea for a parent-focused university magazine was viable. In talking with the staff of the Office of Parent Relations at CU, she learned that because it is a public entity, the university can't put out a guide that endorses specific businesses. However, university personnel told

SARAH SCHUPP

Founder, University Parent
University of Colorado
BS, Leeds School of Business, 2004

Best part of being a student	First entrepreneurial experience	What I do when I'm not working
Support from faculty	*Published coupon book for college students*	*Play tennis*

After studying this chapter you should be ready to:

L E A R N I N G

Objectives

1. Explain entrepreneurship and discuss its importance.

2. Describe corporate entrepreneurship and its use in established firms.

3. Discuss three main reasons people decide to become entrepreneurs.

4. Identify four main characteristics of successful entrepreneurs.

5. Explain the five common myths regarding entrepreneurship.

6. Explain how entrepreneurial firms differ from salary-substitute and lifestyle firms.

7. Discuss the changing demographics of entrepreneurs in the United States.

8. Discuss the impact of entrepreneurial firms on economies and societies.

9. Identify ways in which large firms benefit from the presence of smaller entrepreneurial firms.

10. Explain the entrepreneurial process.

Schupp that if she put together a magazine or guide that was helpful to parents, CU would make it available to parents at university events. After kicking around the idea with her professors at CU and other people as well, she started a company, named University Parent, to produce an advertising-supported magazine for CU parents. To sell ads, she literally went door-to-door among the motels, hotels, restaurants, and shops in Boulder. Many businesses responded positively to her sales effort, largely because they knew the ads would be seen by parents who were from out-of-town and would be looking for a place to eat or stay. She was also able to sell some ads to national advertisers (such as Apple Computer and Marriott) who were interested in targeting college students and their parents.

University Parent's first issue was published in October of 2003 and was distributed during parents' weekend. The issue contained a directory of local motels, hotels, restaurants, and shops, along with a calendar of events and articles of interest to college students and their parents. University Parent's first issue was an immediate success, causing CU to invite Schupp to produce three magazines a year—one to be distributed during summer orientation, one during the fall semester, and the other during the spring semester.

Through research that Schupp and her teammates conducted during the preparation of University Parent's original business plan, they learned that approximately 95 percent of college parents want more information about both the college their child is attending and the community in which it is located. On most campuses there is no publication addressing this set of needs.[4] As a result, following her initial success at CU, Schupp approached other universities about her business idea and is now publishing customized versions of *University Parent* at Colorado State University, Southern Methodist University, Miami University of Ohio, University of Denver, and Kansas State University. Arrangements with several other universities are in the works. At all locations other than CU, the universities mail the magazine to the parents rather than distributing them while the parents are on campus. This approach is particularly attractive to advertisers near those universities. As a rule, universities do not share their mailing lists of parents, so to be able to produce an ad that will be distributed to all the parents of incoming students is very attractive to hotels, motels, restaurants and other businesses in a university town.

Schupp feels that her business fills a need and that University Parent is a win for everyone involved. As to her future, Schupp is expanding University Parent, and hopes to be established on 25 campuses in the near future. "I've always wanted to be an entrepreneur," she said. I'm just trying to grow the business. I'd like to see it be a success."

As you will see by reading this book, there is something unique about how each entrepreneurial venture is launched. However, there are some common features to all launches, including the fact that each venture is started by one or more entrepreneurs who have recognized an opportunity and who develop a plan for how to shape the opportunity into a viable business. The eBay example is particularly instructive because Pierre Omidyar managed this process very effectively and focused on start-up techniques that are emphasized throughout this book. He gained experience before he started eBay, launched it with minimal overhead, built a top-notch management team, won the trust of the investment community, and established partnerships with other firms to help the company grow. He also used information technology to its maximum potential. He took the basic process of a garage sale, put it in an auction format, and figured out a way to move it online.

In this first chapter of your book about the successful launching of an entrepreneurial firm, we define entrepreneurship and discuss why some people decide to become entrepreneurs.

We then look at successful entrepreneurs' characteristics, the common myths surrounding entrepreneurship, the different types of start-up firms, and the changing demographics of entrepreneurs in the United States and in other nations throughout the world. We then examine entrepreneurship's importance, including the economic and social impact of new firms as well as the importance of entrepreneurial firms to larger businesses. To close this chapter, we introduce you to the entrepreneurial process. This process, which we believe is the foundation for successfully launching a start-up firm, is the framework we use to present the book's materials to you.

Introduction to Entrepreneurship

There is tremendous interest in entrepreneurship around the world. Although this statement may seem bold, there is evidence supporting it, some of which is provided by the Global Entrepreneurship Monitor (GEM). GEM, which is a joint research effort by Babson College and the London Business School, tracks entrepreneurship in 35 countries, including the United States. According to the results of the GEM 2005 study, about 330 million, or roughly 14 percent, of adults in the countries surveyed are involved in forming new businesses.[5] Although many of these new businesses will be extremely small, approximately 3 percent to 17 percent (depending on the country) of new business owners expect to employ 20 or more people within 5 years. These percentages may seem small to you; however, the economic impact of firms this size is significant. In fact, research evidence shows that firms that grow to over 20 people are responsible for up to 80 percent of all new jobs created by entrepreneurs.[6]

The GEM report also identifies whether its respondents are starting new businesses to take advantage of attractive opportunities or out of necessity. In other words, it tracks whether people are becoming entrepreneurs because they have recognized what they believe is an attractive opportunity or because they believe that becoming an entrepreneur is the most attractive work-related option available to them. Overall, the vast majority of the individuals in the 35 countries surveyed reported they are starting a business to pursue an attractive opportunity. Unfortunately, in the United States, roughly one-third of all new firms fail within the first 2 years, while another 20 percent fail within 4 years.[7] These statistics show that while many people are motivated to start new firms, motivation alone is not enough; it must be coupled with good information, a solid business idea, and effective execution to maximize chances for success. In this book, we will discuss many examples of entrepreneurial firms and the factors separating successful ventures from unsuccessful ventures.

Many people see entrepreneurship as an attractive career path. Think about your friends and others you know. In all probability, you are acquainted with at least one or two people who want to become an entrepreneur—either now or at some point in the future. The number of books dealing with starting one's own business is another indication entrepreneurship is growing in popularity. Amazon.com, for example, currently lists over 1,900 books dealing with entrepreneurship and over 17,000 books focusing on small business. It is also clear that many people are fascinated by entrepreneurship and related topics, as evidence by the success of ABC's *American Inventor* television show. The purpose of this book is to provide a thorough introduction to the entrepreneurial process as the foundation for successfully launching a new venture.

What Is Entrepreneurship?

The word *entrepreneur* derives from the French words *entre*, meaning "between," and *prendre*, meaning "to take." The word was originally used to describe people who "take on the risk" between buyers and sellers or who "undertake" a task such as starting a new venture.[8] Inventors and entrepreneurs differ from each other. An inventor creates something new. An entrepreneur assembles and then integrates all the resources needed—the money, the people, the business model, the strategy, and the risk-bearing ability—to transform the invention into a viable business.[9]

1. Explain entrepreneurship and discuss its importance.

Entrepreneurship is the process by which individuals pursue opportunities without regard to resources they currently control.[10] The essence of entrepreneurial behavior is identifying opportunities and putting useful ideas into practice.[11] The tasks called for by this behavior can be accomplished by either an individual or a group and typically requires creativity, drive, and a willingness to take risks. Sarah Schupp, the founder of University Parent, exemplified all these qualities. Schupp saw an *opportunity* to create a magazine that would be attractive to parents, universities, and advertisers, she *risked* her career by passing up alternatives to work on University Parent full-time, and she *worked hard* to build a profitable company that delivers a *creative* and *useful* service to its customers.

In this book, we focus on entrepreneurship in the context of an entrepreneur or team of entrepreneurs launching a new business. However, ongoing firms can also behave entrepreneurially. Typically, established firms with an entrepreneurial emphasis are proactive, innovative, and risk-taking. For example, Apple Computer (which celebrated its 30th birthday in 2006) is widely recognized as a firm in which entrepreneurial behaviors are clearly evident. Steve Jobs is at the heart of Apple's entrepreneurial culture. With his ability to persuade and motivate others' imaginations, Jobs continues to inspire Apple's employees as they develop innovative product after innovative product. To consider the penetration Apple has with some of its innovations, think of how many of your friends own an iPod![12] Similarly, studying Cisco Systems' ability to grow and succeed reveals a history of entrepreneurial behavior at multiple levels within the firm.[13] In addition, many of the firms traded on the NASDAQ, such as Yahoo!, Intel, Starbucks, and Google, are commonly thought of as entrepreneurial firms. The NASDAQ is the largest U.S. electronic stock market and with over 3,200 companies listed on the exchange.

We want to note here that established firms with an orientation to acting entrepreneurially practice **corporate entrepreneurship**.[14] All firms fall along a conceptual continuum that ranges from highly conservative to highly entrepreneurial. The position of a firm on this continuum is referred to as its **entrepreneurial intensity**.[15] As we mentioned previously, entrepreneurial firms are typically proactive innovators and are not averse to taking calculated risks. In contrast, conservative firms take a more "wait and see" posture, are less innovative, and are risk averse.

One of the most persuasive indications of entrepreneurship's importance to an individual or to a firm is the degree of effort undertaken to behave in an entrepreneurial manner. Firms with higher entrepreneurial intensity regularly look for ways to cut bureaucracy. For example, Virgin Group, the large British conglomerate, works hard to keep its units small and instill in them an entrepreneurial spirit. Virgin is the third most recognized brand in Britain and is involved in businesses as diverse as airlines and music. In the following quote, Sir Richard Branson, the founder and CEO of Virgin, describes how his company operates in an entrepreneurial manner:

L E A R N I N G

Objective

2. Describe corporate entrepreneurship and its use in established firms.

> Convention . . . dictates that "big is beautiful," but every time one of our ventures gets too big we divide it up into smaller units. I go to the deputy managing director, the deputy sales director, and the deputy marketing director and say, "Congratulations. You're now MD [managing director], sales director and marketing director—of a new company." Each time we've done this, the people involved haven't had much more work to do, but necessarily they have a greater incentive to perform and a greater zeal for their work. The results for us have been terrific. By the time we sold Virgin Music, we had as many as 50 subsidiary record companies, and not one of them had more than 60 employees.[16]

Other large firms are increasingly looking for ways to jump-start their entrepreneurship and innovation-related initiatives. For example, several firms, including Citigroup, Humana, and Coca-Cola, now have executives with the titles Chief Innovation Officer or Vice President of Innovation. Appointing executives with titles such as these sends a clear message to the organization: Innovation is an urgent priority and someone should be held accountable for it.[17]

Steve Jobs is perhaps America's best-known entrepreneur. He co-founded Apple Computer in 1976, and has since built the company into a premier entrepreneurial firm. Apple's latest innovations include the widely popular Apple iTunes Music store and the Apple iPod.

Why Become an Entrepreneur?

The three primary reasons that people become entrepreneurs and start their own firms are to be their own boss, pursue their own ideas, and realize financial rewards.

L E A R N I N G
Objective

3. Discuss three main reasons that people decide to become entrepreneurs.

Be Their Own Boss The first of these reasons—being one's own boss—is given most commonly. This doesn't mean, however, that entrepreneurs are difficult to work with or that they have trouble accepting authority. Instead, many entrepreneurs want to be their own boss because either they have had a long-time ambition to own their own firm or because they have become frustrated working in traditional jobs. The type of frustration that some entrepreneurs feel working in conventional jobs is exemplified by Wendy DeFeudis, the founder of VeryWendy, a company that makes customized social invitations. Commenting on how her experiences working for herself have been more satisfying than working for a large firm, DeFeudis remarked:

> I always wanted to be my own boss. I felt confined by the corporate structure. I found it frustrating and a complete waste of time—a waste to have to sell my ideas to multiple people and attend all kinds of internal meetings before moving forward with a concept.[18]

T. J. Rogers, the founder and longtime CEO of Cypress Semiconductor, an international supplier of computer chips, enjoys being his own boss for a similar, yet slightly different reason. Prior to founding Cypress, Rogers was on the fast track for promotion at Advanced Micro Devices (AMD), one of the world's largest semiconductor firms. When asked why he left AMD to start his own company, Rogers replied:

> Actually, my mother asked me that. Her basic question was—rephrasing it negatively from my perspective—"Now that you're in the rat race and can scramble up the political ladder at Advanced Micro Devices, why give up the sure opportunities and start your own company?" I wanted to start a company since I graduated from college. It was one of my life goals, stated at age 21, that I would start a company by the age 35. Why do people start their own companies? The standard entrepreneurial answer is frustration. You see a company running poorly; you see that it could be a lot better. Like the freshman Congressman who's been around for six months, you realize that the other guys really aren't that good. All of a sudden you understand that you could go build something bigger and more important than where you are. That's a big deal.[19]

Pursue Their Own Ideas The second reason people start their own firms is to pursue their own ideas.[20] Some people are naturally alert, and when they recognize ideas for new products or services, they have a desire to see those ideas realized. Corporate entrepreneurs who innovate within the context of an existing firm typically have a mechanism for their ideas to become known. Established firms, however, often resist innovation. When this happens, employees are left with good ideas that go unfulfilled.[21] Because of their passion and commitment, some employees choose to leave the firm employing them in order to start their own business as the means to develop their own ideas.

This chain of events can take place in noncorporate settings, too. For example, some people, through a hobby, leisure activity, or just everyday life, recognize the need for a product or service that is not available in the marketplace. If the idea is viable enough to support a business, they commit tremendous time and energy to convert the idea into a part-time or full-time firm. In Chapters 2 and 3, we focus on how entrepreneurs spot ideas and determine if their ideas represent viable business opportunities.

Pursue Financial Rewards Finally, people start their own firms to pursue financial rewards. This motivation, however, is typically secondary to the first two and often fails to live up to its hype. The average entrepreneur does not make more money than someone with a similar amount of responsibility in a traditional job. For example, in 1997, only 13.1 percent of the owners of small businesses in the United States made more than $50,000 a year.[22] The financial lure of entrepreneurship is its upside potential. People such as Michael Dell of Dell Inc., Jerry Yang of Yahoo!, and Larry Page and Sergei Brin of Google made hundreds of millions of dollars building their firms. But these people insist that money wasn't their primary motivation. Marc Andreessen, founder of Netscape, said, "[Money] is not the motivator or even the measure of my success."[23] Some entrepreneurs even report that the financial rewards associated with entrepreneurship can be bittersweet if they are accompanied by losing control of their firm. For example, Sir Richard Branson, after selling Virgin Records, wrote, "I remember walking down the street [after the sale was completed]. I was crying. Tears . . . [were] streaming down my face. And there I was holding a check for a billion dollars. . . . If you'd have seen me, you would have thought I was loony. A billion dollars."[24] For Branson, it wasn't just the money—it was the thrill of building the business and of seeing the success of his initial idea.

Characteristics of Successful Entrepreneurs

Although many behaviors have been ascribed to entrepreneurs, several are common to those who are successful. Those in new ventures and those who are already part of an entrepreneurial firm share these qualities, which are shown in Figure 1.1 and described in the following section.

Passion for the Business The number-one characteristic shared by successful entrepreneurs is a **passion for their business**, whether it is in the context of a new firm or an existing business. This passion typically stems from the entrepreneur's belief that the business will positively influence people's lives. Consider Benjamin Tregoe, cofounder of Kepner-Tregoe, a management consulting firm. In describing the purpose of his new venture, he said:

> Tremendously important to me was the feeling that we were doing something that had a significance far beyond building a company or what the financial rewards could be. I was convinced we were doing something that had tremendous importance in the world.[25]

This passion explains why people leave secure jobs to start their own firms and why billionaires such as Bill Gates of Microsoft, Michael Dell of Dell Inc., and Larry Page and Sergei Brin of Google continue working after they are financially secure. They strongly

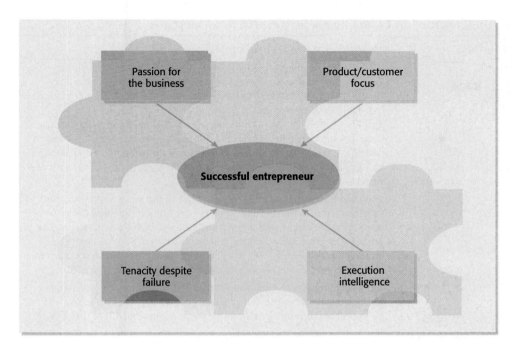

FIGURE 1.1

Four Primary Characteristics of Successful Entrepreneurs

believe that the product or service they are selling makes a difference in people's lives and makes the world a better place to live in.

Passion is particularly important for entrepreneurs because although rewarding, the process of starting and building a new firm is demanding. Entrepreneurship isn't for the person who is only partially committed. Investors watch like hawks to try to determine an entrepreneur's passion for his or her business idea. Michael Rovner, a partner in AV Labs, a venture capital firm in Austin, Texas, expresses this sentiment:

> Everyone has a different concept of what starting a business is like. We look for people who are highly motivated—people who are passionate about providing their solution to customers, people who really want to make a new company fly.[26]

Another reason that passion is important is that in many instances it motivates extraordinary behavior. This outcome is the case with Mary Kent Hearon, the founder of Dragonfly Wellness, a heath food and natural remedy start-up. Remarking on how her passion for her business has helped her become a better writer (she writes a regular newsletter on alternative medicines), Hearon said:

> It gives me so much joy to reach people through my Weekly Beet newsletter, which has about 1,500 subscribers and is growing every day. What I've realized is I'm a good writer. Once you choose the work you love, certain aspects of yourself start to come out that you never knew existed. I didn't do well in English class because I was writing about books that didn't interest me. Now I'm able to better express myself through health.[27]

What this example illustrates, beyond the fact that passion motivates extraordinary behavior, is that entrepreneurs who are passionate about their venture will often invest huge amounts of effort to ensure its healthy functioning. Additional examples of how entrepreneurs view passion are shown in Table 1.1. In each instance, the presence of passion is depicted as an essential characteristic of successful entrepreneurs.

TABLE 1.1 The Importance of "Passion" in Launching a Successful New Venture

Entrepreneur and Company Founded	View on the Importance of Passion
Jared Ross VENA-Fine Italian Takeout Toronto, Canada	My MBA has been invaluable in so many ways. However, one thing business school doesn't teach is how to prepare for the less glamorous, humbling jobs like scrubbing the bathroom floors and driving around the city making deliveries. But it's worth it because I'm passionate about my business. For as long as I can remember, I dreamed of being an entrepreneur. Now my dream is a reality, and the risks are mitigated knowing that I reap all the rewards of my hard work. I love every grueling minute of it and can't wait to go to work tomorrow.
Judi Sheppard Missett Jazzercise Nationwide Fitness Franchise Carlsbad, California	First and foremost, you must be passionate about what you're doing—whether you're leading a large group of people through a step class or massaging the kinks out of an individual's body. Out of passion develops a strong work ethic, and without it you won't succeed. Some people go into fitness careers thinking, "Oh, it will be a nice thing to do and it will keep me fit." These people don't survive because they don't have enough dedication.
Keith Schacht Creative Inventables Chicago, Illinois	Do something you're passionate about. There are a lot of people who start companies about stuff that doesn't personally interest them. . . . It makes all the difference in the world to be doing something you're passionate about.
Laura Gasparis Vonfrolio Educational Enterprises Richmond, Virginia	The only entrepreneurial trait that is universal, in my view, is passion. I've met smart entrepreneurs, stupid entrepreneurs, compulsive entrepreneurs, laid-back entrepreneurs, but they all had passion. Some go into it for the fun, some to make money, some to prove a point, some because they don't want to work for anybody else, but the successful ones all have passion.
Ross Levin Accredited Investors Edina, Minnesota	You could build a business with anything, as long as you can find something that you can be passionate about. I could have been a minister; I bet I would have built a thriving congregation.

Sources: BusinessWeek Online (2006), "The Recipe for Success," available at www.businessweek.com (accessed May 18, 2006); Brent Bowers, *If at First You Don't Succeed* (New York: Doubleday, 2006).

A note of caution is in order here: While entrepreneurs should have passion, they should not wear rose-colored glasses. It would be a mistake to believe that all one needs is passion and anything is possible. It is important to be enthusiastic about a business idea, but it is also important to understand its potential flaws and risks. In addition, entrepreneurs should understand that the most effective business ideas take hold when their passion is consistent with their skills and is in an area that represents a legitimate business opportunity. We examine these points in greater detail in Case 1.1 at the end of the chapter.

Product/Customer Focus   A second defining characteristic of successful entrepreneurs is a **product/customer focus**. This quality is exemplified by Steven Jobs, the cofounder of Apple Computer, who wrote, "The computer is the most remarkable tool we've ever built . . . but the most important thing is to get them in the hands of as many people as possible."[28] This sentiment underscores an understanding of the two most important elements in any business—products and customers. While it's important to think about management, marketing, finance, and the like, none of those functions makes any difference if a firm does not have good products with the capability to satisfy customers.

An entrepreneur's keen focus on products and customers typically stems from the fact that most successful entrepreneurs are, at heart, craftspeople. They are obsessed with making products that can satisfy a customer's need. This is an important point to remember, particularly in an era when it is tempting to envision new businesses resulting from every advance in technology. Michael Dell illustrated this point when he wrote, "We introduce technology that meets the needs of our customers, rather than introducing technology for its own sake."[29]

Watching entrepreneurs create products that meet unfilled needs is fascinating. The idea for the Apple Macintosh, for example, originated in the early 1980s when Steven Jobs and several other Apple employees took a tour of a Xerox research facility. They were astounded to see computers that displayed graphical icons and pull-down menus. The computers also allowed users to navigate desktops using a small, wheeled device called a mouse. Jobs decided to use these innovations to create the Macintosh, the first user-friendly computer. Throughout the two and a half years the Macintosh team developed this new product, it maintained an intense product/customer focus, creating a high-quality computer that is easy to learn, is fun to use, and meets the needs of a wide audience of potential users.[30]

Tenacity Despite Failure Because entrepreneurs are typically trying something new, the failure rate associated with their efforts is naturally high. In addition, the process of developing a new business is somewhat similar to what a scientist experiences in the laboratory. A chemist, for example, typically has to try multiple combinations of chemicals before finding an optimal combination that can accomplish a certain objective. In a similar fashion, developing a new business idea may require a certain degree of experimentation before a success is attained. Setbacks and failures inevitably occur during this process. The litmus test for entrepreneurs is their ability to persevere through setbacks and failures. Ken Nickerson, the cofounder of iBinary, a wireless technology firm and a former Microsoft executive, exemplifies this quality. When asked in an interview "What is the best thing you ever did?" Nickerson responded by saying, "Having high levels of tenacity. For example, bringing Hotmail to Microsoft Network took 18 months, and I just fought that deal through. It was arguably the best Internet thing Microsoft did."[31]

In some instances, tenacity is important because it shows a potential customer the degree of commitment that an entrepreneur has to a new product or service. For example, when his company was just getting started, J. Darius Bikoff, the founder of Gluceau, the company that makes vitaminwater, pounded the streets of New York City trying to drum up interest in his product. When he made a sale he would deliver the product himself, thinking that a personal touch would gain him the loyalty of shopkeepers. "I'll never forget it," Joe Doria, a grocer in Bikoff's New York City neighborhood, recalls. "Darius comes in and says, 'Hey Joe, will you sell this for me?' He was just a customer of the store, but it impressed me that he was delivering the product himself and pushing it. You've got to respect that." Today, Doria's grocery store devotes 12 linear feet of cooler space to vitaminwater, as well as fruitwater and smartwater, two other Gluceau brands. Mr. Doria says he won't sell any other brand of enhanced health water—even Pepsi's Propel, the nation's top seller. "Darius was the first, and I have an allegiance to him." Bikoff's tenacity didn't wane as his company grew, and he continues to make personal deliveries of Gluceau products in select areas. Today, Gluceau bottled water is available in 50,000 outlets, including Albertson's, Safeway, Publix, and a large number of independent stores.[32]

Execution Intelligence The ability to fashion a solid idea into a viable business is a key characteristic of successful entrepreneurs. Rob Adams, a senior partner in AV Labs, calls this ability **execution intelligence**.[33] In many cases, execution intelligence is the factor that determines whether a start-up is successful or fails. An ancient Chinese saying warns, "To open a business is very easy; to keep it open is very difficult."

The ability to effectively execute a business idea means developing a business model, putting together a new venture team, raising money, establishing partnerships, managing finances, leading and motivating employees, and so on. It also demands the ability to translate thought, creativity, and imagination into action and measurable results. As Jeff Bezos, the founder of Amazon.com, once said, "Ideas are easy. It's execution that's hard."[34] For many entrepreneurs, the hardest time is shortly after they launch their firm. This reality was expressed by Jodi Gallaer, the founder of a lingerie company, who said, "The most challenging part of my job is doing everything for the first time."[35]

You might describe an entrepreneur as an independent thinker, an innovator, or perhaps a risk taker. These entrepreneurial employees are passionate enough to work out of their garage if that's what it takes to get the company up and running. Consider Bill Gates, who was so enthusiastic about computers that he dropped out of Harvard University to pursue his vision.

To illustrate solid execution, let's look at Starbucks. Although huge today and still profitably growing, Starbucks' story is that of a successfully launched and managed entrepreneurial venture. The business idea of Howard Schultz, the entrepreneur who purchased Starbucks in 1987, was his recognition of the fact that most Americans didn't have a place to enjoy coffee in a comfortable, quiet setting. Seeing a great opportunity to satisfy customers' needs, Schultz attacked the marketplace aggressively to make Starbucks the industry leader and to establish a national brand. First, he hired a seasoned management team, constructed a world-class roasting facility to supply his outlets with premium coffee beans, and focused on building an effective organizational infrastructure. Then Schultz recruited a management information systems expert from McDonald's to design a point-of-sale system capable of tracking consumer purchases across 300 outlets. This decision was crucial to the firm's ability to sustain rapid growth over the next several years. Starbucks succeeded because Howard Schultz knew how to execute a business idea.[36] He built a seasoned management team, implemented an effective strategy, and used information technology wisely to make his business thrive.[37] In contrast to what Schultz has accomplished at Starbucks, the cost of ignoring execution is high, as explained by Bob Young, the founder of several entrepreneurial firms. When asked "What was your hardest lesson or biggest mistake?" Young replied, "In my first two businesses, my interest was always in 'the new thing,' so I wasn't paying attention to details. As a result of my lack of interest in getting the repetitive stuff right, we never achieved the profitability we should have."[38]

To illustrate the importance of execution intelligence, as well as other factors that are critical in determining a firm's success or failure, we include a boxed feature titled "What Went Wrong?" in each chapter. The feature for this chapter shows how Segway, a maker of light-mode transportation devices, has never reached its desired potential, leaving the firm's survivability in question.

Common Myths About Entrepreneurs

There are many misconceptions about who entrepreneurs are and what motivates them to launch firms to develop their ideas. Some misconceptions are due to the media covering atypical entrepreneurs, such as a couple of college students who obtain venture capital to fund a small business that they grow into a multimillion-dollar company. Such articles rarely state that these entrepreneurs are the exception rather than the norm and that their success is a result of carefully executing an appropriate plan to commercialize what inherently is a solid business idea. Indeed, the success of many of the entrepreneurs we study in each chapter's Opening Profile is a result of carefully executing the different aspects of the entrepreneurial process. Let's look at the most common myths and the realities about entrepreneurs.

Myth 1: Entrepreneurs are born, not made. This myth is based on the mistaken belief that some people are genetically predisposed to be entrepreneurs. The consensus of many hundreds of studies on the psychological and sociological makeup of entrepreneurs is that entrepreneurs are not genetically different from other people. This evidence can be interpreted as meaning that no one is "born" to be an entrepreneur and that everyone has the potential to become one. Whether someone does or doesn't is a function of environment, life experiences, and personal choices.[39] However, there are personality traits and characteristics commonly associated with entrepreneurs; these are listed in Table 1.2. These traits are developed over time and evolve from an individual's social context. For example, studies show that people with parents who were self-employed are more likely to become entrepreneurs.[40] After witnessing a father's or mother's independence in the workplace, an individual is more likely to find independence appealing.[41] Similarly, people who personally know an entrepreneur are more than twice as likely to be involved in starting a new firm as those with no entrepreneur acquaintances or role models.[42] The positive impact of knowing an entrepreneur is explained by the fact that direct observation of other entrepreneurs reduces the ambiguity and uncertainty associated with the entrepreneurial process.

Myth 2: Entrepreneurs are gamblers. A second myth about entrepreneurs is that they are gamblers and take big risks. The truth is, entrepreneurs are usually **moderate risk takers**, as are most people.[43] The idea that entrepreneurs are gamblers originates from two sources.

First, entrepreneurs typically have jobs that are less structured, and so they face a more uncertain set of possibilities than managers or rank-and-file employees.[44] For example, an entrepreneur who starts an e-business consulting service has a less stable job than one working for a state governmental agency. Second, many entrepreneurs have a strong need to achieve and often set challenging goals, a behavior that is sometimes equated with risk taking.

Myth 3: Entrepreneurs are motivated primarily by money. It is naive to think that entrepreneurs don't seek financial rewards. As discussed previously, however, money is rarely the primary reason entrepreneurs start new firms. Considering what motivated him to start Siebel Systems, a successful Silicon Valley firm, Tom Siebel wrote:

Common Traits and Characteristics
TABLE 1.2 of Entrepreneurs

Achievement motivated	Optimistic disposition
Alert to opportunities	Persuasive
Creative	Promoter
Decisive	Resource assembler/leverager
Energetic	Self-confident
Has a strong work ethic	Self-starter
Is a moderate risk taker	Tenacious
Is a networker	Tolerant of ambiguity
Lengthy attention span	Visionary

What Segway Has Learned the Hard Way
www.segway.com

The Segway HT is a two-wheeled, self-balancing transportation device that consists primarily of a set of tall handlebars on top of two disc-like wheels. There are no chains or visible mechanical workings. Riders lean forward to move forward and back to move backward. Turning is done mechanically via hand controls. The devices are driven by quiet, nonpolluting electric motors and can travel up to 10 miles per hour. The name "Segway HT" stands for "Segway Human Transporter."

The Segway was introduced to the marketplace in December 2001 by Dean Kaman, the entrepreneur who invented the product. There was considerable secrecy and hype leading up to the introduction. The initial reaction to the device was enthusiastic. Venture capitalist John Doerr predicted that sales of the Segway would reach $1 billion sooner than any other product in U.S. history. Apple's CEO Steve Jobs forecast that cities would be built around this new form of transportation. To cope with the expected demand for the product, Segway's factory in Bedford, New Hampshire, was designed to build up to 40,000 units per month. Initially sales were targeted at between 10,000 and 50,000 units during the first 12 months. But, after 21 months, only 6,000 units had sold. What went wrong?

As it turned out, several things went wrong when it came to selling the Segway. First, the initial price of the product was $9,000, which put it out of reach for many consumers. Second, despite its technological prowess, it wasn't clear what need the Segway was filling. It was best suited for densely populated areas where people could ride their Segway's to work. But other than places like San Francisco and Manhattan, most affluent people live in suburban areas, making riding a Segway to work impractical. In addition, it was unclear how riding a Segway to work, school, or shop would work. It takes both hands to operate a Segway safely. So, how would a businessperson carry a briefcase or a student carry books? Finally,

Segways are sold on Amazon.com and through other direct channels. There are a few Segway dealers scattered across the United States, but not many. As a result, very few people can see or test-drive a Segway. The lack of a local dealer network also made people wonder where they would get their Segways serviced if they had trouble.

Segway is still in business, but the company is only a shadow of what it hoped to become. Its price has come down to around $5,000, and there are now over 200 Segway dealers. There is a group of Segway enthusiasts that love the product, and Segways are used in some factories, tourist areas, and theme parks. The United States Postal Service, a large potential market for Segway, tested the device for use by mail carriers who still deliver mail by foot. The postal service abandoned the idea after mail carriers complained that they couldn't sort mail or hold an umbrella while operating a Segway.

Questions for Critical Thinking

1. As we've said in this chapter, execution intelligence is critical to entrepreneurial success. How did execution fall short for Segway? What reasons, other than those already mentioned, led to poor sales of the Segway?

2. Why do you think that Dean Kamen and his team didn't do a better job of anticipating the problems that beset the Segway? What would you have done differently to anticipate, in advance, the public's reaction to the Segway?

3. Discuss Segway's value proposition. Did Segway deliver sufficient value to justify its $9,000 sticker price?

4. Do you think the Segway will ever sell to mainstream markets? What niche markets, if any, do you think are the most promising for Segway?

Source: Segway home page, www.segway.com (accessed May 16, 2006); Wikipedia, "Segway HT," (accessed May 16, 2006).

[It] was never about making money. It was never about going public; it was never about the creation of wealth. This was about an attempt to build an incredibly high-quality company. I suppose if I was a great musician that maybe I would play the guitar, if I was a great golfer maybe I would go out on tour, but I can't play the guitar and my golf game is pretty horrible. So what I think, frequently under those circumstances, what you do is do what you do best. And I think that maybe what I do best is start and operate information technology companies.[45]

Some entrepreneurs warn that the pursuit of money can be distracting. Media mogul Ted Turner said, "If you think money is a real big deal . . . you'll be too scared of losing it to get it."[46] Similarly, Debbie Fields, the founder of Mrs. Fields Cookies, said that if you chase money, you'll never get it.[47] And Sam Walton, commenting on all the media attention that surrounded him after he was named the richest man in America by *Forbes* magazine in 1985, said:

> Here's the thing: money never has meant that much to me, not even in the sense of keeping score. . . . We're not ashamed of having money, but I just don't believe a big showy lifestyle is appropriate for anywhere, least of all here in Bentonville where folks work hard for their money. We all know that everyone puts on their trousers one leg at a time. . . . I still can't believe it was news that I get my hair cut at the barbershop. Where else would I get it cut? Why do I drive a pickup truck? What am I supposed to haul my dogs around in, a Rolls-Royce?[48]

Myth 4: Entrepreneurs should be young and energetic. The most active age range for early stage entrepreneurial activity is 25 to 34 years old; established business ownership peaks among those 45 to 54 years old. Later in this chapter, we'll discuss the reality that today, an increasing number of both younger and older individuals are being attracted to the entrepreneurial process.

Although it is important to be energetic, investors often cite the strength of the entrepreneur (or team of entrepreneurs) as their most important criterion in the decision to fund new ventures.[49] In fact, a sentiment that venture capitalists often express is that they would rather fund a strong entrepreneur with a mediocre business idea than fund a strong business idea and a mediocre entrepreneur. What makes an entrepreneur "strong" in the eyes of an investor is experience in the area of the proposed business, skills and abilities that will help the business, a solid reputation, a track record of success, and passion about the business idea. The first four of these five qualities favor older rather than younger entrepreneurs. In addition, many people turn to entrepreneurship in lieu of retirement, as suggested by a researcher's findings that 32 percent of early retirees who return to work start their own business.[50] Before closing this chapter, we'll consider the essence of this finding by discussing the fact that a

It's moments like these that drive the entrepreneurial spirit. When things go right, all the hardwork, sacrifice, and risk seem suddenly worth it.

growing number of seniors (people 55 years of age and older) are choosing to become entrepreneurs.

Myth 5: Entrepreneurs love the spotlight. Indeed, some entrepreneurs are flamboyant; however, the vast majority of them do not attract public attention. In fact, many entrepreneurs, because they are working on proprietary products or services, avoid public notice. Consider that entrepreneurs are the source of the launch of many of the 3,200 companies listed on the NASDAQ; and, many of these entrepreneurs are still actively involved with their firms. But how many of these entrepreneurs can you name? Maybe a half dozen? Most of us could come up with Bill Gates of Microsoft, Steven Jobs of Apple, Michael Dell of Dell, Inc., and maybe Larry Page and Sergei Brin of Google. Whether or not they sought attention, these are the entrepreneurs who are often in the news. But few of us could name the founders of Nokia or GAP even though we frequently use these firms' products and services. These entrepreneurs, like most, have either avoided attention or been passed over by the popular press. They defy the myth that entrepreneurs, more so than other groups in our society, love the spotlight.

Types of Start-Up Firms

As shown in Figure 1.2, there are three types of start-up firms: salary-substitute firms, lifestyle firms, and entrepreneurial firms.

Salary-substitute firms are small firms that yield a level of income for their owner or owners that is similar to what they would earn when working for an employer. Dry cleaners, convenience stores, restaurants, accounting firms, retail stores, and hairstyling salons are examples of salary-substitute firms. The vast majority of small businesses fit into this category. Salary-substitute firms offer common, easily available products or services to customers that are not particularly innovative.

Lifestyle firms provide their owner or owners the opportunity to pursue a particular lifestyle and earn a living while doing so. Lifestyle firms include ski instructors, golf pros, and tour guides. These firms are not innovative, nor do they grow quickly. Commonly, lifestyle companies promote a particular sport, hobby, or pastime and may employ only the owner or just a handful of people. Rocky Mountain River Tours, owned by Dave and Shelia Mills, is an example of a lifestyle firm. The company leads 17 raft trips annually on the Middle Fork tributary to the main Salmon River in Idaho. Buying and owning a raft company was always a dream of the Mills, because it would provide them the lifestyle they desired.[51]

Entrepreneurial firms bring new products and services to market. As we noted earlier in this chapter, the essence of entrepreneurship is creating value and then disseminating that value to customers. In this context, "**value**" refers to worth, importance, or utility. Entrepreneurial firms bring new products and services to market by creating and then seizing opportunities. Google, eBay, and Starbucks are well-known, highly successful examples of entrepreneurial firms. Having recognized an opportunity, companies of this type create products and services that have worth, that are important to their customers, and that provide a measure of usefulness to their customers that they wouldn't have otherwise.

Next, we describe the newly emerging characteristics of today's entrepreneurs. You may be surprised to learn about the types of individuals who are choosing to become entrepreneurs!

FIGURE 1.2

Types of Start-Up Firms

Salary-Substitute Firms	Lifestyle Firms	Entrepreneurial Firms
Firms that basically provide their owner or owners a similar level of income to what they would be able to earn in a conventional job	Firms that provide their owner or owners the opportunity to pursue a particular lifestyle, and make a living at it	Firms that bring new products and services to the market by creating and seizing opportunities regardless of the resources they currently control

Changing Demographics of Entrepreneurs

7. Discuss the changing demographics of entrepreneurs in the United States.

Over the past 10 years, the demographic makeup of entrepreneurial firms has changed in the United States and around the world. Of the 23 million businesses in the United States, a growing number are owned by women, minorities, seniors, and young people. Although there are no solid numbers on how many of the 23 million businesses are entrepreneurial firms rather than salary-substitute or lifestyle firms, there is growing anecdotal evidence that an increasing number of women, minorities, seniors, and young people are becoming actively involved in the entrepreneurial process. This is an exciting development for the entrepreneurial sector of the U.S. economy.

Women Entrepreneurs There were 6.5 million women-owned businesses in 2002, the most recent year the U.S. Census Bureau collected business ownership data. That number is up 20 percent from 1997. Although historically women-owned firms have primarily been in health care and professional services, that emphasis is changing. Between 1997 and 2002, the fastest-growing areas of women-owned firms were construction (30 percent increase), agricultural services (24 percent increase), transportation (20 percent increase), communications (20 percent increase), and public utilities (20 percent increase). In addition, there were 117,069 women-owned firms in 2002 with total sales of $1 million or more. These statistics reflect the growing breadth and economic prowess of women-owned businesses in the United States.[52]

Minority Entrepreneurs There were 1.2 million African-American–owned firms in 2002, up 45 percent from 1997. Similarly, there were 1.6 million Hispanic-owned businesses in 2002, up 31 percent from 1997. There were 1.1 million Asian-owned businesses in 2002, up 24 percent from 1997. There were 206,125 Native-American–owned businesses in 2002. While the majority of minority-owned businesses are in service industries, there are many examples of minority-owned firms in all sectors of the U.S. economy.

Senior Entrepreneurs Although the Census Bureau does not collect data on senior entrepreneurs (people 55 years old and older), there is strong evidence to suggest that the number of older people choosing entrepreneurial careers is increasing rapidly. Unpublished government data obtained by Challenger, Gray & Christmas, an outplacement consulting firm, indicates that 2.1 million Americans 55 years of age and older owned their own businesses in 2005, an increase of 22 percent from 2000.[53] The dramatic increase in the number of senior entrepreneurs is attributed to a number of factors, including corporate downsizing, an increasing desire among older workers for more personal fulfillment in their lives, and growing worries among seniors that they need to earn additional income to pay for future health care services and other expenses.[54] A growing number of seniors may also see themselves as ideal candidates to start their own businesses. Many people in the 55+ age range have substantial business experience, financial resources that they can draw upon, and excellent vigor and health.

Young Entrepreneurs Although the total number of young entrepreneurs is far less than women, minority, or senior entrepreneurs, interest among young people (ages 21 years and younger) in entrepreneurship is growing. At the high school level, a Gallup study revealed that 7 out of 10 high school students want to start their own companies. More specifically, 6 in 10 females, 7 in 10 Hispanics, and 8 in 10 African-American high school students are interested in starting a business.[55] According to the same study, 27 percent of high school students take an entrepreneurial business course and 35 percent take an economics course while in school.

Interestingly, an emphasis on entrepreneurship education is starting to appear in some areas as early as grade school. Harper Arrington Publishing and Media now publishes a series of books titled *The Little Entrepreneur—Takes Flight*. The series is designed to teach kids how to turn their hobbies into businesses and is suitable for children as young as 8. Interest in entrepreneurship is picking up at all levels in K–12 public schools. As evidence of this, the New York City Council recently awarded a $550,000 grant to the National Foundation for Teaching Entrepreneurship to expand youth entrepreneurship education in New York City. The rationale the council gave for making the grant provides insight into the value that policymakers see in entrepreneurship education at an early age:

> "The Council's goal is to give young people the skills and confidence to unlock their true potential so they can improve their lives and their communities," said Council Member Robert Jackson. "Many of our neighborhoods are filled with creative and inspired young people who just needed help finding their talents. By exposing these students to entrepreneurship, we expand their capacity, unleash their creativity, increase their school and community leadership and encourage their individual growth."[56]

On college campuses, interest in entrepreneurship education is at an all time high, as will be described throughout this book. According to a survey by the Ewing Marion Kauffman Foundation, as of Spring 2006, 1,992 two- and four-year colleges and universities were offering at least one course in entrepreneurship, up from 300 in the 1984–85 school years. Although the bulk of entrepreneurship education takes place within business schools, many other colleges and departments are offering entrepreneurship courses as well—including engineering, agriculture, theater, dance, education, law, and nursing. The tide is also turning in regard to the attractiveness of an entrepreneurial career in almost every major. Commenting on this issue, Jerome Katz, a professor of management at St. Louis University who has studied this trend, said, "Twenty years ago students who dared to say they wanted to start their own companies would be sent for counseling. Today, entrepreneurship is the fastest-growing course of study on campuses nationwide."[57]

Entrepreneurship is a particularly attractive option for college students for a number of reasons, including their understanding of the attractiveness of the youth market, their ability to find low-cost labor in the form of other students, their access to resources that are available to them at their colleges or universities, and their intuitive recognition of the reality that if they fail they can pick up where they left off and pursue another venture or a conventional career. In addition, if a student's business was developed through an entrepreneurship program or was competitive in a business plan competition, the business may be seen as less risky than other start-ups. Sarah Schupp, the founder of University Parent featured at the beginning of the chapter, says she feels that the businesses she first approached about advertising in University Parent liked the idea that her business was developed through a college-sponsored entrepreneurship program. The fact that other people, including her professors, had looked at her business and had helped her fine-tune it gave the advertisers an extra measure of assurance that University Parent did indeed have potential.

LEARNING
Objective

8. Discuss the impact of entrepreneurial firms on economics and societies.

Entrepreneurship's Importance

Entrepreneurship has a tremendously positive impact on the economy and on society. In 2005, a report by the Global Entrepreneurship Monitor stated that

> Entrepreneurs are alert individuals who perceive and exploit profit opportunities. In addition to contributing toward market efficiency, entrepreneurs introduce innovations by offering new and unique products or services. As a result, innovative entrepreneurs are also one of the main links between entrepreneurship and economic growth.[58]

Consistent with this set of sentiments, one scholar, commenting on the importance of entrepreneurship at the local level, noted that "entrepreneurship is still the best private vehicle we have to turn around and improve the economic health of a community."[59]

Entrepreneurship's importance to an economy and the society in which it resides was first articulated in 1934 by Joseph Schumpeter, an Austrian economist who did the majority of his work at Harvard University. In his book *The Theory of Economic Development*, Schumpeter argued that entrepreneurs develop new products and technologies that over time make current products and technologies obsolete. Schumpeter called this process **creative destruction**. Because new products and technologies are typically better than those they replace and the availability of improved products and technologies increases consumer demand, creative destruction stimulates economic activity. The new products and technologies may also increase the productivity of all elements of a society.[60]

The creative destruction process is initiated most effectively by start-up ventures that improve on what is currently available. Small firms that practice this art are often called "innovators" or "agents of change." The process of creative destruction is not limited to new products and technologies; it can include new pricing strategies (e.g., discount brokers such as E*Trade), new distribution channels (such as FedEx or Amazon.com), or new retail formats (such as IKEA in furniture).

Now let's look more closely at entrepreneurship's importance.

Economic Impact of Entrepreneurial Firms

For three reasons, entrepreneurial behavior has a strong impact on an economy's strength and stability.

Innovation **Innovation** is the process of creating something new, which is central to the entrepreneurial process.[61] Small entrepreneurial firms are responsible for 55 percent of all innovation in the United States.[62] The most impactful innovations either solve a problem or satisfy a need in a new and cost-effective way. Commenting on this aspect of innovation, Marlo Mazzola, Cisco Systems senior vice president and chief development offier, said, "Innovation is more than just a new idea—it is about taking a new idea and developing it into customer value and positive business impact." [63]

Many innovations help individuals and businesses work more smoothly and efficiently. An example of how one innovative firm, uShip, is helping people cut the cost of shipping large or awkwardly shaped items from one point to another is provided in the boxed feature titled "Savvy Entrepreneurial Firm." In each chapter, this feature will provide an illustration of the exemplary behavior of one or more entrepreneurial firms or will provide an example of a tool or technique that well-managed entrepreneurial firms use to improve their performance.

Job Creation In the past two decades, economic activity has moved increasingly in the direction of smaller entrepreneurial firms, possibly because of their unique ability to innovate and focus on specialized tasks. In fact, over 550,000 new businesses are started in the United States every month.[64] According to the 1997 report of the U.S. Census Bureau (which is the most recent data available), the nation's 17 million small, nonfarm businesses constitute 99.7 percent of all employers, employ 52 percent of the workforce, and generate 51 percent of all sales revenue. A total of 67 percent of young people obtain their first job with a small firm. And between 1994 and 1998, fast-growth young companies, known as **gazelles**, created about two-thirds of all new jobs in the United States.[65] Large firms are increasingly focusing on what they do best, which is usually manufacturing, sales, and service, and are outsourcing the majority of their other tasks to smaller firms.

Globalization Today, 97 percent of all U.S. exporters are small- and medium-sized businesses with fewer than 500 employees. Over two-thirds have fewer than 20 employees. Between 1992 and 2003, the number of small- and medium-sized exporters grew more than twice as fast as the number of large company exporters. Export markets are vital to the U.S. economy and provide outlets for the sale of U.S.-produced products and services.[66]

Entrepreneurial Firms' Impact on Society

The innovations of entrepreneurial firms have a dramatic impact on a society. Think of all the new products and services that make our lives easier, enhance our productivity at work, improve our health, and entertain us. For example, Amgen, an entrepreneurial firm

savvy
entrepreneurial firm

uShip: Helping Individuals and Shippers Move Items More Effectively
www.uship.com

It's easy to ship an envelope or a package, via the United States Postal Service, UPS, or FedEx. But what if you want to ship a larger item, like a piece of furniture, a car, or a boat? There are freight carriers available, but because they are designed to carry heavy and large loads, they are expensive. To ship an individual piece of furniture from North Carolina to California could easily cost as much as the furniture itself, making the idea impractical.

Until now. uShip, which was launched in 2003 in Austin, Texas, is an online marketplace for shipping. It uses a reverse auction system where users can list large or awkward items, like furniture or cars, and shippers can bid on the shipping job. The company claims to have 10,000 registered service providers, most of whom are small movers, freight carriers, van lines, auto and boat haulers, and independent drivers.

uShip was founded by Matt Chasen, who as a student developed the idea as part of a school project while enrolled at the University of Texas. Chasen likes to compare uShip to eBay—"We're just like eBay," he said. "uShip is a venue where people get together. We give customers the tools they need to find the right mover for their stuff. We give them feedback ratings." On any given day, there are thousands of shipments listed on uShip representing millions of dollars in shipping jobs. Here is how the service works. An individual logs onto the uShip Web site and lists a shipping job that needs to be completed. For example, say that a person bought an antique table while vacationing in Virginia, and wants to have it shipped home to Indiana. Shippers would then bid on the job. The shippers are all rated, similar to the way sellers are rated on eBay, and individuals can post positive or negative feedback about a shipper. The shippers that bid typically anticipate having an empty load or excess capacity on a route that passes near the pickup and the delivery locations. The seller will normally accept the lowest bid, assuming that the shipper is satisfactorily rated. uShip makes money by collecting a 7.9 percent commission from the shipper who carries the load.

uShip is building momentum as more people become aware of the service. Its patent-pending search technology connects users and shippers efficiently, and users are typically able to arrange a job for about 50 percent of what it would cost to have a traditional freight company carry the load. The company's feedback system holds drivers accountable for their service and rewards those that perform well. uShip's service is particularly popular among those selling large items on eBay and other auction sites.

Questions for Critical Thinking

1. To what extent do you think uShip's service will make it easier for Internet retailers to sell large, costly items, such as appliances, big-screen televisions, and treadmills? In what ways, if any, does uShip's service have the potential to make a positive impact on the economy, a positive impact on society, and a positive impact on larger firms?

2. Why do you think that a traditional shipping company, like UPS or Yellow Transportation, didn't launch a service similar to uShip's service some time ago? Is it too late for these established firms to launch a service such as this?

3. What steps has uShip taken to excel in the area of execution intelligence?

4. Think of another service that could help make the buying and selling of products more effective. Describe how the service "adds value" for both buyers and sellers.

Sources: uShip, www.uship.com (accessed May 18, 2006); Matt Nauman, "Web Facilitator Brings Together Movers, Shippers," *San Jose Mercury News*, April 21, 2006.

that helped launch the biotech industry, has produced a number of drugs that have dramatically improved people's lives. An example is NEUPOGEN, a drug that decreases the incidence of infection in cancer patients who are undergoing chemotherapy treatment. Sensipar is another one of Amgen's important products. Patients with chronic kidney disease and who are on dialysis take this drug as a secondary treatment of hyperparathyroidism.[67] In addition to improved health care, consider cellular phones, personal computing, Internet shopping, overnight package delivery, digital photography, and microwave ovens. All these products are new to this generation, yet it's hard to imagine our world without them.

However, innovations do create moral and ethical issues with which societies are forced to grapple. For example, bar-code scanner technology and the Internet have made it easier for companies to track the purchasing behavior of their customers, but this raises privacy concerns. Similarly, bioengineering has made it easier to extend the shelf life of many food products, but some researchers and consumers question the long-term health implications of bioengineered foods.

A particularly interesting example of a company that makes a product that is intended for good but some people oppose is VeriChip. VeriChip makes tiny, implantable microchips that hold medical records that can be implanted just beneath a person's skin. Emergency room physicians can scan the chips and gain immediate access to a person's medical records in the event of an emergency. The chips are controversial because they are actually implanted under a person's skin and because they raise privacy concerns. There is a perception in some quarters that the chips could be used to track people, steal their identities, or violate a patient's privacy in other ways.[68] As an individual, how do you react to this product? Would you be willing to use it? Why or why not?

Entrepreneurial Firms' Impact on Larger Firms

In addition to the impact that entrepreneurial firms have on the economy and society, they also have a positive impact on the effectiveness of larger firms. For example, some entrepreneurial firms are original equipment manufacturers, producing parts that go into products that larger firms manufacture and sell. Thus, many exciting new products, such as DVD players, digital cameras, and improved prescription drugs, are not solely the result of the efforts of larger companies with strong brand names, such as Sony, Kodak, and Johnson & Johnson. They were produced with the cutting-edge component parts or research and development efforts provided by entrepreneurial firms.

The evidence shows that many entrepreneurial firms have built their entire business models around producing products and services that help larger firms be more efficient or effective. For example, an increasing number of U.S. firms want to advertise on Spanish sites and purchase media exposure in Latin American companies. Latin Edge, a 2002 start-up, helps its larger clients achieve these objectives. Similarly, many large firms occasionally need temporary labor to facilitate short-term personnel needs. A small firm named IQNavigator has developed software to help Fortune 500 companies quickly hire reliable temporary labor through a network of sources.

In many instances, entrepreneurial firms partner with larger companies to reach mutually beneficial goals. Participation in business partnerships accelerates a firm's growth by giving it access to some of its partner's resources, managerial talent, and intellectual capacities. We examine the idea of partnering throughout this book. In each chapter, look for the boxed feature titled "Partnering for Success," which illustrates how entrepreneurial firms are using business partnerships to boost their chances for success. The feature in this chapter discusses how small, entrepreneurial biotech firms partner with large drug companies to bring their products to market. By working together rather than acting as adversaries, small biotech firms and large drug companies produce the best collective results.

The Entrepreneurial Process

The entrepreneurial process consists of four steps:

Step 1 Deciding to become an entrepreneur

Step 2 Developing successful business ideas

Step 3 Moving from an idea to an entrepreneurial firm

Step 4 Managing and growing the entrepreneurial firm

L E A R N I N G
Objective

9. Identify ways in which large firms benefit from the presence of smaller entrepreneurial firms.

L E A R N I N G
Objective

10. Explain the entrepreneurial process.

FIGURE 1.3

Basic Model of the Entrepreneurial Process

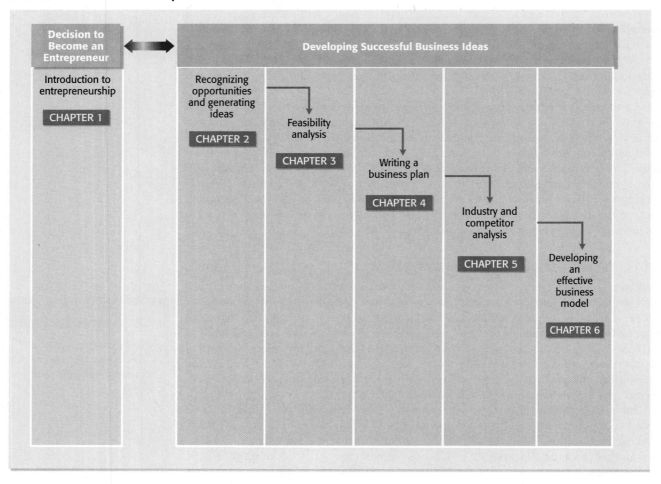

Figure 1.3 models the entrepreneurial process. This process is the guide or framework around which we develop this book's contents. The double-headed arrow between the decision to become an entrepreneur and the development of successful business ideas indicates that sometimes the opportunity to develop an idea prompts a person to become an entrepreneur. Each section of Figure 1.3 is explained in the following sections.

Decision to Become an Entrepreneur (Chapter 1)

As discussed earlier, people become entrepreneurs to be their own boss, to pursue their own ideas, and to realize financial rewards. Usually, a **triggering event** prompts an individual to become an entrepreneur.[69] For example, an individual may lose her job and decide that the time is right to start her own business. Or a person might receive an inheritance and for the first time in his life have the money to start his own company. Lifestyle issues may also trigger entrepreneurial careers. For example, a woman may wait until her youngest child is in school before she decides to launch her own entrepreneurial venture.

Developing Successful Business Ideas (Chapters 2–6)

Many new businesses fail not because the entrepreneur didn't work hard but because there was no real opportunity to begin with. Developing a successful business idea includes opportunity recognition, feasibility analysis, writing a business plan, industry analysis, and the development of an effective business model. Chapter 2 takes a scientific

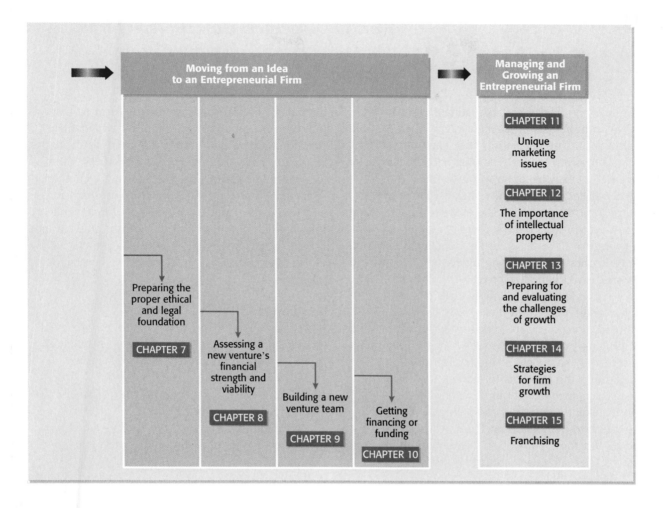

look at how entrepreneurs recognize opportunities and describes how the opportunity recognition process typically unfolds. Chapter 3 focuses on feasibility analysis: the way to determine whether an idea represents a viable business opportunity. Chapter 4 describes how to write a business plan. A **business plan** is a written document that describes all the aspects of a business venture in a concise manner. It is usually necessary to have a written business plan to raise money and attract high-quality business partners. Some entrepreneurs are impatient and don't want to spend the time it takes to write a business plan. This approach is usually a mistake. Writing a business plan forces an entrepreneur to think carefully through all the aspects of a business venture. It also helps a new venture establish a set of milestones that can be used to guide the early phases of the business rollout. Industry and competitor analysis is our concern in Chapter 5. Knowing the industry in which a firm will choose to compete is crucial to an entrepreneur's success. Chapter 6 focuses on the important topic of developing an effective business model. A firm's **business model** is its plan for how it competes, uses its resources, structures its relationships, interfaces with customers, and creates value to sustain itself on the basis of the profits it generates.

Moving from an Idea to an Entrepreneurial Firm (Chapters 7–10)

The first step in turning an idea into reality is to prepare a proper ethical and legal foundation for a firm, including selecting an appropriate form of business ownership. These

partnering for *success*

Working Together: How Biotech Firms and Large Drug Companies Bring Pharmaceutical Products to Market

Large firms and smaller entrepreneurial firms play different roles in business and society and can often produce the best results by partnering with each other rather than acting as adversaries. The pharmaceutical industry is an excellent example of how this works.

It is well known that barriers to entry in the pharmaceutical industry are high. The average new product takes about 7 years from discovery to market approval. The process of discovering, testing, obtaining approval, manufacturing, and marketing a new drug is long and expensive. How, then, do biotech start-ups make it? The answer is that few biotech firms actually take their products to market. Here's how it works.

Biotech firms specialize in discovering and patenting new drugs—it's what they're good at. In most cases, however, they have neither the money nor the know-how to bring the products to market. In contrast, the large drug companies, such as Pfizer and Merck, specialize in developing and marketing drugs and providing information to doctors about them. It's what they are good at. But these companies typically don't have the depth of scientific talent and the entrepreneurial zeal that the small biotech firms do. These two types of firms need one another to be as successful as possible. Often, but not always, what happens is this. The biotech firms discover and patent new drugs, and the larger drug

companies develop them and bring them to market. Biotech firms earn money through this arrangement by licensing or selling their patent-protected discoveries to the larger companies or by partnering with them in some revenue-sharing way. The large drug companies make money by selling the products to consumers.

The most compelling partnership arrangements are those that help entrepreneurial firms focus on what they do best, which is typically innovation, and that allow them to tap into their partners' complementary strengths and resources.

Questions for Critical Thinking

1. In your opinion, what factors in the business environment encourage firms to partner to compete?
2. What risks do small firms face when partnering with large, successful companies? What risks do large companies take when they rely on small firms as a source of innovation?
3. How might government policies affect partnering actions between small and large firms in the pharmaceutical industry?
4. If you worked for an entrepreneurial venture, what would you want to know about a large firm before recommending that your firm form a partnership with that large, established company?

issues are discussed in Chapter 7. Chapter 8 deals with the important topic of assessing a new venture's financial strength and viability. Important information is contained in this chapter about completing and analyzing both historical and pro forma financial statements. Chapter 9 focuses on building a new-venture team. Chapter 10 highlights the important task of getting financing or funding and identifies the options that a firm has for raising money.

Managing and Growing an Entrepreneurial Firm (Chapters 11–15)

Given today's competitive environment, all firms must be managed and grown properly to ensure their ongoing success. This is the final stage of the entrepreneurial process.

Chapter 11 focuses on the unique marketing issues facing entrepreneurial firms, including selecting an appropriate target market, building a brand, and the four Ps—product, price, promotion, and place (or distribution)—for new firms. Chapter 12 examines the important role of intellectual property in the growth of entrepreneurial firms. More and more, the value of "know-how" exceeds the value of a company's physical assets. In addition, we will talk about protecting business ideas through intellectual property statutes, such as patents, trademarks, copyrights, and trade secrets.

Preparing for and evaluating the challenges of growth is the topic of Chapter 13. We'll look at the characteristics and behaviors of successful growth firms. In Chapter 14, we'll study strategies for growth, ranging from new product development to mergers and acquisitions. We conclude with Chapter 15, which focuses on franchising. Not all franchise organizations are entrepreneurial firms, but franchising is a growing component of the entrepreneurial landscape. When you finish studying these 15 chapters, you will have been exposed to all components of the entrepreneurial process—a process that is vital to entrepreneurial success.

Chapter Summary

1. Entrepreneurship is the process by which individuals pursue opportunities without regard to resources they currently control.
2. Corporate entrepreneurship is the conceptualization of entrepreneurship at the organizational level. Entrepreneurial firms are proactive, innovative, and risk taking. In contrast, conservative firms take a more "wait and see" posture, are less innovative, and are risk averse.
3. The three primary reasons that people decide to become entrepreneurs and start their own firms are as follows: to be their own boss, to pursue their own ideas, and to realize financial rewards.
4. Passion for the business, product/customer focus, tenacity despite failure, and execution intelligence are the four primary characteristics of successful entrepreneurs.
5. The five most common myths regarding entrepreneurship are that entrepreneurs are born, not made; that entrepreneurs are gamblers; that entrepreneurs are motivated primarily by money; that entrepreneurs should be young and energetic; and that entrepreneurs love the spotlight.
6. Entrepreneurial firms are the firms that bring new products and services to market by recognizing and seizing opportunities regardless of the resources they currently control. Entrepreneurial firms stress innovation, which is not the case for salary-substitute and lifestyle firms.
7. The demographic makeup of those launching entrepreneurial firms is changing in the United States and around the world. There is growing evidence that an increasing number of women, minorities, seniors, and young people are becoming actively involved in the entrepreneurial process.
8. There is strong evidence that entrepreneurial behavior has a significant impact on economic stability and strength. The areas in which entrepreneurial firms contribute the most are innovation, job creation, and globalization. Entrepreneurial behavior also has a dramatic impact on society. It's easy to think of new products and services that have helped make our lives easier, that have made us more productive at work, that have improved our health, and that have entertained us in new ways.
9. In addition to the impact that entrepreneurial firms have on an economy and society, entrepreneurial firms have a positive impact on the effectiveness of larger firms. There are many entrepreneurial firms that have built their entire business models around producing products and services that help larger firms increase their efficiency and effectiveness.
10. The four distinct elements of the entrepreneurial process, pictured in Figure 1.3, are deciding to become an entrepreneur, developing successful business ideas, moving from an idea to establishing an entrepreneurial firm, and managing and growing an entrepreneurial firm.

Key Terms

Business model, 23
Business plan, 23
Corporate entrepreneurship, 6
Creative destruction, 18
Entrepreneurial firms, 16
Entrepreneurial intensity, 6

Entrepreneurship, 6
Execution intelligence, 11
Gazelles, 19
Innovation, 19
Lifestyle firms, 16
Moderate risk takers, 13

Passion for their business, 8
Product/customer focus, 10
Salary-substitute firms, 16
Triggering event, 22
Value, 16

Review Questions

1. Increasingly, entrepreneurship is being practiced in countries throughout the world. Why do you think this is the case?
2. Which type of new business is more entrepreneurial: a business that is being started to pursue a unique opportunity or a business that is being started out of necessity? Explain your answer.
3. What is entrepreneurship? How can one differentiate an entrepreneurial firm from any other type of firm?
4. What are the three main attributes of firms that pursue high levels of corporate entrepreneurship? Would these firms score high or low on an entrepreneurial intensity scale?
5. What are the three primary reasons people become entrepreneurs?
6. Why is it that people who start their own firms to be independent typically do not grow their firms beyond their immediate control?
7. Some people start their own firms to pursue financial rewards. However, these rewards are often far fewer than imagined. Why is this so?
8. What are the primary traits and characteristics of successful entrepreneurs?
9. Why is passion such an important characteristic of successful entrepreneurs? What is it about passion that makes it particularly compatible with the entrepreneurial process?
10. Why is a product/customer focus an important characteristic of successful entrepreneurs?
11. What is meant by execution intelligence? Why is execution intelligence an important characteristic for entrepreneurs?
12. What are the five common myths of entrepreneurship?
13. What are the major differences among salary-substitute firms, lifestyle firms, and entrepreneurial firms?
14. Are entrepreneurs born or made? Defend your answer.
15. In general, are entrepreneurs high risk takers, moderate risk takers, or low risk takers?
16. What role does money play in motivating people to become entrepreneurs?
17. What did Joseph Schumpeter mean by the term *creative destruction*?
18. In general, what effect does entrepreneurship have on economies around the world?
19. How is the demographic makeup of entrepreneurs changing in the United States? What do you believe is accounting for these changes?
20. Describe several examples of the impact that entrepreneurial firms have on a society.

Application Questions

1. Reread the opening case, then list all the smart or effective moves Sarah Schupp made in the early days of building University Parent. Which three moves were most instrumental in University Parent's early success? Be prepared to justify your selections.
2. Assume that Boise Cascade, the large paper products firm, hired you to assess its level of entrepreneurial intensity. What three factors would you study to determine how entrepreneurial Boise Cascade is at this point in time? How would you determine if these factors were present?
3. Karen Jenkins has a good job working for the city of Charlotte, North Carolina, but is weary of 3 percent per year pay raises. Because she has read magazine articles about

young entrepreneurs becoming extremely wealthy, she decides to start her own firm. Do you think Karen is starting a firm for the right reason? Do you think the money she likely will earn will disappoint her? Do you think Karen's reason for starting a firm will contribute in a positive manner or a negative manner to the stick-to-itiveness that is required to successfully launch an entrepreneurial venture?

4. Pamela, a friend of yours, has always had a nagging desire to be her own boss. She has a good job with AOL but has several ideas for new products that she can't get AOL interested in. Pamela just inherited $200,000 from an elderly relative and has the opportunity to start her own database software firm. She asks you, "Am I crazy for wanting to start my own firm to be my own boss and pursue my own ideas?" What would you tell her?

5. People are sometimes puzzled by the fact that entrepreneurs who have made millions of dollars still put in 60- to 80-hour weeks helping their companies innovate and grow. After reading the chapter, why do you think millionaire and multimillionaire entrepreneurs still get up and go to work every day? If you were one of these entrepreneurs, do you think you would feel the same way? Why or why not?

6. Think about an entrepreneur you know or have read about. Describe how the person either mirrors or contradicts the characteristics of successful entrepreneurs described in the chapter. In your judgment, what is the single most important characteristic that has made the person you are thinking about successful?

7. The Savvy Entrepreneurial Firm boxed feature focuses on uShip, a company that helps people arrange for large or awkwardly shaped items to be shipped at a reduced cost. Is uShip a salary-substitute, a lifestyle, or an entrepreneurial firm? In what ways has uShip demonstrated a product/customer focus? On a scale of 1 to 5 (5 is high), how instrumental has the company's product/market focus been to its early success?

8. You just made a trip home and are visiting with your dad. He is 59 years old and has been in a management position for a public utility for the past 12 years. Prior to that, he served 26 years in the U.S. Air Force. Your father told you that he has always wanted to start his own firm and has an idea about the type of firm to start. He wonders if he is too old to start a firm and if his management experience and his military background will be helpful in a new-venture context. If your dad asked you for your advice, what would you tell him?

9. Shelia Patterson is 26 year old and is thinking about starting a digital media firm. She knows that an increasing number of women are starting their own firms, but doesn't know where to go to learn about the start-up process. She would also like to network with other women, who are approximately her own age, who have started their own firms. Do some Internet research to provide Shelia suggestions about where to go to accomplish her objectives.

10. Jacob Lacy is an MBA student at a Big 12 school in the Midwest. He has an idea to start an Internet-based firm that will help high school students prepare for the SAT exam in an innovative manner. Jacob just talked to a trusted family friend, who told him that college is a poor time and place to launch a firm. The family friend told Jacob, "Try to distance yourself from the college atmosphere before you start your firm." Do you think Jacob is getting good advice? Why or why not?

11. Facebook is an enormously popular social networking site on college campuses. Facebook has been criticized for not doing enough to prevent some of the inappropriate activities that users engage in on its site. In general, do you think Facebook makes a positive or a negative contribution to society? If you were Mark Zuckerberg, the founder and CEO of Facebook, what steps would you take to ensure the site's legitimacy? Are you optimistic or pessimistic about Facebook's future? Why?

12. A friend of yours just bought a Sony digital camera. While showing it to you, he said, "You think entrepreneurial firms are so smart, look at what Sony has done. It has produced a sophisticated digital camera that allows me to take pictures, download them to my PC, and e-mail them to family members. Sony's a big company, not a small entrepreneurial firm. What do you have to say to that?" If you were to defend the role of entrepreneurial firms in developing new technologies, how would you respond?

13. The "You Be the VC 2" feature focuses on Riya, a company that uses face and text search technology to allow people to automatically search digital photos for specific people,

events, or places. What similarities, if any, do you see between Riya and Segway, the company featured in the "What Went Wrong?" boxed feature in the chapter?

14. Go to the Web site of Coldwater Creek, a woman's apparel company that is located in Sandpoint, Idaho, which is on the shores of beautiful Lake Pend Oreille. Spend some time looking at the Web site and reading about Coldwater Creek's history and current offerings. Do you consider Coldwater Creek to be a firm that practices corporate entrepreneurship? If so, what unique value does Coldwater Creek offer to its customers? In what ways, if any, does Coldwater Creek contribute to the economy, to society, and to the success of larger firms?

15. When Jill graduated from college, she opened a small ski shop near Jackson Hole, Wyoming. Although the shop sells some ski equipment, its primary purpose is to give lessons to people who want to learn to ski. Jill likes to tell her friends that she is a "true entrepreneur," just like her father, who started several technology businesses and patented more than 10 products. Do you consider Jill an entrepreneur? If not, what type of firm did she start? If someone bought Jill's business, what steps could they take to make it an entrepreneurial venture?

---

you be the VC 1.1

Company: Cereality
www.cereality.com

Business Idea: Open a chain of small walk-in restaurants (similar to sub-shop restaurants) that serve only cereal. Make the process of buying cereal inviting enough that cereal becomes an alternative to fast food where Cereality stores are located.

Pitch: There are many different forms of fast food, many of which no longer hold much interest for a large group of consumers. In addition, most fast-food restaurants have similar formats and are not fun or appealing destinations.

To address these shortcomings, and to breathe new life into the fast-food industry, Cereality will open small restaurants where customers will be able to walk up to counters to purchase their favorite brand of hot or cold cereal. A consumer can order up to two brands of cereal and a topping, which are mixed together by Cereality employees. The employees are clad in pajamas, to capture the nostalgia associated with cereal. A variety of milk products are available, including skim, 2 percent, whole, and soy. The cereal is placed in take-out-suitable containers, for patrons who want to eat on the run or at home. Several Cereality "signature blends" of cereal are available to show people that mixing different brands of cereal and toppings can make for a delicious meal. For example, the signature blend "Burst O' Berry" is a mixture of Kellogg's Froot Loops, Quaker's Cap'n Crunch Berries, and a dried mixed berry topping.

Cereality stores are bright and pleasant and include a wide selection of cereal from which to make a selection. The company currently has three stores, with the flagship unit located in the Memorial Union Building at Arizona State University in Tempe, Arizona. The other stores are located near the Sears Tower in Chicago and near the University of Pennsylvania in Philadelphia.

Along with selling bowls of cereal, Cereality sells boxes of cereal, which can be mixed any way a customer wants. For example, a box of cereal could include a mixture of Frosted Flakes, Cheerios, and Cocoa Puffs. The boxes can also be customized and include a personalized greeting or artwork on the cover. Smoothie type drinks, made from common cereal toppings like strawberries, bananas, and yogurt, are also available.

Cereality is considering its options for expanding. The three stores it owns are company-owned stores. It has had over 5,000 inquiries for franchise locations. As a result, it is considering selective franchising as a potential growth strategy.

Q&A: Based on the material covered in this chapter, what questions would you ask the firm's founders before making your funding decision? What answers would satisfy you?

Decision: If you had to make your decision on just the information provided in the pitch and on the company's Web site, would you fund this firm? Why or why not?

Company: Riya
www.riya.com

Business Idea: Use face and text search technology to allow people to automatically search their digital photos for specific people, events, or places.

Pitch: How many digital photos do you have—100, 1,000, or maybe even 10,000? If I asked you to find all of your photos of yourself, or of your best friend, or of your ski trip to Colorado, how long would it take you? Admit it—you're probably like most of us, meaning that this task would consume a fair amount of your time.

But there is hope for you and me and others sharing our predicament. While there are lots of online services that help people print, organize, and share their photos, Riya is the first service that helps people automatically search them. Riya is a photo search service that uses face and text technology to look inside digital photos. Here's how it works. Once you have uploaded your photos to Riya, you click on the manual training tab to teach Riya what someone looks like. So, if you have several photos of your best friend Sarah Ryan, you select the photos and move them into a folder named "Sarah Ryan." Riya then "learns" what Sarah looks like. You can then search for Sarah in your library of photos, and Riya will find every photo in which Sarah appears. Riya also has an auto training tab, which takes the service even further. If you click on the auto training tab, Riya will search your photos and will tell you the people in your photos that it already knows. These are the people that someone else

has already taught Riya to recognize. In these instances, you can simply transfer Riya's prior learning to your account.

Riya also can search for locations and for combinations of locations and people. For example, if you tell Riya to show you all the pictures of yourself in Aspen, Colorado, guess what happens? Amazingly, if you're standing next to a ski lift that says "Aspen" Riya will find the picture. Further, if you tell Riya to show you all the pictures of Sarah Ryan and yourself in Aspen, Colorado, you got it. If you and Sarah were photographed while standing next to that same ski lift, Riya will find the picture.

Riya is still in beta mode and the founders like to say, "Riya is like a two-year-old child in terms of its recognition ability," so it's not perfect yet. But Riya is ready for you to give it a try. In terms of its business model, Riya has a number of possibilities for making money. The company is considering advertising, licensing its technology, and a possible acquisition by a larger company.

Q&A: Based on the material covered in this chapter, what questions would you ask the firm's founders before making your funding decision? What answers would satisfy you?

Decision: If you had to make your decision on just the information provided in the pitch and on the company's Web site, would you fund this firm? Why or why not?

CASE 1.1

Dream Dinners: Creating a Business Concept to Help Busy Families at Meal Time

www.dreamdinners.com

Bruce R. Barringer,
University of Central Florida
R. Duane Ireland,
Texas A&M University

Introduction

The best new businesses typically happen when three things converge: someone is passionate about an idea, a market opportunity for the idea exists, and the person with the idea has the skills to implement it. This is exactly what happened in the case of Dream Dinners.

The Birth of Dream Dinners

A stay-at-home mother, Stephanie Firchau regularly prepared meals for her family ahead of time and froze them to use on hectic days. She was so good at doing this that she frequently invited friends over to prepare meals with her. Word spread about what she was doing. "I started getting phone calls and e-mails from (family and friends) asking if they could come," she recalls. To accommodate the growing demand, she rented a commercial kitchen on several occasions, charging people only for the ingredients they used. For Stephanie, the whole idea of preparing meals ahead of time was to reduce

Dream Dinner's Recipe for Success: Passion, Market Opportunity, and the Skills to Make It Happen

Passion
Both founders were passionate about helping families share evening meals together

Market Opportunity
Feedback from customers willing to pay for the service indicated that a market opportunity existed

Skill
Founder Stephanie Firchau's professional background in catering and the business side of cooking

stress for her family around mealtime, yet still feed her family a home-cooked meal. Sure, on particularly busy evenings she could order pizza or serve her family Stouffer frozen dinners. But her preference remained for serving "home-cooked" meals that she had prepared for her family.

All the interest in what she was doing got Stephanie thinking that she might be onto a business idea. She had a background in catering so was familiar with the business side of cooking. To get help fleshing out her idea, she contacted Tina Kuna, a long-time friend and also a stay-at-home mother. The two agreed to start a business around Stephanie's idea, and Dream Dinners was born.

Foundations of Early Success

The structure of Dream Dinners quickly evolved. Like Stephanie's early experiences in the commercial kitchens, each Dream Dinners store is a physical location that provides a setting for its customers to prepare meals. This is how it works. A person registers on the Dream Dinners Web site and picks a 2-hour "session" that works best for her or him. Customers then pick the meals that they would like to prepare from a list of entrees that Dream Dinners is featuring that month. Usually, about 12 entrees can be prepared in a 2-hour session. Each entree serves four to six people. The entrees vary on a month-to-month basis and have included a wide variety of culinary delights, such as Stir-Fried Chicken with Shrimp, Mom's Macaroni & Beef, Deep Dish Chicago-Style Pizza, French Country Chicken, and Apple-Braised Boneless Pork Chops.

When customers arrive at the center, the ingredients for the entrees that they selected are ready to go. The ingredients are precut, and the appropriate measuring cups and spoons are available. The dinners can be customized on the spot—so if a customer's family is particularly fond of cheese, more cheese can be added. Instructions for preparing each dinner are provided and Dream Dinners' employees are on hand to offer advice and answer questions. Once the dinners are prepared, they are placed in

freezer-suitable containers. Dream Dinners even cleans up the mess. The idea is to provide customers the joy and emotional satisfaction of preparing meals for their families without the hassles involved with starting from scratch. The cost of 12 entrees is about $200, or just $3.00 per serving. Dream Dinners also sets up private parties for groups of friends or for co-workers who want to come in at the same time. Once at home, the meals can be heated in an oven or run through the microwave and served in a matter of minutes.

When Dream Dinners first started, the founders were surprised by the interest that people had in their concept. Recalling how intense the interest was, Tina Kuna, one of the cofounders, said, "We've had people e-mail us their FedEx numbers (apparently thinking that they could order premade meals to be shipped). We even had two women from Sacramento, California, fly up, cook over the weekend, and pack everything to ship on the plane home."[70] Looking back, the early success of Dream Dinners can be attributed in part to the three factors mentioned at the beginning of the case converging at the same time: passion for an idea, a market opportunity, and an entrepreneur with the skills needed to implement it. All of these qualities were present in Dream Dinner's rollout as a company. To illustrate this point, the figure titled "Dream Dinners' Recipe for Success: Passion, Market Opportunity, and the Skills to Make it Happen" depicts how these three attributes converged in Dream Dinner's case.

A New Position in the Marketplace

The position that Dream Dinners fills in the marketplace is another important reason for its success. The company basically wants to accomplish two things: (1) help families enjoy an evening meal together and (2) make those members of the family responsible for providing the meals feel good about themselves and their role in preparing the food.

The position that Dream Dinners carved out for itself in the evening meal marketplace is shown in the grid titled "Dream Dinners' Positioning Strategy." Looking at the grid,

Dream Dinner's Positioning Strategy

Combining the Advantages of Moderate Preparation Time and High Emotional Satisfaction Derived from Preparing Meals for Your Family

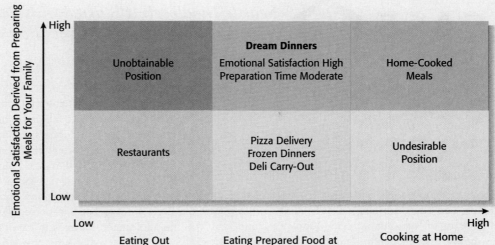

Dream Dinners is the only concept that helps people feel good about their role in preparing dinner for their families and still captures the advantage of relatively short preparation time. A particularly problematic position that Dream Dinners helps its customers avoid is the "Undesirable Position" shown in the lower right-hand portion of the graphic. This position represents incidences in which people take the time to prepare a home-cooked meal but receive little satisfaction from doing so because they feel rushed, they don't have all the ingredients they need, there is stress in the home, or for a variety of other reasons. People who fall into this category all too often are the ideal candidates for Dream Dinners' value proposition.

Future of Dream Dinners

Dream Dinners is now a rapidly growing franchise organization with over 130 franchise locations. Its concept was quickly copied, and there are now several similar companies selling franchises, including Super Suppers, Dinner by Design, and Meal Makers. A trade association has even been started, named the Easy Meal Prep Association, to help companies start meal preparation businesses.

The real question for Dream Dinners and its competitors is whether the concept is just a fad or whether it has real staying power. The company also runs the risk of growing too quickly and finding that it's difficult to provide proper support to all of its franchisees.

Discussion Questions

1. Which of the characteristics of successful entrepreneurs, discussed in this chapter, do you see in Stephanie Firchau and Tina Kuna? To what extent do you believe these characteristics have contributed to Dream Dinners' success?

2. Look at the figure labeled "Dream Dinners' Recipe for Success: Passion, Market Opportunity, and the Skills to Make it Happen." What would have happened if only two of the three attributes represented by the circles in the figure had been present when Dream Dinners was founded? If Stephanie Firchau hadn't had experience in the food business, is there any way that she and her cofounder could have overcome this limitation?

3. To what extent do you think Dream Dinners' basic business idea "adds value" in the lives of its customers? Who is the ideal candidate to be a Dream Dinners' customer?

4. What do you think? Do you think Dream Dinners' concept is just a fad or do you think that Dream Dinners has real staying power? Explain your answer.

Application Questions

1. Study Dream Dinners' Web site and make note of the various ways in which the company supports the communities in which it is located. In your judgment, is the company doing enough in this area? In what ways are the company's initiatives in this area good business as well as philanthropic?

2. Do you have skills in the areas that you are the most passionate about? If so, how could you match your passion and your skills to use a process to pursue viable business opportunities? If your passions and your skills aren't congruent, do you think this could limit your ability to become a successful entrepreneur? Is there anything you can do now to correct this lack of congruence?

Sources: Dream Dinners home page, www.dreamdinners.com (accessed May 7, 2006); A. Y. Pennington, "Two Entrepreneurs Have Put This Question on Ice With Do-It-Yourself Frozen Entrees," *Entrepreneur*, August 2003.

Seattle Biodiesel: It Started with Passion—Its Success Now Hinges on Execution Intelligence
www.seattlebiodiesel.com

Bruce R. Barringer,
University of Central Florida

R. Duane Ireland,
Texas A&M University

Introduction

If you travel to Seattle and sense the smell of popcorn in the air, you'll be disappointed if you think there is a movie theater or an amusement park nearby. Instead, you've probably just encountered a city bus. Seattle's buses are fueled by biodiesel, a clean alternative to diesel fuel. And the fuel has an aroma very similar to popcorn. Environmentalists sing the praises of the biodiesel for being an environmentally friendly substitute for regular diesel fuel.

John Plaza's Passion for Alternative Fuels

The buses in Seattle get their fuel from Seattle Biodiesel, a company that was started in 2003 by John Plaza. Plaza, a former airline pilot, quit his job flying commercial airplanes to pursue an interest in alternative fuels. He points to a single flight that caused him to decide to make a career change. "I was flying a 747 from Anchorage to Tokyo, and I started thinking about how much fuel that flight used," he said. "I figured out that in a 6 1/2 hour flight, we used enough fuel to power my personal vehicle for 42 years. I had to make a change."

The change that Plaza made was to start Seattle Biodiesel. Biodiesel is an alternative fuel for diesel engines and is refined from oils or fats, like the oils found in soybean, mustard, and canola seeds. To start the business, Plaza mortgaged his home, sold his boats and cars, and borrowed against his 401(k) plan. (Taking financial actions such as these are common for entrepreneurs who are passionate about their idea.) To get Seattle Biodiesel's refining operations up and running, Plaza acquired the rights to use a 7,000-square-foot warehouse next to a cement plant near downtown Seattle, which included a set of huge tanks that were formally used by a brewery. Biodiesel works in any diesel engine with few or no modifications. It can be burned pure or in combination with regular diesel fuel. As noted, the use of biodiesel fuel yields significant environmental benefits. It is also attractive because it reduces America's dependence on foreign sources of oil and provides another market for the sale of U.S.-grown crops.

A Fortunate Introduction

Shortly after he launched the company, John Plaza was introduced to Martin Tobias by a mutual friend. Tobias, a partner at Ignition Partners, a Seattle-area venture capital firm, was looking for investment opportunities on behalf of his firm. Through the process of investigating Seattle Biodiesel, Tobias became more and more excited about the company and its mission and started thinking that he might want to become personally involved. In late 2003, he left Ignition Partners to assume leadership of the firm, with Plaza's enthusiastic blessing. Plaza remained on the management team, but recognized the value that Tobias's experience could bring to the firm. Commenting on what attracted him to Seattle Biodiesel, Tobias said:

> As a venture capitalist I've reviewed over 1,200 plans and none have had the impact on me as what I saw from Seattle Biodiesel. I firmly believe the world has enough investors solving software problems, but there aren't enough people solving this country's energy dependency on foreign oil. John Plaza (the founder) and his management team have done an exceptional job bringing Seattle Biodiesel to life and now it's time to take it to the next level.

The way Tobias hopes to take Biodiesel to the next level is by growing the company and finding a way to make its economic model work. This effort will require sharp planning and execution. The biggest disadvantage of biodiesel is that it is more expensive than regular diesel fuel. As a result, the primary consumers of the fuel, to date, have been municipal governments, as part of their efforts to reduce pollution, and environmental enthusiasts. To move biodiesel into the mainstream market, Tobias believes that its price must be comparable to regular diesel.

Tobias's Three-Part Plan

To make biodiesel more price competitive, Tobias has a three-part plan. The plan is summarized in the table labeled "Tobias's Three-Point Plan to Drive Down the Cost of Biodiesel." First, Tobias plans to increase the scale of Seattle Biodiesel and implement process efficiencies. To fund this effort, the company recently attracted $7.5 million in venture capital funding. Second, Tobias plans to shift the way his company sources its raw materials. Currently, the company buys soybean oil from Iowa, which is then shipped by rail to Seattle for refining. To eliminate this step, Tobias is actively involved in an effort to help Washington

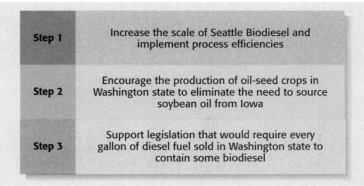

Tobias's Three-Part Plan to Drive Down the Cost of Biodiesel

Step 1	Increase the scale of Seattle Biodiesel and implement process efficiencies
Step 2	Encourage the production of oil-seed crops in Washington state to eliminate the need to source soybean oil from Iowa
Step 3	Support legislation that would require every gallon of diesel fuel sold in Washington state to contain some biodiesel

farmers learn how to integrate oil-seed crops into their crop rotations. If the raw material needed to refine biodiesel could come from local crops rather than from Iowa, a considerable cost savings could be realized. Finally, Seattle Biodiesel is actively involved in supporting legislation that would require every gallon of diesel fuel sold in the state to contain some biodiesel. Last year, the Minnesota legislature passed a law that requires gasoline there to be 20 percent ethanol by 2013. If the Washington legislature would follow suit in regard to diesel fuel, the demand for biodiesel fuel would increase dramatically. An increase in demand would allow Seattle Biodiesel to increase its scale even further, reducing per gallon refining and processing costs.

The Ultimate Importance of Execution Intelligence

The future of Seattle Biodiesel hinges on Plaza's and Tobias's ability to execute this carefully conceived plan. While passion is important, both entrepreneurs know that a process featuring sharp planning and execution must be in place and used to help a venture grow. Looking at the major businesses in Seattle, Tobias sees a bright future for Seattle Biodiesel. Considering that the U.S. diesel market is $160 billion a year, he said, Seattle Biodiesel could be bigger than Microsoft or Boeing.

Discussion Questions

1. What degree of confidence do you have that Tobias will be able to execute his three-part plan? What factors have to come together for the plan to work? What advantages does Seattle Biodiesel have in its efforts to execute Tobias's plan and continue to grow?

2. To what extent did passion play a role in the founding of Seattle Biodiesel and its early success? Do you think that someone without passion for alternative fuels could have successfully founded the firm? Why or why not?

3. Which of the myths of entrepreneurs are dispelled by John Plaza and Martin Tobias's involvement in Seattle Biodiesel?

4. To what extent does Seattle Biodiesel have the potential to (1) make an economic impact on the Seattle area and the state of Washington, (2) make an impact on society, and (3) make an impact on larger firms?

Application Questions

1. To what extent is Seattle Biodiesel creating a network of stakeholders that have a vested interest in seeing the company succeed? Make a list of these people or groups. Comment on how each group's success is linked to Seattle Biodiesel's ultimate success.

2. Make a list of 10 people you know who might help you if you decided to start a firm. Briefly comment on the ways that each individual could offer you assistance. In each case, make a note of what you are doing, or should be doing, to solidify and nurture these relationships.

Sources: W. Cornwall, "Biodiesel Suffers Image Setback," *The Seattle Times*, April 19, 2006; "Biodiesel Production Soars: 2005 Production Expected to Triple Last Year's Figures," *Environmental News Network*, November 9, 2005; "Seattle Biodiesel Closes $2 Million Financing: New CEO With Package," *Green Car Congress*, July 18, 2005.

Endnotes

1. L. Franklin, "Sarah Schupp Helps Parents Get Around In a College Town," *Portfolio* (Alumni Newsletter), Leeds School of Business, University of Colorado-Boulder, Winter, 2004.
2. Ibid.
3. K. Brown, "CU Grad's Magazine Targets Students' Moms, Dads," *The Boulder County Business Report*, November 11–24, 2005, 1–2.
4. I. M. Auggtums, "A Campus Tour For Grownups," *The Dallas Morning News*, December 11, 2005.

5. M. Minniti, W. D. Bygrave, and E. Autio, *Global Entrepreneurship Monitor 2005 Executive Report* (Babson College and London Business School, 2005).
6. E. Autio, *Global Entrepreneurship Monitor 2005 Report on High-Expectation Entrepreneurship* (Babson College and London Business School, 2005).
7. S. Parezo, "Breaking Down Some Small Business Myths," Fiducial homepage, www.fiducial.com (accessed May 18, 2006).
8. B. Bolton and J. Thompson, *Entrepreneurs* (Oxford: Butterworth-Heinemann, 2002).
9. P. Sharma and J. J. Chrisman, "Toward a Reconciliation of the Definitional Issues in the Field of Corporate Entrepreneurship," *Entrepreneurship Theory and Practice* 23, no. 3 (1999): 11–27.
10. H. H. Stevenson and J. C. Jarillo, "A Paradigm for Entrepreneurship: Entrepreneurial Management," *Strategic Management Journal* 11 (1990): 17–27.
11. R. D. Ireland, M. A. Hitt, and D. G. Sirmon, "A Model of Strategic Entrepreneurship," *Journal of Management* 29 (2003): 963–89.
12. C. Kirby and M. Yi. "Apple Turns 30," *San Francisco Chronicle OnLine*, www.sfgate.com (accessed May 22, 2006).
13. M. V. Copeland and O. Malik, "How to Ride the Fifth Wave," *Business 2.0*, July 2005; D. Bunnell, *Making the Cisco Connection* (New York: John Wiley & Sons, 2000).
14. R. D. Ireland, D. F. Kuratko, and M. H. Morris, "A Health Audit for Corporate Entrepreneurship: Innovation At All Levels," *Journal of Business Strategy* 6, no. 2 (2006): 21–30.: J. G. Covin and D. P. Slevin, "A Conceptual Model of Entrepreneurship as Firm Behavior," *Entrepreneurship Theory and Practice* 16 (1991): 7–25.
15. B. R. Barringer and A. C. Bluedorn, "The Relationship Between Corporate Entrepreneurship and Strategic Management," *Strategic Management Journal* 20 (1999): 421–44: M. H. Morris, *Entrepreneurial Intensity Sustainable Advantages for Individuals, Organizations, and Societies* (Westport, CT: Quorum Books, 1998).
16. R. Branson, *Losing My Virginity* (New York: Time Warner, 1999).
17. "Dawn of the Idea Czar," *BusinessWeek*, April 10, 2006.
18. Ladies Who Launch homepage, www.ladieswholaunch (accessed April 12, 2006).
19. R. D. Jager and R. Ortiz, *In the Company of Giants* (New York: McGraw-Hill, 1997).
20. L. Smolin, "Mixed Reactions to No New Einstein," www.physicstoday.org, January 2006; S. Shane, L. Kolvereid, and P. Westhead, "An Exploratory Examination of the Reasons Leading to New Firm Formation Across Country and Gender," *Journal of Business Venturing* 6 (1991): 431–46.
21. C. M. Christensen, *The Innovator's Dilemma* (Boston: Harvard Business School Press, 1997).
22. Office of Advocacy, *The State of Small Business* (Washington, DC: U.S. Government Printing Office, 1998).
23. S. Hamm, "The Education of Marc Andreessen," *BusinessWeek,* Industrial/Technology edition, April 13, 1998: 92.
24. D. Carnoy, "Richard Branson," *Success,* April 1998, 62–63.
25. L. C. Farrell, *Entrepreneurial Age* (New York: Allworth Press, 2001).
26. R. Adams, *A Good Hard Kick in the Ass* (New York: Crown Business, 2002).
27. Ladies Who Launch homepage, www.ladieswholaunch (accessed April 16, 2006).
28. Farrell, *Entrepreneurial Age.*
29. P. Krass, *The Book of Entrepreneurs' Wisdom* (New York: John Wiley & Sons, 1999).
30. Jager and Ortiz, *In the Company of Giants.*
31. S. Baillie, "High Tech Heroes," *Profit,* December 2000/January 2001.
32. G. Bounds, "Move Over, Coke." *The Wall Street Journal*, January 30, 2006, R1.
33. Adams, *A Good Hard Kick in the Ass.*
34. L. Hazleton, "Profile: Jeff Bezos," *Success,* July 1998: 60.
35. Ladies Who Launch homepage, www.ladieswholaunch (accessed April 16, 2006).
36. N. Koehn, *Brand New: How Entrepreneurs Earned Consumers' Trust from Wedgwood to Dell* (Boston: Harvard Business School Press, 2001).
37. Koehn, *Brand New.*
38. Baillie, "High Tech Heroes."
39. J. Cope, "Toward a Dynamic Learning Perspective of Entrepreneurship," *Entrepreneurship Theory and Practice*, 29 (2005): 373–97; Morris, *Entrepreneurial Intensity.*
40. P. Davidsson and B. Honig, "The Role of Social and Human Capital among Nascent Entrepreneurs," *Journal of Business Venturing* 18 (2003): 301–31.
41. F. W. Kellermanns, "Family Firm Resource Management: Commentary and Extensions," *Entrepreneurship Theory and Practice* 29 (2005): 313–19; E. B. Roberts, *Entrepreneurs in High Technology* (New York: Oxford University Press, 1991).

42. P. D. Reynolds, W. D. Bygrave, E. Autio, L. Cox, and M. Hay, *Global Entrepreneurship Monitor 2002 Executive Report* (Kansas City, MO: Kauffman Foundation Center for Entrepreneurship Leadership, 2002).

43. Morris, *Entrepreneurial Intensity.*

44. P. J. Bearse, "A Study of Entrepreneurship by Region and SMSA Size," in *Frontiers of Entrepreneurship Research* (Wellesley, MA: Babson College, 1982), 78–112.

45. T. Siebel, "Betting It All," in *Title,* ed. M. S. Malone (New York: John Wiley & Sons, 2002), 84.

46. C. Williams, *Lead, Follow, or Get Out of the Way* (New York: Times Books, 1981), 111.

47. J. H. Boyett and J. T. Boyett, *The Guru Guide to Entrepreneurship* (New York: John Wiley & Sons, 2001), 16.

48. S. Walton, *Made in America: My Story* (New York: Doubleday, 1992).

49. J. M. Hite, "Evolutionary Processes and Paths of Relationally Embedded Network Ties in Emerging Entrepreneurial Firms," *Entrepreneurship Theory and Practice* 29 (2005): 113–44; R. Quindlen, *Confessions of a Venture Capitalist* (New York: Warner Books, 2000).

50. G. Singh, "Work after Early Retirement" (PhD diss., University of Toronto, 1998).

51. P. Cappell, "Gourmet Meals, 100 Miles of River, and Sold-Out Seats," *The Wall Street Journal,* November 8, 2005, B1.

52. U.S. Census Bureau 2006 Report, U.S. Census Bureau homepage, www.census.gov (accessed May 18, 2006).

53. J. A. Challenger, "As Entrepreneurs, Seniors Lead U.S. Start-Ups," *Franchising World,* August 2005.

54. P. Weber and M. Schaper, "Understand the Grey Entrepreneur," *Journal of Enterprising Culture* 12 (2004), 147–64.

55. SCORE homepage, www.score.org (accessed May 18, 2006).

56. Press Release, "New York City Council Expands NFTE Youth Entrepreneurship Education Programs in City Schools, New York City Council, March 15, 2006.

57. P. B. Gray, "Can Entrepreneurship Be Taught," *Fortune Small Business,* March 10, 2006.

58. M. Minitte, W. B. Bygrave, and E. Autio, *Global Entrepreneurship Monitor 2005 Executive Report,* (Babson College and the London Business School).

59. Reynolds et al., *Global Entrepreneurship Monitor 2002 Executive Report* (Kansas City, MO: Kauffman Foundation Center for Entrepreneurship Leadership, 2002).

60. J. A. Schumpeter, *The Theory of Economic Development* (Cambridge, MA: Harvard University Press, 1994).

61. R. D. Ireland, D. F. Kuratko, and M. H. Morris, "Is Your Firm Ready for Corporate Entrepreneurship?" *Journal of Business Strategy* 27, no. 1 (2006): 10–17; M. Hammer, "Deep Change: How Operational Innovation Can Transform Your Company," *Harvard Business Review* 82, no. 4 (2004): 84–93.

62. U.S. Department of Labor homepage, www.dol.gov (accessed May 18, 2006).

63. E. Viardot, *Successful Marketing Strategy for High-Tech Firms* (New York: Artech House Publishers, 2004), xii.

64. Ewing Marion Kauffman Foundation, "More Than 500,000 Businesses Launched Each Month Says New Kauffman Foundation Study" (Kansas City, MO: The Ewing Marion Kauffman Foundation, September 22, 2005).

65. U.S. Department of Labor homepage, www.dol.gov (accessed May 18, 2006).

66. Commerce Department's Export Database, www.ita.doc.gov (accessed May 19, 2006).

67. "Amgen," *Standard & Poor's Stock Report,* www.standardandpoors.com (accessed April 3, 2004).

68. E. Welsch, "VeriChip IPO Bets an Implant Is in Your Future," *The Wall Street Journal,* January 11, 2006, A12A.

69. S. Downing, "The Social Construction of Entrepreneurship: Narrative and Dramatic Processes in the Coproduction of Organizations and Identities," *Entrepreneurship Theory and Practice* 29 (2005): 185–204.

70. A. Y. Pennington, "Two Entrepreneurs Have Put This Question on Ice With Do-It-Yourself Frozen Entrees." *Entrepreneur,* August 2003.

CHAPTER 2

recognizing *opportunities* and generating ideas

Getting Personal

with **ANAND V. CHHATPAR**

Best advice I've received

Make as many friends as you can as quickly as possible

First entrepreneurial experience

Web development company in high school!

Currently in my iPod

"Winning" by Jack Welch (audiobook)

BrainReactions:

Bringing an External Perspective to Business Organizations

Anand V. Chhatpar, who grew up in India, always aspired to be an entrepreneur. As a teenager, he started a software and Web development company before moving to the United States to pursue an engineering degree at the University of Wisconsin. Shortly after starting classes, Chhatpar met Osman Ozcanil, an international student from Turkey, who he credits with changing his thinking. Ozcanil's imagination and "everything is possible" attitude were very inspiring to Chhatpar.

The engineering college at Wisconsin sponsors a number of contests that provide students an opportunity to try their hand at inventing and writing business plans. Early on, Chhatpar and Ozcanil entered several contests, based on different inventions they had worked on together. In 2002, after several unsuccessful tries, the two won the Tong Prototype Prize for an ergonomically designed stationery binder they had invented. For a short period, Chhatpar and Ozcanil actually produced and sold the binder through a chain of office supply stores in the upper Midwest.

During the summer between his sophomore and junior year in college, Chhatpar landed an internship with Pitney Bowes, the company that makes postal meters. Getting an internship with Pitney Bowes is no easy task, and Chhatpar believes that winning the Tong Prototype Prize sealed the deal. During his internship, Chhatpar was assigned to Pitney Bowes's "concept studio," which is a think tank inside the company that brainstorms new product ideas. The group included a highly diverse array of Pitney Bowes employees, including scientists, engineers, anthropologists, managers, and interns. One thing that struck Chhatpar during their brainstorming sessions was that it was the interns, who were all college students, who came up with the most new ideas. This observation caused Chhatpar to think that maybe people inside an organization are too constrained by conventional thinking to generate novel ideas. If this is a problem, then a solution might be to organize groups of college students to conduct brainstorming sessions on behalf of business organizations.

To implement this idea, Chhatpar started working on a concept called BrainReactions, which would organize groups of college students to conduct brainstorming sessions on behalf of for-profit and not-for-profit business organizations. In Chhatpar's view, a carefully screened group of college

ANAND V. CHHATPAR

Founder & President,
BrainReactions
University of Wisconsin
BS, College of Engineering, 2004

THE UNIVERSITY OF
WISCONSIN
MADISON

What I do when I'm not working	My advice for new entrepreneurs	What I'd like to be doing in 10 years
Hang out with people who inspire me in person or via their books or blogs	*Think about scalability: Make something once—get paid for it over and over*	*Venture capitalist*

After studying this chapter you should be ready to:

L E A R N I N G

Objectives

1. Explain why it's important to start a new firm when its "window of opportunity" is open.

2. Explain the difference between an opportunity and an idea.

3. Describe the three general approaches entrepreneurs use to identify opportunities.

4. Identify the four environmental trends that are most instrumental in creating business opportunities.

5. List the personal characteristics that make some people better at recognizing business opportunities than others.

6. Identify the five steps in the creative process.

7. Describe the purpose of brainstorming and its use as an idea generator.

8. Describe how to use surveys to generate new business ideas.

9. Explain the purpose of maintaining an idea bank.

10. Describe three steps for protecting ideas from being lost or stolen.

students could offer businesses something they'd never achieve in-house—a fresh perspective, no inhibitions, youthful enthusiasm, an understanding of the needs and wants of young people, and close proximity to new technologies. In addition, Chhatpar reasoned, half of the world's population is under the age of 25. By working with college students, businesses could see themselves through the lens of their future (young people), rather than their present and their past.

To validate his concept, Chhatpar partnered with another engineering student and entered BrainReactions into several business plan competitions. In 2003, the plan won fourth place in the G. Steven Burrill Technology Business Plan Competition at the University of Wisconsin. Inspired by the validation of his concept, Chhatpar decided to make BrainReactions his full-time vocation and launched it as a business when he graduated in the spring of 2004.

BrainReactions is now a for-profit entrepreneurial venture organizing brainstorming sessions for businesses. The company, which has developed a proprietary way of screening candidates to participate in the brainstorming sessions, has conducted sessions for a variety of organizations, including Intuit, Bank of America, Quantum Learning Network, the United Nations, and the U.S. Peace Corps. Through its online platform, BrainReactions is able to draw from campuses across the world to put together the ideal set of participants to tackle a company's specific needs. The participants have spanned a wide range of disciplines, including engineering, business, art, theater, music, political science, and journalism. In fact, in its brief history, the company has found that the simplest and most elegant ideas come from students outside engineering, which engineering students then further develop and build on. The deliverables to a participating company include an executive summary, a discussion of the most exciting ideas and themes that emerged from the brainstorming sessions, concept visualizations in the form of sketches and images, and a complete list of the ideas that were generated. The basic BrainReactions package costs $12,000, with an option to upgrade to a $19,800 premium package. The photo at the beginning of the chapter shows a typical BrainReactions brainstorming session. Anand V. Chhatpar is the person in the red shirt seated towards the middle of the group.

Chhatpar is enthused about the future of BrainReactions and the value it can provide to its clients. In terms of whether BrainReactions solves a legitimate business problem, the following client testimonial provides insight for your consideration:

> *You came up with some of the best ideas that we came up with during our brainstorms, plus you gave us lots of new ideas. Also, it's easy for me to get buy-in on these ideas because they're coming from our customers.*[1]

–ZACHARY LYONS, CONSUMER TAX PRODUCT DEVELOPMENT TEAM INTUIT INC.

Identifying and Recognizing Opportunities

Essentially, entrepreneurs recognize an opportunity and turn it into a successful business. An **opportunity** is a favorable set of circumstances that creates a need for a new product, service, or business. Most entrepreneurial ventures are started in one of two ways. Some ventures are externally stimulated. In this instance, an entrepreneur decides to launch a firm, searches for and recognizes an opportunity, and then starts a business, as Jeff Bezos did when he created Amazon.com. In 1994, Bezos quit his lucrative job at a New York City investment firm and headed for Seattle with a plan to find an attractive opportunity and launch an e-commerce company.[2] Other firms are internally stimulated. An entrepreneur

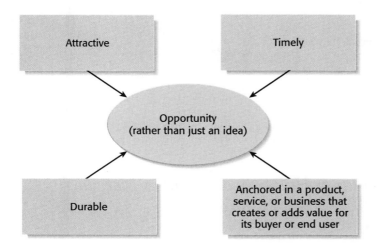

FIGURE 2.1

Four Essential Qualities of an Opportunity

recognizes a problem or an **opportunity gap** and creates a business to fill it. This was the case with BrainReactions.

Regardless of which of these two ways an entrepreneur starts a new business, opportunities are tough to spot. It is difficult to identify a product, service, or business opportunity that isn't merely a different version of something already available. A common mistake that entrepreneurs make in the opportunity recognition process is picking a currently available product or service that they like or are passionate about and then trying to build a business around a slightly better version of it. Although this approach seems sensible, such is usually not the case. The key to opportunity recognition is to identify a product or service that people need and are willing to buy, not one that an entrepreneur wants to sell.[3]

As shown in Figure 2.1, an opportunity has four essential qualities: It is (1) attractive, (2) durable, (3) timely, and (4) anchored in a product, service, or business that creates or adds value for its buyer or end user.[4] For an entrepreneur to capitalize on an opportunity, its **window of opportunity** must be open.[5] The term *window of opportunity* is a metaphor describing the time period in which a firm can realistically enter a new market. Once the market for a new product is established, its window of opportunity opens. As the market grows, firms enter and try to establish a profitable position. At some point, the market matures, and the window of opportunity closes. This is the case with Internet search engines. Yahoo!, the first search engine, appeared in 1995, and the market grew quickly, with the addition of Lycos, Excite, Hotbot, AltaVista, and others. Google entered the market in 1998, sporting advanced search technology. Since then, the search engine market has matured, and the window of opportunity has essentially closed. Today, it would be very difficult for a new start-up search engine firm to be successful unless it was extraordinarily well funded and offered compelling advantages over already established competitors.

It is important to understand that there is a difference between an opportunity and an idea. An **idea** is a thought, an impression, or a notion.[6] An idea may or may not meet the criteria of an opportunity. This is a critical point because, as we noted in Chapter 1, many entrepreneurial ventures fail not because the entrepreneurs that launched them didn't work hard, but rather because there was no real opportunity to begin with. Before getting excited about a business idea, it is crucial to understand whether the idea fills a need and meets the criteria for an opportunity. When it doesn't, it can lead to a disappointing outcome, as illustrated in the boxed feature titled "What Went Wrong?"

Now let's look at the three ways to identify an opportunity, as depicted in Figure 2.2.

1. Explain why it's important to start a new firm when its "window of opportunity" is open.

2. Explain the difference between an opportunity and an idea.

FIGURE 2.2

**Three Ways to Identify
an Opportunity**

Observing Trends	Solving a Problem	Finding Gaps in the Marketplace

Planet Hollywood: An Idea Instead of an Opportunity
www.planethollywood.com

If a seemingly attractive new product or service idea consistently disappoints customers, it's almost sure to fail. The story of a Hollywood-themed restaurant that decided to focus on the lure of Hollywood rather than the quality of its food provides a vivid example of the importance of one of the four qualities of an attractive opportunity; namely, the opportunity must be anchored in a product or service that adds value for its buyer or end user.

In 1991, Planet Hollywood entered the restaurant industry. The idea was to create a Hollywood-themed restaurant chain, where visitors could catch a glimpse of their favorite movie stars. The initial investors, and presumably frequent diners at the restaurants, included Bruce Willis, Demi Moore, Whoopi Goldberg, Sylvester Stallone, and Arnold Schwarzenegger. The chain expanded rapidly and soon had 80 restaurants worldwide. Premier locations were secured in New York City, Chicago, and Los Angeles along with Paris, London, Sydney, and Tokyo.

Regrettably, the concept fell flat. The company has gone bankrupt twice. Although it is still on its feet, it has restaurants in only five U.S. cities. Interestingly, this concept seems to work better internationally in that there are about a dozen Planet Hollywood units located outside the United States. So how could a company with so much hype and so many famous people behind it flop so dramatically? Several things went wrong with Planet Hollywood, all tied to the basic notion that the concept may have been more of an idea than an opportunity to begin with.

First, there was the food. The company never advertised its food, and by most accounts, it was overpriced and average at best. Second, the lure of Planet Hollywood was to catch a glimpse of a movie star—if only for a moment. People would line up outside the restaurants and whisper to one another, "I wonder if Demi Moore or Whoopi Goldberg is inside?" But the stars rarely showed up—leaving guests disappointed. To compensate, the restaurants did display a lot of movie memorabilia. But this facet of Planet Hollywood's approach made it more of a one-time destination rather than a restaurant that people would frequent often.

So Planet Hollywood's customers would consistently overpay for average food and leave disappointed because they didn't see a movie star. As a result, in the end, the experience offered by the company failed one of the key tests of an opportunity: The idea wasn't anchored in a product that created enough value for its customers to represent a legitimate opportunity.

Questions for Critical Thinking

1. Evaluate Planet Hollywood's idea on all four dimensions of an opportunity. On a scale of 1 to 5 (5 is high), how does the idea that was launched as Planet Hollywood rate on each of the four dimensions?

2. If you have dined at a Planet Hollywood, describe your experience. What is your reaction to the food? Did your dining experience create value for you? If you have not dined at one of these units, find a friend who has done so and ask these questions.

3. When Planet Hollywood first started to struggle, what could the founders have done to try to revitalize the chain?

4. Are you surprised that Planet Hollywood turned out to be more of an idea than an opportunity? What, if anything, could the founders of the firm have done to create a different outcome?

Source: Planet Hollywood homepage, *www.planethollywood.com* (accessed June 5, 2006); Matt Haig. *Brand Failures* (London: Kogan Page, 2003).

Observing Trends

The first approach to identifying opportunities is to observe trends and study how they create opportunities for entrepreneurs to pursue. Economic factors, social factors, technological advances, and political action and regulatory statutes are the most important trends to follow. Changes in these areas often provide the impetus for a business opportunity. There are two ways entrepreneurs can get a handle on these trends. First, they can carefully study and observe them. Some entrepreneurs are better at this than others, depending on their personal characteristics and levels of motivation. Entrepreneurs who have industry experience, who have a well-established social network, who are creative, and who are, in general, alert are more likely to spot trends and interpret them correctly.[7] The second way entrepreneurs understand emerging trends is to purchase customized forecasts and market analyses from independent research firms. These tools allow for a fuller understanding of how specific trends create opportunities. Forrester Research, Gartner Group, and Yankee Group are some of the research firms that produce these reports, as illustrated in the boxed feature "Savvy Entrepreneurial Firm."

LEARNING Objective

3. Describe the three general approaches entrepreneurs use to identify opportunities.

savvy entrepreneurial firm
Getting High-Quality Advice on Emerging Trends

Savvy entrepreneurs realize they don't have the time and resources to know everything about emerging trends. This is particularly true of the entrepreneurs in the area of technology, where changes occur daily. So how do entrepreneurs keep up with the latest developments in their industry? Entrepreneurial firms can take advantage of the services offered by professional research firms, such as Forrester Research, Gartner, and Yankee Group. These companies provide conventional consulting services but also provide a variety of other products and services that may be more affordable to young entrepreneurial firms. For example, Forrester Research, which specializes in emerging technologies, offers the following:

- Annual memberships that provide access to research on specific business, industry, and technology topics
- Advisory and consulting services
- Access to global surveys pertaining to consumer attitudes toward and use of technology
- Peer-level executive program, forums, and hands-on boot camps

Other companies (e.g., Gartner) offer publications on emerging trends that can be downloaded from the Internet. The research is cutting-edge and may give a firm important insight that it never would have generated internally.

For entrepreneurial firms, an added benefit of using the services of consulting companies is getting an outside perspective on their current and potential operations. Prudent firms know that their time and field of vision is limited and that investing in a fresh perspective on business trends and developments can often be money well spent.

Questions for Critical Thinking

1. What disadvantages might an entrepreneurial firm experience by relying on outside firms for understanding emerging trends? Are some of these disadvantages more relevant in the short term while others are more relevant for the long term?
2. What options do entrepreneurs have for finding less expensive ways to collect the type of material supplied by a firm like Forrester Research or Gartner?
3. When might it be essential for entrepreneurs to rely on material prepared by an outside firm rather than on their own analysis?
4. Is it possible for aspiring entrepreneurs to become overwhelmed by the rapid pace of environmental changes? What advice would you offer to the person believing that change is too difficult to predict and understand?

Sources: Forrester Research homepage, www.forrester.com (accessed May 28, 2006); Gartner homepage, www.gartner.com (accessed May 28, 2006).

Figure 2.3 provides a summary of the relationship between the environmental factors mentioned previously and identifying opportunity gaps. Next, let's look at how each of these factors helps entrepreneurs spot business, product and service opportunity gaps.

Economic Forces Economic forces affect consumers' level of disposable income. When incomes are high, people are more willing to buy products and services that enhance their lives. Individual sectors of the economy have a direct impact on consumer buying patterns. For example, a drop in interest rates typically leads to an increase in new home construction and furniture sales. Conversely, a rapid decline in the stock market, such as the one in the late 1990s and early 2000s, may lead to a reduction in the demand for luxury goods.

When studying how economic forces affect opportunities, it is important to evaluate who has money to spend. For example, an increase in the number of women in the workforce and the subsequent increase in their disposable income is largely responsible for the number of boutique clothing stores targeting professional women that have opened in the past several years. Anne Fountaine and Tory Burch are examples of these boutiques competing on a national or international scale. Interestingly, a large number of boutiques are local entrepreneurial ventures with locations in a single community. Similarly, as more teens enter the workforce, demand increases for products they buy, such as designer clothing, MP3 players, and concert tickets. Sales of the Apple iPod, for example, took off so rapidly in part because teenagers have increasing levels of cash to spend.

Another trend that is affected by economic factors is pressure on firms to improve their economic performance. In a PricewaterhouseCoopers survey of fast-growth firms, which are companies identified in the media as the fastest-growing U.S. businesses over the past 5 years, 74 percent reported that cost control is one of their top priorities.[8] Many entrepreneurs have taken advantage of this trend by starting firms that help other firms control costs. In the chemical industry, for example, ChemConnect (founded in 1995) provides an online marketplace to make it less expensive for chemical companies to buy and sell chemicals on a global scale.[9]

FIGURE 2.3

Environmental Trends Suggesting Business or Product Opportunity Gaps

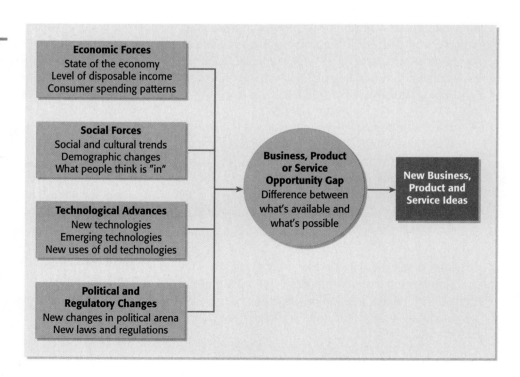

As baby boomers age, opportunities will grow for firms that provide unique products and services to this age group. Look for the resulting expansion of entrepreneurial opportunities in health care, organic food, insurance, travel and entertainment.

Social Forces An understanding of the impact of social forces on trends and how they affect new product, service, and business ideas is a fundamental piece of the opportunity recognition puzzle. The persistent proliferation of fast-food restaurants, for example, isn't due primarily to people's love of fast food but rather to the fact that people are busy—the number of households with both parents working remains high. Similarly, the Sony Walkman was developed not because consumers wanted smaller radios, but because people wanted to listen to music while on the move—while riding the subway, for example, and while exercising. The stress that many people experience while juggling work, family, and other activities provides opportunities for products and services that relieve stress. For example, the number of spa openings in the United States rose 12 percent from 2002 to 2004, with the fastest-growing segment being medical spas or wellness clinics. This increase is attributed to a jump in the number of people trying to deal with the stress in their daily lives, along with paying greater attention to mental health and wellness.[10] Additional recent social trends that allow for new opportunities are the following:

- Family and work patterns (e.g., the number of two-income households and the number of single-parent families)
- The aging of the population
- The increasing diversity in the workplace
- The globalization of industries
- The increasing focus on health care and fitness
- The proliferation of computers and the Internet
- The continual increase in the number of cell phone users
- New forms of music and other types of entertainment

There is an ebb and flow pertaining to how much each of these trends affects the availability of new opportunities. For example, although the number of households that have Internet access continues to grow, the window of opportunity to launch a new Internet search engine, as discussed previously, is essentially closed. Conversely, substantial opportunities may exist in other Internet-related areas, such as wireless Internet access, Web TV, and enhanced encryption software that secures the privacy of computer networks.

Technological Advances Advances in technology frequently dovetail with economic and social changes to create opportunities. For example, the creation of the cell phone is a technological achievement, but it was motivated by an increasingly mobile population that finds many advantages to having the ability to communicate with its co-workers, customers, friends, and families from anywhere and everywhere. Similarly, many e-commerce sites are technological marvels, allowing a customer to order products, pay for them, and choose how quickly they're shipped. But again, it isn't so much the technology that makes e-commerce attractive. The ultimate reason most people buy online is because they are busy and prefer to shop when they have free time rather than being restricted to traditional store hours and store locations.

In addition, technological advances often provide opportunities to help people satisfy basic needs in a better or more convenient way. In many areas people's needs don't change over time. For example, people who shave have always wanted to minimize the number of nicks and shaving time and get as close a shave as possible. These and other shaving-related desires will probably never change. What does change is the degree to which new technologies can better satisfy these needs and desires.

Another aspect of technological advances is that once a technology is created, products often emerge to advance it. For example, RealNetworks was launched to add video capabilities to the Internet, which took the Internet to the next level. The following quote from RealNetwork's Web site explains the impact that it is having on Internet users:

> In 1995, RealNetworks, Inc. pioneered the entire Internet media industry, and continues to fuel its exponential growth. Because the Internet was built to handle text-based information, not audio and video and other rich media, RealNetworks, Inc. foresaw the need for specific solutions that could handle the creation, delivery and consumption of media via the Internet. That led RealNetworks, Inc. to invent and release the RealPlayer and RealAudio in 1995. Today, hundreds of millions of RealPlayers that have been downloaded throughout the world take advantage of RealNetworks, Inc. world-class media creation, delivery and playback technology.[11]

Political Action and Regulatory Changes   Political and regulatory changes also provide the basis for opportunities. For example, new laws create opportunities for entrepreneurs to start firms to help companies comply with these laws. RMS Systems, for example, designed a product called Compliance Suite, which helps its customers track their compliance with Environmental Protection Agency and Occupational Safety and Health Administration regulations. Many firms have benefited by helping others comply with the Sarbanes-Oxley Act of 2002, which requires certain companies to retain all business records, including electronic documents and messages, for at least 5 years. Since the act was put on the books, publicly held companies have spent millions of dollars to meet the new compliance rules. The beneficiaries have been software and hardware companies, which help companies store and manage this data.[12]

Political change also engenders new business and product opportunities. For example, global political instability and the threat of terrorism have resulted in many firms becoming more security conscious. These companies need new products and services to protect their physical assets and intellectual property as well as to protect their customers and employees. The backup data storage industry, for example, is expanding because of this new trend in the tendency to feel the need for data to be more protected than in the past. Companies such as Protect-Data.com and EMC provide data storage services that allow companies to back up their computer data in a secure off-site location.

Table 2.1 offers additional examples of changes in environmental trends that provided fertile soil for opportunities and subsequent concepts to take advantage of them.

Solving a Problem

The second approach to identifying opportunities is to recognize problems and find ways to solve them.[13] These problems can be recognized by observing the challenges that people encounter in their daily lives and through more simple means, such as intuition, serendipity, or chance.[14] There are many problems that have yet to be solved. Commenting

Examples of How Changes in Environmental Trends Provide Openings for New Business
TABLE 2.1 and Product Opportunities

Changing Environmental Trend	Resulting New Business, Product, and Service Opportunities	Companies That Resulted
Economic Trends		
Teenagers with more cash and disposable income	Designer clothes, compact discs, MP3 players, games consoles, handheld computers	GAP, Banana Republic, MTV, Sega, Palm
Increased interest in the stock market	Online brokerage services, stock research services, magazines for investors	BuyAndHold.com, Motley Fool, The Street.com, *Business 2.0* magazine
Social Trends		
Increasing predominance of dual-income families leaves less time to cook at home	Restaurants, microwavable dinners, food delivery services	McDonald's, Stouffer's, Healthy Choice Frozen Dinners, Domino's Pizza, Dream Dinners
Increased interest in fitness, as the result of new medical information warning of the hazards of being overweight	Fitness centers, in-house exercise equipment, weight-loss centers, health food stores	Curves International, Stair Master Fitness Equipment, GNC Nutrition Center, Whole Foods Market, Wild Oats
Increased mobility of the population, as the result of better transportation and increased disposable incomes	Cell phones, laptop computers, handheld computers, phone cards	Nokia, Palm, Handspring, Research in Motion
Technological Trends		
Development of the Internet	E-commerce, improved supply chain management, improved communications	Yahoo!, Amazon.com, Google, Firefox, Travelocity, eBay, Overstock.com
Advances in biotechnology	Biotech-related pharmaceutical products, food products, veterinary products, information services	Genetech, Amgen, Genzyme, BioInform, Bio Online
Political and Regulatory Trends		
Increased EPA and OSHA standards	Consulting companies, software to monitor compliance, products to help ensure compliance	RMS Systems, PrimaTech, Compliance Consulting Services, Inc.

on this issue and how noticing problems can lead to the recognition of business ideas, Philip Kotler, a marketing expert, said:

> Look for problems. People complain about it being hard to sleep through the night, get rid of clutter in their homes, find an affordable vacation, trace their family origins, get rid of garden weeds, and so on. As the late John Gardner, founder of Common Cause, observed: "Every problem is a brilliantly disguised opportunity."[15]

Consistent with this observation, many companies have been started by people who have experienced a problem in their own lives, and then realized that the solution to the problem represented a business opportunity. For example, in 1991, Jay Sorensen dropped a cup of coffee in his lap because the paper cup was too hot. This experience led Sorensen to invent an insulating cup sleeve and to start a company to sell it. Since launching his venture, the company, Java Jacket, has sold over 1 billion cup sleeves.

Some business ideas are gleaned from the recognition of problems in emerging trends. For example, Symantec Corporation created Norton antivirus software to rid computers of viruses, and computer firewall firms such as McAfee developed software to secure computer systems and guard them against attack from hackers or unauthorized users. These companies took advantage of the problems that surface when new technology is introduced. At other times, the process is less deliberate. An individual may set out to solve a practical problem and realize that the solution may have broader market appeal. The most romantic example of this is the founding of Cisco Systems:

> The Cisco legend is the tale of two inhibited sweethearts at Stanford University in the late 1970s. Sandra Lerner of the Stanford University Business School and Leonard Bosack of the computer science department wanted to send love letters to each other via e-mail, but their respective departments used different computer networks. So Len and Sandy, impassioned and determined, invented the router—a mysterious black box consisting of a twist of cable and some agile software. Then they conceived Cisco (which is the last syllable in San Francisco, the city near where they lived). The router made Cisco the fastest-growing company ever. In 2004, 20 years after its founding, Cisco was worth $162 billion.[16]

At still other times, someone may simply notice a problem that others are having and think that the solution might represent an opportunity. Often, however, when you get the whole story, it turns out that the discovery wasn't quite so unanticipated. A **serendipitous discovery** is a chance discovery made by someone with a prepared mind.[17]

Newgistics, an entrepreneurial firm specializing in helping consumers return merchandise they order online and through catalogs is a good example of the serendipity that sometimes surrounds the launching of a new business. The firm was started by Phil Siegel, who had worked at Boston Consulting Group for a decade, where he had acquired a thorough understanding of consumer and retail businesses. Rod Adams, the venture capitalist who provided the early funding for the firm, tells of the auspicious conversation that led to the founding of Newgistics:

> Phil's idea for Newgistics grew out of a conversation with his wife, Lauren, a dedicated Internet and catalog shopper who relished the convenience of online buying. She'd just ordered a blouse from a well-known Internet retailer, and it didn't fit. Now, she'd have to e-mail the site, pack and ship the blouse, and wait until the merchant received it before getting credit toward another order. Why, Lauren lamented, did returning or exchanging these goods have to be so inconvenient? Why wasn't there a way to do it as easily as with a bricks-and-mortar retailer? Phil had a hunch that millions of online and catalog shoppers would second her concern. He resolved to start a company that would streamline the complex product return process—not just for the end consumer but for online and catalog retail merchants as well.[18]

There's no denying that Cartridge World helps solve a problem. Who hasn't cringed at the price of a new ink printer cartridge? A consumer can bring an empty ink cartridge to a Cartridge World store, wait while the cartridge is professionally refilled, and leave with a full cartridge at about half the price of a new one.

Newgistics offers Intelligent Returns Management, a service that provides catalog and Internet shopping customers a simple process for returning items by mail and getting credit for them. Among the first retailers to sign up for the service were Eddie Bauer, Spiegel, and J. Crew.

Newgistics received funding primarily because the company solves a specific problem. Many other colorful examples of people who launched businesses to solve problems are shown in Table 2.2.

There are opportunities that result from a combination of solving a problem and environmental trends. For example, in the mid-1980s, baby boomers (people born between 1945 and 1963) helped create a demand for golf-related products in the United States. This demographic group has been largely responsible for the popularity of golf in the 1980s, 1990s, and early 2000s. The first wave of baby boomers is now in their late 50s and early 60s, and research shows that golfers not only play more as they get older but that their overall spending on golf-related products increases.[19] This suggests that additional opportunities may be available for golf-related products—particularly those that are attractive to older golfers. Radar Golf, the subject of the "You Be the VC 2" feature at the end of the chapter, makes golf balls that have small electronic tags inside making them easy to find when lost. This is an example of a company that not only solves a problem—finding lost golf balls—but capitalizes on a societal trend—aging baby boomers and their interest in golf.

Finding Gaps in the Marketplace

The third approach to identifying opportunities is to recognize a need that customers have that is not being satisfied—by either large, established firms or entrepreneurial ventures. Large retailers like Wal-Mart, Costco, and Home Depot compete primarily on price by serving large groups of customers with similar needs. They do this by offering the most popular items targeted toward mainstream consumers. While this approach allows the large retailers to achieve economies of scale, it leaves gaps in the marketplace. This is the reason that small clothing boutiques and specialty shops exist. The small boutiques, which often sell designer

TABLE 2.2 Businesses Created to Solve a Problem

Entrepreneur(s)	Year	Problem	Solution	Name of Business That Resulted
Julie Aigner-Clark	1997	No method for exposing young children (six months to three years old) to arts and sciences	Created a company to produce videos designed to capture the attention and stimulate the minds of young children	Baby Einstein
Scott Cook	1982	Frustration over traditional process of paying bills and keeping track of personal finances	Developed a software program (Quicken) to make the task easier	Intuit
Lisa Druxman	2002	No fitness routine available to help new mothers stay fit and be with their newborns at the same time	Created a franchise organization that promotes a workout routine (which involves a 45-minute power walk with strollers) that mothers and their newborns can do together	Stroller Strides
Rob Glaser	1995	No way to play audio and video on the Internet	Developed software to play audio and video on the "Net"	RealNetworks
Fred Smith	1973	Inability to get spare parts delivered on a timely basis for his company, a jet aircraft sales firm	Started a new company to help others get packages delivered in a timely manner	Federal Express (now called FedEx)
Jerry Yang and David Filo	1994	No method to find or organize favorite Web sites	Created online directories to find and store favorites	Yahoo!

clothes or clothing for hard-to-fit people, are willing to carry merchandise that doesn't sell in large enough quantities for Wal-Mart or JC Penney to carry. For example, Adelita, a clothing boutique in Seattle, carries eclectic offerings from hard-to-find designers along with stylish handbags, lingerie, yoga wear, and upscale baby clothing. Adelita fills a gap in the marketplace by offering people with particular tastes a line of clothing they would be unlikely to find at a larger store that targets the needs of mainstream customers.

There are also gaps in the marketplace that represent consumer needs that aren't being met by anyone. These gaps are hard to recognize but offer potentially large rewards for those able to fill them. An example of a firm that recognized a gap that fits this profile is Curves International, which is the subject of Case 6.2 later in the book. Curves, which was founded in 1992 by Gary Heavin, is a fitness center just for women. At the time Curves was founded, most fitness centers targeted fitness enthusiasts and included a number of amenities, ranging from showers and towel service to swimming pools. Rather than compete head-to-head against these centers, Heavin opened a fitness center targeted towards an ignored part of the market: overweight women, 30 years old and older, who had never worked out before. Heavin believed that many women in this age group cared deeply about their health and appearance but didn't want to join a fitness center full of people who were already fit. He also felt that if he made the center affordable, which he did by cutting out many of the amenities, it would inspire women to give fitness a try. Heavin's idea was on the mark in that it represented a true opportunity. By targeting a market that had never been served before, Curves captured the attention of a large number of women and generated tremendous positive word of mouth. In fact, until recently, the company spent very little on advertising. Most of its new members come from referrals.[20]

Personal Characteristics of the Entrepreneur

LEARNING Objective

5. List the personal characteristics that make some people better at recognizing business opportunities than others.

How did Michael Dell come up with the idea of a "build it yourself" computer company? How did Howard Schultz, the founder of Starbucks, figure out how to turn a 50-cent cup of coffee and a little skimmed milk into a $3 plus cappuccino?

Researchers have identified several characteristics that tend to make some people better at recognizing opportunities than others. Before we talk about them, there is an important yet subtle difference between two key terms pertaining to this topic. We've already defined opportunity: a favorable set of circumstances that create the need for a new product, service, or business. But, the term **opportunity recognition** refers to the process of *perceiving* the possibility of a profitable new business or a new product or service. That is, an opportunity cannot be taken until it's *recognized*. Now let's look at some specific characteristics shared by those who excel at recognizing an opportunity.

Prior Experience Several studies show that prior experience in an industry helps entrepreneurs recognize business opportunities.[21] For example, a report of the *Inc.* 500 founders revealed that 43 percent of those studied got the idea for their new businesses while working for companies in the same industries.[22] This finding is consistent with research conducted by the National Federation of Independent Businesses.[23] There are several explanations. By working in an industry, an individual may spot a market niche that is underserved. It is also possible that while working in a particular area, an individual builds a network of social contacts in that industry that may provide insights that lead to opportunities.

Once an entrepreneur starts a firm, new venture opportunities become apparent. This is called the **corridor principle**, which states that once an entrepreneur starts a firm, he or she begins a journey down a path where "corridors" leading to new venture opportunities become apparent.[24] The insight provided by this principle is simply that once someone starts a firm and becomes immersed in an industry, it's much easier for that person to see new opportunities in the industry than it is for someone looking in from the outside.

Cognitive Factors Opportunity recognition may be an innate skill or a cognitive process.[25] There are some who think that entrepreneurs have a "sixth sense" that allows them to see opportunities that others miss. This sixth sense is called **entrepreneurial**

alertness, which is formally defined as the ability to notice things without engaging in deliberate search.[26] Most entrepreneurs see themselves in this light, believing they are more "alert" than others.[27] Alertness is largely a learned skill, and people who have more knowledge of an area tend to be more alert to opportunities in that area than others. A computer engineer, for example, would be more alert to needs and opportunities within the computer industry than a lawyer would be.

The research findings on entrepreneurial alertness are mixed. Some researchers conclude that alertness goes beyond noticing things and involves a more purposeful effort.[28] For example, one scholar believes that the crucial difference between opportunity finders (i.e., entrepreneurs) and nonfinders is their relative assessments of the marketplace.[29] In other words, entrepreneurs may be better than others at sizing up the marketplace and inferring the likely implications.

Social Networks The extent and depth of an individual's social network affects opportunity recognition.[30] People who build a substantial network of social and professional contacts will be exposed to more opportunities and ideas than people with sparse networks.[31] This exposure can lead to new business starts.[32] In a survey of 65 start-ups, half the founders reported that they got their business ideas through social contacts.[33] A similar study examined the differences between **solo entrepreneurs** (those who identified their business ideas on their own) and **network entrepreneurs** (those who identified their ideas through social contacts). The researchers found that network entrepreneurs identified significantly more opportunities than solo entrepreneurs but were less likely to describe themselves as being particularly alert or creative.[34]

An important concept that sheds light on the importance of social networks to opportunity recognition is the differential impact of strong-tie versus weak-tie relationships. Relationships with other people are called "ties." We all have ties. **Strong-tie relationships** are characterized by frequent interaction and ties between co-workers, friends, and spouses. **Weak-tie relationships** are characterized by infrequent interaction and ties between casual acquaintances. According to research in this area, it is more likely that an entrepreneur will get a new business idea through a weak-tie than a strong-tie relationship[35] because strong-tie relationships, which typically form between like-minded individuals, tend to reinforce insights and ideas the individuals already have. Weak-tie relationships, on the other hand, which form between casual acquaintances, are not as apt to be between like-minded individuals, so one person may say something to another that sparks a completely new idea.[36] An example might be an electrician explaining to a restaurant owner how he solved a business problem. After hearing the solution, the restaurant owner might say, "I would never have heard that solution from someone in my company or industry. That insight is completely new to me and just might help me solve my problem."

Creativity **Creativity** is the process of generating a novel or useful idea. Opportunity recognition may be, at least in part, a creative process.[37] On an anecdotal basis, it is easy to see the creativity involved in the formation of many products, services, and businesses.

For an individual, the creative process can be broken into five stages, as shown in Figure 2.4.[38] Let's examine how these stages relate to the opportunity recognition process.[39] In the figure, the horizontal arrows that point from box to box suggest that the creative process progresses through five stages. The vertical arrows suggest that if at any stage an individual (such as an entrepreneur) gets "stuck" or doesn't have enough information or insight to continue, the best choice is to return to the preparation stage—to obtain more knowledge or experience before continuing to move forward.

Preparation. Preparation is the background, experience, and knowledge that an entrepreneur brings to the opportunity recognition process. Just as an athlete must practice to excel, an entrepreneur needs experience to spot opportunities. Studies show that 50 to 90 percent of start-up ideas emerge from a person's prior work experience.[40]

LEARNING Objective

6. Identify the five steps in the creative process.

FIGURE 2.4

Five Steps to Generating Creative Ideas

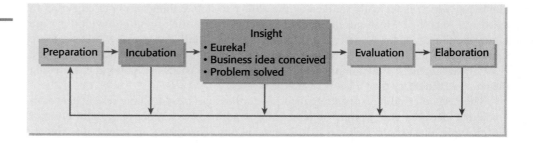

Incubation. Incubation is the stage during which a person considers an idea or thinks about a problem; it is the "mulling things over" phase. Sometimes incubation is a conscious activity, and sometimes it is unconscious and occurs while a person is engaged in another activity. One writer characterized this phenomenon by saying that "ideas churn around below the threshold of consciousness."[41]

Insight. Insight is the flash of recognition—when the solution to a problem is seen or an idea is born. It is sometimes called the "eureka" experience. In a business context, this is the moment an entrepreneur recognizes an opportunity. Sometimes this experience pushes the process forward, and sometimes it prompts an individual to return to the preparation stage. For example, an entrepreneur may recognize the potential for an opportunity but may feel that more knowledge and thought is required before pursuing it.

Evaluation. Evaluation is the stage of the creative process during which an idea is subjected to scrutiny and analyzed for its viability. Many entrepreneurs mistakenly skip this step and try to implement an idea before they've made sure it is viable. Evaluation is a particularly challenging stage of the creative process because it requires an entrepreneur to take a candid look at the viability of an idea.[42] The process of evaluating the feasibility of new business ideas is discussed in Chapter 3.

Elaboration. Elaboration is the stage during which the creative idea is put into a final form: The details are worked out and the idea is transformed into something of value, such as a new product, service, or business concept. In the case of a new business, this is the point at which a business plan is written.

Figure 2.5 illustrates the opportunity recognition process. As shown in the figure, there is a connection between an awareness of emerging trends and the personal characteristics of

FIGURE 2.5

The Opportunity Recognition Process

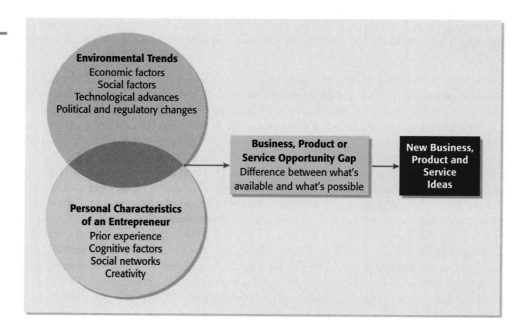

the entrepreneur because the two facets of opportunity recognition are interdependent. For example, an entrepreneur with a well-established social network may be in a better position to recognize emerging technological trends than an entrepreneur with a poorly established social network. Or the awareness of an emerging technology trend, such as digitization, may prompt an entrepreneur to attend conferences or workshops to learn more about the topic, expanding the social network.

Techniques for Generating Ideas

In general, entrepreneurs identify more ideas than opportunities[43] because many ideas are typically generated to find the best way to capitalize on an opportunity. Several techniques can be used to stimulate and facilitate the generation of new ideas for products, services, and businesses. Let's take a look at some of them.

Brainstorming

Brainstorming is used to generate a number of ideas quickly. It is not used for analysis or decision making—the ideas generated during a brainstorming session need to be filtered and analyzed, but this is done later. A brainstorming "session" is targeted to a specific topic about which a group of people are instructed to come up with ideas. The leader of the group asks the participants to share their ideas. One person shares an idea, another person reacts to it, another person reacts to the reaction, and so on. A flip chart or an electronic whiteboard is typically used to record all the ideas.

A productive session is freewheeling and lively. The main objective is to create an atmosphere of enthusiasm and originality where lots of ideas are generated.[44] However, there are four strict rules for conducting brainstorming sessions. If they are not adhered to, it is unlikely that the participants will feel comfortable openly sharing ideas:

- No criticism is allowed, including chuckles, raised eyebrows, or facial expressions that express skepticism or doubt. Criticism stymies creativity and inhibits the free flow of ideas.
- Freewheeling, which is the carefree expression of ideas free of rules or restraints, is encouraged; the more ideas, the better. Even crazy or outlandish ideas may lead to a good idea or a solution to a problem.

LEARNING Objective

7. Describe the purpose of brainstorming and its use as an idea generator.

An increasing number of firms are using whiteboards to record ideas and conduct ongoing branstorming sessions. Here, a Google employee adds a thought or suggestion to a permanent whiteboard at Google's headquarters.

- The session moves quickly, and nothing is permitted to slow down its pace. For example, it is more important to capture the essence of an idea than to take the time to write it down neatly.
- Leapfrogging is encouraged. This means using one idea as a means of jumping forward quickly to other ideas. (The word *leapfrogging* comes from the child's game of leapfrog, in which one player kneels down while the next in line leaps over him or her.)

There are two reasons brainstorming generates ideas that might not arise otherwise. First, because no criticism is allowed, people are more likely to offer ideas than they would in a traditional setting. Criticism is the act of passing judgment and typically stems from intolerance. For example, the manager of a retail store may be skeptical of the Internet. In a normal meeting, he might criticize any suggestion regarding its use. But if the store held a brainstorming session focused on ways to improve customer service, ideas about ways to use the Internet may surface and be discussed. Of course, an employee may be reluctant to suggest an idea that is directly counter to a known position of the boss even though no criticism in the brainstorming session is permitted. To avoid this complication, some firms conduct electronic brainstorming sessions by means of **group support system (or GSS) software**, which allows participants to submit ideas anonymously.

Second, brainstorming sessions can generate more ideas than a traditional meeting because brainstorming focuses on creativity rather than evaluation. Think about a typical meeting. One person suggests an idea, and immediately the rest of the group begins to evaluate it. This happens because most people are better at criticizing ideas than they are at suggesting new ones. The sole purpose of a brainstorming session is to generate ideas, with no evaluation permitted. So if a 2-hour brainstorming session is held, the group will spend 2 hours generating ideas, which almost never happens outside a brainstorming context.[45]

Most brainstorming sessions involve the employees of an organization, but Kodak, for example, hosts pizza-video parties where groups of customers meet with the company's technical people to discuss problems and needs and to brainstorm potential solutions. Similarly, some companies make brief brainstorming sessions a routine part of facility tours.[46]

Focus Groups

A **focus group** is a gathering of 5 to 10 people who are selected because of their relationship to the issue being discussed. Although focus groups are used for a variety of purposes, they can be used to help generate new business ideas.

The strength of focus groups is that they help companies uncover what's on their customers' minds through the give-and-take nature of a group discussion.[47] The weakness is because the participants do not represent a random sample, the results cannot be generalized to larger groups. Usually, focus groups are conducted by trained moderators. The moderator's primary goals are to keep the group "focused" and to generate lively discussion. It is also important that the moderator fully understand the underlying objectives of the study. Much of the effectiveness of a focus group session depends on the moderator's ability to ask questions and keep the discussion on track. For example, a retail establishment in which coffee is sold, such as Starbucks, might conduct a focus group consisting of 7 to 10 frequent customers and ask the group, "What is it that you *don't* like about our coffee shop?" A customer may say, "You sell 1-pound bags of your specialty ground coffees for people to brew at home. That's okay, but I often run out of the coffee in just a few days. Sometimes it's a week before I get back to the shop to buy another bag. If you sold 3-pound or 5-pound bags, I'd actually use more coffee because I wouldn't run out so often. I guess I could buy two or three 1-pound bags at the same time, but that gets a little pricey. I'd buy a 3- or 5-pound bag, however, if you'd discount your price a little for larger quantities." The moderator may then ask the group, "How many people here would buy 3-pound or 5-pound bags of our coffee if they were available?" If five hands shoot up, the coffee shop may have just uncovered an idea for a new product line.

partnering for success

The Growing Role of College Students in Helping Businesses Generate New Ideas

As firms of all sizes continue to search for new business ideas, one trend that is particularly interesting is the growing role of college students in helping businesses formulate new business ideas. This trend is exemplified by BrainReactions, a company started by Anand V. Chhatpar, a former University of Wisconsin student. BrainReactions helps companies innovate new products, services, and marketing concepts by conducting brainstorming sessions with college students. The idea is that college students are enthused, creative, uninhibited, and understand the needs and wants of younger people—an important target customer group for many firms. College students are also up-to-date on new technologies and observe on a daily basis how technology affects people's lives.

While BrainReactions reaches out to companies to offer its services, companies also reach out to colleges and universities to accomplish the same objective. An example is Bold Furniture, a 2000 start-up. This venture is dedicated to designing office furniture that reflects its client's attitudes and cultures. Because the company is fairly young, it doesn't have the deep pockets needed to retain the help of professional design studios when developing new furniture lines. As a result, when the company wanted to design a new line of contemporary office furniture recently, instead of hiring professional help, it partnered with the University of Cincinnati's School of Design. Working with students to help generate new ideas turned out to be a good solution for the company. Commenting on the initiative, Bold Furniture co-owner Todd Folkert, 27, said:

Many designers require retainer fees, and that can be anywhere from a few thousand dollars a month to $10,000 a month. In addition, they'll look for royalties between one percent and five percent of sales. Working with the students, there's really not that significant of an up-front cost. It's pretty much all variable, tied to the success of the product.

To compensate the university and the students for their work, Bold provides internship opportunities and future cash and royalties if the designs pan out.

Other companies are taking similar active roles in partnering with colleges and their students to generate design and product ideas. Recently, Ford Motor Company partnered with students at Carnegie Mellon University, which offers a master's degree in product development, to design interior features for the Ford Escape SUV. BodyMedia, an entrepreneurial start-up that makes body-monitoring devices for medical patients, has worked with several student design programs, including Carnegie Mellon's program. Commenting on his company's experience working with students on design projects, Chris Kasaback, BodyMedia's cofounder, said:

They (college design students) may not necessarily give you the next idea. But they help corroborate ideas you may have already been gravitating (toward), or help prove certain ideas aren't useful.

Questions for Critical Thinking

1. In what ways do you think college students are uniquely capable of helping businesses innovate and come up with new product and service ideas? If you were the CEO of a company like Bold Furniture, would you consider partnering with a university college of design to help develop a new furniture line? What, if any, factors would have a bearing on your decision?

2. Many universities have internship programs that place students in businesses for the purpose of gaining practical experience. How can businesses use their interns to help generate new product and service ideas?

3. Go online and find another example of a business that partners with a college or university in a fashion similar to the companies described in the feature. Describe the partnership.

4. Find out if any of the academic units in your college or university partner with business organizations. Describe the nature of the partnerships and whether they help businesses, even in part, develop new product or service ideas.

Source: Chris Penttila, "Back to School," *Entrepreneur,* January 2006.

Some companies utilize hybrid focus group methodologies to achieve specific insights and goals. An example is "college drop-ins." This approach involves paying a pair of college students to host a party at their campus and providing them a budget to buy food and snacks. During the party, the hosts interview and videotape other students about specific market issues. Everything is up-front—the partygoers are told that the information is being collected for a market research firm (on behalf of a client). Most students are cooperative. One student, commenting on a college drop-in party he attended, said, "Everybody knows it costs a lot to throw a party and if all they have to do is give up 10 minutes of time to offer their opinions, it's a no-brainer!"[48]

Along with college drop-in parties, companies, across a wide spectrum are increasingly turning to college students to help generate new ideas. This subject is the focus of the "Partnering for Success" feature shown nearby.

Surveys

LEARNING

Objective

8. Describe how to use surveys to generate new business ideas.

A **survey** is a method of gathering information from a sample of individuals. The sample is usually just a fraction of the population being studied. Surveys can be conducted over the telephone, by mail, online, or in person. The most effective surveys sample a "random" portion of the population, meaning that the sample is not selected haphazardly or only from people who volunteer to participate. Instead, the sample is chosen in a way that ensures that everyone in the population has an equal chance of being selected, making the results of the survey generalizable to the larger population.

Surveys are taken in a standardized way so that every participant is asked the same questions in the same manner. The intention of a survey is not to describe the experiences or opinions of a particular individual, but rather to obtain a composite profile of the entire population. The quality of survey data is determined largely by the purpose of the survey and how it is conducted. For example, most call-in television surveys or magazine write-in polls are highly suspect because the participants represent what's called a **self-selected opinion poll**. Most people who take the time to participate in a self-selected opinion poll do so because they have either strong positive or strong negative feelings about a particular product or topic.[49]

Surveys generate new product, service, and business ideas because they ask specific questions and get specific answers. For example, a company such as Palm might administer a survey to a randomly selected sample of owners of Palm Pilots and ask the participants which of the following enhancements they would pay extra for if they were added to Palm Pilots: voice capabilities (e.g., a cell phone), text messaging, Internet access, paging, GPS capability, and so on. The survey might also ask how much extra the participants would be willing to pay for each enhancement and how likely it is that they would buy an enhanced product. Some surveys also include open-ended questions to provide the participants an opportunity to add information. For example, at the end of the survey, Palm might ask, "Is there any other product that our company might be uniquely capable of providing that we currently don't provide?" Although the answers to this question won't represent a scientific sample, they sometimes produce interesting leads to new product or service ideas.

Other Techniques

Firms use a variety of other techniques to generate ideas. Some companies set up **customer advisory boards** that meet regularly to discuss needs, wants, and problems that may lead to new ideas. For example, Johnson Controls, a global automotive systems and facility and management control systems company holds an annual event called the "Summit on Building Performance" to bring together customers and industry experts to better understand the impact of building performance on employee productivity.[50] Some advisory boards are conducted online to make it easier for the participants to meet. Other companies conduct varying forms of anthropological research, such as **day-in-the-life research**. A company that practices a variation of this technique is Chaparral Steel, which is an entrepreneurial-minded steel mini-mill. To make sure its customers are satisfied and to probe for new product ideas, the company routinely sends employees to the facilities of their customers.[51] A less expensive tool that some companies use to gain insights into their customer's lives and come up with new product ideas is IDEO Method Cards. IDEO is a design firm in California's Silicon Valley. IDEO Method Cards (which look like a deck of playing cards) show 51 of the methods that IDEO uses to come up with new product and service ideas. Each card has a picture on the front and a corresponding method for coming up with a new idea on the back. The cards are divided into four categories: learn, look, ask, and try. For example, one of the cards (in the look category) pictures an ordinary man on the front. The reverse side of the card, which provides instructions for how to use it, reads as follows:

> A DAY IN THE LIFE (REFERRING TO THE MAN IN THE PICTURE OR ANY OTHER USER OF A COMPANY'S PRODUCTS OR SERVICES)

> How: Catalog the activities and contexts that users (of your product) experience throughout an entire day.

> Why: This is a useful way to reveal unanticipated issues inherent in the routines and circumstances people experience every day.

> Example: IDEO asked potential wearers (or users) of a drug-delivery patch to document their daily behaviors including those that might affect the function of the patch—getting wet, snagging on clothing, etc.[52]

In addition to the techniques described above, some companies approach attendance at trade shows, conferences, and gatherings of industry personnel as intelligence missions to learn what their competition is doing and then use the information to stimulate new product and service ideas. Another technique for generating ideas is to set up an idea or suggestion program for employees. Important attributes of successful suggestion programs are processing suggestions rapidly, giving quality feedback, reacting to useful suggestions and ideas, and offering cash incentives. Suggestion programs vary in terms of their complexity, ranging from simple suggestion boxes to complex programs where ideas are placed in an idea bank for peer review and evaluation.

Encouraging and Protecting New Ideas

In many firms, idea generation is a haphazard process. However, entrepreneurial ventures can take certain concrete steps to build an organization that encourages and protects new ideas. Let's see what these steps are.

Establishing a Focal Point for Ideas

Some firms meet the challenge of encouraging, collecting, and evaluating ideas by designating a specific person to screen and track them—for if it's everybody's job, it may be no one's responsibility.[53] Another approach is to establish an **idea bank** (or vault), which is a physical or digital repository for storing ideas. An example of an idea bank would be a password-protected location on a firm's **intranet** that is available only to qualified employees. It may have a file for ideas that are being actively contemplated and a file for inactive ideas. Other firms do not have idea banks but instead encourage employees to keep journals of their ideas.

Encouraging Creativity at the Firm Level

There is an important distinction between creativity and innovation. Innovation, as mentioned in Chapter 1, refers to the successful introduction of new outcomes by a firm. In contrast, creativity is the process of generating a novel or useful idea but does not require implementation. In other words, creativity is the raw material that goes into innovation. A team of employees may come up with a hundred legitimate creative ideas for a new product or service, but only one may eventually be implemented. Of course, it may take a hundred creative ideas to discover the one that ideally satisfies an opportunity.

L E A R N I N G

Objective

9. Explain the purpose of maintaining an idea bank.

An employee may exhibit creativity in a number of ways, including solving a problem or taking an opportunity and using it to develop a new product or service idea. Although creativity is typically thought of as an individual attribute, it can be encouraged or discouraged at the firm level.[54] The extent to which an organization encourages and rewards creativity affects the creative output of its employees.[55] Table 2.3 provides a list of actions and behaviors that encourage and discourage creativity at both the organizational level and the individual supervisor level.

Protecting Ideas from Being Lost or Stolen

Intellectual property is any product of human intellect that is intangible but has value in the marketplace. It can be protected through tools such as patents, trademarks, copyrights, and trade secrets, which we'll discuss in depth in Chapter 12. As a rule, a mere idea or concept does not qualify for intellectual property protection; that protection comes later when the idea is translated into a more concrete form. At the opportunity recognition stage, however, there are three steps that should be taken when a potentially valuable idea is generated:

L E A R N I N G
Objective

10. Describe three steps for protecting ideas from being lost or stolen.

Step 1 The idea should be put into a tangible form—either entered into a physical idea logbook or saved on a computer disk—and dated. When using a physical logbook, be sure that it is bound so that it cannot be alleged that a page was added. Make all entries in ink and have them witnessed. If an idea has significant potential, the signature of the person who entered the idea into the logbook and the witness should be notarized.

Putting the idea into tangible form is important for two reasons. First, if the idea is in concrete form, is original and useful, and is kept secret or is disclosed only in a situation where compensation for its use is contemplated, the idea may qualify as a "property right" or "trade secret" and be legally protected under a variety of statutes.

Second, in the case of an invention, if two inventors independently come up with essentially the same invention, the right to apply for the patent belongs to the first person who invented the product. A properly maintained idea log provides evidence of the date that the idea for the invention was first contemplated.

TABLE 2.3 Actions and Behaviors That Encourage and Discourage Creativity

Creativity Enhancers	
Organizational Level	Individual Supervisory Level
• Elevating creativity's importance throughout the organization	• Listening attentively in order to acknowledge and provide early support to ideas
• Offering tangible rewards to those generating new ideas	• Dealing with employees as equals to show that status isn't very important
• Investing in resources that help employees sharpen their creative skills	• Speculate, be open, and build on others' ideas
• Hiring people different from those currently working in the company	• Protecting people who make honest mistakes and are willing to learn from them

Creativity Detractors	
Organizational Level	Individual Supervisory Level
• Not attempting to hire creative people	• Being pessimistic, judgmental, and critical
• Maintaining a "stiff" organizational culture with no room for different behaviors	• Punishing mistakes or failed ideas
• Pigeonholing employees; keeping them in the same job for years	• Being cynical or negative and insisting on early precision
• Promoting a mentality suggesting that the best solutions to all problems have already been found	• Being inattentive, acting distant, and remaining silent when employees want to discuss new ideas

Source: Adapted from I. S. Servi, *New Product Development and Marketing* (New York: Praeger, 1990).

Once an invention demonstrates feasibility, a form called a "Disclosure Document," which describes an invention, can be filed with the U.S. Patent and Trademark Office. The purpose of the form is to provide evidence of the date of an invention's conception.[56]

Step 2 The idea, whether it is recorded in a physical idea logbook or saved in a computer file, should be secured. This may seem like an obvious step but is one that is often overlooked. The extent to which an idea should be secured depends on the circumstances. On the one hand, a firm wants new ideas to be discussed, so a certain amount of openness in the early stages of refining a business idea may be appropriate. On the other hand, if an idea has considerable potential and may be eligible for patent protection, access to the idea should be restricted. In the case of ideas stored on a computer network, access to the ideas should be at a minimum password protected.

Step 3 Avoid making an inadvertent or voluntary disclosure of an idea in a way that forfeits your claim to its exclusive rights. In general, the intellectual property laws seek to protect and reward the originators of ideas as long as they are prudent and try to protect the ideas. For example, if two co-workers are chatting about an idea in an elevator in a public building and a competitor overhears the conversation, the exclusive rights to the idea are probably lost.

In summary, opportunity recognition is a key part of the entrepreneurial process. As mentioned, many firms fail not because the entrepreneurs didn't work hard, but because there was no real opportunity to begin with.

Chapter Summary

1. Once an opportunity is recognized, a window opens, and the market to fill the opportunity grows. At some point, the market matures and becomes saturated with competitors, and the window of opportunity closes.

2. An idea is a thought, an impression, or a notion. An opportunity is an idea that has the qualities of being attractive, durable, and timely and is anchored in a product or service that creates value for its buyers or end users. Not all ideas are opportunities.

3. Observing trends, solving a problem, and finding gaps in the marketplace are the three general approaches entrepreneurs use to identify an opportunity.

4. Economic forces, social forces, technological advances, and political action and regulatory changes are the four environmental trends that are most instrumental in creating opportunities.

5. Prior experience, cognitive factors, social networks, and creativity are the personal characteristics that researchers have identified that tend to make some people better at recognizing business opportunities than others.

6. For an individual, the five steps in the creative process are preparation, incubation, insight, evaluation, and elaboration.

7. Brainstorming is a technique used to quickly generate a large number of ideas and solutions to problems. One reason to conduct a brainstorming session is to generate ideas that might represent product, service, or business opportunities.

8. A focus group is a gathering of 5 to 10 people who have been selected on the basis of their common characteristics relative to the issue being discussed. One reason to conduct a focus group is to generate ideas that might represent product or business opportunities.

9. An idea bank is a physical or digital repository for storing ideas.

10. The three main steps that can be taken to protect ideas from being lost or stolen are putting the idea into tangible form by such means as entering it in a logbook or saving it in a computer file, securing the idea, and avoiding making an inadvertent or voluntary disclosure of an idea in a manner that forfeits the right to claim exclusive rights to it if it falls into someone else's hands.

Key terms

Brainstorming, 51
Corridor principle, 48
Creativity, 49
Customer advisory boards, 54
Day-in-the-life research, 54
Entrepreneurial alertness, 48
Focus group, 52
Group support system (or GSS)
    software, 52

Idea, 39
Idea bank, 55
Intellectual property, 56
Intranet, 55
Network entrepreneurs, 49
Opportunity, 38
Opportunity gap, 39
Opportunity recognition, 48
Self-selected opinion poll, 54

Serendipitous discovery, 46
Solo entrepreneurs, 49
Strong-tie relationships, 49
Survey, 54
Weak-tie relationships, 49
Window of opportunity, 39

Review Questions

1. What is a product opportunity gap? How can an entrepreneur tell if a product opportunity gap exists?
2. What is an opportunity? What are the qualities of an opportunity, and why is each quality important?
3. What four environmental trends are most instrumental in creating business opportunities? Provide an example of each environmental trend and the type of business opportunity that it might help create.
4. Explain how "solving a problem" can create a business opportunity. Provide an example that was not mentioned in the chapter of a business opportunity that was created in this way.
5. Explain how finding a gap in the marketplace can create a business opportunity.
6. What is meant by opportunity recognition?
7. In what ways does prior industry experience provide an entrepreneur an advantage in recognizing business opportunities?
8. What is the corridor principle? How does this corridor principle explain why the majority of business ideas are conceived at work?
9. What is entrepreneurial alertness?
10. In what ways does an extensive social network provide an entrepreneur an advantage in recognizing business opportunities?
11. Describe the difference between strong-tie relationships and weak-tie relationships. Is an entrepreneur more likely to get new business ideas through strong-tie or weak-tie relationships? Why?
12. Define creativity. How does creativity contribute to the opportunity recognition process?
13. Briefly describe the five stages of the creative process.
14. Explain the difference between an opportunity and an idea.
15. Describe the brainstorming process. Why is "no criticism" the number one rule for brainstorming?
16. Describe how a focus group is set up and how it is used to generate new business ideas.
17. Describe how surveys can be used to generate new business ideas.
18. What is a self-selected opinion poll? Are self-selected opinion polls an effective or an ineffective way to collect data to help generate new business ideas?
19. What is the purpose of an idea bank? Describe how an idea bank can be set up in a firm.
20. What are the three main steps to protect ideas from being lost or stolen?

Application Questions

1. Kevin, a software engineer, plans to write a memo to his boss describing an idea he has for a new software product. Kevin wants to convince his boss that his idea represents an opportunity the firm should pursue. In your opinion, what should Kevin put in the memo?

2. Melanie is very perceptive and believes she has identified an opportunity for a new business in the fashion industry. She wants to make sure, however, that she isn't just following a hunch—that the opportunity is sound. What criteria can Melanie use to determine whether she has identified an attractive opportunity?

3. Matrix Industries is interested in producing handheld devices similar to the products sold by Palm and Research In Motion. Jim Ryan, the founder of Matrix, remembers hearing about a concept called "window of opportunity." He asks you to explain the concept and how he can use it to help him make his decision. What do you tell him?

4. The "You Be the VC 1" feature focuses on Jingle Networks, a free 411 (directory assistance) service. Does Jingle Networks meet the tests of an opportunity (as opposed to an idea)? Justify your answer.

5. Kim is the founder of a small firm that produces highly specialized components for the semiconductor industry. Sales reps from both Forrester Research and Gartner have called to set up appointments with her to explain how their firms could help identify emerging opportunities that might translate into new product ideas for Kim's company. Keeping on top of emerging trends is important to Kim, and she knows that new product ideas are the lifeblood of high-tech firms. However, her busy schedule makes her reluctant to sit through two sales pitches. Kim explains this dilemma to you and asks whether you think she should take the time to meet with the sales reps. What is your answer?

6. Marshall Hanson, the founder of Santa Fe Hitching Rail, a chain of nine steak restaurants in New Mexico, is considering expanding his menu, which is currently restricted to steak, hamburger, potatoes, and fries. He has just read a book about entrepreneurship and learned that entrepreneurs should study social trends to help identify new product opportunities. List the social trends that might help Martin choose items to add to his menu. Given the trends you list, what items do you suggest Martin add?

7. Make a list of the three to five most compelling "technological advances" that have occurred in the United States or the world since you entered college. Think of at least two new product ideas that have emerged from each of these advances. To what extent do you believe each of these advances will continue to spawn new product ideas?

8. Recognizing a problem and proposing a solution to it is one way entrepreneurs identify opportunities. Think about your current activities as well as others in which you have an interest. Identify a problem with the activity you are considering and recommend a business to solve the problem.

9. Provide an example of a company that was started to fill a gap in the marketplace. Explain the nature of the gap that the company identified and describe how it is filling it.

10. Megan Jones owns a small chain of fitness centers in Kansas City. In general, her centers are successful, but she feels they are getting "stale" and could benefit from new ideas. Suggest to Megan some ways she could generate new ideas for her centers.

11. As mentioned in the chapter, "prior experience" in an industry helps entrepreneurs recognize business opportunities. This concept extends to prior experience in any aspect of life—whether it is in sports, music, or a volunteer activity. In what area or areas do you have a good amount of "prior experience"? How could this position you to start a business drawing on your experiences?

12. Make a list of your strong-tie and weak-tie relationships. (Include at least five names on each list.) Select two names from your list of weak-tie relationships, and speculate on the types of new business ideas that you think these individuals would be uniquely qualified to assist you with.

13. Tom Garrett, the manager of a midsize advertising agency, is planning to conduct several brainstorming sessions to identify new ideas for products and services to offer his clients. The first session is tomorrow, and Tom remembers from your résumé that you took an entrepreneurship class. He calls you into his office to ask whether you know anything about how to conduct brainstorming sessions. Using materials in this chapter, prepare an answer to Tom's question.

14. Delores Jones owns a company that produces a fat-free peanut butter named "Best Choice Peanut Butter." To learn of people's feelings about her product, she stamps an

invitation on each jar that reads, "If you'd like to tell me your opinion of Best Choice, send me a message at the following e-mail address." Is this an effective way to receive quality feedback from customers? In addition, Delores wants to know what other fat-free products her customers would be interested in and is considering sending a survey to 100 of her customers. Provide Delores advice about how to structure and administer the survey.

15. Freedom Electronics is a start-up with about 20 sales representatives. The company has a solid product line but knows that to remain competitive, it must continue recognizing opportunities for new products and services. The firm has not developed a systematic way for its sales staff to report new ideas. Suggest some ways that Freedom can record and protect the idea of its sales representatives.

---

you be the **VC** 2.1 — Jingle Networks
www.jinglenetworks.com

Business Idea: Launch the first free national directory assistance service.

Pitch: As we write this "You be the VC" feature, placing a 411 (directory assistance) call costs you $1.25 if you are a Verizon customer. The same service costs $1.75 with T-Mobile and $3.49 if MCI is your carrier. Regardless of the carrier you are using, directory assistance is expensive.

Not anymore. Jingle Networks, through a service aptly named 1-800-FREE-411, is pioneering the first free to the consumer national directory assistance service. There are currently 6 billion 411 calls made every year in the United States, which represents an $8 billion market. What Jingle Networks has done is taken Google's advertising model and moved it to the telephone. The attractive thing about Google's advertising model is that it directs ads to people at the "point-of-sale." So, if you type "pizza" into the Google search engine, you'll see text ads for pizza restaurants in your area to the right of the search results.

To demonstrate how 1-800-FREE-411 works, here's a transcript of a 411 call you might place through the service. This short example illustrates how the service works for you, the consumer, and the company. Don't worry about manners—remember, you're talking to a computer!

1-800-FREE-411: Welcome to 1-800-FREE-411. What city and state please?

You: Chapel Hill, North Carolina

1-800-FREE-411: Are you looking for a business, government or residential listing?

You: Business

1-800-FREE-411: O.K. What listing?

You: Papa John's Pizza

1-800-FREE-411: While we search for your listing, I'd like to tell you about a great offer from Dominos. Connect now and you get three medium one-topping pizzas for just $5 each. To get connected to Dominos free of charge, press 1, to hear the number you originally requested, press 2.

Jingle Networks calls this short ad a "switch pitch." In early tests, callers have taken the switch pitch offer 6.2 percent of the time. In the cases where a caller asks for the name of a business and there aren't any 1-800-FREE-411 advertisers in the area to build a switch pitch around, the caller is put through to the business, free of charge, with a slight twist. When the call is connected, the person answering the phone hears a brief message that says, "You are receiving a call from 1-800-FREE-411." After the call is completed, someone from Jingle Network's telesales group calls the business to explain how the service works. In early trials, 13 percent of businesses that received a directory assistance call through the 1-800-FREE-411 service and were then contacted by Jingle Networks, eventually became advertisers on the network.

So take a few seconds right now and program 1-800-FREE-411 into your cell phone and give the service a try. With Jingle Networks, you'll never pay for directory assistance again.

Q&A: Based on the material covered in this chapter, what questions would you ask the firm's founders before making your funding decision? What answers would satisfy you?

Decision: If you had to make your decision on just the information provided in the pitch and on the company's Web site, would you fund this firm? Why or why not?

Radar Golf
www.radargolf.com

Business Idea: Place a tiny electronic tag inside golf balls to make them easy to find when lost.

Pitch: What is more frustrating than losing a ball during a round of golf? Not only does a lost ball cost a player a two-stroke penalty but looking for a ball slows down play on a golf course. Slow play is frustrating for all and reduces everyone's enjoyment of the game.

Radar Golf offers a solution to these problems. The company has developed a small electronic tag that can be built into a golf ball during the manufacturing process. The tagged ball looks, feels, and performs like a regular golf ball. When a ball is difficult to find, the golfer pulls out a handheld unit (that has also been developed by Radar Golf), turns it on, points it in the direction of interest, and begins walking toward the ball. Depending on the terrain, it works from up to 100 feet away. By moving the unit from left to right, a pulsed audio tone (from the handheld unit) provides information on ball

location and distance. The golfer quickly walks in the direction of the ball, allowing it to be located within seconds. The system can be adapted to any brand of golf ball. Rather than manufacturing its own balls, Radar Golf plans to license its technology to golf ball manufacturers.

Radar Golf's system is intended to speed up play, improve the golfer's score, and provide an exciting new product to the $44 billion worldwide golf industry. It may also relieve a little of the frustration that most golfers experience on the golf course.

Q&A: Based on the material covered in this chapter, what questions would you ask the firm's founders before making your funding decision? What answers would satisfy you?

Decision: If you had to make your decision on just the information provided in the pitch and on the company's Web site, would you fund this firm? Why or why not?

 *Type 1 and Type 2 Tools and Flavorx: How Solving a Personal Problem Can Trigger the Recognition of a Promising Business Opportunity*
www.type1tools.com; www.flavorx.com

Bruce R. Barringer,
University of Central Florida

R. Duane Ireland,
Texas A&M University

Introduction

Many business opportunities are recognized by people who are trying to find a way to solve a personal problem. The problem can arise in a person's job, because of financial issues, while participating in recreational and/or volunteer activities, or because of an issue affecting family. As many of us would agree, when a problem arises in a person's family for which there isn't an obvious solution, the need to find a solution can become urgent. In these instances, if a creative solution is found, it often represents a solution that other families, facing the same problem, might find useful. In some instances, the solution is compelling enough that it represents the basis for launching a new entrepreneurial venture.

This case provides examples of two firms that were started in this manner. In each case, the recognition of the business opportunity was triggered by a set of parents urgently trying to solve a problem for a member of their family.

Type 1 and Type 2 Tools

Doug and Lisa Powell, who are both graphic designers, live in the Minneapolis area with their two children. The Powells were a typical family until 2004, when their daughter Maya, who was seven at the time, got sick. The Powells took Maya to a doctor, who ran a few tests. Minutes later they were given heart-sinking news: Maya had Type 1 diabetes. Type 1 diabetes, formerly called "insulin-dependent" or "juvenile-onset" diabetes, develops in a very small percentage of children and young adults. A person with Type 1 diabetes has a pancreas that does not produce insulin, a hormone necessary to sustain life. Without insulin, food cannot be utilized by the body. To treat her condition, little Maya would have to prick her finger to test her blood and take insulin one or more times a day for the rest of her life. The reason for the permanent

Tools That Make it Easier for Young Diabetics to Embrace Healthy Eating Habits

FlashCarbs	**FlashCarb Magnets**	**CarbWise Meal Worksheets**
Colorful flashcards help kids and parents learn the carbohydrate counts of common food, making it easier to choose foods wisely	Colorful refrigerator magnets make it fun and easy to learn the carb counts of common foods and provide a quick reference while cooking	Preprinted Post-It notes simplify the process of counting carb choices and calculating the proper insulin dosages at mealtimes
Carb Count Stickers	**DataWise Logbook Set**	**Care Plan Worksheets**
Stickers can be used for labeling leftovers, school lunch items, or any foods packaged without nutritional information	Handy logbooks set contains a year's supply of books that can help parents record and track all diabetes-related data	Preprinted and customized worksheets help parents relay critical information and care directions to adults in charge

need to take insulin is that although taking it allows a person with diabetes to stay alive, it does not cure the disease.

As you can imagine, Doug and Lisa Powell initially felt overwhelmed. As the parents of a seven-year-old Type 1 diabetic, they needed to quickly learn how to calculate insulin dosages, administer shots, calculate the carbohydrate content in foods (which helps a diabetic regulate diet), understand the warning signs of possible trouble, and educate their family and friends about Maya's needs and daily regimens. At the same time, they tried to stay upbeat and reassuring in order to help Maya deal with her condition in a positive manner. They also tried to collect as much information as possible to share with Maya. They wanted their daughter to remain an independent, happy child who was able to care for herself.

To accomplish their goals, the Powells set out to try every device available to help Maya understand her condition and to help her cope with her daily regimen. They tried books, alarms, toys, games, medical alert bracelets, and other devices. After trying all of these items, they were struck by two things. First, almost everything they found related to Type 2 rather than Type 1 diabetes. Type 2 diabetes is more common in adults and represents about 90 percent of diabetes patients. Although the names "Type 1 diabetes" and "Type 2 diabetes" sound similar, they are distinctly different diseases. Many of the tools available for Type 2 diabetics don't work well for people with Type 1 diabetes. The second thing that the Powells noticed was that the vast majority of the material and devices they tried were emotionally cold and intimidating—particularly for a young child. They didn't see how using one or more of the various items could uplift Maya's spirits while teaching her about her disease.

Given what they had discovered, the Powells decided to take action. Using their skills as graphic designers, they started developing their own material to educate and encourage Maya. They developed prototypes of colorful and inviting flash cards, meal worksheets, forms, and charts. As Maya started using the material, the Powells observed how much the material helped her, both physically and emotionally. They started sharing the material with care providers, friends, and other parents whose children had

Type 1 diabetes. The Powells were surprised by how positive the feedback was. As a result, they decided to launch their own firm, named Type 1 Tools, in order to share their materials with others on a more organized basis.

A sample of the types of products that Type 1 Tools sells is shown in the figure pictured above Word about the products quickly got out, and people with Type 2 diabetes started asking the Powells for similar material. The Powells obliged and refocused their company, renaming it Type 1 and Type 2 Tools, to help children and adults with both types of diabetes. The result—the company sold over $500,000 of Type 1 and Type 2 diabetes educational and motivational tools in 2005.

Flavorx

In 1992, Kenny Kramm's second daughter, Hadley, was born premature. As an infant, she developed a medical disorder that required her to take medicine four times a day. The medicine tasted awful, and it was difficult for Kramm and his wife to help Hadley keep it down. The Kramms grew increasingly concerned about this situation. Every time Hadley had a hard time keeping the medicine down, her conditioned worsened. "We were ending up in the emergency room on a weekly basis," Kramm recalls. The situation worsened. There was literally nothing that Hadley's doctors or nurses could do other than to urge the Kramms to help Hadley keep her medicine down—in any way they could.

In a funny twist of fate, Kenny Kramm worked in his parent's pharmacy. To help Hadley, Kenny and his father (a pharmacist for 40 years) started experimenting with concentrated flavors that could be mixed with Hadley's medicine to mask its bitter taste. Eventually, they produced a banana flavor concentrate that they were able to safely mix with the medicine; they were elated when Hadley started accepting the flavored medicine in its entirety. Almost immediately her condition stabilized, both medically and emotionally. Imagine the relief that Kramm and his wife also felt as a result of this positive turn of events.

Over the next 3 years, Kramm and his father continued to experiment with adding flavors to Hadley's various medicines. There were other medicine flavoring products available at the time, but none of them worked well enough to cover the bitter taste of most children's medications. Gradually, Kramm started seeing his pursuit as a business idea. Surely many others parents faced the same challenge that he and his wife had faced with Hadley, he thought. In 1995, he decided to incorporate and named the business Flavorx. To move the business forward, he partnered with one of the largest flavoring companies in the world to help develop custom flavors that could be safely mixed with medicines. After months of testing, Flavorx's first flavor additives were formally approved.

Flavorx's additives are now available in most pharmacies in the United States and are frequently used to improve the taste of both child and adult medicines. Medicines mixed with Flavorx's formulas not only taste better; they improve medicinal compliance and make it possible for some people to take their entire prescribed dosage. Not all Flavorx-treated medicines taste like candy, but they all make medicine taste better. Today, Flavorx offers over 40 flavors. In 2002, *Inc.* magazine reported that in 2001 Flavorx's sales were in the $1.8 million range. Flavorx is a private company and doesn't report its yearly earnings.

As for Hadley, her father's solution was just what she needed. From the time she took her first dose of banana-flavored medicine, she has never had another medicine-related hospital visit.

Discussion Questions

1. What similarities, other than the fact that they both involved medical challenges and children, do you see between the Flavorx and the Type 1 and Type 2 Tools' examples? What does each of these stories teach you about the opportunity recognition process?

2. In the chapter, an opportunity is defined as having the qualities of being (1) attractive, (2) durable, (3) timely, and (4) anchored in a product or service that creates value for its buyer or end user. To what extent do Type 1 and Type 2 Tools and Flavorx meet each of these tests of an opportunity?

3. Refer to the figure titled "Dream Dinners Recipe for Success: Passion, Market Opportunity, and the Skills to Make It Happen" that is pictured in Case 1.1 in the book's first chapter. Think about the point made in that case that resulted in the drawing of the figure—namely, that new businesses typically happen when three things converge: someone is passionate about an idea, a market opportunity for the idea exists, and the person with the idea has the skills to implement it. To what extent were all three of these factors present in the founding of Type 1 and Type 2 Tools and of Flavorx?

4. Why do you think that the types of products that Doug and Lisa Powell developed for Type 1 and Type 2 Tools weren't developed years earlier by a company that sells traditional diabetes treatment supplies? Similarly, why do you think that the products developed by Kenny Kramm weren't developed years earlier by an established drug company?

Application Questions

1. How could Type 1 and Type 2 Tools effectively use focus groups to develop additional diabetes-related products?

2. Think about a challenge in your own life that might represent a business opportunity. If you don't think of something right away, don't give up. Think about the challenges and problems that you have. All of us encounter problems and challenges in our everyday lives that might represent the basis of a promising business opportunity. Be prepared to describe to others the challenge and the business opportunity it presents.

Source: Type 1 Tools homepage (2006) (accessed May 10, 2006); Flavorx homepage (2006) (accessed May 10, 2006); *Minneapolis Star Tribune.* "Type 1 Tools: Helpful Resources for Families Struggling with Diabetes," January 18, 2004.

CASE 2.2 *Intellifit: Is This an Opportunity or Just an Interesting Idea?*
www.intellifit.com

Bruce R. Barringer,
University of Central Florida

R. Duane Ireland,
Texas A&M University

Introduction

What do great-fitting clothes and security scanning have in common? The answer: Small companies in both industries are licensing the same technology—the Millimeter Wave

Holographic Scanning device. The technology, developed by the Pacific Northwest National Laboratory in Richland, Washington, provides a full-body, 360-degree imagery of a person in real time. *R&D* magazine named this technology the most promising innovation of 2004. The technology has many potential applications, such as security screening. In fact SafeView, a security company, has licensed the technology to build a glass booth that people can be asked to step into, and while standing in the booth, the technology can detect whether the person is carrying any weapons, explosives, plastics, or metals. The subject of this case, Intellifit, licensed the technology for an entirely different purpose. People can step into an Intellifit glass booth, and in 10 seconds, a scanner captures their exact body measurements. The measurements can then be compared to garment-sizing data from participating retailers, and in an instant, a person can know exactly what size of jeans will fit best at each retailer. Among other positive benefits, having this knowledge can save a great deal of time for the individual shopper.

Intellifit is currently deploying its system. Its potential customers include malls, large retailers like Levi's and Gap, and specialty retailers like bridal shops and plus-sized stores. Intellifit sees its system as the solution to a major source of frustration for shoppers—poor-fitting clothes. It also sees its system as a solution to a major problem for retailers—returns. The question, which at this point is too early to answer, is whether shoppers and retailers will actually use Intellifit's machines. In addition, the company can't be sure that the problem the firm has identified is compelling enough that shoppers and retailers, in large numbers, will take notice.

So, has Intellifit uncovered a genuine opportunity or does it just have some neat technology and an interesting idea? After reading the case, you decide.

Intellifit

Intellifit was launched in 1999 as Made4Me, a custom-clothing maker. The founder, Albert Charpentier, who is now Intellifit's CEO, felt there was a demand for custom-made clothing. To acquire customers, he sent out 4,000 kits, which included a tape measure, instructions for how to measure yourself, and instructions for how to order custom clothes. Only 40 kits were returned with measurements and orders for custom clothes, so the idea was dropped. In 2002, Charpentier changed the name of his company to Intellifit. Intellifit briefly pilot-tested, at David's Bridal chain and plus-size retailer Catherines, another approach for helping people get better-fitting clothes. This approach required a store's salesperson to use a tape measure to take 38 measurements of a customer's body and feed the measurements into a computer. The computer would then give customers a printout of their exact measurements. This approach was dropped, as retailers reported they didn't have enough salespeople to do the job and they were hesitant to put their customers through such a tedious ordeal. The next year, the scanning technology from the Pacific Northwest National Laboratory was acquired, and work on Intellifit's current measuring system was started.

Interestingly, Charpentier found out about the Pacific Northwest National Lab's technology while he was surfing the Internet one day looking for alternative body-scanning technologies he might use in his business. Intellifit's machine, named The Body Scanner took about 18 months to build and test.

The Body Scanner

The Body Scanner is a fairly generously sized glass booth that a person steps into fully clothed. All a person has to do is remove metal objects, like keys, coins, and cell phones, from pockets before being scanned. The scanner, which is no more invasive than going through a security scanner at an airport, uses safe, low-power radio waves to capture about 200,000 data points on a person's body. A computer in the booth then condenses and analyzes the data and prints out measurements that are accurate to within a quarter-inch. Depending on the retailers that participate, a young woman that gets scanned and is interested in buying jeans might get a printout that says she is a size 4 at Gap, a size 5 at American Eagle, a size 5 at Levi's, and a size 4 at Internet retailer Lands' End.

The technology utilized by Intellifit's system is much less cumbersome than other systems that have been developed to help people get a good fit. Some scanners require shoppers to enter a private booth and partially undress. These machines have never gained traction. Lands' End, the Internet and catalog retailer, introduced a virtual model in 1998. It lets customers try on clothes in a virtual environment (meaning a computer model of a person's body is made and the computer tries clothes on the model). It also lets people see how clothes would fit if they were thinner. To its credit, Lands' End reports that tens of thousands of people have utilized the service. Intellifit sees Lands' End's success as a validation that people will spend time trying to get a better fit. Of course, it also believes that its system is superior to what Lands' End uses.

Markets for Intellifit's Body Scanner

Intellifit has identified three potential market spaces for its Body Scanner.

1. *Malls.* Placing Body Scanners in common areas in malls and manning them with Intellifit employees is the first potential market space. The service would be free to consumers, but retailers would pay Intellifit a monthly fee to have their clothing measurements appear on the printouts. Intellifit could also use this service to collect "blind" data (meaning the data are only reported in aggregate form, no individual measurements are shown) to sell to retailers to help them better understand the most common sizes of shoppers, by age group or some other characteristic, in their areas.

2. *Retail chains.* Another potential market is to sell Body Scanners, which price out at about $50,000 a piece, to retail chains like Levi's and Gap. The chains could use the machines to help shoppers get a good fit and to differentiate themselves from their competitors. If the machines are heavily used, they could also help a retail chain control inventory, improve full-margin sell-through rates, and increase customer satisfaction by providing them with clothing items that fit properly.

3. *Specialty retailers.* The most realistic market, at the outset, may be specialty retailers, like bridal shops, plus-sized retailers, and tall-men clothing stores. These retailers serve people who are particularly concerned about a good fit. A specialty retailer like David's Bridal could advertise that it uses the Intellifit Body Scanning system so brides will be able to have their perfect dress fit perfectly!

An Idea or an Opportunity?

It's too early to tell how successful Intellifit will be. According to an Intellifit press release, Intellifit systems were purchased and placed into select Lane Bryant stores, Catherines stores, David's Bridal stores, and After Hours Formalware stores in late 2004. In fall 2005, Intellifit Body Scanning machines were placed in six malls in Pennsylvania. The first mall to receive the machine was the Willow Grove Park mall, just north of Philadelphia. An article in the *Philadelphia Inquirer* in September 2005 reported the comments of some shoppers who used the service in the mall—with mixed results. One teenager said, "American Eagle gave me too small of a size. It said I'm a double zero. I'm not a double zero, I'm a 2." Another shopper, the mother of a 15-year-old girl who was scanned by the Intellifit machine, said she hopes the data will help her minimize the number of items she buys for her daughter and has to return. Her only complaint was that many of her favorite retailers were not yet participating in the service. Having more stores carry the Intellifit machine would solve this complaint. In mid-2006, additional stores (such as Levi Stores in Washington D.C. and Dallas, Texas) were carrying Intellifit's product.

Discussion Questions

1. According to the chapter, what are the attributes of an opportunity? Use these attributes to evaluate Intellifit.

Based on your evaluation, is Intellifit an opportunity or just an interesting idea?

2. What environmental trends are working in Intellifit's favor? If Intellifit has uncovered a promising business opportunity, what environmental trends have made Intellifit's system possible and potentially attractive to consumers?

3. On two previous occasions, Intellifit (as Intellifit and Made4Me) developed approaches for helping people get better-fitting clothes that didn't work out. What is different about Intellifit's current approach? What, if anything, gives Intellifit's current approach a better chance of succeeding?

4. Which of the three potential markets that Intellifit has identified for its device do you believe is the most promising? Which is the least promising? If Intellifit decides to place a large number of its machines in malls, how important is it that a large percentage of the retailers in the mall participate?

Application Questions

1. Think about the scanning technology that Intellifit licensed from the Pacific Northwest National Laboratory. To what uses, other than security scanning and helping people find better-fitting clothing, could this technology be applied?

2. Look at the "You Be the VC 2" feature, which focuses on Radar Golf, a company that helps people find golf balls. In your judgment, is Radar Golf a promising business opportunity? Explain the basis for your answer.

Sources: Intellifit homepage (accessed May 10, 2006); J. Graybeal, "Fit a Suit, Screen For Weapons," *Innovation: America's Journal of Technology Communications*, February/March, 2005; W. Tanaka, "Fit To Be Tried," *The Philadelphia Inquirer*, September 12, 2005; D. Clark, "Tech Devices Add Oomph to TV, Cars, Games," *The Wall Street Journal*, February 14, 2005.

Endnotes

1. BrainReactions homepage, www.brainreactions.com, (accessed May 30, 2006).
2. Amazon.Com Company Report, *Standard and Poor's Stock Report*, May 27, 2006; *Time*, "Amazing Person.com," December 27, 1999.
3. A. Ulwich, *What Customers Want* (New York: McGraw-Hill, 2005).
4. J. E. Cliff, P. D. Jennings, and R. Greenwood, "New to the Game and Questioning the Rules: The Experiences and Beliefs of Founders Who Start Imitative versus Innovative Firms," *Journal of Business Venturing* 21: (2006): 633–63; J. A. Timmons, "Opportunity Recognition," in *The Portable MBA in Entrepreneurship*, ed. W. D. Bygrave (New York: John Wiley & Sons, 1997), 27.
5. D. N. Sull, "The Three Windows of Opportunity," *Harvard Business School Working Knowledge*, June 6, 2005.
6. D. B. Audretsch and E. Lehmann, "Entrepreneurial Access and Absorption of Knowledge Spillovers: Strategic Board and Managerial Composition for Competitive Advantage," *Journal of Small Business Management* 44, no. 2, (2006): 155–166; *New Webster's Dictionary* (New York: Delair Publishing, 1981).
7. A. Ardichvili, R. Cardozo, and S. Ray, "A Theory of Entrepreneurial Opportunity Identification and Development," *Journal of Business Venturing* 18, no. 1 (2003): 105–23.
8. PricewaterhouseCoopers, "Fast Growth Companies Have Two Big Priorities, PricewaterhouseCoopers Finds," in *Trendsetter Barometer* (New York: PricewaterhouseCoopers, 2000).
9. M. Perin, "ChemConnect to Provide Energy Closing Prices to Dow Jones," *Houston Business Journal Online*, www.houston.bizjournals.com, February 15, 2006; S. H. Diorio, *Beyond "e": 12 Ways Technology Is Transforming Sales and Marketing Strategy* (New York: McGraw-Hill, 2002).
10. H. K. Kinnersley, "Searching for a Stress Buster," *The Wall Street Journal*, March 30, 2006, D6.
11. RealNetwork homepage, www.realnetworks.com (accessed June 5, 2006).
12. J. L. Koehn and S. C. DelVecchio, "Revisiting the Ripple Effects of the Sarbanes-Oxley Act," *The CPA Journal*, www.nysscpa.org, May 2006; Donna Fuscaldo, "For Tech Firms, Sarbanes-Oxley Provides Revenue Opportunities." *The Wall Street Journal*, December 1, 2004, B2A.
13. D. Smagalla, "The Truth About Software Startups," *MIT Sloan Management Review* (Winter 2004): 7.
14. D. A. Shepherd and D. R. DeTienne, "Prior Knowledge, Potential Financial Reward, and Opportunity Identification," *Entrepreneurship Theory and Practice* 29, no. 1 (2005): 91–112.
15. P. Kotler, *Marketing Insights from A to Z* (New York: John Wiley & Sons, 2003), 128.
16. Hoovers, www.hoovers.com (accessed June 24, 2004).
17. C. M. Crawford and C. A. Di Benedetto, *Product Management*, 6th ed. (Boston: Irwin McGraw-Hill, 2000).
18. R. Adams, *A Good Hard Kick in the Ass* (New York: Crown Business, 2002), 76.
19. C. Malta and L. Suttora *What to Sell on eBay* (New York: McGraw-Hill, 2006).
20. Curves homepage, www.curves.com (accessed May 22, 2006).
21. G. D. Markham and R. A. Baron, "Person–Entrepreneurship Fit—Why Some People Are More Successful as Entrepreneurs Than Others," *Human Resource Management Review* 13, no. 2 (2003): 281–301.
22. J. Case, "The Origins of Entrepreneurship," *Inc.*, June 1989.
23. A. C. Cooper, W. Dunkelberg, C. Woo, and W. Dennis, *New Business in America: The Firms and Their Owners* (Washington, DC: National Federation of Independent Business, 1990).
24. R. Ronstadt, "The Educated Entrepreneurs: A New Era of Entrepreneurial Education Is Beginning," *American Journal of Small Business* 10, no. 1 (1985): 7–23.
25. G. T. Lumpkin and B. B. Lichtenstein, "The Role of Organizational Learning in the Opportunity-Recognition Process," *Entrepreneurship Theory and Practice* 29, no. 4 (2005): 451–72.
26. I. M. Kirzner, *Perception, Opportunity, and Profit: Studies in the Theory of Entrepreneurship* (Chicago: University of Chicago Press, 1979).
27. S. A. Alvarez and J. B. Barney, "Entrepreneurial Alertness," in *The Blackwell Encyclopedia of Management—Entrepreneurship*, eds. M. A. Hitt and R. D. Ireland, (Malden, MA: Blackwell Publishing, 2005), 63–64.
28. C. M. Gaglio and J. A. Katz, "The Psychological Basis of Opportunity Identification: Entrepreneurial Alertness," *Small Business Economics* 16, no. 2 (2001): 95–111.

29. I. M. Kirzner, "The Primacy of Entrepreneurial Discovery," in *The Prime Mover of Progress*, ed. A. Seldon (London: Institute of Economic Affairs, 1980), 5–30.

30. G. Kingsley and E. J. Malecki, "Networking for Competitiveness," *Small Business Economics* 23, no. 1 (2004): 71–84.

31. A. C. Cooper and X. Yin, "Entrepreneurial Networks," in *The Blackwell Encyclopedia of Management—Entrepreneurship*, eds. M. A. Hitt and R. D. Ireland (Malden, MA: Blackwell Publishing, 2005), 98–100.

32. P. Davidsson and B. Honig, "The Role of Social and Human Capital among Nascent Entrepreneurs," *Journal of Business Venturing* 18, no. 3 (2003): 301–31.

33. R. H. Koller, "On the Source of Entrepreneurial Ideas," in *Frontiers of Entrepreneurship Research* (Wellesley, MA: Babson College, 1988), 194–207.

34. Hills et al., "Opportunity Recognition,"168–72.

35. R. P. Singh, G. E. Hills, R. C. Hybels, and G. T. Lumpkin, "Opportunity Recognition through Social Network Characteristics of Entrepreneurs," in *Frontiers of Entrepreneurship Research* (Wellesley, MA: Babson College, 1999), 228–38.

36. C. J. Medlin, "Self and Collective Interests in Business Relationships," *Journal of Business Research* 59, no. 7 (2006): 858–65; M. Granovetter, "The Strength of Weak Ties," *American Journal of Sociology* 78, no. 6 (1973): 1360–80.

37. A. Ardichvili, R. Cardozo, and S. Ray, "A Theory of Entrepreneurial Opportunity Identification and Development," *Journal of Business Venturing* 18, no. 1 (2003): 105–23.

38. J. J. Kao, *Entrepreneurship, Creativity, and Organization* (Upper Saddle River, NJ: Prentice Hall, 1989).

39. G. E. Hills, R. C. Shrader, and G. T. Lumpkin, "Opportunity Recognition as a Creative Process," in *Frontiers of Entrepreneurship Research* (Wellesley, MA: Babson College, 1999), 216–27.

40. W. Bygrave, "The Entrepreneurial Process," in *The Portable MBA in Entrepreneurship,* ed. William B. Bygrave (New York: John Wiley & Sons, 1997), 1–26.

41. M. Csikszentmihalyi, *Creativity* (New York: HarperCollins, 1996).

42. E. Edmonds and L. Candy, "Creativity, Art Practice, and Knowledge," *Communications of the ACM* 4, no. 10 (2002): 91–95.

43. J. S. Park, "Opportunity Recognition and Product Innovation in Entrepreneurial High-Tech Start-Ups: A New Perspective and Supporting Case Study," *Technovation* 2, no. 7 (2005): 739–52; R. P. Singh, *Entrepreneurial Opportunity Recognition* (New York: Garland Publishing, 2000).

44. E. F. Rietzschel, B. A. Nijstad, and W. Stroebe, "Productivity is Not Enough: A Comparison of Interactive and Nominal Brainstorming Groups on Idea Generation and Selection," *Journal of Experimental Social Psychology* 42, no. 2 (2006): 244–51.

45. R. G. Cooper, *Winning at New Products: Accelerating the Process from Idea to Launch*, 2nd ed. (Reading, MA: Addison-Wesley, 1993).

46. R. G. Cooper and S. J. Edgett, *Product Development for the Service Sector* (Cambridge, MA: Perseus Books, 1999).

47. American Statistical Association, *What Are Focus Groups?* (Alexandria, VA: American Statistical Association, 1997), 1.

48. S. Gold, "Have Insights, Will Party," *The Hub Magazine*, November 9, 2005, p. 18.

49. American Statistical Association, Web site section on survey research methods, www.bios.unc.edu/~kalsbeek/asa/survpamphlet.html (accessed June 3, 2002).

50. Johnson Controls homepage, www.johnsoncontrols.com (accessed June 5, 2006).

51. T. S. Foster, *Managing Quality: An Integrative Approach* (Upper Saddle, NJ: Prentice Hall, 2001).

52. IDEO homepage, www.ideo.com (accessed May 25, 2006).

53. A. Majchrzak, D. Logan, R. McCurdy, and M. Kirchmer, "Four Keys to Managing Emergence," *MIT Sloan Management Review* 47, no. 2 (2006): 14–18.

54. J. A. Goncalo and B. M. Staw, "Individualism-Collectivism and Group Creativity," *Organizational Behavior and Human Decision Processes* 100 (May 2006): 96–109.

55. S. H. Thomke, "Capturing the Real Value of Innovation Tools," *MIT Sloan Management Review* 47, no.2 (2006): 24–32; A. Cummings and G. R. Oldham, "Enhancing Creativity: Managing Work Contexts for the High Potential Employee," *California Management Review* 40, no. 1 (1997): 22–38.

56. United States Patent and Trademark Office, "Disclosure Document Program," www.uspto.gov/web/offices/pac/disdo.html (accessed June 4, 2002).

Getting Personal

with

DAVID BATEMAN

What I'd like to be doing in 10 years

Doing a start-up of course

Best advice I've received

Recruit people whose strengths are your weaknesses

My biggest surprise as an entrepreneur

Trusting your instincts is key for success—even if it means disagreeing with partners/investors

Property Solutions:
The Value of Validating a Business Idea

In 2002, David Bateman was quite busy. Not only was he taking classes in the College of Business at Brigham Young University (BYU), he was running a company he started called DearElder.com. The idea for DearElder.com came to Bateman after he spent a year in Honduras as a Mormon missionary. One thing that's hard for missionaries is to get letters and packages from home on a reliable basis. DearElder.com provided a service that made it much easier for families to keep in touch with their loved ones in the mission field.

At the same time Bateman was busy with school and DearElder.com, his wife, Amanda, was equally busy, working as a property manager at an apartment complex in Provo, Utah, where BYU is located. Bateman recalls visiting his wife at work and being struck by the huge stacks of paper ledgers on her desk. Most of the bookkeeping for the complex was done by using very basic accounting software. As is common in the apartment rental industry, tenants where Amanda worked paid their monthly rent by check or in cash. Bateman remembers thinking that his small company DearElder.com was more technologically sophisticated than the much larger apartment complex business.

This experience got Bateman thinking. He remembered that his idea for DearElder.com was prompted by one of his professors, who, in explaining the basis for a promising business idea, said to try to find a pain in the marketplace and come up with an idea to ease the pain. While in Honduras, Bateman often waited 3 to 4 weeks to get letters and packages from home—the pain that DearElder.com was founded to ease. To ease the pain that tenants and apartment complex owners felt in dealing with the cumbersome task of collecting rent, Bateman envisioned a Web-based environment where apartment complexes could collect rent online and offer other services. This approach, Bateman reasoned, would be a win-win for both tenants and apartment complex owners. The tenants would win by having a more convenient way to pay their rent, and apartment complexes would win by

DAVID BATEMAN

Founder, Property Solutions
BS, Brigham Young University, 2004

Hardest part of getting funding	What I do when I'm not working	Currently in my iPod
Giving up equity	*Sleep*	*Counting Crows*

After studying this chapter you should be ready to:

Objectives

1. Explain what a feasibility analysis is and why it's important.

2. Discuss the proper time to complete a feasibility analysis when developing an entrepreneurial venture.

3. Describe the purpose of a product/service feasibility analysis and the two primary issues that a proposed business should consider in this area.

4. Identify three primary purposes of concept testing.

5. Explain a concept statement and its contents.

6. Define the term *usability testing* and explain why it's important.

7. Describe the purpose of industry/market feasibility analysis and the three primary issues to consider in this area.

8. Explain the difference between primary research and secondary research.

9. Describe the purpose of organizational feasibility analysis and list the two primary issues to consider in this area.

10. Explain the importance of financial feasibility analysis and list the most critical issues to consider in this area.

collecting rent in a more efficient manner and by offering additional online service to attract and retain good-quality tenants.

To take the idea beyond the thinking state, Bateman and his wife, with the cooperation of student groups at BYU in Provo and BYU-Idaho in Rexburg, Idaho, took three actions. First, they put together a survey and then solicited opinions from 450 apartment complex managers working in the western United States. The survey affirmed their belief that most apartment complex managers were dissatisfied with the way they were collecting rent and would be open to considering more efficient solutions. In fact, not one of the 450 apartment complex managers surveyed allowed their tenants to pay rent online. Second, they surveyed a large number of students who were currently living in apartments to ask if they would pay their rent online if a capability to do so was made available to them. Many students said they would take advantage of such a capability. Finally, the Batemans and those working with them conducted a number of focus groups with both tenants and apartment managers to explore the types of features that both groups would like to see in an online environment for apartment complexes.

Buoyed by the results of these tests, which affirmed the feasibility of his basic idea, Bateman wrote a business plan, naming his business Property Solutions while doing so. He asked two of his classmates, Benjamin Zimmer and Michael Trionfo, to join his team. To get additional feedback on the idea, the group entered Property Solutions into the BYU business plan competition in 2003 and later into a national business plan competition sponsored by *Fortune Small Business* magazine. They won both competitions—each of which was accompanied by a $50,000 prize including a mixture of cash and in-kind services.

The money and notoriety that resulted from winning the competitions prompted Bateman and his team to launch Property Solutions as a business. The group put together an advisory board and started accepting investment dollars on a careful and limited basis. Bateman also invested a considerable share of the money he had made from DearElder.com. The first priority for the company was to build the software needed to accomplish the company's ambitions. Bateman recalls this work as being grueling and tedious. The biggest financial commitment the firm made at the outset was to hire trained programmers to help complete this task. Overhead was kept low, and the company operated out of modest facilities.

Today, Property Solutions is a fully functioning company and is providing a Web-based environment to over 1,200 apartment communities that are run by over 170 property management companies. The company's product allows tenants to go online and pay rent, make maintenance requests, view community announcements, purchase renter's insurance, and perform other tasks. The availability of these benefits not only helps apartment complexes collect rent and other data in a more efficient manner but also helps them retain tenants and boost occupancy rates.

The Property Solutions case illustrates a set of activities that is fundamental to the launch of a successful entrepreneurial venture—determining if the business idea is feasible. In David Bateman's case, he didn't commit to launching Property Solutions as a business before he had a reasonable degree of certainty that the business idea itself was feasible. He tested the idea by conducting surveys and hosting focus groups with both apartment complex managers and apartment tenants. He further tested the idea by entering business plan competitions and by subjecting the idea, the potential market, the capabilities of himself and his initial management team, and the financial aspects of the business to panels of discriminating judges.[1]

In this chapter, we'll discuss the importance of feasibility analysis and look at its four key areas: product/service feasibility, industry/market feasibility, organizational feasibility, and financial feasibility. Failure to conduct a feasibility analysis can result in disappointing outcomes, as illustrated in this chapter's "What Went Wrong?" feature (which deals with satellite phones as a product offering).

Feasibility Analysis

Feasibility analysis is the process of determining if a business idea is viable. As a preliminary evaluation of a business idea, a feasibility analysis is completed to determine if an idea is worth pursuing and to screen ideas before spending resources on them. It follows the opportunity recognition stage but comes before the development of a business plan, as illustrated in Figure 3.1. When a business idea is deemed unworkable, it should be dropped or rethought. If it is rethought and a slightly different version of the original idea emerges, the new idea should be subjected to the same level of feasibility analysis as the original idea.

Although the sequence pictured in Figure 3.1 makes perfect sense, statistics show that the majority of entrepreneurs do not follow this pattern before launching their ventures.[2] Several studies have investigated why this is the case. The consensus of the research is that entrepreneurs tend to underestimate the amount of competition there will be in the marketplace and tend to overestimate their personal chances for success.[3]

Once a business idea is determined to be feasible, much work remains to be done to completely flesh out the idea when preparing to write the business plan and launch the venture. In Table 3.1 we show you the chapters of this book in which the various components of a feasibility analysis are discussed. A positive feasibility analysis gives a green light to an entrepreneur to further pursue a business idea. Each area of the feasibility analysis must then be completely explored in anticipation of launching the new venture.

A business idea developed by Trakus, Inc. provides an example of the importance of conducting a feasibility analysis. Unlike Iridium, Trakus effectively used feasibility analysis to determine that a business idea wasn't feasible before spending a lot of time and effort on it. Let's investigate this matter a bit more.

LEARNING Objective

1. Explain what a feasibility analysis is and why it's important.

LEARNING Objective

2. Discuss the proper time to complete a feasibility analysis when developing an entrepreneurial venture.

FIGURE 3.1

Role of Feasibility Analysis in Developing Successful Business Ideas

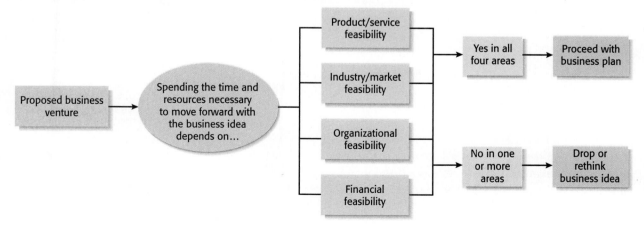

what went wrong?

Satellite Phones: How Feasible Were They?

When Barry Bertiger's wife couldn't reach her clients via her cell phone while vacationing in the Caribbean, the Motorola engineer had an idea. He envisioned placing a constellation of 66 low-orbiting satellites in space that would allow subscribers to make phone calls from anywhere on earth. Although satellite phones were already available while Bertiger was considering this idea, there were problems: They used satellites at high altitudes, they were heavy, and they involved annoying quarter-second voice delays. By using low-altitude satellites, the phones could be smaller and the voice delay would be imperceptible. Bertiger called his solution Iridium.

Sound like a good idea? Unfortunately, it wasn't. Let's see why.

To build the satellites and put them in orbit, Motorola established Iridium LLC as a separate company in 1991. The cost of putting the satellites in orbit was enormous, meaning that the company started with significant debt. The service was launched on November 1, 1998, in a ceremony at which Vice President Al Gore made the first call using Iridium. Iridium charged $3,000 for a handset and $3 to $8 per minute for a call. Iridium knew that its phone would be too large (they were the size of a brick) and that its service would be too expensive to compete with traditional cellular service, so its target market was people who traveled or worked in areas where cellular wasn't available. This group included international business travelers, construction workers in remote areas, those working on ships at sea, military forces around the world, and offshore oil rig workers. Iridium's chief executive officer (CEO), Edward Staiano, predicted that by the end of 1999, the company would have 500,000 subscribers. But by July 1999, the company had only 20,000 subscribers. It needed 52,000 subscribers just to meet its loan obligations. The next month, Iridium defaulted on $1.5 billion in loans and filed for bankruptcy. What went wrong?

Well, several things. First, because of the complexity of its technology, it took 11 years for the Iridium concept to be fully developed, and traditional cell phone service spread much more quickly than Iridium had anticipated. By the time Iridium was available, a good share of its target market could meet its needs via traditional cell phones—which were cheaper and lighter and worked better in most areas. Second, because Iridium's technology depended on line of sight between the phone's antenna and an orbiting satellite, the functionality of the phone was limited. It couldn't be used inside moving cars, inside buildings, or in many urban areas where tall buildings obstructed the line of sight between the phone and the satellite. Dartmouth College professor Sydney Finkelstein, who wrote about Iridium in his book *Why Smart Executives Fail*, said that in studying the failure of Iridium, a top industry consultant told him, "You can't expect a CEO traveling on business in Bangkok to leave a building, walk outside to a street corner, and pull out a $3,000 phone." Iridium had other annoying limitations as well. For example, in remote areas where electricity wasn't available, the battery charger required special solar-powered accessories, which made it unappealing to busy travelers.

One has to wonder what type of feasibility analysis Iridium engaged in before it spent billions of dollars to so spectacularly fail. Another passage from Professor Finkelstein's book, quoting Iridium's second CEO, John Richardson, makes one wonder further:

We're a classic MBA case study in how not to introduce a product. First we created a marvelous technological achievement. Then we asked how to make money on it.

Questions for Critical Thinking

1. Why do you think that those who were leading Iridium continued to push the concept forward despite all the difficulties being encountered in the early stages of the venture's life? Would you have pulled the plug on this venture sooner than actually happened? If so, at what point?

2. One of Iridium's problems was rapidly advancing cell phone technologies. As an entrepreneur, what would you do to remain abreast of technological developments and to monitor their meaning?

3. Why do you think the founders of Iridium and its financial backers didn't conduct a more thorough feasibility analysis before over

Originally named Retailing Insights, Trakus was founded in 1997. The company's business idea was to build computerized shopping carts for grocery stores called Videocarts. Using wireless technologies, Videocarts would know where each cart was in a store and would alert shoppers to specials and provide other useful information on a video display attached to the cart. If a shopper were in the cereal aisle, for example, the Videocart would show advertisements for cereals and let the shopper know what brands were on sale. The Videocart had other useful features, too, such as providing recipes and locating needed items in the store.

Another company's earlier attempt to build a Videocart failed, primarily because of poor execution. Retailing Insights vowed to do it right and equipped its carts with all the latest technology. The company obtained $50,000 of seed money from an angel investor. **Seed money** is the initial investment made in a firm. The investor insisted that Retailing Insights conduct a feasibility analysis of the market for the product before using resources for product development. In response to this request, the company developed a very detailed description of the Videocart, which included all the product's benefits for both the grocery store retailers and grocery products' manufacturers. They showed this description to both retailers and manufacturers and were surprised by what they found. In fact, they discovered that neither party had an interest in the product. The previous cart's bad reputation was a major concern for retailers, who were wary of trying another version of something that had already failed. Retailing Insights knew then that it would have to establish multiple test sites (at its own expense) to convince retailers that the carts were reliable. Manufacturers told the company that they would be willing to consider a new medium of advertising only if sufficient scale were established to justify the cost of producing ads and incurring related expenses. This stipulation led Retailing Insights to realize that the firm would have to sign up a significant portion of all grocery stores in the United States to get manufacturers excited about its product.

After considering these obstacles, the idea for the Videocart was abandoned. The company still thought it had core competencies, however, and after a brainstorming session decided to go in a completely different direction. A **core competency** is a resource or capability that serves as a source of a firm's competitive advantage over its rivals.[4] A new idea was conceived, based on Retailing Insight's core competency in the area of miniature

Locations in This Book of Additional Information
TABLE 3.1 **About Each Component of Feasibility Analysis**

Component of Feasibility Analysis	More Complete Discussion of Topic
Product/service feasibility	Chapter 3 (this chapter)
Industry/market feasibility	Chapter 5: Industry and Competitor Analysis
Organizational feasibility	Chapter 6: Developing an Effective Business Model
	Chapter 9: Building a New-Venture Team
Financial feasibility	Chapter 8: Assessing a New Venture's Financial Strength and Viability
	Chapter 10: Getting Financing or Funding

electronics, to build rugged little transmitters that could be put on athletes (in their helmets or on their clothing) that, together with a set of antennas in a stadium, could determine where every athlete was at any given time during a sports contest. The devices would generate real-time statistics during the course of a game, such as the percentage of time that a defensive lineman spent on his opponent's side of the line of scrimmage during a football game. Such data could be fed to broadcasters to liven up the information they provided during the game's broadcast, or it could even be displayed on the television screen. To test the product feasibility of the idea, Research Insights changed its name to Trakus and showed a detailed description and simulation of the device to its potential clientele. This time, the reception the company received was overwhelmingly positive. The only real concern was whether the device could actually be built. Trakus has since received venture capital financing and has tested the devices in National Hockey League games and in thoroughbred horse racing events.[5] There are several fascinating streaming videos available on Trakus's Web site (www.trakus.com), under the "news" heading, that show how the device works.

Trakus could have spent millions of dollars fully developing the Videocart only to find that the product had no real value in the marketplace. The feasibility analysis accomplished exactly what it was supposed to—it gave the company a candid assessment of the viability of its business idea *before* it consumed resources such as money. To its credit, the company responded by shifting to a different and viable product, causing the firm to move in a more promising direction.

A similar affirmation of the importance of feasibility analysis is provided by Jim Clark, the founder of Silicon Graphics and cofounder of Netscape. Clark is very blunt in the value he places on feasibility analysis—particularly the importance of getting out and talking to potential customers about the merits of a business idea:

> The reason so few companies are successful is that most people don't have a lot of common sense about what will sell and what won't. You need to be very pragmatic about whether people will pay for a product based on your great idea. "This should be great and I am sure the world will beat a path to my door." Once you have an idea for a product or service, you need to test the market. Talk to your potential customers about what they want. And don't try to make the product do everything for everyone. Engineers often make this mistake. It's the Swiss Army knife mentality. They want to put everything into it. Don't. Go out and talk to customers as quickly as you can and put a copy of the product in front of them to get their feedback. When we went out to sell our first product at Silicon Graphics, people came back and said, "We don't want this." We sold them what they wanted.[6]

Now let's turn our attention to the four areas of feasibility analysis. The first area we'll discuss is product/service feasibility.

L E A R N I N G

Objective

3. Describe the purpose of a product/service feasibility analysis and the two primary issues that a proposed business should consider in this area.

Product/Service Feasibility Analysis

Product/service feasibility analysis is an assessment of the overall appeal of the product or service being proposed. Before rushing a prospective product or service into development, a firm should be confident that it's what customers want and that the product or service will have an adequate market. In launching a new venture, it is easy for an entrepreneur to get caught up in activities such as raising money, hiring employees, buying computer equipment, signing leases, writing press releases, and so on. This is understandable, in that these are indeed important activities. However, for most firms, the number one success factor is delivering a superior product or service.[7] The importance of knowing the feasibility of a new product or service idea is affirmed by R. G. Cooper, a widely published author in the area of product development, who wrote,

Often, the most effective thing an entrepreneur can do while completing a product/service feasibility analysis is hit the streets and talk to potential customers. Here, a young entrepreneur collects feedback from a prospective customer about a new product idea.

New product success or failure is largely decided in the first few plays of the game—in those critical steps and tasks that precede the actual development of the product. The upfront homework defines the product and builds the business case for development.[8]

Table 3.2 provides a summary of the benefits of conducting a detailed and thorough product/service feasibility analysis. As shown in the table, the benefits and rewards of conducting the analysis are well worth the effort. Two primary tests—concept testing and usability testing—constitute product/service feasibility analysis.

Concept Testing. A **concept test** involves showing a preliminary description of the product or service idea to prospective customers to gauge customer interest, desirability, and purchase intent.[9] It was after the concept test that Retailing Insights abandoned its plans to build the Videocart. There are three primary purposes for a concept test, as shown in Figure 3.2.[10] The first purpose is to validate the underlying premise of the product or service idea. This is done by showing the concept test to potential customers and asking them to complete a short questionnaire. The questionnaire should

4. Identify three primary purposes of concept testing.

TABLE 3.2 Benefits of Conducting a Product/Service Feasibility Analysis

Benefit	Explanation
Getting the product right the first time	You know what customers want because you asked them. You also tested a product's usability and the quality of the user's experience.
A beta (or early adopter) community emerges	The firms or individuals that participate in the feasibility analysis often become a company's first customers or "adopters." These early customers provide additional feedback as the product or service rolls out.
Avoiding any obvious flaws in product or service design	By asking prospective customers to test the usability of a product or the ease of use of a service, obvious design flaws are usually uncovered.
Using time and capital more efficiently	Because you have a better idea of what customers want, you won't spend as much time or money chasing ideas that customers don't want.
Gaining insight into additional product and service offerings	Often, conducting a feasibility analysis for one product or service prompts the recognition of the need for additional products or services.

FIGURE 3.2

Three Primary Purposes for a Concept Test

Validate the Underlying Premise of the Product or Service Idea	Help Develop the Idea	Try to Estimate Sales
This is accomplished by showing the concept test to potential customers and asking them to complete a short questionnaire and offer comments and suggestions on how the idea can be strengthened.	Based on the results of the initial concept test, many entrepreneurs tweak their idea and then show a revised concept statement to another group of potential customers. This process can be repeated several times to help develop and strengthen the idea.	Some type of buying intention question appears in almost every concept test to try to determine how many people will actually buy the product or service.

include questions pertaining to product features, price, location (if applicable), and suggestions for improving the concept.[11] The second purpose of the concept test is to help develop the idea. For example, a firm may show a product idea to a prospective group of customers, get feedback, tweak the idea, and then show it to another group of customers for additional feedback. This process can be repeated several times to help develop and strengthen the idea. The third purpose of the concept test is to estimate the potential market share the product or service might command.

Some type of buying intention question appears in almost every concept test, usually in the form of a survey questionnaire that looks something like this:

How likely would you be to buy a product like this, if we make it?[12]

1. Definitely would buy
2. Probably would buy
3. Might or might not buy
4. Probably would not buy
5. Definitely would not buy

The number of people who definitely would buy and probably would buy are typically combined and used as a gauge of customer interest. One caveat is that people who say that they intend to purchase a product don't always follow through, so the numbers resulting from this activity are almost always optimistic. Nonetheless, the numbers do give a business an indication of the degree of consumer interest in a firm's product or service.

If a firm's potential customers are geographically dispersed, the concept test can be completed by mail or online. There are many affordable and easy-to-use online platforms for collecting survey data. An example is Zoomerang (www.zoomerang.com). Zoomerang provides services ranging from administering basic online surveys to consulting services regarding how to select the participants in a survey and statistically analyze the results.[13]

A well-designed concept test, which is usually called a **concept statement**, includes the following:

■ *A Description of the Product or Service Being Offered:* This section details the features of the product or service and may include a sketch of it as well. A computer-generated simulation of the functionality of the product or service is also helpful.
■ *The Intended Target Market:* This section lists the businesses or people who are expected to buy the product or service.
■ *The Benefits of the Product or Service:* This section describes the benefits of the product or service and includes an account of how the product or service adds value and/or solves a problem.

L E A R N I N G
Objective

5. Explain a concept statement and its contents.

■ *A Description of How the Product will be Positioned Relative to Similar Ones in the Market:* A company's position describes how its product or service is situated relative to competitors.

■ *A Description of How the Product or Service will be Sold and Distributed:* This section specifies whether the product will be sold directly by the manufacturer or through distributors or franchisees.

The concept statement for a fictitious company named New Venture Fitness Drinks is provided in Figure 3.3. New Venture Fitness Drinks sells a line of nutritious fitness drinks and targets sports enthusiasts. Its strategy is to place small restaurants, similar to smoothie restaurants, near large sports complexes. It is important to keep a concept statement relatively short (no more than one page) to increase the likelihood that it will be read.

Rather than developing a formal concept statement, sometimes entrepreneurs conduct their initial product/service feasibility analysis by simply talking through their ideas with people and gathering informal feedback. This approach was pursued by Jeremy Jaech, the founder of Trumba.com, an online calendar service. In describing how his company conducted its initial product/service feasibility analysis, Jaech recalls:

> The first thing we (did) was to go out and talk to a lot of different people. We talked to about 25 couples about their calendaring, and what they did to manage all the different aspects of their lives. The first hurdle was determining if our idea held water with this broader group of people, what they were using today, and how difficult we thought it would be to switch them over to our solution.[14]

FIGURE 3.3

New Venture Fitness Drinks' Concept Statement

New Business Concept
New Venture Fitness Drinks Inc.

Product

New Venture Fitness Drinks will sell delicious, nutrition-filled, all-natural fitness drinks to thirsty sports enthusiasts. The drinks will be sold through small storefronts (600 sq. ft.) that will be the same size as popular smoothie restaurants. The drinks were formulated by Dr. William Peters, a world-renowned nutritionist, and Dr. Michelle Smith, a sports medicine specialist, on behalf of New Venture Fitness Drinks and its customers.

Target Market

In the first three years of operation, New Venture Fitness Drinks plans to open three or four restaurants. They will all be located near large sports complexes that contain soccer fields and softball diamonds. The target market is sports enthusiasts.

Why New Venture Fitness Drinks?

The industry for sports drinks continues to grow. New Venture Fitness Drinks will introduce exciting new sports drinks that will be priced between $1.50 and $2.50 per 16-ounce serving. Energy bars and other over-the-counter sports snacks will also be sold. Each restaurant will contain comfortable tables and chairs (both inside and outside) where sports enthusiasts can congregate after a game. The atmosphere will be fun, cheerful, and uplifting.

Special Feature—No Other Restaurant Does This

As a special feature, New Venture Fitness Drinks will videotape select sporting events that take place in the sports complexes nearest its restaurants and will replay highlights of the games on video monitors in their restaurants. The "highlight" film will be a 30-minute film that will play continuously from the previous day's sporting events. This special feature will allow sports enthusiasts, from kids playing soccer to adults in softball leagues, to drop in and see themselves and their teammates on television.

Management Team

New Venture Fitness Drink is led by its cofounders, Jack Petty and Peggy Wills. Jack has 16 years of experience with a national restaurant chain, and Peggy is a certified public accountant with seven years of experience at a Big 4 accounting firm.

While not a complete approach, there is merit to the give-and-take that entrepreneurs like Jaech experience by talking with prospective customers rather than just handing them a concept statement and asking them to complete a questionnaire. As a result, the ideal combination is to have a written concept statement, like the one shown in Figure 3.3, with a questionnaire that the participants can complete but also engage in verbal give-and-take with as many of the participants as is practical.

L E A R N I N G

Objective

6. Define the term *usability testing* and explain why it's important.

Usability Testing. A concept test is usually followed by the development of a prototype or model of the product, as appropriate and necessary. A **prototype** is the first physical depiction of a new product, which is usually still in a rough or tentative mode.[15] For products, like a new board game, a prototype is needed to get more substantive feedback than can be gleaned from a concept statement. It is also necessary to have a prototype if feedback will be solicited from potential licensees of a product or the attendees at an industry trade show. There are many ways to get a prototype made if the process requires specialized equipment or expertise. For example, the ThomasRegister (www.thomasnet.com), a directory of all the manufacturers in the United States, has a listing of rapid prototyping services. Similarly, the American Institute of Graphic Arts (www.aiga.org) lists designers and prototype engineers looking for work. Individual projects can also be listed on more general job sites like Craigslist.com and Monster.com. In some instances, a virtual prototype, which is cheaper than a physical prototype, is sufficient.[16] A **virtual prototype** is a computer-generated 3D image of an idea. It displays an invention as a 3D model that can be viewed from all sides and rotated 360 degrees.

It is a judgment call on the part of an entrepreneur regarding when to incur the expense of having a prototype made. One of the main advantages of having a prototype available is that it permits usability testing to take place. **Usability testing** is a form of product/service feasibility analysis, which measures a product's ease of use and the user's perception of the experience. Usability tests are sometimes called user tests, beta tests, or field trials, depending on the circumstances involved. There are many forms of usability tests. Some entrepreneurs, working within limited budgets, develop a fairly basic prototype and ask friends and colleagues to use the product, then complete an evaluation form or give verbal feedback. Although fairly rudimentary, this approach is superior to the decision to not do any testing at all. Other companies have elaborate usability testing programs and facilities.

Usability testing is particularly important for software and Web site design. According to one survey, 36 percent of all Web site owners in the United States conduct usability research.[17] Figure 3.4 illustrates the way in which concept and usability testing unfolds at Activision, a maker of electronic games. Activision calls it the "green light process." As a product passes through the various stages of testing, it must receive a "green light" before it is allowed to progress to the next stage. At any point in the process, a product can also receive a "red light" and be terminated or sent back for further development and review.

FIGURE 3.4

Role of Feasibility Analysis in the Development of Successful Business Ideas at Activision

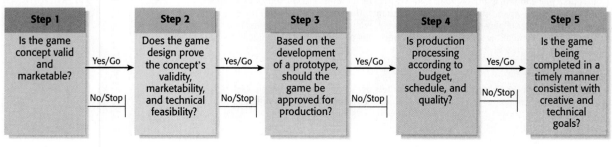

Companies such as Fisher-Price, which makes toys for young children, appreciate the importance of usability testing. Fisher-Price has set up this usability testing lab to observe how children use and interact with its products.

The boxed feature titled "Partnering for Success" describes an approach to usability testing employed at Salesforce.com.

Industry/Market Feasibility Analysis

Industry/market feasibility analysis is an assessment of the overall appeal of the market for the product or service being proposed. For feasibility analysis, there are three primary issues that a proposed business should consider: industry attractiveness, market timeliness, and the identification of a niche market.[18]

LEARNING Objective

7. Describe the purpose of industry/market feasibility analysis and the three primary issues to consider in this area.

partnering for *success*

Salesforce.com: Partnering with Customers in a "User-Centric" Fashion to Build Software Products That Work

www.salesforce.com

Typically, firms don't consider their customers "partners." But Salesforce.com has adopted an approach to product development and usability testing that is so customer-centric the customer is a true partner in the company's efforts. Here's Salesforce.com's story and how its approach to usability testing works.

Salesforce.com was founded in 1999 by former Oracle executive Marc Benioff to pioneer the idea of "software as a service." Traditionally, companies have bought software and then run it on their own computers. Salesforce.com's idea was to let companies rent software and run it on their servers. The niche that Salesforce.com selected was customer relationship management (CRM) software. As a result, the company's business model was to build CRM software, run it on its

computers, and sell access to the software via the Internet as a service. CRM software helps organizations keep track of current and prospective customers.

At the time Salesforce.com was started, CRM software was being sold by Siebel Systems, Oracle, IBM, and other large firms. The constant complaint from users was that the software was unwieldy, difficult to use, updated infrequently, and could only be accessed through a firm's proprietary computer systems. Salesforce.com set out to counter these complaints by making more user-friendly software, and because it hosted its own software on the Web, the software could be updated frequently and users could log onto their company's account anywhere an Internet connection and Web browser were available. The biggest objection that Salesforce.com had to overcome was the fact that it would be hosting its customers' sensitive sales and customer data. Most companies consider their sales and customer data to be highly proprietary, and it was unclear whether they would trust another firm to store it.

Ultimately, Salesforce.com was able to overcome this objection and is now a vibrant, growing, publicly traded firm. What ultimately swayed its customers and won the day was its products' ease of use and low prices and the company's "user-centric" approach to software design and improvement. From the beginning, Salesforce.com adopted a "user-centric" approach, meaning that the company consistently involved small groups of users in the design and usability testing of its products—an approach that is still being utilized today. The company also listens to its users and studies their behavior. To illustrate how this works, Pip Coburn, in his book *The Change Function*, lists Salesforce.com's eight-step approach to utilizing user feedback and behavior:

Step 1 *Salesforce.com translates customer complaints and requests into possible new features.*

Step 2 *They also watch the activity in the applications—which they can do since Salesforce.com hosts them. They can see what is and isn't used.*

Step 3 *They formulate new features and iterate current features based on this information.*

Step 4 *They test new features with real live clients who might come in to talk for a while about it. In return, Salesforce.com personnel might say thanks tons and give their clients a $10 Starbucks gift card.*

Step 5 *Design and development gets more feedback.*

Step 6 *Salesforce.com iterates until they are set to deploy*

Step 7 *They ask their users for permission to include any changes—functionality is never forced.*

Step 8 *Then they start all over again, repeating a fairly straightforward low-risk, community-enhancing process.*

Performing these steps results in a self-perpetuating cycle. As the company reacts to the suggestions and behaviors of its customers, those customers become more willing to provide suggestions and be more transparent in the way they use software online. Along with getting good feedback on the quality and usability of its products, as an added benefit, the company is also creating a community of Salesforce.com users. A community of users is likely to remain more loyal and committed to a company than a more diverse set of customers and is more likely to spread the word about the advantages of using a company's products.

Questions for Critical Thinking

1. What benefits do customers experience by becoming heavily involved in the development and usability testing of their vendor's products? Why would a customer or potential customer of Salesforce.com take the time necessary to help develop and test its products?

2. Do you think Salesforce.com would be willing to reciprocate with its partners? In other words, if your small entrepreneurial venture developed a prototype of a product that Salesforce.com might be able to use, do you think the company would be interested in partnering with you to test its feasibility? What would you do to try to convince Salesforce.com to work with you in this manner if its initial response to your request was negative?

3. What can an entrepreneurial venture conducting its first feasibility analysis learn from the Salesforce.com approach to product development and usability testing?

4. Provide at least three additional examples of companies that sell software as a "service" rather than as a physical product. Do you think selling software as a service is a trend that will continue to gain momentum? What are the biggest advantages and disadvantages to this approach to selling software?

Sources: Salesforce.com homepage, www.salesforce.com (accessed August 4, 2006); Pip Coburn, *The Change Function* (New York: Portfolio, 2006).

Industry Attractiveness. Industries vary considerably in terms of their growth rate, as shown in Table 3.3. Typically, an industry that is growing is more attractive because it is more receptive to new entrants and new product introductions. A primary determinant of a new venture's feasibility is the attractiveness of the industry it chooses. This is why many venture capitalists, such as Don Valentine of Sequoia Capital, first assess the attractiveness of a start-up's industry when considering funding a new venture.[19] In general, the most attractive industries are characterized by the following:

- Being large and growing (with growth being more important than size).
- Being important to the customer. These markets typically sell products or services that customers "must have" rather than "would like to have." As you recall from economics, these attractive products have inelastic demand curves.
- Being fairly young rather than older and more mature. These markets tend to be early in their product life cycle, when price competition is not intense.
- Having high rather than low operating margins. These markets are simply more profitable for entry and competition purposes.
- Not being crowded. A crowded market, with lots of competitors, is typically characterized by fierce price competition and low operating margins.

Although this is admittedly an ideal list, the extent to which a new business's proposed industry's growth possibilities satisfy these criteria should be taken seriously. For example, an entrepreneur may have an idea for a new product or service that would ideally suit the needs of a particular customer. The market may not be big enough, however, to support a business. On the flip side, sometimes entrepreneurs err by placing too much weight on the overall size and attractiveness of the industry they are entering, which makes the issue of industry attractiveness a careful balancing act. This point is vividly illustrated by Michael A. Cusumano, a Distinguished Professor in the Sloan School of Management at MIT and an author of several books on the software industry:

> One of the worst ways for entrepreneurs to explain potential market attractiveness is to describe some huge market or segment (such as how much U.S. financial institutions spent the previous year on information technology and content, or how much U.S. firms spent the previous year in software contracting) and they argue that, if they could get only 1 or 2 percent of the multibillion-dollar market, they would have a viable business. Size alone does not make a market or a business proposition attractive. There is no guarantee that a start-up will get *any* percentage of a market unless the start-up has some real advantage over its competitors, good access to customers, and some way of preventing imitation, among other things.[20]

TABLE 3.3 Three-Year Industry Growth in Revenues

Industry	Three-Year Revenue Growth (%)
Accounting and Financial Software	6.7
Apparel and Accessories Retail	6.3
Appliances	(10.6)
Biotechnology	23.6
Consumer Electronics & Appliance Retail	5.1
Footware	5.1
Internet Auctions	18.8
Internet Content Providers	72.2
Magnetic Disk Storage	4.3
Newspaper Publishing	6.9
Outsourced Human Resource Services	8.0
Personal Computers	16.3
Sauces & Condiments	1.1
Semiconductors	13.4
Specialty Eateries	31.8
Toys & Games	1.2

Source: Adapted from Hoovers Online, **www.hoovers.com,** Three-Year Industry Growth in Revenues (1999–2002), August 1, 2006.

8. Explain the difference between primary research and secondary research.

This quotation is a sobering reminder that industry attractiveness is only one of many factors that lead to entrepreneurial success.

To fully understand the dynamics of the industry a firm plans to enter, an entrepreneur should conduct both primary and secondary research. **Primary research** is original research and is collected by the entrepreneur. In assessing the attractiveness of a market, this typically involves talking to potential customers and key industry participants. **Secondary research** probes data that are already collected. The sources of secondary research include industry-related publications, government statistics, competitors' Web sites, and industry reports from respected research firms, such as Forrester Research. There are also many authoritative sources of industry-related data available online or in hard copy, as shown in Table 3.4. Most universities buy licenses or subscriptions to these resources and provide free access to their students, faculty, and staff. As evidence that primary and secondary research has been completed, entrepreneurs should have concrete numbers relative to the market size and projected growth rate of the industry that they plan to enter. When looking for funding, for example, it is not enough for an entrepreneur to simply say that the research supports that the firm will be participating in a "large and growing market." Instead, an entrepreneur should have hard data to support such a claim.

A caveat to this discussion is that it is impossible to analyze markets that don't exist. This is a challenge confronting entrepreneurs trying to bring breakthrough products or services to market. **Breakthrough products and services** establish new markets or new market segments.[21] Most new products and services feature incremental improvements to existing ones, such as a slightly better DVD player or computer program, while examples of breakthrough products and services include Yahoo! and Internet search engines, eBay and online auctions, and Intuit and personal finance software. Each of these companies pioneered the market it entered. In these instances, it is particularly important that a firm conduct primary research to determine if there is a sufficient market for its product or service.[22]

Market Timeliness. A second consideration in regard to the industry/market feasibility of a business idea is the timeliness of the introduction of a particular product or service.

TABLE 3.4 Resources to Facilitate an Industry Analysis

Source	Description
Dunn & Bradstreet Business Rankings	Ranks U.S. businesses (public and private) within state and industry categories by sales and number of employees.
Encyclopedia of American Industries	Provides an industry overview, relevant trends, and statistical data for over 1,000 industries at the 4-digit SIC code level.
Hoover's Online	Brief histories and financial information on companies, industries, people, and products.
Mergent Online	The "Industry Search" capability allows the user to obtain reports on a wide range of industry sectors and to limit the search by geographic area.
Plunkett's Industry Almanac Series	Each volume covers a specific industry, with competitive intelligence, market research, market and industry analysis, industry statistics, and industry trends.
Standard & Poor's Industry Surveys	A quarterly review and analysis of over 50 major industry groups, searchable by industry in the online version, indexed by industry and company in the print version.
U.S. Industrial Outlook	Does not cover individual companies, but does analyze over 200 manufacturing and nonmanufacturing industries, with a discussion of each one's size, trade position, and growth history.
U.S. Industry Profiles	Profiles the leading 100 industries, including construction, transportation, and entertainment, with analysis of both current and future industry outlooks.
The Wall Street Journal	Financial newspaper offering in-depth coverage of financial markets along with business and industry news.

Source: University of Central Florida Library, **http://library.ucf.edu/Reference/Guides/** (accessed July 30, 2006).

The factors to consider vary, depending on whether a prospective business is planning to introduce a breakthrough new product or service or one that is an improvement on those currently available.

If the product or service is an improvement on those already available in the marketplace, the first consideration is to determine whether the window of opportunity for the product or service is open or closed. As explained in Chapter 2, some markets, such as the one for Internet search engines, are either saturated with competitors or dominated by competitors with sufficient market power that they are essentially closed to new entrants. Other markets, such as specialty eateries, are characterized by windows of opportunity that are wide open and are receptive to new entrants. The second consideration is to study the simple economics of a marketplace to determine the current dynamics of the industry and whether the timing for a new business is good. For example, the personal computer industry is currently consolidating—look at Hewlett-Packard's acquisition of Compaq in 2001, Gateway's acquisition of eMachines in 2004, and Dell's acquisition of Alienware (a high-end gaming machine) in 2006. When an industry consolidates, a handful of large firms acquire or force out of business the smaller firms in the industry and take over the majority of the business. This trend in the personal computer industry suggests that it is not a good time to launch a new personal computer firm.

For new businesses that are developing a potential breakthrough product or service, the issue of whether to try to capture a first-mover advantage is vitally important. A **first-mover advantage** is a sometimes insurmountable advantage gained by the first significant company to move into a new market.[23] Whether getting to market first is truly an advantage remains an active topic for debate. Proponents of first-mover advantage argue that first movers can set the standard for an industry and typically have an advantage in terms of brand recognition and market power.[24] There are many examples of first movers who have captured these advantages, including Palm, Yahoo!, and Nokia. Others argue that there are an equal number of disadvantages to being first to market, such as high research-and-development costs, the risk of seeing whether the product or service will catch on, and the risk that a competitor will study the first-mover's product or service and quickly come out with a slightly better version of essentially the same thing.[25] This last disadvantage is compelling. In fact, the term **second-mover advantage** is used to describe the advantage that the second rather than the first entrant has in entering a market. The second mover has the advantage of studying all the mistakes that were made by the first mover, something that observers believe helps the second mover build a better product or service.[26]

Identifying a Niche (or Vertical) Market. The final step in industry/market feasibility analysis is identifying a niche market in which the firm can participate. A **niche market** is a place within a larger market segment that represents a narrower group of customers with similar interests.[27] Most successful entrepreneurial firms do not start by selling to broad markets. Instead, most start by identifying an emerging or underserved niche within a larger market, as discussed in more detail in Chapter 11.[28] Another useful way of thinking about this topic is to distinguish between vertical and horizontal markets. A **vertical market**, which is analogous to a niche market, focuses on similar businesses that have specific and specialized needs. For instance, a start-up might focus on providing accounting software designed specifically for specialty eateries, like small coffee or smoothie restaurants. A **horizontal market** meets the specific need of a wide variety of industries, rather than a specific one. A start-up that tried to market an accounting software product to all small businesses would be trying to sell into a horizontal market.

For a new firm, selling to a niche or vertical market makes sense for at least two reasons. First, it allows a firm to establish itself within an industry without competing against major participants head-on. Second, a niche strategy allows a firm to focus on serving a specialized market very well instead of trying to be everything to everybody in a broad market, which is nearly impossible for a new entrant. An example is Prometheus Laboratories, a firm selling diagnostic services to the 15,000 doctors in the United States specializing in gastroenterology and rheumatology. Explaining his firm's strategy of developing world-class expertise in a specialized area, Prometheus CEO Michael Walsh said, "We want to be an inch wide and a mile deep."[29]

The challenge in identifying an attractive niche or vertical market is that it must be large enough to support a proposed business yet small enough to avoid initial direct head-to-head competition with industry leaders. If a clearly defined niche market cannot be identified, it is difficult to envision the industry/market feasibility of a new business venture.

More information about the value of vertical versus horizontal markets for start-up firms is provided in the "Savvy Entrepreneurial Firm" feature in this chapter.

savvy entrepreneurial firm

Online Social Networks: Winning by Occupying Vertical Rather Than Horizontal Markets

For the first week of July 2006, what do you think was the single most visited Web site in the United States? Yahoo!? Google? Microsoft's MSN Hotmail? The answer is no to all the above. The winner: MySpace.com—a social networking site.

Social networking is a growing phenomenon on the Internet. Social networking is based on the ability of people to connect to one another via technology, a trend most observers feel is here to stay. It's important from a business standpoint, because sites like MySpace.com and Facebook, which are relatively new, have garnered tremendous market share in terms of people's time and mindshare. Just a few short years ago, it would have been unfathomable to think that a social networking start-up would pass Google and Yahoo! as the most visited site on the Internet.

For the purpose of this chapter, the types of social networking sites that are gaining the most traction and those that aren't are the focal point of interest. There are basically two categories of social networking Web sites. The first is horizontal sites, which are very broad in their appeal and try to connect people of all interests and age groups. This group includes Friendster, Hi5, Tribe.net, and Orkut, which is Google's social networking site. The second category is vertical sites, which focus on more narrow and tightly focused target markets. The biggest is MySpace.com, which is ostensibly about music but is now intensely focused on the teenage demographic. Facebook, which helps connect students at colleges and universities, is another large vertical site. Other vertical sites that have surfaced over the past couple of years include sites that focus on niches such as art, tennis, football, soccer, dating, and even cosmetic surgery. Interesting examples of tightly focused vertical social networking sites include Dogster (www.dogster.com), Catster (www.catster.com), and Craftster.org (www.craftster.org).

The most successful social networking sites, by far, have been the vertical sites, which focus on a specific area of interest. In comparison, the two most heavily touted horizontal sites, Friendster and Tribe.com, have both struggled. David Beisel, a prominent Boston, Mass., venture capitalist, believes that the horizontal sites have struggled because their primary mission, which is basically to sign people up so they can demonstrate that they have friends, lacks emotion and isn't very compelling. The vertical sites, in contrast, focus on things that people care about, a focus that is more compelling, whether it's connecting to other college students or talking about training hunting dogs. People like to share their experiences about something they are passionate about, and the vertical sites give individuals the opportunity to talk directly to like-minded people. It's much harder for the horizontal sites, which try to be all things to all people, to elicit the same degree of passion.

Ironically, it typically is more expensive to try to gain market share in a horizontal market than a vertical market, even though in many cases the vertical markets offer more realistic opportunities for success.

Questions for Critical Thinking

1. What does this feature teach start-up entrepreneurs about the value of vertical versus horizontal markets?
2. Why might a social networking site that appeals to a vertical market, like dog owners or cancer patients, actually have more business potential (for targeted ads or e-commerce) than a broader-based horizontal site with many more members?
3. Why do you think Facebook has been so popular on college campuses? What can entrepreneurs preparing to launch their ventures learn from studying Facebook and what has made it successful?
4. If you launched a social networking site to target a vertical market, what market would you target? What would you expect the demographic makeup of your user group to be?

Sources: CNN.com, "Report: MySpace Top Single U.S. Web Site," July 12, 2006; D. Beisel, Genuine VC blog www.genuinevc.com/archives/2006/02/vertical_social.htm (accessed August 3, 2006).

Organizational Feasibility Analysis

Organizational feasibility analysis is conducted to determine whether a proposed business has sufficient management expertise, organizational competence, and resources to successfully launch its business. There are two primary issues to consider in this area: management prowess and resource sufficiency.

Management Prowess. A firm should candidly evaluate the prowess, or ability, of its management team. Because this requires detailed introspection, the entrepreneur must complete a self-assessment. Two of the most important factors in this area are the passion that the solo entrepreneur or the management team has for the business idea and the extent to which the management team or solo entrepreneur understands the markets in which the firm will participate.[30] There are no practical substitutes for strengths in these areas.[31] Although financing, for example, is important, it is not as important as passion for the business and knowledge of the customer. Scott Cook, the founder of Intuit, makes this point:

> Financing is really not the most important issue. If you have a great business, know your customer, and know that what you are doing is superior to what's on the market— that's what it takes to win. But if you have a lousy business idea, financing won't turn it into a good one. Getting money is a necessary requirement, but I really wouldn't focus on the financing. I would focus on knowing the customer cold.[32]

An example of a company that suffered by having a management team that was unfamiliar with the industry it entered is illustrated in the "What Went Wrong?" feature in Chapter 9. The feature focuses on an Internet start-up named Garden.com, which was launched in 1995 to sell gardening supplies on the Internet. None of Garden.com's three founders had any experience in garden retailing, nor were they knowledgeable gardeners. The firm failed after losing many millions of dollars of its investors' money.

Several other factors should be considered regarding management prowess. Managers with extensive professional and social networks have an advantage in that they are able to reach out to colleagues and friends to help them plug experience or knowledge gaps. In addition, a potential new venture should have an idea of the type of new-venture team that it can assemble. A **new-venture team** is the group of founders, key employees, and advisers that either manage or help manage a new business in its start-up years. If the founder or founders of a new venture have identified several individuals they believe will join the firm after it is launched and these individuals are highly capable, that knowledge lends credibility to the organizational feasibility of the potential venture. The same rationale applies for highly capable people who a new venture believes would be willing to join its board of directors or board of advisers.

Resource Sufficiency. The second area of organizational feasibility analysis is to determine whether the potential new venture has sufficient resources to move forward to successfully develop a product or service idea. The focus in organizational feasibility analysis should be on nonfinancial resources, in that financial feasibility is considered separately. Several areas should be examined, including the availability of office space, the quality of the labor pool in the area where the business will be located, and the possibility of obtaining intellectual property protection on key aspects of the new business (intellectual property is discussed in detail in Chapter 12). Some start-ups are able to minimize their initial facility expenses and gain access to resources that they wouldn't have access to otherwise by locating themselves in a community- or university-sponsored business incubator.

One resource sufficiency issue that new firms should consider is their proximity to similar firms. There are well-known **clusters** of high-tech firms, for example, in the Silicon Valley of California, on Route 128 around Boston, and in the Cambridge region in the United Kingdom. Clusters arise because they increase the productivity of the firms participating in them. Because these firms are located near one another, it is easy for their employees to

An important part of organizational feasibility analysis is assessing the degree of passion that a sole entrepreneur or team of entrepreneurs has for a business idea. A good indication of passion is the willingness of a young team to do what it takes to complete a sound feasibility analysis for a business idea.

network with each other, and it is easy for the firms to gain access to specialized suppliers, scientific knowledge, and technological expertise indigenous to the area. A semiconductor start-up that decided to locate in Kansas City, Missouri, for example, would be at a significant disadvantage to a semiconductor start-up in Silicon Valley, which already has a cluster of semiconductor firms. Researchers have found that small manufacturing firms benefit more than larger firms by being physically close to a cluster of similar firms.[33]

To test resource sufficiency, it is suggested that a prospective firm list the 6 to 12 most critical nonfinancial resources that will be needed to move its business idea forward and to assess the feasibility of securing those resources for the business. If critical resources are not available in key areas, it may be impracticable to proceed with a business idea.

Financial Feasibility Analysis

Financial feasibility analysis is the final stage of a comprehensive feasibility analysis. For feasibility analysis, a quick financial assessment is usually sufficient. More rigor at this point is typically not required because the specifics of the business will inevitably evolve, making it impractical to spend a lot of time early on preparing detailed financial forecasts. The most important issues to consider at this stage are total start-up cash needed, financial performance of similar businesses, and the overall financial attractiveness of the proposed venture. If a proposed new venture moves beyond the feasibility analysis stage, it will need to complete pro forma (or projected) financial statements that demonstrate the firm's financial viability for the first 1 to 3 years of its existence. In Chapter 8, we'll provide you with specific instructions for preparing these statements.

Total Start-Up Cash Needed. This first issue refers to the total cash needed to prepare the business to make its first sale. An actual budget should be prepared that lists all the anticipated capital purchases and operating expenses needed to generate the first $1 in revenues. Very few new ventures qualify for either bank financing or equity funding early on, as will be explained in Chapter 10, so a cursory "I'll borrow the money" or "I plan to bring equity investors on board" won't do. Instead, the financial feasibility analysis should state specifically where the money will come from to fund the venture's start-up costs.

If the money will come from friends and family or is raised through other means, such as credit cards or a home equity line of credit, a reasonable plan should be envisioned to pay the money back. In the small number of cases where a bank loan or equity investors are involved, the case should be made that sufficient funds will be available to cover start-up costs and get

L E A R N I N G

Objective

10. Explain the importance of financial feasibility analysis and list the most critical issues to consider in this area.

the firm to the point where its cash flow is positive. Showing how a new venture's start-up costs will be covered is an important issue. Many entrepreneurial ventures look promising as ongoing concerns, but have no way of raising the money to get up-and-running, or are never able to recover from the costs involved. When projecting start-up expenses, it is better to over-estimate rather than underestimate the costs involved. Murphy's Law is prevalent in the start-up world—things will go wrong. It is a rare start-up that doesn't have some setbacks getting up-and-running—whether it involves unanticipated expenses or delays getting to market.

In terms of raising the money needed to start a firm, you will read many anecdotes through-out this book of savvy and creative ways that entrepreneurs cover their start-up costs. For exam-ple, as we discussed earlier, David Bateman, the founder of Property Solutions, raised $100,000 in cash and in-kind services by winning two prestigious business plan competitions. Similarly, Derek Gregg and Justin Swick, the entrepreneurs featured at the beginning of Chapter 10, raised over $250,000 through business plan competitions and grants to get their firm, Vandalia Research, off the ground. While participating in business plan competitions and applying for grants is hard work, in many instances these and similar types of efforts make the difference between a successful start-up and an idea that has to be dropped because of lack of funding.

Financial Performance of Similar Businesses. The second component of financial feasibility analysis is estimating a proposed start-up's potential financial performance by comparing it to similar, already established businesses. Obviously, this effort will result in approximate rather than exact numbers. There are several ways of doing this, all of which involve a little ethical detective work. First, there are many reports available, some for free and some that require a fee, offering detailed industry trend analysis and reports on thousands of individual firms. The most promising sources are shown in Table 3.5. Bizstats.com (www.bizstats.com), for example, provides a wealth of information for free. On the Bizstats Web site, entrepreneurs can type in the projected revenue of their firm, by industry classification, and receive a mock income statement in return that shows the average profitability and expense percentages of U.S. small businesses in the same category. Similarly, Bizminer.com (www.bizminer.com), which is a for-profit company, sells a wide variety of industry-related data and statistics. A portion of the company's Web site is designed specifically for start-ups and provides information to help entrepreneurs understand how businesses similar to theirs are doing financially. Substantive reports can be purchased for as little as $99.

There are also ways that entrepreneurs can track sales data, in particular, through sim-ple observation and reviewing public records. For example, the fictitious firm New Venture Fitness Drinks, discussed earlier in the chapter, could gauge the type of sales to expect by estimating the number of people, along with the average purchase per visit, who patronize similar restaurants, like smoothie shops, in their area. A very basic way of doing this is to

Resources to Help Entrepreneurs Understand How Businesses Similar to Their
TABLE 3.5 Proposed New Venture Are Doing Financially

Source	Description	Cost
Bizminer.com	Has a wide variety of industry-related data, statistics, and other information. A section of its site is dedicated to new ventures.	Fee-based
Bizstats.com	Has a variety of detailed financial data on various retail categories. On the site, entrepreneurs can type in the projected revenue of their firm, by industry classification, and receive a mock income statement in return that shows the average profitability and expense percentages of U.S. small businesses in the same category.	Free
Hoover's Online	Brief histories and financial information on companies, industries, people, and products. Provides access to detailed financial information and 10-K reports for publicly traded firms.	Typically free if accessed from a college, university, or public library.
Marketresearch.com	In-depth research on industries and various retail categories. Provides data on more difficult-to-understand industries, such as biotechnology, health care, and all forms of technology.	Fee-based

frequent these stores and count the number of customers who come in and out of the stores during various times of the day. Another technique, which may be less precise for a start-up, is to study the annual reports and 10-K forms of similar publicly traded firms. For example, some restaurant chains actually report their average sales per restaurant. This type of information could help the owners of New Venture Fitness Drinks sharpen their own sense of the financial potential of their firm.

The purpose of this entire effort is to get a general sense of how firms that are similar to a proposed new venture are doing financially and whether the financial performance of similar firms is excellent, good, moderate, or poor. This is admittedly harder to do for a start-up that's unique and doesn't have a good set of peer firms. But for a start-up like New Venture Fitness Drinks, there is plenty of information available to get a good sense of how small beverage restaurants are doing. The information collected to complete this stage of feasibility analysis can also be used in preparing pro forma financial statements at a later time.

Overall Financial Attractiveness of the Proposed Venture. A number of other factors are associated with evaluating the financial attractiveness of a proposed venture. Typically, these evaluations are based primarily on a new venture's projected financial rate of return (i.e., return on assets, return on equity, and return on sales). At the feasibility analysis stage, the projected return is a judgment call and is based primarily on comparing a proposed venture to similar businesses, as just discussed. A more precise estimation can be computed by preparing pro forma (or projected) financial statements, including 1- to 3-year pro forma statements of cash flow, income statements, and balance sheets (along with accompanying financial ratios). This work can be done if time and circumstances allow, but is typically done at the business plan stage rather than the feasibility analysis stage of a new venture's development. Detailed information about how to prepare pro forma financial statements is provided in Chapter 8.

At a macro level, the following factors should be considered to determine whether the projected return is adequate to justify the launch of the business:

- The amount of capital invested
- The amount of time required to earn the return
- The risks assumed in launching the business
- The existing alternatives for the money being invested
- The existing alternatives for the entrepreneur's time and efforts

There are conclusions that can be reached from evaluating these factors. Opportunities demanding substantial capital, requiring long periods of time to mature, and having a lot of risk involved make little sense unless they provide high rates of return. For example, it simply makes no economic sense for a group of entrepreneurs to invest $10 million in a capital-intense risky start-up that offers a 5 percent rate of return. Five percent interest can be earned through a money market fund, with essentially no risk. The adequacy of returns also depends on the alternatives the individuals involved have. For example, an individual who is thinking about leaving a $150,000-per-year job to start a new firm requires a higher rate of return than the person thinking about leaving a $50,000-per-year job.[34]

A number of other financial factors are associated with financially promising business opportunities. Again, in the feasibility analysis stage, the extent to which a proposed business

TABLE 3.6 Financial Feasibility

- Steady and rapid growth in sales during the first 5 to 7 years in a clearly defined market niche
- High percentage of recurring revenue—meaning that once a firm wins a client, the client will provide recurring sources of revenue
- Ability to forecast income and expenses with a reasonable degree of certainty
- Internally generated funds to finance and sustain growth
- Availability of an exit opportunity (such as an acquisition or an initial public offering) for investors to convert equity into cash

appears positive relative to each factor is based on an estimate or forecast rather than actual performance. Table 3.6 provides a list of the factors that pertain to the overall financial feasibility of a business opportunity.

In summary, feasibility analysis is a vital step in the process of developing successful business ideas. Many entrepreneurs, in their haste to get their idea to market, neglect to conduct a thorough feasibility analysis. This approach is almost always a mistake and, more often than not, results in failure.

Chapter Summary

1. Feasibility analysis is the process of determining whether a business idea is viable. It is a preliminary evaluation of a business idea, conducted for the purpose of determining whether the idea is worth pursuing.
2. The proper time to conduct a feasibility analysis is early in thinking through the prospects for a new business idea. It follows opportunity recognition but comes before the development of a business plan.
3. Product/service feasibility analysis is an assessment of the overall appeal of the product or service being proposed. Concept testing and usability testing are the two primary issues that a proposed business should consider in this area.
4. A concept statement is a preliminary description of a product idea.
5. The three primary purposes of concept testing are to validate the underlying premises behind a product or service idea, to help develop an idea rather than just test it, and to estimate the potential market share the potential product or service might command.
6. Usability testing is a method by which users of a product or service are asked to perform certain tasks in order to measure the product's ease of use and the user's perception of and satisfaction with the experience.
7. Industry/market feasibility analysis is an assessment of the overall appeal of the market for the product or service being proposed. For feasibility analysis, there are three primary issues that a proposed business should consider: industry attractiveness, market timeliness, and the identification of a niche market.
8. Primary research is original research and is collected by the entrepreneur. In assessing the attractiveness of a market, this typically involves an entrepreneur talking to potential customers and/or key industry participants. Secondary research is examined to discover meaning in or from data already collected.
9. Organizational feasibility analysis is conducted to determine whether a proposed business has sufficient management expertise, organizational competence, and resources to successfully launch its business. There are two primary issues to consider in this area: management prowess and resource sufficiency.
10. Financial feasibility analysis is a preliminary financial analysis of whether a business idea is prudent. The most important issues to consider are capital requirements, financial rate of return, and overall attractiveness of the investment.

Key Terms

breakthrough products and
   services, 82
clusters, 85
concept statement, 76
concept test, 75
core competency, 73
feasibility analysis, 71
financial feasibility analysis, 86
first-mover advantage, 83

follow-me-home testing, 96
horizontal market, 83
industry/market feasibility
   analysis, 79
new-venture team, 85
niche market, 83
organizational feasibility
   analysis, 85
primary research, 82

product/service feasibility
   analysis, 74
prototype, 78
secondary research, 82
second-mover advantage, 83
seed money, 73
usability testing, 78
vertical market, 83
virtual prototype, 78

Review Questions

1. What is a feasibility analysis? What is it designed to accomplish?
2. Briefly describe each of the four areas that a properly executed feasibility analysis explores.
3. What is a product/service feasibility analysis?
4. What is a concept statement?
5. What is a concept test, and what does it accomplish? What are the three primary purposes for it?
6. What is a usability test, and what does it accomplish?
7. Define prototyping.
8. Describe what a virtual prototype is and how it differs from a physical prototype.
9. What is industry/market feasibility analysis?
10. Describe the attributes of an attractive industry for a new venture.
11. Describe the difference between primary and secondary research. Provide an example of each.
12. What is a breakthrough new product or service? Provide several examples.
13. Identify the pluses and minuses of trying to capture a first-mover advantage.
14. Why is it important for a new venture to identify a niche market in which it can participate?
15. What is organizational feasibility analysis?
16. Briefly describe each of the two primary issues to consider when conducting an organizational feasibility analysis.
17. What is a new-venture team?
18. Why is it usually to a firm's advantage to be located near similar firms in its industry?
19. What is financial feasibility analysis?
20. Briefly describe the three primary issues to consider when conducting a financial feasibility analysis.

Application Questions

1. Jason Palmer has an idea for a new approach to personal finance software. He plans to use the $200,000 inheritance he recently received to produce the product and bring it to market. When you ask Jason if he has conducted a feasibility analysis, he acts alarmed and says, "I knew I'd have to write a business plan, but I'm not familiar with what you are calling a feasibility analysis. I don't want to blow the $200,000 I just inherited, so if a feasibility study is necessary, I'm game. Can you tell me how to conduct one?" What would you tell Jason?
2. A good friend of yours, Abby Franklin, has decided to open a sporting goods store geared toward adults 55 years of age and older. As far as she knows, her store will be the only sporting goods store in the United States focused specifically on older adults. Using your imagination, write a concept statement for Abby's proposed venture.
3. Assume that you were one of the recipients of New Venture Fitness Drink's concept statement. What type of feedback would you have given the company about the viability of its product idea? If the concept statement included a survey asking you how likely you would be to purchase some of New Venture Fitness Drink's products, what would you have said and why?
4. Ann O'Neil, who has considerable experience in the home security industry, is planning to launch a firm that will sell a new line of home security alarms that she believes will be superior to anything currently on the market. She is weighing whether to take the time to conduct a product/service feasibility analysis, given the amount of industry experience that she has. If she asked you for your advice, what would you tell her are the benefits of conducting a product/service feasibility analysis?

5. The "You Be the VC 2" feature for this chapter focuses on Bones In Motion, a company that hopes to turn any cell phone into an automatic journal that allows walkers, runners, and bikers to record their activities and benefit from the motivational aspect of keeping track of their progress. How would you go about conducting a product feasibility analysis for this company's product?

6. Marc Blair is planning to open a fitness center that will feature a set of exercise machines that he designed himself. He would like to do some usability testing of the machines but doesn't know how to go about it. If Marc asked you for your advice, what would you tell him?

7. Carrie Wells is planning to open a store to sell DVDs in Nashville. As part of her feasibility study, she hands out a questionnaire to 500 people in her trade area, asking them to indicate whether they would shop at her store. Carrie is pleased to find that 75 percent of the people surveyed said they would either "definitely" or "probably" shop in her store at least once a month. Should Carrie plan her business based on the 75 percent figure? Why or why not?

8. Recently, you were telling a friend about Intuit, in particular about the company's "follow-me-home" usability testing methodology. This methodology is discussed in Case 3.2 in this chapter. Skip ahead to read about this methodology as you prepare your answer to this question. Your friend, who plans to launch a business to sell and make modifications on all-terrain vehicles (ATVs), was intrigued by the story. Describe how your friend could use the follow-me-home methodology to improve the quality of usability testing for his business.

9. Steve Ambrose, who is a physical therapist, is thinking about starting a firm in the medical instruments industry. He would like to know more about the industry, however, before proceeding. Provide Steve with suggestions for conducting primary and secondary research on the industry.

10. The "You Be the VC 1" feature at the end of Chapter 1 focuses on Cereality, a chain of small walk-in restaurants serving only Cereal. How would you have conducted an industry/market feasibility analysis for this company?

11. Kate Wilson has developed an innovative suite of software products for grades K–12. She is wondering if now is a good time to launch a business to sell her products. What factors should Kate consider in making this determination?

12. Wayne Baker has invented a new type of skateboard. He is anxious to get it to market to capture first-mover advantages. Wayne seemed somewhat puzzled when you told him that there are both advantages and disadvantages of capturing a first-mover advantage. Explain to Wayne what you meant by your statement.

13. According to the section of the chapter that focuses on organizational feasibility analysis, two of the most important factors in the area of management prowess are the passion that a solo entrepreneur or the management team has for the business idea and the extent to which the management team or sole entrepreneur understands the markets in which the firm will participate. If you were an investor evaluating the organizational feasibility of a proposed venture, how would you evaluate passion? How would you assess whether the solo entrepreneur or management team behind the proposed venture had sufficient passion to launch a successful firm?

14. Kelly Simon is thinking about opening an electronics store that will feature an innovative floor plan and creative ways of displaying and featuring merchandise. As part of his financial feasibility analysis, Kelly wants to collect data on the level of sales and profitability for other electronics stores in the United States. How would you suggest that Kelly approach this task?

15. What are some of the "red flags" that would suggest that the overall financial attractiveness of a proposed new venture is poor?

3.1   Sundia
www.sundiacorp.com

Business Idea: Produce and sell the first "branded" watermelons and watermelon juice.

Pitch: Many people enjoy watermelon but find shopping for one to be a frustrating experience. There is no "branded" watermelon available to ensure consistent quality, like Sunkist provides for oranges and Chiquita has done for bananas. Surprisingly, there is also no premier watermelon juice available. Watermelon juice is extremely healthy. It is fat and cholesterol free and is high in many essential nutrients and vitamins. Lycopene, the pigment that gives watermelon its red color, has been linked to a lower risk of many types of cancer, heart disease, and even cataracts.

Sundia aims to deal with these watermelon-based gaps in the market. The company has started selling a Sundia-branded watermelon and is aggressively signing up watermelon growers to achieve national distribution and brand awareness. The company employs strict standards for its watermelons, which will each feature a removable label, similar to the labels found on Chiquita bananas. In addition to its watermelons, Sundia has formulated and developed a patented watermelon juice. The juice, which will be sold in attractive single-serve containers, has a sweet taste and a pulpy consistency and has fared extremely well in taste tests. The market for watermelon juice is promising. According to a recent study by Euromonitor, sales of traditional fruit juice, like orange, apple, and cranberry, have declined in recent years while sales of "other flavors" have increased. Watermelon juice, which enjoys immense popularity in other countries, particularly in Asia, falls squarely in the "other flavors" category. In addition, the sales of a juice are typically 2 to 10 times higher than the sales of their corresponding fruit. Watermelon sales in the United States topped $700 million in 2005, which could translate into impressive sales for Sundia's watermelon juice in the future.

Q&A: Based on the material covered in this chapter, what questions would you ask the firm's founders before making your funding decision? What answers would satisfy you?

Decision: If you had to make your decision on just the information provided in the pitch and on the company's Web site, would you fund this firm? Why or why not?

3.2   Bones in Motion
www.bonesinmotion.com

Business Idea: Turn nearly any cell phone into an automatic journal that allows walkers, runners, and bikers to record their activities and benefit from the motivational aspects of keeping track of their progress.

Pitch: Most people know that they need to exercise to first improve and then maintain their health. But simply buying a pair of running shoes or a bicycle is rarely the answer. People must be motivated to stay committed to an exercise plan. One thing that sports psychologists have found helps people stay committed is to keep track of their daily progress. It's also very motivating to people to graphically see the results of their exercise efforts and to be able to share their progress with their family and friends.

Bones in Motion was created to fit this exact need. In the first of what it hopes will be many outdoor applications, the company has turned the ordinary cell phone into a virtual coach using a software application called BiMActive. BiMActive is an online service, which is currently available to Sprint and Nextel cell phone customers, that costs $9.99 per month. Bones in Motion is negotiating with other cell phone service providers and hopes to sign up more of them soon.

Here's how the service works. When you start the application, you have to wait for a few seconds for it to hone in on your GPS location. (You do need a GPS-equipped cell phone.) For the GPS to work you need to be outdoors with a view of the sky. Once you start to run, walk, or bike, it records your distance, speed, pace, location, elevation, and estimated amount of calories burned. All you need to do is keep your cell phone with you. Once finished exercising, your workout data is wirelessly uploaded to a Web page, with the route you just covered superimposed on a Google map. A complete set of stats for your workout are available, including the distance covered, splits, and estimated calories burned. You can also keep track of the distance you've covered by week, month, or year.

If you're community minded you can share your results with other BiMActive members. You can also post the route you just covered for other BiMActive members to see. The route's difficulty is rated by BiMActive based on topography, changes in elevation, and other data. You can also look at the routes that other BiMActive members have posted.

Q&A: Based on the material covered in this chapter, what questions would you ask the firm's founders before making your funding decision? What answers would satisfy you?

Decision: If you had to make your decision on just the information provided in the pitch and on the company's Web site, would you fund this firm? Why or why not?

CASE 3.1

Palapa Azul: Benefiting from a "Hands-On" Approach to Product Feasibility Analysis
www.palapaazul.com

Bruce R. Barringer,
University of Central Florida
R. Duane Ireland,
Texas A&M University

Introduction

After fruitful careers at Black & Decker, Disney, Hewlett-Packard, and United Distillers, along with a couple of Internet start-ups, Michel Algazi and Roni Goldberg wanted to launch a food company. It's what they always wanted to do. As kids growing up in Mexico, they had rich memories of enjoying tasty Mexican treats. As they grew older, they became very proud of their native country's rich cuisines and flavorsome dishes.

One thing that helped influence Algazi and Goldberg to start a food company were signs that Americans were increasingly receptive to good-quality Mexican food. It was 2002. Two very successful restaurant chains, Chipotle and Baja Fresh, featured Mexican cuisines. They were also influenced by Haagen-Dazs' decision in 1997 to introduce an ice cream flavor called Dulce de leche. Dulce de leche is a traditional candy in Mexico and South America. The name literally means "milk candy" in Spanish. Since its introduction, Dulce de leche has become one of Haagen-Dazs' top-selling brands.

After considering several alternatives and partly in light of Haagen-Dazs' positive experience, Algazi and Goldberg decided to create a line of Mexican-style frozen desserts. But they weren't in a hurry. They knew it would be painful to go through a period with no income while they got their company started, but they wanted to do it right. Since coming to America, they had seen many food brands rushed to market by companies who then had to scramble and regroup as they reacted to market tastes. In contrast to this approach, Algazi and Goldberg committed themselves to a process of product feasibility analysis, market testing, and branding that would give them the best possible chance of getting it right the first time.

Developing the Product and Picking a Name

As kids in Mexico, one of Algazi and Goldberg's most salient memories was going to fruit stands and treating themselves to sliced fruits and vegetables that were sprinkled with lime, salt, and chili. This experience influenced the early flavors and formation of their frozen dessert bars. From the outset, the founders wanted to produce a high-quality treat. Their frozen desserts included no added color, artificial ingredients, or high fructose corn syrup. Instead, they used traditional Mexican recipes with fresh fruit and high-end ingredients. The bars averaged around 80 fat-free calories. About 30 flavors were initially made, ranging from prickly pear to watermelon. Algazi and Goldberg figured they could sell their bars in the $2.00 range.

At the same time the two founders were working on the frozen desserts themselves, they set out to pick a name for the company. They considered over 100 names, including Botana, Hamaca, and La Playa. To make their final selection, they walked the streets of Los Angeles, asking people to position various possible names on a spectrum from cheap to expensive. They also asked people to say what "images" particular brand names brought to mind. After collecting over 200 opinions, they settled on the name Palapa Azul. When put together, the words *Palapa* (a palm umbrella found on warm Mexican beaches) and *Azul* (the Spanish word for blue) made people think of Mexico, fruit, food, and quality. This was exactly the set of attributes that the founders wanted people to associate with their product.

In something akin to a concept statement, Algazi and Goldberg boiled Palapa Azul's core value proposition down to one paragraph. The single paragraph defined the company's target market and the benefits and features of its products. Having a short description of the company and its products was helpful in presenting them to others. They also developed a mission statement to further clarify their ultimate purpose: "Our mission is to become the most unique, irresistible, and high-quality ethnic Mexican frozen desserts brand known to U.S. consumers."

Learning from Customers

After Palapa Azul's first frozen bars were ready to be sold, Algazi and Goldberg set up food stands at every farmers market in the Los Angeles area they could find. One advantage of being in Los Angeles is that different areas of the city are populated by different ethnic groups, so it was easy for Algazi and Goldberg to observe how people from different ethnicities reacted to their product. They noticed patterns, such as a preference for the tart flavors plum and kiwi among Asian customers. One particularly humorous anecdote, about gender preferences, was reported in a *Fortune Small Business* article:

> More interestingly, we noticed a gender difference: We could offer two dozen flavors, and still most men would want strawberry. Women, however,

Nine Flavors of Palapa Azul Frozen Fruit Bars

English	Spanish
Mango	Mango
Watermelon	Sandia
Cantaloupe	Melon
Strawberry	Fresa
Mango Chile	Mango Con Chile
Cucumber Chile	Pepino Con Chile
Grapefruit	Toronja
Mexican Papaya	Papaya
Pineapple	Pina

were much more adventurous and willing to try new flavors. Women would say, "You have mango-chile? Interesting! I'd like to try that." Men would say, "You have mango-chile. Interesting? I'd like strawberry." So we targeted our brand strategy to better address women's needs.

Eventually, the company whittled its 30 flavors down to 9. Not everything turned out as expected. Algazi and Goldberg never dreamed that cucumber-chili would be customers' favorite flavor—but in hindsight it makes sense. It is an authentic Mexican flavor, and clearly differentiates Palapa Azul's product from those available from other companies' brands.

The Present

A defining moment for Palapa Azul came in 2004 at the Fancy Food Show, which is a high-profile yearly trade show for confection (candy) and fancy foods. It was the first time Palapa Azul was on a national stage. After the show, Costco, Whole Foods, and several other specialty retailers started carrying the firm's products. In 2005, Palapa Azul introduced ice creams and sorbets, and the company continues to expand.

Looking back, Algazi and Goldberg are convinced that their early product feasibility analysis and customer interaction set the company on the right track. Summing up their experience, the two founders said, "Large companies often hire external agencies to do their research, and what they get in the end is a very filtered report. By doing everything ourselves, we got a richness of information we'd never seen before."

Discussion Questions

1. What, if anything, would the founders of Palapa Azul have lost had they hired a professional market research

firm to pick a name for the company and do its market research?

2. The case focuses primarily on product feasibility analysis for Palapa Azul. How would you have conducted an industry/market feasibility analysis, an organizational feasibility analysis, and a financial feasibility analysis for the company?

3. Develop a one-half-page to one-page concept statement for Palapa Azul.

4. Were the founders of Palapa Azul more interested in conducting primary research or secondary research in regard to their product feasibility analysis? In your judgment, did they make the right call? Explain your answer.

Application Questions

1. The "You Be the VC 1" feature for this chapter focuses on Sundia, a company that is trying to produce and sell the first branded watermelon and watermelon juice in the Unites States. How would you go about conducting a product feasibility analysis for this company? What similarities do you see between the challenges and opportunities that the founders of Palapa Azul experienced and the challenges and opportunities that lie ahead for the founders of Sundia?

2. Come up with a suggestion for a product with a rich Spanish heritage that isn't currently being sold in the United States but could be, or is currently being sold in the United States but in your opinion could be sold in a much more upscale manner.

Sources: M. Algazi and R. Goldberg, "Play It Cool," *Fortune Small Business*, October 2005; HispanicBusiness.com, "Palapa Azul Announces the Newest Addition to the Product Line, Ice Creams and Sorbets, Inspired From Flavors of Mexico," April 2006 (accessed April 28, 2006).

Bruce R. Barringer,
University of Central Florida
R. Duane Ireland,
Texas A&M University

Introduction

Intuit is the leading provider of financial management software and related services in the United States. Its flagship products—Quicken, QuickBooks, and Quicken TurboTax—simplify personal finance, small-business management, payroll processing, and tax preparation. The company prides itself first on its customer focus and second on its technological prowess. Its customer focus is directly tied to its culture of ongoing product/service feasibility analysis and usability testing.

Intuit's Founding

Intuit's founding is an excellent example of how a strong business idea, coupled with properly executed feasibility analysis, leads to business success. Scott Cook, a business consultant, started the company in 1983. After watching his wife painstakingly pay bills by hand, Cook wondered whether a software product could be developed to help people manage their personal finances. He drew up a preliminary business plan and partnered with Tom Proulx, a computer science student at Stanford University, to found Intuit and develop a product that was to be named Quicken.

Cook's background in consumer marketing was a true advantage during the product's development. Cook spent several years as a brand manager with Procter & Gamble earlier in his career and had a thorough understanding of feasibility analysis and marketing research as a result. Cook insisted that he and Proulx first determine exactly what consumers wanted in a personal finance program before any initial prototypes were developed. When asked how he approached this task, Cook answered,

> The only way to find that information was to talk to households. So I'd make calls and I got my sister-in-law to call households. We asked upper-income consumers—they were the only people buying computers—about their financial lives. We did this to build a real gut knowledge about how real people did their finances: their behaviors, their likes, and their dislikes. We looked at behavioral data as well. It became very clear to us that people wanted a way to take the hassle out of doing their finances. Who likes to pay bills and write in checkbooks?

An important component of Cook's approach was a keen understanding that because personal financial management software was a product that consumers hadn't seen before, it wouldn't work to simply ask them what they would like in this type of product. So, in addition to the phone interviews, Cook and Proulx actually watched people managing their finances. Quicken was developed only after they were confident that they knew what consumers needed to make personal financial management easier. Cook said this about understanding a customer's needs:

> The key to business success is knowing your customer cold. We had spent time understanding the customer. We clearly understood customer behavior and had data showing that our solution was vastly better according to customers' decision-making criteria.

Since it's founding, Intuit has developed or employed a number of techniques to determine customers' needs and ensure that its products are easy to use and meet customer expectations. Its most useful techniques, which serve as models for all firms to consider, are as follows.

In-House Usability Testing

Intuit didn't invent the notion of usability testing, but was the first company to apply usability testing to software products. The goal of usability testing is to design products in a way that best meets customer needs. To meet this goal, one thing Intuit does is invite both users and nonusers of its products to visit its usability-testing lab at its California headquarters. At the lab, participants are seated in front of PCs and are asked to work with software products that are being developed. A soundproof room is attached to the lab, where Intuit programmers and designers observe the participants. A "logger" is typically assigned to record usability problems or any comments participants make during the test, and the sessions are taped for further review. The participants are usually given copies of Intuit products in appreciation for their time and efforts. The objective of the testing is to uncover and work out problems relating to Intuit products "before" rather than after they reach the marketplace.

Follow-Me-Home Test

A hybrid form of usability testing that Scott Cook invented is referred to as **follow-me-home testing**. In the early days of Intuit, Cook's committed focus on understanding customers' needs found him going into stores where Intuit's software was being sold and waiting for someone to buy one of his products. He would then ask if he could follow the customer home and watch while the customer installed the software and tried to use it.

Over the years, this form of testing at Intuit has become more formalized but retains the original spirit of Cook's early efforts. The company routinely sends teams of testers to the homes and businesses of its users, to see how its products are working. A team typically consists of three Intuit employees, including someone from the User Experience Group, someone from Quality Assurance, and someone from Engineering or Technical Documentation. Technically, the program is a form of ethnography, which is research based on first-hand observation of how people behave in a certain situation. According to Cook, who has participated in many follow-me-home tests, "You watch their eyebrows, where they hesitate, where they have a quizzical look. Every glitch, every momentary hesitation is our fault." The testing helps the company uncover areas needing improvement that potentially couldn't be uncovered in any other way.

A side benefit of the follow-me-home program is that it demonstrates to users the extent to which Intuit is serious about meeting their needs and is genuinely open to their comments and suggestions. This sentiment was affirmed by Wendy Padmos, a Quicken user, who volunteered to participate in the follow-me-home program in 2004. Commenting on her experience, Padmos said,

> When the Quicken team came to my house, I thought they just wanted to find out how they could better advertise to me and people like me, but it wasn't that at all. It was much more customer-focused. They wanted to know how I use the product, what was important to me, and what was not important to me. I told them I would like the ability to see my current spending against my average spending over the last 12 months, and now it's in the product!

Other Techniques

Intuit utilizes a variety of other techniques to better understand its customers and test its products. The company routinely runs surveys to see how its products are doing. Similarly, the company has a beta tester program that it recruits for on an ongoing basis. The program allows customers to test prerelease software products and then provide Intuit software engineers real-world quality and usability feedback. It is a hands-on program that facilitates a dialogue between Intuit and its users during rather than after the development of a software product. Users aren't paid for their participation—instead they are provided the opportunity to help shape the design of Intuit products and in some cases are able to buy Intuit products at a discount.

Intuit Today

Today, Intuit is one of the largest software companies in the world with over $2 billion in annual sales. In 2005, the company grew over 9 percent and is consistently ranked by *Fortune* magazine as one of the "Top 100 Companies to Work For" in America. All of the programs described here are active and are part of Intuit's ongoing efforts to better understand its customers and their needs.

Discussion Questions

1. Refer to Table 3.2 in the chapter. To what extent does Intuit capture each of the benefits of conducting a product/service feasibility analysis listed in the table?
2. Compare Intuit's approach to feasibility analysis and usability testing to Salesforce.com's approach. (Salesforce.com is the subject of the "Partnering for Success" feature in this chapter.) In what ways are their approaches similar and in what ways are they different?
3. To what extent do you think Intuit's industry is attractive? If Intuit conducted an industry/market feasibility analysis on the main industries in which it participates, what do you believe would be the outcome?
4. Why do you think Intuit puts so much effort into collecting primary research about its users and their experiences? Would it be cheaper for Intuit to hire a marketing research firm to collect data on user preferences? What would Intuit lose if it pursued this approach?

Application Questions

1. The "You Be the VC 2" feature at the end of the chapter focuses on Bones in Motion, the company that hopes to turn cell phones into journals that allow walkers, runners, and bikers to record their activities. Which of the forms of Intuit's feasibility analysis and usability testing do you think would work for Bones in Motion? Describe how you would adapt Intuit's practices to help Bones in Motion better understand its users and test its products.
2. Would you enjoy participating in Intuit's beta tester program? Locate information about the program on Intuit's Web site and read more about it. What aspects of the program, if any, would motivate you to participate?

Sources: Intuit homepage, www.intuit.com (accessed August 2, 2006); "Show Me the Money: Quicken 2006 Provides Instant Insights Into Spending Habits; Personal Finance Software Boasts 121 New Features and Improvements Including Ability to Attach Electronic Documents and Statements," *TMCnet*, August 1, 2005; R. D. Jager and R. Ortiz, *In the Company of Giants* (New York: McGraw-Hill, 1997).

Endnotes

1. Personal Interview with David Bateman, June 28, 2006.
2. A. V. Bhide, *The Origin and Evolution of New Businesses* (Oxford: University Press, 2000).

3. S. Goel and R. Karri, "Entrepreneurs, Effectual Logic, and Over-Trust," *Entrepreneurship Theory and Practice* 30 (2006): 477–93.

4. M. A. Hitt, R. D. Ireland, and R. E. Hoskisson, *Strategic Management: Competitiveness and Globalization*, 7th ed. (Mason, OH: South-Western College Publishing, 2007).

5. Trakus homepage, www.trakus.com (accessed July 30, 2006).

6. "The World According to Clark," *Business 2.0*, May 2005.

7. M. Augier and D. J. Teece, "Understanding Complex Organization: The Role of Know-How, Internal Structure, and Human Behavior in the Evolution of Capabilities," *Industrial and Corporate Change* 15 (2006): 395–416.

8. R. G. Cooper, *Product Leadership: Creating and Launching Superior New Products* (Reading, MA: Perseus Books, 1998), 99.

9. R. R. Klink and G. A. Athaide, "An Illustration of Potential Sources of Concept-Test Error," *Journal of Product Innovation Management*, 23 (2006) 359–70.

10. C. M. Crawford and C. A. Benedetto, *New Product Management*, 6th ed. (New York: McGraw-Hill, 2000).

11. R. R. Klink and G. A. Athaide, "An Illustration of Potential Sources of Concept-Test Error," *Journal of Product Innovation Management* 23 (2006): 359–70.

12. Crawford and De Benedetto, *New Product Management*.

13. Zoomerang homepage, www.zoomerang.com (accessed August 1, 2006).

14. N. C. Kaiser, "Jeremy Jaech, CEO of Trumba.com," nPost.com, www.npost.com (accessed August 8, 2005).

15. American Marketing Association Dictionary of Marketing Terms, www.marketingpower.com (accessed August 1, 2006).

16. R. McCoy, "Virtual Prototyping: The Perfect Solution," *Inventor's Digest*, May/June, 1998.

17. The Usability Company homepage, www.theuseabilitycompany.com (accessed July 9, 2002).

18. T. K. McKnight, *Will It Fly?* (London: Financial Times, Prentice Hall, 2004).

19. P. A. Gompers and J. Lerner, *The Money of Invention: How Venture Capital Creates New Wealth* (Boston: Harvard Business School Press, 2001).

20. Michael A. Cusumano, *The Business of Software* (New York: Free Press, 2004).

21. O. Gassman, P. Sandmeier, C. H. Wecht, "Extreme Customer Innovation in the Front-End: Learning from a New Software Paradigm," *International Journal of Technology Management* 33 (2006): 46–66.

22. A. Phene, K. Fladmoe-Lindquist, and L. Marsh, "Breakthrough Innovations in the U.S. Biotechnology Industry: The Effects of Technological Space and Geographic Origin," *Strategic Management Journal* 27 (2006): 369–88.

23. M. B. Liberman and D. B. Montgomery, "First-Mover Advantages," *Strategic Management Journal*, Summer Special Issue, 9 (1988): 41–58.

24. G. Pawlina and P. M. Kort, "Real Options in an Asymmetric Duopoly: Who Benefits from Your Competitive Disadvantage?" *Journal of Economics and Management Strategy* 15 (2006): 1–35; R. A. Kerin, P. R. Varadarajan, and R. A. Peterson, "First-Mover Advantage: A Synthesis, Conceptual Framework, and Research Propositions," *Journal of Marketing* 56, no. 4 (1992): 33–52.

25. M. Coutler, *Strategic Management in Action* (Upper Saddle River, NJ: Prentice Hall, 2002).

26. S. Dixon, "Multinational Corporations, Stackelberg Leadership, and Tariff-Jumping," *Review of International Economics* 14 (2006): 414–26.

27. C. Markides, "Disruptive Innovation: In Need of Better Theory," *Journal of Product Innovation Management* 23 (2006): 19–25.

28. J. L. Nesheim, *High Tech Start Up: The Corporate Handbook for Creating Successful New High Tech Companies* (New York: Free Press, 2000).

29. "*Inc.* 500 List," *Inc.*, January 2004, 64.

30. M. S. Cardon, C. Zietsma, P. Saparito, B. P. Matherne, and C. Davis, "A Tale of Passion: New Insights into Entrepreneurship from a Parenthood Metaphor, *Journal of Business Venturing* 20 (2005): 23–45.

31. M. Vivarelli, "Are All the Potential Entrepreneurs So Good?" *Small Business Economics* 23, no. 1 (2004): 41–49.

32. R. D. Jager and R. Ortiz, *In the Company of Giants* (New York: McGraw-Hill, 1997).

33. M. Rogers, "Networks, Firm Size and Innovation," *Small Business Economics* 22, no. 2 (2004): 141–53.

34. J. R. Van Slyke, H. H. Stevenson, and M. J. Roberts, "How to Write a Winning Business Plan," in *The Entrepreneurial Venture*, ed. W.A. Sahlman and H. H. Stevenson (Boston: Harvard Business School Press, 1992), 127–37.

4 writing a *business* plan

Getting Personal

with **ERICA FAND**

My biggest worry as an entrepreneur

Putting your heart into your product and not having it well received by others

Currently in my iPod

Keith Urban

My advice for new entrepreneurs

You don't get unless you ask

Fresh Cut Florals:
Proceeding on the Strength of a Winning Business Plan

When Erica Fand and Shelley Kohan enrolled in Entrepreneurship and Emerging Enterprises (EEE) 457 at Syracuse University their senior year, they couldn't have known that the class might change the future direction of their lives. As part of the class, students are challenged to develop a business idea and write a business plan based on their idea. Fand and Kohan partnered with three classmates to propose a venture named Fresh Cut Florals. Now, the two are seriously considering launching Fresh Cut Florals as an entrepreneurial venture. In the picture, Erica Fand is pictured on the right and Shelley Kohan is on the left.

The idea for Fresh Cut Florals emerged during a brainstorming session shortly after the start of EEE 457 during the fall 2005 semester. Fand and Kohan were in their apartment kicking around business ideas. At one point during the discussion, Fand commented that she had returned to college that fall with a bunch of air fresheners, while Kohan, her roommate, had showed up with a bunch of silk flowers. The idea occurred to Fand, along with Kohan, to combine the two products to create silk flowers that emitted a scent that would be similar to the actual smell of their real flower counterparts. Over the next few days, the two excitedly determined that no such product was available on the market, and the idea for Fresh Cut Florals was born.

Through the course of the semester, the team developed a business plan for Fresh Cut Florals, and their excitement for the idea grew. To support the information they were placing in their plan, the group contacted several manufacturers to get information on pricing and distribution. Through their discussions with potential manufacturers and others, the group learned that the real strength of their idea was that it was something that no one had ever considered before. By mixing and matching different silk flowers with different fragrances, customers could essentially "custom design" the floral arrangements and aromas they featured in their homes. Fand recalls that during this period she and her team literally "lived and breathed" their business plan as they continued to learn about the floral industry and build upon their initial idea. She also recalls being constantly challenged by her professor, Eric Alderman, to defend the assumptions

ERICA FAND

Cofounder, Fresh Cut Florals
Syracuse University, BA, Whitman
School of Management, 2006

SHELLEY KOHAN

Cofounder, Fresh Cut Florals
Syracuse University, BA, Whitman
School of Management, 2006

My biggest surprise as an entrepreneur

Being passionate about what you do can take you far

Best part of being a student

Willingness of people to help you

What I do when I'm not working

Pilates and yoga booty ballet

After studying this chapter you should be ready to:

L E A R N I N G

Objectives

1. Explain the purpose of a business plan.

2. Discuss how a business plan can be a dual-use document.

3. Explain how the process of writing a business plan can be as important as the plan itself.

4. Identify the advantages and disadvantages of using software packages to assist in preparing a business plan.

5. Explain the difference between a summary business plan, a full business plan, and an operational business plan.

6. Explain why the executive summary may be the most important section of a business plan.

7. Describe a milestone and how milestones are used in business plans.

8. Explain the purpose of a "sources and uses of funds" statement.

9. Describe a liquidity event.

10. Detail the parts of an oral presentation of a business plan.

made in the plan and to think harder about why the idea for Fresh Cut Florals might work. The semester cumulated with a business plan competition among the teams in the various sections of EEE 457. Fand and her team won the competition, which entitled them to represent Syracuse at the New Ventures World Competition, a business plan competition at the University of Nebraska, in the spring of 2006.

To bolster their chances to place well at the New Ventures World Competition, and other business plan competitions, the Fresh Cut Florals team secured a grant from the Whitman School of Management at Syracuse to hire an industrial design firm to build a prototype of their idea. Working with the industrial design firm, they created an arrangement of six tiger lilies and an arrangement of daisies, magnolias, poppies, and peonies, to show the variety of silk flowers that could be engineered to emit a scent similar to what real flowers of the same type would smell like. At the same time, they persuaded a local attorney, who was a Syracuse alumnus, to submit a patent application for them on a pro bono basis. An important step they took during this period was to approach potential retailers and talk to them about the possibility of carrying Fresh Cuts, which is the name of Fresh Cut Florals' product. In general, the reaction was positive, which was a boost to the morale of the team and further affirmed the strength of their idea.

During the spring of 2006, the team's efforts were rewarded by winning $33,000 in business plan competitions and getting additional feedback on their idea. On April 7, 2006, Fresh Cut Florals won second place, and $3,000, at the 2006 New Ventures World Competition at the University of Nebraska. Then, on April 22, 2006, the students participated in, and won, two additional competitions—the 2006 Venture Adventure Competition at Colorado State University and the 2006 Syracuse Panasci Business Plan Competition at Syracuse University. To pull this off, two members of the team flew to Fort Collins, Colorado, to participate in the Venture Adventure Competition at Colorado State, winning the $5,000 first prize. The remaining three members of the team stayed home and were awarded the $25,000 first-place prize for the Syracuse competition.

Shortly after these competitions concluded, the five members of the Fresh Cut Florals team graduated, and Erica Fand and Shelley Kohan bought out the other three members of the team. The two former students are now carefully considering whether to launch Fresh Cut Florals as an entrepreneurial venture, and commit full-time to making their business plan for the company a reality.[1]

This chapter discusses the importance of writing a business plan. Although some new ventures simply "wing it" and start doing business without the benefit of formal planning, it is hard to find an expert who doesn't recommend preparing a business plan. A **business plan** is a written narrative, typically 25 to 35 pages long, that describes what a new business intends to accomplish and how it intends to accomplish it. For most new ventures, the business plan is a dual-purpose document used both inside and outside the firm. Inside the firm, the plan helps the company develop a "road map" to follow in executing its strategies and plans. Outside the firm, it introduces potential investors and other stakeholders to the business opportunity the firm is pursuing and how it plans to pursue it.[2]

To begin this chapter, we discuss issues with which entrepreneurs often grapple when facing the challenge of writing a business plan. Topics included in the first section of the chapter are reasons for writing a business plan, a description of who reads the business plan and what they're looking for, and guidelines to follow when preparing a written business plan. In the chapter's second section, we present an outline of a business plan with a description of the material in each section of the plan. The third section of the chapter deals with strategies for how to present the business plan to potential investors.

The Business Plan

As illustrated in the basic model of the entrepreneurial process, shown in Chapter 1, the time to write a business plan is midway through the stage of the entrepreneurial process titled "Developing Successful Business Ideas." It is a mistake to write a full business plan too early. The business plan must be substantive enough and have sufficient details about the merits of the new venture to convince the reader that the new business is exciting and should receive support. Much of this detail is accumulated in the feasibility analysis stage of investigating the merits of a potential new venture.

Entrepreneurs should understand what a business plan is and what it isn't. It isn't a contract, an agreement, or a budget. Instead, it is a narrative description of a new business. Steve Jurvetson, the founder of Hotmail and now a prominent venture capitalist, captures this sentiment: "The business plan is not a contract in the way a budget is. It's a story. It's a story about an opportunity, about the migration path, and how [a business] is going to create and capture value."[3]

A large percentage of entrepreneurs do not write business plans for their new ventures. In fact, only 31 percent of the 600 entrepreneurs that participated in a recent Wells Fargo/Gallup Small Business Study indicated that they had started their venture with a business plan.[4] This statistic should not deter an entrepreneur from writing a business plan, however. Consider that we do not know how many of the entrepreneurs participating in the Wells Fargo/Gallup Small Business study who didn't write a business plan now wish they had. Many entrepreneurs say that the day-to-day pressures of getting a company up and running leave them little time for planning. This is short-sighted thinking, though, in that there are clear advantages to writing a business plan. We'll identify these advantages in this chapter's various sections.

Why a Business Plan Is Important

A business plan is important for two major reasons. First, a business plan is an internal document that helps a new venture flesh out its business model and solidify its goals. It should convince the reader that the business idea is viable and that the venture being created to exploit that idea has a bright future. When prepared carefully, the business plan acts as an important road map for the venture's initial management team and employees. This sentiment is affirmed by David Beattle, the founder of Enterprise Food Group, a British firm, who has come to rely on his business plan as a road map to follow more than he originally thought he would:

> When I first started (Enterprise Food Group), the business plan was something you put together to show the bank and then it went in the filing cabinet never to be looked at again. Now I think it is a really good tool, something I look at every month. It tells me what I need to do and what I have done. It is not set in stone, but at least you (the management team of the firm) can get together and look at why something hasn't been done or what problems it (a new initiative) might create in the future.[5]

The second reason a business plan is important is because it is a selling document for a company. It provides a mechanism for a young company to present itself to potential investors, suppliers, business partners, and key job candidates[6] by showing how all the pieces of a new venture fit together to create an organization capable of meeting its goals and objectives.[7]

Imagine that you have enough money to invest in one new business. You chat informally with several entrepreneurs at a conference for start-ups and decide that there are two new ventures that you would like to know more about. You contact the first entrepreneur and ask for a copy of his business plan. The entrepreneur hesitates a bit and says that he hasn't prepared a formal business plan but would love to get together with you to discuss his ideas. You contact the second entrepreneur and make the same request. This time, the entrepreneur says

1. Explain the purpose of a business plan.

2. Discuss how a business plan can be a dual-use document.

that she would be glad to forward you a copy of a 30-page business plan, along with a 10-slide PowerPoint presentation that provides an overview of the plan. Ten minutes later, the PowerPoint presentation is in your e-mail in-box with a note that the business plan will arrive by FedEx the next morning. You look through the slides, which are crisp and to the point and do an excellent job of outlining the strengths of the business opportunity. The next day, the business plan arrives just as promised and is equally impressive.

Which entrepreneur has convinced you to invest in his or her business? All other things being equal, the answer is obvious—the second entrepreneur. The fact that the second entrepreneur has a business plan not only provides you with detailed information about the venture but also suggests that the entrepreneur has thought through each element of the business and is committed enough to the new venture to invest the time and energy necessary to prepare the plan. Consistent with this notion, a leading authority on business plans writes about the importance of having a business plan when trying to obtain bank financing:

> A business plan helps set you apart from the crowd. I've had a number of bankers tell me that while their banks don't require business plans, companies that submit plans immeasurably improve their chances of getting the funds they seek.
>
> Keep in mind that bankers are nervous, averse to risk. A written business plan carries an important message even before it is read: It says the company's executives are serious enough to do formal planning. That's an important message because bankers believe that those individuals who plan are better risks than those who don't, and more deserving of bank funds.[8]

Who Reads the Business Plan—And What Are They Looking For?

There are two primary audiences for a firm's business plan. Let's look at each of them.

A Firm's Employees   A clearly written business plan, which articulates the vision and future plans of a firm, is important for both the management team and the rank-and-file employees. The management team sometimes argues that it's a waste of time to write a business plan because the marketplace changes so rapidly that any plan will become quickly outdated. Although it's true that marketplaces can and often do change rapidly, the process of writing the plan may be as valuable as the plan itself. Writing the plan forces the management team to think through every aspect of its business and agree on its most important priorities and goals.[9] Just imagine the managers of a new firm sitting at a conference table hammering out the content of their business plan. In most instances, many heated discussions are likely to take place as the firm's founders reach agreement on the most important aspects of their operations.

A clearly written business plan also helps a firm's rank-and-file employees operate in sync and move forward in a consistent and purposeful manner. The existence of a business plan is particularly useful for the functional department heads of a young firm. For example, imagine that you are the newly hired vice president for management information systems for a rapidly growing start-up. The availability of a formal business plan that talks about all aspects of the business and the business's future strategies and goals can help you make sure that what you're doing is consistent with the overall plans and direction of the firm.

The confidentiality of a firm's business plan should be protected to avoid the possibility of the plan falling into the hands of a competitor. Many firms restrict the number of copies of their business plan that can be made. These companies assign specific copies to specific people and require that the plans be secured in locked file cabinets or desks when not in use. In addition, most companies stamp the front page of their business plans "Confidential—Do Not Reprint without Permission." While these measures may not prevent the intentional theft of a firm's business plan by a disgruntled employee, they can prevent the inadvertent loss of a copy of the plan. These measures are tightened considerably when a start-up is working on a product or service that is highly sensitive or proprietary. Companies that formulate their initial business plans in secret refer to themselves as operating in "*stealth mode*." For example, during the time that Dean Kamen was developing the Segway, the self-balancing two-wheeled human transporter discussed in Chapter 1, the project was code-named "Ginger." Great lengths were taken to keep secret what the company was doing until its patents were applied for and it was ready to unveil its product.[10]

Investors and Other External Stakeholders External stakeholders, such as investors, potential business partners, potential customers, and key employees who are being recruited to join a firm, are the second audience for a business plan. To appeal to this group, the business plan must be realistic and not reflective of overconfidence on the firm's part.[11] Overly optimistic statements or projections undermine a business plan's credibility, so it is foolish to include them. At the same time, the plan must clearly demonstrate that the business idea is viable and offers potential investors financial returns greater than lower-risk investment alternatives. The same is true for potential business partners, customers, and key recruits. Unless the new business can show that it has impressive potential, there is little reason to become involved as an investor.

A firm must validate the feasibility of its business idea and have a good understanding of its competitive environment prior to presenting its business plan to others. Sophisticated investors, potential business partners, and key recruits will base their assessment of the future prospects of a business on facts, not guesswork or platitudes. The most compelling facts a company can provide in its business plan are the results of its own feasibility analysis and the articulation of a distinctive and competitive business model. (We discuss business models in Chapter 6.) A business plan rings hollow if it is based strictly on an entrepreneur's predictions and estimates of a business's future prospects.

In addition to the previously mentioned attributes, a business plan should disclose all resource limitations that the business must meet before it is ready to start earning revenues. For example, a firm may need to hire service people before it can honor the warranties for the products it sells. It is foolhardy for a new venture to try to downplay or hide its resource needs. One of the main reasons new ventures seek out investors is to obtain the capital needed to hire key personnel, further develop their products or services, lease office space, or fill some other gap in their operations. Investors understand this, and experienced investors are typically willing to help the firms they fund plug resource or competency gaps. Consider Don Valentine, the famous Silicon Valley venture capitalist. Valentine and his firm, Sequoia Venture Capital, had funded many successful entrepreneurial firms during the 1980s and 1990s, including Cisco Systems and Yahoo! Reflecting on how his firm helped Cisco and Yahoo! plug their competency gaps, Valentine wrote:

> There's a great similarity between the two companies. When we encountered the Cisco start-up team, there were actually five employees. The thing that struck me was the cleverness of the people at Cisco—they had an appreciation of what they were really good at, and a profound recognition of what they knew nothing about. Our relationship was struck on the basis that Sequoia would provide management, a management process, and $2.5 million, and Cisco would provide the technical side of things.
>
> Interestingly, we began Yahoo! on the same basis. We encountered two individuals (Jerry Yang and David Filo) whose greatest strength was the recognition of their weaknesses and their lack of experience. And we struck the same kind of arrangement. We would go out and develop the management team and the management process, and we would put up the start-up money. They would work at what they were interested in and very good at.[12]

A summary of who reads business plans and what they're looking for appears in Table 4.1.

TABLE 4.1 Who Reads a Business Plan, and What Are They Looking For?

Audience	What Are They Looking For?
Internal Audience	
Company founders and initial management team	This is the group that typically writes the plan. The process of writing a business plan forces the firm's initial management team to think through every aspect of the business and to reach a consensus regarding the most important priorities.
Rank-and-file employees	This group will be looking for a clear description of what the entrepreneurial venture intends to accomplish and how it intends to accomplish it. Information on these topics helps employees make sure that what they are doing is consistent with the company's objectives and intended direction.
Board of directors	For firms that have a board of directors, the business plan establishes a benchmark against which the top management team's performance can be measured.
External Audience	
Potential investors	For investors, the business plan provides evidence of the strength of the business opportunity, the quality of the firm's top management team, and other relevant information. Investors will also be looking for how they will receive a return on their investment, whether through an initial public offering, the sale of the company, or a management buyback.
Potential bankers	Bankers are interested in how and when money loaned to a start-up would be repaid and whether the start-up has collateral available to secure a loan. Bankers are also interested in how a company would survive potential setbacks.
Potential alliance partners and major customers	High-quality alliance partners and major customers are generally reluctant to enter into arrangements with unknown companies. A convincing business plan can help lessen their doubts.
Key recruits for jobs with the new firm	Key recruits will be looking primarily at the excitement of the business opportunity, the compensation scheme for key employees, and the future prospects of the firm.
Merger and acquisition candidates	Companies grow through acquisitions and engage in divestitures as a way of gaining liquidity. In either case, a potential merger or acquisition candidate will typically ask a company for a copy of its business plan to use as a first screening tool.

LEARNING

Objective

3. Explain how the process of writing a business plan can be as important as the plan itself.

LEARNING

Objective

4. Identify the advantages and disadvantages of using software packages to assist in preparing a business plan.

Guidelines for Writing a Business Plan

There are several important guidelines that should influence the writing of a business plan. It is important to remember that a firm's business plan is typically the first aspect of a proposed venture that will be seen by an investor. If the plan is incomplete or looks sloppy, it is easy for an investor to infer that the venture itself is incomplete and sloppy.[13] It is important to be sensitive to the structure, content, and style of a business plan before sending it to an investor or anyone else who may be involved with the new firm. Table 4.2 lists some of the "red flags" that are raised when certain aspects of a business plan are insufficient or miss the mark.

Structure of the Business Plan To make the best impression, a business plan should follow a conventional structure, such as the outline shown in the next section. Although some entrepreneurs want to demonstrate creativity in everything they do, departing from the basic structure of the conventional business plan format is usually a mistake. Typically, investors are very busy people and want a plan where they can easily find critical information. If an investor has to hunt for something because it is in an unusual place or just isn't there, he or she might simply give up and move on to the next plan.[14]

Many software packages are available that employ an interactive, menu-driven approach to assist in the writing of a business plan. Some of these programs are very helpful. However, entrepreneurs should avoid a boilerplate plan that looks as though it came from a "canned" source. The software package may be helpful in providing structure and saving time, but the information in the plan should still be tailored to the individual business. Some businesses

TABLE 4.2 **Red Flags in Business Plans**

Red Flag	Explanation
Founders with none of their own money at risk	If the founders aren't willing to put their own money at risk, why should anyone else?
A poorly cited plan	A plan should be built on hard evidence and sound research, not guesswork or what an entrepreneur "thinks" will happen. The sources for all primary and secondary research should be cited.
Defining the market size too broadly	Defining the market for a new venture too broadly shows that the true target market is not well defined. For example, saying that a new venture will target the $550-billion-per-year pharmaceutical industry isn't helpful. The market opportunity needs to be better defined. Obviously, the new venture will target a segment or a specific market within the industry.
Overly aggressive financials	Many investors skip directly to this portion of the plan. Projections that are poorly reasoned or unrealistically optimistic lose credibility. In contrast, sober, well-reasoned statements backed by sound research and judgment gain credibility quickly.
Sloppiness in any area	It is never a good idea to make a reader wade through typos, balance sheets that don't balance, or sloppiness in any area. These types of mistakes are seen as inattention to detail, and hurt the credibility of the entrepreneur.

hire consultants or outside advisers to write their business plans. Although there is nothing wrong with getting advice or making sure that a plan looks as professional as possible, a consultant or outside adviser shouldn't be the primary author of the plan. Along with facts and figures, a business plan needs to project a sense of anticipation and excitement about the possibilities that surround a new venture—a task best accomplished by the creators of the business themselves.[15] Plus, savvy venture capitalists learn important things about entrepreneurs on the basis of their writing style, choice of words, and so forth.

Content of the Business Plan The business plan should give clear and concise information on all the important aspects of the proposed venture. It must be long enough to provide sufficient information yet short enough to maintain reader interest. For most plans, 25 to 35 pages are sufficient. Supporting information, such as the résumés of the founding entrepreneurs, can appear in an appendix.

After a business plan is completed, it should be reviewed for spelling and grammar and to make sure that no critical information has been omitted. There are numerous stories about business plans sent to investors that left out important information, such as significant industry trends, how much money the company needed, or what the money was going to be used for. One investor even told the authors of this book that he once received a business plan that didn't include any contact information for the entrepreneur. Apparently, the entrepreneur was so focused on the content of the plan that he or she simply forgot to provide contact information on the business plan itself. This was a shame, because the investor was interested in learning more about the business idea.[16]

Style or Format of the Business Plan The appearance of the plan must be carefully thought out. It should look sharp but not give the impression that a lot of money was spent to produce it. Those who read business plans know that entrepreneurs have limited resources and expect them to act accordingly. A plastic spiral binder including a transparent cover sheet and a back sheet to support the plan is a good choice. When writing the plan, avoid getting carried away with the design elements included in word-processing programs, such as boldfaced type, italics, different font sizes and colors, clip art, and so forth. Overuse of these tools makes a business plan look amateurish rather than professional.[17]

One of the most common questions that the writers of business plans ask is, How long and detailed should it be? The answer to this question depends on the type of business plan

5. Explain the difference between a summary business plan, a full business plan, and an operational business plan.

FIGURE 4.1

Types of Business Plans

Summary Business Plan	Full Business Plan	Operational Business Plan
10–15 pages	25–35 pages	40–100 pages
Works best for new ventures in the early stages of development that want to "test the waters" to see if investors are interested in their idea	Works best for new ventures who are at the point where they need funding or financing; serves as a "blueprint" for the company's operations	Is meant primarily for an internal audience; works best as a tool for creating a blueprint for a new venture's operations and providing guidance to operational managers

that is being written. There are three types of business plans, each of which has a different rule of thumb regarding length and level of detail. Presented in Figure 4.1, the three types of business plans are as follows:

- *Summary plan:* A **summary business plan** is 10 to 15 pages and works best for companies that are very early in their development and are not prepared to write a full plan. The authors of a summary business plan may be asking for funding to conduct the analysis needed to write a full plan (such as a feasibility analysis). Ironically, summary business plans are also used by very experienced entrepreneurs who may be thinking about a new venture but don't want to take the time to write a full business plan. For example, if someone such as Meg Whitman, the chief executive officer (CEO) of eBay, was thinking about starting a new business, she might write a summary business plan and send it out to selected investors to get feedback on her idea. Most investors know about Ms. Whitman's success at eBay and don't need detailed information.

- *Full business plan:* A **full business plan**, which is the assumed focus of our discussions to this point in the chapter, is typically 25 to 35 pages long. This type of plan spells out a company's operations and plans in much more detail than a summary business plan, and it is the format that is usually used to prepare a business plan for an investor. As we've mentioned, the readers of business plans are usually busy people, and a long, drawn-out plan simply will not be read. In fact, the sharper and more concise a full business plan is, the better. Detailed information, such as the résumés of the founders or pictures of product prototypes, can appear in an appendix.

- *Operational business plan:* Some established businesses will write an **operational business plan**, which is meant primarily for an internal audience. An operational business plan is a blueprint for a company's operations. Commonly running between 40 and 100 pages in length, these plans can obviously feature a great amount of detail. An effectively developed operational business plan can help a young company provide guidance to operational managers.

A cover letter should accompany a business plan sent to an investor or other stakeholders through the mail. The cover letter should briefly introduce the entrepreneur and clearly state why the business plan is being sent to the individual receiving it. As discussed in Chapter 10, if a new venture is looking for funding, it is a poor strategy to obtain a list of investors and blindly send the plan to everyone on the list. Instead, each person who receives a copy of the plan should be carefully selected on the basis of being a viable investor candidate.

Regardless of the type of business plan that is written, many plans rely on the establishment of partnerships to make them work. An example is a company named Ideas United, founded by four Emory University students. Ideas United sponsors movie-making contests, called Campus MovieFest, on college campuses across the country. The extent to which Campus MovieFest events rely on partnerships to make them work is depicted in this chapter's "Partnering for Success" feature.

partnering for *success*

Campus MovieFest: Making Partnering an Essential Part of a Business Plan
www.campusmoviefest.com

In 2000, four students at Emory University, led by David Roemer and Dan Costa, had an unusual idea. They decided to host a movie-making contest by giving all freshman dorm halls an Apple laptop computer, a camcorder, some movie-making software, and a week to make their own short movies. Working in teams of about 10, each floor produced a 5-minute film, with 1,000 students participating overall. The outcome: 1,500 students packed Glenn Memorial Auditorium on the Emory campus to see the final products.

Based on their initial success, the four decided to focus on writing a business plan and to flesh out what it would take to translate their idea for hosting movie-making contests on college campuses into a for-profit venture. To flesh out their ideas, the four worked with the entrepreneurship faculty at Emory and entered several business plan competitions. Eventually, a sensible plan came together, and shortly after graduation, in the spring of 2002, the four founded a company named Ideas United to host movie-making contests on college campuses. The contests were originally dubbed iMovieFest, and are now called Campus MovieFest.

After leaving college, the real work to make Campus MovieFest a success began. Integral to the success of the business was the ability to establish partnerships. The contests, along with access to the equipment necessary to make movies, would be free to the students involved, so the founders knew they would have to rely on corporate sponsors to fund their events. In addition, they would need the cooperation of the universities to help promote the events and provide auditorium space and would need to provide incentives to students to participate. In other words, Campus MovieFest would need lots of partners to make its business plan work.

To move forward, the four hit the street and basically "pitched" their idea to a number of potential corporate partners. The founders knew that the corporations they were targeting are approached by many organizations for money and support, so they knew their pitch would have to be financially sound and creatively convincing. The one advantage they knew they had was that their clientele, college-aged students, is a coveted demographic among many corporations. They also drew upon their network of acquaintances to get introductions. Things went well, and they landed their first corporate sponsor—Delta Airlines. Delta was a natural fit because it is headquartered in Atlanta (where Emory is located), is interested in the college-age demographic, and has connections with Emory. In time, additional sponsors followed, including Apple, Coca-Cola, The History Channel, and Virgin Mobile. David Roemer, one of the venture's founders, interned at Apple during his time at Emory.

Fast forward to the present. Campus MovieFest has been extremely successful. The company is now hosting movie-making contests on college campuses across the country. Since its beginning, it has hosted contests on 30 campuses involving more than 50,000 students. The finals are impressive events, with searchlights, red carpets, and many of the elements of a Hollywood movie premier. All the short movies made during Campus MovieFest contests are posted on the company's Web site (www.campusmoviefest). Spend a few minutes and browse the site, and watch a couple of the short movies made by college students. You'll be amazed at the quality of the movies and the creativity involved.

Although there are many elements that make a start-up a success, a key ingredient to Campus MovieFest's success has been its ability to forge and maintain successful business partnerships. Many of its sponsors, including Delta and Apple, have been with it since the beginning. Without the support of its corporate sponsors and the participation of its host universities, Campus MovieFest wouldn't exist.

Questions for Critical Thinking

1. If you had been one of the founders of Campus MovieFest, what would have been the essence of your "pitch" to corporate sponsors to get the company started?

2. What do you think are the primary factors that motivate Delta, Apple Computer, Krispy Kreme, and Campus MovieFest's other corporate sponsors to participate?

3. If you were part of the top management team of Campus MovieFest, how would you show your appreciation to your partners (i.e., corporate sponsors, host universities, etc.) for supporting your business?

4. Spend some time on Campus MovieFest's Web site and watch a couple of the short movies. What do you think? If you were the CEO of a company that wanted to appeal to college-aged students, would you consider sponsoring a Campus MovieFest event? Why or why not?

Sources: Personal interview with David Roemer, August 6, 2006.

Outline of the Business Plan

A suggested outline of the full business plan appears in Table 4.3. Specific plans may vary, depending on the nature of the business and the personalities of the founding entrepreneurs. Most business plans do not include all the elements introduced in Table 4.3; we include them here for the purpose of completeness. Each entrepreneur must decide which specific elements to include in his or her business plan.

A business plan is intended to be a living document that can change if the situation warrants. As discussed throughout this book, new ventures must often bob and weave to keep in step with a changing environment. Many businesses update their business plans on an annual or semiannual basis to maintain the plan's effectiveness.

Exploring Each Section of the Plan

Cover Page and Table of Contents The cover page should include the name of the company, its address, its phone number, the date, the contact information for the lead entrepreneur, and the company's Web site address if it has one. Given today's technologies, the contact information should include a land-based phone number, an e-mail address, and a cell phone number. This information should be centered at the top of the page. Because the cover letter and the business plan could get separated, it is wise to include contact information in both places. The bottom of the page should include information alerting the reader to the confidential nature of the plan. If the company already has a distinctive trademark, it should be placed somewhere near the center of the page. A table of contents should follow the cover letter. It should list the sections and page numbers of the business plan and the appendices.

Campus MovieFest is moving forward with a business plan that relies largely on its ability to develop sustainable partnerships with corporate sponsors such as Apple Computer, Delta Airlines, and Coca-Cola. Since it was founded in 2000, Campus MovieFest has sponsored movie-making contests at more than 30 universities involving over 50,000 students.

TABLE 4.3 Business Plan Outline

Cover Page

Table of Contents

I. Executive Summary

    A. The Opportunity
- Problem to solve or need to be filled

    B. The Description of the Business
- How the proposed business solves the problem or fills the need

    C. Competitive Advantage
- Description of the business model

    D. The Target Market

    E. The Management Team

    F. Brief Summary of the Financial Projections
- The amount of capital needed and what the capital will be used for, if the plan is going to a potential investor

    G. Description of What the Business Needs

    H. Exit Strategy for Investors (if the plan is going to investors)

II. The Business

    A. The Opportunity
- Problem to solve or need to be filled

    B. The Description of the Business
- How the proposed business solves the problem or fills the need
- Brief company history or background
- Company mission and objectives

    C. Competitive Advantage
- Description of the business model
- How the business will create a sustainable competitive advantage

    D. Current Status and Requirements
- Description of where the business stands today
- Description of what the business needs to move forward

III. Management Team

    A. Management Team
- Management experience
- Management ability
- Technical expertise

    B. Board of Directors
- Number of directors
- Composition of the board

    C. Board of Advisers
- Number of advisers
- Composition of the advisory board
- How the advisory board will be used

    D. Key Professional Service Providers
- Law firm
- Accounting firm
- Business consultants

IV. Company Structure, Intellectual Property, and Ownership

    A. Organizational Structure
- Organizational chart
- Description of organizational structure

    B. Legal Structure
- Legal form of organization
- Ownership structure of the business

    C. Intellectual Property
- Patents, trademarks, and copyrights applied for or approved

V. Industry Analysis

    A. Industry description
- Industry trends
- Industry size
- Industry attractiveness (growing, mature, or in decline)
- Profit potential

    B. Target Market
- Description of target market

    C. Competitive position within target market
- Competitor analysis

VI. Marketing Plan

    A. Product Feasibility and Strategy
- Product strategy
- Concept testing
- Usability testing

    B. Pricing Strategy

    C. Channels of Distribution

    D. Promotions and Advertising

VII. Operations Plan

    A. Method of Production or Service Delivery

    B. Availability of Qualified Labor Pool

    C. Business Partnerships
- Types of business partnerships
- Purposes of business partnerships

    D. Quality Control

    E. Customer Support
- Customer support strategies
- Customer support obligations

VIII. Financial Plan

    A. Capital Requirements for the Next 3 to 5 Years
- Sources and uses of funds

    B. Overview of Financial Projections
- Explanation of how financial projections are prepared (assumption sheet)

    C. Income Statements

    D. Cash Flow Projections

    E. Balance Sheets

    F. Payback and Exit Strategy (if the business plan is sent to potential investors)

(Cont'd.)

TABLE 4.3 Business Plan Outline (*Continued*)

IX. Critical Risk Factors
    A. Management Risks
    B. Marketing Risks
    C. Operating Risks
    D. Financial Risks
    E. Intellectual Property Infringement
    F. Other Risks as Appropriate

X. Appendix
    A. Supporting Documents
      • Résumés of founders and key employees
      • Picture of product prototypes
      • Other documents as appropriate

L E A R N I N G
Objective

6. Explain why the executive summary may be the most important section of a business plan.

Executive Summary The **executive summary** is a short overview of the entire business plan; it provides a busy reader with everything that needs to be known about the new venture's distinctive nature.[18] In many instances, an investor will first ask for a copy of a firm's executive summary and will request a copy of the full business plan only if the executive summary is sufficiently convincing. The executive summary, then, is arguably the most important section of the business plan[19] in that if it fails to attract investors' interest, they are unlikely to read the remainder of the plan. After reading the executive summary, investors should have a relatively good understanding of what will be presented in greater detail throughout the plan. The most important point to remember when writing an executive summary is that it is not an introduction or preface to the business plan. Instead, it is meant to be a one- to two-page summary of the plan itself.[20]

If the new venture is seeking financing or funding, the executive summary should state the amount of funds being requested. Some plans will state how much equity a business is willing to surrender for a certain amount of investment capital. In these instances, the executive summary will conclude with a statement such as "The firm is seeking $250,000 in investment capital in exchange for a 15 percent ownership position." Other entrepreneurs are more leery about how much equity they are willing to surrender and leave their plans intentionally vague on this point.

Although the executive summary appears at the beginning of the business plan, it should be created after the plan is finished. Only then can an accurate overview of the plan be written.[21]

The Business The most effective way to introduce the business is to describe the opportunity the entrepreneur has identified—that is, the problem to be solved or the need to be filled—and then describe how the business plans to address the issue. This is the initial "hook" that captures the interest of the reader of a business plan. The description of the opportunity should be followed by a brief history of the company, along with the company's mission statement and objectives. An explanation of the company's competitive advantage and a brief description of the business model follow. The section should conclude with a summary of the firm's current status and a description of what it needs to move forward.

Using milestones is one particularly effective way of describing where a business stands today and what it needs for its future. A **milestone**, in a business plan context, is a noteworthy event in the past or future development of a business. A business could describe where it stands today by listing the date it was founded as its first significant milestone and then summarizing the company's history by referring to the major milestones that were achieved. The future of the business could be described in terms of projected milestones. The first projected milestone might be receiving the funding requested by the business plan. Additional projected milestones would then illustrate what could be accomplished with the funding in place and provide a time line for the future major events in the life of the firm.[22]

L E A R N I N G
Objective

7. Describe a milestone and how milestones are used in business plans.

Management Team As mentioned earlier, one of the most important things investors want to see when reviewing the viability of a new venture is the strength of its management team. If the team doesn't "pass muster," most investors won't read further. Primus Venture Partners, a venture capital firm based in Cleveland, Ohio, is most interested in the following features when considering an investment: (1) proven management, (2) meaningful management ownership, (3) attractive market opportunity and economics, and (4) multiple liquidity options.[23] Note that the second attribute focuses on the amount of money that the management team has invested in the venture. This amount of money is often called "**skin in the game**." Investors are wary of investing in a venture if the founders and the key members of the management team haven't put some of their own money (or "skin") into the venture, as depicted in Table 4.2 The management team of the venture should own a large-enough equity stake to ensure that they are adequately motivated to weather the demands of building a successful firm.

The material in this section should include a brief summary of the qualifications of each key member of the management team, including employment and professional experience, significant accomplishments, educational background, and the relevance of team members' backgrounds to their position in the new firm.[24] Managers' résumés should appear in an appendix if they add useful information. If management team members have worked together before, that work-related experience should be emphasized. There is always a risk that people, regardless of how talented they are, won't be able to work together effectively. Management teams that have a track record of success are a lower risk to investors than a group of people who are new to one another.

The next portion of this section should include material on the board of directors if the firm has or plans to have one (in most cases it will). The composition of the board should be described. For example, if a firm plans to have five directors, the business plan should specify the sources (i.e., from inside the firm or from different places outside the firm) from which those directors would be drawn. A typical scenario for a new venture with five directors is to allocate two director slots to insiders (company founders and/or key management personnel), two director slots to outsiders (people who do not work for the firm), and one director slot for the investor. As we discuss in Chapter 9, many new ventures also have an advisory board.

This section should conclude by listing the professional service providers the firm works with—its law firm, its accounting firm, and any consulting firms. How these professionals have helped the firm achieve its initial objectives and milestones should be described.

Company Structure, Ownership, and Intellectual Property This section should begin by describing the structure of the new venture, including the reporting relationships among the top management team members. A frequent source of tension in new ventures, particularly if two or more founders start out as "equals," is a failure to delineate areas of responsibility and authority.[25] To demonstrate that the founders have sorted out these issues, an organizational chart should be included. An **organizational chart** is a graphic representation of how authority and responsibility are distributed within a company.[26] A short narrative description should supply information on the most important reporting relationships shown in the chart.

The next part of this section should explain how the firm is legally structured in terms of whether it is a sole proprietorship, a partnership, a C corporation, a subchapter S corporation, a limited liability company, or some other form. This issue is discussed in detail in Chapter 7. The ownership structure of the business should also be revealed. If a founders' agreement exists, it should be included in an appendix.

The third portion of this section should discuss the intellectual property the firm owns, or has applied for, including patents, trademarks, and copyrights. This is an extremely important issue. Intellectual property forms the foundation for the valuation and competitive advantage of many entrepreneurial firms. Any significant patents, trademarks, and copyrights a firm has in its intellectual property pipeline should also be revealed unless the information is highly proprietary. If it is highly proprietary, the company should assert that it is operating in **stealth mode** with intellectual property issues.[27] The importance of intellectual property is discussed in detail in Chapter 12.

Industry Analysis This section should begin by discussing the major trends in the industry in which the firm intends to compete along with important characteristics of the industry, such as its size, attractiveness, and profit potential. This section should also discuss how the firm will diminish or sidestep the forces that suppress its industry's profitability. The firm's target market should be discussed next, along with an analysis of how the firm will compete in that market. To show how a firm's products or services stack up against the competition, the plan should include a competitor analysis (discussed in Chapter 5). A competitive analysis grid provides a visual way for an investor to quickly ascertain the major strengths and distinctive attributes of a new venture's product or service offerings compared to its competitors.

After reading the industry analysis, an investor should have a good grasp of the future prospects of the industry (or industries) in which the firm intends to compete along with an understanding of the target market the firm will pursue and how it will defend its position. One thing the business plan shouldn't include is a long-winded description of an industry, particularly if the plan will be sent to people who are already familiar with the industry. For example, a venture capitalist specializing in the electronic games industry doesn't need a lengthy description of the industry from an entrepreneur. Unnecessary content diminishes the value and appearance of a business plan. It is important for a firm to think carefully about the industry in which it will compete and the target market it will pursue in developing its business plan. These points are illustrated in this chapter's "Savvy Entrepreneurial Firm" feature dealing with Red Bull, a company that makes energy drinks.

Marketing Plan The marketing plan should immediately follow the industry analysis and should provide details about the new firm's products or services. This section of the business plan typically is carefully scrutinized. It is very important to investors, in particular, to be confident that a new venture has a product that people will buy and has a realistic plan for getting that product to market. Information about the unique marketing issues facing new ventures is provided in Chapter 11.

This section should begin with a fuller description of the products the firm will sell than has been provided in previous sections of the plan. The results of the feasibility analysis should be reported, including the results of the concept tests and the usability tests, if applicable. A diagram or digital image of the product or the product prototype should be included if it can be done tastefully. An alternative is to include the diagram or image in an appendix to the plan. If the product is small or inexpensive enough—such as a type of nonperishable food—a sample of the product itself could be provided with the business plan. If the product is technologically sophisticated, it should be explained in everyday terms. Investors usually aren't scientists, so technical jargon and industry slang should be avoided. The plan should fully explain any request for funds to more fully develop a product or service. After the product has been described, the other elements of the firm's marketing mix, including pricing, channels of distribution, and promotions, should be addressed.[28] After reading this section of the plan, an investor should be confident that the firm's overall approach to its target market and its product strategy, pricing strategy, channels of distribution, and promotions strategy are in sync with one another and make sense.[29]

If a new venture wants to include more in its business plan than space allows or if the business plan is not a suitable format for providing certain information, the plan can refer the reader to the company's Web site. However, it is vital that all technological aspects of the Web site work flawlessly throughout the time the business plan is being distributed.

Operations Plan This section of the plan deals with the day-to-day operations of the company. The section should begin by describing how the firm plans to manufacture its first product and how realistic the estimates are in this area.[30] The reader will want to know how much of the manufacturing the firm will do itself and how much will be contracted out to others. The location of the manufacturing facility should be specified, along with the availability of a qualified labor pool. Another important issue is how much inventory will need to be carried to meet customer needs. If the company is a service organization, similar information should be provided.

savvy entrepreneurial firm

Red Bull: Showing the Value of a Tightly Focused Target Market
www.redbull.com

In 1982, Dietrich Mateschitz, an Austrian, was sitting in a hotel in Hong Kong when he learned about products called "tonic drinks," which athletes used to boost their energy. The drinks were popular in Asia at the time but were not marketed in Europe or the United States. The idea intrigued Mateschitz, and in 1984 he launched a company called Red Bull to market his version of the Asian tonic drinks. To get attention, he packaged the drink uniquely—Red Bull comes in a sleek, distinctively colored, 8.3-ounce can with a red bull on the side. The drinks promised to provide athletes increased physical stamina, concentration, and vigilance to help them endure the rigors of their sports. The caffeine in one Red Bull is a little less than that found in an average cup of coffee but twice as much found in a 12-ounce can of Coke.

Red Bull quickly caught on in Austria and spread to neighboring countries. In 1992, Red Bull entered Hungary, which was the firm's first foreign market. The drink was introduced in the United States in 1997. Rather than setting out to capture the entire U.S. market, however, Red Bull's business plan concentrated on a much tighter target market. The company began its U.S. efforts by focusing on 16- to 29-year-olds involved in sports. The company then rolled out its campaign one region at a time, learning what worked best before going on to the next region. Today, Red Bull is sold in over 100 countries around the world. In total, customers now consume nearly 2 billion cans of Red Bull annually, making Red Bull the world's most popular energy drink.

There were a couple of other nifty aspects to Red Bull's U.S. business plan that set it apart from its competitors. One particularly successful tactic was to create buzz about the product before it even hit the market by offering free samples through sports clubs and other places in which athletes congregated. When the product finally hit the shelves, it sold quickly. The company also shopped for the hungriest distributors to keep its costs down. Finally, as demand grew, the company never took its eye off its target market: young athletes. Today, Red Bull still focuses on young athletes and sponsors many who are involved in extreme sports.

Red Bull's energy drinks are now making their way into the mainstream market, but the company's early success in the United States was due largely to its decision to focus on a clearly defined target market. By doing so—and by building excitement for the product before it was placed in stores, rolling out the product region by region, and learning as it went—Red Bull executed its U.S. business plan in an exemplary manner.

Questions for Critical Thinking

1. Why do you think Red Bull has been so successful in maintaining market share, given the dozens of competing beverages, backed by companies like PepsiCo and Coca-Cola, that are now trying to appeal to its target market?

2. Go to Red Bull's Web site (www.redbull.com). Do you like the design of the site—given Red Bull's target audience? What changes, if any, would you make to the site?

3. Do you think the energy drink market is still a good place for entrepreneurial start-ups, or do you think the market is too saturated with entrenched competitors like Red Bull? If you were an entrepreneur and wanted to launch a new firm in the energy drink market, how would you go about it?

4. At what point do you think Red Bull will start developing additional products to extend its brand and expand its target market? Do you think a brand-extension strategy would be a good move at this time? Why or why not?

Sources: Red Bull homepage, www.redbull.com (accessed September 1, 2006); K. A. Dolan, "The Soda With Buzz," *Forbes*, March 28; "A Bull's Market," *Brandweek*, May 28, 2001.

An overview of the manufacturing plan should be followed by a description of the network of suppliers, business partners, and service providers that will be necessary to build the product or produce the service the firm will sell. As is discussed in more detail in Chapter 6, all firms are embedded in a network of partnerships that help bring their products and services to market. The major relationships should be described. Investors are suspicious of firms that try to do everything themselves.

A firm's quality control procedures should also be explained. It isn't necessary to go into detail, but the plan should indicate what monitoring or inspection processes will be built into the manufacturing process to ensure high quality. Customer support strategies should then be discussed. If a firm is obligated to provide after-sale support to its customers through a call center or other means, these obligations should be clearly described. Any risks and regulations pertaining to the operations of the firm should be disclosed, such as nonroutine regulations regarding waste disposal and worker safety. This issue becomes important when a firm is producing waste products subject to Environmental Protection Agency regulations. A firm can incur substantial liability if its waste products are not disposed of appropriately.

An increasingly common feature of many business plans for start-ups is a reliance on outsourcing certain functions to third parties as a way of allowing the start-up to focus on its distinctive competencies.

Financial Plan The financial section of a business plan must demonstrate the financial viability of the business. A careful reader of the plan will scrutinize this section. The financial plan should begin with an explanation of the funding that will be needed by the business during the next 3 to 5 years along with an explanation of how the funds will be used. This information is called a **sources and uses of funds statement**.[31] It is also helpful to demonstrate where the money to fund the business has come from to date. Some business plans offer a time line of when money was infused into the business. The time line then typically shows the need for an additional infusion of capital (which is why the investor or banker is reading the plan) along with how the business will further progress if the additional capital is made available.

The next portion of this section includes financial projections, which are intended to further demonstrate the financial viability of the business. The financial projections should include 3 to 5 years of pro forma income statements, balance sheets, and statements of cash flows, as described in Chapter 8. It is crucial that an assumption sheet, which is also described in Chapter 8, precede the projections. As you will learn, an assumption sheet explains the basis for the numbers included in the pro forma financial statements. It is important to remember that a business plan should be based on realistic projections. If it is not and the company gets funding or financing, there will most certainly be a day of reckoning. Investors and bankers hold entrepreneurs accountable for the numbers in their projections. If the projections don't pan out and it becomes obvious to the investors or bankers that the numbers were too optimistic to begin with, the long-term credibility of the entrepreneurs involved will be damaged.

If the business plan is being sent to investors, the financial projections should be followed by a discussion of the rate of return that the investors can expect and how they will get their money back. A venture capital firm will typically want to reclaim an investment in a fairly short period of time (3 to 5 years); a private investor, a business angel, or an institutional investor may have a longer-term investment horizon. Investors get their money back through a **liquidity event**, an occurrence that converts some or all of a company's stock into cash. The three most common liquidity events for a new venture are to go public, find a buyer, or merge with another company. For example, when a firm goes public, its stock starts trading on one of the major exchanges, such as the NASDAQ or the New York Stock Exchange. Once this happens, an investor can sell stock through the exchange—thereby converting the stock to cash. It is much harder for an investor to find a buyer for stock that isn't traded on a major exchange.

Although it may seem odd to talk about selling a company at the time it is being founded, it is just good planning to have an **exit strategy** in mind.[32] Commenting on this topic, Edwin A. Goodman, cofounder of Milestone Venture Partners in New York, said:

> From a venture and an astute entrepreneur's standpoint, you want to think about the endgame when you enter. An entrepreneur's emphasis should always be, "I have a good idea, here's the market and here's how I can address it and build a solid company." And as a secondary matter, [an entrepreneur] should say, "When we achieve those goals, we'll sell the company."[33]

LEARNING Objective

8. Explain the purpose of a "sources and uses of funds" statement.

LEARNING Objective

9. Describe a liquidity event.

Critical Risk Factors Although a variety of potential risks may exist (see the business plan outline in Table 4.3), a business should tailor this section to depict its truly critical risks. One of the most important things that a business plan should convey to its readers is a sense that the venture's management team is on the ball and understands the critical risks facing the business.

The critical risks a new business may face depend on its industry and its particular situation. For example, a business may be counting on the U.S. Patent and Trademark Office to grant a patent to protect its exclusive right to manufacture a product and to provide a barrier to entry for its competition. What if the patent isn't approved? Similarly, a business may be looking for an experienced chief financial officer to manage the growing financial complexities of its operations. A critical risk factor in this context would be the venture's inability to find a suitable candidate for this job on a timely basis. Most plans will include alternative courses of action.

One start-up that did not assess its critical risk effectively was Webvan, one of the most spectacular failures during the dot-com bust. While there are many reasons that firms fail, Webvan's failure was due largely to an overly ambitious business plan, and an apparent absence of an awareness of the critical risk factors confronting the firm. A brief overview of Webvan and the reasons it failed are provided in the "What Went Wrong" feature.

what went wrong?

Webvan: Did a Flawed Business Plan and an Absence of Attention to Critical Risk Factors Sink an Otherwise Good Idea?
www.freshdirect.com

Webvan was an online grocery store that promised to revolutionize the grocery business. The company, which was launched in the late 1990s, delivered grocery store items to customers' homes within a 30-minute window of their choosing. The basic idea behind Webvan's business plan was that the company could lower the costs of selling groceries by storing and sorting groceries in huge warehouses and making home deliveries rather than incurring the costs involved with running traditional grocery stores. The company reasoned that consumers would flock to its service because it relieved them of the time-intensive task of grocery shopping.

The strength of its business idea allowed Webvan to get off to a fast start. In fact, Webvan attracted more venture capital funding than any other Internet company, other than Amazon.com. In 1999, Webvan went public, raising $375 million. At its peak, it was valued at $8.45 billion and its stock was traded at $30 per share. The company hired George Shaheen, the former head of Anderson Consulting, to be its CEO. To accommodate its aggressive 26-city expansion plan, the company signed a $1 billion contract with Bechtel in the early 2000s to build warehouses. Less then 2 years later, Webvan went broke, laying off 2,000 employees and losing all of its investors' money. What went wrong?

Webvan's basic business idea wasn't the chief culprit, as established retailers and other start-ups have proven with profitable and growing Internet grocery concepts. It also wasn't a failure with regard to customer service. In the nine markets that Webvan serviced before its fall, it actually had good customer service ratings, with an 89 percent approval rating on Epinions.com. The primary mistake that Webvan made was that the company's growth far outstripped the demand for its service. Rather than patiently building its infrastructure to accommodate growing demand, Webvan rushed ahead with its expansion plans, based on what Pip Coburn, the author of *The Change Function*, called a "build-it-and-pray-they-will-come" business model. Apparently, the obvious risk of lower-than-expected consumer demand wasn't accounted for in Webvan's business plan. Everything about Webvan's operations was built to accommodate scale, so when the lower-than-expected demand materialized, it worked to Webvan's disadvantage in multiple ways. For example, in some cases Webvan drivers were driving 30 miles to make a single delivery. The end result was that the company simply ran out of money, and its investors had no appetite to invest additional funds.

As a postscript, although the online grocery market is still in its infancy, it does have successes. An example is FreshDirect, an online grocer that delivers to residences, offices, and commuter rail stops in the

New York City area. Unlike Webvan, the company's expansion has been slow, and it is only now moving beyond New York City. In 2005, FreshDirect's sales totaled $150 million, an increase of 25 percent from sales of $120 million in 2004.

Questions for Critical Thinking

1. What do you think were the fundamental flaws in Webvan's business plan? Do some Internet research to expand your knowledge of Webvan beyond the scope of this feature.

2. Do some Internet research on FreshDirect. Why do you think FreshDirect has been successful? Why do you think the company has been reluctant to expand outside the New York City area?

3. Why do you think the venture capitalists that invested in Webvan guessed so wrong regarding the strength of the venture's business plan and its ultimate prospects for success?

4. What can other companies, like Electronic Arts, the company featured at the beginning of this chapter, learn from Webvan's experience?

Source: Wikipedia, Webvan, http://en.wikipedia.org/wiki/Webvan (accessed September 1, 2006); Pip Coburn, *The Change Function* (New York: Portfolio, 2006); Internet Retailer, "FreshDirect Casts a Wider Distribution Net," February 8, 2006.

Appendix Any material that does not easily fit into the body of a business plan should appear in an appendix—résumés of the top management team, photos or diagrams of product or product prototypes, certain financial data, and market research projections. The appendix should not be bulky and add significant length to the business plan. It should include only the additional information vital to the plan but not appropriate for the body of the plan itself.

Putting It All Together In evaluating and reviewing the completed business plan, the writers should put themselves in the reader's shoes to determine if the most important questions about the viability of their business venture have been answered. Table 4.4 lists the 10 most important questions a business plan should answer. It's a good checklist for any business plan writer.

Presenting the Business Plan to Investors

If the business plan successfully elicits the interest of a potential investor, the next step is to meet with the investor and present the plan in person. The investor will typically want to meet with the firm's founders. Because investors ultimately fund only a few ventures, the founders of a new firm should make as positive an impression on the investor as possible.

Webvan was one of the biggest flameouts of the dot-com era, losing over $1 billion of its investors' money. One has to wonder how sound Webvan's business plan was to begin with.

TABLE 4.4 The 10 Most Important Questions a Business Plan Should Answer

1. Is the business just an idea, or is it an opportunity with real potential?

2. Does the firm have an exciting and sensible business model? Will other firms be able to copy its business model, or will the firm be able to defend its position through patents, copyrights, or some other means?

3. Is the product or service viable? Does it add significant value to the customer? Has a feasibility analysis been completed? If so, what are the results?

4. Is the industry in which the product or service will be competing growing, stable, or declining in nature?

5. Does the firm have a well-defined target market?

6. How will the firm's competitors react to its entrance into their markets?

7. Is the management team experienced, skilled, and up to the task of launching the new firm?

8. Is the firm organized in an appropriate manner? Are its strategy and business practices legal and ethical?

9. Are the financial projections realistic, and do they project a bright future for the firm? What rate of return can investors expect?

10. What are the critical risks surrounding the business, and does the management team have contingency plans in place if risks become actual problems?

The first meeting with an investor is generally very short, about 1 hour.[34] The investor will typically ask the firm to make a 20- to 30-minute presentation using PowerPoint slides and use the rest of the time to ask questions. If the investor is impressed and wants to learn more about the venture, the presenters will be asked back for a second meeting to meet with the investor and his or her partners. This meeting will typically last longer and will require a more thorough presentation.

The Oral Presentation of a Business Plan

When asked to meet with an investor, the founders of a new venture should prepare a set of PowerPoint slides that will fill the time slot allowed for the presentation portion of the meeting. The first rule in making an oral presentation is to follow instructions. If an investor tells an entrepreneur that he or she has 1 hour and that the hour will consist of a 30-minute presentation and a 30-minute question-and-answer period, the presentation shouldn't last more than 30 minutes. The presentation should be smooth and well rehearsed. The slides should be sharp and not cluttered with material.

The entrepreneur should arrive at the appointment on time and be well prepared. If any audiovisual equipment is needed, the entrepreneur should be prepared to supply the equipment if the investor doesn't have it. These arrangements should be made before the meeting. The presentation should consist of plain talk and should avoid technical jargon. Start-up entrepreneurs may mistakenly spend too much time talking about the technology that will go into a new product or service and not enough time talking about the business itself. Another mistake entrepreneurs often make is not having the right material at their fingertips. For example, suppose that an entrepreneur has an exciting new product and has submitted a patent application to prevent others from producing the same product. If an investor asks, "When did you submit your patent application?" it makes a poor impression if the entrepreneur answers, "I can't remember the exact date, but I think it was in January or February of last year." Because the patent represents an essential part of the firm's ability to protect its competitive advantage, the entrepreneur should know or be able to locate within seconds the exact date the patent application was filed. The most important issues to cover in the presentation and how to present them are shown in Table 4.5. This presentation format calls for the use of 10 slides. A common mistake entrepreneurs make is to prepare too many slides and then try to rush through them during a 30-minute presentation.

Questions and Feedback to Expect from Investors

Whether in the initial meeting or on subsequent occasions, an entrepreneur will be asked a host of questions by potential investors. The smart entrepreneur has a good idea of what to expect and is prepared for these queries. Because investors often come across as being very

L E A R N I N G
Objective

10. Detail the parts of an oral presentation of a business plan.

TABLE 4.5 Ten PowerPoint Slides to Include in an Investor Presentation

Topic	Explanation
1. Title slide	Introduce the presentation with the company name, the names of the founders, and the company logo if available
2. Problem	Briefly state the problem to be solved or the need to be filled
3. Solution	Explain how the firm will solve the problem or how it will satisfy the need to be filled.
4. Business model	Briefly explain how the company will make money and the essence of its business model
5. Management team	Explain each manager's qualifications and how these qualifications strengthen the new firm
6. Industry and target market	Define the industry the firm will be competing in, along with the segment of the industry the firm will target and how it will be positioned within its target market.
7. Competition	Explain specifically the firm's competitive advantage in the marketplace and how it will compete against more established competitors
8. Intellectual property	Explain the intellectual property the firm owns or will own pending approval
9. Financial projections	Briefly discuss the financials. Stress when the firm will achieve profitability, how much capital it will take to get there, and when its cash flow will break even.
10. Current status, amount of money requested, and the projected use of funds	Discuss the current status of the firm, its accomplishments to date, the amount of money requested, and the projected use of funds. Some experts also recommend that the firm discuss its exit strategy.

Adapted from G. Kawasaki, *The Art of the Start* (New York: Portfolio, 2004).

critical,[35] it is easy for an entrepreneur to get discouraged, particularly if the investor seems to be poking holes in every aspect of the business plan. It helps if the entrepreneur can develop a thick skin and remember that on most occasions investors are simply doing their job. In fact, an investor who is able to identify weaknesses in a business plan does a favor for the entrepreneur. This is because the entrepreneur can take the investor's feedback to heart and use it to improve the product or service. Sometimes, a potential investor's feedback helps the entrepreneur learn how to prepare a more effective presentation. In both of these cases, the investor who seems particularly negative may benefit the entrepreneur.

In the first meeting, investors typically focus on whether a real opportunity exists and whether the management team has the experience and skills to pull off the venture. The investor will also try to sense whether the managers are highly confident in their own venture. The question-and-answer period is extremely important. Here investors are typically looking for how well entrepreneurs think on their feet and how knowledgeable they are about the business venture. Michael Rovner, a partner of Rob Adam's at AV Labs, put it this way: "We ask a lot of peripheral questions. We might not want answers—we just want to evaluate the entrepreneur's thought process."[36]

Chapter Summary

1. A business plan is a written narrative that describes what a new business intends to accomplish and how it plans to achieve its goals.
2. For most ventures, the business plan is a dual-purpose document used both inside and outside the firm. Inside the firm, it helps the company develop a road map to follow in executing its strategies. Outside the firm, it acquaints potential investors and other stakeholders with the business opportunity the firm is pursuing and describes how the business will pursue that opportunity.
3. Writing a business plan can be as valuable as the plan itself. The work required to write a business plan forces the management team to think through every aspect of the business and to establish the most important priorities.
4. Many software packages can assist in the writing of a business plan. These packages provide structure and can save time. However, entrepreneurs should avoid using

business plan software that produces boilerplate material. The information in the plan should always be tailored to the individual business.

5. A summary business plan is 10 to 15 pages and works best for companies in the early stages of development. These companies don't have the information needed for a full business plan but may put together a summary business plan to see if potential investors are interested in their idea. A full business plan, typically 25 to 35 pages, spells out a company's operations and plans in much more detail than a summary business plan and is the usual format for a business plan prepared for an investor. An operational business plan is usually prepared for an internal audience. It is 40 to 100 pages long and provides a blueprint for a company's operations.

6. The executive summary is a quick overview of the entire business plan and provides a busy reader everything that needs to be known about the distinctive nature of the new venture. In many instances, an investor will ask for a copy of a firm's executive summary and will request a copy of the full business plan only when the executive summary is sufficiently convincing.

7. One particularly effective way of describing where a business stands today and what it needs to move forward is to use milestones. A milestone, in a business plan context, is a signpost of a noteworthy event in the past or the future development of a business.

8. The financial portion of a business plan should begin with an explanation of the funding that will be needed by the business during the next 3 to 5 years, along with an explanation of how the funds will be used. This information is called a sources and uses of funds statement.

9. Investors get their money back from investing in a firm through a liquidity event, which is an occurrence that converts some or all of a company's stock into cash. The three most common liquidity events for a new venture are going public, finding a buyer, or merging with another company.

10. When asked to meet with an investor, the managers of a new venture should prepare a set of PowerPoint slides that will fill the time slot allowed for the presentation portion of the meeting. The key topics to cover include the company, the opportunity, the strength of the management team, intellectual property (if there is any), industry analysis, financials, and offering, payback, and exit strategy.

Key Terms

business plan, 100
executive summary, 110
exit strategy, 114
full business plan, 106
liquidity event, 114

milestone, 110
operational business plan, 106
organizational chart, 111
skin in the game, 111

sources and uses of funds
  statement, 114
stealth mode, 111
summary business plan, 106

Review Questions

1. What is a business plan? What are the advantages of preparing a business plan for a new venture? Explain your answer.
2. When is the appropriate time to write a business plan?
3. What are the two primary reasons for writing a business plan?
4. A business plan is often called a selling document for a new company. It what ways does a business plan provide a mechanism for a young company to present itself to potential investors, suppliers, business partners, and key job candidates?
5. It is often argued that the process of writing a business plan is as important as the plan itself, particularly for the top management team of a young firm. How is this so?

6. What are some of the ways to protect the confidentiality of a business plan?

7. What does a company mean when it says it is operating in stealth mode?

8. Why is it necessary for a business plan to be realistic? How will investors typically react if they think a business plan is based on unsubstantiated predictions and estimates rather than on careful thinking and facts? Explain your answer.

9. Why is it important for a business plan to be honest in regard to any gaps (or limitations) that the business has to fill before it is ready to begin earning revenues?

10. Who reads the business plan, and what are they looking for?

11. Why is it important for a business plan to follow a conventional structure rather than be highly innovative and creative?

12. Can business planning software packages be used effectively in preparing a business plan? What are the things to avoid when using such software packages?

13. What are the differences among a summary business plan, a full business plan, and an operational business plan?

14. What should be included on a business plan's cover page? Why is it important to include contact information on the first page of a business plan if the same information is included in the cover letter that accompanies the plan?

15. Many people argue that the executive summary is the most important section in a business plan. What is the basis of this argument? Do you think the executive summary is the most important section in a business plan, or do you think this argument is overstated? Why?

16. Why is it important for a firm to describe the industry in which it intends to compete as part of its business plan? What are the most important topics to discuss in this section?

17. What is the purpose of a sources and uses of funds statement? Why is it important to include this statement in the financial section of a business plan? Explain your answer.

18. What is the purpose of an assumption sheet? Why is it important to include an assumption sheet in a business plan's financial section?

19. What is a liquidity event? Why are investors interested when a new venture thinks that a liquidity event will occur?

20. Why is it important for a business plan to address critical risk factors?

Application Questions

1. Brad Jones is the chief financial officer of an electronic games start-up venture located in San Diego. His firm has decided to apply for venture capital funding and needs a business plan. Brad told Phil Bridge, the firm's CEO, that he could have the plan done in 2 weeks. Phil looked at Brad with surprise and said, "Wouldn't it be better if the entire management team of our firm worked on the plan together?" Brad replied, "The only reason we're writing the plan is to get funding. Getting a lot of people involved would just slow things down and be a waste of their time." Do you agree with Brad? Why or why not?

2. Christina Smith, who lives near Seattle, just left her job with Microsoft to start a business that will sell a new type of fax machine. She knows she'll need a feasibility analysis, a well-articulated business model, and a business plan to get funding, but she can't decide which project to tackle first. If Christina asked you for your advice, what would you tell her, and what rationale for your decision would you provide to Christina?

3. A good friend or yours, Patsy Ford, has decided to leave her teaching job to launch a private tutoring company for grade school and middle school children. She is putting together her business plan and asks you, "I have lots of books and articles that tell me how to write a business plan, but I'm wondering if there is anything in particular I should be careful to avoid in putting my plan together?" How would you respond to Patsy's question?

4. Suppose you have been asked by your local chamber of commerce to teach a 2-hour workshop on how to write an effective business plan. The workshop will be attended by

people who are thinking about starting their own business but don't currently have a business plan. Write a one-page outline detailing what you'd cover in the 2-hour session.

5. John Brunner is a biochemist at a major university. He is thinking about starting a business to commercialize some animal vaccines on which he has been working. John just registered for a biotech investment conference in San Francisco. A number of venture capitalists are on the program, and John hopes to talk to them about his ideas. John hasn't written a business plan and doesn't see the need to write one. When asked about this issue, he told a colleague, "I can sell my ideas without the hassle of writing a business plan. Besides, I'll have plenty of time to talk to investors at the conference. If they need additional information, I can always write something up when I get home." Explain to John why his approach to the development of a business plan is unwise.

6. Imagine you just received an e-mail message from a friend. The message reads, "Just wanted to tell you that I just finished writing my business plan. I'm very proud of it. It's very comprehensive and is just over 100 pages. The executive summary alone is 9 pages. I plan to start sending it out to potential investors next week. Do you have any words of advice for me before I start sending it out? Be honest—I really want to get funding." How would you respond to your friend's request for feedback?

7. Joan Barnes, who is launching a telecommunications start-up, just completed her business plan. She showed it to a close friend who read it and told Joan that she was somewhat surprised by some of the omissions in the plan. Joan's friend told her, "The plan is well written, but it doesn't say anything about the things you need to get your business up and running. The plan makes it sound like you have everything in place. You told me you need to hire a chief technology officer, you need to hire a patent attorney to file your patent applications, and you need to find an outside contractor to build your product." Joan replied, "There is no way that I'm going to tell a potential investor or business partner that I need all those things. I don't want them to think that I'm just starting. If I get the money I need, those things will fall into place very quickly." Do you agree with Joan? Do you think she's on the right track, or is she headed for trouble? Explain your answer.

8. Jared Watts, who lives in Topeka, Kansas, is starting a graphic design business and has just started to write his business plan. Jared was telling a couple of friends at lunch that he plans to write a plan like no one has ever seen before. He plans to skip the basic business plan format and write it in a comic book format to try to grab the attention of investors. Jared thinks the creativity of such a plan would really impress those thinking about investing in a graphic design business. Do you think Jared's idea will work? What are the advantages and disadvantages of Jared's approach?

9. Do some Internet research on business plans. Make a list of at least 10 locations on the Internet that provide access to high-quality advice about how to write an effective business plan, and be prepared to discuss why you find the locations you chose helpful.

10. SureTechRide is the name of an Internet Service Provider start-up that includes a founding team of five entrepreneurs. The founders spent the past 3 weeks writing a business plan that runs 77 pages. They aren't sure if they should go ahead and send it out or if they should try to revise it to make it shorter. The lead entrepreneur, Sally Davis, thinks they should go ahead and send it out, arguing, "The length of the plan will show investors that we really have a grip on things. They will appreciate our hard work." Do you agree with Sally? Should they go ahead and send out the plan, or should they revise it and try to make it shorter? Why?

11. Peter Ford, who lives in Fort Collins, Colorado, has read several books on how to raise money to fund a new venture. All of them say that investors focus on the strength of the top management team. Peter can't figure out why this is true. Recently, he wrote a letter to the editor of *Inc.* magazine and asked, "Why do investors put so much stock in the strength of the top management team of a start-up? If the start-up's product and marketing strategy isn't any good, what is the value of a strong top management team?" If you were the editor of *Inc.*, how would you reply to Peter's letter?

12. Recently, Jill, Diane, and Steven, the founders of a digital photography start-up, presented their business plan to a group of investors in hopes of obtaining funding. One of the

investors asked the three, "How much of your personal money do you each have invested in the venture?" Is this an appropriate question? Why would an investor want to know how much of their personal money Jill, Diane, and Steven had invested in the start-up?

13. Tom Popper, who is launching a designer-clothing start-up, recently met with a consultant to talk about the process of writing a business plan. The consultant emphasized that the financial projections in the business plan should be based on a set of well-thought-out assumptions that can be clearly explained in the plan. If after the meeting Tom asked you why it is important to base the financial projections in a business plan on well-thought-out assumptions, what would you tell him?

14. Tracey Williams just got off the phone with an angel investor and is ecstatic because the investor asked her and her management team to present their business plan next Thursday at 1:00 P.M. The investor said the meeting would last 1 hour and that 30 minutes would be devoted to the presentation of the business plan and that the remaining 30 minutes would be devoted to a question-and-answer session. Tracey wants to make the best of this opportunity and has turned to you for advice. How would you advise Tracey to prepare for this meeting?

15. Suppose you are asked to serve as a judge for a local business plan competition. In preparing for the competition, the organizer has asked you to write a very brief article titled "What the judges of business plan competitions look for" that she plans to pass along to the entrepreneurs who enter the competition. Write a 500- to 600-word article to accommodate this request.

MooBella
www.moobella.com

Business Idea: Use patented new technologies to produce fresh, made-to-order scoops of ice cream that are dispensed from a vending machine in 45 seconds.

Pitch: MooBella is pioneering a new and exciting sales channel for fresh, made-to-order ice cream. The ice cream is dispensed through attractive, state-of-the-art vending machines that are suitable for any location. The company's technologies enable the machines to make ice cream on the spot. The customer orders by choosing from 12 flavors and three kinds of mix to create one of 96 possible combinations of ice cream and mix. The combinations include "Low Fat Vanilla with Walnuts" and "Premium Strawberry with Chocolate Chips." The ice cream is made right on the spot, through a combination of patented technologies that interact, aerate, flavor, mix, and flash-freeze the ingredients just inside the vending machine. While the ice cream is being made, the customer is kept abreast of the process through a checklist shown on the front of the machine. Each of the following steps illuminates when the customer's scoop is passing through the step:

✓ Adding ice cream
✓ Adding flavor
✓ Adding mix
✓ Forming scoop

This approach provides the machines an entertainment value as customers watch and imagine how their ice cream is being made. The ice cream is dispensed in roughly 40 seconds.

Each MooBella machine is equipped with Internet wireless capabilities that allow the machines to track sales data, monitor inventory, and issue maintenance alerts. As part of the company's branding campaign, each vending machine and ice cream cup prominently displays the company's tagline, which captures the essence of the MooBella experience: Quick. Fresh. Now. Wow!

MooBella's vending machines should be attractive to host locations because the premium price charged increases margins for both MooBella and its hosts. The company is rolling out its first machines in the Boston area and will go nationwide after completing its pilot tests.

Q&A: Based on the material covered in this chapter, what questions would you ask the firm's founders before making your funding decision? What answers would satisfy you?

Decision: If you had to make your decision on just the information provided in the pitch and on the company's Web site, would you fund this firm? Why or why not?

 **VC** **4.2**

Zillow
www.zillow.com

Business Idea: Help people make smarter real estate decisions by providing them free, fast, and accurate estimates of the values of the properties they are interested in.

Pitch: If you've ever looked for a home, you know what a hassle it can be. It's hard to know if a particular property is undervalued or overvalued and if the real estate agent is being forthright. It's also hard to know where to go to get good information if you want to do your own research. Most people only buy homes, or investment properties, a few times in their lives. As a result, it's not practical to become an expert on real estate valuations.

Zillow is an online real estate service that was created to help solve these problems. It helps people obtain objective home value estimates for free. To use Zillow, all you have to do is go to the company's Web site and type in the address of the property you're interested in. In a few seconds you will get an estimate—or "zestimate"—of the value of the home. (Go ahead and try it for the home you were raised in. Is the estimated value about what you expected?) The service offers several other features as well, including value changes of homes in a given time frame, aerial views of homes (using Google maps), and the prices of the homes in the surrounding area. It also provides basic data on homes, such as square footage and the number of bedrooms and bathrooms.

The way Zillow generates its values is by buying massive amounts of real estate information from commercial data collectors, including home addresses, tax assessments, square footage, number of bedrooms, prior sales, and so on. The company's computers then identify similar homes that recently sold in the same neighborhood and use mathematical models to create an "estimated market value" for each individual home. The number is only meant to be an estimate. The data the company collects is stronger in some areas than in others. Zillow plans to make money through online advertising.

By the way, if you're wondering where the name Zillow came from, wonder no more. Even though the company is about data, a home is much more—it's where you lay your head to rest at night, like on a pillow. Thus, "Zillow" was born.

Q&A: Based on the material covered in this chapter, what questions would you ask the firm's founders before making your funding decision? What answers would satisfy you?

Decision: If you had to make your decision on just the information provided in the pitch and on the company's Web site, would you fund this firm? Why or why not?

CASE **4.1**

Kazoo & Company: You Can Compete Against the Big Guys—If You Have the Right Plan

www.kazootoys.com

Bruce R. Barringer,
University of Central Florida

R. Duane Ireland,
Texas A&M University

Introduction

There is no denying it. It's tough for an independent toy store to compete against Wal-Mart, Target, Toys "Я" Us, and other large retailers selling products that entertain children and adults alike. So how is it that Kazoo Toys, an independent toy store in Denver, Colorado, is thriving? It's thriving because of two things—the firm has a doggedly determined entrepreneur at the helm and it has a good business plan. After you read about Kazoo Toys,

you'll nod your head and think to yourself, yup—that's a good plan!

Diana Nelson

In the early 1990s, Diana Nelson left the corporate world with the intention of spending more time with her two young sons. In 1998, she decided to reenter the workforce, but this time as an entrepreneur. Rather than starting a company from scratch, she set out looking for a business to buy. After ruling out fast food and flower shops, she came across a toy store named Kazoo & Company. She saw untapped potential in the store and decided to buy it. It wasn't easy to get the money together to close the deal. To finance the purchase, she cashed out her retirement accounts, put $25,000 on credit cards, borrowed money from her father, and set up a $500,000 SBA-guaranteed bank loan. "I gambled everything to buy a toy store," she says. The actions Nelson took to finance her venture demonstrate the courage that characterizes virtually all entrepreneurs.

From the outset, Nelson had no illusions that owning a toy store would be easy. When she bought Kazoo, independent toy stores were being tattered to pieces by Wal-Mart, Toys "Я" Us, and other large retailers. So, she knew that the only way to beat them was to outthink them. In this regard, Nelson saw her challenge as that of designing and then implementing a business plan that would make a small toy store competitive. Here's how she did it.

Kazoo's Business Plan

The essence of Kazoo's business plan was to not try to be like Wal-Mart or Toys "Я" Us. Instead, Nelson set out to build a business that would offer unique products and services to its clientele. The mistake that many small businesses make, in Nelson's thinking, is that they set themselves up to compete against the chains (e.g., Toys "Я" Us) or a supercenter (Wal-Mart) by trying to duplicate what they do. In these instances, the best an entrepreneurial venture can expect to do is to come close to being as effective at what the "big boys" are skilled at doing. Instead of falling into that trap, Nelson took Kazoo in a different direction. "We changed our whole merchandise mix to not carry the same product (as the nationwide chains did)," she recalls, "so price competition isn't an issue." As a result of this strategy, Kazoo doesn't carry Mattel, Crayola, or Fisher-Price. Instead, the store sells unique items like Gotz Dolls from Germany and a wide range of educational toys. The key to making this strategy work, Nelson found, is to build strong relationships with vendors. To help do this, Nelson invites many of Kazoo's vendors to demo and test new products in her store. Doing this gives Kazoo first crack at many of the new products that its vendors make. While they are in her store, the vendors also tip their hand from time to time regarding what the big retailers are buying. This gives Nelson and Kazoo a heads-up about what not to buy.

In 1999, Nelson opened a Yahoo! store online, which has evolved into Kazoo's online store, Kazoo.com. The site sells the same type of toys being sold in the store. Internet sales were slow at first but now represent about 40 percent of the company's income. Nelson's strong relationships with her vendors paid off again as a driver of business to the firm's Web site. Because of a strong and positive relationship, some of the products that Kazoo sells online are drop-shipped directly by the manufacturer to Kazoo's customers. In addition, some specialty toy makers who don't have their own e-commerce sites refer customer inquires directly to the Kazoo site.

At one point, Nelson considered franchising Kazoo but decided to pass on the idea. Instead, she felt it was better to preserve Kazoo's "destination" image and build the e-commerce site.

Points of Differentiation

Through all of this, Kazoo has established strong points of differentiation between itself and its much larger competitors, which has been the heart of Kazoo's business plan from the beginning. Along with carrying different products than its competitors, Kazoo is different from Wal-Mart, Toys "Я" Us, and other large toy retailers in the following ways.

1. The company welcomes professionals, like speech therapists, to bring their patients into the store, to play with them and identify specific toys that might help them progress in their treatments. Observing professionals work with their patients (i.e., young children that have some type of disability) also helps Kazoo's staff know what to recommend when a parent comes in looking for a similar solution.
2. Kazoo's store design is unique. While the store itself is still fairly small, it is further broken down into smaller, more intimate departments. "When a particular consumer goes into a Toys "Я" Us it has departments, but it's like a big warehouse," Nelson explains. "Here, it's very small. It's intimate, but it's also departmentalized, so you actually have a Playmobil department, and you have a Thomas the Tank Engine department."
3. The company focuses intently on customer service. This facet of Kazoo's operations is particularly apparent in its e-commerce site. As evidence of this, the following comment was posted recently on a Yahoo! bulletin board site, where a consumer wrote a comment about his experience shopping at Kazoo.com:

   > Old-fashioned friendly service. When I called to check the delivery date of a little piano I had ordered for my grandson, I was actually speaking to a person that was friendly, polite, courteous, and just delightful. I will continue to buy from this company. They have a real interest in giving top-quality service. It has been a most enjoyable experience.

4. The company's specialty is selling educational, nonviolent toys, for birth to 12-year-old children. In fact, Kazoo's focus on selling toys that meet this criterion has won it a loyal clientele.
5. The inventory in the store is freshened up frequently, so regular customers see different toys each time they come into the store. "If you think about your regular customer, they don't want to see the same stuff on the shelf all the time, so we're always changing our inventory and our mix of what we do," Nelson said.

Kazoo's business plan and its sharp execution have paid off. Business is growing, and the company was selected as one of the Top 5 Specialty Retail Toy Stores in North America by the Toy Industry Association in 2002, 2003, and 2004.

Challenges Ahead

Although Kazoo & Company has done well, there are many challenges that lie ahead. For one, a lot of the manufacturers of specialty toys, which have been Kazoo's bread-and-butter since Nelson bought the firm in 1998, are now selling into broader channels. Thus, the toys that at one time only Kazoo and other specialty toy stores could get their hands on will be popping up in other types of stores. Economic pressures, like the high price of gasoline, also tend to hit specialty retailers particularly hard. Tough economic times drive more people to Wal-Mart and Target, as opposed to specialty stores.

As far as Diana Nelson is concerned, she is very content with her decision to become an entrepreneur and the lifestyle that accompanies that decision as the owner of Kazoo & Company. Commenting on how her young sons fared over the years with her decision to buy a toy store, she said, "There friends think—how cool are they that their mom has a toy store and a toy business." How cool indeed!

Discussion Questions

1. To what extent do you sense that Diana Nelson got up to speed quickly on the dynamics of the toy industry when she took over Kazoo & Company in 1998? What impact would it have had on the ultimate success of Kazoo if Diana had spent more time initially focused on the specifics of her business (i.e., store layout, hiring personnel, placing ads in local newspapers, writing press releases, setting up the accounting

system, and so on) rather than gaining a complete understanding of the toy industry as part of her work to carefully develop a business plan?

2. When she first bought the store do you think that Diana Nelson could have convinced an investor that Kazoo & Company could successfully compete against the likes of giants such as Wal-Mart, Target, and Toys "Я" Us? If not, who needed to believe that the business plan would work? How does an entrepreneur's level of belief in his or her own business plan affect how successful the business is, particularly in the early years?

3. Based on the information contained in the case, write the one-page executive summary of Kazoo's original business plan.

4. What is drop-shipping? What are the advantages and the risks for a company like Kazoo & Company to engage in drop-shipping arrangements with its vendors?

Application Questions

1. If you had taken over Kazoo & Company in 1998 instead of Diana Nelson, would you have thought of all the things that Diana did? Would you have been able to write Kazoo's original business plan? If your answer is *no* to these questions, what steps can you take now to better prepare yourself for the day that you might become an entrepreneur? Make your answer as specific as possible.

2. If you decided to buy a specialty store that competes against Wal-Mart, Target, or another big-box retailer, what type of store would you like to own? How would you differentiate your store from your larger competitors?

Source: B. Ruggiero, "Kazoo & Company Reaches Top 5 . . . Again," *TD Monthly*, June 2005; J. M. Webb, "When the Tools of the Trade Are Toys," *TD Monthly*, March 2006.

Pandora: How a Willingness to Let Its Business Plan Evolve Helped a Music Company Move Forward When the Timing Was Right
www.pandora.com

Bruce R. Barringer,
University of Central Florida
R. Duane Ireland,
Texas A&M University

Introduction

If you like music you'll be delighted to learn about Pandora. Pandora is a Web site that allows its members

to express their musical preferences and then create "radio stations" (or streaming music stations) that play only the type of music that they like. There are two versions of the service—one that costs $3.00 per month and one that is free. So if you like Shania Twain, you can log onto Pandora, click one button, and listen to Shania Twain and artists that have similar vocal qualities as Shania Twain for hours on end, without touching your computer again. And if you hear a song you're not familiar with, a quick glance at Pandora will tell you who the artist is and what CD the song came from.

Although Pandora's service is fairly new, the company has been around since 1999. While its basic mission and goals haven't changed, the company sputtered in the early 2000s trying several approaches to execute its business plan. Rather than panic, the founder and management team remained patient, waiting for the time when the market was right to launch its service. That time arrived in 2005 and the company hasn't looked back since. The following explanation of what Pandora is, and why the timing was right to move the company forward in 2005, illustrates how patience and a willingness to let its business plan evolve allowed Pandora to move forward at exactly the right time.

Tim Westergren and The Music Genome Project

Pandora is the creation of Tim Westergren, a musician and composer. In the 1990s, he was employed as a film composer, writing the music that underlies the motion in a film. Film directors would often come to him with a couple of songs and say, "I like this sound for a particular scene. Can you compose music that has the same qualities as these songs for the scene in my film?" This process got Westergren thinking that every song has a certain set of attributes that define the type of sound that results. These thoughts were going through Westergren's mind in the late 1990s when online music was just starting to explode. Westergren started thinking, "Wow, if I could automate the process of breaking down the attributes of a song, and then use those attributes to help find similar songs, that could really be a powerful medium." Westergren speculated that the process could help a person that likes Metallica, for example, find other bands that sound just like Metallica, but no one knows about. As a musician, and a member of several rock bands when he was younger, one thing that always frustrated Westergren and his colleagues was how to get noticed. Westergren felt that the service he was contemplating could help people find new music they liked and help unknown artists become noticed.

To develop a methodology to identify the attributes in a song, Westergren created "The Music Genome Project," which is a think tank so to speak, and put it inside a for-profit company he named Pandora. The purpose of The Music Genome Project was to develop the methodology for breaking down the attributes of individual songs. A total of 400 attributes were identified that deal with specific aspects of melody, harmony, form, rhythm, instrumentation, vocal quality, and lyrical content. Musicians were hired to evaluate and classify

individual songs. The science moved forward and Westergren and his team developed a solid methodology for identifying the attributes of individual songs (and individual artists) and for employing that knowledge to find similar songs.

Early Failures

Pandora's basic business plan was to use its proprietary methodology to (1) help people find new music, (2) help unknown artists get noticed, and (3) make money in the process. Early on, it tried and failed twice to achieve these objectives. Its first attempt was to build an e-commerce company and sell music online. That approach was quickly abandoned. Its second attempt was to license its technology to retailers that had some type of music service. That approach was abandoned as well. The company hung on in 2002 and 2003, which were tough years for most start-up firms.

A New Direction

At the beginning of 2004, Pandora raised some venture capital funding, based on the strength of its technology, and was finally able to take a breath. Its mission and goals remained intact, and a new approach to implementing its business plan was starting to emerge. It was becoming increasingly clear to Westergren that the company should focus on online "listening" (like a music radio station does) as its core value proposition. Fortunately, several factors were converging that hadn't been in place before. More and more people were using the Internet, most users were converting to high-speed Internet connectivity, and the music industry was looking for positive ways to promote its music. These developments breathed new life into Pandora and Pandora as we know it today was born.

How Pandora Works

The way Pandora now works is like this. A user logs on to the site and types in the name of a favorite song or artist and then hits go (after registering on the site, which is free). As soon as the go button is hit, Pandora scans its entire database and identifies the songs that have the same musical genome (or DNA) as the song or artist the user chose. If the user stops here, Pandora will play songs that are similar to the song (or artist) the users selected for hours on end free of charge. The user can tweak the service in a number of ways, such as giving individual songs a thumbs-up or a thumbs-down. This process helps Pandora actually "learn" what an individual user likes, which improves the likelihood that subsequent songs will be more to the user's taste. For variety, a user can set up multiple music "stations" to listen to. A particular type of song or an individual artist is a station. The unique thing about this service is that it exposes users to songs and musicians that they wouldn't have know about before.

Pandora makes money in three ways. First, the free service is advertiser supported. Ads appear alongside the music results. Second, a user can eliminate the ads by paying a $3.00 per month subscription fee. Finally, if a user likes a particular song that Pandora is playing, the user can click through to Amazon.com and buy the CD or to iTunes and buy the individual song. Pandora receives an affiliate fee from Amazon.com and iTunes for each purchase that is made.

Lessons Learned and Pandora's Future

Although Pandora isn't yet profitable, it has high hopes for the future. It receives an enormous amount of correspondence from its users, who rave about the service. In general, the record companies have been supportive of Pandora's service and are now routinely sending Pandora all of their new music. The general notion is that if Pandora can get more people listening to music, that's good for the industry. All told, it seems that Pandora has created a win-win business model for everyone involved.

A lesson that can be learned from Pandora's experience is that sometimes a company must let its business plan evolve. When Pandora was founded in 1999, the service it has today wouldn't have been possible. There simply weren't enough Internet users with high-speed Internet connections at the time to make the service practical. (A high-speed Internet connection is needed to make Pandora work.) Another lesson to be learned is that a business plan should be a living, breathing document that can be changed. Parts of Pandora's business plan have never changed from the day the company was launched. The parts of the plan dealing with the company's business model, and how it was to be implemented, obviously did change—to Pandora's ultimate benefit.

Pandora's future is now a numbers game. The question is whether the company can attract a large-enough critical mass of users to cover its overhead and provide an adequate return on its investment.

Discussion Questions

1. Go to Pandora's Web site and give it a try. (Nothing will be downloaded onto your computer—Pandora's service runs off your Internet browser.) What do you think? Do you think Pandora will attract a large number of users? Will you use the service again? Explain your answers.

2. What are the most critical risk factors associated with Pandora's current business plan?

3. What do you think motivated Pandora's investors to put money into the company in 2004, even though Pandora had failed to effectively monetize its technology on two separate occasions?

4. Pandora has investors who will no doubt want their money back plus a handsome return at some point in the not-to-distant future. What is the most likely liquidity event in Pandora's future?

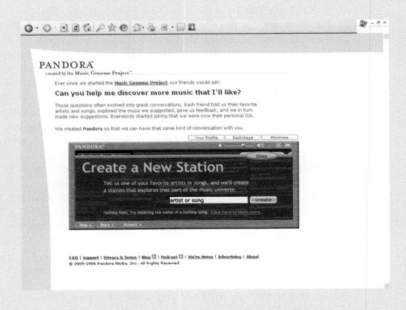

Application Questions

1. Make a list of the parties with a vested interest in Pandora's success. How can each of these parties (i.e., independent musicians, record companies, etc.) help make Pandora successful? Make your list as complete as possible.

2. Think of a time in your life when (1) you committed yourself to achieve something substantial, (2) your first few attempts to achieve it failed, and (3) you eventually found a way to be successful. What made you persevere despite your early failures? Compare your experience to Tim Westergren's experience with Pandora.

Source: Pandora homepage, www.pandora.com (accessed May 6, 2006); L. Laporte A. MacArthur, and T. Westergren. "Inside the Net 006: Tim Westergren, Pandora." Inside the Net Podcast, January 6, 2006.

Endnotes

1. Personal interview with Erica Fand, August 30, 2006.
2. *Entrepreneur's Toolkit* (Boston: Harvard Business School Publishing, 2005).
3. S. Barlett, "Seat of the Pants," *Inc.*, October 15, 2002: 38–40.
4. Wells Fargo, "How Much Money Does It Take to Start a Small Business?" Wells Fargo/Gallup Small Business Index, August 15, 2006.
5. *Sunday Herald*, "The Mentor's Steps to Success," April 16, 2006.
6. Ernst & Young, *Outline for a Business Plan* (New York: Ernst & Young, 1997).
7. Adam Jolly, *From Idea to Profit* (Kogan Page: London, 2005).
8. Deloitte & Touche, *Writing an Effective Business Plan* (New York: Deloitte & Touche, 2003).
9. R. W. Price, *Roadmap to Entrepreneurial Success* (New York: AMACOM, 2004).
10. S. Kemper, *Code Name Ginger: The Story Behind Segway and Dean Kamen's Quest to Invent a New World* (Boston: Harvard Business School Press, 2003).
11. D. Valentine, "Don Valentine: Sequoia Capital," in *Done Deals: Venture Capitalists Tell Their Stories*, ed. U. Gupta (Boston: Harvard Business School Press, 2000), 173.
12. S. R. Rich and D. E. Gumpert, "How to Write a Winning Business Plan," in *The Entrepreneurial Venture,* eds. W. A. Sahlman and H. H. Stevenson (New York: McGraw-Hill, 1992), 127–37.
13. Deloitte & Touche, *Writing an Effective Business Plan.*
14. G. Kawasaki, *The Art of the Start* (New York: Portfolio, 2004).
15. J. L. Nesheim, *The Power of Unfair Advantage* (New York: Free Press, 2005).
16. Personal conversation with Michael Heller, January 20, 2002.
17. *Entrepreneur's Toolkit* (Boston: Harvard Business School Publishing, 2005).
18. U. Looser and B. Schlapfer, *The New Venture Adventure* (New York: Texere, 2001).
19. S. Rogers, *The Entrepreneur's Guide to Finance and Business* (New York: McGraw-Hill, 2003).
20. *Entrepreneur's Toolkit* (Boston: Harvard Business School Publishing, 2005).
21. *Entrepreneur's Toolkit* (Boston: Harvard Business School Publishing, 2005).
22. S. C. Harper, *The McGraw-Hill Guide to Starting Your Own Business*, 2nd ed. (New York: McGraw-Hill, 2003).
23. Primus Venture homepage, www.primus.com (accessed August 29, 2006).
24. A. Afuah, *Business Models* (Boston: McGraw-Hill, 2004).
25. R. Abrams, *The Successful Business Plan* (Palo Alto, CA: Running 'R' Media, 2000).
26. Investorwords.com, www.investorwords.com (accessed March 3, 2003).
27. *Entrepreneur's Toolkit* (Boston: Harvard Business School Publishing, 2005).
28. Abrams, *The Successful Business Plan.*
29. Looser and Schlapfer, *The New Venture Adventure.*
30. J. L. Nesheim, *High-Tech Start Up* (New York: Free Press, 2000).
31. Abrams, *The Successful Business Plan.*
32. Harper, *The McGraw-Hill Guide to Starting Your Own Business.* 2nd ed. (New York: McGraw-Hill, 2003).

33. S. Eng, "Impress Investors with Your Firm's Endgame," www.startup.wsj.com (accessed November 28, 2001).

34. Nesheim, *High-Tech Start Up.*

35. Nesheim, *High-Tech Start Up.*

36. R. Adams, *A Good Hard Kick In the Ass* (New York: Crown Books, 2002), 150.

asrbiz.com

Zone 57 Inc.

Getting Personal

with **EVAN SHAPIRO**

What I do when I'm not working	My advice to new entrepreneurs	Best part of being a student
Playing my guitar or basketball or hang out with my girlfriend	*Be persistent on your path, but open to new ideas*	*It's easier than being an entrepreneur*

Blue Maze Entertainment:

Occupying a Unique Position in a Difficult Industry—and Thriving

The music industry may be one of the worst industries in which to start a new firm. It is plagued by low-profit margins, fierce competition, and piracy—factors that have created a poor environment for start-ups. It is also in the midst of change, and has been since music was digitized and the Internet has enabled people to share music online. The emergence of Apple's iTunes Music Store and similar services that allow people to buy individual songs has also been a big change.

In the midst of all of these changes, Evan Shapiro and Mitch Towbin, two business students at Emory University in Atlanta, started a music company. Their company, Blue Maze Entertainment, was launched in 2000 while Shapiro, who is shown in the picture, was still in college. The initial plan was to build an all-purpose music company, with elements of production, promotion, and distribution. That plan never fully panned out. By 2003, Shapiro and Towbin repositioned Blue Maze, and it is now a profitable, branded music company.

To understand how Blue Maze reached its current stage of development, a little background information is in order. In 1999, Evan Shapiro, who was then a junior, took a break from his studies at Emory and interned at a record label in New York City. That was a pivotal experience for Shapiro. It exposed him to the music industry and gave him the desire to start a music company of his own.

Back at Emory, it didn't take Shapiro long to follow through on his ambition. In 2000, he started Blue Maze with recent graduate Mitch Towbin. The initial plan to make Blue Maze an all-purpose music company turned out to be a

EVAN SHAPIRO

Cofounder, Blue Maze Entertainment
Goizueta Business School
Emory University, 2003

EMORY
UNIVERSITY

MITCH TOWBIN

Cofounder, Blue Maze Entertainment
Goizueta Business School
Emory University, 2003

Currently in my iPod	My biggest surprise as an entrepreneur	First entrepreneurial experience
Incubus, Chili Peppers and Atmosphers	*How quickly markets can change*	*Trading baseball cards*

After studying this chapter you should be ready to:

L E A R N I N G

Objectives

1. Explain the purpose of an industry analysis.

2. Identify the five competitive forces that determine industry profitability.

3. Explain the role of "barriers to entry" in creating disincentives for firms to enter an industry.

4. Identify the nontraditional barriers to entry that are especially associated with entrepreneurial firms.

5. List the four industry-related questions to ask before pursuing the idea for a firm.

6. Identify the five primary industry types and the opportunities they offer.

7. Explain the purpose of a competitor analysis.

8. Identify the three groups of competitors a new firm will face.

9. Describe ways a firm can ethically obtain information about its competitors.

10. Describe the reasons for completing a competitive analysis grid.

tough go. Although Blue Maze experienced some success, 2001 and 2002 were difficult years in the industry, and there wasn't a clear need for another all-purpose music company. Rather than give up, the two decided to reposition Blue Maze as a branded music company—an area in which they had had good success. Branded music is a fairly new concept that combines music with a company's brand to create a unique promotional product. An example is a clothing company that attaches a tag to every pair of blue jeans that it sells. The tag contains a music download card that allows the buyer to download one or more songs for free. The songs are carefully selected to enhance the company's brand and create buzz surrounding its products.

Blue Maze is now in the business of creating branded music products and managing branded music campaigns. Its clients set up their campaigns as either branded, value-added incentives (like the blue jeans example just mentioned) or as memorable gift-with-purchase programs. The music is distributed via a limited run of CDs or DVDs or through music download cards. The recipients of the music vary depending on the nature of the campaign. In some instances, the music is distributed to everyone who attends an event or buys a product. In other cases, it is limited to contest winners, opinion leaders, or trendsetters. One competitive advantage that Blue Maze maintains is its access to the freshest progressive urban sounds. It is the latest music that cannot yet be found on the radio or in a record store. For example, Blue Maze produced a CD titled *21st Century Style*. This product featured tracks from today's top emerging and established progressive-urban artists and was used as a free promotional incentive and branding vehicle at retail and live fashion and music events. The CDs were cobranded by Blue Maze and Enyce, a designer of men's and women's urban fashions and one of Blue Maze's customers. Blue Maze makes money by producing branded music on an a-la-carte basis or by managing entire campaigns.

Another differentiator for Blue Maze, and a particularly promising product that the company has created, is called The Virtual CD (VCD). It is a digital representation of a CD, which emulates the process of opening a CD and flipping through the booklet inside. It is placed on a Web site and contains both streaming music and music downloads, as well as links to e-commerce opportunities. By presenting a robust, self-contained format, The Virtual CD provides innovative product placement opportunities while associating the presenting brand with the hottest music. It also includes a "Send VCD to a Friend" feature, which allows users to share the application with friends, in a viral manner. A sample of a Virtual CD is shown on Blue Maze's Web site.[1]

Today, Shapiro and Towbin feel Blue Maze is well positioned for the future. Rather than slugging it out with the major record labels, as they intended to do when their company was founded as an all-purpose music company, Blue Maze is now firmly positioned in a growing niche in the music industry. As such, Blue Maze is able to service both brands and record labels in a harmonious fashion.

In this chapter, we'll look at industry analysis and competitor analysis. The first section of the chapter considers **industry analysis**, which is business research that focuses on the potential of an industry. An **industry** is a group of firms producing a similar product or service, such as music, fitness drinks, or electronic games. Once it is determined that a new venture is feasible in regard to the industry and market in which it will compete, a more in-depth analysis is needed to learn the ins and outs of the industry the firm plans to enter. This analysis helps a firm determine if the niche or vertical markets it identified during its feasibility analysis are accessible and which ones represent the best point of entry for a new firm.

The second section of the chapter focuses on competitor analysis. A **competitor analysis** is a detailed evaluation of a firm's competitors. Once a firm decides to enter an industry and chooses a market in which to compete, it must gain an understanding of its competitive environment. We'll look at how a firm identifies its competition and the importance of completing a competitive analysis grid.

Industry Analysis

When studying an industry, an entrepreneur must answer three questions before pursuing the idea of starting a firm. First, is the industry accessible—in other words, is it a realistic place for a new venture to enter? Second, does the industry contain markets that are ripe for innovation or are underserved? Third, are there positions in the industry that will avoid some of the negative attributes of the industry as a whole? It is useful for a new venture to think about its **position** at both the company level and the product or service level.

The importance of knowing the competitive landscape, which is what an industry is, may have been first recognized in the fourth century B.C. by Sun-tzu, a Chinese philosopher. Reputedly he wrote *The Art of War* to help generals prepare for battle. However, the ideas in the book are still used today to help managers prepare their firms for the competitive wars of the marketplace. The following quote from Sun-tzu's work points out the importance of industry analysis:

> We are not fit to lead an army on the march unless we are familiar with the face of the country—its pitfalls and precipices, its marshes and swamps.[2]

These words serve as a reminder to entrepreneurs that regardless of how eager they are to start their businesses, they are not adequately prepared until they are "familiar with the face of the country"—that is, until they understand the industry or industries they plan to enter.

The Importance of Industry Versus Firm-Specific Factors

To illustrate the importance of the industry a firm chooses to enter, research has shown that both firm- and industry-specific factors contribute to a firm's profitability.[3] Firm-level factors include a firm's assets, products, culture, teamwork among its employees, reputation, and other resources. Industry-specific factors include the threat of new entrants, rivalry among existing firms, the bargaining power of suppliers, and other factors discussed in this chapter. A number of studies have tried to determine whether firm-specific or industry-specific factors are more important when it comes to affecting a firm's potential to generate profits. Virtually all the studies have concluded that firm-specific factors are the most important, although the industry a firm chooses is important too.[4] In various studies, researchers have found that from 8 to 30 percent of the variation in firm profitability is directly attributable to the industry in which a firm competes. In a recent study, two researchers, including Harvard University professor Michael Porter, the author of the five competitive forces framework discussed in the next section, found that 19 percent of the variation in firm profitability is attributable to stable industry effects. Commenting on the 19 percent figure, Porter concluded, "This result provides strong support for the idea that industry membership has an important influence on [firm] profitability."[5] The industry a firm is in may matter even more for firms that are not well positioned in their industries and do not have products or services that are clearly differentiated from the pack—an unenviable position on both counts. In these instances, the firms involved basically ride the tide of an industry's economic fortunes, because they are not able to insulate themselves from an industry's ups and downs.[6] An example of firm that lost a favorable position in its industry, and the consequences it suffered as a result, is provided in the "What Went Wrong" feature nearby.

LEARNING

Objective

1. Explain the purpose of an industry analysis.

Bath & Body Works: How One Company Lost a Favorable Position in an Industry

www.bathandbodyworks.com

Once a company establishes a favorable position in an industry, it must remain vigilant or its position can be lost. This is what happened to Bath & Body Works in the early 2000s. For over 10 years, the company had been selling, with great success, midprice body and personal care products, primarily through stores in malls. From 1993 to 2000, the company grew at an incredible rate of 51 percent per year, soaring to nearly $2 billion in annual sales. But then the bottom fell out. The company's revenues dropped 19 percent from 2000 to 2002, and it lost nearly 40 percent of its pretax income. What went wrong? The company simply lost its favorable position in the marketplace. Here's how it happened.

Bath & Body Works was launched in 1990 by Leslie Wexner, founder of The Limited. The hunch was that there was a favorable position in the health and beauty products market just waiting to be filled—a position just above the drug store and just below the department store in terms of pricing. Bath & Body Works moved into this position and opened a chain of cheerful and wholesome stores, brimming over with fruit- and flower-scented soaps, creams, oils, scented candles, and other accessories. For millions of shoppers, Bath & Body Works' positioning was just right. It offered attractive and fun products at a price that was high enough to be enticing but low enough to be affordable. The company grew from 15 stores in 1990 to more than 1,300 in 2000.

By the year 2000, however, things had turned sour. Competing retailers, such as Aveda, Sephora, and Origins began opening stores in malls—Bath & Body Works' turf—and started offering fresh new products, like all-natural and organic compounds. Their stores were well organized and pleasant, with signature music always playing. More importantly, they offered a different approach to beauty than the homey approach offered by Bath & Body Works. Their product lines wove together elements of science, design, fitness, relaxation, and psychology, which resonated with consumers. People were willing to spend a little more for their fresher and more sophisticated offerings, particularly in the area of facial creams and makeup. At the same time this was happening, Target, Wal-Mart, and the other big-box retailers were nipping at Bath & Body Works from the low end, particularly in the area of body lotions,

soaps, and accessories. The big boxes started carrying products that looked just like those sold at Bath & Body Works, but were cheaper.

As the result of these factors, which unfolded quickly, Bath & Body Works lost its edge and was no longer seen as distinctive and special. The company was outflanked by Aveda, Sephora, and others at the top end of the market and by Target, Wal-Mart, and others at the bottom end. To counter its slipping sales, Bath & Body Works started to rely more and more on discounts, promotions, and sales. According to Neil Fiske, the company's newly hired CEO, "In 2002, during our critical holiday time period, there were twenty-two in-store deals at Bath & Body Works. It was like a garage sale with deal signs all over." Stated plainly, Bath & Body Works lost the favorable position it had occupied in the bath and beauty products industry for over 10 years. It was essentially stuck in the middle, with no discernible competitive advantage.

Fortunately, Bath & Body Works' leaders recognized its rapidly deteriorating plight and hired Neil Fiske, a Boston Consulting Group veteran, to revive the company and reestablish its position in the marketplace. Fiske started by reconnecting the company with its customers and refashioning its product line based on more contemporary customer preferences and tastes. As a result, over time, a bevy of new partners have been brought on board, enabling the company to enhance its product offerings and update its stores. Shoppers may now purchase many non-Bath & Body Works brands in the stores, which has created a marketplace that brings together all kinds of offerings at many price points, to appeal to a broad cross section of mall shoppers. This new strategy seems to be working. The company is growing again and has returned to profitability.

Questions for Critical Thinking

1. What steps, if any, could Bath & Body Works have taken to prevent the loss of its favorable position in the bath and beauty products marketplace in the early 2000s?

2. Look at the Web sites of Bath & Body Works and Sephora, one of the other firms mentioned in the feature. How would you describe the positioning

differences between Bath & Body Works and Sephora today? Which firm do you think has the most distinct positioning strategy?

3. Why do you think Bath & Body Works seemed to get caught off-guard by emerging competition at the top end from Sephora and others and the bottom end from Target and Wal-Mart?

4. Use Table 5.2 to complete an industry analysis on the bath and beauty products industry today. Is it an attractive industry? Would it be a good or poor industry for a start-up firm to enter?

Sources: Bath & Body Works homepage, www.bathandbodyworks.com, (accessed August 8, 2006); M. J. Silverstein and J. Butman, *Treasure Hunt* (New York: Portfolio).

Because both firm- and industry-level factors are important in determining a firm's profitability, there are firms that do well in unattractive or moderately attractive industries, as illustrated in the JetBlue case, if they are well positioned. Still, the overall attractiveness of an industry should be part of the equation when an entrepreneur decides whether to pursue a particular business opportunity. A new venture can use the five forces model shown below to assess the overall attractiveness of the industry it plans to enter and to determine if a favorable position to occupy exists in that industry.

The Five Competitive Forces That Determine Industry Profitability

The five competitive forces model is a framework for understanding the structure of an industry and was developed by Harvard professor Michael Porter. Shown in Figure 5.1, the framework is comprised of the forces that determine industry profitability.[7] These forces—the threat of substitutes, the entry of new competitors, rivalry among existing firms, the bargaining power of suppliers, and the bargaining power of buyers—determine the average rate of return for the firms in an industry.

Each of Porter's five forces impacts the average rate of return for the firms in an industry by applying pressure on industry profitability. Well-managed companies try to position their firms in a way that avoids or diminishes these forces—in an attempt to beat the average rate of return for the industry. For example, the rivalry among existing firms in the airline industry is high. JetBlue diminished the impact of this threat to its profitability by avoiding head-to-head competition with the major carriers in most markets.

LEARNING Objective

2. Identify the five competitive forces that determine industry profitability.

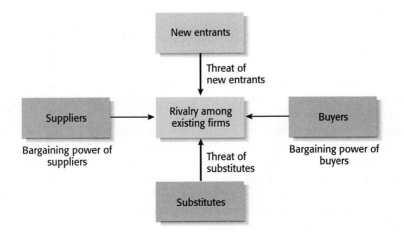

FIGURE 5.1

Forces That Determine Industry Profitability

Source: M. Porter, *Competitive Strategy: Techniques for Analyzing Industries and Competitors* (New York: Free Press, 1980).

In his book *Competitive Advantage*, Porter points out that industry profitability is not a function of *only* a product's features. Although it was written in 1985 and the dynamics of the industries mentioned have changed, Porter's essential point remains correct:

> Industry profitability is not a function of what the product looks like or whether it embodies high or low technology but of industry structure. Some very mundane industries such as postage meters and grain trading are extremely profitable, while some more glamorous, high-technology industries such as personal computers and cable television are not profitable for many participants.[8]

The five competitive forces that determine industry profitability are described next.

Threat of Substitutes   In general, industries are more attractive when the threat of substitutes is low. This means that products or services from other industries can't easily serve as substitutes for the products or services being made and sold in the focal firm's industry. For example, there are few if any substitutes for prescription medicines, which is one of the reasons the pharmaceutical industry is so profitable. When people are sick, they typically don't quibble with the pharmacist about the price of a medicine. In contrast, when close substitutes for a product do exist, industry profitability is suppressed because consumers will opt not to buy when the price is too high. Consider the price of movie tickets. If the price gets too high, consumers can easily switch to watching rented videos or pay-per-view. Similarly, if the price of glass bottles gets too high, manufacturers can easily switch to aluminum cans, plastic bottles, or other alternatives.[9]

The extent to which substitutes suppress the profitability of an industry depends on the propensity for buyers to substitute alternatives. This is why the firms in an industry often offer their customers amenities to reduce the likelihood of their switching to a substitute product, even in light of a price increase. Let's look at the coffee restaurant industry as an example of this. The coffee sold at Starbucks is relatively expensive. A consumer could easily find a less expensive cup of coffee at a convenience store or brew coffee at home rather than pay more at Starbucks. To decrease the likelihood that customers will choose either of these alternatives, Starbucks offers high-quality fresh coffee, a pleasant atmosphere, and good service. Some Starbucks restaurants even offer their customers access to computers and the Internet as a way of motivating them to remain loyal to Starbucks. Starbucks doesn't do this just so its customers don't go to a different coffee restaurant. It offers the service so its customers won't switch to substitute products as well.

L E A R N I N G
Objective

3. Explain the role of "barriers to entry" in creating disincentives for firms to enter an industry.

Threat of New Entrants   In general, industries are more attractive when the threat of entry is low. This means that competitors cannot easily enter the industry to copy what the industry incumbents are doing. There are a number of ways that firms in an industry can keep the number of new entrants low. These techniques are referred to as barriers to entry. A **barrier to entry** is a condition that creates a disincentive for a new firm to enter an industry.[10] Let's look at the six major sources of barriers to entry:

■ *Economies of scale:* Industries that are characterized by large economies of scale are difficult for new firms to enter, unless they are willing to accept a cost disadvantage. **Economies of scale** occur when mass-producing a product results in lower average costs. For example, Intel has huge microchip factories that produce vast quantities of chips, thereby reducing the average cost of a chip. It would be difficult for a new entrant to match Intel's advantage in this area.

■ *Product differentiation:* Industries such as the soft-drink industry that are characterized by firms with strong brands are difficult to break into without spending heavily on advertising. For example, imagine how costly it would be to compete head-to-head against Pepsi or Coca-Cola. Another way of achieving differentiation is through exclusive licensing agreements. For example, in 2004, Electronic Arts inked a 5-year exclusive deal with the National Football League, making it the only company that can produce electronic games involving NFL players, teams, or stadiums.[11]

■ *Capital requirements:* The need to invest large amounts of money to gain entrance to an industry is another barrier to entry. The airline industry is characterized by large capital requirements, although JetBlue, which launched in 1999, was able to overcome this barrier and raise substantial funds by winning the confidence of investors through the strength of its business model and its management team. Similarly, it currently takes about 2 years and $4 million to develop a single electronic game (such as those sold by Electronic Arts and Activision).[12] Many new firms do not have the capital to compete at this level.

■ *Cost advantages independent of size:* Entrenched competitors may have cost advantages not related to size that are not available to new entrants. Commonly, these advantages are grounded in the firm's history. For example, the existing competitors in an industry may have purchased land and equipment in the past when the cost was far less than new entrants would have to pay for the same assets at the time of their entry.

■ *Access to distribution channels:* Distribution channels are often hard to crack. This is particularly true in crowded markets, such as the convenience store market. For a new sports drink to be placed on a convenience store shelf, it typically has to displace a product that is already there.

■ *Government and legal barriers:* In knowledge-intensive industries, such as biotechnology and software, patents, trademarks, and copyrights form major barriers to entry. Other industries, such as banking and broadcasting, require the granting of a license by a public authority.

When a new firm tries to enter an industry with powerful barriers to entry, it must have a plan to overcome those barriers. Scott McNealy, the cofounder of Sun Microsystems, says that Sun was able to overcome the barriers to entry in many of its industries primarily through a program of partnering with other firms:

Initially, Sun's business model was no different from that of its rivals. We wanted to beat our competitors, grow internally, build manufacturing plants, create new distribution channels, acquire promising new start-ups, and so on. What happened was that we realized we couldn't do it alone. The markets were vast, our competitors were huge, barriers to entry to some segments were overwhelming, we didn't have

Starbucks doesn't just sell coffee. It also offers its patrons a convenient and pleasant place to meet, socialize, and study. Starbucks offers these amenities in part to decrease the likelihood that its customers will "substitute" their Starbucks coffee for a less expensive alternative.

enough cash, and the pace of change in the industry was too fast. What we did was purely instinctive. We reached out to other companies that could help us. We leveraged their expertise and specialty products by forming strategic alliances.[13]

LEARNING

Objective

4. Identify the nontraditional barriers to entry that are especially associated with entrepreneurial firms.

When start-ups create their own industries or create new niche markets within existing industries, they must create barriers to entry of their own to reduce the threat of new entrants. It is difficult for start-ups to create barriers to entry that are expensive, such as economies of scale, because money is usually tight. The biggest threat to a new firm's viability, particularly if it is creating a new market, is that larger, better-funded firms will step in and copy what it is doing. The ideal barrier to entry is a patent, trademark, or copyright, which prevents another firm from duplicating what the start-up is doing. Apart from these options, however, start-ups have to rely on nontraditional barriers to entry to discourage new entrants, such as assembling a world-class management team that would be difficult for another company to replicate. A list of nontraditional barriers to entry, which are particularly suited to start-up firms, is provided in Table 5.1.

Rivalry Among Existing Firms In most industries, the major determinant of industry profitability is the level of competition among the firms already competing in the industry. Some industries are fiercely competitive to the point where prices are pushed below the level of costs. When this happens, industry-wide losses occur. In other industries, competition is much less intense and price competition is subdued. For example, the personal computer industry is so competitive that profit margins are extremely thin. In contrast, the market for specialized medical equipment is less competitive, and profit margins are higher.

There are four primary factors that determine the nature and intensity of the rivalry among existing firms in an industry:

■ **Number and balance of competitors:** The more competitors there are, the more likely it is that one or more will try to gain customers by cutting its prices. Price-cutting causes problems throughout the industry and occurs more often when all the competitors in an industry are about the same size and when there is no clear market

TABLE 5.1 Nontraditional Barriers to Entry

Barrier to Entry	Explanation	Example
Strength of management team	If a start-up puts together a world-class management team, it may give potential rivals pause in taking on the start-up in its chosen industry.	JetBlue
First-mover advantage	If a start-up pioneers an industry or a new concept within an existing industry, the name recognition the start-up establishes may create a formidable barrier to entry.	Facebook
Passion of management team and employees	If the key employees of a start-up are highly motivated by its unique culture, are willing to work long hours because of their belief in what they are doing, and anticipate large financial gains through stock options, this is a combination that cannot be replicated by a larger firm. Think of the employees of a biotech firm trying to find a cure for a disease.	Amgen
Unique business model	If a start-up is able to construct a unique business model and establish a network of relationships that make the business model work, this set of advantages creates a barrier to entry.	Dell
Internet domain name	Some Internet domain names are so "spot-on" in regard to a specific product or service that they give a start-up a meaningful leg up in terms of e-commerce opportunities. Think of www.1800flowers.com, www.1800gotjunk.com, and www.bodybuilding.com.	www.1800contacts.com
Inventing a new approach to an industry and executing the idea in an exemplary fashion	If a start-up invents a new approach to an industry and executes it in an exemplary fashion, these factors create a barrier to entry for potential imitators.	Wikipedia

leader. In industries where there is a clear market leader, such as Intel in the semiconductor industry, the leader maintains price discipline and keeps the industry from engaging in destructive price wars.

■ *Degree of difference between products:* The degree to which products differ from one producer to another affects industry rivalry. For example, commodity industries such as paper products producers tend to compete on price because there is no meaningful difference between one manufacturer's products and another's.

■ *Growth rate of an industry:* The competition among firms in a slow-growth industry is stronger than among those in fast-growth industries. Slow-growth industry firms, such as insurance, must fight for market share, which may tempt them to lower prices or increase quality to get customers. In fast-growth industries, such as pharmaceutical products, there are enough customers to go around to fill the capacity of most firms, making price-cutting less likely.

■ *Level of fixed costs:* Firms that have high fixed costs must sell a higher volume of their product to reach the break-even point than firms with low fixed costs. Once the break-even point is met, each additional unit sold contributes directly to a firm's bottom line. Firms with high fixed costs are anxious to fill their capacity, and this anxiety may lead to price-cutting.

Bargaining Power of Suppliers In general, industries are more attractive when the bargaining power of suppliers is low. In some cases, suppliers can suppress the profitability of the industries to which they sell by raising prices or reducing the quality of the components they provide. If a supplier reduces the quality of the components it supplies, the quality of the finished product will suffer, and the manufacturer will eventually have to lower its price. If the suppliers are powerful relative to the firms in the industry to which they sell, industry profitability can suffer.[14] For example, Intel, with its Pentium chip, is a powerful supplier to the PC industry. Because most PCs feature Pentium chips, Intel can command a premium price from the PC manufacturers, thus directly affecting the overall profitability of the PC industry. Several factors have an impact on the ability of suppliers to exert pressure on buyers and suppress the profitability of the industries they serve. These include the following:

■ *Supplier concentration:* When there are only a few suppliers to provide a critical product to a large number of buyers, the supplier has an advantage. This is the case in the pharmaceutical industry, where relatively few drug manufacturers are selling to thousands of doctors and their patients.

■ *Switching costs:* Switching costs are the fixed costs that buyers encounter when switching or changing from one supplier to another. If switching costs are high, a buyer will be less likely to switch suppliers. For example, suppliers often provide their largest buyers with specialized software that makes it easy to buy their products. After the buyer spends time and effort learning the supplier's ordering and inventory management systems, it will be less likely to want to spend time and effort learning another supplier's system.

■ *Attractiveness of substitutes:* Supplier power is enhanced if there are no attractive substitutes for the products or services the supplier offers. For example, there is little the computer industry can do when Microsoft and Intel raise their prices, as there are relatively few if any practical substitutes for these firms' products.

■ *Threat of forward integration:* The power of a supplier is enhanced if there is a credible possibility that the supplier might enter the buyer's industry. For example, Microsoft's power as a supplier of computer operating systems is enhanced by the threat that it might enter the PC industry if PC makers balk too much at the cost of its software or threaten to use an operating system from a different software provider.

Bargaining Power of Buyers In general, industries are more attractive when the bargaining power of buyers (a start-up's customers) is low. Buyers can suppress the profitability of the industries from which they purchase by demanding price concessions or increases in quality. For example, the automobile industry is dominated by a handful of large automakers that buy products from thousands of suppliers in different industries. This enables the automakers to suppress the profitability of the industries from which they buy by demanding price reductions. Similarly, if the automakers insisted that their suppliers provide better-quality parts for the same price, the profitability of the suppliers would suffer. Several factors affect buyers' ability to exert pressure on suppliers and suppress the profitability of the industries from which they buy. These include the following:

■ *Buyer group concentration:* If the buyers are concentrated, meaning that there are only a few large buyers, and they buy from a large number of suppliers, they can pressure the suppliers to lower costs and thus affect the profitability of the industries from which they buy.

■ *Buyer's costs:* The greater the importance of an item is to a buyer, the more sensitive the buyer will be to the price it pays. For example, if the component sold by the supplier represents 50 percent of the cost of the buyer's product, the buyer will bargain hard to get the best price for that component.

■ *Degree of standardization of supplier's products:* The degree to which a supplier's product differs from its competitors' affects the buyer's bargaining power. For example, a buyer who is purchasing a standard or undifferentiated product from a supplier, such as the corn syrup that goes into a soft drink, can play one supplier against another until it gets the best combination of features such as price and service.

■ *Threat of backward integration:* The power of a buyer is enhanced if there is a credible threat that the buyer might enter the supplier's industry. For example, the PC industry can keep the price of computer monitors down by threatening to make its own monitors if the price gets too high.

The bargaining power of buyers is such a pervasive threat that some new ventures opt out of particular industries when the extent of the bargaining power of buyers becomes clear. This scenario changed the course of history for the Sony Corporation, as explained in the boxed feature titled "Savvy Entrepreneurial Firm."

The Value of the Five Forces Model

Along with helping a firm understand the dynamics of the industry it plans to enter, the five forces model can be used in two ways: (1) to help a firm determine whether it should enter a particular industry and (2) whether it can carve out an attractive position in that industry. Let's examine these two positive outcomes.

First, the five forces model can be used to assess the attractiveness of an industry or a specific position within an industry by determining the level of threat to industry profitability for each of the forces, as shown in Table 5.2. This analysis of industry attractiveness should be more in-depth than the cursory analysis conducted during feasibility analysis. For example, if a firm filled out the form shown in Table 5.2 and several of the threats to industry profitability were high, the firm may want to reconsider entering the industry or think carefully about the position it will occupy in the industry. In the restaurant industry, for example, the threat of substitute products, the threat of new entrants, and the rivalry among existing firms are high. For certain restaurants, such as fresh-seafood restaurants, the bargaining power of suppliers may also be high (the number of seafood suppliers is relatively small compared to the number of beef and chicken suppliers). Thus, a firm that enters the restaurant industry has several forces working against it simply because of the nature of the industry. To help sidestep or diminish these threats, it must establish a favorable position. One firm that has accomplished this is Panera Bread, as discussed in Case 5.1 in this chapter. By studying the restaurant industry, Panera found that some consumers have tired of fast food but don't

savvy entrepreneurial firm

How the Bargaining Power of Buyers Changed the Fate of Sony in Its Start-Up Years
www.sony.com

There are many variables that shape a company in its start-up years, but perhaps none are as powerful as Porter's five forces. Many companies, for example, establish strong brands or differentiate themselves in creative ways, primarily to establish barriers to entry and stem the tide of new entrants. Other companies, such as Starbucks, offer amenities in their places of business to discourage customers from switching to less expensive substitute products. The story of Sony, however, tops them all. When Sony was a start-up, it changed its entire approach to doing business as the result of the bargaining power of buyers. In fact, if Sony hadn't responded to this threat in the way it did, it wouldn't be a household name today.

Sony was established in 1946 by Masaru Ibuka and Akio Morita, two Japanese businessmen, to make communication equipment for the reconstruction of Japan after World War II. One thing Ibuka and Morita learned quickly was that to make a sale, they had to win the confidence of the purchasing officers in the government agencies with whom they were dealing. This task often proved difficult, but their hard work typically paid off in orders from these purchasing officers. One day, however, early in the life of Sony, a purchasing agent who Morita had worked particularly hard to win over was transferred to a new position. This was frustrating to Morita because he had to start from square one to win the confidence of the purchasing officer's replacement.

After this scenario repeated itself several times, Morita considered the problem. While he liked the fact that large orders could be granted by the purchasing agents of government agencies and large firms, he was leery of the fact that Sony's sales hinged on the decisions of such a small number of people. After discussing this concern with Ibuka, Morita decided to take Sony in a different direction. Instead of placing the future of Sony in the hands of a few purchasing agents, Morita decided that Sony would go after the consumer market. "In other words, we decided to do business with unspecified millions of individuals instead of with a specific few. On this basis we started to produce the first tape recorders and tapes in Japan," Morita later recalled.

This remarkable story illustrates the compelling nature of the real bargaining power of buyers. This clout is most formidable when there are only a few buyers and many sellers. Morita redirected Sony's entire future to avoid this threat. Today, as it has throughout the majority of its history, Sony's future lies in the hands of the millions of people who buy its products rather than in the hands of just a few powerful buyers.

Questions for Critical Thinking

1. Analyze the electronics industry using Porter's five forces model. What do you think are the biggest threats to the electronics industry today? What is Sony doing to try to deter these threats?
2. Think of examples of at least two other companies that are in industries that are subject to the strong bargaining power of buyers. Do you think the profitability of these firms is being suppressed by the strong bargaining power of their buyers? What, if anything, can these firms do to neutralize this threat?
3. How would you describe Sony's positioning strategy in the electronics industry?
4. What single industry do you think suffers the most from the bargaining power of buyers? How about the bargaining power of suppliers? Are entrepreneurial start-ups able to enter these industries? If so, how?

Source: A. Morita, "Moving Up in Marketing by Getting Down to Basics," in *The Book of Entrepreneurs' Wisdom*, ed. Peter Krass (New York: John Wiley & Sons, 1999), 315–23.

always have the time to patronize a sit-down restaurant. To fill the gap, Panera helped to pioneer a new category called "fast casual," which combines relatively fast service with high-quality food. Panera has been very successful in occupying this unique position in the restaurant industry. You'll learn more about Panera Bread's success while reading Case 5.1.

Panera Bread offers a variety of alternatives to the typical burger and fries offered at many fast-food restaurants. In addition to a selection of fresh baked bread, Panera is also known for bagels, pastries, soups, sandwiches, salads, and coffee.

LEARNING

Objective

5. List the four industry-related questions to ask before pursuing the idea for a firm.

The second way a new firm can apply the five forces model to help determine whether it should enter an industry is by using the model pictured in Figure 5.2 to answer several key questions. By doing so, a new venture can assess the thresholds it may have to meet to be successful in a particular industry:

Question 1: Is the industry a realistic place for our new venture to enter? This question can be answered by looking at the overall attractiveness of an industry, as depicted in Table 5.2, and by assessing whether the window of opportunity is open. It is up to the entrepreneur to determine if the window of opportunity for the industry is open or closed.

Determining the Attractiveness of an Industry
TABLE 5.2 Using the Five Forces Model

Competitive Force	Threat to Industry Profitability		
	Low	Medium	High
Threat of substitutes			
Threat of new entrants			
Rivalry among existing firms			
Bargaining power of suppliers			
Bargaining power of buyers			

Instructions:

Step 1	Select an industry.
Step 2	Determine the level of threat to industry profitability for each of the forces (low, medium, or high).
Step 3	Use the table to get an overall feel for the attractiveness of the industry.
Step 4	Use the table to identify the threats that are most often relevant to industry profitability.

FIGURE 5.2

Using the Five Forces Model to Pose Questions to Determine the Potential Success of a New Venture

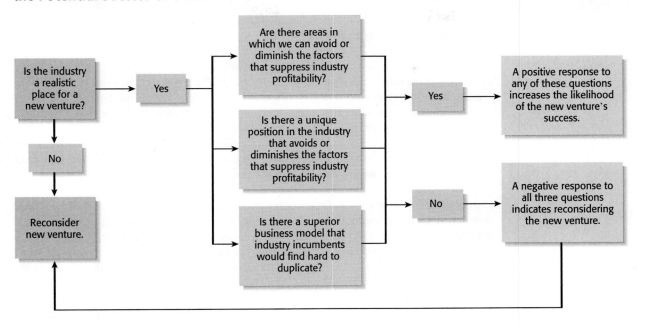

Question 2: If we do enter the industry, can our firm do a better job than the industry as a whole in avoiding or diminishing the impact of the forces that suppress industry profitability? A new venture can enter an industry with a fresh brand, innovative ideas, and a world-class management team and perform better than the industry incumbents. This was the case when Google entered the Internet search engine industry and displaced Yahoo! as the market leader. Outperformance of industry incumbents can also be achieved if a new venture brings an attractive new product to market that is patented, preventing others from duplicating it for a period of time.

Question 3: Is there a unique position in the industry that avoids or diminishes the forces that suppress industry profitability? As we've described, this is the advantage that JetBlue and Panera Bread have captured.

Question 4: Is there a superior business model that can be put in place that would be hard for industry incumbents to duplicate? Keep in mind that the five forces model provides a picture of an industry "as is," which isn't necessarily the way a new venture has to approach it. Sometimes the largest firms in an industry are trapped by their own strategies and contractual obligations, providing an opening for a start-up to try something new. For example, when Dell started selling computers directly to consumers, its largest rivals—Hewlett-Packard, Compaq, and IBM—were not able to respond. They were locked into a strategy of selling through retailers. If they had tried to mimic Dell and sell directly to end users or customers, they would have alienated their most valuable partners—retailers such as Sears, Circuit City, and Best Buy.

The steps involved in answering these questions are pictured in Figure 5.2. If the founders of a new firm believe that a particular industry is a realistic place for their new venture, a positive response to one or more of the questions posed in Figure 5.2 increases the likelihood that the new venture will be successful.

Industry Types and the Opportunities They Offer

Along with studying the factors discussed previously, it is helpful for a new venture to study industry types to determine the opportunities they offer.[15] The five most prevalent industry types, depicted in Table 5.3, are emerging industries, fragmented industries, mature industries, declining industries, and global industries.[16] There are unique opportunities offered by each type of industry.

Emerging Industries An **emerging industry** is a new industry in which standard operating procedures have yet to be developed. The firm that pioneers or takes the leadership of an emerging industry often captures a first-mover advantage, which is a sometimes insurmountable advantage gained by the firm initiating the first significant move into a new market, as explained in Chapter 3.

Because a high level of uncertainty characterizes emerging industries, any opportunity that is captured may be short-lived. Still, many new ventures enter emerging industries because barriers to entry are usually low and there is no established pattern of rivalry.

Fragmented Industries A **fragmented industry** is one that is characterized by a large number of firms of approximately equal size. The primary opportunity for start-ups in fragmented industries is to consolidate the industry and establish industry leadership as a result of doing so. In **industry consolidation**, the smaller companies are typically acquired or go out of business to give way to a handful of larger companies that take over the majority of the business. This is what Blockbuster did in the video rental industry. Prior to Blockbuster's arrival, thousands of small video stores were scattered throughout the United States. Through internal growth and acquisitions, Blockbuster grew quickly, consolidating a previously fragmented industry.

Mature Industries A **mature industry** is an industry that is experiencing slow or no increase in demand, has numerous repeat (rather than new) customers, and has limited product innovation. Occasionally, entrepreneurs introduce new product innovations to mature industries, surprising incumbents who thought nothing new was possible in their industries. An example is Steve Demos, the founder of White Wave, a company that

TABLE 5.3 Industry Structure and Opportunities

Industry Type	Industry Characteristics	Opportunities	Examples of Entrepreneurial Firms Exploiting These Opportunities
Emerging industries	Recent changes in demand or technology; new industry standard operating procedures have yet to be developed	First-mover advantage	• Apple with its iTunes Music Store • XM Satellite Radio with its satellite radio service • MySpace.com with its online social networking Web site
Fragmented industries	Large number of firms of approximately equal size	Consolidation	• Starbucks in coffee restaurants • Movie Gallery in video rentals • Geeks on Call in home computer repairs
Mature industries	Slow increases in demand, numerous repeat customers, and limited product innovation	Process and after-sale service innovation	• Whole Foods Markets in groceries • 1-800-GOT-JUNK? in trash and junk removal • ProFlowers in flower delivery
Declining industries	Consistent reduction in industry demand	Leadership, niche, harvest, and divest	• Nucor in steel • JetBlue in airlines • Circus du Soleil in circuses
Global industries	Significant international sales	Multidomestic and global	• Nike in athletic shoes • Electronic Arts in electronic games

makes vegetarian food products and is further described in Case 11.1. In 1996, the company introduced Silk Soymilk, which has quickly become the best-selling soymilk in the country. Soymilk isn't really milk at all—it's a soybean-based beverage that looks like milk and has a similar texture. Still, it has made its way into the dairy section of most supermarkets in the United States and has positioned itself as a healthy substitute for milk. Who would have thought that a major innovation was possible in the milk industry?

Declining Industries A **declining industry** is an industry that is experiencing a reduction in demand. Typically, entrepreneurs shy away from declining industries because the firms in the industry do not meet the tests of an attractive opportunity, described in Chapter 2. There are occasions, however, when a start-up will do just the opposite of what conventional wisdom would suggest and, by doing so, stakes out an industry position that isn't being hotly contested.

Entrepreneurial firms employ three different strategies in declining industries. The first is to adopt a **leadership strategy**, in which the firm tries to become the dominant player in the industry. This is a rare strategy for a start-up in a declining industry. The second is to pursue a **niche strategy**, which focuses on a narrow segment of the industry that might be encouraged to grow through product or process innovation. The third is a **cost reduction strategy**, which is accomplished through achieving lower costs than industry incumbents through process improvements. Nucor Steel, a small steel company that revolutionized the steel industry through the introduction of the "minimill" concept, is an example of an entrepreneurially minded firm that pursued this strategy. Most steel mills in the United States use large blast furnaces that produce a wide line of products and require enormous throughput in order to be profitable. Nucor's minimills are smaller and produce a narrower range of products. They are, however, energy efficient and make high-quality steel.[17] Nucor proved its concept and quickly found growth markets within the largely declining U.S. steel industry.

Global Industries A **global industry** is an industry that is experiencing significant international sales. Many start-ups enter global industries and from day one try to appeal to international rather than just domestic markets. The two most common strategies pursued by firms in global industries are the multidomestic strategy and the global strategy. Firms that pursue a **multidomestic strategy** compete for market share on a country-by-country basis and vary their product or service offerings to meet the demands of the local market. In contrast, firms pursuing a **global strategy** use the same basic approach in all foreign markets. The choice between these two strategies depends on how similar consumers' tastes are from market to market. For example, food companies typically are limited to a multidomestic strategy because food preferences vary significantly from country to country. Firms that sell more universal products, such as athletic shoes, have been successful with global strategies. A global strategy is preferred because it is more economical to sell the same product in multiple markets.[18]

Competitor Analysis

After a firm has gained an understanding of the industry and the market in which it plans to compete, the next step is to complete a competitor analysis. A competitor analysis is a detailed analysis of a firm's competition. It helps a firm understand the positions of its major competitors and the opportunities that are available to obtain a competitive advantage in one or more areas. These are important issues, particularly for new ventures.[19] In the words of Sun-tzu, quoted earlier in this chapter, "Time spent in reconnaissance is seldom wasted."

First we'll discuss how a firm identifies its major competitors, and then we'll look at the process of completing a competitive analysis grid, which is a tool for organizing the information a firm collects about its primary competitors.

L E A R N I N G
Objective

7. Explain the purpose of a competitor analysis.

Identifying Competitors

The first step in a competitive analysis is to determine who the competition is. This is more difficult than one might think. For example, take a company such as 1-800-FLOWERS. Primarily, the company sells flowers. But 1-800-FLOWERS is not only in the flower business. Because flowers are often given for gifts, the company is also in the gift business. If the company sees itself in the gift business rather than just the flower business, it has a broader set of competitors—and opportunities—to consider.

The different types of competitors a business will face are shown in Figure 5.3. The challenges associated with each of these groups of competitors are described here:

- *Direct competitors:* These are businesses that offer products identical or similar to the products of the firm completing the analysis. These competitors are the most important because they are going after the same customers as the new firm. A new firm faces winning over the loyal followers of its major competitors, which is difficult to do, even when the new firm has a better product.
- *Indirect competitors:* These competitors offer close substitutes to the product the firm completing the analysis sells. These firms' products are also important in that they target the same basic need that is being met by the new firm's product. For example, when people told Roberto Goizueta, the late CEO of Coca-Cola, that Coke's market share was at a maximum, he countered by saying that Coke accounted for less than 2 percent of the 64 ounces of fluid that the average person drinks each day. "The enemy is coffee, milk, tea [and] water," he once said.[20]
- *Future competitors:* These are companies that are not yet direct or indirect competitors but could move into one of these roles at any time. Firms are always concerned about strong competitors moving into their markets. For example, think of how the world has changed for Barnes & Noble since Amazon.com was founded.

It is impossible for a firm to identify all its direct and indirect competitors, let alone its future competitors. However, identifying its top 5 to 10 direct competitors and its top 5 to 10 indirect and future competitors makes it easier for the firm to complete its competitive analysis grid.

If a firm does not have a direct competitor, it shouldn't forget that the status quo can be the toughest competitor of all. In general, people are resistant to change and can always keep their money rather than spend it.[21] A product or service's utility must rise above its cost, not only in monetary terms but also in terms of the hassles associated with switching or learning something new, to motivate someone to buy a new product or service.[22]

Although most of the time the firms in an industry compete against one another, there are occasions when competitors unite for the good of the industry as a whole. On these occasions, it is typically to the advantage of a new venture to cooperate. If it doesn't, it may find itself trying to sell a product or service that doesn't comply with evolving industry norms. The chapter's "Partnering for Success" feature offers an example of this scenario. As you'll see, this segment deals with an organization called Digital Living Network Alliance.

FIGURE 5.3

**Types of Competitors
New Ventures Face**

**Direct
Competitors**

Businesses
offering identical or
similar products

**Indirect
Competitors**

Businesses
offering close
substitute
products

**Future
Competitors**

Businesses
that are not yet
direct or indirect
competitors but
could be at any time

partnering for *success*

Tech Industry Unites to Create Common Standards for Home Networks
www.dlna.org

Although most of the time firms in an industry compete with one another, there are occasions when firms unite for the good of the industry as a whole. An example is the creation of the Digital Living Network Alliance (DLNA), which is a nonprofit organization founded to create a set of rules aimed at making gadgets communicate better with each other through home networks. Gateway, Hewlett-Packard, Intel, Microsoft, Sony, Nokia, and 11 other firms that create products for home networks created the organization. Today, the organization has over 250 members.

Many people have a growing collection of electronic devices in their homes and would like to network them together. They want to share music, pictures, and video, for example, among their PCs, televisions, sound systems, and mobile devices. However, it is often difficult to network these different devices together because they are seldom perfectly compatible. To make the problem more difficult, many forms of digital music and movies are based on proprietary formats that work on some devices but not on others.

The purpose of the Digital Living Network Alliance is to solve this problem. The belief is that all technology-intensive firms will benefit if their devices easily network with each other and if consumers can feel confident that when they buy a new device, it will seamlessly integrate with the other devices in their homes. The Digital Living Network Alliance has established guidelines to ensure that these goals will be met. For example, a cell phone with a digital camera that adheres to the guidelines will be able to transmit pictures wirelessly to PCs or television sets.

Philip Kotler, a marketing expert and highly respected business professor,, has made the statement that for a firm to be an effective competitor, it must also be "an effective cooperator." The firms that established the Digital Living Network Alliance adhere to the spirit of Professor Kotler's observation.

Questions for Critical Thinking

1. What do you think Professor Kotler means when he says that "firms must be effective cooperators to be effective competitors"? Given what you've read in this book and learned from your other courses, do you agree with Kotler's statement? Why or why not?

2. In general, is it easier for direct competitors or indirect competitors to cooperate? Explain your answer.

3. Do you think the adoption of uniform standards that will enable electronic devices used in homes to better network with one another will make it easier or harder for new firms to enter the industries that make electronic devices for homes? Explain your answer.

4. Research the term *open standards* as it applies to electronics and firm competitiveness. What does "open standards" mean in the context of this feature? In your judgment, are open standards a good thing for consumer electronic firms? Do you think we are likely to see more or less open standards in the electronics industry in the future?

Sources: Digital Living Network Alliance homepage, www.dlna.org (accessed August 8, 2006); P. Kotler, *Marketing Insights from A to Z* (New York: John Wiley & Sons, 2002), 24, and "Tech Giants Unite on Gadget Standard for Home Networks," *The Wall Street Journal*, 2003, B4.

Sources of Competitive Intelligence

To complete a meaningful competitive analysis grid, a firm must first understand the strategies and behaviors of its competitors. The information that is gathered by a firm to learn about its competitors is referred to as **competitive intelligence**. Obtaining sound competitive intelligence is not always a simple task. If a competitor is a publicly traded firm, a description of the firm's business and its financial information is available through annual reports filed with the Securities and Exchange Commission (SEC). These reports are public records and are available at the SEC's Web site (www.sec.gov). If one or more of the competitors is a private company, the task is more difficult. Private companies are

LEARNING Objective

9. Describe ways a firm can ethically obtain information about its competitors.

Many companies attend trade shows to display their products and see what their competitors are up to. This is a shot of the Consumer Electronics Trade Show, held in Las Vegas, which is America's largest annual trade show of any kind.

not required to divulge information to the public. There are a number of ways that a firm can ethically obtain information about its competitors:

- *Attend conferences and trade shows:* Most industries have conferences and trade shows at which firms talk about the latest trends in the industry and display their products.
- *Read industry-related books, magazines, and Web sites, along with general business magazines, such as Inc. and Business Week:* In addition, many industries and associations publish magazines and newsletters that contain information about competitors.
- *Talk to customers about what motivated them to buy your product as opposed to your competitors':* Customers can provide a wealth of information about the advantages and disadvantages of competing products.
- *Purchase competitors' products to understand their features, benefits, and shortcomings:* The process of purchasing the product will also provide data about how the competitor treats its customers.
- *Study competitors' Web sites:* Many companies put a lot of information on their Web sites, including their company's history, profiles of their management teams, product information, and the latest news about the company.

There are a number of additional resources available to help entrepreneurs collect competitive intelligence. A sample of these resources in shown in Table 5.4.

Completing a Competitive Analysis Grid

L E A R N I N G

Objective

10. Describe the reasons for completing a competitive analysis grid.

As we mentioned previously, a **competitive analysis grid** is a tool for organizing the information a firm collects about its competitors. It can help a firm see how it stacks up against its competitors, provide ideas for markets to pursue, and, perhaps most importantly, identify its primary sources of competitive advantage. To be a viable company, a new venture must have at least one clear competitive advantage over its major competitors.

An example of a competitive analysis grid is provided in Table 5.5. This grid is for Activision, a company that makes electronic games. The company's products cover the action, adventure, action sports, racing, role-playing, simulation, and strategy games categories. These products operate on both PCs and game consoles such as the Nintendo GameCube. According to Activision, the main competitive factors in the electronics games industry are product features and playability, brand-name recognition, compatibility of

TABLE 5.4 Resources to Help Entrepreneurs Complete a Competitor Analysis

Source	Description	Cost
Hoover's Online (www.hoovers.com)	Provides a brief history, financial information, and list of competitors for each company in its vast database. For publicly traded firms, a detailed comparison of the company's financial results to industry averages is also provided.	Typically free if accessed from a college, university, or public library.
InfoUSA (www.infousa.com)	InfoUSA, a publicly traded company, provides access to lists of companies within industries. A leading supplier of information for ethical competitive intelligence.	Fee-based
LexisNexis (www.lexisnexis.com)	Offers subscribers access to thousands of sources— including newspapers, magazines, journal articles, and public records—that can be used to gather information on companies and individuals.	Portions of LexisNexis are typically free if accessed from a college, university, or public library. Full access available on a subscription basis.
LookSmart Find Articles (www.findarticles.com)	A search engine specifically designed to find articles on businesses. Links to the articles are provided.	Free
Wall Street Journal Online (www.wsj.com)	Very powerful search engine for searching for company performance within a particular industry.	You need to subscribe to *The Wall Street Journal*
ZapData (www.zapdata.com)	ZapData is a Dun & Bradstreet service that, like InfoUSA, allows you to create lists of companies within industries. The lists can be used to generate sales leads or to research competitors.	Fee-based

products with popular platforms (e.g., Microsoft's Xbox), access to distribution channels, quality of products, ease of use, price, marketing support, and quality of customer service.[23] These factors are placed on the vertical axis of Activision's competitive analysis grid. The horizontal axis contains Activision and its five main competitors. In each box, Activision would rate itself compared to its main competitors. The purpose of this exercise is for a company to see how it stacks up against its competitors and to determine if any opportunities exist that it may have overlooked. For example, if Activision judged itself superior to its competitors in the category "ease of use," it might use this knowledge to highlight this advantage in its advertising and promotions.

In summary, it is extremely important for a new venture to have a firm grasp of the industry it plans to enter and of the companies it will be competing against on a day-to-day basis. By carefully studying these important areas, a new venture can position itself correctly in its industry and be fully aware of its competitors' strengths and weaknesses as its makes its own decisions about the best way to compete against those competitors.

TABLE 5.5 Competitive Analysis Grid for Activision

Name	Activision	Electronic Arts	Take-Two	LucasArts	Eidos	THQ
Product features and playability						
Brand-name recognition						
Compatibility of products with popular platforms						
Access to distribution channels						
Quality of products						
Ease of use						
Price						
Marketing support						
Quality of customer service						

Chapter Summary

1. Industry analysis is business research that focuses on an industry's potential. The knowledge gleaned from an industry analysis helps a firm decide whether to enter an industry and if it can carve out a position in the industry that will provide it a competitive advantage.
2. The threat of substitutes, the threat of new entrants, rivalry among existing firms, the bargaining power of suppliers, and the bargaining power of buyers are the five competitive forces that determine an industry's profitability.
3. The threat of new entrants is one of the five forces that determine industry profitability. Firms try to keep other firms from entering their industries by erecting barriers to entry. A barrier to entry is a condition that creates a disincentive for a new firm to enter an industry. Economies of scale, product differentiation, capital requirements, cost advantages independent of size, access to distribution channels, and government and legal barriers are examples of barriers to entry.
4. The nontraditional barriers to entry that are particularly well suited to entrepreneurial firms include strength of the management team, first-mover advantage, passion of the management team and employees, unique business model, special internet domain name, and inventing a new approach to an industry and executing the approach in an exemplary manner.
5. The four industry-related questions that a firm should ask before entering an industry are the following: Is the industry a realistic place for a new venture? If we do enter the industry, can our firm do a better job than the industry as a whole in avoiding or diminishing the threats that suppress industry profitability? Is there a unique position in the industry that avoids or diminishes the forces that suppress industry profitability? Is there a superior business model that can be put in place that would be hard for industry incumbents to duplicate?
6. The five primary industry types and the opportunities they offer are as follows: emerging industry/first-mover advantage; fragmented industry/consolidation; mature industry/emphasis on service and process innovation; declining industry/leadership, niche, harvest, and divest; and global industry/multidomestic strategy or global strategy.
7. A competitor analysis is a detailed analysis of a firm's competition. It helps a firm understand the positions of its major competitors and the opportunities that are available to obtain a competitive advantage in one or more areas.
8. The three groups of competitors a new firm will face are direct competitors, indirect competitors, and future competitors.
9. There are a number of ways a firm can ethically obtain information about its competitors, including attending conferences and trade shows; reading industry-related books, magazines, and publications; talking to customers about what motivated them to buy your product as opposed to those of your competitors; purchasing competitors' products to understand their features, benefits, and shortcomings; and studying competitors' Web sites.
10. A competitive analysis grid is a tool for organizing the information a firm collects about its competitors. This grid can help a firm see how it stacks up against its competitors, provide ideas for markets to pursue, and, perhaps most importantly, identify its primary sources of competitive advantage.

Key Terms

barrier to entry, 136
competitive analysis grid, 148
competitive intelligence, 147
competitor analysis, 133
cost reduction strategy, 145
declining industry, 145
economies of scale, 136
emerging industry, 144
fragmented industry, 144
global industry, 145
global strategy, 145
industry, 132

Review Questions

1. What is an industry? Provide an example of an industry and several firms in it.
2. What is the purpose of industry analysis?
3. Identify the five competitive forces that determine industry profitability.
4. Describe how the threat of substitute products has the potential to suppress an industry's profitability.
5. How does the threat of new entrants have the potential to suppress an industry's profitability?
6. What is meant by the term *barrier to entry*? Describe the six major sources of barriers to entry that firms use to restrict entry into their markets.
7. Identify the nontraditional barriers to entry that are particularly suitable for entrepreneurial firms.
8. Describe the four primary factors that play a role in determining the nature and intensity of rivalry among an industry's existing firms. How does rivalry among existing firms have the potential to suppress an industry's profitability?
9. Describe how the bargaining power of suppliers has the potential to suppress an industry's profitability.
10. Describe the four major factors that affect suppliers' ability to exert pressure on buyers and suppress the profitability of the industries to which they sell.
11. In what way does the bargaining power of buyers have the potential to suppress an industry's profitability?
12. Describe the four major factors that affect buyers' ability to exert pressure on suppliers and suppress the profitability of the industries from which they buy materials.
13. Describe the characteristics of a fragmented industry. What is the primary opportunity for new firms in fragmented industries?
14. Describe the characteristics of a mature industry. What is the primary opportunity for new firms in a mature industry?
15. What is a global industry? Describe the two most common strategies pursued by firms in global industries.
16. Describe the purpose of a competitor analysis. Make your answer as complete as possible.
17. Describe the differences between direct competitors, indirect competitors, and future competitors.
18. What is meant by the term *competitive intelligence*? Why is it important for firms to collect intelligence about their competitors?
19. Identify three sources of competitive intelligence.
20. What is the purpose of completing a competitive analysis grid?

Application Questions

1. Linda Williams is thinking about starting a firm in the electronic games industry. When asked by a potential investor if she had studied the industry, Linda replied, "The electronic games industry is so full of potential, it doesn't need formal analysis." Will Linda's answer satisfy the investor? In what ways will Linda limit her potential if her current attitude about the importance of industry analysis doesn't change?

2. The "You Be the VC 2" feature in this chapter focuses on DayJet. Spend some time studying DayJet's Web site and other information about the company. How would you describe DayJet's positioning strategy? What steps is the company taking to avoid some of the negative attributes of the airline industry?

3. Your friend Lisa Ryan is opening a smoothie shop that will sell a variety of smoothie drinks in the $3 to $4 price range. When you ask her if she is worried that the steep price of smoothies might prompt potential customers to buy a soda or a sports drink instead of a smoothie, Lisa answers, "You're right. Someone could substitute a soda or a sports drink for a smoothie and save a lot of money. Is there anything I can do to discourage that?" What do you tell her?

4. Jose Gonzales has been investigating the possibility of starting a package delivery service but is frustrated by the amount of money it takes to get into the industry. He is particularly concerned about getting the cash to buy the trucks he would need. Which of the five forces in Porter's five forces model is strongly affecting Jose's potential business? How can Jose overcome this obstacle?

5. Peter Jones is in the process of starting a business in the restaurant industry. In a recent *Fortune* magazine article, he read that in industries where the bargaining power of suppliers is high, industry profitability suffers. What criteria can Peter use to determine if the bargaining power of suppliers is high in the industry in which he has an interest?

6. Look at Table 5.1 in the chapter and read Case 5.2, which focuses on Cirque du Soleil and Curves International. Which of the nontraditional barriers to entry have been the most helpful to Cirque du Soleil and Curves in terms of deterring new entrants into their industries?

7. Think of at least three entrepreneurial firms, not listed in Table 5.1, that benefit greatly from their Internet domain names. In each case, to what extent do you think the strength of their Internet domain names is instrumental to their ability to limit the number of new entrants in their industries?

8. As mentioned in this chapter, White Wave Inc. produces Silk Soymilk, a product that has done surprisingly well in the mature milk industry. Based on the material we've covered so far, why do you think Silk Soymilk has been so successful?

9. Troy Pearson is starting a medical products business in Albany, New York. He knows he should put together a competitor analysis but doesn't know how to go about it. If Troy turned to you for advice, what would you tell him?

10. Susan Willis is planning to launch an advertising agency in Tampa, Florida. She knows that she needs to complete a competitor analysis but doesn't know where to obtain information about her competitors. Provide Susan with several suggestions on how to proceed.

11. M. B. Jenkins is the founder of a new firm in the electronics industry. A friend of his owns an electronic business in a neighboring state and has invited him to be his guest at a large electronics industry trade show. M. B. can't decide whether to take the time to attend the trade show. In the context of the material presented in this chapter, what are the arguments in favor of attending the trade show?

12. Dana Smith will soon be opening a fitness club in Tucson, Arizona. Having identified his competitors, he wants to display the information he has collected in a way that will help him determine how he'll stack up against his competitors and pinpoint his sources of competitive advantage. Describe to Dana a technique that he could use to help achieve his objectives.

13. Look at Table 5.4 in the chapter. Describe how a company could use a service like InfoUSA to conduct ethical competitive intelligence.

14. Complete Activision's competitive analysis grid, which is pictured in Table 5.5.

15. Access Panera Bread's most recent 10-K report (www.sec.gov/edgar.searchedgar.companysearch.html). Determine from the report what Panera believes are the primary competitive factors in its industry. Complete a competitive analysis grid for Panera Bread. (See Case 5.1 for additional information on Panera.)

you be the VC 5.1

Eclipse Aviation
www.eclipseaviation.com

Business Idea: Build a jet airplane that is so small and inexpensive to operate that a new class of air taxi services will emerge to make private jet travel more readily accessible to middle-class individuals and companies.

Pitch: Private jet service is safe and convenient but is also very expensive. To remedy this problem, Eclipse Aviation, a start-up in Albuquerque, New Mexico, has designed and constructed a six-passenger jet that has been successfully flown and tested. Eclipse plans to sell the jet for approximately $1 million, which is about one-fourth the cost of the least expensive corporate jet on the market. And it's engineered to be very cheap to operate: less than $1 per mile, which is one-third to one-fifth what it costs to fly other small jets. Eclipse's first jet is dubbed the Eclipse 500 Very Light Jet (VLJ). Eclipse hopes to sell the jet to individuals, corporations, and regional airlines or "taxi services" that will use it to shuttle individuals to and from municipal airports. An advantage of the Eclipse 500 is that it can land on a runway as short as 3,000 feet, compared to 4,000 to 5,000 feet needed by the smallest jets now in service. This advantage will allow the Eclipse 500 to service many of the small airports that currently can't accommodate jets. The

Eclipse 500 is expected to be certified for commercial flight by the FAA in the near future.

The way Eclipse is able to keep the sale price of the Eclipse 500 so low is through ultra-efficient manufacturing techniques that reduce costs and allow for high-volume manufacturing. An individual jet is made in 5 days and can be delivered 10 days later.

As an added bonus, the Eclipse 500 will boast an optional safety feature no jetliner can match: a parachute big enough to float the plane gently down to the ground. The parachute is made by Ballistic Parachute Systems (www.brsparachutes.com), which is a company that develops and deploys parachute systems for small aircraft.

Q&A: Based on the material covered in this chapter, what questions would you ask the firm's founders before making your funding decision? What answers would satisfy you?

Decision: If you had to make your decision on just the information provided in the pitch and on the company's Web site, would you fund this firm? Why or why not?

you be the VC 5.2

DayJet
www.dayjet.com

Business Idea: Offer a new and affordable form of air travel that provides "air-taxi" services to individuals and groups that accommodate their schedules and is able to reach out-of-the way places.

Pitch: Busy individuals and business travelers have two choices when it comes to air travel: booking a flight on a commercial airline or owning or chartering a private jet. Neither of these choices is very attractive. Commercial airline travel comes with lots of hassles, like checking bags, standing in line at security, crowded airplanes, and either no food at all, food that often just doesn't taste very good, or food offered at a high cost to the customer. At the same time, only the superrich and large companies can afford to charter or own a private jet. To further complicate matters, it's hard to get to and from places that have small airports. For example, take the challenge of trying to travel by air from Columbia, South Carolina, to Gainesville, Florida, in an efficient manner.

DayJet's mission is to fill this void. The company, made possible largely by the emergence of affordable "very light jets," like the Eclipse 500, is rolling out an air-taxi service unlike any service currently available. The service will be a "per-seat, on-demand" service, which will resemble a taxicab service but will take travelers from point to point on very light jets. The service will operate between specific airports called DayPorts. DayPorts are mostly regional and community airports that have little or no scheduled airline service. And customers will pay only for the seats they require, not the whole plane.

The cost of a flight on DayJet will range from $1 to $3 per mile. That compares to 50 cents per mile on a commercial airline and $10 per mile on a chartered jet. The big advantage of DayJet will be time savings and convenience. A business executive who flies from South Florida to Raleigh, North Carolina, to visit a client could easily make the round-trip in a single day using DayJet's service.

The same trip on a commercial airline could take parts of three days, and require two nights in a hotel room, if the executive had to leave the night before the visit and return the morning after.

Q&A: Based on the material covered in this chapter, what questions would you ask the firm's founders before making your funding decision? What answers would satisfy you?

Decision: If you had to make your decision on just the information provided in the pitch and on the company's Web site, would you fund this firm? Why or why not?

CASE 5.1

Panera Bread: Occupying a Favorable Position in a Highly Competitive Industry
www.panera.com

Bruce R. Barringer,
University of Central Florida
R. Duane Ireland,
Texas A&M University

Introduction

If you analyzed the restaurant industry using Porter's five forces model, you wouldn't be favorably impressed. Three of the threats to profitability—the threat of substitutes, the threat of new entrants, and rivalry among existing firms—are high. Despite these threats to industry profitability, one restaurant chain is moving forward in a very positive direction. St. Louis–based Panera Bread Company, a chain of specialty bakery-cafés, has grown from 602 company owned and franchised units in 2003 to over 877 today. In 2005 alone, its sales increased by 33.6 percent and its net income increased by 35.2 percent. So what's Panera's secret? How is it that this company flourishes while its industry as a whole is experiencing difficulty? As we'll see, Panera Bread's success can be explained in two words: positioning and execution.

Changing Consumer Tastes

Panera's roots go back to 1981, when it was founded under the name of Au Bon Pain Co. and consisted of three Au Bon Pain bakery-cafés and one cookie store. The company grew slowly until the mid-1990s, when it acquired Saint Louis Bread Company, a chain of 20 bakery-cafes located in the St. Louis area. About that time, the owners of the newly combined companies observed that people were increasingly looking for products that were "special"—that were a departure from run-of-the-mill restaurant food. Second, they noted that although consumers were tiring of standard fast-food fare, they didn't want to give up the convenience of quick service. This trend led the company to conclude that consumers wanted the convenience of fast food combined with a higher-quality experience. In slightly different words, they wanted good food served quickly in an enjoyable environment.

The Emergence of Fast Casual

As the result of these changing consumer tastes, a new category in the restaurant industry, called "fast casual," emerged. This category provided consumers the alternative they wanted by capturing the advantage of both the fast-food category (speed) and the casual dining category (good food), with no significant disadvantages. The owners of Au Bon Pain and Saint Louis Bread Company felt that they could help pioneer this new category, so they repositioned their restaurants and named them Panera Bread. The position that Panera moved into is depicted in the graphic titled "Positioning Strategy of Various Restaurant Chains." A market positioning grid provides a visual representation of the positions of various companies in an industry. About Panera's category, industry expert T. J. Callahan said, "I don't think fast casual is a fad; I think it's a structural change starting to happen in the restaurant industry."

Panera's Version of Fast Casual

To establish itself as the leader in the fast-casual category and to distinguish itself from its rivals, Panera (which is Latin for "time for bread") added a bonus to the mix—specialty food. The company has become known as the nation's bread expert and offers a variety of artisan and other specialty breads, along with bagels, pastries, and baked goods. Panera Bread's restaurants are open for breakfast, lunch, and dinner and also offer hand-tossed salads, signature sandwiches, and hearty soups served in edible sourdough bread bowls, along with hot and cold coffee drinks. The company also provides catering services through its Via Panera catering business. Its restaurants provide an inviting neighborly atmosphere, adding to their appeal. Panera even suggests a new time of day to eat specialty foods, calling the time between lunch and dinner "chill-out" time.

Positioning Strategy of Various Restaurant Chains

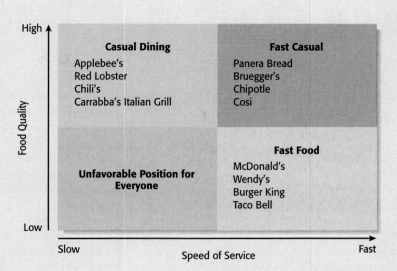

With high hopes for future expansion, Panera Bread is now the acknowledged leader in the fast-casual category. Systemwide sales were $640 million in 2005. Its unique blend of fast-casual service and specialty foods also continues to gain momentum. This sentiment is captured in the following quote from Mark von Waaden, an investor and restaurateur who recently signed an agreement to open 20 Panera Bread restaurants in the Houston, Texas, area. Commenting on why he was attracted to Panera Bread as opposed to other restaurant chains, Mr. von Waaden said,

> My wife, Monica, and I fell in love with the fresh-baked breads and the beautiful bakery-cafés. We think the Panera Bread concept of outstanding bread coupled with warm, inviting environment is a natural fit with the sophistication that the Houston market represents.

The spirit of von Waaden's statement captures the essence of Panera's advantage. It isn't just another restaurant. By observing trends and listening to customers, its leaders helped the firm carve out a unique and favorable position in a difficult industry.

Present Status and Goal for the Future

Panera's leadership in the fast-casual category and its financial performance has drawn considerable attention to the company. As evidence of this, in early 2006 Panera was recognized by the *Wall Street Journal*'s Shareholder Scorecard as the top performer in the restaurant category for one-, five-, and ten-year returns to shareholders.

The company's goal remains to make Panera a leading national brand. The company is counting on its unique positioning strategy, its signature foods, and savvy execution to make this goal a reality.

Discussion Questions

1. How has Panera Bread establish a unique position in the restaurant industry? How has this unique position contributed to its success? Do you think Panera Bread will reach its goal of becoming a leading national brand in the restaurant industry? Why or why not?

2. Analyze the restaurant industry using Porter's five forces model. In what ways has Panera Bread successfully positioned itself against the forces that are suppressing the profitability of the restaurant industry as a whole?

3. What barriers to entry has Panera Bread created for potential competitors? How significant are these barriers?

4. What are Panera Bread's primary sources of competitive advantage? In your judgment, are these sources of advantage sustainable? Why or why not?

Application Questions

1. What are the ways that Panera Bread can conduct ethical and proper forms of competitive analysis to learn about potential competitors entering the fast-casual category?

2. Think of at least two other businesses that have established unique positions in their industries. How have their unique positions contributed to their success?

Sources: Panera Bread homepage, www.panera.com, (accessed May 18, 2006); Panera Bread Annual Report (2005); "Industry by Industry: A Look at the Start, Their Stocks—and Their Latest Picks, *The Wall Street Journal*, May 12, 2003, R8.

CASE 5.2

Cirque du Soleil and Curves International: Succeeding in Unattractive Industries Via Blue Ocean Strategies
www.cirquedusoleil.com, www.curves.com

Bruce R. Barringer,
University of Central Florida
R. Duane Ireland,
Texas A&M University

Introduction

At first glance, Cirque du Soleil and Curves International have little in common. One is a high-end entertainment company with only five permanent locations. The other is a fitness center for women, with close to 10,000 locations worldwide. But when it comes to this chapter's topic, industry and competitor analysis, the two have similar start-up stories as well as current performance-related outcomes. Indeed, although both companies were launched in what would be called unattractive industries, both are thriving today, primarily by attracting new customers to their industries and by changing the rules of competition in their respective industries.

Examining these firms shows that both Cirque du Soleil and Curves have started companies in what W. Chan Kim and Renee Mauborgne call "blue oceans." In their book *Blue Ocean Strategy*, Kim and Mauborgne ask their readers to imagine a market universe composed of two types of oceans: blue oceans and red oceans. In the red oceans, industry boundaries are well defined and the rules of the game are known. Companies slug it out for market share, and as the market gets increasingly crowded, prospects for growth and profits diminish, and cutthroat competition turns the oceans red. In contrast, blue oceans are defined by untapped market space and the opportunity for highly profitable growth. Most blue oceans are actually created within red oceans by expanding existing industry boundaries. When this happens, the industries experience a flood of new customers that rarely, if ever, participated before.

Although not all industries are ripe for blue ocean strategies, Cirque du Soleil and Curves are extraordinary examples of firms that rejuvenated unattractive industries by changing the rules of the game. They have succeeded *not* by taking customers away from their rivals, but by unlocking huge untapped markets in previously unattractive industries. Read on to see how they did it.

Cirque du Soleil

Cirque du Soleil (French for "circus of the sun") was started in Montreal, Canada, in 1984 by Guy Lailberte, a 23-year-old Montreal fire breather, and Daniel Gauthier, a 24-year-old hotel manager. At the time the circus industry was in decline. There was a growing sentiment against the use of animals in circuses and alternative forms of entertainment were increasing. The existing circus companies were focused on maximizing their share of the existing demand by tweaking their acts. This meant hiring more famous clowns and more spectacular circus acts, which resulted in higher costs with little or no corresponding increase in revenue and, subsequently, income.

Rather than trying to create a circus with better fun and more thrilling acts, Cirque du Soleil decided to redefine the boundaries of the circus by offering people at the same time (1) the thrill of the circus and (2) the artistic richness and the intellectual sophistication of the theater. By adopting this approach, Cirque du Soleil was able to eliminate many of the negatives associated with traditional circuses and add the positives associated with more upscale theater productions. In the process, it did away with animal shows, hiring star performers, aisle concession sales, and the "three rings" of the three-ring circus. Animals are expensive to maintain and are controversial in a circus setting. The so-called "circus stars" paled in popularity to movie stars and professional athletics. And the "three rings" of the three-ring circus not only created angst among spectators, who rapidly switched their attention from one ring to another, but drove costs up as well.

To the founders of Cirque du Soleil, the lasting allure of the circus came down to three essential elements: the tent, the clowns, and the acrobatic acts. So they retained these elements and dressed them up. To expand the richness and the boundaries of the circus, they added new elements, such as a story line, a refined environment, artistic music and dance, and permanent venues. In addition, a key decision made early in the life of the company set its direction in terms of quality. As word spread about Cirque du Soleil's early success, offers flooded in from agents and production companies wanting to finance touring renditions of the show. But the founders refused. The supply of world-class circus performers was just too limited, they reasoned, to put dozens of Cirque du Soleil–branded shows on the road. Instead, they decided to strictly limit the number of shows they produced to avoid diluting their talent.

To visually see how Cirque du Soleil redefined the circus industry, refer to the figure titled "How Cirque du Soleil and Curves International Redefined the Industries in Which They Compete." This figure shows the factors that Cirque du Soleil eliminated from the traditional circus and

How Cirque du Soleil and Curves Redefined the Industries in Which They Compete

Cirque du Soleil

Eliminated from Traditional Circuses	Unique Additions to the Circus Concept
• Star performers • Animal shows • Aisle concession sales • Multiple show arenas	• Theme • Refined environment • Artistic music and dance • Multiple productions

Curves International

Eliminated from Traditional Fitness Centers	Unique Additions to the Fitness Center Concept
• Full range of aerobic and strength machines • Locker room and showers • Aerobic classes • Juice bars	• Just for women • A tightly structured 30-minute workout • Affordable prices • Advocacy for women

the factors that it added. The company presently has five permanent venues, four in Las Vegas and one in Orlando, and five touring shows. Each venue features a unique show, which includes a distinct story line, an original musical score, and a masterfully choreographed series of acrobatic acts and spiritual dances. By offering the best of both the circus and the theater, the company has drawn people to its performances that would never have considered attending a traditional circus. Its prices, which range from $40 to $125 per ticket, are comparable to Broadway shows.

Cirque de Soleil's unique approach has created a blue ocean and a new form of live entertainment—which is neither circus nor theater. In just over 20 years, the company has brought in as much revenue as it took Barnum & Bailey and Ringling Brothers a combined 100 years to obtain. To date, its shows have been seen by over 40 million people in 90 cities around the world.

Curves International

In the early 1990s, most fitness centers in the United States targeted people between the ages of 20 and 30. They focused on fitness and sports and typically offered exercise equipment and classes such as aerobics. Amenities ranged from towel service and showers to massages, swimming pools, and child care. Most centers sold annual or monthly memberships. Some of these memberships were expensive, running at high as $1,800 per year.

Like the founders of Cirque du Soleil, Gary and Diane Heavin, who founded Curves in 1992, had a different idea. They wanted to open a fitness center targeted at an underserved part of the market: overweight women who had never worked out before. The Heavins believed that many women 30 and older cared deeply about their health and appearance but didn't want to join a fitness center full of people who were already fit. They also figured that if they made the center convenient and affordable, and restricted it to females, it would inspire middle-aged women to give fitness a try.

To implement their idea, the Heavins stripped the fitness center concept down to what they felt would appeal to the emotional and physical needs of women and would fit into their budgets and busy lives. They started by eliminating many of the factors that drive up the cost of a fitness club membership and provide little value to many women: multiple aerobic and strength machines, locker rooms and showers, aerobic classes and juice bars. In their place, they implemented a tightly structured 30-minute workout on 8 to 12 exercise machines. The machines are located in a circle, and a recorded voice tells a member when to move from one machine to another. A member walks in, works out, and walks out, all in just over half an hour. This approach gives busy women the ability to participate without sacrificing a large portion of their day. It also allows them to shower and dress in the privacy of their homes.

What Curves has eliminated, and has uniquely added to the fitness center concept, is shown in the figure referred to earlier. As shown in the figure, the additions go beyond the workout itself. By creating a fitness center designed specifically for women, the company explicitly and implicitly told this group, "We know how you feel. We know it is not easy to go to a fitness center if you're a little embarrassed about how you look. You're important enough that we've created a company just for you. We care." By positioning itself in this way, Curves became an advocate for women 30 and older and expanded the boundaries of the fitness industry. "What Curves has done is broken through the perception that you have to be fit, coordinated and thin to go to a gym," says Bill Howland, director of research for the International Health, Racquet and Sports Association. "They've carved out a niche within the population that had never been served." In different words, Curves has created a blue ocean out of an existing red ocean.

There are now close to 10,000 Curves locations worldwide with sales exceeding the $1 billion mark. Through its unique approach, Curves has attracted a large number of women to the fitness industry who would never have joined a fitness center before. Its unique approach has also made the opening of a Curves franchise affordable for a wider range of potential franchisees. A curves franchise can be opened for between $35,000 and $50,000. By comparison, a full-service fitness center can cost up to $1 million to build and fully equip.

Discussion Questions

1. What are the primary lessons learned from the Cirque du Soleil and the Curves cases? How do these lessons help the founders of a start-up better appreciate and understand the dynamics of the industry that they are about to enter?

2. What barriers to entry have both Cirque du Soleil and Curves established to deter competitors? Has capturing a first-mover advantage helped these firms deter new entrants from expanding their respective industries in the same ways that Cirque du Soleil and

Curves did? Which company has established stronger barriers to entry—Cirque du Soleil or Curves?

3. Which of the nontraditional barriers to entry, shown in Table 5.1, were utilized by Cirque du Soleil and which were utilized by Curves? To what extent have these nontraditional barriers to entry contributed to each company's success?

4. Develop a competitive analysis grid for Curves. Replicate the grid shown in Table 5.4, replacing the information provided for Activision with similar information for Curves.

Application Questions

1. Provide an example of a company, other than Cirque du Soleil or Curves, that has expanded the market boundaries (that is, that has created a blue ocean) out of an unattractive industry (that is, from a red ocean). Briefly tell this company's story.

2. Do you think a fitness center designed specifically for men could be as successful in drawing new people into the fitness center industry as Curves has been with its fitness centers designed specifically for women? Explain your answer.

Sources: W. C. Kim and R. Mauborge, *Blue Ocean Strategy* (Boston: Harvard Business School Press, 2005); Cirque du Soleil homepage, www.cirquedusoleil.com (accessed May 8, 2006); Curves International homepage, www.curves.com (accessed May 8, 2006); H. W. Tesoriero, "A Slim Gym's Fat Success," *Time,* June, 2003.

Endnotes

1. Personal Interview with Evan Shapiro, July 25, 2006.
2. Sun-tzu, *The Art of War* (Mineola, NY: Dover Publications, 2002), chap. 7.
3. R. P. Rumelt, "How Much Does Industry Matter?" *Strategic Management Journal* 12, no. 3 (1991): 167–85.
4. Y. E. Spanos, G. Zaralis, and S. Lioukas, "Strategy and Industry Effects on Profitability: Evidence From Greece," *Strategic Management Journal* 25 (2004), 139–65.
5. A. M. McGahan and M. Porter, "How Much Does Industry Matter, Really?" *Strategic Management Journal* 18, special issue (1997): 15–30.
6. G. Hawawini, V. Subramanian, and P. Verdin, "Is Performance Driven By Industry Or Firm-Specific Factors? A Reply to McNamara, Aime, and Vaaler," *Strategic Management Journal* 26 (2006), 1083–86.
7. M. Porter, *Competitive Strategy: Techniques for Analyzing Industries and Competitors* (New York: Free Press, 1980).
8. Porter, *Competitive Strategy.*
9. J. W. Mullins, *The New Business Road Test* (London: Financial Times Prentice Hall, 2003).
10. Porter, *Competitive Strategy.*
11. T. Surette and C. Feldman, "Big Deal: EA and NFL Ink Exclusive Licensing Agreement," *Gamespot News,* www.gamespot.com (accessed December 13, 2004).
12. G. Keighley, "Could This Be the Next Disney?" *Business 2.0,* December 2002.

13. S. McNealy, "A Winning Business Model," in *The Book of Entrepreneurs' Wisdom*, ed. Peter Krass (New York: John Wiley & Sons, 1999), 171–89.
14. M. Porter, "How Competitive Forces Shape Strategy," *Harvard Business Review* 57, no. 2, (1979), 137–45.
15. Geoffrey A. Moore, *Dealing With Darwin* (New York: Portfolio, 2005).
16. J. A. Barney and W. Hesterly, "Organizational Economics: Understanding the Relationship Between Organizations and Economic Analysis," in *Handbook of Organization Studies*, eds. Steward R. Clegg, Cynthia Hardy, and Walter R. Nord (London: Sage, 1996), 115–47.
17. J. Rodengen, *The Legend of Nucor Corporation* (Ft. Lauderdale, FL: Write Stuff Enterprises, 1997).
18. T. Levitt, *The Marketing Imagination* (New York: Free Press, 1986).
19. M-J. Chen, "Competitor Analysis and Inter-Firm Rivalry: Toward a Theoretical Integration," *Academy of Management Review* 21, no. 1 (1996): 100–34.
20. P. Kotler, *Marketing Insights from A to Z* (Hoboken, NJ: Wiley, 2003), 23.
21. P. Coburn, *The Change Function* (New York: Portfolio, 2006).
22. J. L. Nesheim, *The Power of Unfair Advantage* (New York: Free Press, 2005).
23. Activision 10-K Report for the Fiscal Year Ending March 31, 2006.

Courtesy of Ethan Fieldman.

Getting Personal
with ETHAN FIELDMAN

Currently in my iPod

Blink (Audiobook)

My advice for new entrepreneurs

Just remember: It's not "work" if you enjoy it. Consider it your 80-hour-per-week hobby

My biggest surprise as an entrepreneur

Everything cost much more than you would expect. Everything

TutoringZone:
Providing a Needed Service to College Students

If you're a student at the University of Florida, or know someone who is, it is likely that you or your friend have heard of TutoringZone. Launched at the University of Florida, TutoringZone is a tutoring service geared toward college students. The company has expanded and now offers its services on additional campuses, such as the University of Georgia. At the University of Florida (UF), the service currently employs more than 50 tutors who help students grasp the fine points of 40 different courses, from physics to macroeconomics to trigonometry.

TutoringZone was started by Ethan Fieldman and Matt Hintze—two students well qualified to mentor others academically. Fieldman, who is shown in the picture, graduated with highest honors from UF (4.0 overall GPA) with a BS in business administration, majoring in finance with a minor in economics. Hintze earned an undergraduate degree with honors from UCLA in business economics, before moving to UF to complete an MBA, graduating first in his class (4.0 overall GPA).[1]

The idea for TutoringZone emerged from Fieldman's need to earn a little extra money during his sophomore year. He started tutoring students one-on-one and soon began receiving requests from other students who wanted to "sit in" on his tutoring sessions. These requests prompted Fieldman to start tutoring students in groups and to start offering weekly "review" sessions for particularly difficult classes that he had already taken or with which he was familiar. At the same time this was happening, Hintze was tutoring students for the UF Athletic Association, where he says he realized there is a social element to studying, and also started tutoring students in groups. "It wasn't like these people were doing this alone, but they were talking to each other, collecting into small groups," Hintze recalls.[2]

Fieldman and Hintze eventually crossed paths, hit it off, and decided to combine their efforts and start TutoringZone. While they saw tutoring businesses like Sylvan Learning Center and Kaplan available for K–12 students in Gainesville, the town where UF is located, they didn't see any structured tutoring service available for college students. TutoringZone was launched to fill this gap in the marketplace.

ETHAN FIELDMAN

Cofounder, Tutoring Zone
BSBA, College of Business,
University of Florida, 2003

MATT HINTZE

Cofounder, Tutoring Zone
MBA, College of Business,
University of Florida, 1997

UF | UNIVERSITY of FLORIDA

What I do when I'm not working	Best part of being a student	My biggest worry as an entrepreneur
Golf, Ski, Travel, Workout, Go out with friends, Watch Tivo	*Florida Gator Football*	*If the business fails, I'll have to lay off friends (employees). I can't imagine anything worse*

After studying this chapter you should be ready to:

L E A R N I N G

Objectives

1. Describe a business model.

2. Explain business model innovation.

3. Discuss the importance of having a clearly articulated business model.

4. Discuss the concept of the value chain.

5. Identify a business model's two potential fatal flaws.

6. Identify a business model's four major components.

7. Explain the meaning of the term *business concept blind spot*.

8. Define *core competency* and describe its importance.

9. Explain the concept of supply chain management.

10. Define the term *target market*.

A unique business model was at the core of launching TutoringZone. The company has a menu of tiered services, where students can spend as little as $60 per semester per class for 4-hour monthly review sessions in a classroom setting, to $300 per semester per class for weekly reviews conducted in small group settings. Since founding TutoringZone, Fieldman and Hintze have carefully documented how much value the service provides to the students who participate. At the end of each final exam review session, a questionnaire is distributed to all students, asking them what grade they "think" they will receive in that particular course. The students are also asked what grade they believe they would have gotten without the help of TutoringZone. On average, students increase their grades by 1.2 grade points as a result of using TutoringZone's services.

There are two other important elements of TutoringZone's business model. First, the company is very careful in terms of how it selects its tutors. In fact, Fieldman and Hintze consider their selection methods to be a trade secret, because of the impressive results they produce. The tutors all receive training before they are put in front of a group of students, and strict ethical and professional guidelines are followed. For example, tutors never solve homework problems for students, even as part of a group discussion. Instead, the tutors focus on fundamentals and teach the students how to solve similar problems, so they can do their homework on their own. The tutors are also trained to mix their instruction with levity and humor, as appropriate, to make the sessions as comfortable yet instructive as possible. The second distinctive aspect of TutoringZone's business model is the manner in which the company interfaces with its student clients. While the tutoring itself is serious, Fieldman and Hintze are keenly aware of the social aspects of learning and college life in general. For example, the company recently moved all of its tutoring sessions into a building formally occupied by a large grocery store. The building has been renovated to make it suitable for tutoring sessions, but also includes a coffee bar, free Internet access, and comfortable areas for students to simply "hang out" while they study and socialize. While TutoringZone is a business, it also wants to be a vibrant, positive part of the college communities in which it locates.

How is TutoringZone's business model performing? The company is profitable, and over 4,000 students per semester take advantage of TutoringZone's service at the University of Florida alone. In fact, Fieldman estimates that 60 to 80 percent of all students enrolled in a course for which TutoringZone provides services at UF will attend one or more of TutoringZone's review sessions sometime during their college program.

This chapter introduces the business model and explains why it's important for a new venture to develop a business model early in its life. In everyday language, a model is a plan that's used to make or describe something. More formally, a **business model** is a firm's plan or diagram for how it competes, uses its resources, structures its relationships, interfaces with customers, and creates value to sustain itself on the basis of the profits it earns.[3] As you'll see later in this chapter, a successful business model has four components.

The term business model first came into use with the advent of the PC and the spreadsheet. The spreadsheet made sensitivity analysis possible, giving managers the ability to ask "what-if" questions. A manager could sit at a computer, manipulate an item such as sales, and see how a shortfall or an upswing in sales would affect every other aspect of the business. In other words, a manager could "model" the behavior of the business.[4] Today, "business model" is used in a much broader context to include all the activities that define how a firm competes in the marketplace.[5]

It's important to understand that a firm's business model takes it beyond its own boundaries. Almost all firms partner with others to make their business models work. In Dell's case, it needs the cooperation of its suppliers, shippers, customers, and many others to make its business model possible. For example, if Dell's suppliers weren't willing to deliver up-to-date parts to the company on a just-in-time basis, Dell would have higher inventory costs and wouldn't be able to ship its customer's state-of-the-art products or be as price competitive. Dell works closely with its suppliers and keeps them motivated to participate. Working with Dell this way can also help a supplier operate profitably in that the size of Dell's orders may account for a major portion of a supplier's production. This could be significant in that Dell is known to be loyal to its suppliers and to help their cash flow by paying them quickly for their delivered products.

Thus, as is the case for TutoringZone, a company's business model involves its network of partners along with its products. It encompasses the capabilities of multiple individuals and entities, all of which must be willing and motivated to play along. Some early e-commerce firms that had plausible business models on paper failed because they couldn't get key partners to participate. An example is online beauty retailer Eve.com. The company struggled largely because many of the high-profile suppliers of women's beauty products wouldn't sell their products on its Web site. The suppliers were concerned that if they sold through Eve.com, they would offend their traditional channel partners, such as Nordstrom and Saks. Eve.com's business model never coalesced, and the firm eventually went out of business.

In this chapter, we'll first discuss business models and their importance. Then we'll look at how business models emerge and examine some of their potential "fatal flaws." Finally, we'll examine the components of effective business models.

Business Models

There is no standard business model, no hard-and-fast rules that dictate how a firm in a particular industry should compete. In fact, it's dangerous for the entrepreneur launching a new venture to assume that the venture can be successful by simply copying the business model of another firm—even if that other firm is the industry leader. This is true for two reasons. First, it is difficult to precisely understand all of the components of another firm's business model. Second, a firm's business model is inherently dependent on the collection of resources it controls and the capabilities it possesses. For example, if Dell Inc. employs the best group of supply chain managers in the country and has established long-term trusting relationships with key suppliers, it may be the only company in the world that can effectively implement its business model. No other firm would have this unique set of capabilities, at least initially.

To achieve long-term success though, all business models need to be modified across time. The reason for this is that competitors can eventually learn how to duplicate the benefits a particular firm is able to create through its business model. In late 2006, for example, financial returns suggested that competitors such as Hewlett-Packard were beginning to understand how to duplicate some of the benefits Dell historically created by using its business model. To prevent duplication of a successful business model, firms engage in **business model innovation**, which refers to initiatives that are undertaken with the intention of revolutionizing how a particular product is produced, sold, and supported after the sale.[6] Figure 6.1 depicts Dell's approach to selling computers versus traditional manufacturers', which represented a business model innovation in the computer industry. As we've noted, some competitors seem to be closer to duplicating the benefits of Dell's model today than they have been over the years. Nonetheless, at the time of its introduction, Dell's business model was definitely revolutionary.

The development of a firm's business model follows the feasibility analysis stage of launching a new venture. If a firm has conducted a successful feasibility analysis and knows that it has a product or service with potential, the business model stage addresses how to surround it with a core strategy, a partnership model, a customer interface, distinctive resources, and an approach to creating value that represents a viable business.

LEARNING Objective

1. Describe a business model.

LEARNING Objective

2. Explain business model innovation.

FIGURE 6.1

Dell's Approach to Selling PCs versus Traditional Manufacturers'

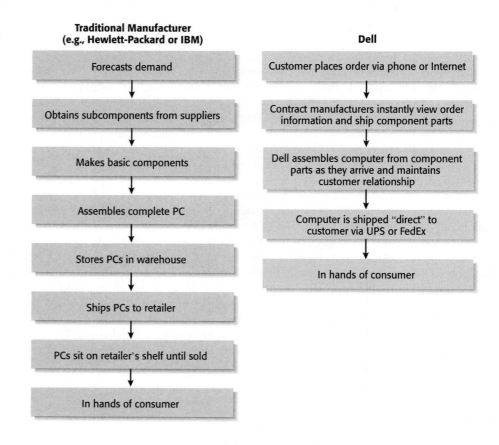

At the business model development stage, it is premature for a new venture to raise money, hire a lot of employees, establish partnerships, or implement a marketing plan. A firm needs to have its business model in place before it can make additional substantive decisions. Failure to develop a well-designed business model generally stems from a naive understanding about the nature of how businesses operate or a rush to get a new product or service idea to market. Matt Ragas, a marketing expert, said this about neglecting to design a thorough business model:

> A killer new product or service without a well-thought-out business model is a lot like a sailor lost at sea without navigational charts. Think about it. Suppose we packed a dream team of yachtsmen onto a ship and told them to set sail and find a new route to Asia. Being pros, they'd give it their best shot, but without charts to guide their journey, they'd end up drifting on the oceans endlessly. Eventually they'd run out of supplies and more than likely not survive. Companies that create innovative products or services without well-crafted business models act much the same way. [They] believe they can succeed in the marketplace merely by throwing their new product or service over the side and hoping it will swim.[7]

Entrepreneurs must do much more than "hope their new ideas can swim." Indeed, a great product or service idea that isn't supported by a carefully crafted business model will likely become an unfulfilled promise of success. Now, let's look more specifically at why a business model is important.

The Importance of a Business Model

Having a well-thought-out business model is important for several reasons. Although some models are better than others, it is dangerous to link the performance of a firm solely to the configuration of its business model. In most cases, performance is a function of both the *choice* of a business model and how effectively a firm *uses* its model. The problem that befell many of the early e-commerce companies was that they thought that by selecting an Internet-based business model, they could sit back and watch the money roll in. But entrepreneurship is not that simple. These companies neglected to pay attention to *how they performed* within that business model. A company must craft a strategy, use resources efficiently, develop a partnership model, and interface with customers effectively to be successful.

Having a clearly articulated business model is important because it does the following:

■ Serves as an ongoing extension of feasibility analysis (a business model continually asks the question, Does the business make sense?)
■ Focuses attention on how all the elements of a business fit together and constitute a working whole
■ Describes why the network of participants needed to make a business idea viable is willing to work together
■ Articulates a company's core logic to all stakeholders, including the firm's employees

LEARNING Objective

3. Discuss the importance of having a clearly articulated business model.

A good way to illustrate the importance of these points is to describe a business model that *didn't* work. WebHouse Club was launched by Priceline.com founder Jay Walker in the fall of 1999 and failed just a year later after eating up nearly $350 million of its investors' money. Priceline.com allows customers to "bid" for airline tickets, hotel rooms, and home mortgages. WebHouse was set up to mimic Priceline.com's business model and extend it to grocery store items. WebHouse worked like this: A shopper obtained a plastic card with a unique number and a magnetic strip from a local grocery store or a newspaper insert. The card was used to activate an account on the WebHouse Internet site. Once an account was established, the shopper could then make a bid for a supermarket item, say $3.75 for a box of toasted corn flakes cereal. The shopper could specify the price but not the brand. In seconds, the shopper would learn whether a maker of toasted corn flakes cereal was willing to accept the price. If so, the shopper would pay WebHouse for the cereal with a credit card and would then pick up the cereal at a participating store using the WebHouse card. The cereal could be Kellogg's, General Mills, or any other brand.

Behind the scenes, WebHouse followed the same formula that Priceline.com had invented to sell airline tickets and hotel rooms. By aggregating shopper demand for products such as cereal, tuna, or diapers, WebHouse could go to producers such as Kellogg's and General Mills and negotiate discounts. The company could then pass along the discounts to consumers and take a small fee for bringing buyers and sellers together.[8]

Why didn't this business model work for WebHouse? Actually, several reasons describe the business model's failure in grocery stores. First, it assumed that companies such as Kellogg's would be willing to participate—not a wise assumption when you consider that Kellogg's has spent millions of dollars convincing consumers that Kellogg's Corn Flakes is better than competing brands. The WebHouse model teaches consumers to select products strictly on the basis of price rather than brand identity. So why would Kellogg's or any other producer want to help WebHouse do that? Second, the WebHouse model assumed that millions of shoppers would take the time to sit down at their computers and bid on grocery store items. It's easy to see why a consumer might take the time to get a better deal on an airline ticket or a stay in a four-star hotel room. But how many people have the time to sit down, log on to their computer, and interact with a Web site to save 50 cents on a box of cereal without even being able to choose the brand? As it turned out, not many people were willing to do so.

Ultimately, WebHouse failed because its business model was flawed. The company just couldn't motivate its suppliers or customers to participate at a sufficient scale to support the overhead of the business. WebHouse was asking suppliers to act against their self-interest and was asking shoppers to take too much time to save too little money. As busy as people are today, shoppers want to make the very best use of their limited time, meaning that they'll likely reject a time-consuming process that doesn't create obvious value for them.

WebHouse illustrates the importance of articulating a business model in the early life of a new venture. Once the model is clearly determined, the entrepreneur should diagram it on paper (to the extent possible), examine it, and ask the following questions:

- Does my business model make sense?
- Will the businesses I need as partners participate?
- If I can get partners to participate, how motivated will they be? Am I asking them to work for or against their self-interest?
- How about my customers? Will it be worth their time to do business with my company?
- If I do get customers, how motivated will they be?
- Can I motivate my partners and customers at a sufficient scale to cover the overhead of my business and make a profit?
- How distinct will my business be? If I'm successful, will it be easy for a larger competitor to step in and steal my idea?

If the answer to each of these questions isn't satisfactory, then the business model should be revised or abandoned. Ultimately, a business model is viable only insofar as the buyer, the seller, and the partners involved see it as an appropriate method of selling a product or service.[9]

How Business Models Emerge

4. Discuss the concept of the value chain.

The value chain is a model developed by an academic researcher[10] that many businesspeople as well as entrepreneurs use to identify opportunities to enhance their competitive strategies. The value chain also explains how business models emerge and develop. The **value chain** is the string of activities that moves a product from the raw material stage, through manufacturing and distribution, and ultimately to the end user. Depicted in Figure 6.2, the value chain consists of primary activities and support activities. The primary activities have

FIGURE 6.2

The Value Chain

Source: Competitive Advantage: Creating and Sustaining Superior Performance by Michael E. Porter. © 1995, 1998 by Michael E. Porter. All rights reserved. Reprinted with permission of The Free Press, a Division of Simon & Schuster Adult Publishing Group.

to do with the physical creation, sale, and service of a product or a service, while the support activities provide reinforcement for the primary activities. Individual parts of the chain either add or do not add value as a product moves through the different stages of the value chain. The final product or service is an aggregate of the individual contributions of value made at the different stages of the chain.

By studying a product's or service's value chain, an organization can identify ways to create additional value and assess whether it has the means to do so. For example, Dell learned that it has customers who want technical support available on a 24-hour-per-day basis, 7 days a week (24/7) and that these customers are willing to pay extra to get it. Dell realized that it could "add value" to the value chain for selling computers by beefing up the "service" segment to include 24/7 technical support. This would work, however, only if Dell had enough trained personnel to offer the 24/7 support and could make money doing so. Additionally, if Dell could offer the 24/7 support and its competitors couldn't, the 24/7 service would become a point of profit-generating differentiation between Dell and its competitors. In late 2006, Dell was allocating additional resources to its support services in order to create more value for its customers. This example illustrates why the value chain has been widely adopted as a tool for developing firm strategy and analyzing firm competitiveness.

Value chain analysis is also helpful in identifying opportunities for new businesses and in understanding how business models emerge. Many scholars now have a wider view of the value chain than the original conceptualization pictured in Figure 6.2. A key reason this expanded view has evolved is that most products and services are produced in a complex supply chain that involves many companies rather than a single firm. Variations of the value chain have been created to depict the production of goods and services through "value networks" or "value systems" rather than a single-firm value chain.[11] Because of this, a value *chain* tends to be identified more with a product (e.g., a computer) or service (e.g., tax preparation) than a particular company (e.g., Dell or tax preparation firm Jackson Hewitt).

Entrepreneurs look at the value chain of a product or a service to pinpoint where the value chain can be made more effective or to spot where additional "value" can be added in some meaningful way. This type of analysis may focus on (1) a single primary activity of the value chain (such as marketing and sales), (2) the interface between one stage of the value chain and another (such as the interface between operations, which are the activities required to manufacture a product, and outbound logistics, which are the activities required to warehouse and ship it), or (3) one of the support activities (such as human resource management). If a product's value chain can be strengthened in any one of these areas, it may represent an opportunity for the formation of a new firm to perform that activity. Table 6.1 provides examples of entrepreneurial firms that have enhanced the value chain of an existing product or service by focusing on one of the three previously mentioned areas.

A firm can be formed to strengthen the value chain for a product, however, only if a viable business model can be created to support it. For example, Michael Dell's idea of selling computers directly to end users wouldn't have been possible if it weren't for low-cost shippers, such as UPS and FedEx, and manufacturers of computer components who were willing to sell their products to him. Similarly, TutoringZone's service wouldn't be possible if the firm couldn't locate enough qualified tutors to conduct its review sessions.

Finally, some start-ups are launched with the defined purpose of providing the missing link in a potentially lucrative value chain that currently isn't plausible because of technical or economic limitations. An example is PepperCoin, a company that is establishing an affordable way for magazines, musicians, and a multitude of others to sell products over the Internet for small amounts of money. One problem that has plagued e-commerce is that it hasn't been affordable for a Web site to sell products for small amounts of money. For example, a musician might want to offer downloads of individual songs for 50 cents apiece, but it might cost 40 cents or more per transaction to collect the money via debit cards, credit cards, or through an online service like PayPal. To solve this problem, PepperCoin is developing a superefficient way to process small payments (which are called "micropayments") for purchases made on the Internet. The upside potential of this technology for PepperCoin's potential customers is huge. Many sites could flourish if they could charge 25 cents for a newsletter, 50 cents to watch a movie trailer, or a dollar to play

TABLE 6.1 Firms Founded to Enhance the Value Chain of an Existing Product or Service

New Venture's Current Name	Value Chain Activity	Reason New Venture was Started
	Primary Activities	
BAX Global, DHL, Maersk Logistics	Inbound logistics	To provide efficient material management, warehousing, and inventory control
Celestica, Flextronics, Solectron	Operations	To provide efficient contract manufacturing services for companies such as IBM, Microsoft, and Ericsson
FedEx, Ryder, UPS	Outbound logistics	To provide new ways to warehouse and move goods effectively to the end user
Costco, Staples, Wal-Mart	Marketing and sales	To provide new ways to market and sell products
EDS, Infosys, TellMe	Service	To provide efficient call center, e-mail, and Web-based customer contact services
	Support Activities	
Accenture, Booz Allen, Boston Consulting Group	Firm infrastructure	To provide management support
Administaff, Paychex, TeamStaff	Human resource management	To provide payroll, tax, benefits administration, and other human resource services
Booz Allen, Perot Systems, Unisys	Technology development	To help firms integrate emerging technologies into existing business systems
BASF, Georgia-Pacific, Grainger	Resource procurement	To help firms procure the raw materials and supplies needed for their production processes
	The Interface Between One Stage of the Value Chain and Another	
Ariba, ChemConnect, i2 Technologies	Inbound logistics/operations	To help firms with the interface between inbound logistics and operations
Con-way Inc., DHL Worldwide Express, UPS	Operations/outbound logistics	To help firms with the interface between operations and outbound logistics
Affiliated Warehouse, Interstate Cold Storage, Specialized Warehousing Services	Outbound logistics/marketing and sales	To help firms with the interface between outbound logistics and marketing and sales
ExpressScripts, Liberty Medical	Marketing and sales/service	To help firms with the interface between marketing and sales/service

an electronic game. Commenting on the potential of its technology for providing the missing link that will enable other business models to be possible, Perry Solomon, an executive of PepperCoin remarked:

> Advertising was dominant through 2001 [as a source of revenue for Internet companies] [but] there wasn't an efficient way for content producers (like the creators of online games) to make their content available on a pay-as-you-go basis. We enable a way for content companies to be able to build profitable businesses through pay-per-use and subscriptions. We see our service as rounding out the business model of online content producers.[12]

Potential Fatal Flaws of Business Models

5. Identify a business model's two potential fatal flaws.

Two fatal flaws can render a business model untenable from the beginning: a complete misread of the customer and utterly unsound economics. Business models that fall victim to one of these two flaws have lost the race before leaving the starting gate.

In plain terms, a product must have customers to be successful. In the previously mentioned WebHouse example, the savings that were possible by bidding on grocery store items just weren't large enough to make it worthwhile for enough people to participate. The product had no customers. A similar misread of the customer sank Pets.com, a high-profile

Pets.com was known for its "spokespuppet," which appeared in Super Bowl ads and even in the Macy's Thanksgiving Day parade in New York City. The company's ads were larger than life, but when it came down to basic customer satisfaction, Pets.com missed the mark, revealing fatal flaws in the company's business model. Pets.com closed its doors in early 2001.

e-commerce flameout. Although it was convenient for consumers to have pet food and supplies delivered directly to their homes, the orders took several days to arrive—too long for customers who have access to the same products at the grocery store and at pet superstores such as PetSmart. Pets.com didn't realize that fast delivery was essential to its customers.

The second fatal flaw is pursuing unsound economics, as shown by the failure of Iridium, the satellite telephone company that was featured in Chapter 3. The idea behind Iridium was to target people who traveled to or worked in areas where traditional cellular service was unavailable. Unfortunately, the cost of putting satellites into orbit was so high that literally hundreds of thousands of people would have had to subscribe to Iridium's service to make it economically viable. As you'll recall, this never happened. Although satellite telephone service is still available, skeptics wonder if it will ever be economically viable.

A substantive example of a business model that failed because of a fatal flaw is depicted in this chapter's "What Went Wrong" feature.

Components of an Effective Business Model

Although not everyone agrees precisely about the components of a business model, many agree that a successful business model has a common set of attributes. For example, one team of academics thinks of a business model as a coordinated plan to design strategy along three vectors: customer interaction, asset configuration, and knowledge leverage.[13] Similarly, a noted business professor and writer, Gary Hamel, believes that a business model consists of four components: core strategy, strategic resources, customer interface, and value network.[14] We'll adopt a similar view and talk about a business model consisting of the following components:

L E A R N I N G
Objective

6. Identify a business model's four major components.

- Core strategy (how a firm competes)
- Strategic resources (how a firm acquires and uses its resources)
- Partnership network (how a firm structures and nurtures its partnerships)
- Customer interface (how a firm interfaces with its customers)

Each of these components has several subcomponents that we'll explore. We provide a summary of each component and its respective subcomponents in Figure 6.3.

MobileStar's Mistaken Belief: "If We Build It, They Will Come"

In 1997, MobileStar was launched to manufacture, sell, and install wireless "hotspot" networks. A hotspot is in an area in which high-speed wireless Internet connectivity is available. The idea behind MobileStar was to install hotspots in public places, such as hotel lobbies and restaurants, where business travelers and others could log on to the Internet via their laptop computers.

To capture first-mover advantages, MobileStar moved quickly to secure venues for its networks. It struck deals with a number of companies, including Hilton Hotels, American Airlines Admirals Clubs, Columbia Sussex Hotels, and its biggest prize, Starbucks, which allowed it to install networks in 500 of its locations. A key element of MobileStar's business model was its formula for making money. Rather than charging the restaurants and hotels in which it built its networks, it charged the end users of its service. The price of its service was $15.95 to $59.95 for a monthly subscription (the nature of the subscriptions varied by location) and around $2.95 per hour for people who bought prepaid minutes cards.

Unfortunately, in late 2001, MobileStar failed. What went wrong? As it turned out, MobileStar's business model just wasn't viable. Here's why.

First, by taking on all the costs associated with installing the networks, MobileStar incurred substantial up-front expenditures. This meant that it needed to entice a large number of people to use its service to cover its overhead. By adopting this approach, critics say that MobileStar engaged in a classic "if we build it, they will come" mentality. But the customers didn't come. In its eagerness to get into prized locations, it didn't ask companies such as Starbucks or Hilton to share any of the costs or risk. When its numbers fell below their projections, it ended up with huge costs and meager income.

Second, by charging the end user for its service rather than the locations that the service was placed in, MobileStar didn't motivate the owners or employees of the locations to sell the service. The number of customers of Starbucks who used the MobileStar network had no effect on the profits of Starbucks. Starbucks agreed to host MobileStar as a service to its customers, but it didn't have a financial stake in whether the service succeeded or failed. This factor turned out to be MobileStar's fatal flaw in many of its locations.

The hotspot industry is still alive, and an increasing number of restaurants, hotels, airports, and other public places are offering wireless Internet connectivity. The new companies, however, are sporting new business models that avoid MobileStar's miscues. The companies are charging the venues in which they place their networks a fee for their services and are letting the venues themselves charge the end users.

Questions for Critical Thinking

1. First-mover advantages are thought to benefit firms. Was MobileStar's first-mover advantage beneficial for the firm? If not, why not?

2. Did MobileStar succumb to one of the potential fatal flaws of business models discussed in the chapter? If so, which one?

3. Skip ahead in the book and read Case 13.2, which focuses on Captivate Networks, a firm that places video screens in elevators. What mistake did MobileStar make that Captivate Networks avoided?

4. Make a list of the lessons you've learned from reading about MobileStar's experiences.

FIGURE 6.3

Components of a Business Model

Core Strategy	Strategic Resources	Partnership Network	Customer Interface
• Business mission • Product/market scope • Basis for differentiation	• Core competencies • Strategic assets	• Suppliers • Partners • Other key relationships	• Target customer • Fulfillment and support • Pricing structure

Core Strategy

The first component of a business model is the **core strategy**, which describes how a firm competes relative to its competitors.[15] The firm's mission statement, the product/market scope, and the basis for differentiation are the primary elements of a core strategy.

Mission Statement A firm's mission, or **mission statement**, describes why it exists and what its business model is supposed to accomplish.[16] Table 6.2 provides examples of the mission statements of five firms from very different industries. To varying degrees, the statements articulate the overarching priorities of the firms and set criteria to measure performance. It is fairly easy to discern the intent of all five organizations by looking at their mission statements. The statement of Southwest Airlines, although slightly less concise than some of the others, provides a clear sense of what the company is about and how it intends to compete.

It is important that a firm's mission not be defined too narrowly. If it is, the business model that evolves may become too singularly focused and resistant to change. Take Xerox, for example. The firm styled itself as "The Document Company," with an implicit mission that focused on copiers and copying. This mission created what some call a **business concept blind spot**, which prevents a firm from seeing an opportunity that might fit its business model. Xerox viewed itself as a company that *reproduced* documents that already existed, causing the firm to be a late entrant into the market for computer printers, which print original documents stored electronically. This narrow focus allowed Hewlett-Packard to gain control of the printer market.[17]

Product/Market Scope A company's **product/market scope** defines the products and markets on which it will concentrate. First, the choice of product has an important impact on a firm's business model. For example, Amazon.com started out as an online bookseller but has evolved to sell many other product lines, including CDs, DVDs, jewelry, apparel, and even groceries. Its business model has expanded to now include the challenge of

L E A R N I N G

Objective

7. Explain the meaning of the term business concept blind spot.

TABLE 6.2 Examples of Mission Statements

Google

Organize the world's information and make it universally accessible and useful.

Intel

Delight our customers, employees, and shareholders by relentlessly delivering the platform and technology advancements that become essential to the way we work and live.

Panera Bread

A loaf of bread in every arm.

Starbucks

Establish Starbucks as the premier purveyor of the finest coffee in the world while maintaining our uncompromising principles as we grow. The following six guiding principles will help us measure the appropriateness of our decisions:

- Provide a great work environment and treat each other with respect and dignity
- Embrace diversity as an essential component in the way we do business
- Apply the highest standards of excellence to the purchasing, roasting, and fresh delivery of our coffee
- Develop enthusiastically satisfied customers all the time
- Contribute positively to our communities and our environment
- Recognize that profitability is essential to our future success

Southwest Airlines

The mission of Southwest Airlines is dedication to the highest quality of customer service delivered with a sense of warmth, friendliness, individual pride, and company spirit.

managing relationships with a number of vendors and partners beyond those connected with books. Similarly, Yahoo! started as a company offering free Internet search services in an attempt to generate enough traffic to sell advertising space on its Web site. This business model worked until the e-commerce bubble burst in early 2000 and advertising revenues declined. Yahoo! is continually revising its business model to include additional subscription services to generate a more consistent income stream.

The markets on which a company focuses are also an important element of its core strategy. For example, Dell targets business customers and government agencies, while Hewlett-Packard targets individuals, small businesses, and first-time computer buyers. For both firms, their choices have had a significant impact on the shaping of their business models.

New ventures should be particularly careful not to expand their product/market offerings beyond their capabilities. Even Dell had to resist this temptation, as illustrated by Michael Dell in his book *Direct from Dell*:

> Growing a company much faster than the industry is growing is great, but when your company grows by as much as 127 percent in one year, you can quickly outstrip your ability to manage it effectively. Our problem was not that Dell was in serious decline or that our customers didn't want to buy our products. Quite the opposite, we learned that it was possible to grow too quickly. The problem was that we had been over enthusiastically pursuing every opportunity that presented itself. We needed to learn that not only did we not have to jump at each and every one, as we once did—but that we couldn't or shouldn't, for our overall well-being.[18]

One mistake in the area of product/market scope new firms are prone to make is to assume that their product and/or market offerings must be more ambitious or expansive than incumbent firms' to have a chance of succeeding. This sentiment isn't always the case. There are many successful firms that have very simple and straightforward business models, which stand out because of their simplicity rather than their complexity. Two firms that fit this profile are In-N-Out Burger and Craigslist, as illustrated in this chapter's "Savvy Entrepreneurial Firm" feature.

Basis for Differentiation   It is important that a new venture differentiate itself from its competitors in some way that is important to its customers and is not easy to copy.[19] If a new firm's products or services aren't different from those of its competitors, why should anyone try them?[20]

From a broad perspective, firms typically choose one of two generic strategies (cost leadership and differentiation) to establish a defensible position in the marketplace. Firms

In-N-Out Burger and Craigslist: Standing Out from the Crowd Because of Simplicity Rather Than Complexity
www.in-n-out.com
www.craigslist.com

One mistake that young firms are prone to make is to develop business models that are overly complex. Typically, new ventures suffer when they do this. The area that is most commonly overreached is product/market scope, where a firm assumes that it must produce more complex products or reach more distant markets than industry incumbents to have a chance of succeeding. This isn't always true. There are many examples of firms that, from their outset, have differentiated themselves along the lines of simplicity rather than complexity and have benefited as the result of doing so. In-N-Out Burger and Craigslist fit this profile. At first glance, neither of these firms is very impressive—in fact, they both seem fairly ordinary compared to some of their jazzier competitors. Yet, both In-N-Out Burger and Craigslist are extremely successful and stand out because of their simplicity rather than their complexity. Let's see how this is the case for each firm.

In-N-Out Burger

In-N-Out Burger operates about 200 fast-food restaurants in three states—California, Nevada, and Arizona. The company is privately owned by the Synder family, who founded In-N-Out Burger in 1948 and owns and operates all of the restaurants. In many ways, the basic look and feel of the restaurants has not changed much since the first In-N-Out Burger was opened almost 60 years ago. Take a minute and look at the company's Web site to get a feel for In-N-Out Burger's somewhat nostalgic and "throwback to an easier era" persona and appeal.

There are three distinctive attributes to In-N-Out's simple and straightforward business model. First, it has an extremely simple menu: cheeseburgers and hamburgers with a variety of combinations of condiments, french fries, three milk shakes (chocolate, vanilla, and strawberry), and a limited variety of beverages. That's it. Nothing on the menu costs more than $2.75 and there are no combo meals. Second, the company is fanatical about quality. For example, the company's personnel select, hand-cut, and grind all of the beef used in its hamburgers, which is free of additives, fillers, and preservatives. The lettuce is hand-leafed at each store and the french fries are cut from potatoes delivered to each restaurant from neighboring farms. The milk shakes contain 100 percent pure ice cream. Finally, everything at In-N-Out Burger is cooked to order. It takes at least 30 minutes to order and eat a meal.

The result: At lunchtime everyday, lines snake through each of In-N-Out Burger's 200 restaurants. No one seems to mind the wait. Many of the company's customers eat at an In-N-Out Burger several times a week. It doesn't offer a wide menu, like Panera Bread or Cosi, doesn't offer quick service, like Burger King or McDonald's, and it doesn't offer "lighter-fare meals" for health or diet enthusiasts. Yet it is busy every day. It is elegant via its simplicity and has garnered a loyal following as a result.

Craigslist

Craigslist is a centralized network of online communities, featuring free classified advertisements and forums sorted by various topics. Although its market scope is impressive—it offered classified ads for 310 cities in the United States and abroad as of June 2006—its product scope and the general look and feel of its Web site are very ordinary. In fact, its Web site has been written about many times as a result of its plainness rather than its impressive functionality or appeal. The company, for example, doesn't even have a logo.

Craigslist was founded in 1995 by Craig Newmark. It originally offered classified ads in the San Francisco Bay area and over the years has expanded to other cities and countries. Its sole source of revenue is paid job ads in select cities and paid broker apartment listings in New York City. Similar to In-N-Out Burger, the company seems to thrive as the result of its simplicity rather than complexity. Although the company may be leaving money on the table by not running banner ads or expanding its product offerings, it seems undeterred. According to Wikipedia, the online encyclopedia, Newmark says that Craigslist works because it gives people a voice, a sense of community trust and even intimacy. Other factors Newmark cites for his firm's success are consistency of down-to-earth values, customer service, and simplicity.

The results, for Craigslist, are impressive. The company serves over 4 billion page views per month, putting it among the 30 top-visited Web sites in the world. Although the company does not disclose financial information, it is thought to be profitable and growing on a monthly basis.

Questions for Critical Thinking

1. Do you think In-N-Out Burger and Craigslist would benefit by adopting more aggressive and contemporary business models? What would be the upside and the downside of this shift for both companies?
2. What do you think is appealing to customers about the inherent simplicity of the business models of In-N-Out Burger and Craigslist?
3. Write a mission statement for either In-N-Out Burger or Craigslist. Briefly explain the rationale for the statement you wrote.
4. Think of another successful company that has a very simple and straightforward business model. Explain the essence of the company's business model and why you think it has been successful. Similarly, think of a company that you believe has an overly complex business model. Make some suggestions for how the company could benefit by integrating more simplicity into its business model.

Sources: MJ. Silverstein and J. Butman, *Treasure Hunt* (New York: Portfolio 2006.); Craigslist homepage, www.craigslist.com, (accessed August 17, 2006); Wikipedia search for Craigslist, www.http://en.wikipedia.org/wiki/Craigslist (accessed August 17, 2006).

that have a **cost leadership strategy** strive to have the lowest costs in the industry, relative to competitors' costs, and typically attract customers by offering them a low, if not the lowest, price for the products they sell. In contrast, firms using a **differentiation strategy** compete on the basis of providing unique or different products, typically on the basis of quality, service, timeliness, or some other dimension that is important to customers.[21] Historically, it has been difficult for a new venture to use a cost leadership strategy because cost leadership typically requires economies of scale that take time to develop. This reality is changing with the advent of the Internet, which has made low cost a viable option for some Web-based start-ups. An example is LogoWorks, the online designer of business logos discussed in the "Partnering for Success" feature later in the chapter. LogoWorks has a very low cost structure, which enables it to provide businesses custom-designed logos for a very affordable price.

Firms within the same industry often use different generic strategies. In the retail clothing industry, for example, Ross follows a cost leadership strategy by offering slightly out-of-date merchandise at a deep discount. In contrast, Abercrombie & Fitch uses a differentiation strategy. It rarely cuts prices and instead competes on the basis that its products are different and stylish enough that they should command a premium price.

The strategy that a firm chooses greatly affects its business model.[22] A cost leadership strategy requires a business model that is focused on efficiency, cost minimization, and large volume, as you will see in the LogoWorks feature. As a result, a cost leader's facilities typically aren't fancy, as the emphasis is on keeping costs low rather than on comfort. Conversely, a differentiation strategy requires a business model focused on developing products and services that are unique in ways that are important to targeted customers and that command a premium price. In addition, differentiators typically work hard to create **brand loyalty**, wherein customers become loyal to a particular company's product, such as Levis jeans or Apple computers. Brand loyalty is a valuable asset in that it causes customers to buy a firm's product or service time and time again. We provide additional information about brand loyalty in Chapter 11.

Strategic Resources

A firm is not able to implement a strategy without adequate resources. This reality means that a firm's resources substantially affect how its business model is used. For a new venture, its strategic resources may initially be limited to the competencies of its founders, the opportunity they have identified, and the unique way they plan to service their market. The two most important resources are a firm's core competencies and its strategic assets.

Amazon.com *proved an exception to the rule that new ventures can't compete on price. As an entrepreneurial firm,* *Amazon.com,* *led by Jeff Bezos, combined its solid business model with the Internet's capabilities to capture market share through low price.*

Core Competencies As defined in Chapter 3, a **core competency** is a resource or capability that serves as a source of a firm's competitive advantage over its rivals. It is a unique skill or capability that transcends products or markets, makes a significant contribution to the customer's perceived benefit, and is difficult to imitate.[23] Examples of core competencies include Sony's competence in miniaturization and Dell's competence in supply chain management. A firm's core competencies determine where it creates the most value. In distinguishing its core competencies, a firm should identify the skills it has that are (1) unique, (2) valuable to customers, (3) difficult to imitate, and (4) transferable to new opportunities.[24]

A firm's core competencies are important in both the short and the long term. In the short term, it is a company's core competencies that allow it to differentiate itself from its competitors and create unique value. For example, Dell's core competencies historically have included supply chain management, efficient assembly, and serving corporate customers, so its business model of providing corporate customers computers that are price competitive, are technologically up-to-date, and have access to after-sale support makes sense. If Dell suddenly started assembling and selling musical instruments, analysts would be skeptical of the new strategy and justifiably ask, "Why is Dell pursuing a strategy that is outside its core competency?"

In the long term, it is important to have core competencies to grow and establish strong positions in complementary markets. For example, Dell has taken its core competencies in the assembly and sale of PCs and has moved them into the market for computer servers and other electronic devices. This process of adapting a company's core competencies to exploit new opportunities is referred to as **resource leverage**.

There is growing evidence that firms benefit from developing core competencies and focusing their efforts on core businesses. This trend means that firms are concentrating on smaller and smaller segments of a product or service's value chain and becoming experts at servicing their respective segments. A Bain and Company study of over 1,800 public companies in seven countries found that 80 percent of the companies that sustained both value creation and at least 5.5 percent annual growth over 10 years had one core business with clear market leadership. This evidence validates the belief that it's better to be really good at one or two things than mediocre at many things.[25]

Strategic Assets **Strategic assets** are anything rare and valuable that a firm owns. They include plant and equipment, location, brands, patents, customer data, a highly qualified staff, and distinctive partnerships. A particularly valuable strategic asset is a company's brand, which is discussed in detail in Chapter 11. Starbucks, for example, has worked hard to build the image of its brand, and it would take an enormous effort for another coffee retailer to achieve this same level of brand recognition. Companies ultimately try to combine their core competencies and strategic assets to create a **sustainable competitive advantage**. This factor is one to which investors pay close attention when evaluating a business.[26] A sustainable competitive advantage is achieved by implementing a value-creating strategy that is unique and not easy to imitate.[27] This type of advantage is achievable when a firm has strategic resources and the ability to use them in unique ways that create value for a group of targeted customers.[28]

Partnership Network

A firm's network of partnerships is the third component of a business model. New ventures, in particular, typically do not have the resources to perform all the tasks required to make their businesses work, so they rely on partners to perform key roles.[29] In most cases, a business does not want to do everything itself because the majority of tasks needed to build a product or deliver a service are not core to a company's competitive advantage.[30] For example, Dell differentiates itself from its competitors through its expertise in assembling computers but buys chips from others, primarily from Intel. Dell could manufacture its own chips, but it doesn't have a core competency in this area. Similarly, Dell relies on UPS and FedEx to deliver its products because it would be silly for Dell to build a nationwide system

L E A R N I N G

Objective

8. Define the term *core competency* and describe its importance.

to deliver its computers. Firms also rely on partners to supply intellectual capital needed to produce complex products and services, as illustrated in the following observation from two authorities on business partnerships:

> Neither Boeing nor Airbus has one-tenth of the intellectual capital or coordination capacity to cost-effectively mine metals, create alloys, make fasteners, cast and machine parts, design avionics, produce control systems, make engines, and so on. The complex systems we call airplanes come together through the voluntary agreements and collaborations of thousands of companies operating in the global marketplace.[31]

A firm's partnership network includes suppliers and other partners. Let's look at each of them.

Suppliers A **supplier** (or vendor) is a company that provides parts or services to another company. Intel is Dell's primary supplier for computer chips, for example. A **supply chain** is the network of all the companies that participate in the production of a product, from the acquisition of raw materials to the final sale. Almost all firms have suppliers who play vital roles in the functioning of their business models.

Traditionally, firms maintained an arm's-length relationship with their suppliers and viewed them almost as adversaries. Producers needing a component part would negotiate with several suppliers to find the best price. Over the past two decades, however, firms have increasingly moved away from contentious relationships with their suppliers and are now partnering with them to achieve mutually beneficial goals.[32] This shift resulted from competitive pressures that motivated managers to look up and down their value chains to find opportunities for cost savings, quality improvement, and improved speed to market. More and more, managers are focusing on **supply chain management**, which is the coordination of the flow of all information, money, and material that moves through a product's supply chain. The more efficiently an organization can manage its supply chain, the more effectively its entire business model will perform.[33]

Firms are developing more collaborative relationships with their suppliers, finding ways to motivate them to perform at a higher level. Many firms are reducing the number of

LEARNING
Objective

9. Explain the concept of supply chain management.

Dell relies on a network of partners worldwide to make its business model work. Here, Dell founder and CEO Michael Dell displays a Dell shipping carton before a map of the world at the company's headquarters in Round Rock, Texas.

their suppliers and working more closely with a smaller group. Dell, for example, maintains close relationships with its suppliers and uses sophisticated software to enhance the performance of its supply chain. Dell has accomplished a level of rigor in its supply chain that supports its core strategy of offering technologically up-to-date computers at affordable prices. The following comes from a case study about Dell, posted on the Web site of i2 Technologies, Dell's provider of supply chain management software:

> Using Factory Planner (a supply chain management software product), a new manufacturing schedule is generated every two hours to reflect customer orders that have been downloaded since the last schedule two hours earlier. Using i2 TradeMatrix Buy Solution (another software product), Dell alerts the supplier hubs as to what specific materials are needed and directs them to deliver those materials to a specific building and dock door, so the materials can then be fed into a specific manufacturing line. Factory Planner also allows for order prioritization based on material availability from the supplier. The schedule is sent to the factory floor, so the orders are being built while exact materials required for the next set of customer orders are being packaged and shipped to the Dell facility.[34]

Other Key Relationships   Along with its suppliers, firms partner with other companies to make their business models work. As described in Table 6.3, strategic alliances, joint ventures, networks, consortia, and trade associations are common forms of these partnerships. A survey by PricewaterhouseCoopers found that more than half of America's fastest-growing companies have formed multiple partnerships to support their business models. According to the research, these partnerships have "resulted in more innovative products, more profit opportunities, and significantly high growth rates" for the firms involved.[35]

An entrepreneur's ability to launch a firm that achieves a sustainable competitive advantage may hinge as much on the skills of the partners that are involved as the skills within the firm itself. Partnerships also help firms stay nimble and focus on their core competencies, as mentioned earlier in this chapter. And top-notch firms are able to choose the best partners. These are the reasons Dell decided to form partnerships early on, as explained by Michael Dell:

> Leveraging our suppliers [who Dell early on described as alliance partners] has allowed us to scale our business very quickly without having to become an expert in surface-mount technology, semi-conductor manufacturing, or building motherboards and other electrical assemblies, all of which would require an enormous commitment

TABLE 6.3 The Most Common Types of Business Partnerships

Partnership Form	Description
Joint venture	An entity created by two or more firms pooling a portion of their resources to create a separate, jointly owned organization
Network	A hub-and-wheel configuration with a local firm at the hub organizing the interdependencies of a complex array of firms
Consortia	A group of organizations with similar needs that band together to create a new entity to address those needs
Strategic alliance	An arrangement between two or more firms that establishes an exchange relationship but has no joint ownership involved
Trade associations	Organizations (typically nonprofit) that are formed by firms in the same industry to collect and disseminate trade information, offer legal and technical advice, furnish industry-related training, and provide a platform for collective lobbying

Source: B. Barringer and J. Harrison, "Walking a Tightrope: Creating Value through Interorganizational Relationships," *Journal of Management* 26, no. 3 (2000): 367–403.

of intellectual and monetary capital. Traditional industry mentality dictates that if you don't build your own components, you'll never have enough control over the process. But by working with outside suppliers, we've found that you actually gain more control over the quality of your products than if you were to do everything yourself. How? You can choose among the best providers in the world.[36]

There are other important motivations for firms to partner with each other. These include gaining economies of scale, risk and cost sharing, gaining access to foreign markets, learning, speed to market, flexibility, and neutralizing or blocking competitors.[37]

There *are* risks involved in partnerships, particularly if a single partnership is a key component of a firm's business model. Many partnerships fall short of meeting the expectations of the participants for a variety of reasons. In recent years, through studies they have conducted, the international accounting firms of PricewaterhouseCoopers[38] and KPMG[39] have estimated that the failure rate for business alliances is 50 percent and 60 to 70 percent, respectively. Many of the failures result from poor planning or the difficulties involved with meshing the cultures of two or more organizations to achieve a common goal. There are also potential disadvantages to participating in alliances, including loss of proprietary information, management complexities, financial and organizational risks, risk of becoming dependent on a partner, and partial loss of decision autonomy.[40]

Still, for the majority of start-ups, the ability to establish and effectively manage partnerships is a major component of their business models' success. For some firms, the ability to manage partnerships is the essence of their competitive advantage and ultimate success. This is the case with LogoWorks, the company illustrated in the chapter's "Partnering for Success" feature.

Customer Interface

Customer interface—how a firm interacts with its customers—is the fourth component of a business model. The type of customer interaction depends on how a firm chooses to compete. For example, Amazon.com sells books solely over the Internet, while Barnes & Noble sells through both its traditional bookstores and online. In the computer industry, there are several customer interface models. Dell sells strictly online and over the phone, while Hewlett-Packard and IBM sell primarily through retail stores. Gateway, like Dell, sells primarily online and over the phone.

For a new venture, the customer interface that it chooses is central to how it plans to compete and where it is located in the value chain of the products and services it provides.[41] The three elements of a company's customer interface are target market, fulfillment and support, and pricing structure. Let's look at each of these elements closely.

10. Define the term *target market*.

Target Market A firm's **target market** is the limited group of individuals or businesses that it goes after or tries to appeal to, as discussed earlier in this book. The target market a firm selects affects everything it does, from the strategic resources it acquires to the partnerships it forges to its promotional campaigns. For example, the clothing retailer Abercrombie & Fitch targets 18- to 22-year-old men and women who are willing to pay full price for trendy apparel. So the decisions it makes about strategic resources, partnerships, and advertising will be much different from the decisions made by Chico's, a clothing store that targets 30- to 60-year-old women.

Typically, a firm greatly benefits from having a clearly defined target market. Because of the specificity of its targeted customer, Abercrombie & Fitch can keep abreast of the clothing trends for its market, it can focus its marketing and promotional campaigns, and it can develop deep core competencies pertaining to its specific marketplace. A company such as Gap has a larger challenge because its stores appeal to a broader range of clientele. In fact, when a retailer such as Gap starts offering too many products, it typically begins breaking itself down into more narrowly focused markets so

partnering for success

LogoWorks: Making Partnering the Essence of its Competitive Advantage and Business Model
www.logoworks.com

For many start-ups, once the name for the business has been selected, the next step is to hire a graphic designer or an advertising firm to help design a logo. While having a logo is important, going back and forth on design ideas with a graphic designer or an advertising firm can easily cost several thousand dollars. This reality forces many start-ups to design their own logos, with hit-and-miss results.

LogoWorks was launched in 2001 to provide an alternative to these approaches. The company, which is an Internet-based firm, provides its customers a variety of logos to choose from in an expedient manner and at an affordable price. Here's how the service works.

LogoWorks has assembled a network of over 200 freelance graphic designers who are spread out across the country. Many of them work in their homes and do work for LogoWorks as a supplement to a full-time income. To get a logo designed, and several alternatives to choose from, a customer fills out a form, called a "creative brief," describing the type of logo design that is desired. Once the creative brief is completed, LogoWorks distributes the request to two to five graphic designers, who have 3 days to come up with one or more designs. LogoWorks has tiered levels of services available, ranging from $299 for two designers, 4 logos, and two revision rounds, to $599 for five designers, 10 logos and unlimited revision rounds. The pay scale for the designers fluctuates, depending on whether they are designated expert, mid-level, or entry-level designers, based on a point scale of 0 to 100. They all start at entry level, and their points go up and down based on how often their designs are selected and by the strength of peer reviews of their designs. Most designers get paid $25 to $50 per project, with a bonus going to the designer whose design is chosen. A number of examples of impressive logos that LogoWork's freelance designers have produced are posted on the company's Web site.

This "freelance" approach to generating logos helps LogoWorks minimize costs, because it doesn't actually employ the designers. In addition, the online nature of the business has allowed the company to locate its corporate headquarters in Lindon, Utah, where the cost of doing business is comparatively low. LogoWorks passes along a portion of its cost savings to its customers in the form of lower prices.

While business is currently booming for LogoWorks, the key to its future is to keep its network of freelance graphic designers, which LogoWork's considers to be its partners, motivated to continue to participate. Managing these partnerships is the essence of LogoWork's competitive advantage and its business model.

Questions for Critical Thinking

1. What are the benefits and the risk of LogoWork's approach to using freelance graphic designers to create logo designs for its clients?
2. From the material provided in the case, describe LogoWork's core strategy and its customer interface.
3. Go to LogoWork's Web site and read the "Our Story" section listed under the "About Us" tab. After reading the story, does LogoWork's business model make more sense to you? Do you consider what LogoWorks is doing to be an example of "business model innovation?" Why or why not?
4. Spend some time looking at LogoWork's Web site. Are you impressed with the examples of the logo designs that the company has posted on its Web site? If you started a firm, would you consider using LogoWork's service? Why or why not?

Sources: LogoWorks homepage, www.logoworks.com (accessed August 21, 2006); "Firm Offers Designers Talent for Logos at Bargain Prices," *The Wall Street Journal*, June 13, 2005.

---

that it can regain the advantages that are enjoyed by a singularly focused retailer such as Abercrombie & Fitch. Gap has done this successfully and now has a more diversified collection of stores, including Gap, GapKids, BabyGap, GapBody, GapMaternity, Banana Republic, Old Navy, and Gap Outlet stores.

Fulfillment and Support **Fulfillment and support** describes the way a firm's product or service "goes to market," or how it reaches its customers. It also refers to the channels a company uses and what level of customer support it provides.[42] All these issues impact the shape and nature of a company's business model.

Firms differ considerably along these dimensions. Suppose that a new venture developed and patented an exciting new cell phone technology. In forming its business plan, the firm might have several options regarding how to take its technology to market. It could (1) license the technology to existing cell phone companies such as Nokia and Ericsson, (2) manufacture the cell phone itself and establish its own sales channels, or (3) partner with a cell phone company such as Motorola and sell the phone through partnerships with the cell phone service providers such as Cingular and Verizon. The choice a firm makes about fulfillment and service has a dramatic impact on the type of company that evolves and the business model that develops. For example, if the company licenses its technology, it would probably build a business model that emphasized research and development to continue to have cutting-edge technologies to license to the cell phone manufacturers. In contrast, if it decides to manufacture its own cell phones, it needs to establish core competencies in the areas of manufacturing and design and needs to form partnerships with cell phone retailers such as Cingular, Sprint, and Verizon.

The level of customer support a firm is willing to offer also impacts its business model. Some firms differentiate their products or services and provide extra value to their customers through high levels of service and support. Customer service can include delivery and installation, financing arrangements, customer training, warranties and guarantees, repairs, layaway plans, convenient hours of operation, convenient parking, and information through toll-free numbers and Web sites.[43] Dell, as mentioned earlier, has a broad menu of tiered services available to provide its corporate clients the exact level of support they need and for which they are willing to pay. Making this choice of services available is a key component of Dell's business model.

Pricing Structure A third element of a company's customer interface is its pricing structure, a topic that will be discussed in more detail in Chapter 11. Pricing structures vary, depending on a firm's target market and its pricing philosophy. For example, some rental car companies charge a daily flat rate, while others charge so much per mile. Similarly, some consultants charge a flat fee for performing a service (e.g., helping an entrepreneurial venture write a business plan), while others charge an hourly rate. In some instances, a company must also choose whether to charge its customers directly or indirectly through a service provider.

Firms differentiate themselves on the basis of their pricing structure in both common and unusual ways. In general, it is difficult for new ventures to differentiate themselves on price, which is a common strategy for larger firms with more substantial economies of scale, as discussed earlier in the chapter. There are exceptions, such as Amazon.com, Domino's in pizza, and LogoWorks in business logos, which have been price leaders since their inception. In contrast, there are several examples of firms that have started primarily on the basis of featuring innovative pricing models. The most noteworthy is Priceline.com, which pioneered the practice of letting customers explicitly set prices they are willing to pay for products and services. Another example is Carmax, which features a "no-haggle" pricing policy and sells new and used cars through its showrooms and Web site. The company's slogan is "The Way Car Buying Should Be." Carmax offers its customers a low-stress environment by presenting them with what it believes to be a fair price, with no negotiations.

In summary, it is very useful for a new venture to look at itself in a holistic manner and understand that it must construct an effective "business model" to be successful. Everyone that does business with a new firm, from its customers to its partners, does so on a voluntary basis. As a result, a firm must motivate its customers and partners to play along. The primary elements of a firm's business model are its core strategy, strategic resources, partnership network, and customer interface. Close attention to each of these elements is essential for a new venture's success.

Chapter Summary

1. A firm's business model is its plan or diagram for how it intends to compete, use its resources, structure relationships, interface with customers, and create value to sustain itself on the basis of the profits it generates.
2. Business model innovation refers to initiatives such as those undertaken by Michael Dell that revolutionize how products are sold in an industry.
3. The main reasons that having a clearly articulated business model is important are as follows: It serves as an ongoing extension of feasibility analysis, it focuses attention on how all the elements of a business fit together, it describes why the network of participants who are needed to make a business idea viable would be willing to work together, and it articulates the core logic of a firm to all its stakeholders.
4. The value chain shows how a product moves from the raw-material stage to the final consumer. The value chain helps a firm identify opportunities to enhance its competitive strategies and to recognize new business opportunities.
5. A complete misread of the customer and utterly unsound economics are the two fatal flaws that can make a business model a failure from the outset.
6. Core strategy, strategic resources, partnership networks, and customer interface are the four major components of a firm's business model.
7. A business concept blind spot prevents a firm from seeing an opportunity that might fit its business model.
8. A core competency is something that a firm does particularly well. It is a resource or capability that serves as a source of a firm's competitive advantage over its rivals.
9. Supply chain management refers to the flow of all information, money, and material that moves through a product's supply chain. The more efficiently an organization can manage its supply chain, the more effectively its entire business model will perform.
10. A firm's target market is the limited group of individuals or business that it goes after or tries to appeal to at a point in time.

Key Terms

brand loyalty, 174
business concept blind spot, 171
business model, 162
business model innovation, 163
core competency, 175
core strategy, 171
cost leadership strategy, 174

customer interface, 178
differentiation strategy, 174
fulfillment and support, 180
mission statement, 171
product/market scope, 171
resource leverage, 175
strategic assets, 175

supplier, 176
supply chain, 176
supply chain management, 176
sustainable competitive
     advantage, 175
target market, 178
value chain, 166

Review Questions

1. Define the term business model. How can entrepreneurial firms benefit by developing and using a business model?
2. Explain what business model innovation means. Provide an example of business model innovation other than the Dell Inc. example given in this chapter.
3. Why is it dangerous for a company to assume that it can be successful by simply copying the business model of the industry leader?
4. Briefly describe the value chain concept. How does the value chain help firms identify business opportunities?
5. How does an understanding of the value chain help explain how business models emerge?
6. What are the two fatal flaws that can render a business model untenable?

7. What are the four primary components of a firm's business model? Briefly describe the importance of each component.
8. Describe what is meant by the term *core strategy* and why it is important.
9. Describe the purpose of a mission statement.
10. What is meant by the term *business model blind spot*? Provide an original example of a firm that suffered as the result of having a business model blind spot.
11. What is a firm's product/market scope? Why is the concept of product/market scope important in regard to crafting a successful business model?
12. Why is it important for firms to differentiate themselves from competitors?
13. In what ways does a focus on a cost leadership strategy lead to a very different business model than a focus on a differentiation strategy?
14. Define the term *core competency* and describe why it's important for a firm to have one or more core competencies. How do a company's core competencies help shape its business model?
15. What is meant by the term *resource leverage*? How does an understanding of this term help a firm exploit new product or service opportunities?
16. What is meant by the term *strategic asset*? Provide examples of the strategic assets of three well-known firms.
17. Why do firms typically need partners to make their business models work?
18. What is meant by the term *supply chain management*?
19. What is meant by the term *customer interface*? Explain how Dell and Hewlett-Packard differ from each other on this core dimension.
20. Describe the impact of a firm's pricing structure on its business model.

Application Questions

1. Write a brief critique of TutoringZone's business model. What do you think are the strengths and weaknesses of the model? Do you think that TutoringZone has a sustainable competitive advantage? Why or why not?
2. Given the information in this chapter about Dell Inc., write a brief description of Dell's business model.
3. Jim Payne is a writer for the business section of a major newspaper in Colorado. Recently, he wrote an article with the following headline: "Why Bother with Business Models?" The gist of the article was that most firms exist in such competitive environments that any business model put in place today will probably be outdated tomorrow. Do you agree or disagree with Jim's assessment? Explain the rationale for your answer.
4. Carol Schmidt plans to open a company that will make accessories for cell phones. She has read that having a clearly articulated business model will help "all the elements of her business fit together." Carol isn't quite sure what that statement means. If Carol asked you to explain it to her, what would you say?
5. Provide an example of a company, not mentioned in the chapter, that has introduced a business model innovation into the marketplace. Describe the nature of the business model innovation and how it has changed the industry's competitive landscape.
6. Jane Rowan is an experienced business consultant. Through working with clients, she has noticed that many companies have "business concept blind spots." How can having a business concept blind spot affect the strength of a firm's business model?
7. Write a mission statement for Peerflix, the subject of the "You Be the VC 2" feature in the chapter. Describe how the statement you just wrote is consistent with the core strategy of the firm.
8. Select one of the following companies: Amazon.com, Google, or eBay. For the company you selected, identify its core competency and explain how its core competency strengthens its business model and contributes to its competitive advantage.
9. Using the same firm you selected for question 8, make a list of the firm's strategic assets. How does each of its strategic assets strengthen its business model?

10. Rich Matthews has a successful electronics company that makes components for DVD and MP3 players. In fact, in the past several years, Rich's company has won several awards for manufacturing excellence. Rich wants to expand his business to increase revenues. He has heard about "resource leverage" but doesn't really understand what it means. If Rich asked you to explain this concept to him and how he could use it in his business, what would you tell him?

11. Six months ago, Peter Wilcox retired as an engineer with NASA and used some of his retirement savings to open a chain of three video stores near the Kennedy Space Center in Florida. Peter had never been in the video store business before but likes the retail environment and enjoys watching videos. So far, the business hasn't done very well. Peter recently went to a bank to get a loan for the business and was startled when the banker told him, "It's no wonder your business isn't thriving. As far as I can tell, it doesn't have a core competency." Peter can't figure out what the banker means by this comment. What would you tell Peter if he asked you to interpret the banker's comment? What core competencies might be particularly important for Peter's type of business?

12. Jill Hopkins just received an e-mail message from an investor who has agreed to listen to her pitch her business idea. The investor said, "Your timing is good—I just happen to be sitting on $500,000 that I'm anxious to invest. One thing I'll warn you about ahead of time, however, is that you must show me that your business has the potential to achieve a sustainable competitive advantage. If you can't show me that, I won't invest." Jill has read about sustainable competitive advantage but is still a little hazy about the concept. Can you explain the concept to Jill?

13. Tom Sanders is a software engineer for Orbitz, the online reservation service for airlines and hotels. He is planning to leave Orbitz to sell a software product that he has developed for the travel industry. Tom's goal is to create a business that achieves a sustainable competitive advantage. Of the four main components of a business model, the area with which Tom is the least acquainted is "customer interface." Based on Tom's business idea, explain the choices that he has available in this area.

14. The "You Be the VC 1" feature at the end of the chapter focuses on StuffBak, a company that helps people recover items that have been misplaced or lost. Describe the "customer interface" component of StuffBak's business model, and explain how its customer interface strengthens its business model and contributes to its success.

15. Do some research on the company 1-800-CONTACTS. Describe its business model. Do you consider 1-800-CONTACTS to be a business model innovator? Why or why not?

you be the VC 6.1   StuffBak
www.stuffbak.com

Business idea: Create a service that allows the owners of lost items to get their stuff back.

Pitch: Every day, thousands of portable devices are inadvertently left behind in airports, taxicabs, restaurants, hotels, and other public venues. Unfortunately, many of the devices are lost forever. Anyone who has ever lost a cell phone, digital camera, or PDA knows how frustrating the experience can be (has this happened to you?). Certainly for today's businessperson (and who among us is not busy?), the loss of data is often more agonizing than the time and money it takes to buy a replacement device and reenter the information.

StuffBak has an answer to this problem. The company sells personal identification stickers that help consumers recover lost items. Here's how it works. A consumer buys a pack of StuffBak labels. The labels include an identification number, StuffBak's toll-free phone number, and an offer of a reward if the item is found. The service makes it easy for Good Samaritans, lost & found personnel, and police departments to return lost or stolen items to their rightful owners. StuffBak immediately notifies the owner when the lost item is found and coordinates the recovery process between finder and owner. Strict confidentiality is maintained for both parties. The owner pays $14.95 plus a shipping fee to get an item back. The person that found the item gets $20 worth of StuffBak labels and often a reward from the owner.

StuffBak claims that its clients get their lost items back approximately 70 percent of the time. This claim is supported by a *Reader's Digest* experiment in which 1,000 wallets were "lost" worldwide to test StuffBak's service. Seventy percent were returned.

Q&A: Based on the material covered in this chapter, what questions would you ask the firm's founders before

making your funding decision? What answers would satisfy you?

Decision: If you had to make your decision on just the information provided in the pitch and on the company's Web site, would you fund this firm? Why or why not?

you be the VC 6.2

Peerflix
www.peerflix.com

Business idea: Launch a legal online peer-to-peer trading platform—first for DVDs and then for other items.

Pitch: Why create a peer-to-peer service to trade DVDs? Sales of DVDs are skyrocketing. In the United States alone, over 1.6 billion DVDs were sold in 2005. That amounts to an average of a bit over 19 DVDs for every household that has one or more DVD players. Oddly enough, at the same time that DVD sales are going up, people are spending less time watching them. As a result, most American households have a growing stack of DVDs gathering dust, with no meaningful secondary market available. Is this the case for you? Have you bought a few DVDs that you aren't watching and that you would be willing to take out of your collection of DVDs? If so, enjoy what you will read next.

Now there is an alternative to letting DVDs pile up. Peerflix is a peer-to-peer online trading platform that allows its users to trade DVDs across a large membership network. You get started by building two lists—one of the DVDs you have and the other of the DVDs you want to see. Peerflix, using a sophisticated computer network, makes the appropriate matches. The only costs involved to the traders are

99 cents for each trade (which goes to Peerflix) and the price of a first-class stamp. The way you mail your DVDs to Peerflix or the intended recipient (it depends on whether the recipient is on your "friends" list) is really slick. Once you agree to make a trade, you are asked to click on a print icon. Two pieces of paper are printed. By following the instructions provided, the papers can be folded and turned into a self-mailer. Because you are instructed to mail only the DVD, and not the case it came in, the DVD can be mailed for the price of a first-class stamp. If any of the DVDs you send are damaged or lost, you are provided a full refund of your money by Peerflix.

For Peerflix, trading DVDs is just the start. In the months and years ahead, Peerflix plans to open its platform for the trading of music, stamps, baseball cards, or anything else its members want to trade.

Q&A: Based on the material covered in this chapter, what questions would you ask the firm's founders before making your funding decision? What answers would satisfy you?

Decision: If you had to make your decision on just the information provided in the pitch and on the company's Web site, would you fund this firm? Why or why not?

CASE 6.1

Meetup: Changing Its Business Model in Hopes of Achieving Increased Revenue and Success
www.meetup.com

Bruce R. Barringer,
University of Central Florida
R. Duane Ireland,
Texas A&M University

Introduction

Scott Heiferman, Matt Meeker, and Peter Kamali launched Meetup in 2002. The idea behind the company was to create an online platform to help get people off-line. The inspiration for Meetup was a book titled *Bowling Alone*, by

Harvard sociologist Robert Putnam. In a nutshell, Putnam argued in what became a widely read book that America is at a dangerous crossroad, as advances in technology, transportation, and changing lifestyles have caused people to become more disconnected from their families, friends, and communities. Putman used bowling as an example throughout the book. Years ago, he wrote, thousands of people belonged to bowling leagues. Today, however, people are more likely to bowl alone.

Heiferman and his cofounders were moved by Putnam's story and created Meetup as a way for people to reconnect.

Meetup is an online platform that allows individuals to organize local community groups via the Web. Once a group is formed, its members "meet up" on a regular basis off-line. The service has struck a popular chord. There are currently over 13,000 Meetup groups worldwide with close to 3 million people participating on a regular basis. The topics of the groups vary widely, from book clubs, to cancer support groups, to stay-at-home moms, to groups focused on pets. You can easily find the groups that meet in your area, or form your own group, by visiting Meetup's Web site.

Examples of Local Meetup Groups

- The Portland Spanish Language Meetup Group
- The Iowa City Moms Meetup Group
- The Philadelphia Yoga Meetup Group
- The Chicago Entrepreneurs Meetup Group
- The Tulsa Singles Meetup Group
- The Seattle Scrabble Meetup Group
- The Raleigh Cat Meetup Group
- The San Antonio Podcasting Meetup Group

On April 12, 2005, Meetup made a bold move. The company changed its business model from a free site that relied primarily on online advertising to a fee-based service that requires each Meetup group to pay a monthly fee to be listed on its Web site. In the short term, the company lost over half its business. Let's discuss the rationale behind Meetup's decision and how changing its business model has affected the company's prospects for the future.

Meetup's Original Business Model

Meetup's original business model reflected what was possible in 2002 for an Internet start-up. Although it had several ways of making money (including a premium service that members could pay for), it relied primarily on online advertising. This approach made the service basically free for the vast majority of groups that organized through the Meetup Web site.

From 2002 to 2004, the combination of a free service and an attractive offering made Meetup one of the fastest-growing online social networks in the world. During this time, the critical mass of people using the Internet also grew at an accelerating pace. This made it possible to get more groups organized. For example, in 2002, there simply may not have been enough people in Minneapolis online to get a group together to go hiking. Today, there are over 90 people in the Minneapolis Meetup Hiking Group.

As the result of its founders' passion, its mission to reconnect people on a local basis, and its early success, Meetup was able to attract venture capital funding and to form an impressive board of directors (which includes former NBA star Bill Bradley and eBay founder Pierre Omidyar). However, as the costs associated with supporting Meetup's growing number of groups continued to increase, its founders and investors started questioning whether its advertising-supported business model was sustainable. In early 2005, the decision was made to start charging groups a monthly fee to be listed on the Meetup Web site. The decision was not motivated strictly by potential financial gain. In fact, at one point, Meetup's founders and its board talked about becoming a nonprofit organization. There was just a growing sense among Meetup's management team and its investors that the company needed to be on a stronger financial foundation to ensure that it could continue to fulfill its mission and support its users.

Meetup's New Business Model

Meetup's new business model was fashioned in part by eBay's earlier experiences. At several points during its growth as a company, eBay migrated portions of its site from free offerings to fee-based services. What eBay found was that participation initially dropped when fees were introduced but gradually recovered, presumably as a result of the inherent value eBay was providing its members. Meetup, of course, had no way of knowing if its users would respond in a similar fashion.

In May 2005, Meetup made the switch and started charging a monthly fee to the groups listed on its Web sites. It also required each group to designate an "organizer" who would pay the fee and take responsibility for the group. Initially, the company lost over half of its members, which was a painful pill to swallow. Meetup was also sharply criticized by many of its members for making the switch. Rather than panicking, however, Meetup and its founders remained resolute and patiently continued to improve the quality of the site's offerings. The fee, which is in the $15 per month range, not only permits a group to be listed on the company's Web site but also provides access to a number of tools that help groups stay together. Still, as 2005 unfolded, the company didn't know what the future held. It desperately wanted to remain a viable platform for groups to organize. It saw no turning back, however, from remaining a fee-based service.

Discussion Questions

1. What do you think happened? Do you think Meetup's evolution to a fee-based business model has been a success, or do you think the company has continued to lose members? Explain the rationale for your answer.

2. On a scale of 1 to 10 (10 is high), how risky do you think Meetup's decision was to switch from a free service to a fee-based business model? What alternatives, if any, did Meetup have to adopting a fee-based business model?

3. Write a mission statement for Meetup.

4. Based on the material contained in the case, briefly describe Meetup's business model in the context of each of the four components of a business model introduced in the chapter.

Application Questions

1. Make a list (up to 20) of the Meetup groups in your area. Which, if any, of these groups are of interest to you? Would you be willing to pay a small monthly fee to belong to one of these groups? Why or why not?

2. In what ways do you think Meetup can use its alliance with eBay to promote and expand its service? What others types of partnerships make sense for Meetup?

Sources: Meetup homepage, www.meetup.com (accessed July 20, 2006); S. Heiferman, A. Fendelman, and B. Spirrison, "ePrairie Podcast 6: Meetup.com Founder Scott Heiferman," July 17, 2006; G. Galant and S. Heiferman, "VV Show #6—Scott Heiferman of Meetup." Venture Voice Podcast, July 28, 2005.

IKEA and ProFlowers: Reconfiguring Industry Value Chains to Create Competitive Business Models
www.ikea.com; www.proflowers.com

Bruce R. Barringer,
University of Central Florida
R. Duane Ireland,
Texas A&M University

Introduction

Although there are no hard-and-fast rules that dictate how a firm in a particular industry should compete, many industries have a standard way of doing business that most participants follow. When the tendency to follow these standards is strong, there is an opportunity for new entrants or industry incumbents to create new business models that revolutionize how products are sold in an industry. This practice is defined in the chapter as "business model innovation."

Both IKEA and ProFlowers are business model innovators. By reconfiguring the value chains in their respective industries, both companies have revolutionized the selling of products. The following case explains how they did it.

IKEA

IKEA is a Swedish furniture company that is known for its brightly colored furniture and its approach of requiring customers to assemble their furniture for themselves. As of July 2006, Ikea had 236 stores that were located in 34 countries, including the United States. The firm is famous for its functional yet stylish products that are sold at a very competitive price.

IKEA was founded in Almhult, Sweden, in 1943 by Ingvar Kamprad, who was then 17. The company's name is a composite of the first letters in his name in addition to the first letters of the names of the property and the village in which he grew up: **I**ngvar **K**amprad **E**lmtaryd **A**gunnaryd. Initially, the firm sold pens, wallets, picture frames, watches, and similar items. Furniture was added to IKEA's product lines in the late 1940s.

When IKEA first considered selling furniture, it closely studied the furniture industry value chain. In Sweden, furniture was manufactured and sold in the late 1940s much the same way it is still manufactured and sold throughout the world today. As shown in the following figure, furniture typically flows through a value chain, with all, or most, of the steps completed by the same company. After a piece of furniture is designed, the parts are typically made by the same company, which then assembles the parts and ships the finished product to a warehouse. The completed furniture then sits in a warehouse until it is delivered to a retail store or is delivered directly to a consumer. The only significant deviation from this process is that furniture companies are increasingly outsourcing the production and assembly of the furniture they sell. Still, the furniture industry value chain depicted in the figure has prevailed largely intact throughout most of IKEA's history.

To create a competitive advantage, IKEA decided to reconfigure the furniture value chain. The bottom part of the figure shows how they did it. IKEA still owns furniture design but outsources the manufacture of parts to a contract manufacturer. The "parts" (the disassembled pieces of the furniture) are then shipped in boxes to IKEA retail stores, where they are stacked on shelves in a large warehouse environment. Customers make their selections by looking at display models and then buy the furniture, still in the box, to assemble later on their own. Customers are also responsible for transporting the furniture to their home.

This reconfiguration of the furniture value chain gives IKEA several distinct advantages. First, by outsourcing the manufacture of the parts, it does not have to incur the cost of maintaining manufacturing facilities. The company also basically "outsources" the assembly and delivery of furniture to the customer. This approach creates substantial cost savings for IKEA, which passes on a portion of the savings to customers. It also allows IKEA to target a segment of the market that is looking for a good value and doesn't mind assembling furniture. To make its offering even more unique, IKEA's stores feature playrooms for children and Swedish cuisine restaurants.

Analysts view IKEA's efforts as a resounding success. Because it is a private company, it doesn't release profitability figures. Although we don't know about the firm's profitability, we do know that according to Hoover's reports, the firm's sales increases 17.3 percent from 2004 to 2005. With effective control of its cost of goods sold, the increase in sales suggests that IKEA is earning profits.

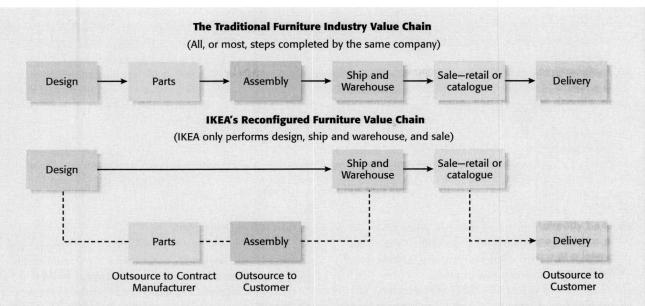

The Traditional Furniture Industry Value Chain

(All, or most, steps completed by the same company)

Design → Parts → Assembly → Ship and Warehouse → Sale—retail or catalogue → Delivery

IKEA's Reconfigured Furniture Value Chain

(IKEA only performs design, ship and warehouse, and sale)

Design → Ship and Warehouse → Sale—retail or catalogue

Parts → Assembly → Delivery

Outsource to Contract Manufacturer   Outsource to Customer   Outsource to Customer

Sources: Adapted from N. Thornberry, *Lead Like an Entrepreneur* (New York: McGraw-Hill, 2006).

ProFlowers

Launched in 1998, ProFlowers is an online retailer that sells and ships fresh flowers for all occasions. It is a subsidiary of Provide Commerce, which operates similar Web sites that sell and ship fresh fruit baskets, steak and seafood, and fresh desserts. Provide Commerce was started in 1997 by Jared Schutz Polis, the son of SPS Studios founders Stephen Schutz and Susan Polis Schutz. SPS Studios created Bluemountain.com, the first Web site to offer free online greeting cards in 1996.

Like IKEA, ProFlowers has created a competitive advantage by reconfiguring its industry's value chain. The traditional value chain for flowers is depicted in the following figure. Flowers are raised by growers and then typically pass through the hands of an importer (or distributor), wholesaler, and retailer before they are sold to the customer. This process typically takes between 7 and 12 days. As a flower passes through the process, temperature and humidity often change, which degrades the flower's appearance and shortens its vase life. ProFlowers has sharply reduced the number of steps a flower must go through as it travels from the grower to the customer, as depicted in the figure. The advantage to the customer is fresher, higher-quality flowers that are normally delivered within 3 days and last longer once delivered. In addition, ProFlowers is able to offer a wider selection than most florists because it doesn't have to take physical possession of its flowers. The advantage to the grower (or supplier) is increased margins, broader customer reach, and better inventory management.

The way ProFlowers has made its approach work is by contracting with a global network of flower growers and suppliers. When an order is received via its Web site, ProFlowers routes the order to the appropriate grower. In turn, the grower fills the order and ships it via either FedEx or UPS utilizing proprietary technology provided by ProFlowers. This approach results in a considerable savings by eliminating steps in the traditional flower value chain. The savings ProFlowers captures are in part passed along to its customers through lower prices. It's difficult to quantify the value of the "freshness factor" made possible by ProFlower's approach. Flowers are often an emotional purchase, with the sender wanting the flowers to be delivered to the recipient in the best shape possible, because quality is intertwined with sincerity. To tout its freshness advantage, ProFlowers basically explains how it has reconfigured its industry's value chain in its advertising and promotions.

To date, ProFlowers has captured only a small portion of the $19 billion total market for flowers and related products in the United States, although its sales are increasing. Provide Commerce, ProFlower's parent company, was profitable in both 2004 and 2005. ProFlower's database of customers has grown from 69,000 in 1999 to approximately 4.3 million in 2005, and its percentage of repeat customers is increasing.

Provide Commerce was purchased by Liberty Interactive Group in December 2005 for $477 million. Liberty Interactive Group includes home shopping network QVC, along with an assortment of online and off-line properties.

Discussion Questions

1. At the beginning of this chapter, the statement is made that "in everyday language, a model is a plan that's used to make or describe something." Do you think IKEA and ProFlowers have plans that effectively describe what the firms offer to customers? How could these firms' models be changed so they would be more appealing?

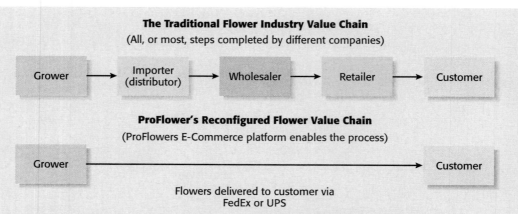

The Traditional Flower Industry Value Chain
(All, or most, steps completed by different companies)

Grower → Importer (distributor) → Wholesaler → Retailer → Customer

ProFlower's Reconfigured Flower Value Chain
(ProFlowers E-Commerce platform enables the process)

Grower → Customer

Flowers delivered to customer via
FedEx or UPS

2. What is IKEA's core competency? What are its strategic assets? Is there anything about IKEA's business model that makes what the company is doing hard to replicate? Explain your answer.

3. Suppose that you are the CEO of ProFlowers. You just received an e-mail from Carolyn Andersen, a highly reputable and sought-after rose grower, who is interested in learning more about your company. In her e-mail message to you, Ms. Andersen asks the following question: "Describe to me your business model. Convince me that your organization has a good story and I should be part of it." How would you respond to this request?

4. How does ProFlower's business model motivate its customers and partners (such as its contract growers) to participate in its business? On a scale of 1 to 10 (10 is high), rate how motivated you think each group is to do business with ProFlowers and help it succeed. Answer the same questions for IKEA.

Application Questions

1. Which industries, other then furniture and flowers, are ripe for business model innovation? Provide an example of a product or a service with a value chain that could be reconfigured in a manner similar to the way that IKEA reconfigured the value chain of the furniture industry or ProFlowers reconfigured the value chain of the flower industry. Discuss how a start-up or an industry incumbent could benefit by reconfiguring its industry's value chain in this manner.

2. The "You Be the VC 2" feature focuses on Peerflix, a company that hopes to revolutionize the way people acquire DVDs to watch in their homes. To what extent to you think Peerflix is a business model innovator?

Sources: IKEA homepage, www.ikea.com (accessed July 20, 2006); ProFlower's homepage, www.proflowers.com (accessed July 20, 2006); Provide Commerce Form 10-K, for the Fiscal Year Ended June 30, 2005; Hoover's Online, www.hoovers.com (accessed July 20, 2006); N. Thornberry, *Lead Like an Entrepreneur* (New York: McGraw-Hill, 2006).

Endnotes

1. Personal Interview with Ethan Fieldman, August 10, 2006.
2. M. Blomberg, "Coaching Students," Gainseville.com, www.gainsville.com (accessed August 10, 2006).
3. A. J. Slywotzky, *Value Migration* (Boston: Harvard Business Review Press, 1996).
4. J. Magretta, "Why Business Models Matter," *Harvard Business Review* 80, no. 5 (2002): 86–94.
5. M. Morris, M. Schindehutte, and J. Allen, "The Entrepreneur's Business Model: Toward a Unified Perspective, *Journal of Business Research* 58 (2005): 726–35.
6. G. Hamel, *Leading the Revolution* (New York: Plume, 2002).
7. M. Ragas, *Lessons from the E-Front* (Roseville, CA: Prima Venture, 2001).
8. N. Wingfield, "New Battlefield for Priceline Is Diapers, Tuna," *The Wall Street Journal*, September 20, 1999, B1.
9. R. Hawkins, *The "Business Model" as a Research Problem in Electronic Commerce* (Delft, The Netherlands: TNO Institute for Strategy, Technology and Policy, 2001).
10. M. Porter, *Competitive Advantage: Creating and Sustaining Superior Performance* (New York: Free Press, 1985).
11. C. B. Stabell and O. D. Fjeldstad, "Configuring Value for Competitive Advantage: On Chains, Shops and Networks," *Strategic Management Journal* 19 (1998): 413–37.

12. Interview conducted by N. C. Kaiser, "Perry Solomon, Executive of PepperCoin, nPost.com homepage, www.npost.com, (accessed August 17, 2006).

13. N. Venkataraman and J. C. Henderson, "Real Strategies for Virtual Organizations," *Sloan Management Review* 40, no. 1 (1998): 33–48.

14. Hamel, *Leading the Revolution*.

15. M. E. Porter, *On Competition* (Boston: Harvard Business School Press, 1996).

16. R. D. Ireland and M. A. Hitt, "Mission Statements: Importance, Challenge, and Recommendations for Development," *Business Horizons* 35, no. 3 (1992): 34–42.

17. Hamel, *Leading the Revolution*.

18. M. Dell, *Direct from Dell* (New York: HarperBusiness, 1999), 57.

19. R. Amit and C. Zott, "Value Creation in E-Business." *Strategic Management Journal* 22 (2001): 493–520.

20. Hamel, *Leading the Revolution*.

21. Porter, *Competitive Advantage*.

22. J. Hedman and T. Kalling, "The Business Model Concept: Theoretical Underpinnings and Empirical Illustrations," *European Journal of Information Systems* 12 (2003): 49–59.

23. C. K. Prahalad, "A New View of Strategy," in *Business: The Ultimate Resource* (Cambridge, MA: Perseus, 2002), 140–41.

24. Hamel, *Leading the Revolution*.

25. R. S. Kaplan and D. P. Norton, "How to Implement a New Strategy Without Disrupting Your Organization," *Harvard Business Review* 84, no. 3 (2006): 100–109; C. Zook and J. Allen, *Profit from the Core* (Boston: Harvard Business School Press, 2001).

26. R. Adner and P. Zemsky, "A Demand-Based Perspective on Sustainable Competitive Advantage," *Strategic Management Journal* 27 (2006): 215–39; J. Nesheim, *High Tech Start Up: The Complete Handbook for Creating Successful New High Tech Companies* (New York: Free Press, 2000).

27. C. Mitreanu, "Is Strategy a Bad Word?" *MIT Sloan Management Review* 47, no. 2 (2006): 96; J. Barney, "Firm Resources and Sustained Competitive Advantage," *Journal of Management* 17, no. 1 (1991): 99–120.

28. G. Hamel, "Management Innovation," *Harvard Business Review* 84, no. 2 (2006): 72–84; G. S. Day and R. Wensley, "Assessing Advantage: A Framework for Diagnosing Competitive Superiority," *Journal of Marketing* 52, no. 2 (1988): 1–20.

29. F. T. Rothaermel and D. L. Deeds, "Alliance Type, Alliance Experience and Alliance Management Capability in High-Technology Ventures," *Journal of Business Venturing* 21 (2006): 429–60; W. C. Kim and R. Mauborgne, "Knowing a Winning Business Idea When You See One," *Harvard Business Review* 78, no. 5 (2000): 129–38.

30. G. Moore, *Living on the Fault Line* (New York: HarperBusiness, 2002).

31. E. Pinchot and G. Pinchot, "Leading Organizations into Partnerships," in *Partnering*, eds. L. Segil, M. Goldsmith, and J. Belasco (New York: AMACOM Books, 2002), 41–55.

32. B. Barringer, "The Effects of Relational Channel Exchange on the Small Firm: A Conceptual Framework," *Journal of Small Business Management* 35, no. 2 (1997): 65–79.

33. L. Xu and B. M. Beamon, "Supply Chain Coordination and Cooperation Mechanisms: An Attribute-Based Approach," *Journal of Supply Chain Management* 42, no. 1 (2006): 4–12.

34. i2 Technologies, "Dell's Supply Chain: Improving on a World-Class Process," www.i2Technologies.com (accessed August 20, 2006).

35. PricewaterhouseCoopers, "Partnerships Have Big Payoffs for Fast-Growth Companies," *Trendsetter Barometer*, August 26, 2002.

36. Dell, *Direct from Dell*, 173.

37. B. Barringer and J. Harrison, "Walking a Tightrope: Creating Value through Interorganizational Relationships," *Journal of Management* 26, no. 3 (2000): 367–403.

38. Coopers & Lybrand Consulting, *Alliances* (New York: Coopers & Lybrand Consulting, 1997).

39. G. Kok and L. Widleman, "High Touch Partnering: Beyond Traditional Selection Perspectives" (white paper published by KPMG, Amsterdam, 1999).

40. Barringer and Harrison, "Walking a Tightrope."

41. F. Reichheld, "The Microeconomics of Customer Relationships," *MIT Sloan Management Review* 47, no. 2 (2006): 73-78; C. Markides, "A Dynamic View of Strategy," *Sloan Management Review* 40, no. 3 (1999): 55–63.

42. J. C. Anderson, J. A. Narus, and W. van Rossum, "Customer Value Propositions in Business Markets," *Harvard Business Review* 84, no. 3 (2006): 90–99.

43. E. Anderson and V. Onyemah, "How Right Should the Customer Be?" *Harvard Business Review* 84, no. 7/8 (2006): 58–67.

C H A P T E R

7

preparing the proper *ethical and legal* foundation

Courtesy of Vail B. Horton.

Getting Personal

with **VAIL HORTON**

Best advice I've received	My biggest worry as an entrepreneur	My biggest surprise as an entrepreneur
Trust is the easiest to lose and hardest to earn	*What are all the people going to do if the company goes under*	*Working for people is what the CEO does*

Keen Mobility:

Getting Off to a Good Start—Ethically and Legally

The founding and growth of Keen Mobility is a heartwarming story. The company was started in 2001 by Vail Horton, an entrepreneurship student at the University of Portland. Born without legs, as a boy Horton was told repeatedly by doctors that he belonged in a wheelchair. Preferring the added mobility offered by crutches, he resisted the doctors' advice and, with the help of his grandfather, located a team of doctors that fitted him with prosthetic legs, making the use of crutches possible.

As a college student, Horton began to develop medical problems associated with prolonged crutch usage. As anyone who has walked with crutches for even a short time knows, crutches are uncomfortable and unforgiving, particularly when it comes to shoulder and back pain. Rather than give up and submit to a wheelchair, Horton decided to create a company to build more comfortable and supportive crutches. To do this, he sought out fellow students who were studying engineering and product design. Keen Mobility was launched in 2001, Horton's junior year, with the assistance of two University of Portland classmates, who helped him build his first prototypes. Today, the company, which has expanded its product line, has over $2 million in annual sales. A short streaming video of Vail Horton, on stage with President Bush at a high school assembly in Beaverton, Oregon, is available at www.vailhorton.com. In the video, the president asks Horton to tell the story of Keen Mobility and compliments him for overcoming the obstacles he has experienced in his life.

During the early development of the company, two areas of utmost concern to Horton and his management team had been getting the company off to a good start ethically and legally. Keen is a values-driven company, which guides both its overall philosophy and its day-to-day activities. Although it's a for-profit company, with investors who expect a healthy return, it is driven by a desire to help people with disabilities become more mobile and lead better lives. This sentiment is reflected in the company's vision statement, which is "To increase the safety, mobility and comfort of the elderly, disabled and injured, so they contribute more to society." The company also sees itself filling a gap in the marketplace. There is no real incentive for large crutch manufacturers to innovate, because they are reimbursed for the vast majority of their sales by Medicare

VAIL HORTON

Founder, Keen Mobility
BA, College of Business,
University of Portland, 2002

THE
UNIVERSITY OF
PORTLAND

What I'd like to be doing in 10 years	What I do when I'm not working	Hardest part of getting funding
Living in the middle of the California redwoods	*Husbanding and fathering*	*Being real and honest*

After studying this chapter you should be ready to:

L E A R N I N G

Objectives

1. Describe how to create a strong ethical culture in an entrepreneurial venture.

2. Explain the importance of having a code of conduct and an ethics training program.

3. Explain the criteria important to selecting an attorney for a new firm.

4. Discuss the steps necessary to ethically depart from an employer.

5. Discuss the importance of nondisclosure and noncompete agreements.

6. Discuss the importance of a founders' agreement.

7. Provide several suggestions for how entrepreneurial ventures can avoid litigation.

8. Discuss the differences among sole proprietorships, partnerships, corporations, and limited liability companies.

9. Explain why most fast-growth entrepreneurial ventures organize as corporations or limited liability companies rather than sole proprietorships or partnerships.

10. Explain double taxation.

at a fixed rate. As a result, prior to Keen Mobility, no real innovation in crutch comfort or design had taken place for decades. Keen Mobility is fiercely innovative, and its products are designed to increase both the mobility and the comfort of its customers.

In regard to legal issues, Keen has played it straight from the start. Horton consulted an attorney before launching his company to make certain that the company was complying with all local and state regulations and in order to put the firm on a sound legal foundation. The company was incorporated as a limited liability company (LLC) but later changed to a C corporation when it accepted money from accredited investors. Keen currently has 12 patents (in various stages of approval) and retained a patent attorney to do the legal work. Horton recalls that he did quit a bit of networking to find the most qualified patent attorney in his area.

Reflecting on his experiences regarding legal considerations and launching a firm, Horton offers the following advice: (1) Don't be shy about shopping for an attorney—find the attorney that represents the best fit for your firm; (2) take the advice of your attorney but don't neglect to learn about legal issues yourself; (3) regardless of how smart you think your attorney is, don't be afraid to get multiple opinions on important issues; (4) get things in writing; (5) be ethical—the business world is very competitive and doesn't always promote doing the right thing—do the right thing anyway; and (6) don't focus on legal issues so much you're not focused on sales. Put legal issues in their proper perspective.

The ethical and legal challenges involved with starting a firm are complicated. It is extremely important that entrepreneurs understand these issues and avoid costly mistakes. This chapter begins by discussing the most important initial ethical and legal issues facing a new firm, including establishing a strong ethical organizational culture, choosing a lawyer, drafting a founders' agreement, and avoiding litigation. The chapter next discusses the different forms of business organization, including sole proprietorships, partnerships, corporations, and limited liability companies.

Chapter 12 discusses the protection of intellectual property through patents, trademarks, copyrights, and trade secrets. This topic, which is also a legal issue, is becoming increasingly important as entrepreneurs rely more on intellectual property rather than physical property as a source of a competitive advantage. Chapter 15 discusses legal issues pertaining to franchising.

Initial Ethical and Legal Issues Facing a New Firm

As the opening case suggests, new ventures must deal with important ethical and legal issues at the time of their launching. Ethical and legal errors made early on can be extremely costly for a new venture down the road. And there is a tendency for entrepreneurs to overestimate their knowledge of the law. In one study, researchers examined the information that some 279 early-stage entrepreneurs sought from a Small Business Student Legal Clinic. They concluded that entrepreneurs underestimate the amount of legal support they will need in the early stages of launching a business. In fact, 44 percent of the new ventures in the study altered or abandoned their original business strategy after they obtained a fuller understanding of the legal issues involved.[1] In a similar study, 254 small retailers and service company owners were asked to judge the legality of several business practices.[2] A sample of the practices included in the survey is shown next. Which practices do you think are legal and which ones do you think aren't legal?

- Avoiding Social Security payments for independent contractors
- Hiring only experienced help
- Preempting potential competition with prices below costs
- Agreeing to divide a market with rivals

The first two practices are legal, while the second two are illegal. How did you do? For comparison purposes, you might want to know that the participants in the survey were wrong 35 percent of the time about these four practices. Neither of these studies implies that entrepreneurs break the law intentionally or that they do not have ethical intentions. What the studies do suggest is that entrepreneurs tend to overestimate their knowledge of the legal complexities involved with launching and running a business.

As a company grows, the legal environment becomes even more complex. A reevaluation of a company's ownership structure usually takes place when investors become involved. In addition, companies that go public are required to comply with a host of Securities and Exchange Commission (SEC) regulations, including regulations spawned by the Sarbanes-Oxley Act of 2002. We provide more information about the Sarbanes-Oxley Act in Chapter 10.

Against this backdrop, the following sections discuss several of the most important ethical and legal issues facing the founders of new firms.

Establishing a Strong Ethical Culture for a Firm

The single most important thing the founders of an entrepreneurial venture can do is establish a strong ethical culture for their firms. The data regarding business ethics are not encouraging. For example, 54 percent of the 2002 *Inc.* 500 CEOs surveyed thought that unethical business practices were as common among small private companies as large organizations.[3] Similarly, in 2005 the National Business Ethics Survey, conducted by the Ethics Resource Center, surveyed more than 3,000 American workers regarding ethics-related issues. A total of 52 percent of the employees surveyed said they had observed at least one type of ethical misconduct in the past year. Of the employees who observed misconduct at work, just over half (55 percent) reported it to management.[4]

In analyzing the results of its survey, which also measured 18 dimensions of ethical culture, the Ethics Resource Center concluded that the most important thing an organization can do to combat the figures its study revealed is to establish a strong ethical culture. But strong ethical cultures don't emerge by themselves. It takes entrepreneurs who make ethics a priority and organizational policies and procedures that encourage ethical behavior (and punish unethical behavior) to make it happen. The following are specific steps that an entrepreneurial organization can take to build a strong ethical culture.

Lead By Example The most important thing that any entrepreneur, or team of entrepreneurs, can do to build a strong ethical culture in their organization is to lead by example. The following results from the 2005 National Business Ethics Survey, which measured the influence that leaders and peers have on the ethical behavior of employees, demonstrate this point:

- Where top management displays certain ethics-related actions, employees are 50 percent less likely to observe misconduct.
- Ethics-related actions of co-workers can increase employee willingness to report misconduct, by as much as 10 percent.
- When employees perceive that others are held accountable for their actions, their overall satisfaction increases by 32 percent.
- Employees in organizations with strong ethical cultures and full formal programs (like codes of conduct and ethics training programs) are 36 percent less likely to observe misconduct than employees in organizations with a weak culture and full formal programs.

These data vividly demonstrate the salient role that the founders or top managers of a firm have on the ethical behavior of employees.[5]

Establish a Code of Conduct A **code of conduct** (or code of ethics) is a formal statement of an organization's values on certain ethical and social issues.[6] The advantage of having a code of conduct is that it provides specific guidance to managers and employees

LEARNING

Objective

1. Describe how to create a strong ethical culture in an entrepreneurial venture.

LEARNING

Objective

2. Explain the importance of having a code of conduct and an ethics training program.

As part of building an ethical culture, many entrepreneurial firms are becoming more proactive in regard to helping address social needs. Here, Bill Gates, the chairman of Microsoft, gives a baby an oral polio drop at a community health clinic in India. Bill Gates is the driving force behind the Bill & Melinda Gates Foundation, which is now the largest charitable foundation in the world.

regarding what is expected of them in terms of ethical behavior. Consider what Google has done in this area. The company's informal corporate motto is "Don't be evil," but it also has a formal code of conduct, which explicitly states what is and isn't permissible in the organization. The table of contents for Google's code of conduct is shown in Table 7.1. It illustrates the ethical issues that Google thinks can be bolstered and better explained to employees via a written document to which they are required to adhere. A copy of Google's full code of conduct is available at http://investor.google.com/conduct.html.

TABLE 7.1 Table of Contents of Google's Code of Conduct

I. Serving our Users
   a. Usefulness
   b. Honesty
   c. Responsiveness
   d. Taking Action

III. Avoiding Conflicts of Interest
   a. Openness
   b. Personal Investments
   c. Gifts and Entertainment
   d. Business Relationships
   e. Friends and Relatives

V. Maintaining Books and Records
   a. Business Transactions
   b. Reporting Procedures
   c. Reporting Irregularities

VII. Obeying the Law
   a. The Foreign Corrupt Practices Act
   b. Export Controls
   c. Antitrust Laws

II. Respecting Each Other
   a. Equal Opportunity Employment
   b. Harassment and Discrimination
   c. Drug and Alcohol Use
   d. Weapons and Workplace Violence
   e. Our Dog Policy

IV. Preserving Confidentiality
   a. Confidential Information
   b. Trademarks, Logos and Copyrights
   c. Google Partners
   d. Competitors' Information
   e. Outside Communication

VI. Protecting Google's Assets
   a. Company Equipment
   b. Computer and Other Communication Resources
   c. Third Party Suppliers
   d. Company Contracts

VIII. Using Our Code

Source: Google Web site, http://investor.google.com/conduct.html (accessed July 29, 2006). Google Code of Conduct © Google Inc. and is used with permission.

In practice, some codes of conduct are very specific, like Google's. Other codes of conduct set out more general principles about an organization's beliefs on issues such as product quality, respect for customers and employees, and social responsibility. The 2005 National Business Ethics Survey, already referred to, found that the percentage of firms that have written codes of conduct is up almost 20 percent from a similar survey conducted in 1994. Many observers feel that having a strong code of conduct (or code of ethics) in place is an important element in establishing a strong ethical culture in a firm.

Implement an Ethics Training Program Firms also use ethics training programs to promote ethical behavior. **Ethics training programs** teach business ethics to help employees deal with ethical dilemmas and improve their overall ethical conduct. An **ethical dilemma** is a situation that involves doing something that is beneficial to oneself or the organization, but may be unethical. Most employees confront ethical dilemmas at some point during their careers.

Ethics training programs can be provided by outside vendors or can be developed inhouse. For example, one organization, Character Training International (CTI), provides ethics training programs for both large organizations and smaller entrepreneurial firms. The company offers a variety of ethics-related training services, including on-site workshops, speeches, a train-the-trainer curriculum, videos, and consulting services. A distinctive attribute of CTI is its focus on the moral and ethical roots of workplace behavior. In workshops, participants talk about the reasons behind ethical dilemmas and are provided practical, helpful information about how to prevent problems and how to deal appropriately with the ethical problems and temptations that do arise. The hope is that this training will significantly cut down on employee misconduct and fraud and will increase morale.[7]

In summary, ethical cultures are built through both strong ethical leadership and administrative tools that reinforce and govern ethical behavior in organizations. There are many potential payoffs to organizations that act and behave in an ethical manner. A sample of the potential payoffs appears in Figure 7.1.

FIGURE 7.1

Potential Payoffs for Establishing a Strong Ethical Culture

Choosing an Attorney for a Firm

It is important for an entrepreneur to select an attorney as early as possible when developing a business venture. Table 7.2 provides guidelines to consider when selecting an attorney. It is critically important that the attorney be familiar with start-up issues and that he or she has successfully shepherded entrepreneurs through the start-up process before. It is not wise to select an attorney just because she is a friend or because you were pleased with the way he prepared your will. For issues dealing with intellectual property protection, it is essential to use an attorney who specializes in this field, such as a patent attorney, when filing a patent application.[8]

LEARNING

Objective

3. Explain the criteria important in selecting an attorney for a new firm.

TABLE 7.2 How to Select an Attorney

1. Contact the local bar association and ask for a list of attorneys who specialize in business start-ups in your area.

2. Interview several attorneys. Check references. Ask your prospective attorney whom he or she has guided through the start-up process before and talk to the attorney's clients. If an attorney is reluctant to give you the names of past or present clients, select another attorney.

3. Select an attorney who is familiar with the start-up process. Make sure that the attorney is more than just a legal technician. Most entrepreneurs need an attorney who is patient and is willing to guide them through the start-up process.

4. Select an attorney who can assist you in raising money for your venture. This is a challenging issue for most entrepreneurs, and help in this area can be invaluable.

5. Make sure your attorney has a track record of completing his or her work on time. It can be very frustrating to be prepared to move forward with a business venture, only to be stymied by delays on the part of an attorney.

6. Talk about fees. If your attorney won't give you a good idea of what the start-up process will cost, keep looking.

7. Trust your intuition. Select an attorney who you think understands your business and with whom you will be comfortable spending time and having open discussions about the dreams you have for your entrepreneurial venture.

8. Learn as much about the process of starting a business yourself as possible. It will help you identify any problems that may exist or any aspect that may have been overlooked. Remember, it's your business start-up, not your attorney's. Stay in control.

Entrepreneurs often object to the expense of hiring an attorney when there are many books, Web sites, and other resources that can help them address legal issues on their own. However, these alternatives should be chosen with extreme caution. Many attorneys recognize that start-ups are short on cash and will work out an installment plan or other payment arrangement to get the firm the legal help it needs without starving it of cash. This is particularly true if the attorney senses that the new venture has strong commercial potential and may develop into a steady client in the future. There are also ways for entrepreneurs to save on legal fees and to increase the value of their relationship with their attorney. The following are several ways for entrepreneurs to achieve these dual objectives:

- *Group together legal matters:* It is typically cheaper to consult with an attorney on several matters at one time rather than schedule several separate meetings. For example, in one conference, a team of start-up entrepreneurs and their attorney could draft a founders' agreement, decide on a form of business organization, and discuss how to best draft nondisclosure and noncompete agreements for new employees. (We discuss these issues later in the chapter.)

- *Offer to assist the attorney:* There are excellent resources available to help entrepreneurs acquaint themselves with legal matters. An entrepreneur could help the attorney save time by writing the first few drafts of a founders' agreement or a contract or by helping gather the documents needed to deal with a legal issue.

- *Ask your attorney to join your advisory board:* Many start-ups form advisory boards (discussed in Chapter 9). Advisory board members typically serve as volunteers to help young firms get off to a good start. An attorney serving on an advisory board becomes a coach and a confidant as well as a paid service provider. However, entrepreneurs must be careful not to give the impression that the attorney was asked to serve on the advisory board as a way of getting free legal advice.

- *Use nonlawyer professionals:* Nonlawyer professionals can perform some tasks at a much lower fee than a lawyer would charge. Examples include management consultants for business planning, tax preparation services for tax work, and insurance agents for advice on insurance planning.

It is important for an entrepreneur to select an attorney as early as possible when developing a business venture. It is best to select an attorney who is familiar with start-up issues.

One thing entrepreneurs should guard themselves against, as expressed in the opening case, is ceding too much control to an attorney. While an attorney should be sought out and relied upon for legal advice, the major decisions pertaining to the firm should be made by the entrepreneurs. Entrepreneurs should also develop a good working knowledge of business law. This notion is affirmed by Constance E. Bagley, a professor at Harvard University, who wrote, "Just as a lawyer needs a sufficient understanding of how business operates and the strategies for success to be an effective partner (in an attorney–client relationship with an entrepreneur), the manager and entrepreneur need to have some knowledge of legal nomenclature and the legal principles most relevant to their business."[9]

Ethically Departing from an Employer

Although some entrepreneurial firms are started by students or by self-employed individuals, people holding traditional jobs start the majority of new ventures. After leaving a job to start a new firm, many entrepreneurs are surprised to find themselves in the midst of a dispute with their former employer. The following are the two most important guidelines when leaving an employer to start your own firm.

LEARNING

Objective

4. Discuss the steps necessary to ethically depart from an employer.

Behave in a Professional Manner First, it is important that an employee give proper notice of an intention to quit and that the employee perform all assigned duties until the day of departure. Quitting on a moment's notice typically doesn't sit well with an employer. In addition, an employee shouldn't spend the last few days on a job making arrangements for the launch of the new venture. This type of behavior is unprofessional and is an improper use of the current employer's time and resources.

If an employee is leaving a job to start a firm in the same industry, it is vital not to take information that belongs to the current employer. Employers have a right to protect their trade secrets (e.g., client lists, marketing plans, product prototypes, and acquisition strategies) from theft or from inappropriate transfer from the office to an employee's home. In addition, an employee should be aware of the general spirit of the law regarding loyalty and employer–employee relationships. According to the legal principle referred to as the **corporate opportunity doctrine**, key employees (such as officers, directors, or managers) and skilled employees (such as software engineers, accountants, and marketing specialists) owe a special duty of loyalty to their employer.[10] The corporate opportunity doctrine most often kicks in when employees divert to themselves an opportunity that rightfully belongs to the employer. An employee may make plans to compete with an employer while still on the job (on off-duty time) but may not divert opportunities, solicit employees to work for the new business, or actually start a competing business until the employment relationship has ended.[11]

TABLE 7.3 Practices to Follow When Leaving a Job

1. Give notice of an intention to leave a job at least 2 weeks in advance.

2. Remain committed to your current job until you leave. Do not spend time on your current job making arrangements for your new venture.

3. Don't talk to co-workers about joining your new firm until you have left your job and get the go-ahead from your attorney.

4. Don't redirect business opportunities that belong to your current employer to your new firm while you are still employed by your current employer.

5. Don't actually start your new firm while you are still employed by your current employer, especially if your new firm competes in any way with your current employer.

6. Take nothing with you except your personal belongings. Don't spend a lot of time at the copy machine or in your office after hours regardless of how innocent your activity may be.

7. Don't use the e-mail account provided by your current employer to make arrangements for the new business even if you're using the account after hours.

8. Do everything you can to prevent the impression that you're taking any information from your current employer. Don't do anything out of the ordinary.

To leave a job ethically and pleasantly and to avoid any suspicion of inappropriate behavior, a departing employee should follow the practices shown in Table 7.3.

Honor All Employment Agreements It is also important that employees be fully aware of the employment agreements that they have signed and honor them. In most cases, key employees have signed nondisclosure and noncompete agreements. A **nondisclosure agreement** is a promise made by an employee or another party (such as a supplier) to not disclose a company's trade secrets. An employee should strictly adhere to this document during employment and after leaving a firm. Many employees have also signed a **noncompete agreement**, which prevents an individual from competing against a former employer for a specific period of time. In making an ethical departure from a firm, an employee should adhere to this agreement if one has been signed.

Sometimes, regardless of how careful an individual is to make an ethical departure from a former employer, disputes arise. An example might be someone who leaves a personal finance software company to start a company that makes financial management software for small businesses. The personal software company may sue the former employee for violation of the noncompete agreement, arguing that some small businesses use its personal finance software rather than more expensive business software. An attorney can help an entrepreneur anticipate and avoid such claims and help mount a defense if one is necessary.

A sample nondisclosure and noncompete agreement is shown in Figure 7.2.

Drafting a Founders' Agreement

It is important to ensure that founders are in agreement regarding their interests in the venture and their commitment to its future. It is easy for a team of entrepreneurs to get caught up in the excitement of launching a venture and fail to put in writing their initial agreements regarding the ownership of the firm. A **founders' agreement** (or shareholders' agreement) is a written document that deals with issues such as the relative split of the equity among the founders of the firm, how individual founders will be compensated for the cash or the "sweat equity" they put into the firm, and how long the founders will have to remain with the firm for their shares to fully vest.[12] The items typically included in a founders' agreement are shown in Table 7.4.

An important issue addressed by most founders' agreements is what happens to the equity of a founder if the founder dies or decides to leave the firm. Most founders' agreements include a **buyback clause**, which legally obligates departing founders to sell to the remaining founders their interest in the firm if the remaining founders are interested.[13] In most cases, the agreement also specifies the formula for computing the dollar value to be paid. The presence of a buyback clause is important for at least two reasons. First, if a

L E A R N I N G
Objective

5. Discuss the importance of nondisclosure and noncompete agreements.

L E A R N I N G
Objective

6. Discuss the importance of a founders' agreement.

Nondisclosure and Noncompetition. (a) At all times while this agreement is in force and after its expiration or termination, [employee name] agrees to refrain from disclosing [company name]'s customer lists, trade secrets, or other confidential material. [Employee name] agrees to take reasonable security measures to prevent accidental disclosure and industrial espionage.

(b) While this agreement is in force, the employee agrees to use [his/her] best efforts to [describe job] and to abide by the nondisclosure and noncompetition terms of this agreement; the employer agrees to compensate the employee as follows: [describe compensation]. After expiration or termination of this agreement, [employee name] agrees not to compete with [company name] for a period of [number] years within a [number] mile radius of [company name and location]. This prohibition will not apply if this agreement is terminated because [company] violated the terms of this agreement.

Competition means owning or working for a business of the following type: [specify type of business employee may not engage in].

(c) [Employee name] agrees to pay liquidated damages in the amount of $[dollar amount] for any violation of the covenant not to compete contained in subparagraph (b) of this paragraph.

IN WITNESS WHEREOF, [company name] and [employee name] have signed this agreement.

_____

[company name]

_____

[employee's name]
Date: _____

Source: Office Depot

FIGURE 7.2

Sample Nondisclosure and Noncompete Agreement

TABLE 7.4 Items Included in a Founders' (or Shareholders') Agreement

- Nature of the prospective business
- A brief business plan
- Identity and proposed titles of the founders
- Legal form of business ownership
- Apportionment of stock (or division of ownership)
- Consideration paid for stock or ownership share of each of the founders (may be cash or "sweat equity")
- Identification of any intellectual property signed over to the business by any of the founders
- Description of the initial operating capital
- Buyback clause, which explains how a founder's shares will be disposed of if she or he dies, wants to sell, or is forced to sell by court order

founder leaves the firm, the remaining founders may need the shares to offer to a replacement person. Second, if founders leave because they are disgruntled, the buyback clause provides the remaining founders a mechanism to keep the shares of the firm in the hands of people who are fully committed to a positive future for the venture.

Avoiding Legal Disputes

Most legal disputes are the result of misunderstandings, sloppiness, or a simple lack of knowledge of the law. Getting bogged down in legal disputes is something that an entrepreneur should work hard to avoid. It is important early in the life of a new business to establish practices and procedures to help avoid legal disputes. Legal snafus, particularly if they are coupled with management mistakes, can be extremely damaging to a new firm, as illustrated in this chapter's "What Went Wrong?" feature.

There are several steps entrepreneurs can take to avoid legal disputes and complications, as discussed below.

Meet All Contractual Obligations It is important to meet all contractual obligations on time. This includes paying vendors, contractors, and employees as agreed and

7. Provide several suggestions for how entrepreneurial ventures can avoid litigation.

How Legal and Management Snafus Can Kill a Business
www.jambiajuice.com

In 1990, Jambia Juice started in San Luis Obispo, California. The company, which sells smoothie drinks, got off to a good start, opened two more cafés in 1993, and now has hundreds of outlets all the way from Hawaii to Boston. In fact, Jambia Juice is somewhat unusual in that at one point during its growth, it obtained venture capital funding, which is normally reserved for high-tech or biotech firms. Apparently, Benchmark Capital, the venture capital firm involved, felt that smoothie drinks were a good bet.

In 1994, two entrepreneurs, Sean Nicholson and Aaron Souza, who had watched Jambia Juice grow, decided to try their own hands at opening a smoothie restaurant and started Green Planet Juicery. Nicholson and Souza were impressed with Jambia Juice and followed its lead in several areas. For example, Jambia Juice located its cafés near college campuses, where smoothie drinks were popular, so Green Planet's first café opened near the University of California, Davis. The café was a hit. In months, it was earning a profit, and its first-year sales figure exceeded $500,000.

Three years later, Green Planet Juicery was broke. What went wrong? It wasn't the market for smoothie drinks. In fact, Jambia Juice is growing faster than ever. Instead, what killed Green Planet were legal and management snafus. Here's the full story.

First, Green Planet tried to grow too quickly. Unlike Jambia Juice, which waited 3 years to open its second café, Green Planet moved more quickly and opened three additional cafés within 2 years of its founding. In the process, it abandoned the idea of locating near college campuses and opened all its new outlets in nearby Sacramento. Two of the three new outlets struggled and, in hindsight, were poorly located. The first was located near a high school (where the students were not allowed to leave the premises during lunchtime), and the second was opened near a discount store. The third outlet was a hit and rivaled the sales of the original café. To open it, though, Green Planet had to form a partnership with an investor and received only a portion of the café's profits.

Second, at the same time Green Planet was struggling with its growth, Jambia Juice sued Green Planet for copyright infringement. According to Jambia Juice, Green Planet copied from its menu or other literature descriptions of such nutritional smoothie additives as algae, tofu, bee pollen, and brewer's yeast. Jambia Juice also alleged that Green Planet copied its promotional slogan for nutritional additives: "If you're green inside, you're clean inside." Green Planet admitted guilt and settled with Jambia Juice for an undisclosed sum.

Green Planet Juicery never fully recovered from these blunders and eventually went out of business. Its story provides a vivid reminder of the damage that can be caused by legal and management snafus, especially early in the life of a venture.

Questions for Critical Thinking

1. To what extent do you believe establishing a strong ethical culture could have helped Green Planet avoid its legal difficulties?

2. Imagine you were given the job of writing a code of conduct for Greet Planet when the company was founded. Using the table of contents of Google's code of conduct as a guide (Table 7.1), construct the table of contents for Green Planet's code of conduct. Make Green Planet's code of conduct fit its industry and individual circumstances.

3. If you had been one of the entrepreneurs founding Great Planet Juicery, what would you have done differently compared to the actions described in this feature?

4. Go to Jambia Juice's Web site (www.jambiajuice. com). Does it appear to you that Jambia Juice is still a successful firm? If so, given what you've studied at the Web site, what do you believe accounts for the firm's continuing success?

Sources: Jambia Juice homepage, www.jambajuice.com (accessed July 27, 2006); M. Selz, "Starting Too Fast: Green Planet Rushed to Add More Stores—Often in the Wrong Places," *The Wall Street Journal*, September 25, 2000, 18.

delivering goods or services as promised. If an obligation cannot be met on time, the problem should be communicated to the affected parties as soon as possible. It is irritating to a vendor, for example, not only to not get paid on time but also to have no explanation for the delay. Commenting on this issue, David Preiser, the managing director of an investment banking company in Los Angeles, says, "Credibility and confidence are built slowly but destroyed rapidly."[14] Preiser recommends being forthright with vendors or creditors if an obligation cannot be met and providing the affected party or parties a realistic plan for repaying the money as a way of retaining their confidence.

Avoid Undercapitalization If a new business is starved for money, it is much more likely to experience financial problems that will lead to litigation.[15] A new business should raise the money it needs to effectively conduct business or should stem its growth to conserve cash. Many entrepreneurs face a dilemma regarding this issue. It is the goal of most entrepreneurs to retain as much of the equity in their firms as possible, but equity must often be shared with investors to obtain sufficient investment capital to support the firm's growth. This issue is discussed in more detail in Chapter 10.

Get Everything in Writing Many business disputes arise because of the lack of a written agreement or because poorly prepared written agreements do not anticipate potential areas of dispute. Although it is tempting to try to show business partners or employees that they are "trusted" by downplaying the need for a written agreement, this approach is usually a mistake. Disputes are much easier to resolve if the rights and obligations of the parties involved are in writing. For example, what if a new business agreed to pay a Web design firm $5,000 to design its Web site? The new business should know what it's getting for its money, and the Web design firm should know when the project is due and when it will receive payment for its services. In this case, a dispute could easily arise if the parties simply shook hands on the deal and the Web design firm promised to have a "good-looking Web site" done "as soon as possible." The two parties could easily later disagree over the quality and functionality of the finished Web site and the project's completion date.

The experiences and perspectives of Maxine Clark, the founder of Build A Bear Workshop, provide a solid illustration of the practical benefits of putting things in writing, even when dealing with a trusted partner:

> While I prefer only the necessary contracts (and certainly as few pages as possible), once you find a good partner you can trust, written up-front agreements are often a clean way to be sure all discussed terms are acceptable to all parties. It's also a good idea after a meeting to be sure someone records the facts and agree-to points, and distribute them to all participants in writing. E-mail is a good method for doing this. Steps like this will make your life easier. After all, the bigger a business gets, the harder it is to remember all details about every vendor, contract, and meeting. Written records give you good notes for doing follow-up, too.[16]

Set Standards Organizations should also set standards that govern employees' behavior beyond what can be expressed via a code of conduct. For example, four of the most common ethical problem areas that occur in an organization are human resource ethical problems, conflicts of interest, customer confidence, and inappropriate use of corporate resources. Policies and procedures should be established to deal with these issues. In addition, as reflecting in the "Partnering for Success" boxed features throughout this book, firms are increasingly partnering with others to achieve their objectives. Because of this, entrepreneurial ventures should be vigilant when selecting their alliance partners. A firm falls short in terms of establishing high ethical standards if it is willing to partner with firms that behave in a contrary manner. This chapter's "Partnering for Success" feature illustrates how two firms, Patagonia and Build A Bear Workshop, deal with this issue.

partnering for success

Patagonia and Build A Bear Workshop: Picking Trustworthy Partners
www.patagonia.com, www.buildabear.com

Patagonia

Patagonia sells rugged clothing and gear to mountain climbers, skiers, and other extreme-sport enthusiasts. The company is also well known for its environmental stands and its commitment to product quality. Patagonia has never owned a fabric mill or a sewing shop. Instead, to make a ski jacket, for example, it buys fabric from a mill, zippers and facings from other manufacturers, and then hires a sewing shop to complete the garment. To meet its own environmental standards and ensure product quality, it works closely with each partner to make sure the jacket meets its rigid standards.

As a result of these standards, Patagonia does as much business as it can with as few partners as possible and chooses its relationships carefully. The first thing the company looks for in a partner is the quality of its work. It doesn't look for the lowest-cost provider, who might sew one day for a warehouse outlet store such as Costco and try to sew the next day for Patagonia. Contractors that sew on the lowest-cost basis, the company reasons, wouldn't hire sewing operators of the skill required or welcome Patagonia's oversight of its working conditions and environmental standards. What Patagonia looks for, more than anything, is a good fit between itself and the companies it partners with. It sees its partners as an extension of its own business, and wants partners that convey Patagonia's own sense of product quality, business ethics, and environmental and social concern.

Once a relationship is established, Patagonia doesn't leave adherence to its principles to chance. Its production department monitors its partners on a consistent basis. The objective is for both sides to prosper and win. In fact, in describing the company's relationship with its partners, Patagonia founder Yvon Chovinard says, "We become like friends, family—mutually selfish business partners; what's good for them is good for us."

Build A Bear Workshop

A similar set of beliefs and actions describe Build A Bear Workshop. Build A Bear lets its customers, who are usually children, design and build their own stuffed animals, in a sort of Santa's Workshop setting. Like Patagonia, Build A Bear is a very socially conscious organization, and

looks for partners that reflect its values. Affirming this point, Maxine Clark, the company's founder, said, "The most successful corporate partnerships are forged between like-minded companies with similar cultures that have come together for a common goal, where both sides benefit from the relationship."

Also similar to Patagonia, Build A Bear thinks of its partners as good friends. Reflecting on her experiences in this area, Clark said, "I tend to think of partners as good business friends—companies and people who would do everything they could to help us succeed and for whom I would do the same." In a book she wrote about founding and building Build A Bear into a successful company, Clark attributes having good partners to careful selection. She also likens business partnership to a marriage, which has many benefits but also takes hard work: "Good business partnerships are like successful marriages. To work, they require compatibility, trust and cooperation. Both parties need to be invested in one another's well-being and strive for a common goal."

Both Patagonia and Build A Bear make extensive use of partnerships and are leaders in their respective industries

Questions for Critical Thinking

1. To what extent do you believe that Patagonia and Build A Bear Workshop's ethical cultures drive their views on partnering?
2. Assume you were assigned the task of writing a code of conduct for Patagonia. Write the portion of the code of conduct that deals with business partnership relationships.
3. List the similarities that you see between the partnership philosophies of Patagonia and Build A Bear Workshop.
4. Spend some time studying Patagonia, by looking at the company's Web site and via other Internet searches. Describe Patagonia's general approach to business ethics, social responsibility, and environmental concerns. What, if anything, can start-ups learn from Patagonia's philosophies and its experiences?

Sources: M. Clark, *The Bear Necessities of Business* (New York: Wiley, 2006); Y. Chovinard, *Let My People Go Surfing* (New York: The Penguin Press, 2005).

When legal disputes do occur, they can often be settled through negotiation or mediation, rather than more expensive and potentially damaging litigation. **Mediation** is a process in which an impartial third party (usually a professional mediator) helps those involved in a dispute reach an agreement. At times, legal disputes can also be avoided by a simple apology and a sincere pledge on the part of the offending party to make amends. An example that illustrates this point is provided by Harvard Professor Constance E. Bagley, who was quoted earlier in this chapter.[16] In regard to the role a simple apology plays in resolving legal disputes, Professor Bagley refers to a *Wall Street Journal* article in which the writer commented about a jury awarding $2.7 million to a woman who spilled scalding hot McDonald's coffee on her lap.

A jury awarded $2.7 million to a woman who spilled scalding hot McDonald's coffee on her lap. Although this case is often cited as an example of a tort (legal) system run amok, the *Wall Street Journal* faulted McDonald's for not only failing to respond to prior scalding incidents but also for mishandling the injured woman's complaints by not apologizing.[17,18]

A final issue important in promoting business ethics involves the manner in which entrepreneurs and managers demonstrate accountability to their investors and shareholders. This issue, which we discuss in greater detail in Chapter 10, is particularly important given the rash of corporate scandals in the early 2000s.

Choosing a Form of Business Organization

When a business is launched, a form of legal entity must be chosen. Sole proprietorship, partnerships, corporations, and limited liability companies are the most common legal entities from which entrepreneurs make a choice. Choosing a legal entity is not a one-time event. As a business grows and matures, it is necessary to periodically review whether the current form of business organization remains appropriate. In most cases, a firm's form of business entity can be changed without triggering adverse tax implications.

There is no single form of business organization that works best in all situations. It's up to the owners of a firm and their attorney to select the legal entity that best meets their needs. The decision typically hinges on several factors, including the cost of setting up and maintaining the legal form, the extent to which an entrepreneur can shield personal assets from the liabilities of the business, tax considerations, and the number and types of investors that an entrepreneur wants to attract. It is important to be careful in selecting a legal entity for a new firm because each form of business organization involves trade-offs among these factors and because an entrepreneur wants to be sure to achieve the founders' specific objectives.

This section describes the four forms of business organization and discusses the advantages and disadvantages of each. A comparison of the four legal entities, based on the factors that are typically the most important in making a selection, is provided in Table 7.5.

Sole Proprietorship

The simplest form of business entity is the sole proprietorship. A **sole proprietorship** is a form of business organization involving one person, and the person and the business are essentially the same. Sole proprietorships are the most prevalent form of business organization. The two most important advantages of a sole proprietorship are that the owner maintains complete control over the business and that business losses can be deducted against the owner's personal tax return.[19]

Setting up a sole proprietorship is cheap and relatively easy compared to the other forms of business ownership. The only legal requirement, in most states, is to obtain a license to do business. If the business is a retail business, the state will also require a sales

L E A R N I N G

Objective

8. Discuss the differences among sole proprietorships, partnerships, corporations, and limited liability companies.

L E A R N I N G

Objective

9. Explain why most fast-growth entrepreneurial ventures organize as corporations or limited liability companies rather than sole proprietorships or partnerships.

TABLE 7.5 Comparison of Forms of Business Ownership

Factor	Sole Proprietorship	Partnership General	Partnership Limited	Corporation C-Corporation	Corporation S-Corporation	Limited Liability Company
Number of owners allowed	1	Unlimited number of general partners allowed	Unlimited number of general and limited partners allowed	Unlimited	Up to 100	Unlimited number of "members" allowed
Cost of setting up and maintaining	Low	Moderate	Moderate	High	High	High
Personal liability of owners	Unlimited	Unlimited for all partners	Unlimited for general partners; limited partners only to extent of investment	Limited to amount of investment	Limited to amount of investment	Limited to amount of investment
Continuity of business	Ends at death of owner	Death or withdrawal of one partner unless otherwise specified	Death or withdrawal of general partner	Perpetual	Perpetual	Typically limited to a fixed amount of time
Taxation	Not a taxable entity; sole proprietor pays all taxes	Not a taxable entity; each partner pays taxes on his or her share of income and can deduct losses against other sources of income	Not a taxable entity; each partner pays taxes on his or her share of income and can deduct losses against other sources of income	Separate taxable entity	No tax at entity level; income/loss is passed through to the shareholders	No tax at entity level if properly structured; income/ loss is passed through to the members
Management control	Sole proprietor is in full control	All partners share control equally, unless otherwise specified	Only general partners have control	Board of directors elected by the shareholders	Board of directors elected by the shareholders	Members share control or appoint manager
Method of raising capital	Must be raised by sole proprietor	Must be raised by general partners	Sale of limited partnerships, depending on terms of operating agreement	Sell shares of stock to the public	Sell shares of stock to the public	It's possible to sell interests, depending on the terms of the operating agreement
Liquidity of investment	Low	Low	Low	High, if publicly traded	Low	Low
Subject to double taxation	No	No	No	Yes	No	No

tax license. Starting up gets more complicated if the business will deal with hazardous material, such as asbestos, or if it wants to sell alcoholic beverages or tobacco products. In these instances, additional licenses are required. In some cases, primarily because of government regulations, obtaining these licenses can be difficult and time-consuming.

If the business will be operated under a trade name (e.g., Rocky Mountain Consulting) instead of the name of the owner (say, Janice Ryan), the owner will have to file an assumed or fictitious name certificate with the appropriate local government agency. This step is required to ensure that there is only one business in an area using the same name and provides a public record of the owner's name and contact information.

A sole proprietorship is not a separate legal entity. For tax purposes, the profit or loss of the business flows through to the owner's personal tax return, and the business ends at the owner's death or loss of interest in the business. The sole proprietor is responsible for all the liabilities of the business, and this is a significant drawback. If a sole proprietor's business is sued, the owner could theoretically lose all the business's assets along with personal assets. The liquidity of an owner's investment in a sole proprietorship is typically low. **Liquidity** is the ability to sell a business or other asset quickly at a price that is close to its market value.[20] It is usually difficult for a sole proprietorship to raise investment capital because the ownership of the business cannot be shared. Unlimited liability and difficulty raising investment capital are the primary reasons entrepreneurs typically form corporations or limited liability companies as opposed to sole proprietorships. Most sole proprietorships are salary-substitute or lifestyle firms (as described in Chapter 1) and are typically a poor choice for an aggressive entrepreneurial firm.

To summarize, the primary advantages and disadvantages of a sole proprietorship are as follows:

Advantages of a Sole Proprietorship

- Creating one is easy and inexpensive.
- The owner maintains complete control of the business and retains all the profits.
- Business losses can be deducted against the sole proprietor's other sources of income.
- It is not subject to double taxation (explained later).
- The business is easy to dissolve.

Disadvantages of a Sole Proprietorship

- Liability on the owner's part is unlimited.
- The business relies on the skills and abilities of a single owner to be successful. Of course, the owner can hire employees who have additional skills and abilities.
- Raising capital can be difficult.
- The business ends at the owner's death or loss of interest in the business.
- The liquidity of the owner's investment is low.

Partnerships

If two or more people start a business, they must organize as a partnership, corporation, or limited liability company. Partnerships are organized as either general or limited partnerships. In the business world, people merging their skills and interests to form a company is a common occurrence, as reflected in this chapter's "Savvy Entrepreneurial Firm" feature.

General Partnerships A **general partnership** is a form of business organization where two or more people pool their skills, abilities, and resources to run a business. The primary advantage of a general partnership over a sole proprietorship is that the business isn't dependent on a single person for its survival and success. In fact, in most cases, the partners have equal say in how the business is run. Most partnerships have a partnership agreement, which is a legal document that is similar to a founders' agreement. A **partnership agreement** details the responsibilities and the ownership shares of the partners involved with an organization. The business created by a partnership ends at the death or withdrawal of a partner, unless otherwise stated in the partnership agreement. General partnerships are typically found in service industries. In many states, a general partnership must file a certificate of partnership or similar document as evidence of its existence. Similar to a sole proprietorship, the profit or loss of a general partnership flows through to the partner's personal tax returns. If a business has four general partners and they all have equal ownership in the business, then one-fourth of the profits or losses would flow through to each partner's individual tax return.[21] The partnership files an informational tax return only.

savvy entrepreneurial firm

Student and Former Professor Collaborate to Launch Honest Tea
www.honesttea.com

In 1995, Seth Goldman, a second-year master's student at Yale School of Management, was completing a case study on the beverage industry. Goldman was struck by the fact that the beverage industry consisted primarily of high-calorie, sugary drinks on one end and no-calorie bottled water at the other end, with little in between. "What if we created a beverage that had a few calories, so that it had taste, but didn't have all the junk in it?" he wondered at the time. Goldman shared his idea with Barry Nalebuff, one of his professors. Although Nalebuff was intrigued, neither he nor Goldman followed through at the time.

Two years later, Goldman remembered his idea after a jog through New York City's Central Park. He was thirsty but couldn't find a drink that appealed to him. So Goldman dropped an e-mail message to Nalebuff, his former professor, to rekindle his interest in the idea. The two met and hit on the beverage they felt the market lacked: bottled tea. The two decided to start a company to produce organic bottled tea and call it Honest Tea—a name that fit well with Goldman's personal interests in social causes.

In early 1998, Goldman left his job with a mutual fund company and started working on Honest Tea full-time. Nalebuff kept his teaching job but contributed $200,000 in investment capital and used his contacts to find additional funds. Goldman refined the initial Honest Tea flavors in his kitchen, working hard to find retailers who would stock his product while doing so. An early break came through a meeting that Goldman had with the marketing director of Fresh Fields, a food chain in the Washington, D.C., area that agreed to stock Honest Tea's drinks. Not coincidentally, the marketing director was also a former student of Barry Nalebuff, Goldman's partner.

In the ensuing years, Honest Tea has done extremely well and is now the best-selling and fastest-growing organic bottled tea company in the United States; it is available in all 50 states. Goldman remains the company's president and TeaEO (as he calls it). The company is known not only for the quality of its drinks but also for its socially responsible mission and its willingness to give back a portion of its profits to the foreign nations from which it purchases its tea leaves. In fact, today, "Honest Tea can be found in bags, bottles, unsweetened, barely sweetened, or even 'a tad sweet' in stores across the U.S. The company has applied its passion for social responsibility to initiatives in the environment and to creating partnerships with the growers, cultures, and communities behind the teas."

Questions for Critical Thinking

1. Think of all the teachers or professors from whom you've taken classes during your education. From the list you've generated, select the one with whom you would be most likely to form a partnership. What are the traits or characteristics that make that person an attractive partner for a business venture?

2. As explained in this feature, ethical business practices are important to Seth Goldman as he serves as Honest Tea's TeaEO. Earlier in this chapter, we talked about the importance of establishing a strong ethical culture in a firm, and even showed the table of contents of Google's code of conduct (Table 7.1). Given what you've read about Honest Tea and Seth Goldman, develop a list of values you believe are important to him as he leads his company.

3. If you had been advising the founders of Honest Tea when the company started, what types of steps would you have suggested to avoid legal disputes and set high ethical standards for the firm?

4. Finish reading the chapter before answering this question. At the time Honest Tea was founded, what form of business ownership do you think was the most appropriate? What do you think is the most appropriate form of business ownership for Honest Tea today? What factors affected your opinions?

Sources: "Our Story," Honest Tea's homepage, www.honesttea.com (accessed August 5, 2006); J. Yang, "On the Steep Path to Success: Honest Tea's Journey from Business School to Store Shelves," *Washington Post*, March 11, 1999, E01; J. Hyman, "Honest Tea Company Fills Niche with Natural Low-Cal Alternative," *Washington Times*, September 14, 1998, D8.

The primary disadvantage of a general partnership is that the individual partners are liable for all the partnership's debts and obligations. If one partner is negligent while conducting business on behalf of the partnership, all the partners may be liable for damages. Although the nonnegligent partners may later try to recover their losses from the negligent one, the joint liability of all partners to the injured party remains. It is typically easier for a general partnership to raise money than a sole proprietorship simply because more than one person is willing to assume liability for a loan. One way a general partnership can raise investment capital is by adding more partners. Investors are typically reluctant to sign on as general partners, however, because of the unlimited liability that follows each one.

In summary, the primary advantages and disadvantages of a general partnership are as follows:

Advantages of a General Partnership

- Creating one is relatively easy and inexpensive compared to a corporation or limited liability company.
- The skills and abilities of more than one individual are available to the firm.
- Having more than one owner may make it easier to raise funds.
- Business losses can be deducted against the partners' other sources of income.
- It is not subject to double taxation (explained later).

Disadvantages of a General Partnership

- Liability on the part of each general partner is unlimited.
- The business relies on the skills and abilities of a fixed number of partners. Of course, similar to a sole proprietorship, the partners can hire employees who have additional skills and abilities.
- Raising capital can be difficult.
- Because decision making among the partners is shared, disagreements can occur.
- The business ends at the death or withdrawal of one partner unless otherwise stated in the partnership agreement.
- The liquidity of each partner's investment is low.

Limited Partnerships A **limited partnership** is a modified form of a general partnership. The major difference between the two is that a limited partnership includes two classes of owners: general partners and limited partners. There are no limits on the number of general or limited partners permitted in a limited partnership. Similar to a general partnership, the general partners are liable for the debts and obligations of the partnership, but the limited partners are liable only up to the amount of their investment. The limited partners may not exercise any significant control over the organization without jeopardizing their limited liability status.[22] Similar to general partnerships, most limited partnerships have partnership agreements. A **limited partnership agreement** sets forth the rights and duties of the general and limited partners, along with the details of how the partnership will be managed and eventually dissolved.

A limited partnership is usually formed to raise money or to spread out the risk of a venture without forming a corporation. Limited partnerships are common in real estate development, oil and gas exploration, and motion picture ventures.[23]

Corporations

A **corporation** is a separate legal entity organized under the authority of a state. Corporations are organized as either C corporations or subchapter S corporations. The following description pertains to C corporations, which are what most people think of when they hear the word *corporation*. Subchapter S corporations are explained later.

C Corporations A **C corporation** is a separate legal entity that, in the eyes of the law, is separate from its owners. In most cases, the corporation shields its owners, who are called

shareholders, from personal liability for the debts and obligations of the corporation. A corporation is governed by a board of directors, which is elected by the shareholders (more about this in Chapter 9). In most instances, the board hires officers to oversee the day-to-day management of the organization. It is usually easier for a corporation to raise investment capital than a sole proprietorship or a partnership because the shareholders are not liable beyond their investment in the firm. It is also easier to allocate partial ownership interests in a corporation through the distribution of stock. Most C corporations have two classes of stock: common and preferred. **Preferred stock** is typically issued to conservative investors who have preferential rights over common stockholders in regard to dividends and to the assets of the corporation in the event of liquidation. **Common stock** is issued more broadly than preferred stock. The common stockholders have voting rights and elect the board of directors of the firm. The common stockholders are typically the last to get paid in the event of the liquidation of the corporation, that is, after the creditors and the preferred stockholders.[24]

Establishing a corporation is more complicated than a sole proprietorship or a partnership. A corporation is formed by filing **articles of incorporation** with the secretary of state's office in the state of incorporation. The articles of incorporation typically include the corporation's name, purpose, authorized number of stock shares, classes of stock, and other conditions of operation.[25] In most states, corporations must file papers annually, and state agencies impose annual fees. It is important that a corporation's owners fully comply with these regulations. If the owners of a corporation don't file their annual paperwork, neglect to pay their annual fees, or commit fraud, a court could ignore the fact that a corporation has been established and the owners could be held personally liable for actions of the corporation. This chain of effects is referred to as "**piercing the corporate veil**."[26]

A corporation is taxed as a separate legal entity. In fact, the "C" in the title "C corporation" comes from the fact that regular corporations are taxed under subchapter C of the Internal Revenue Code. A disadvantage of corporations is that they are subject to **double taxation**, which means that a corporation is taxed on its net income and, when the same income is distributed to shareholders in the form of dividends, is taxed again on shareholders' personal income tax returns. This complication is one of the reasons that entrepreneurial firms often retain their earnings rather than paying dividends to their shareholders. The firm can use the earnings to fuel future growth and at the same time avoid double taxation. The hope is that the shareholders will ultimately be rewarded by an appreciation in the value of the company's stock.

Another advantage of corporations is the ease of transferring stock. It is often difficult for a sole proprietor to sell a business and even more awkward for a partner to sell a partial interest in a general partnership. If a corporation is listed on a major stock exchange, such as the New York Stock Exchange or the NASDAQ, an owner can sell shares at almost a moment's notice. This advantage of incorporating, however, does not extend to corporations that are not listed on a major stock exchange. As we mentioned earlier in this book, there are approximately 2,700 companies listed on the New York Stock Exchange and 3,200 listed on the NASDAQ. These firms are **public corporations**. The stockholders of these 5,900 companies enjoy a **liquid market** for their stock, meaning that the stock can be bought and sold fairly easily through an organized marketplace. It is much more difficult to sell stock in closely held or private corporations. In a **closely held corporation**, the voting stock is held by a small number of individuals and is very thinly or infrequently traded.[27] A **private corporation** is one in which all the shares are held by a few shareholders, such as management or family members, and are not publicly traded.[28] The vast majority of the corporations in the United States are private corporations. The stock in both closely held and private corporations is fairly **illiquid**, meaning that it typically isn't easy to find a buyer for the stock.

A final advantage of organizing as a C corporation is the ability to share stock with employees as part of an employee incentive plan. Because it's easy to distribute stock in small amounts, many corporations, both public and private, distribute stock as part of their employee bonus or profit-sharing plans. Such incentive plans are intended to help firms attract, motivate, and retain high-quality employees.[29] **Stock options** are a special form of

LEARNING
Objective

10. Explain double taxation.

incentive compensation. These plans provide employees the option or right to buy a certain number of shares of their company's stock at a stated price over a certain period of time. The most compelling advantage of stock options is the potential rewards to participants when (and if) the stock price increases.[30] Many employees receive stock options at the time they are hired and then periodically receive additional options. As employees accumulate stock options, the link between their potential reward and their company's stock price becomes increasingly clear. This link provides a powerful inducement for employees to exert extra effort on behalf of their firm in hopes of positively affecting the stock price.[31]

To summarize, the advantages and disadvantages of a C corporation are as follows:

Advantages of a C Corporation

- Owners are liable only for the debts and obligations of the corporation up to the amount of their investment.
- The mechanics of raising capital is easier.
- No restrictions exist on the number of shareholders, which differs from subchapter S corporations.
- Stock is liquid if traded on a major stock exchange.
- The ability to share stock with employees through stock option or other incentive plans can be a powerful form of employee motivation.

Disadvantages of a C Corporation

- Setting up and maintaining one is more difficult than for a sole proprietorship or a partnership.
- Business losses cannot be deducted against the shareholders' other sources of income.
- Income is subject to double taxation, meaning that it is taxed at the corporate and the shareholder levels.
- Small shareholders typically have little voice in the management of the firm.

Subchapter S Corporation A **subchapter S corporation** combines the advantages of a partnership and a C corporation. It is similar to a partnership in that the profits and losses of the business are not subject to double taxation. The subchapter S corporation does not pay taxes; instead, the profits or losses of the business are passed through to the individual tax returns of the owners. It is also similar to a corporation in that the owners are not subject to personal liability for the behavior of the business. An additional advantage of the subchapter S corporation pertains to self-employment tax. By electing the subchapter S corporate status, only the earnings actually paid out as salary are subject to payroll taxes. The ordinary income that is disbursed by the business to the shareholders is not subject to payroll taxes or self-employment tax.

Because of these advantages, many entrepreneurial firms start as subchapter S corporations. There are strict standards that a business must meet to qualify for status as a subchapter S corporation:

- The business cannot be a subsidiary of another corporation.
- The shareholders must be U.S. citizens. Partnerships and C corporations may not own shares in a subchapter S corporation. Certain types of trusts and estates are eligible to own shares in a subchapter S corporation.
- It can have only one class of stock issued and outstanding (either preferred stock or common stock).
- It can have no more than 100 members. Husbands and wives count as one member, even if they own separate shares of stock. In some instances, family members count as one member.
- All shareholders must agree to have the corporation formed as a subchapter S corporation.

The primary disadvantages of a subchapter S corporation are restrictions in qualifying, expenses involved with setting up and maintaining the subchapter S status, and the fact that a subchapter S corporation is limited to 100 shareholders.[32] If a subchapter S corporation wants to include more than 100 shareholders, it must convert to a C corporation or a limited liability company.

Limited Liability Company

The **limited liability company (LLC)** is a form of business organization that is rapidly gaining popularity in the United States. The concept originated in Germany and was first introduced in the United States in the state of Wyoming in 1978. Along with the subchapter S corporation, it is a popular choice for start-up firms. As with partnerships and corporations, the profits of an LLC flow through to the tax returns of the owners and are not subject to double taxation. The main advantage of the LLC is that all partners enjoy limited liability. This differs from regular and limited partnerships, where at least one partner is liable for the debts of the partnership. The LLC combines the limited liability advantage of the corporation with the tax advantages of the partnership.[33] DreamWorks SKG, the movie studio started by Steven Spielberg, Jeffrey Katzenberg, and David Geffen was an LLC until it went public in late 2004.

Some of the terminology used for an LLC differs from the other forms of business ownership. For example, the shareholders of an LLC are called "members," and instead of owning stock, the members have "interests." The LLC is more flexible than a subchapter S corporation in terms of number of owners and tax-related issues. An LLC must be a private business—it cannot be publicly traded. If at some point the members want to take the business public and be listed on one of the major stock exchanges, it must be converted to a C corporation.

The LLC is rather complex to set up and maintain, and in some states the rules governing the LLC vary. Members may elect to manage the LLC themselves or may designate one or more managers (who may or may not be members) to run the business on a day-to-day basis. The profits and losses of the business may be allocated to the members anyway they choose. For example, if two people owned an LLC, they could split the yearly profits 50–50, 75–25, 90–10, or any other way they choose.[34]

In summary, the advantages and disadvantages of an LLC are as follows:

Advantages of a Limited Liability Company

- Members are liable for the debts and obligations of the business only up to the amount of their investment.
- The number of shareholders is unlimited.
- An LLC can elect to be taxed as a sole proprietor, partnership, S corporation or corporation, providing much flexibility.
- Because profits are taxed only at the shareholder level, there is no double taxation.

Disadvantages of a Limited Liability Company

- Setting up and maintaining one is more difficult and expensive.
- Tax accounting can be complicated.
- Some of the regulations governing LLCs vary by state.
- Because LLCs are a relatively new type of business entity, there is not as much legal precedent available for owners to anticipate how legal disputes might affect their businesses.
- Some states levy a franchise tax on LLCs—which is essentially a fee the LLC pays the state for the benefit of limited liability.

Chapter Summary

1. The single most important thing the founders of an entrepreneurial venture can do is establish a strong ethical culture in their firms. Three important ways to do this are: lead by example, establish a code of conduct, and implement an ethics training program.
2. A code of conduct and ethics training programs are two techniques entrepreneurs use to promote high standards of business ethics in their ventures or firms. A code of conduct describes the general value system, moral principles, and specific ethical rules that govern a firm. An ethics training program provides employees with instructions for how to deal with ethical dilemmas when they occur.

3. The criteria important for selecting an attorney for a new firm are shown in Table 7.2. Critical issues include selecting an attorney familiar with the start-up process, selecting an attorney who can assist you in raising money, and making certain that the attorney has a track record of completing work on time.

4. Behaving in a professional manner and honoring all employment agreements are the two most important issues to consider when leaving an employer to launch an entrepreneurial venture.

5. A nondisclosure agreement is a promise made by an employee or another party (such as a supplier) not to disclose a company's trade secrets. A noncompete agreement prevents an individual from competing against a former employer for a specific period of time.

6. It is important to ensure that a venture's founders agree on their relative interests in the venture and their commitment to its future. A founders' (or shareholders') agreement is a written document dealing with issues such as the split of equity between or among the founders of the firm, how individual founders will be compensated for the cash or the "sweat equity" they put into the firm, and how long the founders will have to stay with the firm for their shares to fully vest.

7. Suggestions for how new firms can avoid litigation include meeting all contractual obligations, avoiding undercapitalization, getting everything in writing, and promoting business ethics in the firm.

8. The major differences among sole proprietorships, partnerships, corporations, and limited liability companies are shown in Table 7.5. These forms of business organization differ in terms of the number of owners allowed, cost of setting up and maintaining, personal liability of owners, continuity of the business, methods of taxation, degree of management control, ease of raising capital, and ease of liquidating investments.

9. Fast-growth firms tend to organize as corporations or limited liability companies for two main reasons: to shield the owners from personal liability for the behavior of the firm and to make it easier to raise capital.

10. A disadvantage of C corporations is that they are subject to double taxation. A C corporation is taxed on its net income, and when the same income is distributed to shareholders in the form of dividends, it is taxed again on the personal income tax returns of the shareholders.

Key Terms

articles of incorporation, 208
buyback clause, 198
C corporation, 207
closely held corporation, 208
code of conduct, 193
common stock, 208
corporate opportunity doctrine, 197
corporation, 207
double taxation, 208
ethical dilemma, 195
ethics training programs, 195

founders' agreement, 198
general partnership, 205
illiquid, 208
limited liability company (LLC), 210
limited partnership, 207
limited partnership agreement, 207
liquid market, 208
liquidity, 205
mediation, 203
noncompete agreement, 198

nondisclosure agreement, 198
partnership agreement, 205
piercing the corporate veil, 208
preferred stock, 208
private corporation, 208
public corporations, 208
shareholders, 208
sole proprietorship, 203
stock options, 208
subchapter S corporation, 209

Review Questions

1. When should your friend, who is considering launching a consulting firm to provide tax advice to small businesses, think about the ethical climate she wants to establish in her venture?

2. In general, do entrepreneurs tend to overestimate or underestimate their knowledge of the laws that pertain to starting a new firm? What does the answer to this question suggest that entrepreneurs do before they start a firm?

3. Why is it important for an entrepreneur to build a strong ethical culture for the firm? What are some of the specific steps that an entrepreneurial venture can take to build a strong ethical culture?

4. Some argue that entrepreneurs who "lead by example" tend to establish a strong ethical culture in their firm. What are some outcomes achieved in firms with strong ethical cultures that support this argument?

5. Describe what is meant by the terms *code of conduct* and *ethics training programs*. What is their purpose?

6. What are some of the more important criteria to consider when selecting an attorney for a new firm?

7. Describe several ways an entrepreneur can save on legal fees without compromising the value of a relationship with an attorney.

8. If an entrepreneur is quitting a traditional job to start a new firm, what are the two things that should be kept in mind in order to leave the employer ethically?

9. Describe the purpose of a nondisclosure agreement and the purpose of a noncompete agreement.

10. Describe what a founders' agreement is and why it's important for a team of entrepreneurs to have one in place when launching a venture.

11. Describe several ways entrepreneurial ventures can avoid legal disputes.

12. The following statement appears in this chapter: "Choosing a legal entity (for an entrepreneurial venture) is not a one-time event." Why isn't choosing a legal entity a one-time event? What might trigger a firm's decision to change how it is legally organized?

13. What are the advantages and disadvantages of organizing a new firm as a sole proprietorship? Is a sole proprietorship an appropriate form of ownership for an aggressive entrepreneurial firm? Why or why not?

14. Describe the differences between a general partnership and a limited partnership. Is a general partnership an appropriate form of ownership for two people pooling their resources to start a high-growth entrepreneurial firm?

15. What are the major advantages and disadvantages of a C corporation? How is a C corporation subject to double taxation?

16. What is the difference between preferred stock and common stock? Who gets paid first in the event of liquidation—the preferred stockholders or the common stockholders?

17. What is meant by the term *piercing the corporate veil*? What are the implications for the owners of a corporation if the corporate veil is pierced?

18. What are the differences between a public corporation, a closely held corporation, and a private corporation? Which type of corporation enjoys the highest level of liquidity for its stock?

19. What are stock options? Why would a corporation offer stock options to its employees?

20. What are the advantages and disadvantages of a limited liability company? Is a limited liability company an appropriate form of ownership for an aggressive entrepreneurial firm?

Application Questions

1. Assume you have been asked by the founders of NuRide, the focus of the "You Be the VC 1" feature at the end of the chapter, to help the company write a code of conduct. Given your understanding of NuRide's business model and its priorities, put together a table of contents for NuRide's code of conduct.

2. A good friend of yours, Tim Jensen, is starting a new firm. He asked you if you know any good attorneys, and you tell him that you used an attorney to draw up a will a couple of years ago and had good luck. Tim asked you for the attorney's name and phone number. Is Tim using a good strategy to select an attorney to help launch a new venture? If not, what would be a better strategy for Tim to use to select an attorney?

3. Jason, Martin, and Marie are working on an idea for a new company, which they hope to launch within 3 months. Marie is pressuring Jason and Martin to accompany her to see an attorney to draw up a founders' agreement for their firm. Both Jason and Martin think

Marie is jumping the gun and don't see the need to spend money for a founders' agreement until the firm has been operating for a few weeks. If you were asked to weigh in on this disagreement, would you side with Marie or Jason and Martin? Explain your decision.

4. Stacey Miller currently works for Green Mountain Coffee in Waterbury, Vermont. She has given Green Mountain Coffee her 30-day notice and plans to open a coffee restaurant of her own in a neighboring community after leaving her current job. She's excited about the next 30 days because she won't be starting any new projects at work, so she figures she can spend most of her time working on her new business idea, recruiting Green Mountain Coffee employees to work for her after she leaves, and thinking about how she can use Green Mountain Coffee's strategies in her new business. Does Stacey have a good, ethical strategy for leaving her current job? If not, what should Stacey be doing differently?

5. Kelly Peterson owns an electronics firm in Pittsburgh. He has told you that he has been suffering some cash flow problems, but has avoided having to borrow money by letting some of his bills run late and by cutting corners on meeting some of his contractual obligations. When you raised your eyebrows as he told you this, he said, "Don't worry; I'm really not nervous about it. I have some big orders coming in, and am confident I can catch up on my bills and renegotiate my contracts then." Do you think Kelly has a sound strategy? What could he be doing differently? What are the downsides to what Kelly is currently doing?

6. Nancy Wills is purchasing a business named Niagara Laser Optics near Buffalo, New York. The business has had several brushes with the law during the past several years, dealing with claims of false advertising and wrongful termination of employees. As a result, Nancy is very concerned about the ethical culture of the firm. What specific techniques could Nancy use to increase the emphasis placed on business ethics when she takes control of the firm?

7. Tom Mills just launched an e-commerce company to sell accessories for cell phones. When you asked him about his form of business ownership, he said that he was organized as a sole proprietor. When you asked why, he said that his father owned a business as a sole proprietor for 35 years, and never had any problems. Do you think Tom is making a wise choice? Why or why not?

8. Ted Peterson has saved money his entire life. He currently has $260,000 in savings, a $225,000 house that is free of debt, and over $20,000 in college savings funds for each of three kids. Taking advantage of an early retirement program, he just left a staff job with Ford Motor and plans to open a restaurant. He can't quite decide on the form of legal entity for his restaurant. He wants to shield his personal assets from the liabilities of the restaurant and also plans to bring on some investors to open a second restaurant if the first succeeds. Advise Ted on the form of business organization that might make the most sense for his new firm.

9. For a entrepreneurial start-up, what situation would favor organizing as a subchapter S corporation rather than a limited liability company? What situation would favor a limited liability company over a subchapter S corporation?

10. Karen and Jessica are general partners in a chain of women's clothing stores. The stores are called K&J Women's Shop and are located in Des Moines, Iowa. Recently, Karen was at a school event for her daughter and was explaining her business to one of her daughter's teachers. The teacher told Karen, "I don't want to seem nosey, but is your business really organized as a general partnership?" Karen said, "Yes, why would you ask?" The teacher replied, "My father and Uncle Ken own a chain of clothing stores in Minnesota and almost lost everything, including their cars and houses, when a customer slipped on a patch of ice near the entryway to one of the stores several winters ago and sued my dad and uncle. They settled the lawsuit out of court and immediately incorporated the business to shield their personal assets from the liabilities of their business." Karen thought, "Maybe I should see an attorney to see if Jessica and I should incorporate our business." Do you think Karen and Jessica should see an attorney? If so, why?

11. Brian just formed a C corporation. The shareholders of the corporation will be he and his wife Carrie and his father Bob, who put $35,000 of cash into the business. Brian explained to his wife and dad that he organized the business as a C corporation because

of the ease of transfer of ownership of the stock. He said that if any of the three of them wanted his or her money out of the corporation, that person could simply find a buyer for the stock, just like the shareholders of Microsoft and other large public corporations do, and transfer the ownership. Does Brian have realistic expectations regarding the ease of getting out of his investment if he wants to? Why or why not?

12. You have been approached by a close family friend, who is putting together a limited liability company to purchase a condominium complex near Cocoa Beach in Florida. He is asking you along with a number of family members and friends to each invest $10,000 in his company. The condominium complex is for sale for 5 million dollars. Your friend hopes to convince 50 people to invest $10,000 apiece, which will raise $500,000, and borrow the remaining $4.5 million to close the deal. You told your friend, "I don't mind investing the $10,000, but I'm really nervous about being on the hook for a $4.5 million loan if the deal goes bad. Your friend insists that all you will have at risk is your $10,000 and won't be liable for anything else, no matter what happens. Is your friend right or wrong? Explain your answer.

13. Determine specifically what the requirements are for starting a C corporation in your state. Indicate what forms need to be filed, where they can be obtained, how the filing process works, and what fees are involved.

14. Laura just took a job with Cisco Systems in San Jose, California. One of things that attracted her to Cisco was the stock option plan that Cisco offers its employees. Explain what is meant by a stock option plan and why a company such as Cisco Systems would offer stock options to its employees.

15. The "You Be VC 2" feature in this chapter focuses on LatinoHire (a Web-based platform) and *Buena Chamba* (a weekly periodical) that connect Spanish-speaking Latino workers with employers. What do you think is the most appropriate form of business ownership for both LatinoHire and *Buena Chamba*? Should they be one entity or separate entities? Why?

you be the **VC 7.1**

NuRide
www.nuride.com

Business Idea: Reduce traffic congestion, air pollution caused by cars, and wear and tear on the nation's highways by paying people to carpool.

Pitch: Many of us live in areas where traffic congestion is a way of life. Not only is congestion stressful but it causes air pollution and takes a toll on our nation's highways, which in turn creates a need for additional tax revenues to complete needed repairs.

Now, one company is doing something about these problems. NuRide, located in Washington D.C., is pioneering the concept of a ride-sharing program. The service is currently being tested in Washington D.C., parts of New York, and Houston, Texas. For commuters in these areas, here's how the service works. A commuter logs on to the NuRide Web site to sign up for the service. You must have a business or a university e-mail address to participate, to give your fellow riders some level of confidence that you are who you say you are. You then specify where you want to go, and where you are coming from, just like you do when you buy airline tickets online. NuRide then matches riders up. Riders usually

meet at a location close to all of their points of departure and then share rides to and from work. The best part is that along with saving money on gas and wear and tear on your car, NuRide pays you to participate. For each one-way trip, you get 100 NuRide points, which is equivalent to $1.00. So if you share rides to and from work for a week, totaling 10 rides, you would get 1,000 points, or the equivalent of $10. The NuRide points can be redeemed for gift cards at participating merchants, which include Old Navy, Home Depot, XM Satellite Radio, Shell Oil, and Starbucks. A rider can redeem up to $500 worth of NuRide points per year.

To make its service appealing, NuRide has taken a number of steps to ensure the safety and compatibility of its drivers. For example, riders can request to ride with men or women, smokers or nonsmokers, and so on. The company also asks riders to rate the drivers that they ride with. Each driver then receives a certain number of stars, which are posted on NuRide's Web site, similar to the way sellers are rated on eBay.

NuRide makes money by contracting with state and local governments to deploy its service in their area. The potential upside for governmental agencies is tremendous. The U.S. Department of Transportation estimates that a 10 percent increase in ride sharing has the potential to decrease congestion by 50 percent in a given area.

Q&A: Based on the material covered in this chapter, what questions would you ask the firm's founders before making your funding decision? What answers would satisfy you?

Decision: If you had to make your decision on just the information provided in the pitch and on the company's Web site, would you fund this firm? Why or why not?

LatinoHire.com and *Buena Chamba*
http://latinohire.com

Business Idea: Create a Web-based platform (LatinoHire.com) and a weekly periodical (*Buena Chamba*) that make it easy and affordable for businesses to hire Spanish-speaking Latino workers.

Pitch: Last year, more than 1 million Latino workers were hired in the United States, with most of the positions filled through informal networks. While helpful, informal networks only reach so far. It is difficult for workers and employers to find the optimal match if broader-based mechanisms aren't available to assist in the job placement process.

This is where LatinoHire.com and *Buena Chamba* come in. The company's mission is to create a two-tier platform that makes it easy and affordable for businesses to hire Spanish-speaking Latino workers. The concept is quick and easy. The first tier is the LatinoHire.com Web site. Job postings cost $49 and can be easily posted in an intuitive Web-based environment. If the posting is in English, it is automatically translated into Spanish. This feature is meant to help employers who have minimal or no Spanish-speaking capabilities.

The second tier is the weekly *Buena Chamba* publication. *Buena Chamba* means "great work" or "great job" in

Spanish. A job that is posted on the LatinoHire Web site is automatically included in the *Buena Chamba* publication at no extra charge. The publication, which will be advertiser-supported, will be widely distributed in Spanish-speaking neighborhoods. Along with job listings, the periodical will include articles and other material. As the service grows, postings will expand to include categories such as real estate, furniture, and cars.

LatinoHire.com and *Buena Chamba* are currently active in New York City. The parent company, Emerging Demographics, hopes to expand LatinoHire.com and *Buena Chamba* into nationwide services by 2007. The size of the potential market is attractive, in that Latinos are the fastest-growing group of minority workers in the United States.

Q&A: Based on the material covered in this chapter, what questions would you ask the firm's founders before making your funding decision? What answers would satisfy you?

Decision: If you had to make your decision on just the information provided in the pitch and on the company's Web site, would you fund this firm? Why or why not?

CASE 7.1

Preparing a Proper Legal Foundation: A Start-up Fable

Bruce R. Barringer,
University of Central Florida
R. Duane Ireland,
Texas A&M University

Introduction

Jack Peterson and Sarah Jones are planning to start a business. Their plan is to locate and operate 10 kiosks in malls and other high-traffic areas to sell accessories for Apple

iPods. To complement their accessory sales, the two have created a series of short videos that help users learn how to make better use of their iPods. The videos will be sold or used as value-added promotions and will be delivered via streaming video on Jack and Sarah's Web site. Customers will be provided access codes to retrieve the videos from the Web site, which will also sell additional iPod accessories.

The tentative name for the business is iUser Accessories. Jack and Sarah like to use the word *tentative* because they aren't completely sold on the name. The Internet domain name, www.iuseraccessories.com was available, so they registered it on GoDaddy.com. Part of their start-up funding will be used to hire a trademark attorney to do a formal trademark search before they use the name or do any advertising.

Jack and Sarah met in an introduction to entrepreneurship course at their local university. They hit it off while working on the initial business plan for iUser Accessories, which they completed as an assignment for the class. Their senior year, they refined the plan by working on it during a business planning class. They took first place in a university-wide business plan competition just before graduation. The win netted them $5,000 in cash and $5,000 in "in-kind" services for the business. Their plan was to use the money to establish a relationship with an accountant affiliated with the university.

Feasibility Analysis and Business Plan

As part of their business plan, Jack and Sarah completed a product feasibility analysis for iUser Accessories. They first developed a concept statement and distributed it to a total of 16 people, including professors, electronic store owners, iPod users, and the parents of young iPod users. The responses were both positive and instructive. The idea to distribute the videos dealing with how to better use your iPod, via streaming video over the Internet, and providing customers access codes to retrieve the videos, came directly from one of the concept statement participants. Jack and Sarah's original idea was to distribute this material in a more conventional manner. The person who came up with the idea wrote on the bottom of the concept statement, "Not only will this approach save you money (by not having to distribute actual videos) but it will drive traffic to your Web site and provide you with additional e-commerce opportunities."

Following the concept statement, Jack and Sarah surveyed 410 people in their target market, which is 15–35-year-olds. They did this by approaching people wherever they could and politely asking them to complete the survey. They persuaded one of their marketing professors to help them with the survey's design, to make sure it generalized to a larger population. They learned that 52 percent of the people in their target market own an iPod or plan to get one soon. The survey also listed a total of 26 iPod accessories, which are available through vendors that Jack and Sarah have access to. The results affirmed Jack and Sarah's notion that the vast majority of people in their target market don't realize the number of iPod accessories that exist, let alone know where to get them. They also were pleased with the high degree of interest expressed by the survey participants in learning more about many of the accessories.

Start-up Capital

As part of their business plan, Jack and Sarah completed 1- and 3-year pro forma financial statements, which

demonstrate the potential viability of their business. They have commitments for $66,000 of funding from friends and family. According to their projections, they should be cash-flow positive within 4 months and will not need any additional infusions of cash, unless they expand the business beyond the scope of their original business plan. The projections include salaries of $32,000 per year for both Jack and Sarah, who will both work 40+ hours a week manning the kiosks and running the business.

Jack and Sarah are fortunate in that they are able to each contribute $3,000 to the business personally and were able to get commitments of $30,000 each from their respective groups of friends and family. A year or so ago, they had sat in a class offered by their local Small Business Development Center (SBDC) about how to start a business and remembered an attorney saying that's it all right to talk to people about funding prior to talking to an attorney but don't actually accept any money until you have your legal ducks in order. As a result, other than their own money, Jack and Sarah didn't actually have the $66,000 yet. They can accumulate it within 30 days once they are confident that the business is a go.

Preparing for the Meeting with the Attorney

Jack and Sarah plan to launch their business on September 15, just 2 months prior to the start of the busy Christmas season. They spent some time quizzing around the business school and the technology incubator attached to their university to identify the name of a good small-business attorney. They identified an attorney and made the appointment. The appointment was scheduled for 2:15 P.M. on July 16 at the attorney's office.

Another take-away that Jack and Sarah gleaned from the SBDC class was to plan carefully the time you spend with an attorney, to make best use of your time and minimize expenses. As a result, prior to the meeting, Jack and Sarah planned to spend several evenings at a local Borders bookstore, looking at books that deal with forms of business ownership and other legal issues and making a concise list of issues to discuss with the attorney. They had also gone over this material in preparing their business plan. In the meeting with the attorney, they want to be as well informed as possible and actually lead the discussion and make recommendations. Sarah's dad is a real estate agent and had dealt with many attorneys during his career. One thing he told her, in helping her prepare for this meeting, is that attorneys are helpful and necessary but shouldn't make your decisions for you. Sarah shared this insight with Jack, and they were both determined to follow that advice in their upcoming meeting.

Jack and Sarah's Recommendations

To put their list on paper and get started, Jack created the following document.

Jack Peterson and Sarah Jones
Founders, iUser Accessories
List of Legal Issues to Discuss with Attorney

Issue	Jack and Sarah's Recommendation

Jack and Sarah spent the next several evenings completing this list and talking about their business. When they made the call to set up the meeting with the attorney, the attorney told them that she wasn't an intellectual property lawyer, and if it looked like the business was a go after their meeting, she could arrange for them to talk to one of her partners who specialized in patent and trademark law. As a result, Jack and Sarah knew that this meeting would focus more on forms of business ownership and general legal issues, and they would address their intellectual property questions at another meeting.

The Day Arrives

The day for the meeting arrived, and Jack and Sarah met at the attorney's office at 2:15 P.M. They had e-mailed the attorney

their list of issues along with their recommendations a week prior to the meeting. The attorney greeted them with a firm handshake and opened a file labeled "iUser Accessories, Jack Peterson and Sarah Jones." Seeing their names like that, on an attorney's file, made it seem like their company was already real. The attorney looked at both of them and placed a copy of the list they had e-mailed in front of her. The list already had a number of handwritten notes on it. The attorney smiled and said to Jack and Sarah, "Let's get started."

Discussion Questions

1. Complete Jack and Sarah's list for them, including the issues you think they will place on the list along with their recommendations. Which of the issues do you think will stimulate the most discussion with the attorney, and which issues do you think will stimulate the least?
2. Make a list of the things you think Jack and Sarah did right in preparing for their meeting with the attorney.
3. Comment on the product feasibility analysis that Jack and Sarah completed. Do you think the way Jack and Sarah approached this task was appropriate and sufficient?
4. What advantages do Jack and Sarah have starting iUser Accessories together, rather than one of them starting it as a sole entrepreneur? What challenges do you think Jack and Sarah will have keeping their partnership together?

Application Questions

1. Suggest an alternative to iUser Accessories for the name of Jack and Sarah's firm. Check to see if the ".com" version of the Internet domain name is available. If it isn't, select another name and continue selecting names until you can match a name with an available domain name.
2. Do you think it is too early for Jack and Sarah to start laying an ethical foundation for their firm? What steps can they take now to lay a solid ethical foundation for their firm?

 **CASE 7.2** *What's in a Business Name?: A Lot of Trouble If You Aren't Careful*

Bruce R. Barringer,
University of Central Florida
R. Duane Ireland,
Texas A&M University

Introduction

While at first glance, naming a business may seem like a minor issue, it is an extremely important one. A company's

name is one of the first things people associate with a business, and it is a word or phrase that will be said thousands or hundreds of thousands of times during the life of a firm. A company's name is also the most critical aspect of its branding strategy. A company brand is the unique set of attributes that allow consumers to separate it from its competitors. As a result, it is important that a business choose its name carefully so that it will facilitate rather than hinder how the business wants to differentiate itself in the marketplace.

If an entrepreneur isn't careful, the process of naming a business can also result in a peck of trouble. There are a number of legal issues involved in naming a business, which should be taken seriously. If a business selects a name and later finds out that it's already been legally taken, the business may have to (1) amend its articles of incorporation, (2) change its Internet domain name, (3) obtain new listings in telephone and other directories, (4) purchase new stationery and business cards, (5) redo signage and advertising, and (6) incur the expense and potential embarrassment of introducing a new name to its customers. These are complications that no entrepreneur wants to endure. The following case describes the strategies for naming a business along with the legal issues involved.

Strategies for Naming a Business

The primary consideration in naming a company is that the name should complement the type of business the company plans to be. It is helpful to divide companies into four categories to discuss this issue.

Consumer-driven companies

If a company plans to focus on a particular type of customer, its name should reflect the attributes of its clientele. For example, a high-end clothing store that specializes in small sizes for women is called La Petite Femme. Similarly, the company described in Case 2.1, "Type 1 Tools," helps children with Type 1 diabetes cope with their disease. These companies have names that were chosen to appeal specifically to their target market or clientele.

Product- or service-driven companies

If a company plans to focus on a particular product or service, its name should reflect the advantages that its product or service brings to the marketplace. Examples include Jiffy Print, ServiceMaster, and 1-800-FLOWERS. These names were chosen to reflect the distinctive attributes of the product or service the company offers, regardless of the clientele.

Industry-driven companies

If a company plans to focus on a broad range of product or services in a particular industry, its name should reflect the category it is participating in. Examples include General Motors, Bed Bath and Beyond, and Home Depot. These companies have names that are intentionally broad and are not limiting in regard to target market or product selection.

Personality- or image-driven companies

Some companies are founded by individuals who put such an indelible stamp on the company that it may be smart to name the company after the founder. Examples include Liz Claiborne, Walt Disney, Charles Schwab, The Trump Organization, and Magic Johnson Enterprises. These companies have names that benefit from a positive association with a popular or distinctive founder. Of course, this strategy can backfire if the founder falls out of favor in the public's eye.

While names come to some business owners easily, for others it's a painstaking process. It was a painstaking process for JetBlue, as described in the book *Blue Streak*, which is a chronology of the early years of JetBlue. According to Barbara Peterson, the book's author, David Neeleman, the founder of JetBlue, and his initial management team agonized over what to name the company and considered literally hundreds of names before settling on JetBlue. JetBlue was launched in 1999. Neeleman felt that a strong brand would surmount the handicap of being a new airline and believed that the company's name was the key to building its brand. A list of some of the alternative names that Neeleman and his management team seriously considered for JetBlue is shown here. Today, it's hard to think of JetBlue as anything other than JetBlue, which illustrates the power of branding.

Names That Were Seriously Considered for Jet Blue

Air Hop	*Egg*
Scout Air	*It*
Competition	*Blue*
Home	*Fair Air*
Air Taxi	*Scout*
Avenues	*Hi! Way*
Civilization Airways	*True Blue*

Legal Issues Involved in Naming a Business

The general rule for business names is that they must be unique. In other words, in most instances, there may not be more than one business per name per state. In addition, a business may not have a name that is confusingly similar to another business. This regulation prevents a software company from naming itself Macrosoft, for example, which Microsoft would undoubtedly claim is confusingly similar to its name.

To determine whether a name is available in a particular state, the entrepreneur must usually contact the secretary of state's office to see if a particular name is available. The inquiry can typically be accomplished over the phone or by mail. If the name is available, the next step is to reserve it in the manner recommended by the secretary of state's office. Many attorneys and incorporation services include this step in the fee-based services they offer to entrepreneurs and their ventures.

Once a name that is available has been chosen, it should be trademarked. The process for obtaining a trademark is straightforward and relatively inexpensive, given the protection it provides. A full explanation of how to obtain a trademark is provided in Chapter 12 of this book.

The entire process of naming a business is often very frustrating for entrepreneurs, because it is becoming increasingly difficult to find a name that isn't already taken. For example, if an entrepreneur was planning to open a new quick-printing service, almost every possible permutation of the word *printing* with words like *quick*, *swift*, *fast*, *rapid*, *speedy*, *jiffy*, *express*, *instant*, and so forth are taken. In addition, sometimes names that work in one culture don't work in another, which is something that should be taken into consideration. The classic example of this is the Chevy NOVA. After much advertising and fanfare, the car received a very cool reception in Mexico. It turned out that the phrase *No Va* in Spanish means "Doesn't Go." Not surprisingly, the NOVA didn't sell well in Mexico.

As a result of these complications, and for other reasons, entrepreneurs use a variety of other strategies when naming their business. Some names are simply made up, because the firm wants a name that is catchy or distinctive, or because it needs to make up a name to get an Internet domain name that isn't already taken (more about this later). Examples of names that were made up include Exxon, Cingular, Verizon, eBay, Google, and Xerox. Some of these names are made up with the help of marketing research firms that use sophisticated methodologies such as an evaluation of the "linguistic properties" (will a consumer read the name properly?), the "phonetic transparency," (is it spelled as it sounds?), and the "multilingual functionality" (is it as intelligible in Japanese as in English?) of a particular name. All of these issues are potentially important. Several years ago Anderson Consulting changed its name to Accenture. The pronunciation of "Accenture" isn't obvious, which has been a problem for the firm ever since.

Internet Domain Names

A final complicating factor in selecting a name for a company is registering an Internet domain name. A domain name is a company's Internet address (e.g., www.intel.com). Most companies want their domain name to be the same as their company's name. It is easy to register a domain name through an online registration services such as Go Daddy.com (www.godaddy.com). The standard fee for registering and maintaining a domain name is about $9 per year.

Because no two domain names can be exactly the same, frustrations often arise when a company tries to register its domain name and the name is already taken. There are two reasons that a name may already be taken. First, a company may find that another company with the same name has already registered it. For example, if an entrepreneur started a company called Delta Semiconductor, it would find that the domain name www.delta.com is already taken by Delta Airlines. This scenario plays itself out every day and represents a challenge for new firms that have chosen fairly ordinary names. The firm can either select another domain name (such as www.deltasemiconductor.com) or try to acquire the name from its present owner. However, it is unlikely that Delta Airlines would give up www.delta.com for any price. The second reason that a domain name may already be taken is that it might be in the hands of someone who has registered the name with the intention of using it at a later date or of someone who simply collects domain names in hopes that someone will want to buy the name at a higher price. In addition, all of the 1,000 most common English words have been registered, along with the U.S. Census Bureau's list of the 1,219 most common male names, the 2,814 most common female names, and the 10,000 most common surnames.

Still, a little imagination goes a long was in selecting a company name and an Internet domain name. For example, we (your book's authors) made up the name iUser Accessories for the business described in Case 7.1. The Internet domain name www.iuseraccessories.com was available, which we registered on Go Daddy.com for $8.95 per year. What might we do with this Internet domain name? We aren't certain. But, another party deciding to launch an entrepreneurial venture with this name will discover that the hoped-for name is already registered.

Discussion Questions

1. What do you see as the biggest obstacle in naming a business? Is it legal or practical?
2. Look at the secretary of state's Web site for the state where your college or university is located. Determine the specific regulations for naming a business in your state.
3. Some businesses change their names on purpose—as in the case of Anderson Consulting changing its name to Accenture. Make a list of potentially sound reasons that might motivate a company to voluntarily change its name.
4. Provide examples of two businesses that you think have particularly good (or effective) names and two businesses that you think have poor (or ineffective names). What are the characteristics of the names that make them either good or poor in your mind?

Application Questions

1. If you decided to start a business, how would you go about selecting its name?

2. Look at the alternative names for JetBlue. Which alternative do you like the best? Check to see if the Internet domain name for this name is available. Suggest three additional potential names for an airline. Pick one of the names and make the argument that it is a reasonable name for an airline.

Sources: B. Peterson, *Blue Streak: Inside JetBlue, the Upstart That Rocked An Industry* (New York: Portfolio Trade, 2006); L. Gomes, "All The Good Ones Have Been Taken in Domain Names Too," *The Wall Street Journal*, July 19, 2006; K. B. Nathan and A. H. Magos, *Incorporate*! (New York: McGraw-Hill, 2003).

Endnotes

1. C. A. Brown, C. H.. Colbourne, and W. E. McMullen, "Legal Issues in New Venture Development," *Journal of Business Venturing* 3, no. 4 (1988): 273–86.
2. R. T. Peterson, "Small Retailers and Service Company Accuracy in Evaluating the Legality of Specified Practices," *Journal of Small Business Management* 39, no. 4 (2001): 312–19.
3. C. Caggiano, "A Strategic Misalliance," *Inc.*, October 2002.
4. National Business Ethics Survey, *How Employees View Ethics in Their Organizations 1994–2005* (Washington, DC: Ethics Resource Center, 2005).
5. National Business Ethics Survey, *How Employees View Ethics in Their Organizations 1994–2005*.
6. Wikipedia, www.wikipedia.org, "Ethics Code" (accessed July 29, 2006).
7. Character Training International homepage, www.character-ethics.org (accessed July 27, 2006).
8. T. Monosoff, *The Mom Inventors Handbook* (New York: McGraw-Hill, 2005).
9. C. E. Bagley, *Legal Aspects of Entrepreneurship: A Conceptual Framework* (Cambridge, MA: Harvard Business School Publishing, 2002).
10. *Black's Law Dictionary*, 6th ed. (St. Paul, MN: West, 2002), 340.
11. K. V. W. Stone, "Thinking and Doing—The Regulation of Workers' Human Capital in the United States," *Socio-Economic Review* 4, no. 1 (2006): 121–38; R. P. Mandel, "Legal and Tax Issues," in *The Portable MBA in Entrepreneurship*, ed. William D. Bygrave (New York: John Wiley & Sons, 1997), 285–326.
12. *Black's Law Dictionary*, 2002.
13. K. W. Clarkson, R. L. Miller, G. A. Jentz, and F. B. Cross, *West's Business Law* (New York: West Educational Publishing, 1998).
14. J. A. Fraser, "Cash Flow: When a Cash Crisis Strikes," *Inc.*, February 1, 1996, 104.
15. A. J. Sherman, *Fast-Track Business Growth* (Washington, DC: Kiplinger Washington Editors, 2001).
16. M. Clark, *The Bear Necessities of Business* (New York: Wiley, 2006), 112.
17. C. E. Bagley, *Legal Aspects of Entrepreneurship: A Conceptual Framework* (Cambridge, MA: Harvard Business School Publishing, 2002), 17.
18. A. Gerlin, "A Matter of Degree: How a Jury Decided That a Coffee Spill is Worth $2.7 Million, *Wall Street Journal*, September 1, 1994.
19. H. R. Cheeseman, *The Legal Environment of Business and Online Commerce* 5th ed. (Upper Saddle River, NJ: Pearson, 2007).
20. M. C. Ehrhardt and E. F. Brigham, *Corporate Finance* (Cincinnati: South-Western, 2003).
21. "General Partnership," homepage of TraderStatus.Com, www.traderstatus.com (accessed on August 5, 2006); A. J. Sherman, *The Complete Guide to Running and Growing Your Business* (New York: Random House, 1997).
22. *Black's Law Dictionary*.
23. Sherman, *The Complete Guide to Running and Growing Your Business*.
24. R. A. Brealty and S. C. Myers, *Financing and Risk Management* (New York: McGraw-Hill, 2003).
25. *Black's Law Dictionary*.
26. Clarkson et al., *West's Business Law*.
27. Investorwords.com, www.investorwords.com (accessed July 26, 2006).
28. Investorwords.com, www.investorwords.com (accessed July 26, 2006).
29. M. A. Williams and R. P. Rao, "CEO Stock Options and Equity Risk Incentives," *Journal of Business Finance and Accounting* 33 (2006), 26–33.
30. P. K. Zingheim and J. R. Schuster, *Pay People Right!* (San Francisco: Jossey-Bass, 2000).

31. D. O'Donnell, D. McGuire, and C. Cross, "Critically Challenging Some Assumptions in HRD," *International Journal of Training and Development* 19, no. 1 (2006): 4–16.
32. C. E. Bagley and C. E. Dauchy, *The Entrepreneur's Guide to Business Law* (New York: West Educational Publishing, 1998).
33. Ehrhardt and Brigham, *Corporate Finance*.
34. Sherman, *The Complete Guide to Running and Growing Your Business*.

Getting Personal

with

DEL SEGURA

What I do when I'm not working

Compete in NHRA Drag Racing

Best advice I've received

Decide what you want to do and figure out a way to get someone to pay you to do it

My biggest surprise as an entrepreneur

The speed of our success in the world market

Innovention Toys LLC:

Keeping a Sharp Eye on the Financials from the Start

Del Segura's entrepreneurial journey started in a classroom at Tulane University in New Orleans. Segura, who returned to graduate school after working in the automotive industry for several years, was enrolled in a product development class taught by Dr. Michael Larson. As part of the requirements for the class, Dr. Larson divided the class into two-person teams and asked each team to come up with an idea for a new toy. Once an idea was selected, the team would investigate and discuss the necessary steps to get the idea patented, how a prototype could be made, how the idea could be introduced to the market-place, and so on. Segura was partnered with Luke Hooper, and their idea was for an innovative new type of board game—called Khet (originally Deflexion). As the semester progressed, Segura and Hooper, along with Dr. Larson, started to wonder if the game might have commercial potential beyond the scope of class.[1] Khet is a chess-like board game that utilizes built-in lasers and movable Egyptian-themed game pieces, some of which are equipped with mirrors. Surrounding the board is a raised frame into which are built two low-power lasers, one for each player. The basic idea is to arrange your pieces so that the laser's beam bounces off their mirrored sides in a path that lights your opponent's pharaoh, and prevents your opponent from lighting up your pharaoh. The laser beams are not powerful enough to have any effect on humans.

DEL SEGURA

Cofounder, Innovention Toys LLC
Masters Degree in Mechanical Engineering
College of Engineering
Tulane University, 2004

LUKE HOOPER

Cofounder, Innovention Toys LLC
Masters Degree in Mechanical Engineering
College of Engineering
Tulane University, 2005

DR. MICHAEL LARSON

Cofounder, Innovention Toys LLC
Associate Professor
University of Colorado–Colorado Springs

After the class ended, in the fall of 2004, Segura, Hooper, and Dr. Larson built a rough prototype of the game, using a rapid-prototyping facility at Tulane, and tested it among friends and other students. After gaining confidence in the game, the three located a contract manufacturer in China, through a mutual acquaintance, who built a prototype of what the game would look like if it was offered for sale. The first attempt to build a more suitable prototype turned out to be flawed and wasn't useable, which was a big disappointment. After some scrambling, the same manufacturer agreed to make a higher-quality prototype at a discounted price, and a useable prototype was made. Commenting on his decision to collaborate with two former students to actually build a high-quality prototype of a product developed in one of his classes, Larson said "After teaching product design for 12 years, I decided to finally put an idea into action."[2]

My biggest worry as an entrepreneur	Hardest part of getting funding	First entrepreneurial experience
All the math: Too few sales = too much inventory = too much debt	*Obtaining credit with little company history*	*Picking and selling pecans at age seven*

After studying this chapter you should be ready to:

LEARNING
Objectives

1. Explain the two functions of the financial management of a firm.

2. Identify the four main financial objectives of entrepreneurial ventures.

3. Explain the difference between historical and pro forma financial statements.

4. Explain the purpose of an income statement.

5. Explain the purpose of a balance sheet.

6. Explain the purpose of a statement of cash flows.

7. Discuss how financial ratios are used to analyze and interpret a firm's financial statements.

8. Discuss the role of forecasts in projecting a firm's future income and expenses.

9. Explain what a completely new firm bases its forecasts on.

10. Explain what is meant by the term *percent of sales method*.

To determine if Khet had commercial appeal, in February 2005, Segura, Hooper, and Dr. Larson took the prototype of the game to the American International Toy Fair in New York City. The reception was very positive. The three collected a number of business cards of toy retailers, wholesalers, and distributors who expressed interest in selling the game. The founders received a big boost when several favorable articles were written about Khet following the American International Toy Fair. One article, which appeared in *BusinessWeek*, was particularly complimentary, and ended by saying, "the threesome get my vote"—referring to Segura, Hooper, Dr. Larson, and their chances for success with Khet. Collectively, these articles prompted a number of inquiries from toy stores and distributors wondering how they could carry the game.[3] The photo accompanying this story pictures, from left to right, Luke Hooper, Dr. Michael Larson and Del Segura at the American International Toy Fair in 2006.

The positive buzz generated by the 2005 American International Toy Fair, and the articles mentioned above, led to a $12,580 grant from the National Collegiate Inventors & Innovators Alliance (NCIIA) to partially fund the initial order for 3,500 copies of the games. During this time, even though Khet was taking shape as a company, the three founders had other jobs, primarily because the company hadn't generated any income and its future was still unclear. The first order was placed in August of 2005, and the games were scheduled to be manufactured and shipped promptly, so they would be available well before the 2005 Christmas season. Hurricane Katrina, which took place in late August of 2005, shut down the Port of New Orleans for several weeks, delaying the arrival of the games. The games finally arrived in October 2005. The first 3,500 copies of Khet were taken off the container ship and stored in Segura's garage near Baton Rouge, Louisiana.

The first 3,500 copies of Khet sold in 3 weeks, based on the willingness of the founders to painstakingly follow up on the inquiries generated by the favorable articles written about the game and the business cards collected at the American International Toy Fair. Since that time, sales have accelerated, and Innovention Toys LLC, the name the founders selected for the company, has taken shape as a permanent entity.* Segura and Hooper are now working on Innovention Toys full-time, and Dr. Larson stays plugged in from his new teaching job at the University of Colorado–Colorado Springs. Khet is now being sold at over 300 toy stores nationwide and via the company's Web site. The favorable press surrounding the game has continued, and in March 2006 *Popular Science* named it one of the 10 coolest toys/gadgets of the year. Segura and his partners project sales of 75,000 to 100,000 copies of Khet in 2006, and higher sales beyond.

What's particularly interesting about Innovention Toys, for the purpose of this chapter, is the way the company took shape financially. From the beginning, costs were minimized and the founders kept a keen eye on the financials. The initial commercial quality prototype, the trip to New York City in 2005 to attend the American International Toy Fair, and the initial order for 3,500 copies of Khet were funded from the founders' personal funds and the grant from the NCIIA. In addition, rather than renting warehouse space, the initial copies of the game were stored and shipped from Segura's garage. Similarly, instead of hiring wholesalers or buying expensive advertising, the initial sales were made by following up on inquiries generated from the 2005 American International Toy Fair.

The founders remain committed to managing Innovention Toys in a financially prudent manner. Because the games are made in China, they return a healthy margin when sold at retail. Operating expenses remain low. The founders, who remain the sole owners

---

*The original name of the company was Deflexion, LLC (same as the original name of the game). The new company name, as of June 2006, is Innovention Toys, LLC and the name of the game has changed from Deflexion to Khet.

and only employees of the firm, have divided up the responsibilities for the operations and the financial management of the company, and Dr. Larson manages the finances and keeps the books. He uses Quickbooks to record the day-to-day income and expenses of the firm and to generate financial reports, and the three talk periodically about the financial affairs of the company. Future games, beyond Khet, are now in the works.

In this chapter, we'll look at how new ventures manage their finances and assess their financial strength and viability. For the purposes of completeness, we'll look at how both existing firms and entrepreneurial ventures accomplish these tasks. First, we'll consider general financial management and discuss the financial objectives of a firm and the steps involved in the financial management process. **Financial management** deals with two things: raising money and managing a company's finances in a way that achieves the highest rate of return.[4] We cover the process of raising money in Chapter 10. This chapter focuses on how a company manages its finances in an effort to increase its financial strength and earn the highest rate of return. Next, we'll examine how existing firms track their financial progress through preparing, analyzing, and maintaining past financial statements. Finally, we'll discuss how both existing firms and start-up ventures forecast future income and expenses and how the forecasts are used to prepare pro forma (i.e., projected) financial statements. Pro forma financial statements, which include the pro forma income statement, the pro forma balance sheet, and the pro forma statement of cash flows, are extremely helpful to firms in financial planning.

L E A R N I N G

Objective

1. Explain the two functions of the financial management of a firm.

Introduction to Financial Management

An entrepreneur's ability to pursue an opportunity and turn the opportunity into a viable entrepreneurial firm hinges largely on the availability of money. Regardless of the quality of a product or service, a company can't be viable in the long run unless it is successful financially. Money either comes from external sources (such as investors or lenders) or is internally generated through earnings. It is important for a firm to have a solid grasp of how it is doing financially.

Entrepreneurs and those managing established companies must be aware of how much money they have in the bank and if that amount is sufficient to satisfy their firm's financial obligations. Just because a firm is successful doesn't mean that it doesn't face financial challenges.[5] For example, many of the small firms that sell their products to larger companies such as IBM, General Electric, and Home Depot don't get paid for 30 to 60 days from the time they make a sale. Think about the difficulty this scenario creates. The small firm must buy parts, pay its employees, pay its routine bills, ship its products, and then wait for 1 to 2 months for payment. Unless a firm manages its money carefully, it is easy to run out of cash, even if its products or services are selling like hotcakes.[6] Similarly, as a company grows, its cash demands often increase to service a growing clientele. It is important for a firm to accurately anticipate whether it will be able to fund its growth through earnings or if it will need to look for investment capital or borrowing to raise needed cash.

The financial management of a firm deals with questions such as the following on an ongoing basis:

- How are we doing? Are we making or losing money?
- How much cash do we have on hand?
- Do we have enough cash to meet our short-term obligations?
- How efficiently are we utilizing our assets?
- How do our growth and net profits compare to those of our industry peers?
- Where will the funds we need for capital improvements come from?
- Are there ways we can partner with other firms to share risk and reduce the amount of cash we need?
- Overall, are we in good shape financially?

A properly managed firm stays on top of the issues suggested by these questions through the tools and techniques that we'll discuss in this chapter.

FIGURE 8.1

Primary Financial Objectives of Entrepreneurial Firms

Profitability	Liquidity	Efficiency	Stability
A company's ability to make a profit	A company's ability to meet its short-term obligations	How productively a firm utilizes its assets	The overall health of the financial structure of the firm, particularly as it relates to its debt-to-equity ratio

LEARNING

Objective

2. Identify the four main financial objectives of entrepreneurial ventures.

Financial Objectives of a Firm

Most entrepreneurial firms—whether they have been in business for several years or they are start-ups—have four main financial objectives: profitability, liquidity, efficiency, and stability. Understanding these objectives sets a firm on the right financial course and helps it track the answers to the previously posed questions. Figure 8.1 describes each of these objectives.

Profitability is the ability to earn a profit. Many start-ups are not profitable during their first 1 to 3 years while they are training employees and building their brands, but a firm must become profitable to remain viable and provide a return to its owners.

Liquidity is a company's ability to meet its short-term financial obligations. Even if a firm is profitable, it is often a challenge to keep enough money in the bank to meet its routine obligations in a timely manner. To do so, a firm must keep a close watch on accounts receivable and inventories. A company's **accounts receivable** is money owed to it by its customers. Its **inventory** is its merchandise, raw materials, and products waiting to be sold. If a firm allows the levels of either of these assets to get too high, it may not be able to keep sufficient cash on hand to meet its short-term obligations.[7]

Efficiency is how productively a firm utilizes its assets relative to its revenue and its profits. Southwest Airlines, for example, uses its assets very productively. Its turnaround time, or the time that its airplanes sit on the ground while they are being unloaded and reloaded, is the lowest in the airline industry. As Southwest officials are quick to point out, "Our planes don't make any money sitting on the ground—we have to get them back into the air."[8]

Stability is the strength and vigor of the firm's overall financial posture. For a firm to be stable, it must not only earn a profit and remain liquid but also keep its debt in check. If a firm continues to borrow from its lenders and its **debt-to-equity ratio**, which is calculated by dividing its long-term debt by its shareholders' equity, gets too high, it may have trouble meeting its obligations and securing the level of financing needed to fuel its growth.

Many high-tech entrepreneurial firms use state-of-the-art manufacturing facilities to increase efficiency and reduce costs. Linksys, for example, has been known since its entrepreneurial beginnings for its efficient manufacturing techniques, which is one of the reasons the company has been so successful since its founding in 1988. Linksys makes computer networking products for consumers and small businesses. Linksys' success led to its acquisition by Cisco Systems in 2003.

An increasingly common feature of many new businesses is a reliance on outsourcing certain functions to third parties as a means of freeing up resources to focus on its core competencies and as a way of minimizing the number of employees needed to generate sales. These outcomes have the potential to improve a firm's financial position on all four of the factors just mentioned. One of the most common areas that new firms outsource is human resource management, as illustrated in this chapter's "Partnering for Success" feature.

partnering for *success*

Outsourcing Human Resource Management: An Increasingly Common Feature of the Financial Plans of New Firms

As mentioned in Chapter 6, new ventures typically do not have the resources to perform all the tasks required to make their businesses work, so they rely on partners to perform key roles. An increasingly common role that new ventures pay others to perform is the management of their human resources. Managers of start-ups are very busy and need to focus their energies on the core business issues facing their firms. In addition, outsourcing noncore business activities helps a firm minimize its personnel expenses and the amount of cash and capital it needs. Human resource management issues, such as screening job applicants, training, payroll, benefits administration, and regulatory compliance, are very labor-intensive activities. In the minds of many start-up managers, hiring people to deal with these issues makes no sense when there are professional human resource management firms that are experts at performing these tasks and that can do them at an affordable price.

Start-ups vary in terms of the amount of the human resource functions they outsource to others. Some firms outsource only administrative tasks, such as payroll processing and benefits administration. These firms partner with a payroll accounting firm such as Paychex or Ceridian. Paychex, in particular, focuses on small and medium-size businesses and currently processes the payrolls of more than 543,000 clients. In fact, its average client has just 17 employees. In addition to payroll, Paychex is capable of administrating its clients' benefits program, tax payment services, workers' compensation, and other routine human resource management functions.

Some start-ups outsource a broader range of their human resource management functions and partner with a company such as Automatic Data Processing or Administaff. These companies are called professional employer organizations (PEO) and act like an off-site human resource department for a small firm. Along with doing everything that Paychex does, PEOs can help a start-up with hiring, firing, training, regulatory compliance, and other more in-depth related issues. Outsourcing these tasks can minimize a firm's investment in human resource management personnel and support (such as software products).

Questions for Critical Thinking

1. Do you think human resource management is an appropriate area for outsourcing for a start-up firm? Of the following human resource management functions, which ones would you be comfortable outsourcing if you were the founder/CEO of a new entrepreneurial venture: payroll, benefits administration, regulatory compliance, tax preparation, screening job applicants, training, hiring and firing? What factors influenced your answer to this question?

2. In an effort to improve the financial position of their firms, do you think the majority of entrepreneurs spend an equal amount of time focusing on (1) cost cutting and (2) increasing revenues? If not, which of the two do you think they spend more time on and why?

3. How can a firm increase its efficiency (one of the four financial objectives of a firm) by outsourcing part or all of its human resource management tasks?

4. Assume you intend to launch a venture to sell organic fertilizer that you and your partner have developed. While developing the operations and financial part of your business plan, you and your partner started to discuss outsourcing as a way to control costs. For your proposed venture, what activities would you be willing to outsource and what activities do you believe shouldn't be outsourced, even if it results in a cost savings?

The Process of Financial Management

To assess whether its financial objectives are being met, firms rely heavily on analyses of financial statements, forecasts, and budgets. A **financial statement** is a written report that quantitatively describes a firm's financial health. The income statement, the balance sheet, and the statement of cash flows are the financial statements entrepreneurs use most commonly. **Forecasts** are an estimate of a firm's future income and expenses, based on its past performance, its current circumstances, and its future plans.[9] New ventures typically base their forecasts on an estimate of sales and then on industry averages or the experiences of similar start-ups regarding the cost of goods sold (based on a percentage of sales) and on other expenses. **Budgets** are itemized forecasts of a company's income, expenses, and capital needs and are also an important tool for financial planning and control.[10]

The process of a firm's financial management is shown in Figure 8.2. It begins by tracking the company's past financial performance through the preparation and analysis of financial statements. These statements organize and report the firm's financial transactions. They tell a firm how much money it is making or losing (income statement), the structure of its assets and liabilities (balance sheet), and where its cash is coming from and going (statement of cash flows). The statements also help a firm discern how it stacks up against its competitors and industry norms. Most firms look at 2 to 3 years of past financial statements when preparing forecasts.

The next step is to prepare forecasts for 2 to 3 years in the future. Then forecasts are used to prepare a firm's pro forma financial statements, which, along with its more fine-tuned budgets, constitute its financial plan.

The final step in the process is the ongoing analysis of a firm's financial results. **Financial ratios**, which depict relationships between items on a firm's financial statements, are used to discern whether a firm is meeting its financial objectives and how it stacks up against its industry peers. These ratios are also used to assess trends. Obviously, a completely new venture would start at step 2 in Figure 8.2. It is important that a new

FIGURE 8.2

The Process of Financial Management

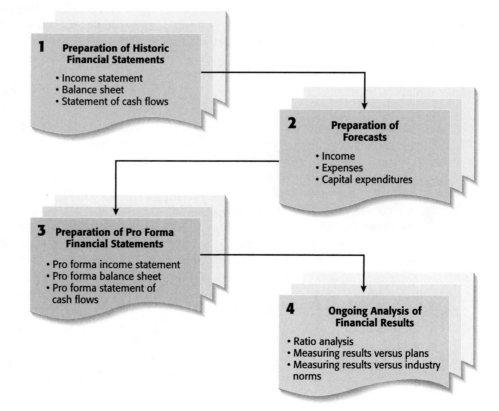

1 **Preparation of Historic Financial Statements**
- Income statement
- Balance sheet
- Statement of cash flows

2 **Preparation of Forecasts**
- Income
- Expenses
- Capital expenditures

3 **Preparation of Pro Forma Financial Statements**
- Pro forma income statement
- Pro forma balance sheet
- Pro forma statement of cash flows

4 **Ongoing Analysis of Financial Results**
- Ratio analysis
- Measuring results versus plans
- Measuring results versus industry norms

venture be familiar with the entire process, however. Typically, new ventures prepare financial statements quarterly so that as soon as the first quarter is completed, the new venture will have historic financial statements to help prepare forecasts and pro forma statements for future periods.

It is important for a firm to evaluate how it is faring relative to its industry. Sometimes raw financial ratios that are not viewed in context are deceiving. For example, a firm's past 3 years' income statements may show that it is increasing its sales at a rate of 15 percent per year. This number may seem impressive—until one learns that the industry in which the firm competes is growing at a rate of 30 percent per year, showing that the firm is steadily losing market share.

Many experienced entrepreneurs stress the importance of keeping on top of the financial management of a firm. In the competitive environments in which most firms exist, it's simply not good enough to shoot from the hip when making financial decisions. Reinforcing this point, Bill Gates, the founder of Microsoft, said,

> The business side of any company starts and ends with hard-core analysis of its numbers. Whatever else you do, if you don't understand what's happening in your business factually and you're making business decisions based on anecdotal data or gut instinct, you'll eventually pay a big price.[11]

Financial Statements and Forecasts

Historical financial statements reflect past performance and are usually prepared on a quarterly and annual basis. Publicly traded firms are required by the Securities and Exchange Commission (SEC) to prepare financial statements and make them available to the public. The statements are submitted to the SEC through a number of required filings. The most comprehensive filing is the **10-K**, which is a report similar to the annual report except that it contains more detailed information about the company's business.[12] The 10-K for any publicly traded firm is available through the U.S. Securities and Exchange Commission's Web site (www.sec.gov/index.htm).

Pro forma financial statements are projections for future periods based on forecasts and are typically completed for 2 to 3 years in the future. Pro forma financial statements are strictly planning tools and are not required by the SEC. In fact, most companies

L E A R N I N G

3. Explain the difference between historical and pro forma financial statements.

The first step toward prudent financial management is keeping good records. This young entrepreneur, who is the owner of a coffee shop, records her income and expenses at the end of each business day, to keep her records up-to-date. Good recordkeeping is essential for tax reporting and the generation of accurate financial statements.

consider their pro forma statements to be confidential and reveal them to outsiders, such as lenders and investors, only on a "need-to-know" basis.

To illustrate how these financial instruments are prepared, let's look at New Venture Fitness Drinks, a fictitious sports drink company first introduced in Chapter 3. New Venture Fitness Drinks has been in business for 5 years. Targeting sports enthusiasts, the company sells a line of nutritional fitness drinks. It opened a single location in 2003, added a second location in 2006, and plans to add a third in 2007. The company's strategy is to place small restaurants, similar to smoothie restaurants, near large outdoor sports complexes. The company is profitable and is growing at a rate of 25 percent per year.

Historical Financial Statements

Historical financial statements include the income statement, the balance sheet, and the statement of cash flows. The statements are usually prepared in this order because information flows logically from one to the next. In start-ups, financial statements are typically scrutinized closely to monitor the financial progress of the firm. On the rare occasion when a company has not used financial statements in planning, it should prepare and maintain them anyway. If a firm goes to a banker or investor to raise funds, the banker or investor will invariably ask for copies of past financial statements to analyze the firm's financial history. If a firm does not have these statements, it may be precluded from serious consideration for an investment or a loan. Let's look at each of these statements.

LEARNING Objective

4. Explain the purpose of an income statement.

Income Statement The **income statement** reflects the results of the operations of a firm over a specified period of time.[13] It records all the revenues and expenses for the given period and shows whether the firm is making a profit or is experiencing a loss (which is why the income statement if often referred to as the "profit-and-loss statement"). Income statements are typically prepared on a monthly, quarterly, and annual basis. Most income statements are prepared in a multiyear format, making it easy to spot trends.

The consolidated income statement for the past 3 years for New Venture Fitness Drinks is shown in Table 8.1. The value of the multiperiod format is clear. It's easy to see that the company's sales are increasing at the rate of about 25 percent per year, it is profitable, and its net income is increasing. The numbers are used to evaluate the effect of past strategies and to help project future sales and earnings.

Consolidated Income Statements for New Venture
TABLE 8.1 Fitness Drinks, Inc. (all data in dollars)

	December 31, 2006	December 31, 2005	December 31, 2004
Net sales	586,600	463,100	368,900
Cost of sales	268,900	225,500	201,500
Gross profit	317,700	237,600	167,400
Operating expenses			
Selling, general, and administrative expense	117,800	104,700	90,200
Depreciation	13,500	5,900	5,100
Operating income	186,400	127,000	72,100
Other income			
Interest income	1,900	800	1,100
Interest expense	(15,000)	(6,900)	(6,400)
Other income (expense), net	10,900	(1,300)	1,200
Income before income taxes	184,200	119,600	68,000
Income tax expense	53,200	36,600	18,000
Net income	131,000	83,000	50,000
Earnings per share	1.31	0.83	0.50

The three numbers that receive the most attention when evaluating an income statement are the following:

- *Net sales:* **Net sales** consist of total sales minus allowances for returned goods and discounts.
- *Cost of sales (or cost of goods sold):* **Cost of sales** includes all the direct costs associated with producing or delivering a product or service, including the material costs and direct labor. In the case of New Venture Fitness Drinks, this would include the ingredients that go into the fitness drinks and the labor needed to produce them.
- *Operating expenses:* **Operating expenses** include marketing, administrative costs, and other expenses not directly related to producing a product or service.

One of the most valuable things that entrepreneurs and managers do with income statements is to compare the ratios of cost of sales and operating expenses to net sales for different periods. For example, the cost of sales for New Venture Fitness Drinks, which includes the ingredients for its fitness drinks and the labor needed to make them, has been 55, 49, and 46 percent of sales for 2004, 2005, and 2006, respectively. This is a healthy trend. It shows that the company is steadily decreasing its material and labor costs per dollar of sales. This is the type of trend that can be noticed fairly easily by looking at a firm's multiyear income statements.

One ratio of particular importance in evaluating a firm's income statements is profit margin. A firm's **profit margin**, or return on sales, is computed by dividing net income by net sales. For the years 2004, 2005, and 2006, the profit margin for New Venture Fitness Drinks has been 13.6, 17.9, and 22.3 percent, respectively. This is also a healthy trend. A firm's profit margin tells it what percentage of every dollar in sales contributes to the bottom line. An increasing profit margin means that a firm is either boosting its sales without increasing its expenses or that it is doing a better job of controlling its costs. In contrast, a declining profit margin means that a firm is losing control of its costs or that it is slashing prices to maintain or increase sales.

One ratio that will not be computed for New Venture Fitness Drinks is price-to-earnings ratio, or P/E ratio. New Venture Fitness Drinks is incorporated, so it has stock, but its stock is not traded on a public exchange such as the NASDAQ or the New York Stock Exchange. **P/E** is a simple ratio that measures the price of a company's stock against its earnings.[14] Generally, the higher a company's price-to-earnings ratio goes, the greater the market thinks it will grow. In 2006, New Venture Fitness Drinks earned $1.31 per share. If it was listed on the NASDAQ and its stock was trading at $20 per share, its P/E would be 15.3. This is what is meant when you hear that a company is selling for "15 times earnings."

The importance of looking at several years of income statements rather than just one is illustrated in this chapter's "Savvy Entrepreneurial Firm" feature.

Balance Sheet Unlike the income statement, which covers a specified *period* of time, a **balance sheet** is a snapshot of a company's assets, liabilities, and owners' equity at a specific *point* in time.[15] The left-hand side of a balance sheet (or the top, depending on how it is displayed) shows a firm's assets, while the right-hand side (or bottom) shows its liabilities and owners' equity. The assets are listed in order of their "liquidity," or the length of time it takes to convert them to cash. The liabilities are listed in the order in which they must be paid. A balance sheet must always "balance," meaning that a firm's assets must always equal its liabilities plus owners' equity.[16]

The major categories of assets listed on a balance sheet are the following:

- *Current assets:* **Current assets** include cash plus items that are readily convertible to cash, such as accounts receivable, marketable securities, and inventories.
- *Fixed assets:* **Fixed assets** are assets used over a longer time frame, such as real estate, buildings, equipment, and furniture.
- *Other assets:* **Other assets** are miscellaneous assets, including accumulated goodwill.

L E A R N I N G
Objective

5. Explain the purpose of a balance sheet.

savvy
entrepreneurial firm

Know the Facts
Behind the Numbers

Let's say that New Venture Fitness Drinks was interested in hiring a new chief executive officer (CEO) and was interviewing the CEOs of three small restaurant chains. To get a sense of how savvy each candidate was at managing a firm's finances, the board of directors of New Venture Fitness Drinks asked each person to submit the 2006 income statement for his or her current firm. An analysis of an abbreviated version of each firm's income statement is shown here.

	Candidate 1: CEO of New Venture Soup and Salad	Candidate 2: CEO of New Venture Beef	Candidate 3: CEO of New Venture Sea Food
Net sales	$326,400	$281,200	$486,700
Cost of sales	150,500	143,900	174,700
Gross profit	175,900	137,300	312,000
All expenses, including taxes and depreciation	114,200	112,400	150,000
Net income	61,700	24,900	162,000

By glancing at these statements, it would appear that the shrewdest financial manager of the three is the CEO of New Venture Sea Food. The company's net income is more than double that of the other two firms. In addition, New Venture Sea Food's costs of sales were 35.9 percent of net sales in 2006, compared to 46.1 percent for New Venture Soup and Salad and 51 percent for New Venture Beef. Similarly, New Venture Sea Food's expenses were 30.9 percent of sales, compared to 35.0 percent for New Venture Soup and Salad and 40 percent for New Venture Beef.

Fortunately, one of the board members of New Venture Fitness Drinks asked a series of questions during the personal interviews of the candidates and uncovered some revealing information. As it turns out, New Venture Sea Food was in the hottest segment of the restaurant industry in 2006. Seafood restaurants of comparable size produced about 1.5 times as much net income as New Venture Seafood did. So if candidate 3 had done his job properly, his company's net income should have been in the neighborhood of $240,000 instead of $162,000. New Venture Soup and Salad was in a slow-growth area and at midyear feared that it might not meet its financial targets. So the CEO pulled several of his best people off projects and reassigned them to marketing with the charge to develop new menu items. In other words, the

company borrowed from its future to make its numbers work today.

As for New Venture Beef, the CEO found herself in a market that was losing appeal. Several reports that gained national publicity were published early in the year warning consumers of the risks of eating red meat. To compensate, the CEO quickly implemented a productivity improvement program and partnered with a local beef promotion board to counter the bad press with more objective research results about beef's nutritional value. The company also participated in several volunteer efforts in its local community to raise the visibility of its restaurants in a positive manner. If the CEO of New Venture Beef hadn't moved quickly to take these actions, its 2006 performance would have been much worse.

Ultimately, New Venture Fitness Drinks decided that candidate 2, the CEO of New Venture Beef, was the best candidate for its job. This example illustrates the need to look at multiple years of an income statement rather than a single year to fairly assess how well a firm is performing financially. It also illustrates the need to look beyond the numbers and understand the circumstances that surround a firm's financial results.

Questions for Critical Thinking

1. Show the income statements for the three candidates to two or three friends who are majoring in business. Ask them to select the best CEO from among these three people on the basis of these income statements. In addition, ask your friends to explain their choices to you. Did your friends choose the same candidate? If not, what do you think caused the differences in their choices?

2. Based on material presented in this chapter, earlier chapters in this book, and your general business knowledge, where would you go to find information about the growth of the different segments of the restaurant industry? Where would you go to find information about the profitability of the restaurant industry in general?

3. What would have been the appropriate financial information to request from the three candidates for the job?

4. What are the three most important insights you gained from studying this feature? Which of these insights surprised you, and why?

The major categories of liabilities listed on a balance sheet are the following:

- *Current liabilities:* **Current liabilities** include obligations that are payable within a year, including accounts payable, accrued expenses, and the current portion of long-term debt.
- *Long-term liabilities:* **Long-term liabilities** include notes or loans that are repayable beyond 1 year, including liabilities associated with purchasing real estate, buildings, and equipment.
- *Owners' equity:* **Owners' equity** is the equity invested in the business by its owners plus the accumulated earnings retained by the business after paying dividends.

Balance sheets are somewhat deceiving. First, a company's assets are recorded at cost rather than fair market value. A firm may have invested $500,000 in real estate several years ago that is worth $1 million today, but the value that is reflected on the firm's current balance sheet is the $500,000 purchase price rather than the $1 million fair market value. Second, intellectual property, such as patents, trademarks, and copyrights, receive value on the balance sheet in some cases and in some cases they don't, depending on the circumstances involved. In many cases, a firm's intellectual property will receive no value on its balance sheet even though it may be very valuable from a practical standpoint.[17] Third, intangible assets, such as the amount of training a firm has provided to its employees and the value of its brand, are not recognized on its balance sheet. Finally, the goodwill that a firm has accumulated is not reported on its balance sheet, although this may be the firm's single most valuable asset.

The consolidated balance sheet for New Venture Fitness Drinks is shown in Table 8.2. Again, multiple years are shown so that trends can be easily spotted. When evaluating a balance sheet, the two primary questions are whether a firm has sufficient short-term assets

Consolidated Balance Sheets for New Venture
TABLE 8.2 Fitness Drinks, Inc. (all data in dollars)

Assets	December 31, 2006	December 31, 2005	December 31, 2004
Current assets			
Cash and cash equivalents	63,800	54,600	56,500
Accounts receivable, less allowance			
for doubtful accounts	39,600	48,900	50,200
Inventories	19,200	20,400	21,400
Total Current Assets	122,600	123,900	128,100
Property, plant, and equipment			
Land	260,000	160,000	160,000
Buildings and equipment	412,000	261,500	149,000
Total property, plant, and equipment	672,000	421,500	309,000
Less: accumulated depreciation	65,000	51,500	45,600
Net property, plant and equipment	607,000	370,000	263,400
Total Assets	729,600	493,900	391,500
Liabilities and shareholders' equity			
Current liabilities			
Accounts payable	30,200	46,900	50,400
Accrued expenses	9,900	8,000	4,100
Total current liabilities	40,100	54,900	54,500
Long-term liabilities			
Long-term debt	249,500	130,000	111,000
Long-term liabilities	249,500	130,000	111,000
Total liabilities	289,600	184,900	165,500
Shareholders' equity			
Common stock (100,000 shares)	10,000	10,000	10,000
Retained earnings	430,000	299,000	216,000
Total shareholders' equity	440,000	309,000	226,000
Total liabilities and shareholders' equity	729,600	493,900	391,500

to cover its short-term debts and whether it is financially sound overall. There are two calculations that provide the answer to the first question. In 2006, the **working capital** of New Venture Fitness Drinks, defined as its current assets minus its current liabilities, was $82,500. This number represents the amount of liquid assets the firm has available. Its **current ratio**, which equals the firm's current assets divided by its current liabilities, provides another picture of the relationship between its current assets and current liabilities and can tell us more about the firm's ability to pay its short-term debts.

New Venture Fitness Drink's current ratio is 3.06, meaning that it has $3.06 in current assets for every $1.00 in current liabilities. This is a healthy number and provides confidence that the company will be able to meet its current liabilities. The company's trend in this area is also positive. For the years 2004, 2005, and 2006, its current ratio has been 2.35, 2.26, and 3.06, respectively.

Computing a company's overall debt ratio will give us the answer to the second question, as it is a means of assessing a firm's overall financial soundness. A company's debt ratio is computed by dividing its total debt by its total assets. The present debt ratio for New Venture Fitness Drinks is 39.7 percent, meaning that 39.7 percent of its total assets are financed by debt and the remaining 60.3 percent by owners' equity. This is a healthy number for a young firm. The trend for New Venture Fitness Drinks in this area is also encouraging. For the years 2004, 2005, and 2006, its debt ratio has been 42.3, 37.4, and 39.7 percent, respectively. These figures indicate that, over time, the company is relying less on debt to finance its operations. In general, less debt creates more freedom for the entrepreneurial firm in terms of taking different actions.

The numbers across all the firm's financial statements are consistent with one another. Note that the $131,000 net income reported by New Venture Fitness Drinks on its 2006 income statement shows up as the difference between its 2006 and 2005 retained earnings on its 2006 balance sheet. This number would have been different if New Venture Fitness Drinks had paid dividends to its stockholders, but it paid no dividends in 2006. The company retained all of its $131,000 in earnings.

LEARNING

Objective

6. Explain the purpose of a statement of cash flows.

Statement of Cash Flows   The **statement of cash flows** summarizes the changes in a firm's cash position for a specified period of time and details why the change occurred. The statement of cash flows is similar to a month-end bank statement. It reveals how much cash is on hand at the end of the month as well as how the cash was acquired and spent during the month.

The statement of cash flows is divided into three separate activities: operating activities, investing activities, and financing activities. These activities, which are explained in the following list, are the activities from which a firm obtains and uses cash:

- *Operating activities:* **Operating activities** include net income (or loss), depreciation, and changes in current assets and current liabilities other than cash and short-term debt. A firm's net income, taken from its income statement, is the first line on the corresponding period's cash flow statement.
- *Investing activities:* **Investing activities** include the purchase, sale, or investment in fixed assets, such as real estate, equipment, and buildings.
- *Financing activities:* **Financing activities** include cash raised during the period by borrowing money or selling stock and/or cash used during the period by paying dividends, buying back outstanding stock, or buying back outstanding bonds.

Interpreting and analyzing cash flow statements takes practice. On the statement, the *uses* of cash are recorded as negative figures (which are shown by placing them in parentheses) and the *sources* of cash are recorded as positive figures. An item such as depreciation is shown as a positive figure on the statement of cash flow because it was deducted from net income on the income statement but was not a cash expenditure. Similarly, a decrease in accounts payable shows up as a negative figure on the cash flow statement because the firm used part of its cash to reduce its accounts payable balance from one period to the next.

The statement of cash flows for New Venture Fitness Drinks is shown in Table 8.3. As a management tool, it is intended to provide perspective on the following questions: Is the firm generating excess cash that could be used to pay down debt or returned to stockholders in the form of dividends? Is the firm generating enough cash to fund its investment activities from earnings, or is it relying on lenders or investors? Is the firm generating sufficient cash to pay down its short-term liabilities, or are its short-term liabilities increasing as the result of an insufficient amount of cash?

Again, a multiperiod statement is created so that trends can easily be spotted. A large increase in a firm's cash balance is not necessarily a good sign. It could mean that the firm is borrowing heavily, is not paying down its short-term liabilities, or is accumulating cash that could be put to work for a more productive purpose. On the other hand, it is almost always prudent for a young firm to have a healthy cash balance.

Table 8.3 shows the consolidated statement of cash flows for New Venture Fitness Drinks for 2 years instead of 3 because it takes 3 years of balance sheets to produce 2 years of cash flow statements. The statements show that New Venture Fitness Drinks is funding its investment activities from a combination of debt and earnings while at the same time it is slowly decreasing its accounts receivable and inventory levels (which is good—these items are major drains on a company's cash flow). It is also steadily increasing its cash on hand. These are encouraging signs for a new venture.

Ratio Analysis The most practical way to interpret or make sense of a firm's historical financial statements is through ratio analysis. Table 8.4 is a summary of the ratios used to evaluate New Venture Fitness Drinks during the time period covered by the previously provided financial statements. The ratios are divided into profitability ratios, liquidity ratios, and overall financial stability ratios. These ratios provide a means of interpreting the historical financial statements for New Venture Fitness Drinks and provide a starting point for forecasting the firm's financial performance and capabilities for the future.

Comparing a Firm's Financial Results to Industry Norms Comparing its financial results to industry norms helps a firm determine how it stacks up against its

L E A R N I N G
Objective

7. Discuss how financial ratios are used to analyze and interpret a firm's financial statements.

Consolidated Statement of Cash Flows for New Venture
TABLE 8.3 Fitness Drinks, Inc. (all data in dollars)

	December 31, 2006	December 31, 2005
Cash flows from operating activities		
Net income	131,000	83,000
Additions (sources of cash)		
Depreciation	13,500	5,900
Decreases in accounts receivable	9,300	1,300
Increase in accrued expenses	1,900	3,900
Decrease in inventory	1,200	1,000
Subtractions (uses of cash)		
Decrease in accounts payable	(16,700)	(3,500)
Total adjustments	9,200	8,600
Net cash provided by operating activities	140,200	91,600
Cash flows from investing activities		
Purchase of building and equipment	(250,500)	(112,500)
Net cash flows provided by investing activities	(250,500)	(112,500)
Cash flows from financing activities		
Proceeds from increase in long-term debt	119,500	19,000
Net cash flows provided by financing activities		19,000
Increase in cash	9,200	(1,900)
Cash and cash equivalents at the begisnning of year	54,600	56,500
Cash and cash equivalents at the end of each year	63,800	54,600

TABLE 8.4 Ratio Analysis for New Venture Fitness Drinks, Inc.

Ratio	Formula	2006	2005	2004
Profitability ratios: associate the amount of income earned with the resources used to generate it				
Return on assets	ROA = net income/average total assets[a]	21.4%	18.7%	14.7%
Return on equity	ROE = net income/average shareholders' equity[b]	35.0%	31.0%	24.9%
Profit margin	Profit margin = net income/net sales	22.3%	17.9%	13.6%
Liquidity ratios: measure the extent to which a company can quickly liquidate assets to cover short-term liabilities				
Current	Current assets/current liabilities	3.06	2.26	2.35
Quick	Quick assets/current liabilities	2.58	1.89	1.96
Overall financial stability ratio: measures the overall financial stability of a firm				
Debt	Total debt/total assets	39.7%	37.4%	42.3%
Debt to Equity	Total liabilities/owners' equity	65.8%	59.8%	73.2%

[a] Average total assets = beginning total assets + ending total assets ÷ 2.
[b] Average shareholders' equity = beginning shareholders' equity + ending shareholders' equity ÷ 2.

competitors and if there are any financial "red flags" requiring attention. This type of comparison works best for firms that are of similar size, so the results should be interpreted with caution by new firms. Many sources provide industry-related information. For example, Hoovers provides industry norms to which a new firm can compare itself and is typically free of charge if accessed from a university library that subscribes to Hoover's premium service. To access this information, simply go to www.hoovers.com. Hoovers also provides comparison data for publicly traded firms. For example, the comparison data for Dell Inc. (the subject of Case 8.1) for the 2005–2006 fiscal year is listed at Hoovers as follows:

Comparison Data (2005–2006 Fiscal Year)	Dell Inc.	Industry Median[a]	Market Median[b]
Gross profit margin	17.50%	34.00%	51.80%
Net profit margin	6.00%	3.00%	4.80%
Return on equity (ROE)	75.6%	10.3%	9.50%
Return on assets (ROA)	14.9%	3.5%	1.6%
12-month revenue growth	11.1%	10.7%	12.3%

[a] Industry: computer hardware.
[b] All firms listed on the major stock exchanges.

These data cast Dell in a favorable light and raise no immediate red flags. Reliable data are harder to come by for private firms. One source is BizStats (http://bizstats.com), a Web site that provides industry data in a variety of formats. Using information gleaned from BizStats, the owners of New Venture Fitness Drinks could make the following comparisons for its most current reporting period:

Comparison Data (Most Current Data Available)	New Venture Fitness Drinks	All Incorporated Restaurants[a]
Sales	100%	100%
Cost of sales	45.8%	42.9%
Net operating income	22.3%	1.3%
Current ratio	3.05%	1.1%
Debt-to-equity ratio	0.65%	4.5%

[a] Industry: eating and drinking establishments.

Note the comparison is for all incorporate restaurants rather than just publicly traded corporations (forms of business ownership are discussed in Chapter 7). These firms represent a better comparison group to New Venture Fitness Drinks than publicly traded firms. The comparisons cast New Venture Fitness Drinks in a positive light and raise no immediate red flags. Cost of sales is higher than industry norms, which may be attributed to the nutritionally rich ingredients that New Venture Fitness Drinks uses in its products. By collecting this information on a periodic basis, New Venture Fitness Drinks could keep track of how its numbers compare to industry norms over time. This type of analysis may be particularly important to New Venture Fitness Drinks as it grows, and the firm must continually assess how its growth is affecting its financials.

Another comparison that New Venture Fitness Drinks can make, to test the efficiency of its operations (or how productively it uses its assets), is to compare its sales per square foot to comparable restaurants. Bizstats has an analysis of the sales per square foot for popular restaurants for 2002. Although it's not ideal to work with old data, we'll work with this information because it's the most current available. We'll use the data as a point of comparison with New Venture Fitness Drink's average sales per square foot for 2004. New Venture Fitness Drinks had one 720- square-foot restaurant in 2004.

Company	Year	Average Sales per Square Feet
Petts Coffee	2002	$696
McDonalds	2002	$543
Starbucks Coffee	2002	$521
New Venture Fitness Drinks	2004	$512
Panera Bread	2002	$418
Ruby Tuesdays	2002	$377

This analysis shows that New Venture Fitness Drink's sales per square foot are within industry averages, although several of its more established competitors are more efficient, probably as a result of their higher daily sales volume and the time they have had to perfect their operating techniques. Again, while it's not optimal to compare New Venture Fitness Drink's 2004 data to its competitors' 2002 data, sometimes financial analysis is more of an art than a science, and compromises have to be made. If the 2002 data is the most current data available, the only alternative to the analysis shown here would be to not do the analysis, which isn't an optimal solution either.

Forecasts

As depicted in Figure 8.2, the analysis of a firm's historical financial statement is followed by the preparation of forecasts. Forecasts are predictions of a firm's future sales, expenses, income, and capital expenditures. A firm's forecasts provide the basis for its pro forma financial statements. A well-developed set of pro forma financial statements helps a firm create accurate budgets, build financial plans, and manage its finances in a proactive rather than a reactive manner.

As mentioned earlier, completely new firms typically base their forecasts on a good-faith estimate of sales and on industry averages (based on a percentage of sales) or the experiences of similar start-ups for cost of goods sold and other expenses. As a result, a completely new firm's forecast should be preceded in its business plan by an explanation of the sources of the numbers for the forecast and the assumptions used to generate them. This explanation is called an **assumption sheet**. Investors typically study assumption sheets like hawks to make sure the numbers contained in the forecasts and the resulting financial projections are realistic. For example, the assumption sheet for a new venture may say that its forecasts are based on selling 500 units of its new product the first year, 1,000 units the second year, and 1,500 units the third year and that its cost of goods sold will remain stable (meaning that it will stay fixed at a certain percentage of net sales) over the 3-year period.

L E A R N I N G
Objective

8. Discuss the role of forecasts in projecting a firm's future income and expenses.

L E A R N I N G
Objective

9. Explain what a completely new firm bases its forecasts on.

FIGURE 8.3

Historical and Forecasted Annual Sales for New Venture Fitness Drinks

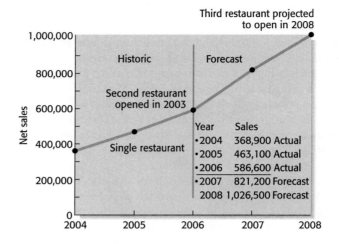

Year	Sales	
• 2004	368,900	Actual
• 2005	463,100	Actual
• 2006	586,600	Actual
• 2007	821,200	Forecast
2008	1,026,500	Forecast

It's up to the reader of the plan to determine if these numbers are realistic.[18] If the reader feels they are not, then the credibility of the entire plan is called into question.

Sales Forecast A **sales forecast** is a projection of a firm's sales for a specified period (such as a year), though most firms forecast their sales for 2 to 5 years into the future.[19] It is the first forecast developed and is the basis for most of the other forecasts.[20] A sales forecast for an existing firm is based on (1) its record of past sales, (2) its current production capacity and product demand, and (3) any factor or factors that will affect its future production capacity and product demand. To demonstrate how a sales forecast works, Figure 8.3 is a graph of the past sales and the forecasted future sales for New Venture Fitness Drinks. The company's sales increased at a rate of about 26 percent per year from 2004 to 2006 as the company became established and more people became aware of its brand. In forecasting its sales for 2007 and 2008, the company took into consideration the following factors:

■ The fitness craze in America continues to gain momentum and should continue to attract new people to try its fitness drinks.

■ The interest in intramural sports, especially soccer, baseball, and softball, should continue to provide a high level of traffic for its restaurants, which are located near large intramural sports complexes.

■ The company expanded from a single location in 2003 to two locations in 2006 (the second restaurant was added in November of 2006), and this should increase its capacity to serve fitness drinks by approximately 50 percent. The second restaurant is smaller than the first and is located in an area where the company is not as well known. The company will be actively promoting the new restaurant but knows it will take time to win market share.

■ The general economy in the city where the company is located is flat—it is neither growing nor shrinking. However, layoffs are rumored for a larger employer near the location of the new restaurant.

The combination of these factors results in a forecast of a 40 percent increase in sales from 2006 to 2007 and a 25 percent increase in sales from 2007 to 2008. It is extremely important for a company such as New Venture Drinks to forecast future sales as accurately as possible. If it overestimates the demand for its products, it might get stuck with excess inventory and spend too much on overhead. If it underestimates the demand for its product, it might have to turn away business, and some of its potential customers might get into the habit of buying other firms' fitness drinks.

Note that sophisticated tools are available to help firms project future sales. One approach is to use **regression analysis**, which is a statistical technique used to find relationships between variables for the purpose of predicting future values.[21] For example, if

New Venture Fitness Drinks felt that its future sales were a function of its advertising expenditures, the number of people who participate in intramural sports at the sports complexes near its restaurants, and the price of its drinks, it could predict future sales using regression analysis as long as it had historical data for each of these variables. If the company used simpler logic and felt that its future sales would increase a certain percentage over its current sales, regression analysis could be used to generate a more precise estimate of future sales than was predicted from the information contained in Figure 8.3. For a new firm that has limited years of "annual data," monthly data could be used to project sales.

Forecast of Costs of Sales and Other Items Once a firm has completed its sales forecast, it must forecast its cost of sales (or cost of goods sold) and the other items on its income statement. The most common way to do this is to use the **percent-of-sales method**, which is a method for expressing each expense item as a percentage of sales.[22] For example, in the case of New Venture Fitness Drinks, its cost of sales has averaged 47.5 percent over the past 2 years. In 2006, its sales were $586,600 and its cost of sales was $268,900. The company's sales are forecast to be $821,200 in 2007. Therefore, based on the percent-of-sales method, its cost of sales in 2005 will be $390,000, or 47.5 percent of projected sales. The same procedure could be used to forecast the cost of each expense item on the company's income statement.

L E A R N I N G

Objective

10. Explain what is meant by the term *percent-of-sales method*.

Once a firm completes its forecast using the percent-of-sales method, it usually goes through its income statement on an item-by-item basis to see if there are opportunities to make more precise forecasts. For example, a firm can closely estimate its depreciation expenses, so it wouldn't be appropriate to use the percent-of-sales method to make a forecast for this item. In addition, some expense items are not tied to sales. For those items, reasonable estimates are made.

Obviously, a firm must apply common sense in using the percent-of-sales method. If a company is implementing cost-cutting measures, for example, it might be able to justify projecting a smaller percentage increase in expenses as opposed to sales. Similarly, if a firm hires an administrator, such as a chief financial officer, toward the end of the year and plans to pay the person $75,000 the next year, that $75,000 may have no immediate impact on sales. In this case, the firm's forecast for administrative expenses may have to be adjusted upward beyond what the percent-of-sales method would suggest.

If a firm determines that it can use the percent-of-sales method and it follows the procedure described previously, then the net result is that each expense item on its income statement (with the exception of those items that may be individually forecast, such as depreciation) will grow at the same rate as sales. This approach is called the **constant ratio method of forecasting**. This approach will be used in preparing the pro forma financial statements for New Venture Fitness Drinks in the next section.

A summary of the forecasts used to prepare the pro forma financial statements for New Venture Fitness Drinks is provided in Table 8.5.

In addition to computing sales forecasts, when a company like New Venture Fitness Drinks considers opening a new restaurant or producing a new product, it often calculates a break-even analysis to determine if the proposed initiative is feasible. The **break-even point** for a new restaurant or product is the point where total revenue received equals total costs associated with the output of the restaurant or the sale of the product.[23] In the case of opening a new restaurant, New Venture Fitness Drinks could use break-even analysis as one way of determining whether the proposed initiative is feasible. The formula for break-even analysis is as follows: Total fixed costs/(price – average variable costs). As a result, if the total fixed cost associated with opening a new restaurant is $101,000 per year, the average price for a fitness drink is $2.75, and the variable cost for each drink is $1.10, then the break-even point for the new restaurant is as follows:

$101,000 (total fixed costs)/($2.75 − $1.10) or $1.65 = 61,212 units

The number means that the new restaurant will have to sell 61,212 "units" or fitness drinks per year to "break even" at the current price of the drinks. That number breaks down to the sale of 170 fitness drinks per day, on average, based on a 360-day year. To determine whether opening the new restaurant is feasible, the managers of New Venture Fitness Drinks would compare this number against the historic sales figures for their other restaurants, making adjustments as appropriate (e.g., the new restaurant may have a better or worse location than the existing restaurants). If selling 170 fitness drinks per day seems unrealistic, then the managers of New Fitness Drinks might opt to not open the new restaurant, or find ways to lower fixed or variable costs or increase revenues. An obvious way to increase revenues is to raise the price of the fitness drinks, if that option is realistic given the competitive nature of the marketplace.

In the context of lowering costs, one thing a new venture should guard itself against is becoming overly optimistic about cutting costs by switching to a supplier that promises to deliver the same quality at a lower cost or by buying supplies through a B2B (business-to-business) exchange. Often, these tactics represent false hopes for cost savings, as illustrated in this chapter's "What Went Wrong?" feature.

Pro Forma Financial Statements

A firm's pro forma financial statements are similar to its historical financial statements except that they look forward rather than track the past. New ventures typically offer pro forma statements, but well-managed established firms also maintain these statements as part of their routine financial planning process and to help prepare budgets. The preparation of pro forma statements also helps firms rethink their strategies and make adjustments if necessary. For example, if the pro forma statements predict a downturn in profitability, a firm can make operational changes, such as increasing prices or decreasing expenses, to help prevent the decrease in profitability from actually happening.[24]

A firm's pro forma financial statements should not be prepared in isolation. Instead, they should be created in conjunction with the firm's overall planning activities. The following sections explain the development of pro forma financial statements for New Venture Fitness Drinks.

Pro Forma Income Statement

Once a firm forecasts its future income and expenses, the creation of the **pro forma income statement** is merely a matter of plugging in the numbers. Table 8.6 shows the pro forma income statement for New Venture Fitness Drinks. Recall that net sales for New Venture Fitness Drinks are forecast to increase by 40 percent from 2006 to 2007 and by 25 percent from 2007 to 2008 and that its cost of sales has averaged 47.5 percent of net sales. In the pro forma income statement, the constant ratio method of forecasting is used to forecast the cost of sales and general and administrative expense, meaning that these items are projected to remain at the same percentage of sales in the future as they were in the past (which is the mathematical equivalent of saying that they will increase at the same rate of sales). Depreciation, other income, and several other items that are not directly tied to sales are figured separately—using reasonable estimates. The most dramatic change is "other income," which jumps significantly from 2006 to 2007. New Venture Fitness Drinks anticipates a significant increase in this category as the result of the renegotiation of a licensing agreement for one of its fitness drinks that is sold by another company.

Pro Forma Balance Sheet

The **pro forma balance sheet** provides a firm a sense of how its activities will affect its ability to meet its short-term liabilities and how its finances will evolve over time. It can also quickly show how much of a firm's money will be tied up in accounts receivable, inventory, and equipment. The pro forma balance sheet is also used to project the overall financial soundness of a company. For example, a firm may have a very aggressive set of pro forma income statements that project rapidly increasing growth and profitability. However, if this rapid growth and profitability push the firm's debt ratio to 75 percent (which is extremely high), investors may conclude that there is too much risk involved for the firm to be an attractive investment.

Forecasts Used to Prepare Pro Forma Financial Statements
TABLE 8.5 **for New Venture Fitness Drinks, Inc.**

Pro Forma Income Statements

Net sales

Historic	Average sales increase of 25% per year
2007	Increase to 40% as the result of increased brand awareness and the opening of a second service location
2008	Increase 25% as the result of increased brand awareness (a third service location will be opened late in the year)

Cost of goods sold (COGS)

Historic	Average of 47.5% of sales the past 2 years
2007	47.5% of sales
2008	47.5% of sales

Selling, general, and administrative expense

Historic	Average 22% of sales the past 2 years
2007	Increase to 25% of sales as the result of the opening of a second service location (the increase will not be any larger as the result of increased operating efficiencies)
2008	25% of sales

Interest expense

Historic	6% to 7% of long-term debt
2007	7% of long-term debt
2008	7% of long-term debt

Other income

Historic	Licensing income of $10,900 per year
2007	Licensing income will increase to $20,000 as the result of the renegotiation of the licensing contract
2008	Licensing income will be $20,000

Pro Forma Balance Sheets

Accounts receivable

Historic	Accounts receivable have trended down to 7% of sales in 2003 from 13.6% of sales in 2001
2007	7% of sales
2008	7% of sales

Inventories

Historic	Inventories have trended down to 3.3% of sales in 2003 from 5.8% of sales in 2002
2007	4% of sales (reflecting slight increase over 2003 as the result of the opening of a second service location)
2008	4% of sales

Land, buildings, and equipment

2007	$100,000 in equipment purchases and capital improvements made to existing buildings
2008	$275,000 in capital improvements, including a $100,000 real estate purchase and $175,000 in buildings and equipment

Accounts payable

Historic	Accounts payable have trended down to 5% of sales in 2003 from 13.6% of sales in 2001 because of the implementation of more effective collection methods (a slightly higher level of accounts payable will be projected for the future)
2007	7% of sales
2008	7% of sales

Long-term debt

2007	$75,000 reduction in long-term debt from earnings
2008	$150,000 will be borrowed to finance $275,000 to acquire land, equipment, and buildings (the balance of the acquisition costs will be funded from earnings)

what went wrong?

B2B Exchanges: A False Hope for Cost Savings?

A B2B (business-to-business) exchange is an online marketplace that connects the buyers and the sellers in an industry. The goal of these connections is to improve the efficiency of the supply chain and save money for everyone. ChemConnect is an example of a B2B exchange. ChemConnect helps companies that purchase chemicals locate the suppliers they need and negotiate a favorable price. True to the nature of an effective online exchange, ChemConnect has helped many companies find suppliers for the raw materials they need and buyers for the products they sell that they would never reach otherwise. In fact, as of mid-2006, ChemConnect's international community of members included more than 9,000 companies from over 150 countries worldwide.

In the early days of e-commerce, experts predicted that B2B exchanges would change the way companies interacted with their buyers and suppliers. Unfortunately, the majority of online exchanges have not worked out as well as ChemConnect. In fact, a study conducted by George Day, Adam Fein, and Gregg Ruppersberger tracked the number of B2B exchanges from 1,500 in 2001 to fewer than 700 in 2002 to an estimated 180 in 2003. The study notes that this kind of shakeout has occurred in new technology markets before, but usually over a 20- to 30-year period. Although the number of B2B exchanges is higher today than in 2003, the numbers are still well below initial expectations. So what went wrong, so fast, with B2B exchanges?

Well, several things. First, even though many B2B exchanges were proficient in helping firms find the supplier with the lowest price, price isn't everything. Most suppliers want to establish a relationship with the companies they sell to rather than make a one-time sale motivated strictly by price. In fact, many advisers counsel firms to limit the number of their suppliers to develop trusting relationships and ensure the delivery of high-quality products or parts. B2B exchanges encourage just the opposite by emphasizing price as the most important buying criterion.

Second, rather than seeing B2B exchanges as making the supply chain more efficient, many firms see the exchanges as adding one more layer of cost. Once a supplier and seller get together and start doing business with each other, they can easily avoid the exchange and eliminate the exchange's commission. As Art Jahnke, writing in *CIO* magazine, put it,

> *Neither (the buyer and the seller) is prepared to dance to the tune of an intermediary who had a bright idea a few years back, and who wants to sit back and take a percentage forever.*

Third, the technology involved with B2B exchanges seldom lived up to the promise. A common complaint from both buyers and sellers was the functionality of B2B Web sites.

Although some exchanges, such as ChemConnect, are doing well, the jury is still out on the future of B2B exchanges. The majority of the exchanges have not been able to overcome the obstacles described here and, in the end, have represented a false hope for cost savings.

Questions for Critical Thinking

1. Choose two companies in your community with which you are familiar. Make an appointment with a top-level manager in each company. Ask the managers to describe the criteria they deem most important when working with their suppliers. Is price the most important criterion for the people you are interviewing? If so, why? If not, are relationships important? If relationships are important to your interviewees, how do they go about establishing and maintaining those relationships?

2. Given the knowledge you've acquired from studying this book as well as from other academic courses and work experience, develop a list of advantages and disadvantages associated with entrepreneurs deciding to rely on B2B transactions. For entrepreneurs, do the advantages of B2B transactions outweigh the disadvantages, or is the reverse true, and why?

3. What would you anticipate the attributes are of the B2B exchanges that have survived?

4. List some ways, other than B2B exchanges, that entrepreneurs are leveraging the power of the Internet to cut costs.

Sources: J. K. Shim, *Dictionary of Business Terms* (Mason, OH: Thomson Higher Education, 2006); G. S. Day, A. J. Fein, and G. Ruppersberger, "Shakeouts in Digital Markets: Lessons from B2B Exchanges," *California Management Review* 45, no. 2 (2003): 131–50; and A. Jahnke, "What Was Wrong with B2B Exchanges?" *CIO*, June 20, 2002.

Many entrepreneurs work with financial analysts and accountants to better understand their financial progress. Entrepreneurs who keep on top of the financial aspects of their company make strong decisions. A good accountant can also offer an entrepreneur invaluable advice in the areas of financial management and control.

TABLE 8.6 Pro Forma Income Statement for New Venture Fitness Drinks, Inc. (all data in dollars)

	2006 Actual	2007 Projected	2008 Projected
Net sales	586,600	821,200	1,026,500
Cost of sales	268,900	390,000	487,600
Gross profit	317,700	431,200	538,900
Operating expenses			
Selling, general, and administrative expense	117,800	205,300	256,600
Depreciation	13,500	18,500	22,500
Operating income	186,400	207,400	259,800
Other income			
Interest income	1,900	2,000	2,000
Interest expense	(15,000)	(17,500)	(17,000)
Other income (expense), net	10,900	20,000	20,000
Income before income taxes	184,200	211,900	264,800
Income tax expense	53,200	63,600	79,400
Net income	131,000	148,300	185,400
Earnings per share	1.31	1.48	1.85

The pro forma balance sheet for New Venture Fitness Drinks is shown in Table 8.7. Note that the company's projected change in retained earnings each year is consistent with its projected net income for the same period on its pro forma income statements. The same approach was used to construct the pro forma balance sheets as the pro forma income statements. For each item listed under current assets and current liabilities, the item's historical percentage of sales was used to project its future percentage of sales. Several of the numbers were adjusted slightly upward, such as inventory levels and accounts payable, to reflect the potential impact of the opening of the second restaurant.

In regard to property, plant, and equipment, New Venture Fitness Drinks plans to invest $100,000 in 2007 and $275,000 in 2008. The pro forma balance sheet shows a corresponding increase in valuation in this category for 2007 and 2008, respectively. The company's projected long-term debt for 2007 and 2008 reflects changes resulting from principal reductions from cash flow and increased borrowing to fund the property, plant,

Pro Forma Balance Sheets for New Venture Fitness Drinks,
TABLE 8.7 **Inc. (all data in dollars)**

Assets	December 31, 2006	2007 Projected	2008 Projected
Current assets			
Cash and cash equivalents	63,800	53,400	80,200
Accounts receivable, less			
allowance for doubtful accounts	39,600	57,500	71,900
Inventories	19,200	32,900	41,000
Total current assets	122,600	143,800	193,100
Property, plant, and equipment			
Land	260,000	260,000	360,000
Buildings and equipment	412,000	512,000	687,000
Total property, plant, and equipment	672,000	772,000	1,047,000
Less: accumulated depreciation	65,000	83,500	106,000
Net property, plant, and equipment	607,000	688,500	941,000
Total assets	729,600	832,300	1,134,100
Liabilities and shareholders' equity			
Current liabilities			
Accounts payable	30,200	57,500	71,900
Accrued expenses	9,900	12,000	14,000
Total current liabilities	40,100	69,500	85,900
Long-term liabilities			
Long-term debt	249,500	174,500	274,500
Total long-term liabilities	249,500	174,500	274,500
Total liabilities	289,600	244,000	360,400
Shareholders' equity			
Common stock (100,000 shares)	10,000	10,000	10,000
Retained earnings	430,000	578,300	763,700
Total shareholders' equity	440,000	588,300	773,700
Total liabilities and			
shareholders' equity	729,600	832,300	1,134,100

and equipment purchases just mentioned. These transactions are reflected in the pro forma statement of cash flows for New Venture Fitness Drinks.

Pro Forma Statement of Cash Flows

The **pro forma statement of cash flows** shows the projected flow of cash into and out of the company during a specified period. The most important function of the pro forma statement of cash flows is to project whether the firm will have sufficient cash to meet its needs. As with the historical statement of cash flows, the pro forma statement of cash flows is broken into three activities: operating activities, investing activities, and financing activities. Close attention is typically paid to the section on operating activities because it shows how changes in the company's accounts receivable, accounts payable, and inventory levels affect the cash that it has available for investing and finance activities. If any of these items increases at a rate that is faster than the company's annual increase in sales, it typically raises a red flag. For example, an increase in accounts receivable, which is money that is owed to a company by its customers, decreases the amount of cash that it has available for investment or finance activities. If accounts receivable gets out of hand, it may jeopardize a company's ability to fund its growth or service its debt.

The pro forma consolidated statement of cash flows for New Venture Fitness Drinks is shown in Table 8.8. The figures appearing on the statement come directly, or are calculated directly, from the pro forma income statement and the pro forma balance sheet. The one exception is that the last line of each statement of cash flows, which reflects the company's

TABLE 8.8 Pro Forma Statement of Cash Flows for New Venture Fitness Drinks, Inc. (all data in dollars)

	December 31, 2006	Projected 2007	Projected 2008
Cash flows from operating activities			
Net income	131,000	148,300	185,400
Changes in working capital			
Depreciation	13,500	18,500	22,500
Increase (decrease) in accounts receivable	9,300	(17,900)	(14,400)
Increase (decrease) in accrued expenses	1,900	2,100	2,000
Increase (decrease) in inventory	1,200	(13,700)	(8,100)
Increase (decrease) in accounts payable	(16,700)	27,300	14,400
Total adjustments	9,200	16,300	16,400
Net cash provided by operating activities	140,200	164,600	201,800
Cash flows from investing activities			
Purchase of building and equipment	(250,500)	(100,000)	(275,000)
Net cash flows provided by investing activities	(250,500)	(100,000)	(275,000)
Cash flows from financing activities			
Proceeds from increase in long-term debt	119,500	—	100,000
Principle reduction in long-term debt		(75,000)	
Net cash flows provided by financing activities			
Increase in cash	9,200	(10,400)	26,800
Cash and cash equivalents at the beginning of the year	54,600	63,800	53,400
Cash and cash equivalents at the end of the year	63,800	53,400	80,200

cash balance at the end of the period, becomes the first line of the company's balance sheet for the next period. The pro forma statement of cash flows for New Venture Fitness Drinks shows healthy cash balances at the end of each projected period and shows that investment activities are being funded more by earnings than by debt. This scenario reflects a company that is generating sufficient cash flow to fund the majority of its growth without overly relying on debt or investment capital.

In regard to dividends, the pro forma statement of cash flows shows that New Venture Fitness Drinks is not planning to pay a dividend to its stockholders in 2007 and 2008. Recall that New Venture Fitness Drinks is incorporated and has stockholders even through it is not traded on an organized exchange. If New Venture Fitness Drinks were planning to pay a dividend, the projected dividend payments would show up under financing activities and would reduce the amount of cash available for investing and financing activities. It is common for a new firm to invest the majority of its cash in activities that fund its growth, such as property, plant, and equipment purchases, rather than pay dividends.

Ratio Analysis

The same financial ratios used to evaluate a firm's historical financial statements should be used to evaluate the pro forma financial statements. This work is completed so the firm can get a sense of how its projected financial performance compares to its past performance and how its projected activities will affect its cash position and its overall financial soundness.

The historical financial ratios and projected ratios for New Venture Fitness Drinks are shown in Table 8.9. The profitability ratios show a slight decline from the historical period to the projected. This indicates that the projected increase in assets and corresponding sales will not produce income quite as efficiently as has been the case historically. Still, the numbers are strong, and no dramatic changes are projected.

The liquidity ratios show a consistently healthy ratio of current assets to current liabilities, suggesting that the firm should be able to cover its short-term liabilities without difficulty. The

TABLE 8.9 **Ratio Analysis of Historical and Pro Forma Financial Statements for New Venture Fitness Drinks, Inc.**

	Historical			Projected	
Ratio	2004	2005	2006	2007	2008
Profitability ratios					
Return on assets	14.7%	18.7%	21.4%	19.0%	18.9%
Return on equity	24.9%	31.0%	35.0%	28.9%	27.2%
Profit margin	13.6%	17.9%	22.3%	18.1%	18.1%
Liquidity ratios					
Current	2.35	2.26	3.05	2.07	2.24
Quick	1.96	1.89	2.58	1.60	1.78
Overall financial stability ratios					
Debt	42.3%	37.4%	39.7%	29.3%	31.8%
Debt to equity	73.2%	59.8%	65.8%	41.5%	46.6%

overall financial stability ratios indicate promising trends. The debt ratio drops from an actual of 39.7 percent in 2006 to a projected 31.8 percent in 2008. The debt-to-equity ratio shows an even more dramatic drop, indicating that an increasing portion of the firm's assets is being funded by equity rather than debt.

In summary, it is extremely important for a firm to understand its financial position at all times and for new ventures to base their financial projections on solid numbers. As mentioned earlier, regardless of how successful a firm is in other areas, it must succeed financially to remain strong and viable.

Chapter Summary

1. Financial management deals with two things: raising money and managing a company's finances in a way that achieves the highest rate of return.
2. Profitability, liquidity, efficiency, and stability are the four main financial objectives of entrepreneurial firms.
3. Historical financial statements reflect past performance. Pro forma financial statements are projections for expected performance in future periods.
4. An income statement reflects the results of a firm's operations over a specified period of time. It records all the revenues and expenses for the given period and shows whether the firm is making a profit or is experiencing a loss.
5. A balance sheet is a snapshot of a company's assets, liabilities, and owners' equity.
6. A statement of cash flows summarizes the changes in a firm's cash position for a specified period of time.
7. Financial ratios depict relationships between items on a firm's financial statement and are used to discern if a firm is meeting its financial objectives and how it stacks up against its competitors.
8. Forecasts are predictions of a firm's future sales, expenses, income, and capital expenditures. A firm's forecasts provide the basis for its pro forma financial statements.
9. Completely new firms typically base their forecasts on a good-faith estimate of sales and on industry averages (based on a percentage of sales) or the experiences of similar start-ups for cost of goods sold and other expenses.
10. Once a firm has completed its sales forecast, it must forecast its costs of sales as well as the other items on its income statement. The most common way to do this is to use the percent-of-sales method, which is a method for expressing each expense item as a percentage of sales.

Key Terms

accounts receivable, 226
assumption sheet, 237
balance sheet, 231
break-even point, 239
budgets, 228
constant ratio method of forecasting, 239
cost of sales, 231
current assets, 231
current liabilities, 233
current ratio, 234
debt-to-equity ratio, 226
efficiency, 226
financial management, 225
financial ratios, 228

financing activities, 234
fixed assets, 231
forecasts, 228
historical financial statements, 229
income statement, 230
inventory, 226
investing activities, 234
liquidity, 226
long-term liabilities, 233
net sales, 231
operating activities, 234
operating expenses, 231
other assets, 231
owners' equity, 233
P/E, 231

percent-of-sales method, 239
pro forma balance sheet, 240
pro forma financial statements, 229
pro forma income statement, 240
pro forma statement of cash flows, 244
profit margin, 231
profitability, 226
regression analysis, 238
sales forecast, 238
stability, 226
statement of cash flows, 234
10-K, 229
working capital, 234

Review Questions

1. What are the two primary functions of the financial management of a firm?
2. What are the four main financial objectives of a firm?
3. Why is it important for a company to focus on its liquidity? What special challenges do entrepreneurial firms have in regard to remaining liquid?
4. What is meant by the term *efficiency* as it relates to the financial management of a firm?
5. What is meant by the term *stability* as it relates to the financial management of a firm?
6. What is the purpose of a forecast? What factors does a firm use to create its forecasts of future income and expenses?
7. On what factors or conditions do completely new firms base their forecasts?
8. What is the purpose of an income statement? What are the three numbers that receive the most attention when evaluating an income statement? Why are these numbers important?
9. How does a firm compute its profit margin? What is the significance of this ratio?
10. How does a firm compute its price-to-earnings ratio? Why does a high price-to-earnings ratio indicate that the stock market thinks the firm will grow?
11. What is the purpose of a balance sheet?
12. What are the major categories of assets and liabilities on a balance sheet? Briefly explain each category.
13. What is meant by the term *working capital*? Why is working capital an important consideration for entrepreneurial firms?
14. How does a firm compute its current ratio? Is this a relatively important or unimportant financial ratio? Explain your answer.
15. What is the purpose of a statement of cash flows?
16. What are the three separate categories of activities that are reflected on a firm's statement of cash flows? Briefly explain the importance of each activity.
17. What is the purpose of financial ratios? Why are financial ratios particularly useful in helping a firm interpret its financial statements?
18. What is the purpose of an assumption sheet?
19. Describe why a firm's sales forecast is the basis for most of the other forecasts.
20. Explain what is meant by the percent-of-sales method as it relates to forecasts.

Application Questions

1. Trevor Smith has developed a new wireless application that he feels will revolutionize the communications industry. He has been turned down by several potential investors

who seemed to like his idea but who insisted on seeing pro forma financial statements as part of a business plan. Trevor doesn't think it's a good use of time to develop pro forma financial statements. He believes, "If the product is good enough, the financials will take care of themselves." Why is Trevor's thinking unwise? In your opinion, how common is the position Trevor is taking about financial statements?

2. Kirsten, a friend of yours, plans to start a business in the advertising industry. She told you that she leafed through several books on how to prepare forecasts and pro forma financial statements but that the books were geared toward existing firms that have several years of historical financial statements on which to base their projections. If Kirsten asked you your advice for how to prepare forecasts for a completely new firm in the advertising industry, what would you tell her?

3. Dustin Berg is the owner of a company, located in Oxford, Mississippi, that sells security systems to luxury car owners. He keeps good records but has never completed financial statements. He wants to expand his business and has been told that he'll need both historical and pro forma financial statements to complete a business plan. Dustin isn't sure he understands the difference between historical and pro forma financial statements. If he asked you to explain the distinction, what would you tell him?

4. Sheila Clark just retired from a career with British Petroleum, cashing out a sizable retirement fund at the time of doing so. To start a second career, she is looking at the possibility of buying three different businesses. She has the historical financial statements for each business and has been pouring over the numbers. She was puzzled when she read this footnote attached to one of the balance sheets: "Assets are valued at purchase price rather than fair market value." If Sheila asked you to explain this statement, what would you tell her?

5. Tim Phillips, who owns a digital photography start-up in Sioux Falls, South Dakota, plans to expand his business in 2 to 3 years, by servicing clients in Minneapolis, Minnesota, and Des Moines, Iowa. He hopes to get a bank loan to fund the expansion, so he wants to do everything he can to strengthen his financial statements before he applies for a loan. One thing that he read recently is that banks focus intently on a firm's current ratio and its overall debt/asset ratio when considering loan requests. Explain to Tim why these two ratios are critical indicators of the financial strength of a business.

6. Chipotle Mexican Grill is a publicly traded company. Calculate the firm's price-to-earnings ratio (P/E). What does Chipotle's P/E ratio tell you about investors' expectations regarding the company's growth?

7. Jarrett Baker is the founder of an enterprise software company located in Philadelphia. By looking at the income statements for Jarrett's business over the past 3 years, you see that its working capital has declined from $42,400 in 2004 to $17,900 in 2005 to $3,100 in 2006. If this trend continues, in what ways could it jeopardize the future of Jarrett's business?

8. Jorge Martinez is thinking about buying an existing printing business and has been carefully studying the records of the business to get a good handle on its historical financial performance. Jorge heard that you are taking a class in entrepreneurship and asks you, "What suggestions do you have for me to make the best use of this financial information (i.e., three years of audited income statements, balance sheets, and statements of cash flow)?" What suggestions would you give Jorge for making the maximum use of the financial statements?

9. Casey Cordell is the owner of a digital photography service in Madison, Wisconsin. The company has been profitable every year of its existence. Its debt ratio is currently 68 percent, its current ratio is 1.1, and its debt-to-equity ratio is 72.2 percent. Do these financial numbers cause any reason to be concerned? Why or why not?

10. Brian Baker is thinking about starting his own company and has been doing some reading about the differences among income statements, balance sheets, and statements of cash flow. One thing that has Brian stumped is a statement that he read in a book he picked up at Borders. The statement reads, "While the income statement reflects the operations of a firm over a specific period of time, the balance sheet is a snapshot of a company's assets, liabilities, and owners' equity at a specific point in time." Brian has asked you to explain this statement. What would you say?

11. Go to Hoovers (www.hoovers.com) and analyze how the financials of Panera Bread, the company that is the focus of Case 5.1 in Chapter 5, compare to other firms in the

restaurant industry in the same manner as Dell Inc. was compared to other firms in the computer industry in this chapter. Evaluate the financial performance of Panera Bread as it compares to industry norms.

12. Megan Mesker owns a company that is in the health services industry. She is planning to expand her business and is working on a business plan to present to investors. A friend of Megan's suggested that she compare the past financial results of her firm to industry norms. Megan is not sure why her friend made that suggestion and doesn't know where to start to find the relevant information. If Megan asked you for your assistance, how would you help her?

13. The "You Be the VC 1" feature focuses on H2O Audio, the company that plans to provide people who enjoy water sports the ability to listen to their Apple iPod and other MP3 players while in the water. If the founders of H2O Audio asked you to help them complete a break-even analysis for their business, how would you go about it?

14. Josh Lee has owned a fitness center for the past 4 years. He has historical financial statements but has never put together a set of pro forma financial statements. He just applied for a bank loan and has been told he needs a set of pro forma financial statements for the next 2 years. If Josh asked you to help him, how would you tell him to proceed?

15. Brenda Wilson owns a restaurant chain named Rhapsody Cuisine. She is planning to expand her chain from 9 restaurants to 15. Brenda is now working to put together a set of pro forma financial statements for an investor who expressed interest in her expansion project. Brenda used a combination of common sense and industry norms to project her future income and expenses. Shortly after she submitted the financial statements, she received them back with a handwritten note from the investor, who wrote, "I'm comfortable with your sales forecasts but think you would be on firmer ground if you used the percent-of-sales method to forecast expenses. Please redo the statements." If Brenda asked you what the investor was talking about, what would you tell her?

H2OAudio
www.H2OAudio.com

Business Idea: Provide people who enjoy water sports the ability to listen to their Apple iPod and other MP3 players while in the water.

Pitch: People who participate in water sports are usually out of luck when it comes to listening to music while they enjoy their sport. While walkers, runners, bikers, and other sports enthusiasts enjoy their music while they work out, swimmers, surfers, and scuba divers are left out. This reality struck the founders of H2OAudio as unfair—so they set out to do something about it.

What emerged is H2OAudio, a company that makes sealed waterproof housings for the Apple iPod and the iPod Mini music players. The company has also designed a set of headphones that work underwater. To accommodate skiers and snowboarders, the housings and headphones also work in a snowy environment. The housings are rated to keep an iPod safe in up to 10 feet of water. The housings are also shock resistant. This helps when a swimmer dives into the water or when a snowboarder or

skier wipes out. The waterproof housing and accompanying headphones sell in the $150 range.

For scuba divers, H2OAudio has a separate housing, which is compatible with iRiver's iFP-300 flash-based MP3 player. Rated as waterproof up to 200 feet, this system has a special set of headphones that are needed to amplify sound at deeper depths. This set sells in the $200 range.

There are many potential markets for H2OAudio's products beyond water enthusiasts. Runners and bikers in rainy locations, like the Seattle area, have trouble keeping their iPods dry or simply don't chance it on rainy days. Similarly, people who take long baths or have a hot tub may find H2OAudio's products appealing.

Q&A: Based on the material covered in this chapter, what questions would you ask the firm's founders before making your funding decision? What answers would satisfy you?

Decision: If you had to make your decision on just the information provided in the pitch and on the company's Web site, would you fund this firm? Why or why not?

Virgin Galactic
www.virgingalactic.com

Business Idea: Offer suborbital spaceflights and later orbital spaceflights to the paying public.

Pitch: This company is no spoof. It is deadly serious—and has very credible people behind it. Virgin Galactic is a company that was launched by Sir Richard Branson's Virgin Group and plans to start offering spaceflights to paying customers by the end of 2008.

Designs for the spaceship that will carry the company's passengers are progressing at a facility led by Burton Rutan, the visionary behind the maiden voyage of SpaceShipOne in 2004. Recall that SpaceShipOne successfully traveled to sub-orbital space and back twice in late 2004, reaching an altitude of over 67 miles. The company is now deeply involved in comprehensive and detailed R&D efforts. The purpose of these efforts is to take what was learned from SpaceShipOne's trips to space and create a new, more robust spaceship called Virgin Galactic. Sir Richard's vision to build a space tourism business and Burt Rutan's technical knowledge and passion for the future of manned spaceflight create an ideal combination to launch an entrepreneurial venture. Articulating his personal passion for Virgin Galactic, Richard Branson is quoted on the company's Web site as saying: "We hope to create thousands of astronauts over the next few years and bring alive their dreams of seeing the majestic beauty of our planet from above, the stars in all their glory and the amazing sensation of weightlessness and space flight."

The mechanics of how this product will work are interesting. The Virgin Galactic spacecraft will be carried under the belly of a large plane until around 52,000 feet, where it will be released and will then rocket into space. After spending several precious moments in space, it will glide back to earth and will land at its point of departure. Safety is being emphasized in every aspect of the ship's design, to create a robust, reusable craft that inspires confidence. The spacecraft will be flown by a professional pilot, and passengers will need about 1 week of training before the flight. Virgin Galactic is currently taking $25,000 deposits from people who want to reserve seats during the first years of flights. The ticket price has been set at $200,000.

To illustrate how much confidence serious people have in Virgin Galactic's ability to turn its dream into a reality, the state of New Mexico recently committed $200 million in order to build a spaceport in the southern part of the state. Virgin Galactic has agreed to locate its world headquarters and mission control in New Mexico.

Q&A: Based on the material covered in this chapter, what questions would you ask the firm's founders before making your funding decision? What answers would satisfy you?

Decision: If you had to make your decision on just the information provided in the pitch and on the company's Web site, would you fund this firm? Why or why not?

Dell Inc.: How Its Business Model Sweetens Its Financial Statements
www.dell.com

Bruce R. Barringer,
University of Central Florida
R. Duane Ireland,
Texas A&M University

Introduction

As we've mentioned in other chapters, there are many reasons that Dell Inc.'s sales approach has been so successful. One of the most profound reasons revolves around the effect that selling directly to the end user has had on Dell's financial

structure. Conventionally, a business forecasts its demand and then schedules its production. The sales forecast that it sets reverberates throughout the supply chain. A company such as Hewlett-Packard (HP) shares its forecasts with its component manufacturers, which set their production schedules accordingly. If sales fall short, everyone gets stuck with inventory that's hard to unload. If fact, an often-told joke in the PC industry is that unsold inventory is like unsold vegetables—it spoils quickly. If sales go better than expected, everyone has to scramble to meet demand. Think of the financial implications that this way of doing business has for computer manufacturers and their suppliers. Forecasting, inventory levels, and unsold, obsolete products are just some of the challenges.

Financial Advantages of Dell's Business Model

Dell's business model sidesteps these problems through its direct-sales approach. Building to order (BTO) means producing a unit after the customer's order is transmitted to the factory floor. There's not much forecasting to do because the tempo of sales is determined in real time. Component suppliers who also build to order get information electronically from Dell as customers place orders. They deliver parts that Dell quickly places into production. Shippers, such as UPS and FedEx, cart the products away as soon as they exit the production process. This process compresses the amount of time it takes from order to delivery and forces everyone in the supply chain to be extremely efficient. Dell can take an order, build a computer, and have it to its customer within a week. Now think about the financial implications of doing business *this* way. Dell has very little forecasting to do and has little inventory to worry about. It gets its money before rather than after the sale. And it can focus its attention on manufacturing and customer service rather than trying to find ways to unload stale inventory.

As an added benefit, Dell's model significantly improves its inventory turnover, which is an important financial metric for an assembly company. Inventory turnover is determined by the following formula:

$$\text{Inventory Turnover} = \frac{\text{Cost of Good Sold}}{\text{Average Inventories}}$$

A high inventory turnover means that a company is converting its inventory into cash quickly. Dell turns its inventory over about every 5 days on average. This advantage enables Dell to generate a tremendous amount of cash that it uses to fund its growth. It also enables Dell to introduce new technology more quickly than many of its rivals, which use slower-moving, indirect distribution channels.

Along with crunching numbers, savvy managers assess the impact of their financial strategies on their overall goals and levels of customer satisfaction. Ultimately, it doesn't matter that a company has pretty financial statements if its customers are starting to go elsewhere. Dell's business model shines in this area too. Because it turns its inventory over quickly, it offers its customers the latest technologies rather than saddling them with products that are going out-of-date. It can also pass along the advantages of falling component costs quicker than its competitors can.

It's hard to quantify how much long-term benefit a firm receives by passing along advantages to its customers. Positive "buzz" is a hard thing to put a price tag on. If you were the CEO of HP or Lenovo, it would also be hard to know how to respond. Companies such as HP can't simply scrap unsold inventory just because it's getting a little out-of-date. And Dell doesn't have unsold inventory sitting at Best Buy or Circuit City to worry about.

The Downside of Pushing Cost Savings Too Far

Although the majority of the decisions that Dell has made have both sweetened its financial statements and pleased its customers, Dell is learning the hard way that cost savings can be pushed too far. In the early 1990s, partly in response to the challenges imposed by its rapid growth, Dell started outsourcing the majority of its call center activities to low-wage countries in Asia and Central America. This strategy led to a chorus of growing complaints about long wait times for customer service calls and poor postsales support. In response, Dell has spent over $100 million to revive its customer service, including an effort to increase the percentage of full-time Dell employees who man customer service support lines and reduce its use of part-time and contract workers. The jury is still out on whether Dell has done enough to stem the tide of customer dissatisfaction. One indicator that Dell's efforts are working is that its level of overall customer satisfaction improved from 2005 to 2006. In fact, according to the University of Michigan's American Customer Satisfaction Index, Dell finished second behind Apple for computer companies with a customer satisfaction score of 78 (out of 100), which is a 5.4 percent improvement from the previous year. In the same period, Dell's primary rival, Hewlett-Packard, scored 72.

Discussion Questions

1. Investigate the financial ratio of inventory turnover. Find current information about Dell (www.hoovers.com is a good starting place) and report whether its inventory turnover is still as impressive as the number mentioned in the case. How does Dell's current inventory turnover ratio compare to that of its competitors?
2. Locate Dell's most recent 10-K and compute the financial ratios for Dell that are shown in Table 8.4. Comment on Dell's strength or weakness as suggested by these ratios.
3. If you were the CEO of HP, how would you respond to Dell's direct approach to selling?
4. What lessons can a young entrepreneurial firm learn from Dell's experiences?

Application Questions

1. Do some Internet research to see if Dell has successfully stemmed the tide of customer complaints regarding its call center management and after-sales support. What long-term adverse affect, if any, do you think that Dell's decision to cut costs by outsourcing the majority of its call center operations in the early 1990s will have on the firm's reputation and level of customer satisfaction?
2. Look at the most recent 10-K report of Hewlett-Packard. Study the report carefully, and comment on any statements or claims that HP is making regarding how it is improving the efficiency of its supply chain. Also, do an Internet search to see if others have written about HP's efforts to improve its supply chain. Based on your

investigation, do you think HP is making meaningful strides in "catching up" to Dell in terms of supply chain management? If so, how is HP doing this?

Sources: Dell Inc. 10-K Report to the Securities and Exchange Commission, filed on March 15, 2006; CNNMoney.com, "Customer Satisfaction Growing, Survey Says," August 15, 2006; D. Sims, "Dell Call Center Déjà Vu," TMCnet, August 19, 2006.

 *Managing the Left Side as Well as the Right Side of the Balance Sheet*

Bruce R. Barringer,
University of Central Florida
R. Duane Ireland,
Texas A&M University

Introduction

Many firms focus on managing their liabilities, or the right side of their balance sheet. By closely managing its liabilities, a firm can build a healthy working capital balance, keep its overall debt ratio low, and make sure its accounts payable are paid on time. Along with managing the right side of their balance sheets, however, firms must manage the left side, or the assets side, too. By reducing the assets they need to produce a dollar of sales, firms can reduce their need for debt, improve their cash flow, and increase their overall profitability.

Examples of Savvy Asset Management

There are many ways firms reduce the assets they need to produce a dollar of sales, and the possibilities are limited only by the imagination. For example, Netflix, the online DVD subscription service, stocks over 55,000 DVDs—one of the most appealing aspects of its business model. Paradoxically, the company doesn't own a large inventory of DVDs. Instead, it has revenue-sharing agreements with a number of studios and distributors that provide DVDs in exchange for a share of the subscription revenue. Similarly, eBags, an online retailer of name-brand bags and similar items, sells over 300 brands and 18,000 products, including backpacks, suitcases, wallets, and MP3/iPod cases. The company, however, stocks very little of what it sells. When it receives an order, it is electronically transmitted to the manufacturer or the distributor of the product, who ships the item directly to the purchaser through a process called "drop shipping," as explained in Chapter 11. The product is even shipped in boxes with the eBags logo. This approach lets eBags offer a huge selection of products without the cost and risk of maintaining a large inventory. "It's probably one of the most important reasons why we survived," says eBags cofounder Peter Cobb.

Other firms have been equally creative in finding ways to minimize the amount of assets they need to grow their operations. For example, the reservation agents for airlines JetBlue and Midwest Air work out of their homes instead of in company facilities. This allows JetBlue and Midwest Air to avoid the cost of building, purchasing, or leasing office space for these employees. Sometimes the insights into how to minimize expenses come more by accident than by deliberate planning. For example, in the mid-1990s, Cisco Systems started using an Internet-based system that provided its customers the opportunity to post technical problems and questions for the Cisco tech staff to answer. What the company didn't expect was that as soon as the posting capability was made available, its customers started responding to each other's questions. A single posting would often prompt several suggestions, solutions, and work-arounds without ever involving a Cisco engineer. As a result of this phenomenon, Cisco was able to get through its explosive growth years without significantly bolstering its call center staff. In fact, if it weren't for this site, a Cisco executive once determined, the company would have had to hire up to 10,000 engineers to maintain pace with answering the volume of questions that its customers answered for each other. Similarly, eBay doesn't have to hire a staff of people to monitor the performance of its buyers and sellers. Buyers and sellers rate each other, and the cumulative ratings are posted on eBay's Web site.

Entrepreneurial firms also do a large amount of outsourcing, in part to reduce the amount of staff and assets they have to maintain. Outsourcing is work done by someone other than a firm's full-time employees. The most common activities that are outsourced are administrative activities, such as payroll and benefits management, and internal operations, such as building maintenance and information technology services. Most companies outsource to save money, free up time to focus on the core competencies of the firm, and gain access to technical expertise. Although a controversial practice in the United States, largely because many jobs are being outsourced to companies in other nations, outsourcing can contribute to an entrepreneurial firm's success, especially during its infancy. As illustrated in Case 8.1, a firm must be careful that outsourcing does not erode customer satisfaction.

Finally, firms reduce the amount of assets they need through alliances and other types of partnerships. By partnering with a larger firm, a smaller firm can in effect co-opt a portion of the larger firm's resources and managerial expertise. An example is Pixar's former alliance with Disney. At the time Pixar made *Toy Story* (its first full-length animated film), it needed money to finance production costs. Disney provided the money for the production of *Toy Story* in exchange for a percentage of the profits. Although Disney acquired Pixar in 2006, the partnership played an important role in Pixar's success during the 1990s. Similar arrangements are common in the biotech industry. In fact, the vast majority of biotech firms would never be able to fund the years of research and development it takes to develop a new drug without access to the financial resources of large drug companies through revenue-sharing agreements.

The Results

Firms in all industries can often benefit as much by managing their assets as they do by managing their liabilities.

Discussion Questions

1. Describe the items that receive the most scrutiny on the left side and the right side of a firm's balance sheet. In regard to each of these items, what are the most important factors that a new venture should focus on to maintain its overall financial health?

2. Make a list of the advantages and disadvantages of Netflix's strategy of avoiding the cost of owning DVDs through revenue-sharing agreements with major studios and distributorships.

3. What are the potential downsides of eBag's strategy of acting strictly as a storefront and allowing the

manufacturers and distributors of the products it sells to ship the products to its customers?

4. What are the potential downsides of outsourcing as a way of cutting costs?

Application Questions

1. Make a list of the ways that the firms mentioned in the case have saved money by minimizing the amount of assets they need to produce revenues or maintain customer satisfaction. Next to each item in your list, briefly comment on how important this item is to the overall competitive advantage of the firm.

2. The "You Be the VC 1" feature focuses on H2OAudio, a company that provides people who enjoy water sports the ability to listen to their iPod and other MP3 players when in the water. Make a list of the ways in which H2OAudio can improve its financial position by carefully managing the "left side" of its balance sheet.

Sources: eBag's homepage, www.ebags.com (accessed August 26, 2006); Netflix 10-K Report to the Securities and Exchange Commission, filed May 16, 2006; T. Abate, *The Biotech Investor* (New York: Times Books, 2004); D. Bunnell, *Making the Cisco Connection* (New York: John Wiley & Sons, 2000).

Endnotes

1. Personal Interview with Del Segura, July 26, 2006.
2. Caroline Politz, "Deflexion: Success Brewed Right Here at Tulane," *tulanehullaboloo* (A Tulane University Publication) 96, no. 3 (March 11, 2005).
3. L. Gard, "Tales From the 2005 Toy Fair," *BusinessWeek*, February 25, 2005.
4. P. G. Bergeron, *Finance: Essentials for the Successful Professional* (New York: South-Western, 2002).
5. J. A. Tracey, *The Fast Forward MBA in Finance* (New York: John Wiley & Sons, 2002).
6. J. A. Tracy, *How To Manage Profit and Cash Flow* (New York: John Wiley & Sons, 2004).
7. R. Stutely, *The Definitive Guide to Managing the Numbers* (New York: Financial Times Prentice Hall, 2003).
8. J. H. Gittell, *The Southwest Airlines Way* (New York: McGraw-Hill, 2003), 7.
9. M. J. Lane, *Advising Entrepreneurs* (New York: John Wiley & Sons, 2001).
10. D. E. Vance, *Financial Analysis and Decision Making* (New York: McGraw-Hill, 2003).
11. B. Gates, *Business @ the Speed of Thought* (New York: Time Warner, 1999), 214.
12. SEC homepage, www.sec.gov (accessed July 22, 2006).
13. J. C. Leach, *Entrepreneurial Finance* (Mason, OH: Thomson Higher Education, 2006).
14. J. K. Shim, *Dictionary of Business Terms* (Mason, OH: Thomson Higher Education, 2006).
15. J. C. Leach, *Entrepreneurial Finance*.
16. A. Damodaran, *Applied Corporate Finance* (New York: John Wiley & Sons, 2006).
17. A. K. Arrow, "Managing IP Financial Assets," in *From Ideas to Assets*, ed. B. Berman (New York: John Wiley & Sons, 2002), 111–37.
18. W. Lasher, *The Perfect Business Plan Made Simple* (New York, Broadway Books, 2005).
19. R. Stutely, *The Definitive Guide to Managing the Numbers* (New York: Financial Times Prentice Hall, 2003).
20. R. Reider and P. B. Heyler, *Managing Cash Flow: An Operational Focus* (Hoboken, NJ: John Wiley & Sons, 2003).
21. D. R. Anderson, D. J. Sweeney, and T. A. Williams, *Statistics for Business and Economics*, 9th ed. (Mason, OH: South-Western College Publishing, 2005).
22. E. F. Brigham and J. F. Houston, *Fundamentals of Financial Management,* 11th ed. (Cincinnati: South-Western College Publishing, 2006).
23. A. Damodaran, *Applied Corporate Finance* (New York: John Wiley & Sons, 2006).
24. J. C. Leach, *Entrepreneurial Finance* (Mason, OH: Thomson Higher Education, 2006).

building a *new-venture* team

Currently in my iPod

K.T. Tunstall

**Importance of insanely
good salespeople**

**My biggest surprise as an
entrepreneur**

**What I'd like to be doing in
10 years**

*Opening dozens of stores
nationwide each year*

Spark Craft Studios:
Hitting the Ground Running

Spark Craft Studios is the creation of Jan Stephenson and Amy Appleyard. The two met in 2002 during the first year of their MBA program at Boston University and then got better acquainted when they worked on a project together the second year. The project, which was part of a social entrepreneurship class, required Stephenson and Appleyard, along with another classmate, to develop a business plan for a company that would be for-profit but also have redeeming social value.[1] Stephenson is pictured to the left and Appleyard to the right in the photograph accompanying this Opening Profile.

The idea the group developed was to create a studio where young, cosmopolitan women could engage in crafts such as knitting, crocheting, and jewelry making in a comfortable and uplifting setting where they could socialize and network with one another. The price point, per visit, would be in the $30 range. The idea was to create an upscale setting where women could sip wine and socialize while working on crafts. As part of their plan, Stephenson and Appleyard pointed toward trends indicating that women were showing a renewed interest in this type of activity. The trends also showed there was a gap in the marketplace that they could fill. Although stores like Michael's and Jo-Ann's sold crafts, they weren't targeting younger women and weren't focused on the socializing and networking aspects of making crafts. In addition, most craft stores, Stephenson and Appleyard observed, are retailers first and offer classes second. They planned to flip that set of priorities by making classes and socializing the most important part of the Spark Craft Studios' offering.

Both Stephenson and Appleyard had careers before they entered the Boston University MBA program. Appleyard had worked as a theatrical lighting designer with a variety of companies across the United States, and Stephenson was a fund-raiser for a large non-profit organization. They both saw themselves remaining in traditional careers after they graduated. However, the business plan they wrote for Spark Craft Studios changed their perspectives. Recalling this pivotal time in her life, Appleyard said to Ladies Who Launch, a Web site dedicated to supporting female entrepreneurs:

JAN STEPHENSON

Cofounder, Spark Craft Studios
MBA, Boston University, 2004

AMY APPLEYARD

Cofounder, Spark Craft Studios
MBA, Boston University, 2004

Best part of being a student

Learning from my peers

My advice for new entrepreneurs

Stay the course, but be flexible

What I do when I'm not working

Make jewelry or spend time outdoors

As we started to develop the idea for Spark Craft Studios, we realized this was a once-in-a-lifetime opportunity. So we decided to go for it. While most of our friends were settling into potential careers, we realized we were going to make (Spark Craft Studios) happen.[2]

Their complementary experiences and skills were a key motivator for Stephenson and Appleyard to launch their business together. Stephenson was strong in marketing, planning, public relations, and sales, while Appleyard was strong in finance and accounting. From the outset, the two have also relied on advice from others. At the end of the social entrepreneurship class where they became better acquainted, they presented their business plan for Spark Craft Studios to a group of judges. Two of the judges, who were angel investors, took an interest in their plan and later invested. They were also quick to hire an attorney and an accountant to provide professional services and give them advice about their entrepreneurial venture. Although the company doesn't have a formal board of advisers, that is something Stephenson and Appleyard are considering. Stephenson is currently the CEO of the company while Appleyard is the COO.

To prepare for their formal opening, Stephenson and Appleyard drew on their personal acquaintances and network of advisers to put together an initial list of potential clientele. When they opened their doors in January 2005, they had over 500 names on the list. Since then, the business has grown at a measured pace. To expand Spark Craft Studio's sphere of influence, one thing Stephenson and Appleyard have done is partner with well-established organizations, like the Boston Young Professionals Association and the Harvard Business School Partners Group. These organizations bring in large groups of customers while providing valuable feedback regarding how Spark Craft Studios can improve its offerings.

Spark Craft Studios, which now has over 6,000 customers, is poised to grow and expand beyond its original location. This will require key hires and an expansion of the firm's new-venture team. Stephenson and Appleyard are also considering franchising as an option for growing the business. When asked by Ladies Who Launch to give advice about picking a partner, which is the beginning of any business started by two or more people, Appleyard responded in the following manner:

Find a business partner who may or may not be a friend. Jan and I partnered on this venture because we have complementary skills. It's an added bonus that we have also become really good friends in the process.[3]

In this chapter, we'll focus on how the founders of an entrepreneurial venture build a new-venture team as well as the importance of the team to the firm's overall success. A **new-venture team** is the group of founders, key employees, and advisers that move a new venture from an idea to a fully functioning firm. Usually, the team doesn't come together all at once. Instead, it is built as the new firm can afford to hire additional personnel. The team also involves more than paid employees. Many firms have a board of directors, a board of advisers, and other professionals on whom they rely for direction and advice.

In this chapter's first section, we discuss the role of an entrepreneurial venture's founder or founders and emphasize the substantial effect that founders have on their firm's future. We then turn our attention to a discussion about how the founders build a new-venture team, including the recruitment and selection of key employees and the forming of a board of directors. The chapter's second section examines the important role of advisers and other professionals in shaping and rounding out a new-venture team.

As we note throughout this book, new ventures have a high propensity to fail. The high failure rate is due in part to what is known as the **liability of newness**, which refers to the fact that companies often falter because the people who start them aren't able to adjust quickly enough to their new roles and because the firm lacks a "track record" with outside buyers and suppliers.[4] Assembling a talented and experienced new-venture team is one path firms can take to overcome these limitations. Indeed, experienced management teams that get up to speed quickly are much less likely to make a novice's mistakes. In addition, firms able to persuade high-quality individuals to join them as directors or advisers quickly gain legitimacy with a variety of individuals, such as some of those working inside the venture as well as some people outside the venture (e.g., suppliers, customers, and investors). In turn, legitimacy opens doors that otherwise would be closed.

Another way entrepreneurs overcome the liability of newness is by attending entrepreneurship-focused workshops, speaker series, boot camps and similar events. These types of activities are often sponsored by local universities, small business development centers, and economic development commissions. Attending events such as these can yield unexpected positive results, as illustrated in this chapter's "Partnering for Success" boxed feature.

Creating a New-Venture Team

Those who launch or found an entrepreneurial venture have an important role to play in shaping the firm's business concept. Stated even more directly, it is widely known that a well-conceived business plan cannot get off the ground unless a firm has the leaders and personnel to carry it out. As one expert put it, "People are the one factor in production . . . that animates all the others."[5] Often, several start-ups develop what is essentially the same idea at the same time. When this happens, the key to success is not the idea but rather the ability of the initial founder or founders to assemble a team that can execute the idea better than anyone else.

The way a founder builds a new-venture team sends an important signal to potential investors, partners, and employees. Some founders like the feeling of control and are reluctant to involve themselves with partners or hire managers who are more experienced than they are. In contrast, other founders are keenly aware of their own limitations and work hard to find the most experienced people available to bring on board. Similarly, some new firms never form an advisory board, whereas others persuade the most important (and influential) people they can find to provide them with counsel and advice. In general, the way to impress potential investors, partners, and employees is to put together as strong a team as possible.[6] Investors and others know that experienced personnel and access to good-quality advice contributes greatly to a new venture's success.

The elements of a new-venture team are shown in Figure 9.1. We'll look at each of these elements in the next section. While reading these descriptions, remember that entrepreneurial ventures vary in how they use the elements.

The Founder or Founders

A founder's or founders' characteristics and their early decisions have a significant effect on the way an entrepreneurial venture is received and the manner in which the new-venture team takes shape. The size of the founding team and the qualities of the founder or founders are the two most important issues in this matter.

Size of the Founding Team The first decision that most founders face is whether to start a firm on their own or whether to build an initial **founding team**. Studies show that more than one individual starts 50 to 70 percent of all new firms.[7] It is generally believed that new ventures started by a team have an advantage over those started by an individual because a team brings more talent, resources, ideas, and professional contacts to a new venture than does a sole entrepreneur.[8] In addition, the psychological support that cofounders of a new business can offer one another is an important element in the firm's success.[9] Srivats Sampath, the founder of McAfee.com and a serial entrepreneur, uses a

1. Identify the primary elements of a new-venture team.

2. Explain the term *liabilities of newness*.

partnering for *success*

How Attending an Entrepreneurship Boot Camp Netted One Aspiring Entrepreneur Funding and a Business Partner

www.helixfiber.com

Two of the most consistent themes that appear in books and magazines about entrepreneurship are the importance of education and networking. It is also extremely beneficial for new or aspiring entrepreneurs to spend time with individuals who have started one or more successful firms. One format that is used to expose new or aspiring entrepreneurs to these types of activities is an entrepreneurship boot camp. A boot camp is an immersion experience, where a group of people come together to learn basic skills quickly. Various groups sponsor entrepreneurship boot camps throughout the United States, where the participants spend one to several days studying all the aspects of the entrepreneurial process.

Luke Pinkerton, who has a master's degree in engineering from the University of Michigan and an MBA from Georgia Tech, was working on a business idea in the summer of 2003 when he decided to attend an entrepreneurship boot camp at the University of Michigan. His idea, which he was working on with a former professor at Michigan, was to put small twisted pieces of wire into concrete mix to strengthen the concrete for use in blast-resistant and earthquake-resistant structures. The boot camp was a week-long activity and was sponsored by the Tech Transfer Office at the University of Michigan. As part of the activities, each participant was matched with a mentor who was to shepherd the mentoree through the program and react to their business ideas. Pinkerton was matched with Bill Orabone, an experienced entrepreneur. According to Pinkerton, when Orabone first heard his idea to use small pieces of twisted wire to strengthen concrete, he "told me I was crazy for three hours." But then, as Pinkerton recalls, a funny thing happened. The next day Orabone returned with suggestions for how to improve the idea. During the remainder of the boot camp, the two engaged in a number of heated discussions about the viability of Pinkerton's idea.

Pinkerton and Orabone continued their discussions following the boot camp. Something clicked, and they eventually formed a partnership to bring the product to market. The company the two founded, Helix, is now manufacturing the product and is shipping it throughout the upper Midwest. Orabone invested in the company and is now the company's CEO while Pinkerton is the CTO (chief technology officer).

Questions for Critical Thinking

1. Do you think Pinkerton and Orabone would have ever found each other if Pinkerton hadn't attended the boot camp? If you are an aspiring entrepreneur, what lessons can be learned from Pinkerton's experience about the importance of attending entrepreneurship-related educational and networking events?

2. What advantages did Pinkerton experience by maintaining his ties with the University of Michigan? If you were to launch an entrepreneurial venture, do you anticipate maintaining an ongoing relationship with your college or university? In what ways do you think maintaining a relationship with your college or university can benefit both you (personally) and your new firm?

3. Look at Helix's Web site at the address shown at the beginning of this feature. Briefly report on the progress that Helix has made since this feature was written. Are both Pinkerton and Orabone still with the firm? Have their roles changed in any substantive ways?

4. When Pinkerton enrolled in the boot camp offered at the University of Michigan, he was planning to start Helix on his own. In what ways has Pinkerton reduced the liabilities of newness for his new firm by attending the boot camp? How important are these reductions to Helix's future success?

Source: Personal Interview with Luke Pinkerton, July 14, 2006.

---

military metaphor to explain the advantage of starting with a team of people who already trust one another:

Starting and building a company is like going into battle—and I always prefer to go into battle with a team that is loyal to one another and to the cause. At Mercora [Sampath's

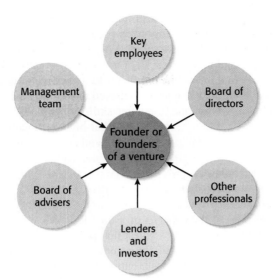

FIGURE 9.1

**Elements of a
New-Venture Team**

latest start-up] most of us have worked together for 6 to 10 years, and the trust and loyalty we have for one another makes an extremely difficult task enjoyable.[10]

Several factors affect the value of a team that is starting a new firm. First, teams that have worked together before, as opposed to teams that are working together for the first time, have an edge. If people have worked together before and have decided to partner to start a firm together, it usually means that they get along personally and trust one another.[11] They also tend to communicate with one another more effectively than people who are new to one another.[12] Second, if the members of the team are **heterogeneous**, meaning that they are diverse in terms of their abilities and experiences, rather than **homogeneous**, meaning that their areas of expertise are very similar to one another, they are likely to have different points of view about technology, hiring decisions, competitive tactics, and other important activities. Typically, these different points of view generate debate and constructive conflict among the founders, reducing the likelihood that decisions will be made in haste or without the airing of alternative points of view.[13] A founding team can be too big, causing communication problems and an increased potential for conflict. A founding team larger than four people is typically too large to be practical.[14]

3. Discuss the difference between heterogeneous and homogeneous founding teams.

There are two potential pitfalls associated with starting a firm as a team rather than as a sole entrepreneur. First, the team members may not get along. This is the reason investors favor teams consisting of people who have worked together before. It is simply more likely that people who have gotten along with one another in the past will continue to get along in the future. Second, if two or more people start a firm as "equals," conflicts can arise when the firm needs to establish a formal structure and designate one person as the chief executive officer (CEO). If the firm has investors, the investors will usually weigh in on who should be appointed CEO. In these instances, it is easy for the founder that wasn't chosen as the CEO to feel slighted. This problem is exacerbated if multiple founders are involved and they all stay with the firm. At some point, a hierarchy will have to be developed, and the founders will have to decide who reports to whom. Some of these problems can be avoided through the development of a founder's agreement, which was described in Chapter 7.

Qualities of the Founders The second major issue pertaining to the founders of a firm is the qualities they bring to the table. The past several chapters have illustrated the importance that investors and others place on the strength of the firm's founders and initial management team. One reason the founders are so important is that in the early days of a firm, their knowledge, skills, and experiences are the most valuable resource the firm has. Because of this, new firms are judged largely on their "potential" rather than their current assets or current performance. In most cases, this results in people judging the future prospects of a firm by evaluating the strength of its founders and initial management team.

Several features are thought to be significant to a founder's success. The level of a founder's education is important because it's believed that entrepreneurial abilities such as search skills, foresight, creativity, and computer skills are enhanced through obtaining a college degree. Similarly, some observers think that higher education equips a founder with important business-related skills, such as math and communications. In addition, specific forms of education, such as engineering, computer science, management information systems, physics, and biochemistry, provide the recipients of this education an advantage if they start a firm that is related to their area of expertise.[15]

Prior entrepreneurial experience, relevant industry experience, and networking are other attributes that strengthen the chances of a founder's success. Indeed, the results of research studies somewhat consistently suggest that **prior entrepreneurial experience** is one of the most consistent predictors of future entrepreneurial performance.[16] Because launching a new venture is a complex task, entrepreneurs with prior start-up experience have a distinct advantage. The impact of **relevant industry experience** on an entrepreneur's ability to successfully launch and grow a firm has also been studied, as illustrated in the feature on Garden.com titled "What Went Wrong?"[17] Entrepreneurs with experience in the same industry as their current venture, which wasn't the case with the founders of Garden.com, will have a more mature network of industry contacts and will have a better understanding of the subtleties of their respective industries.[18] The importance of this factor is particularly evident for entrepreneurs who start firms in technical industries such as biotechnology. The demands of biotechnology are sufficiently intense that it would be virtually impossible for someone to start a biotech firm while at the same time learning biotechnology. The person must have an understanding of biotechnology prior to launching a firm through either relevant industry experience or an academic background.

A particularly important attribute for founders or founding teams is the presence of a mature network of social and professional contacts.[19] Founders must often "work" their social and personal networks to raise money or gain access to critical resources on behalf of their firms.[20] **Networking** is building and maintaining relationships with people whose interests are similar or whose relationship could bring advantages to a firm. The way this

what went wrong?

Garden.com: Why Experience Counts

Launching a new venture is a complex task. Research shows that founders with experience in the industry in which they are starting a firm have a distinct advantage. There is no better story illustrating the importance of this point than Garden.com. Let's see what happened to this entrepreneurial venture as it was launched.

In May 1995, three new MBAs, Cliff Sharples, Lisa Sharples, and Jamie O'Neill, each in their early 30s, met in one of their homes. They were all working for Trilogy, a software firm in Austin, Texas. They wanted to start a

company together but didn't know what to do. Though none of them had any experience in garden retailing, they picked the gardening industry and decided to launch a gardening e-commerce site: Garden.com. At that time, Amazon.com and Yahoo! were new, and there was a huge buzz about the Internet's capabilities to deliver value to customers in a virtually endless array of products and services. The $50-billion gardening industry was fragmented, and no one was selling gardening supplies on the Internet. Seizing on what the founders thought was a golden opportunity, Garden.com was formed to offer a way for gardeners to purchase plants and supplies online. The company launched its Web site in March 1996. Over the next 4 years, as the dot-com bubble expanded, Garden.com raised over $50 million in funding. Soon, in addition to gardening supplies, it was selling a range of other products, such as furniture, candles, cookware, soap, tea, perfume, and Christmas ornaments. In September 1999, the company went public. Two years later, it was out of business. What went wrong?

Well, several things. First, its business model may have been fundamentally flawed. Garden.com's only means of attracting customers to its Web site was advertising, which made it extremely expensive to get people to look at its offerings. In fact, the company spent 56.7 percent of the money it raised through its initial public offering on various forms of advertising, including glossy catalogs and full-page magazine advertisements. Commenting on Garden.com's high customer acquisition costs, John Thornton, a member of the company's board of directors, later said, "They [Garden.com's management team] did not understand what it would cost to attract the traffic." Second, the Internet bubble burst in early 2000, making it impossible for Garden.com to raise additional funds. Because the company wasn't even close to being profitable (it lost $19 million in its fiscal year that ended June 30, 1999), it couldn't continue without raising money. The company's plan was to drive costs down and increase revenues to the point where it was profitable and wouldn't need any more investment capital, which it felt it was within 2 years of achieving. But after the Internet bubble burst, investors closed their checkbooks. This series of events left the company with no way to continue financially.

Third, the entrepreneurs behind Garden.com had no background in gardening or retailing and had no prior entrepreneurial experience. Although it's hard to know how much difference this made, it is a point worth serious consideration. For example, after studying the demise of Garden.com for a book titled *Buy, Lie, and Sell High: How Investors Lost Out on Enron and the Internet Bubble*, D. Quinn Mills, a Harvard Business School professor, wrote,

> Gardeners for this book observed that the Garden.com *Web site was difficult to use, and offered the opinion that the people running the company seemed to know little or nothing about gardening.*

In making his own assessment, Professor Mills observed that Garden.com's business premise hinged not on gardening products but on trying to introduce a new way for people to buy gardening products and supplies. Yet its founders didn't have any background in the gardening industry or have any prior knowledge about customer behavior as it relates to gardening products. The traditional criterion that investors use when funding a venture is that the founders have some experience in the area in which they are working or at least related experience. In the excitement that surrounded the Internet bubble, this criterion wasn't applied in the case of Garden.com. Garden.com's failure is indeed a vivid reminder of the importance of relevant industry experience for those launching an entrepreneurial venture.

Questions for Critical Thinking

1. Based on information contained in this feature, would you classify Cliff Sharples, Lisa Sharples, and Jamie O'Neill as a homogeneous founding team or as a heterogeneous founding team? Given your choice, how do you believe the founding team's diversity or lack of diversity affected the firm's ability to succeed?

2. In your opinion, is it possible for entrepreneurs to overcome the problems that surface when they lack experience in the industry in which they intend to launch a new venture? Even more particularly, what could Garden.com's three entrepreneurs have done to reduce the negative effect their lack of industry experience created for their venture?

3. Is there any evidence in the feature that the founders of Garden.com took steps to overcome the liabilities of newness that often affect new ventures? If not, what steps could the founders of Garden.com have taken to address this issue?

4. Refer to the "Partnering for Success" feature that appeared earlier in the chapter. Contrast the founding team for Helix, the company referred to in the feature, with the founding team of Garden.com. Do you think Helix had a better chance of succeeding from the beginning than Garden.com did? If so, why?

Sources: D. Q. Mills, *Buy, Lie and Sell High: How Investors Lost Out on Enron and the Internet Bubble* (Upper Saddle River, NJ: Prentice Hall, 2002) and "Wilted," *Texas Monthly*, February 1, 2001.

TABLE 9.1 Preferred Attributes of the Founder or Founders of an Entrepreneurial Venture

Attribute	Explanation
Firm started by a team	New ventures that are started by a team can provide greater resources, a broader diversity of viewpoints, and a broader array of items than ventures started by individuals.
Higher education	Evidence suggests that important entrepreneurial skills are enhanced through higher education.
Prior entrepreneurial experience	Founders with prior entrepreneurial experience are familiar with the entrepreneurial process and are more likely to avoid costly mistakes than founders new to the rigors of the entrepreneurial process.
Relevant industry experience	Founders with experience in the same industry as their new venture will most likely have better-established professional networks and more applicable marketing and management expertise than founders without relevant industry experience.
Broad social and professional network	Founders with broad social and professional networks have potential access to additional know-how, capital, and customer referrals.

might play out in practice is that a founder calls a business acquaintance or friend to ask for an introduction to a potential investor, business partner, or customer. For some founders, networking is easy and is an important part of their daily routine. For others, it is a learned skill.

Table 9.1 shows the preferred attributes of the founder or founders of a firm. Start-ups that have founders or a team of founders with these attributes have the best chances of early success.

Recruiting and Selecting Key Employees

Once the decision to launch a new venture has been made, building a management team and hiring key employees begins. Start-ups vary in terms of how quickly they need to add personnel. In some instances, the founders work alone for a period of time while the business plan is being written and the venture begins taking shape. In other instances, employees are hired immediately. However, evidence suggests that finding good employees today is not an easy task. Consider the results of a recent survey by PricewaterhouseCoopers as evidence of this. In the PWC survey, the CEOs of 312 rapid-growth firms were asked if finding qualified workers was a concern. A total of 49 percent of the CEOs reported that a lack of qualified workers is a potential barrier to growth for their firms over the next 12 months.[21] A study conducted by the Council for Entrepreneurial Development, which is an organization that supports entrepreneurship in the Research Triangle area of North Carolina, resulted in a similar finding. When asked to rank the key factors in growing a firm, entrepreneurs in the Research Triangle area selected "Availability of Qualified Technical and Non-Technical Workers" as the no. 1 factor.[22]

5. Explain an executive-search firm's actions.

Founders differ in their approach to the task of recruiting and selecting key employees. Some founders draw on their network of contacts to identify candidates for key positions; others use executive-search firms. An **executive-search firm** is a company that specializes in helping other companies recruit and select key personnel. There are two reasons a new venture might take this route. First, the process of recruiting and screening job candidates is time-consuming, reducing the amount of time founders have to spend on other important tasks. Second, the initial hires that new ventures make are often critical to their eventual success. For example, some founders may decide to hire a CEO rather than give this position to one of the founding members and may need someone with a unique set of attributes and skills. It may take the experience and network of contacts of an executive-search firm to find the right candidate.

Many founders worry about hiring the wrong person for a key role. Because most new firms are strapped for cash, every team member must make a valuable contribution, so it's not good enough to hire someone who is well intended but who doesn't precisely fit the

Pierre Omidyar, the founder of eBay, wasn't reluctant to hire Meg Whitman, a seasoned executive, to take the reigns of the company in 1998, just 3 years after it was founded. Omidyar recognized that eBay was entering a rapid-growth phase and wanted the day-to-day operations of the company to be run by an experienced hand. With Whitman on board, Omidyar turned his attention to the company's strategic direction and its community of users.

job. Alisa Nessler, the founder of Lane15, a software start-up, emphasizes this point in the following remarks:

> One of the first things you learn in a start-up is that it's very expensive to make a bad hire. In a large company, people sometimes tend to think that when you have somebody who fits into the bucket labeled "Heart's in the right place," or the one labeled "Good attitude but just not getting it done," you can work around it. Maybe it's because in an established organization, it's easier to lose sight of the contributions each individual is making. In a start-up, you simply can't do that. Everyone is important. Every team member's work has to have a direct impact on value, or the person has to go.[23]

On some occasions, key hires work out perfectly and fill the exact roles that the founders of the firm need. For example, Dave Olsen was one of the first hires made by Starbucks founder Howard Schultz. At the time of his hiring, Olsen was the owner of a popular coffeehouse in the university district of Seattle, the city where Starbucks was launched. In his autobiography, Schultz recalls the following about the hiring of Olsen:

> On the day of our meeting, Dave and I sat on my office floor and I started spreading the plans and blueprints out and talking about my idea. Dave got it right away. He had spent ten years in an apron, behind a counter, serving espresso drinks. He had experienced firsthand the excitement people can develop about espresso, both in his café and in Italy. I didn't have to convince him that this idea had big potential. He just knew it in his bones. The synergy was too good to be true. My strength was looking outward: communicating the vision, inspiring investors, raising money, finding real estate, designing the stores, building the brand, and planning for the future. Dave understood the inner workings: the nuts and bolts of operating a retail café, hiring and training baristas (coffee brewers), ensuring the best quality coffee.[24]

Dave Olsen went on to become a key member of the Starbucks new-venture team and remains with the company today, where he serves as the senior vice president for culture and leadership development.

Some founders develop a formal hiring plan; others approach the task more informally and hire personnel as funds become available and opportunities emerge. One attribute investors value in founders is a willingness to be flexible and assume the role that makes the most sense for them in their venture rather than insisting on being the CEO. This is a difficult task for some founders who become entrepreneurs to "be their own boss" or put their distinctive stamp on a firm. Founders who do remain flexible, however, often have an easier time obtaining financing or funding. The way many founders look at this issue is that it is better to be the vice president of a $100-million firm than the CEO of a $10-million firm. An example of a group of founders who decided at the outset to hire an outside CEO is provided in Case 9.2 in this chapter.

The Roles of the Board of Directors

L E A R N I N G

Objective

6. Describe a board of directors and explain the difference between inside directors and outside directors.

If a new venture organizes as a corporation, it is legally required to have a **board of directors**—a panel of individuals who are elected by a corporation's shareholders to oversee the management of the firm.[25] A board is typically made up of both inside and outside directors. An **inside director** is a person who is also an officer of the firm. An **outside director** is someone who is not employed by the firm. A board of directors has three formal responsibilities: (1) appoint the firm's officers (the key managers), (2) declare dividends, and (3) oversee the affairs of the corporation. In the wake of corporate scandals such as Enron and WorldCom and others, the emphasis on the board's role in making sure the firm is operating in an ethical manner continues to become stronger. One outcome of this movement is a trend toward putting more outsiders on boards of directors, because people who do not work for the firm are usually more willing to scrutinize the behavior of management than insiders who work for the company. Most boards meet formally three or four times a year. Large firms pay their directors for their service. New ventures are more likely to pay their directors in company stock or ask them to serve without direct compensation—at least until the company is profitable. The boards for publicly traded companies are required by law to have audit and compensation committees. Many boards also have nominating committees to select stockholders to run for vacant board positions.

If handled properly, a company's board of directors can be an important part of its new-venture team. Providing expert guidance and legitimacy in the eyes of others (e.g., customers, investors, and even competitors) are two ways a board of directors can help a new firm get off to a good start and develop what, it is hoped, will become a sustainable competitive advantage.

L E A R N I N G

Objective

7. Identify the two primary ways in which the nonemployee members of a start-up's new-venture team help the firm.

Provide Guidance Although a board of directors has formal governance responsibilities, its most useful role is to provide guidance and support to the firm's managers.[26] Many CEOs interact with their board members frequently and obtain important input. The key to making this happen is to pick board members with needed skills and useful experiences who are willing to give advice and ask insightful and probing questions. An illustration of what can happen when a board functions in this way is provided by Sam Eichenfield, the CEO of the FINOVA Group:

> An effective board is one that is available to me and other members of the management team when we have questions that their expertise could assist in. Also, when we contemplate certain kinds of strategic activities, I want them to be available for consultation. . . . I also value the questions the board asks. We're in the finance business, but our board members are from manufacturing, insurance, academia. Very often their questions will open our eyes to a different way of looking at things.[27]

Because managers rely on board members for counsel and advice, the search for outside directors should be purposeful, with the objective of filling gaps in the experience and background of the venture's executives and the other directors. For example, if two computer programmers started a software firm and neither one of them had any marketing experience, it would make sense to place a marketing executive on the board of directors. Indeed, a board of directors has the foundation to effectively serve its organization when its members represent many important organizational skills (e.g., manufacturing, human resource management, and financing) involved with running a company. Sometimes companies error by not being thoughtful enough about the people they place on their boards. Bob Weissman, a former executive of several companies, makes this point in the following statement:

> Let's assume I am the CEO of Netscape and I'm dealing with the typical mix of business issues—changes in the marketplace, the competitive mix, changes in cost dynamics being driven externally. If I have on my board five experienced, intelligent people, all of whom have spent thirty years working in a slow-moving, regulated industry, they won't be able to help me much. Not that they're incompetent or disinterested. They just won't understand my market, my customers, or the dynamics of a highly fragmented and competitive marketplace simply because they have no experience with it.[28]

This complication can be avoided by carefully selecting board members who have experience in the areas in which the firm needs guidance and advice the most.

Lend Legitimacy Providing legitimacy for the entrepreneurial venture is another important function of a board of directors. Well-known and respected board members bring instant credibility to the firm. For example, just imagine the positive buzz a firm could generate if it could say that Eric Schmidt of Google or Steven Jobs of Apple had agreed to serve on its board of directors. This phenomenon is referred to as **signaling**. Without a credible signal, it is difficult for potential customers, investors, or employees to identify high-quality start-ups. Presumably, high-quality individuals would be reluctant to serve on the board of a low-quality firm because that would put their reputation at risk. So when a high-quality individual does agree to serve on a board of a firm, the individual is in essence "signaling" that the company has potential to be successful.[29]

Achieving legitimacy through high-quality board members can result in other positive outcomes. Investors like to see new-venture teams, including the board of directors that have people with enough clout to get their foot in the door with potential suppliers and customers. Board members are also often instrumental in helping young firms arrange financing or funding. As we will discuss in Chapter 10, it's almost impossible for an entrepreneurial venture's founders to get the attention of an investor without a personal

8. Describe the concept of signaling and explain it's importance.

Entrepreneurs often meet with a member of their advisory board personally to obtain valuable business advice. With a carefully selected advisory board, entrepreneurs can tap into a wide range of experience and expertise.

TABLE 9.2 Guidelines for Forming an Effective Board of Directors

Guideline	Explanation
Aim high	Select directors with the following characteristics: • Experience running successful companies • Possessing competencies the new venture needs • Well known and respected in their fields
Composition	Select a board with the following characteristics: • Diversity • In tune with the technology and the markets in which the new venture will participate • Composed of both inside and outside directors
Establish ground rules pertaining to decisions	Establish the following ground rules: • Routine decisions to be handled by those leading and managing the venture • Significant personnel, operational, and financial decisions to be taken to the board for approval
Share information	Practice the following communication protocols: • Consistently update the board about the venture's activities • Do not blindside the board with bad news (one thing board members loathe is being blind-sided by unexpected bad news that has been withheld from them)
Use committees	Implement the following approach to committees: • Recognize that boards do their best work in committees • Maintain statutory committees, such as the audit, compensation, and nomination committees • Establish additional committees on an "as needed" basis
Motivate board members	Motivate board members to provide exemplary service through the following: • Some form of financial incentive, such as company stock or stock options • The opportunity to be part of an exciting new project
Address liability issues	Disclose to board members the following: • Advise members that they have a fiduciary duty to the new venture's shareholders • Verify that the members are aware of their points of potential liability • Make legal and accounting experts available to board members for counsel and advice

introduction. One way firms deal with this challenge is by placing individuals on their boards who are acquainted with people in the investment community.

Table 9.2 contains a list of guidelines for assembling an effective board of directors.

Rounding Out the Team: The Role of Professional Advisers

Along with the new-venture team members we've already identified, founders often rely on professionals with whom they interact for important counsel and advice. In many cases, these professionals become an important part of the new-venture team and fill what some entrepreneurs call "talent holes."

Next, we discuss the roles that boards of advisers, lenders, investors, and other professionals play in rounding out new-venture teams.

Board of Advisers

9. Discuss the purpose of forming an advisory board.

A growing number of start-ups are forming advisory boards to provide them direction and advice. An **advisory board** is a panel of experts who are asked by a firm's managers to provide counsel and advice on an ongoing basis. Unlike a board of directors, an advisory board possesses no legal responsibility for the firm and gives nonbinding advice.[30] An advisory board can be established for general purposes or can be set up to address a specific issue or need. For example, some firms have customer advisory boards specifically to help identify new product and service ideas. Other companies have advisory boards to help them enter international markets or deal with an emerging challenge, such as how to make better use of the Internet. Andrea Lyons, the founder of Goddess Granola, which is a natural-ingredients snack-food company, strongly believes that establishing an advisory board is important. Lyon's testimonial reflects both her satisfaction in setting up an advisory board and the type of advice that an advisory board can offer:

> One of the most important things I did was create a dynamo advisory board. It's about getting advice from people who have done what you want to do and who are ready to roll up their sleeves and help you. Some of my members include the founder of No Pudge! Brownies and the author of *The Idiot's Guide to Brand Management* and a leader who has worked within the nation's largest food brokerage for years. From them, I learned that I had to build a premium brand and take the crunch out of granola. I had to take it (the new line of granola snacks) to places it hadn't been before because you're not going to get decent margins from the grocery store.[31]

The fact that a venture has a board of directors does not preclude it from establishing one or more advisory boards. For example, Coolibar, a maker of sun proactive clothing, has a board of directors and a medical advisory board.[32] Similarly, Intouch Health, a medical robotics company, has a board of directors along with a business and strategy advisory board, an applications and clinical advisory board, and a scientific and technical advisory board.[33] Many people are more willing to serve on a company's board of advisers than on its board of directors because it requires less time and there is no potential legal liability involved. In this way, they can still provide a company's managers counsel and advice and can lend credibility to the firm.[34]

Boards of advisers interact with each other and with a firm's managers in several ways. Some advisory boards meet three or four times a year at the company's headquarters or in another location. Other advisory boards meet in an online environment. In some cases, a firm's board of advisers will be scattered across the country, making it more cost-effective for a firm's managers to interact with the members of the board on the telephone or via e-mail rather than to bring them physically together. In these situations, board members don't interact with each other at all on a face-to-face basis yet still provide high levels of counsel and advice.

Most boards of advisers have between 5 and 15 members. Companies typically pay the members of their board of advisers a small honorarium for their service either annually or on a per meeting basis.

Ugobe, the subject of the "You Be the VC 1" feature in this chapter, is a start-up that makes sophisticated robotic toys that relate to humans through a wide range of simulated emotions. Pleo, which is a 1-week-old long-neck dinosaur, is the venture's first robotic toy. Ugobe has a five-person advisory board that consists of the following members:

■ Steven Mayer—Co-founder, Atari Computer and Activision. Mayer has more than 30 years of experience in the computer, television, and electronic entertainment industries. For the past several years, he has been an adviser to Intel, Nintendo, and other companies regarding business and technical issues.

■ Curtis Sasaki—Vice President, Sun Microsystems. Sasaki's responsibilities at Sun include strategy, business development, content, and execution. Before joining Sun in 1996, Sasaki served in various senior management positions at General Magic, NeXT Computer and Apple Computer.

■ Phil Schlein—Partner, U.S. Venture Partners. Schlein joined U.S. Venture Partners in 1985 after a successful 28-year career as an operating executive in the retailing industry. Since joining U.S. Venture Partners, Schlein has originated a number of investments in the consumer/retail sector, including PETsMART, Fresh Choice, and The House of Blues.

■ Abraham Wei—Senior Managing Director, Chinavest Merchant Bank. In his current position, Wei has been actively working with high-technology firms. He has held a number of key executive management positions in publicly traded companies.

Additionally, he has been involved in several start-up companies that culminated in two successful IPOs and two successful mergers.

■ Bill Hillard—Managing Partner, Hillard Equities/Sonn-Hill Consulting. Hillard has grown four companies and/or corporate divisions to market-leading positions and profitability and has developed and launched OEM products in China, Japan, Korea, Taiwan, Europe, and the United States. Through Hillard Equities/Son-Hill Consulting, Hillard assists start-ups and emerging growth companies with risk capital, fund-raising, and management guidance.[35]

This example provides an illustration of the breadth of talent and expertise that a firm can have available when it creates a board of advisers. Imagine the combined network of friends and business acquaintances that Ugobe's board of advisers has and the number of referrals they can make to people who are in a position to help Ugobe become successful.

There are several guidelines to organizing a board of advisers. First, a board of advisers should not be organized just so a company can boast of it. Advisers will become quickly disillusioned if they don't play a meaningful role in the firm's development and growth. Second, a firm should look for board members who are compatible and complement one another in terms of experience and expertise. Unless the board is being set up for a specific purpose, a board that includes members with varying backgrounds is preferable to a board of people with similar backgrounds. Third, when inviting a person to serve on its board of advisers, a company should carefully spell out to the individual the rules in terms of access to confidential information.[36] Some firms ask the members of their advisory board to sign nondisclosure agreements, which are described in Chapter 7. Finally, firms should caution their advisers to disclose that they have a relationship with the venture before posting positive comments about it or its products on blogs or in Internet chat rooms. A potential conflict of interest surfaces when a person says positive things about a company without disclosing an affiliation with the firm, particularly if there is a financial stake in the company. This issue has become more important as participation in Internet blogging has skyrocketed.[37]

One of the biggest challenges in managing an advisory board is finding a time when all the board members can meet. To deal with this challenge, those leading entrepreneurial ventures must often find innovative ways to make it more convenient for the board members to meet. An example is using the Internet as a vehicle for getting board members together, as illustrated in this chapter's "Savvy Entrepreneurial Firm" feature.

Lenders and Investors

As emphasized throughout this book, lenders and investors have a vested interest in the companies they finance, often causing them to become very involved in helping the firms they fund. It is rare that a lender or investor will put money into a new venture and then simply step back and wait to see what happens. In fact, the institutional rules governing banks and investment firms typically require that they monitor new ventures fairly closely, at least during the initial years of a loan or an investment.[38]

The amount of time and energy a lender or investor dedicates to a new firm depends on the amount of money involved and how much help the new firm needs. For example, a lender with a well-secured loan may spend very little time with a client, whereas a venture capitalist may spend an enormous amount of time helping a new venture refine its business model, recruit management personnel, and meet with current and prospective customers and suppliers. In fact, evidence suggests that an average venture capitalist is likely to visit each company in a portfolio 19 times a year.[39] This number denotes a high level of involvement and support.

As with the other nonemployee members of a firm's new-venture team, lenders and investors help new firms by providing guidance and lending legitimacy and assume the natural role of providing financial oversight.[40] In some instances, lenders and investors also work hard to help new firms fill out their management teams. Sometimes this issue is

savvy entrepreneurial firm

Can't Get Your Advisory Board Together? Move the Meeting Online

Finding a place and time for a meeting that is convenient for all parties is one of the challenges in maintaining an active board of advisers. Because board members are volunteers and are usually either unpaid or paid a modest honorarium, it's not easy to ask them to travel long distances or take too much time from their schedules to meet. Conducting meetings online is one way to bring the board together and to avoid the issues associated with a face-to-face meeting. Some firms tried this approach early in the development of the Internet and were disappointed by the somewhat tacky appearance of the first generation of chat rooms and discussion boards. Fortunately, there are now extremely good collaboration software tools available that provide firms a number of options when conducting online meetings.

Facilitate.com, for example, is one of many companies selling software that helps firms conduct effective meetings using the Internet as a communication medium. Here are the details of what an advisory board meeting might look like using FacilitatePro, the company's latest iteration of collaboration software. This particular board is a customer advisory board that meets to brainstorm new product ideas and to discuss customer service issues. On the day of the meeting, the participants sign on to a designated Web site that combines a Web conferencing service and the collaboration software. To start the meeting, you propose an agenda. You can pick from a number of agenda templates or customize your own. The first item on the agenda might be, for example, to brainstorm new product ideas. Each board member is asked to contribute ideas that flow onto an electronic flip chart that everyone can see. The flip chart can identify the contributions by the participant's name or record the contributions anonymously. After a few minutes, you lead the group in a verbal discussion of the ideas and assign them to categories that are displayed in real time on everyone's screen. You now quickly change the flip chart to a ranking system and ask the group to rank the ideas according to profit potential and feasibility. The results are immediately shown in both numeric and graphic form. The real payoff from the meeting occurs in the final step, when a company official takes the recommendations provided and builds them into action plans with roles, responsibilities, and time lines.

The same type of approach is used to discuss customer service issues and to reach a consensus among the group on each of them. At the end of the meeting, each participant receives a complete set of meeting notes.

Questions for Critical Thinking

1. Imagine that you are a member of a board of advisers using Facilitate.com's software to conduct a meeting. How would you react to this type of experience? Do you feel that you could be effective using this technology? Why or why not?

2. Under what circumstances might it be best to record suggestions on the electronic flip charts in an anonymous manner rather than identifying the contribution by the participant's name? In what ways does the ability to record ideas and suggestions anonymously make online brainstorming potentially more effective than conducting brainstorming sessions in person?

3. Choose two or three entrepreneurial firms or start-up ventures in your local community. Set up a meeting with each firm's top manager. During the meeting, ask your contact person if the venture has established one or more board of advisers. If such boards have been formed, ask for feedback about how effective they've been for the venture. If such boards haven't been formed, ask why they haven't been established. Finally, ask all the managers to comment about their view of the effectiveness of having a board of advisers meet online to conduct business.

4. Suggest other ways that entrepreneurs can creatively network and communicate with their board of advisers.

Source: Facilitate.com homepage, www.Facilitate.com (accessed July 14, 2006).

so important that a new venture will try to obtain investment capital not only to get access to money but also to obtain help hiring key employees.

For example, during its beginning stages, eBay's partners, Pierre Omidyar and Jeff Skoll, decided to recruit a CEO. They wanted someone who was not only experienced but also had the types of credentials that Wall Street investors value. They soon discovered that every experienced manager they tried to recruit asked if they had venture capital backing— which at that time they did not. For a new firm trying to recruit a seasoned executive, venture capital backing is a sort of seal of legitimacy. To get this valuable seal, Omidyar and Skoll obtained funding from Benchmark Venture Capital, even though eBay didn't really need the money. Writer Randall Stross recalls this event as follows:

> eBay was an anomaly: a profitable company that was able to self-fund its growth and that turned to venture capital solely for contacts and counsel. No larger lesson can be drawn. When Benchmark wired the first millions to eBay's bank account, the figurative check was tossed into the vault—and there it would sit, unneeded and undisturbed.[41]

This strategy worked for eBay. Soon after affiliating with Benchmark, Bob Kagle, one of Benchmark's general partners, led eBay to Meg Whitman, an executive who had experience working for several top firms, including Procter & Gamble, Disney, and Hasbro. Meg Whitman remains eBay's chairman and CEO today.

Experienced investors can also assist new ventures in the hiring process by helping them structure compensation packages that are fair to both the firm and the new hires. An illustration of this advantage is provided by Alisa Nessler, CEO of Lane15, a firm backed by venture capital:

> If you're looking to recruit that all-important CEO, investors can be a particular boon. They know how much a CEO should earn, cash- and stock-wise. They can help you negotiate a package that fits your capital and equity structures, while also motivating the CEO to build a world-class company.[42]

Bankers also play a role in establishing the legitimacy of new ventures and their initial management teams. Research evidence rather consistently suggests that the presence of bank loans is a favorable signal to other capital providers.[43] Investors often take a seat on the boards of directors of the firms they fund to provide oversight and advice. It is less common for a banker to take a seat on the board of directors of an entrepreneurial venture, primarily because bankers provide operating capital rather than large amounts of investment capital to new firms.

There are additional ways that lenders and investors add value to a new firm beyond financing and funding. These roles are highlighted in Table 9.3.

Other Professionals

At times, other professionals assume important roles in a new venture's success. Attorneys, accountants, and business consultants are often good sources of counsel and advice. The role of lawyers in helping firms get off to a good start is discussed in Chapter 7, and the role of accountants is discussed in Chapter 8. So here, let's take a look at the role a consultant may play.

Consultants   A **consultant** is an individual who gives professional or expert advice. New ventures vary in terms of how much they rely on business consultants for direction. In some ways, the role of the general business consultant has diminished in importance as businesses seek specialists to get advice on complex issues such as patents, tax planning, and security laws.[44] In other ways, the role of general business consultant is as important as ever; it is the general business consultant who conducts in-depth analyses on behalf of a firm, such as preparing a feasibility study or an industry analysis. Because of the time it would take, it would be inappropriate to ask a member of a board of directors or board of advisers to take on one of these tasks on behalf of a firm. These more time-intensive tasks must be performed by the firm itself or by a paid consultant.

TABLE 9.3 Beyond Financing and Funding: Ways Lenders and Investors Add Value to an Entrepreneurial Venture

- Help identify and recruit key management personnel
- Provide insight into the industry and markets in which the venture intends to participate
- Help the venture fine-tune its business model
- Serve as a sounding board for new ideas
- Provide introductions to additional sources of capital
- Recruit customers
- Help to arrange business partnerships
- Serve on the venture's board of directors or board of advisers
- Provide a sense of calm in the midst of the emotional roller-coaster ride that many new-venture teams experience

Those leading an entrepreneurial venture often turn to consultants for help and advice because while large firms can afford to employ experts in many areas, new firms typically can't. If a new firm needs help in a specialized area, such as building a product prototype, it may need to hire an engineering consulting firm to do the work. The fees that consultants charge are typically negotiable. If a new venture has good potential and offers a consulting firm the possibility of repeat business, the firm will often be willing to reduce its fee or work out favorable payment arrangements.

Consultants fall into two categories: paid consultants and consultants who are made available for free or at a reduced rate through a nonprofit or government agency. The first category includes large international consulting firms, such as Bearing Point (formerly KPMG), Accenture, IBM Global Services, and Bain & Company. These firms provide a wide array of services but are beyond the reach of most start-ups because of budget limitations. But there are many smaller, localized firms. The best way to find them is to ask around for a referral.

Consultants are also available through nonprofit or government agencies. SCORE, for example, is a nonprofit organization that provides free consulting services to small businesses. SCORE currently has over 10,500 volunteers with about 1,300 of these individuals serving as e-counselors—people who answer questions via the Internet. Commonly, SCORE volunteers are retired business owners who counsel in areas as diverse as finance, operations, and sales.[45] And the Small Business Administration, a government agency, provides a variety of consulting services to small businesses and entrepreneurs, primarily through its network of Small Business Development Centers (SBDC), which are spread throughout the United States. There is evidence that these centers are effective in providing advice and helping entrepreneurial ventures get off to a good start. For example, one study found that the rates of survival, growth, and innovation of SBDC-counseled firms are higher than the population of start-ups in general.[46]

In summary, putting together a new-venture team is one of the most critical activities that a founder or founders of a firm undertake. Many entrepreneurs suffer by not thinking broadly enough or carefully enough about this process. Ultimately, people must make any new venture work. New ventures benefit by surrounding themselves with high-quality employees and advisers to tackle the challenges involved with launching and growing an entrepreneurial firm.

Chapter Summary

1. A new-venture team is the group of people who move a new venture from an idea to a fully functioning firm. The primary elements of a new-venture team are the company founders, key employees, the board of directors, the board of advisers, lenders and investors, and other professionals.
2. The liability of newness refers to the fact that entrepreneurial ventures often falter or even fail because the people who start them can't adjust quickly enough to their new roles and because the firm lacks a "track record" with customers and suppliers. These limitations can be overcome by assembling a talented and experienced new-venture team.
3. A heterogeneous founding team has members with diverse abilities and experiences. A homogeneous founding team has members who are very similar to one another.

4. The personal attributes that affect a founder's chances of launching a successful new firm include level of education, prior entrepreneurial experience, relevant industry experience, and the ability to network. Networking is building and maintaining relationships with people who are similar or whose friendship could bring advantages to the firm.

5. An executive-search firm is a company specializing in helping other companies recruit and select key personnel.

6. The two primary ways in which the nonemployee members of a start-up's new-venture team help the firm are by providing guidance and lending legitimacy.

7. A board of directors is a panel of individuals who is elected by a corporation's shareholders to oversee the management of the firm. It is typically made up of both inside and outside directors. An inside director is a person who is also an officer of the firm. An outside director is someone who is not employed by the firm.

8. When a high-quality individual agrees to serve on a company's board of directors, the individual is in essence expressing an opinion that the company has potential (why else would the individual agree to serve?). This phenomenon is referred to as signaling.

9. An advisory board is a panel of experts who are asked by the management of a firm to provide counsel and advice on an ongoing basis.

10. The primary reason that new ventures turn to consultants for help and advice is that while large firms can afford to employ experts in many areas, new firms typically can't. Consultants can be paid or can be part of a nonprofit or government agency and provide their services for free or for a reduced rate.

Key Terms

advisory board, 266
board of directors, 264
consultant, 270
executive-search firm, 262
founding team, 257

heterogeneous team, 259
homogeneous team, 259
inside director, 264
liability of newness, 256
networking, 260

new-venture team, 256
outside director, 264
prior entrepreneurial experience, 260
relevant industry experience, 260
signaling, 265

Review Questions

1. What is a new-venture team? Who are the primary participants in a start-up's new-venture team?

2. What is liability of newness? What can a new venture do to overcome the liability of newness?

3. Describe the difference between a heterogeneous and a homogeneous founding team.

4. List several factors that enhance the value of a new-venture team.

5. Describe the two potential pitfalls of using a team to start a firm.

6. What are the personal attributes that affect a founder's chances of launching a successful new firm? In your judgment, which of these attributes are the most important? Why?

7. Explain why having prior entrepreneurial experience helps the founder of a firm.

8. Define the term *networking*. Why is it important for an entrepreneur to have a vibrant social and professional network?

9. What are the two reasons that prompt new ventures to use executive-search firms to help them identify and screen key employees?

10. What is a board of directors? What is the difference between inside and outside directors?

11. Describe the three formal responsibilities of a board of directors.

12. Explain why recruiting a well-known and highly respected board of directors lends legitimacy to a firm.

13. Define the term *signaling*.

14. Discuss the purpose of forming an advisory board. If you were the founder of an entrepreneurial firm, would you set up an advisory board? Why or why not?

15. Describe the different ways that advisory boards meet and conduct their business.
16. Describe several of the guidelines to setting up a board of advisers.
17. In what ways do lenders and investors lend legitimacy to a firm?
18. Explain why new ventures often turn to consultants for advice.
19. Describe the purpose of SCORE. What type of advice and counsel do SCORE volunteers provide?
20. As noted in the chapter, SBDCs (Small Business Development Centers) seem to contribute positively to the launch of an entrepreneurial venture. In your opinion, what accounts for this positive relationship? If you were launching an entrepreneurial venture today, would you seek the services of a SBDC? Why or why not?

Application Questions

1. Reread the opening case. What factors did Jan Stephenson and Amy Appleyard have working in their favor and what factors did they have working against them as the founders of Spark Craft Studios?
2. Amy Snell works for Coldwater Creek, a catalog retailer for women's apparel in Sandpoint, Idaho. She is thinking about leaving Coldwater Creek to move to Boise to open a store that sells hiking, fishing, and camping gear. She wants to find a partner to help her start the firm. What qualities should Amy look for in a potential partner or "cofounder" for her new firm?
3. Early in the chapter, under the section titled "Creating a New-Venture Team," a quote is provided that reads as follows: "People are the one factor in production . . . that animates all others." In the context of everything you know and have learned about entrepreneurship, what does this quote mean to you?
4. According to the chapter, prior entrepreneurial experience, relevant industry experience, and networking are attributes that strengthen a person's chances of launching a successful venture. Think about the type of company that you might launch someday. Which of these attributes do you currently possess? What steps can you take now to build strengths in each of these areas?
5. Read Case 9.1 and focus specifically on John Patton, the founder of Nektar Therapeutics. On a scale of 1 to 10 (10 is high), rate Patton's suitability to launch Nektar and be prepared to explain your rating.
6. Tom Ryan is part of a group of four individuals who recently left IBM to launch a computer consulting firm. They are trying to recruit a CEO but haven't had any luck finding someone with the credentials they want. Tom has suggested to his partners that they hire an executive-search firm to help, but his partners think that executive-search firms are too expensive. If you were Tom, what arguments would you use to persuade your cofounders that hiring an executive-search firm might be money well spent?
7. Bill Carroll plans to start a chain of fitness clubs in Virginia. He has considered establishing a board of directors and a board of advisers but has decided to shield himself from the advice of others so that he can stay focused on his objectives. Why is Bill making a poor decision?
8. Peggy Armstrong is in the process of starting an educational software company. She has incorporated the business and has 22 stockholders. She next needs to set up a board of directors but doesn't know how to proceed. How would you advise Peggy?
9. Andrew Powell recently launched a tutoring service to help high school students prepare for college entrance exams. Andrew is very ambitious and plans to have 100 centers open within 2 years. He recently put together his board of directors. The board consists of himself, his cofounder, his chief financial officer, and two college buddies with whom he plays golf occasionally. Do you think Andrew has formed a board with a high chance of being effective? If not, what would be a better approach for Andrew?
10. Study HydroPoint, the subject of the "You Be the VC 2" feature at the end of the chapter. If the company asked you for advice in setting up a six-person board of advisers, what types of people would you suggest be included?

11. Examine the board of advisers set up by Ugobe, the company described in this chapter's first "You Be the VC" feature. Briefly comment on the potential of each board member to help this venture.

12. Reneé Coombs, a professional investor, was having lunch with a colleague recently and said, "Do you remember Phil Moore, the entrepreneur we met the other day, who has invented a new kind of computer keyboard? I checked up on him, and he has all the right personal attributes to be a successful entrepreneur." Renee's dinner companion said, "Really, tell me about him." What do you think Reneé would say if she were describing a person who had all the right personal attributes to be a successful entrepreneur?

13. Jim Lane is an executive with General Motors. A former co-worker of his recently started a company and raised $3 million from a well-known investor even though he didn't need the money to launch the business. Jim thinks his friend is foolish and can't think of one reason to take money from an investor if you don't need it. If you were talking to Jim, what would you tell him about this situation?

14. Melanie Atkins is preparing to launch a software firm near Minneapolis. She is very capable but is worried about the amount of money she'll need to spend paying consultants to help her launch and grow her business. Does Melanie have to rely strictly on paid consultants to help her launch and grow her business? If not, what alternatives does Melanie have?

15. Refer to this chapter's "Partnering for Success" feature. Do some research, and determine what types of educational and networking opportunities for new and aspiring entrepreneurs are available in your community during the next 6 months. Which of these events do you think you could benefit from attending?

you be the VC 9.1 — Ugobe
www.ugobe.com

Business Idea: Create sophisticated robotic toys that relate to humans through a wide range of simulated emotions and relate to their environments in very human-like ways.

Pitch: Ugobe is a robotics company that is dedicated to making unique robotic products. The company's first product, a toy named Pleo, is designed to resemble a 1-week-old, long-neck dinosaur—a sauropod. If you type "Pleo" into Google or Yahoo!, you can quickly find pictures of Pleo and streaming videos of Pleo demonstrations.

It is a treat to watch Pleo move about, and you'll find yourself showing Pleo to others. Rather than having lots of functions and features, what's unique about Pleo is his ability to emulate human emotion. If Pleo walks to the side of a table, he'll peek over the side and back up a step to avoid falling off. If you call out Pleo's name, he'll turn in the direction of your voice. If you play with Pleo, he will play back. And if you quit playing with Pleo, in a few minutes he will act sad because he has no one to play with.

Ugobe took 5 years to design Pleo and solicited input from robotics experts, animators, scientists, biologists, and computer programmers. Inside his body, Pleo has 40

sensors to detect light, motion, touch, and sound. The sensors feed information about Pleo's environment to processors that can collectively handle 60 million calculations per second. A complex computer program then determines how Pleo behaves. Ugobe has two target markets for Pleo. The first is kids ages 6 to 12 who will treat Pleo like a pet. The second is adults who are interested in customizing and adding to the base emotions of their Pleos. The company says Pleo will learn and adapt to certain behaviors of its owner. As time goes on, the owner can also alter Pleo's personality by buying upgrades to the operating system, known as "personality modules." The upgrades will be sold through a SD memory card expansion or using a standard USB connection to download updates from the Internet. Pleo will initially sell for around $200.

Ugobe has other products on the drawing board. It says that all of its products must obey three laws. They must simulate the feeling and displaying of emotion, they must be aware of themselves and their environment, and they must be able to evolve over time (through upgrades). Making all of its products upgradeable is important part of

Ugobe's business model. This tactic will provide the company recurring revenue from people who purchase its robotics products.

Q&A: Based on the material covered in this chapter, what questions would you ask the firm's founders before making your funding decision? What answers would satisfy you?

Decision: If you had to make your decision on just the information provided in the pitch and on the company's Web site, would you fund this firm? Why or why not?

HyrdoPoint
www.hydropoint.com

Business Idea: Build a system that provides real-time weather data wirelessly to the controllers (which are electronic boxes) or irrigation systems to permit the systems to adjust their irrigation schedule according to the expected weather in the area.

Pitch: Have you ever seen a homeowner, a golf course, or an office building watering its lawn during a rainstorm or shortly before or after it rained? If you have, you've witnessed a growing problem, as more and more people and businesses are irrigating their properties. Overwatering damages the environment, ruins lawns, wastes water, and can cause serious runoff problems. With growing shortages of water on a global basis, these are indeed serious matters.

Using a patented system called WeatherTRAK, HydroPoint has developed a system that addresses this challenge. Every day, the WeatherTRAK data service transmits location-specific weather data, wirelessly, to irrigation systems that are equipped with its controllers. Controllers are electronic boxes that regulate the timing and flow of water through an irrigation system. WeatherTRAK's controllers, which can be installed in new

irrigation systems or retrofitted into existing ones, are suitable for both residential and commercial systems. On the basis of the weather forecast it receives, a WeatherTRAK controller automatically calculates the proper watering schedule for an irrigation system to which it is connected. The system has been proven to work during 5 years of independent field testing.

The timing couldn't be better for this device. Many municipalities are struggling with maintaining a proper water supply and often impose watering restrictions during periods of low rainfall. WeatherTRAK's system conserves water by reducing overwatering. The system also helps customers save money by eliminating overwatering and keeping lawns and landscapes healthy.

Q&A: Based on the material covered in this chapter, what questions would you ask the firm's founders before making your funding decision? What answers would satisfy you?

Decision: If you had to make your decision on just the information provided in the pitch and on the company's Web site, would you fund this firm? Why or why not?

CASE 9.1   *Nektar Therapeutics: How One Company Built an Unusual But Highly Effective New-Venture Team*
www.nektar.com

Bruce R. Barringer,
University of Central Florida
R. Duane Ireland,
Texas A&M University

Introduction

In 1990, John Patton, a scientist working for Genentech, had an ambitious dream—to rid Type 2 diabetics of having

to take insulin shots every day. If you've ever known a diabetic, who must have a shot on a daily basis, you can sympathize with Patton's dream. The task of administering insulin shots is both tedious and painful and can continue for a person's entire life.

Patton's solution to this problem was to develop a system that allowed diabetics to receive their insulin through an inhaler, similar to the type of inhaler asthma patients use. The idea of replacing shots with an inhaler isn't new;

in fact, scientists have kicked it around for over 80 years. What was new is that Patton, who at the time was the head of Genentech's drug delivery team, felt that he was on the verge of a breakthrough in making an insulin inhaler a reality. But when he brought his work before Genentech's product development committee, to get funding, he was turned down. He recalls that they said, "This looks like a great idea, but we would rather put that money into a brand-new molecule (or drug)."

Not to be deterred, Patton left Genentech, a major drug company, in 1990 to start his own firm. It was a bold move. Patton recalls, "I had three kids ready for college and my wife wasn't working. I had to leave Genentech to start this company and I sold my stock options so we'd have something to live on." At this point, Patton had limited resources, no team, no partners, and no product. What he did have were two things: a license from Genentech to continue the work he had started at the firm and a passion to fulfill his dream of making and selling a product that could relieve the daily suffering that diabetic patients endured.

Fast-forward from 1990 to the present. In January 2006, Patton's dream came true. United States and European regulators approved Exubera, the first inhaled form of insulin for use by diabetic patients. Exubera is the brainchild of Nektar Therapeutics, the company Patton started. It took 16 long years and $500 million for Patton to help Exubera become a reality, but it will soon be available to diabetic patients.

What's particularly interesting about Patton's entrepreneurial journey is how Patton built the team that made Exubera a reality, the subject of this case. The following narrative provides a loose chronology and a sense of how Patton built his team. Some of the key hires and partnerships he and his firm developed may surprise you. As you will see, though, these partnerships were critical to his venture's success.

Building a New-Venture Team

Step 1: Taking on a Partner
The first thing Patton did was take on a partner. Patton selected Robert Platz, an aerosol specialist from Stanford University's Research Institute, to cofound Nektar with him. The two had corresponded for some time. Platz had come up with the idea of spray-drying the essential elements of insulin, which was a potentially important piece of the solution to the problem Patton was trying to solve. As was the case with Patton, Platz had little business experience but had a passion for helping diabetic patients.

Step 2: Taking on Investors
Because they had no money, Patton and Platz wrote a business plan and immediately started cold-calling venture capitalists with it. They found this to be a tedious and lengthy process. Patton recalls, "Each time we had a meeting, the VCs would say, 'Go away, make these changes and come back.' I was running out of money." The biggest objection Patton and Platz continually ran into was the sentiment that if their idea was so good, why wasn't Genentech, or some other large drug company pursuing it. Money became so tight that the partners almost dissolved the firm, and Patton nearly took a job as a marine biologist in Baltimore. Eventually, Patton and Platz met Terry Opdendyk and Rob Kuhling, partners at Onset Ventures. The entrepreneurs and the VCs clicked, and Onset offered to provide Nektar seed funding. Reflecting back on their meeting with Onset's partners, Patton said, "At first Terry and Rob were cautious, too. But when all the other VCs were saying 'too risky,' Terry was saying 'that's a great idea.' I can honestly say that without Terry (one of the Onset partners), Inhale (the original name of the company) never would have happened." At this time the company also started building its board of directors.

Step 3: Hiring Co-CEOs
The first thing that Patton and Platz's venture capitalists did after providing them funding was to help them hire a CEO. It was clear that Patton and Platz's time would be best spent working on the technology rather than running the business side of the company. As it turned out, they hired two people to serve as co-CEOs—Robert Chess, the former president of a dermatological company, and Ajit Gill, an electrical engineer with a background in software. Gill may seem like an odd choice, given his background, but the passion he demonstrated for Nektar's vision won the day. "I decided I wanted to work for a company where I really cared about the product," he recalls. "I happened to know Rob Chess, and I happened to know the investors who provided the seed financing. And the timing just happened to work out."

Step 4: Key Hires
Particularly interesting are some of the first key hires that Patton and Platz made, along with Nektar's newly appointed co-CEOs, early in the firm's life. Adrian Smith, a mechanical engineer who had designed ink-jet printers for Hewlett-Packard and medical devices at IDEO (a highly respected design firm) was one of the earliest hires. A critical challenge that ink-jet printer designers have is developing a product that is capable of shooting ink through the small jets in the head of a printer cartridge in just the right manner. Nektar would face a similar challenge in forcing insulin mist through the small jets in the nozzle of an inhaler. Smith helped Nektar recruit an eclectic and highly diverse group of additional early hires, including the following people:

David Lechuga-Ballesteros, from Mexico, had a Ph.D. in pharmaceutics and experience at Abbott Laboratories

Herman Snyder, from the United States, a combustion scientist who had worked at a Caterpillar subsidiary designing gas turbine engines

James Park, from the United States, a mechanical engineer who had designed equipment to make intricately packaged items like electronic components

Carlos Schuler, from Venezuela, had a Ph.D. in fluid mechanics and aerodynamics and had experience working with NASA and analyzing the aerodynamics of disk drives at IBM

Step 5: Partnerships

By 1993, Nektar's team had a prototype of their device ready and started clinical trials. The device worked like a little air gun. The gun released a small cloud of insulin particles into a person's mouth. As soon as the particles hit the moist linings of an individual's lungs, they dissolve. Once the prototype was ready to be shown to others, Nektar's team approached most of the insulin companies in the world with the purpose of forming partnerships with them to move their work forward. They were repeatedly turned down. The big fear was that the insulin particles delivered by the inhaler would have an adverse long-term affect on a patient's lungs. Some initial clinical results actually reinforced these concerns, which caused Nektar's stock price to tumble and a nearly completed partnership agreement with Genentech to be cancelled. Ultimately though, Nektar was able to forge a major partnership with Pfizer, which believed in the long-term prospects for Exubera and helped fund its ongoing development.

Step 6: More Personnel and Products Via Acquisition

Nektar's next move was to expand its core technology to round out the competencies needed to make Exubera a reality. To accomplish this objective, it acquired some particle-processing intellectual property from San Diego-based Alliance Pharmaceuticals in 1999 and acquired two small firms, United Kingdom-based Bradford Particle Design and Alabama-based Shearwater Inc., in 2001. These moves markedly helped Nektar acquire the final capabilities and personnel needed to bring Exubera to its current state. At this point, Nektar was also looking at leveraging its core competencies to create inhalers that could treat diseases other than diabetes. The competencies acquired through the acquisitions bolstered this ambition.

Nektar Today

Today, analysts predict that sales of Exubera, Nektar's diabetic inhaler, could hit $3 billion per year. Of course, Nektar will have to share the revenue with Pfizer. Pfizer, for its part, will be richly rewarded for partnering with Nektar

when others wouldn't. Exubera will be introduced to the market as a Pfizer-branded product.

Beyond financial rewards, the most important thing for John Patton and his team is that the 21 million Americans who have Type 2 diabetes have new hope for managing their daily regimens. Some diabetics have to inject insulin up to five times a day. Imagine their relief if Exubera reaches its full potential as a substitute for traditional insulin shots.

Nektar is now broadening its focus and is working on additional products. One product that Nektar is working on in partnership with a company called Zelos may enable people who are injected with a drug to slow the progress of osteoporosis to receive the same medication via an inhaler. Products with similar capabilities are also in the pipeline.

Discussion Questions

1. Evaluate the suitability of John Patton and Ronald Platz as the founders of Nektar. Why do you think they were repeatedly turned down in their initial attempts to get venture capital funding for their firm? Why do you think Patton and Platz were able to eventually get funding and to form the new-venture team described in the case?

2. Make a list of all the members of Nektar's new-venture team. Briefly comment on the potential strengths and weaknesses of each person. One component of Nektar's team that was only briefly touched on in the case is its board of directors. If you had been on Nektar's founding team, which type of board of directors would you have put together? Why?

3. Comment on the diversity and the eclectic nature of Nektar's initial key hires. Why do you think Patton and Platz, along with their newly appointed co-CEOs, selected such a diverse group? Make your answer as thoughtful and substantive as possible.

4. If Nektar had set up a board of advisers early in the life of the firm, what type of board of advisers would have been the most appropriate?

Application Questions

1. If you decided to start a firm to tackle a difficult technological challenge, like John Patton did, what lessons could you learn by reading this case?

2. Look at the "You Be the VC 1" feature in this chapter. What type of new-venture team should Ugobe be assembling? Make up a simulated new-venture team for Ugobe that would be capable of taking the company from a regional to a nationwide firm.

Sources: K. Philipkoski, "He and His CEO Inhaled," *Wired News*, March 28, 2006; Onset Ventures homepage, "John Patton" (accessed May 11, 2006); L. J. Sellers, "Special Delivery," *Pharmaceutical Executive*, April 1, 2004.

CASE 9.2 Neterion: What Comes First—The CEO or the Funding?

www.neterion.com

Bruce R. Barringer,
University of Central Florida
R. Duane Ireland,
Texas A&M University

Introduction

Neterion, which was originally named S2io Technologies, was founded in 2001 by five former Nortel Networks and Alteon employees. The mission of the firm was to develop and market an integrated circuit, or chip, that would boost the processing power of servers for data networks.

Since its founding, Neterion has been largely successful in fulfilling its mission. It now delivers 10-gigabit Ethernet hardware and software solutions, which help original equipment manufacturers (OEMs) solve their customers' high-end networking problems.

Early in the life of Neterion, the founders faced two critical milestones: (1) hiring a CEO and (2) raising venture capital funding. They knew they would have to achieve both of these objectives to gain the traction needed to be a player in their industry. But which objective should they pursue first? Should they hire a CEO and then go after funding? Or should they get funding first and then seek a high-quality CEO? This issue is the heart of this case.

Fortunately for Neterion, the firm was able to achieve both of its objectives. They were able to hire David Zabrowski, with the assistance of a small executive-search firm named Cross Creek Systems. Zabrowski (who is still Neterion's CEO) was the type of executive who confidently takes the reins of a company such as Neterion. At the time, he was 39 years old and had 16 years of broad experience with Hewlett-Packard in both finance and marketing. More importantly, he had "connections" and knew his way around Silicon Valley. There are few things more coveted in the start-up world than landing an executive who already has a network of acquaintances among investors, suppliers, government officials, and potential customers.

Neterion was also able to meet its objective of obtaining funding. In November 2001, the company obtained $9 million in initial funding from a prominent venture capital firm. In October 2002, it raised a second round of $18 million in funding, and in June 2003 raised a third round of $15 million. As an interesting aside, Neterion changed its name from S2io Technologies to Neterion in late 2004.

According to CEO David Zabrowski, the name failed the "Missouri Mother" test. "I have worked for S2io for two years and my mother never got the name right," he says. And Neterion? According to Zabrowski, the name combines the company's network heritage and the "promise of discovery and infinite possibilities."

Hiring Zabrowski as CEO and obtaining venture capital funding put Neterion on a path that has resulted in the success it enjoys today. But back to the issue that lies at the heart of this case: What came first—the CEO or the funding? Here is what the two alternatives looked like to the founders of Neterion in 2001.

Alternative 1: Hiring a CEO Before Getting Funding

Hiring a well-known CEO first would give Neterion more credibility with lenders and investors. "Back then, our biggest challenge was getting someone to pay attention to us," said Ed Roseberry, one of the company's founders. "Start-up companies don't have any clout." The founders realized that having a first-rate CEO would bring legitimacy to the firm and open doors that wouldn't open otherwise, exposing them to a broader range of funding choices. By hiring a CEO first, the business plan presented to investors could be strengthened. The CEO could also help the firm develop a strategy for obtaining multiple rounds of funding.

In addition, a well-connected CEO brings a broad network of industry-related contacts, so a strong CEO might gain commitments from initial customers and might enable partnerships to be formed. These types of initiatives could strengthen Neterion's business plan and increase the likelihood of obtaining favorable funding from a top-tier venture capital firm.

Alternative 2: Getting Funding Before Hiring a CEO

The second approach provided seemingly equal advantages. To attract a high-quality CEO, a start-up needs all the positive attributes it can muster, and a firm with access to funding would certainly make itself more attractive to a potential CEO. Getting funding not only provides a firm the capital it needs but also is a seal of legitimacy, suggesting that a firm is a serious contender. One downside to this approach is that the founders knew that once they got funding, pressure to perform would become more acute. This meant that they would have progressively less time to devote to a search for a CEO.

Getting funding before hiring a CEO would also enable Neterion's investors to assist in the CEO recruitment and selection process. One of the biggest assets that investors bring to a start-up, other than money, is their connections. The founders also wondered what would happen if they hired a CEO and the person they hired didn't pass muster with the venture capitalists. They didn't want to ruin their chances with the VCs by prematurely placing someone in the CEO role in their firm. They also didn't want to go through the awkward process of replacing a CEO shortly after they hired one.

The Decision

In the end, the decision boiled down to the age-old "what came first, the chicken or the egg" type of quandary. Hiring an experienced CEO would help Neterion get funding, while at the same time having funding would help Neterion get an experienced CEO.

If you had been one of the founders of Neterion in 2001, which alternative would you have argued in favor of? Which alternative do you think the company selected?

Discussion Questions

1. How common do you think the issue is that faced Neterion's founders? If you were to launch an entrepreneurial venture within the next year, would you pursue Alternative 1 or Alternative 2, as explained in this case? What is the reasoning for your choice of one of these two alternatives??

2. Rather than hiring a CEO, one of the founders of Neterion could have moved into the CEO position.

Do you think this would have been a good idea? Why or why not?

3. Go to Neterion's Web site and look at the composition of its board of directors. Write a short critique of its board on the basis of the preferred attributes of directors discussed in this chapter.

4. No information is provided in the case about whether Neterion had a board of advisers when the company was founded. Do you think the firm should have had a board of advisers? If so, what role could the board of advisers have played in helping the company recruit a CEO and in obtaining venture capital funding?

Application Questions

1. What are the advantage and the disadvantage of having a large founding team? (Neterion had five founders.) If you had to err on one side, would you want your founding team to be too big or too small? Make your answers as thoughtful and substantive as possible.

2. Go online and find three executive-search firms. Write a brief summary of the services that each firm offers. Do you think using an executive-search firm was a good choice for Neterion? What are the advantages and disadvantages of executive-search firms for young entrepreneurial firms?

Sources: Neterion homepage, www.neterion.com (accessed May 15, 2006); "S2io Becomes Neterion." *ByteandSwitch*, January 25, 2005; J. Sterline, "How Do You Know Whether to Hire a CEO? *The Wall Street Journal*, March 17, 2003, R6.

Endnotes

1. Personal Interview with Jan Stephenson, June 14, 2006.
2. Ladies Who Launch homepage, www.ladieswholaunch (accessed June 12, 2006).
3. Ladies Who Launch homepage, www.ladieswholaunch (accessed June 12, 2006).
4. M. Hager, J. Galaskiewicz, W. Bielefeld, and J. Pins, "Takes From the Grave: Organizations' Accounts of Their Own Demise," *American Behavioral Scientist* 39, no. 8 (2006): 975–94; A. Stinchcombe, "Social Structure and Organization," in *Handbook of Organizations*, ed. James G. March (Chicago: Rand McNally, 1965), 142–93.
5. C. Read, J. Ross, J. Dunleavy, D. Schulman, and J. Bramante, *eCFO* (Chichester, UK: John Wiley & Sons, 2001), 117.
6. M. Jaaskelainen, M. Maula, and T. Seppa, "Allocation of Attention to Portfolio Companies and the Performance of Venture Capital Firms," *Entrepreneurship Theory and Practice* 30 (2006): 185–206.
7. M. Gruber and J. Henkel, "New Ventures Based on Open Innovation—An Empirical Analysis of Start-up Firms in Embedded Linux," *International Journal of Technology Management* 33 (2006): 356–72; H. Fesser and G. Willard, "Founding Strategy and Performance: A Comparison of High and Low Growth Tech Firms," *Strategic Management Journal* 11, no. 2 (1990): 87–98.
8. D. P. Forbes, P. S. Borchert, M. E. Zellmer-Bruhn, and H. J. Sapienza, "Entrepreneurial Team Formation: An Exploration of New Member Addition," *Entrepreneurship Theory and Practice*

30 (2006): 225–48; E. B. Roberts, *Entrepreneurs in High Technology: Lessons From MIT and Beyond* (New York: Oxford University Press, 1991).

9. A. Lockett, D. Ucbasaran, and J. Butler, "Opening Up the Investor-Investee Dyad: Syndicates, Teams, and Networks," *Entrepreneurship Theory and Practice*, 30, 2006: 117–130; Fesser and Willard, "Founding Strategy and Performance."

10. *Business 2.0*, "Loyalty Counts as Much as Smarts," December 2, 2005.

11. K. Eisenhardt and C. Schoonhoven, "Organizational Growth: Linking Founding Team, Strategy, Environment, and Growth among U.S. Semiconductor Ventures, 1978–1988," *Administrative Science Quarterly* 35 (1990): 504–29.

12. T. Zenger and B. Lawrence, "Organizational Demography: The Differential Effects of Age and Tenure Distribution on Technical Communication," *Academy of Management Journal* 32 (1989): 353–76.

13. Eisenhardt and Schoonhoven, "Organizational Growth."

14. B. Clarysee and N. Moray, "A Process Study of Entrepreneurial Team Formation: The Case of a Research-Based Spin-Off," *Journal of Business Venturing* 19 (2004): 55–79.

15. D. Ravasi and C. Turati, "Exploring Entrepreneurial Learning: A Comparative Study of Technology Development Projects," *Journal of Business Venturing* 20 (2005): 137–64; A. C. Cooper, F. J. Gimeno-Gascon, and C. Y. Woo, "Initial Human and Financial Capital as Predictors of New Venture Performance," *Journal of Business Venturing* 9, no. 5 (1994): 371–95.

16. D. Politis, "The Process of Entrepreneurial Learning: A Conceptual Framework," *Entrepreneurship Theory and Practice* 29 (2005): 399–424.

17. Clarysee and Moray, "A Process Study of Entrepreneurial Team Formation."

18. C. Hienerth and A. Kessler, "Measuring Success in Family Businesses: The Concept of Configurational Fit," *Family Business Review* 19 (2006): 115–34; I. MacMillian, L. Zemann, and P. N. S. Narasimha, "Criteria Distinguishing Successful from Unsuccessful Ventures in the Venture Screening Process," *Journal of Business Venturing* 2 (1987): 123–37.

19. D. M. DeCarolis and P. Saparito, "Social Capital, Cognition, and Entrepreneurial Opportunities: A Theoretical Framework," *Entrepreneurship Theory and Practice* 30 (2006): 41–56; A. Ardichvili, R. Cardozo, and S. Ray, "A Theory of Entrepreneurial Opportunity Recognition and Development," *Journal of Business Venturing* 18 (2004): 105–23.

20. F. Welter and D. Smallbone, "Exploring the Role of Trust in Entrepreneurial Activity," *Entrepreneurship Theory and Practice* 30 (2006): 465–75.

21. PricewaterhouseCooopers, "Fast-Growth CEOs More Optimistic, But Increasingly Concerned About Availability of Qualified Workers and Pressure For Increased Wages, PricewaterhouseCoopers Finds." *Trendsetter Barometer*, June 7, 2006.

22. Council of Entrepreneurial Development, "Entrepreneurial Satisfaction Survey Report" (Raleigh-Durham, NC, 2004).

23. R. Adams, *A Good Hard Kick in the Ass* (New York: Crown Business, 2002), 240.

24. H. Schultz, *Pour Your Heart into It* (New York: Hyperion, 1997), 82.

25. D. Yermack, "Boards and Market Value," *Financial Markets and Portfolio Management* 20 (2006): 33–47; Investorwords.com homepage, www.investorwords.com (accessed June 1, 2004).

26. M. K. Fiegener, "Determinants of Board Participation in the Strategic Decisions of Small Corporations," *Entrepreneurship Theory and Practice*, September 2005, 627–50.

27. R. Charan, *Boards at Work* (San Francisco: Jossey-Bass, 1998), 29.

28. Charan, *Boards at Work*, 73.

29. L. W. Busenitz, J. O. Fiet, and D. D. Moesel, "Signaling in Venture Capitalist–New Venture Team Funding Decisions: Does It Indicate Long-Term Venture Outcomes?" *Entrepreneurship Theory and Practice* 29 (2005): 1–12; S. Certo, C. Daily, and D. Dalton, "Signaling Firm Value through Board Structure: An Investigation of Initial Public Offerings," *Entrepreneurship Theory and Practice* 26, no. 2 (2001): 33–50.

30. A. Sherman, *Fast-Track Business Growth* (Washington, DC: Kiplinger Books, 2001).

31. "Meet Andrea Lyons," Ladies Who Launch homepage, www.ladieswholaunch.com (accessed July 7, 2006).

32. Coolibar homepage, www.coolibar.com (accessed July 8, 2006).

33. Intouch Health homepage, www.intouch-health.com (accessed July 9, 2006).

34. R. Kenny, "Rediscovering Advisory Boards," *IEEE Engineering Management Review*, Fourth Quarter (2000): 24–27.

35. Ugobe homepage, www.ugobe.com (accessed July 7, 2006).

36. S. Schmidt and M. Brauer, "Strategic Governance: How to Assess Board Effectiveness in Guiding Strategy Execution," *Corporate Governance: An International Review* 14 (2006): 13–22.

37. R. Buckman, "Blog Buzz on High-Tech Start-Up Causes Some Static," *The Wall Street Journal*, February 9, 2006, B4.

38. D. Dimov and D. De Clercq, "Venture Capital Investment Strategy and Portfolio Failure Rate: A Longitudinal Study," *Entrepreneurship Theory and Practice* 30 (2006): 207–23; J. Lerner, "Venture Capitalists and the Oversight of Private Firms," *Journal of Finance* 50, no. 1 (1995): 301–18.

39. M. Gorman and W. A. Sahlman, "What Do Venture Capitalists Do?" *Journal of Business Venturing* 4, no. 4 (1989): 231–48.

40. A. Davila, G. Foster, and M. Gupta, "Venture Capital Financing and the Growth of Startup Firms," *Journal of Business Venturing* 18 (2004): 689–708.

41. R. Stross, *eBoys* (New York: Crown Books, 2000), 29.

42. Adams, *A Good Hard Kick in the Ass*, 173.

43. D. Cumming, "Adverse Selection and Capital Structure: Evidence from Venture Capital," *Entrepreneurship Theory and Practice* 30 (2006): 155–83.

44. H. H. Stevenson and W. A. Sahlman, "How Small Companies Should Handle Advisors," in *The Entrepreneurial Venture*, ed. William A. Sahlman and Howard H. Stevenson (Boston: Harvard Business School Publications, 1992), 295–302.

45. SCORE homepage, www.score.org (accessed July 24, 2006).

46. J. J. Chrisman and W. E McMullan, "A Preliminary Assessment of Outsider Assistance as a Knowledge Resource: The Longer-Term Impact of New Venture Counseling," *Entrepreneurship Theory and Practice* 24 (2000): 37–53.

10 getting *financing* or funding

Getting Personal

with **DEREK GREGG**

My biggest worry as an entrepreneur	What I'd like to be doing in 10 years	Hardest part of getting funding
Making sales and raising more funding	*Starting or running another company*	*Being responsible for so much money*

Vandalia Research:
Raising Money Through a Variety of Sources

In the spring of 2003, Derek Gregg and Justin Swick, both freshmen, enrolled in a class called "Technology and Innovation" at Marshall University. It was an experimental class, funded by a grant from the NCIIA (National Collegiate Inventors and Innovators Alliance). The purpose of the grant was to help Marshall University develop a curriculum blending science and entrepreneurship. The students in the class, taught by Dr. Elizabeth Murray and Dr. Herbert Tesser, were split into teams. The challenge to each team was to try to solve a vexing scientific problem. As a team, Gregg and Swick were challenged to learn how to duplicate DNA more efficiently.[1] Swick is pictured to the left and Gregg to the right in the photograph accompanying this Opening Profile.

Over the course of the class, Gregg and Swick developed a novel approach to solving their assigned problem. DNA represents the basic building blocks of life. All forms of life, including humans, animals, and plants, have DNA, which basically determines the physical characteristics that they inherit. An original sample of DNA can be reproduced in a laboratory—a procedure that has a number of applications in health care and other industries. Gregg and Swick came up with an idea for a machine that could reproduce DNA faster and more effectively than any device currently available. The design seemed plausible to Dr. Murray, who showed the design to Dr. Mike Norton, a chemistry professor and colleague, who was also intrigued. "It was one of those things that seemed so simple that it had probably been done, but our research of the patent database concluded that it hadn't," said Dr. Murray.[2] Toward the end of the class, Gregg and Swick, along with Murray and Norton, decided to continue working together with the objective of launching an entrepreneurial venture to build the device.

From the beginning, the four individuals knew that funds would have to be raised to purchase lab equipment, hire personnel and build a working prototype if they were to actually launch a company to take the product to market. The initial work on the project was funded through a combination of bootstrapping and grants. In June 2003, just a month after the class ended, Gregg and Swick received a $15,000 grant from a program sponsored by the state of West Virginia.

DEREK GREGG
Cofounder, Vandalia Research
Undergraduate Student
College of Science
Marshall University

MARSHALL UNIVERSITY

JUSTIN SWICK
Cofounder, Vandalia Research
Undergraduate Student
College of Science
Marshall University

Best advice I've received

Make as many decisions as fast as you can

My biggest surprise as an entrepreneur

Selling is really, really hard

First entrepreneurial experience

Selling stuff door-to-door as a kid

After studying this chapter you should be ready to:

L E A R N I N G

Objectives

1. Explain why most entrepreneurial ventures need to raise money during their early life.

2. Identify the three sources of personal financing available to entrepreneurs.

3. Provide examples of how entrepreneurs bootstrap to raise money or cut costs.

4. Identify the three steps involved in properly preparing to raise debt or equity financing.

5. Explain the role of an elevator speech in attracting financing for an entrepreneurial venture.

6. Discuss the difference between equity funding and debt financing.

7. Describe the difference between a business angel and a venture capitalist.

8. Explain why an initial public offering (IPO) is an important milestone in an entrepreneurial venture.

9. Discuss the SBA Guaranteed Loan Program.

10. Explain the advantages of leasing for an entrepreneurial venture.

A couple of months later, the NCIIA approved a grant for $18,500. This money was used to start working on a prototype of the DNA replication device, file a patent application, and fund the operating expenses of the endeavor. In early 2004, the four entrepreneurs decided to incorporate, launching Vandalia Research as a result. Later that year, the company moved off campus and occupied lab space owned by another Marshall professor, who made the space available for free. The company operated on the grant money the founders had already received, along with several additional grants, while work progressed on the prototype and several related initiatives. Altogether, more than $250,000 was raised through grants and similar sources.

An important part of Vandalia's start-up story involves how the founders went about laying the groundwork for more serious funding. As soon as the company was launched, the founders started talking to local angel investors about their vision for the company and what they hoped to accomplish. In June 2004, Gregg and Swick were introduced to Selby Wellman, a retired Cisco Systems executive and Marshall alumnus. Williams took an interest in the pair and their vision for Vandalia Research and helped them write a formal business plan. In September 2005, with Wellman's help, Gregg and Swick, along with Vandalia's other founders, held a meeting for local investors to present their business plan and ask for investments. Prior to the meeting, they met with an attorney, who put together a proposal for funding. Selby Wellman, the retired Cisco Systems executive, presented the business plan on the founders' behalf. The meeting went well, and to the founders and the presenter's surprise, approximately $925,000 was raised that evening from about 40 local investors.

Vandalia Research is now selling an educational product for high schools and college courses as a means of generating revenue while work on the DNA replication device is finished. The founders anticipate they will need one more round of funding in the $1.5-million range, which they hope to obtain from local angel investors. Once the DNA replication device is fully operational, Vandalia will sell its technology as a service and will perform DNA replication services for others on a fee basis. The company has determined that it is not practical to sell the device, because of the costs involved in establishing a manufacturing system and because its potential clients may not find it cost-effective to purchase a machine they may only use on an occasional basis.

As start-ups go, Vandalia Research and its founders have been fortunate. Although it hasn't been easy, the company has been able to raise the money it has needed to fund the development of its product and its operations. It still has one round of funding to go, which may represent it biggest challenge to date.

In general, start-ups often have difficulty raising money because they are unknown and untested. Founders must frequently use their own money or try to secure grants or go to friends and family for help. This effort is often a grueling endeavor. Many entrepreneurs hear "no" many times before they match up successfully with a banker or investor. To Derek Gregg and Justin Swick's credit, this pair of entrepreneurs has led a founding team that has been largely successful in its fund-raising efforts.

In this chapter, we focus on the process of getting financing or funding. We begin by discussing why firms raise capital. We follow this with a description of personal financing and the importance of personal funds, capital from friends and family, and bootstrapping in the early life of a firm. We then turn to the different forms of equity, debt, and creative financing available to entrepreneurial ventures. We also emphasize the importance of preparing to secure these types of financing.

The Importance of Getting Financing or Funding

Few people deal with the process of raising investment capital until they need to raise capital for their own firm. As a result, many entrepreneurs go about the task of raising capital haphazardly because they lack experience in this area and because they don't know much about their choices.[3] This shortfall may cause a business owner to place too much reliance on some sources of capital and not enough on others.[4] Entrepreneurs need to have as full an understanding as possible of the alternatives that are available in regard to raising money. And raising money is a balancing act. Although a venture may need to raise money to survive, its founders usually don't want to deal with people who don't understand or care about their long-term goals.

The need to raise money catches some entrepreneurs off-guard, in that many of them launch their firms with the intention of funding all their needs internally. Commonly, though, entrepreneurs discover that operating without investment capital or borrowed money is more difficult than they anticipated. Because of this, it is important for entrepreneurs to understand the role of investment capital in the survival and subsequent success of a new firm.

Why Most New Ventures Need Funding

There are three reasons that most entrepreneurial ventures need to raise money during their early life: cash flow challenges, capital investments, and lengthy product development cycles. These reasons are laid out in Figure 10.1. Let's look at each reason so we can better understand their importance.

Cash Flow Challenges As a firm grows, it requires an increasing amount of cash to serve its customers. Often, equipment must be purchased and new employees hired and trained before the increased customer base generates additional income. The lag between spending to generate revenue and earning income from the firm's operations creates cash flow challenges, particularly for new, often small ventures as well as for ventures that are growing rapidly.

If a firm operates in the red, its negative real-time cash flow, usually computed monthly, is called its burn rate. A company's **burn rate** is the rate at which it is spending its capital until it reaches profitability. Although a negative cash flow is sometimes justified early in a firm's life—to build plant and equipment, train employees, and establish its brand—it can cause severe complications. A firm usually fails if it burns through all its capital before it becomes profitable. This is why inadequate financial resources is one of the primary reasons new firms fail.[5] A firm can simply run out of money even if it has good products and satisfied customers.

To prevent their firms from running out of money, most entrepreneurs need investment capital or a line of credit from a bank to cover cash flow shortfalls until their firms can begin making money. It is usually difficult for a new firm to get a line of credit from a bank (for reasons discussed later). So new ventures often look for investment capital, bootstrap their operations, or try to arrange some type of creative financing.

Capital Investments Firms often need to raise money early on to fund capital investments. Although it may be possible for the venture's founders to fund its initial

LEARNING Objective

1. Explain why most entrepreneurial ventures need to raise money during their early life.

Cash Flow Challenges	Capital Investments	Lengthy Product Development Cycles
Inventory must be purchased, employees must be trained and paid, and advertising must be paid for before cash is generated from sales.	The cost of buying real estate, building facilities, and purchasing equipment typically exceeds a firm's ability to provide funds for these needs on its own.	Some products are under development for years before they generate earnings. The up-front costs often exceed a firm's ability to fund these activities on its own.

FIGURE 10.1

Three Reasons Start-Ups Need Funding

Being an entrepreneur in the biotech industry requires a lot of determination and patience. In the case of Scios, a biopharmaceutical company located in Freemont, California, that "tortoise-like pace" paid off. Scios's Natrecor has posted monumental sales and is a ground-breaking treatment for acute heart failure.

activities, it becomes increasingly difficult for them to do so when it comes to buying property, constructing buildings, purchasing equipment, or investing in other capital projects. Many entrepreneurial ventures are able to delay or avoid these types of expenditures by leasing space or co-opting the resources of alliance partners. However, at some point in its growth cycle, the firm's needs may become specialized enough that it makes sense to purchase capital assets rather than rent or lease them.

Lengthy Product Development Cycles   In some industries, firms need to raise money to pay the up-front costs of lengthy product development cycles. For example, it takes about 2 years and $4 million to develop an electronic game.[6] In the biotech industry, it often takes a decade or more to get a new medicine approved. For example, Scios, a biotech firm that was founded in 1982, got its first medicine approved in 2001, close to 20 years after its founding.[7] This tortoise-like pace of product development takes substantial up-front investment before the anticipated payoff is realized. Although the biotech industry is an extreme example, lengthy product development cycles are the realities ventures face in many industries.

Sources of Personal Financing

LEARNING

Objective

2. Identify the three sources of personal financing available to entrepreneurs.

Typically, the seed money that gets a company off the ground comes from the founders' own pockets. There are three categories of sources of money in this area: personal funds, friends and family, and bootstrapping. These sources are depicted in Figure 10.2 and are explained next.

Personal Funds   The vast majority of founders contribute personal funds, along with sweat equity, to their ventures. **Sweat equity** represents the value of the time and effort that a

FIGURE 10.2

Sources of Personal Financing

Personal Funds	**Friends and Family**	**Bootstrapping**
Involves both financial resources and sweat equity. Sweat equity represents the value of the time and effort that a founder puts into a firm.	Often comes in the form of loans or investments, but can also involve outright gifts, foregone or delayed compensation, or reduced or free rent.	Finding ways to avoid the need for external financing through creativity, ingenuity, thriftiness, cost-cutting, obtaining grants, or any other means.

founder puts into a new venture. Because many founders do not have a substantial amount of money to put into their ventures, it is often the sweat equity that makes the most difference.

Friends and Family Friends and family are the second source of funds for many new ventures. This type of contribution often comes in the form of loans or investments but can also involve outright gifts, forgone or delayed compensation (if a friend or family member works for the new venture), or reduced or free rent. For example, Cisco Systems, the giant producer of Internet routers and switches, started in the house of one of its cofounder's parents. Similarly, Ted Waitt, the founder of Gateway Computer, got his start with a $10,000 loan from his grandmother. One potential hazard associated with accepting help from friends or family is that it can strain relationships if the new venture doesn't pan out.

Bootstrapping A third source of seed money for a new venture is referred to as bootstrapping. **Bootstrapping** is finding ways to avoid the need for external financing or funding through creativity, ingenuity, thriftiness, cost-cutting or any means necessary.[8] (The term comes from the adage "pull yourself up by your bootstraps.") Because it's hard for new firms to get financing or funding early on, many entrepreneurs bootstrap out of necessity.[9] There are many well-known examples of entrepreneurs who bootstrapped to get their companies started. Legend has it that Steve Jobs and partner Steve Wozniak sold a Volkswagen van and a Hewlett-Packard programmable calculator to raise $1,350, which was the initial seed capital for Apple Computer.

An illustration of how adept some entrepreneurs are at bootstrapping is provided by Michelle Madhok, the founder of SheFinds, a company that helps busy women (through a twice-weekly e-mail newsletter) keep in touch with fashion trends and find good values on the Internet. In describing how she combined her personal savings with bootstrapping to start her company, Madhok said:

> I financed SheFinds myself and have spent about $5,000 of my own money to get the business off the ground. The most expensive items were forming the LLC, legal costs and public relations. My [Web] site was built for about $250 by a guy in the Ukraine who I found on craigslist (www.craigslist.org). My photos were done for barter and I got a good deal on the illustrations on my site because the artist had downtime. I work with many independents—my lawyer is an independent, because I don't see the value in paying for a big, fancy firm. And I look for discount resources on the Internet—if you search around, you can find companies that will make quality color copies for about 20 cents a copy.[10]

There are many ways entrepreneurs bootstrap to raise money or cut costs. Some of the more common examples of bootstrapping are provided in Table 10.1.

LEARNING

Objective

3. Provide examples of how entrepreneurs bootstrap to raise money or cut costs.

TABLE 10.1 Examples of Bootstrapping Methods

- Buy used instead of new equipment
- Coordinate purchases with other businesses
- Lease equipment instead of buying
- Obtain payments in advance from customers
- Minimize personal expenses
- Avoid unnecessary expenses, such as lavish office space or furniture
- Buy items cheaply but prudently through discount outlets or online auctions such as eBay, rather than at full-price stores
- Share office space or employees with other businesses
- Obtain grants

Preparing to Raise Debt or Equity Financing

Once a start-up's financial needs exceed what personal funds, friends and family, and boot-strapping can provide, debt and equity are the two most common sources of funds. The most important thing an entrepreneur must do at this point is determine precisely what the company needs and the most appropriate source to use to obtain those funds. A carefully planned approach to raising money increases a firm's chance of success and can save an entrepreneur considerable time.

The steps involved in properly preparing to raise debt or equity financing are shown in Figure 10.3 and are discussed next.

Step 1 **Determine precisely how much money the company needs** Constructing and analyzing documented cash flow statements and projections for needed capital expenditures are actions taken to complete this step. This information should already be in the business plan, as described in Chapter 4.

Knowing exactly how much money to ask for is important for at least two reasons. First, a company doesn't want to get caught short, yet it doesn't want to pay for capital it doesn't need. Second, entrepreneurs talking to a potential lender or investor make a poor impression when they appear uncertain about the amount of money required to support their venture.

Step 2 **Determine the most appropriate type of financing or funding** The two most common alternatives for raising money are equity and debt financing. **Equity financing** (or funding) means exchanging partial ownership in a firm, usually in the form of stock, for funding. Angel investors, private placement, venture capital, and initial public offerings are the most common sources of equity funding (we discuss all these sources later in the chapter). Equity funding is not a loan—the money that is received is not paid back. Instead, equity investors become partial owners of the firm. Some equity investors invest "for the long haul" and are content to receive a return on their investment through dividend payments on their stock. More commonly, equity investors have a 3- to 5-year investment horizon and expect to get their money back, along with a substantial capital gain, through the sale of their stock. The stock is typically sold following a liquidity event (described in Chapter 4).

Because of the risks involved, equity investors are very demanding and fund only a small percentage of the business plans they consider.[11] An equity investor considers a firm that has a unique business opportunity, high growth potential, a clearly defined niche market, and proven management to be an ideal candidate. In contrast, businesses that don't fit these criteria have a hard time getting equity funding. Many entrepreneurs are not familiar with the standards that equity investors apply and get discouraged when they are repeatedly turned down by venture capitalists and angel investors. Often, the reason they don't qualify for venture capital or angel investment isn't because their business proposal is poor, but because they don't meet the exacting standards equity investors usually apply.[12]

Debt financing is getting a loan. The most common sources of debt financing are commercial banks and Small Business Administration (SBA) guaranteed loans. The types of bank loans and SBA guaranteed loans available to entrepreneurs are discussed later in this chapter. In general, banks lend money that must be repaid with interest. Banks are not investors. As a result, bankers are interested in minimizing risk, properly collateralizing loans, and repayment, as opposed to return on investment and capital gains. The ideal candidate for a bank loan is a firm with a strong cash flow, low leverage, audited financial statements, good management, and a

FIGURE 10.3

Preparation for Debt or Equity Financing

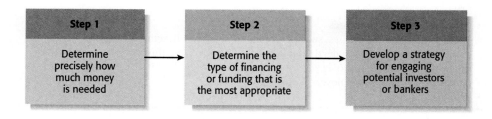

Step 1	Step 2	Step 3
Determine precisely how much money is needed	Determine the type of financing or funding that is the most appropriate	Develop a strategy for engaging potential investors or bankers

Matching an Entrepreneurial Venture's Characteristics
TABLE 10.2 with the Appropriate Form of Financing or Funding

Characteristics of the Venture	Appropriate Source of Financing or Funding
The business has high risk with an uncertain return: Weak cash flow High leverage Low-to-moderate growth Unproven management	Personal funds, friends, family, and other forms of bootstrapping
The business has low risk with a more predictable return: Strong cash flow Low leverage Audited financials Good management Healthy balance sheet	Debt financing
The business offers a high return: Unique business idea High growth Niche market Proven management	Equity

healthy balance sheet. A careful review of these criteria demonstrates why it's difficult for start-ups to receive bank loans. Most start-ups are simply too early in their life cycle to have the set of characteristics bankers want.

Table 10.2 provides an overview of three common profiles of new ventures and the type of financing or funding that is appropriate for each one. This table illustrates why most start-ups must rely on personal funds, friends and family, and bootstrapping at the outset and must wait until later to obtain equity or debt financing. Indeed, most new ventures do not have the characteristics required by bankers or investors until they have proven their product or service idea and have achieved a certain measure of success in the marketplace.

Step 3 **Developing a strategy for engaging potential investors or bankers** There are three steps to developing a strategy for engaging potential investors or bankers. First, the lead entrepreneurs in a new venture should prepare an **elevator speech (or pitch)**—a brief, carefully constructed statement that outlines the merits of a business opportunity. Why is it called an elevator speech? If an entrepreneur stepped into an elevator on the 25th floor of a building and found that by a stroke of luck a potential investor was in the same elevator, the entrepreneur would have the time it takes to get from the 25th floor to the ground floor to try to get the investor interested in the business opportunity. Most elevator speeches are 45 seconds to 2 minutes long.

There are many occasions when a carefully constructed elevator speech might come in handy. For example, many university-sponsored centers for entrepreneurship hold events that bring investors and entrepreneurs together. Often, these events include social hours and refreshment breaks designed specifically for the purpose of allowing entrepreneurs looking for funding to mingle with potential investors. An outline for a 60-second elevator speech is provided in Table 10.3.

L E A R N I N G
Objective

5. Explain the role of an elevator speech in attracting financing for an entrepreneurial venture.

The second step in developing a strategy for engaging potential investors or bankers is more deliberate and requires identifying and contacting the best prospects. First, the new venture should carefully assess the type of financing or funding it is likely to qualify for, as depicted in Table 10.2. Then, a list of potential bankers or investors should be compiled. If venture capital funding is felt to be appropriate, for example, a little legwork can go a long way in pinpointing likely investors. A new venture should identify the venture funds that

TABLE 10.3 Guidelines for Preparing an Elevator Speech

The elevator speech is a very brief description of your opportunity, product idea, qualifications, and market. Imagine that you step into an elevator in a tall building and a potential investor is already there; you have about 60 seconds to explain your business idea.

Step 1: Describe the opportunity or problem that needs to be solved	20 seconds
Step 2: Describe how your product or service meets the opportunity or solves the problem	20 seconds
Step 3: Describe your qualifications	10 seconds
Step 4: Describe your market	10 seconds
Total	60 seconds

are investing money in the industry in which it intends to compete and target those firms first. To do this, look to the venture capital firms' Web sites. These reveal the industries in which the firms have an interest. Sometimes, these sites also provide a list of the companies the firm has funded. For an example, access Sequoia Capital's Web site (www.sequoia.com), a well-known venture capital firm.

A cardinal rule for approaching a banker or an investor is to get a personal introduction. Bankers and investors receive many business plans, and most of them end up in what often becomes an unread stack of paper in a corner in their offices. To have your business plan noticed, find someone who knows the banker or the investor and ask for an introduction. This requirement is explained in blunt terms by Randall Stross, the author of *eBoys*, a book about the venture capital industry. Stross spent 2 years observing the day-to-day activities at Benchmark Venture Capital, a prominent Silicon Valley venture capital firm. According to Stross,

> The business plan that comes in from a complete stranger, either without the blessing of someone the venture capital firm knows well or without professional recommendations that render an introduction superfluous, is all but certain not to make the cut. In fact, knowing that this is the case becomes a tacit requirement from the perspective of a venture guy: Anyone whom I don't know who approaches me directly with a business plan shows me they haven't passed Entrepreneurship 101.[13]

The third step in engaging potential investors or bankers is to be prepared to provide the investor or banker a completed business plan and make a presentation of the plan if requested. We looked at how to present a business plan in Chapter 4. The presentation should be as polished as possible and should demonstrate why the new venture represents an attractive endeavor for the lender or investor. This point is emphasized by Irene Smith, founder of The Business Center, a provider of services to businesses, including word processing and graphic design. Smith is also the author of *Diary of a Small Business*, in which she provides a candid assessment of her experiences as an entrepreneur. Commenting on the challenges involved with raising money, Smith said,

> I came to the conclusion that seeking outside financing, whether debt financing (borrowing money) or equity capital financing (sale of stock), is not a simple business problem. It is a marketing problem. Just as you must market your product or service to make it appealing to your potential customers, you must present your business to potential lenders or investors in a way that will make it an attractive investment for them. You must speak eloquently in a language to which they will respond—and that language is profit.[14]

6. Discuss the difference between equity funding and debt financing.

Sources of Equity Funding

The primary disadvantage of equity funding is that the firm's owners relinquish part of their ownership interest and may lose some control. The primary advantage is access to capital. In addition, because investors become partial owners of the firms in which they invest, they often try to help those firms by offering their expertise and assistance. Unlike a loan, the money received from an equity investor doesn't have to be paid back. The investor receives a return on the investment through dividend payments and by selling the stock.

The three most common forms of equity funding are described next.

Business Angels

Business angels are individuals who invest their personal capital directly in start-ups. The term "angel" was first used in connection with finance to describe wealthy New Yorkers who invested in Broadway plays. The prototypical business angel, who invests in entrepreneurial start-ups, is about 50 years old, has high income and wealth, is well educated, has succeeded as an entrepreneur, and is interested in the start-up process.[15] These investors generally invest between $10,000 and $500,000 in a single company and are looking for companies that have the potential to grow 30 percent to 40 percent per year before they are acquired or go public.[16] Jeffrey Sohl, the director of the University of New Hampshire's Center for Venture Research, estimates that only 10 percent to 15 percent of private companies meet that criterion.[17] Many well-known firms have received their initial funding from one or more business angels. For example, Apple Computer received its initial investment capital from Mike Markkula, who obtained his wealth as an executive with Intel. In 1977, Markkula invested $91,000 in Apple and personally guaranteed another $250,000 in credit lines. When Apple went public in 1980, his stock in the company was worth more than $150 million.[18] Similarly, in 1998 Google received its first investment from Sun Microsystems cofounder Andy Bechtolsheim, who gave Larry Page and Sergey Brin (Google's cofounders) a check for $100,000 after they showed him an early version of Google's search engine.[19] Can you image what Bechtolsheim's investment was worth when Google went public in 2005?

The number of angel investors in the United States, which is estimated to be around 227,000, has increased dramatically over the past decade.[20] The rapid increase is due in part to the high returns that some angels report. In 2005, angels invested $23.1 billion in 49,500 small companies.[21] By comparison, during that same period, venture capital funds invested about $22.1 billion in 3,008 deals.[22] In exchange for their investment, angels expect a rather hefty annual return—usually in the neighborhood of 35 to 40 percent.[23] They also usually fill a seat on the board of directors of the firms in which they invest and provide varying levels of managerial input.

Business angels are valuable because of their willingness to make relatively small investments. This gives access to equity funding to a start-up that needs just $50,000 rather than the $1 million minimum investment that most venture capitalists require. Many angels are also motivated by more than financial returns; they enjoy the process of mentoring a new firm. Oron Strauss is a 1995 Dartmouth College graduate who received angel funding. Recalling an experience with his angel investor, Strauss said,

> About a year ago, when I was having a particularly bad week, I fired off a long, heartfelt e-mail message to my angel. I explained, in great detail, the difficulties I faced and my thoughts about them. His response was succinct: "All sounds normal. You're handling it well. Keep up the good work." My first reaction was disappointment over what struck me as a curt response. Then I realized that the angel had given me the best possible response. He understood that what I was going through was normal and that I would make it.[24]

Most angels remain fairly anonymous and are matched up with entrepreneurs through referrals. To find a business angel investor, an entrepreneur should discretely work a network of acquaintances to see if anyone can make an appropriate introduction. An advantage that college students have in regard to finding business angels is that many angels judge college- or university-sponsored business plan competitions. For example, while at Boston University, Jan Stephenson and Amy Appleyard presented their idea for

Spark Craft Studios, the subject of the opening profile for Chapter 9, to a panel of judges in a business plan competition connected with their social entrepreneurship class. Two of the judges, who were angel investors, took an interest in the contents of their plan and later invested.

The number of organized groups of angels continues to grow. Typically, each group consists of 10 to 150 angel investors in a local area that meet regularly to listen to business plan presentations. In 1996, there were only about 10 of these types of groups; now there are more than 200.[25] The Angel Capital Education Foundation provides a list of angel groups in the United States and Canada on its Web site (www.angelcapitaleducation.org). In many areas, local governments and nonprofit organizations are active in trying to bring entrepreneurs and angel investors together. Some communities are very creative in this regard. For example, FundingUtah, an organization that promotes entrepreneurship in Utah, periodically sponsors "speedpitching" luncheons for small groups of entrepreneurs and angel investors. At speedpitching luncheons, entrepreneurs give 5-minute pitches of their business ideas to several small groups of business angels, rotating from group to group in a fast-paced, speed-dating type of fashion.[26]

Venture Capital

LEARNING
Objective

7. Describe the difference between a business angel and a venture capitalist.

Venture capital is money that is invested by venture capital firms in start-ups and small businesses with exceptional growth potential.[27] There are about 650 venture capital firms in the United States, which provide funding to about 3,000 firms per year. As mentioned, in 2005, venture capital firms invested $22.1 billion in just over 3,000 companies.[28] The peak year for venture capital investing was 2000, when $106.6 billion was invested at the height of the e-commerce craze. A distinct difference between angel investors and venture capital firms is that angels tend to invest earlier in the life of a company, whereas venture capitalists come in later. In 2005, nearly 55 percent of angel investments were to "seed" or start-up companies, while only 6 percent of venture deals were to these types of firms. The majority of venture capital money goes to follow-on funding for businesses originally funded by angel investors, government programs (which are discussed later in the chapter), or by some other means.

Venture capital firms are limited partnerships of money managers who raise money in "funds" to invest in start-ups and growing firms. The funds, or pools of money, are raised from wealthy individuals, pension plans, university endowments, foreign investors, and similar sources. A typical fund is $75 million to $200 million and invests in 20 to 30 companies over a 3- to 5-year period.[29] The venture capitalists that manage the fund receive an annual management fee in addition to 20 to 25 percent of the profits earned by the fund. The percentage of the profits the venture capitalists get is called the **carry**. So if a venture capital firm raised a $100 million fund and the fund grew to $500 million, a 20 percent carry means that the firm would get, after repaying the original $100 million, 20 percent of the $400 million in profits, or $80 million. The investors in the fund would get the remainder. Venture capitalists shoot for a 30 to 40 percent annual return on their investment or more and a total return over the life of the investment of 5 to 20 times the initial investment.[30]

Because of the venture capital industry's lucrative nature and because in the past venture capitalists have funded high-profile successes such as Google, Cisco Systems, eBay, and Yahoo!, the industry receives a great deal of attention. But actually, venture capitalists fund very few entrepreneurial ventures in comparison to business angels and relative to the number of firms needing funding. Remember, venture capitalists fund about 3,000 companies per year, compared to 50,000 funded by business angels. As mentioned earlier in this chapter, many entrepreneurs become discouraged when they are repeatedly rejected for venture capital funding, even though they may have an excellent business plan. Venture capitalists are looking for the "home run." This target causes VCs to reject the majority of the proposals they consider.

Venture capitalists know that they are making risky investments and that some investments won't pan out. In fact, most venture firms anticipate that about 15 to 25 percent of their investments will be home runs, 25 to 35 percent will be winners, 25 to 35 percent will break even, and 15 to 25 percent will fail.[31] The home runs must be sensational to make up for the break-even firms and the failures.

Still, for the firms that qualify, venture capital is a viable alternative to equity funding. An advantage to obtaining this funding is that venture capitalists are extremely well connected in the business world (by this we mean that they have a large number of useful contacts with customers, suppliers, government representatives, and so forth) and can offer a firm considerable assistance beyond funding. Firms that qualify typically obtain their money in stages that correspond to their own stage of development. Once a venture capitalist makes an investment in a firm, subsequent investments are made in **rounds** (or stages) and are referred to as **follow-on funding**. Table 10.4 shows the various stages in the venture capital process, from the seed stage to buyout financing.

An important part of obtaining venture capital funding is going through the **due diligence** process, which refers to the process of investigating the merits of a potential venture and verifying the key claims made in the business plan. Firms that prove to be suitable for venture capital funding should conduct their own due diligence of the venture capitalists with whom they are working to ensure that they are a good fit. An entrepreneur should ask the following questions and scrutinize the answers to them before accepting funding from a venture capital firm:

- Do the venture capitalists have experience in our industry?
- Do they take a highly active or passive management role?
- Are the personalities on both sides of the table compatible?
- Does the firm have deep enough pockets or sufficient contacts within the venture capital industry to provide follow-on rounds of financing?
- Is the firm negotiating in good faith in regard to the percentage of our firm they want in exchange for their investment?

Along with traditional venture capital, there is also **corporate venture capital**. This type of capital is similar to traditional venture capital except that the money comes from corporations that invest in start-ups related to their areas of interest.[32]

Initial Public Offering

Another source of equity funding is to sell stock to the public by staging an **initial public offering** (IPO). An IPO is the first sale of stock by a firm to the public. Any later public issuance of shares is referred to as a **secondary market offering**. When a company goes

L E A R N I N G

Objective

8. Explain why an initial public offering (IPO) is an important milestone in an entrepreneurial venture.

TABLE 10.4 Stages (or Rounds) of Venture Capital Funding

Stage or Round	Purpose of the Funding
Seed funding	Investment made very early in a venture's life to fund the development of a prototype and feasibility analysis.
Start-up funding	Investment made to firms exhibiting few if any commercial sales but in which product development and market research are reasonably complete. Management is in place, and the firm has completed its business model. Funding is needed to start production.
First-stage funding	Funding that occurs when the firm has started commercial production and sales but requires additional financing to ramp up its production capacity.
Second-stage funding	Funding that occurs when a firm is successfully selling a product but needs to expand both its production capacity and its markets.
Mezzanine financing	Investment made in a firm to provide for further expansion or to bridge its financing needs before launching an IPO or before a buyout.
Buyout funding	Funding provided to help one company acquire another.

public, its stock is typically traded on one of the major stock exchanges. Most entrepreneurial firms that go public trade on the NASDAQ, which is weighted heavily toward technology, biotech, and small-company stocks.[33] An IPO is an important milestone for a firm.[34] Typically, a firm is not able to go public until it has demonstrated that it is viable and has a bright future.

Firms decide to go public for several reasons. First, it is a way to raise equity capital to fund current and future operations. Second, an IPO raises a firm's public profile, making it easier to attract high-quality customers, alliance partners, and employees. Third, an IPO is a liquidity event that provides a mechanism for the company's stockholders, including its investors, to cash out their investments. Finally, by going public, a firm creates another form of currency that can be used to grow the company. It is not uncommon for one firm to buy another company by paying for it with stock rather than with cash.[35] The stock comes from "authorized but not yet issued stock," which in essence means that the firm issues new shares of stock to make the purchase. In fact, a large percentage of Cisco System's 70-plus acquisitions were paid for in this manner.

Although there are many advantages to going public, it is a complicated and expensive process and subjects firms to substantial costs related to SEC reporting requirements. Many of the most costly requirements were initiated by the **Sarbanes-Oxley Act** of 2002. The Sarbanes-Oxley Act is a federal law that was passed in response to corporate accounting scandals involving prominent corporations, like Enron and WorldCom. This wide-ranging act established a number of new or enhanced reporting standards for public corporations.

The first step in initiating a public offering is for a firm to hire an investment bank. An **investment bank** is an institution, such as Credit Suisse First Boston, that acts as an underwriter or agent for a firm issuing securities.[36] The investment bank acts as the firm's advocate and adviser and walks it through the process of going public. The most important issues the firm and its investment bank must agree on are the amount of capital needed by the firm, the type of stock to be issued, the price of the stock when it goes public (e.g., $12 per share), and the cost to the firm to issue the securities.

There are a number of hoops the investment bank must jump through to assure the Securities and Exchange Commission (SEC) that the offer is legitimate. During the time the SEC is investigating the potential offering, the investment bank issues a **preliminary prospectus** that describes the offering to the general public. The preliminary prospectus is also called the "red herring." After the SEC has approved the offering, the investment bank issues the **final prospectus**, which sets a date and issuing price for the offering.

In addition to getting the offering approved, the investment bank is responsible for drumming up support for the offering. As part of this process, the investment bank typically takes the top management team of the firm wanting to go public on a **road show**, which is a whirlwind tour that consists of meetings in key cities where the firm presents its business plan to groups of investors.[37] Until December 1, 2005, the presentations made during these road shows were seen only by the investors physically present in the various cities; an SEC regulation went into effect at that time requiring that road show presentations be taped and made available to the public. Road show presentations can now be viewed online at www.retailroadshow.com. If enough interest in a potential public offering is created, the offering will take place on the date scheduled in the prospectus. If it isn't, the offering will be delayed or canceled.

Timing and luck play a role in whether a public offering is successful. For example, a total of 332 IPOs raised about $50 billion in 1999, the height of the Internet bubble. When the bubble burst in early 2001, the IPO marketplace all but dried up, particularly for technology and telecom stocks. Since then, the market has recovered some, although it is still not robust, and most firms cannot count on an IPO to raise capital or as an exit strategy. There were 75 IPOs in 2002, followed by 71 in 2003, 205 in 2004, and 190 in 2005.[38] The vitality of the IPO market hinges largely on the state of the overall economy and the mood of the investing public. However, when facing a strong economy and a positive mood toward investing, an entrepreneurial venture should guard itself against becoming caught up in the euphoria and rushing its IPO. The problems that can result from this approach are illustrated in the boxed feature titled "What Went Wrong?"

what went wrong?

Why Rushing an IPO Isn't Such a Good Idea
www.akamai.com

In the late 1990s and the early 2000s, the Internet bubble was at its height. The bubble was created by the public's enthusiasm over the Internet and the proclamation from many quarters that the Internet was going to "change everything," including how businesses would be funded and operate. The height of the bubble was July 1999 to February 2001—a time when money flowed into technology companies at a breathtaking rate. Venture capitalists invested about $80 billion in start-ups during this period, and the NASDAQ Composite Index rose by 74.4 percent. Investor euphoria was at an all-time high. At least two new terms—day trading and day trader—entered the vocabulary. Some people were so caught up in investing that they literally spent their entire days trading stocks. There was talk of soon reaching "Dow 30,000," an expectation that proved to be pure fantasy.

In the spring of 2001, the bubble burst. Investors and the public at large realized that the Internet wasn't going to change everything. Many investors took heavy losses. But it wasn't just investors who were hurt. Many start-ups would have been better off if the bubble had never happened. Why? In some cases, firms rushed their public offerings to catch the wave of the rising stock market, and when the bubble burst, their share prices fell faster than they had earlier risen. This chain of events caused tremendous heartache among the firms that were affected. Akamai Technologies was one of these firms. (Today, this firm's official name is Akamai.)

A team of entrepreneurs from the Massachusetts Institute of Technology launched Akamai Technologies in August 1998. The firm was established with the intention of finding a solution to the growing problem of congestion on the Internet. The company got off to a good start. In its first few months, it hired a seasoned CEO, attracted the attention of customers, and applied for patents on its core technologies. In October 1999, Akamai went public, just 14 months after it started. Its stock price, which debuted at $26 per share, quickly ran up to $345 per share. By early 2001, it had 1,300 employees and was managing 9,700 servers in 56 countries.

Then, in early 2001, the Internet bubble burst. Although Akamai was growing, it wasn't yet profitable and fell out of favor with investors. By the fall of 2001, its stock price had fallen to less than $4 per share. Its customers, suppliers, and employees were startled by this turn of events and became nervous about Akamai's ability to survive. Moreover, rumors circulated that the company was for sale.

What went wrong at Akamai? While part of its troubles may have been due to management blunders, the company was primarily a victim of the general loss of confidence in technology companies following the burst of the dot-com bubble. The fact that it went public so early contributed to its problems. The rapid increase in its stock price, followed by its rapid decline, drew attention to the company and frightened its stakeholders. In reality, in the midst of everything that was happening, the company was patiently executing its business model and following its plan. Nothing it did justified a stock price of $345 per share or a price of $4 per share. But it's hard for the public to believe that when a company's stock price is high it isn't doing something spectacular and that when its stock price is low it isn't in trouble. As a result, when Akamai's stock price sank to $4 per share, it lost the confidence of the people it needed the most to build its business. Right or wrong, people judged Akamai on the basis of its stock price rather than on the quality of its products and services.

Akamai has recovered and is now a strong company, and its stock is trading in a healthy range. In the second quarter of 2006, for example, the company generated over $100 million in sales and recorded over $11 million in net income. At the close of the third quarter of 2006, Akamai's stock was selling at over $51 per share.

The lesson to be learned from this case is that it's dangerous for a firm to rush its IPO, particularly if it is new and its true value is unknown. If Akamai had waited to launch its IPO until its business model was better understood and its customers, suppliers, and employees had a better sense of the firm's long-term potential, its stock price probably would not have suffered as severe gyrations as it did, even in a volatile market.

Questions for Critical Thinking

1. As a potential entrepreneur, what have you learned by reading this case in addition to the mistake of rushing to the IPO stage? List three or four lessons you are taking away from reading about the experiences of Akamai Technologies.

2. What alternatives for raising capital did Akamai Technologies have other than launching a public offering? Do you think raising capital was the primary motivation for going public? If not, what do you think Akamai's primary reasons were?

3. As the founder of Akamai Technologies or as the firm's seasoned CEO, what could you have said to customers, suppliers, and shareholders to alleviate their concerns as the price of the company's stock was rapidly sinking?

4. Go to Akamai's Web site (www.akamai.com). How has its business changed since going public in 1999? What is the price of a share of Akamai today? Using data from the Web site, evaluate the firm's current financial performance.

Source: Akamai homepage, www.akamai.com (accessed July 20, 2006); D. Mills, *Buy, Lie, and Sell High: How Investors Lost Out on Enron and the Internet Bubble* (Upper Saddle River, NJ: Financial Times Prentice Hall, 2002).

A variation of the IPO is a **private placement**, which is the direct sale of an issue of securities to a large institutional investor. When a private placement is initiated, there is no public offering, and no prospectus is prepared.

Sources of Debt Financing

Debt financing involves getting a loan or selling corporate bonds. Because it is virtually impossible for a new venture to sell corporate bonds, we'll focus on obtaining loans.

There are two common types of loans. The first is a **single-purpose loan**, in which a specific amount of money is borrowed that must be repaid in a fixed amount of time with interest. The second is a **line of credit**, in which a borrowing "cap" is established and borrowers can use the credit at their discretion. Lines of credit require periodic interest payments.

There are two major advantages to obtaining a loan as opposed to equity funding. The first is that none of the ownership of the firm is surrendered—a major advantage for most

April 12, 2002 was a special day for the employees and investors in JetBlue. The company went public on the NASDAQ and posted a 67 percent gain its first day of trading. A public offering is a major milestone for an entrepreneurial firm. Here, JetBlue founder and CEO David Neeleman and his staff celebrate the company's first day of trading at the NASDAQ stock exchange in New York City.

entrepreneurs. The second is that interest payments on a loan are tax deductible in contrast to dividend payments made to investors, which aren't.

There are two major disadvantages of getting a loan. The first is that it must be repaid, which may be difficult in a start-up venture in which the entrepreneur is focused on getting the company off the ground. Cash is typically "tight" during a new venture's first few months and sometimes for a year or more. The second is that lenders often impose strict conditions on loans and insist on ample collateral to fully protect their investment. Even if a start-up is incorporated, a lender may require that an entrepreneur's personal assets be collateralized as a condition of the loan.

The two most common sources of debt financing available to entrepreneurs are described next.

Commercial Banks

Historically, commercial banks have not been viewed as practical sources of financing for start-up firms.[39] This sentiment is not a knock against banks; it is just that banks are risk averse, and financing start-ups is risky business. Instead of looking for businesses that are "home runs," which is what venture capitalists seek to do, banks look for customers who will reliably repay their loans. As shown in Table 10.2, banks are interested in firms that have a strong cash flow, low leverage, audited financials, good management, and a healthy balance sheet. Although many new ventures have good management, few have the other characteristics, at least initially. But banks are an important source of credit for small businesses later in their life cycles.

There are two reasons that banks have historically been reluctant to lend money to start-ups. First, as mentioned previously, banks are risk averse. In addition, banks frequently have internal controls and regulatory restrictions prohibiting them from making high-risk loans. So when an entrepreneur approaches a banker with a request for a $250,000 loan and the only collateral the entrepreneur has to offer is the recognition of a problem that needs to be solved, a plan to solve it, and perhaps some intellectual property, there is usually no practical way for the bank to help. Banks typically have standards that guide their lending, such as minimum debt-to-equity ratios that work against start-up entrepreneurs.

The second reason banks have historically been reluctant to lend money to start-ups is that lending to small firms is not as profitable as lending to large firms, which have historically been the staple clients of commercial banks. If an entrepreneur approaches a banker with a request for a $50,000 loan, it may simply not be worth the banker's time to do the due diligence necessary to determine the entrepreneur's risk profile. Considerable time is required to digest a business plan and investigate the merits of a new firm. Research shows that a firm's size is an important factor in determining its access to debt capital.[40] The $50,000 loan may be seen as both high risk and marginally profitable (based on the amount of time it would take to do the due diligence involved), making it doubly uninviting for a commercial bank.[41]

Despite these historical precedents, some banks are starting to engage start-up entrepreneurs—although the jury is still out regarding how significant these lenders will become. When it comes to start-ups, some banks are rethinking their lending standards and are beginning to focus on cash flow and the strength of the management team rather than on collateral and the strength of the balance sheet. Entrepreneurs should follow developments in this area closely.

SBA Guaranteed Loans

Approximately 50 percent of the 9,000 banks in the United States participate in the **SBA Guaranteed Loan Program**. The most notable SBA program available to small businesses is the **7(A) Loan Guaranty Program**. This program accounts for 90 percent of the SBA's loan activity. The program operates through private-sector lenders who provide loans that are guaranteed by the SBA. The loans are for small businesses that are unable to

L E A R N I N G

Objective

9. Discuss the SBA Guaranteed Loan Program.

The SBA Guaranteed Loan Program is a viable source of financing for many entrepreneurs. Since its inception, the program has helped make $280 billion in loans to nearly 1.3 million businesses—more than any other source of funding. Approximately 50 percent of the 9,000 banks in the United States participate in the program.

secure financing on reasonable terms through normal lending channels. The SBA does not currently have funding for direct loans, nor does it provide grants or low-interest-rate loans for business start-ups or expansion.

Almost all small businesses are eligible to apply for an SBA guaranteed loan. The SBA can guarantee as much as 85 percent (debt to equity) on loans up to $150,000 and 75 percent on loans of over $150,000. In most cases, the maximum guarantee is $1.5 million. A guaranteed loan can be used for working capital to expand a new business or start a new one. It can also be used for real estate purchases, renovation, construction, or equipment purchases. To obtain an SBA guaranteed loan, an application must meet the requirements of both the SBA and the lender. Individuals must typically pledge all of their assets to secure the loan.[42]

Although SBA guaranteed loans are utilized more heavily by existing small businesses than start-ups, they should not be dismissed as a possible source of funding. Since its inception, the SBA has helped make $280 billion in loans to nearly 1.3 million businesses—more money than any other source of financing.[43] Diane Nelson, the woman who built Kazoo & Company into a successful business and is the subject of Case 4.1, got her start through a $500,000 SBA guaranteed loan. John and Caprial Pence, who own several businesses in Portland, Oregon, have relied on the SBA guaranteed loan program twice for funding. The Pence's story, which is related in the following "The Savvy Entrepreneurial Firm" feature, illustrates the important role that the SBA loan program plays in funding small businesses and entrepreneurs. The Pence's own the types of businesses that typically don't qualify for equity funding. In their case, the SBA program enabled them to build the thriving businesses that they own today.

Creative Sources of Financing and Funding

Because financing and funding are difficult to obtain, particularly for start-ups, entrepreneurs often use creative ways to obtain financial resources. Even for firms that have financing or funding available, it is prudent to search for sources of capital that are less expensive than traditional ones. The following sections discuss three of the more common creative sources of financing and funding for entrepreneurial firms.

savvy entrepreneurial firm

John and Caprial Pence: How the SBA Guaranteed Loan Program Helped Two Entrepreneurs Get the Financing They Needed

John and Caprial Pence are two of Portland, Oregon's finest cooks and busiest entrepreneurs. The two run a growing number of ventures in the Portland area, all focused around fine food. A distinctive aspect of their story is the role that the Small Business Administration (SBA) Guaranteed Loan Program has played in their success. The Pences have utilized the SBA loan program twice, and it has been instrumental in helping them build their businesses.

John and Caprial grew up on opposite coasts and met at the Culinary Institute of America in Hyde Park, N.Y., where they were both attending school to become chefs. In the mid-1980s, following graduation, they moved to Seattle, where they launched their careers. In 1990, Caprial won the 1990 James Beard Award for Best Chef in the Pacific Northwest. At the same time, she was working on her first cookbook, teaching classes, and appearing on local TV. By 1992, the Pences were able to write their own ticket, and they moved to Portland.

In Portland, the Pences bought the old Westmoreland Bistro with private financing. In 1998, they decided to remodel and expand the Bistro, when space became available next door. The Pences considered several options for financing. The most realistic alternative, based on the advice of their banker, was an SBA guaranteed loan. The Pences agreed, and the bank facilitated a $260,000, seven-year SBA guaranteed loan. The loan enabled the couple to expand the seating capacity of their restaurant from 26 to 70.

Following the expansion of their restaurant, the Pences decided to diversify and leverage their cooking expertise by opening a cooking school and a cookware shop. A second SBA guaranteed loan, for an identical amount as the first one ($260,000), made these objectives a reality. All three locations, the restaurant, the school, and the shop, are located near one another, making it easy for their customers to visit more than one location in a single trip. The addition of the cooking

school and the cookware shop has tripled the Pence's annual revenue.

The future for the Pences and their ventures looks bright. The restaurant initially brought in around $1,000 a day, but now brings in $4,000 to $5,000 on an average weekday. The cooking school offers classes and demonstrations nearly every evening, where participants pay from $35 to $135 for hands-on classes or to view special cooking demonstrations. Just recently, the Pences started broadcasting a television show from the cooking school, and Caprial celebrated the printing of her eighth cookbook. Commenting on their experiences borrowing money to fund their growing operations, John Pence remarked, "We learned to get into this business (cooking) at the lowest debt level and have a cushion of working capital."

Questions for Critical Thinking

1. When the Pences decided to expand and remodel their restaurant in 1998, what sources of funding or financing were realistically available to them?

2. Do some research to find out what it takes to qualify for an SBA guaranteed loan. What criteria do the SBA and the participating lenders typically apply when evaluating candidates for loans?

3. Based on the material provided here, any additional information you can garner from the Pences Web site, and your general knowledge of entrepreneurship, write a short analysis of why you think the Pences have been successful.

4. Do you think the Pences would be where they are today if they hadn't been made aware of the SBA Guaranteed Loan Program? Do you think most entrepreneurs are aware of the program?

Sources: Caprial and John's Kitchen homepage www.caprialandjohnskitchen.com (accessed July 24, 2006); Shelly Herochik, "Restaurateurs Fit More on Their Plate with Help of Loan Program," *Bizjournals*, www.bizjournals.com/sba/1 (accessed January 31, 2006).

Leasing

A **lease** is a written agreement in which the owner of a piece of property allows an individual or business to use the property for a specified period of time in exchange for payments. The major advantage of leasing is that it enables a company to acquire the use of assets with very little or no down payment. Leases for facilities and leases for equipment are the

LEARNING Objective

10. Explain the advantages of leasing for an entrepreneurial venture.

two most common types of leases that entrepreneurial ventures undertake.[44] For example, many new businesses lease computers from Dell Inc. The advantage for the new business is that it can gain access to the computers it needs with very little money invested up-front.

There are many different players in the leasing business. Some vendors, such as Dell, lease directly to businesses. As with banks, the vendors look for lease clients with good credit backgrounds and the ability to make the lease payments. There are also **venture-leasing firms** that act as brokers, bringing the parties involved in a lease together. These firms are acquainted with the producers of specialized equipment and match these producers with new ventures that are in need of the equipment. One of the responsibilities of these firms is conducting due diligence to make sure that the new ventures involved will be able to keep up with their lease payments.

Most leases involve a modest down payment and monthly payments during the duration of the lease. At the end of an equipment lease, the new venture typically has the option to stop using the equipment, purchase it at fair market value, or renew the lease. Lease deals that involve a substantial amount of money should be negotiated and entered into with the same amount of scrutiny as when getting financing or funding. Leasing is almost always more expensive than paying cash for an item, so most entrepreneurs think of leasing as an alternative to equity or debt financing. Although the down payment is typically lower, the primary disadvantage is that at the end of the lease, the lessee doesn't own the property or equipment.[45] Of course, this may be an advantage if a company is leasing equipment, such as computers or copy machines that can rather quickly become technologically obsolete.

Government Grants

The Small Business Innovation Research (SBIR) and the Small Business Technology Transfer (STTR) programs are two important sources of early stage funding for technology firms. These programs provide cash grants to entrepreneurs who are working on projects in specific areas. The main difference between the SBIR and the STTR programs is that the STTR program requires the participation of researchers working at universities or other research institutions. For the purpose of the program, the term *small business* is defined as an American-owned for-profit business with fewer than 500 employees. The principle researcher must also be employed by the business.[46]

The **SBIR Program** is a competitive grant program that provides over $1 billion per year to small businesses for early stage and development projects. Each year, 10 federal departments and agencies are required by the SBIR to reserve a portion of their research and development funds for awards to small businesses. The agencies that participate, along with the types of areas that are funded, are shown in Table 10.5. Guidelines for how to apply for the grants are provided on each agency's Web site, along with a description of the types of projects the agencies are interested in supporting. The SBIR is a three-phase program, meaning that firms that qualify have the potential to receive more than one grant to fund a particular proposal. These three phases, along with the amount of funding available for each phase, are as follows:

- *Phase I* is a 6-month feasibility study in which the business must demonstrate the technical feasibility of the proposed innovation. Funding available for Phase I research ranges from $75,000 to $100,000, depending on the agency involved.
- *Phase II* awards are made for up to $750,000 for as long as 2 years to successful Phase I companies. The purpose of a Phase II grant is to develop and test a prototype of Phase I innovations. Funding available for Phase II research ranges from $300,000 to $750,000, depending on the agency involved. Some agencies have **fast-track programs** where applicants can simultaneously submit Phase I and Phase II applications.
- *Phase III* is the period during which Phase II innovations move from the research and development lab to the marketplace. No SBIR funds are involved. At this point,

TABLE 10.5 Small Business Innovation Research: Three-Phase Program

Phase	Purpose of Phase	Duration	Funding Available (varies by agency)
Phase I	To demonstrate the proposed innovation's technical feasibility.	Up to 6 months	$75,000–$100,000
Phase II	Available to successful phase I companies. The purpose of a phase II grant is to develop and test a prototype of the innovation validated in phase I.*	Up to 2 years	$300,000–$750,000
Phase III	Period in which phase II innovations move from the research and development lab to the marketplace.	Open	No government funding involved. At this point, businesses must find private funding or financing to commercialize the product.

*Some agencies have a fast-track program where applicants can submit phase I and phase II applications simultaneously. Government agencies that participate in this program include the following: Department of Agriculture, Department of Commerce, Department of Defense, Department of Education, Department of Energy, Department of Health and Human Services, Department of Homeland Security, Department of Transportation, Environmental Protection Agency, NASA, and the National Science Foundation.

the business must find private funding or financing to commercialize the product or service. In some cases, such as with the Department of Defense, the government may be the primary customer for the product.

Historically, less than 15 percent of all Phase I proposals are funded, and about 30 percent of all Phase II proposals are funded. The payoff for successful proposals, however, is high. The money is essentially free. It is a grant, meaning that it doesn't have to be paid back and no equity in the firm is at stake. The recipient of the grant also retains the rights to the intellectual property developed while working with the support provided by the grant. The real payoff is in Phase III if the new venture can commercialize the research results.

The **STTR Program** is a variation of the SBIR for collaborative research projects that involve small businesses and research organizations, such as universities or federal laboratories. More information about the STTR program can be obtained from the SBA.

Strategic Partners

Strategic partners are another source of capital for new ventures.[47] Indeed, strategic partners often play a critical role in helping young firms fund their operations and round out their business models.

Biotechnology companies, for example, rely heavily on partners for financial support. Biotech firms, which are typically fairly small, often partner with larger drug companies to conduct clinical trials and bring products to market. Most of these arrangements involve a licensing agreement. A typical agreement works like this. A biotech firm licenses a product that is under development to a pharmaceutical company in exchange for financial support during the development of the product and beyond. This type of arrangement gives the biotech firm money to operate while the drug is being developed. The downside to this approach is that the larger firm ultimately markets the drug and retains a large share of the income for itself. Sometimes strategic partnerships take on a different role in helping biotech firms take products to market and allows them to keep a larger share of the income than licensing arrangements permit. This scenario is depicted in this chapter's "Partnering for Success" feature.

partnering for success

Biogen Idec Inc.: How the Smart Use of Alliances Helped a Biotech Firm Avoid the Need for Additional Funding

www.biogen.com

Biogen, one of the two firms that merged in late 2003 to form Biogen Idec Inc., is a biotechnology company. During the 1980s and 1990s, Biogen developed a number of pharmaceutical products that it licensed to larger drug companies. Licensing products to larger companies is a mixed blessing for a company like Biogen. Although in many instances it is the only practical way to take a drug to market, licensing deals force biotech firms to give up the lion's share of their income to the larger companies.

In the early 1990s, Biogen started working on a drug called AVONEX, which slows the progression of physical disabilities resulting from multiple sclerosis (MS). In 1994, the company received a positive response from the Food and Drug Administration (FDA) to its phase III trials of the product, meaning that the product was nearing final approval. The company was elated, because only about 1 out of every 250 drugs that enter formal testing concludes successful phase III trials.

This opportunity presented a challenge. Even though Biogen was a publicly traded firm, at the time it got the FDA's letter regarding AVONEX it was still a fairly small company with modest capabilities. This set of circumstances placed Biogen at a critical juncture. Would it continue to license its most promising products to large pharmaceutical companies or would it become a real operating drug company itself?

Confident that AVONEX would receive final approval, Biogen felt that it had three options in regard to bringing AVONEX to market:

Option 1: License the product to a large company like Pfizer or Merck, which would manufacture AVONEX and bring it to market.

Option 2: Build all the capabilities needed to bring AVONEX to market itself.

Option 3: Put together a network of alliance partners and outsource providers to perform the majority of activities needed to bring AVONEX to market, but retain all rights to the product.

Option 1 was rejected because Biogen felt that the economic potential of AVONEX was simply too large to give away most of the profits to Pfizer or Merck. Option 2 wasn't realistic, simply because the company lacked the time and money to build all the capabilities it needed. Option 3 was the only viable choice, which involved a challenging combination of bootstrapping, partnering, and outsourcing to work around the time constraints and financial hurdles involved.

The rest of the story is a legend in the biotech industry. The first thing the company did was evaluate the four steps in a drug's production and distribution:

Step 1   *Production (in a qualified manufacturing facility)*

Step 2   *Formulation (AVONEX needed to be freeze-dried and warehoused in cold storage)*

Step 3   *Packaging and labeling*

Step 4   *Distribution to retailers, physicians, and patients*

The company determined that it could manufacturer AVONEX in its existing facilities, but needed partners to complete steps 2, 3, and 4. Although it was a demanding task, Biogen succeeded in putting together the partnership network it needed. In each instance, the company found an alliance partner that excelled at what it did (whether it involved step 2, 3, or 4 of the process) but was still small enough to consider Biogen an important customer.

The final approval for AVONEX was granted to Biogen by the FDA on May 17, 1996. AVONEX became the U.S. market share leader for treating MS patients within 6 months of launch and now accounts for more than half the company's $1 billion in annual revenues. Rather than pursing a licensing deal or additional sources of funding to bring AVONEX to market, Biogen accomplished the task through ingenuity and smart partnering.

Questions for Critical Thinking

1. Why do you think Biogen didn't try to go to a large bank to try to get the money to bring AVONEX to market? What would have been the advantages and disadvantages of bank financing as opposed to the course that Biogen chose?

2. If Biogen had licensed AVONEX to a larger drug company, do you think it would be a $1 billion company today? Why or why not?

3. Make a list of five specific things that Biogen did "right" in regard to successfully bringing AVONEX to market through the savvy use of alliances.

4. What can be learned from this case about the role that alliances can play in raising the capital needed to fund the growth of an entrepreneurial firm?

Sources: Biogen homepage, www.biogen.com (accessed July 20, 2006); T. Abate, *The Biotech Investor* (New York: New York Times Books, 2003); D. Bovet and J. Martha, *Value Nets: Breaking the Supply Chain to Unlock Hidden Profits* (New York: John Wiley & Sons, 2000).

Finally, many partnerships are formed to share the costs of product or service development, to gain access to a particular resource, or to facilitate speed to market.[48] In exchange for access to plant and equipment and established distribution channels, new ventures bring an entrepreneurial spirit and new ideas to these partnerships. These types of arrangements can help new ventures lessen the need for financing or funding.

Alliances also help firms round out their business models and conserve resources. For example, as we discussed in Chapter 5, Dell Inc. can focus on its core competency of assembling computers because it has assembled a network of partners that provides it critical support. Intel and AMD provide chips, Microsoft provides software, UPS provides access to shipping, and so forth. Dell is a familiar example, but savvy new ventures also work hard to find partners to perform functions that would be expensive and distracting for them to perform themselves.

Chapter Summary

1. For three reasons—cash flow challenges, capital investment needs, and the reality of lengthy product development cycles—most new firms need to raise money at some point during the early part of their life.

2. Personal funds, friends and family, and bootstrapping are the three sources of personal financing available to entrepreneurs.

3. Entrepreneurs are often very creative in finding ways to bootstrap to raise money or cut costs. Examples of bootstrapping include minimizing personal expenses and putting all profits back into the business, establishing partnerships and sharing expenses with partners, and sharing office space and/or employees with other businesses.

4. The three steps involved in properly preparing to raise debt or equity financing are as follows: Determine precisely how much money is needed, determine the type of financing or funding that is most appropriate, and develop a strategy for engaging potential investors or bankers.

5. An elevator speech is a brief, carefully constructed statement outlining a business opportunity's merits.

6. Equity funding involves exchanging partial ownership in a firm, which is usually in the form of stock, for funding. Debt financing is getting a loan.

7. Business angels are individuals who invest their personal capital directly in start-up ventures. These investors tend to be high-net-worth individuals who generally invest between $25,000 and $150,000 in a single company. Venture capital is money that is invested by venture capital firms in start-ups and small businesses with exceptional growth potential. Typically, venture capitalists invest at least $1 million in a single company.

8. An initial public offering (IPO) is an important milestone for a firm for four reasons: It is a way to raise equity capital, it raises a firm's public profile, it is a liquidity event,

and it creates another form of currency (company stock) that can be used to grow the company.

9. The main SBA program available to small businesses is referred to as the 7(A) Loan Guaranty Program. This program operates through private-sector lenders providing loans that are guaranteed by the SBA. The loans are for small businesses that are unable to secure financing on reasonable terms through normal lending channels.

10. A lease is a written agreement in which the owner of a piece of property allows an individual or business to use the property for a specified period of time in exchange for payments. The major advantage of leasing is that it enables a company to acquire the use of assets with very little or no down payment.

Key Terms

bootstrapping, 287
burn rate, 285
business angels, 291
carry, 292
corporate venture capital, 293
debt financing, 288
due diligence, 293
elevator speech (or pitch), 289
equity financing, 288
fast-track programs, 300

final prospectus, 294
follow-on funding, 293
initial public offering, 293
investment bank, 294
lease, 299
line of credit, 296
preliminary prospectus, 294
private placement, 296
road show, 294
rounds, 293

Sarbanes-Oxley Act, 294
SBA Guaranteed Loan Program, 297
SBIR Program, 300
STTR Program, 301
secondary market offering, 293
7(A) Loan Guaranty Program, 297
single-purpose loan, 296
sweat equity, 286
venture capital, 292
venture-leasing firm, 300

Review Questions

1. What are the three most common reasons most entrepreneurial ventures need to raise money in their early life?

2. What is meant by the term *burn rate*? What are the consequences of experiencing a negative burn rate for a relatively long period of time?

3. What is meant by the term *sweat equity*?

4. To what extent do entrepreneurs rely on their personal funds and funds from friends and families to finance their ventures? What different forms do funds from friends and family take?

5. What is bootstrapping? Provide several examples of how entrepreneurs bootstrap to raise money or cut costs. In your judgment, how important is the art of bootstrapping for an entrepreneurial venture?

6. Describe the three steps involved in properly preparing to raise debt or equity financing.

7. Briefly describe the difference between equity funding and debt financing.

8. Describe the most common sources of equity funding.

9. Describe the most common sources of debt financing.

10. What is the purpose of an elevator speech? Why is preparing an elevator speech one of the first things an entrepreneur should do in the process of raising money?

11. Why is it so important to get a personal introduction before approaching a potential investor or banker?

12. Describe the three steps required to effectively engage potential investors or bankers.

13. Identify the three most common forms of equity funding.

14. Describe the nature of business angel funding. What types of people typically become business angels, and what is the unique role that business angels play in the process of funding entrepreneurial firms?

15. Describe what is meant by the term *venture capital*. Where do venture capital firms get their money? What types of firms do venture capitalists commonly want to fund? Why?

16. Describe the purpose of an initial public offering (IPO). Why is an initial public offering considered to be an important milestone for an entrepreneurial firm?

17. What is the purpose of the investment bank in the initial public offering process?

18. In general, why are commercial banks reluctant to loan money to start-ups?

19. Briefly describe the SBA's 7(A) Loan Guaranty Program. Do most start-up firms qualify for an SBA guaranteed loan? Why or why not?

20. What is a Small Business Innovation Research (SBIR) grant? Why would a firm want to apply for such as grant if it so qualified?

Application Questions

1. Write a 60-second elevator speech for PrintDreams, which is the "You Be the VC1" feature in this chapter.

2. Doug Malone is a computer programmer at Activision, a maker of electronic games. In a year or so, Doug plans to leave Activision in order to launch his own firm. A colleague of Doug's recently asked him, "Where do you plan to get the money to fund your new venture?" Doug replied, "I really don't think I'll need to raise any money. I have $35,000 in the bank, and I think I can fund the start-up and growth of the firm myself." Do you think Doug is being realistic? If not, what steps should he plan to take to properly fund his firm?

3. Tina Russell is in the early stages of launching a new firm and has been attending seminars to get information about funding. Several of the seminars have had business angels and venture capitalists on the program. Tina has casually spoken with several of these individuals but has only made small talk. A friend of Tina suggested that she develop an elevator speech to use when she runs into potential investors. If Tina asked you, "What in the world is an elevator speech, and why would I need one?" what would you say to her?

4. John Baker is in the midst of starting a computer hardware firm and thinks he has identified a real problem that his company will be able to solve. He has put together a management team and has invested $250,000 of his own money in the project. John feels that time is of the essence and has decided to try to obtain venture capital funding. How should he go about it?

5. One criticism of the venture capital industry is that the majority of the money is invested in a small number of geographic areas in the United States. In fact, in 2005, over 58 percent of the investments were made in just two states. Do some research on the venture capital industry, and determine which two states are the perennial leaders for venture capital funding.

6. Study the two "You Be the VC" features at the end of this chapter. In your judgment, which of the two firms is the better candidate for venture capital funding? Justify your answer.

7. YouTube (www.youtube.com) is a Web site that allows users to upload, view, and share video clips. In the short time since it was founded (February 2005), it has become one of the most popular sites on the Internet and now streams more than 100 million videos per day. As of mid-2006, YouTube had obtained over $11.5 million in venture capital funding. Many observers are skeptical that YouTube has a

viable business model and wonder if the VCs involved got caught up in the hype surrounding YouTube's rapid success. Study YouTube and describe the company's business model. Do you think the venture capitalists that funded YouTube made prudent investments? How does Google's late-2006 decision to acquire YouTube influence your judgment about the venture capitalists' investments? Explain your answers.

8. Cathy Mills has spent the past 5 years bootstrapping a very successful consumer software company. Her company now has strong cash flow and a healthy balance sheet, and she has put together an impressive management team. Cathy has decided to branch out into business software and needs $175,000 to start her new division. Given Cathy's situation, what type of funding or financing do you think she would be eligible for? Explain your answer.

9. Bill Ryan, who lives near Michigan State University, has just opened a chain of salad and soup restaurants. He needs capital to expand his business. If Bill asked you which of his alternatives would be the most likely to offer him financing or funding, what information would you need from Bill to provide him an informed opinion?

10. Patricia Rob is the CEO of a medical equipment company that is on the verge of going public. She recently decided to write an e-mail message to her entire workforce to explain the reasons the company was going public. If you were Patricia, what would you include in the message? Explain your answer.

11. Go to the Web site www.retailroadshow.com and watch one of the IPO road shows currently available for viewing (they last about 30 minutes). Briefly describe the company involved, including its reasons for wanting to go public. Did the company make a compelling case for going public? If you were an investor, would you invest in the company's IPO? Why or why not?

12. In early 2006, Chipotle Mexican Grill (www.chipotle.com) launched a very successful public offering. This is despite the fact that the market for IPOs was not particularly robust at that time. Study Chipotle Mexican Grill and determine why Chipotle was a good candidate for launching a public offering.

13. Ed Sayers just returned from a meeting with his banker with a frustrated look on his face. He tosses his keys on the kitchen counter and tells his wife, "I just can't understand where my banker is coming from. I have a great idea for a new firm, but the bank isn't interested in helping me with a loan. Tomorrow, I'm going to visit a couple of other banks to see if I have better luck." Do you think Ed will have any better luck with the second and third banks he visits? Why or why not?

14. Pam Sherman, who lives near Galveston, Texas, is in the process of setting up a manufacturing facility that will produce highly specialized equipment for the oil drilling industry. The high cost of equipment is an issue with which Pam is struggling. She has talked to several investors who have balked at funding the equipment. Pam has thought about leasing instead of buying but isn't quite sure if leasing is the way to go. If Pam asked you your advice, what would you tell her?

15. Alex Gondolas is in the early stages of developing a new laser optics technology that may be of interest to the U.S. Department of Defense. Alex recently attended a seminar for start-ups and was advised to apply for a Small Business Innovation Research grant to fund his project. Alex thought about applying for the grant but decided it was too much hassle and paperwork. If you were advising Alex, would you tell him to rethink his decision? Why or why not?

you be the VC 10.1 PrintDreams
www.PrintDreams.com

Business Idea: Establish a global de facto standard for mobile pocket printers based on PrintDream RMPT (Random Movement Printing Technology).

Pitch: Although PDAs, cell phones, and laptop computers are handy to use while on the go, these devices are usually not attached to a printer—particularly when a person is away from the office. This complication can be problematic for businesspeople working in the field, or for ordinary computer users, who may need to print one or more documents while away from their home or office printer.

To solve this problem, PrintDreams has developed a technology that makes mobile printing a reality. This is how the technology works. The PrintBrush, which is the product's name, is about the size of a cell phone. Text and pictures can be loaded onto the PrintBrush from a PDA or other mobile device using Bluetooth wireless technology. Then the PrintBrush is swept by hand across any type of paper (the paper is not in the printer) regardless of its size, shape, or

thickness. The PrintBrush prints the text and images as it goes. PrintDreams will produce its own printer and will license the patented PMPT technology to other manufacturers.

A demonstration of how the product works is provided on the firm's Web site. To envision how the product works without visiting the Web site, try this. Pretend that you have downloaded a document to your PrintBrush. Take your cell phone, place it on the left side of a sheet of paper, and slowly move the phone from left to right across the paper. If your cell phone were a PrintBrush, it would have printed out the material you downloaded on the paper as it moved across it.

Q&A: Based on the material covered in this chapter, what questions would you ask the firm's founders before making your funding decision? What answers would satisfy you?

Decision: If you had to make your decision on just the information provided in the pitch and on the company's Web site, would you fund this firm? Why or why not?

you be the VC 10.2 No-Cal Soda Pop
www.no-calsoda.com

Business Idea: Create a fun, fresh, and clearly differentiated new entry into the diet soda industry.

Pitch: No-Cal was originally launched in 1952 as the first zero-calorie soft drink in America. The brand disappeared from the market in the 1960s, unable to compete with emerging diet drinks offered by Coke, Pepsi, and others. No-Cal is now back and is being positioned as a nostalgic, fun, and fresh new beverage in the diet soda category. Diet soda is one area of the beverage industry that is still growing, and No-Cal is an almost perfect descriptive name. No-Cal will sport four innovative and fun flavors: cherry lime, chocolate, vanilla crème, and Clementine. Each No-Cal flavor will be packaged in 12-ounce glass longneck bottles for $1.50 per bottle or $3.99 for a four-pack carrier. The bottles are stylish and vaguely reminiscent of the original brand.

To promote a sense of adventure and fun, each No-Cal flavor has its own cartoon character, with a little story that will be told through the flavor's advertising and promotional

activities. For example, "Gilbert the Jazz Player" is shown playing his saxophone on the vanilla cream soda bottle, and "Sullivan the Cop" is the Clementine-flavored character. One thing No-Cal prides itself on, and will reinforce in its branding, is that it is strictly a diet soda and focuses all of its efforts on its diet soda flavors. Diet Pepsi, Diet Coke, and the majority of other diet sodas are "stepchildren" of their parent brands (Coke, Pepsi, etc.) and often don't taste as good as the original beverage. No-Cal believes that there is a sufficient number of customers who want to purchase their preferred diet cola from a firm specializing in that type of product.

Q&A: Based on the material covered in this chapter, what questions would you ask the firm's founders before making your funding decision? What answers would satisfy you?

Decision: If you had to make your decision on just the information provided in the pitch and on the company's Web site, would you fund this firm? Why or why not?

Zazzle: Will the Company Disappoint or "Dazzle" Its Investors?

www.zazzle.com

Bruce R. Barringer,
University of Central Florida
R. Duane Ireland,
Texas A&M University

Introduction

Zazzle is an online service that allows its customers to upload images that can be printed on T-shirts, stamps, posters, cards, coffee mugs, and a variety of other items. In addition, customers can choose from Zazzle's library of over 500,000 images, including 3,500 pictures of 130 characters from The Walt Disney Company. Zazzle's expansive library also includes historical images from the Library of Congress, the California State Library, the Boston Public Library, and similar institutions.

Zazzle also allows the creators of digital images to place their images on its Web site. If someone buys the image, the creator of the image is paid a 10 percent royalty. The royalty jumps to 17 percent if the buyer of the image was referred to Zazzle by its creator.

This service provides a marketplace for artists, freelance photographers, and photo hobbyists to sell their work.

In the spring of 2005, Zazzle raised $16 million in venture capital (VC) funding from Kleiner Perkins Caufield & Byers and Sherpalo Ventures. While the venture capitalists that led the funding, John Doerr at Kleiner Perkins and Ram Shriram at Sherpalo Ventures, expressed confidence in Zazzle's future, a number of journalists and bogglers were puzzled by the investment. "What's so unique about Zazzle?" and "How can a company that sells T-shirts get $16 million in funding?" were common observations.

We tell the Zazzle story in the following paragraphs. Eventually, will the venture capitalists or the critics of their investment be proven correct? Read about Zazzle, and then you decide!

Zazzle's Start-up Story

Zazzle was founded in 1999 by Bobby and Jeff Beaver, two Stanford University students. Their father, Robert Beaver, was a serial entrepreneur (a serial entrepreneur is a person who launches one entrepreneurial venture after another). While at Stanford, the two brothers became interested in the Internet, which was all the buzz at the time, and decided to start an Internet company of their own when they graduated. Their goal was to identify an online opportunity that wasn't currently being pursued, was meaningful, and was something they could build a real business around. For a number of reasons, they started talking about the printed apparel industry. Printed apparel, which includes products like Mickey Mouse T-shirts and Boston Red Sox and New York Yankees' sweaters, is a $25–$30 billion industry. At the time, there was no dominant Internet company servicing the industry. As a result, the Beavers decided to focus their efforts on starting a company in the Internet printed apparel industry.

The reason there wasn't an Internet company focused on the printed apparel industry, the Beavers soon learned, is that the industry was plagued by antiquated technology. The only effective way to make high-quality printed T-shirts, and other apparel products, was through a process called silk-screening. Although silk-screening produces a high-quality product, it is very labor-intensive. As a result, to justify the cost, most manufacturers must make lots of 100 or more of the same product. An alternative is to iron on designs. Although quicker, iron-on designs are not of high quality.

The vision that the Beavers fashioned was to create a company that could print T-shirts one at a time at an affordable price. The idea was to create an "on-demand" (one at a time) printing company where a customer could send the company a digital picture of a newborn baby, for example, and order just a few shirts with the baby's picture to distribute to family and friends. In addition, the Beavers wanted to guarantee 24-hour delivery, so the shirts could be distributed by the new parents right away. Another piece of the Beavers' vision was to provide aspiring artists, freelance photographers, and photo hobbyists a marketplace to sell their work. Most of these folks never got their work on a T-shirt or a sweater because they would have to make 100 or more of them at a time and store the product as inventory. Some images may sell only a few T-shirts or sweaters, let alone 100, making the prospects impractical.

The Beavers set out to make this happen and named their company Zazzle. Their dad, who joined the firm, had good connections in the Silicon Valley. He relied on these connections to help his sons put together a small team of people to tackle the technological challenge of printing T-shirts and other apparel products on demand at an affordable price. It took 3 years of bootstrapping and painstaking work to do it, but the small Zazzle team persevered. They developed a proprietary way of reengineering the silk-screening process to automate it and drive down the costs, making producing a high-quality individual T-shirt or other apparel product on demand practical.

The Zazzle Web site was launched in 2003. Orders quickly began flowing to the company, with the pace quickening as more people learned about the service.

Financially, the company never ran large deficits, as did many start-ups. In fact, it teetered on profitability from the beginning. Zazzle's business model was very similar to Dell's. It had essentially no inventory costs, except for the physical disk space needed to store digital images and a supply of paper and ink. Its customers paid by credit card before an order was processed and shipped. And its suppliers, the independent artists and companies that placed images on Zazzle's site, didn't get paid until Zazzle did.

Enter the VCs

Incredibly, a year or so after Zazzle's Web site was up and running, the company was contacted by a venture capital firm. The founders remember being "shocked, humbled, and thrilled" that a venture capital firm would be interested in their business. As luck would have it, one of Zazzle's first key hires, Matt Wilsey, knew Brook Byers, a partner at Kleiner Perkins, through their kids, who went to the same school. Byers became interested in what Zazzle was doing and encouraged his partners to check it out. This initial overture caused the Beavers to do their own due diligence on the venture capital process, and they discussed funding with several firms. Kleiner Perkins and Sherpalo offered to invest $16 million, so the decision boiled down to whether Zazzle wanted to accept the VCs' terms if they were to accept the money.

The Pros and Cons of Accepting the Money

As is typically the case with a relationship between an entrepreneurial venture and a venture capitalist, there were pros and cons to accepting the money. On the pro side, partnering with two prestigious venture capital firms would lend Zazzle tremendous credibility. The founders also liked the two lead venture capitalists, John Doerr and Ram Shriram. Both were early investors in Google and had successful track records. The Zazzle team also felt comfortable with their potential investors. They shared a common vision for the future of Zazzle, and both Doerr and Shriram had reputations for being "hands-on" investors.

Zazzle could also grow much more quickly with $16 million available to build its infrastructure, hire more employees, and build the firm's brand. The major con or disadvantage to accepting the money was that Zazzle would be forced into a fast-growth mode. The founders knew that anytime a company accepts venture capital funding the pace of activity quickens, overhead gets bigger, larger returns are expected, and scrutiny is increased. They would also be giving up in exchange for the money a sizeable piece of the company that they had spent 4 long years building.

In the end, Zazzle took the money, thinking that the opportunity to take the company to the next level, and the opportunity to partner with two prestigious venture

capital firms, was just too good to pass up. Commenting on why the investment made sense, Bobby Beaver, one of Zazzle's founders said,

> Their (Kleiner Perkins and Sherpalo Ventures) support will help us expand our marketplace, as we drive to provide all individuals with an outlet where they can create and share products limited only by imagination.

In a *Seattle Times* article that was written shortly after the funding was announced, John Doerr, the venture capitalist, expressed nothing short of wild enthusiasm for Zazzle's future. "This will be a smash success" he predicted. Commenting on Zazzle's founders, Bobby and Jeff Beaver, Doerr said "They are Googlesque in their energy and their ability to think big."

The Aftermath

After Zazzle's funding was announced, several bloggers and journalists weighed in, discussing the merits of the investments. One blogger, Jason Ball, who is a London-based venture capitalist and writes a blog called TechBytes, wrote:

> A $16 million Series A round for a T-shirt site? With all due respect to KPCB (Kleiner Perkins), because they deserve it, an investment of this size in this space baffles me. From a London perspective, it looks like they're partying like it's 1999 all over again in California.

Similar comments were posted expressing surprise that Zazzle was able to raise so much money from its venture capitalists.

For its part, Zazzle's growth has accelerated as a result of the funding, and the company continues to expand its partnership and its business. The company claims that its online galleries now contain hundreds of thousands of totally unique, user-submitted photos, along with a growing library of photos from sources as diverse as Build-A-Bear Workshop and Twentieth-Century Fox's *Family Guy* television series.

Discussion Questions

1. So what do you think? Do you think Kleiner Perkins and Sherpalo Ventures made a wise decision investing $16 million in Zazzle? Three years from now, do you think that Zazzle will have disappointed or dazzled its investors? Why?

2. Look at Table 10.2 in the chapter. At the time that Zazzle raised venture capital funding, to what extent did it resemble the ideal candidate for venture capital funding as stipulated by the materials in the table?

3. Evaluate Jason Ball's (the blogger's) criticism of Kleiner Perkins' investment in Zazzle. Do you think Ball makes some good points or do you think his arguments are off-base? Explain your answer.

4. What do you think is Zazzle's exit strategy? How will Kleiner Perkins and Sherpalo Ventures recoup their investment?

Application Questions

1. One of the criticisms of Zazzle is that its service is almost identical to a similar venture-backed company called Café Press. Look at Zazzle's and Café Press's (www.cafepress.com) Web sites. What points of differentiation, if any, do you see between Café Press and Zazzle?

2. Spend some time on Zazzle's Web site creating a T-shirt (you don't have to actually buy it). Did you find the site to be easy to navigate and Zazzle's product offering appealing? What is it that you liked about the experience and what did you not like? Did your experience influence your perception of the wisdom of Kleiner Perkins' and Sherpalo's investment in Zazzle?

Sources: R. Beaver and J. Beaver, "Stanford Technology Ventures Go Entrepreneurial Thought LeadersPodcast," December 2005; "Why Zazzle Dazzles John Doerr," *BusinessWeek*, July 2005; M. Liedtke, "Early Investors in Google Expect Zazzle to Dazzle," *The Seattle Times*, July 2005; J. Ball, TechBytes blog dated April 19, 2005.

CASE 10.2

Google: An Interesting and Instructive Funding Journey
www.google.com

Bruce R. Barringer,
University of Central Florida
R. Duane Ireland,
Texas A&M University

Introduction

Although Google is now a strong, vibrant, publicly traded company, its beginnings were rather humble. It began with two Stanford graduate students who recognized an opportunity and, through hard work, and a patient yet methodical approach to raising money, built a successful entrepreneurial firm.

Today, Google is the most popular search engine on the Internet. Its main Web site, at www.google.com, conducts over 91 million searches a day. The firm's name is a play on words. The word *googol* refers to the number 1 followed by 100 zeros. As far as scientists know, there isn't a googol of anything in the universe—not stars, grains of sand, or particles of dust. Still, the name reflects the company's mission to organize the seemingly endless material on the World Wide Web. Somehow, "googol" became "Google," which is now one of the world's most commonly recognized names. In fact, the name is so well known that the verb, google (i.e., "I'm going to google him") was recently added to both the *Merriam-Webster Collegiate Dictionary* and the *Oxford English Dictionary* in July 2006.

As a company, Google is universally admired. It is technologically savvy, treats its employees well, is highly profitable, and is financially strong. The firm is known for its democratic culture in which employees are encouraged to spend roughly 20 percent of their time working on any project they believe will best benefit the company. Founders Sergey Brin and Larry Page assert that their firm isn't a conventional place to work and that they never intend for it to become so.

Google is also a somewhat peculiar firm in an admirable sort of way. It was launched in the midst of the Internet bubble but never overextended itself, particularly regarding its finances. Unlike many of its Silicon Valley peers, it has moved with deliberation, didn't rush its IPO, and, until recently, has slowly built its business. In fact, the way Google has funded its operations is quite impressive. The company has utilized a variety of sources of funding, yet has done so in an objectively prudent and disciplined fashion.

Google's Funding Journey

Larry Page and Sergey Brin, two computer science graduate students at Stanford University, founded Google in 1998. The two met in 1995 and by 1996 started collaborating on a search engine technology. As with most students, Page and Brin didn't have much money and had to scrounge around campus to find the hardware they needed to work on their project. They realized they were on to something and started trying to license their search technology to major portals. They didn't have any luck, so they decided to try to make a go of it on their own as a stand-alone company.

To get Google off the ground, Page and Brin needed money to move out of Page's dorm room, which acted as Google's first data center, and pay off credit card debt they had run up to buy equipment. So they put their PhDs on hold and started looking for an angel investor. They targeted Andy Bechtolsheim, a friend of a faculty member and one of the founders of Sun Microsystems. Bechtolsheim invested $100,000 after seeing a demo of Google's search technology. According to company lore, the $100,000 check that Bechtolsheim wrote was made out to Google Inc. instead of Page and Brin. This caused a small dilemma since there was no Google Inc. at the time. The check sat in Page's desk for a couple of weeks while the founders scrambled to set up a corporation. Page and Brin also went to family and friends to raise more money. In total, they raised almost $1 million to get Google off the ground.

On September 7, 1998, Google opened its doors in Menlo Park, California, in a small office attached to the garage of a friend. Google quickly outgrew that facility and moved into more adequate surroundings. By early 1999, the company's search engine was processing 500,000 queries per day even though it was still being tested. Interest in Google was also growing, and articles about the company were starting to appear in magazines. People were initially somewhat perplexed by Google's plain Web site yet outstanding performance. On June 7, 1999, the company announced that it had secured $25 million in venture capital funding from Sequoia Capital and Kleiner Perkins Caufield & Byers, two of the Silicon Valley's most prestigious venture capital firms.

Google hired more people, but its surroundings didn't change much; the company stayed in modest facilities. It incentivized its employees through stock options rather than large salaries. Eventually, Google moved to its current headquarters in Mountain View, California, which is called the Googleplex, and the company has continued to grow. On June 26, 2000, Google and Yahoo! announced a partnership that solidified Google's reputation. In the months that followed, more partnership deals were announced, further propelling Google's standing. In early 2002, Google signed an agreement with AOL to provide Web search services to AOL users. Google's revenue model also started to shift from licensing income for its search technology to paid listings. A paid listing delivers an advertiser's message alongside a search result. For example, if you type the words "computer games" into a search engine, you will see listings of paid ads at the top of the page (highlighted in blue) and to the side of the search results. Google's pact with AOL boosted its prominence in this market. According to Google CEO Eric Schmidt, who was hired in the summer of 2001, "The AOL deal (put) Google on the map for paid listings."

By carefully managing its resources, Google avoided the need for additional funding beyond what it received from the venture capitalists in 1999 until it went public in August 2004. It also steadily rose in stature and generated income, in contrast to many of its dot-com peers that never made money and failed. Google's IPO was executed in an unconventional manner, which ruffled some feathers on Wall Street. Rather than following the traditional approach, Google set up a modified Dutch auction. In a Dutch action, a company reveals the maximum amount of shares it is willing to sell and a potential selling price. Investors then privately state the number of shares they want at what price. Once a minimum price has been established (by the auction), investors who bid at least that price are awarded shares. Investors that bid lower than the minimum price are out of luck. The rationale behind this approach is to find the true "market value" of the stock.

Frequently, firms go public and their shares rapidly increase in price. When this happens, firms kick themselves because it means that the offering price could have been higher.

Google went public on August 19, 2004 at $85 per share and raised $1.67 billion. It only partially achieved its objectives, because its stock price quickly rose to over $100 per share. In October 2006, the price of a share of Google stock was over $420. Despite all of its success, including its financial successes, the firm remains located in relatively modest facilities (by public company standards), and its more than 450,000 servers are basically racks of low-cost computers running stripped-down versions of Linux. It has used the money it raised in its public offering to buy small companies with products or technologies it liked, to build products internally, and to fund its growing operations. This combination of efforts has resulted in a range of new products that complement the Google search engine, such as Gmail, Google Maps, Froogle, Google Video, and Google Talk.

The Lesson

What once was just a couple of doctoral students working together on a research project is now a publicly traded company with worldwide brand recognition and tremendous momentum. The momentum, however, has not been created by rounds and rounds of funding. On the contrary, careful founders, able managers, and outstanding technology have created this momentum—a momentum desired by all founders of start-up ventures.

Discussion Questions

1. Draw a time line of Google's history in terms of raising money. Start the time line in 1998 (when the company was founded) and extend it through the period covered by the case. Write a short critique of Google's performance in the area of raising money.

2. Look at Table 10.2 in the chapter. At the time Google raised venture capital funding, to what extent did it resemble the ideal candidate for such funding, as stipulated in the table?

3. How many of the different sources of funding and financing discussed in the chapter did Google utilize? To what degree do you think Google was prudent, rather than reckless, in its approach to funding? How would Google's story have changed if it had received round after round of venture capital funding in the late 1990s and early 2000s to more quickly build its business? How would its story have changed if it had rushed to launch an IPO, instead of waiting until late 2004?

4. What lessons can be learned from Google's experience by other start-ups?

Application Questions

1. Although this topic is not covered in detail in the case, to what extent do you think Google's strategic partners have helped it avoid the need to obtain additional funding or financing? What role has Google's strategic partners played in its overall success?
2. Google's start-up story has been widely reported on the Internet, in books, and in periodicals. Do some research on Google's story, and find an interesting anecdote or fact about Google, preferably during its early years, that isn't mentioned in the case. Briefly explain how the anecdote or fact helps us better understand Google's start-up story.

Sources: Google homepage, www.google.com/corporate (accessed July 21, 2006); Wikipedia, www.wikipedia.com (accessed July 21, 2006); J. Battelle, *The Search* (New York: Portfolio, 2005); M. Mangalindan and J. Angwin, "Google Lands Pact with AOL, Strengthening IPO Prospects," *The Wall Street Journal*, May 2, 2002, B5.

Endnotes

1. Personal Interview with Derek Gregg, July 24, 2006.
2. S. Kerns, "IDEAs," *Spotlight*, Summer 2004.
3. J. W. Mullins and D. Forlani, "Missing the Boat or Sinking the Boat: A Study of New Venture Decision Making," *Journal of Business Venturing* 20 (2005): 47–69.
4. D. Cumming, "Adverse Selection and Capital Structure: Evidence from Venture Capital," *Entrepreneurship Theory and Practice* 30 (2006): 155–83.
5. K. Soufani, D. Vrontis, and P. Poutziouris, "Private Equity for Small Firms: A Conceptual Model of Adaptation Versus Standardisation Strategy," *International Journal of Entrepreneurship and Small Business* 3 (2006): 498–515.
6. G. Keighley, "Could This Be the Next Disney?" *Business 2.0*, December 2002, 110–18.
7. T. Abate, *The Biotech Investor* (New York: Times Books, 2003).
8. J. Ebben and A. Johnson, "Bootstrapping in Small Firms: An Empirical Analysis of Change Over Time," *Journal of Business Venturing* (2006), in press.
9. G. Gianforte, *Bootstrapping Your Business* (Avon, MA: Adams Media, 2005).
10. "Meet Michelle Madhok," Ladies Who Launch homepage, www.ladieswholaunch (accessed July 20, 2006).
11. A. Lockett, D. Ucbasaran, and J. Butler, "Opening Up the Investor–Investee Dyad: Syndicates, Teams, and Networks," *Entrepreneurship Theory and Practice* 30 (2006): 117–30; G. Benjamin and J. Margulis, *Angel Financing* (New York: John Wiley & Sons, 2000).
12. J. Florin, "Is Venture Capital Worth It? Effects on Firm Performance and Founder Returns," *Journal of Business Venturing* 20 (2005): 113–35.
13. R. Stross, *eBoys* (New York: Crown Business, 2000), 25.
14. I. Smith, "Money: The Truth about Financing a Growing Small Business," in *The Book of Entrepreneurs' Wisdom*, ed. P. Krass (New York: John Wiley & Sons, 1999), 121–29.
15. A. Riding, "Financing Entrepreneurial Firms: Research Paper for the Task Force on the Future of the Canadian Financial Services Sector," Carleton University, September 1998.
16. J. Melloan, "Angels With Angels," *Inc.*, July 2005.
17. Melloan, "Angels With Angels."
18. ASAP, *Forbes*, June 1, 1998, 24.
19. J. Battelle, *The Search* (New York: Portfolio, 2005).
20. Center for Venture Research, "The Angel Investor Market in 2005: The Angel Market Exhibits Modest Growth," (Durham: University of New Hampshire, 2005).
21. Center for Venture Research, "The Angel Investor Market in 2005."
22. J. E. Solh, *Testimony in Support of the Access to Capital for Entrepreneurs Act of 2006* (HR 5198), May 10, 2006. House Small Business Committee, 109th Congress, 2nd session.
23. PricewaterhouseCoopers, (CE: www.pwcglobal.com) "The Second Key: Writing the Business Plan," www.pwcglobal.com (accessed July 30, 2006).
24. O. Strauss, "Toughed by an Angel," Entrepreneur's Byline, www.entreworld.org (accessed March 20, 2003).
25. Melloan, "Angels With Angels."
26. Utah Business homepage, "Speed-Dating and Venture Funding Collide at Speedpitching Luncheon," www.utahbusiness.com (accessed July 20, 2006).
27. Investorwords, www.investorwords.com (accessed March 20, 2003).

28. Solh, *Testimony in Support of the Access to Capital for Entrepreneurs Act of 2006* (HR 5198).
29. PricewaterhouseCoopers, *Three Keys to Obtaining Venture Capital* (New York: PricewaterhouseCoopers, 2001).
30. PricewaterhouseCoopers, *Three Keys to Obtaining Venture Capital*.
31. D. Laurie, *Venture Catalyst* (Cambridge, MA: Perseus, 2001).
32. G. Dushnitsky and M. J. Lenox, "When Do Firms Undertake R&D by Investing in New Ventures?" *Strategic Management Journal* 26 (2005): 947–65.
33. J. M. Nelson, "Intangible Assets, Book-to-Market, and Common Stock Returns," *The Journal of Financial Research* 29 (2006): 21–41.
34. C. M. Daily, S. T. Certo, and D. R. Dalton, "Investment Bankers and IPO Pricing: Does Prospectus Information Matter?" *Journal of Business Venturing* 20 (2005): 93–111.
35. M. A. Hitt, R. D. Ireland, and R. E. Hoskisson, *Strategic Management: Competitiveness and Globalization*, 7th ed. Mason, OH: (South-Western College Publishing., 2007)
36. Investorwords, www.investorwords.com (accessed July 6, 2006).
37. F. Lipman, *The Complete Going Public Handbook* (Roseville, CA: Prima Publishing, 2000).
38. WilmerHale, 2005 IPO Report, *2005 IPO Report* (Baltimore, MD: Wilmer, Cutler, Pickering, Hale, and Dorr, LLP), 2–5.
39. S. Marlow and D. Patton, "All Credit to Men? Entrepreneurship, Finance, and Gender," *Entrepreneurship Theory and Practice* 29 (2005): 717–35.
40. G. Haines and L. Riding, "Loan Guarantee Programs for Small Firms: Recent Canadian Experience on Risk, Economic Impacts, and Incrementality," *Frontiers of Entrepreneurship Research* 16 (1995): 422–36.
41. Riding, "Financing Entrepreneurial Firms."
42. SBA homepage, www.sba.gov (accessed July 20, 2006).
43. G. Bounds, "Fed Fund," *The Wall Street Journal*, November 29, 2004.
44. J. Nesheim, *High Tech Start Up: The Complete Handbook for Creating Successful New High Tech Companies* (New York: Free Press, 2000).
45. A. Sherman, *Raising Capital* (Washington, DC: Kiplinger Books, 2000).
46. SBA homepage, www.sba.gov (accessed July 20, 2006).
47. S. A. Alvarez, R. D. Ireland, and J. J. Reuer, "Entrepreneurship and Strategic Alliances," *Journal of Business Venturing* 21 (2006): 401–404.
48. B. Barringer and J. Harrison, "Walking a Tightrope: Creating Value through Interorganizational Relationships, " *Journal of Management* 26 (2000): 367–403.

Hardest part of getting funding	My advice for new entrepreneurs	Best part of being a student
Convincing the first investor to give money	*To be prepared for high risks and stress, which is a tradeoff for living your dream*	*Becoming friends with people from all backgrounds*

ino del Sol:
Creating a New Brand in the Wine Industry

As an undergraduate student at Vanderbilt University, Matt Hedges (shown in the photograph accompanying this Opening Profile) spent one semester of his junior year as an exchange student at the University of Buenos Aires in Argentina. During his time in Argentina in 2001, he fell in love with the country's rich culture, language, and geographic beauty. He also learned to appreciate and love Argentine wine. Argentina is very sunny and dry, which allows its wine makers to control the amount of moisture their vineyards receive through irrigation. This creates an almost perfect setting for producing grapes that make full-bodied fine wines.[1]

After returning from Argentina and finishing his degree at Vanderbilt, Hedges decided to pursue an MBA at the University of Mississippi. While at Mississippi, he started working on the business plan for Vino del Sol, the company he hoped to create to bring Argentine wine to the United States. The first indication that Hedges had a realistic and potentially exciting idea came in March 2004, when he and classmate Andrew Jones won the "Best Company" award at the Babcock Elevator (pitch) Competition at Wake Forest University. The pair had 2 minutes to pitch the idea for Vino del Sol to a panel of venture capitalists. The pitch proved good enough to win top honors over teams from Yale, Wharton, Carnegie Mellon, and almost 20 other universities. Buoyed by the elevator pitch competition win, Hedges decided to go for it and launched Vino del Sol in late 2004 with start-up capital that had been raised from private investors. Fluent in Spanish, Hedges had actually been working on the Vino del Sol business plan since returning from Argentina in 2001. While in Buenos Aires, Hedges learned that less than 2 percent of the $22 billion of wine sold annually in the United Sates comes from Argentina. Hedges felt that he had uncovered a gap in the marketplace and that Americans would be attracted to Argentina's clean, fruity-tasting wines. His instincts were right. Vino del Sol is now a successful young business and Hedges is realizing his dream of bringing Argentine wine to the United States.

MATT HEDGES

Founder, Vino del Sol

MBA, University of Mississippi, 2004

UNIVERSITY OF
MISSISSIPPI

What's interesting about Vino del Sol, for the purposes of this chapter, is that many of the most important elements of its early success revolve around its marketing program. Initially, Hedges planned to sell Argentine wine directly to

Currently in my iPod	What I do when I'm not working	Best advice I've received
Pink Floyd	*Spend time with my wife and daughter*	*Working with good people and being a good partner is the most important ingredient*

U.S. wholesalers, but that idea was determined to be too expensive. Instead, the company struck a deal with Epic Wines of Aptos, California, an established importer, to sell its wine through its network of more than 50 distributors. Establishing this partnership was a big break for Vino del Sol. It eliminated the cost of marketing to wholesalers and renting warehouse space, which has helped the company keep its prices competitive: $6.99 to $24.00 a bottle at retail. It also gave Vino del Sol access to Epic Wines' distribution network and vast resources.

Two other major marketing-related decisions Vino del Sol made early on involved branding and the manner in which the company supports its wineries in Argentina and distributors in the United States. In terms of branding, all of the different Argentine wines the company sells carry its distinctive "The Best of Argentina" brand, which builds consistency across the company's family of wineries and wines. This strategy makes selling through Vino del Sol more attractive for wineries (by becoming part of a "brand" rather than just a distribution network), makes it easier for the sales reps to sell to retailers, and provides added confidence for consumers when they buy a "The Best of Argentina" branded wine. In terms of supporting its wineries in Argentina and distributors in the United States, the company excels in these areas. Vino del Sol is located in Argentina, which permits it to work closely with its wineries and oversee the production and logistics of moving the wine to the United States. It also allows the company to build a level of trust with its wineries that it feels is rare in the wine industry. In terms of supporting its U.S distributors, Vino del Sol personnel are constantly traveling across the country, providing education and sales tools to the distributors and sales reps who are responsible for finding shelf space for Vino del Sol branded wines.

As Vino del Sol moves forward, its biggest challenges will be to continue to build its brand, so when people shop for wine, they have confidence when they see an Argentine wine with the Vino del Sol logo attached. The company will also have to continually remain vigilant in regard to all the elements of its marketing mix, including product, pricing, promotion, and distribution.

As for Matt Hedges, he seems to be having the time of his life. Recently, he returned to the University of Mississippi to give the School of Business Administration $20,000 worth of Vino del Sol stock. According to Hedges, "the Ole Miss MBA program has been a big help. The quality of the class work is outstanding, and it really gave me the fundamentals of business that I apply every day. The little things that I remember, the strategies I should tackle . . . the school has been so supportive."[2]

In this chapter, we'll look at the marketing challenges confronting entrepreneurial firms. Marketing involves a range of issues, from promotions to selecting a target market to managing distribution channels. Marketing is a broad subject, and there are many books dedicated to marketing and its subfields. However, in this chapter, we zero in on the marketing challenges that are most pressing for young entrepreneurial firms. The reason for doing this is that marketing is an essential component to the success of a start-up firm.[3]

We begin this chapter by discussing how firms define and select their target markets. Next, we discuss two issues that are particularly important for new firms—selling benefits rather than features and establishing a brand. The chapter concludes by discussing the four key facets of marketing as they relate to young entrepreneurial firms. These four facets, commonly referred to as the "4Ps" of marketing, are product, price, promotion, and place (or distribution).

Selecting a Market and Establishing a Position

In order to succeed, a new firm must address this important question: Who are our customers, and how will we appeal to them?[4] A well-managed start-up uses a three-step approach to answer these questions: segmenting the market, selecting or developing a niche within a target market, and establishing a unique position in the target market. These steps are shown in Figure 11.1. In each step, the entrepreneurial venture must answer an important question that will help it pinpoint its market and determine how to attract customers in that market. Gary Heavin, the founder of Curves, the fitness center exclusively for women described in Case 5.2, addressed these issues when he crafted the initial strategy for his company. When asked about the importance of having a clearly defined target market in the fitness industry, he said,

> There are so many fitness companies that it is dog-eat-dog in the general fitness industry. The only hope for the average small fitness provider is that they focus on something and do that better than anything else.[5]

As noted in Chapter 3, a firm's **target market** is the limited group of individuals or businesses that it goes after or to which it tries to appeal. It is important that a firm first choose its target market and position itself within its target market because virtually all its marketing decisions hinge on these critical initial choices. If other marketing decisions are made first, such as choosing an advertising campaign, there is a danger the firm will not send a clear message to its target customers.

Segmenting the Market

The first step in selecting a target market is to study the industry in which the firm intends to compete and determine the different potential target markets in that industry. This process is called **market segmentation**. Market segmentation is important because a new firm typically has only enough resources to target one market segment, at least initially.[6] Markets can be segmented in a number of different ways, including product type, price point, and customers served.[7] For example, the computer industry can be segmented by product type (i.e., handheld computers, laptops, PCs, minicomputers, and mainframes) or customers served (i.e., individuals, businesses, schools, and government).[8] A firm will typically select the segment that represents the best prospects for entry, as discussed in Chapter 3, and that is the most compatible with its core competencies. There are several important objectives an entrepreneurial venture should try to accomplish as part of its market segmentation process:[9]

1. Explain the purpose of market segmentation.

- The process should identify one or more relatively homogeneous groups of target customers within the industry the firm plans to enter in regard to their wants and needs.

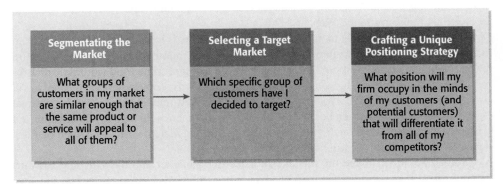

FIGURE 11.1

The Process of Selecting a Target Market and Positioning Strategy

■ Differences within the segment the firm chooses should be small compared to differences across segments.

■ The segment should be distinct enough so that its members can be easily identified. Once identified, advertising and promotional campaigns can be established to appeal specifically to the target market.

■ It should be possible to determine the size of the segment so that a firm knows how large its potential market is before it aggressively moves forward. A firm's growth can quickly plateau if its market segment is too small—even if the people in its segment are very satisfied with its product or service.

As mentioned previously, markets can be segmented a number of ways, including by product type, price point, and customers served. Sometimes a firm will segment its market on more than one dimension to drill down to a specific market niche that it thinks it is uniquely capable of serving. Curves segments its market first on customers serviced and second on price (it is less expensive to join than most fitness centers). Following the lead of Curves, there are now firms serving other previously underserved segments of the fitness market. An example is My Gym Children's Fitness Center, a franchise organization designed to help children aged 3 months to 9 years develop physically, cognitively, and emotionally.

Despite the importance of market segmentation, it is a process entrepreneurs commonly overlook. Overlooking this important activity can result in a faulty assessment of the size of the potential market for a new product or service. For example, on a global basis, approximately $300 billion is spent annually by small and medium-sized businesses on information technology (IT). If a start-up planned to introduce a new IT product to the market, it would be incorrect to say that the total market potential for the product is $300 billion. Obviously, the market opportunity needs to be better defined. The start-up needs to identify the different segments in the $300 billion worldwide IT market so it can target the segment it feels it is uniquely capable of serving.[10]

Selecting a Target Market

L E A R N I N G
Objective

2. Describe the importance of selecting a target market.

Once a firm has segmented the market, the next step is to select a target market. As discussed in Chapters 3 and 5, the market must be sufficiently attractive, and the firm must be able to serve it well. Typically, a firm (especially a start-up venture) doesn't target an entire segment of a market because many market segments are too large to target successfully. Instead, most firms target a niche or a vertical market within the segment. For example, one segment of the computer industry is handheld computers (or personal digital assistants, as they are sometimes called). Within this segment, there are several smaller niche markets that are targeted by different companies. A **niche market** is a place within a market segment that represents a narrower group of customers with similar interests. Two of the largest companies in the market for handheld computers, Research in Motion (RIM) and Palm, serve different niches. Historically, RIM has served business users who want their handheld devices to have wireless connectivity so that they can send and receive e-mail and browse the Web while on the run. In contrast, Palm has traditionally served the consumer part of the handheld computer market, which is more concerned with the ability to store and retrieve information, such as addresses and appointments, rather than send and receive e-mail or browse the Web.[11]

In most cases, the secret to appealing to a niche market is to understand the market and meet its customers' needs better than those needs can be met by firms targeting an entire market segment. As an example of this, consider the fact that some food wholesale distributors serve only businesses located in small communities and others service businesses in communities of all sizes. By focusing on a clearly defined market, a firm can become an expert in that market and then be able to provide its customers with high levels of value and service. This advantage is one of the reasons why Philip Kotler, a world-renowned marketing expert, says that "there are riches in niches."[12]

Sometimes firms make the mistake of selecting a market and then rushing forward without fully understanding that market or its customers, as discussed in Chapter 3. Other

The niche market on which Research in Motion (RIM) focuses is the business professional. RIM's success is rooted in its ability to understand the needs of its customers in that target segment. A businessperson is constantly on the run—to and from meetings, conference calls, and the airport. RIM's product helps these individuals keep in touch with their home office and organize their contacts and calendars.

times, firms try to appeal to multiple markets simultaneously and spread themselves too thin, not becoming an expert in any specific market. Firms that determine and then focus on a single niche have a better chance of becoming experts in that market and reaping the accompanying rewards.

The biggest challenge a new firm faces when selecting a target market is choosing a market that is attractive enough to be interesting but is different enough that the firm isn't just another face in the crowd. A firm's choice of target markets must also be in sync with its business model and the backgrounds and skills of its founders and other personnel. A firm must also continually monitor the attractiveness of its target market. Societal preferences change, a fact that sometimes causes a target market to lose its attractiveness for a firm and the product or service it has to offer customers.

Establishing a Unique Position

After selecting a target market, the firm's next step is to establish a "position" within it that differentiates it from its competitors. As we discussed in Chapter 5, position is concerned with how the firm is situated relative to competitors. In a sense, a position is the part of a market or of a segment of the market the firm is claiming as its own. A firm's market position can be understood by studying the features of its goods or services. For example, BMW's position (luxury) in the automobile market differs from Chevrolet's position (functional). Clearly, these products differ from each other in substantial ways. Even within the luxury automobile market, BMW's position (more sports-driving oriented) differs from that of Lexus (more luxury-features oriented). The term *differentiation* was introduced in Chapter 6, where we emphasized that a firm's position in the marketplace determines how it is situated relative to its competitors. From a marketing perspective, this translates into the image of the way a firm wants to be perceived by its customers and answers the question, "Why should someone in our target market buy our product or service instead of our competitors'?"[13] Of course, once a firm positions itself in a certain way, it must be able to follow through with a product or service offering that lives up to the image it has created. However, no amount of positioning will help when customers have tried the firm's product or service and are dissatisfied with their experience.

A firm's decision about how to position itself relative to its competitors starts with a product or service idea that is tested and refined through feasibility analysis and marketing research, as we discussed in earlier chapters. To underscore the importance of getting this

L E A R N I N G
Objective

3. Explain why it's important for a start-up to establish a unique position in its target market.

TABLE 11.1 Match the Company to Its Tagline

Company	Tagline
Google	Connecting people
Flavorx	Made from the best stuff on earth
Netflix	We make medicine a lot less yucky
Panera Bread	Have it your way
MySpace	It's about time
Snapple	To organize the world's information
Burger King	There's always a movie to watch at home
Nokia	Fresh bread makes friends
Day Jet	A place for friends

process right, venture capitalists estimate that as many as 60 percent of business failures could be prevented through better prelaunch marketing research.[14]

Oakley, the sunglasses company, has done an excellent job of positioning itself and delivering on its promises. We discuss Oakley in this chapter's "Savvy Entrepreneurial Firm."

Firms often develop a **tagline**—a phrase that is used consistently in a company's literature, advertisements, promotions, stationery, and even invoices and thus becomes associated with that company—to reinforce the position they have staked out in their market. An example is Nike's familiar "Just do it." The Nike tagline, which was introduced in 1988, implies that people don't need to be told they should exercise—they already know that. The challenge is to "Just do it." The beauty of this simple three-word expression is that it applies equally to a 21-year-old triathlete and a 65-year-old mall walker. This clever tagline, along with Nike's positioning strategy, helped the firm expand its product line beyond running shoes to athletic products for all age groups.[15]

Table 11.1 is a short matching quiz that asks you to match several well-known companies with their taglines. A company has created a successful tagline if the message makes you think immediately of its products or services and the position it has established in its market.

Key Marketing Issues for New Ventures

There are indeed many marketing issues with which entrepreneurial ventures must grapple. However, the selling of benefits rather than features and establishing a brand are very critical to a new venture's early success. A lack of attention to either of these issues can cripple a firm's marketing efforts by sending confusing messages to the firm's intended customers.

Selling Benefits Rather Than Features

4. Describe the importance of the ability to position a company's products on benefits rather than features.

Many entrepreneurs make the mistake of positioning their company's products or services on features rather than benefits. A positioning or marketing strategy that focuses on the features of a product, such as its technical merits, is usually much less effective than a campaign focusing on the merits of what the product can do.[16] Consider a cell phone manufacturer that claims, "Our cell phones are equipped with sufficient memory to store 100 phone numbers." The ability to store 100 phone numbers is a feature rather than a benefit. While features are nice, they typically don't entice someone to buy a product. A better way for the manufacturer to market the same cell phone would be to say, "Our cell phone lets you store up to 100 phone numbers, giving you the phone numbers of your family and your friends at your fingertips." This statement focuses on benefits. It tells prospects how buying the product will enhance their life.

savvy entrepreneurial firm

Oakley: Stamping a Strong Image in Customers' Minds
www.oakley.com

Although sunglasses had been around for a long time before Oakley arrived on the scene, the company has created a category and market position that are virtually its own and has achieved impressive growth as a result of doing so. Oakley (named after its founder's dog) started as a company that sold handgrips and goggles for motorcycle racing. In the mid-1980s, the firm started selling sunglasses. Since that time, it has grown substantially, achieving a sales volume of over $648 million in 2005. Oakley is now a recognized leader in the sunglasses industry.

Much of Oakley's success can be attributed to its positioning. Rather than producing typical sunglasses, Oakley's glasses are innovative, state-of-the art products that are both high quality and visually appealing. Oakley also projects a brash counterculture persona, similar in sprit to the persona projected by Harley-Davidson. In its ads and promotions, Oakley says that its foundation is built on three fundamental precepts or attributes: find opportunity, solve with technology, wrap in art.

By adhering to these principles, Oakley has stamped an image of itself in the minds of its customers as a creative, technologically savvy, and independent (i.e., answering only to itself) company. This position resonates with a particular set of customers who want to perceive themselves as similarly "hip"—at least part of the time. Because of the position it commands, Oakley can charge a premium price for its glasses. Most of Oakley's sunglasses sell in the $65 to $375 range,

depending on the style and features. Even the names of Oakley's sunglasses reinforce the company's brash image. For example, its metal-frame glasses include choices that are named Romeo 2.0, Polarized Juliet, X Metal XX, and Penny. Oakley is currently branching into high-performance athletic shoes, watches, and apparel and is patterning its positioning strategy in these markets after its experience with sunglasses.

Questions for Critical Thinking
1. Do you think Oakley's attempt to position itself in athletic shoes, watches, and apparel in ways similar to how it is positioned in the sunglasses market will work? Why or why not?
2. Develop a list of attributes for Oakley's sunglasses that differs from the list you would develop to describe the attributes of sunglasses you could purchase in Wal-Mart and Target. What are the primary attributes of Oakley's sunglasses for which customers are willing to pay?
3. Describe Oakley's target market. Do you think its branding and positioning choices reflect a sensible approach to reaching its target market?
4. If you had to write a tagline for Oakley, what would it be? Does the tagline you wrote speak to you as a customer? Why or why not?

Sources: Oakley homepage, www.oakley.com (accessed August 17, 2006).

One of the most successful advertising campaigns ever launched by McDonald's contained ads that featured the jingle, "You deserve a break today—at McDonald's." McDonald's could have stressed the cleanliness of its stores or the speed of its service, both of which are features. Instead, it struck a chord with people by focusing on one of the biggest benefits of eating at McDonald's—not having to cook. Although not as obvious in today's society, not having to cook a meal at home was a major advantage when McDonald's started using this tagline.

Entrepreneurs should tout a product or service's benefits before describing its features. Sometimes this is hard to do. For example, it is easy to see why an engineer who has just invented a new product wants to talk about that product's technical specifications. Similarly, it is natural for a company that has just developed an improved digital camera to want to point out all the bells and whistles that its camera has that other cameras don't. However, one of the most fundamental precepts of marketing is that "customers don't buy features, they buy benefits."[17] The first thing most customers want to know is how the product or service will help them accomplish their goals or improve their lives.

5. Illustrate the two major ways in which a company builds a brand.

Establishing a Brand

A **brand** is the set of attributes—positive or negative—that people associate with a company. These attributes can be positive, such as trustworthy, innovative, dependable, or easy to deal with. Or they can be negative, such as cheap, unreliable, arrogant, or difficult to deal with. The customer loyalty a company creates through its brand is one of its most valuable assets. Lending support to this sentiment, Russell Hanlin, the CEO of Sunkist Growers, said, "An orange is an orange . . . is an orange. Unless . . . that orange happens to be a Sunkist, a name 80 percent of consumers know and trust."[18] By putting its name on an orange, Sunkist is making a promise to its customers that the orange will be wholesome and fresh. It is important that Sunkist not break this promise. Some companies monitor the integrity of their brands through **brand management**, which is a program used to protect the image and value of an organization's brand in consumers' minds. This means that if Sunkist discovered that some of its oranges weren't fresh, it would take immediate steps to correct the problem.

Table 11.2 lists the different ways people think about the meaning of a brand. All the sentiments expressed in the table are similar, but they illustrate the multifaceted nature of a company's brand.

Start-ups must build a brand from scratch, which starts with selecting the company's name, as described in Case 7.2. One of the keys to effective branding is to create a strong personality for a firm, designed to appeal to the chosen target market.[19] Southwest Airlines, for example, has created a brand that denotes fun. This is a good fit for its target market: people traveling for pleasure rather than business. Similarly, Starbucks has created a brand that denotes an experience framed around warmth and hospitality, encouraging people to linger and buy additional products. A company ultimately wants its customers to strongly identify with it—to see themselves as "Southwest Airlines flyers" or "Starbucks coffee drinkers." People won't do this, however, unless they see a company as being different from competitors in ways that create value for them.

So how does a new firm develop a brand? On a philosophical level, a firm must have meaning in its customers' lives.[20] It must create value—something for which customers are willing to pay. Imagine a father shopping for airline tickets so that he can take his three children to see their grandparents for Christmas. If Southwest Airlines can get his family to their destination for $75 per ticket cheaper than its competitors, Southwest has real meaning in the father's life. Similarly, if a teenage boy enjoys playing Madden football with his friends and always wants the latest version of the game, Electronic Arts, the maker of the game, has real meaning in his life. Firms that create meaning in their customers' lives stand for something in terms of benefits, whether it is low prices, fun, fashion, quality, friendliness, dependability, or something else. This meaning creates a bond between a company and its customers.

TABLE 11.2 **What's a Brand? Different Ways of Thinking about the Meaning of a Brand**

- A brand is a promise.
- A brand is a guarantee.
- A brand is a pledge.
- A brand is a reputation.
- A brand is an unwritten warrantee.
- A brand is an expectation of performance.
- A brand is a presentation of credentials.
- A brand is a mark of trust and reduced risk.
- A brand is a collection of memories.
- A brand is a handshake between a company and its customers.

Source: Adapted from D. Travis, *Emotional Branding: How Successful Brands Gain the Irrational Edge* (Roseville, CA: Prima Ventures, 2000).

iRobot produces the popular Roomba vacuum cleaner. Although iRobot is enjoying much success as a smaller and newer company, it will eventually face the challenge of having to establish a strong brand image for its product if it is to continue growing. Expanding the business will be challenging because iRobot will be competing against bigger and more established corporations such as Electrolux and DirtDevil.

On a more practical level, brands are built through a number of techniques, including advertising, public relations, sponsorships, support of social causes, and good performance. A firm's name, logo, Web site design, and even its letterhead are part of its brand. It's important for start-ups, particularly if they plan to sell to other businesses, to have a polished image immediately so that they have credibility when they approach their potential customers. Affirming all of these points, Dan Byrne, the CEO of Byrne Specialty Gases, a company that provides specialized gases to laboratories, sums up what his company has done to build a strong brand during its 20 years of existence:

> It is all based on trust, reliability, responsiveness, quality, etc. It is all these infinitesimal details that drive a company's brand. We have the attitude that everything matters. We lost a large customer once that went to a discount provider. Three months later the customer called us back almost hat in hand. Our level of service reinforces our brand and keeps customers coming back to us.[21]

Most experts warn against placing an overreliance on advertising to build a firm's image. A more affordable approach is to rely on word of mouth, the media, and ingenuity to create positive buzz about a company. Creating **buzz** means creating awareness and a sense of anticipation about a company and its offerings.[22] This process can start during feasibility analysis, when a company shows its concept statement or product prototype to prospective buyers or industry experts. Unless a company wants what it is doing to be kept secret (to preserve its proprietary technology or its first-mover advantage), it hopes that people start talking about it and its exciting new product or service.[23] In addition, newspapers, magazines, and trade journals are always looking for stories about interesting companies. If a new company can get a favorable review of its products or services in a magazine or a trade journal, that lends a sense of legitimacy to a firm that would be hard to duplicate through advertisements. Case 11.1 focuses on how two companies, PowerBar and White Wave, created buzz surrounding their products.

Focusing too much on the features and benefits of their products is a common mistake entrepreneurs make when trying to gain attention from the media. Journalists are typically skeptical when entrepreneurs start talking about how great their products are relative to those of their competitors. What journalists usually prefer is a human interest story about why a firm was started or a story focused on something that's distinctly unique about the start-up. For example, MyGoals.com, a Web-based company that helps people set and manage goals, has been particularly proficient in generating free publicity surrounding its goal of helping other people reach their goals. Since it was founded in the late 1990s, the company has been featured on CNN (at least six times), CNN Financial, CBS Early Show, and *Time* magazine as well as several other media outlets. Greg Helmstetter, the cofounder of MyGoals.com, says the majority of its business (it offers a subscription-based service) has resulted from these features.[24] Imagine the amount of money that the company would have had to spend on advertising to generate the same amount of publicity and visibility.

Sometimes entrepreneurs go out on a limb and try innovative tactics to get their firm noticed. An example is what Zach Nelson, the founder of MyCIO.com (now called McAfee ASaP), did when his firm was first launched:

> One of the great things we did when we first launched MyCIO.com is that we draped our entire eleven-story building on Highway 101 with the MyCIO.com logo. It was the world's largest billboard. The City of San Jose wasn't very happy with us for doing it, but they let us keep it up for a month. Everyone that I called after we ran that giant billboard I received a return call back from.[25]

Tactics such as these are a little tricky, and the wisdom of them must be considered on a case-by-case basis. What Nelson was trying to do for MyCIO.com was to get people talking about his company and wondering what it was trying to do.

Ultimately, a strong brand can be a very powerful asset for a firm. Fifty-two percent of consumers say that a known and trusted brand is a reason to buy a product.[26] As a result, a brand allows a company to charge a price for its products that is consistent with its image. A successful brand can also increase the market value of a company by 50 to 75 percent.[27] This increased valuation can be very important to a firm if it is acquired, merges with another firm, or launches an initial public offering. **Brand equity** is the term that denotes the set of assets and liabilities that are linked to a brand and enable it to raise a firm's valuation.[28] It is important for firms to understand brand equity and how to use it to create value. As explained in this chapter's "What Went Wrong" feature, companies sometimes fail to effectively execute when it comes to this activity.

Although the assets and liabilities that make up a firm's brand equity will vary from context to context, they usually are grouped into the following five categories:

- Brand loyalty
- Name recognition
- Perceived quality (of a firm's products and services)
- Brand associations in addition to quality (e.g., good service)
- Other proprietary assets, such as patents, trademarks, and high-quality partnerships

One technique that companies use to strengthen their brands is to enter into a cobranding arrangement with other firms. **Cobranding** refers to a relationship between two or more firms where the firms' brands promote each other. A well-known example of cobranding is the "Intel Inside" campaign. If a computer has Intel components inside, the positive image associated with Intel will rub off on the computer and help sell it. Intel wins too because the more computers that are sold, the more demand there is for Intel products.

Before a firm (including an entrepreneurial venture) enters into a cobranding arrangement, it should consider the following three questions:

- Will the cobranding arrangement maintain or strengthen my brand image?
- Do I have adequate control over how my partner will display or use my brand?
- Are their tangible benefits associated with attaching my brand to my partner's brand? For example, will my partner's brand have a positive effect on my brand and actually increase my sales?

If the answer to each of these questions is yes, then a cobranding arrangement may be a very wise marketing approach.

what went wrong?

Quaker Oats' Botched Acquisition of Snapple: The Price of Failing to Understand the Real Meaning of a Company's Brand

www.snapple.com

Many entrepreneurial firms are acquired at some point during their corporate lives, or the founders leave or retire and turn over the day-to-day management of the company to a new management team. On these occasions, it is important that the new owners or the new managers of the company fully understand the meaning of the company's brand. If they don't, they can make decisions that inadvertently diminish the value of the brand. There is no better story to illustrate this point than Quaker Oats' failed acquisition of Snapple.

Snapple was created in 1972 by Leonard Marsh, Hyman Golden, and Arnold Greenberg, three beverage entrepreneurs. The name "Snapple" originated from the snapping sound the early versions of the drink made when the cap was removed. From the outset, Snapple was positioned as a quirky, fashionable alternative to standard soft-drink brands. Its flavors, which over time grew to include teas, diet drinks, juice drinks, and lemonades, included stylish and eccentric names, such as Lime Green Tea, White Tea, Diet Cranberry Raspberry, Kiwi Strawberry, and Super Sour Lemonade. The company's slogan—"Made from the best stuff on earth"—referred to its all natural ingredients. In the early 1990s, the company hired Rush Limbaugh and Howard Stern as celebrity endorsers. In 1993, Wendy Kauffman, one of Snapple's employees, was recruited to be the commercial spokesperson for the brand. Kauffman had taken it upon herself to answer letters that were coming into the company with questions about the product. The quirky ads centered on Kauffman reading letters out loud and delivering comical responses. The commercials were so popular and well received, that Kauffman became affectionately known as the "Snapple Lady."

In 1994, food giant Quaker Oats bought Snapple for $1.7 billion. In 1997, just 3 short years later, the company sold Snapple to a private investment group for $300 million, losing an astounding $1.4 billion in the process. What went wrong? As many observers have written, plenty—starting with branding.

The consensus view among those that observed Quaker Oats' handling of Snapple is that the company simply didn't understand what the Snapple brand was all about. From the outset, Quaker saw Snapple as an all-around sports drink, similar to Gatorade, rather than the eclectic drink it was. This perception led to two strategic marketing blunders, both of which worked to Snapple's disadvantage.

Blunder #1: Distribution. Prior to the Quaker Oats' acquisition, Snapple was sold primarily through small shops and gas stations. This distribution approach made Snapple a drink that had to be sought out or was available as a "treat" for travelers or someone who wanted a satisfying drink after filling their car with gas. Once Quaker Oats got hold of Snapple, it mainlined Snapple into its mass merchandise channels and suddenly it was available everywhere. This switch took the uniqueness away from Snapple in terms of distribution. It was now just another beverage among dozens of others on grocery store shelves.

Blunder #2: Promotion. Quaker Oats did away with Snapple's celebrity endorsers, Rush Limbaugh and Howard Stern, and silenced Wendy Kaufman, the Snapple Lady. In their place, Quaker launched an advertising campaign boasting that Snapple would be happy to be third behind Coca-Cola and Pepsi in the beverage market. The ads fell flat.

The combined impact of these blunders was a rapid erosion of Snapple's once strong brand. Prior to the acquisition, Snapple's brand stood for fun, quirkiness, uniqueness, feeling good, and good nutrition. Snapple was a treat to be savored and enjoyed. Quaker Oats did nothing to support those elements of Snapple's appeal. Instead, it in effect "rebranded" Snapple into a mainline brand, with little differentiation from other beverages on store shelves. The result was a continuous slide in sales, until Quaker eventually gave up and sold Snapple to Triarc in 1997. Triarc returned Snapple to its roots by reintroducing Wendy Kauffman (the Snapple Lady) in its promotions and reinvigorating the positive attributes of Snapple's original positioning strategy and brand. Gradually, Snapple's original customers returned and the brand increased in value. In 2000, Cadbury Schweppes bought Snapple for $1 billion, and Snapple is now almost fully restored after its rocky ride.

Questions for Critical Thinking

1. Why do you think Snapple was successful prior to its acquisition by Quaker Oats?

2. Why do you think Quaker Oats didn't work harder to more fully understand the nature of Snapple's brand before it made the changes described here?

3. How would you describe Snapple's positioning strategy before the Quaker Oats' acquisition? How would you describe the way that Quaker Oats tried to position Snapple?

4. Provide an example of what you think is a very cleverly branded product. What has the company that makes the product done to make its branding distinctive and effective?

Sources: Snapple homepage, www.snapple.com (accessed August 17, 2006); M. Haig, *Brand Failures* (London: Kogan Page, 2003).

The 4Ps of Marketing for New Ventures

6. Identify the four components of the marketing mix.

Once a company decides on its target market, establishes a position within that market, and establishes a brand, it is ready to begin planning the details of its marketing mix. A firm's **marketing mix** is the set of controllable, tactical marketing tools that it uses to produce the response it wants in the target market.[29] Most marketers organize their marketing mix into four categories: product, price, promotion, and place (or distribution). For an obvious reason, these categories are commonly referred to as the 4Ps.

The way a firm sells and distributes its product dramatically affects a company's marketing program. This effect means that the first decision a firm has to make is its overall approach to selling its product or service. Even for similar firms, the marketing mix can vary significantly, depending on the way the firms do business. For example, a software firm can sell directly through its Web site or through retail stores, or it can license its product to another company to be sold under that company's brand name. A start-up that plans to sell directly to the public would set up its promotions program in a much different way than a firm planning to license its products to other firms. A firm's marketing program should be consistent with its business model and its overall business plan.

Let's look more closely at the 4Ps. Again, these are broad topics on which entire books have been written. In this section, we focus on the aspects of the 4Ps that are most relevant to entrepreneurial ventures.

Product

7. Explain the difference between a core product and an actual product.

Although all elements of the marketing mix are important, the success of a marketing program starts with a good-quality product that people need or enjoy. The Apple iPod is a product that has brought happiness and joy to millions of people since it was first introduced in 2001.

A firm's **product**, in the context of its marketing mix, is the good or service it offers to its target market. Technically, a product is something that takes on physical form, such as an Apple iPod, an electronic game, or a laptop computer. A **service** is an activity or benefit that is intangible and does not take on a physical form, such as an airplane trip or advice from an attorney. But when discussing a firm's marketing mix, both products and services are lumped together under the label "product."

Determining the product or products to be sold is central to the firm's entire marketing effort. As stressed throughout this book, the most important attribute of a product is that it adds value in the minds of its target customers. Let's think about this by comparing vitamins with pain pills, as articulated by Henry W. Chesbrough, a professor at Harvard University:

> We all know that vitamins are good for us and that we should take them. Most of us, though, do not take vitamins on a regular basis, and whatever benefits vitamins provide do not seem to be greatly missed in the short term. People therefore pay relatively very little for vitamins. In contrast, people know when they need a pain killer. And they know they need it now, not later. They can also tell quite readily whether the reliever is working. People will be willing to pay a great deal more for a pain reliever than they pay for a vitamin. In this context, the pain reliever provides a much stronger value proposition than does a vitamin—because the need is felt more acutely, the benefit is greater and is perceived much more quickly.[30]

This example illustrates at least in part why investors prefer to fund firms that potentially have breakthrough products, such as a software firm that is working on a product to eliminate e-mail spam or a biotech firm that is working on a cure for a disease. These products are pain pills rather than vitamins because their benefits would be felt intensely and quickly. In contrast, a new restaurant start-up or a new retail store may be exciting, but these types of firms are more akin to a vitamin than a pain pill. The benefits of these businesses would not be felt as intensely.

As the firm prepares to sell its product, an important distinction should be made between the core product and the actual product. While the core product may be a CD that contains an antivirus software program, the actual product, which is what the customer buys, may have as many as five characteristics: a quality level, features, design, a brand name, and packaging.[31] For example, the Norton antivirus program is an actual product. Its name, features, warranty, ability to upgrade, packaging, and other attributes have all been carefully combined to deliver the benefits of the product: protecting computers and their contents against damage and protecting computer users against work interruption. When first introducing a product to the market, an entrepreneur needs to make sure that more than the core product is right. Attention also needs to be paid to the actual product—the features, design, packaging, and so on that constitute the collection of benefits that the customer ultimately buys. Anyone who has ever tried to remove a product from a frustratingly rigid plastic container knows that the way a product is packaged is part of the product itself. The quality of the product should not be compromised by missteps in other areas.

The initial rollout is one of the most critical times in the marketing of a new product. All new firms face the challenge that they are unknown and that it takes a leap of faith for their first customers to buy their products. Some start-ups meet this challenge by using reference accounts. A **reference account** is an early user of a firm's product who is willing to give a testimonial regarding his or her experience with the product. For example, imagine the effect of a spokesperson for Dell Inc. saying that Dell used a new computer hardware firm's products and was pleased with their performance. A testimonial such as this would pave the way for the salesforce of this new firm's hardware, and the new firm could use it to reduce fears that it was selling an untested and perhaps ineffective product.

To obtain reference accounts, new firms must often offer their product to an initial group of customers for free or at a reduced price in exchange for their willingness to try the product and for their feedback. There is nothing improper about this process as long as everything is kept aboveboard and the entrepreneur is not indirectly "paying" someone to offer a positive endorsement. Still, many entrepreneurs are reluctant to give away products, even in exchange for a potential endorsement. But there are several advantages to getting a strong set of endorsements: credibility with peers, noncompany advocates who are willing to talk to the press, and quotes or examples to use in company brochures and advertisements.

L E A R N I N G

Objective

8. Contrast cost-based pricing and value-based pricing.

Price

Price is the amount of money consumers pay to buy a product. It is the only element in the marketing mix that produces revenue; all other elements represent costs.[32] Price is an extremely important element of the marketing mix because it ultimately determines how much money a company can earn. The price a company charges for its products also sends a clear message to its target market. For example, Oakley positions its sunglasses as innovative, state-of-the art products that are both high quality and visually appealing. This position in the market suggests the premium price that Oakley charges. If Oakley tried to establish the position described previously and charged a low price for its products, it would send confusing signals to its customers. In addition, the lower price wouldn't generate the sales revenue Oakley requires to continuously differentiate its sunglasses from competitors' products in ways that create value for customers.

Most entrepreneurs use one of two methods to set the price for their products: cost-based pricing or value-based pricing.

Cost-Based Pricing In **cost-based pricing**, the list price is determined by adding a markup percentage to a product's cost. The markup percentage may be standard for the industry or may be arbitrarily determined by the entrepreneur. The advantage of this method is that it is straightforward, and it is relatively easy to justify the price of a good or service. The disadvantage is that it is not always easy to estimate what the costs of a product will be. Once a price is set, it is difficult to raise it, even if a company's costs increase in an unpredicted manner. In addition, cost-based pricing is based on what a company thinks it should receive rather than on what the market thinks a good or service is worth. It is becoming increasingly difficult for companies to dictate prices to their customers, given customers' ability to comparison shop on the Internet to find what they believe is the best bargain for them.[33]

Value-Based Pricing In **value-based pricing**, the list price is determined by estimating what consumers are willing to pay for a product and then backing off a bit to provide a cushion. What a customer is willing to pay is determined by the perceived value of the product and by the number of choices available in the marketplace. Sometimes, to make this determination, a company has to work backwards by testing to see what its target market is willing to pay. A firm influences its customers' perception of the value through positioning, branding, and the other elements of the marketing mix. Most experts recommend value-based pricing because it hinges on the perceived value of a product or service rather than cost-plus markup, which, as stated previously, is a formula that ignores the customer.[34] A gross margin (a company's net sales minus its costs of goods sold) of 60 to 80 percent is not uncommon in high-tech industries. An Intel chip that sells for $300 may cost $50 to $60 to produce. This type of markup reflects the perceived value of the chip. If Intel used a cost-based pricing method instead of a value-based approach, it would probably charge much less for its chips and earn less profit.

Most experts also warn entrepreneurs to resist the temptation to charge a low price for their products in the hopes of capturing market share. This approach can win a sale but generates little profit. In addition, most consumers make a **price-quality attribution** when looking at the price of a product. This means that consumers naturally assume that the higher-priced product is also the better-quality product.[35] If a firm charges a low price for its products, it sends a signal to its customers that the product is low quality regardless of whether it really is.

A company can't charge premium prices, however, without delivering on its positioning and branding promises and unless the circumstances are right. As explained in Chapter 5, some industries have very low barriers to entry and intense competition, making it difficult for a firm to charge high prices regardless of how differentiated its good or service is. To charge a premium price, one or more of the following circumstances must be present:

- Demand for the product is strong relative to supply.
- Demand for the product is inelastic (people will buy at any price).

- The product is patent protected and has a clearly defined target market.
- The product offers additional features that are valued (e.g., a strong warranty).
- A new technology is being introduced.
- The product serves a compelling need (it is a pain pill rather than a vitamin).
- The product is positioned as a luxury item.

The ability to charge a premium price is an issue that a firm should consider when developing its positioning and branding strategies.

Promotion

Promotion refers to the activities the firm takes to communicate the merits of its product to its target market. Ultimately, the goal of these activities is to persuade people to buy the product. There are a number of these activities, but most start-ups have limited resources, meaning that they must carefully study promotion activities before choosing the one or ones they'll use. Let's look at the most common activities entrepreneurs use to promote their products.

Advertising **Advertising** is making people aware of a product in hopes of persuading them to buy it. Advertising's major goals are to do the following:

- Raise customer awareness of a product
- Explain a product's comparative features and benefits
- Create associations between a product and a certain lifestyle

These goals can be accomplished through a number of media, including direct mail, magazines, newspapers, radio, the Internet, television, and billboard advertising. The most effective ads tend to be those that are memorable ("Dude, you're getting a Dell!") and support a product's brand. However, advertising has some major weaknesses, including the following:

- Low credibility
- The possibility that a high percentage of the people who see the ad will not be interested
- Message clutter (meaning that after hearing or reading so many ads, people simply tune out)
- Relative costliness compared to other forms of promotions
- The perception that advertising is intrusive[36]

L E A R N I N G
Objective

9. Explain the differences between advertising and public relations.

Because of these weaknesses, most start-ups do not advertise their products broadly. Instead, they tend to be very frugal and selective in their advertising efforts, such as limiting their print ad dollars to industry trade journals or using highly focused pay-per-click advertising provided by Google, Yahoo!, or another online firm. Pay-per-click advertising represents a major innovation in advertising and has been embraced by firms of all sizes. Google has two pay-per-click programs—AdWords and AdSense. AdWords allows an advertiser to buy keywords on Google's home-page (www.google.com), which triggers text-based ads to the side (and sometimes above) the search results when the keyword is used. So, if you type "soccer ball" into the Google search bar, you will see ads that have been paid for by companies that have soccer balls to sell. Many advertisers report impressive results utilizing this approach, presumably because they are able to place their ads in front of people who are already searching for information about their product. Google's other pay-per-click program is called AdSense. It is similar to AdWords, except the advertiser's ads appear on other Web sites instead of Google's homepage. For example, an organization that promotes soccer might allow Google to place some of its client's ads on its Web site. The advertiser pays on a pay-for-click basis when its ad is clicked on the soccer organization's site, just like it does with AdWords. Google shares the revenue generated by the advertisers with the sponsoring site. Table 11.3 provides a summary of the Google AdWords and Google AdSense programs. Yahoo!'s program, which is very similar to Google's, is called Yahoo! Search Marketing (formally Overture).

TABLE 11.3 Description of Google AdWords and AdSense Programs for Advertisers and Web Site Owners

AdWords	AdSense
Allows advertisers to buy keywords on the Google Home Page	Allows advertisers to buy ads that will be shown on other Web sites instead of Google's Home Page.
Triggers text-based ads to the side (and sometimes above) search results when the keyword is used.	Google selects sites of interest to the advertiser's customers.
Advertisers are charged on a pay-per-click basis.	Advertisers are charged on a pay-per-click or per-thousand impression basis.
The program includes local, national, and international distribution.	Advertisers are not restricted to text-based ads. Choices include text, image, and video advertisements.
Advertisers specify the maximum amount they are willing to pay per click. The ordering of the paid listings on the search results depends on other advertisers' bids and the historical click-through rates of all ads shown for a given search.	Advertisers benefit because their ads are seen as less intrusive than most banner ads, because the content of the ad is often relevant to the Web site.
Advertisers have the option of enabling their ads to be displayed on Google's partner network. This network includes AOL, Ask.com, and Netscape.	Web site owners benefit by using the service to monetize their Web sites.
Advertisers benefit because they are able to place their ads in front of people who are already searching for information about their product.	A companion to the regular AdSense program, AdSense for Search lets Web site owners place the Google search box on their Web site. Google shares any ad revenues it makes from those searches.

As an aside, the Google AdSense program has allowed many Web sites that didn't have a source of income to monetize their sites by participating in the program. For example, there is a Web site named SeatGuru.com, which was started by a flying enthusiast and lists the best seats and the worst seats (in terms of comfort) for each airline by type of aircraft. Prior to the advent of the Google AdSense program, the site had no practical way of making money. Now, the site is viable as a result of participating in the Google AdSense program. If you look at the site, you will see a number of targeted ads sponsored by the Google AdSense program. Google gets the ads, places them on the site, and shares the revenue generated by the ads with the owners of SeatGuru.com.

The steps involved in putting together an advertisement are shown in Figure 11.2. Typically, for start-up firms, advertisements are the most effective if they're part of a

FIGURE 11.2

Steps Involved in Putting Together an Advertisement

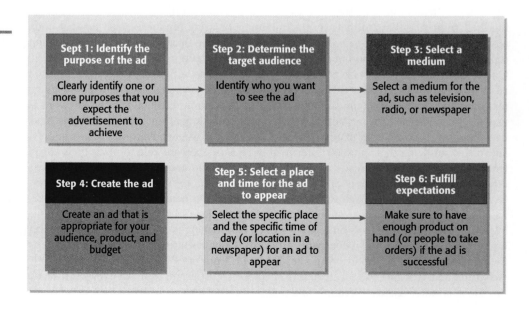

coordinated marketing campaign.[37] For example, a print ad might feature a product's benefits and direct the reader to a Web site for more information. The Web site might offer access to coupons or other incentives if the visitor fills out an information request form (which asks for name, address, and phone number). The names collected from the information request form could then be used to make sales calls. Some companies also benefit by hiring celebrities to endorse their products. This alternative is illustrated in Case 11.2, which focuses on Proactiv, a company that sells acne prevention cream. Proactiv has made very effective use of celebrity endorsers, although this approach is expensive and is appropriate on a case-by-case basis. Another alternative that is illustrated in the Proactiv case is the use of infomercials. An **informercial** is a television commercial that runs as long as a television show and usually includes a pitch selling an item directly to the public.[38] Informercials can be very effective in specialized cases, as illustrated in the Proactiv example.

Entrepreneurs should be aware that a poorly crafted ad runs the risk of irritating the firm's target audience. In fact, in direct response to advertising, negative terms such as *junk mail*, *spam*, and *telemarketing* (which is not in itself a negative word, although many people associate it with being interrupted) have become part of our standard language. The "mute" button on a television remote was designed primarily to silence ads. There are no easy ways for advertisers to meet these challenges, but they point out the importance of making sure that an advertisement is carefully crafted, that it is consistent with the brand image a firm wants to convey, and that it is geared to its target market.

Public Relations One of the most cost-effective ways to increase the awareness of the products a company sells is through public relations. **Public relations** refer to efforts to establish and maintain a company's image with the public. The major difference between public relations and advertising is that public relations is not paid for—directly. The cost of public relations to a firm is the effort it makes to network with journalists and other people to try to interest them in saying or writing good things about the company and its products. Several techniques fit the definition of public relations, as shown in Table 11.4.

Many start-ups emphasize public relations over advertising primarily because it's cheaper and helps build the firm's credibility. In their book *The Fall of Advertising and the Rise of PR*, Al and Laura Ries argue that in launching a new product, it is better to start with public relations than advertising because people view advertising as the self-serving voice of a company that's anxious to make a sale. Advertising, according to the authors, is largely discounted. In contrast, public relations allows a firm to tell its story through a third party, such as a magazine or a newspaper. If a magazine along the lines of *Inc.* or *BusinessWeek* publishes a positive review of a new company's products, consumers are likely to believe that those products are at least worth a try. They think that because these magazines have no vested interest in the company, they have no reason to stretch the truth or lie about the usefulness or value of a company's products.[39]

There are many ways in which a start-up can enhance its chances of getting noticed by the press. One technique is to prepare a **press kit**, which is a folder that contains background information about the company and includes a list of its most recent accomplishments. The kit is normally distributed to journalists and made available online. Another technique is to be present at industry trade shows and other events. A **trade show** is an event at which the goods or services in a specific industry are exhibited and demonstrated. Members of the media often attend trade shows to get the latest industry news. For example, the largest trade show for consumer electronics is International CES, which is held in Las Vegas every January. Many companies wait until this show to announce their most exciting new products. They do this in part because they have a captive media audience that is eager to find interesting stories to write about. A recent International CES show is pictured in Chapter 5.

Other Promotions-Related Activities There are many other activities that help a firm promote and sell its products. Some firms, for example, give away free samples of

TABLE 11.4 Public Relations Techniques

Technique	Description
Press release	An announcement made by a firm that is circulated to the press. Start-ups typically circulate a press release when something positive happens, such as the launch of a new product or the hiring of a new executive.
Media coverage	Any coverage in print or broadcast media. In most cases, start-ups try to cultivate media coverage, as long as it is positive.
Articles in industry press and periodicals	Articles in industry press and periodicals are particularly coveted because they are read by people already interested in the industry in which the start-up is participating.
Blogging	A blog is a type of Web site where entries (similar to journal or diary entries) are displayed in reverse chronological order (with the most recent entries first). There are blogs that cover most industries. Outwardly talking about the merits of one's own products or services is considered spamming but making thoughtful and substantive contributions to a blog is a public service. When you sign (i.e., identify yourself online) your entry, include your company's Web site address so people who are interested in your contributions can refer back to you and your company.
Monthly newsletter	Many companies stay in touch with their potential target audience by producing and distributing a monthly or quarterly newsletter. Along with containing updates on a firm's products and services, the newsletter should contain more general information of interest to the reader. Companies should avoid sending out newsletters that simply brag about their products. These types of newsletters are often seen as too self-serving.
News conference	A new conference is the live dissemination of new information by a firm to invited media. A start-up might call a news conference to announce a breakthrough new product or service innovation.
Civic, social, and community involvement	Start-ups often try to create a positive image of their organization by sponsoring local events or asking their employees to be involved in civic clubs such as the Chamber of Commerce or the Rotary Club.

their products. This technique is used by pharmaceutical companies that give physicians free samples to distribute to their patients as appropriate. Many food companies distribute free samples in grocery and discount stores. A similar technique is to offer free trials such as a 3-month subscription to a magazine or a 2-week membership to a fitness club to try to hook potential customers by exposing them directly to the product or service.

Another technique is event sponsorships. Many firms sponsor sporting events, enter floats in parades, or sponsor civic events, such as a concert series, to align their names with something of interest to their target markets. Whether these types of techniques are cost-effective is usually unclear; it's difficult to determine how much a firm gains from sponsoring a Little League baseball team or a concert series.

A fairly new technique that has received quite a bit of attention is **viral marketing**, which facilitates and encourages people to pass along a marketing message about a particular product. The most well-known example of viral marketing is Hotmail. When Hotmail first started distributing free e-mail accounts, it put a tagline on every message sent out by Hotmail users that read "Get free e-mail with Hotmail." Within less than a year, the company had several millions users. Every e-mail message that passed through the Hotmail system was essentially an advertisement for Hotmail. The success of viral marketing depends on the pass-along rate from person to person. Very few companies have come close to matching Hotmail's success with viral marketing. However, the idea of designing a promotional campaign that encourages a firm's current customers to recommend its product to future customers is well worth considering.

Place (or Distribution)

Place, or distribution, encompasses all the activities that move a firm's product from its place of origin to the consumer. A **distribution channel** is the route a product takes from the place it is made to the customer who is the end user.

The first choice a firm has to make regarding distribution is whether to sell its products directly to consumers or through intermediaries (such as wholesalers and retailers). Within most industries, both choices are available, so the decision typically depends on how a firm believes its target market wants to buy its product. For example, it would make sense for a recording company that is targeting the teen market to produce digital recordings and sell the recordings directly over the Web. Most teens have access to a computer and know how to download music. In contrast, it wouldn't make nearly as much sense for a recording company targeting retirees to use the same distribution channel to sell its music offerings. A much smaller percentage of the retiree market has access to computers and knows how to download music from the Web. In this instance, it would make more sense to produce CDs and sell them through retail outlets where retirees shop.

Figure 11.3 shows the difference between selling direct and selling through an intermediary. Let's look at the strengths and weaknesses of each approach.

Selling Direct Many firms sell direct to customers. Being able to control the process of moving their products from their place of origin to the end user instead of relying on third parties is a major advantage of direct selling. Examples of companies that sell direct are Abercrombie & Fitch, which sells its clothing exclusively through company-owned stores, and Amway, Avon, and Mary Kay, which sell their products through home or office sales parties.

The disadvantage of selling direct is that a firm has more of its capital tied up in fixed assets because it must own or rent retail outlets or must field a salesforce to sell its products. It must also find its own buyers rather than have distributors that are constantly looking for new outlets for the firm's products.

The advent of the Internet has created new opportunities for firms to sell direct. Companies such as Amazon.com and Travelocity have built their entire business models around selling direct, and many firms that once sold their products exclusively through retail stores are now also selling directly online. The process of eliminating layers of middlemen, such as distributors and retailers, to sell directly to customers is called **disintermediation**. This is a tricky process, particularly if a firm wants to sell online and through its traditional distribution channels simultaneously. For example, if a firm has traditionally sold its products through electronics stores and is now offering the same

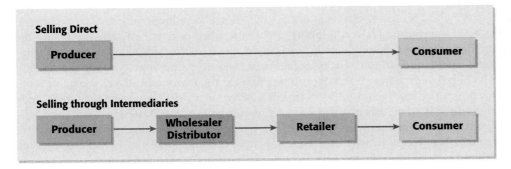

FIGURE 11.3

Selling Direct Versus Selling Through Intermediaries

products for sale online, the electronics stores may refuse to stock the products or may insist that they be sold online for the same price offered in the stores. This problem is referred to as channel conflict. **Channel conflict** occurs when two or more separate marketing channels (e.g., online sales and retail sales) are in conflict over their roles in selling a firm's products.

Selling Through Intermediaries Firms selling through intermediaries typically pass off their products to wholesalers who place them in retail outlets to be sold. An advantage of this approach is that the firm does not need to own as much of the distribution channel. For example, if a company makes MP3 players and the players are sold through retail outlets such as Best Buy and Circuit City, the company avoids the cost of building and maintaining retail outlets. It can also rely on its wholesalers to manage its relationship with Best Buy and Circuit City and to find other retail outlets to sell its products.

The disadvantage of selling through intermediaries is that a firm loses distribution-related control of its product. There is no guarantee that Best Buy and Circuit City will talk up the firm's product as much as the manufacturer would if it had its own stores. At times, it may also be more costly to sell through wholesalers than to sell direct. Just because a firm eliminates the middlemen in its supply chain by selling direct doesn't mean that it eliminates the functions they perform. Companies such as Abercrombie & Fitch that sell direct still have to get their products from the place they are produced to the customer. On a related note, some companies have built their entire business models around changing their industry's value chains to eliminate the need for intermediaries, and thus lower costs. An example is Dell, which pioneered the idea of selling built-to-order computers direct to the consumer, bypassing the retail store.[40] Another example is ProFlowers, which facilitates the sale of flowers directly from growers to consumers, as illustrated in Case 6.2.

Some firms enter into exclusive distribution arrangements with channel partners. **Exclusive distribution arrangements** give a retailer or other intermediary the exclusive rights to sell a company's products in a specific area for a specific period of time. The specific area is usually a county or a metropolitan area. The advantage to giving out an exclusive distribution agreement is to motivate a retailer or other intermediary to make a concerted effort to sell a firm's products without having to worry about direct competitors. For example, if Nokia granted Cingular the exclusive rights to sell a new type of cell phone, Cingular would be more motivated to advertise and push the phone than if many or all cell phone companies had access to the same phone.

One choice that entrepreneurs are confronted with when selling through intermediaries is how many channels to sell through. The more channels a firm sells through, the faster it can grow. But there are two problems associated with selling through multiple channels, particularly early in the life of a firm. First, a firm can lose control of how its products are being sold. For example, the more retailers through which Liz Claiborne sells its clothing, the more likely it is that one or more retailers will not display the clothes in the manner the company wants. Second, the more channels a firm sells through, the more opportunity there is for channel conflict. If a trendy store in a mall is selling Liz Claiborne clothes and a discount outlet at the edge of town starts selling the same clothes for half the price, do you think the store in the mall will be upset?

A hybrid model of sales and distribution that some entrepreneurs utilize for online sales is referred to as drop shipping. **Drop shipping** is a type of retailing where the retailer does not keep products in stock, but instead passes customers' orders and shipment details to distributors or manufacturers, who then ship directly to the customer.[41] The biggest advantage of this approach is that the retailer doesn't have to keep items in inventory. Instead, the inventory is maintained by the distributor or manufacturer, which ships directly to the buyer. Drop shipping requires close cooperation between the retailers and the manufactures involved, as illustrated in the nearby "Partnering for Success" feature. The feature focuses on eBags, a successful online retailer of luggage and related products.

partnering for *success*

eBags: Utilizing Drop Shipping as an Important Part of a Successful Online Marketing Strategy

www.ebags.com

In 1998, Jon Nordmark left an executive position at Samsonite and cofounded eBags, an online retailer of luggage, briefcases, backpacks, and other types of bags. Through frugal management and good customer service, eBags weathered the dot-com storm and has established itself as a premier online merchant. The company is also considered to be an innovative leader in Web site design and online marketing. Recently, eBags won the coveted "Website of the Year" award at the 2006 Multichannel Merchant Awards. It also won the award in 2001, 2002, and 2004.

One of the keys to eBags success is its distribution strategy. The company currently features over 200 brands and 12,000 products from well-known names including Samsonite, JanSport, The North Face, and Nike. Normally, offering that many products would cost a fortune in warehousing. It would also require eBags to assume the risk of trying to anticipate consumer demand. To keep its costs down and to avoid this risk, eBags uses a simple yet innovative strategy to manage its inventory: It has none. Instead, eBags employs drop shipping. As explained in this chapter, drop shipping allows eBags and other online merchants to maintain little or no inventory. Instead, they rely on manufacturers and wholesalers to ship products directly to consumers. Profit margins on drop-shipped items tend to be lower because the retailer shares the profits of the sale with the manufacturer or distributor. But for eBags, drop shipping has been a great deal.

Here's how it works. eBags takes an order that is then electronically transmitted to the appropriate manufacturer, such as Samsonite. Samsonite then packages and ships the item, usually in a day or so. The product is shipped in a box with eBag's logo and name, and the buyer never knows the difference.

The risk with drop shipping is that the seller has to rely on the goodwill of the drop shipper to get the product to the customer on time and in a professional manner. If a customer buys a Samsonite handbag through eBags, for example, and Samsonite fails to get the handbag to the customer in a timely manner, the customer will be upset with eBags, not Samsonite. For all the customer knows, the bag was in eBags' warehouse, and eBags caused the delay. As a result, it's important for a retailer that utilizes drop shipping to maintain a close working relationship with its drop shippers and do everything possible to motivate its drop shippers to perform effectively. In some cases, retailers install elaborate forms of oversight to make sure their drop shippers perform and assess penalties for late shipments or other adverse customer service issues.

Questions for Critical Thinking

1. Spend some time looking at eBags' Web site. What are the primary risks that eBags would be running if it stocked its own inventory, rather than relying on drop shipping as its primary method for inventory management and shipping?

2. If you were the CEO of eBags, what types of oversight mechanisms, if any, would you put in place to hold your drop shippers accountable for performing all of their activities as agreed?

3. Not all online merchants utilize drop shipping in the manner that eBags does. In fact, Zappos.com, a popular online seller of shoes and bags, maintains an inventory of all of the products it sells and does all of its own shipping. Make the argument in favor of Zappos.com's approach as opposed to eBags' approach.

4. What are the fundamental attributes of the positioning strategy of eBags and its brand? Do you think eBags' positioning and branding strategies will continue to be effective? Why or why not?

Sources: eBags homepage, www.ebags.com (accessed August 17, 2006).

Chapter Summary

1. The first step in selecting a target market is to study the industry in which the firm intends to compete and determine the different potential target markets within that industry. This process is called market segmentation. Markets can be segmented in a number of ways, including product type, price point, and customers served.

2. A firm typically only has enough resources to target one market segment—at least initially. By focusing on a clearly defined target market, a firm can become an expert in that market and by doing so provide its customers high levels of value and service.

3. After a firm has selected its target market, the next step is to establish a "position" within it that differentiates it from its competitors. The term *position* was introduced in Chapter 5, where it was emphasized that a firm's position in the marketplace determines how it is situated relative to its competitors. From a marketing perspective, this translates into the image of the way a firm wants to be perceived by its customers. Importantly, position answers the question, "Why should someone in our target market buy our good or service instead of our competitors?"

4. Many entrepreneurs make the mistake of creating a strategy that focuses on the features of a product, such as its technical merits. This approach is usually less effective than a campaign focusing on the benefits of owning the product, such as convenience or being able to keep in better touch with family or friends.

5. A company's brand is the set of attributes people associate with it. On a philosophical level, a firm builds a brand by having it create meaning in customers' lives. It must create value. On a more practical level, brands are built through advertising, public relations, sponsorships, supporting social causes, and good performance.

6. A firm's marketing mix is the set of controllable, tactical marketing tools that it uses to produce the response it wants in its target market. Most marketers organize their marketing mix around the 4Ps: product, price, promotion, and place (or distribution).

7. The product itself is a firm's core product, such as the CD that contains an antivirus program. The actual product, which is what the customer buys, is more encompassing. It may have as many as five characteristics: a quality level, features, design, a brand name, and packaging.

8. In cost-based pricing, the list price is determined by adding a markup percentage to the product's cost. In value-based pricing, the list price is determined by estimating what consumers are willing to pay for a product and then backing off a bit to provide a cushion.

9. Advertising is making people aware of a good or service in hopes of persuading them to buy it. Public relations refers to efforts to establish and maintain a company's image with the public. The major difference between the two is that advertising is paid for, and public relations isn't—at least directly. The cost of public relations to a firm is the effort it makes to network with journalists and other people to try to interest them in saying and/or writing good things about the company.

10. The first choice a firm must make regarding distribution is whether to sell its products directly to consumers or through intermediaries (e.g., wholesalers and retailers). An advantage of selling direct is that it allows a firm to maintain control of its products rather than relying on third parties. The disadvantage is that it ties up more capital in fixed assets because the firm must own (or rent) retail outlets or must field a salesforce to sell its products. An advantage of selling through intermediaries is that a firm doesn't have to own much of its distribution channel (e.g., trucks and retail outlets). A disadvantage of this approach is that a firm loses some control of its product in that there is no guarantee that the retailers it sells through will talk up and push its products as much as the manufacturer would if it had its own stores.

Key Terms

advertising, 329
brand, 322
brand equity, 324
brand management, 322
buzz, 323
channel conflict, 334
cobranding, 324
cost-based pricing, 328
disintermediation, 333
distribution channel, 333
drop shipping, 334

exclusive distribution
   arrangements, 334
infomercial, 331
market segmentation, 317
marketing mix, 326
niche market, 318
place, 333
press kit, 331
price, 328
price-quality attribution, 328

product, 326
promotion, 329
public relations, 331
reference account, 327
service, 326
tagline, 320
target market, 317
trade show, 331
value-based pricing, 328
viral marketing, 332

Review Questions

1. What is a target market? Why is it important for a firm to choose its target market carefully?
2. Explain the importance of market segmentation. Describe several ways in which markets can be segmented.
3. Why is market segmentation the first step in the process of selecting a target market?
4. What is a niche market? Provide examples of niche markets in the food and beverage industries.
5. Describe what is meant by a firm's positioning strategy.
6. Describe how a firm decides to position itself relative to its competitors.
7. What is a tagline? What is your favorite tagline? Why?
8. Why is it important for firms to sell the benefits of its products rather than the features?
9. What is a brand? Provide an example of a brand that you buy frequently and describe the mental image that pops into your mind when you hear or see the brand's name.
10. What is the purpose of brand management?
11. What is the difference between a company's brand and its positioning strategy?
12. Why is it important for a company to have meaning in its customers' lives? What does this concept have to do with successfully establishing a brand?
13. What is buzz? Provide an example of a firm that has created effective buzz for its product.
14. Describe the difference between a core product and an actual product.
15. What is a reference account? How can having a reference account help a new firm?
16. Contrast cost-based pricing and value-based pricing.
17. What is meant by the phrase "price-quality attribution"? How does an understanding of this phrase help an entrepreneur know how to price a product?
18. Contrast the roles of advertising and public relations in promoting a firm and its products.
19. What is the purpose of a press release?
20. Contrast the advantages of selling direct versus the advantages of selling through an intermediary.

Application Questions

1. Reread the Opening Profile. After doing this, make a list of all the things that you think that Matt Hedges has done right in building Vino del Sol's marketing program.
2. Paul Bustamante is in the process of opening a music store in Tallahassee, Florida. After touring the store, a friend asked him, "Who's your target market?" Paul

shrugged and said, "Kids who go to Florida State I guess, but I haven't given it much thought." What could Paul gain by thinking more carefully about his target market and how important would those insights be?

3. If you decided to start a small-business consulting service in Columbus, Ohio, how would you approach the following topics: market segmentation, selecting a target market, and developing a positioning strategy?

4. Reread the Blue Maze feature at the beginning of Chapter 5. How do you think Blue Maze segmented the music industry? Describe the company's positioning strategy.

5. The "What Went Wrong" feature focuses on Snapple and the blunders that Quaker Oats made when it purchased Snapple in 1994. At the same time that Quaker Oats (which has since been purchased by PepsiCo) owned Snapple, it owned Gatorade, which seemed to be well positioned and branded. Why do you think Quaker Oats did a better job with Gatorade than Snapple? Is there anything about Quaker Oats that makes you think it might have been better suited to position and brand Gatorade than Snapple?

6. Assume that you just invented a new type of computer printer that can be easily folded up and carried like a laptop computer. You have decided to start a company to produce the computer. Select a name and a tagline for your new company.

7. Derek Smith just opened a new restaurant that focuses on healthy food, such as salads, soups, and smoothie drinks, made from natural ingredients. He named the restaurant Derek's Health Escape. The jingle that Derek wrote for his first ad is "Fiber, nutrition, vitamins, and low-fat, that's what Derek's Health Escape is all about." Do you like Derek's jingle? If so, explain why. If not, suggest an alternative and explain why your jingle is better than Derek's.

8. Make a list of things that Derek Smith could do to create buzz about Derek's Health Escape.

9. Tammy Ryan has developed a new type of nutritional bar. What are the different ways that Tammy can create interest in her product and legitimize it before she tries to sell it?

10. The "You Be the VC 1" feature focuses on Massive, the company that enables advertisers to place targeted ads within video games. Consider each of the 4Ps and comment on the most important issues for Massive to consider in each area.

11. Jim has just developed a new computer program that will help computer networks recognize and eliminate e-mail spam. Jim doesn't know how to price this product. Describe to Jim the two most common methods of pricing and give him your recommendation for how to price his product.

12. Provide several examples of cobranding relationships, other than those involving Intel. Describe how the relationship benefits the companies involved.

13. Kelly Andrews has developed a new line of jewelry that has created some positive buzz among friends and some business stores in her local community. When asked by a reporter, "Where do you plan to sell your jewelry?" Kelly said, "Hopefully everywhere—jewelry stores, Target, Wal-Mart, gift shops, online, through catalogs, and a dozen other places." Write a critique of Kelly's approach.

14. Peter Sanders is interested in iPods and for some time has supported a Web site that provides information for iPod enthusiasts. Although Peter thoroughly enjoys running the site, it has become a financial burden and he is thinking about shutting it down. Provide some suggestions to Peter for ways to avoid shutting down the site for financial reasons.

15. Dogster.com, first mentioned in Chapter 3, is the name of a social networking site for dog enthusiasts. Visit the company's Web site. Comment on the company's overall marketing strategy, including positioning, the selection of a target market, branding, and the 4Ps. To what extent do you think that Dogster.com's overall approach to marketing has contributed to the company's success?

you be the VC 11.1

Massive
www.massiveincorporated.com

Business Idea: Create a technology that allows video game producers, whose games are connected to the Internet, to place targeted ads within video games. The innovation that Massive brings to the market is that the ability to change ads on the fly (rather than set when the game is made), and advertisers will be charged based on how many game players actually see the ads and how often they see them.

Pitch: Up to now, advertisers have paid flat fees to place ads in video games, and once the games started shipping, the ads were set. This approach has caused many potential advertisers to be leery of in-game advertising, because ads can quickly get stale, and they were never sure of how often their ads would be seen.

Enter Massive. For video games connected to the Internet, Massive aims to revolutionize the in-game advertising model by allowing advertisers to change ads on the fly and by charging advertisers based on how many times their ads are actually seen. Massive, along with the video game producers, is betting that this new approach will appeal to a much larger "mass" of advertisers. The predominant market for online videogames is 18- to 34-year-old males. This is an audience that is particularly coveted by many mainline advertisers.

In-game ads don't appear as commercials. Instead, the ads are placed on billboards or on the sides of buildings that are part of the scenery in the game. Massive's strategy will allow the same billboard to have different ads at different times of the day, or different days of the week. A key element of Massive's strategy will be to sell video game ads the way TV networks sell 30-second spots, based on the demographic group that is most likely to be playing a particular game and based on premium times of day. As a result of this strategy, Massive is hoping to persuade companies that typically place ads during professional football games, for example, to place ads within online football video games, like Madden 2007.

Q&A: Based on the material covered in this chapter, what questions would you ask the firm's founders before making your funding decision? What answers would satisfy you?

Decision: If you had to make your decision on just the information provided in the pitch and on the company's Web site, would you fund this firm? Why or why not?

you be the VC 11.2

Visible World
www.visibleworld.com

Business Idea: Produce television ads that can target a specific neighborhood or a specific area of town, with the intent of delivering ads that are the most appropriate for the demographic group in the targeted area.

Pitch: A consistent complaint about television advertising is that many of the people who see a particular ad have no interest in the product being advertised or couldn't afford to buy it if they did. Visible World has developed a partial solution to this problem. Through its patent-pending technology an advertiser can deliver television ads that are targeted to a specific zip code, area of town, or similar criteria. This approach allows a Denver car dealer, for example, to air ads for its luxury brands in affluent neighborhoods, while directing ads for less expensive models in areas of town where residents may have less purchasing power.

Visible World's technology also allows its users to update their ads continuously. As a result, an ad for Disney World in Florida could run in Boston during the winter, and the ad could say, "Do you realize that it is 63 degrees warmer at Disney World this minute than it is in downtown Boston?" The 63-degree difference figure could change as the temperature changes in the two locations. An advertiser could even merge the ability to update ads continuously with the ability to target ads to specific locations. For example, the Disney World ad just described could feature the real-time difference between the temperature in downtown Boston and Disney World in Florida and could show different scenes from Disney World based on the area of town in which the ad is shown. A scene of Disney's Epcot Center, for example, could be shown in neighborhoods with a high percentage of retirees, because Epcot appeals to an older demographic. In contrast, a scene of children enjoying the rides at Disney's Magic Kingdom could be shown in areas with a high percentage of families with young children.

Through its unique approach and technology, Visible World hopes to rejuvenate the television advertising industry. Television advertising has been losing ad dollars to more tightly focused point-of-sale advertising by online companies like Google and Yahoo!. Visible World believes that its technology is the pathway through which these losses can be stemmed.

Q&A: Based on the material covered in this chapter, what questions would you ask the firm's founders before

making your funding decision? What answers would satisfy you?

Decision: If you had to make your decision on just the information provided in the pitch and on the company's Web site, would you fund this firm? Why or why not?

CASE 11.1

PowerBar and White Wave: How to Create "Buzz" Around a Product Launch

www.powerbar.com; www.whitewave.com

Bruce R. Barringer,
University of Central Florida
R. Duane Ireland,
Texas A&M University

Introduction

"Creating buzz" means creating awareness and a sense of anticipation about a company and its offerings. Many start-ups live or die based on their ability to create buzz, because at the time of launch, they can't afford expensive print or media advertising. This case provides examples of how two firms created buzz around their initial product offerings. In each instance, the creation of effective buzz was instrumental in a product's success.

PowerBar

PowerBar is the brainchild of the late Brian Maxwell, who was a marathon runner. During a race he was leading in 1983, he developed stomach cramps and started falling back. The disappointment of that race led Maxwell to develop a food product for athletics that was easy to digest and nutritious. The product was actually developed in his kitchen with the help of his girlfriend, Jennifer Biddulph, who later became his wife. He decided to call the product PowerBar.

PowerBar was the first energy bar on the market. Maxwell didn't have much of an advertising budget, so the question was "how to get noticed." The approach he decided to pursue was to launch what he called a "grassroots seeding" effort. Maxwell decided to spread the word about PowerBar by word of mouth, but in a savvy and purposeful way.

The first thing Maxwell did, with Biddulph's help, was to go to every sporting event in the San Francisco area (which is where they lived) and talk to people about the product. Between the two of them, they spoke to over 1,200 people. Once the product was ready, Maxwell sent the people they talked to a little box containing five

PowerBars and a follow-up survey. This effort got people talking about PowerBar and sharing the product with their friends. The next move is legendary. To stimulate word of mouth in other areas of the country, Maxwell sent a letter to his existing customers offering to send five PowerBars on their behalf to anyone in the United States for just a $3.00 shipping fee. "We would even put a note in [such as] "To Charlie from Amy in San Francisco," Maxwell says. This effort jump-started word of mouth about PowerBar in different parts of the country.

As the buzz surrounding PowerBar grew, Maxwell turned his focus to "seeding" various sports. He knew that runners were talking about PowerBar, but he wasn't as confident regarding other sports. There is an interesting psychological tendency people have that's called homophily, or the tendency for people to associate with people who are similar to themselves. An awareness of this tendency prompted Maxwell to suspect that each sport has its own social network, so buzz doesn't automatically spread from one sport to another. He suspected that golfers talk to golfers, basketball players talk to basketball players, and so forth. So Maxwell hired people within each sport to spread the word about PowerBar. He gave each "seeder" a certain number of bars to give away and a marketing budget. This effort stimulated buzz surrounding PowerBar in multiple sports.

At one point in the early life of PowerBar, Maxwell experienced a bit of luck. He was approached by the captain of the U.S. cycling team that was preparing to represent the United States at the Tour de France. The person asked Maxwell to donate 1,000 PowerBars to the team. Maxwell hesitated but agreed. On a Saturday, 3 weeks later, right in the middle of the Tour de France, CBS, which was covering the event, did a 3-minute segment on PowerBar, a new "energy bar" the U.S. team was eating. Maxwell couldn't believe his good fortune. That single broadcast created buzz about PowerBar in thousands of different places.

Over the years, Maxwell continued his seeding efforts. He started "PowerBar Team Elite" and hired thousands of lead athletes to spread the word about PowerBar. Each team member would receive money when her or his picture appeared in the media eating a PowerBar or wearing PowerBar-branded gear. To this day, athletes approach PowerBar and ask to be signed up as a PowerBar Team Elite member. It's often difficult for athletes in minor sports, like cycling and snowboarding, even if they are professionals, to make a full-time living performing their sport. The PowerBar Team Elite program gives these athletes a source of income, so they are typically highly motivated to be photographed wearing their PowerBar gear.

PowerBar, which remained an independent company through the 1980s and 1990s, was purchased by Nestlé in 2000. PowerBar is now sold worldwide through Nestlé's global distribution network.

White Wave

White Wave sells soymilk. You've probably seen White Wave's colorful cartons in the dairy case at your local supermarket. Actually, soymilk isn't milk at all; rather, it's a milk substitute. The story of how White Wave got its milk substitute product in supermarkets' refrigerated dairy sections, and in front of millions of consumers, is quite a tale.

Soymilk is not a new product. Some people are lactose-intolerant and can't drink milk. Others simply don't like milk, but want a product that serves a similar function (like eating it with breakfast cereal). Soymilk has appealed to this clientele for years. The most common way that soymilk was sold, until White Wave came along, was in a square-shaped container on grocery store shelves. Lactose-intolerant people knew to look for soymilk there, but it never caught the attention of a broad audience. Who would think to look for a milk substitute somewhere other than in the milk aisle?

In 1996, White Wave, a producer of soymilk with a history of innovation, came up with a new idea for selling soymilk. It would produce a dry soy mixture, ship it to dairies that produced regular milk, and pay the dairies to add water, package the resulting soymilk in milklike containers, and distribute the product. Most dairies were willing to do this because they were looking for additional sources of income.

Initially, the going was slow. The company caught a big break in October 1999 when the FDA announced that soy was considered a heart-healthy substance that could lower cholesterol. This announcement provided White Wave the legitimacy it needed to take its soymilk mainstream, which was its goal from the beginning. The company didn't have a large advertising budget, so, similar to PowerBar's experience, the question was "how to get noticed."

Recognizing the potential enormity of the opportunity, White Wave set out to create buzz about soymilk and its particular brand of soymilk called Silk. The company developed a five-point plan to dramatically increase awareness of soymilk and its particular product.

1. Sample Silk soymilk aggressively in stores. This step was necessary to get people to try the product. The Silk soymilk was sampled in small half-pint containers, like the milk cartons that kids get at school. The FDA approval appeared in bold letters on the cartons to reinforce the product's legitimacy.
2. Sample the product at health-focused fund-raising and charity events, where health-conscious people congregate. This step was intended to get health-focused people, who are always on the lookout for good products, to try Silk soymilk and start talking about it among their family and friends.
3. To get grocery stores to go along, White Wave offered a guarantee that if its product didn't sell a specified number of units a week, White Wave would buy it back. Being able to buy a new product on a consignment basis such as White Wave made possible appeals to stores when they try an untested item.
4. The sides of the cartons that Silk soymilk were sold in contained interesting facts about soymilk and educational and amusing material. The purpose of this strategy was to get people to read the cartons while they enjoyed breakfast, so they could tell their friends and family what they learned about soymilk.
5. In select cities, White Wave purchased outdoor billboards and signage on buses and sponsored programming on public radio. The company felt that the audience that listened to public radio was the same audience that would be most likely to try soymilk.

In addition to these tactics, a particularly clever thing that the company did to create buzz was to lease the sides of a number of trucks and place large ads for Silk soymilk on them. People traveling down the highway would see the trucks and naturally think that Silk soymilk was being distributed in the area. Most of the trucks didn't contain Silk soymilk, they just advertised it. White Wave used the trucks to create rolling billboards to spread the word about its product across the nation.

The buzz campaign worked. White Wave went from having a negligible share of the soymilk market in 1996 to 85 percent in 2003. The company's rapid rise as a soymilk distributor didn't go unnoticed. In 2001, White Wave was acquired by Dean Foods and has been a subsidiary of Dean Foods since. The company's propensity to generate buzz hasn't let up. It is currently generating buzz on its Horizon Organic Milk product, which you'll also find in your grocery store's refrigerated dairy section.

Discussion Questions

1. It's easy to see how a company can build buzz about a product when it is first introduced. But after a product

has been out for a couple of years, how does a company keep buzz alive? If you were asked to advise White Wave, how would you recommend that the company keep buzz alive for Silk soymilk?

2. Both PowerBar and White Wave benefited from a specific single incident, mentioned in the case, that helped them jump-start the buzz for each firm's product. For each company, what was the incident that had a positive effect on its success? To what extent do you think luck or good fortune plays a roll in one product taking off in the market place while another product dies?

3. What is PowerBar's tagline? Do you like it? Why or why not? Propose an alternative tagline for PowerBar.

4. PowerBar and White Wave were both acquired by larger firms in the early 2000s. To what extent do you think PowerBar and White Wave's ability to create buzz and build the market shares of their respective products made them attractive to the larger companies?

Application Questions

1. Look at the "You Be the VC 1" feature for this chapter. It focuses on Massive, a company that places ads inside video games. If you were given the job of creating a buzz campaign for Massive, how would you go about it? How do you think Massive can best create buzz for its service?

2. Many companies actually hire people to help create buzz about their products. What do you think are the ethical boundaries of this practice? Would you be upset if you found out that a friend who recommended a product to you was being paid to make the recommendation? Would you feel comfortable engaging in a similar process yourself?

Sources: J. F. Kelly, *The Breakaway Brand* (New York: McGraw-Hill, 2005); E. Rosen, *The Anatomy of Buzz* (New York: Doubleday, 2000).

CASE 11.2 — *Proactiv: How Three Critical Marketing Decisions Shaped a New Venture's Future*

www.proactiv.com

Bruce R. Barringer,
University of Central Florida
R. Duane Ireland,
Texas A&M University

Introduction

In 1995, two dermatologists, Dr. Katie Rodan and Dr. Kathy Fields, developed what they believed was a medical breakthrough in fighting acne. Their mission: to help millions of people rid themselves of acne and acne-related problems. They named their product Proactiv Solutions. This name was chosen because the product could heal existing blemishes and *proactively* help prevent new ones from forming.

Today, Proactiv is the #1-selling acne product in the United States, even though it's not available in most stores. It's sold primarily through infomercials, the company's Web site, a subscription service called the "Proactiv Solution Clear Skin Club," and in select upscale boutiques. The way Proactiv reached the point it currently occupies is an interesting story. Early in its life, Proactiv was shaped by three critical marketing decisions, from which the company has not wavered, even to this day. This case recounts these decisions and discusses how the decisions shaped this entrepreneurial venture's future.

How It Started

Katie Rodan and Kathy Fields met while they were working summer jobs at a cardiovascular research lab in Los Angeles.

The lab was developing a drug to treat post-heart attack patients. Both Rodan and Fields enjoyed the exciting pace of the work as well as the camaraderie they shared with the lab's researchers and doctors. After earning their college degrees, they both went to medical school and became dermatologists. They stayed in touch and often shared with one another how surprised they were at the number of acne patients they were seeing. At the time, the medical research said that only 3 percent of the adult population had acne, but Rodan and Fields became convinced that the number was higher. They were each seeing acne patients on a daily basis, and they weren't just seeing teenagers. They were seeing women in their 20s, 30s, 40s, and even in their 50s who were suffering from acne and acne-related problems.

Rodan and Fields decided to form a partnership to investigate the acne issue further. They started by talking to their patients, asking them a wide range of acne-related questions. What they found was that the vast majority of their patients hated the acne products on the market. The most common complaints were that the products were very drying and they were very irritating. Worst of all, patients told Rodan and Fields, the available products flat did not work. At this point, the two physicians started thinking there might be an opportunity for them to create a better product.

Rodan and Fields spent the next couple of years thoroughly investigating the acne products on the market.

After testing many of the products on their patients, they made what they believed was a shocking discovery. All of the products on the market were designed to spot-treat a pimple—none were designed to stop the pimple from forming in the first place. This just didn't make sense to the two dermatologists—from both a practical and a medical standpoint. By the time you see a pimple, whatever treatment you administer, it's too little too late. In their judgment, not taking steps to prevent acne from developing was akin to not brushing your teeth and going to the dentist to fill cavities. Why not brush your teeth and floss and try to prevent the cavities from developing in the first place?

This revelation motivated Rodan and Fields to start working on a product of their own—one that would be more proactive in preventing acne and acne-related problems. They hired a chemist, and the three worked together for another couple of years. Finally, they had a product they were happy with and that seemed to work and to satisfy their patients.

Important Revelations

To get ideas about how to market and develop their product, which didn't have a name yet, Rodan hosted dinner parties at her house and conducted brainstorming sessions with the guests. The guests included business executives, market researchers, marketing consultants, an FDA regulatory attorney, the chief financial officer of a major company, and others. One of the things the participants in these sessions stressed to Rodan and Field was the importance of marketing research. In particular, the group urged Rodan and Fields to hire an unbiased third party to validate their findings. Rodan and Fields took this advice to heart and hired an outside consultant. In focus groups that the consultant led, Rodan and Fields learned two important things about older women. First, many women who medically *do* have acne refuse to believe it. Second, people don't like to talk about their acne with others. Rodan and Fields also learned that their product still needed work. There were several aspects of the product that needed improvement, a need that Rodan and Fields fully intended to take care of.

Three Critical Marketing Decisions That Shaped the Future of the Firm

Critical Marketing Decision #1: We're a Skincare Company.
After Rodan and Fields reformulated the product again, they hired another marketing consultant to advise them as to how they should proceed to successfully market their product. The first piece of advice they got from the consultant was to think of their product as a skin care rather than as an acne product. At the time, the acne market in the

United States was about $250 million a year, a low number by consumer products standards. In contrast, the skin care market was several billion dollars a year, making it much more attractive. The consultant told Rodan and Fields to think of their product as a skin care system that just happens to treat acne, rather than an acne medication alone. This recommendation obviously caused Rodan and Fields to have a much broader vision for the scope of the market for their product.

Critical Marketing Decision #2: Our Name is Proactiv.
After Rodan and Fields started thinking of their product as part of the skin care market, they got advice from a marketing specialist about what to name their product. The name the specialist recommended was Proactiv (proactive without the e). Looking back, Rodan and Fields admit that initially they didn't get the reason for this recommendation. They were hoping for a more cosmetic-sounding name, like Dermo-Beautiful. The name Proactiv turned out to be perfect. It captured the essence of what Rodan and Fields were trying to accomplish—to create a product that would be *proactive* (rather than *reactive*) in dealing with acne and acne-related issues. In other words, the name Proactiv captured the entrepreneurs' interest in signaling to customers that their product was intended to prevent the occurrence of additional acne-related problems for them.

Critical Marketing Decision #3: Infomercials.
To get their product on the market, Rodan and Fields initially tried to raise investment capital. They were repeatedly turned down. The biggest objection they encountered was the sentiment that if their product was so good and so obvious, why hadn't Procter & Gamble or Johnson & Johnson already thought of it? Surely, they must have dermatologists on their advisory boards telling them what to do, was the comment repeatedly expressed to Rodan and Fields as they talked to those with investment capital. After giving up on raising capital, Rodan and Fields approached Neutrogena to try to get a licensing deal. Neutrogena passed on the deal but did make a suggestion that resonated with Rodan and Fields. Neutrogena said that the most effective way to sell the product would be via infomercials. Initially, Rodan and Fields were shocked, because they had a fairly low opinion of infomercials. But there was one company, according to the folks at Neutrogena, named Guthy Renker, that made high-quality infomercials for professional products like Proactiv. Rodan and Fields also got to thinking that an infomercial might be the best way to educate people about their product. The following table lays out the points in favor of using infomercials to sell a product in which Rodan and Fields had a great deal of confidence.

Why infomercials Have Worked for Proactiv (Infomercials are 30–60 minute programs that are paid for by an advertiser)

- People need to be reeducated about how to treat acne
- The reeducation can't be done in a 30-second or 60-second television commercial, or in a print ad
- Acne is an embarrassing problem, so people will be most open to learning about it in the privacy of their homes
- The demographic group that spends the most time watching infomercials, women in their 20s, 30s and 40s, are Proactiv's market
- Infomercials provide Proactiv the opportunity to show heartfelt testimonials of people who have used the product. Showing "before" and "after" pictures of people who have used the product and have experienced dramatic results has been a particularly persuasive tactic.

Guthy Renker

After being turned down by Neutrogena, Rodan and Fields were about ready to throw in the towel when they met, simply by chance, a person that introduced them to Guthy Renker, the infomercial company that people at Neutrogena recommended highly. After several meetings, Guthy Renker offered to license Proactiv and to create an infomercial to sell the product. It also put up the money to buy the media time needed for the infomercial to be tele-vised. The initial infomercial was targeted toward women in the age group most ignored by the present providers of acne products. The 30-minute spot carefully explained what acne is, how it can affect older women, and how Proactiv was the only product available that potentially pre-vented acne from occurring. It also offered a complete money-back guarantee. The first infomercial sold twice as much Proactiv as expected, and Guthy Renker and Proactiv remain close partners today.

It was also Guthy Renker's idea to get celebrity endorsements for Proactiv. The first celebrity endorser was Judith Light. Light was followed by Vanessa Williams, and now a number of other celebrities (including Elle Macpherson) endorse the product.

Proactiv Today

Today, Proactiv is strong. The first Guthy Renker infomercial ran in 1994, and the product has steadily gained market share since. Proactiv is now being sold in Europe and Asia as well as in the United States. Neither the product nor the sales strategy has changed since Proactiv was first intro-duced. The three marketing decisions described here set the direction for the company, and the company remains fully committed to taking only the actions suggested by these decisions.

Discussion Questions

1. Does Proactiv sell features or benefits? Provide evidence from the case to support your conclusion.
2. Discuss the things that Rodan and Fields learned, prior to meeting Guthy Renker, that persuaded them that infomercials were the best way to sell Proactiv. If Proactiv hadn't developed infomercials in partnership with Guthy Renker, do you think Proactiv would be in existence today? Describe why infomercials were a bet-ter choice than print or media advertising for Proactiv when the company was first being introduced.
3. Describe Proactiv's positioning strategy. To what extent did the three critical marketing decisions discussed in the case shape the evolution of Proactiv's positioning strategy?
4. What is the difference between Proactiv's core prod-uct and its actual product? Describe its actual product and your assessment of whether the actual product provides an attractive mix of characteristics.

Application Questions

1. In your judgment, why doesn't Proactiv sell through mainline retail stores along with the direct-to-consumers' channel? Make your answer as thoughtful and substantive as possible.
2. Use materials included in Chapter 1 to identify the characteristics of successful entrepreneurs you see in Katie Rodan and Kathy Fields. To what extent do you believe these characteristics have contributed to Proactiv's success?

Sources: Proactive homepage, www.proactiv.com (accessed May 10, 2006); K. Rodan, Stanford Technology Ventures Entrepreneurial Thought Leaders Podcast, April 2006.

Endnotes

1. Personal correspondence with Matt Hedges, August 15, 2006.
2. D. Jackson, "Sweet Smells of Success," *BusinessFirst*, Spring 2005.
3. J. Nesheim, *The Power of Unfair Advantage* (New York: Free Press, 2005).

4. R. McKanna, *Relationship Marketing: Strategies for the Age of the Customer* (New York: Basic Books, 2006).

5. P. Kufahl, "Get into the Niche," *Club Industry,* December 1, 2002.

6. D. L. Rainey, *Product Innovation* (Cambridge, UK: Cambridge University Press, 2005).

7. A. Weinstein, "A Strategic Framework for Defining and Segmenting Markets," *Journal of Strategic Marketing* 14, no. 2 (2006): 115–27.

8. J. Kurtzman and G. Rifkin, *Startups That Work* (New York: Portfolio, 2005).

9. O. Walker, H. Boyd, J. Mullins, and J. Larreche, *Marketing Strategy: A Decision-Focused Approach* (Boston: McGraw-Hill, 2003).

10. R. W. Price, *Roadmap to Entrepreneurial Success* (New York: AMACOM, 2004).

11. A. Hesseldahl, "Palm Goes Low," *Forbes,* October 6, 2002.

12. P. Kotler, *Marketing Insights from A to Z* (New York: John Wiley & Sons, 2003), 65.

13. K. J. Clancy and P. C. Krieg, *Counterintuitive Marketing: Achieve Great Results Using Uncommon Sense* (New York: Free Press, 2000).

14. L. M. Lodish, H. L. Morgan, and A. Kallianpur, *Entrepreneurial Marketing* (New York: John Wiley & Sons, 2001).

15. A. Venkatesh and L. A. Meamber, "Arts and Aesthetics: Marketing and Cultural Production," *Marketing Theory 6,* no. 1 (2006): 11–39; S. Bedbury, *A New Brand World* (New York: Penguin, 2002).

16. F. Reichheld, "Microeconomics of Customer Relationships," *MIT Sloan Management Review* 47, no. 2 (2006): 73–78; R. M. McMath, What Were They Thinking? (New York: Times Books, 1999).

17. Lodish et al., *Entrepreneurial Marketing.*

18. Kotler, *Marketing Insights from A to Z,* 65.

19. M. J. Kay, "Strong Brands and Corporate Brands," *European Journal of Marketing* 40, nos. 7 & 8 (2006): 742–60; P. B. Seybold, The Customer Revolution (New York: Crown Business, 2001).

20. S. Zyman, *Building Brandwidth: Closing the Sale Online* (New York: HarperCollins, 2000).

21. N. C. Kaiser, "Dan Byrne, CEO of Byrne Specialty Gases," nPost.com (www.nPost.com), from the nscript of an interview conducted April 29, 2004.

22. D. Debelak, *Bringing Your Product To Market in Less Than a Year,* 2nd ed. (New York: John Wiley & Sons, 2005).

23. E. Rosen, *The Anatomy of Buzz* (New York: Random House, 2000).

24. N. C. Kaiser, "Greg Helmstetter, CEO of MyGoals.com," nPost.com (www.nPost.com), from the transcript of an interview conducted April 24, 2003.

25. M. W. Ragas, *Lessons from the eFront* (New York: Prima Publishing, 2001), 181.

26. N. J. Hicks, "From Ben Franklin to Branding: The Evolution of Health Services Marketing," in *Branding Health Services,* ed. G. Bashe, N. J. Hicks and A. Ziegenfuss (Gaithersburg, MD: Aspen Publishers, 2000), 1–18.

27. Hicks, "From Ben Franklin to Branding."

28. B. B. Stern, "What Does *Brand* Mean? Historical Analysis Method and Construct Definition," *Journal of the Academy of Marketing Science* 34 (2006): 216–23.

29. P. Kotler and G. Armstrong, *Principles of Marketing* (Upper Saddle River, NJ: Prentice Hall, 1999).

30. H. W. Chesbrough, *Open Innovation* (Boston: Harvard Business School Press, 2003).

31. Kotler and Armstrong, *Principles of Marketing.*

32. Kotler and Armstrong, *Principles of Marketing.*

33. M. J. Silverstein, *Treasure Hunt* (New York: Portfolio, 2006).

34. J. H. Boyett and J. T. Boyett, *The Guru Guide to Marketing* (New York: John Wiley & Sons, 2003).

35. T. Foster, *Managing Quality* (Upper Saddle River, NJ: Prentice Hall, 2001).

36. R. A. Nykiel, *Marketing Your Business: A Guide to Developing a Strategic Marketing Plan* (New York: Best Business Books, 2003).

37. B. Barton, "Integrating Advertising with Other Campaigns," in *Business: The Ultimate Resource* (New York: Bloomsbury Publishing, 2003).

38. American Marketing Association, Dictionary of Marketing Terms, www.marketingpower.com (accessed August 10, 2006).

39. A. Ries and L. Ries, *The Fall of Advertising and the Rise of PR* (New York: HarperBusiness, 2002).

40. M. Dell, *Direct From Dell* (New York: HarperCollins, 2006).

41. Wikipedia, http://en.wikipedia.org/wiki/Drop_shipping (accessed August 16, 2006).

Getting Personal

with RYAN O'DONNELL

My advice for new entrepreneurs

Never give up. My first startup failed, but paved the way for BullEx

What I do when I'm not working

Spend time in the Adirondack Mountains with my wife Staci

Best advice I've received

It's all about the team

BullEx Digital Safety:
The Key Role of Intellectual Property in its Early Success

As an engineering student at Rensselaer Polytechnic Institute (RPI) in New York State, Ryan O'Donnell learned a lot about the importance of intellectual property protection. In particular, one class, called the Inventor's Studio, drove home the importance of patents. This class helps seniors use the technical knowledge they learned in their engineering classes to come up with new product ideas. The students, who are organized into teams, are then required to file provisional patent applications on their product ideas. In the recent history of the course, which is taught by RPI lecturer Burt Swersey, five patents have been or are about to be issued, and several other issuances are pending.

O'Donnell, who graduated from RPI in the spring of 2004, has put the knowledge he learned in the Inventor's Studio as well as many of his other classes to good use. In March of 2005, he founded a company, called BullEx Digital Safety, with two of his classmates, John Blackburn and Tom Rossi. BullEx Digital Safety sells an innovative fire extinguisher training system, which is described next. What's particularly interesting about the company, for the purposes of this chapter, is the role that intellectual property considerations played in the firm's development. During his senior year at RPI, there were several product ideas that O'Donnell and his colleagues considered. The decision to move forward with the BullEx Digital Safety idea, rather than any other one, hinged largely on the perception that the idea could obtain solid patent protection.

The BullEx fire extinguisher training system works like this. Many companies are required by OSHA to train their employees to use fire extinguishers. The training is typically done in a parking lot or on a grass field, where a small fire is started and employees take turns discharging a fire extinguisher to put out the fire. The problems with this approach are that it cost $20 to $30 per person (which is spent primarily on recharging extinguishers), the process itself creates a mess, and it is not environmentally friendly. What BullEx has done is create a product that looks and feels just like a fire extinguisher but is charged with air and water rather than fire retardants. In addition, the company has created a propane device that creates a very controlled fire and has special sensors that can detect whether and simulated fire extinguisher is being

RYAN O'DONNELL
Founder & President,
BullEx Digital Safety
Rensselaer Polytechnic Institute[*]
BS College of Engineering, 2004

 Rensselaer

[*]The information contained in this Profile was not furnished by Rensselaer Polytechnic Institute, was not reviewed by Rensselaer for accuracy and Rensselaer makes no representation as to its accuracy.

Best part of being a student	My biggest surprise as an entrepreneur	Currently in my iPod
Seemingly endless possibilities	*How quickly things can happen*	*Johnny Cash, Hair of the Dog*

After studying this chapter you should be ready to:

L E A R N I N G

Objectives

1. Define the term *intellectual property*, and describe its importance.

2. Discuss the four major forms of intellectual property: patents, trademarks, copyrights, and trade secrets.

3. Specify the rules of thumb for determining whether a particular piece of intellectual property is worth the time and expense of protecting.

4. Describe the six-step process for obtaining a patent.

5. Identify the four types of trademarks.

6. Identify the types of material that are eligible for copyright protection.

7. Discuss the legal environment that facilitates trade secret protection.

8. Identify the most common types of trade secret disputes.

9. Describe some of the physical measures that firms take to protect their trade secrets.

10. Explain the two primary reasons for conducting an intellectual property audit.

used correctly to try to put out its fire. The system, called the Intelligent Training System, costs only about $2.00 per employee (which is spent primarily on propane), isn't messy, and is environmentally sound. All told, the BullEx system reduces the cost to perform live fire extinguisher training by over 90 percent. The company has gotten off to a quick start and counts General Electric, Northrop Grumman, and Stanford University among its initial customers.[1] O'Donnell is pictured in the yellow shirt in the photo accompanying this feature, helping someone learn how to use Intelligent Training System.

To protect its system against potential imitators BullEx has applied for a patent, which in mid-2006 was in the final stages of approval. One thing that made the system attractive from a business standpoint is that after an exhaustive search by a patent attorney, it was determined that the BullEx system is truly unique, and that there are no even remotely similar devices or systems that have been patented. This is a very positive finding for two reasons. First, it means that the BullEx system won't infringe on any other patents. Second, it means that it will be extremely difficult for another firm to sell a similar fire extinguisher training system without infringing on BullEx's patent. To illustrate the importance of these factors, prior to coming up with the BullEx idea, O'Donnell and his colleagues considered two other business ideas: a stovetop fire suppression system and a smart fire extinguisher that could sense where a fire was and provide verbal cues to the operator of the extinguisher. The first idea, the fire suppression system, was eventually rejected, primarily because there are already fire suppressions systems on the market, which would have made it difficult to present unique claims in a patent application. The second idea, the smart fire extinguisher, was also rejected, not so much because intellectual property protection couldn't have been obtained, but because the device would have entered a crowded marketplace, and would have had to compete head-to-head against products produced by mainstream fire extinguisher manufacturers. Only the BullEx idea was truly unique and could be protected by a highly defensible patent.[2]

Along with its patent application, O'Donnell and his cofounders have thought holistically about BullEx's entire intellectual property strategy. All of the company's distinctive marks, like its logo, have been trademarked. Much of its printed material, such as its operating manuals, has been copyrighted. As is the case with many savvy firms, however, not all of its intellectual property is legally protected. The software code and algorithms that control the flames in its propane device, for example, are trade secrets and are not protected by patents or copyrights. It is virtually impossible for a competitor to learn this information by reverse engineering BullEx's products. As a result, rather than disclosing this information, which would be necessary in the case of a patent, BullEx has decided to keep it secret and protect it internally.

BullEx Digital Safety is now moving forward as a business with its intellectual property securely intact. As a validation of its business idea and its early success, the company won the $100,000 Tech Valley (New York) business plan competition in early 2006. In 2005, BullEx won a similar competition at the collegiate level.[3]

Many entrepreneurial firms have valuable intellectual property. In fact, virtually all businesses, including start-ups, have knowledge, information, and ideas that are critical to their success.

For at least three reasons, it is important for businesses to recognize what intellectual property is and how to protect it. First, the intellectual property of a business often represents its most valuable asset.[4] Think of the value of the Google trademark, the Nike "swoosh" logo, or the Microsoft Windows operating system. All of these are examples of intellectual property, and because of intellectual property laws, they are the exclusive properties of the firms that own them. Second, it is important to understand what intellectual property is and how to protect it to avoid unintentional violations of intellectual property laws. For example, imagine the hardship facing an entrepreneurial start-up if it selected a name for its business, heavily advertised that name, and was later forced to change the name because it was infringing on a trademark. Finally, intellectual property can be licensed or sold, providing valuable licensing income.

We begin this chapter by defining intellectual property and exploring when intellectual property protection is warranted. There are costs involved with legally protecting intellectual property, and the costs sometimes outweigh the benefits, at least in the short term. Next, we discuss the four key types of intellectual property. The chapter ends with a discussion of the importance of conducting an intellectual property audit, which is a proactive tool an entrepreneurial firm can use to catalog the intellectual property it owns and determine how its intellectual property should be protected.

The Importance of Intellectual Property

Intellectual property is any product of human intellect that is intangible but has value in the marketplace. It is called "intellectual" property because it is the product of human imagination, creativity, and inventiveness.[5] Traditionally, businesses have thought of their physical assets, such as land, buildings, and equipment, as their most important assets. Increasingly, however, a company's intellectual assets are the most valuable. In the case of BullEx Digital Safety, intellectual property consists of intangible assets such as an invention, a business's logo, and a company's Internet domain name. All these assets can provide a business with a competitive advantage in the marketplace, and the loss of such assets can be just as costly (if not more so) to a business as the loss of physical property or equipment.

Not all firms are as intellectual property savvy as BullEx Digital Safety. In fact, common mistakes that entrepreneurial firms make are not properly identifying all their intellectual property, not fully recognizing the value of their intellectual property, not using their intellectual property as part of their overall plan of success, and not taking sufficient steps to protect it. These challenges are presented in Figure 12.1. It can be difficult, however, to determine what qualifies as intellectual property and whether it should be legally protected. Every facet of a company's operations probably owns intellectual property that

L E A R N I N G

Objective

1. Define the term *intellectual property*, and describe its importance.

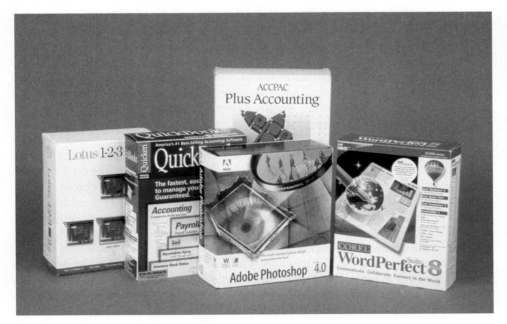

If you purchase the latest version of Adobe Photoshop, the $125 or so you pay is not for the CD-ROM and discs themselves. The value you are paying for is the access you now have to the intellectual property contained on the disc.

FIGURE 12.1

Common Mistakes Firms Make in Regard to Intellectual Property

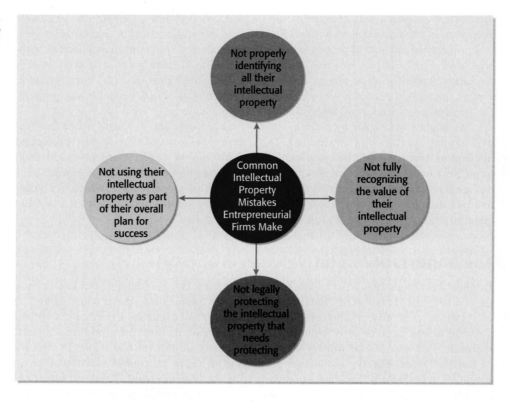

should be protected. To illustrate this point, Table 12.1 provides examples of the intellectual property that typically resides within the departments of midsize entrepreneurial firms.

Intellectual property is also an important part of our nation's economy and its competitive advantage in the world marketplace. "It's a huge issue," U.S. Commerce Secretary Carlos Gutierrez said. "There is so much of our economy that is linked to branded products, patented products, copyrights. So much of our economy thrives on creativity."[6]

Determining What Intellectual Property to Legally Protect

There are two primary rules of thumb for deciding if intellectual property protection should be pursued for a particular intellectual asset. First, a firm should determine if the intellectual property in question is directly related to its competitive advantage. For example, Amazon.com has a business method patent on its "one-click" ordering system, which is a nice feature of its Web site and is arguably directly related to its competitive advantage. Similarly, when Yahoo! launched a Web site specifically designed for children and named it Yahooligans, it would have been foolish for the company not to trademark the Yahooligans name. In contrast, if a business develops a product or business method or produces printed material that isn't directly related to its competitive advantage, intellectual property protection may not be warranted.

The second primary criterion for deciding if intellectual property protection should be pursued is to determine whether an item has value in the marketplace. A common mistake that young companies make is to invent a product, spend a considerable amount of money to patent it, and find that the market for the product does not exist or that the existing market is too small to be worthy of pursuit. As discussed in Chapter 3, business ideas should be properly tested before a considerable amount of money is spent developing and legally protecting them. Owning the exclusive right to something no one wants is of little value. Similarly, if a company develops a logo for a special event, it is probably a waste of money to register it with the U.S. Patent and Trademark Office if there is a good chance the logo will not be used again.

On other occasions, obtaining intellectual property protection is crucial, because if appropriate forms of protection are not obtained, the value of the intellectual property can be lost. This was the crux of the disagreement between the music industry and Napster, which evolved into one of the most famous copyright infringement cases in history, as

TABLE 12.1 Examples of Intellectual Property That Typically Resides Within a Midsized Entrepreneurial Firm's Departments

Department	Forms of Intellectual Property Typically Present	Usual Methods of Protection
Marketing	Names, slogans, logos, jingles, advertisements, brochures, pamphlets, ad copy under development, customer lists, prospect lists, and similar items	Trademark, copyright, and trade secret
Management	Recruiting brochures, employee handbooks, forms and checklists used by recruiters in qualifying and hiring candidates, written training materials, and company newsletters	Copyright and trade secret
Finance	Contractual forms, PowerPoint slides describing the company's financial performance, written methodologies explaining how the company handles its finances, and employee pay records	Copyright and trade secret
Management information systems	Web site design, Internet domain names, company-specific training manuals for computer equipment and software, original computer code, e-mail lists	Copyright, trade secret, and Internet domain name registry
Research and development	New and useful inventions and business processes, improvements to existing inventions and processes, and laboratory notes documenting invention discovery dates and charting the progress on various projects	Patents and trade secrets

depicted in this chapter's "What Went Wrong" feature. As indicated in the feature, the courts ultimately pulled the plug on Napster, because of the music industry's diligence in enforcing the intellectual property laws that protected its music.

Why the Courts Pulled the Plug on Napster
www.napster.com

In May 1999, Shawn Fanning and Sean Parker, two college students, cofounded Napster and instantly created one of the Internet's hottest sites. Using Napster software, Internet users could access music files stored on other users' computers that were connected to the Internet. Although Napster didn't actually provide a library of songs itself, it made a search engine available to users that listed the names and computer locations of songs on its users' computers, making possible peer-to-peer swapping of music files, including those that were copyrighted, for free. At its peak, Napster had over 50 million users who were sharing over 3 billion songs each month.

So what went wrong? For some time, the recording industry had been concerned about the swapping of copyrighted music online. However, prior to Napster, this activity was confined primarily to amateur Web sites. Napster was much more professional and moved the science of swapping music to a new level. As Napster's user base continued to grow, the industry started to take notice. It was clear that people were acquiring millions of songs every day, and the recording industry wasn't being paid anything for its products.

To put a halt to this, most of the world's biggest record labels, led by the Recording Industry Association of America, sued Napster in December 1999. The heavy metal band Metallica and rapper Dr. Dre joined the lawsuit. Metallica went so far as to submit a list of 300,000 users who had downloaded its music through Napster and demanded that their Napster privileges be revoked. Napster defended its position, arguing that it wasn't doing anything illegal. In fact, it argued not only that its Web site was perfectly legal but also that it was doing the recording industry a favor by promoting artists and encouraging sales. It also argued that sharing music was legal for consumers who weren't doing it to make a profit. After all, the argument went, who hasn't borrowed a compact disc or other recording from a friend or family member and copied it for personal use? Napster alleged that it was simply facilitating this sharing process on a broader level.

On February 12, 2001, a day Napster loyalists dubbed "the day the music died," the federal court of appeals gave an almost total victory to the record companies. Although the court did not hold that Napster was an actual copyright infringer, the court did find Napster liable for contributory copyright infringement in violation of federal copyright law. The court stated that Napster "knowingly encourages and assists in the infringement of copyrights" by others. When Napster tried to argue that it did not know of its users' infringing conduct, the court cited a document written by Napster cofounder Sean Parker that mentioned "the need to remain ignorant of users' real names and IP addresses since they are exchanging pirated music."

Although there is nothing inherently illegal about creating a software program that allows for the swapping of files over the Internet, the bulk of files transferred through Napster were songs protected under the U.S. Copyright Act. The courts had no choice but to rule against Napster as an active participant in helping its users gain access to this material. From Napster's point of view, it was never able to work around this complication. Napster obeyed the court and shut down its file-swapping service after the ruling. Later, it announced that it planned to launch a legal music download service with backing from Bertelsmann, a German music company. Regrettably, there was simply too much bad blood between Napster and the major record labels for the new service to come together. Eventually, Napster liquidated.

Ironically, Roxio, a company best known for its software that allows users to create their own compact discs, paid $5 million in November 2002 to buy the Napster name and trademark. Roxio renamed itself

Napster and launched a legal music download subscription site. The new Napster, which claims to have over 600,000 subscribers, sells its subscribers the right to download an unlimited number of songs, but the files can only be played while their subscription is current. The company broadened its offerings in 2006 and now sells audio files that can be purchased individually and downloaded, similar to Apple's iTunes music service.

Questions for Critical Thinking

1. Who do you think was right in this dispute—Napster or the music industry? Explain your answer.

2. In your view, could the federal court of appeals have ruled in any other way than it did? What implication, for both the music industry and intellectual property laws in general, would have resulted if the court had ruled in favor of Napster? If the court had ruled in favor of Napster, do you think Apple would have launched iTunes? To what extent has iTunes been responsible for the success of the iPod?

3. You may know of individuals who still download songs or movies from sites that are similar to Napster and are still in existence. In your opinion, are these individuals violating copyright law? Explain your answer.

4. To what extent do strong intellectual property laws, and courts willing to defend them, bolster the entrepreneurial sector of the U.S. economy?

Sources: Napster homepage, www.napster.com (accessed June 6, 2006); "Napster Opens U.K. Site," *The Wall Street Journal Online*, www.wsj.com (accessed May 21, 2004); H.R. Cheeseman, *Contemporary Business and E-Commerce Law* (Upper Saddle River, NJ: Prentice Hall, 2003); A. Mathews and D. Clark, "Roxio to Buy Pressplay and Revive Napster Name," *The Wall Street Journal*, May 19, 2003, B4; *A&M Records v. Napster, Inc.*, 239 F.3d 1004 (9th Cir. 2001).

The Four Key Forms of Intellectual Property

LEARNING

Objective

2. Discuss the four major forms of intellectual property: patents, trademarks, copyrights, and trade secrets.

Patents, trademarks, copyrights, and trade secrets are the four key forms of intellectual property. We discuss each form of intellectual property protection in the following sections. Intellectual property laws exist to encourage creativity and innovation by granting individuals who risk their time and money in creative endeavors exclusive rights to the fruits of their labors for a period of time. Intellectual property laws also help individuals make well-informed choices. For example, when a consumer sees a Panera Bread restaurant, she knows exactly what to expect because only Panera Bread is permitted to use the Panera Bread trademark for soups, signature sandwiches, and bakery products.

One special note about intellectual property laws is that it is up to entrepreneurs to take advantage of them and to safeguard their intellectual property once it is legally protected. Police forces and fire departments are available to quickly respond if an entrepreneur's buildings or other physical assets are threatened, but there are no intellectual property police forces or fire departments in existence. The courts prosecute individuals and companies that break intellectual property laws. However, it is up to the individual entrepreneur to understand intellectual property laws, safeguard intellectual property assets, and initiate litigation if intellectual property rights are infringed upon or violated.

LEARNING
Objective

3. Specify the rules of thumb for determining whether a particular piece of intellectual property is worth the time and expense of protecting.

Patents

A **patent** is a grant from the federal government conferring the rights to exclude others from making, selling, or using an invention for the term of the patent.[7] The owner of the patent is granted a legal monopoly for a limited amount of time. However, a patent does not give its owner the right to make, use, or sell the invention; it gives the owner only the right to exclude others from doing so. This is a confusing issue for many firms. If a company is granted a patent for an item, it is natural to assume that it could start making and selling the item immediately. But it cannot. A patent owner can legally make or sell the patented invention only if no other patents are infringed on by doing so.[8] For example, if an inventor obtained a patent on a computer chip and the chip needed technology patented earlier by Intel to work, the inventor would need to obtain permission from Intel to make and sell the chip. Intel may refuse permission or ask for a licensing fee for the use of its patented technology. Although this system may seem odd, it is really the only way the system could work. Many inventions are improvements on existing inventions, and the system allows the improvements to be patented, but only with the permission of the original inventors, who usually benefit by obtaining licensing income in exchange for their consent.[9]

Patent protection has deep roots in U.S. history and is the only form of intellectual property right expressly mentioned in the original articles of the U.S. Constitution. The first patent was granted in 1790 for a process of making potash, an ingredient in fertilizer. The patent was signed by George Washington and was issued to a Vermont inventor named Samuel Hopkins. Patents are important because they grant inventors temporary, exclusive rights to market their inventions. This right gives inventors and their financial backers the opportunity to recoup their costs and earn a profit in exchange for the risks and costs they incur during the invention process. If it weren't for patent laws, inventors would have little incentive to invest time and money in new inventions. "No one would develop a drug if you didn't have a patent," Dr. William Haseltine, the chief executive officer (CEO) of Human Genome Sciences, a biotech firm, once said.[10]

Since the first patent was granted in 1790, the U.S. Patent and Trademark Office has granted over 7 million patents. Some inventors, and companies, are very prolific and have multiple patents. There is increasing interest in patents, as shown in Table 12.2, as advances in technology spawn new inventions. The U.S. Patent and Trademark Office, the sole entity responsible for granting patents in the United States, is strained. At the end of 2005, there were 885,002 patent applications pending, and it took an average of 29.1 months to get a patent application approved. As shown in the table, the last several years have seen the number of patent applications continue to increase while the number of patents granted decreases, reflecting the increasing complexity of the patent application process.

TABLE 12.2 Growth in Patent Applications in the United States

	2003	2004	2005
Applications received	355,394	378,984	409,532
Patents issued	189,597	187,170	165,485
Total patents pending	674,691	756,604	885,002
Average time for approval	26.7 months	27.6 months	29.1 months

Source: United States Patent & Trademark Office, Performance and Accountability Report for Fiscal Year 2005.

Types of Patents

There are three types of patents: utility patents, design patents, and plant patents. As shown in Figure 12.2, there are three basic requirements for a patent to be granted: The subject of the patent application must be (1) useful, (2) novel in relation to prior arts in the field, and (3) not obvious to a person of ordinary skill in the field.

Utility patents are the most common type of patent and cover what we generally think of as new inventions. Patents in this category may be granted to anyone who "invents or discovers any new and useful process, machine, manufacture, or composition of matter, or any new and useful improvement thereof."[11] The term of a utility patent is 20 years from the date of the initial application. After 20 years, the patent expires, and the invention falls into the public domain, which means that anyone can produce and sell the invention without paying the prior patent holder. Consider the pharmaceutical industry. Assume a drug produced by Pfizer is prescribed for you and that, when seeking to fill the prescription, your pharmacist tells you there is no generic equivalent available. The lack of a generic equivalent typically means that a patent owned by Pfizer protects the drug and that the 20-year term of the patent has not expired. If the pharmacist tells you there is a generic version of the drug available that typically means the 20-year patent has expired and other companies are now making a drug chemically identical to Pfizer's. The price of the generic version of the drug is generally lower because the manufacturer of the generic version of the drug is not trying to recover the costs Pfizer (in this case) incurred to develop the product (the drug) in question.

A utility patent cannot be obtained for an "idea" or a "suggestion" for a new product or process. A complete description of the invention for which a utility patent is sought is required, including drawings and technical details. In addition, a patent must be applied for within one year of when a product or process was first offered for sale, put into public use, or was described in any printed publication—or the right to file a patent application is forfeited. The advantage of this provision is that it gives an inventor one year to test-market an invention before having to decide whether to file for a patent. The downside is that sometimes entrepreneurs forget about the provision or lose track of time, and then at the last minute realize that the product or process can never be patented unless the company finds a patent attorney willing to work feverishly to put together a filing in a short period of time to meet the **one year after first use** deadline. You can image how expensive that would be for the forgetful entrepreneur!

Recently, utility patent law has added business method patents, which have been of particular interest to Internet firms. A **business method patent** is a patent that protects an invention that is or facilitates a method of doing business. Patents for these purposes were not allowed until 1998, when a federal circuit court issued an opinion allowing a patent for a business method, holding that business methods, mathematical algorithms, and software are patentable as long as they produce useful, tangible, and concrete results. This ruling opened a Pandora's box and has caused many firms to scramble to try to patent their business methods. Since 1998, the most notable business methods patents awarded have been Amazon.com's one-click ordering system, Priceline.com's "name-your-price" business model, and Netflix's method for allowing customers to set up a rental list of movies they want mailed to them.

FIGURE 12.2

Three Basic Requirements for a Patent

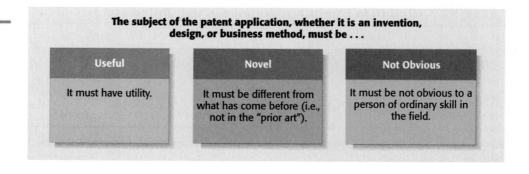

The subject of the patent application, whether it is an invention, design, or business method, must be . . .

Useful	Novel	Not Obvious
It must have utility.	It must be different from what has come before (i.e., not in the "prior art").	It must be not obvious to a person of ordinary skill in the field.

Design patents are the second most common type of patent and cover the invention of new, original, and ornamental designs for manufactured products.[12] A design patent is good for 14 years from the grant date. While a utility patent protects the way an invention is used and works, a design patent protects the way it looks. As a result, if an entrepreneur invented a new version of the computer mouse, it would be prudent to apply for a utility patent to cover the way the mouse works and for a design patent to protect the way the mouse looks. Although all computer mice perform essentially the same function, they can be ornamentally designed in an infinite number of ways. As long as each new design is considered by the U.S. Patent and Trademark Office to be novel and nonobvious, it is eligible for design patent protection. This is not a trivial issue in that product design is increasingly becoming an important source of competitive advantage for many firms producing many different types of products.

Plant patents protect new varieties of plants that can be reproduced asexually. Such plants are reproduced by grafting or crossbreeding rather than by planting seeds. The new variety can be different from previous plants in its resistance to disease or drought or in its scent, appearance, color, or productivity. Thus, a new color for a rose or a new type of hybrid vegetable would be eligible for plant patent protection. The term for plant patent protection is 20 years from the date of the original application.

Table 12.3 provides a summary of the three forms of patent protection, the types of inventions the patents cover, and the duration of the patents.

Who Can Apply for a Patent?

Only the inventor of a product can apply for a patent. If two or more people make an invention jointly, they must apply for the patent together. Someone who simply heard about the design of a product or is trying to patent something that is in the public domain may not apply for a patent.

There are notable exceptions to these rules. First, if an invention is made during the course of the inventor's employment, the employer typically is assigned the right to apply for the patent through an **assignment of invention agreement** signed by the employee as part of the employment agreement. A second exception is that the rights to apply for an invention can be sold. This option can be an important source of revenue for entrepreneurial firms. If a firm has an invention that it doesn't want to pursue on its own, the rights to apply for a patent on the invention can be sold to another party.

The Process of Obtaining a Patent

Obtaining a patent is a six-step process, as illustrated in Figure 12.3 and as we discuss here. The total cost of applying for a patent ranges from $5,000 to $50,000, depending on the situation.[13]

L E A R N I N G

Objective

4. Describe the six-step process for obtaining a patent.

Step 1 **Make sure the invention is practical.** As mentioned earlier, there are two rules of thumb for making the decision to patent. Intellectual property that is worth protecting typically is directly related to the competitive advantage of the firm seeking the protection or has independent value in the marketplace.

Summary of the Three Forms of Patent Protection, the Types of Inventions
TABLE 12.3 **the Patents Cover, and the Duration of the Patents**

Type of Patent	Types of Inventions Covered	Duration
Utility	New or useful process, machine, manufacture, or composition of material or any new and useful improvement thereof	20 years from the date of the original application
Design	Invention of new, original, and ornamental designs for manufactured products	14 years from the date of the original application
Plant	Any new varieties of plants that can be reproduced asexually	20 years from the date of the original application

Step 2 **Document when the invention was made.** Put together a set of documents clearly stating when the invention was first thought of, dates on which experiments were conducted in perfecting it, and the date it was first used and found to operate satisfactorily. Inventors should get in the habit of filling out an "invention logbook" on a daily basis to record their activities. An **invention logbook** documents the dates and activities related to the development of a particular invention. As soon as an inventor has an idea for an invention, a complete description of the invention should be written down, sketches should be made of it, and how it works should be described in detail. The inventor should then sign and date the documents and indicate that he or she is the inventor. If possible, a notary or another party without a financial interest in the invention should witness the inventor's signature. This step is important because if two inventors independently develop essentially the same invention, the right to apply for the patent belongs to the person who came up with it first. The United States adheres to the **first-to-invent** rule rather than the first-to-file rule, meaning that the first person to invent an item or process is given preference over another person who is first to file a patent application. If there is a dispute regarding who was first to invent a product, the dispute is resolved in an administrative proceeding known as an **interference** that is presided over by a judge at the U.S. Patent & Trademark Office.

Step 3 **Hire a patent attorney.** It is highly recommended that an inventor work with a patent attorney. Even though there are "patent-it-yourself" books and Web sites on the market, it is generally naive for an entrepreneur to think that the patent process can be successfully navigated without expert help. As an indication of the difficulty of writing a patent application, the U.S. Patent and Trademark Office requires all attorneys and agents to pass a tough exam before they can interact with the agency on behalf of a client.

Step 4 **Conduct a patent search.** To be patentable, an invention must be novel and different enough from what already exists. A patent attorney typically spends several hours searching the U.S. Patent and Trademark Office's database (which is available online at www.uspto.gov) to study similar patents. After the search is completed and the patents that are similar to the invention in question have been carefully studied, the patent attorney renders an opinion regarding the probability of obtaining a patent on the new invention.

Step 5 **File a patent application.** The fifth step, if the inventor decides to proceed, is to file a patent application with the U.S. Patent and Trademark Office (PTO) in Washington, D.C. Unlike copyright and trademark applications, which can be prepared and filed easily by their owners, patent applications are highly technical and almost always require expert assistance. Approximately 80 percent of inventors retain patent attorneys or agents to prepare and file their patent applications.[14]

Step 6 **Obtain a decision from the U.S. Patent and Trademark Office.** When the U.S. Patent and Trademark Office receives a patent application, it is given a serial number, assigned to an examiner, and then waits to be examined. The patent

FIGURE 12.3

The Process of Obtaining a Patent

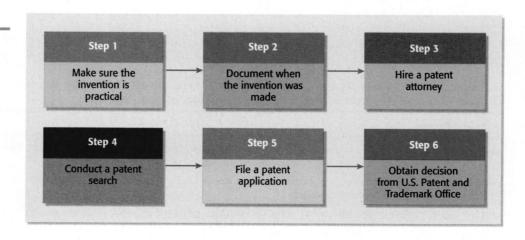

examiner investigates the application and issues a written report ("Office Action") to the applicant's patent attorney, often asking for modifications to the application. Most of the interactions that applicants have with the U.S. Patent and Trademark Office are by mail. Occasionally, an inventor and a lawyer will meet face to face with a patent examiner to discuss the invention and the written report. There is room to negotiate with the patent office to try to make an invention patentable. Eventually, a yes-or-no decision will be rendered. A rejected application can be appealed, but appeals are rare and expensive.

One provision of patent law that is particularly important to entrepreneurs is that the U.S. Patent and Trademark Office allows inventors to file a **provisional patent application**, pending the preparation and filing of a complete application. This part of the law grants "provisional rights" to an inventor for up to one year, pending the filing of a complete and final application.

Patent Infringement

Patent infringement takes place when one party engages in the unauthorized use of another party's patent. A typical example of an infringement claim was that initiated by Alacritech, a start-up firm, which claimed that Microsoft violated two of its patents on technology used to speed the performance of computers connected to networks. According to court documents, Alacritech showed its technology to Microsoft in 2003, hoping that Microsoft would license it. But Microsoft passed on the offer and later announced a surprisingly similar technology, called Chimney. Alacritech again offered to license the technology to Microsoft but was rebuffed. In response, Alacritech filed suit against Microsoft in 2004. Microsoft claimed that its technology was developed independently.[15] In April of 2005, the U.S. District Court in San Francisco sided with Alacritech and filed a preliminary injunction against Microsoft, preventing it from shipping products that contained the contested technology. In mid-2005, the suit was settled out of court, with Microsoft agreeing to license Alacritech's technology.[16]

The tough part about patent infringement cases is that they are costly to litigate, which puts start-up firms and their entrepreneurs at quite a disadvantage. While there is no way of knowing how much it cost Alacritech to sue Microsoft, a typical patent-infringement suit, according to *Fortune Small Business*, cost each side at least $500,000 to litigate.[17]

Trademarks

A **trademark** is any word, name, symbol, or device used to identify the source or origin of products or services and to distinguish those products or services from others. All businesses want to be recognized by their potential clientele and use their names, logos, and other distinguishing features to enhance their visibility. Trademarks also provide consumers with useful information. For example, consumers know what to expect when they see an Abercrombie & Fitch store in a mall. Think of how confusing it would be if any retail store could use the name Abercrombie & Fitch.

As is the case with patents, trademarks have a rich history. Archaeologists have found evidence that as far back as 3,500 years ago, potters made distinctive marks on their articles of pottery to distinguish their work from others. But consider a more modern example. The original name that Jerry Yang and David Filo, the cofounders of Yahoo!, selected for their Internet directory service was "Jerry's Guide to the World Wide Web." Not too catchy, is it? The name was later changed to Yahoo!, which caught on with early adopters of the Internet and now is one of the most recognizable trademarks in America.

The Four Types of Trademarks

There are four types of trademarks: trademarks, service marks, collective marks, and certification marks (see Table 12.4). Trademarks and service marks are of the greatest interest to entrepreneurs.

5. Identify the four types of trademarks.

This flag, which depicts Cisco Systems' trademark, flies in front of the company's headquarters in San Jose, California. Companies like Cisco Systems fiercely protect their trademarks, which are the most compelling aspects of their brands. To be thorough, Cisco Systems has separately trademarked its name and its familiar rendition of the Golden Gate Bridge, which appears below its name on the flag. Cisco Systems has also trademarked its tagline, which is "Empowering the Internet Generation."

TABLE 12.4 Summary of the Four Forms of Trademark Protection, the Type of Marks the Trademarks Cover, and the Duration of the Trademarks

Type of Trademark	Type of Marks Covered	Duration
Trademark	Any word, name, symbol, or device used to identify and distinguish one company's goods from another	Renewable every 10 years, as long as the mark remains in use
	Examples: *Dell, Nokia, Oracle, Palapa Azul, Sun Microsystems, Type 1 and Type 2 Tools*	
Service mark	Similar to trademarks; are used to identify the services or intangible activities of a business, rather than a business's physical products	Renewable every 10 years, as long as the mark remains in use
	Examples: *1-800-FREE-411; Ameritrade, Amazon.com, Dream Dinners, eBay, Overstock.com, Pandora*	
Collective mark	Trademarks or service marks used by the members of a cooperative, association, or other collective group	Renewable every 10 years, as long as the mark remains in use
	Examples: *Information Technology Industry Council, International Franchise Association, Rotary International*	
Certification mark	Marks, words, names, symbols, or devices used by a person other than its owner to certify a particular quality about a good or service	Renewable every 10 years, as long as the mark remains in use
	Examples: *Canadian Standards Association, Florida Oranges, ISO 9000, Underwriters Laboratories*	

Trademarks, as described previously, include any word, name, symbol, or device used to identify and distinguish one company's products from another's. Trademarks are used in the advertising and promotion of tangible products, such as Nokia for cell phones, Nike for athletic shoes, and Electronic Arts for electronic games.

Service marks are similar to ordinary trademarks, but they are used to identify the services or intangible activities of a business rather than a business's physical product. Service marks include *The Princeton Review* for test prep services, eBay for online auctions, and Cingular for cell phone service.

Collective marks are trademarks or service marks used by the members of a cooperative, association, or other collective group, including marks indicating membership in a union or similar organization. The marks belonging to the American Bar Association,

The International Franchise Association, and the Entrepreneurs' Organization are examples of collective marks.

Finally, **certification marks** are marks, words, names, symbols, or devices used by a person other than its owner to certify a particular quality about a product or service. The most familiar certification mark is the UL mark, which certifies that a product meets the safety standards established by Underwriters Laboratories. Other examples are the Good Housekeeping Seal of Approval, Stilton Cheese (a product from the Stilton region in England), and Carneros Wines (from grapes grown in the Napa Valley of northern California).

What Is Protected Under Trademark Law?

Trademark law, which falls under the **Lanham Act,** passed in 1946, protects the following items:

- ▪ *Words:* All combinations of words are eligible for trademark registration, including single words, short phrases, and slogans. Pixar Animation Studios, and the National Football League are examples of words and phrases that have been registered as trademarks.
- ▪ *Numbers and letters:* Numbers and letters are eligible for registration. Examples include 3M, MSNBC, and AT&T. Alphanumeric marks are also registerable, such as 1-800-FREE-411.
- ▪ *Designs or logos:* A mark consisting solely of a design, such as the Golden Gate Bridge for Cisco Systems or the Nike swoosh logo, may be eligible for registration. The mark must be distinctive rather than generic. As a result, no one can claim exclusive rights to the image of the Golden Gate Bridge, but Cisco Systems can trademark its unique depiction of the bridge. Composite marks consist of a word or words in conjunction with a design. An example is the trademark for Zephyrhill's bottled water, which includes the Zephyrhill's name below a picture of mountain scenery and water.
- ▪ *Sounds:* Distinctive sounds can be trademarked, although this form of trademark protection is rare. The most recognizable examples are the MGM's lion's roar, the familiar four-tone sound that accompanies "Intel Inside" commercials, and the Yahoo! yodel.
- ▪ *Fragrances:* The fragrance of a product may be registerable as long as the product is not known for the fragrance or the fragrance does not enhance the use of the product. As a result, the fragrance of a perfume or room deodorizer is not eligible for trademark protection, whereas stationery treated with a special fragrance in most cases would be.
- ▪ *Shapes:* The shape of a product, as long as it has no impact on the product's function, can be trademarked. The unique shape of the monitor on Apple's iMac computer is protectable. The Coca-Cola Company has trademarked its famous curved bottle. The shape of the bottle has no effect on the quality of the bottle or the beverage it holds; therefore, the shape is not functional.
- ▪ *Colors:* A trademark may be obtained for a color as long as the color is not functional. For example, Nexium, a medicine pill that treats acid reflux disease, is purple and is marketed as "the purple pill." The color of the pill has no bearing on its functionality; therefore it can be protected by trademark protection.
- ▪ *Trade dress:* The manner is which a product is "dressed up" to appeal to customers is protectable. This category includes the overall packaging, design, and configuration of a product. As a result, the overall look of a business is protected as its trade dress. In a famous case, *Two Pesos, Inc., v. Taco Cabana International Inc.*, the U.S. Supreme Court protected the overall design, colors, and configuration of a chain of Mexican restaurants from a competitor using a similar decor.

Trademark protection is very broad and provides many opportunities for businesses to differentiate themselves from one another. The key for young entrepreneurial firms is to trademark their products and services in ways that draw positive attention to them in a compelling manner.

Exclusions from Trademark Protection

There are notable exclusions from trademark protection that are set forth in the U.S. Trademark Act:

- **Immoral or scandalous matter:** A company cannot trademark immoral or scandalous matter, including profane words.
- **Deceptive matter:** Marks that are deceptive cannot be registered. For example, a food company couldn't register the name "Fresh Florida Oranges" if the oranges weren't from Florida.
- **Descriptive marks:** Marks that are merely descriptive of a product or service cannot be trademarked. For example, an entrepreneur couldn't design a new type of golf ball and try to obtain trademark protection on the words *golf ball*. The words describe a type of product rather than a brand of product, such as Titleist or MaxFli, and are needed by all golf ball manufacturers to be competitive. This issue is a real concern for the manufacturers of very popular products. Recently, Xerox was in danger of losing trademark protection for the Xerox name because of the common use of the word *Xerox* as a verb (e.g., "I am going to Xerox this").
- **Surnames:** A trademark consisting primarily of a surname, such as Anderson or Smith, is typically not protectable. An exception is a surname combined with other wording that is intended to trademark a distinct product, such as William's Fresh Fish or Smith's Computer Emporium.

The Process of Obtaining a Trademark

As illustrated in Figure 12.4, selecting and registering a trademark is a three-step process. Once a trademark has been used in interstate commerce, it can be registered with the U.S. Patent and Trademark Office for a renewable term of 10 years and can theoretically remain registered forever as long as the trademark stays in use.

Technically, a trademark does not need to be registered to receive protection and to prevent other companies from using confusingly similar marks. Once a mark is used in commerce, such as in an advertisement, it is protected. There are several distinct advantages, however, in registering a trademark with the U.S. Patent and Trademark Office: Registered marks are allowed nationwide priority for use of the mark, registered marks may use the federal trademark registration symbol (®), and registered marks carry with them the right to block the importation of infringing goods into the United States. The right to use the trademark registration symbol is particularly important. Attaching the trademark symbol to a product (e.g., My Yahoo!®) provides notice of a trademark owner's registration. This posting allows an owner to recover damages in an infringement action and helps reduce an offender's claim that it didn't know that a particular name or logo was trademarked.

There are three steps in selecting and registering a trademark:

Step 1 **Select an appropriate mark.** There are several rules of thumb to help business owners and entrepreneurs select appropriate trademarks. First, a mark, whether it is a name, logo, design, or fragrance, should display creativity and strength. Marks that are inherently distinctive, such as the McDonald's Golden Arches; made-up words, such as *Google* and *eBay*; and words that evoke particular images, such as *Double Delight Ice Cream*, are strong trademarks. Second, words that create a favorable

FIGURE 12.4

The Process of Obtaining a Trademark

Step 1	Step 2	Step 3
Select an appropriate mark	Perform a trademark search	Create rights in the trademark

impression about a product or service are helpful. A name such as *Safe and Secure Childcare* for a day care center positively resonates with parents.

Step 2 **Perform a trademark search.** Once a trademark has been selected, a trademark search should be conducted to determine if the trademark is available. If someone else has already established rights to the proposed mark, it cannot be used. There are several ways to conduct a trademark search, from self-help searches to hiring a firm specializing in trademark clearance checks. The search should include both federal and state searches in any states in which business will be conducted. If the trademark will be used overseas, the search should also include the countries where the trademark will be used.

Although it is not necessary to hire an attorney to conduct a trademark search, it is probably a good idea to do so. Self-searches can also be conducted. A simple-to-use search engine is available at the U.S. Patent and Trademark Office's Web site (www.uspto.org). Using this Web site, a person can check the agency's database of 3.0 million registered, abandoned, canceled, and expired marks and pending applications. Adopting a trademark without conducting a trademark search is risky. If a mark is challenged as an infringement, a company may have to destroy all its goods that bear the mark (including products, business cards, stationery, signs, and so on) and then select a new mark. The cost of refamiliarizing customers with an existing product under a new name or logo could be substantial.

Step 3 **Create rights in the trademark.** The final step in establishing a trademark is to create rights in the mark. In the United States, if the trademark is inherently distinctive (think of Starbucks, iTunes, or Nokia), the first person to use the mark becomes its owner. If the mark is descriptive, such as BUFFERIN for buffered aspirin, using the mark merely begins the process of developing a secondary meaning necessary to create full trademark protection. **Secondary meaning** arises when, over time, consumers start to identify a trademark with a specific product. For example, the name CHAP STICK for lip balm was originally considered to be descriptive, and thus not afforded trademark protection. As people started to think of CHAP STICK as lip balm, it met the threshold of secondary meaning and was able to be trademarked.

There are two ways that the U.S. Patent and Trademark Office can offer further protection for firms concerned about maintaining the exclusive rights to their trademarks. First, a person can file an **intent-to-use trademark application**. This is an application based on the applicant's intention to use a trademark. Once this application is filed, the owner obtains the benefits of registration. The benefits are lost, however, if the owner does not use the mark in business within 6 months of registration. Further protection can be obtained by filing a formal application for a trademark. The application must include a drawing of the trademark and a filing fee (ranging from $275 to $375, depending on how the application is filed). After a trademark application is filed, an examining attorney at the U.S. Patent and Trademark Office determines if the trademark can be registered.

Copyrights

A **copyright** is a form of intellectual property protection that grants to the owner of a work of authorship the legal right to determine how the work is used and to obtain the economic benefits from the work.[18] The work must be in a tangible form, such as a book, operating manual, magazine article, musical score, computer software program, or architectural drawing. If something is not in a tangible form, such as a speech that has never been recorded or saved on a computer disk, copyright law does not protect it.

Businesses typically possess a treasure trove of copyrightable material, as illustrated earlier in Table 12.1. A work does not have to have artistic merit to be eligible for copyright protection. As a result, things such as operating manuals, advertising brochures, and training videos qualify for protection. The Copyright Revision Act of 1976 governs copyright law in the United States. Under the law, an original work is protected automatically from the time it is created and put into a tangible form whether it is published or not. The first copyright in the United States was granted on May 31, 1790, to a Philadelphia educator named John Barry for a spelling book.

L E A R N I N G
Objective

6. Identify the types of material that are eligible for copyright protection.

What Is Protected by a Copyright?

Copyright laws protect "original works of authorship" that are fixed in a tangible form of expression. The primary categories of material that can be copyrighted follow:

- *Literary works:* Anything written down is a literary work, including books, poetry, reference works, speeches, advertising copy, employee manuals, games, and computer programs. Characters found in literary works are protectable if they possess a high degree of distinctiveness. A character that looks and acts like Garfield, the cartoon cat, would infringe on the copyright that protects Garfield.
- *Musical compositions:* A musical composition, including any accompanying words, that is in a fixed form (e.g., a musical score, a cassette tape, a CD, or an MP3 file) is protectable. The owner of the copyright is usually the composer and possibly a lyricist. **Derivative works**, which are works that are new renditions of something that is already copyrighted, are also copyrightable. As a result of this provision, a musician who performs a unique rendition of a song written and copyrighted by Aerosmith or by Metallica can obtain a copyright on his or her effort. Of course, Aerosmith or Metallica would have to consent to the infringement on its copyright of the original song before the new song could be used commercially, which is a common way that composers earn extra income.
- *Computer software:* In 1980, Congress passed the **Computer Software Copyright Act**, which amended previous copyright acts. Now, all forms of computer programs are protected.
- *Dramatic works:* A dramatic work is a theatrical performance, such as a play, comedy routine, newscast, movie, or television show. An entire dramatic work can be protected under a single copyright. As a result, a dramatic work such as a television show doesn't need a separate copyright for the video and audio portions of the show.
- *Pantomimes and choreographic works:* A pantomime is a performance that uses gestures and facial expressions rather than words to communicate a situation. Choreography is the arrangement of dance movements. Copyright laws in these areas protect ballets, dance movements, and mime works.
- *Pictorial, graphic, and sculptural works:* This is a broad category that includes photographs, prints, art reproductions, cartoons, maps, globes, jewelry, fabrics, games, technical drawings, diagrams, posters, toys, sculptures, and charts.

Other categories of items covered by copyright law include motion pictures and other audiovisual works, sound recordings, and architectural works.

As can be seen, copyright law provides broad protection for authors and the creators of other types of copyrightable work. The most common mistake entrepreneurs make in this area is not thinking broadly enough about what they should copyright.

Exclusions from Copyright Protection

There are exclusions from copyright protection. The main exclusion is that copyright laws cannot protect ideas. For example, an entrepreneur may have the idea to open a soccer-themed restaurant. The idea itself is not eligible for copyright protection. However, if the entrepreneur writes down specifically what the soccer-themed restaurant will look like and how it would operate, that description is copyrightable. The legal principle describing this concept is called the **idea–expression dichotomy**. An idea is not copyrightable, but the specific expression of an idea is.

Other exclusions from copyright protection include facts (e.g., population statistics), titles (e.g., *Introduction to Entrepreneurship*), and lists of ingredients (e.g., recipes).

How to Obtain a Copyright

As mentioned, copyright law protects any work of authorship the moment it assumes a tangible form. Technically, it is not necessary to provide a copyright notice or register work with the U.S. Copyright Office to be protected by copyright legislation. The following steps can be taken, however, to enhance the protection offered by the copyright statutes.

First, copyright protection can be enhanced for anything written by attaching the copyright notice, or **"copyright bug"** as it is sometimes called. The bug—a "c" inside a circle—typically appears in the following form: © [first year of publication] [author or copyright owner]. Thus, the notice at the bottom of a magazine ad for Dell Inc.'s computers in 2007 would read © 2007 Dell Inc. By placing this notice at the bottom of a document, an author (or company) can prevent someone from copying the work without permission and claiming that they did not know that the work was copyrighted. Substitutes for the copyright bug include the word "Copyright" and the abbreviation "Copr."

Second, further protection can be obtained by registering a work with the U.S. Copyright Office. Filing a simple form and depositing one or two samples of the work with the U.S. Copyright Office completes the registration process. The need to supply a sample depends on the nature of the item involved. Obviously, one could not supply one or two samples of an original painting. The current cost of obtaining a copyright is $30 per item. Although the $30 fee seems modest, in many cases it is impractical for a prolific author to register everything he or she creates. In all cases, however, it is recommended that the copyright bug be attached to copyrightable work and that registration be contemplated on a case-by-case basis. A copyright can be registered at any time, but filing promptly is recommended and makes it easier to sue for copyright infringement.

Copyrights last a long time. According to current law, any work created on or after January 1, 1978, is protected for the life of the author plus 70 years. For works made for hire, the duration of the copyright is 95 years from publication or 120 years from creation, whichever is shorter. For works created before 1978, the duration times vary, depending on when the work was created. After a copyright expires, the work goes into the public domain, meaning it becomes available for anyone's use.

Copyright Infringement

Copyright infringement is a growing problem in the United States and in other countries, with estimates of the costs to owners at more than $20 billion per year. For example, less than a week after the film was released in the United States, bootleg video discs of the original Harry Potter movie were reported to be for sale in at least two Asian countries.[19] **Copyright infringement** occurs when one work derives from another or is an exact copy or shows substantial similarity to the original work. To prove infringement, a copyright owner is required to show that the alleged infringer had prior access to the copyrighted work and that the work is substantially similar to the owner's.

There are many ways to prevent infringement. For example, a technique frequently used to guard against the illegal copying of software code is to embed and hide in the code useless information, such as the birth dates and addresses of the authors. It's hard for infringers to spot useless information if they are simply cutting and pasting large amounts of code from one program to another. If software code is illegally copied and an infringement suit is filed, it is difficult for the accused party to explain why the (supposedly original) code included the birth dates and addresses of its accusers. Similarly, some publishers of maps, guides, and other reference works will deliberately include bits of phony information in their products, such as fake streets, nonexistent railroad crossings, and so on, to try to catch copiers. Again, it would be pretty hard for someone who copied someone else's copyrighted street guide to explain why the name of a fake street was included.[20]

Current law permits limited infringement of copyrighted material. Consider **fair use**, which is the limited use of copyrighted material for purposes such as criticism, comment, news reporting, teaching, or scholarship. This provision is what allows textbook authors to repeat quotes from magazine articles (as long as the original source is cited), movie critics to show clips from movies, and teachers to distribute portions of newspaper articles. The reasoning behind the law is that the benefit to the public from such uses outweighs any harm to the copyright owner. Other situations in which copyrighted material may be used to a limited degree without fear of infringement include parody, reproduction by libraries, and making a single backup copy of a computer program or a digital music file for personal use.

There are limits, however, to the extent that fair use can be legitimately claimed, as illustrated in this chapter's "Savvy Entrepreneurial Firm" feature.

savvy entrepreneurial firm

Protecting Intellectual Property: Elvis's Memory, and Intellectual Property, Live On
www.elvis.com

Savvy owners of intellectual property are always on the lookout for people who infringe on their intellectual property and take legal action when necessary. In 2003, this scenario played out in a dispute involving a company named Passport Video and the copyright holders of music and videos produced by the late Elvis Presley.

Elvis, affectionately known as "The King" of rock and roll, was a musical icon for more than 20 years, until his death on August 16, 1977. During his career Elvis was very prolific, and a wide variety of people own the copyrights to his music, videos, and films. In the early 2000s, Passport Video, a video production company, produced a video documentary of Elvis's life, named *The Definitive Elvis*. The documentary, which included 16 1-hour episodes, focused on every aspect of Elvis's life, and was priced at $99.00. Each episode contained shots of Elvis performing—many of which were taken from sources that are copyrighted and owned by Elvis Presley Enterprises or others. Passport did not get permission to use the material. As a result, the copyright holders, who caught wind of the production of the video, got together and in August of 2003 decided to sue Passport for copyright infringement.

Passport mounted a defense, claiming that its use of the copyrighted material was fair use and that it had spent over $2 million producing and marketing the documentary. Fair use is a doctrine in U.S. copyright law that allows limited use of copyrighted material without requiring permission from the copyright holder. In general, the following uses are protected under this doctrine:

- Quotation of the copyrighted work for review or criticism or in a scholarly or technical work
- Use in a parody or satire
- Brief quotation in a news report
- Reproduction by a teacher or a student of a small part of the work to illustrate a lesson
- Incidental reproduction of a work in a newsreel or broadcast of an event being reported
- Reproduction of a work in a legislative or judicial proceeding

After listening to both sides, the U.S. District Court ruled in favor of the plaintiffs, saying that fair use didn't apply and Passport should have obtained the appropriate copyright permissions.

Passport persisted, appealing the decision to the Ninth Circuit Court of Appeals, arguing that its documentary of Elvis's life constituted scholarly research and should therefore be protected under fair use. The U.S. District Court disagreed and affirmed the ruling of the lower court. In its ruling, the court said, "The King is dead. His legacy, and those that wish to profit from it, remain very much alive." The court found that Passport's documentary was for commercial use rather than scholarly research, although the commercial nature of the project was not the deciding factor. Instead, the extent to which the copyrighted material was used tipped the decision for the court, which referred to the lower court's original assessment in its ruling. In its decision, the Ninth Circuit Court of Appeals, quoting from the decision of the lower court, said:

> *Passport's use of clips from television appearances, although in most cases of short duration, were repeated numerous times throughout the tapes. While using a small number of clips to reference an event for biographical purposes seems fair, using a clip over and over will likely no longer serve a biographical purpose. Additionally, some of the clips were not short in length. Passport's use of Elvis' appearance on* The Steve Allen Show *plays for over a minute and many more clips play for more than just a few seconds.*

The ruling prevented Passport from moving forward with the sale of its documentary.

In this case, the copyright law did exactly what it is designed to do: protect the legal owners of Elvis's material from copyright infringement.

Questions for Critical Thinking
1. Do you agree with the Ninth Circuit Court's ruling? Why or why not?
2. Why do you think the copyright holders of Elvis's work objected to Passport's video?
3. What can the founder or founders of an entrepreneurial firm learn from this case?

4. Do you think Passport Video acted ethically and honestly and believed that its production was protected by fair use, or do you think the firm was simply using fair use as a way of avoiding paying royalties for the copyrighted material it was using?

Source: H. R. Cheeseman, *The Legal Environment of Business and Online Commerce,* 5th ed. (Upper Saddle River, NJ: Prentice Hall, 2007); Ruling by the United States District Court for the Central District of California in the case of *Elvis Presley Enterprises v. Passport Video,* November 6, 2004.

The rampant illegal downloading and sharing of music—copyright infringement—is a major challenge the music industry is trying to overcome. Hackers are always looking for a new way to skirt the law.

Copyrights and the Internet

Every day, vast quantities of material are posted on the Internet and can be downloaded or copied by anyone with a computer. Because the information is stored somewhere on a computer or Internet server, it is in a tangible form and probably qualifies for copyright protection. As a result, anyone who downloads material from the Internet and uses it for personal purposes should be cautious and realize that copyright laws are just as applicable for material on the Internet as they are for material purchased from a bookstore or borrowed from a library. Because the Internet is still fairly new, the courts have been busy sorting out Internet-related copyright issues.

Copyright laws, particularly as they apply to the Internet, are sometimes difficult to follow, and it is easy for people to dismiss them as contrary to common sense. For example, say that a golf instructor in Phoenix posted a set of "golf tips" on his Web site for his students to use as they prepare for their lessons. Because the notes are on a Web site, anyone can download the notes and use them. As a result, suppose that another golf instructor, in Dallas, ran across the golf tips, downloaded them, and decided to distribute them to his students. Under existing law, the second golf instructor probably violated the intellectual property rights of the first. Arguably, he should have gotten permission from the first golf instructor before using the notes even if the Web site didn't include any information about how to contact the first instructor. To many people, this scenario doesn't make sense. The first golf instructor put his notes on a public Web site, didn't include any information about how to obtain permission to use them, and didn't even include information about how he could be contacted. In addition, he made no attempt to protect the notes, such as posting them on a password-protected Web page. Still, intellectual property rights apply, and the second instructor runs the risk of a copyright infringement suit.

There are a number of techniques available for entrepreneurs and Webmasters to prevent unauthorized material from being copied from a Web site. Password protecting the portion of a site containing sensitive or proprietary information is a common first step. In addition, there are a number of technical protection tools available on the market that limit access to or the use of online information, including selected use of encryption, digital watermarking (hidden copyright messages), and digital fingerprinting (hidden serial numbers or a set of characteristics that tend to distinguish an object from other similar objects).

Trade Secrets

7. Discuss the legal environment that facilitates trade secret protection.

Most companies, including start-ups, have a wealth of information that is critical to their success but does not qualify for patent, trademark, or copyright protection. Some of this information is confidential and needs to be kept secret to help a firm maintain its competitive advantage. An example is a company's customer list. A company may have been extremely diligent over time tracking the preferences and buying habits of its customers, helping it fine-tune its marketing message and target past customers for future business. If this list fell into the hands of one or more of the company's competitors, its value would be largely lost, and it would no longer provide the firm a competitive advantage over its competitors.

A **trade secret** is any formula, pattern, physical device, idea, process, or other information that provides the owner of the information with a competitive advantage in the marketplace. Trade secrets include marketing plans, product formulas, financial forecasts, employee rosters, logs of sales calls, and laboratory notebooks. The medium in which information is stored typically has no impact on whether it can be protected as a trade secret. As a result, written documents, computer files, audiotapes, videotapes, financial statements, and even an employee's memory of various items can be protected from unauthorized disclosure.

Unlike patents, trademarks, and copyrights, there is no single government agency that regulates trade secret laws. Instead, trade secrets are governed by a patchwork of various state laws. The federal **Economic Espionage Act**, passed in 1996, does criminalize the theft of trade secrets. The **Uniform Trade Secrets Act**, which was drafted in 1979 by a special commission, attempted to set nationwide standards for trade secret legislation. Although the majority of states have adopted the act, most revised it, resulting in a wide disparity among states in regard to trade secret legislation and enforcement.

What Qualifies for Trade Secret Protection?

Not all information qualifies for trade secret protection. In general, information that is known to the public or that competitors can discover through legal means doesn't qualify for trade secret protection. If a company passes out brochures at a trade show that are available to anyone in attendance, nothing that is in the brochure can typically qualify as a trade secret. Similarly, if a secret is disclosed by mistake, it typically loses its trade secret status. For example, if an employee of a company is talking on a cell phone in a public place and is overheard by a competitor, anything the employee says is generally exempt from trade secret protection. Simply stated, the general philosophy of trade secret legislation is that the law will not protect a trade secret unless its owner protects it first.

Companies can maintain protection for their trade secrets if they take reasonable steps to keep the information confidential. In assessing whether reasonable steps have been taken, courts typically examine how broadly the information is known inside and outside the firm, the value of the information, the extent of measures taken to protect the secrecy of the information, the effort expended in developing the information, and the ease with which other companies could develop the information. On the basis of these criteria, the strongest case for trade secret protection is information that is characterized by the following:

■ Is not known outside the company
■ Is known only inside the company on a "need-to-know" basis

- Is safeguarded by stringent efforts to keep the information confidential
- Is valuable and provides the company a compelling competitive advantage
- Was developed at great cost, time, and effort
- Cannot be easily duplicated, reverse engineered, or discovered.

Trade Secret Disputes

Trade secret disputes arise most frequently when an employee leaves a firm to join a competitor and is accused of taking confidential information along. For example, a marketing executive for one firm may take a job with a competitor and create a marketing plan for the new employer that is nearly identical to the plan being worked on at the previous job. The original employer could argue that the marketing plan on which the departed employee was working was a company trade secret and that the employee essentially stole the plan and took it to the new job. The key factor in winning a trade secret dispute is that some type of theft or misappropriation must have taken place. Trade secrets can be lawfully discovered. For example, it's not illegal for one company to buy another company's products and take them apart to see how they are assembled. In fact, this is a relatively common practice, which is another reason companies continuously attempt to innovate as a means of trying to stay at least one step ahead of competitors.

A company damaged by trade secret theft can initiate a civil action for damages in court. The action should be taken as soon after the discovery of the theft as possible. In denying the allegation, the defendant will typically argue that the information in question was independently developed (meaning no theft took place), was obtained by proper means (such as with the permission of the owner), is common knowledge (meaning it is not subject to trade secret protection), or was innocently received (such as through a casual conversation at a business meeting). Memorization is not a defense. As a result, an employee of one firm can't say that "all I took from my old job to my new one was what's in my head" and claim that just because the information conveyed wasn't in written form, it's not subject to trade secret protection. If the courts rule in favor of the firm that feels its trade secret has been stolen, the firm can stop the offender from using the trade secret and obtain substantial financial damages.

Trade Secret Protection Methods

Aggressive protection of trade secrets is necessary to prevent intentional or unintentional disclosure. In addition, one of the key factors in determining whether something constitutes a trade secret is the extent of the efforts to keep it secret. Companies protect trade secrets through physical measures and written agreements.

Physical Measures There are a number of physical measures firms use to protect trade secrets, from security fences around buildings to providing employees access to file cabinets that lock to much more elaborate measures. The level of protection depends on the nature of the trade secret. For example, although a retail store may consider its inventory control procedures to be a trade secret, it may not consider this information vital and may take appropriate yet not extreme measures to protect the information. In contrast, a biotech firm may be on the cusp of discovering a cure for a disease and may take extreme measures to protect the confidentiality of the work being conducted in its laboratories.

The following are examples of commonly used physical measures for protecting trade secrets:

- *Restricting access:* Many companies restrict physical access to confidential material to only the employees who have a "need to know." For example, access to a company's customer list may be restricted to key personnel in the marketing department.
- *Labeling documents:* Sensitive documents should be stamped or labeled "confidential," "proprietary," "restricted," or "secret." If possible, these documents should be

LEARNING
Objective

8. Identify the most common types of trade secret disputes.

LEARNING
Objective

9. Describe some of the physical measures that firms take to protect their trade secrets.

secured when not in use. Such labeling should be restricted to particularly sensitive documents. If everything is labeled "confidential," there is a risk that employees will soon lose their ability to distinguish between slightly and highly confidential material.

■ *Password protecting confidential computer files:* Providing employees with clearance to view confidential information by using secure passwords can restrict information on a company's computer network, Web site, or intranet. Companies can also write-protect documents to ensure that employees can read but do not modify certain documents.

■ *Maintaining logbooks for visitors:* Visitors can be denied access to confidential information by asking them to sign in when they arrive at a company facility, wear name badges that identify them as visitors, and always be accompanied by a company employee.

■ *Maintain logbooks for access to sensitive material:* Many companies maintain logbooks for sensitive material and make their employees "check out" and "check in" the material.

■ *Maintaining adequate overall security measures:* Commonsense measures are also helpful. Shredders should be provided to destroy documents as appropriate. Employees who have access to confidential material should have desks and cabinets that can be locked and secured. Alarms, security systems, and security personnel should be used to protect a firm's premises.

Some of these measures may seem extreme. However, unfortunately we live in a world that is not perfect, and companies need to safeguard their information against both inadvertent disclosure and outright theft. Steps such as shredding documents may seem like overkill at first glance but may be very important in ultimately protecting trade secrets. Believe it or not, there have been a number of cases in which companies have caught competitors literally going through the trash bins behind their buildings looking for confidential information.

Written Agreements It is important for a company's employees to know that it is their duty to keep trade secrets and other forms of confidential information secret. For the best protection, a firm should ask its employees to sign nondisclosure and noncompete agreements, as discussed in Chapter 6.

Intellectual property, and the problems that underlie the need for intellectual property to be created, are important enough that firms have been started strictly for the purpose of helping companies solve problems and obtain the intellectual property that they need. An example of a firm that was started for this purpose is InnoCentive, as illustrated in the boxed feature titled "Partnering for Success."

Conducting an Intellectual Property Audit

10. Explain the two primary reasons for conducting an intellectual property audit.

The first step a firm should take to protect its intellectual property is to complete an intellectual property audit. This is recommended for firms regardless of size, from start-ups to mature companies. An **intellectual property audit** is conducted to determine the intellectual property a company owns.

The following sections describe the reasons for conducting an intellectual property audit and the basic steps in the audit process. Some firms hire attorneys to conduct the audit, whereas others conduct the audit on their own. Once an audit is completed, a company can determine the appropriate measures it needs to take to protect the intellectual property that it owns and that is worth the effort and expense of protecting.

Why Conduct an Intellectual Property Audit?

There are two primary reasons for conducting an intellectual property audit. First, it is prudent for a company to periodically determine whether its intellectual property is being properly protected. As illustrated in Table 12.5, intellectual property resides in every department in a firm, and it is common for firms to simply overlook intellectual property that is eligible for protection.

partnering for success

InnoCentive: Helping Firms Solve Problems and Obtain the Intellectual Property That They Need
www.innocentive.com

Imagine if a company's R&D lab could tap into the brainpower of scientists all over the world. That's exactly the capability offered by InnoCentive, a start-up spun out of pharmaceutical giant Eli Lilly & Company.

The service works a little bit like eBay in that it brings buyers and sellers together. On InnoCentive's Web site, a company, called a "seeker," can post a technological problem it is trying to solve and offer a cash award to anyone who can solve the problem. The service was launched in 2001 and can already point to a long list of difficult technology problems that have been solved through its site. Initially, about 400 scientists, called "solvers," signed up to participate. That number has swelled to over 80,000, from all over the world. In fact, the top four solver communities, in terms of numbers, are China, the United States, India, and Russia. The problem that is posed by a seeker is called a "challenge."

The biggest advantage of the service is that it helps companies pose their toughest challenges to a worldwide audience of scientists. No matter how prominent a company's R&D staff is, it can't know everything. This reality played itself out in a story told by Ali Hussein, the vice president of marketing for InnoCentive. A large multinational company was struggling to solve a problem. The company's chief scientist posted the problem on InnoCentive's Web site, and 72 hours later a solution was posted from a petroleum engineer in Kazakhstan. "He had worked on this problem, but neither knew about the other," said Hussein. "We are looking for the uniquely prepared mind."

Here is how the service works. The identity of both the seekers and the problem solvers is known only to InnoCentive. InnoCentive determines whether the criterion of a challenge has been met. Once a match has been made between a seeker and a problem solver, InnoCentive collects the award money, which is exchanged for the intellectual property rights associated

with the solution, and passes it along to the problem solver. Awards range from $20,000 to $100,000, depending on the problem involved. InnoCentive is paid anywhere from a percentage of the award to an amount equaling the award, depending on the circumstances involved. According to a *BusinessWeek* article, the award money that InnoCentive's clients have paid to have problems solved is about one-sixth of what it would have cost to have the same problem solved in-house.

Questions for Critical Thinking

1. To what extent does InnoCentive's service level the playing field between large companies and smaller entrepreneurial firms? Would this leveling effect, if you think it exists, have been possible without the invention of the Internet? Explain your answer.
2. What factors do you think are motivating companies to continually turn to outside sources to innovate on their behalf and help them solve technological problems?
3. If you were the founder of a small entrepreneurial firm, what would be the arguments for and against using services like InnoCentive to innovate on your behalf and solve technological problems, as opposed to building your own R&D capabilities?
4. In general, InnoCentive helps companies solve chemistry-related and biology-related problems. Make a list of other types of problems that could be solved by InnoCentive, or another firm that adopted InnoCentive's business model. If you were starting a firm similar to InnoCentive, what types of problems would your firm try to help its clients solve?

Sources: InnoCentive homepage, www.innocentive.com (accessed June 5, 2006); L. Sanford, "Businesses Must Learn to Let Go," *BusinessWeek*, January 6, 2006; N. Grossman, "InnoCentive is Problem Solver, Inks Deal With Indian Institute," *IndUS Business Journal*, March 15, 2005.

The second reason for a company to conduct an intellectual property audit is to remain prepared to justify its value in the event of a merger or acquisition. Larger companies purchase many small, entrepreneurial firms primarily because the larger company wants the small firm's intellectual property. When a larger company comes calling, the smaller firm should be ready and able to justify its valuation.

TABLE 12.5 Types of Questions to Ask When Conducting an Intellectual Property Audit

Patents	Copyrights
• Are products under development that require patent protection? • Are current patent maintenance fees up to date? • Do we have any business methods that should be patented? • Do we own any patents that are no longer consistent with our business plan that could be sold or licensed? • Do our scientists properly document key discovery dates?	• Is there a policy in place regarding what material needs the copyright bug and when the bug is to be put in place? • Is there a policy in place regarding when copyrightable material should be registered? • Is proper documentation in place to protect the company's rights to use the material it creates or pays to have created? • Are we in compliance with the copyright license agreements into which we have entered?

Trademarks	Trade Secrets
• Are we using any names or slogans that require trademark protection? • Do we intend to expand the use of trademarks in other countries? • Do we need additional trademarks to cover new products and services? • Is anyone infringing on our trademarks?	• Are internal security arrangements adequate to protect the firm's intellectual property? • Are employees that do not have a "need to know" routinely provided access to important trade secrets? • Is there a policy in place to govern the use of nondisclosure and noncompete agreements? • Are company trade secrets leaking out to competitors?

The Process of Conducting an Intellectual Property Audit

The first step in conducting an intellectual property audit is to develop an inventory of a firm's existing intellectual property. The inventory should include the firm's present registrations of patents, trademarks, and copyrights. Also included should be any agreements or licenses allowing the company to use someone else's intellectual property rights or allowing someone else to use the focal company's intellectual property.

The second step is to identify works in progress to ensure that they are being documented in a systematic, orderly manner. This is particularly important in research and development. As mentioned earlier, if two inventors independently develop essentially the same invention, the right to apply for the patent belongs to the person who invented the product first. Properly dated and witnessed invention logbooks and other documents help prove the date an invention was made.

The third step of the audit is to specify the firm's key trade secrets and describe how they are being protected. Putting this information in writing helps minimize the chance that if a trade secret is lost, someone can claim that it wasn't really a trade secret because the owner took no specific steps to protect it.

Chapter Summary

1. Intellectual property is any product of human intellect that is intangible but has value in the marketplace. It is called intellectual property because it is the product of human imagination, creativity, and inventiveness.
2. Patents, trademarks, copyrights, and trade secrets are the major forms of intellectual property. A common mistake companies make is not thinking broadly enough when identifying their intellectual property assets. Almost all companies, regardless of size or age, have intellectual property worth protecting. But to protect this property, firms must first identify it.
3. There are two rules of thumb for determining whether intellectual property is worth the time and expense of protecting. First, a firm should determine whether the intellectual property in question is directly related to its current competitive advantage or could facilitate the development of future competitive advantages. Second, it's important to know whether the intellectual property has independent value in the marketplace.

4. Obtaining a patent is a painstaking, six-step process that usually requires the help of a patent attorney. A patent can be sold or licensed, which is a common strategy for entrepreneurial firms.

5. Trademarks, service marks, collective marks, and certification marks are the four types of trademarks. Trademark law is far-reaching, helping businesses be creative in drawing attention to their products and services. Examples of marks that can be protected include words, numbers and letters, designs and logos, sounds, fragrances, shapes, and colors. Immoral or scandalous matter, deceptive matter, descriptive marks, and surnames are ineligible for trademark protection.

6. Copyright law protects original works of authorship that are fixed in a tangible form of expression. This is a broad definition and means that almost anything a company produces that can be written down, recorded, or videotaped or that takes a tangible form itself (such as a sculpture) is eligible for copyright protection. Examples of copyrightable material include literary works, musical compositions, dramatic works, and pictorial, graphic, and sculptural works.

7. Unlike patents, trademarks, and copyrights, there is not a single government agency that regulates trade secret laws. Instead, trade secrets are governed by a patchwork of various state laws. The federal Economic Espionage Act does criminalize the theft of trade secrets.

8. Trade secret disputes arise most frequently when an employee leaves a firm to join a competitor and is accused of taking confidential information along. Firms protect their trade secrets through both physical measures and written agreements.

9. There are a number of physical measures that firms use to protect trade secrets. These include restricting access, labeling documents, password protecting computer files, maintaining logbooks for visitors, and maintaining adequate overall security measures.

10. There are two primary reasons for conducting an intellectual property audit. First, it is prudent for a company to periodically assess the intellectual property it owns to determine whether it is being properly protected. Second, a firm should conduct a periodic intellectual property audit to remain prepared to justify its value in the event of a merger or acquisition.

Key Terms

assignment of invention
  agreement, 355
business method patent, 354
certification marks, 359
collective marks, 358
Computer Software
  Copyright Act, 362
copyright, 361
copyright bug, 362
copyright infringement, 363
derivative works, 362
design patents, 355

Economic Espionage Act, 366
fair use, 363
first-to-invent rule, 356
idea–expression dichotomy, 362
intellectual property, 349
intellectual property audit, 369
intent-to-use trademark
  application, 361
interference, 356
invention logbook, 356
Lanham Act, 359
one year after first use deadline, 354

patent, 353
patent infringement, 357
plant patents, 355
provisional patent application, 357
secondary meaning, 361
service marks, 358
trademark, 357
trade secret, 366
Uniform Trade Secrets Act, 366
utility patents, 354

Review Questions

1. What distinguishes intellectual property from other types of property, such as land, buildings, and inventory? Provide several examples of intellectual property and describe its importance to a firm.

2. What are the two primary rules for determining whether intellectual property protection should be pursued for a particular intellectual asset?

3. Who is responsible for finding out if one firm is infringing on the intellectual property rights of another? What happens once a case of infringement is discovered?

4. What are the major differences between utility patents and design patents? Provide an example of each.

5. What is a business method patent? Provide an example of a business method patent and explain how having such a patent can provide a firm a competitive advantage in the marketplace.

6. Give an example of a design patent. Explain how having a design patent can provide a firm a competitive advantage in the marketplace.

7. Describe the purpose of an assignment of invention agreement. Is it a good idea for firms to ask their employees to sign assignment of invention agreements?

8. What are the six steps in applying for a patent? Make your answer as thorough as possible.

9. What is a trademark? Provide several examples of trademarks, and describe how they help a firm establish a competitive advantage in the marketplace.

10. What are the three steps involved in selecting and registering a trademark?

11. What is meant by the term *trade dress*?

12. What is a copyright?

13. In the context of copyright law, what is meant by the term *derivative work*? Provide an example of when this concept is important for the creators of copyrightable material.

14. If an entrepreneur has an idea for a themed restaurant based on television game shows (such as *Jeopardy*, *Who Wants to Be a Millionaire?*, or *Hollywood Squares*), is the idea itself eligible for copyright protection? Why or why not?

15. What is a copyright bug? Where would one expect to find the bug, and how is it used?

16. What is meant by the phrase *copyright infringement*? Would you characterize copyright infringement as a minor or as a major problem in the United States and in other countries? Explain.

17. What is a trade secret? Provide an example of a trade secret, and describe how it helps a firm establish a competitive advantage in the marketplace.

18. What information does not qualify for trade secret protection? Make your answer as thorough as possible.

19. What types of physical measures do firms take to protect their trade secrets?

20. What are the two primary purposes of conducting an intellectual property audit? What risks does a company run if it doesn't periodically conduct an intellectual property audit?

Application Questions

1. Amy Rozinski owns a small optics firm named Northland Optics. About 11 months ago, the company invented a new product that has sold extremely well to consumers in a localized area. Amy has decided to wait a year to see how the product does and will then apply for a patent if the product appears to have a good future. Is this a good approach for Amy to follow? Why or why not?

2. Pete Aguilar just invented a new computer mouse that helps relieve the stress that people sometimes feel in their hand after using a computer all day. A friend told Pete to apply for a design patent in order to protect the functionality of his device. Is Pete's friend right?

3. Search the U.S. Patent & Trademark database and determine how many patents Donald E. Weder of Highland Park, Illinois has received. In what area are most of his patents?

4. Tyler Simms just invented a new product that he is convinced is unique and will make him wealthy. The product is a toothbrush with a tube of toothpaste attached to the handle. Tyler is anxious to file a patent application on the product, but when he tells you about the idea, you say—"whoa, lets do a preliminary patent application search first to see if someone else has already patented this idea." What do you find when you help Tyler with the preliminary search?

5. Pam Tarver just opened an information technology consulting company and has thought for a long time about what to name it. She finally settled on the fictitious

name Infoxx. Infoxx is not a word; it is just a bunch of letters that Pam thought looked good together and that her customers would remember. Is Pam's made-up word trademarkable?

6. Search the U.S. Patent & Trademark database to determine if the name Infoxx is available. Is it? If it is available, describe how Pam would go about obtaining a trademark on Infoxx or any other name.

7. Rick Sanford lives in a small community in northern Minnesota. He is planning to open the only fried chicken restaurant in his area and would like to trademark the words *fried chicken*. Because of his special circumstances, can he do this?

8. Helen Downey just finished writing a book about Google, including how the company was started and how it helped pioneer the rapid growth of the Internet. In the book, Helen doesn't reveal anything new about that company and in many cases simply retells stories about the early days of Google that others have told. Still, Helen wrote the book, which took considerable research and work on her part. Can Helen copyright her book?

9. Jackson Blair is the CEO of a small computer company but makes his living going around the country delivering motivational speeches at conventions and corporate events. Although his standard speech isn't written down and hasn't been recorded, Jackson has it committed to memory, which makes it easy for him as he travels from event to event. Is Jackson's speech copyrightable?

10. Maggie Simpson has always admired her Grandmother Thompson's cooking and has considered putting together a cookbook titled *Grandma Thompson's Favorite Recipes*. Some of Grandma's recipes are truly original, and before she writes the book, Maggie would like to copyright several of the most original ones. Can she do this?

11. Jason Scott is the CEO of a small graphic design company in Orlando, Florida. Several months ago, he spent an entire day searching the Web site of Dolphin Graphics, a larger graphics design firm in Miami. From its Web site, Jason was able to put together a list of Dolphin's major customers and is using the list to prospect new customers for his firm. After discovering what he is doing, Dolphin has threatened to sue Jason if he doesn't stop using its customer list, which it claims is a trade secret. Is Jason infringing on Dolphin's trade secrets?

12. Melanie Hays owns a firm near Austin, Texas. Her firm, Secure Plus Health Care, makes disk drives for computers that are used in the health care industry. Recently, Melanie found out that her largest competitor bought several of her disk drives, took them apart to see how they were manufactured, and now plans to integrate into its disk drives some of her disk drive's most innovative features. Melanie is thinking about suing the company for stealing trade secrets. Do you think Melanie's suit will be successful? Why or why not?

13. After working for Prime Optics for 5 years, Sarah Simic went to work for Tech Optical, one of Prime's major competitors. A year later, Tech came out with a new product that made a big splash in the marketplace. Prime Optics sued Sarah, complaining that when Sarah worked at Prime, she was part of a team that developed a nearly identical product that Prime planned to roll out later that year. Sarah said that she lived up to her nondisclosure agreement with Prime and didn't take any documents from Prime to Tech. The only thing that she told her new colleagues at Tech, Sarah said, were the things she remembered about the project she was working on at Prime. Is Sarah in the clear? Why or why not?

14. Two years ago, Mike Carini opened a restaurant called Mike's Italian. To his horror, Mike just found out that several disgruntled customers have launched a Web site with the Internet address www.avoidmikesitalian.com. The site contains testimonials by people who have eaten at Mike's and have not been satisfied. Is there anything that Mike can do to shut down the Web site?

15. The "You Be the VC 1" feature in this chapter focuses on Expresso Fitness, the company that makes Spark, a new type of exercise bike. Make a complete list of the types of intellectual property protection that Expresso Fitness should have on Spark in order to be able to successfully defend the proprietary aspects of its bike and operations.

you be the VC 12.1

Expresso Fitness
www.expressofitness.com

Business Idea: Produce an exercise bike that keeps its users engaged and motivated by turning the bike into a sort of video game.

Pitch: According to the National Center for Health Statistics, 66.5 percent of Americans who are 20 years old or older are overweight or obese. To lose weight and improve their fitness, many people join gyms and start working out on exercise machines, like stationary bikes, treadmills, and Stairmasters. However, for many people, there's one big drawback to this approach: It's boring. The main complaint of people who use exercise bikes or walk on treadmills is that it's hard to stay motivated, because the daily grind of using these types of machines is just too dull.

To combat this problem, Expresso Fitness has designed a stationary bike called the Spark. The new twist that the bike brings to the market is that it helps its riders stay motivated by turning the bike into a sort of video game. The Spark has a built-in computer and flat-panel monitor that allow a user to race against virtual opponents through a variety of simulated outdoor courses, including one that simulates portions of the latest Tour de France course. Unlike the typical exercise bike, the Spark has moveable handlebars to steer you through trails on the screen and a gearshift for tackling hills. And, just like on a real bike,

when you climb a hill on the screen, you have to downshift the bike to keep the pedaling from getting harder. If you're having a particularly good ride and are coming close to a personal record (the bike keeps a record of all of your rides), a cyclist in a yellow jersey will appear and set the pace to help you meet the goal.

The Spark also has a built-in television and built-in music channels, but its main feature is its competitive riding courses. The machine is attached to the Internet so its owners can troubleshoot directly with the company in case of problems. It also allows the company to download new courses to its machines periodically and to keep track of which courses are the most popular. The bike sells in the $5,000 range, plus shipping and installation. Although the bike is designed primarily for gyms and fitness clubs, Expresso Fitness expects the Spark to appeal to highly motivated exercise enthusiasts as well.

Q&A: Based on the material covered in this chapter, what questions would you ask the firm's founders before making your funding decision? What answers would satisfy you?

Decision: If you had to make your decision on just the information provided in the pitch and on the company's Web site, would you fund this firm? Why or why not?

you be the VC 12.2

Major League Gaming
www.mlgpro.com

Business Idea: To establish a professional league for the world's fastest-growing sport—video gaming.

Pitch: More Americans play video games than participate in sports. Although that statement seems astounding, it is backed up by hard data. According to the Entertainment Software Association, 50 percent of all Americans play video games. In addition, 53 percent of those who play video games expect to be playing as much or more in 10 years than they play today.

As interest in video gaming has heated up nationwide, so have organized competitions between video game players. Many people are passionate about video games and spend enormous amounts of time mastering certain games. Naturally, these people like to get together to compete against one another.

Major League Gaming was founded to take advantage of these trends. The company, which is a for-profit professional sports league, has positioned itself as the international sanctioning body for professional video gaming. The main purpose of the organization is to set standards for video game competitions and to sponsor video game tournaments across the country. The company currently sponsors a seven-city tour of matches, which culminates in a final championship game every year. At the matches, individuals and teams battle against each other in video games like Microsoft's Halo 2 for prize money. The matches are set up in hotel conference rooms or convention centers, where as many as 1,200 competitors assemble before 1,000 spectators to play each other. Up to $100,000 in prize money is awarded per tournament.

Major League Gaming will make money through gate receipts, sponsorships, and the selling of television rights to broadcast the tournaments. Some of the early deals the company has inked are promising, including a Cable TV deal with USA Networks. Similar to what the World Poker Tour has done for poker and NASCAR has done for auto racing, the company's ultimate goal is to bring the viewing of video game tournaments to the mass market.

Q&A: Based on the material covered in this chapter, what questions would you ask the firm's founders before making your funding decision? What answers would satisfy you?

Decision: If you had to make your decision on just the information provided in the pitch and on the company's Web site, would you fund this firm? Why or why not?

CASE 12.1 *You Make the Call: Can a Company Patent How It Makes a Peanut Butter and Jelly Sandwich?*
www.smuckers.com; www.albies.com

Bruce R. Barringer,
University of Central Florida
R. Duane Ireland,
Texas A&M University

Introduction

Here's a question that a panel of judges recently decided: Can a company patent how it makes a peanut butter and jelly sandwich? More specifically, in this instance, judges considered whether J. M. Smucker's method of making Uncrustables—which is a crustless peanut butter and jelly sandwich sealed inside soft bread—is worthy of legal protection against imitators. While the nature of this case is interesting, the legal rulings resulting from the case have broader implications. At stake is how generous the patent office should be in awarding patents—an issue with solid arguments on both sides.

There were actually two cases leading up to the case that resulted in the final verdict. The three cases are designated Round 1, Round 2, and Round 3 of Smucker's battle to patent the peanut butter and jelly sandwich.

The case involves Smucker's Uncrustables sandwich. Uncrustables are found in the frozen food section of most grocery stores. They are 2-ounce peanut butter and jelly pockets that come in two flavors—grape and strawberry—and are sealed inside soft bread. They come in boxes of 4, 10, or 18 sandwiches per box. To make an Uncrustables ready to eat, the customer simply needs to let it thaw for 30–60 minutes after being taken out of the freezer.

The Uncrustables was developed in 1995 by David Geske, of Fargo, North Dakota and Len Kretchman, of Fergus Falls, Minnesota. The two started mass-producing them for Midwestern schools. Smucker's took note of their success and bought Geske and Kretchman's company in 1999. The purchase of the company included a general patent on crustless peanut butter and jelly sandwiches (Patent No. 6,004,596) that Geske and Kretchman had obtained.

Round 1: Smucker's vs. Albie's Foods

It wasn't long before Smucker's was defending its turf. In 2001, Smucker's ordered a much smaller firm, Albie's Foods, to stop selling its own crustless peanut butter and jelly sandwich. Albie's was selling the sandwich to a local school district. Albie's fought back and the case was eventually dismissed. In its arguments, Albie's contended that the "pasty"—a meat pie with crimped edges, which the company saw its crustless peanut butter and jelly sandwich as a variation of—had been a popular food in northern Michigan since the immigration of copper and iron miners from England in the 1800s.

Round 2: Smucker's and the Patent Office

Stung by its experience with the case it brought against Albie's, Smucker's returned to the U.S. Patent & Trademark Office to try to get its general patent on crustless peanut butter and jelly sandwiches broadened as a means of being able to better defend the Uncrustables. The patent office rejected the application. The gist of Smucker's argument was that its sandwich's sealed edge is unique and its layering approach, which keeps the jelly in the middle of the sandwich, is one-of-a-kind, and as such, should be protected by law. The patent office disagreed with this view. It said that the crimped edge, which was one of the things Smucker's argued was unique about its sandwich, is similar to the crimped edges in ravioli and pie crusts. In addition, the patent office determined that putting jelly in the middle of a peanut butter and jelly sandwich is hardly unique, and as evidence cited a 1994 *Wichita* (Kansas) *Eagle* newspaper article on back-to-school tips that suggested just this approach.

Round 3: Smucker's Appeals

Smucker's appealed the patent office's decision to the U.S. Court of Appeals. During the court hearings the attorney representing Smucker's argued that the method for making the Uncrustables is unique because the two slices of bread are sealed by compression but are not "smashed" as they are in tarts or ravioli. (Recall, the patent office's original decision compared the process of making Uncrustables to that of making ravioli.) Smucker's further argued that it wouldn't be fair to let other companies simply copy the Uncrustables and benefit from the hard work of Smucker's scientists and the money that the company had invested to produce what it believed was a unique product. The Uncrustables is also a big seller for Smucker's. According to a *Wall Street Journal* article, the product generated sales of $27.5 million in 2004.

Broader Issues Involved

The Smucker's case was watched closely because of the broader issues involved. Critics of the U.S. patent process contend that the U.S. Patent and Trademark Office is too generous when awarding patents—a generosity that they say stifles innovation and drives up the cost for consumers. More than 400,000 patents are filed each year, and nearly 65 percent of them are granted. In the Smucker's case, the critics would argue that Smucker's shouldn't get the patent, because it will deter other food companies from making their own versions of peanut butter and jelly sandwiches, which will keep the price of the Uncrustables high. Advocates of the U.S. patent process argue the opposite—that patents motivate a company like Smucker's to invest in new-product innovation, and that absent patent protection, a company like Smucker's would have no incentive to develop a product like the Uncrustables.

The Court's Ruling

In mid-April 2005, after listening to all the arguments, the U.S. Court of Appeals ruled on whether Smucker's should get the patent it was requesting. Which way do you think the court ruled?

Discussion Questions

1. Go to the U.S. Patent & Trademark Office's Web site (www.uspto.gov) to look up Patent No. 6,004,596. Read the patent. After reading the patent, are you more inclined or less inclined to side with the Smucker's point of view?

2. Type "Uncrustables" into the Google search engine and look at the Uncrustables sandwich. Spend a little time reading about the Uncrustables on Smucker's Web site. Again, after looking over the Web site, are you more inclined or less inclined to side with the Smucker's point of view?

3. In regard to the arguments espoused by the "critics" of the U.S. patent system and the "advocates" of the U.S. patent system, which of the points of view do you agree with? Thinking as an entrepreneur, use your own words to state why you think the critics or the advocates have a stronger point of view.

4. So what do you think happened? Do you think Smucker's did or didn't get the patent it was requesting?

Application Questions

1. What would be the impact, if any, on the entrepreneurial sector of the U.S. economy if patents became increasingly hard to get? Would it help or hurt the majority of entrepreneurial companies? Why?

2. Based on the material in the chapter, are there facets of the U.S. patent system and, in particular, the operations of the U.S. Patent and Trademark Office that you think need to be improved or changed? What are these facets? Using the perspective of an entrepreneur, what changes do you believe should be made?

Source: S. Munzo, "Patent No. 6,004,596: Peanut Butter and Jelly Sandwich." *The Wall Street Journal*, April 5, 2005.

CASE 12.2
A Classic Trademark Dispute: Harley-Davidson versus The Hog Farm
www.harley-davidson.com; www.the-hog-farm.com

Bruce R. Barringer,
University of Central Florida
R. Duane Ireland,
Texas A&M University

Introduction

If you live near Buffalo, New York, and own a motorcycle that needs to be fixed, you're in luck. Just down the road, in West Seneca, New York, you'll find The Hog Farm, a business that is owned by Ron Grottanelli. All the repairs you might want are available from this store. Ron, who likes to be called "Grott," opened The Hog Farm in 1969. From the beginning, the business serviced all makes and models of motorcycles and even built "custom bikes." The custom bikes, according to Grott, have always been particularly special, especially in the early days. They had fancy paint, long front ends, and lots of chrome and were affectionately called "hogs."

As time passed, The Hog Farm grew, becoming a place for motorcycle enthusiasts to gather and enjoy one another's company. To facilitate this, The Hog Farm started hosting a series of yearly events, including flea markets and celebrations over holiday weekends. To brand its events, the company started using the word *hog* more and more often. For example, it began hosting a "Hog Holiday" in July and a "Hog Labor Day Holiday" in September. It also started attaching the word *hog* to many of its products. For example, the company sells an engine degreaser called "Hog Wash."

Of course, from the early days of its existence, Harley-Davidson was one of the motorcycle brands on which The Hog Farm personnel worked the most. Grott remembers the bleakest days in Harley-Davidson's history, during the late 1960s and the early 1970s, when it looked as though the company might go under. During this period, Grott helped keep his customers fired up about motorcycles and feels like he helped keep the Harley-Davidson flame alive. Harley-Davidson recovered, reestablishing itself as a premier motorcycle manufacturer.

As motorcycles continued to gain popularity in the United States, everything was looking good for the Grottanellis and their business until a series of events took place that landed them and The Hog Farm in court opposite, of all companies, Harley-Davidson. In the 1980s, Harley started taking control of the word *hog*, including registering it as a trademark in 1987. Following the registration, Harley started scouring the country looking for shops and companies that used the word when referring to motorcycles. To Harley-Davidson, a hog was a Harley, and no one else was entitled to use that name when referring to a motorcycle. When Harley finally caught up with The Hog Farm, it asked that it change its name and quit using the "hog" when referring to motorcycles or related products.

The Trial

Rather than giving in, however, Grott decided to fight, and a classic trademark dispute took shape. "You certainly have a memory lapse," Grott wrote to the company when it started demanding that he stop using the "hog." "In the 50s, 60s, and 70s, you wanted no association [with the word *hog*]," he wrote. "You cringed whenever Harleys were included in discussions about motorcycles called hogs by the people that rode them; they were a means of escape from the square world." Harley didn't back down, and the case came to a head in federal district court near Buffalo. The courtroom was quite a scene and on opening day was packed with bikers supporting The Hog Farm's right to keep its operations as they had been established. To try to diffuse the image of a big corporation trying to squash the little guy,

a Harley attorney, in an interview outside the courtroom, said, "Harley-Davidson is not trying to hurt these people. All they are trying to do is protect their trademark." The trial, which went on for several days, basically boiled down to Harley's assertion that, by virtue of its trademark, it has exclusive rights to the word *hog* in reference to motorcycles. Grott argued that Harley's assertion was unreasonable because "hog" had been used to refer to motorcycles long before Harley trademarked it in 1987.

The Court's Decision

In announcing its decision, the court reviewed the trial and related the following facts. First, the court found that several periodicals and books have used the term *hog* to refer to motorcycles. The earliest source was a 1935 issue of *Popular Mechanics* that used "Hog Heaven" in the caption of a picture of some large motorcycles. Similarly, in 1965, a *Newsweek* article noted that the motorcycle gang Hell's Angels used the word *hog* to refer to big motorcycles. Further, the court pointed out that several American dictionaries and slang dictionaries defined the word *hog* as a form of large motorcycle.

In addition, the court found that throughout the 1970s and 1980s, many motorcycle enthusiasts began using the word *hog* when referring to Harley-Davidson motorcycles. Initially, Harley attempted to distance itself from any association of that word with its products. It was not until 1981 that Harley-Davidson began to use the word *hog* in its promotions and advertisements. The court found that Harley-Davidson itself recognized that the word referred in a generic sense to large motorcycles before it trademarked the word in 1987. The court therefore concluded that Harley-Davidson couldn't prevent The Hog Farm from using the word *hog* in connection with motorcycles. In essence, the court ruled that Harley-Davidson couldn't appropriate a term that was already in the public domain and turn it into its own private property.

The Hog Farm Lives to See Another Day

So, The Hog Farm lives to see another day, and the Hog Holidays sponsored by the Grottanellis and their company continue without a name change. However, Grott remains irritated with the Harley-Davidson company and the actions it took against his firm. His anger and disappointment are suggested by the following comment, which recently appeared on his firm's Web site: "The Hog Farm celebrates 100 years of the Harley-Davidson motorcycle we love, and the company we hate!" This case provides an important lesson in trademark law, particularly as it pertains to the protection of generic names from becoming the exclusive property of a single company.

Discussion Questions

1. Do you agree or disagree with the court's decision? Why or why not?

2. To what extent do you believe that The Hog Farm would have been harmed if it had lost the decision? If you were Ron Grottanelli and the decision had gone against you, how would you have rebranded your company?

3. What can other companies as well as entrepreneurs who are interested in trademark law learn from the case of Harley-Davidson versus The Hog Farm?

4. For a company like Harley-Davidson, how important a factor is its intellectual property in enabling it to maintain a sustainable competitive advantage? How about The Hog Farm?

Application Questions

1. List several examples of names that are currently controlled by companies that you think are becoming "generic" enough that their trademark protection may be in jeopardy. What can a company do to prevent this from happening?

2. The "You Be the VC 2" feature in this chapter focuses on Major League Gaming, the company that is starting a professional sports league for video gaming. Write a short intellectual property protection plan for this company. Include in the plan all facets of Major League Gaming and its operations that should be protected, and the form of intellectual property protection that should be used in each instance.

Sources: The Hog Farm homepage, www.the-hog-farm.com (accessed May 15, 2006); M. Beebe, "Hog Farm Trial Less Than Easy Ride," *Buffalo News*, October 27, 1996, B1; R. Grottanelli, "History of the Hog Farm," www.the-hog-farm.com (accessed January 28, 2002 and July 21, 2004).

Endnotes

1. BullEx homepage, www.bullexsafety.com (accessed June 21, 2006).
2. Personal interview with Ryan O'Donnell, June 21, 2006.
3. "BullEx Wins Kudos As 'Rising Star' of Business Community at TechConnex Ceremony," *The Business Review,* May 5, 2006.
4. H. R. Cheesman, *The Legal Environment of Business and Online Commerce*, 5th ed. (Upper Saddle River, NJ: Prentice Hall, 2007).
5. R. Ramcharan, "Singapore's Emerging Knowledge Economy: Role of Intellectual Property and Its Possible Implications for Singaporean Society," *The Journal of World Intellectual Property* 9, no. (3 (2006): 316–43; D. E. Bouchoux, *Intellectual Property* (New York: AMA-COM Books, 2001).
6. A. Murray, "Protecting Ideas Is Crucial for U.S. Businesses," *The Wall Street Journal*, November 9, 2005, A2.
7. A. Esteve, "Patent Protection of Computer-Implemented Inventions Vis-À-Vis Open Source Software," *The Journal of World Intellectual Property* 9, no. 3 (2006): 276–300; Bouchoux, *Intellectual Property*.
8. H. J. Knight, "Intellectual Property '101,'" in *From Ideas to Assets*, ed. B. Berman (New York: John Wiley & Sons, 2002), 3–25.
9. Knight, " *Intellectual Property* '101. '"
10. G. Wolff, *The Biotech Investor's Bible* (New York: John Wiley & Sons, 2001).
11. U.S. Patent and Trademark Office, www.uspto.gov (accessed January 10, 2002).
12. Bouchoux, *Intellectual Property*.
13. T. E. Garabedian, "*Primer on Patent Law*," (2004), Wiggin and Dana homepage, www.wiggin.com (accessed January 15, 2006).
14. Bouchoux, *Intellectual Property*.
15. P. Thurrott, "Start-Up Cleans Microsoft's Chimney in Court," *WindowsITPro*, April 14, 2005.

16. A. Gilbert, "Microsoft Settles Infringement Suit," *ZDNet*, July 14, 2005.

17. "Protection Money," *Fortune Small Business*, October 2005.

18. C. E. Bagley and C. E. Dauchy, *The Entrepreneur's Guide to Business Law*, 2nd ed. (Cincinnati: South-Western College Publishing, 2002).

19. *Los Angeles Times*, November 20, 2001.

20. *Wired*, November 11, 2005.

CHAPTER

13

preparing for and
evaluating
the challenges of growth

Getting Personal

with

ANTHONY CASALENA

Best advice I've received

Learn to say no. Saying no means you have focus. You can't pursue all of your ideas

What I'd like to be doing in 10 years

What I'm doing now

Best part about being a student

Not having to worry about living in the real world

Squarespace:
Preparing for Growth Carefully

Midway through his undergraduate program in computer science at the University of Maryland, Anthony Casalena decided to create a personal Web site. He wanted to build a site that would allow him to post photos, start a journal, blog, and accomplish a number of other objectives. Although he was computer savvy, he was frustrated by the Web-site building programs available in that none of the programs were capable of integrating all of the things he wanted to do. So, out of sheer frustration, he created his own Web-site building program to develop his site.[1]

Shortly after the program was finished, a friend of his looked at the program, and offered Casalena $500 for a copy of it. This incident started Casalena thinking that perhaps his program filled a gap in the marketplace—between relatively simple Web-development tools that are for sale at Circuit City and Best Buy and more sophisticated content management solutions that involve professional programmers and run into the thousands of dollars. His program was sophisticated but was also user-friendly and could potentially be sold at a very affordable price.

Casalena took this idea and created a company called Squarespace. Initially, he worked out of his dorm room at Maryland and was in no hurry to start selling the product. Instead of rushing to the marketplace, Casalena wanted to make his product as solid and strong as possible before he tried to sell it. Through some contacts at school, he also became aware of the Hinman CEO program at Maryland. The "CEO" in the title stands for "campus entrepreneurial opportunities." The program, which was formed in the fall of 2000, is designed to create an environment where students can develop business plans, network with the program's corporate partners, and encourage one another's entrepreneurial ambitions. Maryland has even set aside a dorm floor for the program's participants.[2]

Casalena became involved in the Hinman CEO program and moved into the dorm. He continued to work on Squarespace and further develop the product. In November 2003, he tried the product with 300 beta testers—potential customers who volunteer to give the product a try. After incorporating feedback from the beta testers, the product was formally launched in

ANTHONY CASALENA

Founder, Squarespace
University of Maryland
BS Computer Science, 2004

UNIVERSITY OF
MARYLAND

Hardest part of getting funding	First entrepreneurial experience	My advice for new entrepreneurs
Institutional funding? Don't worry about it. Bootstrap your ideas	*Working at an Internet startup company during the tech boom*	*Solve your own problems. Don't try to fix problems that aren't your own*

January 2004. The early stages of the company were managed from Casalena's dorm room until he finished his computer science program at Maryland in December 2004.

Squarespace is now a fully launched company. The product is a robust, yet affordable, Web-site development and management program. Growth has come quickly, which for most entrepreneurs is both a blessing and a curse. To prepare for growth, Casalena has continued to minimize expenses, which has eased cash flow pressures. As a result, Squarespace is profitable and has been able to fund its growth primarily from its earnings. One thing that has been particularly striking to Casalena during his company's early growth phase is the number of requests he has received from individuals and companies that want to partner with Squarespace in some manner. Casalena has passed on most of these offers and has been careful to avoid initiatives that might distract his company from its core mission or force it to move in too many different directions.

A particularly fruitful approach that Casalena has used to help his company grow is purchasing keywords on Google AdWords. As discussed in Chapter 11, when entering a search term into Google, a person sees paid ads at the top (highlighted in blue) and to the right and the search results in the middle of the page. The ads are linked to the topic of the search. If you type "blog" into Google's search box, you will more than likely see a paid ad for Squarespace at the top or to the side of the page. Casalena has found this approach to be a particularly cost-effective way to sell his product.

Squarespace is now serving clients "in the thousands" according to Casalena. Its overhead and headcount remain low (important attributes for the early success of an entrepreneurial venture). Although Casalena is considering adding other products to his company's product mix, he is in no rush to do so. He is committed to growing the company in an even-paced, careful manner and doesn't anticipate any significant departures from the current growth trajectory.

The Starbucks case is encouraging in that the company has gotten off to a good start and has achieved growth in a well-executed manner. It has been able to achieve sustained growth, which is growth in both revenues and profits over a sustained period of time. Evidence shows that relatively few (perhaps as few as one in seven companies) generate sustained, profitable growth.[3] The figures are even lower for rapid-growth firms. According to the National Commission on Entrepreneurship, a rapid-growth firm is a firm that grows its employment by at least 15 percent per year. A study by the commission found that only 4.7 percent of businesses that existed in 1991 grew their employment by at least 15 percent per year or at least doubled their employment over the 5 years from 1992 to 1997.[4] Using this data as a foundation, we consider a **rapid-growth firm** to be one that maintains a growth rate of at least 20 percent per year for 5 consecutive years. We believe that a firm growing at this rate for at least a period of 60 months is truly meeting a full set of expectations in terms of "growing rapidly."

Although challenging, as the data offered indicates, most entrepreneurial ventures try to grow and see it as an important part of their ability to remain successful.[5] This sentiment was expressed by Hewlett-Packard (HP) cofounder David Packard, who wrote that while HP was being built, he and cofounder Bill Hewlett had "speculated many times about the optimum size of a company." The pair "did not believe that growth was important for its own sake" but eventually concluded that "continuous growth was essential" for the company to remain competitive.[6] When HP published a formal list of its objectives in 1996, one of the seven objectives was growth.[7] For HP, acquiring Compaq Computer Corporation contributed to the firm's continuing commitment to growth. Although a controversial strategic decision, acquiring Compaq seems to have provided HP with the breadth and depth it needed to improve its ability to compete against strong computer competitors such as Dell Inc.

Growth is important for a number of additional reasons, as we will explain later in this chapter. For example, it is often necessary for firms to grow to have sufficient promotional opportunities available to retain high-performing employees. Similarly, as a firm's customer base grows, it is often necessary for the firm itself to grow to maintain sufficient scale to meet its customers' needs.

In Chapter 14, we'll introduce you to specific growth strategies. Before considering those materials though, it is necessary for us to describe how firms prepare for growth as well as the important dynamics of the growth process. To do this, we begin this chapter with a general overview of growth and discuss benchmarking as a technique for learning the tactics of successful growth firms. In the second section, we discuss the challenges of growth, including the managerial capacity problem, the day-to-day challenges of growing a firm, and the importance of developing and maintaining professional business practices. Finally, we look at the attributes of successful growth firms. Although growth is difficult to achieve, firms with specific attributes increase their chances of achieving and sustaining profitable growth and of becoming a successful rapid-growth firm.

1. Explain the term *sustained growth.*

Preparing for Growth

Most entrepreneurial firms want to grow. Especially in the short term, growth in sales revenue is an important indicator of an entrepreneurial venture's potential to survive today and be successful tomorrow. Growth is exciting and fast-paced and for most businesses is an indication of success. And, researchers continue to suggest that growth is the single most important indicator of business success.[8] Many entrepreneurial firms have grown quickly and have produced impressive results for their employees and owners: Consider Starbucks, Amgen, Google, and eBay, among others as examples of this.

Growth, however, is a double-edged sword. Indeed, if not managed properly, growth can threaten the stability of a firm's operations in every area, from human resources to finance. Finding the right growth strategy is tricky. Just months after Amazon.com announced that it intended to become "a place where you can buy anything for anyone" (denoting an aggressive growth strategy), the company laid off 15 percent of its workforce and started eliminating product lines under the slogan "Get the Crap Out." In the final analysis, entrepreneurs should remember that growth is a path with the potential to increase the venture's profitability—it is not an end objective itself. Next, we examine some of the specific reasons entrepreneurs decide to try to grow their ventures with the hope of increasing their profitability as a result of their efforts.

2. Describe the potential downsides to firm growth.

Reasons for Firm Growth

Sustained, profitable growth is a result of deliberate intentions. That is not to say, however, that firms can always choose the pace of their growth. A firm's **pace of growth** is the rate at which it is growing on an annual basis. Sometimes firms are forced into a high-growth mode sooner than they would like. For example, when a firm develops a product or service that satisfies a need for many customers such that orders roll in very quickly, it must adjust quickly or risk faltering. In other instances, a firm experiences unexpected competition and must grow to maintain its market share.

This section examines the seven primary reasons firms try to grow to increase their profitability and valuation, as depicted in Figure 13.1.

3. Discuss the seven most common reasons firms pursue growth.

Capturing Economies of Scale   **Economies of scale** are generated when increasing production lowers the average cost of each unit produced. This phenomenon occurs for two reasons. First, if a company can get a discount by buying component parts in bulk, it can lower its variable costs per unit as it grows larger. **Variable costs** are the costs a company incurs as it generates sales. Second, by increasing production, a company can spread its fixed costs over a greater number of units. **Fixed costs** are costs that a company incurs whether it sells something or not. For example, it may cost a company $10,000 per

Although its primary engine of growth has always been expanding the number of its specialty coffee restaurants, Starbucks is increasingly relying on related products like its Frappuccino Coffee Drink to increase sales. Bottled Frappuccino is now available in select grocery and convenience stores as well as in Starbucks' restaurants.

FIGURE 13.1

Appropriate Reasons for Firm Growth

- Economies of scale
- Economies of scope
- Execute a scalable business model
- Market leadership
- Influence, power, and survivability
- Need to accommodate the growth of key customers
- Ability to attract and retain talented employees

month to air-condition its factory. The air-conditioning cost is fixed; cooling the factory will cost the same whether the company produces 10 or 10,000 units per month.

A related reason firms grow is to make use of unused labor capacity or other resources. For example, a firm may need exactly 2.5 full-time salespeople to fully cover its trade area. Because a firm obviously can't hire 2.5 salespeople, it may hire 3 salespeople and expand its trade area.[9]

Capturing Economies of Scope   Economies of scope are similar to economies of scale, except the advantage comes through the scope (or range) of a firm's operations rather than from its scale of production. For example, a company's salesforce may be able to sell 10 items more efficiently than 5, because the cost of travel and the salesperson's salary is spread out over 10 products rather than 5. Similarly, a company like Dell Inc. captures economies of scope in its advertising when the same advertises computers along with printers, other computer-related accessories, and extended warranty plans.

Executing a Scalable Business Model   Some companies have an incentive to grow because they have a scalable business model. A **scalable business model** is one in which increased revenues cost less to deliver than current revenues, so profit margins increase as sales go up. This is typically found in companies that have large up-front costs but have

LEARNING

Objective

4. Explain the advantages of having a scalable business model.

products or services with small per-unit variable costs. The classic example of a scalable business model is computer software. Developing software is very expensive, but delivering a copy of a software program to a consumer is relatively inexpensive. It may cost a software company such as Electronic Arts $10 million to develop a software program, but the per-unit cost of producing and selling the program is small from that point forward, so the profit margin increases as more and more copies are sold. This is why selling downloadable products over the Internet continues to create excitement. It may cost a publisher $1 million to produce a book and pay for an advertising campaign to promote it. If the customer can then download the book, the publisher's cost of goods sold falls to almost zero. Costs involved with printing, shipping, warehousing, and retailing the book are avoided by selling over the Internet.

The catch to having a scalable business model that actually works is having sufficient demand for a product or service to continually drive revenues up. Many of the Internet companies that purportedly had scalable business models never were able to generate enough interest in their products to make the scalability portion of the formula work. In some cases, the up-front costs were also just too high. For example, a firm that is launched to produce computer games that will be sold online has a business model that is theoretically very scalable. The business plan will say that the costs associated with developing the games will be covered by sales that involve low variable costs and that margins will increase as more and more copies of the games are sold. This works, however, only if increasing numbers of consumers buy the games.

Market Leadership **Market leadership** occurs when a firm holds the number-one or the number-two position in an industry or niche market in terms of sales volume. Many firms work hard to achieve market leadership, to realize economies of scale and economies of scope, and to be recognized as the brand leader. Being the market leader also permits a firm to use slogans such as "Number 1 Software Producer in America" in its promotions, helping it win customers and attract talented employees as well as business partners.

Research evidence confirms the importance of market leadership to achieving growth. In each of the industries included in the study, the market leader grew faster than the industry growth rate. For example, in the athletic shoe industry, Nike's 27 percent yearly growth rate outpaced the industry growth of 6 percent per year for the period 1987–1997. A similar pattern was observed for Coca-Cola and Harley-Davidson in their respective industries.[10]

Influence, Power, and Survivability Larger businesses usually have more influence and power than smaller firms in regard to setting standards for an industry, getting a "foot in the door" with major customers and suppliers, and garnering prestige. In addition, larger businesses can typically make a mistake yet survive more easily than entrepreneurial ventures. Commenting on this issue, Jack Welch, GE's former CEO, once said, "Size gives us another big advantage; our reach and resources enable us to go to bat more frequently, to take more swings, to experiment more, and unlike a small company, we can miss on occasion and get to swing again."[11]

A firm's capacity for growth affects its survival in additional ways. For example, a firm that stays small and relies on the efforts and motivation of its founder or a small group of people is vulnerable to the loss of their skills or interest in the firm. Once a firm grows, however, and has a larger staff and more products and services to offer, it usually gains momentum and is no longer as dependent on the efforts and motivation of a small number of founders or employees.

Need to Accommodate the Growth of Key Customers Sometimes firms are compelled to grow to accommodate the growth of a key customer. For example, if Intel has a major account with an electronics firm buying a large number of its semiconductor chips and the electronics firm is growing at a rate of 20 percent per year, Intel may have to add capacity each year to accommodate the growth of its customer or else risk losing some or all of its business.

Ability to Attract and Retain Talented Employees The final reason that firms grow is to attract and retain high-quality personnel. It is natural for talented employees to want to work for a firm that can offer opportunities for promotion, higher salaries, and increased levels of responsibility. Growth is a firm's primary mechanism to generate promotional opportunities for employees, while failing to retain key employees can be very damaging to a firm's growth efforts. High turnover is expensive, and in knowledge-based industries in particular, such as biotechnology and film production, a company's number-one asset is the combined talent, training, and experience of its employees. In less knowledge-intensive settings, turnover may not be as critical, but it is still costly. Based on estimates from Merck & Company, Hewlett-Packard, and *Fortune* magazine, the average cost of turnover is 1.5 times the employee's salary.[12] Entrepreneurial ventures rarely have the excess financial capital needed to support the unfavorable relationship between employee hiring and turnover.

Although each of the reasons for growth just discussed are important, a firm should be careful to grow prudently. Establishing a relationship with Wal-Mart or Costco might seem like a dream come true for a consumer products firm, but the relationship might cripple the firm if it isn't a good fit or the large retailer captures the majority of the venture's profits. This scenario played itself out at Timbuk2, a manufacturer of urban shoulder bags. Timbuk2 forged a relationship with CompUSA to carry its bags. Timbuk2 quickly realized it had made a mistake and exited the relationship, as described in this chapter's "Savvy Entrepreneurial Firm" boxed feature.

Benchmarking Against Successful Growth Firms

5. Describe the basic idea behind benchmarking and how benchmarking can be used to help a firm execute a successful growth strategy.

By **benchmarking**, a firm improves the quality of an activity by identifying and copying the methods of other firms that are particularly successful in that activity. Firm growth provides an excellent opportunity for benchmarking. For example, if a small agricultural products firm in the Midwest decided to start exporting to Europe, it would be wise to identify other agricultural products firms in the Midwest that are successfully exporting to Europe so that it could study their methods and experiences. Usually, if the firm that a company is trying to "benchmark against" doesn't see it as a competitor, it will be helpful and supportive of the benchmarking effort. There are many well-known examples of firms that have successfully "benchmarked" against one another. For example, Ford Motor Company fashioned its Internet-based enterprise FordDirect.com along the lines of Dell's highly successful built-to-order concept.

While benchmarking typically involves copying the methods of a specific firm, a broader approach to benchmarking includes collecting information from a variety of sources about how firms meet specific challenges. The broader approach, which has been made possible largely as the result of the Internet, is exemplified by Nicole Pitell, the founder of Total Chaos Fabrication, a company that builds suspension parts for off-road vehicles. Pitell routinely surfs off-road Web sites and chat rooms where she picks up valuable industry information, such as which supplier's suspensions are holding up and how much discretionary income off-road racers are spending on their trucks. As the result of information she collected via this method, Pitell decided to reposition her company as a fabricator of high-end custom parts (rather than more generic parts)—a niche that has differentiated her company from its competitors and has contributed to higher sales and profits. "Benchmarking, Pitell concludes, "is the reason our company still exists."[13]

Challenges of Growth

Although growth has many advantages for the entrepreneurial firm, including broader access to markets, an enhancement in a firm's reputation and the opportunity to work with

savvy entrepreneurial firm

Timbuk2: Bagging the Right Customers Rather Than the Biggest Ones
www.timbuk2.com

In early 2003, Mark Dwight, the CEO of Timbuk2, was on the top of the world. Timbuk2, the San Francisco-based manufacturer of urban shoulder bags, had just inked a deal with CompUSA to carry its bags. "I thought it was our big break," Dwight recalls.

Yet just 3 months later, Dwight had second thoughts. It wasn't the sales. Sales were booming. But financially, Timbuk2 was being squeezed by the relationship. CompUSA's slim margins and high-volume demand were difficult for Timbuk2 to cope with. In addition, Dwight feared that selling through a mainstream retailer like CompUSA would change how consumers viewed his company. He wanted to see his company increase sales, but he didn't want it to lose its quirkiness and unique appeal either.

So Dwight cancelled the CompUSA deal and refocused Timbuk2. In refocusing the company, he compared Timbuk2 to Coach, which is a billion-dollar company but sells primarily through specialty stores. Specialty stores, like the Sharper Image, the Discovery Channel Store, and the Apple Computer Store, appeal to consumers who prioritize quality and brand image over price. This attribute of specialty stores allows vendors like Timbuk2 to earn higher margins (than they would earn at a big-box retailer like CompUSA), which compensates for lower-volume sales. Selling simultaneously through specialty stores and big-box retailers is difficult for a firm like Timbuk2. The large retailers invariably insist on a lower price point then the specialty retailer, which forces the vendor to either undercut the sales price of the specialty

retailers or enhance the product sold through the large retailer in some way to increase the price. In Timbuk2's case, the bags it sold through CompUSA were bundled with extra accessories to avoid undercutting the sales prices of its other retailers.

The results of Dwight's decision have been impressive. Timbuk2's sales have more than doubled since 2003. The company has an increasingly attractive product line, which is sold both online and through specialty stores throughout the United States.

Questions for Critical Thinking

1. Do you think Timbuk2 made the right decision in canceling the deal with CompUSA? What were the pluses and minuses of making this decision?
2. According to the feature, Timbuk2's CEO Mark Dwight worried that selling through CompUSA would change the way consumers viewed his company. Describe, in more detail, what you think Dwight was worried about in this area.
3. Which of the seven reasons for firm growth are the most motivating for Timbuk2?
4. Identify another consumer products firm that sells primarily through specialty retailers rather than big-box stores like CompUSA, Wal-Mart, and Target. Briefly describe whether you think the retailer would be hurt by selling through a big-box store.

Sources: Timbuk2 homepage, www.timbuk2.com (accessed on July 7, 2006); A. Tilin, "Bagging the Right Customers," *Business 2.0*, May 2005, 56–57.

---

larger and more experienced channel partners, growth is a challenging and rigorous process.[14] Firm growth typically involves raising additional capital, recruiting new employees, learning how to supervise a larger organization, and accepting more risk. To illustrate how fast some companies grow, Siebel Systems, a company that makes customer relationship management (CRM) software, started in 1993 with $50,000. Just 5 years later, in 1998, the company had $391 million in revenue. At the end of 2005, Siebel reported $1.42 billion in sales.

The challenges of growth impose an emotional toll on entrepreneurs and managers as well. A PricewaterhouseCoopers *Trendsetter Barometer* surveyed CEOs of America's fastest-growing firms. Thirty-two percent of those interviewed said that their own inability to manage or reorganize their business could be an impediment to growth over the next 12 months. In the press release announcing the results of the survey, a Pricewaterhouse Coopers spokesman speculated on the reasons for this finding:

> Consider how much more complex management has become. In addition to running day-to-day operations and planning for the future, CEOs of growing companies must navigate their way through the challenges of strategic alliances, outsourcing, joint ventures, mergers and acquisitions, the worker shortage, and the Federal Reserve Board's next move, just to name a few.[15]

This type of sentiment should not discourage entrepreneurs but should alert them to the challenges involved. Let's look more closely at these challenges.

Managerial Capacity

6. Describe the managerial capacity problem and how it inhibits firm growth.

In her thoughtful book *The Theory of the Growth of the Firm*, Edith T. Penrose argues that firms are collections of productive resources that are organized in an administrative framework.[16] As an administrative framework, the primary purpose of a firm is to package its resources together with resources acquired outside the firm for the production of products and services at a profit. As a firm goes about its routine activities, the management team becomes better acquainted with the firm's resources and its markets. This knowledge leads to the expansion of a firm's **productive opportunity set**, which is the set of opportunities the firm feels it's capable of pursuing. The opportunities might include the introduction of new products, geographic expansion, licensing products to other firms, exporting, and so on. The pursuit of these new opportunities causes a firm to grow.

Penrose points out, however, that there is a problem with the execution of this simple logic. The firm's administrative framework consists of two kinds of services that are important to a firm's growth—entrepreneurial services and managerial services. **Entrepreneurial services** generate new market, product, and service ideas, while **managerial services** administer the routine functions of the firm and facilitate the profitable execution of new opportunities. However, the introduction of new product and service ideas requires substantial managerial services (or managerial "capacity") to be properly implemented and supervised. This is a complex problem because if a firm has insufficient managerial services to properly implement its entrepreneurial ideas, it can't simply quickly hire new managers to remedy the shortfall. It is expensive to hire new employees, and it takes time for new managers to be socialized into the firm's culture, acquire firm-specific skills and knowledge, and establish trusting relationships with other members of their firms.[17] When a firm's managerial resources are insufficient to take advantage of its new product and services opportunities, the subsequent bottleneck is referred to as the **managerial capacity problem**. James Vincent, former CEO of Biogen Inc., an entrepreneurial biotech firm, has argued convincingly in interviews that this capacity issue is his firm's number-one growth constraint.[18]

As the entrepreneurial venture grows, it encounters the dual challenges of adverse selection and moral hazard. **Adverse selection** means that as the number of employees a firm needs increases, it becomes increasingly difficult for it to find the right employees, place them in appropriate positions, and provide adequate supervision.[19] The faster a firm grows, the less time managers have to evaluate the suitability of job candidates and the higher the chances are that an unsuitable candidate will be chosen. **Moral hazard** means that as a firm grows and adds personnel, the new hires typically do not have the same ownership incentives as the original founders, so the new hires may not be as motivated as the founders to put in long hours or may even try to avoid hard work. To make sure the new hires are doing what they are employed to do, the firm will typically hire monitors (i.e., managers) to supervise the employees. This practice creates a hierarchy that is costly and isolates the top management team from its rank-and-file employees.

The basic model of firm growth articulated by Penrose is shown in Figure 13.2, and Figure 13.3 shows the essence of the growth-limiting managerial capacity problem.[20] Figure 13.3 indicates that the ability to increase managerial services is not friction free. It is constrained or limited by (1) the time required to socialize new managers, (2) how

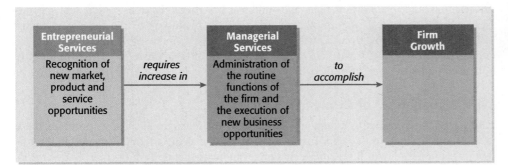

FIGURE 13.2

Basic Model of Firm Growth

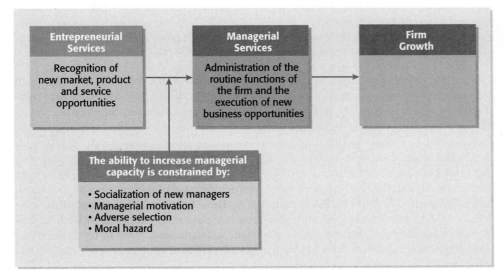

FIGURE 13.3

The Impact of Managerial Capacity

Source: Based on material in E. T. Penrose, *The Theory of the Growth of the Firm* (Oxford: Basil Blackwell, 1959).

motivated entrepreneurs and/or managers are to grow their firms, (3) adverse selection, and (4) moral hazard.

The reality of the managerial capacity problem is one of the main reasons that entrepreneurs and managers worry so much about growth. Growth is a generally positive thing, but it is easy for a firm to overshoot its capacity to manage growth in ways that will enhance the venture's sales revenues and profits.

180s is an example of a company that mismanaged its growth. The firm makes sports apparel and accessories and was made famous by its patented ear warmers that wrap around the back of a person's head and fold into tiny disks. Throughout the 1990s, the company, backed by nearly $3.5 million in funding, grew and added an innovative yet somewhat eclectic list of products to go along with the ear warmers. The products included a radio-controlled kite-glider, a collapsible beach mat, and a talking children's lunch bag. To accelerate its growth, 180s established a separate brand, Kelsyus, to develop and sell additional products, which included sunglasses, beach towels, pool flotation devices, and a line of collapsible beach chairs that turned into backpacks. Firm sales increased from $1 million in 1999 to $7.4 million in 2000, and the number of employees almost doubled.

But behind the scenes things weren't going so well. The growth didn't produce profits and the company was continually raising funds to fuel its rising sales. The company also changed its distribution strategy in 2003—from selling through large sporting goods stores to specialty shops. The idea was to earn high margins through the specialty stores and then as products aged, pass them along to the larger retailers. As part of the new strategy, 180s also decided to sponsor a team of nonprofessional athletes—Team 180s—which proved to be very expensive.

In early 2004, sales stalled, partly because of the shift in distribution strategy. At the same time, the company finances were stretched to their limit, as the result of mounting debt and an ongoing effort to introduce still new products. By mid-2004, the company was no longer able to sustain itself financially and was bought out by a distressed debt specialist. As an indication of the amount of pressure the managers of the firm were under just prior to the buyout, Brian Le Gette, one of the 180s founders, told one of the venture capitalists involved that it was like "being in the jaws of (a) monster."[21] The firm literally collapsed under the weight of its own growth.

Typical Challenges of Growing a Firm

7. Discuss the day-to-day challenges of growing a firm.

Along with the overarching challenges imposed by the managerial capacity problem, there are a number of day-to-day challenges involved with growing a firm, discussed in the following sections. As you'll see, these challenges indicate that no firm operates in a competitive vacuum. By this we mean that the actions one firm takes to grow will cause reactions from competitors. In turn, the firm trying to grow will respond to its competitors' responses, generating what is called a series of action–reaction competitive moves. Thus, entrepreneurs must recognize that the efforts they take to grow their firms will be recognized and that responses to those actions by competitors will be forthcoming.

Cash Flow Management As discussed in Chapters 8 and 10, as a firm grows, it requires an increasing amount of cash to service its customers. In addition, a firm must carefully manage its cash on hand to make sure it maintains sufficient liquidity to meet its payroll and cover its other short-term obligations. Growth usually increases rather than decreases the challenges involved with cash flow management because an increase in sales means that more cash will be flowing into and out of the firm. Some firms deal with potential cash flow shortfalls by establishing a line of credit at a bank or by raising investment capital. Other firms deliberately restrict the pace of their growth to avoid cash flow challenges. The latter option is preferred by Dave Schwartz, the founder of Rent-A-Wreck, a discount car rental company, who grew his firm through earnings rather than debt or investment capital. Commenting on this issue, Schwartz said, "One of the main things I tell people starting out is not to grow too quickly. Often it's better to grow slowly, and when you do expand, try to grow with cash flow."[22]

Price Stability If firm growth comes at the expense of a competitor's market share, a price war can result. For example, if an entrepreneur opens a video store near a Blockbuster that begins to erode Blockbuster's market share, Blockbuster will probably fight back by lowering prices. Because a price war (especially a longer-term one) typically helps no one but the customer, any growth strategy should consider competitors' responses and their effect on price stability.

Quality Control Growth is typically accomplished by an increase in activity. This means that a firm must handle more service requests and paperwork and contend with more customers, stakeholders, and vendors. If a firm does not properly increase its resources to manage these challenges, then product or service quality may decline. Part of the key to having sufficient resources to maintain quality during periods of high activity is to focus a firm's operations on the most important tasks and to avoid becoming distracted. Affirming this point, Rich Field, the founder of Rick's Picks, a New York company specializing in homemade pickles, said, "Focus is everything—and I'm cognizant of spreading myself too thin at times."[23]

Capital Constraints Capital constraints are an ever-present problem for growing firms. Several of the strategies for firm growth that we discuss in Chapter 14, including strategic alliances and licensing, are attractive because they help meet this challenge.

Developing and Maintaining Professional Business Practices

Many firms grow quickly and do not take the time to develop formal management systems or procedures. Although this approach may work for a while, it is rarely, if ever, sustainable. In fact, the four basic functions of management—planning, leading, organizing, and controlling—may be more important in growth firms than in any other type of organization.

As a firm grows, it often needs new facilities and employees to manage the growth. Here, a group of entrepreneurs studies the floor plan for a new building. While often necessary, constructing a building and hiring employees place a strain on the finances of an entrepreneurial firm.

Sustainable growth is difficult and challenging and takes a lot of savvy to pull off, and growth-oriented firms are typically strapped for resources and can ill afford management miscues that waste limited or constrained financial capital.

Some firms recognize too late that they need to professionalize their business practices and stumble badly under the weight of rapid growth. Oracle, which develops information management software, almost made this mistake. Commenting on his firm's experience, Ray Lane, Oracle's former chief operating officer, said,

> We were at a billion dollars in revenue, and you cannot run a billion dollar company the way we were doing it. We had to make sure the business was run using professional business practices. This place is basically under control now, we understand our business pipeline, and we have a professional relationship with our customers, instead of the "*run-and-shoot*" offense we had in the 1980s.[24]

The need for an organization to grow must be tempered by the need to maintain control of growth. The trick is to find the right balance between the ability to move quickly and seize market opportunities and the need for a well-managed growth plan and professional business practices. These issues are germane to our analysis of LA Gear in this chapter's "What Went Wrong" feature.

Myths About Growth

There are several common myths about firm growth that have the potential to confuse or misdirect entrepreneurs and managers. Let's look at the three most pervasive ones.

Myth 1: Growth companies are predominantly computer software and health care companies Because so much attention has been paid to how quickly some well-known technology and health care companies have grown, such as Cisco Systems, Google, and Amgen, it is easy to get the idea that growth companies are predominantly technology and health care companies. Although technology and health care companies are represented in any list of rapid-growth firms, they do not necessarily dominate. For example, the 2006 *Fortune* list of the 100 fastest-growing publicly traded small firms in America included just 21 health care firms and 10 software companies. Industries such as energy (10 firms), industrial equipment (six firms), and consumer products (seven firms) were also well represented on the list.[25]

LEARNING Objective

8. Identify the three myths surrounding firm growth.

LA Gear: How Managing Growth Poorly Can Cost a Firm Its Business
www.lagear.com

LA Gear was launched in 1979 as a manufacturer of sweatshirts and jeans. In the early 1980s, however, the firm's leaders become very impressed by Reebok's success with aerobics shoes, causing the firm to begin selling its own line of shoes—with a distinctive, "hip" Los Angeles style. LA Gear's initial products were enormous hits. First, it produced a line of "Valley Girl" sneakers for teen girls and young women. The shoes were made of denim or patent leather and were adorned with feminine fringes. Then, in the mid-1980s, the company created children's shoes and walking shoes with small lights in the heels that blinked when the walker's soles hit the ground. The shoes, dubbed L.A. Lights, flew off the shelves, and it seemed as though LA Gear couldn't miss. In fact, the company's sales increased from $11 million in 1985 to $820 million in 1990.

This early success with customers caught the attention of investors, causing LA Gear to become the quintessential hot stock. After going public in 1986, the stock's split-adjusted price of $3 a share in 1987 soared to $50 a share within 2 years. But just as quickly as LA Gear heated up, it turned cold. The company filed for Chapter 11 bankruptcy protection in January 1998. This is a pretty astonishing turn of events, don't you think? Given its success, what did go wrong for LA Gear? Three things, all related to the hazards of rapid growth, sealed the company's fate.

First, instead of focusing its efforts on marketing research and product quality, rapid growth was LA Gear's first priority. When Robert Greenberg, one of the company's cofounders, saw an opportunity for LA Gear to expand, he took it regardless of whether convincing marketing research was available. Later, after being forced from the company in the early 1990s, Greenberg admitted, "I love to build. That's why I get in trouble; building too much." Second, in its thirst for growth, LA Gear quickly moved beyond producing shoes for teen girls and young women and rolled out a full line of sneakers to appeal to a broad spectrum of customers—including high-performance shoes for serious athletes. At the same time, the company branched into athletic clothing and accessories. Without doing anything to change its brand, which most people still associated with teenagers and young girls, LA Gear was now trying to be all things to all people. Quality started to suffer. In fact, in a particularly embarrassing moment for the company, one of the company's high-performance athletic shoes, worn by a

Marquette University basketball player, lost its sole during a nationally televised game.

Finally, LA Gear found that a company that lives by the notion of "cool" can also die by that notion. As a result of failing to change its image before it branched out, the company produced shoes that just didn't sell. Most people still saw LA Gear as a company that was good at making feminine-looking shoes for young girls regardless of how many markets it entered. As a result, by 1991, LA Gear had 12 million shoes in its warehouses that nobody wanted and only $1.5 million in cash. Although the company tried various strategies through the early and mid-1990s to survive, it never fully recovered. Today, LA Gear is a relatively minor player in athletic products. However, it continues to try to provide what it calls "the ultimate Los Angeles gear" for customers and the games they want to play. In 2004, LA Gear signed Luke Walton (son of the famous Bill Walton) to wear the firm's basketball shoes. This was a Los Angeles–specific decision in that Luke Walton is from the area and played his rookie season in 2004 with the Los Angeles Lakers.

LA Gear's experiences illustrate the many hazards of growth. In retrospect, even though LA Gear suffered from some obvious miscues, even under the best of circumstances rapid growth has to be managed carefully and prudently to be successful.

Questions for Critical Thinking
1. Using materials in this chapter, develop a list of actions LA Gear could have taken to better manage its growth during the 1980s and 1990s.
2. Do you think that the issues of moral hazard and adverse selection could have contributed to LA Gear's problems as described in this feature? If so, how?
3. What do you think LA Gear could have done to grow successfully?
4. Talk to some of your friends who are involved with sports. See if they are familiar with LA Gear and its products. If they are, how satisfied are they with those products? If they aren't satisfied, ask if there is anything the firm could do to entice them to buy more of its products.

Sources: LA Gear homepage, www.lagear.com (accessed July 7, 2006); W. Joyce, N. Nohria, and B. Roberson, *What Really Works* (New York: HarperBusiness, 2003); D. Darlin, "Getting Beyond a Market Niche," *Forbes*, November 22, 1993, 106.

Myth 2: Rapid-growth firms emerge only in rapid-growth industries Another common belief is that rapid-growth firms emerge primarily in rapid-growth industries. Of course, rapid-growth firms do exist in rapid-growth markets, but there are many examples of firms in fairly ordinary industries that have maintained impressive growth rates. For example, Momentum Marketing Services, a 1995 start-up, is consistently ranked on lists of rapid-growth firms. Momentum is in the advertising and marketing industry, which is a relatively low-growth industry. Its secret is that it develops innovative promotional campaigns. For example, Momentum was hired by GE Financial Services to help it introduce its Web site. Instead of running ordinary ads, the company dropped 5,000 wallets in office lobbies, elevators, and train stations in 10 cities. People who picked up a wallet and opened it were invited to visit GE Financial Service's Web site to see if they had won a prize. (The company even discreetly filmed people's behavior when they noticed the wallets on the floor; several news programs aired the footage.)[26]

For most firms such as Momentum Marketing Services, rapid growth is dependent more on the ability to be creative and establish a leadership position within a chosen target market than on the ability to ride the wave of a rapidly growing market. In fact, rapidly growing markets are not always healthy markets for long-term participation in that they often burn out relatively quickly as capacity catches up with demand and consumers move on to the next fad or new technology.[27]

Myth 3: To grow quickly, you must have a first-mover advantage As discussed in Chapter 3, a first-mover advantage is not always advantageous. Several firms have pioneered industries and grown quickly, such as Yahoo! in the Internet search engine industry and Cisco Systems in routers, but many firms have grown quickly by entering an industry later on. FedEx in overnight delivery, Nucor in steel, Google in Internet search, and Southwest Airlines in air travel are examples of non-first-mover firms that have been exceptionally successful. More specifically, while these companies were not first in their industries, they have sustained impressive growth rates.[28]

Attributes of Successful Growth Firms

Many firms cannot effectively manage the complexities and demands associated with the growth process, in part because entrepreneurs and their advisers are not fully aware of the attributes of successful growth firms. Let's look at the systematic differences that tend to exist between growth firms and firms that are unable to achieve and sustain growth. These attributes—summarized in Table 13.1—also offer a solution, at least in part, to the challenges of growth described previously.

LEARNING Objective

9. Identify the most prevalent growth-related firm attributes.

TABLE 13.1 Growth-Related Firm Attributes

Attribute	Description
Growth-oriented vision	A growth-oriented vision and/or mission statement clearly communicate to stakeholders the importance of growth to an organization.
Commitment to growth	A drive and commitment to achieve growth is frequently mentioned as a necessary precursor for successful growth.
Business growth planning	Planning helps a firm organize for growth and address the relevant managerial and strategic issues necessary to maintain growth.
Participation in business alliances	Business alliances help firms share costs, increase speed to market, gain economies of scale, and gain access to essential resources, knowledge, and foreign markets.
Geographic location that facilitates knowledge absorption	A firm located in a geographic area that is in close proximity to important external sources of knowledge will have better access to the knowledge and will be able to substitute a portion of the externally derived knowledge for more expensive internally generated knowledge.

Growth-Related Firm Attributes

The presence of certain firm attributes, or qualities, facilitates the growth process. The attributes are discussed in the following sections.

Growth-Oriented Vision A **growth-oriented vision**, whether it is articulated through a vision statement, a mission statement, a values statement, or some other means, helps a firm crystallize the importance of growth for its stakeholders and ensures that its major decisions are made with growth in mind.[29] It is not uncommon for a firm to formally articulate its vision for growth. A study by two Deloitte consultants reported that nearly 60 percent of the rapid-growth firms they are acquainted with have put their growth vision in writing. In contrast, only 15 percent of the slow-growth firms they are familiar with had done the same.[30]

The importance of documenting a growth-oriented vision is supported by a broad-based global study by A. T. Kearney. Of the companies surveyed, 83 percent of the firms that are growing have a growth vision that is well defined and well communicated. In addition, more than half the growth firms said that articulating a growth vision was the turning point that drove them toward new found growth.[31]

10. Describe the importance of having a commitment to growth.

Commitment to Growth The less clear or more vague concept of **commitment to growth** deals with the extent to which a firm is committed to pursuing growth. For growth to take place on a continual basis, it must be a deliberate choice made by the firm's owners/entrepreneurs and managers.[32] Thomas L. Doorley III, founder of Braxton Associates, an international consulting firm, has emphasized the importance of both a growth-oriented vision and a commitment to growth. Drawing on the experiences of his consulting practice, Doorley wrote, "We find that companies that grow actually take time to write down something that hammers out the growth theme in their vision, mission, or values statement." He quotes one chief operating officer who wrote this growth mission as saying, "We want to take advantage of our key assets—our brands, technologies, people, and alliances—to lead our key competitors in profitable market share growth." This mission is effective, says Doorley, "because it is high-level, yet tactical—any person can understand it."[33]

Business Growth Planning **Business growth planning** is the process of setting growth-related goals and objectives, then mapping out a plan to achieve those goals and objectives.[34] The literature on planning suggests that firms that plan in a conscientious, thorough manner increase their chances of reaching their growth objectives.[35] The literature also suggests that planning helps entrepreneurs make decisions more quickly than trial-and-error—an attribute that is likely to be important when an entrepreneur is faced with a growth-related decision.[36]

Part of business growth planning involves selecting a market niche in which firm growth can realistically compete. An awareness of this issue led Philip McCaleb, the founder of Genuine Scooter Company, to focus on selling scooters rather than motorcycles. Scooters, which were pop-culture icons in the 1950s and 1960s, are making a comeback, particularly in large cities. Commenting on his decision to focus on scooters rather than motorcycles, which reflects a conscientious plan for firm growth, McCaleb said:

> I always wanted to grow and compete but there is no way we can compete, or want to compete, with the Hondas or the Yamahas. We carefully look to compete on a scale that focuses on niche, on service, and quality."[37]

Participation in Business Partnerships As emphasized in the "Partnering for Success" features throughout this book, participation in business partnerships also spurs growth. These relationships include joint ventures, networks, consortia, strategic alliances, trade associations, and interlocking directorates. In the case of joint ventures, networks, and strategic alliances, the consensus view is that participation in these types of business alliances accelerates a firm's growth by providing it access to a portion of its partner's resources, managerial talent, and intellectual capacities.[38]

Some partnership arrangements do not fit into any of the categories mentioned here; instead, they are entrepreneurial in their own right and help the companies involved further their objectives in ways that no one company could do on its own. An example is the Lodi-Woodbridge Winegrape Commission, which is described in the chapter's "Partnering for Success" feature.

partnering for success

Lodi-Woodbridge Winegrape Commission: Helping Local Wineries Get the Attention They Desire

www.lodiwine.com

The wine country in Northern California is known as one of the finest wine-growing regions in the world. The best-known area is the region north of San Francisco, which includes the famous Napa Valley and Sonoma Valley. But there are other areas of Northern California that produce fine wine too. One is the wine country surrounding Lodi and Woodbridge, California, which is about 90 miles east of San Francisco. Although this area doesn't have the same brand magnetism of Napa or Sonoma, its wineries produce rich wine that its residents are very proud of.

In 1991, the local growers of Lodi and Woodbridge decided to band together in an attempt to step out of the shadow of Napa and Sonoma. They created the Lodi-Woodbridge Winegrape Commission to promote the area's wineries and provide ongoing education to local growers. Since its inception, the commission, which is backed by over 800 local winegrowers and has a $1 million annual budget, has made a difference in the following ways:

- Over the past 10 years, the acreage of winegrapes in the Lodi-Woodbridge area has nearly doubled while the crop value has quadrupled.

- The number of "Lodi" labeled wines (which is the area's distinctive trademark) has grown from only a handful when the commission was formed to over 100 Lodi brands today.

- The commission has launched the industry's most successful districtwide sustainable viticultural programs to reduce pesticide and herbicide use and sustain the area's vineyards for generations to come. (Viticultural is the study of grapes.)

- The commission recently spearheaded the opening of the Lodi Wine & Visitor Centre, one of the newest and most exciting regional wine-tasting centers in California.

The Lodi Wine & Visitor Centre has been a particularly effective initiative spearheaded by the commission. The center gives tastings and sells bottles of local wines. It also refers visitors to local vineyards, whose sales have increased thanks to the center. Most importantly, it has helped the Lodi-Woodbridge wine country become a "destination" for tourists and visitors, helping it better compete with Napa and Sonoma.

Questions for Critical Thinking

1. Make a list of the things the Lodi-Woodbridge Winegrape Commission can accomplish for local growers and wineries that those businesses couldn't accomplish on their own.

2. Spend some time looking at the Web site of the Lodi-Woodbridge Winegrape Commission. In your judgment, does it seem that the financial support provided to the commission by local growers and wineries is money well spent? Does the commission strike you as a well-managed or poorly managed partnership amongst local businesses?

3. What is the most prevalent agricultural product grown in the area surrounding your college or university? Find out whether the local growers have banded together in any way. If they have, describe the nature of their partnership and how the partnership benefits the local growers.

4. What other types of partnerships do you think the wine growers and the wineries in the Lodi-Woodbridge area have banded together to create? What other types of partnerships would you recommend?

Source: Lodi-Woodbridge Winegrape Commission homepage, www.lodiwine.com (accessed July 7, 2006); T. S. Bernard, "Small Wineries Unite in Marketing Efforts," *StartupJournal*, www.startupjournal.com (accessed July 7, 2006).

Geographic Location That Facilitates Knowledge Absorption Locating in a geographic area that facilitates the absorption of knowledge from external sources, as described in Chapter 3, is typically to a firm's advantage. By being physically located near similar firms, a company can gain access to these firms' specialized suppliers, scientific knowledge, and technological expertise.[39]

Chapter Summary

1. Sustained growth is defined as growth in both revenues and profits over an extended period of time.
2. Although most firms endeavor to grow, there are potential downsides to growth. Growth is a two-edged sword that can threaten the stability of a firm's operations in every area, from human resources to finance, if it is not managed properly.
3. Growth is not a random or chance event. It is something firms pursue deliberately. The seven most common reasons that firms grow in an effort to increase their profitability and valuation are as follows: to capture economies of scale; to capture economies of scope; to execute a scalable business model; to achieve market leadership; to maintain influence, power, and survivability; to accommodate the growth of key customers; and to maintain an ability to attract and retain talented employees.
4. A scalable business model is one in which increased revenues cost less to deliver than current revenues. As a result, profit margins increase as sales go up.
5. The basic idea behind benchmarking is that a firm can improve the quality of an activity by identifying and copying the methods of other firms that have been particularly successful in that area. Firm growth is an excellent opportunity for benchmarking.
6. The managerial capacity problem suggests that firm growth is limited by the managerial capacity (i.e., personnel, expertise, and intellectual resources) that firms have available to implement new business ideas. The basic idea is that it does a firm little good to have exciting ideas about growth when it lacks the managerial capacity to implement its ideas.
7. The day-to-day challenges of managing growth include cash flow management, price stability, quality control, and capital constraints.
8. The three most pervasive myths about firm growth are that growth companies are predominantly technology companies, that rapid-growth firms emerge only in rapid-growth industries, and that to grow quickly, the firm must have a first-mover advantage.
9. The firm attributes that are most commonly related to firm growth include a growth-oriented vision, a commitment to growth, participation in business alliances, business growth planning, and a geographic location that facilitates the absorption of knowledge from external sources.
10. The variable commitment to growth deals with the extent to which a firm is committed to pursuing growth as a deliberate, ongoing strategy. The idea is that for growth to take place on a continual basis, it must be a deliberate choice made by the owners/managers of the firm.

Key Terms

adverse selection, 388
benchmarking, 386
business growth planning, 394
commitment to growth, 394
economies of scale, 383
entrepreneurial services, 388

fixed costs, 383
growth-oriented vision, 394
managerial capacity problem, 388
managerial services, 388
market leadership, 385
moral hazard, 388

pace of growth, 383
productive opportunity set, 388
rapid-growth firm, 382
scalable business model, 385
sustained growth, 382
variable costs, 383

Review Questions

1. What is sustained growth? Why is it important?
2. Are most firms rapid-growth firms? Explain your answer.
3. What are the potential downsides to firm growth?
4. Provide an example that describes why a firm might be forced to grow faster than it prefers.
5. Describe economies of scale and economies of scope as rationales for firm growth.
6. Define the phrase "scalable business model." Provide an example of an industry that lends itself to scalable business models.
7. List three reasons firms work hard to achieve market leadership.
8. How does a firm's growth rate affect its ability to attract and retain talented employees?
9. Describe the basic idea behind benchmarking and how benchmarking can help a firm achieve its growth objectives.
10. Give a brief overview of the managerial capacity problem.
11. What are the differences between a firm's entrepreneurial services and its managerial services? How are these two services linked in regard to a firm's growth efforts?
12. Explain what is meant by adverse selection and moral hazard. What roles do these concepts play in facilitating or hindering a firm's growth efforts?
13. Explain why cash flow management, price stability, and quality control are important issues for a venture that is entering a period of rapid growth.
14. Why is it important for growth firms to develop and maintain professional business practices? Make your answer as substantive and thoughtful as possible.
15. In what industries do rapid-growth firms emerge? Explain your answer.
16. Why is it important for a firm to have a growth-oriented vision?
17. Why is it important for a firm to engage in business growth planning?
18. How does participation in business alliances facilitate firm growth?
19. How does participation in business alliances help a firm solve the managerial capacity problem?
20. Why is it to an entrepreneurial venture's advantage to locate in a geographic area that is populated by similar firms?

Application Questions

1. Pete Martin just purchased a copy of *Inc.* magazine's annual issue that ranks the top 500 fastest-growing privately owned companies in America. Pete was amazed by some of the stories in the article and is more encouraged than ever to start his own art restoration firm. As is the case for many entrepreneurs leading many of the *Inc.* 500 firms, Pete believes his firm can grow 1,000 percent or more per year. He is ready to cash out his savings and get started. Is Pete starting this venture with realistic expectations? If not, what should his expectations be?
2. Twelve months ago, Brittany Nelson launched a chain of stores that sell accessories for wireless communications devices. Her first store was in Memphis, and she is now expanding into northern Mississippi and western Tennessee. Brittany's company has grown quickly from 1 store to 5, and she hopes to add 10 to 20 stores per year during the next 5 years. Recently, a friend told Brittany that perhaps she should slow down a bit because a company can grow "too fast." Brittany brushed the suggestion aside, simply noting that things were going fine and that growth was "no problem." Do you think Brittany should think again about her friend's advice? What are the pitfalls of growing too quickly?
3. Patty Stone owns an industrial equipment company named Get Smart Industrial that sells three products in the oil services industry. Get Smart's products are sold via a

direct salesforce. Patty wants to grow the firm by adding new products but has run into resistance from her chief financial officer (CFO), who argues that adding new products will increase inventory costs. While Patty is sensitive to her CFO's concerns, what arguments can she make in favor of adding new products as a way of effectively growing her firm?

4. BUZZ OFF, a company that makes insect repellent clothing, is the focus of the "You Be the VC 1" feature for this chapter. Which of the reasons for firm growth mentioned in the chapter are likely to be the most compelling in BUZZ OFF's case? What steps, if any, has BUZZ OFF taken to lessen the impact of the managerial capacity problem?

5. Brian Ward is a computer software engineer. He has an idea for a software product that he thinks could constitute the initial product for a new business. Brian recently read that software companies can grow quickly because software lends itself to a "scalable business model." Brian doesn't quite know what a scalable business model is and has asked you for an explanation. He would also like to know if there are any potential hazards in launching a business that is founded on a scalable business model. What would you tell him?

6. Three years ago, Chris Dees launched a medical products company that specializes in providing products for people with diabetes. His company is number one in its industry. Recently, a couple of competitors have entered the picture, and Chris is wondering if it is worth the fight to remain number one. In terms of firm growth, what advantages are there to being the market leader?

7. Troy Milton owns a successful consumer products firm in Oakland, California. The firm has a number of talented employees who have contributed significantly to the company's success. The company has stalled in terms of growth. Curiously, Troy doesn't seem to be concerned, and a couple of his top employees have even observed that Troy seems to be enjoying the slower pace. In terms of his ability to retain his most talented employees, what risks does Troy run by letting his firm stall in terms of growth?

8. Ian Khalid lives in Tallahassee, Florida, and has owned a fiber-optics company for 5 years. Although the company is profitable, he is worried about it because it isn't growing. Ian has heard about the concept of benchmarking and has asked you if benchmarking could play a role in helping him identify ways to grow his firm. What would you tell him? What types of firms should Ian attempt to benchmark against?

9. Doug Rypien owns a small electronics firm in central Ohio. He is thinking about trying to grow the firm outside its immediate trade area. He is even thinking about approaching some customers in Cincinnati, believing that he has a good chance of making some sales. What are some of the day-to-day challenges that Doug will probably experience if he tries to grow his company? Given the nature of Doug's business, which of the challenges do you think will be the most demanding, and why?

10. AutoCart, the company that hopes to operate the first "drive-thru" chain of grocery stores where customers will stay in their cars while their orders are filled, is the focus of the "You Be the VC 2" feature in this chapter. To what extent do you think AutoCart will capture a first-mover advantage if its idea works, and what do you think will be its most compelling growth-related challenges?

11. Kevin Owens is thinking about starting a natural foods company in Springfield, Missouri, and hopes to grow the company fairly quickly throughout the Midwest. He just talked to a business consultant, however, who told him to forget it. The consultant said, "The only types of companies that grow quickly are software and health care companies." Do you agree with Kevin's consultant? Why or why not?

12. Meredith Colella is a food products engineer who has developed an innovative approach for the packaging of meat. Her approach will extend the shelf life of most meat products by about 30 percent. Meredith is getting ready to try to sell the idea to

investors. What could Meredith tell the investors that would give them confidence that she is prepared to cope with the challenges of rapid growth?

13. Claudia Jones is the owner of a graphic design firm in Baton Rouge, Louisiana. She wants to grow her firm and has been told that it is a good idea to write down her "vision for growth" and share the vision with her employees. Claudia wonders if it's really worth her time to write out a formal vision for growth—she would rather just talk to her employees about growth in broad terms. Do you think it's worth Claudia's time to write out a formal vision for growth? Why or why not?

14. Stacey Williams owns a medical products firm in Durham, North Carolina. She just attended a seminar, where one of the speakers said, "Participating in business partnerships can help firms lessen the impact of the managerial capacity problem." Stacey's not sure what the speaker meant by that statement. Can you help Stacey understand how participating in business partnerships can help firms lessen the impact of the managerial capacity problem?

15. Look at the Web site of Home Swimmer (www.homeswimmer.com). As you'll see, this firm makes products that help people complete aerobic workouts in their swimming pools. Spend some time familiarizing yourself with Home Swimmer's products and its business model. Home Swimmer is about to launch an aggressive growth strategy. Write a one-page set of recommendations for Home Swimmer that outlines some of the issues it should be aware of as it launches its growth initiative.

you be the VC 13.1 BUZZ OFF
www.buzzoff.com

Business Idea: Partner with branded apparel manufacturers to provide consumers access to safe and effective insect-repellent clothing.

Pitch: Who likes mosquito bites, and who wants to run the risk of acquiring Lyme disease or other mosquito-spread maladies? Insect repellents, like Off!, help but are often unavailable or don't seem to work when needed most. In addition, even though health officials say that insect repellents are safe, many people are leery of spraying chemicals on their bodies and worry about the long-term health effects. Other people simply don't like the mess or odor that goes along with aerosol or topical cream repellents.

BUZZ OFF offers a solution to these concerns and problems. The company partners with branded clothing manufacturers and retailers, like Orvis, L.L. Bean, Oxford Golf, and Tommy Hilfiger, to produce insect-resistant clothing. The clothing, which includes shirts, pants, gloves, socks and hats in adult and child sizes, contains the insecticide permethrin, which the Environmental Protection Agency considers safe and effective when applied to fabrics. Unlike the ingredients in insect repellents, which keep bugs at bay, permethrin actually stuns or kills them. This factor makes BUZZ

OFF–treated clothing more effective in preventing potentially dangerous and irritating bug bites.

BUZZ OFF is courting diverse markets for its patented insecticide-treated clothing technologies, which illustrates the broad appeal of its product. The company recently entered into a strategic partnership with Oxford Golf Group, which will produce a line of BUZZ OFF insect-repellent apparel for men. This apparel will be marketed under the labels of Tommy Hilfiger and Oxford Golf and will be sold in the finest golf shops and resorts in the country. In addition, BUZZ OFF is partnering with Rocky Brands, an apparel retailer that sells clothing to fishermen and hunters. Rocky Brands plans to sell a line of BUZZ OFF–treated camouflage clothing, including shirts, pants, jackets, T-shirts, caps, gloves, bandanas, and socks.

Q&A: Based on the material covered in this chapter, what questions would you ask the firm's founders before making your funding decision? What answers would satisfy you?

Decision: If you had to make your decision on just the information provided in the pitch and on the company's Web site, would you fund this firm? Why or why not?

AutoCart
www.autocart.com

Business Idea: Operate the first "drive-thru" chain of grocery stores where customers will stay in their cars while their orders are filled and delivered to their vehicles.

Pitch: It takes about 45 minutes for the average shopper to pick up 21 items at a grocery store. In addition, most trips to the store involve a frustrating search for a hard-to-find item. AutoCart has a solution to these problems. The company will soon open its first "drive-thru" grocery store in Albuquerque, New Mexico, with more stores to follow. Each store will consist of a 130,000-square-foot warehouse and about 70,000 square feet of drive-thru space. The drive-thru space will have 30 order stations. To put the size of the facility into perspective, the average Wal-Mart Discount Store is about 100,000 square feet.

Here's how it works. Upon arrival at the store, a customer pulls up to an order station and grabs a 15-inch touch-screen computer, which is attached to a tether and can be taken into the car. While parked, the customer makes selections from the screen. In addition to groceries, the stores will feature DVD/game rentals, a pharmacy, dry cleaning, office supplies, and a florist. After the order is placed, the customer will be directed to a pickup station to pay for the order and watch television on a large screen until the order arrives. The order arrives through an automated system and is placed in the car by the customer prior to departure. Customers can also e-mail or fax orders, which will be waiting for them when they arrive.

Behind the scenes, the customer's order is filled by a patented state-of-the-art product-handling system and by a team of loaders, who scurry about the warehouse placing items on conveyor belts. The system is designed to maximize vehicle throughput while providing the customer quick and convenient service. AutoCart estimates that it can cut the 45 minutes shopping time needed to fill a 21-item grocery list down to just 16 minutes. The company plans to open up to 1,500 AutoCart stores in North America over the next 10 years.

Q&A: Based on the material covered in this chapter, what questions would you ask the firm's founders before making your funding decision? What answers would satisfy you?

Decision: If you had to make your decision on just the information provided in the pitch and on the company's Web site, would you fund this firm? Why or why not?

CASE 13.1

CD Baby: Using the Tale of the Fox and the Hedgehog to Guide its Philosophy for Growth
www.cdbaby.com

Bruce R. Barringer,
University of Central Florida
R. Duane Ireland,
Texas A&M University

Introduction

CD Baby has the largest catalog of music in the world, even though you've probably never heard of the majority of its musicians. The company is an online music store for independent bands and musicians. Since its founding in 1997, CD Baby has maintained a laserlike focus on its primary mission—to provide a way for independent musicians to sell their music at a profit. The results have been impressive. Over 100,000 independent musicians now sell their music through the CD Baby Web site.

One thing that is extraordinary about CD Baby is that with the exception of partnering with Apple's iTunes and the other online music services, CD Baby has built its business without expanding beyond its core service. Derek Sivers, the company's founder and CEO, likes to use the fable of the Hedgehog and the Fox to explain why.

The Founding of CD Baby

CD Baby was founded by Derek Sivers, a musician and former circus performer, in 1997. The company was founded partly by accident. Sivers, the leader of a rock band, wanted to start selling his band's music online but couldn't find an online music store who would take him. At that time, the online stores would only work with bands who had the backing of a record label or who had a major distributor agreement. When he would ask an online store why he couldn't simply send them a box of CDs for them to sell, they would remind him that they were basically the storefront for the record labels and distributors, and without backing they couldn't help him.

CD Baby's Distribution Arrangement with Its Client Musicians

1. Clients will be paid once a week, no matter what.

2. CD Baby will provide its clients the full name and address of everyone who buys their CDs.

3. No client (i.e., musician or band) will ever be kicked off the CD Baby Web site for not selling enough.

4. There will never be any paid placement (which refers to a musician "paying" to be listed at the top of a chart).

To get around this complication, Sivers decided to put a shopping cart on his own band's Web site and start selling his CDs. Back in 1997, this task was much harder than it is today. It took Sivers 3 months of painstaking work to make the shopping cart functional and to secure a credit card merchant account. Once he started selling CDs, he invited some of his friends, who also had bands, to start selling their CDs on his site, to avoid all the hassles that he just went through. At this point, Sivers had no intention of turning the site into a full-time business. It was just a way to sell CDs for his band and to help a few friends do the same thing.

Word of mouth about what he was doing quickly grew, and Sivers started getting phone calls from people he didn't know asking how they could start selling CDs on his site. Sivers started a separate Web site, which he called CD Baby, to accommodate the requests. At this point, he knew that CD Baby represented a viable business idea.

CD Baby's Business Philosophy

CD Baby quickly grew, largely because the service solved a problem for the firm's clients—how to sell their CDs online. The way the company was set up was influenced by an experience that Sivers had when he was younger. After graduating from college, Sivers worked for several years for Warner Music in New York City. He says that it was a good job, but he was put off by the way the music industry focused most of its attention on a few large stars, at the expense of emerging musicians. He also saw many promising artists struggle to make ends meet, because their income was irregular or they simply weren't selling enough albums to keep the record labels interested. As a result, CD Baby developed a unique business philosophy that approached things from the musician's point of view. The key to the philosophy was to offer its clients (i.e., the independent musicians that sold music through its Web site) a distribution arrangement that favored them—rather than CD Baby. The distribution arrangement is highlighted in the table titled "CD Baby's Distribution Arrangement with Its Client Musicians." Through this agreement, CD Baby became an advocate for its clients. Advocacy for its clients

remains in place today at CD Baby and is at the heart of the reason for the firm's success.

CD Baby's Growth Philosophy

Although CD Baby has experienced exceptional growth, it has not strayed from its original purpose, to be an online music store. Sivers says that the company gets inquiries every week about potential business opportunities, including starting a radio station, becoming a booking agency, launching a magazine, and sponsoring a tour of the "best-of-the-best" of its independent musicians. It has passed on all of these potential opportunities. In a recent interview, Sivers was asked why the company passes on so many opportunities, and he replied by referring to an essay titled "The Hedgehog and the Fox" by Isaiah Berlin, which he was reminded of while reading Jim Collin's book *Good to Great*. Collins retells the fable of the fox and the hedgehog. Because he is sly, cunning, and strong, everyone thinks that the fox is better than the hedgehog. All the lowly hedgehog knows how to do is one thing—curl up in a ball, with its spikes out, to deter intruders. The ironic thing is that no matter what the fox does, and no matter how many of its 100 tricks it tries to use, the hedgehog always wins, because it knows how to do one thing particularly well—roll up in a ball and stick its spikes out. In *Good to Great*, Collins says businesses that are successful over the long hall are like hedgehogs—they find their niche or market space and learn how to do one thing exceptionally well.

Sivers has taken Collins's advice to heart and has centered CD Baby's growth philosophy on one thing—being an online music store. The only exception that CD Baby has made is to participate with Apple's iTunes and the other online music service by funneling its clients' music to the online services for sale. As a result, CD Baby is now the largest single distributor of songs that are listed on iTunes. The CD Baby iTunes partnership is a win–win for both companies. It's a win for iTunes, because when independent artists contact the company and inquires about listing their songs on iTunes, it can simply refer the artist to CD Baby. It's a win for CD Baby and its clients because it provides another channel through which independent artists are able to sell their songs.

As a result, if you know anyone who wants to get music listed on iTunes, all they have to do is ship their music to CD Baby (CD Baby accepts music from any band or musician). CD Baby will take care of all the technical and legal necessities of getting the music listing on the iTunes Web site.

Future Growth Plans

CD Baby plans to continue growing in the same way it has been growing, with no changes in its basic growth philosophy planned. The company finds itself in the enviable position of controlling the largest music catalog in the world. As a result, almost any new online service that comes along will have to work with CD Baby to gain access to its catalog.

Discussion Questions

1. Do you think CD Baby's distribution arrangement with its clients is fair for both parties? What, if any, modifications would you recommend for the arrangement and why?
2. Do you think CD Baby has an effective growth strategy? If so, explain what you like about the strategy. If

you don't think the company's growth strategy is effective, explain your concerns.
3. Which of the "growth-related firm attributes" discussed in the chapter are exemplified in this case?
4. In what ways is CD Baby's business model scalable? How has the scalability of CD Baby's business model contributed to the company's success?

Application Questions

1. In terms of their growth strategies, provide an example of a business you are familiar with that acts like a fox and a business that acts like a hedgehog. Discuss the differences between the businesses. Which business do you think will be the most successful in the long run and why?
2. Apply the fable of the hedgehog and the fox to your life. Do you act more like a fox or a hedgehog? If you act more like a fox, are there lessons you could learn from the hedgehog? What are those lessons?

Source: G. Galant, and D. Sivers, "VV Show #19—Derek Sivers of CD Baby." Venture Voice Podcast, November 2005.

CASE 13.2 — *Captivate Networks: How Four Critical Decisions Shaped One Firm's Path to Growth*
www.captivate.com

Bruce R. Barringer,
University of Central Florida
R. Duane Ireland,
Texas A&M University

Introduction

In 1996, Michael DiFranza, a young technology executive, was restless. He had just gone through a program at Harvard, which caused him to think about starting his own firm. He would often jot down business ideas, but for one reason or another, would then rule them out. One morning, after returning from the West Coast on a red-eye flight, he stopped by his office in downtown Boston. As usual, he looked at the people already there as he stepped into the elevator and the door closed. They were fidgeting, looking at their shoes, staring at the floor numbers as they lit up, and glancing at their watches. He thought—what if you put flat-screen displays inside elevators so people had something to watch while waiting to reach their destination? Would this work? Is this a viable business idea?

After spending some time thinking about his idea, DiFranza decided to proceed and founded Captivate Networks. Today, Captivate (get it?—people are "captive" when they are in elevators) has more than 6,600 wireless, digital screens located in the elevators of premier office

towers in 21 of North America's top markets. The company estimates that its screens are seen by over 2 million people every day. Although very successful today, Captivate's future and success were anything other than certain in the company's early days. The founders were faced with a number of critical decisions that shaped the future direction of the company. Here, we focus on four critical decisions that DiFranza and his team faced.

Critical Decision 1: Are We a Technology Company or a Media Company?

Prior to starting Captivate Networks, DiFranza worked for Mentor Graphics, a company that makes software that helps engineers design and test electronic components. One thing that DiFranza learned from his colleagues at Mentor is that it's not enough for a company to focus on technology. A company must also focus on how its technology creates value for the end user.

The reason this issue was important for Captivate is because the leaders of the company had to find the answer to a fundamental question: At its core, was Captivate a technology company or a media company? The answer to the question made a difference. If Captivate was a technology company, its efforts should focus intently on the technology, with hopes of eventually licensing the technology to an elevator company like Otis. If Captivate was a media company, than a different set of priorities would take precedence. The company would need to clearly define its audience. It would also have to assemble sufficient data to persuade building owners to install flat-panel displays in their elevators and advertisers to pay to run ads on the displays.

DiFranza and his team decided to be a media company. The essence of the company's vision was to place ads and other programming on flat-panel displays in elevators—the technology was simply a means to an end. Although the company still had the challenge of creating the flat-panel displays and the technology needed to support them, from that point forward, Captivate was thought of as a media company first and foremost.

Critical Decision 2: Should We Hire Nielsen Media or Do Our Own Market Research?

Using its own preliminary research, Captivate identified that its audience, people riding elevators in large office buildings, had an average income of $100,000, compared to $54,000 for the general population. The demographic was professional, split 50/50 between males and females, managerial, and difficult to reach through traditional media.

Its advertisers would also catch people when they were making decisions to buy, during the heart of the business day, when it is difficult to get these people's attention otherwise.

Based on these findings, DiFranza and his team felt that it would be a no-brainer for many advertisers to try out Captivate's service.

But there was a catch: No one had ever placed flat-panel displays in elevators before, so know one knew for sure how effective the advertising would be. Because of this, DiFranza and his team approached Nielsen Media to see how much they would charge to conduct a market research study of the concept. Nielsen wanted $200,000, which was a lot of money for a start-up. The idea behind having Nielsen do the work is that it would validate the data it collected. DiFranza's fear was that if Captivate collected the data itself it would appear to be self-serving and be less believable to its potential customers—building owners and potential advertisers.

Ultimately, DiFranza and his team hired Nielsen to do the research, and the data it collected was compelling. According to the research, the average person in a large office building takes six elevator trips per day, with each trip averaging a minute. As a result, the average person was spending 120 minutes a month in elevators, or 24 hours a year. This data, along with other data Nielsen collected, armed DiFranza and his team with verified, unbiased data to support their business concept.

Critical Decision 3: Should We Take Otis's Offer?

When Captivate started installing its flat-panel displays in elevators, the first displays went into Otis elevators. Otis was so impressed with the technology that it asked

Captivate to be an exclusive provider of flat-screen displays for its elevators. This offer would mean that Captivate had Otis in its corner. However, the potential downside to this arrangement was that Captivate was not allowed to install its systems in any other elevators.

It was a tough decision, but DiFranza and his team decided to pass. Although Otis was the largest elevator company in the world, the firm had only a 25 percent market share. Captivate didn't want 25 percent of the market, it wanted all of the market (or as much as it could get). In addition, because Captivate thought of itself as a media company, it saw building owners and advertisers as its primary customers, rather than elevator companies. Still, Otis's offer was hard to pass up at the time. In reflecting on this decision, DiFranza is quoted in the book *Startups That Work* by Joel Kurtzman as saying:

> Here we were. We had no revenue, very little funding, a cool technology, and an idea. And here's the largest elevator company in the world that wants to partner with us, and we said, "No."

Critical Decision 4: Should We Give the Building Owners a Cut of the Profits?

The fourth critical decision that Captivate faced was the development of its business model, and specifically how much of its revenue it should share with its partners. The most important piece of the equation was the building owners. On the one hand, Captivate could make the case that it was providing building owners a service and not offer them any revenue-sharing agreement. In addition, at the time that Captivate was rolling out its service, there was a lot of consolidation going on in the office building industry. Major owners, like Equity Office Properties and Boston Properties, were accumulating lots of buildings. Captivate felt that it could help these owners "brand" their properties by having Captivate flat panels in their elevators. On the other hand, Captivate wanted building owners to feel like they were a participant in its business rather than just bystanders. DiFranza and his team instinctively knew if building owners were offered a cut of the profits, when a problem occurred with a display, the building owners would see it as a problem that they should help fix, rather than just call Captivate or ignore the problem all together.

Ultimately, Captivate decided to offer the building owners a cut of the profits, along with several other amenities. For example, some building owners used the flat-panel displays to make announcements to their tenants, like when fire drills would be held.

Present-Day Growth Path

Captivate's service is now more popular than ever, and the demand for flat-panel displays in elevators is strong. The tragic events of September 11, 2001 have increased demand even further, as building owners look for additional ways to pass safety information along to occupants in times of emergency. Captivate's flat-panel displays are now featured in some of the most famous buildings in the world, including the Prudential Tower in Boston, the Sears Building in Chicago, and the Empire State Building in New York City. Captivate was purchased by Gannett in 2004, affirming the company's decision to become a media rather than a technology company. It now operates independently as a wholly owned subsidiary of Gannett.

Discussion Questions

1. Which of the four decisions discussed in the case do you think was the most critical? What would have happened to Captivate if it had made the opposite decision in this circumstance?
2. Why do you think that Captivate has been able to sustain its growth? What, if anything, will eventually slow the growth of the company?

3. Of the day-to-day challenges of managing growth discussed in the chapter, which of the challenges do you think were the most difficult for Captivate to deal with during the firm's early years?
4. Why do you think Gannett purchased Captivate?

Application Questions

1. How do you think Captivate would have evolved if DeFranza and his team had seen the company as a technology company rather than a media company? Make your answer as detailed and substantive as possible.
2. Think of your professional life as a student or as an employee, if you currently have a job. List four major decisions that you made that have put you on the track that you're currently on. Reflecting back, would you change any of the decisions that you made? If so, why?

Source: Captivate Networks home page, (accessed May 4, 2006); J. Kurtzman, *Startups That Work* (New York: Penguin Group, 2005).

Endnotes

1. Personal Interview with Anthony Casalena, July 14, 2006.
2. G. A. Lohr, "University of Maryland Student in a Class by Himself," *Washington Business Journal*, April 23, 2004.
3. T. M. Welbourne, "Learning About Leadership and Firm Growth Through Monthly Data Collection and Dialogue with Entrepreneurs," *International Entrepreneurship and Management Journal* 2, no. 1 (2006): 39–55; C. Zook and J. Allen, *The Facts about Growth* (New York: Bain & Company, 1999).
4. National Commission on Entrepreneurship, *High Growth Companies: Mapping America's Entrepreneurial Landscape*, July 2001.
5. R. W. Price, *Roadmap to Entrepreneurial Success: Powerful Strategies for Building a High-Profit Business* (New York: AMACOM, 2004).
6. D. Packard, *The HP Way: How Bill Hewlett and I Built Our Company*, ed. D. Kirby with Karen Lewis (New York: HarperBusiness, 1996).
7. Packard, *The HP Way*.
8. J. G. Covin, K. M. Green, and D. P. Slevin, "Strategic Process Effects on the Entrepreneurial Orientation—Sales Growth Rate Relationship," *Entrepreneurship Theory and Practice* 30, no. 1 (2006): 57–81.
9. E. Garnsey, E. Stam, and P. Heffernan, "New Firm Growth: Exploring Processes and Paths," *Industry and Innovation* 13, no. 1 (2006): 1–20; A. V. Bhide, *The Origin and Evolution of New Businesses* (Oxford: Oxford University Press, 2000).
10. C. Zook, J. Allen, and J. Smith, "Strategies for Corporate Growth," *European Business Journal* 12, no. 2 (2000), 3–10.
11. J. Welch, "Growth Initiatives," *Executive Excellence* 16, no. 6 (1999): 8–9.
12. "Strategic HR Intelligence Key to Employee Retention," *The Biotech HR Pulse* 1, no. 14 (November 12, 2003): 1–4.
13. M. Mehler, "The Success Factor," *Priority*, January/February, 2003.
14. H. Littunen and M. Virtanen, "Differentiating Growing Ventures from Non-Growth Firms," *International Entrepreneurship and Management Journal* 2, no. 1 (2006): 93–109; R. W. Price, *Roadmap to Entrepreneurial Success* (New York: AMACOM, 2004).
15. PricewaterhouseCoopers, "One-Third of Fast-Growth CEOs Grapple with Self-Doubt, PricewaterhouseCoopers Finds," *Trendsetter Barometer*, May 22, 2000.

16. E. T. Penrose, *The Theory of the Growth of the Firm*, 3rd ed. (Oxford: Oxford University Press, 1995).

17. E. T. Penrose, *The Theory of the Growth of the Firm* (New York: John Wiley & Sons, 1959).

18. C. Zook, *Profit from the Core* (Boston: Harvard Business School Press, 2001).

19. D. Cumming, "Adverse Selection and Capital Structure: Evidence from Venture Capital," *Entrepreneurship Theory and Practice* 30, no. 2 (2006): 155–83; D. C. Hambrick and R. M. Crozier, "Stumblers and Stars in the Management of Rapid Growth," *Journal of Business Venturing* 1 (1985): 31–45.

20. Penrose, *The Theory of the Growth of the Firm* (1959).

21. J. Anderson, "The Company That Grew Too Fast," *Inc.*, November 2005, 104–110.

22. D. Bartholomew, "The Perfect Pitch," *Priority*, December/January, 2004.

23. J. Walker, "Learn From Entrepreneurs' Mistakes," *Deseret Morning News*, January 22, 2006.

24. B. Jaruzelski, K. Volkholz, and G. Horkan, *The High-Tech Challenge: Sustaining Rapid and Profitable Growth* (New York: Booz-Allen & Hamilton, 2002), 4.

25. *Fortune* homepage, www.fortune.com (accessed July 5, 2006).

26. "America's Fastest-Growing 500 Private Companies," *Inc.*, January, 2004, 28.

27. T. Ahrens, *High-Growth Companies: Driving the Tiger* (Hampshire: Gower, 1999).

28. A. J. Sherman, *Fast-Track Business Growth* (Washington, DC: Kiplinger Books, 2001).

29. T. L. Doorley and J. M. Donovan, *Value-Creating Growth* (San Francisco: Jossey-Bass, 1999).

30. Doorley and Donovan, *Value-Creating Growth.*

31. A. T. Kearney, Inc., *Sustaining Corporate Growth* (Boca Raton, FL: St. Lucie Press, 2000).

32. Ahrens, *High-Growth Companies.*

33. T. L. Doorley, quoted in *Value-Creating Growth: Goals, Strategies, Foundations* (New York: The Conference Board, Inc., 1997), 6.

34. Sherman, *Fast-Track Business Growth.*

35. G. C. Reid and J. A. Smith, "What Makes a New Business Start-Up Successful?" *Small Business Economics* 14 (2000): 165–82.

36. F. Delmar and S. Shane, "Does Business Planning Facilitate the Development of New Ventures?" *Strategic Management Journal* 24 (2003): 1165–85.

37. T. S. Bernard, "Scooter Maker Sees a Chance for Growth," *StartupJournal* homepage, www.startupjournal.com (accessed June 28, 2006).

38. B. R. Barringer and J. S. Harrison, "Walking a Tightrope: Creating Value Through Interorganizational Relationships," *Journal of Management* 26 (2000): 367–403.

39. D. B. Audretsch and E. Lehmann. "Entrepreneurial Access and Absorption of Knowledge Spillovers: Strategic Board and Managerial Composition for Competitive Advantage," *Journal of Small Business Management* 44, no. 2 (2006): 155–66.

Courtesy of Christian Marin

Superior
SCIENTIFIC, Ltd.

**Superior Scientific
is a leading supplier of tools for
the bioscience industry**

**The first company created through
the Biotechnology subset of the
Science Entrepreneurship Program,
Superior Scientific was created
by scientists, for scientists**

perior-scientific.com

...tific is a low-cost
...quality
...tials

Getting Personal

with **CHRISTIAN MARIN**

My advice for new entrepreneurs	My biggest worry as an entrepreneur	What I do when I'm not working
You are the image you project	*Getting stuck in a rut*	*Bodybuilding and boxing*

Product Development

Cleveland-based
mpany seeks to provi
sonal se
titutions
veland a

ustom De
Milling, Lat
anually pe

Computer Numerical Contr

PLC/PAC Integration

Superior Scientific:
Gradually Pursuing Additional Strategies for Growth

When Christian Marin finished his undergraduate degree in molecular biology from the Florida Institute of Technology (FIT), he knew that he didn't want to pursue a research career. Instead, he was more interested in the business side of science. Rather than pursuing a job, however, an alternative caught his eye. The alternative was the Science and Technology Entrepreneurship Program at Case Western Reserve University. The program, which was launched in 2000, offers a master's degree that combines a specific science discipline with entrepreneurship. The program started by offering a degree in physics and entrepreneurship and has since expanded to offer combined degrees in entrepreneurship and biology, chemistry, mathematics and computation, and statistics. Marin saw the Biology Entrepreneurship Program as a perfect fit for what he needed and desired. While he knew biology, he readily admitted that he didn't know the first thing about business or entrepreneurship and was highly motivated to learn as much as he could.[1]

Marin started the program at Case Western in the fall of 2003. His wife, Adele, was already enrolled in the Physics Entrepreneurship program. Both programs offer instruction in their individual science discipline, along with second-year MBA classes that teach students how to innovate, commercialize technology, and launch new businesses. The goal of both programs is to graduate scientists who develop new businesses, either as start-up entrepreneurs or as corporate entrepreneurs working within the boundaries of an existing company.

Once he got involved in the program, Marin started thinking about new business ideas. His first idea was to license a technology owned by Johns Hopkins University, involving kits that enable labs to detect genetic mutations. His business would market and sell the kits. He was enthused enough about the idea that he started talking to potential customers. Although his idea fell somewhat flat, his discussions took a surprising twist. What he continually heard from people in the industry was a desire to obtain basic laboratory supplies at a more affordable price. This need resonated with Marin, who thought to himself, "That is something I can do." To further investigate this idea, Marin partnered with another student in the program, Chris Mizer, a serial entrepreneur who got his

CHRISTIAN MARIN

Founder, Superior Scientific

Master's Degree

Biology Entrepreneurship

Program

Case Western Reserve

University, 2006

CASE
CASE WESTERN RESERVE UNIVERSITY

First entrepreneurial experience

Paper route as a kid

Currently in my iPod

10,000 Maniacs

Best advice I've received

Don't do it if you're not having fun

407

MBA about 20 years ago but was attracted to Case's Biology Entrepreneurship program to bolster both his scientific and business knowledge. After investigating the need further, the two launched Superior Scientific, an online laboratory supply company.

Superior Scientific sells basic laboratory supplies, like gloves, Petri dishes, centrifuge tubes, and microscopes. Its competitive advantage, which Marin and Mizer articulated in their original business plan, is to offer customers deep discounts on lab equipment while providing high levels of customer service. The way the company is able to accomplish this seemingly impossible combination of advantages is through careful positioning and cost control. Rather than trying to stock every conceivable item a laboratory might need, as its larger competitors do, Superior Scientific sells a smaller number of items, which reduces the complexity and cost of doing business.[2] Marketing expenses are kept to a minimum, primarily by utilizing Google's AdWords, which the company has found to be particularly effective in selling laboratory supplies. Early on, Marin and Mizer partnered with a supplier in China to manufacture their own line of products. The supplier has been invaluable in providing high-quality supplies at a low cost. Finally, the company operates with very few employees and low overhead.

Marin graduated from Case's Biology Entrepreneurship program in the spring of 2006. Superior Scientific, which has moved beyond the start-up stage, is now in a growth mode. Working through its Chinese partner, the company has produced specialized products for specific customers, a means of growth that may accelerate in the future. International expansion has already begun, another means of growth that may gather speed. Although the company has focused primarily on organic growth up until now, several external growth strategies are being pursued. Superior Scientific is in the process of acquiring its first company. It is also working with several universities to license technology they have developed and sell the technology through its channels.

Superior Scientific is a typically young entrepreneurial firm. As it picks up momentum as a company, it is starting to use additional methods to leverage its core competencies and accelerate its growth. This chapter discusses the most common strategies firms use to grow. The growth strategies are divided into internal strategies for growth and external strategies for growth, as shown in Figure 14.1.

Internal Growth Strategies

Internal growth strategies involve efforts taken within the firm itself, such as new product development, other product-related strategies, and international expansion with the purpose of increasing sales revenue and profitability. Many businesses, such as Starbucks and Olive Garden, are growing through internal growth strategies. The distinctive attribute of internally generated growth is that a business relies on its own competencies, expertise, business practices, and employees. Internally generated growth is often called **organic growth** because it does not rely on outside intervention.

Effective though it can be, there are limits to internal growth. As a company matures, it becomes more difficult to sustain its growth strictly through internal means. This is the challenge facing a company such as Starbucks. Even though it is still opening new restaurants and is developing new products, it is increasingly relying on partnerships with companies such as Dryers, which produces a Starbucks-branded ice cream, and PepsiCo, which distributes Starbucks ready-to-drink coffee products, to fuel its growth. Table 14.1 lists the distinct advantages and disadvantages of internal growth strategies.

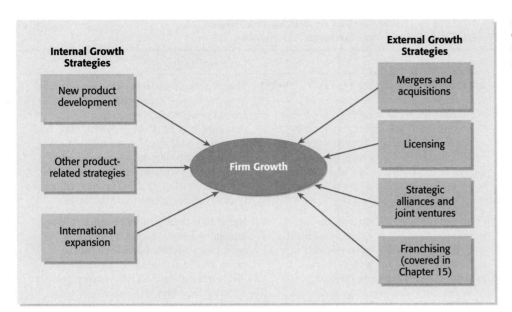

FIGURE 14.1

Internal and External Growth Strategies

New Product Development

New product development involves designing, producing, and selling new products (or services) as a means of increasing firm revenues and profitability. In many fast-paced industries, new product development is a competitive necessity. For example, the average product life cycle in the computer software industry is 14 to 16 months. Because of this, to remain competitive, software companies must always have new products in their pipelines. For some companies, continually developing new products is the essence of their existence. The official vision of 3M, for example, is to be "the most innovative enterprise in the world."[3]

Although developing new products can result in substantial rewards, it is a high-risk strategy. The key is developing innovative new products that aren't simply "me-too" products that are entering already crowded markets. A recent PricewaterhouseCoopers survey reported that the chief executive officers (CEOs) from two-thirds of America's fastest-growing companies say that innovation is an organization-wide priority, and almost all say it has had a significant, positive impact on their business. Over the past 5 years, the more innovative firms in the survey have increased revenues by an average of 346 percent, versus only 138 percent for all others.[4]

When developing new products is properly executed, there is tremendous upside potential. Many biotech and pharmaceutical companies, for example, have developed products that not only improve the quality of life for their customers but also provide reliable revenue streams. In most cases, the products are patented, meaning that no one else can make them, at least until the patents expire. Successful new products can also provide sufficient cash flow to fund a company's operations and provide resources to support developing additional new products. For example, Amgen, which is by far the biggest and most profitable biotech company, has two stellar pharmaceutical products, Epogen and Neupogen. Epogen is used for the treatment of anemia associated with chronic renal failure in dialysis patients, and Neupogen helps prevent infection in cancer patients undergoing certain types of chemotherapy. These products have provided the company sufficient revenue to cover its overhead, fund new product development, and generate profits for an extended period of time.

The keys to effective new product and service development, which are consistent with the material on opportunity recognition (Chapter 2) and feasibility analysis (Chapter 3) follow:

- *Find a need and fill it:* Most successful new products fill a need that is presently unfilled. "Saturated" markets should be avoided. For example, in the United States as well as in most developed countries, consumers have a more-than-adequate selection

1. Explain the difference between internal growth strategies and external growth strategies.

2. Identify the keys to effective new product development.

TABLE 14.1 Advantages and Disadvantages of Internal Growth Strategies

Advantages	Disadvantages
Incremental, even-paced growth. A firm that grows at an even pace can continually adjust to changing environmental conditions to fine-tune its strategies over time. In contrast, a firm that doubles its size overnight through a merger or acquisition is making a much larger commitment at a single point in time.	**Slow form of growth.** In some industries, an incremental, even-paced approach toward growth does not permit a firm to develop competitive economies of scale fast enough. In addition, in some industries, it may not be possible for a firm to develop sufficient resources to remain competitive. A high level of merger and acquisition activity typically characterizes these industries.
Provides maximum control. Internal growth strategies allow a firm to maintain control over the quality of its products and services during the growth process. In contrast, firms that grow through collaborative forms of growth, such as alliances or joint ventures, must share the oversight function with their business partners.	**Need to develop new resources.** Some internal growth strategies, such as new product development, require a firm to be innovative and develop new resources. While internal innovation has many positive attributes, it is typically a slow, expensive, and risky strategy.
Preserves organizational culture. Firms emphasizing internal growth are not required to blend their organizational culture with another organization. As a result, the venture can grow under the auspices of a clearly understood, unified corporate culture.	**Investment in a failed internal effort can be difficult to recoup.** Internal growth strategies, such as new product development, run the risk that a new product or service idea may not sell, making it difficult to recoup the development cost the firm incurred.
Encourages internal entrepreneurship. Firms that grow via internal growth strategies are looking for new ideas from within the business rather than from outside stakeholders or acquisition targets. This approach encourages a climate of internal entrepreneurship and innovation.	**Adds to industry capacity.** Some internal growth strategies add to industry capacity, and this can ultimately help force industry profitability down. For example, a restaurant chain that grows through geographic expansion may ultimately force industry profitability down by continuing to open new restaurants in an already crowded market.
Allows firms to promote from within. Firms emphasizing internal growth strategies have the advantage of being able to promote within their own organizations. The availability of promotional opportunities within a firm is a powerful tool for employee motivation.	

of appliances, tires, credit cards, and cell phone plans. These are crowded markets with low profit margins. The challenge for entrepreneurs is to find unfilled needs in attractive markets and then find a way to fill those needs.

- *Develop products that add value:* In addition to finding a need and filling it, the most successful products are those that "add value" for customers in some meaningful way.
- *Get quality right and pricing right:* Every product represents a balance between quality and pricing. If the quality of a product and its price are not compatible, the product may fail and have little chance for recovery. To put this in slightly different terms, customers are willing to pay higher prices for higher-quality products and are willing to accept lower quality when they pay lower prices.

- *Focus on a specific target market:* Every new product and service should have a specific target market in mind, as discussed in Chapter 11. This degree of specificity gives the innovating entrepreneurial venture the opportunity to conduct a focused promotional campaign and select the appropriate distributors. The notion that "it's a good product, so somebody will by it" is a naive way to do business and often contributes to failure.
- *Conduct ongoing feasibility analysis:* Once a product or service is launched, the feasibility analysis and marketing research should not end. The initial market response should be tested in focus groups and surveys, and incremental adjustments should be made when appropriate.

There is also a common set of reasons that new products fail. These include inadequate feasibility analysis, overestimation of market potential, bad timing (i.e., introducing the product at the wrong time), inadequate advertising and promotion, and poor service.

One thing firms must guard against is testing the feasibility of a new offering at the time it is introduced and then failing to retest it periodically to ensure that it continues to fill a need. If a firm's business environment changes, it may need to change its product offerings quickly to remain relevant.

3. Explain the common reasons new products fail.

Other Product-Related Strategies

Along with developing new products, firms grow by improving existing products or services, increasing the market penetration of an existing product or service, or pursuing a product extension strategy.

Improving an Existing Product or Service Often, a business can increase its revenue by **improving an existing product or service**—enhancing quality, making it larger or smaller, making it more convenient to use, improving its durability, or making it more up-to-date. Improving an item means increasing its value and price potential from the customer's perspective. Consider a business that uses a new technology to switch from processing film from 2 days to 1 hour. By increasing the convenience of its service, the business will most likely increase its film processing revenue potential. Similarly, software firms routinely increase revenues by coming out with "updated" versions of an existing software product.

A mistake many businesses make is not remaining vigilant enough regarding opportunities to improve existing products and services. It is typically much less expensive for a firm to modify an existing product or service and extend its life than to develop a new product or service from scratch. To do this, entrepreneurs should continually ask themselves and those working with their venture, "what could we do to our product or service that would create more value for customers?"

Increasing the Market Penetration of an Existing Product or Service A **market penetration strategy** involves actions taken to increase the sales of a product or service through greater marketing efforts or through increased production capacity and efficiency. An increase in a product's market share is typically accomplished by increasing advertising expenditures, offering sales promotions, lowering the price, or increasing the size of the salesforce. Consider Proactiv, the skin-care company that is the focus of Case 11.2. Since its inception in 1994, Proactiv has relied on celebrity endorsers to demonstrate and promote its product. Judith Light and Vanessa Williams were the firm's first celebrity endorsers. Over the years, the company has added additional celebrity endorsers, including Anthony Robbins, Jessica Simpson, and Jane Seymour, to appeal to a broader and more diverse clientele. Dr. Kathie Rodan, a cofounder of Proactiv, points to the celebrity endorser program as one of the savviest actions the company has taken to build market share.[5] Another example is Starbucks, which has created a card, called "The Starbucks' Card, that permits customers to prepay from $10 to $100 for Starbucks items. By making it more convenient for its customers to purchase its products, Starbucks is hoping to increase revenues and profits. The ultimate objective of a market penetration

4. Discuss a market penetration strategy.

strategy is to increase net income along with total revenues. If an initiative costs more than the additional net income it generates, then the strategy would obviously be ineffective.

Increased marked penetration can also occur through increased capacity or efficiency, which permits a firm to have a greater volume of product or service to sell. In a manufacturing context, an increase in product capacity can occur by expanding plant and equipment or by outsourcing a portion of the production process to another company. **Outsourcing** is work that is done for a company by people other than the company's full-time employees. For example, a firm that previously manufactured and packaged its product may outsource the packaging function to another company and as a result free up factory space to increase production of the basic product. Firms should always outsource to companies that are particularly skilled at completing a certain activity.

Extending Product Lines A **product line extension strategy** involves making additional versions of a product so that it will appeal to different clientele or making related products to sell to the same clientele. For example, a company may make another version of a low-end product, that is a little better and then make another version of it that represents the top of the line to appeal to different clientele. This is a strategy that allows a firm to take one product and extend it into several products without incurring significant additional development expense. Computer manufacturers provide a good example of how to execute a product line extension strategy. Each manufacturer sells several versions of its desktop and laptop computers. The different versions of the same computer typically represent good, better, and best alternatives based on processor speed, memory capacity, monitor size, graphic capabilities, and other features. In regard to making related products to sell to the same clientele, many firms start by offering one product or service and then expand into related areas. For example, Payday Inc., an Albuquerque, New Mexico, payroll management firm, started by offering payroll services to its clients. To spur its growth, it now offers benefits administration and human resource consulting services to the same clientele.[6]

Firms also pursue product extension strategies as a way of leveraging their core competencies into related areas. For example, Abercrombie & Fitch has applied the expertise it developed through its Abercrombie and Hollister stores to the launching of RUEHL, a chain of stores aimed at customers (22 to 30 years old) who have outgrown their other stores. Similarly, Curves, the fitness center for women, recently announced that it will offer a 6-week weight-management class to nonmembers as well as members, as a way of further leveraging its expertise and facilities. An account of the history of Oracle, a computer database software company, provides a particularly interesting example of the potential payoff of a product extension strategy. The example demonstrates that product extension strategies can take time and patience to pay off but can lead to breakthrough growth strategies:

> As Ellison [Oracle's CEO] recognized that he had sold a database to almost every one of the biggest companies in the world, he knew he would need new products to sell. That is how he came up with the idea of applications. Oracle applications would sit on top of and use Oracle databases to perform functions such as inventory management, personnel record keeping, and sales tracking. The proof of his thinking took almost seven years, but by 1995, the company generated nearly $300 million in license revenues from application products and an additional $400 million in applications-related services.[7]

Another firm that has done a good job of executing a product extension strategy is OSI Restaurant Partners, the parent company for Outback Steakhouse and Carrabba's Italian Grill, as illustrated in the "Savvy Entrepreneurial Firm" feature for this chapter.

Geographic Expansion **Geographic expansion** is another internal growth strategy. Many entrepreneurial businesses grow by simply expanding from their original location to additional geographic sites. This type of expansion is most common in retail settings. For example, a small business that has a successful retail store in one location may expand by opening a second location in a nearby community. GAP, Walgreens, and

FedEx Kinko's are examples of firms that have grown through geographic expansion. Of course, McDonald's, which now has over 31,800 locations, is the classic example of incredibly successful growth through geographic expansion. The keys to successful geographic expansion follow:

- **Perform successfully in the initial location:** Additional locations can learn from the initial location's success.
- **Establish the legitimacy of the business concept in the expansion locations:** For example, a particular type of fitness center may be well accepted in its original location because it has been there a long time and has a loyal clientele. However, potential clientele in a neighboring community may be completely unfamiliar with its unique products and services. A common mistake an entrepreneurial venture makes when it expands from one community to another is to assume that if something works in one community, it will automatically work in another.
- **Don't isolate the expansion location:** Sometimes the employees in an expansion location feel isolated and that they are not receiving adequate training and oversight from the headquarters location. It is a mistake to believe that an expansion location can excel without the same amount of attention and nurturing that it took to build the business in the original location.

International Expansion

International expansion is another common form of growth for entrepreneurial firms. According to a recent PricewaterhouseCooper's survey of rapid-growth entrepreneurial firms, 46 percent of the 350 firms surveyed sell in international markets.[8] A look at the world's population and purchasing power statistics affirms the importance of international markets for growth-minded firms. Approximately 95 percent of the world's population and two-thirds of its total purchasing power are located outside the United States. Influenced by these data, an increasing number of the new firms launched in the United States today are international new ventures.

International new ventures are businesses that, from inception, seek to derive significant competitive advantage by using their resources to sell products or services in multiple countries.[9] From the time they are started, these firms, which are sometimes called "global start-ups," view the world as their marketplace rather than confine themselves to a single country. Amazon.com, for example, was an international firm from its inception and now generates 44 percent of its sales from international markets.[10] Other new firms are not

The pursuit of international markets is an important part of Yahoo!'s growth strategy. Yahoo! currently generates approximately 30 percent of its revenues and 23 percent of its income from international sales.

international from the start, but choose to enter international markets shortly after they gain product acceptance in the United States. For example, Slingbox, which makes a product that lets people watch TV on their computers while they are away from home (and is the subject of the "You Be the VC 1" feature at the end of the chapter), was founded in 2004. Having gained favorable reaction to its product in the United States, the company started testing a beta version of its product in Europe in 2006.[11]

savvy entrepreneurial firm

OSI Restaurant Partners: Making a Product Extension Strategy Work
www.osirestaurantpartners.com

Understanding entrepreneurs is sometimes difficult. If you had started a restaurant chain in the cholesterol-conscious 1980s, what would you have put on the menu? Chicken? Fish? Pasta? Salads? Apparently, none of these ideas appealed to Chris Sullivan and Robert Bashman, the founders of Outback. Of all things, they started a steakhouse.

In fairness to Sullivan and Bashman, they actually had a sensible business idea. Despite the consciousness about the fat content of foods that was prominent during the 1980s, they noticed that steakhouses were still doing well. What they needed was an attractive niche, so they positioned their first steakhouse, which opened in Tampa, Florida, in 1988, between the "high-end" steakhouses that charged $25 for a steak and the "low-end" steakhouses that charged $6.99 for a steak and salad. Along with offering an attractive price for a good meal, they did a lot of other things right. They created a unique atmosphere for their restaurant chain based on an Australian theme. As a way of keeping their employees "fresh," their restaurants are open only for the evening meal. They also made Outback Steakhouses fun. The restroom doors, for example, are labeled "Blokes" and "Aussies" instead of "Men" and "Women." Menu items include "Shrimp on the Barbie" and "Bloomin' Onion." While at times these unusual names confuse some customers, they also help create a lighthearted atmosphere that is perfect for casual dining.

The number of Outback steakhouses has grown rapidly. Today, OSI Restaurant Partners Inc., Outback's parent company, operates in all 50 states in the United States as well as in 20 other countries. The company, however, hasn't relied exclusively on its steakhouses to fuel its overall growth. Over time, the company has built on its experience of filling a "midrange niche" by developing a family of restaurant chains to grow revenues and profits. The

OSI Restaurant Partners' family of restaurants includes Outback Steakhouse, Carrabba's Italian Grill, Roy's, Fleming's Prime Steakhouse & Wine Bar, Lee Roy Selmon's, and Cheeseburger in Paradise. In looking for new restaurant ideas, the company tries to identify concepts that fill a niche and have broad appeal. All their restaurants also offer a good value and, as is the case with Outback Steakhouse, are fun, lighthearted, and creative.

OSI Restaurant Partners has created a savvy new-product development strategy that builds on what the company does best: run restaurants. The strategy has also consistently placed OSI's restaurant chains in the midprice range of attractive dining categories, which is proving to be a very profitable position.

Questions for Critical Thinking

1. Do you think OSI Restaurant Partners has an effective product extension strategy? Why or why not?

2. Conduct a survey of your friends who have eaten at Outback Steakhouse. What competitive threats do your friends see for this firm? In light of those threats, what do you think Outback should do to successfully deal with them? Could outsourcing be of any value to this firm in terms of controlling its costs and increasing its profitability? Why or why not?

3. To what extent does OSI Restaurant Partners' family of restaurants favorably reflect current trends in the eating and dining preferences of American consumers? Are future prospects for OSI's restaurants favorable or unfavorable based on these criteria? Do you think the firm's growth prospects are favorable or unfavorable in markets outside the United States? Why?

4. What other product-related strategies, if any, make sense for OSI Restaurant Partners?

Source: OSI Restaurant Partners homepage, www.osirestaurantpartners. com (accessed July 5, 2006).

Although there is vast potential associated with selling overseas, it is a fairly complex form of firm growth. Let's look at the most important issues that entrepreneurial firms should consider in pursuing growth via international expansion.

Assessing a Firm's Suitability for Growth Through International Markets
Table 14.2 provides a review of the issues that should be considered, including management/organizational issues, product and distribution issues, and financial and risk management issues, when a venture considers expanding into international markets. If these issues can be addressed successfully, growth through international markets may be

TABLE 14.2 Evaluating a Firm's Overall Suitability for Growth Through International Markets

Management/Organizational Issues

Depth of management commitment. A firm's first consideration is to test the depth of its management commitment to entering international markets. Although a firm can "test the waters" by exporting with minimal risk, other forms of internationalization involve a far more significant commitment. A properly funded and executed international strategy requires top management support.

Depth of international experience. A firm should also assess its depth of experience in international markets. Many entrepreneurial firms have no experience in this area. As a result, to be successful, an inexperienced entrepreneurial firm may have to hire an export management company to familiarize itself with export documentation and other subtleties of the export process. Many entrepreneurial firms err by believing that selling and servicing a product or service overseas is not that much different than doing so at home. It is.

Interference with other firm initiatives. Learning how to sell in foreign markets can consume a great deal of entrepreneurs' or managers' time. Overseas travel is often required, and selling to buyers who speak a different language and live in a different time zone can be a painstaking process. Overall, efforts must be devoted to understanding the culture of the international markets the venture is considering. Thus, a firm should weigh the advantages of involvement in international markets against the time commitment involved and the potential interference with other firm initiatives.

Product and Distribution Issues

Product issues. A firm must first determine if its products or services are suitable for overseas markets. Many pertinent questions need to be answered to make this determination. For example, are a firm's products subject to national health or product safety regulations? Do the products require local service, supplies, or spare parts distribution capability? Will the products need to be redesigned to meet the specifications of customers in foreign markets? Are the products desirable to foreign customers? All these questions must have suitable answers before entering a foreign market is advisable. A firm can't simply "assume" that its products are salable in foreign countries.

Distribution issues. How will the product be transported from the United States to a foreign country? Alternatively, how would a product produced in The Netherlands be transported to a U.S. market? Is the transportation reliable and affordable? Can the product be exported from the venture's home operation, or will it have to be manufactured in the country of sale?

Financial and Risk Management Issues

Financing export operations. Can the foreign initiative be funded from internal operations, or will additional funding be needed? How will foreign customers pay the firm? How will the firm collect bad debts in a foreign country? These questions must obtain appropriate answers before initiating overseas sales.

Foreign currency risk. How will fluctuations in exchange rates be managed? If the entrepreneurial firm is located in America and it sells to a buyer in Japan, will the American firm be paid in U.S. dollars or in Japanese yen?

an excellent choice for an entrepreneurial firm. The major impediment in this area is not fully appreciating the challenges involved.

Foreign Market Entry Strategies The majority of entrepreneurial firms first enter foreign markets as exporters, but firms also use licensing, joint ventures, franchising, turnkey projects, and wholly owned subsidiaries to start international expansion.[12] These strategies, along with their primary advantages and disadvantages, are explained in Table 14.3.

CNET Networks is a media company that reports technology news through Web sites, print media, and radio. Its flagship Web sites are CNET.com and ZDnet.com. CNET is an example of an entrepreneurial firm using multiple methods to increase its revenues in foreign markets. For example, the company currently has a Web presence in the United States and 12

TABLE 14.3 Primary Advantage and Disadvantage of Various Foreign-Market Entry Strategies

Foreign-Market Entry Strategy	Primary Advantage	Primary Disadvantage
Exporting. Exporting is the process of producing a product at home and shipping it to a foreign market. Most entrepreneurial firms begin their international involvement as exporters.	Exporting is a relatively inexpensive way for a firm to become involved in foreign markets.	High transportation costs can make exporting uneconomical, particularly for bulky products.
Licensing. A licensing agreement is an arrangement whereby a firm with the proprietary rights to a product grants permission to another firm to manufacture that product for specified royalties or other payments. Proprietary services and processes can also be licensed.	The licensee puts up most of the capital needed to establish the overseas operation.	A firm in effect "teaches" a foreign company how to produce its proprietary product. Eventually, the foreign company will probably break away and start producing a variation of the product on its own.
Joint ventures. A joint venture involves the establishment of a firm that is jointly owned by two or more otherwise independent firms. Fuji-Xerox, for example, is a joint venture between an American and a Japanese firm.	Gaining access to the foreign partner's knowledge of local customs and market preferences.	A firm loses partial control of its business operations.
Franchising. A franchise is an agreement between a franchisor (the parent company that has a proprietary product, service, or business method) and a franchisee (an individual or firm that is willing to pay the franchisor a fee for the right to sell its product, service, and/or business method). U.S. firms can sell franchises in foreign markets, with the reverse being true as well.	The franchisee puts up the majority of capital needed to operate in the foreign market.	Quality control.
Turnkey projects. In a turnkey project, a contractor from one country builds a facility in another country, trains the personnel that will operate the facility, and *turns* over the *keys* to the project when it is completed and ready to operate.	Ability to generate revenue.	It is usually a one-time activity, and the relationships that are established in a foreign market may not be valuable to facilitate future projects.
Wholly owned subsidiary. A firm that establishes a wholly owned subsidiary in a foreign country has typically made the decision to manufacture in the foreign country and establish a permanent presence.	Provides a firm total control over its foreign operations.	The cost of setting up and maintaining a manufacturing facility and permanent presence in a foreign country can be high.

foreign countries, including wholly owned operations in Australia, France, Germany, Japan, Russia, Switzerland, and the United Kingdom. It also has a number of joint ventures and licensees around the world, including South Korea and China. In China, CNET operates through a variety of entities, some of which are owned by Chinese employees in order to comply with local ownership and regulatory licensing requirements.[13]

Selling Overseas Many entrepreneurial firms first start selling overseas by responding to an unsolicited inquiry from a foreign buyer. It is important to handle the inquiry appropriately and to observe protocols when trying to serve the needs of customers in foreign markets. Following are several rules of thumb for selling products in foreign markets:

- Answer requests promptly and clearly. Do not ignore a request just because it lacks grammatical clarity and elegance. Individuals using a nonnative language to contact a business located outside their home nation often are inexperienced with a second language.
- Replies to foreign inquires, other than e-mail or fax, should be communicated through some form of airmail or overnight delivery. Ground delivery is slow in some areas of the world.
- A file should be set up to retain copies of all foreign inquiries. Even if an inquiry does not lead to an immediate sale, the names of firms that have made inquiries will be valuable for future prospecting.
- Keep promises. The biggest complaint from foreign buyers about U.S. businesses is failure to ship on time (or as promised). The first order is the most important. It sets the tone for the ongoing relationship.
- All correspondence should be personally signed. Form letters are offensive in some cultures.
- Be polite, courteous, friendly, and respectful. This is simple common sense, but politeness is particularly important in some Asian cultures. In addition, avoid the use of business slang that is indigenous to the United States, meaning that the slang terms lack meaning in many other cultures. Stated simply, be sensitive to cultural norms and expectations.
- For a personal meeting, always make sure to send an individual who is equal in rank to the person with whom he or she will be meeting. In some cultures, it would be seen as inappropriate for a salesperson from a U.S. company to meet with the vice president or president of a foreign firm.

External Growth Strategies

External growth strategies rely on establishing relationships with third parties, such as mergers, acquisitions, strategic alliances, joint ventures, licensing, and franchising. Thus, joint ventures, licensing, and franchising are strategic options entrepreneurial firms use to both enter foreign markets (as explained above) and accomplish external growth. Each of these strategic options is discussed in the following sections, with the exception of franchising, which we consider separately in Chapter 15.

An emphasis on external growth strategies results in a more fast-paced, collaborative approach toward growth than the slower-paced internal strategies, such as new product development and expanding to foreign markets. External growth strategies level the playing field between smaller firms and larger companies.[14] For example, Pixar, the small animation studio that produced the animated hits *Cars*, *Finding Nemo*, and *Toy Story*, had a number of key strategic alliances with Disney, before it was acquired by Disney in 2006. By partnering with Disney, Pixar effectively co-opted a portion of Disney's management savvy, technical expertise, and access to distribution channels. The relationship with Disney helped Pixar grow and enhance its ability to effectively compete in the marketplace, to the point where it became an attractive acquisition target. Similarly, by acquiring other companies, relatively young firms such as Pixar can gain access to patents and proprietary techniques that take larger firms years to develop on their own.

There are distinct advantages and disadvantages to emphasizing external growth strategies, as shown in Table 14.4.

Mergers and Acquisitions

Many entrepreneurial firms grow through mergers and acquisitions. A **merger** is the pooling of interests to combine two or more firms into one. An **acquisition** is the outright purchase of one firm by another. In an acquisition, the surviving firm is called the **acquirer**, and the firm that is acquired is called the **target**. This section focuses on acquisitions rather than mergers because entrepreneurial firms are more commonly involved with acquisitions than mergers. In most cases, the entrepreneurial firm is the target, meaning that it is the firm being acquired, but not always, in that there are certainly instances in which entrepreneurial firms have grown by acquiring other firms.

Acquiring another business can fulfill several of a company's needs, such as expanding its product line, gaining access to distribution channels, achieving economies of scale, or expanding the company's geographic reach. In most cases, a firm acquires a competitor or a company that has a product line or distinctive competency that it needs. Red Hawk Industries is an example of an entrepreneurial firm acquiring other companies to obtain new products. Red Hawk specializes in financial security systems, ranging from integrated

L E A R N I N G
Objective

6. Discuss the objectives a company can achieve by acquiring another business.

TABLE 14.4 Advantages and Disadvantages of Emphasizing External Growth Strategies

Advantages	Disadvantages
Reducing competition. Competition is lessened when a firm acquires a competitor. This step often helps a firm establish price stability by eliminating the possibility of getting in a price war with at least one competitor. By turning potential competitors into partners and through alliances and franchises, the firm can also reduce the amount of competition it experiences.	**Incompatibility of top management.** The top managers of the firms involved in an acquisition, an alliance, a licensing agreement, or a franchise organization may clash, making the implementation of the initiative difficult.
Getting access to proprietary products or services. Acquisitions or alliances are often motivated by a desire on the part of one firm to gain legitimate access to the proprietary property of another.	**Clash of corporate cultures.** Because external forms of growth require the combined effort of two or more firms, corporate cultures often clash, resulting in frustration and subpar performance.
Gaining access to new products and markets. Growth through acquisition, alliances, or franchising is a quick way for a firm to gain access to new products and markets. Licensing can also provide a firm an initial entry into a market.	**Operational problems.** Another problem that firms encounter when they acquire or collaborate with another firm is that their equipment and business processes may not be fully compatible.
Obtaining access to technical expertise. Sometimes, businesses acquire or partner with other businesses to gain access to technical expertise. In franchise organizations, franchisors often receive useful tips and suggestions from their franchisees.	**Increased business complexity.** Although the vast majority of acquisitions and alliances involve companies that are in the same or closely related industries, some entrepreneurial firms acquire or partner with firms in unrelated industries. This approach vastly increases the complexity of the combined business. The firm acquiring a brand or partnership with another company to gain access to its brand may subsequently fail to further develop its own brand and trademarks. This failure can lead to an increased dependency on acquired or partnered brands, reducing the firm's ability to establish and maintain a unique identity in the marketplace.
Gaining access to an established brand name. A growing company that has good products or services may acquire or partner with an older, more established company to gain access to its trademark and name recognition.	
Economies of scale. Combining two or more previously separate firms, whether through acquisition, partnering, or franchising, often leads to greater economies of scale for the combined firms.	**Loss of organizational flexibility.** Acquiring or establishing a partnership with one firm may foreclose the possibility of acquiring or establishing a partnership with another one.
Diversification of business risk. One of the principal driving forces behind all forms of collaboration or shared ownership is to diversify business risk.	**Antitrust implications.** Acquisitions and alliances are subject to antitrust review. In addition, some countries have strict antitrust laws prohibiting certain business relationships between firms.

security systems to safes and ATM machines. To keep its product line current and comprehensive, Red Hawk has acquired 16 smaller financial security firms since 1999. Once an acquisition is made, Red Hawk either folds the acquired firm's products into its catalog of offerings or boosts the sales of the acquired firm's products by assimilating them into its robust distribution network.[15]

what went wrong?

The Perfect Storm: The Aftermath of Movie Gallery's Acquisition of Hollywood Video
www.moviegallery.com

In April 2005, Movie Gallery boldly acquired rival Hollywood Video for $1.2 billion. It looked like a blockbuster deal. By combining its existing stores with Hollywood Video's outlets, Movie Gallery became the No. 2 video rental company in the country. The acquisition also blocked Blockbuster's bid to get bigger. Blockbuster fought hard to acquire Hollywood Video, with the purpose being to widen its already sizable lead in the video rental market.

Movie Gallery was founded in 1985 by Joseph Malugen, who remains the company's CEO. The company prospered through the 1980s and 1990s by focusing on rural and secondary markets, rather than competing head-to-head against Blockbuster and Hollywood Video in metropolitan areas. One thing the entrepreneurial venture became skilled at doing was acquisitions. It furthered its strategy of focusing on rural and secondary markets partly by opening new stores but also by acquiring dozens of smaller video chains. The strategy paid off. Since it went public in 1994 and prior to the Hollywood Video acquisition, it grew at a rate of 16.3 percent per year. During that same period, the video rental industry grew at a rate of 6.1 percent per year.

Clearly, Movie Gallery was on a roll—until the impact of the Hollywood Video acquisition started to be felt. Since the acquisition, a literal perfect storm of unfavorable events have plagued the company and have stretched its finances literally to the brink. Here's what's happened.

First, the Hollywood Video deal left Movie Gallery deeply in debt. Its debt is so burdensome, company Senior Vice President Thomas Johnson told *BusinessWeek* magazine in May of 2006 that it couldn't afford to launch an online video rental service to compete against Netflix and similar firms. Second, the rise of online video rental services, like Netflix, is taking sales from all the brick-and-mortar video rental chains. The fact that Movie Gallery is now larger, as the result of the Hollywood Video acquisition, makes this complication even more pronounced than

it would have been before. Finally, 2005, the year of the acquisition, was a weak year for new video releases. There were no new blockbuster films to bring large numbers of customers into video rental stores. All of these negatives have had a dramatic impact on Movie Gallery's bottom line, along with its ongoing operations. The company lost over $552.7 million in 2005. To save money, it is now closing unprofitable outlets and laying off employees.

Movie Gallery doesn't count itself out and is restructuring its debt and taking steps to try to reinvigorate its video rental stores. Still, the Hollywood Video acquisition demonstrates how an ill-advised or poorly timed acquisition can take a company that's on a roll to a screeching halt.

Questions for Critical Thinking

1. Developing economies of scale is one of the reasons Movie Gallery acquired Hollywood Video. Explain why having economies of scale in the video rental industry, at this point in time, may not enhance Movie Gallery's profitability.

2. What internal growth strategy or strategies could Movie Gallery have pursued instead of acquiring Hollywood Video as a way to try to increase revenues and profitability?

3. If you were Movie Gallery's CEO, what could you do now that your firm has purchased Hollywood Video? In other words, is there a way to make this acquisition more successful than it seems to be at this point? If so, what actions should be taken and why?

4. Netflix is another entrepreneurial venture competing in the video rental industry. Do you think that Netflix might want to buy Movie Gallery in order to have brick-and-mortar stores as another distribution channel? Why or why not?

Sources: Hoovers Online, www.hoovers.com (accessed July 7, 2006); Brian Grow, "Nightmare on Main Street," *BusinessWeek*, May 8, 2006.

Although it can be advantageous, the decision to grow the entrepreneurial firm through acquisitions should be approached with caution.[16] Many firms have found that the process of assimilating another company into their current operation is not easy and can stretch finances to the brink. Primarily for this reason, 65 to 70 percent of acquisitions fail to deliver anticipated results.[17] In this chapter's "What Went Wrong" feature, we describe Movie Gallery's troubled acquisition of Hollywood Video. While reading this feature, assess the degree to which you believe Movie Gallery's top-level managers carefully considered the issues, presented next, that are critical to evaluate when pursuing an acquisition strategy.

L E A R N I N G

Objective

7. Identify a promising acquisition candidate's characteristics.

Finding an Appropriate Acquisition Candidate If a firm decides to grow through acquisition, it is extremely important for it to exercise extreme care in finding acquisition candidates. Many acquisitions fail not because the companies involved lack resolve, but because they were a poor match to begin with. There are typically two steps involved in finding an appropriate target firm. The first step is to survey the marketplace and make a "short list" of promising candidates. The second is to carefully screen each candidate to determine its suitability for acquisition. The key areas to focus on in accomplishing these two steps are as follows:

- The target firm's openness to the idea of being acquired and its ability to obtain key third-party consent. The third parties from whom consent may be required include bankers, investors, suppliers, employees, and key customers.
- The strength of the target firm's management team, its industry, and its physical proximity to the acquiring firm's headquarters.
- The perceived compatibility of the target company's top management team and its corporate culture with the acquiring firm's top management team and corporate culture.
- The target firm's past and projected financial performance.
- The likelihood that the target firm will retain its key employees and customers if it is acquired.
- The identification of any legal complications that could impede the purchase of the target firm and the extent to which it has protected its intellectual property through patents, trademarks, and copyrights.
- The extent to which the acquiring firm understands the business and industry of the target firm.

The screening should be as comprehensive as possible to provide the acquiring firm sufficient data to determine realistic offering prices for the firms under consideration. A common mistake among acquiring firms is to pay too much for the businesses they purchase. Firms can avoid this mistake by basing their bids on hard data rather than on guesses or intuition.

Steps Involved in an Acquisition Completing an acquisition is a nine-step process, as illustrated in Figure 14.2:

Step 1 **Meet with the top management team of the acquisition target:** The acquiring firm should have legal representation at this point to help structure the initial negotiations and help settle any legal issues. The acquiring firm should also have a good idea of what it thinks the acquisition target is worth.

Step 2 **Assess the mood of the acquisition target:** If the target is in a "hurry to sell," it works to the acquiring firm's advantage. If the target starts to get cold feet, the negotiations may become more difficult.

Step 3 **Identify sources of financing for the transaction:** The acquiring firm should be financially prepared to complete the transaction if the terms are favorable.

Step 4 **Continue negotiations:** If a purchase is imminent, obtain all necessary shareholder and third-party consents and approvals.

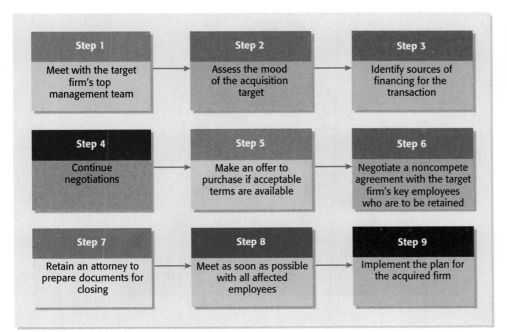

FIGURE 14.2

The Process of Completing the Acquisition of Another Firm

Step 5 **Make an offer to purchase if acceptable terms are available:** Both parties should have the offer reviewed by attorneys and certified public accountants that represent their interests. Determine how payment will be structured.

Step 6 **Negotiate a noncompete agreement with the target firm's key employees who are to be retained after the acquisition:** This agreement, as explained in Chapter 6, limits the rights of the key employees of the acquired firm to start the same type of business in the acquiring firm's trade area for a specific amount of time.

Step 7 **Retain an attorney to prepare the documents for closing:** Complete the transaction.

Step 8 **Meet as soon as possible with all affected employees:** A meeting should be held as soon as possible with the employees of both the acquiring firm and the target firm. Articulate a vision for the combined firm and ease employee anxiety where possible.

Step 9 **Implement the plan for the acquired firm:** In some cases, the acquired firm is immediately assimilated into the operations of the acquiring firm. In other cases, the acquired firm is allowed to operate in a relatively autonomous manner.

Licensing

Licensing is the granting of permission by one company to another company to use a specific form of its intellectual property under clearly defined conditions. Virtually any intellectual property a company owns that is protected by a patent, trademark, or copyright can be licensed to a third party. Licensing can be a very effective way of earning income, particularly for intellectual property–rich firms, such as software and biotech companies.

The terms of a license are spelled out through a **licensing agreement**, which is a formal contract between a licensor and a licensee. The **licensor** is the company that owns the intellectual property. The **licensee** is the company purchasing the right to use it. A license can be exclusive, nonexclusive, for a specific purpose, and for a specific geographic area.[18] In almost all cases, the licensee pays the licensor an initial payment plus an ongoing royalty for the right to use the intellectual property. There is no set formula for determining the amount of the initial payment or the royalties—these are issues that are part of the process of negotiating a licensing agreement.[19] Entrepreneurial firms often press for a relatively large initial payment as a way of generating immediate cash to fund their operations.

LEARNING
Objective

8. Explain "licensing" and how licensing can be used as a growth strategy.

eBay has engaged in a number of acquisitions to fuel its growth. Two of its largest and perhaps most important acquisitions have been PayPal and Skype. ebay CEO Meg Whitman and Skype cofounder and CEO Niklas Zennstrom share a light moment at Skype's headquarters in London, England.

Along with generating income, another distinct advantage of licensing for entrepreneurial firms is that it spreads the risk and cost of developing new technologies. An ever-present danger in licensing (and its most compelling disadvantage) is that a licensor may inadvertently create a competitor that quits licensing its products and starts selling something just dissimilar enough that it does not infringe on the licensing agreement. Another potential disadvantage associated with licensing is that by licensing its technology to one firm, a company may preclude itself from licensing to others or even making the product or service to which the technology pertains. This was one of the dilemmas facing Captivate Networks, the subject of Case 13.2. Recall, Captivate places digital screens inside elevators that display programming and advertising throughout the course of a day. Its first prototypes went into Otis Elevators. Otis was so taken with Captivate's product that it asked the company for an exclusive licensing arrangement. Although it was tempted to accept the offer, Captivate ultimately passed because it would have precluded it from installing its systems in the elevators of Otis's competitors.

There are two principal types of licensing: technology licensing and merchandise and character licensing.

Technology Licensing   **Technology licensing** is the licensing of proprietary technology that the licensor typically controls by virtue of a utility patent. This type of licensing agreement typically involves one of two scenarios. First, firms develop technologies to enhance their own products and then find noncompetitors to license the technology to spread out the costs and risks involved. Second, companies that are tightly focused on developing new products pass on their new products through licensing agreements to companies that are more marketing oriented and that have the resources to bring the products to market. Qualcomm is a perfect example of technology licensing. It invents and designs chips and software for cell phones. It then licenses the chips and software to larger, more marketing-oriented companies, such as Ericsson, Motorola, and Nokia that produce the cell phones and bring them to market.

Striking a licensing agreement with a large firm can involve tough negotiations. An entrepreneur should carefully investigate potential licensees to make sure they have a track record of paying licensing fees on time and are easy to work with. To obtain this information, it is appropriate to ask a potential licensee for references. It is also important that an entrepreneur not give away too much in regard to the nature of the proprietary technology in an initial meeting with a potential licensee. This challenge means finding the right balance of piquing a potential licensee's interest without revealing too much. Nondisclosure agreements, described in Chapter 7, should be used in discussing proprietary technologies with a potential licensee.

Merchandise and Character Licensing **Merchandise and character licensing** is the licensing of a recognized trademark or brand that the licensor typically controls through a registered trademark or copyright. For example, Harley-Davidson licenses its trademark to multiple companies that place the Harley trademark on T-shirts, jackets, collectibles, gift items, jewelry, watches, bike accessories, and so on. By doing this, Harley not only generates licensing income but also promotes the sale of Harley-Davidson motorcycles. Similarly, entrepreneurial firms such as Yahoo!, eBay, and Starbucks license their trademarks not only to earn licensing income but also to promote their products or services to a host of current and potential customers. According to the International Licensing Industry Merchandisers' Association, this type of licensing generates $110 billion annually in retail sales.[20]

The key to merchandise and character licensing is to resist the temptation to license a trademark too widely and to restrict licensing to product categories that have relevance and that appeal to a company's customers. If a company licenses its trademark too broadly, it can lose control of the quality of the products with which its trademark is identified. This outcome can diminish the strength of a company's brand. For example, consumers expect a certain level of quality when they purchase a Starbucks-branded product. If Starbucks started licensing its trademark indiscriminately, it would inevitably end up on products that disappoint consumers and result in a gradual loss of confidence in the Starbucks brand. To prevent this from happening, companies should restrict their licensing to product categories that have relevance and appeal to their customers and that reflect the quality image the company is trying to convey. For example, a company such as Liz Claiborne might license its trademark to a watch manufacturer that is interested in producing a line of "Liz Claiborne" men's and women's watches. Liz Claiborne would want to make sure that the watches bearing its trademark were fashionable, were of similar quality to its clothing, and were appealing to its clientele. Liz Claiborne can enforce these standards through the terms of its licensing agreements.

Strategic Alliances and Joint Ventures

The increase in the popularity of strategic alliances and joint ventures has been driven largely by a growing awareness that firms can't "go it alone" and succeed. According to a recent *Trendsetter Barometer* survey, released by PricewaterhouseCoopers, more than half of the 339 rapid-growth firms surveyed say that strategic alliances and joint ventures will be critical to their success over the next 3 years.[21] As with all forms of firm growth, strategic alliances and joint ventures have advantages and disadvantages. We present these points in Table 14.5.

Character licensing represents a major source of income and growth for a film company like Pixar, the creator of many memorable animated characters. Here, the two main characters from the animated hit Toy Story, *Woody and Buzz Lightyear, adorn the bedspread in a child's bedroom.*

TABLE 14.5 Advantages and Disadvantages of Participating in Strategic Alliances and Joint Ventures

Advantages	Disadvantages
Gain access to a particular resource. Firms engage in strategic alliances and joint ventures to gain access to a particular resource, such as capital, employees with specialized skills, or modern production facilities.	**Loss of proprietary information.** Proprietary information can be lost to a partner who is already a competitor or will eventually become one. This is a common worry.
Economies of scale. In many industries, high fixed costs require firms to find partners to expand production volume as a means of developing economies of scale.	**Management complexities.** Because strategic alliances and joint ventures require the combined effort of two or more firms, managing them can be challenging. Frustrations and costly delays often occur as a result.
Risk and cost sharing. Strategic alliances and joint ventures allow two or more firms to share the risk and cost of a particular business endeavor.	**Financial and organizational risks.** The failure rate for strategic alliances and joint ventures is high.
Gain access to a foreign market. Partnering with a local company is often the only practical way to gain access to a foreign market.	**Risk becoming dependent on a partner.** A power imbalance arises if one partner becomes overly dependent on the other. This situation increases the potential for opportunism on the part of the stronger partner. Opportunistic behavior takes advantage of a partner.
Learning. Strategic alliances and joint ventures often provide the participants the opportunity to "learn" from their partners.	**Partial loss of decision autonomy.** Joint planning and decision making may result in a loss of decision autonomy.
Speed to market. Firms with complementary skills, such as one firm being technologically strong and another having strong market access, partner to increase speed to market in hopes of capturing first-mover advantages.	**Partners' cultures may clash.** The corporate cultures of alliance partners may clash, making the implementation and management of the alliance difficult.
Neutralizing or blocking competitors. Through strategic alliances and joint ventures, firms can gain competencies and market power that can be used to neutralize or block a competitor's actions.	**Loss of organizational flexibility.** Establishing a partnership with one firm may foreclose the possibility of establishing a partnership with another firm.

Source: Adapted from B. R. Barringer and J. S. Harrison, "Walking a Tightrope: Creating Value Through Interorganizational Relationships," *Journal of Management* 26, no. 3 (2002): 367–403.

LEARNING Objective

9. Explain "strategic alliances" and describe the difference between technological alliances and marketing alliances.

Strategic Alliances A **strategic alliance** is a partnership between two or more firms that is developed to achieve a specific goal. Various studies show that participation in alliances can boost a firm's rate of patenting,[22] product innovation,[23] and foreign sales.[24] Alliances tend to be informal and do not involve the creation of a new entity (such as in a joint venture). An example of a firm that has made alliances a central portion of its growth strategy is 1-800-FLOWERS, as illustrated in this chapter's "Partnering for Success" boxed feature.

Technological alliances and marketing alliances are two of the most common forms of alliances.[25] **Technological alliances** feature cooperation in research and development, engineering, and manufacturing. Research-and-development alliances often bring together entrepreneurial firms with specific technical skills and larger, more mature firms with experience in development and marketing. By pooling their complementary assets, these firms can typically produce a product and bring it to market faster and cheaper than either firm could alone.[26] Pfizer's blockbuster drug Celebrex, for example, was created via a technological alliance. Celebrex is a prescription arthritis medicine. **Marketing alliances** typically match a company with a distribution system with a company that has a product to sell in order to increase sales of a product or service. For example, an American food company may initiate an alliance with Nestlé (a Swiss food company) to gain access to Nestlé's distribution channels in Europe. The strategic logic of this type of alliance for both partners is simple. By finding more outlets for its products, the partner that is supplying the product can increase economies of scale and reduce per unit cost. The partner that supplies the distribution channel benefits by adding products to its product line, increasing its attractiveness to those wanting to purchase a wide array of products from a single supplier.

partnering for *success*

1-800-Flowers.com: 40,000 Partners and Growing
www.1800flowers.com

1-800-Flowers.com sells fresh flowers and gifts for adults and children primarily through its toll-free number and the Internet. As is the case for many companies, it has a number of key partnerships. In the case of 1-800-FLOWERS, it promotes its products through strategic relationships with leading Web sites. The company's relationships include those it has established with America Online, Microsoft, Google, and Yahoo!.

Although this collection of relationships sounds impressive, it might not be the firm's most important category of partnerships. The company also has an extensive affiliate program that has grown to more than 40,000 Web sites operated by third parties. An affiliate program is a way for online merchants to get more exposure by offering a commission to Web sites that are willing to feature ads for their products. In the case of 1-800-FLOWERS, this is how it works. If you have a Web site, you can become part of the 1-800-FLOWERS affiliate program. 1-800-FLOWERS will provide you banner ads and other forms of advertising to place on your site. Each time a visitor from your site clicks through to the 1-800-FLOWERS site and makes a purchase, you earn a commission. If a customer from your site clicks through to 1-800-FLOWERS and doesn't buy anything right away but purchases something within 10 days, you are still credited for the sale.

Well-managed affiliate programs, such as the one featured by 1-800-FLOWERS, are organized in a way that builds trust and ensures that affiliates get paid. For example, LinkShare tracks all 1-800-FLOWERS purchases made via an affiliate and then pays the affiliates at the end of each month. Commissions are paid on a sliding scale, depending on the amount purchased. 1-800-FLOWERS pays a commission of 8 percent for monthly sales up to $2,000 and 10 percent for monthly sales over $2,000. The most attractive aspect of affiliate programs is that they are true win–win situations for all parties involved. 1-800-FLOWERS vastly increases its exposure by placing ads on 40,000+ Web sites, and each time a purchase is made through one of those sites, the owner earns a commission.

1-800-FLOWERS "qualifies" its affiliates before they are admitted to the program. The qualifying step, which is commonly adopted by firms using affiliates, is included to ensure that the company doesn't partner with an affiliate that tarnishes its image or brand. In general, 1-800-FLOWERS is looking for affiliate Web sites that:

- Are aesthetically pleasing
- Do not display content that may be deemed pornographic or offensive
- Are fully up and functional
- Are not personal homepages or personal Web sites

Through its affiliate program, 1-800-FLOWERS has literally created partnerships with the owners of over 40,000 Web sites.

Questions for Critical Thinking

1. All parties to a strategic alliance, such as those 1-800-FLOWERS has formed with various companies, must possess desirable attributes or skills. What does 1-800 FLOWERS "bring to the table" that is attractive to its partners? Prepare as comprehensive a list as possible to answer this question.
2. Study the details of 1-800-FLOWERS' affiliate program at www.affiliate.1800flowers.com/. Does the program seem to be fair for all parties involved? If you were thinking about becoming a 1-800-FLOWERS affiliate, what additional questions would you ask?
3. What risks does 1-800-FLOWERS run by having an affiliate program that involves over 40,000 partners?
4. Ask several of your friends who have used the 1-800-FLOWERS service to describe their experiences. As customers, were they satisfied? If so, why? If not, what aspects of the firm's service disappointed your friends as customers, and what could 1-800-FLOWERS do to avoid those problems in the future?

Sources: 1-800-FLOWERS 2005 10-K filing and 1-800-Flowers homepage, www.1800flowers.com (accessed July 7, 2006).

Both technological and marketing alliances allow firms to focus on their specific area of expertise and partner with others to fill their expertise gaps. This approach is particularly attractive to entrepreneurial firms, which often don't have the financial resources or time to develop all the competencies they need to bring final products to market quickly. Michael Dell describes the early years of Dell Inc.:

> As a small start-up, we didn't have the money to build the components [used to make up a PC] ourselves. But we also asked, "Why should we want to?" Unlike many of our competitors, we actually had an option: to buy components from the specialists, leveraging the investments they had already made and allowing us to focus on what we did best—designing and delivering solutions and systems directly to customers. In forging these early alliances with suppliers, we created exactly the right strategy for a fast-growing company.[27]

Joint Ventures A **joint venture** is an entity created when two or more firms pool a portion of their resources to create a separate, jointly owned organization.[28] An example is Beverage Partners Worldwide, which is a joint venture between Coca-Cola and Nestlé. The joint venture markets ready-to-drink chilled teas and coffees, including Nestea, Nestea Cool, Belte, and Planet Java, in more than 40 countries worldwide.

A common reason to form a joint venture is to gain access to a foreign market.[29] In these cases, the joint venture typically consists of the firm trying to reach a foreign market and one or more local partners. Joint ventures created for reasons other than foreign market entry are typically described as either scale or link joint ventures.[30] In a **scale joint venture**, the partners collaborate at a single point in the value chain to gain economies of scale in production or distribution. This type of joint venture can be a good vehicle for developing new products or services. In a **link joint venture**, the position of the parties is not symmetrical, and the objectives of the partners may diverge. For example, many of the joint ventures between American and Canadian food companies provide the American partner with access to Canadian markets and distribution channels and the Canadian partner with the opportunity to add to its product line.

A hybrid form of joint venture that some larger firms utilize is to take small equity stakes in promising young companies. In these instances, the large companies act in the role of corporate venture capitalists, as explained in Chapter 10. Intel officially established a venture capital program in the early 1990s, named Intel Capital. Investing in private companies, this program seeks to help start-up ventures grow from their initial stages to a point of either issuing an initial public offering or being acquired. As of July 2006, Intel had over 270 active investments fitting this profile.[31] Firms typically make investments of this nature in companies with the potential to be either suppliers or customers in the future. The equity stake provides the large company a "say" in the development of the smaller firm. On occasion, the larger firm that has a small equity stake will acquire the smaller firm. These transactions are called **spin-ins**. The opposite of a spin-in is a **spin-out**, which occurs when a larger company divests itself of one of its smaller divisions and the division becomes an independent company. Hewlett-Packard, for example, spun off its test-and-measurement equipment division in 1999, which became Agilent Technologies.

Chapter Summary

1. Internal growth strategies rely on efforts generated within the firm itself, such as new product development, other product-related strategies, international expansion, and Internet-driven strategies. External growth strategies rely on establishing relationships with third parties, such as mergers, licensing, strategic alliances, joint ventures, and franchising.

2. The keys to effective new product development are as follows: find a need and fill it, develop products that add value, get quality and pricing right, focus on a specific target market, and conduct an ongoing feasibility analysis.

3. The reasons that new products fail include an inadequate feasibility analysis, overestimation of market potential, bad timing (i.e., introducing a product at the wrong time), inadequate advertising and promotion, and poor service.

4. A market penetration strategy seeks to increase the sales of a product or service through greater marketing efforts or through increased production capacity and efficiency.

5. International new ventures are businesses that, from inception, seek to derive significant competitive advantage from the use of resources and the sale of outputs in multiple countries.

6. Acquiring another business can fulfill several of a company's needs, such as expanding its product line, gaining access to distribution channels, achieving competitive economies of scale, or expanding the company's geographic reach.

7. A promising acquisition candidate has the following characteristics: operates in a growing industry, has proprietary products and/or processes, has a well-defined and established market position, has a good reputation, is involved in very little, if any, litigation, is open to the idea of being acquired by another firm, is positioned to readily obtain key third-party consent to an acquisition, and is located in a geographic area that is easily accessible from the acquiring firm's headquarters location.

8. Licensing is the granting of permission by one company to another company to use a specific form of its intellectual property under clearly defined conditions. Virtually any intellectual property a company owns can be licensed to a third party. Licensing can be a very effective way of earning income, particularly for intellectual property–rich firms, such as software and biotech companies.

9. A strategic alliance is a partnership between two or more firms that is developed to achieve a specific objective or goal. Technological alliances involve cooperating in areas such as research and development, engineering, and manufacturing. Marketing alliances typically match one firm with a partner's distribution system that is attractive to the company trying to increase sales of its products or services.

10. A joint venture is an entity that is created when two or more firms pool a portion of their resources to create a separate, jointly owned organization. In a scale joint venture, the partners collaborate at a single point in the value chain to gain economies of scale in production or distribution by combining their expertise. In a link joint venture, the position of the parties is not symmetrical and the objectives of the partners may diverge.

Key Terms

acquirer, 418
acquisition, 418
external growth strategies, 417
geographic expansion, 412
improving an existing product
   or service, 411
internal growth strategies, 408
international new ventures, 413
joint venture, 426
licensee, 421

licensing, 421
licensing agreement, 421
licensor, 421
link joint venture, 426
market penetration strategy, 411
marketing alliances, 424
merchandise and character
   licensing, 423
merger, 418
new product development, 409

organic growth, 408
outsourcing, 412
product line extension strategy, 412
scale joint venture, 426
spin-ins, 426
spin-outs, 426
strategic alliance, 424
target, 418
technological alliances, 424
technology licensing, 422

Review Questions

1. Describe the difference between an internal and an external growth strategy. Provide examples of each strategy and how each one contributes to firm growth.
2. Under what circumstances is new product development a competitive necessity?
3. Describe some of the common reasons new products fail.

4. What is a market penetration strategy? Provide an example of a market penetration strategy, and describe how using it effectively might increase a firm's sales.

5. What is a product line extension strategy? Provide an example of a product line extension strategy, and describe how its effective use might increase a firm's sales.

6. What is a geographic expansion strategy, and what are the keys to implementing a successful geographic expansion strategy for an entrepreneurial firm? Make your answer as complete as possible.

7. What is an international new venture? Explain why it might be to the benefit of an entrepreneurial start-up to position itself as an international new venture from the outset.

8. What are the six foreign-market entry strategies? Briefly describe each strategy.

9. What are several rules of thumb to follow for selling products overseas?

10. Describe the difference between a merger and an acquisition. In what ways can acquisitions help firms fill their needs?

11. What are the characteristics of a promising acquisition candidate?

12. What are the nine steps involved in completing an acquisition?

13. What does the term *licensing* mean? How can licensing be used to increase a firm's revenues?

14. Describe the purpose of a licensing agreement. In a licensing agreement, which party is the licensor, and which is the licensee?

15. Describe the difference between technology licensing and merchandise and character licensing. Provide examples of both types of licensing and how they can increase a firm's sales.

16. Over the past several years, why have strategic alliances and joint ventures become increasingly prevalent growth strategies? Make your answer as thoughtful and as thorough as possible.

17. Describe the difference between technological alliances and market alliances. Provide examples of both types of alliances and how they can increase a firm's sales.

18. What is a joint venture?

19. How does a joint venture differ from a strategic alliance?

20. Describe the difference between a scale joint venture and a link joint venture. Provide examples of both types of joint venture and how their effective use can increase a firm's sales.

Application Questions

1. Ann Beatty owns a database software firm in Portland, Oregon. She currently has three products that are sold through office supply stores in the Northwest. Ann is frustrated because she hasn't increased her revenues during the past 3 years. Provide Ann with some suggestions for growth strategies she might pursue.

2. Taylor Jenkins has developed a new type of athletic shoe. He hopes to sell his product in retailers such as Foot Locker. Before he approaches Foot Locker, however, he wants to make sure that his product has the best chance of being successful. What criteria or rules of thumb can Taylor use to make sure that his product has "all the right stuff" before he takes it to Foot Locker?

3. Sleeptracker, the focus of the "You Be the VC 2" feature in this chapter, has just started to market a device that helps people feel more refreshed when they wake in the morning. If Sleeptracker's initial sales are promising, is it more likely that the firm will pursue internal or external strategies for growth? Explain the rationale for your answer.

4. Karen Paulsen has developed a new piece of computer hardware that she is convinced is a sure hit. She can't imagine that the product could fail. She just remembered that you are taking a course in entrepreneurship, however, and calls you on your cell phone. Her question is "Is there a common set of reasons that cause products to fail? If there is, I'd like to know them so I can make sure to avoid them before I pitch my new product to anyone." What would you tell her?

5. Chad Caldwell manufactures cookware that is sold to restaurants. He isn't really interested in developing new products but has been wondering lately about the options he has for increasing his sales. What advice would you give Chad if he asked you if there are any "product-related strategies short of developing new products" that he could utilize to increase his sales?

6. Jim Morrissey owns a small tool-and-die shop that makes parts for the automobile industry. Lately, he has been wondering about exporting but has no idea whether exporting is a good idea for his firm. Provide Jim with a list of factors to consider in assessing his firm's suitability for growth through international markets.

7. Google, the widely popular Internet search engine, has been on a buying spree in recent years and has acquired a number of smaller companies. Why would a company like Google, which employees hundreds of software engineers and computer programmers, decide to buy other firms to acquire technology and add to its product line, rather than developing the technology and new products in-house?

8. Donna Hawkins owns a small print shop in Sunnyvale, California. She is determined to grow her overall operation. She has decided to grow by acquiring other print shops and related businesses. She would like to start the process by broadly surveying the market to develop a "short list" of promising acquisition candidates. Help Donna make a checklist of the characteristics to evaluate in screening acquisition candidates.

9. Brian Brunner is an entrepreneur who has invented several devices that are used in the telecommunications industry. He has patented the devices, which he manufactues in a job shop in St. Louis. Brian sells the devices directly to AT&T and Sprint. Last week, Brian got a certified letter in the mail from Motorola, indicating that firm's interest in licensing the technology that is represented in one of his devices. Brian doesn't know anything about licensing and has turned to you for help. What would you tell Brian about licensing, and how would you suggest that he respond to Motorola's letter?

10. Imagine that you are the CEO of Burton Snowboards, a company that makes snowboards and related equipment. A clothing company has approached you about licensing your company's name in order to start selling a line of Burton Snowboard–labeled winter clothing, including sweaters, jackets, mittens, socks, and boots. What issues should you consider to evaluate this request?

11. Entrepreneur Mary Phillips is a software engineer and owns a small software company in Murfreesboro, Tennessee. A software firm in Cincinnati that would like to enter into a strategic alliance with her to share the research and development expense of producing a new software product has approached her. Mary has asked you if this type of arrangement is common and if strategic alliances are a legitimate vehicle through which to achieve firm growth. What would you tell her?

12. Peter Cook owns an e-commerce Web site that sells camping and boating supplies. He spends a lot of time on the Internet and sees the phrase "affiliate program" periodically but has never really figured out what an affiliate program is all about. Explain to Peter what an affiliate program is and how he could set up an affiliate program to drive traffic to his Web site.

13. Spend some time studying Slingbox, the focus of the "You Be the VC 1" feature for this chapter. Suppose the company hired you to investigate how strategic alliances and joint ventures could spur its growth. How would you approach the investigation? What types of growth-oriented strategic alliances and joint ventures do you think would be appropriate for Slingbox at this point in its corporate life?

14. Study the popular social networking site MySpace.com. What growth strategies has the company employed? Make recommendations for appropriate growth strategies for the future.

15. Which of the growth strategies discussed in the chapter are the most risky? Which are the least risky? What role should risk play in a company's decision to pursue a particularly growth strategy?

you be the VC 14.1

Slingbox
www.slingbox.com

Business Idea: Produce an affordable device that allows people who are away from home to tap into their home television cable box or satellite receiver and watch any program that is being played at home on their remote computer.

Pitch: Have you ever been away from home and kicked yourself because you were missing a local sporting event or other program that isn't being broadcast where you are? If so, then you are exactly the person that Sling Media wants to reach.

Sling Media has created a product called the Slingbox that lets people watch TV on their computers and Windows Mobile portable devices while they are away from home. The device is remotely connected to a user's television and home Internet connection and can then "sling" the television reception to the user, regardless of where the user is anywhere in the world. All the user has to have is access to an Internet connection and a computer. This arrangement permits someone to watch a hometown sporting event, for example, while traveling in another city. A user can also use the Slingbox to work in various locations in the home. For instance, a user can

watch television in a bedroom by slinging the reception from the cable box in the family room.

The Slingbox device is sleek, making it easy for a traveler to carry. Some hardware and software installation is required and can be accomplished through easy-to-follow instructions. A big plus for the Slingbox, from the user's point of view, is that all the user has to buy is the box itself—there are no monthly service fees. A Macintosh-compatible version of the Slingbox is currently being tested.

One way to think about the Slingbox is that it is one of the few products available that actually "adds value" to the services that you're already paying for. The Slingbox extends the reach of your cable TV or satellite service to alternative locations around the house or around the world.

Q&A: Based on the material covered in this chapter, what questions would you ask the firm's founders before making your funding decision? What answers would satisfy you?

Decision: If you had to make your decision on just the information provided in the pitch and on the company's Web site, would you fund this firm? Why or why not?

you be the VC 14.2

SleepTracker
www.sleeptracker.com

Business Idea: Develop an affordable, easy-to-use device that helps people feel more refreshed when they wake up in the morning.

Pitch: Ever wonder why you feel more refreshed after you wake up some mornings compared to others? The answer may be that you were awakened during a period of deep sleep, which is the worst time to wake up. A much better time to wake up is when you are in a period of light sleep. Interestingly, periods of deep sleep and light sleep are often separated by mere minutes. The difference in how you feel if you wake up during light sleep rather than deep sleep, however, can be dramatic.

Obviously, you can't control whether you wake up during a period of deep sleep or light sleep—until now. To address this problem, SleepTracker has developed a watch that will wake you only when you are in light sleep. The watch, which looks like a large athletic-type watch, monitors

and records brief periods of movement, which are indicative of light stages of sleep. The wearer sets an alarm on the watch and gives the alarm a window of between 10 and 30 minutes to wake up. (For example, between 6:10 AM and 6:30 AM) SleepTracker will then activate its alarm the first time during that window when you are in light sleep. The device has added benefits that can be activated at the user's discretion. For instance, it can be set to record all of your awake moments during the night so you can get an idea of how restful your sleep was.

Getting a good night's sleep is important for reasons beyond feeling refreshed. According to the National Institute of Health, drowsiness causes an estimated 100,000 car accidents each year in the United States. Fatigue-related accidents on the job are a hazard too, particularly in trucking, construction, and health care. Thus, SleepTracker has the potential to help each of us as individuals while also benefiting overall society as a whole.

Q&A: Based on the material covered in this chapter, what questions would you ask the firm's founders before making your funding decision? What answers would satisfy you?

Decision: If you had to make your decision on just the information provided in the pitch and on the company's Web site, would you fund this firm? Why or why not?

CASE 14.1

Cranium: Growing Aggressively But Carefully
www.cranium.com

Bruce R. Barringer,
University of Central Florida
R. Duane Ireland,
Texas A&M University

Introduction

Cranium was founded in 1998 by two former Microsoft executives, Whit Alexander and Richard Tait. While working together at Microsoft, they discovered that they shared a passion for entrepreneurship and set out to start a firm together. They thought about starting an Internet company but decided the market space was too crowded. Then one day, after spending a weekend playing board games with his wife and friends, Tait starting talking about creating a new type of board game. He noticed that different board games favored people with different skills. He was a particularly good Pictionary player, for example, but was only average at Scrabble. What if a game could be created that offered so much variety that everyone looked good when playing it? He shared his idea and his enthusiasm with Alexander, and the two decided to develop just such a game.

The result of Tait and Alexander's efforts was Cranium, a board game for adults. To provide the game a unique position in the marketplace, they decided to engineer it around the "moment," specifically the moment when players feel smart and funny around their family and friends. As a result, they designed Cranium around four decks of cards: Worm Wood, Data Head, Star Performer, and Creative Cat. The game is played by rolling dice (there are two people per team) and going around the board. On each square on which it lands, a team is required to draw a card and either answer the question or perform the activity that's required by the card before the timer runs out. The activities included in the four decks of cards range widely, from unscrambling words, to humming a tune, to answering trivia questions, to playing charades. The idea is that everyone is good at something, so the game makes people feel good about themselves when they complete the task at which they have some skill.

The Company's Origins

Rather than trying to convince toy stores and retailers like Wal-Mart and Target to carry the Cranium board game, the founders (who lived in Seattle) talked Starbucks into featuring the game in its restaurants, which built just the kind of initial buzz that the founders wanted. Soon after, Barnes & Noble (which had never sold a game before) and Amazon.com signed on. They also "seeded" interest in the game by borrowing a trick they learned from the makers of Trivial Pursuit. For $15,000, they recruited 100 radio stations around the country to have their DJs read Cranium questions over the air. The callers who phoned in the correct answers got a copy of the game as a prize.

The results of these efforts were nothing less than astounding. In 2001, Cranium sold 1 million copies, making it the fastest-selling board game in U.S. history. Since then, the company has grown rapidly, but carefully, and has moved forward with a strong sense of purpose and mission as its guide. Its mission is a very positive one and focuses on creating games that "enrich lives and create memories that give everyone a chance to shine." While at Microsoft, both Tait and Alexander were impressed by the way Bill Gates was able to instill Microsoft's mission to the point where any one of the software giant's 22,000 employees could have repeated it without missing a beat: "a computer on every desktop and in every home." Tait and Alexander sought to infuse a similar sense of mission at Cranium and allow the mission to guide its growth strategies.

Although Cranium has grown rapidly, which involves risk, the care that has been taken with its growth initiatives is instructive. The following are the major strategies in Cranium's growth, with an explanation of how the company has approached each one.

New Product Development

Cranium now has 14 board games, targeting the following age groups: ages 3, 4, 5, and up; ages 7 and up; family; and adults and teens. One thing the company has intentionally avoided is the temptation to simply take its flagship Cranium game and develop "age-appropriate" versions of it. Instead, each of the 14 games has been built from the ground up and was extensively tested within its age group. For example, Cadoo is a board game for kids 7 and up. The game fits in a backpack and is designed for two players (instead of four, like the original Cranium) since kids typically have only one friend over at a time.

The company didn't expand beyond board games until 2005, when it released *The Cranium Big Book of Outrageous Fun*. This launch extended the company's brand into an interactive, "game-in-a-book" product. The book will be distributed in partnership with Little, Brown Books for Young Readers, a major publisher of children's books. More recently, Cranium expanded into toys. The toys will include new creations by Cranium and will feature two existing product lines of toys from Big BOING, LLC, who is a Cranium partner. The selection of Big BOING as a partner was a very careful decision, according to Cranium cofounder Whit Alexander. Cranium and Big BOING have a similar sense of mission and a commitment to product quality.

International Expansion

Cranium is now selling products in 30 countries and 10 languages, and its international expansion has been achieved in a deliberate manner. Rather than simply translate its games into other languages, Cranium "localizes" each game for individual markets. As a result, the questions and activities within each game vary to appeal to the local cultures. The company has also created versions of its games that appeal to different ethnicities and regions of the world rather than people in specific countries. For example, in 2006 Cranium introduced a Latin American version of its original board game. The name of the game is *Cranium Edicion Lationamericana*. During the process of developing the game, Cranium put together a team of reviewers, writers, anthropologists, translators, and editors in Latin America to make sure the questions and activities included in the game crossed cultural and geographic lines in an appropriate manner.

Strategic Alliances

Cranium maintains a very lean staff, which has prompted the company to create a number of partnerships on both the operations and the sales sides of the company. On the sales side, Cranium has created a number of strategic alliances designed around "going where the customers are," rather than expecting the customer to find the games. This strategy harkens back to the early days when Cranium was first introduced through Starbucks rather than a traditional retailer. Currently, Cranium has formal alliances with Post Cereal, Bobili (a frozen pizza maker), Clorox, US Airways, Pizza Hut/Dr. Pepper, and Great Clips.

The alliances vary and each is entered into carefully. The Great Clips alliance put three different Cranium games in the waiting areas of Indianapolis Great Clips salons, and each stylist wore a Cranium T-shirt for a specified period of time. Kids visiting the salons were given a Cadoo starter pack to take home and explore. The Boboli alliance featured peel-offs (on the pizza boxes) that highlighted fun, Cranium-style activities that kids could do with their families while baking the pizza.

Future Growth Possibilities

Cranium's growth shows no sign of slowing. The company's products are now sold at more than 10,000 large retail stores and smaller specialty shops in 30 countries. From 2004 to 2005, Cranium's revenue increased 71 percent (55 percent domestically and 181 percent internationally). The company has won numerous awards and is the only company to win the Toy Industry Association's Game of the Year Award 4 years in a row.

There are several socioeconomic trends that may affect Cranium's future growth. While the sales of traditional toys have declined in the past several years, the sales of board games are up. In addition, children and teenagers, in increasing numbers, are moving away from traditional toys and games to video games and the Internet. Although this trend could hurt Cranium, there is a silver lining. (Another way of thinking about this is that along with every threat there comes an opportunity as well.) The company is seeing an increasing number of parents seeking out family-focused board games as an alternative to video games and the Internet for their families.

Discussion Questions

1. Despite its success, do you think Cranium is taking a risk by growing so quickly? What downsides could Cranium experience as a result of its rapid growth?
2. To date, Cranium has not engaged in any mergers or acquisitions. Why do you think this is the case? Would mergers and acquisitions be an effective growth strategy for Cranium? Explain your answer.

3. Which one of the growth strategies covered in this chapter do you think represents the most fruitful strategy for Cranium, moving forward? Why?

4. Is Cranium a good acquisition candidate for a major toy company like Mattel or Hasbro? Do you think Cranium is a good candidate for an initial public offering? Do you think the founder of Cranium would be open to the idea of Cranium being acquired?

Application Questions

1. Make a list of the things that you think Cranium has done "right" in regard to its growth and its growth

strategies. Briefly comment on how each item on the list has contributed to Cranium's successful execution of its overall growth strategy.

2. What can Cranium do to keep teenagers and young adults interested in board games? Develop a three-point plan that Cranium could implement to excite teenagers and young adults about Cranium board games.

Sources: Cranium homepage, www.cranium.com (accessed May 1, 2006); "Cranium, Inc. Builds on Success to Enter Toy Category," Cranium Press Release (May 2006); "Cranium Brings Families Together Morning, Noon and Night," *PRWeb* (November 2005); J. Bick, "Inside the Smartest Little Company in America." *Inc.* (January 2002).

CASE 14.2

Starbucks: Managing Growth in an Exemplary Manner
www.starbucks.com

Bruce R. Barringer,
University of Central Florida
R. Duane Ireland,
Texas A&M University

Introduction

Starbucks is well beyond the start-up stage. However, the manner in which the company has handled its growth over the years provides an excellent model for other firms to consider. The company's growth has been focused in four tightly clustered areas—the Starbucks retail stores, licensed outlets, products, and specialty operations.

Over time, Starbucks has not strayed from these four distinct areas, having turned down many offers that could have weakened its focus on them. In addition, the majority of its growth has been organic, meaning that it has been generated, until recently, by the company itself rather than achieved through mergers, acquisitions, or franchising and alliances. Since it was founded, the company has relied largely on its own initiative and the strength of its brand to achieve its growth.

This case provides a brief recap of (1) the two things Starbucks has done particularly well to set itself up for growth and provide an atmosphere where growth can flourish and (2) the strategies it has used to achieve growth. Although companies must craft their own growth philosophies and strategies, Starbuck's approach to growth provides useful guidance for all firms to consider.

Setting Itself Up for Growth

There are two things that Starbucks has done particularly well to set itself up for growth and to create an environment where growth can flourish. First, from the beginning, the company has focused on hiring and retaining high-quality employees and managers. Early on, for example, Starbucks' founder, Howard Schultz, hired Howard Behar, an experienced manager, to head the company's retail operations and Orin Smith as the company's chief financial officer. Smith was a particularly key hire. With a Harvard MBA and 13 years of consulting experience with Deloitte & Touche (which today is part of the global firm Deloitte Touche Tohmatsu), he brought discipline to the Starbucks operations without inhibiting its entrepreneurial spirit.

Schultz also developed a deep appreciation for the role that his *baristas*, or coffee brewers, played in creating an inviting environment for Starbucks customers. Schultz's appreciation for his employees showed: He spent money on employee benefits and training that could have been spent on advertising. In 1988, Starbucks became one of the first companies to extend full health benefits to part-time employees; in 1991, it became the first privately owned U.S. firm to offer a stock option program (called "bean" stock). Reflecting on his philosophy of managing and rewarding employees, Schultz wrote in his memoirs:

We can be extremely profitable and competitive, with a highly regarded brand, and also be respected for treating our people well. In the end, it's not only possible to do both, but you can't really do one without the other.

Treating employees well has paid off for Starbucks. After the company began offering part-time employees health benefits, the employee turnover rate dropped from as much as 175 percent per year to less than 65 percent. And it was a Starbucks employee in southern California who originally crafted the blended Frappuccino brand of bottled coffee, which has been enormously successful.

The second thing the company has done particularly well to set itself up for growth and create an environment where growth can flourish is to remain true to its guiding principles and strengths, which at times has stymied growth in the short term in the interest of preserving growth for the long term. The simple formula of providing customers high-quality, freshly brewed coffee in a comfortable, secure, and inviting atmosphere is as important as ever and has enabled the company to build a strong brand and move forward with a consistent commitment to providing its customers a quality, Starbucks experience. For example, Starbucks has had many opportunities to sell its coffee through venues such as McDonald's but has consistently rejected these opportunities. Because of its commitment to high quality, it does not want to risk cheapening its brand.

Executing Multiple, Yet Highly Focused, Growth Strategies

As noted, Starbucks' growth has focused on four areas: the Starbucks retail stores, licensed outlets, products, and specialty operations. Although it seems like this set of strategies represents a broad array, the company has actually remained highly focused in its growth efforts. Each of the four areas of focus is straightforward and transparent and represents a sensible and prudent way for the company to extend its brand.

The primary method of growth has been to increase the number of Starbucks retail stores, both domestically

and abroad. (Toward the end of 2006, Starbucks announced that over the long term, it would have a total of 40,000 units on a global basis.) Starbucks does not franchise—with one notable exception. Magic Johnson, the former NBA basketball star, owns an interest in about 75 Starbucks franchises through the Johnson Development Corporation, an organization that helps revitalize urban communities. Instead of franchising, over 60 percent of Starbucks outlets are company-owned stores, with the remaining 40 percent run by licensees (which we will talk about next). Its first international outlet was opened in Tokyo, Japan, in 1992, and the company currently has coffee shops in 36 countries. In most cases, Starbucks has entered international markets by partnering with local companies that know the local communities, issues, and culture. Schultz credits this approach as a key factor in making the international expansion of Starbucks both feasible and practical. Starbucks has also been successful at making its stores a good place to simply hang out, check e-mail, meet a business acquaintance for lunch, or enjoy being with a friend or family member.

The second method of growth has been through licensing. Although the company prefers company-owned stores to licensing, there are locations where company-owned stores are either not allowed or are impractical. As a result, Starbucks has a large number of licensed outlets (5,338 as of October, 2006) in places like Barnes & Nobel bookstores, college campuses, airports, hospitals, grocery stores, and office buildings that are authorized to sell Starbucks drinks.

The third method of growth has been through new products. The number of products that Starbucks sells through its retail stores has grown over the years, helping to increase same-store sales. Rich-brewed coffee, Italian-style espresso beverages, cold blended beverages, a variety of pastries and confections, coffee-related accessories and equipment, other beverages, such as tea, juice, and

Starbucks' Four Strategies for Growth

soda, and carefully selected novelty items, like Cranium board games and Barnes & Noble CDs, are sold in Starbucks' retail stores. The company has also excelled at drawing people into its stores who wouldn't normally have visited a coffee shop. Drinks like White Chocolate Mocha and Chai Eggnog Latte appeal to people who don't normally like coffee. Introducing these types of drinks has helped Starbucks make major inroads in youth and female markets.

The final way that Starbucks has spurred its growth is through its specialty operations. These operations seek to develop the Starbucks brand outside the company-owned retail stores through a number of channels, including business alliances, grocery channel licensing, warehouse club accounts, and other initiatives. An example is the North American Coffee Partnership, which is a 50-50 joint venture between Starbucks and PepsiCo. The joint venture was launched in 1994 to develop and distribute ready-to-drink coffee-based products, such as Frappuccino and Starbucks Doubleshot. Similarly, in 1996 Starbucks and Dryers launched a joint venture to develop and distribute Starbucks' premium ice cream. It also has a grocery retail licensing relationship with Kraft, which has placed a selection of Starbucks coffee beans in grocery stores.

Opportunities and Challenges Ahead

Through its emphasis on employees, commitment to core values, and a premium brand, there is no reason to think that Starbucks won't continue to grow. The company currently has over 12,000 retail stores and is the leading retailer of specialty coffee in the world. A total of 1,672 stores were added in 2005 alone. Beginning in 2006, the company planned to add at least 2,000 units annually for the next several years. Revenues and profits are sound. In 1995, net revenues increased 20 percent to $6.4 billion, while net earnings increased 27 percent to $494 million.

Starbucks' commitment to organic growth, which was in effect during the formative years of the company's development, has eased some in recent years to include carefully targeted acquisitions and partnerships, which are part of the company's specialty operations. The company now owns and franchises the Seattle's Best Coffee and Torrefazione Italia chains in the United States. Starbucks has learned that growth beyond a company's core entails risk. In 2005, the company partnered with Jim Beam to produce a Starbucks coffee liqueur. As a result, Pax World Fund (which is a highly respected socially responsible mutual fund) dropped Starbucks from its investment portfolio, citing a policy of not investing in companies that make money by producing and selling liquor-based products. This is in spite of the fact that

Starbucks has made a major commitment to social responsibility itself. Starbucks supports conservation measures among the nations that supply its coffee beans, encourages farming practices that limit negative impacts on the environment, and engages in a number of other socially responsible initiatives in the United States and abroad.

The biggest challenge that lies ahead for Starbucks will be whether the company's guiding principles will remain the driver of its expansion efforts. Reflecting on this challenge, which most successful entrepreneurial firms face at some point in their life, Howard Schultz remarked:

> There is no doubt in my mind that Starbucks can realize its financial goals. A more fragile issue is whether our values and guiding principles will remain intact as we continue to expand. I for one would consider it a failure if we reach the $2-billion-plus level at the expense of our unique connection with our people.

Discussion Questions

1. In the quote that ends the case, what is Schultz really worried about? What does he mean when he implies that the company risks losing its "unique connection" with its people? How would it hurt Starbucks if this happened?

2. Rank Starbucks' four methods of growth from 1 to 4 (1 is the best), based on which areas you think represent the most fruitful areas for the company, moving forward. Justify your rankings. Are their any areas of growth that Starbucks has neglected? If so, what are they?

3. Why do you think Starbucks never engaged in franchising (with the one exception noted in the case)? Why wouldn't franchising have been a sensible course of growth for the firm during the formative years of its existence?

4. Do you think Starbucks made a mistake by partnering with Jim Beam to produce a Starbucks coffee liqueur? Why or why not?

Application Questions

1. If you've never visited a Starbucks' retail store, visit one. If you have visited a Starbucks, reflect on your experiences. What, if anything, did you notice that's "special" about Starbucks? Was there anything that you noticed during your visit, or during previous visits, that illustrated for you why Starbucks has been so successful?

2. Think about a job you've had or an organization that you've been a part of. Did the company you worked for or the organization that you were a part of (1) treat its employees (or volunteers) well and (2) remain

committed to its core values, even when that resulted in missing out on short-term opportunities? If so, did an adherence to these practices help the company or organization grow? If not, did it hurt the company or organization's growth aspirations? Explain your answer.

Sources: K. W. Wiley, "Taste of Success," *Selling Power* (April 2006); Starbucks homepage (accessed May 8, 2006); R. Gulati, S. Huffman, and G. Neilson, "The Barista Principle: Starbucks and the Rise of Relational Capital," *Strategy and Business* 28 (2002); H. Schultz, *Pour Your Heart Into It* (New York: Hyperion, 1997).

Endnotes

1. Personal Interview with Christian Marin, July 10, 2006.
2. Superior Scientific homepage, www.superior-scientific.com (accessed July 10, 2006).
3. 3M homepage, www.3M.com (accessed July 9, 2006).
4. PricewaterhouseCoopers, "Fast-Growth Companies Make Innovation a Way of Life," *Trendsetter Barometer*, March 15, 2005.
5. K. Rodan, Stanford Technology Ventures Entrepreneurial Thought Leaders, Leaders Podcast, April 20, 2006.
6. PAYDAY Inc. homepage, www.paydayinc.com (accessed April 21, 2006).
7. F. M. Stone, *The Oracle of Oracle* (New York: AMACOM Books, 2002), 125.
8. PricewaterhouseCoopers, "Fast-Growth CEOs Set Revenue Target and Investment Plans Higher, PricewaterhouseCooper's Finds," *Trendsetter Barometer*, August 23, 2005.
9. J. P. Mathews, "Dragon Multinationals: New Players in 21st Century Globalization," *Asia Pacific Journal of Management* 23, no. 1 (2006): 5–27; B. M. Oviatt and P. P. McDougall, "Defining International Entrepreneurship and Modeling the Speed of Internationalization," *Entrepreneurship Theory and Practice* 29, (2005): 537–53.
10. Amazon.com 10-K filing with the Securities & Exchange Commission, February 17, 2006.
11. Slingbox homepage, www.slingmedia.com (accessed June 29, 2006).
12. J. W. Lu and P. W. Beamish, "Partnering Strategies and Performance of SMEs' International Joint Ventures," *Journal of Business Venturing* 21 (2006): 461–86.
13. CNET's 10-K filing with the Securities & Exchange Commission, March 16, 2006.
14. S. A. Alvarez, R. D. Ireland, and J. J. Reuer, "Entrepreneurship and Strategic Alliances," *Journal of Business Venturing* 21 (2006): 401–04.
15. Red Hawk homepage, www.redhawkindustries.com (accessed June 29, 2006).
16. P. Nijkamp and J. V. Ommeren, "Drivers of Entrepreneurial Location as an Innovative Act," *International Journal of Entrepreneurship and Innovation Management* 6 (2006): 256–64.
17. H. A. Schildt and T. Laamanen, "Who Buys Whom: Information Environments and Organizational Boundary Spanning Through Acquisitions," *Strategic Organization* 4, no. 2 (2006): 111–33.
18. D. H. B. Welsh, I. Alon, and C. M. Falbe, "An Examination of International Retail Franchising in Emerging Markets," *Journal of Small Business Management*, 44, no. 1 (2006): 130–149.
19. S. Shane, "Introduction to the Focused Issue on Entrepreneurship," *Management Science* 52, no. 2 (2006): 155–59.
20. "Being Small Can Help Win the Big Contract," StartupJournal.com (accessed June 29, 2006).
21. PricewaterhouseCoopers, "Alliances and Acquisitions Increasingly Important for Fast-Growth Companies, PricewaterhouseCoopers Finds," *Trendsetter Barometer*, May 16, 2006.
22. W. Shan, G. Walker, and B. Kogut, "Interfirm Cooperation and Startup Innovation in the Biotechnology Industry," *Strategic Management Journal* 15 (1994): 387–94.
23. F. T. Rothaermel and D. L. Deeds, "Alliance Type, Alliance Experience and Alliance Management Capability in High-Technology Ventures," *Journal of Business Venturing* 21 (2006): 429–60; D. J. Kelley and M. P. Rice, "Advantage Beyond Founding: Strategic Use of Technologies," *Journal of Business Venturing* 17 (2002): 41–57.
24. M. J. Leiblein and J. J. Reuer, "Building a Foreign Sales Base: The Roles of Capabilities and Alliances for Entrepreneurial Firms," *Journal of Business Venturing* 19 (2004), 285–307.
25. S. Das, P. K. Sen, and S. Sengupta, "Impact of Strategic Alliances on Firm Valuation," *Academy of Management Journal* 41 (1998): 27–41.
26. E. V. Karniouchina, L. Vitorino, and R. Verma, "Product and Service Innovation: Ideas For Future Cross-Disciplinary Research," *Journal of Product Innovation Management* 23 (2006): 274–87; D. L. Deeds and C. W. L. Hill, "Strategic Alliances and the Rate of New Product

Development: An Empirical Study of Entrepreneurial Biotechnology Firms," *Journal of Business Venturing* 11 (1996): 41–55.

27. M. Dell, *Direct from Dell* (New York: HarperBusiness, 1999), 50.

28. A. Madhok, "How Much Does Ownership Really Matter? Equity and Trust Relations in Joint Venture Relationships," *Journal of International Business Studies* 37 (2006): 4–11.

29. R. M. Salomon, "Spillovers to Foreign Market Participants: Assessing the Impact of Export Strategies on Innovative Productivity," *Strategic Organization* 4 (2006): 135–64.

30. J. F. Hennart, "A Transaction Cost Theory of Equity Joint Ventures," *Strategic Management Journal* 9 (1988): 361–74.

31. Intel Capital homepage, www.intel.com/capital (accessed June 29, 2006).

Currently in my iPod

Michael Buble

Hardest part of getting funding

Outside pressures for return

My advice for new entrepreneurs

Be innovative, be nimble

College Nannies & Tutors:

Franchising as a Form of Business Ownership and Growth

Joseph Keeley grew up in a small town in North Dakota. After graduating from high school in 2000, he moved to St. Paul, Minnesota, to attend St. Thomas University. One of Keeley's passions was hockey, which he fulfilled as a member of St. Thomas's varsity hockey team. While playing hockey, he became acquainted with a couple that had two young boys and a girl. As the summer following his freshman year approached, the couple asked him if he'd be interesting in watching their kids as a full-time summer job. Keeley jumped at the chance. While his two roommates spent the summer digging pools for a local contractor, Keeley engaged in fun activities with the children, and acted as their nanny and role model.

The summer job got Keeley to thinking about how young kids need positive role models and how college students are uniquely capable of filling that role. The idea was so compelling that during his sophomore year he launched a company called Summer College Nannies. Matching college students with families that needed part-time or full-time nanny services was the firm's core service. Early on he viewed himself more as a matchmaker than as a potential franchisor, and viewed his business primarily as a way to earn extra cash. But as time went on, two things struck Keeley. First, rather than just a means of earning extra money, he started to see real potential in the college nanny idea. For many parents, there wasn't a service available to help them find a safe and reliable nanny. He also liked the idea of making a positive difference in the lives of families and young children. Second, he found that having an actual business to work on enhanced his classroom experiences. "I feel I had 10 times the education that anyone else did because I had a working, living project everyday," Keeley said, reflecting on this point.[1]

As the business picked up steam, St. Thomas provided Keeley with office space, and he turned Summer College Nannies into a self-made internship. To get advice, he started dropping in on St. Thomas entrepreneurship professors, who urged him to enroll in the entrepreneurship program—which he did. As time went on, Keeley entered and won several business plan competitions with the Summer College Nannies business idea. He also won the 2003 Global Student Entrepreneurship Award, which is presented by the Entrepreneurs' Organization and included a

JOSEPH KEELEY
Founder, College Nannies & Tutors
BS in Entrepreneurship
St. Thomas University, 2003

UNIVERSITY *of* ST. THOMAS
MINNESOTA

What I do when I'm not working

Water & snow ski, ice hockey, enjoy time with my baby daughter and wife

First entrepreneurial experience

Custom car washing service

My biggest surprise as an entrepreneur

The many areas that one must be good at or willing to learn

439

After studying this chapter you should be ready to:

L E A R N I N G

Objectives

1. Explain franchising and how it differs from other forms of business ownership.

2. Describe the differences between a product and trademark franchise and a business format franchise.

3. Explain the differences among an individual franchise agreement, an area franchise agreement, and a master franchise agreement.

4. Describe the advantages of establishing a franchise system as a means of firm growth.

5. Identify the rules of thumb for determining when franchising is an appropriate form of growth for a particular business.

6. Discuss the factors to consider in determining if owning a franchise is a good fit for a particular person.

7. Identify the costs associated with buying a franchise.

8. Discuss the advantages and disadvantages of buying a franchise.

9. Identify the common mistakes franchise buyers make.

10. Describe the purpose of the Uniform Franchise Offering Circular.

$20,000 prize. At the awards ceremony, Keeley met Peter Lytle, an angel investor and well-known Minneapolis entrepreneur. Although he had interviewed for traditional jobs, by this time Keeley had decided that following graduation he would devote his time and energy to his own business venture. Lytle was so impressed with Keeley and his business idea that he offered to invest, and Keeley accepted the offer. At this point, Lytle helped Keeley expand his vision for the business to include tutors, and College Nannies & Tutors was born.

Following graduation, the money Lytle invested provided Keeley the time and resources to more fully develop the College Nannies & Tutors business idea. The company started to generate some buzz, primarily through media coverage and word of mouth. One of the things that interested the media was the fact the Keeley, a male and a recent college graduate, was starting a company in an industry—childcare—that traditionally, females dominated. The first College Nannies & Tutors center was opened in Wayzata, a suburb of Minneapolis. In college, Keeley took a class in franchising, and as Keeley and Lytle fine-tuned their business idea over 2 long years of testing and planning, it became clear that College Nannies & Tutors was franchiseable. Interestingly, part of the firm's franchising process included proprietary ways for screening nannies through background checks, interviews, and psychological assessments and matching them with families. Commenting on the suitability of College Nannies & Tutors for franchising, Keeley remarked, "[And] there's value there as a franchise because we've figured it out. You (a potential franchisee) don't have to go through the learning curve."[2]

College Nannies & Tutors currently has seven franchise locations in three states, including Minnesota, Arizona, and Pennsylvania. The goal is to have 200 locations in 5 years.[3]

Many retail and service organizations find franchising to be an attractive form of business ownership and growth. In some industries, such as restaurants, hotels, and automobile service, franchising is a dominant business ownership form. Franchising is less common in other industries, although franchising is now being used in industries as diverse as Internet service providers, furniture restoration, cellular services, and senior care.

There are instances in which franchising is not appropriate. For example, new technologies are typically not introduced through franchise systems, particularly if the technology is proprietary or complex. Why? Because franchising, by its very nature, involves the sharing of knowledge between a franchisor and its franchisees, and this, in large franchise organizations, can involve thousands of people. The inventors of new technologies typically involve as few people as possible in the process of rolling out their new products or services because they want to keep their trade secrets secret. They typically reserve their new technologies for their own use or license them to a relatively small number of companies, with strict confidentiality agreements in place.[4]

Still, franchising is a common method of business expansion and is growing in popularity. In 1950, fewer than 100 franchisors existed in the United States. Today, there are roughly 2,500 franchise systems in the United States, collectively accounting for about one-third of all retail sales.[5] You can even go to a Web site (www.franchising.com) to examine the array of franchises available for potential entrepreneurs to consider. This Web site groups franchising opportunities by type (e.g., automotive, personal services, specialty retail, and so forth) as well as the total number of dollars a franchisee must invest to get started. These categorizations highlight the breadth of franchising opportunities now available for consideration.

Unfortunately, not all the news about franchising is positive. Because many franchise systems operate in competitive industries and grow quickly, the failure rate is relatively high. It is estimated that three-quarters of all franchise systems fail within 12 years of their founding.[6] Plus, despite its proliferation, franchising is a relatively poorly understood form of business ownership and growth. While most students and entrepreneurs generally know what franchising is and what it entails, franchising has many subtle aspects that can be learned only through experience or careful study.

We begin this chapter, which is dedicated to franchising as an important potential path to entrepreneurship and subsequent venture growth, with a description of franchising and when it is appropriate to use franchising. We then explore setting up a franchise system from the franchisor's perspective and buying a franchise from the franchisee's point of view. Next, we look at the legal aspects of franchising. We close this chapter by considering a few additional topics related to the successful use of franchising.

What Is Franchising and How Does It Work?

Franchising is a form of business organization in which a firm that already has a successful product or service (**franchisor**) licenses its trademark and method of doing businesses to other businesses (**franchisees**) in exchange for an initial franchise fee and an ongoing royalty.[7] Some franchisors are established firms; others are first-time enterprises being launched by entrepreneurs. This section explores the origins of franchising and how franchising works.

L E A R N I N G

Objective

1. Explain franchising and how it differs from other forms of business ownership.

What Is Franchising?

The word *franchise* comes from an old dialect of French and means "privilege" or "freedom." Franchising has a long history. In the Middle Ages, kings and lords granted franchises to specific individuals or groups to hunt on their land or to conduct certain forms of commerce. In the 1840s, breweries in Germany granted franchises to certain taverns to be the exclusive distributors of their beer for the region. Shortly after the U.S. Civil War, the Singer Sewing Machine Company began granting distribution franchises for its sewing machines and pioneered the use of written franchise agreements. Many of the most familiar franchises in the United States, including Kentucky Fried Chicken (1952), McDonald's (1955), Burger King (1955), Midas Muffler (1956), and H&R Block (1958), started in the post–World War II era of the 1940s and 1950s.

The franchise organization Comfort Keepers demonstrates how franchises are started. A year before the company was founded, Kristina Clum, a registered nurse, noticed that her parents were having trouble with ordinary daily chores. She wanted someone to come into their home to help them but was unable to find people willing to do so. So Kristina and her husband Jerry founded a business dedicated to helping seniors cope with everyday nonmedical tasks, such as meal preparation, light housekeeping, grocery shopping, laundry, and errands. The first Comfort Keepers office was opened in Springfield, Ohio, in March 1998, and the second was opened in Dayton a year later.

Smoothie franchises such as Planet Smoothie and Smoothie King are examples of business format franchises. Smoothie King has certainly used this approach to its advantage. It operates more than 425 locations in 38 states and 14 foreign countries and opens new stores on a weekly basis in the United States.

Comfort Keepers is a timely idea that addresses a need for a particular target market. As we've discussed in earlier chapters, having a solid business idea is critical to achieving firm growth. In mid-2005, there were 36.8 million people in the United States over the age of 65. That number is expected to exceed 70 million over the next two decades. The services offered by Comfort Keepers may provide some seniors the option of staying in their homes as opposed to entering more costly assisted living centers.[8] In August 1999, the company began franchising and by 2006 had over 540 franchise outlets. At a total franchise investment cost of between $44,000 and $66,000, Comfort Keepers claimed that it was one of the least expensive franchises available to investors/entrepreneurs.[9]

The Comfort Keepers business idea lends itself to franchising because the company has a good trademark and a good business method. Moreover, because the nature of the business keeps the cost of starting a Comfort Keepers franchise relatively low, there is a substantial pool of people available to purchase the franchise. For Comfort Keepers and its franchisees, franchising is a win–win proposition. Comfort Keepers wins because it is able to use its franchisees' money to quickly grow its business and strengthen its brand. The franchisees win because they are able to start a business in a growing industry relatively inexpensively and benefit by adopting the Comfort Keepers trademark and method of doing business.

How Does Franchising Work?

There is nothing magical about franchising. It is a form of growth that allows a business to get its products or services to market through the efforts of business partners or "franchisees." As described previously, a franchise is an agreement between a franchisor (the parent company, such as College Nannies) and a franchisee (an individual or firm that is willing to pay the franchisor a fee for the right to sell its product, service, and/or business method).[10] Subway, for example, is a very successful franchise system. The franchisor (Subway, Inc.) provides the rights to individual businesspersons (the local franchisees) to use the Subway trademark and business methods. The franchisees, in turn, pay Subway a franchise fee and an ongoing royalty for these privileges and agree to operate their Subway restaurants according to Subway, Inc.'s standards.

There are two distinctly different types of franchise systems: the product and trademark franchise and the business format franchise. A **product and trademark franchise** is an arrangement under which the franchisor grants to the franchisee the right to buy its products and use its trade name. This approach typically connects a single manufacturer with a network of dealers or distributors. For example, General Motors has established a network of dealers that sell GM cars and use the GM trademark in their advertising and promotions. Similarly, British Petroleum (BP) has established a network of franchisee-owned gasoline stations to distribute BP gasoline. Product and trademark franchisees are typically permitted to operate in a fairly autonomous manner. The parent company, such as GM or BP, is generally concerned more with maintaining the integrity of its products than with monitoring the day-to-day activities of its dealers or station owners. Other examples of product and trademark franchise systems include agricultural machinery dealers, soft-drink bottlers, and beer distributorships. Rather than obtaining a royalty or franchise fee, the product and trademark franchisor obtains the majority of its income from selling its products to its dealers or distributors at a markup.

The second type of franchise, the **business format franchise**, is by far the more popular approach to franchising and is more commonly used by entrepreneurs and entrepreneurial ventures. In a business format franchise, the franchisor provides a formula for doing business to the franchisee along with training, advertising, and other forms of assistance. Fast-food restaurants, convenience stores, fitness centers, and tax preparation services are well-known examples of business format franchisees. While a business format franchise provides a franchisee a formula for conducting business, it can also be very rigid and demanding. For example, fast-food restaurants such as McDonald's and Burger King teach their franchisees every detail of how to run their restaurants, from how many seconds to cook french fries to the exact words their employees should use when they greet customers (such as "Will this be dining in or carry out?"). Business format franchisors obtain the majority of their revenues from their franchisees in the form of royalties and franchise fees.

For both product and trademark franchises and business format franchises, the franchisor–franchisee relationship takes one of three forms of a franchise agreement, which are depicted in Figure 15.1. The most common type of franchise arrangement is an individual franchise agreement. An **individual franchise agreement** involves the sale of a single franchise for a specific location. For example, an individual may purchase a CD Warehouse franchise to be constructed and operated at 901 Pearl Street in Boulder, Colorado. An **area franchise agreement** allows a franchisee to own and operate a specific number of outlets in a particular geographic area. For example, a franchisee may purchase the rights to open five CD Warehouse franchises within the city limits of Augusta, Georgia. This is a very popular franchise arrangement, because in most cases it gives the franchisee exclusive rights for a given area. Finally, a **master franchise agreement** is similar to an area franchise agreement, with one major

3. Explain the differences among an individual franchise agreement, an area franchise agreement, and a master franchise agreement.

FIGURE 15.1

Different Types of Franchise Systems

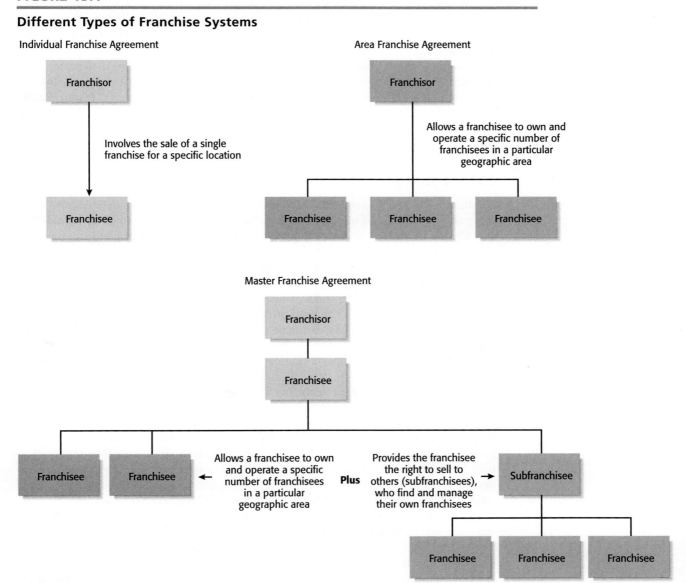

difference. A master franchisee, in addition to having the right to open and operate a specific number of locations in a particular area, also has the right to offer and sell the franchise to other people in its area. For example, Barnie's Coffee & Tea is a coffee restaurant franchise. The company sells master franchise agreements that provide a master franchisee the right to open a certain number of Barnie's Coffee & Tea outlets in a defined geographic area. After its own outlets have been opened, the master franchisee can then sell the rights to open additional Barnie's Coffee & Tea locations in the same area to other individuals. The people who buy franchises from master franchisees are typically called **subfranchisees**.

An individual who owns and operates more than one outlet of the same franchisor, whether through an area or a master franchise agreement, is called a **multiple-unit franchisee**. Multiple-unit franchisees are common in both small and large franchise chains, and this source of growth far outpaces the units added by new franchisees in most franchise organizations.[11] For the franchisee, there are advantages and disadvantages to multiple-unit franchising. By owning more than one unit, a multiple-unit franchisee can capture economies of scale and reduce its administrative overhead per unit of sale. The disadvantages of multiple-unit franchising are that the franchisor takes more risk and makes a deeper commitment to a single franchisor. In general, franchisors encourage multiple-unit franchising. By selling an additional franchise to an existing franchisee, a franchisor can grow its business without adding to the total number of franchisees with whom it must maintain a relationship to conduct its business.

An increasingly common practice among franchise organizations is to partner with one another through co-branding arrangements to increase systemwide sales and decrease costs. This practice is discussed in the "Partnering for Success" feature for this chapter.

Establishing a Franchise System

Establishing a franchise system should be approached carefully and deliberately. While the process is a familiar one to a company such as McDonald's, which as of mid-2006 had 18,420 franchised units worldwide, franchising is quite an unfamiliar process to new businesses, such as Comfort Keepers. Franchising is a complicated business endeavor, which means that an entrepreneur must look closely at all of its aspects before deciding to franchise. Indeed, franchising often involves the managerially demanding tasks of training, supporting, supervising, and nurturing franchisees.

An entrepreneur should also be aware that over the years a number of fraudulent franchise organizations have come and gone and left financially ruined franchisees in their wake. Because of this, franchising is a fairly heavily regulated form of business expansion. Even with this regulation, though, caution is in order for those pursuing franchising as a business opportunity.

Despite the challenges, franchising is a popular form of growth. It is particularly attractive to new firms in retailing and services because it helps firms grow quickly and alleviates the challenge of raising substantial amounts of money. There is some anecdotal evidence, however, that many companies are hasty in putting together their franchise programs and as a result do a poorer job than they might have were they to take their time.[12] Although franchising is often touted as an easy way to rapidly expand a business, an effective franchise system needs to be as consciously initiated, managed, and supported as any other form of business expansion.[13] An example of a franchise organization that has gotten off to a good start via prudent management is Which Wich, a franchise with a new sandwich concept. Which Wich's unique twist is that customers "build their own sandwich" by checking off the ingredients they want on a paper bag with a Sharpie as they enter the restaurant. The company opened its first 12 restaurants in 2004 but didn't sell a franchise until 15 months later, preferring to wait until all the

partnering for *success*

Boosting Sales and Reducing Expenses Through Co-branding

Have you ever stopped at a gas station and caught a quick lunch of an Arbys or a Blimpie sub sandwich inside? Or have you ever noticed that Baskin-Robbins and Dunkin Donuts often share the same building? If either of these two scenarios applies to you, then you have witnessed co-branding first hand.

Co-branding takes place when two or more businesses are grouped together. It is becoming increasingly common among franchise organizations that are looking for new ways to increase sales and reduce expenses. As we describe next, there are two primary types of co-branding arrangement that apply to franchise organizations.

Two Franchises Operating Side by Side

The first type of co-branding arrangement involves two or more franchises operating side by side in the same building or leased space. This type of arrangement typically involves a franchise like a donut shop that is busiest in the morning and a taco restaurant that is the busiest at lunch and dinner. By locating side by side, these businesses can increase their sales by picking up some business from the traffic generated by their co-branding partner and can cut costs by sharing rent and other expenses.

Side-by-side co-branding arrangements are not restricted to restaurants. Sometimes the benefit arises from the complementary nature of the products involved, rather than time of day. For example, a franchise that sells exercise equipment could operate side by side with a business that sells vitamins. By locating side by side, these two businesses could realize the same types of benefits as the donut shop and the taco restaurant.

Two Franchises Occupying the Exact Same Space

The second type of co-branding arrangement involves two franchises occupying essentially the same space. For example, it is increasingly common to see sub shops inside gasoline stations and other retail outlets. The relationship is meant to benefit both parties. The sub shop benefits by opening another location without incurring the cost of constructing a freestanding building or leasing expensive shopping mall space. The gasoline station benefits by having a quality branded food partner to help it attract road traffic and by collecting lease income. Having a sub shop inside its store also helps a gasoline station become a "destination stop" for regular customers rather than simply another gas station serving passing cars.

Important Considerations

Although co-branding can be an excellent way for franchise organizations to partner for success, before a firm enters into a co-branding relationship, it should consider the following three questions:

- Will the co-branding arrangement maintain or strengthen my brand image?
- Do I have adequate control over how my partner will display or use my brand?
- Are their tangible benefits associated with attaching my brand to my partner's brand? For example, will my partner's brand have a positive effect on my brand and actually increase my sales?

If the answer to each of these questions is yes, than a co-branding arrangement may be a very effective way for a franchise organization to boosts sales and reduce expenses.

Questions for Critical Thinking

1. Do you think that co-branding will continue to gain momentum, or do you think it is a fad they will wane in terms of its popularity? Explain your answer.
2. What are the potential downsides of co-branding? What might make a franchise hesitant to enter into a co-branding relationship with another franchise organization?
3. Consider the Cartridge World Profile at the beginning of the chapter. Suggest some co-branding relationships that College Nannies & Tutors might consider forming.
4. Do some research in order to identify at least two additional examples of each of the two types of co-branding relationships just described. Explain how each co-branding relationship benefits the parties involved.
5. Make a list of the types of businesses that might work well together in a co-branding relationship. Several initial examples include: (1) quick oil change and tire store, (2) bakery and a coffee house, (3) and a florist and candy store.

kinks were worked out of its approach. Which Wich now has about 20 franchise outlets and is growing.[14]

Now let's look more closely at the issues to consider when an entrepreneur is trying to decide if franchising is an appropriate approach to growing a business.

When to Franchise

Retail firms grow when two things happen: first, when the attractiveness of a firm's products or services become well known, whether it is a new restaurant or a fitness center, and, second, when a firm has the financial capability to build the outlets needed to satisfy the demand for its products or services.

There are at least two options firms have as a means to grow. Building company-owned outlets is one of these options. However, this choice presents a company with the challenge of raising the money to fund its expansion. As discussed in Chapter 10, this option is typically pursued through debt, investment capital, or earnings, none of which is easy to achieve for a start-up venture.

Franchising is a second growth alternative available to firms. Franchising is perhaps especially attractive to young firms in that the majority of the money needed for expansion comes from the franchisees. Franchising is appropriate when a firm has a strong or potentially strong trademark, a well-designed business model, and a desire to grow. A franchise system will ultimately fail if the franchisee's brand doesn't create value for customers and its business model is flawed or poorly developed.

In some instances, franchising is simply not appropriate. For example, franchising works for Burger King but would not work for Wal-Mart. While Burger King has a large number of franchise outlets, each individual outlet is relatively small and has a limited menu, and policies and procedures can be written to cover almost any contingency. In contrast, although Wal-Mart is similar to Burger King in that it, too, has a strong trademark and thousands of outlets, Wal-Mart stores are much larger, more expensive to build, and more complex to run than Burger King restaurants. It would be nearly impossible for Wal-Mart to find an adequate number of qualified people who would have the financial capital and expertise to open and successfully operate a Wal-Mart store.

Steps to Franchising a Business

Let's assume that as an entrepreneur you have decided to use franchising as a means of growing your venture. What steps should you take to develop a franchise system? As illustrated in Figure 15.2, entrepreneurs should take nine steps in order to successfully set up a franchise system.

Step 1   **Develop a franchise business plan:** The franchise business plan should follow the format of a conventional business plan that we discussed in Chapter 4 and should fully describe the rationale for franchising the business and act as a blueprint for rolling out the franchise operation.

Step 2   **Get professional advice:** Before going too far, a potential franchisor should seek advice from a qualified franchise attorney, consultant, or certified public accountant. If the business is not realistically franchisable, then a qualified professional can save a potential franchisor a lot of time, money, and frustration by urging that the process be stopped. If the business is franchisable, then it is advisable to get professional advice to help direct the entire process.

Step 3   **Conduct an intellectual property audit:** As we discussed in Chapter 12, this step is necessary to determine the intellectual property a company owns and to ensure that the property is properly registered and protected. All original written, audio, and visual material, including operating manuals, training videos, advertising brochures, audiotapes, and similar matter, should be afforded copyright protection. If a firm has a unique business model that includes a unique business method, it should consider obtaining a patent for its

FIGURE 15.2

Nine Steps in Setting Up a Franchise System

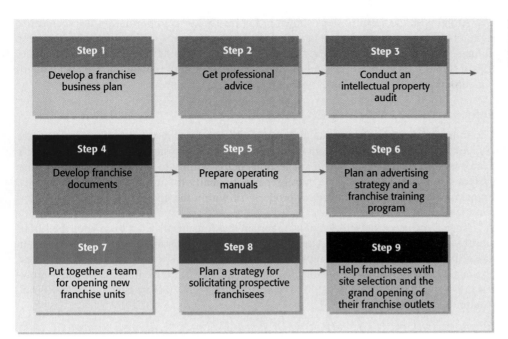

business method. These protective measures are vital because once a company begins franchising, its trademarks and business model and any unique business methods are disseminated, making them more visible to customers and competitors. In addition, a franchisor should make sure that its trademark is not infringing on the trademark of any other firm.

Step 4 **Develop franchise documents:** We will discuss the documents that are required to franchise a business later in this chapter. Here, we can note that at the beginning of the franchise evaluation process, a prospective franchisor should prepare the Uniform Franchise Offering Circular (this circular is explained in detail later in this chapter) and the Franchise Agreement. A franchise attorney can provide specific information regarding the content and format of these documents.

Step 5 **Prepare operating manuals:** Businesses that are suitable for franchising typically have a polished business system that can be fairly easily taught to qualified franchisees. The franchisor should prepare manuals that document all aspects of its business model.

Step 6 **Plan an advertising strategy and a franchisee-training program:** Prospective franchisees will want to see an advertising strategy and a franchisee-training program in place. The scope of each program should match the speed at which the franchisor wants to grow its business.

Step 7 **Put together a team for opening new franchise units:** A team should be developed and prepared to help new franchisees open their franchise units. The team should be well trained and equipped to provide the franchisee a broad range of training and guidance.

Step 8 **Plan a strategy for soliciting prospective franchisees:** There are many channels available to franchisors to solicit and attract potential franchisees. Franchise trade fairs, newspaper ads, franchise publications, and Internet advertising are examples of these channels.

Step 9 **Help franchisees with site selection and the grand opening of their franchise outlet:** Location is very important to most businesses, so a franchisor should be heavily involved in the site selection of its franchisees' outlets. The franchisor should also help the franchisee with the grand opening of the franchise outlet.

Along with the specific steps shown in Figure 15.2, it is important for a franchisor to remember that the quality of relationships that it maintains with its franchisees often defines the ultimate success of the franchise system. It is to the franchisor's advantage to follow through on all promises and to establish an exemplary reputation. This is an ongoing commitment that a franchisor should make to its franchisees.

Selecting and Developing Effective Franchisees

The franchisor's ability to select and develop effective franchisees strongly influences the degree to which a franchise system is successful. For most systems, the ideal franchisee is someone who has good ideas and suggestions but is willing to work within the franchise system's rules. Bold, aggressive entrepreneurs typically do not make good franchisees. Franchisees must be team players to properly fit within the context of a successful franchise system.

Once franchisees are selected, it is important that franchisors work to develop their franchisees' potential. Table 15.1 contains a list of the qualities that franchisors look for in prospective franchisees and the steps that franchisors can take to develop their franchisees' potential. Personality tests are one method for screening prospective franchisees that is growing in popularity. This method is discussed in this chapter's "Savvy Entrepreneurial Firm" feature.

Advantages and Disadvantages of Establishing a Franchise System

LEARNING Objective

4. Describe the advantages of establishing a franchise system as a means of firm growth.

There are two primary advantages to franchising. First, early in the life of an organization, capital is typically scarce, and rapid growth is needed to achieve brand recognition and economies of scale. Franchising helps an organization grow quickly because franchisees provide the majority of the capital.[15] For example, if Comfort Keepers were growing via company-owned outlets rather than franchising, it would probably have only a handful of outlets rather than the more than 540 it has today. Many franchisors even admit that they would have rather grown through company-owned stores but that the capital requirements needed to grow their firms dictated franchising. This sentiment is affirmed by an executive at Hardee's, who wrote the following about the growth of this fast-food chain:

> Hardee's would have preferred not to have franchised a single location. We prefer company-owned locations. But due to the heavy capital investment required, we could only expand company-owned locations to a certain degree—from there we had to stop. Each operation represents an investment in excess of $100,000; therefore, we entered the franchise business.[16]

TABLE 15.1 Selecting and Developing Effective Franchisees

Qualities to Look for in Prospective Franchisees
- Good work ethic
- Ability to follow instructions
- Ability to operate with minimal supervision
- Team oriented
- Experience in the industry in which the franchise competes
- Adequate financial resources and a good credit history
- Ability to make suggestions without becoming confrontational or upset if the suggestions are not adopted
- Represents the franchisor in a positive manner

Ways Franchisors Can Develop the Potential of Their Franchisees
- Provide mentoring that supersedes routine training
- Keep operating manuals up-to-date
- Keep product, services, and business systems up-to-date
- Solicit input from franchisees to reinforce their importance in the larger system
- Encourage franchisees to develop a franchise association
- Maintain the franchise system's integrity

savvy entrepreneurial firm

Using Personality Tests to Identify High-Potential Franchisees

An increasingly common tool that franchisors are using to screen potential franchisees is personality tests. The idea is that each franchise system is unique, and people with certain personality characteristics represent the best fit for a particular franchise organization.

Here's how the process works. A franchisor, like Cartridge World or Comfort Keepers, contracts with a personality assessment company to develop a profile of an ideal franchisee. The profile is usually developed by assessing the personality characteristics of the franchisor's most successful franchisees. Potential franchisees are then administered a personality test, to show how they compare to the chain's ideal franchisee. There are no value judgments made in regard to a person's character. Instead, the tests are designed to predict how well a person will fit into a particular franchise system. For example, a person may be found to be "meticulous and reserved," which might be an ideal fit for a tax preparation service like Jackson Hewitt but a poor fit for a day care or a fitness franchise like Curves. Some tests also assess how a person's personality matches with the management characteristics that are required to lead a specific franchise. For instance, a person who is found to be "aggressive, assertive, ambitious, and goal oriented" may be an ideal candidate for a new franchise system that needs to prove the worth of its product to a skeptical clientele.

Despite their growing popularity, personality tests have their skeptics. Stephen Spinelli, a professor at Babson College and the author of a book on franchising, says, "I've never seen any academic analysis that shows that they [personality tests] work." Others worry that the tests will cause franchisors to pick franchisees who all resemble each other—missing out on the advantages of diversity. Commenting on this issue, Bob Kreisberg, president of Opus Marketing, said, "Franchise companies that say, 'We have one culture. If you don't fit, we don't want you,' are missing out on the advantages that different people bring to the table."

Still, there is mounting anecdotal evidence that personality tests are an effective tool for qualifying high-potential franchisees. In addition, franchisors are increasingly trying to become savvier in selecting franchisees, to maximize the potential of every franchise outlet. The International Franchise Association estimates that 30 percent to 40 percent of the group's 1,000 franchise members now use personality tests, and the number is growing.

Questions for Critical Thinking

1. If you were a franchisor, would you use personality tests to screen prospective franchisees? If you were a prospective franchisee, would you feel comfortable taking the type of test described here? Explain your answers.

2. In your judgment, how compelling are arguments against using personality tests to screen potential franchisees?

3. If you were a franchisor, what methods, other than personality tests, would you use to screen prospective franchisees? How important do you think the process of selecting franchisees is for the ultimate success of a franchise system? Make your answers as thoughtful and substantive as possible.

4. Do some research to determine the attrition rate for the average franchisee. In your view, what are the major factors contributing to franchise failures?

Sources: J. Bennett, "What It Takes to Be a Successful Franchisee," *StartupJournal*, www.startupjournal.com (accessed June 1, 2006); J. Bennett, "Do You Have What It Takes?" *The Wall Street Journal*, September 19, 2005, R11.

Second, a management concept called **agency theory**, which we discussed in Chapter 13, argues that for organizations with multiple units (such as restaurant chains), it is more effective for the units to be run by franchisees than by managers who run company-owned stores. The theory is that managers, because they are usually paid a salary, may not be as committed to the success of their individual units as franchisees, who are in effect the owners of the units they manage.[17]

The primary disadvantage of franchising is that an organization allows others to profit from its trademark and business model. For example, each time Comfort Keepers sells a franchise it gets a $23,200 franchise fee and an ongoing royalty, which is 3 to 5 percent of gross sales. However, if Comfort Keepers had provided its service itself in the same location, it would be getting 100 percent of the gross sales and net profits from the location. This is the main reason some organizations that are perfectly suitable for franchising grow through company-owned stores rather than franchising. An example is Darden Restaurants Inc., the parent company of Red Lobster, Olive Garden, Bahama Breeze, Smokey Bones BBQ, and Seasons 52. With over 1,400 locations, this firm is the world's largest publicly held casual dining restaurant chain.[18] All of Darden's units are company owned. Jamba Juice is another company that is suitable for franchising but does not have any franchise outlets. A more complete list of the advantages and disadvantages of franchising as a means of business expansion is provided in Table 15.2.

When a company decides to investigate franchising as a means of growth, it should ensure that it and its product or service meet several criteria. Businesses that fail to satisfy these criteria are less likely to make effective franchise systems. Before deciding to franchise, a firm should consider the following:

LEARNING

Objective

5. Identify the rules of thumb for determining when franchising is an appropriate form of growth for a particular business.

■ *The uniqueness of its product or service:* The business's product or service should be unique along some dimension that customers value. Businesses with a unique product or service typically have the best potential to expand.

TABLE 15.2 Advantages and Disadvantages of Franchising as a Method of Business Expansion

Advantages	Disadvantages
Rapid, low-cost market expansion. Because franchisees provide most of the cost of expansion, the franchisor can expand the size of its business fairly rapidly.	**Profit sharing.** By selling franchises instead of operating company-owned stores, franchisors share the profits derived from their proprietary products or services with their franchisees. For example, before being acquired by FedEx, Kinko's did not sell franchises, allowing it to retain all its profits.
Income from franchise fees and royalties. By collecting franchise fees, the franchisor gets a fairly quick return on the proprietary nature of its products/services and business model. The franchisor also receives ongoing royalties from its franchisees without incurring substantial risk.	**Loss of control.** It is typically more difficult for a franchisor to control its franchisees than it is for a company to control its employees. Franchisees, despite the rules governing the franchise system, still often view themselves as independent businesspeople.
Franchisee motivation. Because franchisees put their personal capital at risk, they are highly motivated to make their franchise outlets successful. In contrast, the managers of company-owned outlets typically do not have their own capital at risk. As a result, these managers may not be prone to work as hard as franchisees or be as attentive to cost savings.	**Friction with franchisees.** A common complaint of franchisors is dealing with the friction that often develops between franchisors and franchisees. Friction can develop over issues such as the payment of fees, hours of operation, caveats in the franchise agreement, and surprise inspections.
Access to ideas and suggestions. Franchisees represent a source of intellectual capital and often make suggestions to their franchisors. By incorporating these ideas into their business model, franchisors can in effect leverage the ideas and suggestions of their individual franchisees.	**Managing growth.** Franchisors that are in growing industries and have a strong trademark often grow quickly. Although this might seem like an advantage, rapid growth can be difficult to manage. A franchisor provides each of its franchisees a number of services, such as site selection and employee training. If a franchise system is growing rapidly, the franchisor will have to continually add personnel to its own staff to properly support its growing number of franchisees.
Cost savings. Franchisees share many of the franchisors' expenses, such as the cost of regional and national advertising.	**Differences in required business skills.** The business skills that made a franchisor successful in the original business are typically not the same skills needed to manage a franchise system. For example, Sam Jones may be a very effective owner/manager of a seafood restaurant. That does not necessarily mean, however, that he will be an effective manager of a franchise system if he decided to franchise his seafood restaurant concept.
Increased buying power. Franchisees provide franchisors increased buying power by enlarging the size of their business, allowing them to purchase larger quantities of products and services when buying those items.	**Legal expenses.** Many states have specific laws pertaining to franchising. As a result, if a franchisor sells franchises in multiple states, legal expenses can be high to properly interpret and comply with each state's laws. Unfortunately, from the franchisor's point of view, some of the toughest laws are in the most populated states.

■ *The consistent profitability of the firm:* The business should be consistently profitable, and the future profitability of the business should be fairly easy to predict. When developing a franchise system, a company should have several prototype outlets up and running to test and ensure the viability of the business idea. Remember, a franchisee is supposed to be buying a way of doing business (in the form of a business model) that is "proven"—at least to a certain extent. Franchisors that learn how to run their businesses through the trial and error of their franchisees have typically franchised their businesses prematurely (especially from the franchisees' point of view).

■ *The firm's year-round profitability:* The business should be profitable year-round, not only during specific seasons. For example, a lawn and garden care franchise in North Dakota should be set up to provide the franchisee supplemental products and services to sell during off-peak seasons. Otherwise, owning the franchise may not be an attractive substitute for a full-time job. This issue is particularly problematic for some ice cream and smoothie franchises in northern states, which experience a significant decline in sales during winter months.

■ *The degree of refinement of the firm's business systems:* The systems and procedures for operating the business should be polished and the procedures documented in written form. The systems and procedures should also be fairly easy to teach to qualified candidates.

■ *The clarity of the business proposition:* The business proposition should be crystal clear so that prospective franchisees fully understand the business proposition to which they are committing. The relationship between the franchisor and the franchisee should be completely open, and communication between them should be candid.

After determining that the firm satisfies these criteria, the entrepreneur should step back and review all the alternatives for business expansion. No single form of business expansion is the best under all circumstances. For any entrepreneurial venture, the best form of expansion is the one that increases the likelihood that the venture will reach its objectives.

Buying a Franchise

Now let's look at franchising from the franchisee's perspective. Purchasing a franchise is an important business decision involving a substantial financial commitment. Potential franchise owners should strive to be as well informed as possible before purchasing a franchise and should be well aware that it is often legally and financially difficult to exit a franchise relationship. Indeed, an individual franchise opportunity should be meticulously scrutinized. Close scrutiny of a potential franchise opportunity includes activities such as meeting with the franchisor and reading the Uniform Franchise Offering Circular, soliciting legal and financial advice, and talking to former franchisees who have dropped out of the system one is considering. In particularly heavily franchised industries, such as fast food and automobile repair, a prospective franchisee may have 20 or more franchisors from which to make a selection. It is well worth franchisees' time to carefully select the franchisor that best meets their individual needs.[19]

Some franchise organizations are designed to provide their franchisees a part-time, rather than a full-time income, which is attractive to some people. An example is Stroller Strides, a company that gathers new mothers together to do 45-minute power walks with their babies in strollers. The initial franchise fee ranges between $2,500 and $5,000. Owing a Stroller Strides franchise is ideal for a woman who wants to work 2 to 3 hours a day rather than 8 and is passionate about fitness.

LEARNING
Objective

6. Discuss the factors to consider in determining if owning a franchise is a good fit for a particular person.

Is Franchising Right for You?

Entrepreneurs should weigh the possibility of purchasing a franchise against the alternatives of buying an existing business or launching their own venture from scratch. Answering the following questions will help determine whether franchising is a good fit for people thinking about starting their own entrepreneurial venture:

- Are you willing to take orders? Franchisors are typically very particular about how their outlets operate. For example, McDonald's and other successful fast-food chains are very strict in terms of their restaurants' appearance and how the unit's food is prepared. Franchising is typically not a good fit for people who like to experiment with their own ideas or are independent minded.
- Are you willing to be part of a franchise "system" rather than an independent businessperson? For example, as a franchisee you may be required to pay into an advertising fund that covers the costs of advertising aimed at regional or national markets rather than the market for your individual outlet. Will it bother you to have someone use your money to develop ads that benefit the "system" rather than only your outlet or store? Are you willing to lose creative control over how your business is promoted?
- How will you react if you make a suggestion to your franchisor and your suggestion is rejected? How will you feel if you are told that your suggestion might work for you but can be put in place only if it works in all parts of the system?
- What are you looking for in a business? How hard do you want to work?
- How willing are you to put your money at risk? How will you feel if your business is operating at a net loss but you still have to pay royalties on your gross income?

None of these questions is meant to suggest that franchising is not an attractive method of business ownership for entrepreneurs. It is important, however, that a potential franchisee be fully aware of the subtleties involved with franchising before purchasing a franchise outlet.

The Cost of a Franchise

LEARNING
Objective

7. Identify the costs associated with buying a franchise.

The initial cost of a business format franchise varies, depending on the franchise fee, the capital needed to start the business, and the strength of the franchisor. The average initial investment for about 8 of every 10 franchise units operating in the United States is less than $250,000 (excluding the cost of real estate).[20] Capital costs vary. For example, McDonald's typically provides the land and buildings for each franchisee's unit. In contrast, other organizations require their franchisees to purchase the land, buildings, and equipment needed to run their franchise outlets. Table 15.3 shows the total costs of buying

TABLE 15.3 Initial Costs to the Franchisee of a Sample of Franchise Organizations

Franchise Organization	Year Started Franchising	Company-Owned Units	Franchised Units	Franchise Fee	Ongoing Royalty Fee	Total Initial Investment
Comfort Keepers	1999	0	539	$23,200	3%–5%	$46,000–$69,000
Curves	1995	0	9,468	$35,900	5%–6%	$38,400–$53,500
General Nutrition Centers	1988	2,644	2,108	$35,000	6%	$132,700–$182,000
Gold's Gym	1965	38	679	$25,000	3%	$300,000–$2 million
McDonald's	1955	8,135	22,435	$45,000	12.5% +	$506,000–$1.6 million
Play It Again Sports	1988	0	414	$20,000	5%	$185,000–$354,000
Smoothie King	1988	1	389	$25,000	6%	$91,000–$239,000
Subway	1974	0	24,815	$12,500	8%	$70,000–$220,000

Source: Entrepreneur.com, www.entrepreneur.com (accessed June 1, 2006).

into several franchise organizations. As you can see, the total initial cost ranges from a low of $38,400 for a Curves International franchise to more than $2 million for a Gold's Gym franchise.

Also shown in Table 15.3 is a breakdown of the number of company-owned units and the number of franchise units maintained by different organizations. Company-owned units are managed and operated by company personnel, and there is no franchisee involved. Franchise organizations vary in their philosophies regarding company-owned versus franchised units. As we noted earlier in this chapter, some companies (e.g., Subway) are strictly franchisors and have no company-owned units. Other companies, such as General Nutrition Centers, maintain large numbers of both company-owned and franchised units.

When evaluating the cost of a franchise, prospective franchisees should consider all the costs involved. Franchisors are required by law to disclose all their costs in a document called the Uniform Franchise Offering Circular and send it to the franchisee. (We'll talk about this document in more detail later in this chapter.) To avoid making a hasty judgment, a franchisee may not purchase a franchise for 10 days from the time the circular is received. The following costs are typically associated with buying a business format franchise:[21]

- *Initial franchise fee:* The initial franchise fee varies, depending on the franchisor, as shown in Table 15.3.
- *Capital requirements:* These costs vary, depending on the franchisor, but may include the cost of buying real estate, the cost of constructing a building, the purchase of initial inventory, and the cost of obtaining a business license. Some franchisors also require a new franchisee to pay a "grand opening" fee for its assistance in opening the business.
- *Continuing royalty payment:* In the majority of cases, a franchisee pays a royalty based on a percentage of weekly or monthly gross income. Note that because the fee is typically assessed on gross income rather than net income, a franchisee may have to pay a monthly royalty even if the business is losing money. Royalty fees are usually around 5 percent of gross income.[22]
- *Advertising fees:* Franchisees are often required to pay into a national or regional advertising fund, even if the advertisements are directed at goals other than promoting the franchisor's product or service. (For example, advertising could focus on the franchisor's attempt at attracting new franchisees.) Advertising fees are typically less than 3 percent of gross income.
- *Other fees:* Other fees may be charged for various activities, including training additional staff, providing management expertise when needed, providing computer assistance, or providing a host of other items or support services.

Although not technically a fee, many franchise organizations sell their franchisee products that they use in their businesses, such as restaurant supplies for a restaurant franchise. The products are often sold at a markup and may be more expensive than those the franchisee could obtain on the open market.

There are some franchise organizations that use a more hybrid fee structure than the pricing formula shown here. An example is Candy Bouquet, which charges an initial franchise fee starting at $3,500 but has no ongoing royalty fee. Instead, the company charges its franchisees a monthly association fee of $35 to $200, which is not tied to store volume.[23]

The most important question a prospective franchisee should consider is whether the fees and royalties charged by a franchisor are consistent with the franchise's value or worth. If they are, then the pricing structure may be fair and equitable. If they are not, then the terms should be renegotiated or the prospective franchisee should look elsewhere.

Finding a Franchise

There are thousands of franchise opportunities available to prospective franchisees. The most critical step in the early stages of investigating franchise opportunities is for the entrepreneur to determine the type of franchise that is the best fit. For example, it is typically unrealistic for someone who is not a mechanic to consider buying a muffler repair franchise. A franchisor teaches a franchisee how to use the contents of a business model, not a trade. Before buying a franchise, a potential franchisee should imagine operating the prospective franchise or, better yet, should spend a period of time working in one of the franchisor's outlets. After working in a print shop for a week, for example, someone who thought she might enjoy running a print shop might find out that she hates it. This type of experience could help avoid making a mistake that is costly both to the franchisee and to the franchisor.

There are many periodicals, Web sites, and associations that provide information about franchise opportunities. Every Thursday, for example, ads for franchise opportunities appear in special sections of *The Wall Street Journal* and *USA Today*. Periodicals featuring franchise opportunities include *Inc.*, *Entrepreneur* (especially the January issues), *Nation's Business*, and franchise-specific magazines such as *The Franchise Handbook* and *Franchise Opportunities Guide*. Prospective franchisees should also consider attending franchise opportunity shows that are held periodically in major U.S. cities and the International Franchise Exposition, which is held annually in Washington, D.C. The U.S. Small Business Administration is another good source of franchise information.

Because of the risks involved in franchising, the selection of a franchisor should be a careful, deliberate process. One of the smartest moves a potential franchise owner can make is to talk to current franchisees and inquire if they are making money and if they are satisfied with their franchisor. Reflecting on how this approach helped ease her inhibitions about buying a franchise, Carleen Peaper, the owner of a Cruise Planner franchise, said:

> I was really apprehensive about making an investment of my time and money into a franchise, so I e-mailed 50 Cruise Planner agents with a set of questions, asking for honest feedback. Everyone responded. That was a big thing and helped me determine that I wanted to join them.[24]

Table 15.4 contains a list of sample questions to ask a franchisor and some of its current franchisees before investing. Potential entrepreneurs can expect to learn a great deal by studying the answers they receive in response to these questions.

LEARNING Objective

8. Discuss the advantages and disadvantages of buying a franchise.

Advantages and Disadvantages of Buying a Franchise

There are two primary advantages to buying a franchise over other forms of business ownership. First, franchising provides an entrepreneur the opportunity to own a business using a tested and refined business model. This attribute lessens the probability of business failure. In addition, the trademark that comes with the franchise often provides instant legitimacy for a business.[25] For example, an entrepreneur opening a new Curves fitness center would likely attract more customers than an entrepreneur opening a new, independently owned fitness center because many women who are a part of the target market of Curves have already heard of the firm and have a positive impression of it. Second, when an individual purchases a franchise, the franchisor typically provides training, technical expertise, and other forms of support. For example, many franchise organizations provide their franchisees periodic training both at their headquarters location and in their individual franchise outlets.

The main disadvantage of buying a franchise is the cost involved. As mentioned earlier, the franchisee must pay an initial franchise fee. The franchisee must also pay the franchisor an ongoing royalty as well as pay into a variety of funds, depending on the franchise organization. Thus, franchisees have both immediate (i.e., the initial franchise fee) and long-term (i.e., continuing royalty payments) costs. By opening an independent business, an entrepreneur can keep 100 percent of the profits if it is successful.

TABLE 15.4 Questions to Ask before Buying a Franchise

Questions to Ask a Franchisor

- What is the background of the company and its performance record?
- What is the company's current financial status?
- What are the names, addresses, and phone numbers of existing franchisees in my trade area?
- Describe how you train and mentor your franchisees.
- If at some point I decide to exit the franchise relationship, how does the exit process work?
- In what ways do you work with a franchisee who is struggling?

Questions to Ask Current Franchisees

- How much does your franchise gross per year? How much does it net? Are the procedures followed to make royalty payments to the franchisee burdensome?
- Are the financial projections of revenues, expenses, and profits that the franchisor provided me accurate in your judgment?
- Does the franchisor give you enough assistance in operating your business?
- How many hours, on average, do you work?
- How often do you get a vacation?
- Have you been caught off-guard by any unexpected costs or expectations?
- Does your franchisor provide you ongoing training and support?
- If you had to do it all over again, would you purchase a franchise in this system? Why or why not?

Table 15.5 contains a list of the advantages and disadvantages to buying a franchise.

Steps in Purchasing a Franchise

Purchasing a franchise system is a seven-step process, as illustrated in Figure 15.3. The first rule of buying a franchise is to avoid making a hasty decision. Again, owning a franchise is typically costly and labor-intensive, and the purchase of a franchise should be a careful, deliberate decision. Once the decision to purchase a franchise has been nearly made, however, the following steps should be taken. If at any time prior to signing the franchise agreement the prospective franchisee has second thoughts, the process should be stopped until the prospective franchisee's concerns are adequately addressed.

Step 1 ***Visit several of the franchisor's outlets:*** Prior to meeting with the franchisor, the prospective franchisee should visit several of the franchisor's outlets and talk with their owners and employees. During the visits, the prospective franchisee should continually ask, "Is this the type of business I would enjoy owning and operating or managing?"

Step 2 ***Retain a franchise attorney:*** Prospective franchisees should have an attorney who represents their interests, not the franchisor's. The attorney should prepare the prospective franchisee for meeting with the franchisor and should review all franchise documents before they are signed. If the franchisor tries to discourage the prospective franchisee from retaining an attorney, this is a red flag.

Step 3 ***Meet with the franchisor and check the franchisor's references:*** The prospective franchisee should meet with the franchisor, preferably at the franchisor's headquarters. During the meeting, the prospective franchisee should compare what was observed firsthand in the franchised outlets with what the franchisor is saying. Additional references should also be checked. The Uniform Franchise Offering Circular is a good source for references. In section 20 of this document, there is a list of all the franchisees that have dropped out of the system in the past 3 years along with their contact information. Several of these should be called. Although it may seem to be overkill, the mantra for prospective franchisees is to check, double-check, and triple-check a franchisor's references.

Step 4 ***Review all franchise documents with the attorney:*** The franchise attorney should review all the franchise documents, including the Uniform Franchise Offering Circular and the franchise agreement.

TABLE 15.5 Advantages and Disadvantages of Buying a Franchise

Advantages	Disadvantages
A proven product or service within an established market. The most compelling advantage to buying a franchise is that the franchise offers a proven product or service within an established market.	**Cost of the franchise.** The initial cost of purchasing and setting up a franchise operation can be quite high, as illustrated in Table 15.3.
An established trademark or business system. The purchase of a franchise with an established trademark provides franchisees with considerable market power. For example, the purchaser of a McDonald's franchise has a trademark with proven market power.	**Restrictions on creativity.** Many franchise systems are very rigid and leave little opportunity for individual franchisees to exercise their creativity. This is an often-cited frustration of franchisees.
Franchisor's training, technical expertise, and managerial experience. Another important attribute of franchising is the training, technical expertise, and managerial experience that the franchisor provides the franchisee.	**Duration and nature of the commitment.** For a variety of reasons, many franchise agreements are difficult to exit. In addition, virtually every franchise agreement contains a non-compete clause. These clauses vary in terms of severity, but a typical clause prevents a former franchisee from competing with the franchisor for a period of 2 years or more.
An established marketing network. Franchisees who buy into a powerful franchise system are part of a system that has tremendous buying power and substantial advertising power and marketing prowess.	**Risk of fraud, misunderstandings, or lack of franchisor commitment.** Along with the many encouraging stories of franchise success, there are also many stories of individuals who purchase a franchise only to be disappointed by the franchisor's broken promises.
Franchisor ongoing support. One of the most attractive advantages of purchasing a franchise rather than owning a store outright is the notion that the franchisor provides the franchisee ongoing support in terms of training, product updates, management assistance, and advertising. A popular slogan in franchising is that people buy franchises to "be in business for themselves but not by themselves."	**Problems of termination or transfer.** Some franchise agreements are very difficult and expensive to terminate or transfer. Often, a franchisee cannot terminate a franchise agreement without paying the franchisor substantial monetary damages.
Availability of financing. Some franchisors offer financing to their franchisees, although these cases are the exception rather than the rule. This information is available in section 10 of the UFOC.	**Poor performance on the part of other franchisees.** If some of the franchisees in a franchise system start performing poorly and make an ineffective impression on the public, that poor performance can affect the reputation and eventually the sales of a well-run franchise in the same system.
Potential for business growth. If a franchisee is successful in the original location, the franchisee is often provided the opportunity to buy additional franchises from the same franchisor. For many franchisees, this prospect offers a powerful incentive to work hard to be as successful as possible.	**Potential for failure.** Some franchise systems simply fail to reach their objectives. When this happens, franchisees' wealth can be negatively affected. Indeed, when a franchise system fails, it commonly brings its franchisees down with it.

FIGURE 15.3

Seven Steps in Purchasing a Franchise

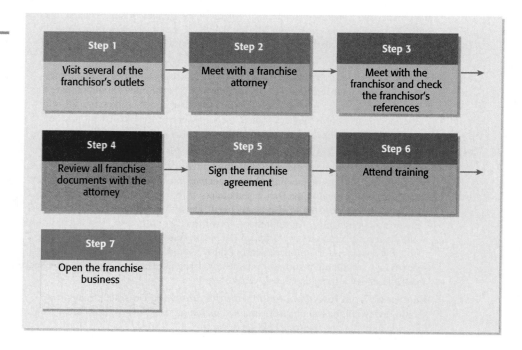

Step 5 *Sign the franchise agreement:* If everything is a go at this point, the franchise agreement can be signed. The franchise agreement is the document in which the provisions of the franchisor–franchisee relationship are outlined. We discuss this agreement in greater detail later in this chapter.

Step 6 *Attend training:* Almost all franchise organizations provide their franchisees training. For example, Comfort Keepers requires each of its new franchisees to attend an intensive 5-day training program at its corporate headquarters, and ongoing opportunities for training are made available.

Step 7 *Open the franchise business:* For many franchises, particularly restaurants, the first 2 to 3 weeks after the business is opened may be its busiest period, as prospective customers "try it out." This is why many franchise organizations send experienced personnel to help the franchisee open the business as smoothly as possible. One goal of a franchisee is generating positive word of mouth about the business right from the start.

Watch Out! Common Misconceptions About Franchising

Despite the abundance of advice available to them, many franchisees make false assumptions about franchising. Part of the explanation for this is that franchising has an attractive lure. It is easy to become enthralled with the promise of franchising and not spend an adequate amount of time examining the potential pitfalls. The following is a list of misconceptions that franchisees often have about franchising:

9. Identify the common mistakes franchise buyers make.

- ■ *Franchising is a safe investment:* Franchising, in and of itself, is no safer an investment than any other form of business ownership.
- ■ *A strong industry ensures franchise success:* Although it is generally important to operate in a growing industry, the strength of an industry does not make up for a poor product, a poor business model, poor management, or inappropriate advertising. There are many firms that fail in growing industries just as there are firms that succeed in unattractive ones.
- ■ *A franchise is a "proven" business system:* A franchisor sells a franchisee the right to use a particular business model. Whether the model is proven or not is subject to the test of time. Obviously, companies such as Subway, Curves, and McDonald's are using models that are polished and that have worked well over time. Most prospective franchisees, however, cannot afford a McDonald's or a Subway unit and will be considering a lesser-known franchise. All too frequently, companies start selling franchises before their systems are anywhere close to being proven—a fact that should cause entrepreneurs to be wary.
- ■ *There is no need to hire a franchise attorney or an accountant:* Professional advice is almost always needed to guide a prospective franchisee through the franchise purchase process. A prospective franchisee should never give in to the temptation to save money by relying solely on the franchisor's advice.
- ■ *The best systems grow rapidly, and it is best to be a part of a rapid-growth system:* While some franchise systems grow rapidly because they have a good trademark and a polished business model, other franchise systems grow quickly because their major emphasis is on selling franchises. It is to a franchisee's benefit to be part of a system that has a solid trademark and business system—as that trademark and system will attract more customers—but some franchise systems grow so quickly that they outrun their ability to provide their franchisees adequate support.
- ■ *I can operate my franchise outlet for less than the franchisor predicts:* The operation of a franchise outlet usually costs just as much as the franchisor predicts.
- ■ *The franchisor is a nice person—he'll help me out if I need it:* Although it may be human nature to rely on the goodwill of others, don't expect anything from your franchisor that isn't spelled out in the franchise agreement.

Because these misconceptions are often hard to detect, some prospective franchisees attend seminars or franchise "boot camps" that teach them the ins and outs of franchising, including the things to watch out for when they talk to prospective franchisors. These types of seminars and boot camps are regularly offered by organizations such as Women in Franchising, the United States Hispanic Chamber of Commerce, and the International Franchising Organization.

Legal Aspects of the Franchise Relationship

According to the Federal Trade Commission, a franchise exists any time that the sale of a business involves (1) the sale of goods or services that bear a trademark, (2) the retention of significant control or assistance by the holder of the trademark on the operation of the business, and (3) royalty payments by the purchaser of the business to the owner of the trademark for the right to use the trademark in the business.

The legal and regulatory environment surrounding franchising is based on the premise that the public interest is served if prospective franchisees are as informed as possible regarding the characteristics of a particular franchisor. The offer and sale of a franchise is regulated at both the state and the federal level. The legal aspects of the franchise relationship are unique enough that some attorneys specialize in franchise law. One law firm, Wiggin & Dana, has even set up a blog that focuses on franchise law. The blog is available at www.FranchiseLawBlog.com.

Federal Rules and Regulations

Except for the automobile and petroleum industries, federal laws do not directly address the franchisor–franchisee relationship. Instead, franchise disputes are matters of contract law and are litigated at the state level. During the 1990s, Congress considered several proposals for federal legislation to govern franchise relationships, but none became law.

However, the offer and sale of a franchise is regulated at the federal level. According to Federal Trade Commission (FTC) Rule 436, franchisors must furnish potential franchisees with written disclosures that provide information about the franchisor, the franchised business, and the franchise relationship. The disclosures must be supplied at least 10 business days before a franchise agreement can be signed or the franchisee pays the franchisor any money.[26] In most cases, the disclosures are made through a lengthy document referred to as

The fitness industry represents one of the most rapidly growing areas of franchising because it caters to all ages and demographics. Here, a young man and a young woman chat while working out on stair-climbing exercise machines at a fitness center in California.

the Uniform Franchise Offering Circular, which is accepted in all 50 states and parts of Canada. The **Uniform Franchise Offering Circular** (UFOC) contains 23 categories of information that give a prospective franchisee a broad base of information about the background and financial health of the franchisor. A summary of the information contained in the UFOC is provided in Table 15.6. A prospective franchisee should fully understand all the information contained in the UFOC before a franchise agreement is signed.

10. Describe the purpose of the Uniform Franchise Offering Circular.

The UFOC requires the franchisor to attach a copy of the franchise agreement and any other related contractual documents to the circular. The **franchise agreement**, or contract, is the document that consummates the sale of a franchise. Franchise agreements vary, but each agreement typically contains two sections: the purchase agreement and the franchise or license agreement. The purchase agreement typically spells out the price, the services to be provided by the franchisor to the franchisee, and the "franchise package," which refers to all the items the franchisee has been told to expect. The franchise or license agreement typically stipulates the rights granted to the franchisee (including the right to use the franchisor's trademark), the obligations and duties of the franchisor, the obligations and duties of the franchisee, trade restrictions, rights and limitations regarding the transfer or termination of the franchise agreement, and who is responsible for attorney fees if disputes arise. Most states have enacted a statute of frauds that requires franchise agreements to be in writing.

The federal government does not require franchisors to register with the Federal Trade Commission (FTC). The offer of a franchise for sale does not imply that the FTC has examined the franchisor and has determined that the information contained in the franchisor's UFOC is accurate. The franchisor is responsible for voluntarily complying with the law, and it is the responsibility of prospective franchisees to exercise due diligence in investigating franchise opportunities. Although most franchisor–franchisee relationships are conducted in an entirely ethical manner, it is a mistake to assume that a franchisor has a fiduciary obligation to its franchisees. What this means is that if a franchisor had a **fiduciary obligation** to its franchisees, it would always act in their best interest, or be on the franchisees' "side." Commenting on this issue, Robert Purvin, an experienced franchise attorney, wrote:

> While the conventional wisdom talks about the proactive relationship of the franchisor to its franchisees, virtually every court case decided in the U.S. has ruled that a franchisor has no fiduciary obligation to its franchisees. Instead, U.S. courts have agreed with franchisors that franchise agreements are "arms length" business transactions.[27]

This quote suggests that a potential franchisee should not rely solely on the goodwill of a franchisor when negotiating a franchise agreement. A potential franchisee should have a lawyer who is fully acquainted with franchise law and should closely scrutinize all franchise-related legal documents.

State Rules and Regulations

In addition to the FTC disclosure requirements, 17 states have laws providing additional protection to potential franchisees. California, Florida, Hawaii, Illinois, Indiana, Maryland, Michigan, Minnesota, New York, North Dakota, Rhode Island, South Dakota, Texas, Utah, Virginia, Washington, and Wisconsin are the states in which these laws have been established. In most of these states, a franchisor is required to file its UFOC with a designated state agency, making the UFOC public record. In these states, the agency typically reviews the UFOC for compliance with the law. In most of these 17 states, a franchisor can be prevented from selling a franchise if the state agency in charge is not satisfied that the UFOC is complete, understandable, and fully in compliance with FTC Rule 436.

By requiring franchisors to file their UFOCs with a state agency, these states provide franchise purchasers important legal protection, including the right to sue a franchisor for violation of state disclosure requirements (if the franchise purchaser feels that full disclosure in the offering circular was not made). For example, if someone purchased a franchise in one of the states fitting the profile described previously and 6 months later discovered that the franchisor did not disclose an issue required by the UFOC (and, as a result, felt that he had

TABLE 15.6 Information Contained in the Uniform Franchise Offering Circular (UFOC) Along with Explanations of Their Meanings

Section and Item	Explanation
1. The franchisor, its predecessors, and affiliates 2. Business experience of the franchisor 3. Litigation experience of the franchisor 4. Bankruptcy on the part of the franchisor	These items provide information about the franchisor's operating history, business affiliations, and past litigation and bankruptcy experience, if any. It is not uncommon for a large company to have experienced some litigation. It would be a red flag, however, if a disproportionate percentage of the litigation involved suits with current or former franchisees.
5. Initial franchise fee 6. Other fees 7. Initial investment	These items specify the fees that the franchisee is subject to along with the franchisees initial investment, which can be quite substantial. The "other fees" section should be carefully studied to avoid any surprises.
8. Restrictions on sources of products and services 9. Franchisee's obligations	These items stipulate the franchisee's obligations, along with restrictions pertaining to where the franchisee is permitted to purchase supplies and services. Some franchise agreements require the franchisee to purchase supplies from the franchisor.
10. Financing available 11. Franchisor's obligations	These items spell out the franchisor's obligations, along with a description of the financing (if any) that the franchisor offers to the franchisee. The franchisor's obligations typically include providing assistance in opening the franchise's unit, ongoing training, and advertising.
12. Territory 13. Trademarks 14. Patents, copyrights, and proprietary information	These items describe the territorial rights granted the franchisee (if any) and the franchisor's right to grant other franchises and open company-owned outlets. In addition, items 13 and 14 specify the principal trademarks, patents, and copyrights and other proprietary information owned by the franchisor and the extent to which these items can be used by the franchisee.
15. Obligation to participate in the actual operation of the franchise business	This section addresses the franchisee's obligation to participate personally in the operation of the franchise. Franchisors typically do not want absentee franchisees.
16. Restrictions on what the franchisee may sell 17. Renewal, termination, transfer, and dispute resolution	These sections deal with what the franchisee may sell and how the franchisor resolves disputes with its franchisees. Item 17 also contains important information about the manner in which franchisees can renew, terminate, and/or transfer their franchise.
18. Public figures	This section lists public figures affiliated with the franchise through advertising and other means.
19. Earnings claim	If a franchisor makes an earnings claim in connection with an offer of a franchise, then certain past and projected earnings information must be provided.
20. List of outlets	This section is quite exhaustive and contains (1) the number of franchises sold by the franchisor, (2) the number of company-owned outlets, (3) the names of all franchisees and the addresses and telephone numbers of all their outlets (within certain limitations), (4) an estimate of the number of franchises to be sold in the next year, and (5) a list of all franchisees (covering the past 3 years) who have dropped out of the system, including their last-known home addresses and telephone numbers.
21. Financial Statements	This section contains the franchisor's previous 2 years of independently audited financial statements.
22. Contracts	These last two sections contain copies of the documents that franchisees have to sign.

23. Receipt
    Attachments:
    Franchise Agreement (or contract)
    Equipment Lease
    Lease for Premises
    Loan Agreement
	These are the common exhibits attached to the UFOC.

been damaged), that person could seek relief by suing the franchisor in state court. All 17 states providing additional measures of protection for franchisees also regulate some aspect of the termination process.[28] Although the provisions vary by state, they typically restrict a franchisor from terminating the franchise before the expiration of the franchise agreement, unless the franchisor has "good cause" for its action.

More About Franchising

There are a number of additional issues pertaining to the franchisor–franchisee relationship. Three important topics, for both franchisors and franchisees, are franchise ethics, international franchising, and the future of franchising as a method of business ownership and growth.

Franchise Ethics

The majority of franchisors and franchisees are highly ethical individuals who are interested only in making a fair return on their investment. In fact, according to a recent FTC report, instances of problems between franchisors and their franchisees tend to be isolated occurrences rather than prevalent practices.[29] There are certain features of franchising, however, that make it subject to ethical abuse. An understanding of these features can help franchisors and franchisees guard against making ethical mistakes. These features are the following:

- *The get-rich-quick mentality:* Some franchisors see franchising as a get-rich-quick scheme and become more interested in selling franchises than in using franchising as a legitimate means of distributing their product or service. These franchisors have a tendency to either oversell the potential of their franchise or overpromise the support they will offer to their franchisees.
- *The false assumption that buying a franchise is a guarantee of business success:* Buying a franchise, as is the case with all other business investments, involves risk. Any statement to the contrary is typically misleading or unethical. A franchisor must steer clear of claims that it has the "key" to business success, and a franchisee needs to be wary of all such claims.
- *Conflicts of interest between franchisors and their franchisees:* The structure of the franchise relationship can create conflicts of interest between franchisors and their franchisees. For example, franchisees benefit from the profits of a unit, while franchisors benefit from increased revenues (recall that a franchisor's royalty is typically paid on a percentage of gross profits rather than net profits). This anomaly in the franchise arrangement can motivate franchisors to take steps that boost revenues for the entire system but hurt profits for individual franchisees. For example, a franchisor might insist that a franchisee sell a product that has high revenue but low margins (or net income). Similarly, a franchisor might sell several franchises in a given geographic area to maximize the revenue potential of the area regardless of the effect on each individual franchisee's net income. These actions can at times be ethically questionable and can often lead to contentious conflicts of interests in franchise systems.

Despite the protection of law and the advocacy of franchise associations, individual franchisors and franchisees must practice due diligence in their relationships. "Buyer beware" is a good motto for franchisors selecting franchisees and prospective franchisees selecting franchisors. Entering into a franchise relationship is a major step for both parties and should be treated accordingly. The metaphor used frequently to describe the franchisor–franchisee relationship is marriage. Similar to marriage, the franchisor–franchisee relationship is typically close, long-term, and painful to terminate. Each side of the franchise partnership should scrutinize the past ethical behavior of the other before a franchise agreement is executed.

International Franchising

International opportunities for franchising are becoming more prevalent as the markets for certain franchised products in the United States have become saturated.[30] Indeed, heavily franchised companies, such as McDonald's, Kentucky Fried Chicken, and Century 21 Real

Estate, are experiencing much of their growth in international markets. For example, Century 21 currently has 1,384 offices in Europe and Asia, including 58 in Hong Kong, 19 in Spain, and 77 in the Belgium, Netherlands and Luxembourg region. The trend toward globalization in many industries is also hastening the trend toward international franchising. Regional initiatives, such as the North American Free Trade Agreement, are making it increasingly attractive for U.S. firms to offer franchises for sale in foreign countries. Many new franchise organizations have made international expansion part of their initial business plans. An example is WSI Internet, which is a U.S. company that was founded in 1995 and now has franchise outlets in 87 countries.

A U.S. citizen who is thinking about buying a franchise abroad may be confronted with the choice of buying from an American company or a foreign company regardless of the location in the world. For U.S. citizens, these are some of the steps to take before buying a franchise in a foreign country:

- *Consider the value of the franchisor's name in the foreign country:* There are very few franchise systems whose names are known worldwide. Beyond a select few—McDonald's, Coca-Cola, and Budweiser come to mind—the majority of trademarks well known to Americans may be known to only a small percentage of the population of a foreign country. When considering the purchase of a U.S.-based franchise in a foreign country, carefully evaluate the value of the trademark in that country.
- *Work with a knowledgeable lawyer:* Many of the legal protections afforded to prospective franchisees in the United States are unavailable in foreign countries, highlighting the need for the purchaser of a franchise in a foreign country to obtain excellent legal advice. All the hazards involved with purchasing a domestic franchise are magnified when purchasing a franchise in a foreign country.
- *Determine whether the product or service is salable in a foreign country:* Just because a product or service is desirable to Americans is no guarantee of success in a foreign culture. Before buying a franchise in a foreign country, determine if sufficient marketing research has been conducted to ensure that the product or service will have a sufficient market in the foreign country.
- *Uncover whether the franchisor has experience in international markets:* It is typically not a good idea to be a franchisor's "test case" to see if the franchisor wants to operate in foreign markets. Be leery of franchisors with aggressive expansion plans but little international experience.
- *Find out how much training and support you will receive from the franchisor:* If your franchise unit will be in a foreign country and the franchisor remains headquartered in the United States, make sure you fully understand the amount of training and support you can expect. Will the franchisor have an area representative in your country? If not, do you have to make an international phone call each time you want to talk to your franchisor? Will your franchisor be willing to travel to the foreign country to offer you training and support? Who pays for the international travel of the franchisor's training staff? Who is responsible for advertising in the foreign country, the franchisor or the franchisee?
- *Evaluate currency restrictions:* Evaluate any restrictions that the foreign country places on the convertibility of its currency into U.S. dollars.

To avoid some of the potential problems alluded to here, U.S. franchisors typically structure their expansion into a foreign country through the following:

- *Direct franchising arrangement:* Under a direct franchise arrangement, the U.S. franchisor grants the rights to an individual or a company (the developer) to develop multiple franchised businesses within a country or territory. For example, if Midas Muffler decided to sell franchises for the first time in Spain, Midas may grant the rights to a Spanish company to develop multiple Midas franchises there.
- *Master franchise agreement:* Under a master franchise arrangement, the U.S. firm grants the right to an individual or company (the master franchisee) to develop one or more franchise businesses and to license others to develop one or more franchise businesses within the country or territory.

■ *Other agreements:* Combinations of other arrangements are also employed by franchisors expanding to foreign markets. Examples include joint-venture arrangements, direct-sales arrangements, or straight franchising agreements.

Even when a company adheres to these safeguards, there is plenty that can go wrong when opening franchise outlets overseas. This topic is addressed in this chapter's "What Went Wrong?" feature.

Watch Out: Plenty Can Go Wrong in Opening Franchise Outlets Overseas

Although the Internet, satellite television, and Hollywood movies have increased the demand for American products and services abroad, franchisors should take care not to rush into opening franchise outlets overseas. Because many of the easiest countries into which U.S. firms can export their products and services, such as Canada and England, are already saturated with U.S. franchised outlets, this leaves only more difficult foreign markets. Differences in language and the customs associated with a nation's culture are examples of factors making franchising very challenging in these more difficult foreign markets. Indeed, plenty can go wrong because of the complexities of operating overseas.

Sometimes, franchisors run into unique challenges in foreign markets, sometimes they simply make mistakes, and sometimes they insist on trying to impose American tastes on overseas markets, which doesn't always work. All of these complications result from a lack of familiarity with the foreign markets the companies are trying to enter. Here are some examples of mistakes U.S. franchisors have made when trying to enter foreign markets:

• Burger King didn't register its trademark in Australia before another restaurant group did. If you walk through the Sydney airport, you'll pass hamburger stands called Burger King and Hungry Jack's. Burger King is a local company—U.S. Burger King sandwiches are sold at Hungry Jack's.

• A donut concept failed in Brazil because people felt the hole meant they were being shortchanged.

• In Malaysia, a company put up a hotel, but no one would go inside because the door was on the wrong side of the building, violating the residents' religious norms.

• The Coca-Cola Company bought one of India's most successful soft-drink companies, which distributed the popular brand Thumbs Up, to get access to its distribution channels. Although this acquisition gave Coca-Cola immediate access to distribution channels, Thumbs Up remained more popular than Coke for many years. Most Indians thought that Coke wasn't fizzy enough.

• TCBY, the yogurt maker, found that it couldn't use its slogan "None of the guilt, all of the pleasure" in Japan because the Japanese culture does not have the same interpretation of the word *guilt* as American culture does.

Fortunately, many U.S franchisors are gaining experience and are making fewer mistakes in foreign countries. Flexibility is increasing too. For example, Domino's, which has almost 3,000 franchises overseas, is now encouraging its owner-operators to tweak menus according to local tastes. As a result, the company's overseas franchisees now offer pizzas topped with squid and peas in Taiwan, lamb and pickled ginger in India, and tuna in Iceland. Amazingly, Iceland is now home to three of Domino's four highest-grossing outlets. Similarly, in China, KFC outlets offer the chain's U.S. menu, plus "Duck Soup" and the "Old Beijing Twister," which is a wrap modeled on the way Peking duck is served, but with fried chicken inside.

Questions for Critical Thinking

1. In this feature, we considered a number of things that can go wrong when trying to pursue what appear to be franchising opportunities in some foreign markets. Using insights you've drawn from this chapter as well as your study of the book's first 14 chapters, prepare a list of reasons firms or entrepreneurs might be willing to accept the risks of establishing a franchise unit in a challenging foreign market. In slightly different words, what are the potential advantages of franchising in challenging international markets?

2. The examples of franchising mistakes made by Burger King and Coca-Cola, as described in this feature, may surprise you. Why is it that large organizations such as Burger King and Coca-Cola sometimes err when pursuing apparent franchising opportunities in difficult or challenging foreign markets? Prepare a list of factors you believe could cause large, long-lived organizations to make these types of mistakes.

3. Unlike Domino's Pizza, some restaurant chains sell the exact same food overseas as they sell in the United States. What are the pluses and the minuses of doing this?

4. Do some Internet research and identify a foreign-owned franchise organization that sells franchises in the United States. Do the company's U.S. franchises sell the same exact product as the company sells in its home country? If not, what types of changes or modification have been made to satisfy American consumers?

Sources: "Giving New Meaning to the Term 'Gross Revenue,'" *Business 2.0*, October 2005, 144; M. Haig *Brand Failures* (London: Kogan Page 2003); J. Bennett, "Some Franchises Don't Translate Well Overseas," *The Wall Street Journal*, www.startupjournal.com (accessed October 28, 2003); J. Bennett, "Why U.S. Franchises Face Problems Abroad," *The Wall Street Journal*, www.startupjournal.com (accessed October 28, 2003).

The Future of Franchising

The future of franchising appears bright. Franchise organizations represent a large and growing segment of the retail and service sectors of U.S. businesses and are in some cases replacing more traditional forms of small business ownership.[31] According to the International Franchise Association (IFA), franchising represents about $1 trillion in annual retail sales in the United States and involves 320,000 franchised outlets in 75 industries. In addition, the IFA estimates that a new franchise outlet opens somewhere in the United States every 8 minutes.[32] More and more college graduates are choosing careers in industries that are heavily dominated by franchising. The availability of digital business tools, which increase the effectiveness of franchise organizations in a variety of ways, is also making franchising more desirable. As franchising continues to become a more pervasive form of business, regulators and franchise associations are likely to intervene in ways that strengthen the viability of the franchise concept.[33]

Chapter Summary

1. A franchise is an agreement between a franchisor (the parent company, such as McDonald's), and a franchisee (an individual or firm that is willing to pay the franchisor a fee for the right to sell its product or service).
2. There are two distinctly different types of franchise systems: the product trademark franchise and the business format franchise. A product trademark franchise is an arrangement under which the franchisor grants to the franchisee the right to buy its products and use its trade name. Automobile dealerships and soft-drink distributorships are examples of product trademark franchises. In a business format franchise, the franchisor provides a formula for doing business to the franchisee along with training, advertising, and other forms of assistance.
3. An individual franchise agreement involves the sale of a single franchise for a specific location. An area franchise agreement allows a franchisee to own and operate a specific number of outlets in a particular geographic area. A master franchise agreement is similar to an area franchise agreement with one major exception. In addition to having the right to operate a specific number of locations in a particular area, the franchisee also has the right to offer and sell the franchise to other people in the area.
4. The advantages of setting up a franchise system include rapid, low-cost market expansion; income from franchise fees and royalties; franchisee motivation; access to ideas and suggestions; cost savings; and increased buying power. The disadvantages of setting up a franchise system include sharing profits with franchisees, loss of control, friction with franchisees, managing growth, differences in required business skills, and legal expenses.

5. The rules of thumb for determining whether franchising is a good choice for growing a business are as follows: The product or service the business sells should be unique; the business should be consistently profitable; the business should be profitable year-round, not only during a specific season; the business system and procedures should be polished; and the business proposition should be clear so that prospective franchisees fully understand the relationship to which they are committing.

6. Preparing answers to the following questions helps the entrepreneur determine if franchising is a good fit as a way to launch a venture: Are you willing to take orders? Are you willing to be part of a franchise system? How will you react if you make a suggestion to your franchisor and your suggestion is rejected? What are you looking for in a business? How willing are you to put your money at risk?

7. The following costs are typically associated with buying a business format franchise: initial franchise fee, capital requirements (such as land, buildings, and equipment), continuing royalty payment, advertising fee, and other fees (depending on the franchise system).

8. The advantages of buying a franchise include a proven product or service within an established market; an established trademark or business system; the franchisor's training, technical expertise, and managerial experience; an established marketing network; ongoing franchisor support; availability of financing; and potential for business growth. The disadvantages of buying a franchise include cost of the franchise; restrictions on creativity; duration and nature of commitment; risk of fraud, misunderstanding, or lack of franchisor commitment; problems of termination or transfer; and the possibility of poor performance on the part of other franchisees.

9. The common mistakes made by franchise buyers include believing that franchising is a completely safe investment, believing that a great industry ensures franchise success, putting too much faith in the idea that a franchise is a "proven" business system, believing that there is no need to hire a franchise attorney or accountant, being overly optimistic about how fast the franchise outlet will grow, believing that "I can operate my franchise outlet for less than the franchisor predicts," and believing that just because the franchisor is a nice person, he or she will always be there to help out when needed.

10. The Uniform Franchise Offering Circular (UFOC) is a document with 23 categories of information. This document provides a prospective franchisee a broad base of information about a franchisor's background and financial health. The UFOC must be provided by the franchisor to a prospective franchisee at least 10 business days before a franchise contract can be signed or the franchisee pays the franchisor any money.

Key Terms

agency theory, 449
area franchise agreement, 443
business format franchise, 442
fiduciary obligation, 459
franchise agreement, 459
franchisees, 441

franchising, 441
franchisor, 441
individual franchise agreement, 443
master franchise agreement, 443
multiple-unit franchisee, 444

product and trademark franchise, 442
subfranchisees, 444
uniform franchisor offering circular, 459

Review Questions

1. What is franchising? How does it differ from other forms of business ownership?
2. Describe the differences between a product and trademark franchise and a business format franchise. Provide an example of both types of franchise arrangements.
3. What is the difference among an individual franchise agreement, an area franchise agreement, and a master franchise agreement?
4. What are the nine basic steps in setting up a franchise system?
5. What are the advantages and disadvantages of establishing a franchise system?

6. What are the rules of thumb for determining whether franchising is a good choice for a particular business? Provide an example of a business that wouldn't be suitable for franchising.

7. What are some of the issues an entrepreneur should consider when answering the question "Is franchising a good choice for me?"

8. What are the costs involved in purchasing a business unit franchise? Are these costs similar across franchise systems, or do they vary widely?

9. Explain why it is to the franchisor's advantage to receive its royalty payment on the gross income rather than net income of its franchise outlets.

10. Describe some of the resources available to prospective franchisees to identify franchise opportunities.

11. What are the principal advantages and disadvantages of buying a franchise?

12. What are the seven steps involved in purchasing a franchise?

13. What are some of the common misconceptions franchisees often have about franchising?

14. What is the purpose of the Uniform Franchise Offering Circular (UFOC)? Are there any regulations regarding when the UFOC must be provided to a prospective franchisee? If so, what are they?

15. What is the purpose of a franchise agreement? Identify the two sections of the franchise agreement and describe the purpose of each one.

16. To date, every court case that has been adjudicated in the United States indicates that franchisors do not have a fiduciary responsibility to their franchisees. What do these rulings suggest to entrepreneurs considering the possibility of buying into a franchise system? Why?

17. What are some of the aspects of franchising that make it subject to ethical abuses?

18. For U.S. citizens, what are the main issues that should be considered before buying a franchise in a foreign country?

19. What are the main reasons that many U.S. franchise systems are expanding into global markets? Do you think this expansion will continue to gain momentum or will decline over time? Explain your answer.

20. Does franchising have a bright or a dim future in the United States? Make your answer as substantive and thoughtful as possible.

Application Questions

1. Reread the opening feature, which focuses on Joseph Keeley and the franchise organization that he founded—College Nannies & Tutors. Think of an activity, other than nanny and tutoring services, that you think college students might be particularly good at and has a defined need and is franchisable. Describe how that activity could be turned into a franchise organization.

2. Several executives from Coca-Cola have decided to leave their jobs to launch a new chain of a Dairy Queen type of restaurant called Thirst Burst Etc. They want to grow quickly. Under what conditions would franchising be a good choice for them?

3. Pick a franchise organization that you admire. Spend some time looking at the company's Web site. Describe how the company is set up. Is it a product and trademark franchise or a business format franchise? Does it sell individual franchise agreements, area franchise agreements, master franchise agreements, or some combination of the three? How many company-owned stores and how many franchise outlets are in the system? Report any particularly interesting or unusual things you learned about the system.

4. Up to this point, Comfort Keepers has not sold master franchise agreements. Would setting up master franchises be an effective course of action for Comfort Keepers? Explain your answer.

5. Select a franchise organization that is located on your campus or near the campus that isn't involved in any co-branding arrangements. Suggest several co-branding relationships that would make sense for this company.

6. Bill Watts has decided to buy a sub shop franchise called Deluxe Subs. He lives in Cedar Falls, Iowa, and will be the first Deluxe Subs franchisee in the state. Along with

buying a Deluxe Subs franchise, Bill would also like to purchase the rights to offer and sell Deluxe Subs franchises to other people in the Cedar Falls area. What type of franchise agreement should Bill negotiate with Deluxe Subs? For Bill, what are the advantages and disadvantages of this type of arrangement?

7. Sarah Gandy works for a computer consulting firm in Salt Lake City. For some time, she has been thinking about either starting her own computer consulting company or buying a computer consulting franchise. She knows that you have been taking a course in entrepreneurship and asks you to tell her a little bit about what a franchise costs and how to identify a good franchise system. What would you tell her?

8. Helen Partridge owns a very successful chain of Web site development businesses. She currently has 21 offices spread across Illinois, Indiana, and Ohio. She is thinking about franchising her business as a means of expanding beyond the Midwest. Helen has always believed in getting professional advice before making a major decision. Who should Helen talk to, and what types of questions should she ask before making the decision to franchise her business?

9. Jason Carpenski is a serial entrepreneur. Although he is only 35, he has already started three businesses. Jason loves launching businesses because he likes being his own boss and enjoys the independence an entrepreneurial career offers him. Recently, Jason sold his latest business, a communications equipment start-up, and is looking for a new opportunity. He just attended a franchise fair and is extremely interested in buying a printing and copying franchise. Do you think Jason is a good candidate to buy a franchise in an established franchise system? Why or why not?

10. Joan Wagner has worked for Walgreen's for several years as a photo processor. She just inherited a nice sum of money and has decided to purchase a Planet Smoothie franchise. Before she signs the franchise agreement, however, she wants to make sure that she fully understands the advantages and disadvantages of buying a franchise. What would you tell Joan if she asked you for this information?

11. Suppose you ran into an old friend who is just about to buy into a handheld computer accessories retail franchise. He tells you that he is excited about the opportunity because the system he is about to buy into (1) is in an industry that virtually guarantees its success, (2) has a "proven" business model, and (3) is operated by people who are so honest that he can skip the expense of hiring a franchise attorney to review the documents he has to sign. If your friend asked you, "Be honest with me now—am I being naive, or does this sound like a great opportunity?" what would you tell your friend? Why?

12. Suppose you saw an ad in your local newspaper for a franchise opportunity that caught your attention. You called the phone number listed in the ad and liked what you heard. As a result, you scheduled a time to meet with a representative of the franchise organization at a nearby Panera Bread restaurant. After learning more about the opportunity, you tell the representative that you're really interested and would like more information. If the opportunity is legitimate and the organization you are dealing with complies with the law, what should you expect from this point forward?

13. Sarah Saladino, a close high school friend, is thinking about buying into a franchise operation that sells expensive clothing that is targeted to middle-aged working women. Although interested in the possibility, Sarah is concerned by the franchisor's request that she take a personality test. "Why in the world should I take such a test?" Because you are a psychology major with a minor in entrepreneurship, Sarah believes that you may be able to help her understand this request. What answer would you give to Sarah regarding her question about the use of personality tests by franchisors?

14. If College Nannies & Tutors decided to start selling franchises in Great Britain and France, which steps should it take to make sure that its concept is suitable for use in those countries? What types of mistakes should it be careful to avoid?

15. Suppose you are an American citizen living in England. You just lost your job with a telecommunications firm that merged with a French company. You would like to stay in England and are thinking about buying a franchise in an American cell phone retail company that is expanding to Europe. What are some of the issues you should evaluate before buying an outlet in an American franchise system that is selling franchises in England?

you be the VC 15.1

Velocity Sports Performance
www.velocitysp.com

Business Idea: Develop a business that helps athletes in every sport, at all ages and skill levels, realize their athletic potential through advanced sports performance training programs scientifically designed to maximize human sports performance.

Pitch: Many people are interested in becoming better athletes. The reasons vary and range from reaching a personal goal, to making the varsity team in high school, to getting a college scholarship. Regrettably, despite their aspirations, many people never reach their full potential as an athlete. The problem often centers on not having sufficient personal strength, speed, and overall athleticism to perform at a high level. Most people can't obtain these attributes on their own. They need fitness education, personal attention, and professional coaching to take themselves to the next level.

Velocity Sports Performance was founded to address this exact set of problems. The company is developing a national chain of training centers to equip athletes of all ages to reach their full potential. Each Velocity Sports Performance Center is a 10,000–30,000-square-foot, climate-controlled facility. Rather than teaching specific skills, like how to throw a football further or how to improve a golf swing, the centers focus on athleticism and fitness. A personal training program is established for each client, and the clients train in small groups, under the direction of coaches. All of Velocity's coaches have at least a bachelor's degree in exercise science or a related field and have coached at least at the collegiate level. The individual

programs that most clients rotate through, with their small groups, are as follows:

- Speed, Agility, and Coordination
- Strength and Power
- Mobility and Flexibility
- Energy Systems
- Injury Prevention

Each program was carefully designed by Loren Seagrave, Velocity's founder and world-renowned speed and sports performance coach. To accommodate clients' personal interests, and to provide training facilities for drop-in college and pro athletes, each Velocity center includes athletic turf fields, running tracks, hard court basketball/volleyball surfaces, and Olympic-style weightlifting equipment.

One particularly fun aspect of the Velocity Sport Performance experience is that many top-notch college and professional athletes train at Velocity facilities, right alongside Velocity's other clients. Wouldn't it be fun to pace yourself against some of the world's finest while completing one or more exercise activities?

Q&A: Based on the material covered in this chapter, what questions would you ask the firm's founders before making your funding decision? What answers would satisfy you?

Decision: If you had to make your decision on just the information provided in the pitch and on the company's Web site, would you fund this firm? Why or why not?

you be the VC 15.2

ZENhome
www.zenhomecleaning.com

Business Idea: Provide unique housecleaning services while remaining conscious of environmental concerns by using only nontoxic, eco-friendly products.

Pitch: Many people pay professional housekeepers to clean their homes. A potential downside to this approach is that most housekeepers use traditional cleaning supplies to do their work. This situation poses a problem for people who prefer to use nontoxic, eco-friendly products in their homes. At the same time, most housecleaning companies are similar in terms of the services they provide. For instance, few if any housecleaning services view

housecleaning as a holistic service that deals with both the physical act of housekeeping and the emotional and spiritual well-being of the client.

ZENhome offers a solution to this problem by changing humdrum cleaning into something special. The company uses only nontoxic, environmentally friendly cleaning products, which appeals to both ecologically aware customers and people with allergies. In addition, ZENhome cleaners burn essential oils while cleaning, spray linens with lavender mist, turn down beds, place organic chocolate bars on pillows, and leave small bowls of potpourri in their clients' homes. The entire effort is meant to help customers feel good about choosing an environmentally friendly cleaning service and feel good about themselves. Not only does ZENhome want its customers to come home to a clean house, they want them to come home to a peaceful, therapeutic setting as well.

ZENhome is currently operating in New York City. The company is thinking about using franchising to expand outside of the city.

Q&A: Based on the material covered in this chapter, what questions would you ask the firm's founders before making your funding decision? What answers would satisfy you?

Decision: If you had to make your decision on just the information provided in the pitch and on the company's Web site, would you fund this firm? Why or why not?

1-800-GOT-JUNK?: How to Turn People's Discards Into a Vibrant Franchise System
www.1800gotjunk.com

Bruce R. Barringer,
University of Central Florida
R. Duane Ireland,
Texas A&M University

Introduction
1-800-GOT-JUNK? advertises itself as the "world's largest junk removal service." If you have junk that needs to be removed from your home or business, all you have to do is call the company's toll-free number, and if you're in one of the markets the company serves, you can schedule an appointment for the junk to be removed at your convenience.

Sound pretty ordinary? It is—and it isn't. There is certainly nothing new about 1-800-GOT-JUNK?'s business idea. Junk removal services have always been around. What is new is the way the company has approached selling its services in the junk removal industry. Impressively, the company's approach has made it a profitable and rapidly growing franchise organization. Let's see how this has happened.

Brian Scudamore
Brian Scudamore started 1-800-GOT-JUNK? in 1989. He remembers the exact moment of inspiration that led to launching his venture. It was three days before his 19th birthday, and he was waiting his turn in a McDonald's drive-through lane. Just ahead of him was a beat-up old pickup truck, filled with old tires and twisted bicycle frames. The hand-painted sign on the door read MARK'S HAULING. Scudamore thought, "I could do that." He figured he could buy a beat-up old truck and haul junk for people as a way of paying for college education.

The next day, Scudamore bought a $700 truck and started a junk removal service. He named it Rubbish Boys. The business started slowly but picked up as time went on, and eventually Scudamore was so busy that he dropped out of college to pursue the business full-time. One of his favorite stories from that time in his life is telling his father that he

dropped out of school to build a junk removal business. His father was, of all things, a liver transplant surgeon. He recalls that his father was not impressed—to say the least. He chuckles when he says that today in that his father is a member of the board of directors for the company his son founded.

In 1998, Scudamore changed the name of his company from Rubbish Boys to 1-800-GOT-JUNK? He wanted a name that was descriptive of his service and was easy for customers to use and remember. Scudamore decided to franchise the business, primarily to avoid having to borrow money to expand. Reflecting on his decision to become a franchisor Scudamore said:

> It's the ultimate leverage model. People pay you a fee up-front to help them grow. Rather than lose control of my vision by going public—I chose franchising. It's the ultimate growth model.

1-800-GOT-JUNK?'s Unique Approach to the Junk Industry
There are three aspects of the way 1-800-GOT-JUNK? has approached the junk industry that have helped the company differentiate itself in the marketplace and build a high-quality franchise organization.

1. Positioning. The company occupies a position in the junk industry that previously wasn't served adequately, if at all. 1-800-GOT-JUNK? fills the sweet stop between city-provided trash removal (provided to most homes for free) and companies like Waste Management, which serve businesses, factories, and apartment complexes. 1-800-GOT- JUNK?'s position is depicted in the figure titled 1-800-GOT-JUNK?'s Positioning Strategy: Occupying the Sweet Spot in the Middle. By occupying this position, the company is filling unmet needs. Think about it. All homeowners have larger items they need to get rid of from time to time, like an old refrigerator, sofa, or dishwasher. City trash collectors typically won't

1-800-GOT-JUNK's Positioning Strategy: Occupying the Sweet Spot in the Middle

Curbside Trash and Garbage Pickup for Homeowners	Larger Items Consumers Have that are Too Big for City Pickup but Too Small for Large Companies	Big Bins with Trash From Businesses, Factories, and Apartment Buildings
Removal Provided by City Governments	**Removal Provided by 1-800-GOT-JUNK** (The sweet spot in the middle)	Removal Provided by Large For-Profit Companies like Waste Management

take these types of items. 1-800-GOT JUNK? provides a pickup service to satisfy these types of needs.

2. **Standardized, high-quality service.** In communities where junk removal services are available, they are typically hit-and-miss. The services are run mostly by independent operators. Many of these operators are fine, but the consumer typically doesn't know what to expect. If a consumer picks a junk removal service out of the yellow pages, it's entirely possible that someone will show up late in a beat-up old truck that may or may not have the capacity to complete the customer's job. In contrast, 1-800-GOT-JUNK? provides a highly standardized, branded service. Its drivers show up on time, in late-model Ford F-450s, Nissan UD 1400s, or Isuzu NPR trucks. The trucks are all painted the same colors (blue and white) and have identical dump boxes. Franchisees are required to wash their trucks once a day. All of the company's employees wear uniforms. A 1-800-GOT-JUNK? employee wears navy slacks, a royal-blue golf shirt (tucked in) with logo, a baseball cap, belt, and boots, all of which must match.

To illustrate Scudamore and his top-management team's commitment to providing customers a high-quality standardized service, CNNMoney.com reported in an article that Scudamore pulled the plug on a Canadian franchisee for driving a muddy truck with a peeling 1-800-GOT-JUNK? decal. According to the article, Scudamore reacted to the incident by saying, "Do you ever see a dirty FedEx truck? I mean, do you ever"?

3. **A savvy mix of low-tech and high-tech.** While hauling junk is a low-tech activity, the company is decidedly high-tech in its behind-the-scenes activities. All the calls that are placed to the company's toll-free number, which is the same as its name (1-800-GOT-JUNK?), are handled by a call center in Vancouver, Canada, which is where the company is headquartered. The requests for service are entered into a proprietary computer program called JunkNet, which is a program the company built from scratch for $500,000. To view a given day's schedule of jobs, all a franchisee has to do is log on to his or her JunkNet account. If a new job comes in during the day, the program automatically sends the applicable franchisee an alert. All of the franchisees are equipped with

Web-enabled cell phones. JunkNet provides other back-end type functionality for the franchisees.

There is also a green, or environmentally friendly, aspect to 1-800-GOT-JUNK?'s business. Franchisees are encouraged to dispose of items at recycling centers, instead of county landfills, when appropriate. Along with helping the environment, this policy has a financial reward. Most landfills charge a fee; dropping items at recycling centers is typically free. Some recycling centers even pay for certain items, like scrap metal. There are also times when people dispose of things that have value. In these instances, the franchisees can take the items and resell them, if the effort is worth the gain.

One thing the company enjoys doing is maintaining a list of the most unusual things they have been asked to dispose of. The list currently includes:

- An 8-foot-long stuffed swordfish
- A ship's compass
- A prosthetic leg
- A Bill Clinton mask
- 18,000 cans of outdated sardines
- Antique rifles

What Lies Ahead

To Scudamore's credit, he has gotten his company off to a good start. The firm has 241 franchisees in the United States, Canada, and Australia, and is still growing. 1-800-GOT-JUNK?'s growth has been bootstrapped entirely from its own cash flow, and Scudamore remains the sole owner of the company. The question for 1-800-GOT-JUNK? now is "What lies ahead?"

Discussion Questions

1. What do you think lies ahead for 1-800-GOT-JUNK? What are some of the things that can go right and what are some of the things that can go wrong as this firm continues to expand?

2. What qualities do you think 1-800-GOT-JUNK? looks for in prospective franchisees? If you were a prospective franchisee, what questions would you ask the company as part of your own due diligence process?

3. Do you think 1-800-GOT-JUNK? is a business concept that lends itself to franchising, or do you think franchising

is inappropriate for this company? Justify your answer. What alternatives did Brian Scudamore have for growing 1-800-GOT-JUNK? other than franchising?

4. In your judgment, would 1-800-GOT-JUNK? be better off pursuing new markets via individual franchise agreements or area franchise agreements? Explain your answer.

Application Questions

1. Do you think 1-800-GOT-JUNK? will stay in its niche as it continues to grow, or do you think the company will eventually expand into markets pictured to the left and markets pictured to the right of its current position

in the figure titled 1-800-GOT-JUNK's Positioning Strategy? (*Note:* Some city governments contract with private firms for curbside trash and garbage removal.)

2. Spend some time looking at 1-800-GOT-JUNK?'s Web site and doing some additional reading about the company. Make a list of what you believe are some of the firm's strengths and weaknesses. In addition, briefly describe what an average day would be like for a 1-800-GOT-JUNK? franchisee.

Sources: 1-800-GOT-JUNK? homepage, (accessed May 10, 2006); S. Allen, (2004). About homepage, "Entrepreneur Success Story: Brian Scudamore of 1-800-GOT-JUNK?" (accessed May 11, 2006); J. Martin, "Cash From Trash," CNNMoney.com (2003).

CASE 15.2

Cartridge World: How Bright Is the Outlook for the Company's Franchisees?
www.cartridgeworld.com

Bruce R. Barringer,
University of Central Florida

R. Duane Ireland,
Texas A&M University

Introduction

There is no denying that Cartridge World's service meets a need. The company, which is a franchise organization, sells franchises to individuals who operate small storefronts that refill ink cartridges. The idea behind the business is to offer consumers an affordable alternative to buying expensive printer replacement cartridges. Haven't you cringed over the prices as you buy a replacement cartridge for your printer?

Cartridge World's concept has caught on so quickly that the company recently passed the 1,000-store threshold worldwide. But there are two threats looming on Cartridge World's horizon that could have a major impact on the company and its franchisees' future. This case describes the history of Cartridge World and then presents the challenges that the company is facing.

Easing a Pain

Cartridge World was launched in Australia in 1988. From the outset, it has been a business that specializes in refilling empty printer cartridges. A consumer can bring an empty ink cartridge to a Cartridge World store, wait while the cartridge is professionally refilled, and leave with a full cartridge at about half the price of a new one. To spur its growth, the company starting selling franchises in 1997. Since then, its growth has taken off. Its roster of 1,000-plus franchised outlets is currently growing by more than one outlet every day.

The essence of Cartridge World's success is clear—the company eases a pain. There is one frustration that almost all computer printer owners have in common: the replacement cost cartridges. To illustrate just how expensive the ink

in a printer cartridge is, Burt Yarkin, the CEO of Cartridge World's North American division, points out that the ink inside a new cartridge from Hewlett-Packard (HP), Lexmark, or Canon costs more per ounce than Chanel No. 5 (perfume) or Dom Perignon champagne. "People know they're getting ripped off," Yarkin recently told *BusinessWeek.* "We're giving consumers and businesses a choice."

Why Cartridge World Sells Franchises

The idea of refilling ink cartridges rather than buying replacements isn't new, but Cartridge World is the first company to set up retail stores that offer ink cartridge refills while you wait. The bet is that consumers will make a habit of getting their existing cartridges refilled, rather than buying new ones, if the process is cheaper, simple, and convenient. To make the process convenient, Cartridge World is selling franchises at an aggressive pace. "We want to be the McDonald's of ink and toner," Burt Yarkin said in a separate interview. "We're going right into people's neighborhoods and becoming part of their daily lives."

Cartridge World turned to franchising primarily as a means of accelerating its growth.

The cost of a Cartridge World franchise is between $105,000 and $175,000. These figures, which include a one-time franchise fee of $25,000 to $35,000 and the capital needed to start up the business, show the beauty of franchising for a company like Cartridge World. If Cartridge World sells 1,000 franchises in the United States in the next 10 years, the company will collect $25 million to $35 million in franchise fees, and its franchisees will invest between $75 million and $145 million for land and equipment to open their stores. This is money that the company would have had to raise through other means if it had decided to expand via company-owned stores rather than franchising.

With a focus on even more growth, Cartridge World offers a range of products, including new ink and laser cartridges, specialty papers for quality photographic prints, copy toners, fax supplies, and printer and cash register ribbons in addition to its core service of cartridge refilling. The idea behind adding products is to become a true one-stop shop for printer supplies.

Threats on the Horizon

Despite its positive momentum, there are two threats looming on Cartridge World's horizon. It is unclear how significant these threats are.

Threat #1: New Entrants.

In early 2006, Walgreens announced that it plans to enter the ink-replacement business and is currently pilot-testing its service. If Walgreens decides to offer the service nationwide, it will become available to customers in more than 1,500 of its stores. Similar offerings are in the works at OfficeMax and Office Depot, along with a number of smaller companies. At Walgreens, consumers will be able to have ink cartridges refilled within 15 minutes, which is similar to the time it takes at Cartridge World. Walgreens says that its price will be around 50 percent less than the price of a new cartridge, which provides it a slight price advantage over Cartridge World.

Along with larger companies offering a similar service, Cartridge World may also be facing new competition from smaller firms that plan to open their own storefronts or put ink-refill service in existing retail locations. For example, Rapid Refill, an Oregon-based franchise organization, presently has 40 cartridge-refill stores and is expanding.

Threat #2: The Cartridge Makers Are Fighting Back.

Obviously, the potential losers in Cartridge World's pursuit to provide consumers a more affordable way to refill their cartridges are the printer cartridge manufacturers. Analysts say that ink and toner supplies made up more than 50 percent of HP's 2004 profits, even though they brought in less than 25 percent of the company's $80 billion in sales. Similar types of proportions between revenue and profit are thought to exist at Canon and Lexmark. The impact of Cartridge World and its peers is being felt. According to a recent *New York Times* article, the migration by consumers to alternative ways of getting their printer cartridges refilled is the primary reason that Lexmark's net income dropped 47 percent in the fourth quarter of 2005.

In response to these developments, the cartridge makers are fighting back in two ways. First, they are using the courts to make sure that Cartridge World and similar firms don't use the same patented ink formulation that they do. For example, HP, which has over 4,000 patents in its printer supply business, went after Cartridge World in October 2005 for using ink that HP alleged infringed on its patents. Similarly, at roughly the same time, HP went after InkCycle, the company that makes cartridge refills under the Staples brand, saying that it had violated three HP patents covering fast-drying ink for paper and methods for preventing color from bleeding on paper. That dispute was settled when InkCycle changed its ink formulation.

The second way that the cartridge manufacturers are fighting back is by arguing that refilled cartridges produce lower-quality printing results and are more expensive for consumers in the long run. Some independent analysts agree that a tangible difference still exists between the results produced by a new cartridge and a refilled one, although many people have a hard time seeing the difference. In regard to costs, the manufacturers say that the original cartridges will print more pages than refilled cartridges, and that the per page cost is actually lower for new cartridges.

A potential third way that HP and the other manufacturers could fight back, but haven't pursued, is to engineer their cartridges in a way that would prevent them from being refilled. This possibility is seen as unlikely as a result of regulatory issues.

Cartridge World's Outlook for the Future

Cartridge World is continuing to aggressively expand and sell new franchises. Two important questions the company must now face are: to what extent should it be concerned about the competitive threats it is facing and what steps should it take to deal with them?

Discussion Questions

1. What do you think? How important are the two competitive threats that Cartridge World is facing? What steps, if any, should Cartridge World take to meet these threats?
2. Of the two major threats facing Cartridge World, which one do you think has the most potential to negatively affect this firm? Explain your answer.
3. Do you think the competitive threats mentioned in the case will slow the pace at which Cartridge World sells franchises? Should they?
4. Do you think that this is a good time or a poor time to start a new company in the cartridge-refill business? If you started a new company in this area, what types of competitive issues would be foremost in your mind?

Application Questions

1. Reflect back on Chapter 5 of this book. What does the Cartridge World case teach us with regard to the impact of Porter's five forces on an industry's profitability? Which of the five forces will be most adversely impacted (in terms of lowering the cartridge-refill industry's profitability) if Walgreens, Office Depot, and OfficeMax establish a significant presence in the market?
2. If Walgreens, Office Depot, and OfficeMax enter Cartridge World's business, how can Cartridge World differentiate itself from these larger firms? Think carefully about your answer. Brainstorm some ways that Cartridge World could remain vibrant by serving its customers in a different, a unique, or a more valuable way as compared to its larger competitors.

Sources: D. Darlin, "New Printer Cartridge or a Refill? Either Way, Ink Is Getting Cheaper," *The New York Times*, February 4, 2006, C1; Pui-Wing Tam, "A Cheaper Way to Refill Your Printer," *The Wall Street Journal*, January 26, 2006, p. D1; P. Burrows, "Ever Wonder Why Ink Costs So Much?" *BusinessWeek*, November 4, 2005, 42–44; Pui-Wing Tam, "Fill'er Up, with Color," *The Wall Street Journal*, August 3, 2004, B1.

Endnotes

1. L. Wolf, "Learning Curve," *Upsizemag.com*, www.upsizemag.com (accessed June 1, 2006).

2. Wolf, "Learning Curve."

3. Personal interview with Joseph Keeley, May 30, 2006.

4. V. K. Jolly, *Commercializing New Technologies* (Cambridge, MA: Harvard Business School Press, 1997).

5. www.franchise.com (accessed June 3, 2006); I. Alon, "The Use of Franchising by U.S.-Based Retailers," *Journal of Small Business Management* 39, no. 2 (2001): 111–22.

6. J. G. Combs, D. J. Ketchen, and R. D. Ireland, "Effective Managing Service Chain Organizations," *Organizational Dynamics* (2007, in press).

7. Wikipedia Encyclopedia, www.wikpedia.com (accessed June 3, 2006).

8. "Breaking the Silver Ceiling," U.S. Congress Report from the Committee on Aging, 2005; Start Your Own Business, "It Pays to Care," *Small Business Opportunities*, Spring 2002.

9. Comfort Keepers homepage, www.comfortkeepers.com (accessed June 1, 2006).

10. P. H. Rubin, "The Theory of the Firm and the Structure of the Franchise Contract," *Journal of Law and Economics* 21 (1978): 223–33.

11. Combs, Ketchen, and Ireland, "Effectively Managing Service Chain Organizations."

12. D. H. B. Welsh, I. Alon, and C. M. Falbe, "An Examination of Retail Franchising in Emerging Markets," *Journal of Small Business Management* 44, no. 1 (2006): 130–49.

13. B. Merrilees and L. Frazer, "Entrepreneurial Franchises Have Hidden Superior Marketing Systems," *Qualitative Market Research* 9, no. 1 (2006): 73–85.

14. R. Sloan, J. Sloan, and J. Sinelli, Startupnation Podcast, March 27, 2006.

15. G. J. Castrogiovanni, J. G. Combs, and R. T. Justis, "Shifting Imperatives: An Integrating View of Resource Scarcity and Agency Reasons for Franchising," *Entrepreneurship Theory and Practice* 39, no. 1 (2006): 23–40.

16. R. Bennett, "To Franchise or Not: How to Decide," in *Franchising Today: 1966–1967*, ed. C. L. Vaughn and D. B. Slater (New York: Matthew Bender and Company, 1967), 20.

17. J. Brickley and F. Dark, "The Choice of Organizational Form: The Case of Franchising," *Journal of Financial Economics* 18 (1987): 401–20.

18. "Darden Restaurants, Inc.," *Standard & Poor's Stock Report*, www.standardandpoors.com (accessed June 4, 2006).

19. J. E. Clarkin and S. M. Swavely, "The Importance of Personal Characteristics in Franchisee Selection," *Journal of Retailing and Consumer Services* 13, no. 2 (2006): 133–42.

20. International Franchising Association, "What Is Franchising?" www.franchise.org (accessed May 27, 2004).

21. Federal Trade Commission, *Consumers Guide to Buying a Franchise* (Washington, DC: U.S. Government Printing Office, 2002).

22. M. Grunhagen and M. Mittlestaedt, "Entrepreneurs or Investors: Do Multi-Unit Franchisees Have Different Philosophical Orientations?" *Journal of Small Business Management* 43, no. 3 (2005): 207–25.

23. Candy Bouquet homepage, www.candybouquet.com (accessed June 1, 2006).

24. J. Bennett, "Cruise Franchisee Says It's Been Smooth Sailing, *StartupJournal.com*, www.startupjournal.com (accessed May 30, 2006).

25. L. Altinay, "Selecting Partners in an International Franchise Organisation," *International Journal of Hospitality Management* 25, no. 1 (2006): 108–28.

26. Federal Trade Commission, "Guide to the FTC Franchise Rule," www.ftc.gov/bcp/franchise/netrule.html (accessed June 1, 2006).

27. R. L. Purvin, *The Franchise Fraud* (New York: John Wiley & Sons, 1994), 7.

28. American Bar Association, *Legal Guide for Small Business* (New York: Random House, 2000).

29. Federal Trade Commission, "Guide to the FTC Franchise Rule."

30. I. Alon and K. Bian, "Real Estate Franchising: The Case of Coldwell Banker Expansion into China," *Business Horizons* 48, no. 3 (2005): 223–31.

31. Federal Trade Commission, "Guide to the FTC Franchise Rule."

32. International Franchise Association, "How Widespread Is Franchising?" www.franchise.org (accessed March 29, 2002).

33. E. Pfister, B. Deffians, M. Doriant-Duban, and S. Saussier, "Institutions and Contracts: Franchising," *European Journal of Law and Economics* 21, no. 1 (2006): 53–78.

Case 1 Matt Grant

William Bygrave and Carl Hedburg, case writer
*Arthur M. Blank Center for Entrepreneurship,
Babson College*

Driving home from work one evening in early January, 2003, 27-year-old Matt Grant was recalling the last time he had asked his wife Margy to "trust me on this one." That fiasco—while not resulting from any miscalculation on his part—had not only caused his wife a lot of aggravation and extra work, but had also interfered with the early trajectory of her own career.

Now, a couple of years later, Matt was planning to ask Margy to support another leap of faith. The difference was that while the first leap had been in response to what had seemed like a solid advancement opportunity within a successful electronics corporation, this second one would involve the standard bearer of business risk: new venture creation.

On the one hand, he had a decent management job with a multinational where the work was as predictable and steady as his paychecks and 401K matches. On the other hand, there was Racer's Resource, a venture that he'd researched and tested enough to know—at least in his gut—that there was a real opportunity there; albeit one with little predictability and even less guarantee of regular, near-term compensation.

Matt had been working on the assumption that he could initially run his magazine venture on the side, but that afternoon—in a bid to trim staff during the tough recession—his boss had come to him with an attractive, sixteen-week severance package. Matt was now at a critical juncture in the road, and he wished that he could be sure that he wasn't favoring the entrepreneurial venture for the wrong reasons—because it was new, exciting, and "out there" on the risk/reward continuum:

> Was Racer's Resource as good as it seemed, or would I be throwing away a perfectly good job—and an established career track—only to realize too late that I'd overestimated the upside potential? And if that happened—if

Carl Hedberg prepared this case under the supervision of Professor William Bygrave, Babson College, as a basis for class discussion rather than to illustrate either effective or ineffective handling of an administrative situation. Funding provided by the F.W. Olin Graduate School of Business and a gift from the class of 2003.

> I put in the time and failed—how likely was it that I could re-enter the corporate world at a level even close to where I am right now?

Important considerations to be sure, but by the time Matt pulled into the driveway, he was back to thinking about how his wife was going to feel about all this. While her work as the in-house counsel for the Massachusetts Association of Realtors came with health benefits and a decent salary, their financial situation would take a drastic turn, if, as an entrepreneur, Matt failed to get up to speed before his severance ran out.

Snow had been in the forecast that night, and Matt watched as the first wispy flakes touched down and dissolved on the windshield. Figuring that Margy was on the computer in their home office, Matt killed the headlights and left the motor running; he needed a few moments to collect his thoughts.

Sprinting Through the Late 90s

In 1996, Matt graduated from the University of New Hampshire with a business degree, and immediately landed a job as a buyer with the Teradyne Corporation. Propelled by a combination of opportunity and hard work, in just two years Matt rose through the ranks to become a purchasing manager. He recalled that for a twenty-three-year-old recent undergraduate, Teradyne was a fun challenge.

> Even though I was now supervising employees with a lot more seniority and higher degrees than I had, I think I managed to earn their respect by working to understand the business, by staying flexible in my leadership style, and by using an honest and open style of communication.
>
> I was on the road a lot, and when I wasn't traveling, it was usual for me to work from six to six, zip out for something to eat, and then go back to work for another three or four hours. It was wild and rewarding, and since I was living alone in Nashua at the time, working like that just seemed natural.

In May of 1998, his desire to give everything that he had to Teradyne changed a bit when he married Margaret Geary, a law student and fellow UNH graduate that he had been dating for four years. By the summer of 1999, the couple had purchased a house in Medfield, Massachusetts, and Matt—still working long hours—was enjoying his reverse commute to and from New Hampshire.

During the summer of 2000, Teradyne announced that it was planning to buy a privately held firm in San Diego. One of Matt's former bosses had been chosen to run the operation, and when he approached Matt with an offer to join him, the young manager jumped at the chance:

Everything became a total whirlwind. I was soon traveling to San Diego almost every week to help oversee the due diligence. After the deal closed in mid-August, I began living out of a hotel room while Margy got our house sold and prepared to join me.

My wife had just graduated from law school and had taken the Bar exam in Massachusetts. Now she would have to wait until February to take the California Bar, which was known to be the hardest one in the country. This was a very tough time for her.

Although he had a strong background in purchasing and planning, Matt soon discovered that his new position included a good deal of frantic on-the-job training:

I had never managed hourly employees before or ever dealt directly with customers, but suddenly there I was, backing up my account managers when they were unable to solve the really tough problems. I'll never forget the first time I was handed the phone with an angry customer on the other end of the line. Oh man; that was truly a baptism by fire!

Matt had always been athletic, but ever since he had stopped playing football in his second year at UNH, he had failed to shed the extra pounds he'd gained to make the team. The challenge, he knew, was that he found personal exercise routines boring; in the absence of competitive sports, he wasn't getting the regular exercise he needed.

All that changed as he quickly warmed to the mild weather and fitness culture of their new home. Prompted by a friendly wager, Matt signed up for a half-marathon. To keep himself motivated as he trained for the event, Matt began to sign up for short and casual road races. These events energized his training with a competitive dynamic that had been missing from his previous attempts to establish a workout regime. Central to this new athletic passion of his was a local event calendar publication called *RacePlace*.

San Diego's *RacePlace*

RacePlace was a free publication that was distributed six times a year. The magazine was a must-have reference for athletic event enthusiasts in Southern California, since it offered—in addition to detailed event schedules—easily removed application forms to a range of competitive venues, including road races, walks, triathlons, biathlons, bicycle tours/races, open track meets and multisport activities. Matt explained that *RacePlace* soon became an important part of his training regime:

They didn't bother to fill up the pages with generic content about proper hydration, carb diet recipes and other stuff that most runners knew all about anyway. *RacePlace* was a no-nonsense resource—just schedules, applications, and ads for fitness-related products and services. I started checking my copy every week to see what races might be fun to enter in the coming weeks—I was so into it that I lost 20 pounds in two months.

RacePlace could be found throughout greater San Diego at over six-hundred locations, including sporting goods stores, public and private workplaces, specialty retailers, health and fitness clubs, restaurants, libraries, and at any event that was featured in the publication. Matt was considering an annual $15 subscription to *RacePlace* when his career with Teradyne suddenly hit a big bump in the road.

The Road Back East

In early 2001, less than six months after he had headed West, it became apparent that the timing of Teradyne's acquisition had coincided with the onset of what some would call a depression in the electronics industry. Massive reductions in demand at key accounts like Cisco, Lucent, and EMC hit the company hard. Almost overnight, it seemed, the extra capacity that had made the San Diego facility such an attractive acquisition had turned the division—and its 540 employees—into a liability. The painful layoff program began in March of 2001 and continued quarterly. Matt explained that as a key member of the San Diego management team, he found himself in a terrible spot:

I had to play a significant role in orchestrating the layoff process, and I agonized over those decisions. These were people who had contributed so much to Teradyne in such a short amount of time, and here we were letting them go. That long period of layoffs and supposed reorganizations took a huge emotional toll on me.

In October 2001, when the decision came down to close the facility, Matt was offered a position as materials manager back at Teradyne's facility in Nashua, New Hampshire. Margy, who had passed the California bar and was working as an attorney in downtown San Diego, was once again obliged to start over. After a rather somber Christmas season in San Diego, Matt and Margy packed up and moved back East.

If a silver lining could be gleaned from this depressing string of events, it was that Babson College was happy to have Matt pick up where he left off in their part-time MBA program. Not only that, but Matt had learned enough about the *RacePlace* business model to be able to seriously explore the idea of developing a similar publication in the Boston area.

Racer's Resource

As the economy continued its slide into early 2002, Matt's new management job at Teradyne became increasingly stressful and tedious. To escape those pressures. Matt found himself devoting more and more of his time to his graduate studies:

Babson was a welcome distraction from all the challenges at my job. That Spring I had decided to begin taking all my electives in entrepreneurship. I had often thought about owning my own business someday, so I figured, why not take a step towards that now by taking advantage of what Babson is best known for?

He added that whenever the subject of innovative new opportunities came up, he always seemed to come back to the same thing:

The whole running experience that I had in San Diego was great; I really missed it after I returned. The *RacePlace* concept was elegantly simple, and satisfied a real need in that market. I knew that there were plenty of road races in the Boston area. I wondered: would there be a similar demand for a free-distribution event calendar here?

Matt decided to find out. He began by attending road races and approaching participants with questions such as:

> *How did you find out about this race?*
>
> *Where do you look for information about events?*
>
> *Do you read any current running magazines?*
>
> *If so, which ones? If not, how come?*

He discovered that word of mouth was the primary conveyance for information about any of the approximately 1,900 race events held in the Boston area each year. Racing event calendars were available online, but few recreational runners appeared to know about them. With regard to the physical publications he'd asked about, racers indicated that although they rarely even glanced at newsy content, they did look over the general advertising for special deals on sneakers, sportswear, nutritional supplements and other products.

Matt also approached event organizers, the primary paying customers of a publication of this sort. They reported spending the bulk of their slim promotional budgets[1] on direct-mail campaigns that targeted past participants or runners who had participated in similar area events. These organizers (who often had little marketing experience and volunteer staffs ranging from small to none) said that while direct mail seemed to be their best option, the effort was time-consuming and frequently failed to attract many new participants. First-annual and one-time events had an even tougher time getting the word out.

When Matt concluded from his research that there were no publications operating a *RacePlace*-type model in the greater Boston market, he was intrigued:

> When demand for such a magazine seemed to be out there, I began to wonder exactly how one would go about producing one. I had accumulated a three-ring binder of various free publications that I had come across—real estate, homes, dating services and the like. The next step was to get in touch with those guys and find out what it was costing them to put those magazines out there.

Production

Since his job at Teradyne was keeping him very busy, it wasn't until the onset of a two-week vacation in July that Matt was finally able to begin his production cost research. As he thumbed through his hefty collection of "take-one" guides, he passed over a number of Boston area firms that were "slick and intimidating." He didn't make a single call until he came across an outfit based in Vermont. Matt recalled that it was a fortuitous connection:

> I figured correctly that people in Vermont would be friendly and helpful. Bob Smith was a guy with more than

thirty years of publishing experience in the free distribution market. That call led to a thirty-minute conversation a couple of days later, which then resulted in a two-hour tour of his office the following week. Bob had a lot of enthusiasm for the idea, and when he said that his staff of graphic designers and printing relationships could offer a turnkey layout and print solution, I swallowed hard and asked how much. I was pleasantly surprised.

Mr. Smith quoted a price of under $2,000 for 16 pages, well within a range that would enable Matt to take this idea a step further.

The Test Issue

When Matt expressed an interest in producing a test issue, Bob Smith put him in touch with a company who could handle the physical distribution of the magazine. Matt spent all of his free time in July assembling a list of over 300 event directors around greater Boston, as well as putting together a mailing to introduce his publication—now named *Racer's Resource*. He offered the directors two options for adding their free listing to the calendar section of the magazine—by sending in the enclosed form or by going online to the basic *Racer's Resource* site that Matt had set up.

After designing a simple MS Word brochure (see Exhibit 1), Matt invited a few friends over for pizza and beer to put the whole thing together. By early August the mailing had produced over fifty calendar listings. As he called each event director to see if they would be interested in placing a display ad or an application form in the publication, Matt quickly learned that direct sales could be a tough business:

> Selling the advertising was a very difficult and time-consuming process. I learned that nothing, no matter how innovative or revolutionary you think it is, is going to sell itself. You make the calls, pound the pavement to meet interested people in person, and then make more calls to try to get a firm commitment. I never would have known how hard it was unless I'd gone out and done it.

As a result of his hard work, Matt took in $1,750 on seven ads. He paid $1,144 for 20,000 copies of *Racer's Resource*, which he then had delivered to 300 locations at a cost of $750. In order to keep the first issue as straightforward as possible, Matt had made no attempt to solicit general advertising from local vendors such as specialty shops and event sponsors. He figured that those efforts would be best served once he could demonstrate that his publication was resonating with event organizers and the running public.

With bundles of his premier issue in hand, Matt hit the road-racing circuit. Eagerly handing them out, he pressed race participants for their honest opinions. The feedback from the athletes on the street was positive, and his paid-event advertisers seemed satisfied with the response they were getting. Matt was ready for more:

> I'd gotten a much better idea of how this business would work. Along the way, I also had established good

---

[1] CoolRunning.com indicated in 2002 that the average promotional budget for running events was $1,500.

EXHIBIT 1   MS Word Three-fold Brochure, Inside Section

ATTRACT MORE RUNNERS TO YOUR EVENT

- Reach more runners. 20,000 runners pick up *each issue* of our magazine.

- Reach new runners. They may be people who have not run in a while or someone interested in running for the first time. They may not be actively seeking a race, but they will pick up an issue of the Racer's Resource and participate in your event!

IT SAVES YOU TIME

- You don't need a fancy advertisement. Simply include a copy of your flyer in the magazine. Runners can just tear it out and send it in.

- Don't have a flyer yet? Let our professional graphic artists help layout your race flyer.

- Our distribution team gets the magazine to more than 300 locations & events in Massachusetts and New Hampshire, far more than you could reach distributing your flyer on your own. Let us do the work for you.

OUR RESULTS ARE GUARANTEED

- Don't take our word for it. If your full-page ad does not pay for itself then we will *pay you* the difference.

ADVERTISING RATES

BLACK & WHITE	1×	2×	6×
Full Page	$625	$575	$500
½ Page	$400	$350	$300
¼ Page	$275	$250	$200
FOUR COLOR	1×	2×	6×
Full Page	$1,100	$800	$700
½ Page	$700	$615	$525
¼ Page	$480	$440	$350

EVENT RATES

	BLACK & WHITE	FOUR COLOR
Cover	N/A	$1,100
Back Cover	N/A	$1,300
Full Page	$475	$650
½ Page	$275	On Request
¼ Page	$175	On Request

Other premium positions are available. Please call for details.

2002–2003 SCHEDULE

Issue	Available	Order Date
Aug/Sept	Aug 15	Aug 1
Oct/Nov	Oct 1	Sept 15
Dec/Jan	Dec 1	Nov 15
Feb/Mar	Feb 1	Jan 15
Apr/May	Apr 1	Mar 15
June/July	June 1	May 15

RATES YOU CAN AFFORD

The Racer's Resource is the most cost effective way to promote your event. Why not call us today?

Call 603-880-9096

THE RACER'S RESOURCE *R*R

P.O. Box 1364 · Nashua, NH 03061
Phone/Fax: 603-880-9096
info@racersresource.net

www.racersresource.net

"Reach More Runners"

---

relationships with customers and suppliers. That fall I signed up for the foundation Entrepreneurship class at Babson. The primary output for that class would be a business plan for a new venture, and I still had a lot of questions about *Racer's Resource* like, "Could the magazine grow to a sufficient size in the Boston market?" and "How could I make sure that this wouldn't end up as some meager-income lifestyle business?" To me, that would be as bad as failing outright; I was looking to create value on a large scale.

Articulating the Plan

Feedback and critical analysis from his fellow MBAs proved invaluable as Matt spent many hours researching and refining the business concept. What came into focus was a growth strategy that would begin with a successful launch of a Greater Boston edition, and then leverage that model to create a national network of *Racer's Resource* publications. Local sales and distribution in each metropolitan area would be overseen by a regional account manager earning 20 percent on sales, while graphics, printing, and—eventually—national advertising contracts would be handled out of the main office in New England.

In his Executive Summary (see Exhibit 2), Matt emphasized that the simplicity of this model—free, useful, and without the usual editorial content—would translate into competitively lower advertising rates and gross margins in the range of 70 percent. By keeping his overhead low and by reinvesting profits as he grew, Matt estimated that he would require funding of about $100,000 to open up eight regions in five years.

The Competition

Event organizers in New England had three primary choices when it came to promoting their races: direct mail, running/sports magazines, and Web sites. Matt determined that relative to these advertising alternatives, *Racer's Resource* would be

EXHIBIT 2 Executive Summary; Racer's Resource

The Running industry is a growing market. Nationwide participation in running has increased by 13% over the past five years. There are now more than 24 million runners in the United States. Frequent participation has increased by more than 30% over the same period. This has contributed to an 18% increase in the number of road races staged per year. This growth in participants and events presents an opportunity to build an organization based on new innovative methods to promote these events and reach these athletes.

The Racer's Resource is focused on this opportunity. Our goal is to provide effective new alternatives to the traditional methods organizations use to communicate advertising messages to runners. These organizations include the organizers of health and fitness events, the manufacturers of products targeted at runners and marketers interested in reaching runners. The primary product is a free distribution, advertiser supported publication. These regional publications contain listings of local health and fitness events, entry forms to events and general advertisements.

The Racer's Resource was launched in July 2002 to test the market's response to this concept. Since then the company has successfully published two trial issues. The initial customer feedback has been very positive and there is already strong interest in the 2003 publication schedule. This publication concept is innovative and effective for several reasons:

- Reach: The free distribution concept allows for greater reach than subscription magazines or direct mail. This reach exposes a larger percentage of the target market to an advertiser's message.

- Response: Compared to editorial content-based magazines, the advertiser-supported concept provides better response to the advertiser's message. The advertisements are the content and therefore the reader pays attention to the advertiser's message.

- Cost: The simplicity of the business model offers a fundamental cost advantage over competitors. This translates into advertising rates 85% lower than competitive publications on a cost per thousand basis while delivering 70% gross margins.

The current competition in this market is fragmented and made up primarily of small privately owned organizations. There is a mix of regional magazines, subscription and free distribution, as well as a loose collection of printers and other service organizations to support direct mailing. The competition has been unable to innovate and introduce new techniques to support this market.

The lack of editorial content significantly reduces overhead and provides a fundamental financial advantage. This allows the company to operate with 70% gross margins and deliver 25% profitability while offering prices significantly below the competition. The lack of editorial content also simplifies the business processes allowing the company to focus on delivering exceptional customer service.

The Racer's Resource currently produces a Boston area publication. The company is seeking financing of $100,000 to fund developing eight additional regional publications over the next five years.

positioned to deliver a greater reach at a lower total cost (see Exhibit 3). Matt offered a critique of the field:

> As I had learned early on, direct mail was not working for event organizers who were on tight budgets—and that was most of them. I was able to find some good race event information online, but because you have to have a computer and know the domain name, those sites are probably not going to be able to reach a broad base of participants. Magazines—especially national ones—are expensive to advertise in, and since they are so filled up with content, modest ads get lost in the shuffle and don't work well. So, with the exception of some niche Web sites, my bi-monthly would be the only free publication in this market specifically designed to give event coordinators a cost-effective way to connect with the running and fitness community.

The number-one question from Babson students and potential investors seemed to be, "If this business is so easy to set up and cheap to run, how will you stay ahead of new entrants?" Matt's reply:

> Racer's Resource will move quickly to establish a branded advantage in New England. I am already pursuing exclusive or primacy of position arrangements at key locations that distribute the magazine—including point-of-sale displays. I am also working on strategic partnerships with companies that have a national reach.

One such company was CoolRunning.com, an Internet business with a steadily growing national readership base.[2] When Matt determined that this Massachusetts-based business was one of the few players with the visibility and clout to mount an immediate and effective response to *Racer's Resource*, he gave them a call.

Racer's Resource was now in talks with the firm to develop a dual-media advertising package that would give Cool Running event clients a presence on the street as well as online. Matt saw this alliance as an excellent way to pave the way for opening new markets for his company, while simultaneously heading off any interest that Cool Running may have had about developing a magazine of their own.

_____

[2] Nationwide, Coolrunning.com was attracting between 100,000 to 200,000 runners per month to its site. Event listings were free, and a link to an event's own Web site was $99. The site offered a range of value-added services to organizers, including entry form blanks, Web site creation, online race registration, and event management consulting.

EXHIBIT 3 Competitive Positioning

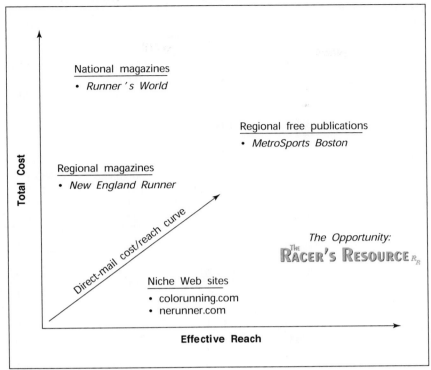

Economics and Projections

By keeping costs down by using event, product, and service advertisers as the sole source of content for his publication, Matt projected that at maturity, a regional magazine like *Racer's Resource* could deliver an annual per market net contribution of just over $100,000 (see Exhibit 4). In each new market, Matt estimated that the ramp-up period to reach this mature phase would be about 10 issues. Sustaining a regional business would require selling around 280 event ads per year.

Matt noted that favorable margins would support an aggressive pricing strategy:

Racer's Resource would enter each market as a low-cost provider and would therefore be able to attract advertisers quickly while the publication built up and proved its local readership base. With each new area we open, that task will get easier since we'll be able to refer to existing regions as proof of concept. Over time I suspect

EXHIBIT 4 Publishing Economics, Mature Magazine Model

			Per Issue	Per Year	
REVENUE:	60 pages	$500/page	$30,000	$180,000	
COST OF SALES:					
Graphics	60 pages	$45/page	2,700	16,200	
Printing	60,000 copies	$.054/copy	3,223	19,338	
Distribution	600 stops	$2.00/stop	1,200	7,200	
Cost of Sales:			7,123	42,738	24%
Gross Profit:			22,877	137,262	76%
Sales Expense	20% Commission		6,000	36,000	
Net Contribution:			$16,877	$101,262	56%

EXHIBIT 5   Pro Forma Statement of Income, Years 1–5

	2003	2004	2005	2006	2007
REVENUE:					
Events	$26,400	$154,400	$400,000	$688,000	$976,000
Advertising	6,600	38,600	100,000	172,000	244,000
Subscriptions	400	1,900	4,600	8,200	11,800
Total Sales	33,400	194,900	504,600	868,200	1,231,800
COST OF SALES:					
Printing	6,556	29,315	64,856	103,532	142,208
Graphics	5,040	23,580	53,280	85,680	118,080
Postage-Subscriptions	60	480	1,380	2,460	3,540
Distribution	3,000	12,263	25,725	40,125	54,525
Cost of Sales	14,656	65,638	145,241	231,797	318,353
Gross Profit	18,744	129,263	359,359	636,403	913,447
EXPENSES:					
Sales and Marketing Expenses	6,000	50,280	127,600	207,400	287,200
General and Admin. Expenses	46,000	96,400	203,500	207,500	207,500
Amortization	—	—	—	—	—
Depreciation	—	1,093	1,193	1,193	1,193
Total Operating Expenses	52,000	147,773	332,293	416,093	495,893
NET INCOME (LOSS) BEFORE TAXES:	(33,256)	(18,511)	27,066	220,310	417,554
Income Tax	(9,977)	(5,553)	8,120	66,093	125,266
Net Income (Loss)	(23,279)	(12,958)	18,946	154,217	292,288
Beginning Cash Balance	—	76,721	24,157	9,462	130,098
ENDING CASH BALANCE	$76,721	$24,157	$9,462	$130,098	$388,804

that we would move to raise our insertion rates to be more comparable with other similar resources in the area.

In the first year of operations Matt expected to produce four issues with combined sales of $33,000. He projected his breakeven would come in year 3 on sales of $504,000, and that he'd reach positive cash flow in the fourth year (see Exhibits 5 and 6). By 2007, the business was expected to have established eight regional publications with a combined net income of just under $300,000.

Funding the Leap

Matt calculated that if he took advantage of Teradyne's exit offer—8 weeks' salary plus 8 weeks of paid vacation time he'd accumulated—his severance would come to approximately $24,000. He also planned to apply for competitively disbursed seed funds available through Babson. If *Racer's Resource* made the cut, Matt could expect to receive between $3,500 and $7,500.

Once incorporated, Matt planned to issue 20,000 shares of stock. By selling 3,500 of those shares to outside investors at $30 each, Matt would retain 55 percent ownership and have a remaining 10 percent equity available to attract key employees and board members. He planned to begin issuing dividends in his first profitable year—paid annually and equal to at least 25 percent of after-tax profits.

Decision Time

A thin blanket of snow was covering his car by the time Matt headed into the house to make a decision with his wife, Margy, that would, for better or for worse, change their lives forever; again.

EXHIBIT 6   Pro Forma Cash Flows, Years 1–5

	2003	2004	2005	2006	2007
OPERATING ACTIVITIES:					
Net Income	$(23,279)	$(12,958)	$18,946	$154,217	$292,288
Depreciation and Amortization	—	1,093	1,193	1,193	1,193
Gross Cash Flow	(23,279)	(11,864)	20,139	155,410	293,481
CHANGES IN WORKING CAPITAL:					
Accounts Receivable	—	(47,400)	(60,000)	(60,000)	(60,000)
Accounts Payable	—	8,738	14,366	14,426	14,426
Accrued Expenses	—	4,212	10,800	10,800	10,800
Net Cash Flow from Operating Activities	(23,279)	(46,314)	(14,695)	120,636	258,707
INVESTING ACTIVITIES:					
Capital Expenditures	—	(6,250)	—	—	—
Net Cash Flow from Investing Activities	—	(6,250)	—	—	—
Financing Activities:					
Changes in Capital Stock	100,000	—	—	—	—
Changes in Bank Borrowings	—	—	—	—	—
Net Cash Flow Provided by (Used In) Financing Activities	100,000	—	—	—	—
Increase (Decrease) in Cash	76,721	(52,564)	(14,695)	120,636	258,707
Beginning Cash Balance	—	76,721	24,157	9,462	130,098
Ending Cash Balance	$76,721	$24,157	$9,462	$130,098	$388,804

Case 2   IDEO Product Development

"I should have had café latte," thought Dennis Boyle as he was sipping his strong espresso at Peet's coffeehouse, just around the corner from his office. Many designers and engineers from his company, IDEO, one of the world's largest and arguably most successful product development firms, often gathered here and talked. It was late summer 1998 in Palo Alto, the heart of California's Silicon Valley, and Boyle gathered his thoughts for a meeting with David Kelley, the head and founder of IDEO.

Boyle had just led his group at IDEO through the development of 3Com's Palm V hand-held computer, which designers and managers at both firms already considered a successful product with very large commercial potential. Now he was being asked to design the competing Visor product by the very same individuals he had worked with previously. The only twist was that these clients themselves now worked at Handspring, a new venture whose goal was to come out with a fully compatible, slightly smaller and less expensive palm-size computer that could easily add functionality. 3Com had even licensed out operating software to Handspring.

Although working on the Palm V challenged IDEO's engineering skills, working with Handspring promised to challenge the very manner in which it operated. It operated on the principle of getting all team members to "fail often to succeed sooner"—a creative process that often looked to outsiders like "spinning wheels." The process usually generated a fountain of absurd-appearing but innovative ideas before the final answer and product miraculously came through a process of discipline and fast decision-making.

The IDEO philosophy melded Californian iconoclasm with a genuine respect for new ideas and invention. For over two decades, the firm contributed to the design of thousands of new products ranging from the computer mouse to the stand-up toothpaste dispenser. (See Exhibit 1 to learn about the important milestones in the firm's development.) IDEO came to national prominence when ABC's Nightline illustrated its innovation process by showing its designers re-engineer a decades-old icon, the supermarket shopping cart, in just five days.

Now Boyle had to decide whether he should suggest to Handspring's management to add more time to a development schedule that was less than half of what it took to design the stunningly beautiful and innovative Palm V. Boyle's group feared that an overly aggressive development schedule would require them to bypass many of the early development stages that the firm was particularly good at and, at the end, deliver a product that could be so much better if they just had more time.

History of IDEO

[David Kelley] and the company he heads, IDEO of Palo Alto, has designed more of the things at our fingertips than practically anyone else in the past 100 years, with the possible exception of Thomas Edison.

—San Francisco Examiner[1]

It was desperation caused by recalcitrant furniture during a college move that drove David Kelley to enter the Carnegie-Mellon campus workshop in search of a saw. The sights and sounds of the strange new world captured the fancy of the electrical engineering major from Ohio. For a while, in fact, he considered switching majors to fine arts but stayed with engineering. The internal switch that flickered on, however, would lead Kelley to leave engineering jobs at Boeing and NCR to embark on the journey that, according to *Fortune* Magazine, would make him "one of the most powerful people in Silicon Valley." But the first thing Kelley would ever actually design of consequence was a telephone that could only ring one number: his own. He presented this to his college girlfriend.

In 1975, Kelley joined the Stanford University program in product design. These were heady days with Kelley finding that "In Silicon Valley everything was new. . . there were no preconceived notions."[2] Through part-time consulting experience, Kelley found to his surprise that most consulting firms consisted of specialists, with technological companies lacking clear access to a general product development firm. In 1978, amid the Silicon Valley boom, Kelley gave up writing his Ph.D. thesis. (Nonetheless, even without a formal Ph.D. he would become a professor at Stanford University.)

Professor Stefan Thomke and Ashok Nimgade, M.D. prepared this case as the basis for class discussion rather than to illustrate either effective or ineffective handling of an administrative situation.

[1] R. Garner, *San Francisco Examiner*, May 23, 1994, p. B-1.
[2] L. Watson, "Palo Alto Product Designer Finds Business Booming," *The San Francisco Chronicle*, August 3, 1992, p. C3.

EXHIBIT 1 Important Milestones

ca. 500 B.C.		Documentation of Egyptian papyrus prototypes for paper, which millennia later remains medium of choice for personal data storage.
1978		David Kelley receives master's degree from Stanford's product design program. Eventually starts up his own company, David Kelley Design.
Mid-1980s		With the advent of Apple Computer's Newton, handheld computing gets its start and meets its near-demise.
1991		IDEO started through a merger between David Kelley Design, ID Two, and Matrix.
1996		Annual IDEO revenues reach $40–50 million.
	March	Engineer-visionary Jeff Hawkins' handheld "Palm Pilot," meant to replace papyrus derivatives rather than computers, finds immediate consumer acceptance.
	Fall	IDEO starts work on the Palm V project, which bears the code name "Razor."
1997	March	Phase I ("Understand") starts on the Palm V project; by May Phase II ("Evaluation and refinement") starts; by fall, Phase III ("Implementation") starts.
1998	Summer	Handspring project starts at IDEO when Jeff Hawkins asks Dennis Boyle for a proposal for proposed handheld computing device with revolutionary "Springboard" slot.
	Fall	Phase IV ends; "Razor" will be released to production. Gearing up for market release starts.
1999	February	First Palm V shipments expected.
	October	Shipment of Handspring Visor planned by Hawkins and Dubinsky, in time for Christmas shopping season.

EXHIBIT 2 Leading Design Firms and Corporations with Industrial Design Excellence Awards

Design Firms	1995–1998 Awards
IDEO	32
ZIBA Design	20
Fitch	18
Frogdesign	12
Altitude	11
Pentagram	10
Design Continuum	10
Lunar Design	9
Herbst Lazar Bell	7
Hauser	6
Ralph Applebaum Associates	6

Corporations	1995–1998 Awards
Apple	9
Black & Decker	13
Compaq	9
Samsung Electronics	7
Hewlett Packard	5
NCR	9
IBM	5
Microsoft	7
Philips Electronics	6
Thomson Consumer Electronics	7

Source: Business Week's 1999 Design Awards, Industrial Designers Society of America

Kelley went on to form and run David Kelley Design for the next decade. IDEO started in 1991 when David Kelley Design merged with two companies: ID Two, led by renowned designer Bill Moggridge, and Matrix, started by Mike Nuttall. The name IDEO came to life when Bill Moggridge scanned his dictionary for suitable names and liked "ideo-" (a Greek word which meant "idea") as it formed the foundation of many important combined words such as *ideo*logy and *ideo*gram. Kelley, whose company was larger than the other two combined, took over as chief executive of the new firm.

The merger brought under one umbrella all services client companies needed to design, develop, and manufacture new products: mechanical and electrical engineering, industrial design, ergonomics, information technology, prototype machining, and even cognitive psychology. IDEO thus pioneered the design version of "concurrent engineering"—a fusion of art and engineering to produce aesthetically pleasing products that were also technically competent.[3] As an example of the utility of concurrent engineering, consider how the decision to add air vents to a computer to prevent overheating might detract from the product's streamlined aesthetics if the designers and engineers failed to work together closely.

The hardest places to practice concurrent engineering, quite understandably, were in devices involving compact and complex design such as automotive components, medical instruments, and small computing devices where small changes

---

[3] J. Lew, "Of mice and Miatas: Design shops shape our lives," *San Francisco Examiner*, August 12, 1992, p. 4.

would have often unforeseeable ripple effects on components far removed. IDEO, with its equal emphasis on design and engineering, took up many of these challenges. In contrast, its leading competitors historically had stressed industrial design over engineering.

Major IDEO clients included Apple Computer, AT&T, Samsung, Philips, Amtrak, Steelcase, Baxter International, and NEC Corp. IDEO's thirst for variety led it to complete thousands of projects, including 50 projects for Apple Computer (including its first mouse), ski goggles, the Avocet Vertech Skiers watch, and a large variety of medical instrumentation. The company also participated in Hollywood film projects, creating scale-model submarines for "The Abyss" and a 25-foot mechanical whale for "Free Willy". In the 1990s, IDEO won more industry awards than any other design firm worldwide (see Exhibit 2).

In the late 1990s, IDEO employed over 300 staff and maintained design centers in Boston, Chicago, San Francisco, London, Palo Alto, Grand Rapids, New York, Milan, Tel Aviv, and Tokyo. The sites were chosen for their stimulating locations. Although all centers operated independently, seeking business locally, they exchanged a high volume of e-mail and often shared talent as needed. Over the years, while his employees focused on designing client products, Kelley increasingly found himself designing and re-designing IDEO. "I'm more interested in the methodology of design . . . ," according to Kelley. "I'm the person who builds the stage rather than performs on it."

Part of this stage-building involved studying the IDEO environment in new ways. Instead of merely relying on employee surveys, the company also studied workplace interactions through suspended video cameras in order to optimize office design.[4] IDEO also sought to improve its own design processes by reviewing all completed projects. According to Kelley, "We pick the things each client does well, and assimilate them into our methodology. We're not good at innovating because of our flawless intellects, but because we've done thousands of products, and we've been mindful."[5]

With corporate downsizing of the 1990s, IDEO and other design firms flourished as companies outsourced more design projects. IDEO's fees generally ran from as little as $40,000 to over $1 million, depending on the scope of the project. The privately held company remained tightlipped about revenues, but in 1996 was known to have revenues of $40-$50 million. Revenues came from about 30% each in medical, consumer, and telecommunications/computers with an additional 10% from industrial products.[6]

IDEO came to national prominence when it allowed ABC to televise a segment showing its designers meeting the challenge of re-engineering the commonplace shopping cart—a virtually unchanged icon for the past several decades, despite its creaky and obdurate wheels and often unwieldy basket—in just five days. The IDEO design replaced the traditional large basket with a system of baskets that allowed consumers to use the shopping cart as a "base camp" for shopping. Innovative new wheels allowed greater maneuverability in the store. Hooks on the frame would allow for bagged items to be transported out to the parking lot. The lack of a central basket removed much of the incentive for stealing the shopping carts.

Design Philosophy and Culture

If a picture is worth a thousand words, a prototype is worth ten thousand.

—IDEO innovation principle

Central to IDEO's design philosophy was the role of prototyping. According to Tom Kelley, general manager and David Kelley's brother, "we prototype more than our clients suspect, and probably more than our competitors." Frequent prototyping served as the most important way for his company to communicate with clients, marketers, experts, and end users. Prototypes ensured everyone was imagining the same design during discussions about a product. All IDEO offices had shops staffed by highly skilled machinists to rapidly produce both simple and sophisticated prototypes. Quite often, according to Whitney Mortimer, a Harvard MBA who joined the firm in the late '90s, "the real 'aha's' in product development occur here."

But in the early stages, perfecting a sophisticated model was considered a waste of time. "You learn just as much from a model that's wrong as you do from one that's right," according to engineer Steve Vassallo. Thus, designers and engineers themselves created early prototypes from readily available material such as cardboard, foamcore, Legos, and Erector sets.

Rapid prototyping at IDEO followed the three "Rs": "Rough, Rapid, and Right!" The final R, "Right," referred to building several models focused on getting specific aspects of a product right. For example, to design a telephone receiver, an IDEO team carved dozens of pieces of foam and cradled them between their heads and shoulders to find the best shape for a handset. "You're not trying to build a complete model of the product you're creating," per Vassallo. "You're just focusing on a small section of it."[7]

Quick and dirty prototyping allowed for a greater number of iterations. "By our method," David Kelley claimed, "you could never design a VCR you couldn't program. [Researchers at larger companies] are afraid of looking bad to management, so they do an expensive, sleek prototype, but then they become committed to it before they really know any of the answers. You have to have the guts to create a straw man." At IDEO, these

---

[4] P. Roberts, P, "Live! From your office! It's. . . ," *Fast Company*, October 1999.

[5] T.S. Perry, "Designing a Culture for Creativity," *Research Technology Management*, March 1995, v. 38(2), pp. 14–17.

[6] R. Rosenberg, *The Boston Globe*, "By design, these firms take on other companies' products," May 11, 1997, p. C1.

[7] T.S. Perry, "Designing a Culture for Creativity," *Research Technology Management*, March 1995, v. 38(2) pp. 14–17.

straw men were repeatedly knocked down, a process which left IDEO's staffers with thick skin. "Failure," Kelley felt, "is part of the culture. We call it enlightened trial and error."[8]

In an allied process, IDEO sought to generate as many ideas as possible early in the design process through almost daily brainstorming sessions. A much-used paraphrased quotation from Einstein epitomized the playfulness of the early stage: "If at first an idea does not sound absurd, then there is no hope for it." The entire process resembled a funnel, with several ideas at the top, three or four at the base, and only one making it all the way through. People were generally not upset if their idea did not become the definitive solution since the act of clipping off ideas brought the entire team closer to the solution—similar to legendary baseball batter Babe Ruth who outlined his strategy once as, "Every strike I make gets me closer to a home run." In addition, discarded ideas were archived and sometimes kept for possible future products.

Sometimes in the course of a project, when progress appeared to come to a standstill, the leader could call for what has come to be known as a Deep Dive® approach. In this process, the team would focus intensively for an entire day to generate a large number of creative concepts, weed out weak ideas, and start prototyping based on the top handful of solutions.

To an outsider, however, the entire process could appear messy. "The nature of the organization is very much like David Kelley's mind," says Arnold Wasserman who was part of IDEO's innovation strategy group. "Both are seriously playful and messy. And both are comfortable with confusion, incomplete information, paradox, irony, and fun for its own sake."[9]

The inherent inability to precisely predict the innovation process' outcome, time and cost made it extremely important to keep clients involved. At the beginning of a new project, IDEO would submit cost and time estimates to potential clients. As a project unfolded and designers came up with innovative ideas and concepts, project managers had to ensure that those concepts were within agreed upon budgets and timelines. However, designers often aimed for perfection which could potentially lead to cost and time overruns—also known as "creeping elegance" in design circles—and clients needed to be aware of those opportunities for further innovation and the cost and time involved. As a result, IDEO required very frequent client meetings where all those issues would be discussed.

After a visit to the company's Palo Alto office, business writer Tom Peters likened IDEO to a veritable playground. In his words, "IDEO is a zoo. Experts of all flavours co-mingle in offices that look more like cacophonous kindergarten classrooms. . . . Walk into the offices of IDEO design in Palo Alto, California, immediately you'll be caught up in the energy, buzz, creative disarray and sheer lunacy of it all. Breach the reception area at XYZ Corp . . . and you'll think you've walked into the city morgue."[10]

In keeping with its playroom atmosphere, on Mondays all company branches held "show-and-tells" where designers and engineers could showcase their latest insights and products. Also, of increasing importance to designers was IDEO's "Tech Box," the company's giant "shoebox" for curiosities and interesting gadgets meant to inspire innovators. Designers could rummage through the contents and play with the switches, buttons, and odd materials in search of new uses. The Tech Box included some 300 objects ranging from an archery bow based on pulleys to heat pipes that would turn uncomfortably hot almost the moment they were placed in a cup of hot water.

The culture itself reflected the importance that management attached to creating a democracy of ideas. Most design firms had less than two dozen employees. Growing IDEO to 300 employees involved keeping each unit small. Thus, growth was achieved by budding out smaller design studios whenever one appeared to grow too large. Much quoted was David Kelley's confident assertion in 1990 that "This company will never be larger than 40 people."[11] Following an amoeboid growth strategy, even in a small section of Palo Alto, found the company in possession of nine different buildings in the late '90s.

Employees were encouraged to design their own workspace to reflect their own personalities. Some strung up their bicycles on pulleys. Rolling doors could quickly seal offices for privacy. Staffers kept personal possessions in portable bookshelves and cabinets so that moves between projects could be accomplished rapidly. One studio suspended the wing of a DC-3 airplane with a blinking red winglight from the ceiling.

In keeping with Silicon Valley informality, the company discouraged formal titles and did not mandate a dress code. Management encouraged employees to leave their desk and walk around, especially during mental blocks. "It's suspicious when employees are at their desk all day," according to general manager Tom Kelley, "because it makes you wonder how they pretend to work." IDEO paid high rent for its prime Silicon Valley location so as to encourage stimulating interactions between employees. Free, unlocked loaner bicycles at the Palo Alto lobbies also facilitated movement between each building. Designers were encouraged to talk to one another or even call a brainstorming session through email.

Management rarely fired employees. "We do a better job of managing good employees than of weeding out lower performing employees," David Kelley admitted. "But with small studios, there's literally nowhere to hide for noncontributors." High-performing employees were rewarded by being given more challenging projects to lead. Each employee was assessed through peer review sessions, with peers chosen by the employee. Management also sought to reward high performers through more shares in its client venture capital base.

Through much of the 1990s, turnover, at less than 5% per year, was shockingly low by Silicon Valley standards. The company typically recruited young individuals out of its own internship programs. Recruiting was a long process, entailing meeting

8 Ibid.
9 R. Garner, *San Francisco Examiner*, May 23, 1994, p. B-1.
10 T. Peters, "The Peters Principles," *Forbes ASAP*, September 13, 1993, p. 180.
11 B. Katz, "A leadership style," *Perspective*, Fall 1999.

with 10 staff members, often over lunch. A disproportionate number of recruits came from Stanford University, where Kelley continued to serve as a professor.

An individual could work on one large project as a principal or on as many as three to four projects as a contributor. IDEO was a flat organization to an extreme. All work was organized into project teams, which formed and disbanded for the life of a project. As a result there were no permanent job assignments or job titles. There were no organization charts or titles to distract from the quality of the work. Project leaders often emerged on the basis of personal excitement about a project. Motivation from peer pressure also spurred employees to put in 50- to 60-hour weeks in creative endeavors.[12]

The lack of hierarchy also avoided the problem of promoting designers and engineers into administrative positions and out of their first love: creating products. But the "no-policy policy" could make for confusion among new recruits. Even proponents of the IDEO culture, including veteran Larry Shubert, admitted that "The culture is partly to be comfortable with ambiguity and confusion. . . . We err on the side of autonomy. There's some discomfort, yes."[13]

But growth appeared to bring its own changes. According to Jeff Smith, president of the Palo Alto-based Lunar Design and an admirer of IDEO, "How well they're able to remain creative and not become bureaucratic and politicized will be very interesting. There's rumor of politics and agendas. . . ." Even David Kelley admitted some increase in bureaucratization. "People are talking about it like it's a company. 'Is it o.k. to invite my wife to this?' Nobody ever asked me that before. . . Or, 'Is it o.k. if I go home and mow the lawn this afternoon?' Of course, it's o.k."[14]

By the late 1990s, however, the turnover had crept up to 10% as the promise of unparalleled high-tech wealth at Internet-based firms beckoned employees. To counter the trend of increasing attrition, IDEO sought to redo its compensation strategy, planning to do more equity deals and seek royalties.

IDEO's Innovation Process

It is inconceivable that the head guy in any organization will know all the answers.

—David Kelley, IDEO founder

If prototyping was central to IDEO's design process, brainstorming was central to its methodology. The two processes, actually, went hand in hand, with brainstorming sessions leading to rapid prototyping or vice versa. The goal was to quickly create a whirlwind of activity and ideas, with the most promising

ideas developed into prototypes in just days. The firm followed several principles of brainstorming: stay focused on the topic; encourage wild ideas; defer judgment to avoid interrupting the flow of ideas; build on the ideas of others (since it was usually more productive than seeking glory for one's own insights); hold only one conversation at a time to ensure that introverts also got their say; go for quantity (very productive brainstorming could generate 150 ideas in 30 to 45 minutes); and be visual, since sketching ideas would help people understand them.

Throughout a single project, the project leader might hold brainstorming sessions, or "brainstormers." No more than eight invitees attended these sessions, which ran under the above rules. IDEO personnel viewed invitations to these sessions as a sign of worth and rarely turned them down. In an organization whose lobbies sported large bowls of M&M chocolates, David Kelley once said "brainstormers are the candy. . . . You are in the middle of a project, handling endless details, and then you get invited to a brainstormer, where you get to have all sorts of good ideas and leave with no responsibility for them. It's cathartic, to dump your ideas."[15]

IDEO's product development process followed several phases (see Exhibit 3 for details). In **Phase 0 ("Understand/ Observe")**, the team sought to understand the client's business and immersed itself in finding out about the feasibility of a product. This involved inhaling everything ever written about the planned product and potential users. By the end of this process, team members tacked to the project center walls pictures and diagrams summarizing major discoveries about the marketplace and users. In the closely related **Phase I ("Visualize/Realize")**, the team ended up choosing a product direction based on ideas, technologies, and market perceptions. The team also gained an understanding of the product context through a gallery of envisioned characters using the product in their daily lives. By the end of Phase I, through close coordination with the client, the team would have rough three-dimensional models of a product and a general idea of the manufacturing strategy to be utilized.

In **Phase II ("Evaluating/Refining")**, the team enhanced design prototypes through testing functional prototypes. Emphasis shifted over the course of this stage from human factors and ergonomics to engineering. Phase II culminated with a functional model as well as a "looks like" design model. Then in **Phase III ("Implement/Detailed Engineering")**, the team completed product design and verified that the final product worked and could be manufactured. Although engineering efforts predominated, continuous low-level involvement with design team members occurred. By the end of this phase, the team delivered a fully functional design model, tooling databases, and technical documentation. Finally, in **Phase IV ("Implement/Manufacturing Liaison")**, the team ensured smooth product release to manufacturing as the product moved from the shop floor to the client's factory lines.

---

[12] T.S. Perry, "Designing a Culture for Creativity," *Reseach Technology Management*, March 1995, v. 38(2) pp. 14–17.
[13] S. Orenstein, "The doyen of design," Stanford: May/June 1996, pp. 74–79.
[14] Ibid.

[15] T.S. Perry, "Designing a Culture for Creativity," *Research Technology Management*, March 1995, v. 38(2) pp. 14–17.

EXHIBIT 3   IDEO's Product Development Process Phases

PHASE 0: Understand/Observe

This phase helps the team determine feasibility of designing a product. It involves understanding everything about a new client and its business. Thus, to design a new home entertainment remote control, for instance, the team might study the history of remote controls and the companies involved in designing them. It would research everything from the cost structure of remote controls to the associated panic incidence of "where is the remote control?" syndrome. The team would buy every different kind of remote controls on the market to take apart in a fashion more gentle and controlled than exhibited by frustrated owners.

In addition to meeting with representatives from marketing and manufacturing, the team might also observe people at home on their couches attempting to use remotes. On the topic of consumer observations, IDEO head David Kelley once noted: "That's where most of the good ideas for a new project come."[16] Although this phase was typically the least expensive part of an entire project, product developers at most companies spent little time here for fear of duplicating efforts of marketing or R&D. By the end of Phase 0, the team created a feasibility record along with major discoveries about the marketplace and users.

PHASE I: Visualize/Realize

In the "Visualize/Realize" phase, the product development team visualized potential solutions through tangible prototypes to the point where a product direction was chosen. Although it involved similar activities as Phase 0 (in fact, Phases 0 and I were often combined), it was more product-focused. This intensive stage required close coordination of efforts with the client to ensure constant feedback. By the end of Phase I, the team aimed for having rough three-dimensional models of a product, an understanding of the context in which the product would be used, and an outline of a manufacturing strategy.

The team combined ideas, technologies, and market perceptions with observations of real world users to investigate potential needs that the product could fill. To do this, IDEO eschewed the traditional reliance on statistical data collected by the marketing team in favor of storyboard depictions of lives of several potential users. Use of these fictional characters concretized the product development process. For instance, while designing a better remote system, the IDEO team might conjure up characters like "Jughead the constantly eating couch potato" or "Archie the swinging bachelor" or "Moose the klutz," or "Veronica the princess." Observations of Jughead or Veronica might lead to thoughts about how to avoid spillage of food or nail polish into the buttons; observations of Moose might lead to ideas about developing drop-proof remotes; observations of either Archie or Veronica on a weekend night might lead to design of a remote with large "glow-in-the-dark" buttons that could be hastily be programmed with just one hand in a darkened room.

PHASE II: Evaluating/Refining

The purpose of this stage was to develop functional prototypes and resolve technical problems as well as problems users faced. The emphasis shifted over the course of this stage from human factors and ergonomics to engineering. Concurrent engineering often occurred, through filling in previously unspecified features using an iterative process. This process, of course, required constant communications between various subgroups to ensure that the final outcomes would mesh well together.

By the end of Phase II, a functional model as well as a "looks like" design model was delivered. The industrial design solutions eventually became documented using CAD tools. With finalization of technical specifications, detailed engineering could occur.

PHASE III: Implement (detailed engineering)

During this phase, the team completed product design and verified that the product worked. It validated the manufacturability and performance of the final product. Although engineering efforts predominated, continuous low-level involvement with design team members occurred. For designers, frequent visits to the machine shops during this phase provided a reality check. By the end of this phase, the team delivered a fully functional design model, tooling databases, and technical documentation. Testing might also be undertaken in this phase to meet government regulations. The team also started selecting vendors.

PHASE IV: Implement (manufacturing liaison)

In this phase, the team resolved issues involving the final design to ensure smooth product release to manufacturing as the product moved from the shop floor to the client's factory lines. The team still supervised production of tooling, regulatory approvals, and construction of pilot runs of the manufacturing line. Testing of manufacturing feasibility was crucial: each day's loss of a production line's output might cost the client company a substantial amount in lost revenues. By the end of this phase, the product would be formally handed over to the client.

Source: IDEO

---

16 Garner, R., *San Francisco Examiner*, May 23, 1994, p. B-1.

But despite the phases delineated above, IDEO had mixed feelings about formalizing any aspect of the innovative process. According to European director Tim Brown, "It's a delicate balance between process and innovation. . . . It's no good if you crank the handle and you know exactly what is going to come out the other end. You also have to be prepared to fail a lot. The great thing about a prototype culture like ours is that we have lots of spectacular failures. We celebrate that."[17]

Nonetheless, armed with the tools of rapid prototyping, brainstorming, and a well-honed product development process, the company viewed itself as being able to provide value to virtually any client. The very diversity and experience of its personnel ensured that it would rarely encounter entirely new problems. Occasionally, however, the company found itself swimming out of familiar water. Once, for instance, the governor of Hawaii asked IDEO about how the state should proceed with its economic reforms.

The Palm V Project

Never go to a client meeting without a prototype.

—"Boyle's Law" (per Dennis Boyle of IDEO; not to be confused with the law of pressure & volume named after 17th century physicist Robert Boyle)

In the mid 1980s, with the advent of Apple Computer's Newton pad, handheld computing got its start and met its near-demise. This revolutionary feature-laden product proved ahead of its time, with consumers frustrated by the sometimes slow and inaccurate handwriting recognition system that was meant to replace the tyranny of the cumbersome keyboard. Users also found the system large and inconvenient. It took until March 1996 before anyone could successfully introduce another general-purpose handheld computing device. This honor belonged to California-based engineer-visionary Jeff Hawkins, whose "Palm Pilot" found almost immediate consumer acceptance. Key to Hawkins' success was the development of critical technologies, including the so-called Graffiti program for handwriting recognition and "syncing," the capability to synchronize data between a handheld computer and a home computer.

Hawkins possessed a maniacal focus on product simplicity. This led him to hone his vision by carrying a crude wood prototype the size of a deck of cards in his pocket while envisioning how typical customers might use the product through the course of a day. Sometimes he would sit through staff meetings scrawling imaginary notes onto the inert wood screen of the prototype. The end result proved a product meant to compete with paper rather than with larger computers. Although it could just store addresses, telephone numbers, a calendar, and a to-do list, it did so rapidly and conveniently.

For all its apparent simplicity, the Palm Pilot became the fastest-selling computer product ever.[18] Hawkins and his staff achieved their feat of design and engineering while working during a period of corporate upheaval that saw their parent company change from Palm Company to U.S. Robotics to 3Com. Understandably, the Palm Pilot success story attracted other start-ups and entrants to the new field, leading to handheld devices touting features such as vibrating alarms, voice recording, increased memory, and so on. One advertisement for the competing Everex Freestyle palm-sized computer, after listing several new features, warned: "Palm Pilot beware!"[19] Microsoft itself was expected to enter the field with a new product that would leapfrog current products by offering eight megabytes of memory.

At the Palm division, while many engineers pondered new ways to retain market share, Hawkins recalled thinking, "Who cares. I don't need eight megabytes; I can't even fill up two. Let's show the world that this isn't about speeds and feeds. . . . It's about simplicity."[20] To avoid being caught up in the battle over new features and minutiae, the Palm division under Hawkins' leadership sought an entirely new approach, one that would also hopefully draw in more female users into a market of predominantly male businessmen.

Palm eventually turned to IDEO to fulfill Hawkins' vision. Within IDEO, the choice of project leader fell naturally to Dennis Boyle, a senior project leader and studio manager who had left his mark on the company with a stream of successful products and the institution of the Tech Box, a natural outgrowth of his tendencies since childhood (to the chagrin of this mother) to collect curios of all sorts in shoeboxes. For Boyle, the fit was natural: the very moment he first saw the Palm Pilot he knew "this will make a big difference" and proceeded to use it, add it to his collection, and discuss it at staff meetings. Palm was to remain Boyle's main client for the duration of the project, with a majority of his billable time dedicated there.

For Hawkins' and Boyle's teams, inspiration came from the sleek Motorola StarTac mobile phone that was introduced in 1996 at the price of $1,000—at a time when many mobile phone makers started giving away their products in return for user subscription fees. Hawkins recalled that, "The StarTac was a radical departure. It looked different, beautiful. It also commanded outrageous prices. We wanted to do the same thing."[21] Other products that inspired the IDEO team, and which Boyle kept in his briefcase, included a metal Canon minicamera, Pentax opera glasses, and a telescoping pair of eyeglasses in a thin metal case used as emergency back-up eyewear.

Each of these small and elegant products made the existing line of Palm Pilots appear stodgy in comparison. This was not surprising given that the computer world had generally ignored design in favor of technical bells and whistles that catered to

---

[17] D. Dearlove, "Innovation from the chaos," *The Times* (U.K.), August 13, 1998.

[18] P.E. Teague, "Special Achievement Award: Jeff Hawkins," *Design News*, March 6, 2000, p. 108.
[19] D. Roth, "Putting fluff over function," *Fortune*, March 15, 1999.
[20] Ibid.
[21] Ibid.

men. Men, after all, comprised the majority of computational gadget users at the time. This mindset was successfully challenged by Apple Computer, which true to its "Think Different" advertisement campaigns, came up with its translucent turquoise iMac computers. Apple President Steve Jobs declared, "for most consumers, color is more important than megahertz."

With similar thoughts in mind, Boyle's team outlined plans for a slimmer, sleeker version of the existing Palm Pilot. This called for reducing the thickness from the current 19mm to 11mm and the weight by one-third. According to Janice Robert, the 3Com vice president in charge of the Palm division at the time of the Palm V release: "We want to appeal to people not just on the rational level but the emotional level."[22]

The team started work on what would become the Palm V project late in 1996.[23] At the outset of the "Understand Phase" (**Phase 0**), which lasted 10–12 weeks, the IDEO team realized that despite the popularity of the Palm III, little data existed on user preferences. Boyle therefore started creating his own observational database by purchasing dozens of the Palm Pilots and giving them to colleagues, business friends, spouses, physicians, and representatives from other walks of life.

The rapidly developing obsession of Boyle's team with Palms spread throughout the company: over 200 IDEO staff members throughout the company eventually started using Palms. Feedback through e-mail or through casual hallway conversations quickly started reaching Boyle's team. The team thus became aware of problems concerning the product's susceptibility to breaking after being dropped, rigidity of the case, placement of the battery and memory doors, and location of the stylus holder.

In March 1997, **Phase I** (visualize and realize) started. At the outset, only three to four IDEO designers and engineers were involved. At the project's height of activity, as many as a dozen staffers would become involved. The diverse team included nationalities ranging from as far afield as Taiwan, the Netherlands, and Israel. Boyle deliberately tapped the talent of two female design engineers including senior designer, Amy Han, in hopes of achieving insights that would attract more female users into a marketplace where 95% of the existing Palm users were men.

Han and her colleague Trae Niest, in turn, obtained feedback from 15 other female colleagues. As a group, they challenged the conventional wisdom that handheld devices, in general, had to be square with block edges and colored a mundane gray. Even the advertisements promoted a corporate monolithic blandness, with, for instance, depictions of businessmen slipping Palms into gray suit pockets. The findings and insights of Han and her group led the industrial designers to make the new product more curvy, with tapering edges. The new project bore the code name "Razor," which indicated the goal of Hawkins' team at Palm to create a "razor thin" product.

The IDEO team met weekly with the Palm division to ensure a constant stream of feedback. Boyle made sure the team never went to a client meeting without a prototype of some type or another. The prototypes varied from being as simple as a keypad button to mockups of subtly different-sized LCD panels to styluses of varying thicknesses, lengths, and contours. This process helped ensure that even the smallest of details would be considered. As a result, for instance, the team designed both sides of the device to accommodate a wide variety of potential add-on covers and styluses. Even left-handed individuals would find the dual rail system accommodating.

To ensure a very thin product, the design teams realized early in the process that traditional batteries would have to give way to thinner rechargeable lithium ion batteries. However, it was not clear, considering recharging times and use patterns, that lithium ion would work in this design. The Palm team under Frank Canova, director of hardware engineering, and IDEO spent much of the first half of 1997 corralling reluctant battery makers to cooperate in this venture. Another sticky issue confronting the entire team concerned the use of anodized aluminum for creating the thin casing—a choice of material based on the limitations of plastics—given that US manufacturers had little experience working with this material. As a result, the Palm V team faced the dual challenge of communicating with Asian manufacturers while simultaneously using anodized aluminum to create the technically difficult thin complex surfaces.[24]

By May 1997, conceptualization and realization of the Palm V project gave way to **Phase II** (evaluation and refinement). This stage involved computer-aided design (CAD) engineering to help create accurate industrial models resembling the proposed end product. In this phase, designers and engineers incorporated observed usage patterns to allow users to recharge the Palm for only brief periods of time without shortening battery lives. The team moved toward a final model, choosing solutions, vendors, and sources. Every part of the mechanical model was machined out as close as possible to the final mass-produced parts. By the end of Phase II, some 20–25 prototypes had been created.

In the fall of 1997, **Phase III**, implementation (detailed engineering), started. Every component was engineered to be functional in terms of the electronics and software. Some three to five production prototypes were created. A number of each of these prototypes were built for drop testing to develop the sturdiest possible electronics. Testing was also undertaken to meet government regulations. By the end of Phase III, prototype models could exceed $30,000 each. The team kept refining those models until just one or two final contestants remained. At the same time, the Palm team grew by leaps and bounds, particularly in the realm of production as well as product promotion. Through regular meetings of increasing sizes, and through a flurry of e-mail exchanges, responsibilities gradually shifted away from IDEO.

---

[22] Ibid.

[23] Many viewed the parallels in nomenclature between the Palm III, V, and VII and the BMW 3, 5, and 7 series as 3Com's tribute to BMW's internationally heralded automotive product line.

[24] D. Roth, "Putting fluff over function," *Fortune*, March 15, 1999.

One of the most bothersome problems confronting the team involved binding the complex 11 mm-wide unit together without a single screw (screws being considered aesthetically and mechanically undesirable by the IDEO designers). The team ultimately committed to using a binding device never before used for handheld computers: industrial glue. At a most inopportune time, however, 3Com's modem card gluers—the only available personnel with experience in using industrial glue—left the company. The remaining team ended up experimenting through trial and error with several different adhesives and bonding parameters before arriving at a satisfactory solution.

By end of **Phase IV**, implementation (manufacturing liaison) and expected late fall 1998, "Razor" would be released to production. The Palm division planned to retain some IDEO personnel for another six months—the amount of time projected for gearing up for market release in February 1999. During this period, pilot production would work on smoothing processes at the production line to ultimately allow for manufacturing up to 5,000 units a day. This was crucial: each day's loss of a production line's output would cost the company a few hundred thousand dollars. Many problems still remained for the Palm manufacturers to address including cracks in the display, electrostatic charge, docking problems, cover imperfections, supplies procurement, and component switching. An aggressive schedule would compound problems that would otherwise be considered routine for products of this complexity. Hundreds of personnel were expected to become involved at the manufacturing sites in Utah, Japan, and Singapore as well as at dozens of vendor sites in Hong Kong, Taiwan, California, Texas, and Singapore.

The Handspring Project

In July 1998, both Hawkins and his business partner Donna Dubinsky, a Harvard MBA who had run the business side of Palm, resigned from 3Com on amicable terms to set up shop in Palo Alto. Part of the reason for the move was the desire for greater autonomy. Despite the success of the Palm line, 3Com as a whole was not doing well enough to reward personnel with stock. The goal of the new company was to come out with a fully compatible, slightly smaller, and less expensive clone of the palm-size computers. A technical motivation behind the new company was to address the Palm's inability to easily add functionality.

Hawkins had already scaled back to part-time work at Palm Computing to turn his attention to a long-time interest of his: writing a book on how the brain works. The temptation to interrupt the academic project to take another pass at building the perfect palm-size device was irresistible for someone universally hailed as the "father of a new industry." In quick order, Hawkins and Dubinsky were joined by the original Palm team of a dozen engineers. People enjoyed working with Hawkins, who, in Boyle's words was "by and large an even-keeled, predictable, normal person despite being a brilliant innovator."

Just a few weeks after starting up, Dubinsky and Hawkins, now chief product officer at Handspring, signed a licensing agreement with 3Com for the right to use the Palm operating system. This agreement would provide any product they developed compatibility with the myriad applications already available for Palm devices. Once again, Hawkins would turn to IDEO for designing a new product.

In July 1998, Hawkins asked Boyle for a proposal. Hawkins felt that the proposed device should be able to easily link-up through so-called "ROM cards" for games, pagers, cell phones, Global Positioning System receivers, voice recorders (the product would have a tiny built-in microphone), wireless modems, MP3 music players, graphing calculators, digital cameras, and even cardiac monitors. A solution for how to do this came to Hawkins when he spotted his child's Nintendo Game Boy, which allowed for changing games simply by inserting interchangeable game cartridges. This led to the so-called "Springboard" slot on the back of the product, which would allow the user to plug in a variety of matchbook-size modules. Hawkins' ten-year-old daughter actually proposed the product name "Visor"—short for "advisor."

The IDEO-Handspring team wanted the modules to be simple to use, with the device operating the moment a module was inserted. Some two dozen third-party developers expressed interest in developing add-on devices for the proposed Visor. Even without a concrete plan, funding flowed easily from venture capitalists eager to duplicate Palm's success with a device that could set a new trend in handheld computing. Publicity, too, would come easily, even in a field replete with new handheld devices. For the meantime, however, the media was kept guessing.

Apart from product features such as price, memory and colors, the Visor team saw little need for market research. According to Dubinsky, "We felt we understood the marketplace pretty well. After all, we invented the product and the category. . . You can't test the concept of a slot; it's too major."[25] The new project, however, was launched at a time when skeptics noted that people used hand-held devices primarily for mundane tasks such as storing addresses and personal calendars, rather than for complex tasks such as accessing e-mail. "People don't want a combination device," according to Ken Dulaney, mobile computing market research specialist at the Gartner Group. "Every time you try to get a computer to do many things, it ends up doing none of them well."[26]

Hawkins and Dubinsky insisted that the Visor's cost be kept to $150—a price far below the $300 commanded by the original Palm Pilot in 1996 and the $450 commanded by the Palm V at its market launch. This price was intended to attract a wider following and consistent with Handspring's strategy of getting a product with the new standard into many hands as quickly as possible. As a result, Hawkins and Dubinsky pushed for a product launch deadline of late 1999, just in time for the holiday gift-giving season and several months less than their already ambitious prior deadline of spring 2000.

[25] K. Hafner, "One More Ultimate Gadget," *The New York Times*, September 16, 1999, Late Edition, p. G1.

[26] Ibid.

This would entail a product development cycle of about 10 months before handing off the product to production in March–April 1999.

Boyle was not worried about meeting this challenging deadline because IDEO could meet difficult deadlines, even if at the eleventh hour and fifty-ninth minute. Furthermore, the team under Boyle had already encountered and worked smoothly with most of the Handspring team through dozens of prior meetings and other encounters during the Palm V project. IDEO and Handspring shared in common a belief in quick prototyping and a consumer-centered mentality. In Hawkins' words, after all, "I'm not down on engineering, but I'm really down on technology for technology's sake. . . . I don't say 'Put the biggest, meanest CPU in here.' I say, 'Make this work well for the consumer.'"[27]

The Handspring project would also require Boyle's team to keep the rest of IDEO, not to mention the rest of Silicon Valley, in the dark about the project. This would make for uncomfortable moments, especially during informal hallway conversations with colleagues, some of whom were still working on the Palm V project.

What concerned Boyle much more, however, was having to sacrifice the IDEO emphasis on innovation and design in order to meet the client's goal. Because of the time and price pressures, Hawkins' proposal would imply running with only "tried-and-true" technology; IDEO would not be able to indulge in the early phases of its legendary development process that differentiated it from other product development firms. Visor would have to sacrifice style and settle on an inexpensive plastic housing, and on AAA batteries instead of the rechargeable lithium-ion battery found in the Palm V.

If they have twice the time, Boyle was confident that his team could help create a killer product that would match the Palm V in design excellence and capability. Should he and Kelley try to persuade Handspring to postpone the Visor launch which would allow the team to follow all the steps of IDEO's legendary innovation process? Or should they just accept the client's request for a very aggressive schedule that would not allow his team to fully engage in early experimentation? He wrestled with these thoughts as he finished his espresso and walked back to the studio to meet David Kelley.

---

[27] R. Merritt, "Palm Pilot designer steers fresh course in handhelds." *Electronic Engineering Times*, October 25, 1999.

Case 3 Eat2Eat.com

Eat2Eat.com

Eat2Eat.com was the most highly rated Internet-based restaurant reservation service covering major cities in the Asia Pacific region. It was the principal business of Singapore-based Eat2Eat Pte Ltd (Eat2Eat). Eat2Eat.com had firmly established its technology, business model and industry relationships. However, after five years of operation, the website's registered user base remained at approximately 12,000 customers. In January 2006, founder and Chief Executive Officer Vikram Aggarwal was considering new ways to promote the company and the website. Eat2Eat had limited resources, so Aggarwal knew his methods would have to be innovative, efficient and effective.

Company Origin

In the late 1990s, Aggarwal had been an investment banker specializing in the high-technology sector at Chase Manhattan in Tokyo. He had seen many entrepreneurs launch their own companies and was confident he could do the same. When Chase Manhattan merged with JP Morgan in 2000, Aggarwal's group was dissolved. He accepted an exit package, voluntarily left the bank and decided to launch his own Internet company.

Aggarwal saw an opportunity in online restaurant bookings. He noticed that airline bookings, hotel reservations and car rentals were highly automated processes, with customers frequently searching for information and transacting business online. However, there was little or no similar automation for restaurant reservations. The technology discrepancy was particularly noticeable in the case of hotel restaurants: a consumer could reserve a room at a hotel online, but not a table

at the hotel's restaurant.[1] Many corporations—particularly large ones—negotiated special room rates for employees at preferred hotels, but did not negotiate discounts at preferred restaurants. Given that business dinners were a common occurrence, Aggarwal wondered why corporations had not extended their purchasing power to restaurants in the same way they exercised it with hotels.

Aggarwal believed there was a value proposition in connecting diners—both corporate and personal—with restaurants. He believed diners could benefit from accessing a wealth of information on restaurant options, conveniently reserving tables online and receiving loyalty points or discounts. Moreover, he believed restaurants could benefit by having a presence on the Internet, an increasingly popular medium.

Establishment and Business Model

In 2000, Aggarwal relocated to Singapore, registered Eat2Eat Pte Ltd and began running the company out of his home. He hired a chief technology officer and a programmer, both based in India, to develop the website and the supporting technology. Aggarwal himself signed up the first participating restaurants. The English version of the website was launched in July 2001. Aggarwal wanted to retain full ownership and control, and subsequently financed the company himself. He invested US$1 million from his personal savings and his exit package from Chase Manhattan. Aggarwal eventually hired two other people to help with the workload, one in Singapore and one in Sydney.

Eat2Eat.com was an Internet-based restaurant portal promoting fine dining in the Asia Pacific region. The website was a guide to the region's best restaurants with an online reservation service. Features included restaurant reviews, recipes, interviews with leading chefs and lists of top establishments in various categories. By January 2006, Eat2Eat.com covered more than 800 restaurants in Bangkok, Hong Kong, Kuala Lumpur, Shanghai, Singapore, Seoul, Sydney, Taipei and Tokyo. The company was also launching in Kyoto, Melbourne and Phuket. The original website appeared in English, but equivalent sites had also been launched in Japanese and Korean to cover the restaurants in Tokyo and Seoul, respectively.

Nigel Goodwin prepared this case under the supervision of Professor Kenneth G. Hardy solely to provide material for class discussion. The authors do not intend to illustrate either effective or ineffective handling of a managerial situation. The authors may have disguised certain names and other identifying information to protect confidentiality.

[1] While the example of hotel restaurants gave birth to the concept in Aggarwal's mind, he believed there were also innumerable restaurants not affiliated with hotels that could also benefit from online reservations.

EXHIBIT 1   Eat2Eat.com Participating Restaurants by City, 2000–2005

	Participating Restaurants (Cumulative)					
	2000	**2001**	**2002**	**2003**	**2004**	**2005**
Bangkok	—	—	12	32	58	98
Hong Kong	—	18	42	84	97	112
Kuala Lumpur	—	6	30	54	66	72
Shanghai	—	—	6	48	60	62
Singapore	—	24	84	102	120	174
Seoul	—	—	—	4	18	72
Sydney	—	30	66	94	98	137
Taipei	—	—	—	—	—	23
Tokyo	—	—	6	14	44	73
Total		78	246	432	561	823

Note: Actual figures have been disguised for the purpose of confidentiality.
Note: Figures do not include Kyoto, Melbourne or Phuket. Eat2Eat was in the process of launching in those cities.
Source: Company files.

Core Business: Restaurant Reservations and Advertisements

Eat2Eat.com allowed diners to reserve tables through the Internet, conveniently and with a wealth of supporting information. Aggarwal met with restaurant managers in cities across the Asia Pacific region and encouraged them to participate. (See Exhibit 1 for participating restaurants by city.) He negotiated discounts for corporate customers and commissions for Eat2Eat, and then listed the restaurants on the website. A registered customer wishing to make a meal reservation visited the website and used a simple booking interface to select a restaurant, date, time and party size.[2] See Exhibit 2 for registered customers by city. The restaurants could be searched by various criteria, including location, ambiance, accessibility for disabled diners, smoking preference, cuisine, price range, quality rating and hotel affiliation (if applicable). Customers received loyalty points that could be redeemed during future restaurant visits.

Eat2Eat contacted the restaurant the day after the reservation date, confirmed that the customer had actually eaten there and invoiced the restaurant for the agreed-upon commission.[3] Commissions varied depending on the restaurant in question, but typically were between seven to 10 per cent of the customer's bill. In 2005, these reservations contributed 40 per cent of Eat2Eat's total revenue of US$478,000. (See Exhibit 3 for annual revenue, profit and loss figures.)

The company also sold website banner advertisements to restaurants wanting additional promotion. In 2005, advertisements on Eat2Eat.com contributed an additional 20 per cent of the company's total revenue.

Eat2Eat.com had received considerable recognition. A poll taken by the Smart Diners Organization in the United States had rated Eat2Eat.com as the top restaurant information and reservation site in the world. In addition, Google and Yahoo! search engines consistently ranked Eat2Eat.com first in search results for Asian restaurant reviews and reservations.

There were other restaurant portals on the Internet, covering Asia Pacific and other regions, but Eat2Eat.com was different. Most of the other portals derived revenue from advertising alone, and subsequently depended on hits and click-through statistics. Also, the other Asia Pacific portals were city-specific, whereas Eat2Eat.com offered regional coverage.

In 2004 Aggarwal adapted Eat2Eat.com to make its content and booking function accessible through WAP-enabled mobile phones.[4] He believed this added accessibility would significantly extend the company's reach and utilization, considering the high penetration of mobile phones in the region. The service became popular in Tokyo and Seoul, but lagged elsewhere. Aggarwal was disappointed the service had not found greater acceptance in cities such as Hong Kong and Singapore. In the latter cities, virtually every person carried a multifunction mobile phone and people were very savvy about applications such as customized ring tones, photographs and games. Aggarwal suspected people in these cities were uncomfortable in actually making transactions using the new technology.

Complementary Business: Third-party Sourcing

Aggarwal also engaged in another, complementary business: negotiating preferred arrangements between credit card companies and restaurants for the benefits of credit card holders.

---

[2] First-time users of the service were required to register as customers and provide some personal details. Registration was free.
[3] Coordination with the restaurants could be automated and conducted online. For restaurants that were not connected to the Internet, the process was conducted using facsimile (fax) machines. Thus, restaurants did not require Internet access to participate, although Internet access made the process more efficient for both the restaurants and for Eat2Eat.com.

[4] WAP, or wireless application protocol, was an open international standard for applications on wireless communication devices. A common example was Internet access on mobile phones.

EXHIBIT 2 Eat2Eat.com New Customer Registrations by City, 2000–2005

	Registered Users (Annual)						
	2000	**2001**	**2002**	**2003**	**2004**	**2005**	**Total**
Bangkok	—	—	30	18	48	100	196
Hong Kong	—	300	324	94	576	804	2,098
Kuala Lumpur	—	60	126	30	324	509	1,049
Shanghai	—	30	65	14	54	70	233
Singapore	—	126	204	42	391	778	1,541
Seoul	—	—	—	84	204	402	690
Sydney	—	48	222	90	120	204	684
Taipei	—	—	—	—	—	300	300
Tokyo	—	152	466	694	1,176	2,580	5,068
Total	—	716	1,437	1,066	2,893	5,747	11,859

Note: Actual figures have been disguised for the purpose of confidentiality.
Note: Figures do not include Kyoto, Melbourne or Phuket. Eat2Eat was in the process of launching in those cities.
Source: Company files.

EXHIBIT 3 Eat2Eat Revenue, Profit and Loss by City, 2000–2005

		Revenue, Profit and Loss (Annual, in US$000's)						
		2000	**2001**	**2002**	**2003**	**2004**	**2005**	**Total**
Bangkok	Revenue	—	—	—	4	6	8	18
	Cost	—	—	18	30	17	30	95
	Profit/(Loss)	—	—	(18)	(26)	(11)	(22)	(77)
Hong Kong	Revenue	—	8	24	6	54	66	158
	Cost	6	28	41	30	24	32	161
	Profit/(Loss)	(6)	(19)	(17)	(24)	30	34	(2)
Kuala Lumpur	Revenue	—	18	31	8	34	56	148
	Cost	4	18	30	30	36	37	155
	Profit/(Loss)	(4)	—	1	(22)	(2)	19	(7)
Shanghai	Revenue	—	—	20	2	24	22	68
	Cost	—	41	66	18	34	44	203
	Profit/(Loss)	—	(41)	(46)	(16)	(10)	(23)	(134)
Singapore	Revenue	—	12	36	18	70	91	227
	Cost	162	180	156	114	144	144	900
	Profit/(Loss)	(162)	(168)	(120)	(96)	(74)	(53)	(673)
Seoul	Revenue	—	—	—	—	12	42	54
	Cost	—	—	—	18	66	36	120
	Profit/(Loss)	—	—	—	(18)	(54)	6	(66)
Sydney	Revenue	—	18	60	48	48	46	220
	Cost	12	96	96	42	36	48	330
	Profit/(Loss)	(12)	(78)	(36)	6	12	(2)	(110)
Taipei	Revenue	—	—	—	—	—	18	18
	Cost	—	—	—	—	—	48	48
	Profit/(Loss)	—	—	—	—	—	(30)	(30)
Tokyo	Revenue	—	—	30	54	90	128	302
	Cost	6	30	70	90	98	114	408
	Profit/(Loss)	(6)	(30)	(40)	(36)	(8)	14	(106)
Total	Revenue	—	56	202	140	337	478	1,213
	Cost	190	392	476	372	455	534	2,419
	Profit/(Loss)	(190)	(336)	(275)	(232)	(118)	(56)	(1,206)

Note: Actual figures have been disguised for the purpose of confidentiality.
Source: Company files.

Credit card companies typically offered special deals and perks for cardholders, including discounts at preferred restaurants, spas, sporting venues and retail stores. The card companies' motivations were to attract and retain cardholders by offering superior value, and to encourage cardholders to use the cards, thereby bolstering loyalty and increasing transaction volume.

The credit card companies did not negotiate the arrangements themselves; instead, their marketing teams outsourced the job to third parties. Because Aggarwal already negotiated with restaurants to sign them up for the website, he found it was a natural extension to source restaurants for credit card companies as well. In 2005, third-party negotiations contributed the remaining 40 per cent of Eat2Eat's revenue.

Segmentation and Approach to Market

Reaching the Restaurants

Aggarwal dealt exclusively with what he described as first-tier restaurants. First-tier restaurants were typically those that accepted reservations, were moderately expensive, or were very popular and busy. Second-tier restaurants did not accept reservations and therefore were of no concern to Aggarwal.

Aggarwal approached the restaurants himself to sign them up as suppliers. This task typically involved traveling to the 12 cities covered by Eat2Eat.com and personally meeting with restaurant managers. In some cities, the restaurants were predominantly chain organizations, while in other cities they were predominantly independently owned. A single chain might have many restaurants, so at first glance a chain-focused approach seemed more efficient. However, it usually took much more time and effort to sign up a chain than a single independent restaurant.

The restaurant reviews posted on Eat2Eat.com were written by Aggarwal and his two employees. He had considered adding reviews by professional restaurant critics, but had decided against it since critics and their publications typically demanded payment for reprinting their reviews. Also, many restaurant reviews in Asia were actually written as promotional pieces on the restaurants' behalf, and Aggarwal felt such reviews were neither independent nor objective. He did consider adding user reviews, as Asia-Hotels.com did for hotels, but had not yet taken any action in that direction.

Market characteristics

As he traveled, Aggarwal gathered information on the different markets. He was particularly interested in population density, dining habits, the presence of first-tier restaurants, broadband Internet penetration and receptivity to new marketing and distribution tactics. The information helped him select new restaurants to pursue as suppliers. See Exhibit 4 for some of Aggarwal's market observations.

Promotional Strategies

In the beginning, Aggarwal focused his promotional efforts on corporate customers. People who planned business dinners invariably made reservations; by contrast, timing and restaurant choice for personal dining were often spontaneous. Also,

Aggarwal thought personal diners were too numerous and, consequently, too difficult and expensive to reach. He thought the corporate approach would bring more value for his efforts and would be the best way to reach customers.

Aggarwal approached large corporations and asked them to encourage their employees to sign up for the service. Because corporations reimbursed their employees for business lunches and dinners, the discounts available for meals reserved through Eat2Eat.com essentially offered the corporations a cost reduction. The service was easy for clients to find, preview and reserve at good restaurants, and users received loyalty points that could be redeemed for free meals in the future.

Aggarwal was pleased with the adoption rates from the targeted corporations. Roughly 80 per cent of the companies he approached endorsed the program. At those companies, typically 15 per cent of employees would register as Eat2Eat.com users with 10 per cent becoming active users. Most of the active users were secretaries and personal assistants to executives because they were the people typically tasked with arranging business functions. They spent most of the workday at their desks with broadband Internet connections, so it was easy for them to access Eat2Eat.com. Also, Eat2Eat.com simplified the task of finding and reserving at an appropriate restaurant.

This approach worked well in most of the cities in question, but Aggarwal found a different strategy worked better in Tokyo. In his opinion, Japanese corporations were reluctant to try new ideas. Also, many first-tier restaurants in Japan had their own websites. Those websites provided information to customers, but did not support online reservations because the required technology was too complex. Eat2Eat.com enabled the reservations for the restaurants' websites, so when a customer viewed a restaurant website and wanted to reserve a table, that customer was redirected to Eat2Eat.com's own booking engine. This model proved to be popular among Tokyo's personal diners.

The adaptation of Eat2Eat.com for mobile phones also bolstered the website's success in Tokyo. As with Korean customers in Seoul, Japanese customers in Tokyo were comfortable finding information and transacting business through that medium.

By the end of 2005, Eat2Eat.com had almost 12,000 registered users. Approximately 43 per cent of those users lived in Tokyo, and most of them were personal customers making reservations for their own dining. The remaining 57 per cent of registered users lived in other markets, and most of them were secretaries or personal assistants reserving tables for corporate dining.

Expanding in the Personal Market

Although Aggarwal had built a solid user base through the corporate market, he knew he would have to tap the personal market (beyond Tokyo) if Eat2Eat were to reach its potential. However, the company did not have the employees or financial resources needed to pursue such a vast market. Aggarwal

EXHIBIT 4 **Market Observations**

City	Description	City	Description
TOKYO	• Fragmented restaurant industry with broad range of dining options • Opportunities primarily in the mature hotel industry, particularly with established chains that E2E has worked with elsewhere • Low Internet penetration • Language issues • Difficult to gain customer acceptance		• Tendency for restaurants to cluster in common areas • Willingness to try any restaurant at least once • Government initiatives to support Internet business • High Internet penetration but reluctance to transact business online • Restaurateurs' resistance to new promotion/distribution channels
HONG KONG	• High Internet penetration but low transaction volume • High population density with easy movement around the island • Many corporate head offices • Many restaurants, but choice normally based on proximity to office • Free local phone calls made it easy to reserve by phone • Language issues	SEOUL	• High WAP acceptance • Busy city with many dining options, so restaurant managers valued the promotional assistance • Many international visitors willing to book tables • Language issues
KUALA LUMPUR	• Broad restaurant base and large dining population • Tendency to choose restaurants by the type of food • High restaurant turnover, which encourage marketing innovations • Customers willing to try new technology • Growing market of visitors from the Middle East • Spontaneity in dining leading to no-shows and multiple bookings • Low Internet penetration	SYDNEY	• Dining well-established as a pastime • Many new restaurants • Many visitors from overseas • Higher margins for Eat2Eat.com • Reluctance to provide personal information over the Internet
		TAIPEI	• Busy city with established dining scene • High Internet penetration • Web-based reservations new and considered trendy • Relatively low number of first-tier restaurants
SHANGHAI	• Rapidly growing local market • Strong business from overseas, with visitors to Shanghai willing to book tables in advance • Unscrupulous restaurant managers posing difficulties for E2E • Busy restaurant not requiring any promotional support • Language issues • Low Internet penetration	TOKYO	• High Internet penetration • Widespread WAP use, and marketing on mobile phones widely practiced and accepted • Huge city with established dining culture and countless restaurants • Widespread acceptance among local population • Major foreign presence in the city as well • Difficulty in growing fast enough and keeping up with the ever-changing environment
SINGAPORE	• Vibrant dining scene, with hotel restaurants and many new eateries opening outside hotels as well		

Note: Information unavailable for Kyoto, Melbourne and Phuket.
Source: Company files.

believed Eat2Eat would have to partner with other companies that already had large, established user bases and "piggyback" with them.

There were many possible options, including airlines, hotel chains, and local and regional newspapers. "There is no end of possible partners we could work with," he commented, "if we only had the time to approach them, convince them and develop the partnerships."

In May and June of 2004, Eat2Eat partnered with leading regional newspaper, *The Asian Wall Street Journal*, for the first Eat! promotion. The promotion tied in with a regular feature of the paper's Friday section in which food critics sought and reviewed the most authentic and exciting eateries in Asia's culinary capitals. This promotion was one of the paper's most popular features, with readers regularly contacting the paper to request more information or suggest additional eateries.

The three-week promotion featured 70 participating restaurants in Hong Kong, Kuala Lumpur and Singapore, with cuisine ranging from Mediterranean to Asian to fusion. The restaurants offered special set menus for lunch and dinner, featuring more variety and value than their regular offerings. Some restaurants also offered complementary glasses of wine or champagne. Diners could view restaurant details and menus and could make reservations online at www.eat2eat.com/awsj. The promotion was held for a second time in September 2005, when, in addition to the original cities, it was expanded to include Seoul and Taipei for a total of 101 participating restaurants.

The Eat! promotion had little immediate impact on Eat2Eat.com reservations and revenue, but it did give the website a great deal of publicity that would likely attract more users and reservations in the longer term. Also, it allowed Aggarwal to expand his restaurant base in current cities and establish his business in new cities, such as Taipei.

Aggarwal thought credit card companies would be another natural avenue for reaching personal customers. He had already negotiated restaurant deals on the companies' behalf so he had the necessary contacts and credibility. He thought it would be logical to extend the arrangements to cover online bookings.

When credit card companies sent monthly statements to cardholders they often included brochures of benefits for cardholders, including discounts at restaurants, spas, hotels and entertainment venues. The credit card companies also maintained websites with the same information, but they were basic information websites and were rarely visited by cardholders. Aggarwal wanted to enhance the websites by tying them to Eat2Eat.com and providing booking functionality.

Credit card companies would benefit from such arrangements by driving more cardholders to their websites. Such interaction would build customer loyalty and also increase transactions on the credit cards, which would be the reason for offering such deals in the first place. Restaurants would likewise benefit by attracting more customers. Finally, Eat2Eat would benefit by leveraging the credit card companies' large user bases. A partnership with a single credit card company might expose Eat2Eat.com to millions of new customers.

The idea made sense to Aggarwal, but he admitted it was hard to convince the credit card companies to buy into it. It required a shift in their thinking, which he was finding difficult to achieve. The marketing teams at credit card companies turned over quickly. Just when Aggarwal made headway with them, the representatives changed and he had to start over with new people. Aggarwal had been trying to negotiate such arrangements for five years and still had not closed any deals, although he felt he was close with at least one company.

Raising Additional Capital

Eat2Eat had established a strong presence with Aggarwal's initial investment, but additional funding would be required to reach the next level. Aggarwal and his two employees spent practically all their time managing the company's day-to-day operations and had little time for additional strategic developments or promotional activities. Aggarwal thought this lack of strategic focus inhibited Eat2Eat's growth and put the company at a competitive disadvantages. As he commented:

> I feel like I'm in a Formula One race with a private entry car. I compete with professional teams with major funding, and I'm always one or two laps behind, just trying to keep up.

Aggarwal hoped to raise US$2 million in additional capital. Roughly 50 per cent of those funds would be allocated to establishing three or four new sales representatives throughout the region. The sales representatives would add more restaurants to the company's inventory. Each representative would be paid US$5,000 to US$6,000 per month and would incur related costs, including computers and travel expenses. It was difficult to estimate the return for investing in new sales representatives, but Aggarwal hoped the additional revenue would outweigh the additional costs by a factor of two to one.

Roughly 40 per cent of the new capital would be spent on public relations and marketing activities to reach the personal dining market segment. Aggarwal planned to hire a well-known public relations firm with regional influence and expertise in the hospitality sector. A public relations campaign would begin in a single market, as a test of its effectiveness, before being rolled out to the rest of the region.

The remaining 10 per cent of the new capital would be spent on a technology upgrade. The Eat2Eat.com website and the supporting software were currently hosted by a third party; Aggarwal wanted to set up his own server and support the website in-house. He also wanted to enhance the company's mobile phone functionality to enable more reservations. While the technology upgrade would not have a direct impact on Eat2Eat.com's revenue, it would support the company as a whole and improve operational efficiency.

Potential Sources for Additional Capital

Aggarwal considered debt financing but quickly dismissed the idea. He believed it would be difficult to obtain bank loans because Eat2Eat had not yet established a profitable track record. In fact, he believed it would be difficult for practically any early-stage Internet company to obtain bank loans for this reason. "If I were a banker," he mused, "I wouldn't loan money to this company."

Aggarwal thought he might find another Internet company willing to purchase a stake in Eat2Eat. He pointed to the recent example of Yahoo! purchasing a major stake in Alibaba.com, the Chinese online business-to-business marketplace.[5] The deal had received a great deal of publicity, and Aggarwal hoped it would galvanize the Asian Internet investment scene and inspire more deals in the sector. However, no other Internet companies had yet expressed an interest in buying into Eat2Eat.

Venture capital was a more likely option, although not necessarily a more favorable one. Aggarwal had been approached by several venture capital firms in recent months, but he had low expectations. He believed venture capitalists and entrepreneurs had inherently opposing objectives. The former wanted to buy into companies cheaply while the latter wanted to maximize investment value, so the two parties would naturally dispute the true value of a company's equity. Furthermore, a venture capitalist typically wantd to crystallize a profit from an investment within five years and wanted a return on investment in the 30 per cent range. The venture capitalist would also impose a set of conditions (covenants) regarding the company's management

---

[5] Alibaba.com operated the world's largest online marketplace for international and domestic China trade, as well as China's most widely used online payment system, AliPay. It has a community of more than 15 million businesses and consumers in more than 200 countries and territories. In 2004, Alibaba.com facilitated more than US$4 billion in trade. In August 2005, Yahoo! Inc. and Alibaba.com announced a long-term strategic partnership in China. The arrangement would promote the Yahoo! Brand in China. Also, Yahoo! purchased US$1 billion of Alibaba.com shares, giving Yahoo! Approximately 40 per cent economic interest in the company.

and financial performance, and Aggarwal believed that in most cases those conditions might be difficult to meet.

Aggarwal had received telephone calls from other Asian restaurant website entrepreneurs trying to sell their businesses to him. Their companies were specific to certain cities, whereas Eat2Eat.com covered the entire region. Aggarwal considered buying or merging with another company to increase his restaurant inventory and user base, but only if such an amalgamation could be accomplished at a reasonable price. However, each of the companies concerned expected several million U.S. dollars for their equity, and Aggarwal was confident he could build or expand his business in any given city organically with a lower investment.

Aggarwal thought he would have to make a decision about new funding in the first half of 2006. He also thought it would be difficult to raise the money. Not only would it be hard to find the right investor, but the task would require more of his time, and his time was already in short supply.

Aggarwal's Challenge

Aggarwal was proud of what Eat2Eat had achieved in its first five years, including its technology, industry recognition and value to both diners and restaurants. However, he knew the company would have to significantly expand its user base in 2006 and beyond. Such growth would be a difficult challenge, considering his limited time and financial capital. Aggarwal reviewed his current promotional strategies and tactics and wondered what he should do in the year ahead.

The Richard Ivey School of Business gratefully acknowledges the generous support of the Lee Foundation in the development of this case as part of THE LEE FOUNDATION ASIAN CASE SERIES.

Case 4 Elderline Communications

William Bygrave and Carl Hedberg, case writer
*Arthur M. Blank Center for Entrepreneurship,
Babson College*

Mark Culinski waved up to his wife and two young sons as the ferry pulled away from the dock, then turned back to his car with a smile. Normally he might have been disheartened at the prospect of missing a lazy mid-summer excursion to his parents' rented beach house, but instead he was keen on using his alone-time to focus on a start-up he had joined in the spring. Elderline Communications, a voice-application technology enterprise founded by two former colleagues, had reached a critical juncture.

While their momentum had been encouraging, the need to conserve cash and raise money had become essential if they were going to survive. Three months prior, in May of 2002, the team had closed a multi-investor seed round of just over $380,000. While it had been a relief to finally compensate employees who had up until then been working on faith, it was evident that things were going to get real tight again, and fast.

The Elderline partners had discovered that venture capitalists, sobered by the dot-com bust and a steadily declining stock market, seemed to be favoring less risky opportunities that could offer—if not actual profits—at least established contracts, clients and revenue. In a move to cast a wider net, the team was in talks with a "finder"—a well-connected funding broker with venture investor contacts throughout the Northeast.

As Mark turned into the driveway of the suburban duplex that Elderline called home, he knew that it was time to make some pivotal decisions.

Early Connections

Mark had met Elderline co-founder, Jorge Santos, when the two were MBA students at Babson College, in Wellesley, Massachusetts. Jorge was recruited by Harvard MBA John Warnick to work for Datalink Networks (DNI), a high-flying

---

venture that would come to epitomize the dazzling rise and slide of the manic dot-com era. In turn, Jorge recruited Mark for the wild ride. In just two years a share of DNI stock fell from a high of nearly $160 to less than the cost of a bottle of drinking water—but not before the exuberant public offering had landed John, Jorge, and Mark with tidy financial windfalls.

John and Jorge exited DNI ahead of Mark and immediately began brainstorming ideas for a "business that could solve a real problem." Drawing on still-vivid memories of attending college while at the same time caring for his elderly grandfather, John decided to focus on developing a technology solution that could ease the challenges faced by caregivers to the elderly.

Suburban Headquarters

In January of 2002, John and Jorge incorporated Elderline. To conserve their paid-in capital, they set up offices on the first floor of a duplex that Jorge owned on a quiet, tree-lined street just over the Massachusetts border in Nashua, New Hampshire. With sales, marketing and finance in the living room, software development in the dining room, executive offices in the kitchen and a conference table in the bedroom, the partners figured that they could grow there for quite some time—or at least until the local zoning board got wind of their operation. Mark, who had left DNI to consider his next move, was intrigued by how the close quarters seemed to contribute to a feeling of unity and mission:

> Honesty is a crucial part of building a business. And there they all were; working in a house, where everyone could hear every single conversation that was going on. There was more of a sense of openness. Everyone understood that there was going to be sacrifice, and that the sacrifice was going to be equally spread.

Adjusting the Focus

The partners soon discovered that their vision for designing automated speech technology to assist caregivers was technically feasible but logistically flawed. Mark recalled that by the time he signed on officially in April, Elderline had adjusted its business model to support a more robust market opportunity:

> The problem with the elder-care market was that it was very fragmented and not easy to penetrate. The biggest account we could have gotten was maybe a thirty-thousand dollar deal, and we'd have had to work really hard to get it.
>
> Then, through one of our employees, we were introduced to a medical director at a PBM [Pharmacy Benefit

Manager]. He told us that there was a big issue with increasing communications with patients around routine areas like refilling prescription drugs and checking in with a patient after surgery. It is cost prohibitive to have a live operator make such calls, but it would be a value-added service if you could figure out how to lower the cost of that communication through automation.

So, we kept the fundamental principle of improved communication between one entity and another, but now the entity is a PBM and the call recipient is the patient on medications or the person recovering from heart surgery who you want to follow up with to make sure they are still feeling all right.

Voice Recognition Technology

While the partners spent the spring of 2002 working to raise seed capital on a pre-money valuation of $1 million, Elderline's talented lead developer Doug McGowan was busy assembling a prototype that was "held together with the software-engineering equivalent of duct tape and bubblegum."

Their solution would utilize a new voice-application technology known as VoiceXML, or simply VXML. VXML had been developed for cold-calling systems that merged recipient data into generalized scripts (Hello <Mary Farmer>, this is Dan at the ABC Corp. calling with an important message for you and your family . . .). These applications were typically used by program managers to automate outbound sales, marketing and research calls to large swaths of the population.

A Call Center of One

In addition to targeting Pharmacy Benefit Managers, the partners also began to look at similar business models such as Clinical Research Organizations (CROs) and Disease Management firms (DMs). They found that firms of this sort primarily used call centers, direct mail and email to collect data and/or influence customer behavior. Live-operator call centers appeared to be effective but very expensive, direct mail programs were economical but largely ineffective, and email technology had not yet been adopted by a significant portion of the elderly community.

EXHIBIT 1 Executive Summary

Elderline at a Glance

Business—Voice Application Service Provider
Target Market—Healthcare

Currently Available Services—

- HealthCast™: Offers Health Enterprises the ability to create customized and interactive telephone messages for thousands of recipients.
- LifeMinder™: Offers caregivers the ability to manage individual patients' medical regimens via personalized telephone messages.

Current Full-Time Employees—Eight

Key Accomplishments—

- Highly effective management team recruited.
- Proprietary SAVVI™ 2.0 software released July 2002.
- Massachusetts General Hospital—Contract signed and Internal Review Board (IRB) approval received for two pilot projects.
- Initial round of seed funding closed.
- In contract negotiation with multiple prospects, strong sales pipeline in target markets

Corporate Overview

- Elderline Communications™ is **a service provider** delivering **voice applications** on a **proprietary software platform** that specifically address the unique issues of **healthcare companies**.
- Elderline is fundamentally changing the economics of driving patient behavior and collecting patient data.
- Elderline's **management team** fuses enterprise services with healthcare industry expertise.

The Opportunity—$3–$5 Billion Market

Voice applications are a rapidly growing component of the $21 Billion healthcare IT market. Much of this spend is driven by increasing pressure to *reduce* operational and marketing costs. Most healthcare enterprises currently have budget allocated for programs to influence behavior and to collect data. Voice applications can provide a more effective and less costly way to execute these programs than methods in use today (such as mail/call center efforts). Elderline is currently focusing its efforts on delivering such value in the Health Enterprise segment—specifically for Pharmacy Benefit Management (PBM) companies. Clinical Research Organizations (CROs) and Managed Care Organizations (MCOs). Several other Health Enterprise market segments (including disease management companies and pharmaceuticals) also have viable applications of Elderline's services. We believe these markets total represent an addressable market of $3–$5 Billion.

Why Elderline?

- **Health enterprises are looking for a better way to run programs.**
  Health enterprises currently run mail/call center-based programs designed to drive patient behavior (e.g., drug refill reminders) or to collect patient data (e.g., drug satisfaction polls). The requirements for these programs are driven by drug and healthcare cost reductions, drug patent expirations, and increasing patient self-management. While critical, they require an exorbitant amount of time to design, are expensive to execute, and are difficult to evaluate in terms of effectiveness. Companies using Interactive Voice Response (IVR) systems as an alternative are unsatisfied with these systems' functionality, speed to deployment, and internal resource requirements.

(continued)

EXHIBIT 1 **Executive Summary** (*continued*)

- **Better, faster, cheaper . . . and easier!**
  Elderline is fundamentally changing the economics of behavior modification and data collection programs. Elderline can drive patient behavior or capture data for a fraction of the cost of mail/call center programs. Beyond impressive cost savings, Elderline's services are more effective and dependable and offer real-time reporting and data collection capabilities that provide immediate effectiveness feedback—unattainable from traditional programs. And our SAVVI™ 2.0 platform allows nontechnical customers to execute their programs—without IT!

  In delivering our application as a service, Elderline eliminates the need for customers to make large investments in IT infrastructure, resources, or upfront costs. Program managers, regardless of their technical background, are able to quickly and easily set up programs. This represents an enormous advantage over the cost and complexity of IVR systems and is consistent with the industry drive to do more with less.

  Finally, Elderline's technology and operations are designed to support our customers' HIPAA compliance efforts and are CFR 21 part 11 compliant—critical for companies doing business in healthcare today.

Elderline is initially bringing two services to market:

Using our SAVVI™ 2.0 platform (Elderline Advanced Visual Voice Interface) we will initially offer two services:

Elderline HealthCast™: Offers Health Enterprises the ability to create customized and interactive telephone messages for thousands of recipients. Using Elderline's Web application and a standard telephone, customers record audio messages, schedule delivery, and define interactivity. This service is ideal for widespread information distribution and data collection efforts and will likely be used for prescription refill programs, drug migration programs, clinical trial polling, and health information dissemination programs.

LifeMinder™: ElderlineLifeMinder is a service that offers caregivers the ability to manage individual customers' medical regimens via personalized telephone messages. Using Elderline's Web application and a standard telephone, caregivers record audio messages, schedule delivery, and define escalation and interactivity functions. This service is ideal for disease management programs, medication compliance programs, and other programs that require a more personal approach to delivering information and collecting data.

When delivering each of these services, Elderline offers its customers: upfront application customization (including custom reporting), user training and technical support, and designated Customer Support resources.

Elderline's Business Strategy:

Elderline is a service provider delivering voice applications that specifically address the unique issues of healthcare companies. Elderline's SAVVI™ 2.0 enables customers to deliver cost-effective, personalized, and interactive telephone messages using their current IT resources and infrastructure.

In order to speed adoption, we have minimized the technical resources our customers have to allocate in order to use our services. Elderline's application can be private-labeled and is designed to meet HIPAA and FDA 21 CFR Part 11 regulations ensuring patient privacy; version control and consistent time-stamping will be standard in all services delivered.

Elderline's sales strategy involves working with decision makers to define a "starting point" project with measurable results and a clearly defined customer ROI. The goal is then to execute successfully and earn projects throughout the organization while constantly maintaining a pipeline of new customers.

The company will charge customers on a per-call/per-minute basis (with minimum volume commitments and an initial customization/data integration fee). Approximate revenue to Elderline will be $0.30 per call and gross margins are estimated at 50%–70%.

Key Accomplishments

- **Highly effective management team recruited.** Elderline's management team forges world-class enterprise services experience with leaders in healthcare and healthcare IT services.
- **Proprietary software application SAVVI™ 2.0.** Production release of 2.0 in July 2002. Successful demonstrations are delivered on a regular basis to customers and investors.
- **Massachusetts General Hospital Internal Review Board (IRB) approval for pilot projects.** Working closely with the head of gerontology, Elderline recently gained IRB approval on two pilot projects allowing end-user use.
- **Initial round of funding closed.** A combination of employees, friends, family, and angel investors contributed to a round of funding which closed May 2002.
- **Multiple advanced sales cycles ongoing.** In contract negotiations with multiple prospects in our target markets. Verbals received from 2 CEOs and 1 Executive VP. Strong follow-on pipeline. First revenue expected in August, 2002.

Factors for Success:

The following factors suggest Elderline is well positioned to achieve its goals:

- **A Compelling Value Proposition:** For health enterprises currently investing in driving patient behavior or collecting patient information, Elderline's services allow health enterprises to run programs much more effectively and at a fraction of their current cost. Elderline reduces the burden on IT resources while ensuring compliance with applicable regulations (such as HIPAA's Final Rule and CFR 21 Part 1).
- **Technology:** A sophisticated custom-built Web and VXML application (SAVVI™ 2.0) is at the heart of Elderline's Services. Our development team has created a one-of-a-kind platform using state-of-the-art, yet reliable, technologies. Our efforts in this area have won high praise from industry experts, customers, and prospects. Production release is scheduled for July 2002.

(continued)

EXHIBIT 1 Executive Summary (*continued*)

- **First-Mover Advantage:** Elderline has the lead in the development of this kind of application. No other company offers a product or service that provides the same functionality while remaining sensitive to the highly unique needs of the healthcare industry. Elderline is positioned to be the first—and best—mover with a technology that is tested, proven, and ready for market.
- **The Right Market at the Right Time:** Healthcare IT spending for 2002 is projected to be $15 Billion. This number is expected to grow to $22 Billion by 2005. A more stringent regulatory environment is encouraging healthcare companies to outsource IT efforts, making Elderline's service model especially attractive. Furthermore, voice application technology is gaining increasing acceptance and is projected to grow from a $5 Billion market to a $41 Billion by 2005.
- **Team:** Elderline's management team fuses IT enterprise services with healthcare industry expertise. The right experience, combined with an unmatched drive to succeed, makes this the right team to capitalize on the opportunity before us:

CEO: IT services and general management background most recently as general manager of primary storage services at Datalink Networks. Experience building and operating new business units for GTE Internet working (now Genuity) and the Indian operations for InterGen (an energy development company owned by Bechtel Corporation). He has an MBA from Harvard University (1993) and an AB from Harvard College (1987).

Chief Operating Officer: IT services, IT management, and healthcare design background. Product-managed Datalink Networks' enterprise-class storage management service offering. Managed the IT department of a division of Houghton Mifflin Company. Six years' experience in healthcare consulting. He has an MBA from Babson College (1999) and Master of Architecture degree from MIT (1990).

Chief Strategy Officer: Co-founder and former CTO of Physicians Online. Served as senior executive or advisor for health-related technology companies, including Vicus.com, VitaSave, Inc., Neurotrax, Inc. Facilitated 21 CFR 11 compliance for a Web-enabled diagnostic system, in addition to product placement strategy in the pharmaceutical industry.

Medical Advisor: Currently a healthcare consultant specializing in managed care for Watson Wyatt Worldwide. Formerly chief medical officer for Express Scripts and served as vice president of health services and national medical director for United HealthCare Corporation. He is a board-certified pediatrician and was educated at the University of Minnesota.

Financial Advisor: Currently a general partner of Telecom Partners III. Served as partner with In Fusion, which advised start-up and early stage technology companies. Formerly chairman and CEO of Andataco, Inc., former CFO and executive vice president at Storage Technology Corporation, held senior positions with BMC Industries, and was partner in the law firm of Oppenheimer, Wolf, Foster, Shepard and Donnel.

Consumer research indicated that automated speech applications via the telephone were well received and effective. Interestingly, it appeared that in the healthcare sector, people responded as well or better to automated voice response systems as they did to live calls from nurses, pharmacists and other clinicians.

For a per-call/per-minute fee, Elderline would provide a turnkey solution, including the voice recognition and speech software, user-friendly Web interface, telephony network, and infrastructure support (see Exhibit 1). The team felt that this outsourcing model made more sense than simply selling a software package that would, in many cases, require the client to make a substantial IT investment. They also reasoned that their "call center of one" approach would enable them to build a client base more quickly by pitching relatively low-risk, low-cost pilot programs.

Friends and Angels

As the founders worked to raise capital and gain some traction in the marketplace, their efforts were supported by a growing number of hard-working, and as-yet, unpaid, employees. Mark, who figured that he could live off his savings for around six months, reflected on their pre-money investment of time and effort:

We are asking everyone to make a pretty significant commitment to make this thing work. A lot of us had already invested in the sense that we'd been working for nothing until we got that funding. . . . One of our developers, for example, had been working two jobs; a full-time gig during the day and then coding for us six hours at night to push this through. This is a true start-up experience where people are working like that just to get the ball rolling.

In May the team closed on a seed round of just over $380,000. Referring to their budget projections (see Exhibit 2), Mark stressed that the money unfortunately did not relieve the pressing need for venture funding:

It was a lot of work to raise money in a down market with everyone's portfolios crashing. For every one of the ten or twelve people that said yes there were one or two that said no. You can do the math to see how many pitches we were making. Not only that, you have to do each pitch several times because you have to convince the person, and their wife, then show it to them again. . . . Everyone who wasn't working for equity needed to be paid, and all of a sudden you discover the burn rate. With full salaries being paid and no revenue coming in, three hundred eighty thousand is both a lot and a little—mostly a little.

EXHIBIT 2   Four-Month Budget

Current Expenditures 7/26/2002

Current Balance	July $220,053	August	Sept.	October	Notes
BUDGET					
CEO	$8,333	$8,333	$8,333	$8,333	
COO	$8,333	$8,333	$8,333	$8,333	
Director BD	$6,667	$6,667	$6,667	$6,667	
Lead Developer	$5,833	$5,833	$5,833	$5,833	
Junior Developer	$2,667	$2,667	$2,667	$2,667	
Junior Developer	$2,667	$2,667	$2,667	$2,667	
Director Marketing	$450	$2,000	$7,200	$7,200	1
CSO	$9,000	$9,000	$9,000	$9,000	
Admin & QA (part time)	$1,500	$1,500	$1,500	$1,500	
Program Management	$—	$—	$—	$3,750	2
Health, Dental, Taxes	$—	$4,000	$4,000	$4,000	
Hosting Site	$4,200	$4,200	$4,200	$4,200	
Hosting Deposit + Install	$5,200	$—	$—	$—	
Health Compliance Consultant	$1,500				
Voice Interface Consultant		$1,800			
Telephony	$500	$500	$765	$1,000	
Rent	$—	$1,200	$1,200	$1,200	
Legal	$1,500	$4,000	$7,500	$4,000	3
Office Supplies	$1,000	$1,000	$1,000	$1,000	4
Insurance	$—	$—	$1,500	$—	
Misc Expenses	$500	$1,000	$1,000	$1,000	
Travel & Entertainment	$3,000	$5,000	$7,500	$4,000	5
Total	$62,850	$69,700	$80,865	$76,350	
End Month Balance	$157,203	$87,503	$6,638	$(69,712)	

Extra / Unknown
Extra Legal
Finance-Related Fees
Auditor
First Revenue—not likely more than $5,000 in Sept., $10,000 in October
Timing of A Round

Notes
1. Maternity Leave—assumes she works 10 hours in July, 45 hours in August, and comes back full time in Sept.
2. 1/2 salary in October—full salary in November
3. Assumes cost increase during period of raising money
4. Postage, printing, professional voices, extra Testing Calls, Web hosting
5. Assumes cost increase during period of raising money

EXHIBIT 3 **Three Year Financial Projections**

INCOME STATEMENT

	Year 1	Year 2	Year 3
Projects	15	35	57
Headcount (end)	21	37	54
Ave. Rev per Project Per Year	$60,132	$199,679	$304,613
Revenue	$901,979	$6,988,750	$17,362,917
Cost of Sales	$429,755	$2,355,325	$5,463,436
Gross Margin	$478,224	$4,633,425	$11,899,481
Gross Margin %	53%	66%	69%
Operating Costs	$1,484,327	$3,483,202	$5,764,188
Operating Income	($1,006,103)	$1,150,223	$6,135,292
Operating Margin %	−112%	16%	35%
Net Profit After Tax	($1,006,103)	$950,963	$3,571,610
	−112%	14%	21%

Key Income Statement Assumptions.

• Years are from May through April
• Each customer represents multiple projects
• Each project is between 12 and 36 months in length
• 90% of projects will renew
• Average selling price will be approximately $0.30 per call/minute, prices will decline 12.5% in Year 2, 25% in Year 3.
• Initial telephony and speech software infrastructure will be outsourced
• In January 2003 telephony and speech software infrastructure will be built

CASH FLOW STATEMENT

	Year 1	Year 2	Year 3
Previous Cash		$3,305,081	$2,129,547
Cash Flow In from Ops.	$511,333	$5,811,469	$15,832,260
Cash Flow Out	($2,587,502)	($6,987,003)	($15,478,891)
Cash Flow In from Financing	$5,381,250		
Net Cash	$3,305,081	$2,129,547	$2,482,917

Key Cash Flow Assumptions:

• A total of $5.4 Million dollars will be raised in 2002
• Accounts receivable average 60 days
• Capital equipment will be purchased

Key Points:

• High-margin business with recurring revenue stream
• November 2002:   Gross margin positive
• May 2003:   First 15 projects
• Q3 2003:   Profitable after tax
• Q3 2004:   Cash flow positive

ADDITIONAL DATA

Project Summary

Number of Projects	12-Month Booking Size	Year 1	Year 2	Year 3
Pilot	$20,000	4	0	0
Small	$50,000	3	2	2

(*continued*)

EXHIBIT 3   Three Year Financial Projection (*continued*)

Number of Projects	12-Month Booking Size	Year 1	Year 2	Year 3
Medium	$150,000	4	5	5
Large	$325,000	2	6	7
Enterprise	$800,000	2	7	8
TOTAL		15	20	22
Total Bookings		$3,080,000	$8,400,000	$9,525,000
Average Booking		$205,333	$420,000	$432,955

HEADCOUNT SUMMARY (YEAR END)

	Year 1	Year 2	Year 3
Sales	3	6	10
Marketing	1	2	3
R&D	5	7	9
IT/Network	1	2	3
Exec	4	4	5
G&A	1	3	3
Program Mgmt	4	9	15
Support	2	4	6
TOTAL	21	37	54

CAPITAL BUDGET

	Year 1	Year 2	Year 3	Total
Number of Ports Required	87	343	645	
Number of Gateways	6	14	15	35
Voice Gateways and SW	$540,000	$1,260,000	$1,350,000	$3,150,000
Support Infrastructure	$228,000	$135,000	$135,000	$498,000
TOTAL	$768,000	$1,395,000	$1,485,000	$3,648,000

The team was certain that their best hope of getting to the next level rested on securing early-stage funding from a venture capitalist with experience in the healthcare industry. After updating their financials (see Exhibit 3), the partners worked the phones and tapped their existing contacts to raise the $5 million they required. By early summer they had managed to land four introductory VC meetings, but each time the response had been the same: given the difficult business environment, seed money was being diverted to more established, less risky opportunities.

A Finder of Funds

In June, Elderline's financial advisor suggested that they contact Jim Cooper, a well-connected investment consultant with experience in raising risk capital. Mark explained that the team was intrigued by the idea of hiring a pro:

While we had all worked in start-ups before, to a degree we were all first-time entrepreneurs. None of us had ever raised VC money and we were thinking that maybe someone who had done this before might be able to do it better—maybe help expand the pool of potential investors and guide us through the process of obtaining capital.

The partners understood that a fund-finder's Rolodex did not come cheap, and that when set as a percentage of monies raised, fees could easily run six figures. They also wanted to avoid paying commissions on investments garnered outside of the direct efforts of Mr. Cooper. Mark noted that the contract they were reviewing (see Exhibit 4) was crafted to address these and other pitfalls:

The reason we were not too concerned was because Jim's salary was capped at twenty-five thousand, and the firms he was going to contact were all identified in writing.

EXHIBIT 4   Contract Highlights

This Letter Agreement (this "Agreement") is to confirm our discussions and the engagement of Jim Cooper ("Consultant") as a consultant to Elderline Communications ("Customer").

1. *Consulting Services:* Consultant will provide to Customer the consulting services described on Schedule A and other consulting services requested by Customer and agreed to by Consultant (the "Consulting Services").

2. *Confidential Information:* In order to perform the Consulting Services, Consultant will need to familiarize himself with the business of Customer related to the Consulting Services. All such information is considered confidential to Customer. Prior to providing such information to Consultant (or other information which Customer may provide in order to permit Consultant to perform Consulting Services under this Agreement), Customer requires execution by Consultant of a Confidentiality Agreement in the form attached as Exhibit A to this Consulting Agreement.

3. *Fees:* Customer will pay consulting fees to Consultant as described on Schedule A. Invoices will be paid within 15 days of receipt by Customer.

4. *Expenses:* Customer will reimburse Consultant for reasonable travel and out-of-pocket expenses incurred in connection with providing Consulting Services under this Agreement. Consultant will request pre-approval from Customer for any expenses anticipated to exceed $500. Reasonable expenses shall include coach (but not first class) airfare. Consultant will invoice Customer for expense reimbursement monthly, and invoices shall include photocopies of receipts. Invoices will be paid within 15 days of receipt by Customer.

5. *Independent Contractor:* Consultant shall not be entitled to any benefits, including social security, unemployment or medical benefits. Consultant will perform all Consulting Services under this Agreement as an "independent contractor" and not as an employee or agent of Customer.

6. *Indemnity:* Customer agrees to defend, indemnify and hold Consultant harmless against any losses, claims, damages and liabilities (and all actions in respect thereof) caused by, related in any way to, or arising out of the provision of the Consulting Services; provided that (a) Consultant shall have promptly provided Customer with any written notice of any claim or threatened claim and reasonable cooperation, information and assistance and (b) Customer shall have control and authority with respect to the defense, settlement or compromise thereof. This provision is in addition to any obligation which Customer might otherwise have to Consultant.

7. *Termination of Engagement:* Consultant's engagement under this Agreement may be terminated by Customer or Consultant at any time, with or without cause, upon prior written notice to the other party; provided that the provisions of Section 2 shall survive such termination for a period of two (2) years and the provisions of Section 6 shall survive indefinitely.

Termination shall not affect Customer's obligations to pay Consulting Fees and expenses incurred prior to the effective date of termination.

Other:

The benefits of this Agreement shall inure to the respective successors and assigns of the parties hereto, and the obligations and liabilities assumed by the parties hereto shall be binding upon their respective successors and assigns.

Customer acknowledges and agrees that Consultant is not an investment banker and is not registered as a broker/dealer and that the engagement of Consultant under this letter agreement is not intended to replace or supplant in any manner investment banking services that might be necessary or appropriate in connection with any transaction undertaken by Customer. Consultant will not perform valuations, make fairness assessments or render fairness opinions with respect to any proposed transaction or target.

Customer expressly acknowledges that all advice (written or oral) given by Consultant to Customer in connection with Consultant's engagement is intended solely for the benefit and use of Customer and Customer agrees that no such advice shall be reproduced, disseminated, quoted or referred to at any time, in any manner or for any purpose, nor shall any public references to Consultant be made by Customer, without the prior written consent of Consultant. Customer expressly acknowledges that Consultant has been retained solely as an advisor to Customer and not as an advisor to or agent of any other person, and that Customer's engagement of Consultant is not intended to confer rights upon any persons not a party hereto (including stockholders, employees or creditors of Customer) as against Consultant.

SCHEDULE A

Consulting Services:

Consultant will assist the Company in identifying private equity investors for a potential Financing as defined in Section 1 under Consulting Fees below. In addition, Consultant will assist the Company in identifying potential customers.

Consulting Fees:

As used in this letter agreement, the term "Financing" means, whether effected in one transaction or a series of transactions, the sale of equity securities of the Company (whether in a private placement offering of common stock, preferred stock, warrants or other equity securities and/or pursuant to a registration statement(s) filed under the Securities Act of 1933, as amended) resulting in gross proceeds to Company of at least $2 million or more (before deducting underwriting commissions, legal fees or other transaction-related expenses).

If, during the period Consultant is retained by the Company or within six months thereafter, a Financing is consummated which includes as investors in the Financing, any of the organizations referenced in Section 2 below, then Company will pay to Consultant $25,000 in the same securities issued to such private equity participants in the Financing:

(continued)

EXHIBIT 4   **Contract Highlights** (*continued*)

Those organizations pursuant to which payment is due to Consultant under Section 1 above shall include Aetna Private Equity, Axiom Venture Partners, CB Health Ventures, Conning Capital Partners, Cutlass Capital, Delphi Ventures, Frontenac Company, GE Capital, Pequot Capital, Schroeder Ventures, the Sprout Group, Still River Fund, Swiss Re Capital, Symphony Capital or any subsidiaries or affiliates thereof.

As used in this letter agreement, Customer means a source of gross or net revenue, as defined under generally accepted accounting principles, to the Company of any amount or type. If, during the period Consultant is retained by the Company or within six months thereafter, Company requests that Consultant provide an introduction to a Customer including any of the organizations referenced in Section 4 below, then Company shall pay Consultant the lesser of (i) 10% of forecast 12 month minimum revenue committed by such Customer in agreements executed with the Company; or (ii) $25,000 in cash per such Customer. Such payment shall be made within 15 days of the first revenue received by the Company from such Customer.

Those organizations pursuant to which payment is due to Consultant under Section 3 above shall include Cardium Health Solutions, CorSolutions, Medco Health Solutions, or Personal Path Systems or any subsidiaries or affiliates thereof.

This was a referral arrangement; capped, and therefore not financially risky.

Time was not on their side, however. Best case, they figured that it would take at least three months following a favorable presentation for a venture group to complete their due diligence and offer a term sheet. Therefore, even if Jim Cooper were able to work magic with his connections, it was clear that immediate steps had to be taken in order to prevent a financial meltdown.

Survival Mode

Mark arrived at Elderline to find the tech staff in the bedroom, on conference call. He swung into the kitchen where the management team was hunkered down around the issues at hand. All were in agreement that unless they were able to secure financial backing while at the same time make fundamental changes to Elderline's cost structure, the opportunity would be lost before the business had even begun.

Case 5   Jim Poss

William Bygrave and Carl Hedburg, case writer
Arthur M. Blank Center for Entrepreneurship,
Babson College

On his way through Logan Airport, Jim Poss stopped at a newsstand to flip through the June 2004 *National Geographic* cover story that declared, "The End of Cheap Oil." Inside was a two-page spread of an American family sitting amongst a vast array of household possessions that were derived, at least in part, from petroleum-based products: laptops, cell phones, clothing, footwear, sports equipment, cookware, and containers of all shapes and sizes. Without oil, the world will be a very different place. Jim shook his head.

> . . . and here we are burning this finite, imported, irreplaceable resource to power three-ton suburban gas-guzzlers with "these colors don't run" bumper stickers!

Jim's enterprise, Seahorse Power Company (SPC), was an engineering start-up that encouraged the adoption of environmentally friendly methods of power generation by designing products that were cheaper and more efficient than twentieth-century technologies. Jim was sure that his first product, a patent-pending solar-powered trash compactor, could make a real difference.

> In the United States alone, 180,000 garbage trucks consume over a billion gallons of diesel fuel a year. . .

By compacting trash on-site and off-grid, the mailbox-sized "BigBelly" could cut pickups by 400 percent. The prototype—designed on the fly at a cost of $10,000—had been sold to Vail Ski Resorts in Colorado for $5,500. The green technology had been working as promised since February, saving the resort lots of time and money on round-trips to a remote lodge accessible only by snow machine.

Carl Hedberg prepared this case under the supervision of Professor William Bygrave, Babson College, as a basis for class discussion rather than to illustrate either effective or ineffective handling of an administrative situation. Funding provided by the F. W. Olin Graduate School of Business and a gift from the class of 2003.

Jim viewed the $4,500 loss on the sale as an extremely worthwhile marketing and proof-of-concept expense. Now that they were taking the business to the next level with a run of twenty machines, Jim and his SPC team had to find a way to reduce component costs and increase production efficiencies.

Jim returned the magazine to the rack and made his way to the New York Shuttle gate. An investor group in the City had called another meeting, and Jim felt that it was time for him to start asking the hard questions about the deal they were proposing. These investors in socially responsible business had to be given a choice: either write him the check they had been promising—and let him run SPC the way he saw fit—or decline to invest altogether so he could concentrate on locating other sources of funding to close this $250,000 seed round. So far, all Jim had received from this group were voices of concern and requests for better terms—it was time to do the deal or move on.

Green Roots

As a kid, Jim Poss was always playing with motors, batteries and electronics. He especially enjoyed fashioning new gadgets from components he had amassed by dismantling all manner of appliances and electronic devices. He also spent a lot of time out of doors cross-country skiing with his father. Jim said that by his senior year in high school, he knew where he was headed:

> I had read *Silent Spring*[1] and that got me thinking about the damage we are doing to the earth. And once I started learning about the severity of our problems—that was it. By the end of my first semester at Duke University, I had taken enough environmental science to see that helping businesses to go green was going to be a huge growth industry.

Jim felt that the best way to get businesses to invest in superior energy system was to make it profitable for them to do so. In order to prepare himself for this path, Jim set up a double major in environmental science & policy, and geology—with a minor degree in engineering. He graduated in 1996 and found

---

[1] *Silent Spring*, written in 1962 by Rachel Carson, exposed the hazards of the pesticide DDT, eloquently questioned humanity's faith in technological progress, and helped set the stage for the environmental movement. Appearing on a CBS documentary shortly before her death from breast cancer in 1964, the author remarked. "Man's attitude toward nature is today critically important simply because we have now acquired a fateful power to alter and destroy nature. But man is a part of nature, and his war against nature is inevitably a war against himself. . . [We are] challenged as mankind has never been challenged before to prove our maturity and our mastery, not of nature, but of ourselves."

work as a hydrologist, analyzing soil and rock samples for a company that engineered stable parking lots for shopping malls. He didn't stay long:

> That certainly wasn't my higher calling. I poked around, and within six months I found a fun job redesigning the production capabilities at a small electronics firm. Soon after that, I started working for this company called Solectria; that was right up my alley.

As a sales engineer at Solectria—a Massachusetts-based designer and manufacturer of sustainable transportation and energy solutions—Jim helped clients configure electric drive systems for a wide range of vehicles. He loved the work, and developed an expertise in using spreadsheets to calculate the most efficient layout of motors, controllers, power converters, and other hardware. By 1999, though, he decided that it was once again time to move on:

> Solectria had a great group of people, but my boss was a micro-manager and I wasn't going to be able to grow. I found an interesting job in San Francisco as a production manager for a boat manufacturing company—coordinating the flow of parts from seven or eight subcontractors. When the [Internet] bubble burst, the boat company wasn't able to raise capital to expand. My work soon became relatively mundane, so I left.

This time though, Jim decided to head back to school:

> I had now worked for a bunch of different businesses and I had seen some things done well, but a lot of things done wrong. I knew that I could run a good company—something in renewable energy, and maybe something with gadgets. I still had a lot to learn, so I applied to the MBA program at Babson College. I figured that I could use the second-year EIT[2] module to incubate something.

Opportunity Exploration

Between his first and second year at Babson, Jim applied for a summer internship through the Kauffman Program. He sent a proposal to the Spire Corporation—a publicly traded manufacturer of highly engineered solar electric equipment—about investigating the market and feasibility of solar-powered trash compactors. Jim had copied his idea to someone he knew on the board, and the same week that the HR department informed him that there were no openings, he got a call from the president of the company:

> Roger Little had talked with the board member I knew and said that while they weren't interested in having me write a case study on some solar whatever-it-was, he said

they'd like me to write some business plans for Spire—based on their existing opportunities and existing operations. I said sure, I'll take it.

That summer, Jim worked with the executive team to complete three business plans. When they asked him to stay on, Jim agreed to work fifteen hours per week—on top of his full-time MBA classes. He mentioned that every month or so he would bring up his idea for a solar-powered trash compactor with the Spire executives, but their answer was always the same:

> I was trying to get them to invest in my idea or partner with me in some way, and these guys kept saying, "It'll never work." So I just kept working on them. I did the calculations to show them that with solar we could do ten compactions a day and have plenty [of electric charge] on reserve for a run of cloudy weather. Finally, they just said that they don't get into end-user applications.

Early in his second year, Jim attended a product design fair featuring young engineers from Babson's new sister school, the Franklin W. Olin School of Engineering. He connected with Jeff Satwicz, an engineering student with extensive experience in remote vehicle testing for the Department of Defense. When Jim got involved with a project that required engineering capabilities, he knew who to call:

> I went up the hill to Olin to ask Jeff if he'd like to help design a folding grill for tailgating—he said sure. It's funny, the two schools are always talking about working together like that, but it doesn't happen until the students sit in the café together and exchange ideas. That's how it works, the faculty wasn't involved—and they didn't really need to be.

Although Jim didn't stay with the grill team, the project had forged a link with an engineer with a penchant for entrepreneurship. Now certain of his trajectory, Jim incorporated the Seahorse Power Company (SPC)—a nod to his ultimate aspiration of developing power systems that could harness the enormous energy of ocean waves and currents.

Understanding that sea-powered generators were a long way off, Jim began to investigate ways to serve well-capitalized ventures that were developing alternative-energy solutions. One idea was to lease abandoned oil wells in California for the purpose of collecting and selling deep-well data to geothermal energy businesses that were prospecting in the area. When Jim sought feedback, he found that even people who liked his concept invariably pointed him in a different direction:

> Everybody kept telling me that wind was where it's at—and they were right; it's the fastest-growing energy source in the world. All the venture capitalists are looking at wind power. I realized though, that if I was going to make wind plants, I'd have to raise two to five hundred million dollars—with no industry experience. Impossible. So instead, I started looking at what these [wind-plant ventures] needed.

---

2 The Entrepreneurship Intensity Track (EIT) was a compressed and highly focused entrepreneurship curriculum for graduate students at Babson College. The program provided a select group of MBAs who intended to become full-time entrepreneurs as soon as they graduated with the necessary skills to take their new venture ideas through the critical stages of exploration, investigation, and refinement, so they could launch their businesses during the spring of their second year.

The DAQ Buoy

Jim discovered that The Cape Wind Project, a company working to build a wind farm on Nantucket Sound, had erected a $2.5 million, two-hundred foot monitoring tower to collect wind and weather data in the targeted area. Jim felt that there was a better way:

Meteorological testing is a critical first step for these wind businesses. I thought, whoa, they've just spent a lot of money to construct a static tower that probably won't accurately portray the wind activity in that 25-square-mile area. And without good data, it's going to be really hard for them to get funding.

My idea was to deploy data buoys that could be moved around a site to capture a full range of data points. I spent about six months writing a business plan on my data acquisition buoy—the DAQ. I figured that to get to the prototype stage I'd need between five and ten million. This would be a pretty sophisticated piece of equipment, and a lot of people worried that if a storm came up and did what storms typically do to buoys, we'd be all done. I was having a hard time getting much traction with investors.

Finding the Waste

Even while he was casting about for a big-concept opportunity, Jim had never lost sight of his solar compactor idea. With the spring semester upon him, he decided to see if that business would work as an EIT[3] endeavor. Although he was sure that such a device would be feasible—even easy—to produce, he didn't start to get excited about the project until he took a closer look at the industry:

I did an independent study to examine the trash industry. I was about a week into that when I looked at the market size and realized that I had been messing around with expensive, sophisticated business models that didn't offer close to the payback this compactor would.

U.S. companies spent $12 billion on trash receptacles in 2000, and $1.2 billion on compaction equipment in 2001. The average trash truck gets less than three miles to the gallon and costs over $100 an hour to operate. There are lots of off-grid sites[4] that have high trash volumes—resorts, amusement parks and beaches—and many are getting multiple pickups a day. That's a tremendous waste of labor and energy resources.

Joining him in the EIT module was first-year MBA candidate Alexander Perera. Alex had an undergraduate degree in Environmental Science from Boston University, as well as industry experience in renewable energy use and energy efficiency measures. The pair reasoned that if a solar compactor could offer significant savings as a trash collection device, then

EXHIBIT 1 Target Customers

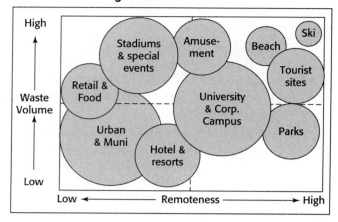

the market could extend beyond the off-grid adopters to include retail and food establishments, city sidewalks, and hotels (see Exhibit 1).

Gearing Up

By the time the spring semester drew to a close, they had a clear sense of the market and the nature of the opportunity—in addition to seed funding of $22,500: $10,000 from Jim's savings, and $12,500 through the hatchery program at Babson College. Since solar power was widely perceived as a more expensive, more complex, and less efficient energy source than grid power, it was not surprising to discover that the competition—dumpster and compaction equipment manufacturers—had never introduced a system like this. Nevertheless, Jim and Alex were certain that if they could devise a reliable, solar-powered compactor that could offer end users significant cost savings, established industry players could be counted on to aggressively seek to replicate or acquire that technology.

Understanding that patent protections were often only as good as the legal minds that drafted them, Jim had sought out the best. The challenge was that most of the talented patent attorneys he met with were far outside his meager budget. In May of 2003, Jim got a break when he presented his idea at an investor forum:

I won $1,500 in patent services from Brown and Rudnick.[5] That might not have taken me too far, but they have a very entrepreneurial mindset. They gave me a flat rate for the patent—which is not something many firms will do. I paid the $7,800 up front, we filed a provisional patent in June, and they agreed to work with me as I continued to develop and modify the machine.

Jim's efforts had again attracted the interest of Olin engineer Jeff Satwicz, who in turn brought in Bret Richmond, a fellow student with experience in product design, welding, and

---

[3] EIT was an acronym for the Entrepreneurship Intensity Track, a Babson College graduate-level program in Entrepreneurship introduced in 2000.
[4] Sites without electrical power.

[5] Brown Rudnick Berlack Israels, LLP, Boston, Massachusetts.

fabrication. When the team conducted some reverse engineering to see if the vision was even feasible, Jim said they were pleasantly surprised:

> I found a couple of kitchen trash compactors in the Want Ads and bought them both for about 125 bucks. We took them apart, and that's when I realized how easy this was going to be . . . of course, nothing is ever as easy as you think it's going to be.

Pitching without Product

Figuring that it was time to conduct some hard field research, they decided to call on businesses that would be the most likely early adopters of an off-grid compactor. Alex smiled as he described an unexpected turn of events:

> We had a pretty simple client-targeting formula; remoteness, trash volume, financial stability, and an appreciation for the environmental cachet that could come with a product like this. Literally the first place I called was the ski resort in Vail, Colorado. Some eco-terrorists had recently burned down one of their lodges to protest their expansion on the mountain, and they were also dealing with four environmental lawsuits related to some kind of noncompliance.
>
> This guy Luke Cartin at the resort just jumped at the solar compactor concept. He said, "Oh, this is cool. We have a lodge at Blue Sky Basin that is an hour and a half round trip on a snow cat. We pick up the trash out there three or four times a week; sometimes every day. We could really use a product like that . . ." That's when you put the phone to your chest and think, *oh my gosh* . . . .

Jim added that after a couple of conference calls, they were suddenly in business without a product:

> I explained that we were students and that we had not actually built one of these things yet (sort of). Luke asked me to work up a quote for three machines. They had been very open about their costs for trash pickup, and I figured that they'd be willing to pay six grand apiece. I also had a rough idea that our cost of materials would fall somewhat less than that.
>
> Luke called back and said that they didn't have the budget for three, but they'd take one. I was actually really happy about that, because I knew by then that making just one of these was going to be a real challenge.

In September, SPC received a purchase order from Vail Resorts. When Jim called the company to work out a payment plan with twenty-five percent up front, Luke surprised them again:

> He said, "We'll just send you a check for the full amount, minus shipping, and you get the machine here by Christmas." That was great, but now we were in real trouble because we had to figure out how to build this thing quickly, from scratch—and on a tight budget.

Learning by Doing

The team set out to design the system and develop the engineering plans for the machine that SPC had now trademarked as the "BigBelly Solar-Powered Trash Compactor." Although his Olin team was not yet versant with computer-aided design (CAD) software, Jim saw that as an opportunity:

> These guys were doing engineering diagrams on paper with pens and pencils—but now we were going to need professional stuff. I said that we could all learn CAD together, and if they made mistakes, great, that's fine; we'd work through it.

Concurrent to this effort was the task of crunching the numbers to design a machine that would work as promised. As they began to source out the internal components, they searched for a design, fabrication and manufacturing subcontractor that could produce the steel cabinet on a tight schedule. Although the team had explained that SPC would be overseeing the entire process from design to assembly, quotes for the first box still ranged from $80,000 to $400,000. Jim noted that SPC had an even bigger problem to deal with:

> On top of the price, the lead times that they were giving me were not going to cut it; I had to get this thing to Colorado for the ski season!
>
> So, we decided to build it ourselves. I went to a local fabricator trade show, and discovered that although they all have internal engineering groups; some were willing to take a loss on the research and development side in order to get the manufacturing contract.
>
> We chose Boston Engineering since they are very interested in developing a relationship with Olin engineers. They gave me a hard quote of $2,400 for the engineering assistance, and $2,400 for the cabinet. By this time we had sourced all the components we needed, and we began working with their engineer to size everything up. Bob Treiber, the president, was great. He made us do the work ourselves out at his facility in Hudson (Massachusetts), but he also mentored us, and his firm did a ton of work pro bono.

Fulfillment and Feedback

As the Christmas season deadline came and went, the days grew longer. By late January 2004, Jim was working through both of the shifts they had set up; from four in the morning to nearly eleven at night. In February, they fired up the device, tested it for three hours, and shipped it off to Colorado (see Exhibit 2). Jim met the device at their shipping dock, helped unwrap it, met the staff, and put a few finishing touches on the machine. Although it worked, even at zero degree temperatures, it had never been tested in the field. Jim left after a few days, and for two weeks, he endured a deafening silence.

Jim wrestled with how he could check in with SPC's first customer without betraying his acute inventor's angst about whether the machine was still working, and if it was, what Vail

EXHIBIT 2 The BigBelly Arrives in Vail

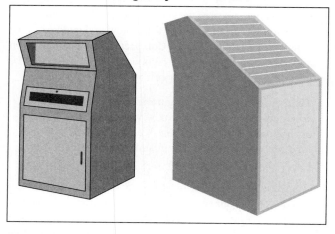

thought about it. Finally, when he could stand it no longer, he placed the call under the guise of soliciting satisfied-customer feedback. The news from Vail nearly stopped his heart:

> They said that they had dropped the machine off a fork lift and it fell on its face. Oh man, I thought; if it had fallen on its back, that would have been okay, but this was bad—real bad. And then Luke tells me that it was a bit scratched—but it worked fine. He told me how happy they were that we had made it so robust. When I asked how heavy the bags were that they were pulling out of the thing, he said, "I don't know; we haven't emptied it yet . . . ." I was astounded.

As it turned out, the Vail crew discovered that the single collection bag was indeed too heavy—a two-bin system would be more user-friendly. The resort also suggested that the inside cart be on wheels, that the access door be in the back, and that there be some sort of wireless notification when the compactor was full.

As the SPC team got to work incorporating these ideas into their next generation of "SunPack" compactors, they were also engineering a second product that they hoped would expand their market reach to include manufacturers of standard compaction dumpsters. The "SunPack Hippo" would be a solar generator designed to replace the 220-volt AC-power units that were used to run industrial compactors. The waste hauling industry had estimated that among commercial customers that would benefit from compaction, between five and twenty percent were dissuaded from adopting such systems because of the set-up cost of electrical wiring. SPC planned to market the system through manufacturing and/or distribution partnerships.

Protecting the Property

While the interstate shipment of the BigBelly had given SPC a legal claim to the name and the technology, Jim made sure to keep his able patent attorneys apprised of new developments and modifications. SPC had applied for a provisional patent in June of 2003, and they had one year to broaden and strengthen those protections prior to the formal filing. As that date approached, the attorneys worked to craft a document that

protected the inventors from infringement, without being so broad that it could be successfully challenged in court.

The SPC patents covered as many aspects of SunPack products as possible, including energy storage, battery charging, energy draw cycle time, sensor controls, and wireless communication. The filing also specified other off-grid power sources for trash compaction such as foot pedals, windmills, and water wheels.

Even without these intellectual property protections, though, Jim felt that they had a good headstart in an industry segment that SPC had created. Now they had to prove the business model.

The Next Generation

While the first machine had cost far more to build than the selling price, the unit had proven the concept and been a conduit for useful feedback. A production run of twenty machines, however, would have to demonstrate that the business opportunity was as robust as the prototype appeared to be. That would mean cutting the cost of materials by more than seventy-five percent to around $2,500 per unit. SPC estimated that although the delivered price of $5,000 was far more expensive than the cost of a traditional trash receptacle, the system could pay for itself by trimming the ongoing cost of collection (see Exhibit 3).

The team had determined that developing a lease option for the BigBelly would alleviate new-buyer jitters by having SPC retain the risk of machine ownership—a move that could increase margins by ten percent. Over the next five years SPC expected to expand its potential customer pool by reducing the selling price to around $3,000—along with a corresponding drop in materials costs (see Exhibit 4).

With steel prices escalating, the SPC team designed their new machines with thirty percent fewer steel parts. They also cut the size of the solar panel and the two-week battery storage capacity in half, and replaced the expensive screw system of compaction with a simpler, cheaper, and more efficient sprocket and chain mechanism (see Exhibit 5).

In order to offer an effective service response capability, the team tried to restrict their selling efforts to the New England area, although "a sale was a sale." One concern that kept cropping up was that this unique device would be a tempting target for vandals. Team members explained that the solar panel on top was protected by a replaceable sheet of Lexan,[6] that all mechanical parts were entirely out of reach, and that the unit had already proven to be quite solid. The general feeling, Jim noted, was that if the machine could be messed with, people would find a way:

> One state park ranger was worried that it would get tossed into the lake, so I assured him that the units would be very heavy. He said, "So they'll sink really fast. . . ."

Jim added that the overall response had been very favorable—so much so that once again, there was a real need for speed:

> We have presold nearly half of our next run to places like Acadia National Park in Maine, Six Flags

---

[6] A clear, high-impact-strength plastic used in many security applications.

EXHIBIT 3 **Customer Economics**

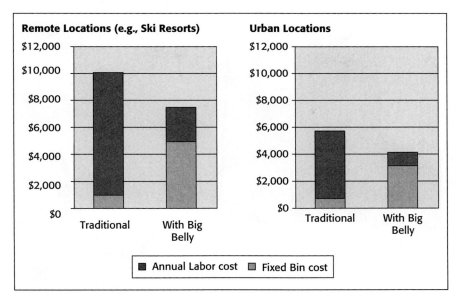

EXHIBIT 4 **BigBelly Economics**

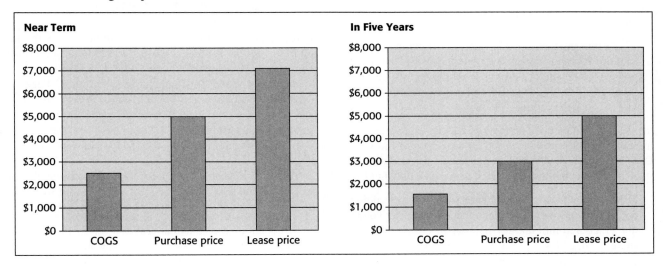

Amusement Park in Massachusetts, Harbor Lights in Boston, beaches on Nantucket, and to Harvard University. Fifty-percent down-payment deposits should be coming in soon, but that won't cover what we'll need to get this done.

Projections and Funding

During this "early commercialization period," Jim was committed to moderating investor risk by leveraging on-campus and contractor facilities as much as possible. The company was hoping to close on an A-round of $250,000 with a pre-money valuation of $2.5 million by early summer to pay for cost-reduction engineering, sales and marketing, and working capital. The following year the company expected to raise a B-round of between $700K and $1 million.

SPC was projecting a positive cash flow in 2006 on total revenues of just over $4.7 million (see Exhibit 6). The team felt that if their products continued to perform well, their market penetration estimates would be highly achievable (see Exhibit 7). Jim estimated that by 2008, SPC would become an attractive merger or acquisition candidate.

In January of 2004, as Jim began work on drafting an SBIR[7] grant proposal, his parents helped out by investing $12,500 in the venture. That same month, while attending a wind energy conference sponsored by Brown and Rudnick, Jim overhead an investor saying that he was interested in putting a

---

[7] The Small Business Innovation Research (SBIR) Program was a source of government grant funding driven by ten federal departments and agencies that allocated a portion of their research and development capital for awards to innovative small businesses in the U.S.

EXHIBIT 5 **BigBelly CAD Schematic**

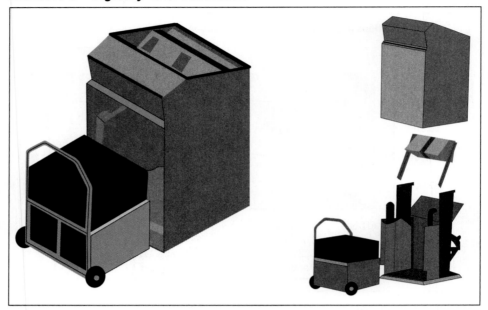

recent entrepreneurial windfall to work in socially responsible ventures. Jim decided it was worth a try:

> I gave him my three-minute spiel on the compactor. He said that it sounded interesting, but that he was into wind power—after all; this *was* a wind-power conference. "Well then," I said, "have I got a business plan for you!"

That afternoon Jim sent the investor the most recent version of the data acquisition buoy business plan. That led to a three-hour meeting where the investor ended up explaining to Jim why the DAQ was such a good idea. Jim said that the investor also understood how difficult it would be to get the venture fully funded:

> [The investor] said, "Well, I sure wish you were doing the Data Acquisition Buoy, but I can also see why you're not." I assured him that my passion was of course, offshore wind, and that it was something I was planning to do in the future. So he agreed to invest $12,500 in the compactor—but only because he wanted to keep his foot in the door for what SPC was going to do later on.

In February, after the folks at Vail had come back with their favorable review, Jim called on his former internship boss at the Spire Corporation. Roger Little was impressed with Jim's progress, and his company was in for $25,000. In April, the team earned top honors in the 2004 Douglas Foundation Graduate Business Plan Competition at Babson College. The prize—$20,000 cash plus $40,000 worth of services—came with a good deal of favorable press as well. The cash, which Jim distributed evenly among the team members, was their first monetary compensation since they had begun working on the project.

Although SPC could now begin to move ahead on the construction of the next twenty cabinets, Jim was still focused on the search for a rather uncommon breed of investor:

> This is not a venture capital deal, and selling this idea to angels can be a challenge because many are not sophisticated enough to understand what we are doing. I had one group, for example, saying that this wouldn't work because most trash receptacles are located in alleys—out of the sun.

EXHIBIT 6 **SPC Financial Projections**

	2004	2005	2006	2007	2008
BigBelly Unit Sales	50	300	1,200	3,600	9,000
BigBelly Revenues	$225,000	$1,200,000	$4,200,000	$10,800,000	$22,500,000
Hippo Royalty Revenues	0	120,000	525,000	1,620,000	3,937,500
Total Income	225,000	1,320,000	4,725,000	12,420,000	26,437,500
COGS	146,250	660,000	2,100,000	4,860,000	9,000,000
Gross Income	78,750	660,000	2,625,000	7,560,000	17,437,500
SG&A	400,000	1,600,000	2,600,000	5,000,000	11,000,000
EBIT	($321,250)	($940,000)	$25,000	$2,560,000	$6,437,500

EXHIBIT 7   Market Size and Penetration

	2004	2005	2006	2007	2008
TOP-DOWN					
SunPack Market* (Billion)	$1.0	$1.0	$1.0	$1.0	$1.0
SunPack % Penetration	0.0%	0.1%	0.5%	1.2%	2.6%
BOTTOM-UP					
Total Potential Customers**	30,000	30,000	30,000	30,000	30,000
Potential units/customer	20	20	20	20	20
Total potential units	600,000	600,000	600,000	600,000	600,000
Cummulative units sold	50	350	1,550	5,150	14,150
Cummulative % penetration	0.0%	0.1%	0.3%	0.9%	2.4%

* Assume $600,000,000 BigBelly market (5% of $12 Billion waste receptacles sold to target segments) plus a $400,000,000 power unit market ($1.2 Billion compacting dumpsters sold/$12,000 average price × $4,000 per power unit).

** Assume 400 resorts, 600 amusement parks, 2,000 university campuses, 5,000 commercial campuses, 2,200 hotels, 4,000 municipalities, 57 National Parks, 2,500 state parks and forests, 3,700 RV parks and campgrounds, and 17,000 fast-food and retail outlets.

Here we have a practical, common-sense business, but since it is a new technology, many investors are unsure of how to value it. How scalable is it? Will our patent filings hold up? Who will fix them when they break?

Earlier that spring Jim had presented his case in Boston to a gathering of angels interested in socially responsible enterprises. Of the six presenters that day, SPC was the only one offering products that were designed to lower direct costs. During the networking session that followed, Jim said that one group in particular seemed eager to move ahead:

> They liked that Spire had invested, and they seemed satisfied with our projections. When I told them that we had a $25,000 minimum, they said not to worry—they were interested in putting in fifty now, and $200K later. In fact, they started talking about setting up funding milestones so that they could be our primary backers as we grew. They wanted me to stop fund-raising, focus on the business, and depend on them for all my near-term financing needs.
>
> At this point I felt like I needed to play hard ball with these guys; show them where the line was. My answer was that I wasn't at all comfortable with that, and that I would be comfortable when I had $200K in the bank—my bank. They backed off that idea, and by the end of the meeting, they agreed to put in the $50,000; but first they said they had to due some more due diligence.

Momentum

By May of 2004, the Seahorse Power Company had a total of six team members.[8] All SPC workers had been given an equity stake in exchange for their part-time services. The investor group expressed deep concern with this arrangement, saying that the team could walk away when the going got tough—and

maybe right when SPC needed them most. Jim explained that it wasn't a negotiable point:

> They wanted my people to have "skin in the game" because they might get cold feet and choose to get regular jobs. I told them that SPC workers are putting in twenty hours a week for free when they could be out charging consulting rates of $200 an hour. They have plenty of skin in this game, and I'm not going to ask them for cash. Besides, if we could put up the cash, we wouldn't need investors, right?

As Jim settled into his seat for the flight to New York, he thought some more about the investors' other primary contention; his pre-money valuation was high by a million:

> These investors—who still haven't given us a dime—are saying they can give me as much early-stage capital as SPC would need, but at a pre-money of $1.5 million, and dependent on us hitting our milestones. With an immediate funding gap of about $50,000, it's tempting to move forward with these guys so we can fill current orders on time and maintain our momentum. On the other hand, I've already raised some money on the higher valuation, and maybe we can find the rest before the need becomes really critical.

---

[8] Three of the most recent equity partners were Richard Kennelly, a former Director at Conservation Law Foundation where he concentrated on electric utility deregulation, renewable energy, energy efficiency, air quality, and global warming; Kevin Dutt, an MBA in Operations Management and Quantitative Methods from Boston University with extensive work experience in improving manufacturing and operational practices in a range of companies; and Steve Delancy, an MBA from The Tuck School at Dartmouth College with a successful track record in fund-raising, business development, market strategy, finance, and operations.

Case 6   Rosa's Palas Franchise

Richard H. Mimick and Elizabeth M.A. Grasby,
case writer

*Richard Ivey School of Business, The University
of Western Ontario*

Harshini Ansari, entrepreneur, was investigating the feasibility of opening a Rosa's Palas (Rosa's) franchise, a well-known Italian chain restaurant, in Denver, Colorado. In the fall of 2003, Ansari had spoken with the franchiser, Latrelle Waller, about the financial investment and the income Ansari could expect from this investment. Ansari had also toured and spoken with other owners of the present Rosa's franchises in Des Moines, Iowa, Sioux City, Iowa, St. Paul, Minnesota, and Omaha, Nebraska, to see if their estimates of sales and costs were similar to those of the franchiser.

Rosa's was a pizza and pasta, sit-down, chain restaurant. Several franchises had been opened in the past five years and considerable success had been experienced by all. Rosa's was particularly recognized for its "Papa's Deep Dish" pizza with triple bacon and mozzarella cheese and for its "Mama's Premium" lasagna with special cheese egg noodles and a secret sauce, layered seven times, between the noodles. The amount of carry-out business varied with each franchise.

Waller had been looking for a franchise in Denver for about one year before Ansari approached him in late 2003.

Waller estimated that the new franchise, if located on the potential site available at the corner of Base Avenue and Tail Road, would produce a sales volume of $1,600,000 in the first year with annual increases in sales of $150,000 for the next two years, at which time he felt the restaurant would reach its peak annual sales volume. These estimates were based on historical

sales generated from other franchises, adjusted for the additional traffic that would surround the Denver store. Waller recommended that Ansari spend $75,000 on advertising in each of the first three years to help achieve these sales goals and to establish the restaurant in its new location.

Waller explained to Ansari that many of the costs were based on the sales volume, and that Ansari could project food costs to be 31 per cent of sales and the payroll costs 17 per cent of sales. He explained that it was normal to have a large percentage of the dollar sales go towards payroll since long hours combined with efficient service were among the franchise's key success factors. Furthermore, Waller reasoned that the flexible nature of restaurant labor reduced the risk to Ansari since no fixed salaries, other than her own, would be carried by the business. Government payroll taxes were roughly 10 per cent of the payroll figure.

As he did with all potential franchisees, Waller had his accountant prepare a list of the franchise's depreciable fixed assets and the corresponding depreciation schedule for the next seven years. See Exhibit 1 for this schedule. At the same time, Waller informed Ansari of other investments she would have to make. One of these was a $50,000 franchise fee,[1] which was a flat fee and had to be paid on the first day of the franchise opening. This fee did not include the additional annual franchise fee, 4 per cent of sales, which was in actuality a royalty on sales volume. A liquor license would cost $1,000 to obtain initially; annual payments of $1,200 would be required to maintain the license. An ongoing inventory of $15,000 would be required to maintain the minimum operational level. As well, in order to take advantage of purchase and/or cash discounts and other short-term needs, Waller recommended that Ansari retain an additional $20,000 cash float to meet emergency working capital at all times.

The building available to Ansari, if she were to go ahead with the franchise, was 3,500 square feet in size. Ansari thought she could rent the building for $20 per square foot per year for a three-year period. Due to the open-ended nature of the lease agreement, a month's deposit would not be required. Payment would be due at the beginning of each month.

Ansari was also informed that paper goods, such as serviettes, glasses, pizza boxes, etc., would be roughly 1.5 per cent of sales, with laundry and maintenance being .6 per cent of sales, and cash short and allowance for bad checks .5 per cent of sales.

---

[1] All fees and licenses were to be amortized over five years.

EXHIBIT 1 **Fixed Asset Depreciation Schedule[1]**

Year	Investment Tax Credit	Double-Declining Balance	Sum-of-Years Digits[2]	Total Depreciation for the Year	Book Value at Year-end
1	$39,000[3]	$100,286		$139,286[4]	$250,714
2		$ 71,633		$ 71,633	$179,081
3			$59,694	$ 59,694	$119,387
4			$47,755	$ 47,755	$ 71,632
5			$35,816	$ 35,816	$ 35,816
6			$23,877	$ 23,877	$ 11,939
7			$11,939	$ 11,939	$ 0

[1]Fixed assets cost is expected to be $390,000. Asset purchase is the responsibility of the franchisee.
[2]An accelerated amortization method.
[3]This is an additional write-off in the first year allowed under U.S. tax laws (investment tax credit).
[4]Under U.S. tax laws, a firm may choose whichever depreciation method produces the greatest depreciation expense for that particular year.

Waller was unable to provide exact figures on utilities, repairs, etc. because each franchise was different; however, Ansari spoke with some of the other franchise managers and found out the following:

	Des Moines Franchise	Sioux City Franchise	St. Paul Franchise
Sales	$1,560,000	$1,200,000	$960,000[2]
Utilities	21,600	42,000[3]	9,600
Repairs	4,800	12,000	15,600
Insurance	6,000	12,000	8,000
Telephone	4,800	10,000	14,400

From this information, Ansari "guesstimated" her utilities to be 70 per cent of Sioux City's bill since electricity costs were running about 30 per cent higher than gas costs. Ansari thought an increase of $2,000 in each successive year was reasonable. Regular maintenance and repairs expense on the building, fixtures, and equipment were estimated by Ansari to be $14,000 annually. Recent inquiries into insurance and telephone expenses indicated these costs would be similar to Sioux City's costs. These expenses were expected to be incurred evenly throughout the year.

Income taxes were calculated at the corporate tax rate of 20 per cent on the first $50,000 of income, 22 per cent on the next $50,000, and 48 per cent on any income over $100,000.

Ansari had recently spoken to a college alumnus who practiced law and who was willing to provide her professional services on a retainer for $3,600 each year.

After discussion with other Rosa's managers, Ansari was warned that Waller tended to be slightly optimistic in his sales predictions, yet accurate in his growth pattern forecasting. Using information from the other franchisees, Ansari figured

that she should discount Waller's annual sales estimates by 20 per cent when projecting statements. Furthermore, Ansari was told that it would be more realistic to project the cost of food at 35 per cent of sales and the payroll at 20 per cent of sales.

Ansari also found out that many sales were made on credit card. According to other franchises, about 60 per cent of all sales were made on credit. Sales made on bank credit cards such as *Visa* and *MasterCard* would be treated like a discounted cash sale since the signed credit card drafts could be deposited directly in the company bank account; however, sales made on non-bank cards such as *EnRoute* and *Diner's Club* would involve receivables. From her interviews, Ansari deduced that 5 per cent of all credit card sales were made with such non-bank cards. From previous experience, Ansari knew that the monies from sales made on these cards would be collected about a

EXHIBIT 2 **Three-Year Projected Income Statement Worksheet: Ansari's Assumptions**

	Year 1	Year 2	Year 3
Sales	———	———	———
Less: Variable Cost	———	———	———
Contribution	———	———	———
Less: Cash Fixed Costs	———	———	———
Less: Non-cash Fixed Costs	———	———	———
Earnings Before Interest and Taxes	———	———	———
Less: Interest	———	———	———
Net Income Before Taxes	———	———	———
Less Taxes	———	———	———
Net Income	———	———	———

[2] 2,400 square feet, 60 per cent carry-out business.
[3] All utilities were electric.

EXHIBIT 3 Annual Cash Budget: Ansari's Assumptions

	March	April	May	June	July	Aug.	Sept.	Oct.	Nov.	Dec.	Jan.	Feb.	Totals
Sales	$106,667	$106,667	$106,667	$106,667	$106,667	$106,667	$106,667	$106,667	$106,667	$106,667	$106,667	$106,667	$1,280,000
INFLOWS:													
Collections	$103,467	$103,467	$103,467	$103,467	$103,467	$103,467	$103,467	$103,467	$103,467	$103,467	$103,467	$103,467	$1,241,600
Non-Bank Credit Cards	—	3,200	3,200	3,200	3,200	3,200	3,200	3,200	3,200	3,200	3,200	3,200	35,200
Capital Infusion	50,000	—	—	—	—	—	—	—	—	—	—	—	50,000
Bank Loan	426,000	—	—	—	—	—	—	—	—	—	—	—	426,000
Total Inflows	$579,467	$106,667	$106,667	$106,667	$106,667	$106,667	$106,667	$106,667	$106,667	$106,667	$106,667	$106,667	$1,752,800
OUTFLOWS:													
Variable Costs	70,080	70,080	70,080	70,080	70,080	70,080	70,080	70,080	70,080	70,080	70,080	70,080	840,960
Fixed Costs													
Util., Repairs, Phone & Ins.	—	5,450	5,450	5,450	5,450	5,450	5,450	5,450	5,450	5,450	5,450	5,450	59,950
Other Cash	15,817	15,817	15,817	15,817	15,817	15,817	15,817	15,817	15,817	15,817	15,817	15,817	189,800
Interest	2,840	2,840	2,840	2,840	2,840	2,840	2,840	2,840	2,840	2,840	2,840	2,840	34,080
Tax	—	—	—	—	—	—	—	—	—	—	—	—	—
Investments	476,000	—	—	—	—	—	—	—	—	—	—	—	476,000
Loan Repayment	—	—	—	—	—	—	—	—	—	—	—	152,010	152,010
Total Outflows	$564,737	$94,187	$94,187	$94,187	$94,187	$94,187	$94,187	$94,187	$94,187	$94,187	$94,187	$246,197	$1,752,800
Net Cash Flow	$14,730	$12,480	$12,480	$12,480	$12,480	$12,480	$12,480	$12,480	$12,480	$12,480	$12,480	$(139,530)	—
Beginning Cash	20,000	34,730	47,210	59,690	72,170	84,650	97,130	109,610	122,090	134,570	147,050	159,530	20,000
Ending Cash	$34,730	$47,210	$59,690	$72,170	$84,650	$97,130	$109,610	$122,090	$134,570	$147,050	$159,530	$20,000	$20,000

EXHIBIT 3 Annual Cash Budget: Ansari's Assumption (continued)

									Year 2				
	March	April	May	June	July	Aug.	Sept.	Oct.	Nov.	Dec.	Jan.	Feb.	Totals
Sales		$116,667	$116,667	$116,667	$116,667	$116,667	$116,667	$116,667	$116,667	$116,667	$116,667	$116,667	$1,400,000
INFLOWS:													
Collections	$113,167	$113,167	$113,167	$113,167	$113,167	$113,167	$113,167	$113,167	$113,167	$113,167	$113,167	$113,167	$1,358,000
Non-Bank Credit Cards	3,200	3,500	3,500	3,500	3,500	3,500	3,500	3,500	3,500	3,500	3,500	3,500	41,700
Total Inflows	$116,367	$116,667	$116,667	$116,667	$116,667	$116,667	$116,667	$116,667	$116,667	$116,667	$116,667	$116,667	$1,399,700
OUTFLOWS:													
Variable Costs	76,650	76,650	76,650	76,650	76,650	76,650	76,650	76,650	76,650	76,650	76,650	76,650	919,800
Fixed Costs													
Util., Repairs, Phone & Ins.	5,450	5,617	5,617	5,617	5,617	5,617	5,617	5,617	5,617	5,617	5,617	5,617	67,233
Other Cash	15,817	15,817	15,817	15,817	15,817	15,817	15,817	15,817	15,817	15,817	15,817	15,817	189,800
Interest													
Tax													
Loan Repayment													
Total Outflows													
Net Cash Flow													
Beginning Cash	20,000												
Ending Cash													

(continued)

EXHIBIT 3 Annual Cash Budget: Ansari's Assumption (*continued*)

Year 3

	March	April	May	June	July	Aug.	Sept.	Oct.	Nov.	Dec.	Jan.	Feb.	Totals
Sales	$126,667	$126,667	$126,667	$126,667	$126,667	$126,667	$126,667	$126,667	$126,667	$126,667	$126,667	$126,667	$1,520,000
INFLOWS:													
Collections	$122,867	$122,867	$122,867	$122,867	$122,867	$122,867	$122,867	$122,867	$122,867	$122,867	$122,867	$122,867	$1,474,400
Non-Bank Credit Cards	3,500	3,800	3,800	3,800	3,800	3,800	3,800	3,800	3,800	3,800	3,800	3,800	45,300
Total Inflows	$126,367	$126,667	$126,667	$126,667	$126,667	$126,667	$126,667	$126,667	$126,667	$126,667	$126,667	$126,667	$1,519,700
OUTFLOWS:													
Variable Costs	83,220	83,220	83,220	83,220	83,220	83,220	83,220	83,220	83,220	83,220	83,220	83,220	998,640
Fixed Costs													
Util., Repairs, Phone & Ins.	5,617	5,783	5,783	5,783	5,783	5,783	5,783	5,783	5,783	5,783	5,783	5,783	69,233
Other Cash	15,817	15,817	15,817	15,817	15,817	15,817	15,817	15,817	15,817	15,817	15,817	15,817	189,800
Interest													
Tax													
Loan Repayment													
Total Outflows													
Net Cash Flow													
Beginning Cash													
Ending Cash													

month after the sale. Ansari also deduced that given Rosa's proposed sales mix, service charges levied by all credit card companies, payable in the month of the sale, would average 2.1 per cent of total sales.

Like most restaurants, which tend to operate on a cash basis, accounts payable would be minimal. Wages and government payroll taxes would all be paid in the year in which they were incurred. All other expenses would also be paid for in cash in the month that they were incurred with the exception of the utilities, telephone, repairs, and insurance bills. These four expenses would be paid about thirty days after the bill came due. In order to conserve cash, the entire income tax payment would be made in one lump sum in April of the following fiscal year.

Under the franchise agreement, Ansari, as manager, could be paid a salary of $40,000 minimum plus 1.5 per cent of sales in excess of a $1,600,000 sales level. The salary and bonus could be written off as an expense. Bonus payments would be disbursed after the books were completed (probably a month and a half after the fiscal year ended). If she went ahead, Ansari hoped to open the franchise on March 1, 1994.

Ansari knew the analysis would be fairly straightforward with the information she had gathered. She wanted to project an income statement, cash budget, and balance sheet for the first three years of operations under her more conservative assumptions. To assist her in her financial planning, Ansari developed worksheets for the three desired projected statements (see Exhibit 2, 3, and 4). Furthermore, Ansari was sincerely interested in the results Waller's assumptions would produce. She thought both sets of estimates would provide the complete spectrum of results she could expect.

Ansari realized that she would require additional financing to fund the venture since she only had $50,000 of her own money to invest in the franchise.[4] She hoped to obtain a bank loan for the additional financing requirements. For her estimates, Ansari decided she would calculate interest, estimated at an annual rate of 8 per cent, based on the opening outstanding balance of the loan. All funds would be borrowed at the beginning of the year. She would pay off as much of the loan as possible only at year-end.

---

[4] Ansari's investment represents 100 shares of common stock.

EXHIBIT 4   Three-Year Projected Balance Sheet Worksheet: Ansari's Assumptions

	Year 1	Year 2	Year 3
ASSETS			
Cash	———	———	———
Receivables	———	———	———
Inventory	———	———	———
Net Fixed Assets	———	———	———
Net Intangibles	———	———	———
Total Assets	———	———	———
LIABILITIES & OWNER'S EQUITY			
Liabilities:			
Accounts Payable	———	———	———
Bonus Payable	———	———	———
Taxes Payable	———	———	———
Bank Loan	———	———	———
Total Liabilities	———	———	———
Equity:	———	———	———
Common Stock	———	———	———
Retained Earnings	———	———	———
Total Equity	———	———	———
Total Liabilities & Owner's Equity	———	———	———

Harshini Ansari thought, after projecting these statements, that she could analyze the results, assess the risk of the franchise by looking at her margin of safety and return on investment, and make a decision.

Glossary

7(A) loan guaranty program. The main Small Business Administration (SBA) program available to small businesses operating through private-sector lenders providing loans that are guaranteed by the SBA; loan guarantees reserved for small businesses that are unable to secure financing through normal lending channels.

10-K. A report that is similar to the annual report, except that it contains more detailed information about the company's business.

accounts receivable. The money owed to a firm by its customers.

acquirer. The surviving firm in an acquisition.

acquisition. The outright purchase of one firm by another.

adverse selection. The challenge a firm must face as it grows such that as the number of employees a firm needs increases, it becomes more difficult to find the right employees, place them in appropriate positions, and provide adequate supervision.

advertising. Making people aware of a product or service in hopes of persuading them to buy it.

advisory board. A panel of experts who are asked by a firm's managers to provide counsel and advice on an ongoing basis; unlike a board of directors, an advisory board possesses no legal responsibilities for the firm and gives nonbinding advice.

agency theory. A management concept that argues that for organizations with multiple units (such as restaurant chains), it is more effective for the units to be run by franchisees than by managers who run company-owned stores.

area franchise agreement. Agreement that allows a franchisee to own and operate a specific number of outlets in a particular geographic area.

articles of incorporation. Documents forming a legal corporation that are filed with the secretary of state's office in the state of incorporation.

assignment of invention agreement. A document signed by an employee as part of the employment agreement that assigns the employer the right to apply for the patent of an invention made by the employee during the course of his or her employment.

assumption sheet. An explanation in a new firm's business plan of the sources of the numbers for its financial forecast and the assumptions used to generate them.

balance sheet. A snapshot of a company's assets, liabilities, and owner's equity at a specific point in time.

barriers to entry. Conditions that create disincentives for a new firm to enter an industry.

benchmarking. The idea that a firm can improve the quality of an activity by identifying and copying the methods of other firms that have been successful in that area.

board of directors. A panel of individuals who are elected by a corporation's shareholders to oversee the management of the firm.

bootstrapping. Using creativity, ingenuity, or any means possible to obtain resources other than borrowing money or raising capital from traditional sources.

brainstorming. A technique used to quickly generate a large number of ideas and solutions to problems; conducted to generate ideas that might represent product or business opportunities.

brand. The set of attributes—positive or negative—that people associate with a company.

brand equity. The set of assets and liabilities that is linked to a brand and enables it to raise a firm's valuation.

brand loyalty. A valuable asset for a particular company wherein customers become loyal to its product or service and will buy its product or service time and time again.

brand management. A program that protects the image and value of an organization's brand in consumers' minds.

break-even point. The point where total revenue received equals total costs associated with the output.

breakthrough products and services. New products and services that establish new markets or new market segments.

budgets. Itemized forecasts of a company's income, expenses, and capital needs that are also important tools for financial planning and control.

burn rate. The rate at which a company is spending its capital until it reaches profitability.

business angels. Individuals who invest their personal capital directly in new ventures.

business concept blind spot. An overly narrow focus that prevents a firm from seeing an opportunity that might fit its business model.

business format franchise. By far the most popular approach to franchising in which the franchisor provides a formula for doing business to the franchisee along with training, advertising, and other forms of assistance.

business growth planning. The process of setting growth-related goals and objectives and then mapping out a plan to achieve those goals and objectives.

business method patent. A patent that protects an invention that is or facilitates a method of doing business.

business model. A company's plan for how it competes, uses its resources, structures its relationships, interfaces with customers, and creates value to sustain itself on the basis of the profits it generates.

business model innovation. Initiative that revolutionizes how products are sold in an industry.

business plan. A written document describing all the aspects of a business venture, which is usually necessary to raise money and attract high-quality business partners.

buyback clause. A clause found in most founders' agreements that legally obligates the departing founder to sell to the remaining founders his or her interest in the firm if the remaining founders are interested.

buzz. An awareness and sense of anticipation about a company and its offerings.

c corporation. A legal entity that in the eyes of the law is separate from its owners.

carry. The percentage of profits that the venture capitalist gets from a specific venture capital fund.

certification marks. Marks, words, names, symbols, or devices used by a person other than its owner to certify a particular quality about a product or service.

channel conflict. A problem that occurs when two or more separate marketing channels (e.g., online sales and retail sales) are in conflict over their roles in selling a firm's products or services.

closely held corporation. A corporation in which the voting stock is held by a small number of individuals and is very thinly or infrequently traded.

clusters. Collections of similar firms in a specific geographic area (i.e., there is a "cluster" of semiconductor firms in the Silicon Valley near San Jose, California).

cobranding. A relationship between two or more firms in which the firms' brands promote each other.

code of conduct. A formal statement of an organization's values on certain ethical and social issues.

collective marks. Trademarks or service marks used by the members of a cooperative, association, or other collective group, including marks indicating membership in a union or similar organization.

commitment to growth. The extent to which a firm's owners and managers have made a deliberate choice to pursue growth.

common stock. Stock that is issued more broadly than preferred stock and that gives the stockholders voting rights to elect the board of directors of the firm.

competitive analysis grid. A tool for organizing the information a firm collects about its competitors to see how it stacks up against its competitors, provide ideas for markets to pursue, and identify its primary sources of competitive advantage.

competitive intelligence. The information that is gathered by a firm to learn about its competitors.

competitor analysis. A detailed evaluation of a firm's competitors.

Computer Software Copyright Act. In 1980, Congress passed this act which amended previous copyright acts; now, all forms of computer programs are protected.

concept statement. A preliminary description of a business that includes descriptions of the product or service being offered, the intended target market, the benefits of the product or service, the product's position in the market, and how the product or service will be sold and distributed.

concept test. A representation of the product or service to prospective users to gauge customer interest, desirability, and purchase intent.

constant ratio method of forecasting. A forecasting approach using the percent of sales method in which expense items of a firm's income statement are expected to grow at the same rate as sales.

consultant. An individual who gives professional or expert advice. Consultants fall into two categories: paid consultants and consultants who are made available for free or at a reduced rate through a nonprofit or governmental agency.

copyright. A form of intellectual property protection that grants to the owner of a work of authorship the legal right to determine how the work is used and to obtain economic benefits of the work.

copyright bug. The letter *c* inside a circle with the first year of publication and the author copyright owner (e.g., © 2007 Dell Inc).

copyright infringement. Violation of another's copyright that occurs when one work derives from another work or is an exact copy or shows substantial similarity to the original copyrighted work.

core competency. A unique skill or capability that transcends products or markets, makes a significant contribution to the customer's perceived benefit, is difficult to imitate, and serves as a source of a firm's competitive advantage over its rivals.

core strategy. The overall manner in which a firm competes relative to its rivals.

corporate entrepreneurship. Behavior orientation exhibited by established firms with an entrepreneurial emphasis that is proactive, innovative, and risk taking.

corporate opportunity doctrine. Legal principle that states that key employees (such as officers, directors, and managers) and skilled employees (such as software engineers, accountants, and marketing specialists) owe a special duty of loyalty to their employer.

corporate venture capital. A type of capital similar to traditional venture capital, except that the money comes from corporations that invest in new ventures related to their areas of interest.

corporation. A separate legal entity organized under the authority of a state.

corridor principle. States that once an entrepreneur starts a firm and becomes immersed in an industry, "corridors" leading to new venture opportunities become more apparent to the entrepreneur than to someone looking in from the outside.

cost-based pricing. A pricing method in which the list price is determined by adding a markup percentage to the product's cost.

cost leadership strategy. Generic strategy in which firms strive to have the lowest costs in the industry relative to competitors' costs and typically attract customers on that basis.

cost reduction strategy. A marketing strategy which is accomplished through achieving lower costs than industry incumbents through process improvements.

cost of sales. All of the direct costs associated with producing or delivering a product or service, including the material costs and direct labor costs (*also* cost of goods sold).

creative destruction. The process by which new products and technologies developed by entrepreneurs over time make current products and technologies obsolete; stimulus of economic activity.

creativity. The process of generating a novel or useful idea.

current assets. Cash plus items that are readily convertible to cash, such as accounts receivable, inventories, and marketable securities.

current liabilities. Obligations that are payable within a year, including accounts payable, accrued expenses, and the current portion of long-term debt.

current ratio. A ratio that equals the firm's current assets divided by its current liabilities.

customer advisory boards. Panel of individuals set up by some companies to meet regularly to discuss needs, wants, and problems that may lead to new product, service, or customer service ideas.

customer interface. The way in which a firm interacts with its customers.

day-in-the-life research. A form of anthropological research used by companies to make sure customers are satisfied and to probe for new product ideas by sending researchers to the customers' homes or business.

debt financing. Getting a loan; most common sources of debt financing are commercial banks and the Small Business Administration (SBA) guaranteed loan program.

debt-to-equity ratio. A ratio calculated by dividing the firm's long term debt by its shareholders' equity.

declining industry. An industry that is experiencing a reduction in demand.

derivative works. Works that are new renditions of something that is already copyrighted, which are also copyrightable.

design patents. The second most common type of patent covering the invention of new, original, and ornamental designs for manufactured products.

differentiation strategy. A strategy that firms use to provide unique or different products to customers. Firms using this strategy typically compete on the basis of quality, service, timeliness, or some other dimension that creates unique value for customers.

disintermediation. The process of eliminating layers of intermediaries, such as distributors and retailers, to sell directly to customers.

distribution channel. The route a product takes from the place it is made to the customer who is the end user.

domain name. A company's Internet address.

double taxation. Form of taxation in which a corporation is taxed on its net income. When the same income is distributed to shareholders in the form of dividends, it is taxed again on shareholders' personal income tax returns.

drop shipping. A type of retailing where the retailer does not keep products in stock, but instead passes customers' orders and shipment details to distributors or manufacturers, who then ship directly to the customer.

due diligence. The process of investigating the merits of a potential venture and verifying the key claims made in the business plan.

Economic Espionage Act. Passed in 1996, an act that makes the theft of trade secrets a crime.

economies of scale. A phenomenon that occurs when mass producing a product results in lower average costs.

efficiency. How productively a firm utilizes its assets relative to its rate of return.

Electronic Signatures in Global and International Commerce Act. Law enacted October 1, 2000, which states that electronic contracts and electronic signatures are just as legal as traditional paper contracts signed in ink.

elevator speech. A brief, carefully constructed statement that outlines the merits of a business opportunity.

emerging industry. A new industry in which standard operating procedures have yet to be developed.

entrepreneurial alertness. The ability to notice things without engaging in deliberate search.

entrepreneurial firms. Companies that bring new products and services to market by creating and seizing opportunities.

entrepreneurial intensity. The position of a firm on a conceptual continuum that ranges from highly conservative to highly entrepreneurial.

entrepreneurial services. Those services that generate new market, product, and service ideas.

entrepreneurship. The process by which individuals pursue opportunities without regard to resources they currently control.

equity financing. A means of raising funds by exchanging partial ownership in a firm, which is usually in the form of stock for funding.

ethical dilemma. A situation that involves doing something that is beneficial to oneself or the organization, but may be unethical.

ethics training program. Programs designed to teach employees how to respond to the types of ethical dilemmas that might arise on their jobs.

exclusive distribution arrangements. An agreement that gives a retailer or other intermediary the exclusive rights to sell a company's products in a specific area for a specific period of time.

execution intelligence. The ability to fashion a solid business idea into a viable business is a key characteristic of successful entrepreneurs.

executive-search firm. A company that specializes in helping other companies recruit and select key personnel.

executive summary. A quick overview of the entire business plan that provides a busy reader everything that he or she needs to know about the distinctive nature of the new venture.

exit strategy. A plan that details how the owners of a firm will sell their interest in the firm, and convert their stock to cash.

external growth strategies. Growth strategies that rely on establishing relationships with third parties, such as mergers, acquisitions, strategic alliances, joint ventures, licensing, and franchising.

fair use. The limited use of copyright material for purposes such as criticism, comment, news reporting, teaching, or scholarship.

fast-track program. A provision in the SBIR Program in which some applicants can simultaneously submit Phase I and Phase II grant applications.

feasibility analysis. A preliminary evaluation of a business idea to determine if it is worth pursuing.

fiduciary obligation. The obligation to always act in another's best interest; it is a mistake to assume that a franchisor has a fiduciary obligation to its franchisees.

final prospectus. Documents issued by the investment bank after the Securities and Exchange Commission (SEC) has approved the offering that sets a date and issuing price for the offering.

financial feasibility analysis. A financial assessment that considers a business idea's capital requirements, financial rate of return, and overall attractiveness of investment.

financial management. The process of raising money and managing a company's finances in a way that achieves the highest rate of return.

financial ratios. Ratios showing the relationships between items on a firm's financial statements that are used to discern whether a firm is meeting its financial objectives and how it stacks up against industry peers.

financial statements. Written reports that quantitatively describe a firm's financial health.

financing activities. Activities that raise cash during a certain period by borrowing money or selling stock, and/or use cash during a certain period by paying dividends, buying back outstanding stock, or buying back outstanding bonds.

first-mover advantage. A sometimes significant advantage gained by the first company to move into a new market because of the opportunity to establish brand recognition and market power.

first-to-invent rule. States that first person to invent an item or process is given preference over another person who is first to file a patent application.

fixed assets. Assets used over a longer time frame, such as real estate, buildings, equipment, and furniture.

fixed costs. The costs that a company incurs in operating a business whether it sells something or not (e.g., overhead).

focus group. A gathering of five to ten people who have been selected based on their common characteristics relative to the issue being discussed; conducted to generate ideas that might represent product or business opportunities.

follow-me-home testing. A product testing methodology in which a company sends teams of testers to the homes or businesses of users to see how its products are working.

follow-on funding. Additional funding for a firm following the initial investment made by investors.

forecasts. Estimates of a firm's future income and expenses, based on its past performance, its current circumstances, and its future plans.

founders' agreement. A written document that deals with issues such as the relative split of the equity among the founders of a firm, how individual founders will be compensated for the cash or the "sweat equity" they put into the firm, and how long the founders will have to remain with the firm for their shares to fully vest (*also* shareholders' agreement).

founding team. A team of individuals chosen to start a new venture; has an advantage over firms started by an individual because a team brings more talent, resources, ideas, and professional contacts to a new venture than does a sole entrepreneur.

fragmented industry. An industry characterized by a large number of firms approximately equal in size.

franchise agreement. The document that consummates the sale of a franchise, which typically contains two sections: (1) the purchase agreement and (2) the franchise or license agreement.

franchisee. A firm that enters into a franchising agreement and pays an initial fee and an ongoing royalty in order to license another firm's successful product or service.

franchising. A form of business organization in which a firm that already has a successful product or service (franchisor), licenses its trademark and method of doing businesses to other businesses (franchisees) in exchange for an initial franchise fee and an ongoing royalty.

franchisor. A firm with a successful product or service that enters into a franchising agreement to license its trademark and method of doing business to other businesses in exchange for fee and royalty payments.

fulfillment and support. The way a firm's product or service "goes to market" or how it reaches its customers; also, the channels a company uses and the level of customer support it provides.

full business plan. A document that spells out a company's operations and plans in much more detail than a summary business plan; the format that is usually used to prepare a business plan for an investor.

gazelles. Fast-growth young companies.

general partnership. A form of business organization in which two or more people pool their skills, abilities, and resources to run a business.

geographic expansion. An internal growth strategy in which an entrepreneurial business grows by simply expanding from its original location to additional geographical sites.

global industry. An industry that is experiencing significant international sales.

global strategy. An international expansion strategy in which firms compete for market share by using the same basic approach in all foreign markets.

group support system (GSS) software. Software that allows participants to submit ideas anonymously during electronic brainstorming sessions.

growth-oriented vision. A plan that helps a firm crystallize the importance of growth for is stakeholders and ensures that its major decisions are made with growth in mind.

heterogeneous team. A team whose individual members are diverse in terms of their abilities and experiences.

historical financial statements. Reflects past performance and are usually prepared on a quarterly and annual basis.

homogenous team. A team whose individual members' areas of expertise are very similar to one another.

horizontal market. A market that meets the specific need of a wide variety of industries, rather than a specific one.

idea. A thought, impression, or notion.

idea bank. A physical or digital repository for storing ideas.

idea-expression dichotomy. The legal principle describing the concept that although an idea is not able to be copyrighted, the specific expression of an idea is.

illiquid. Describes stock in both closely held and private corporations, meaning that it typically isn't easy to find a buyer for the stock.

improving an existing product or service. Enhancing a product or service's quality by making it larger or smaller, making it easier to use, or making it more up-to-date, thereby increasing its value and price potential.

income statement. A financial statement that reflects the results of the operations of a firm over a specified period of time: prepared on a monthly, quarterly, or annual basis.

individual franchise agreement. The most common type of franchise agreement, which involves the sale of a single franchise for a specific location.

industry. A group of firms producing a similar product or service, such as airlines, fitness drinks, or electronic games.

industry analysis. Business research that focuses on the potential of an industry.

industry consolidation. The primary opportunity existing for start-ups in fragmented industries to establish leadership when smaller companies are typically acquired or go out of business to give way to a handful of larger companies that take over the majority of the business.

industry/market feasibility analysis. An assessment of the overall appeal of the market for the product or service being proposed.

infomercial. A television commercial that runs as long as a television show and usually includes a pitch selling an item directly to the public.

initial public offering (IPO). The first sale of a company's stock to the public and an important milestone for a firm for four reasons: it is a way to raise equity capital; it raises a firm's public profile; it is a liquidity event; and it creates another form of currency (company stock) that can be used to grow the company.

innovation. The process of creating something new, which is central to the entrepreneurial process.

inside director. A person on a firm's board of directors who is also an officer of the firm.

intellectual property. Any product of human intellect, imagination, creativity, or inventiveness that is intangible but has value in the marketplace and can be protected through tools such as patents, trademarks, copyrights, and trade secrets.

intellectual property audit. A firm's assessment of the intellectual property it owns.

intent-to-use trademark application. An application based on the applicant's intention to register and use a trademark.

interference. An administrative proceeding if this is a dispute regarding who was first to invent a product; presided over by a judge at the U.S. Patent & Trademark Office.

internal growth strategies. Growth strategies that rely on efforts generated within the firm itself, such as new product development, other product-related strategies, or international expansion.

international new ventures. Businesses that, from inception, seek to derive significant competitive advantage by using their resources to sell products or services in multiple countries.

intranet. A privately maintained Internet site that can be accessed only by authorized users.

invention logbook. Documentation of the dates and activities related to the development of a particular invention.

inventory. A company's merchandise, raw materials, and products waiting to be sold.

investing activities. Activities that include the purchase, sale, or investment in fixed assets, such as real estate and buildings.

investment bank. A financial institution that acts as an underwriter or agent for a firm issuing securities.

joint venture. An entity created when two or more firms pool a portion of their resources to create a separate, jointly owned organization.

Lanham Act. A trademark law passed in 1946 that protects words, numbers and letters, designs and logos, sounds, fragrances, shapes, colors and trade dress.

leadership strategy. A competitive strategy in which the firm tries to become the dominant player in the industry.

lease. A written agreement in which the owner of a piece of property allows an individual or business to use the property for a specified period of time in exchange for regular payments.

liability of newness. Situation that often causes new firms to falter because the people who start the firms can't adjust quickly enough to their new roles, and because the firm lacks a "track record" with customers and suppliers.

licensee. A company that purchases the right to use another company's intellectual property.

licensing. The granting of permission by one company to another company to use a specific form of its intellectual property under clearly defined conditions.

licensing agreement. The formal contract between a licensor and licensee.

licensor. The company that owns the intellectual property in a licensing agreement.

lifestyle firms. Businesses that provide their owners the opportunity to pursue a particular lifestyle and earn a living while doing so (e.g., ski instructors, golf pros, and tour guides).

limited liability company (LLC). A form of business organization that combines the limited liability advantage of the corporation with the tax advantages of the partnership.

limited partnership. A modified form of a general partnership that includes two classes of owners: general partners and limited partners. The general partners are liable for the debts and obligations of the partnership, but the limited partners are liable only up to the amount of the investment. The limited partners may not exercise any significant control over the organization without jeopardizing their limited liability status.

limited partnership agreement. Sets forth the rights and duties of the general and limited partners, along with the details of how the partnership will be managed and eventually dissolved.

line of credit. A borrowing "Cap" is established and borrowers can use the credit at their discretion; require periodic interest payments.

link joint venture. A joint venture in which the position of the parties is not symmetrical and the objectives of the partners may diverge.

liquid market. A market in which stock can be bought and sold fairly easily through an organized exchange.

liquidity. The ability to sell a business or other asset quickly at a price that is close to its market value; also, a company's ability to meet its short-term financial obligations.

liquidity event. An occurrence such as a new venture going public, finding a buyer, or being acquired by another company that converts some or all of a company's stock into cash.

long-term liabilities. Notes or loans that are repayable beyond one year, including liabilities associated with purchasing real estate, buildings, and equipment.

managerial capacity problem. The problem that arises when the growth of a firm is limited by the managerial capacity (i.e., personnel, expertise, and intellectual resources) that a firm has available to implement new business ideas.

managerial services. The routine functions of the firm that facilitate the profitable execution of new opportunities.

marketing alliances. Alliances that typically match a company with a distribution system in order to increase sales of a product or service.

marketing mix. The set of controllable, tactical marketing tools that a firm uses to produce the response it wants in the target market; typically organized around the four Ps—product, price, promotion, and place (or distribution).

market leadership. The position of a firm when it is the number-one or the number-two firm in an industry or niche market in terms of sales volume.

market penetration strategy. A strategy designed to increase the sales of a product or service through greater marketing efforts or through increased production capacity and efficiency.

market segmentation. The process of studying the industry in which a firm intends to compete to determine the different potential target markets in that industry.

master franchise agreement. Similar to an area franchise agreement, but in addition to having the right to operate a specific number of locations in a particular area, the franchisee also has the right to offer and sell the franchise to other people in the area.

mature industry. An industry that is experiencing slow or no increase in demand, has numerous (rather than new) customers, and has limited product innovation.

mediation. A process in which an impartial third party (usually a professional mediator) helps those involved in a dispute reach an agreement.

merchandise and character licensing. The licensing of a recognized trademark or brand, which the licensor typically controls through a registered trademark or copyright.

merger. The pooling of interest to combine two or more firms into one.

milestone. In a business plan context, a noteworthy event in the past or future development of a business.

mission statement. A statement that describes why a firm exists and what its business model is supposed to accomplish.

moderate risk takers. Entrepreneurs who are often characterized as willing to assume a moderate amount of risk in business, being neither overly conservative nor likely to gamble.

moral hazard. A problem a firm faces as it grows and adds personnel; the assumption is that new hires will not have the same ownership incentives or be as motivated to work hard as the original founders.

multidomestic strategy. An international expansion strategy in which firms compete for market share on a country-by-country basis and vary their product or services offerings to meet the demands of the local market.

multiple unit franchisee. An individual who owns and operates more than one outlet of the same franchisor, whether through an area or a master franchise agreement.

net sales. Total sales minus allowances for returned goods and discounts.

network entrepreneurs. Entrepreneurs who identified their idea through social contacts.

networking. Building and maintaining relationships with people whose interests are similar or whose relationship could bring advantages to a firm.

new product development. The creation and sale of new products (or services) as a means of increasing a firm's revenues.

news conference. The live dissemination of news information by a firm to invited media.

new-venture team. The group of founders, key employees, and advisors that move a new venture from an idea to a fully functioning firm.

niche market. A place within a large market segment that represents a narrow group of customers with similar interests.

niche strategy. A marketing strategy that focuses on a narrow segment of the industry.

noncompete agreement. An agreement that prevents an individual from competing against a former employer for a specific period of time.

nondisclosure agreement. A promise made by an employee or another party (such as a supplier) to not disclose a company's trade secrets.

one year after first use deadline. A patent must be applied for within one year of when product or process was first offered for sale, so if it was forgotten about, a patent attorney would have to put together a filing in a short period of time to meet this deadline.

operating activities. Activities that affect net income (or loss), depreciation, and changes in current assets and current liabilities other than cash and short-term debt.

operating expenses. Marketing, administrative costs, and other expenses not directly related to producing a product or service.

operational business plan. A blueprint for a company's operations; primarily meant for an internal audience.

opportunity. A favorable set of circumstances that creates a need for a new product, service, or business.

opportunity gap. An entrepreneur recognizes a problem and creates a business to fill it.

opportunity recognition. The process of perceiving the possibility of a profitable new business or a new product or service.

organic growth. Internally generated growth within a firm that does not rely on outside intervention.

organizational chart. A graphic representation of how authority and responsibility are distributed within a company.

organizational feasibility analysis. A study conducted to determine whether a proposed business has sufficient management expertise, organizational competence, and resources to be successful.

other assets. Miscellaneous assets including accumulated goodwill.

outside director. Someone on a firm's board of directors who is not employed by the firm.

outsourcing. Work that is done for a company by people other than the company's full-time employees.

owner's equity. The equity invested in the business by its owner(s) plus the accumulated earnings retained by the business after paying dividends.

pace of growth. The rate at which a firm is growing on an annual basis.

partnership agreement. A document that details the responsibility and the ownership shares of the partners involved with an organization.

passion for their business. An entrepreneur's belief that his or her business will positively influence people's lives; one of the characteristics of successful entrepreneurs.

patent. A grant from the federal government conferring the rights to exclude others from making, selling, or using an invention for the term of the patent.

patent infringement. This is when one party engages in the unauthorized use of another's patent.

percent of sales method. A method for expressing each expense item as a percent of sales.

piercing the corporate veil. The chain of effects that occurs if the owners of a corporation don't file their yearly payments, neglect to pay their annual fees, or commit fraud, which may result in the court ignoring the fact that a corporation has been established, and the owners could be held personally liable for actions for the corporation.

place. The marketing mix category that encompasses all of the activities that move a firm's product from its place of origin to the consumer (*also* distribution).

plant patents. Patents that protect new varieties of plants that can be reproduced asexually by grafting or crossbreeding rather than by planting seeds.

position. How the entire company is situated relative to its competitors.

preferred stock. Stock that is typically issued to conservative investors, who have preferential rights over common stockholders in regard to dividends and to the assets of the corporation in the event of liquidation.

preliminary prospectus. A document issued by an investment bank that describes the potential offering to the general public while the SEC is conducting an investigation of the offering (*also* red herring).

press kit. A folder typically distributed to journalists and made available online that contains background information about a company and includes a list of the company's most recent accomplishments.

price. The amount of money consumers pay to buy a product; one of the four Ps in a company's marketing mix.

price/earnings (P/E) ratio. A simple ratio that measures the price of a company's stock against its earnings.

price-quality attribution. The assumption consumers naturally make that the higher-priced product is also the better-quality product.

primary research. Research that is original and is collected first hand by the entrepreneur by, for example, talking to potential customers and key industry participants.

prior entrepreneurial experience. Prior start-up experience; this experience has been found to be one of the most consistent predictors of future entrepreneurial performance.

private corporation. A corporation in which all of the shares are held by a few shareholders, such as management or family members, and the stock is not publicly traded.

private placement. A variation of the IPO in which there is a direct sale of an issue of securities to a large institutional investor.

product. The element of the marketing mix that is the good or service a company offers to its target market; often thought of as something having physical form.

product and trademark franchise. An arrangement under which the franchisor grants to the franchisee the right to buy its product and use its trade name.

product/customer focus. A defining characteristic of successful entrepreneurs that emphasizes producing good products with the capability to satisfy customers.

productive opportunity set. The set of opportunities the firm feels it is capable of pursing.

product line extension strategy. A strategy that involves making additional versions of a product so they will appeal to different clientele.

product/market scope. A range that defines the products and markets on which a firm will concentrate.

product/service feasibility analysis. An assessment of the overall appeal of the product or service being proposed.

profitability. The ability to earn a profit.

profit margin. A measure of a firm's return on sales that is computed by dividing net income by average net sales.

pro forma balance sheet. Financial statements that show a projected snapshot of a company's assets, liabilities, and owner's equity at a specific point in time.

pro forma financial statements. Projections for future periods, based on a firm's forecasts, and typically completed for two to three years in the future.

pro forma income statement. A financial statement that shows the projected results of the operations of a firm over a specific period.

pro forma statement of cash flows. A financial statement that shows the projected flow of cash into and out of a company for a specific period.

promotion. The marketing mix category that includes the activities planned by a company to communicate the merits of its product to its target market with the goal of persuading people to buy the product.

prototyping. An iterative process in which the prototype as a model of the product or service is continually refined until the customer and designer agree on the final design.

provisional patent application. A part of patent law that grants "provisional rights" to an inventor for up to one year, pending the filing of a complete and final application.

public corporation. A corporation that is listed on a major stock exchange, such as the New York Stock Exchange or the NASDAQ, in which owners can sell their shares at almost a moment's notice.

public relations. The efforts a company makes to establish and maintain a certain image with the public through networking with journalists and others to try to interest them in saying or writing good things about the company and its products.

rapid-growth firm. A firm that maintains a growth rate of at least 20 percent per year for five consecutive years.

reference account. An early user of a firm's product who is willing to give a testimonial regarding his or her experience with the product.

regression analysis. A statistical technique used to find relationships between variables for the purpose of predicting future values.

relevant industry experience. Experience in the same industry as an entrepreneur's current venture that includes a network of industry contacts and an understanding of the subtleties of the industry.

resource leverage. The process of adapting a company's core competencies to exploit new opportunities.

road show. A whirlwind tour taken by the top management team of a firm wanting to go public; consists of meetings in key cities where the firm presents its business plan to groups of investors.

rounds. Stages of subsequent investments made in a firm by investors.

salary-substitute firms. Small firms that yield a level of income for their owner or owners that is similar to what they would earn when working for an employer (e.g., dry cleaners, convenience stores, restaurants, accounting firms, retail stores, and hair styling salons).

sales forecast. A projection of a firm's sales for a specified period (such as a year); however, although most firms forecast their sales for two to five years into the future.

Sarbanes-Oxley Act. A federal law that was passed in response to corporate accounting scandals involving prominent corporations, like Enron and WorldCom.

SBA Guaranteed Loan Program. An important source of funding for small businesses in general in which approximately 50 percent of the 9,000 banks in the United States participate.

SBIR Program. Small Business Innovation Research (SBIR) competitive grant program that provides over $1 billion per year to small businesses for early-stage and development projects.

scalable business model. A business model in which increased revenues cost less to deliver than current revenues, so profit margins increase as sales go up.

scale joint venture. A joint venture in which the partners collaborate at a single point in the value chain to gain economies of scale in production or distribution.

secondary market offering. Any later public issuance of shares after the initial public offering.

secondary meaning. This arises when, over time, consumers start to identify a trademark with a specific product. For example, the name CHAP STICK for lip balm was originally considered to be descriptive, and thus not afforded trademark protection.

secondary research. Data collected previously by someone else for a different purpose.

second-mover advantage. The advantage the second company has in entering a market. This advantage exists because of the opportunity to study the mistakes made by the first mover.

seed money. The initial investment made in a firm.

self-selected opinion poll. A survey whose participants have not been chosen at random but who have selected themselves to be respondents often because they have either strong positive or negative feelings about a particular product or topic; data may not be representative of the larger population.

serendipitous discovery. A chance discovery made by someone with a prepared mind.

service. An activity or benefit that is intangible and does not take on a physical form, such as an airplane trip or advice from an attorney.

service marks. Similar to ordinary trademarks but used to identify the services or intangible activities of a business rather than a business's physical product.

shareholders. Owners of a corporation who are shielded from personal liability for the debts and obligations of the corporation.

signaling. The act of a high-quality individual agreeing to serve on a company's board of directors, which indicates that the individual believes that the company has the potential to be successful.

single-purpose loan. One common type of loan in which a specific amount of money is borrowed that must be repaid in a fixed amount of time with interest.

"skin in the game." The amount of money the management team has invested in a new venture.

Small Business Technology Transfer Program (STTR). A collaborative program that involves small business and research organizations, such as universities or federal laboratories.

solo entrepreneurs. Entrepreneurs who identified their business idea on their own.

sole proprietorship. The simplest form of business organization involving one person, in which the owner maintains complete control over the business and business losses can be deducted against the owner's personal tax return.

sources and uses of funds statement. The explanation within the financial section of a business plan of the funding that will be needed by the business during the next three to five years, along with details of how the funds will be used.

spin-in. An investment made by a larger firm with a small equity stake by acquiring a smaller firm.

spin-out. The opposite of a spin-in that occurs when a larger company divests itself of one of its smaller divisions.

stability. The strength and vigor of the firm's overall financial posture.

statement of cash flows. A financial statement summarizing the changes in a firm's cash position for a specified period of time and detailing why the changes occurred. Similar to a month-end bank statement, it reveals how much cash is on hand at the end of the month as well as how the cash was acquired and spent during the month.

stealth mode. Formulating initial business plans in secret.

stock options. Special form of incentive compensation providing employees the option or right to buy a certain number of shares of their company's stock at a stated price over a certain period of time.

strategic alliance. A partnership between two or more firms that is developed to achieve a specific goal.

strategic assets. Anything rare and valuable that a firm owns, including plant and equipment, location, brands, patents, customer data, a highly qualified staff, and distinctive partnerships.

strong-tie relationships. Relationships characterized by frequent interaction that form between like-minded individuals such as coworkers, friends, and spouses; these relationships tend to reinforce insights and ideas the individuals already have and, therefore, are not likely to introduce new ideas.

subchapter S corporation. A form of business organization that combines the advantages of a partnership and C corporation; similar to a partnership, in that the profits and losses of the business are not subject to double taxation, and similar to a corporation, in that the owners are not subject to personal liability for the behavior of the business.

subfranchisees. The people who buy franchises from master franchisees.

summary business plan. A business plan 10 to 15 pages long that works best for companies very early in their development that are not prepared to write a full plan.

supplier. A company or vendor that provides parts or services to another company.

supply chain. A network of all the companies that participate in the production of a product, from the acquisition of raw materials to the final sale.

supply chain management. The coordination of the flow of all information, money, and material that moves through a product's supply chain.

survey. A method of gathering information from a sample of individuals usually representing just a fraction of the population being studied.

sustainable competitive advantage. A combination of a company's core competencies and strategic assets achieved by implementing a unique value-creating strategy.

sustained growth. Growth in both revenues and profits over an extend period of time.

sweat equity. The value of the time and effort that a founder puts into a new firm.

tagline. A phrase that is used consistently in a company's literature, advertisements, promotions, stationery, and even invoices to develop and to reinforce the position the company has staked out in its market.

target. In an acquisition, the firm that is acquired.

target market. The limited group of individuals or businesses that a firm goes after or tries to appeal to at a certain point in time.

technological alliances. Business alliances that cooperate in R&D, engineering, and manufacturing.

technology licensing. The licensing of proprietary technology, which the licensor typically controls by virtue of a utility patent.

trademark. Any work, name, symbol, or device used to identify the sources or origin of products or services and to distinguish those products and services from others.

trade secret. Any formula, pattern, physical device, idea, process, or other information that provides the owner of the information with a competitive advantage in the marketplace.

trade show. An event at which the goods or services in a specific industry are exhibited and demonstrated.

triggering event. The event that prompts an individual to become an entrepreneur (e.g., losing a job, inheriting money, accommodating a certain lifestyle).

Uniform Franchise Offering Circular (UFOC). Accepted in all 50 states and parts of Canada, a lengthy document that contains 23 categories of information giving a prospective franchise a broad base of information about the background and financial health of the franchisor.

Uniform Trade Secrets Act. Drafted in 1979 by a special commission in an attempt to set nationwide standards for trade secret legislation; although the majority of states have adopted the act, most revised it, resulting in a wide disparity among states in regard to trade secret legislation and enforcement.

usability testing. Testing that requires the user of a product to perform certain tasks in order to measure the product's ease of use and the user's perception of the experience.

utility patents. The most common type of patent covering what we generally think of as new inventions that must be useful, must be novel in relation to prior arts in the field, and must not be obvious to a person of ordinary skill in the field.

value. Relative worth, importance, or utility.

value-based pricing. A pricing method in which the list price is determined by estimating what consumers are willing to pay for a product and then backing off a bit to provide a cushion.

value chain. The string of activities that moves a product from the raw material stage, through manufacturing and distribution, and ultimately to the end user.

variable costs. The costs that are not fixed that a company incurs as it generates sales.

venture capital. The money that is invested by venture capital firms in start-ups and small businesses with exceptional growth potential.

venture-leasing firms. Firms that act as brokers, bringing the parties involved in a lease together (e.g., firms acquainted with the producers of specialized equipment match these producers with new ventures that are in need of the equipment).

vertical market. Focuses on similar businesses that have specific and specialized needs.

viral marketing. A new marketing technique that facilitates and encourages people to pass along a marketing message about a particular product or service.

virtual prototype. A computer-generated 3D image of an idea.

weak-tie relationships. Relationships characterized by infrequent interaction that form between casual acquaintances who do not have a lot in common and, therefore, may be the source of completely new ideas.

window of opportunity. The time period in which a firm or an entrepreneur can realistically enter a new market.

working capital. A firm's current assets minus its current liabilities.

Name Index

Subject Index

Page numbers followed by *f* or *t* refer to figures or tables respectively.

Company Index